THE MENTALLY RETARDED CITIZEN AND THE LAW

Sponsored by The President's Committee on Mental Retardation

Edited by **MICHAEL KINDRED**, Project Director
JULIUS COHEN
DAVID PENROD
THOMAS SHAFFER

With a Preface by **LAWRENCE A. KANE, JR.**
Chairman, Law and Ethics Work Group,
President's Committee on Mental Retardation

THE FREE PRESS
A Division of Macmillan Publishing Co., Inc.
NEW YORK

Collier Macmillan Publishers
LONDON

The Free Press
A Division of Macmillan Publishing Co., Inc.
866 Third Avenue, New York, N.Y. 10022

Collier Macmillan Canada, Ltd.

Library of Congress Catalog Card Number: 74-21489

Printed in the United States of America

printing number

2 3 4 5 6 7 8 9 10

Library of Congress Cataloging in Publication Data

Main entry under title:

The Mentally retarded citizen and the law.

"The President's Committee on Mental Retardation convened a conference in 1973 . . . Each of the 22 principal papers appear in a chapter of this volume."
  Includes bibliographical references.
  1. Insanity—Jurisprudence—United States—Congresses.   2. Mental health laws—United States—Congresses.   I. Kindred, Michael.   II. United States. President's Committee on Mental Retardation.
[DNLM: 1. Mental retardation—Congresses.   2. Civil rights—Congresses.   WM300 M5545 1973]
KF480.A75M46   346′.73′013   74-21489
ISBN 0-02-916860-0

Robert A. Burt, "Beyond the Right to Habilitation," pp. 418–36, from *The Classification of Exceptional Children*, 1974. Reprinted by permission of Jossey-Bass, Inc.

Stanley Herr, "The Right to an Appropriate Free Public Education," pp. 252–67. This paper is in part an elaboration of material first published in and copyrighted by the *Syracuse Law Review*, Syracuse University, Syracuse, New York, and is printed here with the permission of the Board of Editors of the Review.

Paul Friedman, "Peonage and Involuntary Servitude," pp. 564–82. Copyright 1974 by The Harvard Law Review Association. This paper appeared as a Comment entitled "The Mentally Handicapped Citizen and Institutional Labor." The Comment was an outgrowth of a paper on this topic presented at the conference on the legal rights of the mentally retarded sponsored by the President's Committee on Mental Retardation, Columbus, Ohio, May 3–5, 1973.

Patricia Wald, "Basic Personal and Civil Rights," pp. 3–26. Reprinted with an update by permission of PLI (Practising Law Institute) from their 1973 course handbook, *Legal Rights of the Mentally Handicapped*, originally published as "The Legal Rights of People with Mental Disabilities in the Community: A Plea for Laissez Faire."

THE WHITE HOUSE

WASHINGTON

Opportunity for every individual to develop his
full potential has long been an American ideal.
We judge our success or failure as a Nation by
the norms of justice and equality under the law.
The treatment we have accorded mentally
retarded and other handicapped members of our
society tests our success and challenges our
ideals. Only recently have we sought to assure
the right of mentally retarded citizens to develop
their full potential, to share in the bounty of our
land and to receive equal justice under the law.

The President's Committee on Mental Retardation
has stood for nearly a decade as the symbol of
Presidential dedication to securing these rights
to mentally retarded Americans. This volume,
sponsored by the President's Committee, is a
further step toward the achievement of that goal.
The lawyers, scholars, social scientists, and
parents who have produced this remarkable collection of papers and comments challenge each
of us -- executive, legislator, judge, citizen --
to make our goals of justice, equality, and
opportunity a reality for the mentally retarded
citizens among us.

Gerald R. Ford

Summary Table of Contents

PART FOUR   **The Mentally Retarded Citizen and the Criminal and Correctional Process**

Table of Contents

Editors and Contributors

ALAN ABESON, Ed.D., is Assistant Director of State and Local Governmental Relations for the Council for Exceptional Children (CEC). His publications include *A Continuing Summary of Pending and Completed Litigation Regarding the Education of Handicapped Children (CEC)*.

CHARLES E. ACUFF, Ph.D., is Commissioner of Mental Retardation–Developmental Disabilities Services in Arkansas. He is also past director of the Division of Mental Retardation for the State of Kentucky and past president of the National Association of Coordinators of State Programs for the Mentally Retarded.

RICHARD C. ALLEN, J.D., is Professor of Law and Chairman of the Department of Forensic Sciences at George Washington University in Washington, D.C. He has directed two studies on mental incompetency and mental retardation and the law under the sponsorship of the National Institute of Mental Health and has served as a legal consultant to the President's Committee on Mental Retardation.

PERCY BATES, Ed.D., is Assistant Dean of the University of Michigan School of Education. He was previously a teacher of mentally retarded children, a school psychologist, and director of the Ypsilanti Board of Education Mental Retardation Teacher-Training Program.

MERTON BERNSTEIN, LL.B., is Professor of Law, The Ohio State University, and has written extensively in the field of income material and social legislation. He served as chairman of the Advisory Committee on Research of the Social Security Administration and as a consultant to the U.S. Treasury, U.S. Department of Labor, and the National Science Foundation, and as counsel to subcommittees of the U.S. Senate.

ELIZABETH M. BOGGS, Ph.D., has been a volunteer advocate for the mentally retarded since 1950. She was one of the founders of the National Association for Retarded Citizens in 1950 and its first woman president. She has also served as a member of President Kennedy's Panel on Mental Retardation and the National Advisory Child Health and Human Development Council, and more recently as chairman of the National Advisory Council on Services and Facilities for the Developmentally Disabled.

LOUIS A. BRANSFORD, Ph.D., is Director of Utilization for the Satellite Technology Demonstration of the Federation of Rocky Mountain States. He has extensive experience in public schools and university special education programs and has assisted in implementing changes in school programs directly affecting Chicano students.

MARCIA PEARCE BURGDORF, J.D., is a lecturer at the Notre Dame Law School and was project attorney for the National Center for Law and the Handicapped.

ROBERT A. BURT, J.D., is Professor of Law and Professor of Law in Psychiatry at the University of Michigan. He is co-reporter of the volume on child abuse, neglect, and dependency for the ABA-IJA Juvenile Justice Standards Project, and a member of the Board on Maternal, Child, and Family Health Research of the National Research Council–National Academy of Sciences.

PHILIP CAPER, M.D., is an internist and a member of the professional staff of the United States Senate Sub-committee on Health, chaired by Senator Edward M. Kennedy. He is a member of the visiting faculty at Harvard University and Georgetown University School of Medicine in Washington, D.C.

DAVID CHAMBERS, LL.B., is Professor of Law at the University of Michigan Law School. He is the author of articles on constitutional principles for insisting on the use of alternatives to civil commitment and on systems of effective counsel for persons facing commitment. He currently serves as reporter for a Michigan Supreme Court committee developing rules of procedure for commitment proceedings for the mentally ill and mentally retarded.

JO ANN CHANDLER, J.D., is a Staff Attorney with Public Advocates, Inc., the largest public interest law firm in the western United States. She is counsel in one of the major cases seeking to eliminate zoning restrictions on normal residential opportunities for the mentally retarded and in a right-to-education suit for handicapped children.

FRANKLIN D. CHU, B.A., was Project Director of Ralph Nader's Task Force on the National Institute of Mental Health and is co-author of a study of the federal community mental health centers program. He has served as a consultant for several community mental health centers. Mr. Chu currently attends the Yale Law School.

JAMES CLEMENTS, M.D., is Director of the Georgia Retardation Center, Clinical Assistant Professor of Pediatrics and Psychiatry at Emory University School of Medicine, and Assistant Clinical Professor of Pediatrics and Associate Clinical Professor of Pediatric Neurology at the Medical College of Georgia. He is the current president of the American Association on Mental Deficiency.

FRED COHEN, J.D., is Professor of Law and Criminal Justice, SUNY at Albany, School of Criminal Justice, and is currently serving as Associate Director of the ABA-IJA Juvenile Justice Standards Project and as Visiting Adjunct Professor, New York University School of Law. His article, "The Function of the Attorney and the Commitment of the Mentally Ill," 44 *Tex. L. Rev.* 424 (1966) was the first systematic exploration of the civil commitment of the mentally ill with a primary focus on the role of counsel.

JULIUS S. COHEN, Ed.D., is Deputy Director of the Institute for the Study of Mental Retardation and Related Disabilities at the University of Michigan. His contribution to this volume is as the editor representing the non-legal perspective. Dr. Cohen recently completed a sabbatical program with the President's Committee on Mental Retardation in which he explored legal, ethical, and moral issues facing mental retardation professionals and did a follow-up study on the impact of early cases brought by minority children alleging biased treatment by school systems in the testing, labeling, and placement process.

LOUIS Z. COOPER, M.D., is Director of Pediatric Services at Roosevelt Hospital and Professor of Pediatrics at the College of Physicians and Surgeons of Columbia University. As director of the Rubella Project, he has worked on development, evaluation, and distribution of rubella vaccines, characterization of the disease, and development of improved habilitation programs for young, multihandicapped children.

JOHN M. DEUTCH, Ph.D., is Professor of Chemistry at M.I.T. His participation in this volume is not as an expert but as a private citizen. His views about zoning barriers are shaped by extensive experience in the design, management, and implementation of public social welfare programs as well as the personal experience he recounts.

GUNNAR DYBWAD is the Gingold Professor of Human Development at the Florence Heller Graduate School, Brandeis University. Over the past forty years he has worked in the fields of penology and juvenile delinquency, child welfare and child development, rehabilitation, and mental retardation. In 1972 he and his wife, Dr. Rosemary Dybwad, received the distinguished service award from the International League of Societies for the

Mentally Handicapped and in 1973 he was recipient of the C. Anderson Aldrich Award from the American Academy of Pediatrics for his contributions to the field of child development.

RICHARD W. EFFLAND, LL.B., LL.M., is Professor of Law at Arizona State University. His impact on legislative reform is evidenced by his work as one of the reporters on the Uniform Probate Code and as legislative assistant on the Arizona Probate Code and on revision of the Wisconsin property statutes. He has written extensively in the area of estate planning.

ELEANOR S. ELKIN is a foster parent of a mentally retarded son. She has served as president of the Pennsylvania Association for Retarded Citizens and the National Association for Retarded Citizens (NARC).

BRUCE J. ENNIS, J.D., is plaintiff's counsel in three of the major right to treatment cases, as well as numerous other cases involving the rights of the mentally disabled. He is author of *Prisoners of Psychiatry,* co-author of "Psychiatrists and the Presumption of Expertise," 62 *Calif. Law Review* 693 (1974) and *The Rights of Mental Patients,* and co-editor of *Legal Rights of the Mentally Handicapped.* Mr. Ennis serves as chairperson of the American Bar Association's Subcommittee on the Mentally Disabled, staff counsel to the New York Civil Liberties Union, and staff counsel, trustee, and co-founder of the Mental Health Law Project.

MILTON W. FERRIS is a consultant on mental retardation programs and facilities, with over twenty years experience and background in the field of mental retardation. He is owner–operator of his own consultant agency, and has authored several papers and curricula on training the mentally retarded and supervision of the retarded worker. Mr. Ferris is a member of the President's Committee on Employment of the Handicapped.

J. F. FOLLMANN, JR., is a consultant to the National Institute of Alcoholism and Alcohol Abuse of the Department of Health, Education, and Welfare, the National Institute of Cancer, the Rand Corporation, the American Health Foundation, and other health organizations. Until recently he was vice president of the Health Insurance Association of America, and in 1969 was elected Health Insurance Man of the Year.

SANFORD J. FOX, LL.B., is Professor of Law at Boston College Law School and was the draftsman for the New Hampshire Criminal Code (1973). He is presently completing similar assignments in Maine and Vermont. He is author of many scholarly articles and several books, including the leading casebook on juvenile justice and *Science and Justice,* a study of the impact of the scientific revolution on the Massachusetts witchcraft trials.

HERSCHEL H. FRIDAY, LL.B., is a partner in the Little Rock, Arkansas, law firm of Smith, Williams, Friday, Eldredge and Clark and the parent of a mentally retarded child. Mr. Friday has been involved with the development of virtually all legislation pertaining to mental retardation services in Arkansas since 1957. Mr. Friday has served as a regional vice president, president elect, and president of the AARC.

PAUL R. FRIEDMAN, LL.B., is Managing Attorney of the Mental Health Law Project, and has served as counsel for plaintiffs or amici in a number of cases concerning the rights of the mentally handicapped, including *Souder v. Brennan* and *Dale v. State of New York.* He is author of *Mental Retardation and the Law,* a quarterly report on the status of current court cases published by the President's Committee on Mental Retardation, and co-author of *Legal Rights of the Mentally Handicapped.* He is in training as a research candidate at the Baltimore-District of Columbia Institute for Psychoanalysis and is a member of the American Psychological Association's Commission on Behavior Modification and the Department of Labor's Advisory Committee on Sheltered Workshops.

KENNETH D. GAVER, M.D., is a psychiatrist by training and has served as state mental health and mental retardation director in Oregon, Ohio, and currently, Texas.

THOMAS K. GILHOOL, M.A., LL.B., is Chief Counsel of the Public Interest Law Center of Philadelphia (A bar association sponsored law firm) and director of its Project on the Handicapped, the Elderly and the Law. He was counsel for plaintiffs in *Pennsylvania Association for Retarded Children v. Commonwealth of Pennsylvania.* Mr. Gilhool was the first chairman of the Advisory Committee to the National Center on Law and the Handicapped, and reporter of the Juvenile Justice Standards volume on handicapped children for the American Bar Association-Institute of Judicial Administration.

LINDA L. GLENN, Ph.D., is Executive Director of the Eastern Nebraska Community Office of Retardation (ENCOR). As director of ENCOR, she operated one of the most innovative and comprehensive community based programs for the mentally retarded in the country, serving approximately 1400 clients in a wide array of dispersed and integrated programs, utilizing over ninety facilities in the eastern Nebraska area. She is the co-author of the widely accepted and utilized *Program Analysis of Service Systems: A Quantitative Evaluation of Human Services.* She has testified as an expert witness in many of the leading right to treatment and right to habilitation cases. At twenty-six, she has already achieved notice in *Who's Who in American Women,* as Nebraska's Outstanding Woman of the Year, and as one of the Ten Outstanding Young Women of America for 1974.

BOB GOLTEN, LL.B., has spent the last four years working with the Public Defender Service in Washington, D.C., where he initiated, developed, and managed a mental health division for the public defender. His treatise on the "Role of the Defense Lawyer in the Criminal Commitment Process" appeared in the Spring, 1972, issue of the *American Criminal Law Quarterly.*

DENNIS E. HAGGERTY, LL.B., is in the general practice of law in Philadelphia, Pennsylvania and has a sixteen-year-old retarded son. He conducted an investigation of one of the largest state schools and hospitals in the United States and recommended institution of the first right to education suit *(Pennsylvania Association for Retarded Children v. Commonwealth of Pennsylvania)* in federal court. Mr. Haggerty was subsequently appointed by the court as master to oversee the implementation of the consent decree entered as a result of that suit. He has represented many mentally retarded individuals and has served for eight years as a consultant to the President's Committee on Mental Retardation. He was the first president of the Philadelphia Bar Association's Committee for the Mentally Retarded and the Law, the first such committee in the United States, and later was appointed the first co-chairman of the American Bar Association Family Law Section's Committee on the Mentally Retarded and the Law.

CHARLES HALPERN, LL.B., is Executive Director, Council for Public Interest Law. He was previously the director of the Center on Law and Social Policy and a founder of and attorney with the Mental Health Law Project. Mr. Halpern was plaintiff's counsel in *Rouse v. Cameron,* the first right to treatment case, and was counsel to amici curiae professional and citizen organizations in *Wyatt v. Stickney.* He has written widely on the right to treatment and habilitation.

H. CARL HAYWOOD, Ph.D., is Kennedy Professor of Psychology at George Peabody College for Teachers and Director of its John F. Kennedy Center for Research on Education and Human Development, one of twelve national mental retardation research centers. He is also Professor of Neurology at Vanderbilt University, editor of the *American Journal of Mental Deficiency,* and a member of the Institute of Medicine of the National Academy of Sciences.

MELVIN D. HECKT, J.D., is a Vice President of Richards, Montgomery, Cobb & Bassford, a Minneapolis law firm. He is also a member of the President's Committee on

Mental Retardation, a regional vice president of the National Association for Retarded Citizens, and past president of the Minneapolis and Minnesota Associations for Retarded Citizens. Mr. Heckt has prepared in excess of 200 estate plans for parents of retarded citizens and has represented retarded citizens, their parents, and service organizations in court and before many governmental agencies. His eldest of six children, Janice, is mentally retarded.

STANLEY HERR, LL.B., has been co-counsel in some of the major court cases affecting the retarded citizen's access to habilitation services. As a public interest lawyer in Washington, he participated in several major right to habilitation and right to education cases and wrote and lectured on the rights of children and the mentally handicapped. In 1973 he received the National Association for Retarded Citizens' Rosemary F. Dybwad Award to study recent European experiences in implementing habilitation programs. A Joseph P. Kennedy, Jr., Fellow, he is now at Balliol College, Oxford working on a comparative legal study of some commitment and treatment rights of the retarded.

ROBERT H. JOHNSON is in private practice with the firm of Fitzwilliam, Memering, Stumbos & DeMers in Sacramento, California, specializing in litigation. As a trial attorney for the U.S. Department of Justice, he directed the extensive FBI investigation of Partlow State School in Alabama, and represented the United States at the subsequent trial and appeal of *Wyatt v. Stickney,* the first case to hold that civilly committed mentally retarded citizens have a right to habilitation.

LAWRENCE A. KANE, JR., J.D., is in the private practice of law in Cincinnati, Ohio and is the parent of a retarded child. He is a member of the President's Committee on Mental Retardation and chairman of the committee's Workgroup on Law and Ethics. Mr. Kane also serves as co-chairman of the American Bar Association Family Law Section's Committee on the Mentally Retarded and the Law and as vice-chairman of the Board of Directors of the National Center on Law and the Handicapped.

MICHAEL KINDRED, J.D., M. Comp. L., is Associate Dean at The Ohio State University College of Law and Chief of Legal Affairs of the university's Nisonger Mental Retardation Center. He is project director, editor, and contributor in this volume. He is also the director of a project at Ohio State that provides on-going research and technical assistance in the area of developmental disabilities and the law and has been instrumental in drafting and securing passage of major mental retardation reform legislation in Ohio.

JOHN R. KRAMER, LL.B., is Associate Professor of Law at Georgetown University Law Center in Washington, D.C. where he teaches and helps run the civil litigation clinic. As executive director of the National Council on Hunger and Malnutrition in the United States, he has led the food program lobby and been responsible for drafting most of the major changes in the food stamp and child nutrition laws during the past five years.

KAREN LEBACQZ, Ph.D., is Professor of Ethics at the Pacific School of Religion, a member of the National Commission for the protection of Human Subjects of Biomedical and Behavioral Research and co-founder of the Joint Program in Bioethics, Pacific School of Religion and the University of California Medical School, San Francisco.

LEOPOLD LIPPMAN is the author of *Attitudes Toward the Handicapped: A Comparsion Between Europe and the United States* (1972) and is co-author (with I. Ignacy Goldberg) of *Right to Education: Anatomy of the Pennsylvania Case and Its Implications for Exceptional Children* (1973). Since the early 1950's Mr. Lippman has served successively as an executive of the Washington Association for Retarded Children, executive secretary of the California Study Commission on Mental Retardation, coordinator of mental retardation programs for California, and director of services for the mentally and physically handicapped in New York City.

NORVAL MORRIS, Ph.D., is Dean of the University of Chicago Law School and Julius Kreeger Professor of Law and Criminology. He previously held faculty positions in Australia and England as well as at several American universities. He has served on numerous federal and state governmental and scholarly councils and commissions, as well as on several United Nations committees. Dr. Morris is a fellow of the American Academy of Arts and Sciences and the author of *The Habitual Criminal* (1951), *Studies in Criminal Law* (with Colin Howard, 1964), *The Honest Politician's Guide to Crime Control* (with Gordin Hawkins, 1970), three other books, and over a hundred articles and chapters of books. His most recent book, *The Future of Imprisonment,* was published by the University of Chicago Press in October, 1974.

VIRGINIA DAVIS NORDIN, LL.B., is a member of the bars of California, Michigan, and New York. She has served as a legal consultant to the Institute for the Study of Mental Retardation and Related Disabilities at the University of Michigan and to the President's Committee on Mental Retardation.

DOLORES NORLEY, M.P.A., is a Fellow of the American Association on Mental Deficiency; Special Advisor to the President's Committee on Mental Retardation; Chairman, International Relations Committee, National Association for Retarded Citizens; and Lecturer and Instructor, Florida Atlantic University. She developed a curriculum for police training in recognition and handling of retarded citizens and is now training police and trainers of police in the United States and Canada.

DAVID PENROD, J.D., is an attorney in Harrisonburg, Virginia and an Adjunct Professor of Law at the Washington and Lee University, College of Law.

MONROE E. PRICE, LL.B., is Professor of Law at the University of California, Los Angeles. He has been a member of the Citizens Advisory Council to the Director of the Department of Mental Hygiene of the state of California. He was law clerk to Mr. Justice Potter Stewart and a special assistant to Secretary of Labor W. Willard Wirtz.

PHILIP ROOS, Ph.D., has been the Executive Director of the National Association for Retarded Citizens since 1969. He previously held positions as associate commissioner for mental retardation in the New York State Department of Mental Hygiene and as superintendent of the Austin (Texas) State School. He has also had considerable clinical, administrative, and academic experience in the fields of mental retardation and mental health. He has published and lectured extensively in these areas and has given expert testimony in major litigation on behalf of mentally retarded persons.

DAVID ROSEN, M.S., is Director of the Macomb-Oakland Regional Center in Macomb County, Michigan. He has held positions in both residential and community care programs and has served on many national commissions and organizations concerned with the provisions of services to the mentally retarded. As president of the American Association on Mental Deficiency, Mr. Rosen was an expert witness in a number of right to treatment and involuntary labor suits in 1973–74.

STERLING L. ROSS, JR., J.D., is in private practice in San Francisco specializing in the legal problems of the handicapped. During his third year of law school he worked as the legal consultant for the Institute for the Study of Mental Retardation and Related Disabilities at the University of Michigan, co-authoring Ross, DeYoung, and Cohen, ''Confrontation: Special Education and the Law,'' *Exceptional Children,* September, 1971. He then worked for two years as staff attorney and legislative advocate for the California Association for the Retarded.

DAVID J. ROTHMAN, Ph.D., is Professor of History at Columbia University and Senior Research Associate at the Center for Policy Research. He is a member of the boards of directors of the New York Civil Liberties Union and the Mental Health Law Project. He is the author of *The Discovery of the Asylum* (1971), which received the Albert J. Beveridge Award from the American Historical Association.

BEVERLY A. ROWAN, J.D., is Director of Advocacy at the Joseph P. Kennedy, Jr. Foundation and Associate Research Scholar at the Kennedy Institute for the Study of Human Reproduction and Bioethics at Georgetown University. Ms. Rowan has written and lectured extensively on law and mental retardation and has developed a comprehensive legislative package on behalf of the mentally retarded.

HERMAN SCHWARTZ, LL.B., is Professor of Law at the State University of New York at Buffalo and is an expert on wiretapping and prisoners' rights. He was one of the founders of the ACLU Prisoners' Rights Project and is now a member of the steering committee of the National Prison Project of the American Civil Liberties Foundation. He has personally handled numerous prisoners' rights cases and has written widely in the field.

HUGH J. SCOTT, Ph.D., is currently Dean and Professor in the Division of Programs in Education at Hunter College. Dr. Scott served from 1970–1973 as superintendent of public schools in the District of Columbia. His research findings, related to the problems confronted by and the contributions made by black superintendents, were published in 1975 by Howard University Press.

THOMAS J. SHAFFER, J.D., is Dean of the Law School and Professor of Law at the University of Notre Dame. His publications include: *The Planning and Drafting of Wills and Trusts* (1972), *Death, Property, and Lawyers* (1970), *Problems and Readings in Property Settlement* (1965), and *Readings on the Common Law* (1967). He is an elected member of the American Law Institute, a fellow of the American College of Probate Counsel, and advisory editor of *Life Threatening Behavior* (the official publication of the American Association on Suicidology), the *Journal of Legal Education,* and the *American Journal of Jurisprudence.*

EUNICE KENNEDY SHRIVER has since 1957 been Executive Vice President of the Joseph P. Kennedy, Jr., Foundation, established in 1946 by the Kennedy family to deal with the multiple problems of the mentally retarded. Under her leadership the foundation has extended its activities into the field of medical ethics, supporting major institutes at Georgetown and Harvard Universities.

PETER SIMMONS, LL.B., is Dean of the Rutgers Law School and Visiting Professor of Urban Planning. He served the state of Ohio while on the faculty at The Ohio State University College of Law as chairman of the Land Use Planning Committee, Governor's Housing and Community Development Advisory Commission and the city of Columbus, Ohio, as chairman of the Development Code Advisory Commission and the Housing Code Advisory Commission.

FRANKLIN C. SMITH, Ph.D., is Chariman of the Board of George V. Stennes and Associates, Consulting Actuaries, and Lecturer in Actuarial Science at the University of Minnesota. He is the author of *Mathematics of Finance* and several papers in actuarial journals. He has been active in the Associations for Retarded Citizens and has been chairman of the Insurance Committee of the national Association for many years.

MICHAEL S. SORGEN, LL.B., is Assistant Professor at Hastings College of Law in San Francisco. He is author of *State, School and Family* (1973) a casebook-treatise on law and education which includes a comprehensive overview of legal problems in the education of the handicapped. Professor Sorgen is also attorney for the plaintiffs in a leading case on IQ testing and special class placement of the educable mentally retarded.

ROBERT A. SPRECHER has been a United States Court of Appeals judge for the seventh circuit since 1971. He wrote the opinion in *Lessard v. Schmidt,* 349 F.Supp. 1078 (E.D. Wis. 1972) (three-judge court), vacated and remanded on other grounds, 414 U.S. 473

(1974), judgment re-entered by three-judge court, 379 F.Supp. 1376 (E.D. Wis. 1974), vacated on procedural grounds, 95 S.Ct. 1943 (1975), noted 87 Harv. L. Rev. 1190 (1974) and 68 Nw. U.L. Rev. 585 (1973).

PETER L. STRAUSS, LL.B., is Professor of Law at Columbia University. He previously served as law clerk to Chief Judge David Bazelon of United States Court of Appeals for the District of Columbia and to Supreme Court Justice William J. Brennan, Jr., taught penal law at the Haile Selassie I University Law School in Ethiopia, and was an assistant to the Solicitor General of the United States.

LINDA TARR-WHELAN is the Director of Program Development for the American Federation of State, County and Municipal Employees (AFSCME) which represents 170,000 workers in the health field. She serves as assistant to the president of AFSCME for development of health policy. Ms. Tarr-Whelan is a registered nurse and holds a master's degree in administration of nursing education.

PATRICIA M. WALD, LL.B., is a member of the Mental Health Law Project and has served as co-counsel for plaintiffs in *Mills v. Board of Education* (D.C. right to education for handicapped children) and *Souder v. Brennan* (right of institutional working mental patients to coverage under Fair Labor Standards Act), and counsel for amicus in *Morales v. Turman* (rights of institutionalized delinquent minors, including the mentally retarded). Ms. Wald is a former member or consultant to numerous national commissions and is the author of *Bail in the United States* (1964, with Daniel Freed), *Law and Poverty* (1965), and *Dealing with Drug Abuse* (1972, with Peter Hutt). She is also a member of the ABA-IJA Juvenile Justice Standards Project.

WOLF WOLFENSBERGER, Ph.D., is Professor at Syracuse University, Division of Special Education and Rehabilitation and has had diverse involvements with handicapped and devalued groups. He has worked in public institutions for the disordered, held administrative, research, and training positions in institutions for the mentally retarded, and worked as a researcher and planner in mental retardation, and as a consultant to services for the blind. He is the originator of the citizen advocacy schema, which is now operational in approximately one hundred locales across North America.

J. JERRY WOOD, SR., J.D., is Assistant United States Attorney for the middle district of Alabama and represented the defendants in *Wyatt v. Stickney*. Previously, he was administrator for the department of surgery and assistant to the chief of staff at the University of Alabama Medical Center in Birmingham and the counsel and lobbyist for the Alabama State Medical Association.

VINCENT J. ZICCARDI, LL.B., is Chief Defender of the Defender Association of Philadelphia. Because he sees the office of the defender as having the responsibility to represent all persons whose liberties are in danger, a full-time forensic psychiatrist was added to the Philadelphia defender staff to assist in criminal, juvenile, and involuntary commitment cases.

Foreword

Among certain American Indians, it was considered rude to ask an individual, "Who are you?" or "What is your name?" The reply was both a criticism and a revelation. The Indian would answer, "I am a person." The nameless mentally retarded people of the world give us this same response. And then we are forced to ask ourselves, "What *is* a person?", for mentally retarded individuals are always among the first to have their human rights denied, the first to be experimented upon, to be placed in institutions, to be sterilized, to be allowed to wither, and even to be destroyed.

To restore personhood to the mentally retarded citizen, we must establish a truly comprehensive "Bill of Rights" for them, because even now the rights of mentally retarded citizens are under attack all over the nation.

There has been legislation, for example, considered by the Florida legislature to permit physicians in state hospitals to allow children with Down's syndrome and severely retarded persons to die simply by withholding life-sustaining procedures and drugs. The author of the bill says that of 1,500 severely retarded patients in Florida institutions, 90 percent should be permitted to die. "Why not let them die," urge proponents of such legislation, "when the money for their care could be used for such good social purposes." "Five billion dollars could be saved over the next fifty years in Florida," they argue, "if the mongoloids in our state institutions were permitted to succumb to pneumonia." The sponsor of this bill calls it "Death with Dignity"—by which he means, of course, death with dignity for the mentally retarded person. I suggest that such legislation would mean death without dignity for the moral principles upon which this country has been founded.

This is not, of course, a brand new idea. A number of years ago, a similar plan was put into effect. Doctors were told, "Patients whose illness, according to the most critical application of human judgment, is incurable, can be granted release by euthanasia." This plan was proposed in 1939, and it was signed, Adolph Hitler. Over 100,000 people died as a result of those simple instructions. The authority to kill was expanded to include millions of patients suffering from mental retardation, schizophrenia, epilepsy, encephalitis, and a social disease called Judaism.

Five days prior to the President's Committee's conference from which this volume derives, a helpless mongoloid infant was denied life-saving assistance in a hospital in Decatur, Illinois. The events are becoming tragically familiar. The film "Who Should Survive?", produced by the Kennedy Foundation, related a similar incident that occurred several years ago at the Johns Hopkins Hospital. This film has been shown all over the nation. Newspapers have editorialized on it. The general consensus has been one of horror and repugnance. And yet history has repeated itself, as it is repeating itself day after day in hospitals throughout the country.

These cases are just one more proof that as a nation we have failed in our basic human obligations to the mentally retarded citizen. A "Bill of Rights," human and legal, for mentally retarded citizens is essential. The first right is the right to life itself. The mentally retarded person deserves the right to life, the right to be born, as much as any other human being. While even the right to life is not an absolute right, the principle must remain: The retarded citizen's right to life must be equal to that accorded any other person.

Second, the retarded child must have the right to an education in his or her own community. Class action suits around the nation have established that retarded children—even the severely retarded ones—have a right to education and rehabilitation services. Nonetheless, hundreds of thousands of retarded children are still denied an adequate education. They cannot wait for class action suits in every state. Just as we have a Civil Rights Act to prevent discrimination according to race, color, national origin, or sex, so Congress should pass an Equal Opportunity Act to prevent discrimination based on intellect.

Third, the parent of a mentally retarded child must have the right to a choice of care within the community. In most states, the only available residential placement outside the home is a non-competitive state institution that is large, crowded, far away, old, expensive, lacking education, rehabilitative, and spiritual opportunities and offers little chance for a person to exit into a fruitful life in the community.

Mildly retarded individuals, especially the young, fare far better in the community. Commitment, voluntary or involuntary, of the mildly retarded person is totally unjustified and leads to a serious loss of the common civil and human rights that can be fully appreciated by them. By such action, often without due process, the rights to vote, to marry, to execute a will, to drive, and to make contracts are affected. If the mentally retarded resident of an institution inherits property, the institution can acquire that property to defray the cost of keeping him institutionalized. Even more frightening, the mentally retarded person may have no appeal mechanism, and in many cases may be institutionalized without review for a lifetime.

Fourth, the mentally retarded adult should have the right to work. Mentally retarded persons can do many productive jobs even in our highly industrialized and technological society. The emphasis should be to fit the job to the person and not the person to the job.

Fifth, the mentally retarded citizen should have the right to a sexual and family life. Dr. George Tarjan, a foremost psychiatrist in the field of mental retardation, has pointed out that retarded people are always the first people to be thought of as "surplus" by society, and the most available for "social action" and eugenic experimentation. Indeed, surgical sterilization of mentally retarded persons is permitted by statute in many states, and in most of these states it can be performed without the patient's consent.

On the question of who should and who should not be allowed to have children, there is no equation between high IQ and desirable parental traits or low IQ and undesirable ones. Tests of intelligence are constructed for predicting success or failure in school, not in society. Surely by now we should have learned not to confuse smartness with wisdom or humanity. Or have we learned this lesson?

We have learned that the age old notions about sex and parenthood among mentally retarded citizens must be reexamined. A recent study at a state institution where the sexes were allowed to mix freely found that the mentally retarded residents were in general more responsible, more puritanical, and more sensitive to rules of proper conduct in sexual matters than other individuals. The report stated, "The extra-marital conception rate of our women patients would have given pride to any college president or high school principal."

Sixth, mentally retarded people must have equal protection of the laws. When a retarded person is involved or suspected of involvement in crime, no statutes exist that deny him rights accorded to every other citizen. Yet, in practical operation, the mentally retarded offender is frequently deprived of these rights. The fact is that mentally retarded people are three times as common in the population of federal prisons as in the general population. Such data have sometimes been erroneously interpreted to mean that retardation is characterized by criminal tendencies. In fact, however, these statistics show that the mentally retarded individual is less able than others to protect his legal rights. In a recent study it was shown that mentally retarded suspects, at the time of arrest, have far more frequently waived their constitutional rights against making self-incriminatory statements. They are easily cajoled into confession. They waive the right to counsel and to jury trial far more often than the criminal with average intelligence. Likewise, reduction of the charge is far less frequent with the mentally retarded person. It is infrequent for a judgment or sentence against a mentally retarded defendant to be appealed.

We are finally learning that, with the proper help and by any standards of worth, mentally retarded individuals have great value to our society. In their naive innocence, they believe us when we talk about love, about trust, and about sharing. In their striving to be what they think we are, they are devoted, hardworking, and trusting. In the courage with which they face their handicaps and disabilities, they inspire us all to a new standard of achievement.

It is the obligation of each of us to value and nurture above all the moral principles which teach us that all human beings are equal in law, that those who have the most gifts have the greatest responsibility, that indeed those with the least must be entitled to the most in a compassionate society, and that every human being must count as one whole person.

EUNICE KENNEDY SHRIVER

Executive Vice-President
Joseph P. Kennedy, Jr., Foundation

Preface

The title of this landmark volume is testimony to recent dramatic changes in the law and in public attitudes toward mentally retarded individuals. Today we speak of *citizens* with the rights that accompany citizenship. Until a very few years ago, we spoke euphemistically of all mentally retarded individuals as "children," without regard to their age, abilities, and individual potential. Not long ago, the mentally retarded were treated as objects—and referred to with such derogatory labels as idiots, imbeciles, and feebleminded.

In *The Mentally Retarded Citizen and the Law* over sixty academic and practicing lawyers, educators, mental retardation professionals, social scientists, and concerned citizens explore the legal and social changes that must take place before this concept of citizenship can become reality for all mentally retarded individuals. Too many thousands of these citizens are still housed in giant warehouses, monuments to a bankrupt philosophy. In too many of these inhumane places, the only schooling is still in the lessons of brutality and despair. Too many thousands of mentally retarded individuals are excluded from our systems of "universal" public education. And too many thousands more are placed needlessly in segregated classes and buildings, denying both mentally retarded students and their nonretarded peers the advantages of interacting and learning from each other.

The recent critical reappraisal of legal discrimination against the mentally retarded has been a joint effort. Major credit goes to those parents who after World War II founded the National Association for Retarded Children (now Citizens), with its state and local affiliates. The American Bar Association has played an important role through publication in 1961 and 1972 of *The Mentally Disabled and the Law* and establishment of the Family Law Sub-section on Mental Retardation and the Law and the ABA Commission on the Mentally Disabled. The Association's sponsorship of the National Center on Law and the Handicapped at the University of Notre Dame underscores its commitment. Through these and other organizations, many dedicated men and women have fought for the human dignity and civil rights of mentally retarded Americans. Many of those involved in this struggle have cooperated to create this volume.

The President's Committee on Mental Retardation takes great pride in its sponsorship of *The Mentally Retarded Citizen and the Law*. Intense presidential interest in the rights of mentally retarded citizens has been demonstrated now over four administrations. The President's Panel on Mental Retardation, established by President John F. Kennedy in 1961, was a decisive act on behalf of mentally retarded citizens. In a real sense this volume is the legal profession's response to the work of that panel. The intervening decade has brought great judicial, legislative, and social reform. It is, therefore, only fitting that the President's Committee, successor to the original President's Panel, should provide leadership and support in this reexamination of the legal rights of mentally retarded citizens.

The citizenship of mentally retarded individuals in America has now been recognized. The battle to ensure respect for all the rights inherent in this citizenship will be long and difficult.

"We have miles to go—and promises to keep." The volume discusses some constitutional promises now fulfilled and others still to keep.

LAWRENCE A. KANE, JR.

Chairman, Law and Ethics Work Group
President's Committee on Mental Retardation

Acknowledgments

Primary acknowledgment for inspiration in the production of this volume must go to the mentally retarded citizens and their families who have compelled professional and public recognition of the developmental potential of mentally retarded individuals and of the systematic discrimination, restriction, and exclusion to which they have been subject.

This book represents a massive collaborative effort among many of the legal and non-legal professionals who have played, and continue to play, key roles in the drive to guarantee the legal rights of the mentally retarded. To these contributors the editors extend their appreciation. Their collaboration here stands as a signal of their dedication to equal treatment under the law for all persons. It should be noted that both contributors and editors have foregone any royalty rights for this work in order to permit its widest possible distribution.

The initial conference and this volume would not have been possible without the financial assistance and support of the President's Committee on Mental Retardation and the Office of the Secretary of the U.S. Department of Health, Education, and Welfare under contract number HEW (OS) 73-113 and the logistical support of The Ohio State University and its Research Foundation.

Dozens of individuals have provided vital assistance in this undertaking. Special acknowledgment, however, must be made to Lawrence A. Kane, Jr., who served as initiator and chairperson of the May 1973 President's Committee conference on the Mentally Retarded Citizen and the Law. His critical role in the production of this volume is reflected in his authorship of the preface. Staff members of the President's Committee on Mental Retardation, the Department of Health, Education, and Welfare, and The Ohio State University provided services beyond the requirements of their positions both in the development of these materials as well as in the organization of the conference of which they are a product. Wives and families of editors and contributors have given of their time, and in many cases of their talents as well, in this production. Requiring special mention are the student assistants who worked with the editors on the tedious jobs of honing and cutting text and verifying the accuracy of citations. Directing a team of students at The Ohio State University were Robert Guehl, Daniel Sharpe, and Anthony Lucia. Working with them were Michael Greenberg, Douglass Lee Hayman, Phil Mullin, Fred Green, Bernard J. Schaeff, Gerard Lobosco, Roy Lowenstein, and J. William Sikora. Talbot Young worked as an assistant to Dean Shaffner at the Notre Dame University Law School, and Janice Siegel assisted Dr. Cohen at the University of Michigan.

The many drafts through which this volume has passed have been typed by Martha Brown and E. Ann Levine, without whose tireless devotion this work would not exist.

To all of these, and the many other individuals who have contributed to this work and to the conference from which it grew, we acknowledge our debt and gratitude. THE EDITORS

Introduction

The President's Committee on Mental Retardation convened a conference in 1973 to review recent progress in ensuring the legal rights of mentally retarded citizens and to consider the practical and conceptual obstacles to full realization of those rights. The conference brought together legal and mental retardation professionals who have played key roles in the drive to guarantee all mentally retarded individuals full constitutional protection. This volume is the product of that conference. A major legal paper was prepared in each of twenty-two areas affecting the rights of the retarded; for each area at least two conference participants presented reactions to the papers. Following the conference, papers were refined in light of the reaction comments and conference discussion. Each of the twenty-two principal papers appear in a chapter of this volume. Some reactors' contributions have been completely incorporated in the principal papers; others could not be easily accommodated within the principal papers and so are presented as discrete parts of the appropriate chapters.

The Mentally Retarded Citizen and the Law is intended as a resource work for judges, attorneys, law students, guardians, advocates, and others concerned with the legal rights of mentally retarded citizens. It expands considerably the total literature available on this vital subject. Further information on related legal problems and on mental retardation can be pursued through the references cited herein. The President's Committee on Mental Retardation publishes a periodical which provides extensive information on new cases as they are decided; it is entitled *Mental Retardation and the Law: A Report on the Status of Current Court Cases.*

Recent programs in ensuring the legal rights of mentally retarded citizens has resulted from increased scientific understanding of mental retardation and demonstration that ancient legal restrictions are inconsistent with the factual and conceptual elements of this scientific understanding. Further progress is dependent upon effective communication between lawyers and mental retardation professionals. In every profession, a special form of language evolves that permits members of the group to communicate precisely and easily with others within the group. This professional jargon, however, also can segregate the group from other professions. Editors for this volume were chosen to include both lawyers and an individual with extensive experience in mental retardation, and a major goal of the editors was to lower the language barriers between the lawyers and mental retardation professionals. *The Mentally Retarded Citizen and the Law* should assist lawyers and judges in communicating with personnel in the mental retardation field and help mental retardation professionals better understand, utilize, and communicate with attorneys.

Misconceptions about mental retardation are still common in this society, and these misconceptions are shared by many lawyers, legislators, and judges. Too often legislative and judicial decisions still reflect inappropriate and inaccurate stereotypes and beliefs. A prerequisite to sustained recognition of the legal rights of mentally retarded citizens is increased public and professional education to foster a more realistic view of the great developmental potential of retarded individuals. The legal profession tends to look to medicine, and especially psychiatry, for solutions to mental retardation problems although for almost 90 percent of the individuals labeled mentally retarded medicine plays no greater role than among the general population. This tendency reflects an inaccurate perception of mental retardation as a sickness residing within the mentally retarded individual. Mental retardation is too often perceived as an illness, a problem that the individual has; with appropriate programing and treatment, therefore, the individual can be treated and may be cured. Unfortunately, this view fails to recognize the role of the physical and social environment—an environment that can exacerbate, or even create, the problems of a person labeled mentally retarded.

The interrelationship of mental illness and mental retardation in legal development presents a particularly delicate problem. Scientifically and socially the two are distinct phenomena; nevertheless, both the general public and the legal literature often treat them as the same. In large part this is simply a result of ignorance, but other factors complicate the interrelationship somewhat. First, both mental retardation and mental illness carry the burden of centuries of prejudice, misunderstanding, and discrimination. Second, scientific development in both fields has emphasized the great variety of individuals that carry each of the labels, the potential of individuals to develop and be integrated with the rest of society, and the capacity of community services to obviate any need for restrictive institutionalization. And finally, many legal concepts in the two areas have developed in parallel. As different as the mentally ill and the mentally retarded are, each individual requires due process prior to restriction of liberty, access to general and specialized social services, effective advocacy, and many other legal rights that are taken for granted by other citizens and that have long been denied the mentally ill as well as the mentally retarded. It is essential to beware of old stereotypes and to be faithful to scientific fact in determining when a common legal approach is appropriate to the problems of these two very different categories of individuals.

Considerable attention was paid in the editing of this volume to conceptualizations of mental retardation. The mentally retarded have long been regarded and treated in literature and society as non-human objects; in this volume reference is to *mentally retarded citizens* and *mentally retarded individuals*. The term *retardate* is eschewed because of its almost inanimate connotations. Further, *average* instead of *normal* is used to describe the general population. To use *normal* in this context is to imply that mentally retarded individuals are abnormal. Based on the factor of intelligence, many of the people who read this volume are as normal or abnormal as the mentally retarded. It is merely that their scores vary from the average in the opposite direction. The more accurate categorization is *below average, average,* and *above average.* Language affects conceptualization. If the talk is about normal and abnormal, and if mentally retarded people are seen as abnormal, then it is much easier to deal with them as an undifferentiated group, perhaps somehow less than human. Thus, deprivation, isolation, and the denial of civil and human rights may not appear to be very important. In fact, the idea that mentally retarded persons are citizens with rights equal to those of other citizens may never come to mind. It is only when mentally retarded citizens are seen as more like than different from everyone else in society that appropriate programs of normalization can be instituted for even the most severely limited mentally retarded individuals.

The effect of labeling is critical in the area of mental retardation. When a person is told that another individual is mentally retarded, that person often develops different expectations for the so-called retarded individual, based merely on the label and not on the individual's performance. In time, the "mentally retarded" person begins to act in keeping with these expectations. There is ample evidence in the literature that this phenomenon occurs and that it is a significant factor in limiting the functioning of mentally retarded persons. In school, children perform in ways consistent with teachers' expectations. Examiners who do not expect good performances from poor black children do not get good performances from them. This is not to say that there are no individuals who require special services; it is to say that environmental factors and pre-set expectations have a major impact in determining who is regarded and ultimately labeled as mentally retarded.

By statistical definition, people perceived and labeled mentally retarded are those individuals who function intellectually at the lower 1 to 3 percent of the total population. Using this figure, current estimates for the United States indicate that there are over 6 million mentally retarded persons. Of these, about 250,000 are in institutions, primarily state homes or training schools for the mentally retarded. The definition of mental retardation accepted by the American Association on Mental Deficiency states: "Mental retardation refers to significantly subaverage intellectual functioning which manifests itself during the developmental period and is characterized by inadequacy in adaptive behavior." The mentally retarded population is often divided into several groups or levels based upon the severity of their retardation. The boundaries between mental retardation and average and between any of the levels of mental retardation are not clear or precise; different disciplines use different cutoff points; some words change in meaning, depending on the orientation of the professional using them.

A categorization system frequently used is mild, moderate, severe, and profound. For purposes of example, if a 3 percent incidence is used, this would mean there are 30 mentally retarded persons in a population of 1,000. Of the 30, approximately 25 would fall in the mild classification; the moderately retarded group would include 4; there would be only 1 in the severe or profound level.

The mildly mentally retarded group (25 of the 30 per 1,000) would include individuals who, in all likelihood, are identified by the public school system as retarded. Depending upon the general behavior of these individuals and the programs available in the school system, they may or may not be placed in special classes. Moreover, after completion of school, commonly they are absorbed into the total adult population and are not readily identifiable. These are individuals who generally work in competitive jobs and who, provided they have no physical or emotional problems in addition to their retardation, are able to lead independent lives.

The moderately mentally retarded (4 of the 30 per 1,000) are more limited in their capabilities. Generally, they will be identified before entering school and need special preschool and school programs. These children are most likely to be placed in classes for the trainable mentally retarded. As adults, they usually are able to live and work in the community, but need some type of sheltered environment or supervision in order to function optimally.

The severe and profound levels are represented by only 1 of the 30 individuals per 1,000. These individuals include many whose problems usually can be identified at, or shortly after, birth. Individuals functioning at this level are much more dependent, need more intensive programing, and frequently have physical problems in addition to the retardation in mental development.

Although the different degrees of mental retardation are generally recognized, there often are questions about how a particular individual should be classified and, even more importantly, an expanding debate over the value, if any, of classification. Classification usually provides little or no information of value in developing programs for the individual; that requires factual information about the person's strengths and specific weaknesses and the kinds of support that are most beneficial to the person. Unfortunately, classification systems are used widely and in many instances are written into law or regulations governing programs and services. Thus, it is important to reemphasize that the dividing lines between the various groupings and between the retarded and nonretarded populations are inexact.

There is no mention of IQ levels in this consideration of classification, as an IQ score is one of the least helpful facts available to the professional. It gives little information or guidance although it provides a basis for stereotyping; both work to the disadvantage of the person to be served. An IQ represents the score than an individual obtains on a specific test under certain standardized conditions. The score may predict performance in some areas, but it is of very limited value in most areas of human functioning. A parallel would be to time a person's running speed over a measured distance under specific conditions of temperature, humidity, and wind velocity and then to use the resultant time (score) to determine what the person would be permitted to do. Those with slow times would not be permitted to make contracts, marry, handle their assets, have children, or attend regular classes in public school.

Recent literature emphasizes the relationship of mental retardation to socioeconomic class. It has been noted that the more severely handicapped children who survive tend to be found in families from the middle and upper classes (perhaps because of the better medical care and treatment that is available to them), whereas a larger number of mildly retarded children tends to be found in families from low socioeconomic levels and poor environments. There is increasing evidence that a cause of this imbalance is the biases that are built into IQ tests and into examiners. Tests do not measure the cultural experience that many of these students bring to school. It is absurdly inappropriate to use an English language instrument to determine the intelligence of children for whom English is not their primary language; yet, even this is done. Moreover, the norm groups against which students are compared in intelligence tests have usually been drawn from white middle class populations. Thus, the racial and social class biases of this society have been incorporated into a testing, labeling, and placement system which ensures that a disproportionate number of minority group and economically deprived children will be identified, labeled, and placed as mentally retarded.

If there is anything that readers of this volume should keep in mind, it is that individuals labeled mentally retarded frequently are labeled so inappropriately. Moreover, irrespective of the accuracy of the label, individuals labeled mentally retarded require the same things that others in this society require: first, equal treatment under the law; second, a full enjoyment of their civil rights; third, individualized services designed to meet their specific needs and help ensure their functioning at an optimal level—an impossible objective if they are treated as part of an undifferentiated group; fourth, the provision of services accomplished insofar as possible within general service systems, rather than within specialized systems that highlight differences and isolate mentally retarded citizens from others; and fifth, full opportunities for normalizing experiences—that is, experiences in which the program helps them to become incorporated more fully into the general society.

Some interesting aspects of labeling can be seen in this society's provision of special services for mentally retarded citizens. The school system provides special services, and these services tend either to isolate children labeled as mentally retarded or to exclude such children from school services entirely. Exclusion is probably the highest order of proving that certain children cannot learn within a school setting. The inability to learn is demonstrated by labeling them and then keeping them out of school entirely; once having been excluded, they not surprisingly fail to benefit from school.

The health and mental health systems also have used labeling to ensure that people called mentally retarded are placed in isolated institutions where, historically, the length of stay has been determined by institutional needs rather than by the needs of the individual. Moreover, treatment frequently has not been available or has been deemed inappropriate merely because the person has been labeled mentally retarded.

The mentally retarded person, as any other person, can have physical and mental illnesses, educational and legal needs, and can respond and improve if provided the necessary services and treatment. Basically, as citizens mentally retarded individuals have the same needs as others in the general population, and when their potential is realized they contribute to the society. They need access to systems and services, and they have legal rights assuring this access.

The May 1973 conference sponsored by the President's Committee on Mental Retardation and this resulting volume have brought a diverse group of persons and ideas together. The views expressed in each of the contributions to this volume represents the position of its author and does not necessarily represent the viewpoint of sponsoring institutions, other contributors, or the editors. Nonetheless, readers will find many themes reiterated throughout the volume. These themes may be seen as providing some consensus on the legal rights of mentally retarded citizens.

PART ONE

Personal and Civil Rights of Mentally Retarded Citizens

CHAPTER 1

Basic Personal and Civil Rights

Editorial Introduction

Wald's paper in this first chapter provides a broad overview of rights that are taken for granted by most citizens of the United States and often casually denied to mentally retarded citizens. She groups these rights into two categories: personal rights (to marry, to have a family and sexual relationships, to bear and raise children) and civil and commercial rights (to contract, to work, to sue, to vote, to hold public office, to serve on a jury). These rights are seen as defining the very essence of citizenship and even of the human condition. Wald points out how cherished these rights are in general and how readily the society has denied most or all of them to others as soon as those others are labeled "incompetent" or "mentally retarded."

Wald argues that we have created a two-track legal system based on labels and that recent Supreme Court decisions, as well as common sense and humanity, require that we develop a much more sophisticated and individualized method of restricting these rights where restriction is necessary. Her basic proposition is that laws applicable particularly to the mentally retarded are almost never appropriate. Rather, society must decide generally whether it is willing to place restrictions on these basic personal and civil rights and then apply these restrictions even-handedly to all citizens, whether or not they are mentally retarded. For example, society should have general minimum child care qualifications; it is not appropriate, however, to apply to the mentally retarded a blanket prohibition on the raising of their own children. An individualized determination is required to establish that a given parent, mentally retarded

2

or not, is unfit to raise his children. Wald also argues that many of the rights she discusses fall in the constitutional category of "fundamental rights," so that a compelling state interest is required to justify whatever general restrictions are applied.

Some of the individual rights discussed in this overview are discussed in greater depth elsewhere in this volume. The theme of individualizing determinations of capabilities, rather than labeling, and the theme of providing mentally retarded citizens with equal treatment under general laws applicable to all citizens run throughout most of the volume.

Roos characterizes the traditional legal treatment of the mentally retarded, described by Wald, as exhibiting high levels of denial and supersimplification. Through these mechanisms, the law has condoned the concept of levels of humanity. Roos emphasizes, however, that social scientists must refine their skills of evaluation and prediction if individual legal restrictions are to be placed on basic rights and geared to the capabilities of the individual. Roos closes with a plea for improved communication among lawyers and other professionals in concept development and advocacy.

Haggerty adds strong support to Wald's analysis and notes the irony of having to make a special plea for all citizens to be treated equally under the law. He is highly critical of society's treatment of mentally retarded citizens and assigns a portion of the blame to the legal profession.

PRINCIPAL PAPER

PATRICIA M. WALD

THE PAST FEW YEARS has seen an explosion of litigation on behalf of mentally retarded persons. Most cases have focused on the minimum standards of humaneness and treatment that must be accorded persons who are institutionalized after someone has decided they cannot function in the community. More recently, cases have dealt with demands that all children with mental handicaps be provided an equal opportunity for a publicly supported education by the public school systems. With an increasing acceptance of the principle of "normalization," future litigation probably will involve rights to community services — health care, jobs, housing,

The author is indebted to Dr. Phil Roos, executive director of the National Association for Retarded Citizens, and Dennis Haggerty, Esq., Philadelphia attorney and consultant to the President's Committee on Mental Retardation, for the stimulation provided by their reaction comments. In addition, Erwin Friedman, Ph.D., director of the National Children's Center, Washington, D.C., has generously shared with me his insights and decades of experience in working with retarded persons in and out of institutions.

counseling, and, perhaps the ultimate right, the right not to be condemned to institutions through default of the community's responsibility to provide the support that is necessary for people with disabilities to survive and function. It also will deal with the legal, personal, and civil rights of these special people as they move out into the community.

At present, comparatively little is heard about the personal and civil rights of persons with mental disabilities: the rights to marry, to have and to raise children, to be brought up by one's own family, to make contracts and engage in business and trade, to hold a job, to vote, and to go to court.

These rights define a man or woman as a human being and they spell out the individual's obligations as a member of society. The rest of society perceives each individual as a functional or superfluous man or woman largely on the basis of whether he or she has the option to exercise these rights. Does he or she contribute to, or, in the words of Justice Holmes, "sap the strength of the State"?[1]

At first glance, it would seem that rights as important as these could be denied to no one except under extraordinary circumstances. And this indeed is the thesis of this paper: Only in rare instances do the mentally retarded require a special law or laws — a double-track legal system. This is true even though the aims of such a system are to help and protect. Legally and constitutionally, it must be presumed that all citizens are equal before the law. The Bill of Rights does not speak of competents and incompetents. A presumption in favor of a single-track legal system in the area of fundamental rights has been mandated by the Supreme Court in the last few decades. In a series of decisions the Court has carved out

> a right of personal privacy, or a guarantee of certain areas or zones of privacy [that] exist under the Constitution. [The] right has some extension to activities relating to marriage, . . . procreation, . . . contraception, . . . family relationships, . . . and child rearing and education.[2]

These basic relationships can be interfered with, according to the Court, only where there is a "compelling state interest,"[3] and even then, "legislative enactments must be normally drawn to express only the legitimate state interests at stake."[4] The test of "compelling" justification for denial of fundamental rights to any citizen is a stiffer one than that of showing mere "incompetence" according to normal standards of judgment in certain areas in human functioning. And it should be. Every human being should be presumed to have these rights unless someone can show an almost certain probability of disastrous consequences if he exercises them. If this becomes the test, moreover, it should apply to retarded and nonretarded citizens alike. An even more fundamental legal principle, which also demands a revision of the legal approach toward the mentally disabled, is that of individualization. There appears to be little legal justification for laws now on the books which

---

[1] Buck v. Bell, 274 U.S. 200, 207 (1927) (compulsory sterilization of institutionalized retarded woman upheld): "It would be strange if [society] could not call upon those who already sap the strength of the State for these lesser sacrifices, often not felt to be such by those concerned, in order to prevent our being swamped with incompetence. . . . Three generations of imbeciles are enough."
[2] Roe v. Wade, 410 U.S. 113, 152-53 (1973).
[3] *Id.* at 155.
[4] *Id.*

deny persons with mental disabilities an entire set of rights on one omnibus finding of "incompetency" or "mental retardation."[5]

Mental retardation covers a large human territory. In precise discussion, there must be concern about even using the term "retarded." Although no one has yet supplied a palatable substitute, too frequent use of a generic term leads to narrow thinking about a diverse group of persons. What may be said of some does not apply to all. Retarded people, like all people, vary enormously in talent, aptitude, personality, achievement, and temperament.[6] Like everyone else, some retarded individuals can do some things well, but not others. The point is a simple one. The law presently has no scientific or other basis on which to presume that any mentally retarded individual cannot do any or all things well. Only an individual's capacity to do specific things can be judged. Broadly worded laws are suspect when they place categorical disqualifications and restrictions on persons described as "imbeciles," "idiots," "feebleminded," "weakminded," "mentally deficient," "mentally defective," and "mentally retarded." So are judicial rulings based on unproven presumptions or "common knowledge" that persons with low IQs do or act or feel or react in a peculiar way. Each person's capacities must be judged individually before he can be denied rights of citizenship or humanity. This principle should apply to protective services and helping laws, as well as to the blatant denials of fundamental rights. There is a fundamental right to be left alone, a right to be allowed to succeed or fail,[7] a right to ignore gratuitous advice, a right not to tell every problem to the social worker, and a right not to answer the door. These components

---

[5] For a comprehensive listing of these laws, see THE MENTALLY DISABLED AND THE LAW (rev. ed. S. Brakel & R. Rock eds, 1971) [hereinafter cited as THE MENTALLY DISABLED].

[6] *See, e.g.*, Seeley, *The Law of the Retardate and the Retardation of the Law*, MENTAL RETARDATION: THE BULL. OF THE CANADIAN ASS'N. FOR RETARDED CHILDREN, June 1964, at 6-7:

> For the retardate, as he faces the law, raises clearly (bless him!) a number of vital issues which all men raise indeed but none so clearly and unambiguously. And the clarity of the retardate's case makes more difficult the evasion of the law-man's duty.
>
> The retardate poses the first issues by what he is. A retardate is merely (a) a person classified as belonging to that X% of the population who (b) do certain defined things worst, because (c) they *cannot* do them any better. I put the matter so because I want it to be clear (a) that it is a social classification we are dealing with, and not a "natural fact" like, say, the taste of salt; (b) that the X% is or can be 1%, 2%, 5% or 25% . . . according to social convenience; (c) that the social test depends on what things are socially defined (like schoolwork, say) to be peculiarly important; and (d) that the test that distinguishes those who *cannot* from those who *will not* is itself a very subtle social test. I want to be clear on these points because they are important to seeing clearly what is at stake. The whole question of who is or is not "retarded" depends on social desire (or "need") to classify in this way at all; it depends on the percentage arbitrarily chosen; on the tasks held to be sufficiently vital to justify the discrimination; and on the techniques accredited for distinguishing between "won'ts" and "can'ts."
>
> These points may seem primarily "philosophical" but, as with all well-taken points, they are pre-eminently practical. For "retardation" cannot be "wiped-out," because it is defined in relative terms. If all those presently defined as retarded were wished out of sight tomorrow, then society would simply turn its attention to a new group to whom it would give the same label, the same worry, the same treatment—or neglect.
>
> We must recognize the damage that is done by the defining process itself, in which a human being becomes very largely what he is said to be as a consequence of what is said about him.

[7] This critical "right to fail," which we all need in order ultimately to succeed, is emphasized by Clements, p.437-39, Chapter 14 of this volume. In other areas of the law such as narcotics addiction, we recognize this right in express statutory terms to prevent denials of further treatment when an addict slips during the early phases of treatment. *See* PROPOSED UNIFORM DRUG DEPENDENCE TREATMENT AND REHABILITATION ACT § 211 (1974).

of the right to privacy belong to, and are valued by, all people and must not be taken away from mentally retarded individuals without a particularized showing that they cannot cope by themselves without disastrous consequences. The retarded adult should not be thought of as an eternal child, subject to a lifelong application of *parens patriae*.

The law in its present form cannot cope adequately with the concepts of civil and legal rights of retarded persons in the community. The concept of rights of care and treatment for institutionalized persons is more familiar; retarded people can be dealt with more easily when they are safely tucked away. But when people move about freely in the community, society's notions of legal obligations and rights operate on basic assumptions about these people: They know and understand the consequences of what they do. They can explain to others what they intend to do. They act reasonably in their own interests, and it is morally right that they suffer the consequences of their actions. The law has formulated another set of assumptions for people who do not fit this profile. Such people are "outlaws."

In the past, when the law has had to deal with the reality that some people in the community cannot be held to the "reasonable man standard," its response has been to deny them the legal ability to negotiate the personal and commercial bargains of everyday life. There are other responses that might be tried instead: Laws might require a higher burden of care on those who deal with the mentally disabled commercially, instead of denying the disabled person his right to transact his business. A trend developing in some areas of regulatory law would require a seller to have responsible sensitivity to a buyer's potential for exploitation. Examples include mortgage frauds perpetrated on poor people, television advertising directed to children, and 24-hour optional cancellation periods for the victims of door-to-door salesmen. These rules suggest that the law can develop increased sensitivity to the problems of retarded citizens who live freely in the community.

The remainder of this paper will explore the application of legal counterparts of the "normalization" principle. These counterparts are: (1) a presumption that retarded persons can exercise all civil and personal rights, requiring the state to show a "compelling justification" of denial of these liberties, and (2) a requirement that before the right to be left alone or even to fail can be denied, or "help" compulsorily given, a citizen must be judged by reference to specific narrow and relevant behavior.

PERSONAL RIGHTS

Certainly in human terms the most basic social needs or "rights," if you will, of men and women are the freedom to love, marry, and procreate. Justice Goldberg, in *Griswold v. Connecticut*,[8] talked of the marital relationship as a fundamental area of privacy protected by the ninth amendment.[9] Hence, the state cannot, except

[8] 381 U.S. 479 (1965).
[9] *Id.* at 487 (Goldberg, J., concurring). *Cf.* Loving v. Virginia, 388 U.S. 1 (1967).

in the most unusual situations, say whether its citizens can marry, can have children, must practice birth control, or must undergo sterilization.[10] The state may not dictate to a pregnant woman whether or not she may have an abortion during the first trimester of her pregnancy.[11]

But what about mentally retarded people? Starting from a legal premise that a mentally retarded person is a citizen with the same constitutional rights as any other citizen, a compelling justification must be shown by the state before the retarded individual can be deprived of these or any fundamental rights.[12] The relevant issue then becomes: When does the state have a compelling rationale to deprive a man or woman of rights to privacy, to marriage, sexual intercourse, and procreation?

The Right to Marry

Over 40 states now have some restriction on the right to marry for those classified as "incapable of consenting for want of sufficient understanding," "imbeciles," persons of "unsound mind," "persons who cannot make a civil contract," "idiots," "under guardianship," "mental retardates," "feebleminded," "legally incompetent," "mental defectives," "mental deficients," or "weakminded." A few states allow incompetent women over the age of 45 or those who have been sterilized to marry.[13] It is not possible to know the real deterrent effect of such laws: How many persons with mental deficiencies are not identified as such and marry? How many are told they cannot marry and never challenge that ban? What is known is that official enforcement of such laws is haphazard. Only a few states require any positive proof of mental capacity or check records of incompetency registers before issuing a marriage license. It is often the courthouse clerk, presiding minister or judge, or interfering relative who must raise any question as to mental capacity. The question of whether the applicant has been adjudicated incompetent or institutionalized at any time does, however, appear on many applications to trigger further inquiry about those who answer truthfully. Annulment proceedings can also be brought variously by the incompetent person, his guardian or relative, or the "injured party."[14]

The critical policy question is who among those who function at a lower intellectual and social level present such an intolerable risk to themselves or their mates that they should be forbidden to marry? Some mental retardation experts

---

[10] *See* Eisenstadt v. Baird, 405 U.S. 438 (1972); Skinner v. Oklahoma, 316 U.S. 535 (1942).

[11] *See* Roe v. Wade, 410 U.S. 113 (1973).

[12] No one denies, for instance, that he or she must be given fifth amendment due process before liberty is taken away; that the equal protection of the laws guaranteed under the fourteenth amendment applies; or that he or she cannot be subjected to cruel and unusual punishment under the eighth amendment.

[13] THE MENTALLY DISABLED at 226-49

[14] OGG, SECURING THE LEGAL RIGHTS OF RETARDED PERSONS 10 (Public Affairs Pamphlet No. 492, 1973) cites two instances of retarded couples—one who answered "yes" on the form and were denied a license and one who answered "no" and against whom annulment proceedings were brought—who fought their cases in the courts and won the right to marry.

say categorically, none. Far more refined data than are available currently would be required to make a scientific differential diagnosis.[15] Accurate predictions cannot even be made about how normal people will function in a domestic liaison. One of every four marriages ends in divorce, and an unknown number of the rest generate misery, murder, mayhem, mental breakdowns, and child abuse. On what basis then can retarded persons be told that they cannot marry? Many marry successfully. Either data must be developed which show that some retarded persons (and specifically which ones) will almost certainly injure themselves or others disastrously by entering a marital relationship, or the state must keep its hands off.

If society's fears about retarded couples marrying are honestly examined, they probably will be seen only as intensified reflections of the general worries about marriages: that one party may be unduly influenced by others or by a superficial understanding of what marriage involves; that one partner may exploit or abuse the other; or that the couple may bring into the world children they are unable to care for or who have a high probability of physical or mental abnormality. How many of these fears can be shown as more justified in the case of the retarded?[16] The answer is not known and the data are not available to make confident predictions in the cases of retarded persons[17] any more than in other cases. Certainly the risks vary dramatically with *all* individuals, their partners, their relatives and friends, and their past histories. It must vary, also, with the preparation the individual has been given for learning, understanding, and observing what marriage and home-making entails. The prognosis might be different, too, with a couple who could not have or did not want to have children, or with one who has a degree of economic security or special support from the partners' families. It must be remembered that the poor and the physically handicapped can marry even though they are not self-

[15] *See, e.g.,* the conference comments of Wallace Babbington, that by focusing on a clinical population, we may have been collecting the wrong kind of field data in the past to help expand the rights of retarded persons in the community. Dr. Roos, in his remarks, also stressed that mental retardation experts need to develop better ways of predicting specific behavior on the part of retarded persons to aid their usefulness to courts and legislatures as experts; to answer questions about the "level of competence of particular individuals to engage in specified behavior," the "potentials of danger to self and to others." All this, he pointed out, in turn means an increased commitment to support more research since this kind of community functioning data is simply not available now, and unless bodies such as the National Institute for Neurological Diseases and the National Institute for Child Health and Human Development are supported, the potential source of such data will "atrophy."

[16] Dr. Roos made the telling point that we grossly overreact to the retarded, that there is "a tendency for society to project its own anxieties on a symbolic group—the fears of lack of impulse control and the fears of helplessness, dependency, and vulnerability."

[17] *See, e.g.,* Fotheringham, *The Concept of Social Competence as Applied to Marriage and Child Care in Those Classified as Mentally Retarded,* 104 CANADIAN MEDICAL ASS'N. J. 813, 814-15 (1971) [hereinafter cited as Fotheringham]:

Some evidence, of rather poor quality, indicates that many mildly retarded persons do marry and lead a self-supporting life in the community provided they are not faced with the stresses resulting from the care of children. Certain investigations have suggested that the retarded are frequently inadequate parents, that their offspring suffer neglect, deprivation and indifferent care, and that they have a high proportion of retarded offspring. Such evidence provides general background information but is of little assistance in arriving at decisions in a specific instance. Each individual should be considered on his own demonstrated competence. . . .

Many persons who might be judged incompetent of adequate child care may well be competent in the other responsibilities and duties of a husband or wife. With effective methods of reversible and non-reversible contraception available, why should such individuals be prevented from obtaining the many benefits of marriage other than child-rearing?

supporting; alcoholics and drug addicts can marry even if they are not thought to be suitable parents. Desperately needed are more empirical data on what kinds of special stress (if any) retarded couples encounter and what resources or help can alleviate such stresses.

Denial of the right to marry means condemning the individual to illicit hetero-sexual or homosexual relations or to enforced celibacy. There must at a minimum be an individual judicial determination that the physical danger to one or both of the parties from any marriage is a real and overwhelming one.[18] It is even legally dubious if potential inadequacies as parents should be a legitimate criteria for denying present marriage rights, since, if children do result, there is still time for intervention, if needed, on behalf of the child. The best answer to an unsuccessful marriage is the no-fault concept of divorce.

To sum up, in the present state of non-knowledge, there are no data to justify applying a different rule for marriage of retarded persons. If there are circumstances in which the state can show a compelling justification for interference, the same criteria and procedures should apply to all persons.

The Right to Sexual Freedom Outside Marriage

Marriage is not a prerequisite to sexual activity for either retarded or nonretarded people. And some retarded people as well as nonretarded people may not be likely candidates for marriage. Perhaps the hardest area to regulate is the right to sexual freedom, a right which for normal people has expanded physically by new methods of birth control and psychologically by legal and social acceptance of birth control and abortion. There is a new climate of sexual laissez faire among youth and many adults in this country. Consent — of adults and of adolescents above the age of statu-tory rape — is the passkey to sexual freedom.

What implications does this new freedom have for retarded persons? For decades, mentally retarded persons have been herded into institutions and sexually quarantin-ed to prevent indiscriminate coupling. We know the results: sexual frustration and homosexuality.[19] Society has invented a myth of the retarded person with abnormal or accentuated sexual drives and low impulse control who may either force his atten-

---

[18] The Supreme Court's recent decision in Stanley v. Illinois, 405 U.S. 645 (1972) would seem to demand an individual determination. There the Court nullified a state law that presumed an unmarried father was an unfit parent and required an individualized hearing on whether each such natural father was a fit parent before his children could be taken from him.

    [T]he Constitution recognizes higher values than speed and efficiency. . . .

        Procedure by presumption is always cheaper and easier than individualized determination. But when, as here, the procedure forecloses the determinative issues of competence and care, when it explicitly disdains present realities in deference to past formalities, it needlessly risks running roughshod over the important interests of both parent and child. It therefore cannot stand. 405 U.S. at 656-57.

[19] *See, e.g.,* Friedman, *Missing in the Life of the Retarded Individual — Sex,* 5 J. SPECIAL EDUC. 365 (1971). Dr. Friedman tells us "the maturing mentally handicapped child becomes increasingly bewildered and anxious in an environment filled with concrete and symbolic sexual stimuli. . . . [I]n clinical practice we often see the handicapped youth craving warmth, love and human closeness, which in most cases is provided only in connection with sexual exploitation." *Id.*

tions upon an inappropriate partner (a child, an unwilling recipient) or who may himself or herself be exploited by another. Aside from its fear of retarded offspring,[20] society has recoiled from the idea of sex without "intelligent consent."[21] Retarded adolescents often do not know how to make their genuine sexual needs known or how to deal with the needs themselves. They need instruction in legitimate techniques of sexual expression. Adolescents with mental handicaps have the same sexual needs as other youngsters. They are capable of being taught how to recognize and control them in acceptable ways. Boys can be taught not to thrust their attentions on inappropriate subjects. Girls can be taught to take precautions against unwanted pregnancy and how to repel unwanted overtures. Coed programs for mentally retarded youngsters are being carried on with low incidence of nonconsensual acting out.[22]

A retarded individual should be permitted normal freedom of association with the opposite sex. But he also needs to learn about the ethics and mechanics of sex. Behavior which appears uncontrolled or unduly seductive or aggressive will yield to humane conditioning techniques. However, extreme care must be exercised to insure that a single, socially determined norm is *not* applied to sexual behavior. Limited regimes of tranquilizing drugs may even prove useful at certain times. Girls can be taught to avoid unwanted pregnancies through sex education and birth control instruction and devices. In no case is sexual promiscuity a reason for institutionalization or sterilization of a retarded person if a similar sanction would not be taken against a nonretarded promiscuous person.

Failure to provide sex education in special education programs is a scandal. One recent survey of 53 mentally deficient children showed only 7 percent had received sex education at school, although 20 percent of their parents thought the children were having sexual adjustment difficulties.[23]

Several legal principles support the thesis that sex education and instruction must precede more drastic intrusions on a person's liberty, such as institutionalization or sterilization, and that institutionalization based on sexual misconduct must be directed toward its correction. The first principle is that no one's basic liberty or sexual freedom should be taken from him when a less drastic alternative, such as sex education, may solve the problem.[24] The second principle is that the length and nature of noncriminal commitment must be related to its purpose—institutionalization for sexual misconduct must be tied to an institutional program of education and behavioral modification that will lead to better sexual adjustment in

[20] In Buck v. Bell, 274 U.S. at 205-06, Justice Holmes noted:
  [the state alleged it was] supporting in various institutions many defective persons who if now discharged would become a menace but if incapable of procreating might be discharged with safety and become self-supporting with benefit to themselves and society. . . .
[21] Compare this with the (tacit) acceptance in many circles of using liquor to set up a woman for sexual exploitation.
[22] Conversation with Dr. Erwin Friedman, May 10, 1973.
[23] *See, e.g.,* Turner, *Attitudes of Parents Toward Their Child's Sexual Behavior*, J. SOCIAL HEALTH 548 (1970).
[24] *Cf.* Covington v. Harris, 419 F.2d 617 (D.C. Cir. 1969); Lake v. Cameron, 364 F.2d 657 (D.C. Cir. 1966); Wyatt v. Stickney, 344 F. Supp. 387, 344 F. Supp. 373 (M.D. Ala. 1972), 334 F. Supp. 1341, 325 F. Supp. 781 (M.D. Ala. 1971), *modified sub nom.* Wyatt v. Aderholt, 503 F.2d 1305 (5th Cir. 1974); Lynch v. Baxley, 386 F. Supp. 378, 392 (M.D. Ala. 1974). *See also* Chambers, Chapter 16 of this volume.

the community.[25] Finally, the equal protection clause would seem to say that if normal people may live together without benefit of marriage in the community so can the retarded. This equal protection doctrine may leave some people vaguely uncomfortable. But the alternative is moral righteousness for some citizens and, for others, imprisonment in the artificial and inhumane atmosphere of an institution that will "protect them from themselves."[26]

The Right to Bear Children

The right to have children is a "basic civil right of man."[27] Yet, in 1927 in *Buck v. Bell*,[28] Justice Holmes declared that the state might sterilize an 18-year-old institutionalized retarded mother, whose own mother and illegitimate daughter had also been labeled retarded. *Buck v. Bell* has limited precedental value, if, indeed, it is still good law at all. The most it can stand for is that some institutionalized retarded persons "afflicted with hereditary forms of insanity" may be sterilized against their will under some circumstances. Few would suggest it can be confidently cited as far as due process or legitimate sterilization criteria are concerned.

We are, however, familiar with the heyday of compulsory sterilization laws which that case ushered in. In the intervening years, many thousands of operations have been performed on retarded persons, pursuant to such laws.[29] Twenty-five states still have them on the books.[30] In only eight states, however, does the scope

---

[25] *See* Fotheringham at 814:
> If institutionalization is to be utilized, it should be structured as an educational setting. It should attempt to alter behavior in a desired direction as well as provide protection for the general public. Its goals should be to break up old-established routines and associations, to teach more adaptive techniques of relating to others, to supply basic factual data on sexual and social behavior, to give instructions on adequate contraceptive methods, and to improve the person's ability to evaluate social situations so that he can decide the best courses of action. I am unaware of the existence of any such an institution for the retarded.

> *Cf.* Jackson v. Indiana, 406 U.S. 715 (1972).

[26] *See, e.g.,* N. KITTRIE, THE RIGHT TO BE DIFFERENT 402 (1971). *See also* Fotheringham at 815-16:
> [A]re there not circumstances where it would be appropriate to sanction the sexes living together under varying degrees of supervision? If the possibility of having children is removed temporarily or permanently, why must everyone in our institutions for the incompetent live segregated from the opposite sex as if we were running celibate religious institutions? In the celibate religious setting the residents choose their way of life while in our custodial institution the quality of life is by imposition, not by decision. Surely in this age of "the Pill" we must come to terms with our frequently outmoded and often impractical and unfair puritanical traditions. This is particularly true at a time when we are attempting to retain the adult retarded person in the community, often in small family-like residences. Our ideas on marriage and "the sanctity" of the family must undergo some changes when, for example in the United States, which we so assiduously follow, approximately one in four marriages ends in divorce.

[27] Skinner v. Oklahoma, 316 U.S. 535 (1942). *See also* Eisenstadt v. Baird, 405 U.S. 438, 453 (1972):
> If the right of privacy means anything, it is the right of the *individual*, married or single, to be free from unwarranted governmental intrusion into matters so fundamentally affecting a person as the decision whether to bear or beget a child.

[28] 274 U.S. 200 (1927).

[29] J. Paul, *State Eugenic Sterilization History: A Brief Overview*, in EUGENIC STERILIZATION 25, 25-26, 34 (J. Robitsher ed. 1973).

[30] THE MENTALLY DISABLED at 206-25; OGG, *supra* note 14, at 8-9.

include retarded persons living in the community. Recent surveys have indicated that the number of compulsory sterilizations performed has dropped dramatically over the past decades, to a few hundred per year.[31] On the other hand, so-called voluntary sterilizations are frequent. They are, moreover, often a required condition of release from an institution or a condition for avoiding an institution. Sterilization may even be a condition of entrance or a condition of probation or continued welfare entitlement.[32]

The original rationale for sterilization laws was eugenic—to prevent new generations of mentally defective children. But the scientific data just do not exist to show that most retardation is inheritable.[33] Although there is evidence that in some few kinds of mental deficiency the retarded parent does have a higher than normal chance of having subnormal offspring, nongenetic causes of retardation—birth injuries, infections, poor nutrition, lead paint, poor education, and other environmental assaults—have also been indicated as causes of retardation. It is no coincidence that 75 percent of the mentally retarded come from lower income groups.[34]

Compulsory sterilization laws are vulnerable. Unless there is unusually strong proof that the kind of retardation an individual has is inheritable, it is unlikely that he can be lawfully sterilized against his will.[35] Even in inheritance retardation cases, there is a strong legal and moral question about the right to sterilize. Imagine the

[31] *See* note 29 *supra.*

[32] *See* Relf v. Weinberger, 372 F. Supp. 1196 (D.D.C. 1974):
> Over the last few years, an estimated 100,000 to 150,000 low-income persons have been sterilized annually under federally funded programs. . . . There are no statistics in the record indicating what percentage of these patients were mentally incompetent.
> Although Congress has been insistent that all family planning programs function on a purely voluntary basis, there is uncontroverted evidence in the record that minors and other incompetents have been sterilized with federal funds and that an indefinite number of poor people have been improperly coerced into accepting a sterilization operation under the threat that various federally supported welfare benefits would be withdrawn unless they submitted to irreversible sterilization.

> *See also* Cox v. Stanton, 381 F. Supp. 349 (E.D. N.C. 1974) and N. KITTRIE, *supra* note 26, at 330-33.

[33] *See* THE MENTALLY DISABLED at 211-12; A. DEUTSCH, MENTALLY ILL IN AMERICA 372-73 (2d ed. 1949); M. HUTT & R. GIBBY, MENTALLY RETARDED CHILD 129 (1958).

[34] Fotheringham at 814-15:
> Studies have shown that a proportion of those who are retarded are so as the result of inherited factors. In spite of this, sterilization of a person whose retardation is the result of an identifiable genetic mechanism will be of little consequence as he is likely to be severely retarded, possibly sterile, unattractive and "out of circulation," and hence unlikely to procreate. Also, as most identifiable genetic conditions are recessive in nature, the probability of mating with another person with a similar gene is generally low.
> It has been demonstrated that dull children tend to have dull parents. Various investigations have suggested that the backwardness in children of dull parents is in large measure due to the unfavorable social environment in which they have been reared.

> *See generally* Kramer, pp. 32-59, Chapter 2 of this volume.

[35] *See* THE MENTALLY DISABLED at 220-23. Due process as it has evolved since 1927 would seem to require a judicial hearing with appointed counsel for the subject and rights to confront and cross-examine expert witnesses and to secure an independent evaluation at state expense. A review of the existing laws—reprinted in the addendum to Chapter 6 of THE MENTALLY DISABLED AND THE LAW— shows that only 18 laws require notice to the patient; 19 require notice to relatives; 20 to guardians; 5 require a medical certificate; 5 an independent medical examination; 17 a hearing of any sort; 15 the presence of the patient, if requested; in 5 states the hearing is judicial; in 16 it is administrative; in 19 states there is an appeal to the courts; in 14 there is a right to counsel; in 20 states the only criterion is to prevent procreation; in 8 states it is to improve the patient's condition; in still others there is no specified criterion except "a proper case," the "public good," or the "protection of society." *Id.*

opposition to a law requiring all high-risk parents of children with cystic fibrosis, hemophilia, or cerebral palsy to undergo sterilization.

Two aspects of the situation of retarded persons living in the community deserve comment. The first that should be viewed skeptically is the aspect of "voluntariness" of many sterilizations. No parent should be allowed to "volunteer" his child for such an operation.[36] Too often the parent seeks sterilization out of anxiety about legal responsibility for unwanted grandchildren, or even as a condition for getting a child into an institution. (Institutions in turn seek sterilization for administrative convenience.) When presented with such "voluntary" candidates, doctors and clinics should be required to follow the federal precedent and refuse to perform sterilizations at all on minor children except for medical necessities. In the case of retarded adults, the doctor or clinic should be certain that the individual himself or herself really understands and wants the operation. If there is any question, judicial approval should be sought. The judge's responsibility in such a proceeding is to ensure that the operation is comprehended and desired by the patient, after it has been explained to him by a neutral, detached person, preferably someone accustomed to working with the mentally deficient. Then, whenever possible, reversible sterilization techniques should be used.

But if sterilization is not really desired by the person himself, what remains is the question of when, if ever, involuntary sterilization is warranted in a community case. Should the criteria relate to the patient's health? Is a prognosis of parental unfitness sufficient cause? A past experience of illegitimacy or sexual promiscuity?[37] Many would say *never*. But future laws, at a minimum, should require a record of individual behavior which shows gross sexual irresponsibility and adverse consequences, as well as: (1) the exhaustion of the "less drastic alternatives" of sex education and birth control; (2) a showing of total and lasting incompetence to care for children; and (3) application to *all* persons, not just those with mental defects.

Even so, there will be cases where an individual could perform competently as a parent with supportive services and supervision, even though he might not be able to do the job without help.[38] Perhaps judges should not accept the status quo; perhaps they should not evaluate the individual in the context of community services as they exist when that evaluation means depriving individuals of basic human rights. The principle of the "least restrictive alternative" may include a requirement that the state affirmatively help a person exercise basic rights before the state attempts to take these rights away. Any nonvoluntary sterilization law must give pause for

---

[36] Thirty percent of the sterilizations performed in North Carolina between 1962 and 1964 were of children aged 10 to 19. Children as young as six have been sterilized. At least one state court has already held that a parent cannot compel a retarded child living in the community to undergo sterilization. Frazier v. Levi, 440 S.W. 2d 393 (Tex. Ct. Civ. App. 1969). Between 2,000 and 3,000 minors under 21 (300 under 18) have been sterilized annually in federally funded clinics or programs. And a federal court has held that such federally assisted clinics cannot perform sterilizations at all on minors who are legally incompetent to give consent under state laws. Relf v. Weinberger, 372 F. Supp. 1196 (D.D.C. 1974). *See also* Cox v. Stanton, 381 F. Supp. 439 (E.D. N.C. 1974).

[37] *See* Fotheringham at 813-15.

[38] Thus, retarded couples living in a residential setting with staff support and day care, etc., to ensure proper stimulation of the infant might perform adequately, whereas the same couple isolated from outside help would end up depriving the child or even endangering its well-being.

thought, no matter to whom it applies. Modern contraceptive techniques should make such laws unnecessary in virtually all cases. The state should be required to furnish sex education and training and access to contraceptive advice and devices to all of its citizens, before resorting to such laws.[39]

The Right to Raise Children

The right of a parent to keep and raise his or her child is as basic as his or her right to have the child. The Supreme Court recently recognized this right in the case of unmarried fathers.

> The private interest here, that of a man in the children he has sired and raised, undeniably warrants deference and, absent a powerful countervailing interest, protection. It is plain that the interest of a parent in the companionship, care, custody and management of his or her children "come[s] to this Court with a momentum for respect lacking when appeal is made to liberties, which derive merely from shifting economic arrangements."[40]

Forty states now dispense with the requirement of a parent's consent to adoption if the parent is "incompetent." Only a few states require an additional finding that it is against the child's best interests to be taken away from that parent.[41] Only a few require notice to the "incompetent" parent or a hearing before decision.[42]

Obviously, though, the welfare of the child should be the paramount concern when the state proposes to take a child from its parents, and just as obviously this kind of decision can be determined only on a case-by-case basis. A general finding of "incompetence" based on intellectual deficiencies is inadequate as a criterion for taking away parental rights. There are no data to support a general finding that retarded parents are generally bad parents.[43] *Stanley* requires proof of individualized

---

[39] R. ALLEN, LEGAL RIGHTS OF THE DISABLED AND DISADVANTAGED 21 (1969). A recent three-judge federal court has declared a state compulsory sterilization law unconstitutional as applied to institutionalized retarded persons. It has ordered that before any sterilization can be performed on a resident by state mental health authorities a determination must be made that "no temporary measure of birth control or contraception will adequately meet the needs" of the resident and no sterilization shall be made "on the basis of institutional convenience or purely administrative consideration." No resident under 21 can be sterilized except for medical necessity. No resident can be sterilized without his own written permission based on adequate information unless he is incapable of making such a decision and an institutional review committee composed of nonemployees and a court approves it as in his best interests and he has been represented by counsel throughout the proceedings. Wyatt v. Aderholt, 368 F. Supp. 1383 (M.D. Ala. 1974).

[40] Stanley v. Illinois, 405 U.S. 645, 651 (1972).

[41] Actually there are few data on what it means to a child to be raised by retarded parents. What are the advantages and burdens? Conversely, how many children of retarded parents put up for adoption actually get adopted? These data are required, particularly in view of the policy in some states to allow annulment of the adoption within five years if the child shows signs of retardation. *See* THE MENTALLY DISABLED table 7.3, at 248-49.

[42] *Cf.* Wisconsin v. Yoder, 406 U.S. 205, 224 (1972). (Amish children need not continue in public schools beyond eighth grade). A way of life that is odd or even erratic but interferes with no rights or interests of others is not to be condemned because it is different.

[43] *See, e.g.,* Fotheringham at 816:
> Intellectual retardation is just one of the reasons for personal incompetence within the areas of family life and child-rearing, but is one of the high-risk groups in which the incompetence tends to persist over long periods of time. When one looks around and sees the number of children who are in the care of non-retarded persons who are incompetent for the task, living in squalor, ignorance and suffering, one wonders whether the principles outlined here for dealing with the retarded do not apply equally as well to us all.

neglect,[44] but even individualized determination of competence for child care presents problems. The recent case of *In re MacDonald*[45] is an illustration. The court found that a mother with an IQ of 47 was "simply not able to give these twins the proper care and attention, including, but not limited to, the stimulation which the twins need and to which they responded almost immediately when placed in foster homes."[46] Their father had an IQ of 74. A visiting nurse testified about dirty diapers and propped-up bottles, but she also testified about the husband's efforts to get a domestic day care worker and a mother-in-law's efforts to teach the retarded woman about child care. The court found that a "person with low IQ did not have the same capacity to love and show affection as a person with normal intelligence"[47] and took the children away. Whether or not the facts may have justified the result in this case, the court's general observations are not justified.

Again, what is needed is empirical fieldwork to supplant general allegations that retarded persons are not competent to be mothers and fathers. What background characteristics of the retarded individual point to success or failure as parents? How do the children of retarded parents fare? What kind of help from relatives and the community affects success or failure? Without such data, judges and legislators work in the dark and make cruel mistakes. The general principle is that neglect by retarded parents must be proven in the same way as neglect by any other parents. It may not be presumed from mental retardation. Enlightened family courts now try to keep ordinary families together by providing economic and counseling help. The same route should be followed with retarded people.[48]

The Right to Family Life

The most important part of any child's life is his family.[49] The antithesis of "normal" childhood is to grow up in an institution with changing shifts of counselors, nurses, and custodians—to be one among many. Institutional quarantine or segregation for retarded children has been a failure, especially from the child's point of view. Evolving knowledge of early childhood development confirms that the human organism needs steady personal love and stimulation. This stimulation and warmth is the sine qua non of contentment and of development of cognitive faculties. The child born with a developmental difficulty needs every possible chance to fulfill

---

[44] Stanley v. Illinois, 405 U.S. 645, 657-58 (1972).

[45] 201 N.W. 2d 447 (Iowa 1972).

[46] *Id.* at 448-49.

[47] MENTAL HEALTH LAW PROJECT, OFFICE OF MENTAL RETARDATION COORDINATION, MENTAL RETARDATION AND THE LAW 20 (Feb. 1973) (summarizing the evidence and holding).

[48] C. SCHULTZE, E. FRIED, A. RIVLIN & N. TEETERS, SETTING NATIONAL PRIORITIES: THE 1973 BUDGET 280 (Brookings Institution 1972) (Milwaukee project involving children of mentally retarded low-income mothers who received intensive all-day care and mental stimulation since infancy showed dramatic gains over control groups who received no such services).

[49] *See, e.g.,* Stanley v. Illinois, 405 U.S. at 651 (1972):
The Court has frequently emphasized the importance of the family. The rights to conceive and to raise one's children have been deemed "essential" . . . "basic civil rights of man" . . . and "rights far more precious than property rights" . . . . "It is cardinal with us that the custody, care and nurture of the child reside first in the parents, whose primary function and freedom include preparation for obligations the state can neither supply nor hinder" . . . . The integrity of the family unit has found protection in the Due Process Clause of the Fourteenth Amendment.

his potential. Even children who seem to be severely retarded, if surrounded by a warm and stimulating family, sometimes develop to a borderline level, a level where they can survive in the outside world.

There is, of course, another side to the story. Retarded children often drain their parents, especially parents without ample resources, both financially and emotionally. They can make life tension-ridden for their normal siblings. Professor Allen's fieldwork [50] found that many obstetricians recommended that mothers of retarded babies institutionalize them immediately after birth. The law has accepted the principle that the parents of a retarded child can divest themselves of that child if and when they choose. In fact, the trend of recent years has been toward commitment without a hearing, on the theory that the courtroom is an ordeal for the parents and confusing for the child.[51] These commitments are referred to as "voluntary" even though they signal the end of anything resembling a chance for the child to be happy and to develop to his fullest. These "voluntary" commitments often are forced upon a tortured parent who cannot locate community schooling, baby-sitting services, therapy, or special education for the child.

How can the law accommodate these realities of childrearing and yet at the same time protect the retarded child (or adult) if need be from harassed relatives? First, the fiction that the parent or guardian speaks for the child must be abandoned; it must be recognized that there are personal conflicts of interest in any commitment proceeding. Progress at this point, at least in some states, precludes commitment of mental patients or unruly juveniles merely at the behest of frustrated parents. What is required is an impartial or neutral court to decide whether that institutionalization is warranted for the child's benefit.[52] Second, the doctrine of the "least restrictive alternative" should come into play. Before a parent institutionalizes a retarded child, there ought to be a full judicial inquiry into: (1) the potential of the child to respond to other program alternatives; (2) alternative resources in the community that might be used to help the family care for the child; (3) conditions (personal care and programing) in the institution to which he will be committed; and (4) if the parents are adamant about removal from the home, whether foster homes or small-group settings are available in the community. In such a proceeding, the child needs his own advocate — either one appointed by the court or a volunteer from a child advocacy unit. The irony is that waiting lists for institutions grow as rapidly as Gothic tales of horror grow about their back wards.

A fundamental issue is at stake — whether parents of retarded children have an absolute legal right to turn these children back to society, even though their chances of developing will drop significantly.[53] Society accepts such children pas-

---

[50] R. Allen, *supra* note 39, at 42.

[51] *Cf.* President's Panel on Mental Retardation, National Action to Combat Mental Retardation 152 (1962).

[52] *Cf.* Horacek v. Exon, 357 F. Supp. 71 (D. Neb. 1973), wherein a special guardian *ad litem* to represent the interests of mentally retarded children in a proceeding brought by their parents to obtain better conditions in the institution because of the possibility that the remedy or treatment the parents sought might not always be in the best interests of the children.

[53] The same issue applies to normal children who are put out for adoption by their parent or parents.

sively, but it is not willing to devote the resources necessary to provide a decent substitute for the family home. It could refuse to "take" the retarded child, but some desperate parents might simply abandon the child in such a case. Other parents might take their frustrations out on the child. In each instance society would have to step in. But in other cases parents would at least try harder to care for their child. Big institutions and the lack of community resources make it possible and even necessary for parents to deny their retarded children at home. Cities and counties should: (1) cut back or abandon support for care in large isolated institutions; (2) allocate resources to community-based day care and school programs for the retarded, as well as transportation and home care support; and (3) accept "voluntary" retarded children on a selective basis only, when the parents have no capacity to care for the child. The retarded child would be better off at home in most cases.

Public funds for foster homes for retarded children who must leave their families would help to provide better alternatives when growing up in the natural home is out of the question. As early as 1793 Kentucky provided subsidies for families to rear retarded children. But it is obvious that as more retarded children grow up in the community, community attitudes and tolerance levels for some patterns of behavior will have to change. The benefit to these children would be enormous. The child who in his early years has had his quota of personal attention and stimulation from persons who are involved emotionally with him will be far better off even if he ultimately ends up in an institutional setting.

From a brief survey of the writings of retardation specialists, it is possible to demonstrate that not enough is yet known about how or when to classify a very young child as significantly retarded. Intelligence tests do not provide sufficient or appropriate information; infants or children who do not read, write, or speak cannot be accurately measured. In the few years since severely retarded children have been accorded a right to public education, retardation and education specialists have been amazed at the progress they are able to make in classrooms. Inadequate intellectual functioning can be measured only after the child has accumulated a history and some experience. Surely intelligence must vary with the stimuli and experience the individual is exposed to, as well as the way he is taught, rewarded, and punished.

It is not possible to predict in his earliest years a retarded child's potential for development. How well he functions in the community must depend on whether he is given the opportunity to learn to function in the community. Therefore, the child ought to have every chance to grow up in his own family; and society's laws and resources ought to presume such an arrangement and not legitimize its abdication. A full exploration of the child's needs and the alternatives to family life, in a judicial hearing, ought to follow any proposal to take a child out of his home.[54] This procedure may be hard on parents, but the alternative is even harder on children. The most important right of a retarded child may be the right not to be institutionalized, a right difficult to ensure, especially when there are no treatment resources in the community and when his family is not encouraged or helped to raise him.

[54] *See* Saville v. Treadway, Civil No. 6969 (M.D. Tenn., Mar. 8, 1974).

CIVIL AND COMMERCIAL RIGHTS

There are other rights of an individual outside his person and family that give him meaningful presence in the community. A citizen commands respect when he wields political power through his vote; economic power through his ability to hold a job, spend money, buy and sell goods and property; and the power to demand these rights in court.[55] If he can do none of these, it is more likely than not that he will be seen as a liability, someone to whom attention need not be paid. As one proceeds on the "normalization" principle in the economic area, as well as familial one, it is necessary to try to make the retarded person act and be perceived as normal. It must be assumed that he can exercise the same prerogatives as other citizens until it is proven otherwise or unless there is a huge risk of disaster. In general, there will be no attempt to label him as different at all unless it is absolutely necessary — and then his rights must be preserved and he must receive special services and protection. The capacity to exercise each right must be considered separately since each right requires different capacities and skills and each restriction has different consequences.[56]

The Right to Contract for Goods and Property: Guardianship

In most cases a person has all contract rights or none. He is competent or incompetent to make contracts, sign checks, convey property, make wills. Generally, disqualifications based on retardation are limited to those who have been "adjudged incompetent" and for whom a guardian has been appointed. And generally only when property and money of some size is involved do interested parties have incentive to go to court to have a person adjudged incompetent.[57] The practical result is a kind of legal limbo for most retarded persons in the community. Business people may of course refuse to deal with someone they think incompetent or they may exploit him. Irate relatives may try to cancel transactions after the fact and to contest wills.

How can persons with mental inpairments be helped to function economically

---

[55] Cf. THE MENTALLY DISABLED at 1-4. Historically, the family of the "fool" was entrusted by law with his person and property. Later, Roman magistrates appointed guardians to take care of property, and the "idiot" was not allowed to enter contracts or marry. The Visigothic Code also prohibited the feebleminded to make contracts or testify in court. In England in the thirteenth century, the king took possession of the idiot's lands after providing him with necessaries. By Lord Coke's time the idiot could appear in court in person but he was not allowed to transfer property. A jury decided if a man was an idiot or not. In colonial times, a person of allegedly inferior intelligence required a court hearing before his land could be taken from him. It is useful to remember that in these more primitive societies, standards for labeling retardation were undoubtedly much lower and many persons now considered retarded were only "slow" then.

[56] See, e.g., H.R. 35, 93d Cong., 1st Sess. (1973).

[57] Government benefits such as social security, veterans benefits, welfare checks are, however, often diverted from the retarded recipient through a special "representative payee" arrangement. R. ALLEN, E. FERSTER & H. WEIHOFEN, MENTAL IMPAIRMENT AND LEGAL INCOMPETENCY 2, 8, 73 (1968).

in the community? Under what conditions and limitations should a guardian be appointed for a retarded person so that the effect of such an appointment is not to strip the person of many of the prerequisites of citizenship? In general, the presumption should be that anyone who earns money can spend it.[58] Voluntary counseling and consumer education should exist to help the retarded person in the community avoid exploitation and redress commercial grievances.[59] Citizen advocates can fill the role of financial counselors and ombudsmen as well.[60] It is when the area of coercive guardianship is addressed that most legal problems present themselves. Most states now provide that a guardian may be appointed for an incompetent to manage his person or property.[61] But once appointed, a guardian usually must receive all payments (even pensions, social security, veterans allowances, etc.), make all contracts, dole out all spending money. Usually the stigma of legal incompetence bars other civil rights such as voting, marriage, or driving a car.

If the ward's estate is not sufficient to pay a private guardian, a public agency may perform the guardianship function. Generally, notice of hearing and a specially appointed counsel to represent the alleged incompetent is required before the guardian is appointed. But the finding of "incompetence" is itself often the result of a minutes-long uncontested proceeding initiated by a relative or public official.[62] At least half of the states apply the same law to the mentally ill, alcoholics, addicts, and the mentally retarded. Only a handful have established special guardianship laws for the retarded. It has even been proposed in one state that state authorities act as the guardian of all mentally handicapped persons in all financial transactions.[63]

In 1962, the President's Panel on Mental Retardation recommended a guardianship law that would separate guardians of the property from guardians of the person on the basis of the individual's need for help. The guardianship order in either case would contain individualized terms geared to the specific needs and abilities of the retarded person and would be based on an expert clinical evaluation of the person conducted by a team of doctors, psychologists, special educators, and social workers. Private guardians would be supervised by a state agency which also

---

[58] Obviously, there is a close connection between the kind of education accorded to retarded persons and the resultant capability they will have to exercise the civil rights and prerogatives of normal life; *i.e.,* they must learn to recognize simple signs, understand simple transactions, count, and make themselves understood.

[59] *See* NATIONAL ACTION TO COMBAT MENTAL RETARDATION, *supra* note 51, at 150.

[60] OGG, *supra* note 14, at 14 (citizen advocacy project run by the Capital Association for Retarded Children in Lincoln, Nebraska, furnishes citizen advocates for retarded persons coming back into the community from institutions).

[61] Guardianship laws in the books now paint with a broad brush, authorizing guardians for one "incapable of conducting his affairs," "unable to manage or take care of himself or his property without assistance," "likely to be imposed upon by artful or designing persons," "[who] lacks sufficient control, judgment, and discretion to manage his own property or affairs," "[is] in danger of dissipating or losing such property," "lacks sufficient understanding or capacity to make or communicate responsible decisions concerning either his person or his estate," or "so wastes, spends or lessens his estate or so neglects to attend his business as to expose himself or any of his family to want or suffering, or the town in which he resides to expense for the support of himself or any of his family," or is simply "a mental retardate." *See* THE MENTALLY DISABLED at 266-71.

[62] ALLEN, FERSTER & WEIHOFEN, *supra* note 57, at 82, 83.

[63] Study of Existing Guardianship Laws for the Mentally Retarded, 1970 (unpublished paper prepared for Florida State University School of Social Work).

provided protective service to all retarded persons. And guardianships would be periodically reviewed to determine whether they were needed any longer. Only New York and a very few other states have enacted this sort of limited guardianship law. (In New York, a retarded person retains the right to receive and spend earned wages and to control up to one month's wages or $ 300.)[64] Most states, unfortunately, cling to the older omnibus life-and-death powers of the guardian to control the ward.

The mentally retarded citizen has to be as wary of the protective embrace of the lifelong public guardian as of the possibly predatory or neglectful private one. Laws that automatically put the retarded person in the hands of a state retardation authority, whether he is in an institution or in the community, should be replaced. Guardianship terms should always be individualized and subjected to the "least restrictive alternative" principle. A new role for a guardian — either of the person or of property — ought to be required in future laws. The object should be for the guardian to help the individual care for himself to the optimum degree and for the guardian to be held accountable on this basis. Just as all institutional superintendents should be required to develop and implement an individual plan of treatment and progress toward specified goals, so a community guardian should show a program of assistance, program support, and even experimentation with lesser restrictions whenever appropriate to help the retarded person attain self-fulfillment in the community.[65]

The Right to Work

Under the value system supported by the majority of people in this society, the most urgent need of people is work — work that produces monetary reward and makes so many of life's other options possible. Currently, there is no guarantee of work for anyone in America.[66] Legal employment rights of the retarded person can be approached from two angles. (1) Is he unfairly discriminated against by employers? (2) What should society do for him, over and above putting him in a position to compete for existing jobs?[67]

[64] In some states parents pay annual fees to a trust fund which pays a social worker to plan for and help the retarded child after the parent's death. In New York, the Association for Retarded Children has set up a trust to manage sums left to retarded persons. The New York State Guardianship Statute also allows parents to designate a standby guardian for the retarded child who will take over after their death. If no relatives are available, a non-profit organization can assume the guardianship. N. Y. SURR. CT. PRO. § 1753 (McKinney Supp. 1973).

[65] Article V of the Declaration of General and Specific Rights of the Mentally Retarded states that "no person rendering direct service to the mentally retarded should also serve as his guardian." Reprinted in Int'l. League of Societies for the Mentally Handicapped, Symposium on Guardianship of the Mentally Retarded (1969). The League's symposium is generally an excellent guide to more sensitive guardianship laws and directions for the retarded.

[66] In fact, current governmental policy related to this area requires an unemployment rate. A 4-6 percent unemployment rate appears to be acceptable to those federal employees who are responsible for setting economic policy.

[67] See, e.g., H.R. 420, 93d Cong., 1st Sess. (1973) (bill to amend Civil Rights Act of 1964 by adding "physical or mental handicap" to list of prohibited categories of discrimination). Cf. Section 504, Title V of Rehabilitation Act of 1973, stating that "[n]o otherwise qualified handicapped individual . . . shall, solely by reason of his handicap, be excluded from . . . be denied the benefits of . . . or be subjected to discrimination under any program or activity receiving Federal financial assistance." Pub. L. No. 93-112, 87 Stat. 355 (1974).

There is a firmly established body of law that says discrimination by public or private employers on the basis of color, race, or sex is unlawful. These principles have been expanded to cover unreasonable work qualifications which systematically exclude people of one race, color, or sex; *i.e.,* the unnecessary requirement of a high school diploma for certain jobs, or the absence of an arrest record in communities where a resident is more likely than not to have one. Ex-convicts, ex-addicts, and homosexuals are litigating the equal protection implications of legal provisions that will not allow them access to jobs licensed or supervised by the state or that allow their dismissal from public employment on grounds of status alone.

It is well known and generally accepted that some retarded individuals can do many jobs well, some can do only a very few well, and some are not able to do any well. Jobs that put a premium on reliability, loyalty, attitude, and steadfastness may be rewarding or suitable for many retarded persons. More complex or demanding jobs can also be done by many retarded persons when they are provided with adequate supervision and support. It is practical to begin thinking in terms of stricter legal requirements on the employer; he should be required to show that the applicant's retardation is a specifically disqualifying factor before he may reject that individual. The first step is to enact legislation to bring the mentally retarded, like minority groups and women, under the protection of the Civil Rights Act. In the past, however, it has been difficult for nonretarded individuals discriminated against to show individual prejudice. Suits have to be based on a systematic practice of not hiring such persons. Certainly in the area of retardation, such suits could be contemplated only against an employer who clearly had jobs some or many mentally retarded persons could perform, and who had consistently rejected qualified retarded applicants. Even then the employer might maintain that such factors as job safety or inability to insure make it economically unfeasible to hire retarded people. Thus, insurance companies may have to be required by regulation to insure retarded persons under workmen's compensation laws and health insurance, just as they have to be required to insure allegedly high-risk drivers or homes and businesses in high crime areas.[68] More data are of course required to prove or disprove the assertion that retarded workers are safety risks.[69]

On the affirmative action front, there have been sheltered workshops around for a long time in this country;[70] in the last decade there has been some voluntary

---

[68] Of course, special rates should be permitted only if firm data were available to demonstrate that a mentally retarded employee is, in fact, at greater risk than any other employee in the same situation.

[69] *See, e.g.,* Letter to the editor, in Washington Post, May 20, 1973, § C. at 7, col. 2 (by representatives of several handicapped groups) referring to:

> [T]he well established fact that it sometimes costs extra to arrange a job so that a disabled person can be fully productive.
>
> It is for this reason that joblessness is the rule rather than the exception for disabled people seeking employment in this country. Other contributing factors are consistent discrimination in education, housing, public transportation, and insurance rates; but employment, with normal on-the-job training, advancement, and self-sufficiency, is the most important.
>
> The value of hiring is clear in England and West Germany, where laws favoring the hiring of disabled people have made life for them completely different than it is here. Full mobility in and contribution to society are accepted as the norm for millions of disabled people there.

[70] The letter cited in note 69 *supra* criticizes many of these workshops because they

> . . . train the disabled in unsaleable skills on outmoded equipment and then put them to work in degrading jobs for as little as 10 cents an hour.
>
> If the President's Committee is to be of any real value, it must be restructured to give it power

movement in the federal government and among private employers to hire retarded persons.[71] But there are some even more interesting models of positive government action for the retarded in other countries, especially Great Britain and the Netherlands.[72]

In the Netherlands, 180 supported work projects employing 44,000 disabled workers have been set up and subsidized by the government.[73] These work projects compete for regular contracts in the open market and they are operated on a work-productivity ethic, rather than on a therapy-treatment one. On the premises or nearby, however, are counselors, physicians, physical therapists, and other needed aides. The work is planned for low stress, and minimum wages are paid to all workers except when the worker's productivity falls below one-third of normal. Private industry must set aside 2 percent of its jobs for handicapped workers.

The governments of both Great Britain and the Netherlands are committed to a policy of employing everyone who is not bedridden. This includes the retarded, the brain damaged, the physically disabled, the mentally ill, and the social dropout. In Great Britain, the government requires every employer of over 20 employees to hire 3 percent handicapped. In certain industries, jobs are set aside for the physically and mentally disabled, retarded, or handicapped by designation of the government. Other handicapped persons work in social workshops. The shops are unionized and perform changing jobs ranging from candy wrapping to furniture assembly. Many workers spend nights in institutions or group residences and days at work. REMPLOY, in England, has 86 factories using 7,500 disabled workers, including mildly to severely retarded persons. The average productivity level of an employee in REMPLOY is 50 percent of normal. Work projects present opportunities for employees to gain confidence in their ability to work, attain good work habits and skills, and receive the requisite counseling and assistance they need to succeed in their work. The aim is to move as many people as possible into open industry after they have gained experience and skills. The difference between

---

to act as an advocate for and legal defender of the civil rights of the disabled themselves. But Congress could do the job more effectively by giving these duties immediately to the Civil Rights Commission and the Equal Employment Opportunity Commission.

Disabled people, like blacks and women, are entitled under the Constitution to be evaluated on the basis *only* of their ability to do the job at hand. This can only be done when artificial man-made barriers—in this case both prejudicial and architectural—are removed. This is clearly the responsibility of industry and the government—not the disabled, who are giving their all to live their God-given lives in a rewarding and self-respecting manner. *Id.*

[71] *See, e.g.,* U. S. CIVIL SERVICE COMMISSION, HANDBOOK OF SELECTIVE PLACEMENT IN FEDERAL CIVIL SERVICE EMPLOYMENT (1972). Since 1964, special rules apply to hiring handicapped in the federal government. Certification by a state vocational rehabilitation agency substitutes for competitive examinations. Special procedures for counseling and dismissal are in force. Particular civil service jobs are set aside by agreement with the agency for the handicapped. During the past 8½ years, a total of 7,442 appointments of mentally retarded persons have been made in 40 federal agencies in every state. Fifty-three percent of these persons were still working in 1972; over 3,000 had been employed for at least three years. U.S. CIVIL SERVICE COMMISSION, AN 8½ YEAR RECORD (1972). Some state agencies have followed suit with special hiring programs for the mentally retarded. A few private employers such as W. T. Grant Co. have established affirmative action programs for the retarded. There are 1,100 Grant stores; 73 of them now employ 107 mentally retarded persons.

[72] The remainder of this section is based on Supported Employment Program: The Netherlands, England, Translated to the United States 1971 (unpublished paper of Vera Institute of Justice).

[73] Compare this with the results cited in note 71 *supra.*

contract profit and expense is paid by a combination of local and national government subsidies.

Such a system puts teeth into a commitment to hire the handicapped and deserves serious consideration in this country. Supported work projects are already operational in New York City for addicts, alcoholics, and paroled offenders. They are subsidized by a reallocation of welfare payments. Participants perform community work which would not otherwise be done: cleaning up parks, water-blasting buildings, collecting newspapers. And the workers are paid a minimum wage.

If a similar system were operative nationwide, it could attack employer resistance far more quickly and comprehensively than lawsuits. It could guarantee productivity through the team concept; the team would provide the necessary (and individualized) support for each worker until he reached his optimal level.

One purely economic reason why the right to work is so important to retarded persons is that as such individuals compile their work records, they will be assured of some income in their later years from social security and pension funds. This is an especially important goal for retarded persons and has been emphasized by plaintiffs in the peonage suits.[74]

Institutions are now full of persons working in laundries and kitchens, in janitorial and ground maintenance, who until recently have earned next to nothing and who could perform these same jobs on the outside if there were a genuine official commitment to guarantee them this chance. Under present policy, the national economy will always have some unemployment; it will always be very difficult for many persons to compete on the open market as long as the number of jobs is exceeded by the number of applicants. How much work can be expected for the mentally retarded from private employers remains to be seen. An affirmative action plan for the retarded seems a far better arrangement if positive results actually are desired. A work program for the mentally retarded will take much more than repealing the laws that now formally limit access to employment.[75] A policy of equal and work-related tests for all applicants would provide the solution. An example may be drawn from another area: Anyone who can pass a driving test ought to receive his license; anyone who cannot should not.[76] No other laws are needed.

The Right to Sue

Any person who works or makes contracts may have to go to court to defend or enforce his transactions or to seek relief from his employer. Present laws on access to court

[74] *See* Friedman, pp. 566,572, Chapter 18 of this volume. *See generally* Weidenfeller v. Kidulis, 380 F. Supp. 445 (E.D. Wisc. 1974).

[75] *See* THE MENTALLY DISABLED app. to ch. 9, table 9.3, at 266-67. Disqualifying provisions for "incompetents" apply to medical technicians, nurses, pharmacists, physical therapists, insurance agents, executors, adjustors, solicitors, dentists, chauffeurs, psychologists, cosmetologists, polygraph examiners, architects, dental hygienists, alcoholic beverage license holders, social workers, barbers, manicurists, veterinarians, accountants, engineers, embalmers, chiropodists, beer sellers, pilots, ophthalmic dispensers, justices of the peace, any public officers, attorneys. The licensing board can either initially deny or later revoke the license for incompetency.

[76] *Cf.* Bell v. Burson, 402 U.S. 535 (1971) (state cannot suspend driver's license on basis of accident without any determination of individualized fault).

for retarded persons address themselves almost exclusively to the person adjudged incompetent and insist that such a person's guardian appear for him. If a conflict exists between the ward and guardian or if no guardian exists and the litigant is incompetent, then the court usually appoints a guardian *ad litem*.

The basic premise should be that a person who is considered competent enough to work or to make contracts should be permitted to sue. Given this premise, there is no question that the retarded person needs a new kind of advocacy: (1) preventive legal education so that the citizen knows his rights; (2) a realistic relaxation of rigid ethical rules in client solicitation so that someone can tell him if his rights are being violated or he is being taken advantage of; (3) residential and day programs for the retarded in the community which provide regular access to counsel; and (4) access for retarded persons to group legal insurance programs where they exist. The retarded (along with many other citizens) need someone to explain to them their rights at critical junctures throughout their lives—when they marry, have children, engage in commercial transactions, or are threatened with sterilization and institutionalization. Lawyers who provide this counseling should be sensitized to making clients understand what is happening; they should themselves learn to deal with the other kinds of advocates on whom the retarded depend. With this kind of legal umbrella, there need be no special rules on suits by, for, or against the retarded. Laws disqualifying the incompetent from bringing suit can be discarded.

In the case of the mentally retarded, as with juveniles, the concept of the "next friend" is also a useful one. This envisions a sort of "private attorney general" concept for the retarded, whose rights in the community, and in institutions, may be violated without their comprehension. The "next friend" need not always be a natural or appointed guardian. An advocacy unit for the mentally retarded should be qualified to assume such an obligation as well as to consult with, advise, and represent retarded individuals. Should an individual who does not appear competent to present his case appear in court with no lawyer, the court should be responsible for appointing one to protect the individual's interest.[77] The individual should be permitted to take the witness stand when this would be useful and appropriate. And the judge should assure himself that the suit is being conducted in the retarded party's best interests, especially when great control resides in the lawyer, next friend, or guardian.

In all events, the right of any citizen to gain access to the courts for the vindication of his legal rights is fundamental. It is not to be denied or curtailed without compelling justification.[78] The mentally retarded are among the most vulnerable groups in society. Any denial of their right to redress grievances must be rigidly scrutinized. Public policy should be to treat the retarded individual in the same way as any other citizen with regard to his access to the courts, but to provide the extra aid he needs to make that access meaningful.[79]

[77] This would be going further than present law provides for normal litigants in civil cases, but it seems indispensable if justice is to be done. In some cases where the judge may suspect retardation he should request the plaintiff to submit himself to an expert evaluation.

[78] *See* Boddie v. Connecticut, 401 U.S. 371 (1971).

[79] *Id.* at 380:

> [A] generally valid notice procedure may fail to satisfy due process because of the circumstances of the defendant. . . . The State's obligations under the Fourteenth Amendment are not simply generalized ones; rather, the State owes to each individual that process which, in light of the values of a free society, can be characterized as due.

The Right to Vote, Hold Office, Serve on a Jury

Voting, holding public office, and jury duty are ways a citizen participates in democratic government. Most states prohibit all three rights to "incompetents." In practice there are generally no enforcement controls on these laws unless a person is so deficient he cannot register to vote, or the forms for voting include questions on incompetence or institutionalization, or he has already been declared incompetent and the registrar has a record of it. The right to vote has been held by the Supreme Court to be a fundamental one, not to be curtailed by a state without compelling justification.[80] Retarded individuals may work, pay taxes, and be held legally accountable. There should be a presumption in favor of every citizen's capacity to vote unless it is clearly shown that he does not understand what he is doing. It should be remembered that much of voting is highly irrational even among persons of normal intellectual capacity.[81]

Retarded people have very definite needs and interests in the way government is run. If there is a minimal comprehension test for any voter it should apply for all voters. A citizen may well have the right to choose a President even if he cannot sell property. As far as holding office is concerned, it is not facetious to suggest that anyone who can survive a political campaign certainly ought to be able to hold office. In short, there should be no automatic disqualification of voting or access to elective office for retarded persons. Serving on a jury which makes decisions about another man's life or liberty may involve a more difficult selective judgment. The standard of comprehension may reasonably be higher than for voting, but the same test should be applied to everyone, not just to persons labeled mentally retarded.

CONCLUSION

Human rights to love, marry, and raise children are a vital part of the "normalization" of the mentally retarded. Of course, there may be individuals totally incapable of being wives, mothers, husbands, and fathers. But many, many individuals who do not meet preconceived norms of intellectual and sexual functioning are capable of such relationships. Laws that deny "incompetents" their instinctual relationships are suspect when no individualized determination takes place. They may act subtly as a deterrent and source of discouragement. The structure of the law should be such that these rights cannot be denied anyone until a judicial determination has been made that their exercise will almost certainly result in serious injury to the individual or to someone else. This individualized standard, moreover, should apply not just to the mentally retarded and addicts, alcoholics, and the mentally ill, but to all persons.

---

[80] Harper v. Virginia Bd. of Elections, 383 U.S. 663 (1966).
[81] *Cf.* Klein & Grossman, *Voting Pattern of Mental Patients in a Community State Hospital.* 3 COMMUNITY MENTAL HEALTH J. 149 (1967) (hospitalized mentally ill patients' voting patterns closely resembled normal voters' in the district).

The law must be enforced with an eye to reality. Legal facades of "voluntariness" must be abandoned when parents abrogate parenthood or when parents sterilize children. Retarded people must have their day in court. No one with a potential conflict of interest should be allowed to make vital decisions for them.

The "least restrictive alternative" principle, allowing retarded persons to stay in the community with institutionalization a "last resort only," also should be invoked where sex education can deter promiscuity and where birth control devices will suffice instead of sterilization. Society should not take infants from retarded parents before it tries to supplement their limited resources with instruction, day care, home consultants, or other needed services.

The optimal liaison between mental retardation specialists and lawyers has not yet taken place. To write better laws, to argue better cases, to prevent more injustices to the retarded, what is desperately needed is communication between what specialists know about the capacities and potentialities of the retarded and what lawyers know about the law.

Translating rhetoric into reality for the retarded means overhauling the incompetency and guardianship laws. It means requiring as a prerequisite to taking away any individual's civil or economic rights a full-scale hearing on his ability to exercise that right. Guardianships must be restricted to specific incompetencies and geared toward progress to competency, and they must be periodically evaluated on this basis.

Reform of the law means putting a greater burden on mental retardation specialists to come up with necessary backup data on how to measure functioning in the community and what different levels of functioning a specific retarded individual has proven capable of in the past and can be expected to meet in the future. Study of the institutionalized or clinical population may have to give way to more emphasis on study of retarded persons who cope in the community.

Because of our past inhumanities and underestimations we have little experience with the many retarded persons who live in and cope with the community. We have to begin actively accumulating this kind of experience. We must probe the limits of what retarded persons can do, with help, in the community. Only with such experiential data can we formulate humane and reasonable laws on the legal rights of the retarded. Until we do, the burden should be on those who would deny such rights. And states should begin to overhaul their commercial transaction and property laws, as well as their guardianship concepts, to incorporate retarded people into their citizenry. Along the way we urge the creation of legal advocates for the retarded who regard them as human beings deserving of dignity and respect and having great potential as citizens in our community.

Reaction Comment

PHILIP ROOS

WALD'S PAPER very ably documents the discrepancy between the noble ideals upon which our nation is founded and the primitive reality in which we operate.

I cannot disagree with it in any substantial respect. The existing laws, indeed, embody the characteristic defenses against future shock, which Toffler documented so well in his recent book on this subject.[1] The laws, for example, are replete with the mechanism of denial: the references to voluntary admission to dungeons, to voluntary sterilization, and so forth are obvious denials. The laws, as a matter of fact, have essentially condoned the concept of levels of humanity, thereby belying the Bill of Rights and, indeed, the religious systems which are dominant in our society.

In addition to the mechanism of denial, Wald demonstrates that the legal system relies heavily on supersimplification. I think she has particularly ably documented the evils of labeling, of reducing a highly heterogeneous population to the least common denominator. Instead, she proposes that we endorse the principle of individualization, that we judge each individual on his own merits, that we assume that mentally retarded persons have all the rights of other persons until it is shown to the contrary on an individual basis, and that formal judicial procedures be required to curtail any specific rights. This I see as the legal counterpart of the developmental model of mental retardation which has been widely publicized among mental retardation specialists.

Wald's presentation also suggests to me that the existing laws embody gross overreaction. Essentially, we are witnessing a tendency for society to project its own anxieties on a symbolic group—the fears of lack of impulse control and the fears of helplessness, dependency, and vulnerability. Many of our own existential conflicts are projected, by a rather primitive psychological mechanism, onto this entire population.

Wald's paper is a major challenge to the mental retardation professional and to the representatives of the consumer group. It is obvious that we need to develop better predictions of specific behaviors. The judiciary and the legal profession will ask us more and more to determine the level of competence of particular individuals to engage in specified behavior and to predict the potentials of danger to self and to others. The professional will also be increasingly required to improve his technology, his educational technique, his habilitation technique, and his technique for shaping and modifying behavior. The professional will increasingly be asked to clarify reality, to debunk myths, to provide expertise to the judiciary.

These challenges require that we (1) improve the dialogue between the mental retardation professional and the legal professional and (2) engage in exercises of mutual education. A member of the President's Committee on Mental Retardation, Mr. Aris Mallas, did some pioneer work a couple of years ago in educating county judges throughout the state of Texas in the field of mental retardation. This is the type of design which will need to be developed and refined throughout the nation.

It is also essential that we support research because the data that this paper calls for are largely unavailable to us. We may have been collecting the wrong kind of data. Many of the predictions that we are asked to make we cannot make. And when I speak of more and better research I speak, of course, of increased legislative clout and of the need to support the National Institute for Neurological Diseases and Stroke and the National Institute for Child Health and Human Development. These sources of data, unless we take definitive action, will atrophy.

[1] A. Toffler, Future Shock (1970).

Third, as we work together, we must, I think, be candid enough to recognize and admit our current limitations. We must be able to recognize each other's limitations. It is an exhilarating experience to rise majestically in a courtroom as an expert witness and to lay on the good word. We impress ourselves as expert witnesses and we receive massive reinforcement from our attorneys. Likewise, I suspect that attorneys get a certain amount of reinforcement by laying on the good word to non-attorneys, presenting us with somewhat technical jargon at times, which suggests that they can manipulate the destiny of the human race.

I think another major point of Wald's presentation is the need to develop viable advocacy systems and multiple models of advocacy—agency advocacy, legal advocacy, the ombudsman concept, and the recently developed concept of the citizen advocate. Advocacy is emerging as a major thrust in this field. Indeed, Wald's paper alludes to the potential conflict that may exist between a parent or a guardian and the retarded individual himself. To operate effectively, the system of advocates will need professional support from both the attorney and the mental retardation professional.

In conclusion, there is no question that the mentally retarded citizens of our land will indeed benefit from closer cooperation between the legal and the mental retardation professions. We have, indeed, begun to work together, but we have a long, long way to go.

Reaction Comment

DENNIS HAGGERTY

MY BASIC REACTION to Wald's presentation is "amen." It is an in-depth and scholarly treatment of the plight of the forgotten citizen. One might well ask, "Why is it necessary to write such a paper in the first place? Are not retarded citizens like the rest of us?" It is true that, as a class, they are more like than unlike the rest of us, but the differences (both real and imagined) are sufficient to require special attention, considering the history of deprivation of rights experienced by this special group of citizens. It is necessary, then, to write such a paper, not to advance the notion that mentally retarded citizens need a separate Bill of Rights, but to emphasize that as citizens they have the same rights as all citizens of this society.

The presumption that we all enjoy basic rights such as "life, liberty, and the pursuit of happiness" is dangerous. The presumption that "all men are created equal" is equally dangerous. Quotations from the Declaration of Independence and the Constitution seem to apply to everyone. Yet it is fair to suggest that the authors of these documents did not intend "everyone" to include blacks and Indians. Our task is to ensure that "everyone" does indeed mean everyone.

By what authority has society placed its mentally retarded citizens in a special category of neglect—of unneeded institutionalization? The answer is simple—by an authority devoid of legitimate foundation. Wald places in sharp focus the history of our rights as citizens. What has caused us to rethink our ways of handling retarded citizens? Parents' groups after World War II were early advocates of this cause. Perhaps the atrocities of the war led to greater sensitivity to oppression of minorities. In any case there has been increased concern about guaranteeing the civil rights of minority populations, one of which is composed of retarded citizens. Though long overdue, promotion of the "normalization principle" for the retarded is bringing results.

The retarded have simply not been part of our active community since we traditionally have excluded them. At the birth of a severely mentally retarded child, the medical profession has urged institutionalization: "Put the child away and forget you ever had it." Educators also have kept the "slow learners" out, placing some of these children in special classes. Only now are educators recognizing that all human beings are capable of learning something and that education must follow a zero reject principle, a dedicated commitment to the uplifting of each individual.

The legal profession has practically ignored the vulnerable minority of the mentally handicapped as it played storekeeper with funds of the "estate of the retarded," forgetting "the person of the retarded"; after all, why would the mentally retarded poor need lawyers? Lawyers, sadly, have done little in the field of mental retardation until recently because there has been no money in it. Legal practice has in fact worked against the retarded individual: A declaration of incompetency reduces one to a nonentity; guardianship laws often remove rights the individual is capable of exercising (these laws cry out for revision toward a concept of limited guardianship). Parents, members of legislatures, and others somehow have not given much consideration to retarded citizens. So it is not strange that back wards exist in institutions where humans live in subhuman conditions.

What is needed is a realistic approach. Utopia may be unattainable, but constant vigilance by advocates for mentally retarded citizens can prevent a repeat of past mistakes and perhaps commission of new ones.

"Man's inhumanity to man, makes countless thousands mourn,"[1] said Robert Burns. These words should be engraved over every institution door. Accountability is a must on the part of administrators who run programs as well as among legislators who inadequately fund them. Presumptions that retarded persons "can function" must replace presumptions that they must be "protected." Opportunity to act and develop as a full-fledged citizen must be provided continually. Parents of mentally retarded children should receive support that helps them bear the responsibility of their retarded offspring. Retarded children should be entitled to share in the family experience equally with nonretarded siblings.

It should go without saying that all areas of human experience open to others in this society, such as sexual experience, marriage, and raising children should be available to the mentally retarded. The truth is, however, that this concept must be stated and restated until society actually implements it. Lawyers must take the lead, albeit late, in reducing and removing the arbitrary barriers that face the retarded citizen as he returns to the community.

---

[1] R. Burns, Man Was Made to Mourn st. 4 (1786).

In recent years there has been an awakening to the needs of the retarded citizen. As a result, the medical profession is slowly reconsidering the advisability of institutionalizing all retarded persons. The educational community is beginning to offer a vital learning opportunity to retarded children, allowing them in schools with so-called normal children. From this experience we all learn; the future law enforcement official, the future physician, the future lawyer will not need to be educated as to "what" retarded people are since they will know. They will have seen them during the growing years. Eternal vigilance is the price of liberty and with liberty comes an opportunity for the pursuit of happiness and the fulfillment of one's life. The retarded citizen must be spoken for. Wald has done so eloquently.

CHAPTER 2

The Right Not to Be Mentally Retarded

Editorial Introduction

*K*ramer draws a stark contrast between the scientific data on the environmental causes of mental retardation and the legal system's response to this evidence. He documents the numerous direct and indirect ways in which poverty contributes to mental retardation. Poverty results in malnutrition for pregnant mothers, with resultant mental retardation for babies. Poverty places restrictions on availability of medical services, and lack of medical intervention may result in mental retardation. The damage caused cries out for a legal response, but Kramer describes in painful detail the absence of such a response to date.

Kramer explores the various constitutional theories that might be used to secure judicial intervention — due process, equal protection, right to privacy, even a right to life — and concludes that the courts would have to shift focus dramatically to be of effective assistance. He then looks at the legislative response to the problem and reviews the various programs in existence. He demonstrates the restrictions that limit their effectiveness as a force to ensure the rights of citizens to be born without intellectual impairment.

Cooper's reaction comment is confirmatory of the scientific data presented by Kramer. It emphasizes the connection between poverty and mental retardation and provides a prophetic illustration of this connection. Cooper closes with a call to lawyers to make their impact felt through the legislative process.

PRINCIPAL PAPER

JOHN R. KRAMER

LITIGATING LAWYERS invariably intervene after the fact. After the harm has been done, they compel compensation for the injured. Lawyers normally are not prepared to develop strategies for avoiding the incidence of harm. Perhaps for this reason most legal intervention to date on behalf of the 6 million citizens classified mentally retarded has focused on securing for them the civil rights the rest of society theoretically has, rather than preventing the conditions that led to their impairment and resulting classification.

Lawyers and judges often are understandably reluctant to infringe on someone else's territory, and the prevention of mental retardation would seem to be within the province of the medical profession. If natural hesitancy at venturing into another profession's bailiwick were not enough, there is a guard with a shotgun at the border. As George Tarjan would have it, in his capacity as former president of the American Association on Mental Deficiency and vice-chairman of the President's Panel on Mental Retardation, "the main responsibility for primary and secondary prevention rests with the medical profession."[1]

With deference to the medical profession, lawyers concerned with the rights of mentally retarded citizens as a class might meaningfully divert some of their attention to what is potentially the most fruitful right, the right not to be mentally retarded. This requires exploration of the viability of litigative, legislative, and regulatory approaches to preventing the occurrence of mental retardation, to guaranteeing the human right to be born normal, and indeed, to remain that way. Former President Nixon indicated that a goal of his administration was to reduce the incidence of mental retardation by one-half before the year 2000.[2] This paper evaluates the present utility of the law as an instrument for achieving that goal as the law is now applied by the judicial, legislative, and executive branches of government of this country.

THE CAUSES OF MENTAL RETARDATION:
TARGETS FOR ELIMINATION

Abstractly defined, the legal right to be born and remain intellectually unimpaired is rather open-ended, encompassing as a social ideal the provision of whatever

---

[1] Tarjan, *Prevention—A Program Goal in Mental Deficiency*, in MENTAL RETARDATION 135 (J. Rothstein ed. 1961).
[2] *See* Statement of November 16, 1971, in 7 WEEKLY COMPILATION OF PRESIDENTIAL DOCUMENTS 1530 (1971).

minimum level of goods and services is necessary to enable the fetus and, later, the child to avoid any of the major causes of mental retardation. Unfortunately, the largest category of causes, covering 80 percent or more of all cases of mental retardation, is the catchall one entitled environmental, or more often "unknown."[3] Current medical knowledge is not very helpful in prescribing what the exact contents of the legal inoculation against mental retardation ought to be. Discovery of the full scope of the right must await the results of further etiological research.

This fundamental uncertainty as to cause ought not, however, prompt abandonment of the legal effort to construct and implement a right to be born and remain intellectually unimpaired. There does exist a substantial amount of information isolating several environmental factors as significant causes of mental retardation. Much damage to intellectual functioning that occurs during the prenatal period, the birth process, and the first five to eight years of life has been reliably linked to poverty-induced malnutrition, inadequate prenatal and postnatal medical attention, and environmental poisoning from sources such as lead. The linkages are by no means hard and fast. Percentage figures obtained in particular studies ought not to be recited as absolute facts, but the correlations are undeniably present.

Poverty and Malnutrition

Poverty, malnutrition, and mental retardation form an especially unholy trinity, with an ever-tightening chain of evidence connecting the first with the second and both with the third. The close association between poverty and malnutrition has been asserted for many years. It has now been confirmed rather unambiguously by the Ten-State Nutrition Survey of 30,000 families conducted from 1968 through 1970 by Dr. Arnold Schaefer of the Center for Disease Control in the Department of Health, Education, and Welfare (HEW) pursuant to the Partnership for Health Act of 1967.[4]

The survey evidence revealed that the poor simply do not get enough to eat. The diets of poor families did not vary in quality from those of middle-income families, but total food intake was considerably lower. As a result, the percentage of persons surveyed in the lowest economic quartile census districts of the low-income states of Texas, Louisiana, Kentucky, South Carolina, and West Virginia who had deficient or low levels of hemoglobin, vitamin C, riboflavin, and protein was twice to four times as great as those in the high-income states of California, Washington, Michigan, Massachusetts, and New York. The United States Senate Select Committee on Nutrition and Human Needs had been hearing evidence of the relationship between poverty and malnutrition since 1969, but Dr. Schaefer's final compilation, five years in the making, ended any debate on the matter.

Poverty and malnutrition have their most harmful impact upon pregnant and nursing women. Pregnant and nursing women who are poor cannot afford to purchase a nutritionally adequate diet. Even if they receive food stamps (and only

---

[3]THE PRESIDENT'S COMM. ON MENTAL RETARDATION, MENTAL RETARDATION—DEFINITION, SCOPE, CAUSES, AND IMPACT ON THE AMERICAN FAMILY 5 (1972).

[4]The best available summary of the survey appears in U.S. DEP'T OF HEALTH, EDUCATION AND WELFARE, TEN-STATE NUTRITION SURVEY, 1968-1970, PUB. NO. (HSM) 72-8132 (July 1972).

55 percent of the nation's poor currently are recipients), the average monthly allotment of $37.50 is far less than the $44.10 in food purchasing power the Department of Agriculture estimates (in 1974) a pregnant woman must have to avoid malnutrition or the $51.20 necessary for a woman who is lactating.[5] Thus, poverty, with or without food stamps, leads to serious malnutrition for women who are pregnant or nursing.

Again, the Schaefer survey data confirm the existence of the problem. The most alarming finding was that the low-income black pregnant women who were surveyed had an average daily caloric intake of 1506 calories and protein intake of 60 grams, compared with 2127 calories and 89 grams for the higher income white pregnant women. The 1500 daily caloric level rendered it likely that there would be intrauterine growth retardation, whereas the protein level was borderline deficient, tending to interfere with the development of the brain of the fetus.

The primary visible consequence of poverty-induced malnutrition in the mother is the prematurity and, hence, low birth weight (under five and one-half pounds) of the child. In 1968, the risk of underweight babies in the newborn nonwhite population was nearly double the 7.1 percent rate among whites, whereas middle-class blacks and whites were considerably less prone to prematurity than poor ones.[6] Prematurity, in other words, was directly related to the mother's poor nutrition, which in turn was related to economic status, irrespective of the race of the mother. Further support for this proposition flows from a study of the distribution of legitimate live births by birth weight and family income in 1964-65, which disclosed that at the lowest income level (under $3,000) 10 percent of all infants born weighed 2,500 grams or less (a level considered premature) compared to 8 percent or less at the higher income levels (e.g., 6.2 percent above $10,000).[7]

Babies that are premature not only run the greatest risk of dying in the first year of life;[8] they also are far more likely than normal term babies to be mentally retarded. The President's Panel on Mental Retardation found that:

> 26.3 per cent of those infants with a birth weight of 1,500 grams (3.3 pounds) or less have neurological abnormalities of sufficient degree to cause serious concern about their future development, while comparable figures for the remainder of the premature infants in the sample and for the full-term control groups are 8.2 per cent and 1.6 per cent, respectively. . . .
> Prematurity generally has a deleterious effect, and 50 per cent of these infants have handicaps ranging from minimum neurological damage to severe mental deficiencies and blindness.[9]

[5] AGRICULTURAL RESEARCH SERVICE, U.S. DEP'T OF AGRICULTURE, COST OF FOOD AT HOME ESTIMATED FOR THE ECONOMY FOOD PLAN, MARCH *1974*. U.S. AVERAGE, CFE (Adm.-256).

[6] Gussow, *Bodies, Brains and Poverty: Poor Children and the Schools*, INFORMATION RETRIEVAL CENTER OF THE DISADVANTAGED BULL., No. 3, 1970, at 4 [hereinafter cited as ICR BULL.]. For an excellent overview of all of the evidence on the matter see H. G. BIRCH & J. GUSSOW, DISADVANTAGED CHILDREN—HEALTH, NUTRITION AND SCHOOL FAILURE (1970); R. HURLEY, POVERTY AND MENTAL RETARDATION (1969).

[7] *Senate Select Comm. on Nutrition and Human Needs, to Save the Children*, 93d Cong., 2d Sess., at 8-9 (1974).

[8] *Id.* at 10. The figures are dramatic. Infants from families of all races and income levels whose birthweight was in the premature range (2,500 grams or less) had a death rate of 185.5 per 1,000, whereas infants in the normal range for birthweights (3,001-4,000 grams) had a death rate of 7 per 1,000.

[9] THE PRESIDENT'S PANEL ON MENTAL RETARDATION, A PROPOSED PROGRAM FOR NATIONAL ACTION TO COMBAT MENTAL RETARDATION 51 (1963).

Although not all of the approximately 150,000 children born mentally retarded each year are premature, mental retardation is ten times more likely to occur in the premature than in the full-term infant.[10] All the results are not yet analyzed on the 14-year study sponsored by the National Institute of Neurological Diseases and Stroke, which has followed 56,000 mothers and 40,000 of their children through the first eight years of life, but physicians involved in the study have already begun to reorient previous medical advice given to pregnant women so as to encourage them to gain nearly twice as much weight during pregnancy as was previously considered ideal.[11] The aim is to reduce the possibility of malnutrition in the mother and increase the weight of the baby at birth, thereby limiting the potential of neurological or intellectual harm.

The damage malnutrition can do to the mental development of the fetus and infant is quite substantial. As Dr. Charles Upton Lowe, chairman of the Committee on Nutrition of the American Academy of Pediatrics, summarized the studies:

> [T]he earlier malnutrition exists, the more devastatingly it impinges on growth and development. . . . When a fetus receives inadequate nutrition *in utero*, the infant is born small, the placenta of his mother contains fewer cells than normal to nourish him and his growth will be compromised. . . .
> During the last trimester of pregnancy protein synthesis by the brain is proceeding at a very rapid rate. Immediately upon delivery this rapid rate decreases, although it still continues at a greater pace than at later times of life. In animals, this sharp decrease in protein synthesis immediately after birth occurs in both full-term and premature animals. The decrease in protein synthesis occurring in premature animals in all probability also occurs in premature human infants. If we can extend animal observations to the human situation we have a logical explanation for one of the most distressing concomitants of prematurity. When very small at birth, as many as 50 per cent of the prematurely born infants grow to maturity with an intellectual competence significantly below that which would be expected when compared with siblings and even with age peers.[12]

If Dr. Lowe's 50 percent figure describing the relationship between prematurity and mental retardation is accurate, then prematurity could be deemed the chief factor associated with, if not the major cause of, mental retardation, since there are 330,000 premature births each year and 150,000 births of retarded individuals. But even if the causative relationship is not this direct, it is clear that the last four months of *intra utero* life are critical for the development of the nerve cells, and these cells require protein to grow.

Brain growth is only 40 percent complete at birth. During the next eight to nine months brain cells grow rapidly. By the age of three, the brain is approximately 80 percent of its full-grown size.[13] Thus, brain damage attributable to poverty-produced

---

[10] Wylie, *The Challenge of Infant Mortality,* BULL. OF THE CLEVELAND ACADEMY OF MEDICINE, June 1965, quoted in HURLEY, POVERTY AND MENTAL RETARDATION 55 (1969). *See also* Aldrich, *Liquidation of the Problem Through Research and Training,* in PROCEEDINGS, THE WHITE HOUSE CONFERENCE ON MENTAL RETARDATION 82 (1963).

[11] Auerbach, *Pregnancy Study,* Washington Post, February 19, 1973, § A, at 1, col. 2.

[12] *Hearings on Nutrition and Human Needs Before the Senate Select Comm. on Nutrition and Human Needs,* 90th Cong., 1st Sess., pt. 3, at 1085 (1968) [hereinafter cited as *Senate Select Comm. Hearings*]. *See also Senate Select Comm. Hearings, Maternal, Fetal, and Infant Nutrition, 1973,* 93d Cong., 1st Sess., at 5 (1973).

[13] THE PRESIDENT'S COMM. ON MENTAL RETARDATION, *MR* 71, ENTERING THE ERA OF HUMAN ECOLOGY 7 (U.S. Dep't of Health, Education & Welfare, Pub. No. (OS 72-7, 1972).

malnutrition does not stop at birth. It continues throughout early life, with particular intensity during the first year. "When an infant undergoes severe nutritional deprivation during the first months of life, its brain fails to synthesize protein and develop cells at normal rates and consequently suffers a decrease as great as 20 percent in the cell number."[14] It may be possible for a child born prematurely into an affluent home (whose mother probably had an adequate diet) to overcome low birthweight without any impact upon his mental ability, but the premature child born in a poverty situation is likely to be condemned to less than borderline intelligence.[15]

As previously indicated, malnutrition can produce deleterious effects upon the brain after birth when none existed before. Work in the late 1940s and early 1950s by Dr. David Coursin, director of research at St. Joseph's Hospital in Lancaster, Pennsylvania, demonstrated that were a single nutrient, vitamin B-6 (pyridoxine), to be deficient in an infant formula (60 micrograms instead of 100), the infant population fed that formula could undergo neurological alterations of function resulting in mental retardation.[16] Many other vitamin deficiencies can produce the same result in the absence of therapy. The retardation may lessen if proper care, including food, is received after the deficiency is discovered, but some damage remains.[17]

In 1970, a Memphis newspaper reported the case of a girl born healthy and normal who was brought into St. Jude's Hospital at eight weeks with a gain of only one pound since birth.[18] She was a victim of poverty-caused malnutrition. Her mother worked 40 hours a week as a waitress to earn $ 20 plus tips; the daughter was fed only a watered-down formula. The doctors, noting the disease of malnutrition, prescribed food — no medicine, just food. After six months, the little girl had gained enough height and weight to be above the fiftieth percentile. But her head circumference remained below average and her brain failed to develop fully. She was mentally retarded for life.

The reported evidence of substantial intelligence decline traceable to undernutrition in the first years of life was brought to the attention of the nation in March 1969, when, acting as chairman of the President's Urban Affairs Council, Daniel Moynihan informed the President that, although he suspected that there was no evidence of low nutrition intake causing brain damage in the United States, there was proof of noticeable IQ loss in poor children during the early years of life.[19]

Poverty and Medical Attention

The provision of adequate amounts of nourishing food alone would not eliminate mental retardation among the poor. Poverty also critically influences the availability

[14] *Senate Select Comm. Hearings,* 90th Cong., 1st Sess., pt. 3, at 1085 (1968) (testimony of Dr. Charles Lowe).

[15] Gussow, *Bodies, Brains and Poverty: Poor Children and the Schools,* 6 ICR BULL., No. 3, 1970, at 10.

[16] *See Senate Select Comm. Hearings,* 90th Cong., 1st Sess., pt. 3, at 1105 (1968) (testimony of D. Coursin); Coursin, *Effects of Undernutrition on Central Nervous System Function,* 23 NUTRITION REVIEWS, March 1965, at 65; Coursin, *Undernutrition and Brain Function,* 26 BORDON'S REV. NUTRITION RESEARCH, Jan.-March 1965, at 1.

[17] *Senate Select Comm. Hearings,* 90th Cong., 1st Sess., pt. 3, at 1105 (1968).

[18] DuBois, *Lucy Loses Race Before She Starts It,* Memphis Commercial Appeal, Dec. 27, 1970.

[19] D. Moynihan, Memo to President Nixon, quoted in *Senate Select Comm. Hearings,* 91st Cong., 1st Sess., pt. 8 — *The Nixon Administration Program,* at 2667 (1969).

of prenatal and postnatal health care, the likelihood of difficulties at birth, and the incidence of diseases, all of which may be, directly or indirectly, responsible for producing mental retardation. The poor, even with the advent of Medicaid, tend to have inadequate access to obstetricians, gynecologists, or other providers of prenatal care.[20] If, as Eunice Shriver put it, "pregnant cows are getting better care than pregnant women,"[21] then poor women are not even in the competition. Women who have little or no prenatal care are two or three times more likely to have premature babies than women who have ready access to adequate care. After the child is born, the poor do not get prompt and proper pediatric attention. Thus, brain damage which has been suffered is likely to go undetected and uncorrected,[22] and additional damage may be suffered.

Poor children have mothers who are subject to higher rates of almost every major reproductive abnormality that may result in significant neurological damage.[23] Poor children have mothers who have high rates of infectious syphilis. Poor children are more likely than middle-class children to have mothers who have anemia, toxemia, contracted pelvises, and other problems attending pregnancy that can lead, in the absence of adequate medical attention, to organic damage to the children. Poor children themselves tend to succumb more to those diseases of childhood which, if not treated effectively and with speed, can damage the central nervous system. Poor children are less likely to be inoculated against common childhood diseases. The litany could go on forever, but the point ought to be clear: The environment of poverty and mental retardation are inextricably interlinked.

Environmental Pollution

Pollution of the environment, particularly in the form of lead poisoning, is another isolable cause of mental retardation. The lead may come from many sources: from paint on interior house walls and ceilings, from paint on toys and cribs, from prepared infant milk formulas and evaporated milk products, from kindling materials, from drinking water, from batteries in abandoned cars, and from the atmosphere through industrial pollution and motor vehicle exhaust.[24]

Whatever the source, its impact on the body and specifically on the brain can be quite grave. A study by Dr. Meyer Perlstein in Chicago determined that of 425 children treated for plumbism, or lead poisoning, some 39 percent had some noticeable neurological damage and 22 percent became mentally retarded, including 9 percent who had no clinical symptoms at all at the time of diagnosis, but who had developed

---

[20] THE PRESIDENT'S PANEL ON MENTAL RETARDATION, *supra* note 9, at 52; P. LAWRENCE et al., MEDICAL CARE, HEALTH STATUS AND FAMILY INCOME 3 (1964); REPORT TO THE PRESIDENT— WHITE HOUSE CONFERENCE ON CHILDREN 156 (1971).

[21] Thompson, *The Quality of Human Reproduction,* in PROCEEDINGS, THE WHITE HOUSE CONFERENCE ON MENTAL RETARDATION 88 (1963).

[22] REPORT TO THE PRESIDENT, *supra* note 20, at 156-57.

[23] Gussow, *supra* note 15, at 9-10; R. MASLAND, S. SARASON & T. GLADWIN, MENTAL SUBNORMALITY 19 (1958); Thompson, *supra* note 21, at 87.

[24] *See generally Hearings on S. 3080 Before the Subcomm. on Health of the Senate Comm. on Labor and Public Welfare,* 92d Cong., 2d Sess. (1972) [hereinafter cited as *Hearings on S. 3080*]; *Senate Select Comm. Hearings,* 91st Cong., 2d Sess., pt. 5, at 1458-60 (1970); J. LIN–FU, LEAD POISONING IN CHILDREN (Public Health Service Pub. No. 2108, 1970).

retardation by the time of the follow-up investigation.[25] In a 1971 survey of 473 homes in the ghetto of Roxbury, Massachusetts, 800 children were found to be suffering from lead poisoning, 30 percent of these having permanent brain damage.[26] Similar results with respect to IQ deterioration to the point of mental retardation have been reported in other studies. This information impelled a pediatric consultant with the Maternal and Child Health Service to suggest the likelihood of chronic brain damage flowing from even low levels of exposure to lead despite the absence of clinical symptoms of poisoning.[27]

The President's Committee on Mental Retardation has been convinced by the data that "lead poisoning is an important preventable cause of mental retardation" whether in the overt guise of clinical symptoms usually created by "three to six months of fairly steady ingestion of lead-based paint" or in the subtle form of excessive lead absorption revealed metabolically.[28] How important a cause of retardation lead poisoning may be is suggested by the estimates indicating that 400,000 children get sick from lead each year, with 12,000 to 16,000 actually receiving medical treatment and 50 percent of these left mentally retarded because medical care became available only after the disease was in its advanced stages.[29]

Again, the inevitable poverty linkage appears, tying the leaded environment of substandard housing to mental retardation. The Roxbury study took place exclusively in an impoverished Boston ghetto.[30] Of the Chicago patients, 84 percent were blacks from slum areas.[31] One-fourth of all children tested in a screening program in the model cities area of the District of Columbia during nine months of 1971 had unsafe lead levels in their blood.[32] In New York, 80 percent of all slum apartments surveyed had lead-based paint, while housing facilities and socioeconomic standards were all poor in the districts in which the incidence of lead poisoning was highest.[33]

City by city, area by area, poverty and mental retardation coincide, first with malnutrition, thereafter with lack of adequate medical care, and then with lead poisoning supplementing the impact of the two.

The correlation can be viewed directly as well, short-circuiting the connection between poverty and mental retardation:

> Children of the poor are about ten times more likely to be retarded than children of the middle and upper classes.
> If the children of all population groups had the same rate of mental retardation as those of middle and upper class whites, the prevalence of retardation would decrease by 80 per cent.[34]

[25] Perlstein & Attala, *Neurologic Sequelae of Plumbism in Children,* in *Senate Select Comm. Hearings,* 91st Cong., 2d Sess., pt. 5, at 1704-15 (1970).
[26] *Hearings on S. 3080,* at 114 (testimony of Senator Edward Kennedy).
[27] *Senate Select Comm. Hearings,* 91st Cong., 2d Sess., pt. 5, at 1386 (1970) (testimony of J. Lin-fu).
[28] THE PRESIDENT'S COMM. ON MENTAL RETARDATION, POSITION STATEMENT ON LEAD POISONING (Nov. 1972).
[29] 119 CONG. REC. S1449 (daily ed. Jan. 29, 1973) (remarks of Senator Kennedy).
[30] *Hearings on S. 3080,* at 114, 119 (testimony of Senator Kennedy).
[31] Perlstein & Attala, *supra* note 25, at 1704.
[32] Levy, *D. C. Delays Action on Lead Content in Paint,* Washington Post, Feb. 10, 1973, § D, at 1, col. 5.
[33] Jacobziner, *Lead Poisoning in Childhood: Epidemiology, Manifestations and Prevention,* reproduced in *Senate Select Comm. Hearings,* 91st Cong., 2d Sess., pt. 5, at 1689-1703 (1970). *See also* J. LIN-FU, *supra* note 24, at 2.
[34] THE PRESIDENT'S COMM. ON MENTAL RETARDATION, *supra* note 13, at 27.

CONSTITUTIONAL CURES: IS THERE A FUNDAMENTAL INTEREST IN THE HOUSE?

If poverty manifesting itself in the malnutrition of mothers, fetuses, and infants, in inadequate medical care, and in substandard housing with peeling lead-based paint is the primary, environmental cause of mental retardation, what can be proposed as the legal cure? The need for adequate cash or in-kind income and adequate housing is self-evident. Viewed in this context the right to be born and remain intellectually unimpaired may simply be another way of paraphrasing the demand of "justice" that the state satisfy certain basic needs of every citizen, by guaranteeing that no one is ill-fed, ill-clothed, ill-housed, or forced to live in an otherwise unhealthy environment. The right not to be mentally retarded is tantamount to the right not to be impoverished.

Is this right legally viable? Legal philosophers have attempted to establish this concept of social justice not as requiring the abolition of all inequalities of wealth and income, but as assuring every child at least the minimum welfare that will provide an opportunity for complete self-development.[35] The United Nations General Assembly has recognized this claim upon the state in Article 25 of the Universal Declaration of Human Rights:

> Everyone has the right to a standard of living adequate for the health and well-being of himself and of his family including food, clothing, housing and medical care and the necessary social services, and the right to security in the event of unemployment, sickness, disability, widowhood, old age or other lack of livelihood in circumstances beyond his control.[36]

The General Assembly has also extended this right to the mentally retarded.[37]

Law professors Sparer and Harvith have asserted that there is a "right to life" implicit in the fifth and fourteenth amendments that would encompass the furnishing of income, food, housing, and medical care as predicates to the exercise of other explicit constitutional rights such as free speech and freedom of religion.[38] A three-judge court has found in the Preamble of the Constitution, with its express purposes of ensuring domestic tranquility and promoting the general welfare, the basis for suggesting that receipt of welfare benefits might well become a constitutional right in order "to insure that indigent, unemployable citizens will at least have the bare minimums required for existence, without which our expressed fundamental constitutional rights and liberties frequently cannot be exercised and therefore become meaningless."[39] Congress, too, has used statutory statements of policy to declare its desire to realize "as soon as feasible . . . the goal of a decent home and a suitable living environ-

---

[35] Michelman, *Foreword: On Protecting the Poor Through the Fourteenth Amendment*, 83 HARV. L. REV. 1, 15 (1969). *See generally* J. RAWLS, A THEORY OF JUSTICE (1971).
[36] Universal Declaration of Human Rights § 25 (1), G.A. Res. 217, U.N. Doc. A/810 at 71 (1948).
[37] G.A. Res. 2856, 26 U.N. GAOR Supp. 29, at 93, U.N. Doc. A/8429 (1971).
[38] *See* Sparer, *The Right to Welfare*, in THE RIGHTS OF AMERICANS 65 (N. Dorsen ed. 1971); Harvith, *Federal Equal Protection and Welfare Assistance*, 31 ALB. L. REV. 210, 241-45 (1967).
[39] Rothstein v. Wyman, 303 F. Supp. 339, 346-47 (S.D.N.Y. 1969), *vacated and remanded*, 398 U.S. 275 (1970).

ment for every American family,"[40] "to safeguard the health and well-being of the Nation's population,"[41] by alleviating hunger and malnutrition.

But all the theories, declarations, assertions, and policies put no food on the table, remove no lead paint from the walls, and furnish no prenatal care. The right to life going beyond the mere right not to be executed without due process remains for the most part a praiseworthy abstraction without meaningful adoption or enforcement by the judicial, executive, or legislative branch. The future generation of unborn citizens which presently seeks succor from this right finds only a withered teat.

The Rights of the Unborn

There exist at least three potential sources of constitutional support for the development of the right to be born and remain normal: the due process clauses of the fifth and fourteenth amendments applicable respectively to federal and state governments; the ninth amendment protection against encroachment by any branch of government; and the equal protection clause of the fourteenth amendment applicable only to the states. All four clauses protect only a "person" or "people."

The limited coverage of personality in the constitutional sense means that there is presently no constitutional mandate to accord the unborn due process or equal protection or unspecified retained rights. In the Texas abortion case, *Roe v. Wade*,[42] the Supreme Court determined that the due process clause of the fourteenth amendment did not limit a woman's right to obtain an abortion, in part because "the word 'person,' as used in the fourteenth amendment, does not include the unborn."[43] A fetus could thus be deprived of whatever "life" it had without due process of law.

The Court's definition of "person" applies to the fifth and ninth amendments as well. The Court in *Roe* included the fifth amendment in its canvas of those places in the Constitution in which the word "person" appeared, pointing out that "in nearly all these instances, the use of the word is such that it has application only post-natally."[44] The Court also referred for additional support to its decision in *United States v. Vuitch*,[45] permitting abortion under limited conditions pursuant to the District of Columbia abortion statute, as denying by implication any fourteenth amendment protection for fetuses. In fact, *Vuitch* could only have denied by implication such protection under the fifth amendment, since the validity of District of Columbia legislation is governed by the fifth, not the fourteenth, amendment.[46]

Ninth amendment analysis, especially that of Justice Goldberg, concurring in *Griswold v. Connecticut*,[47] deals with "fundamental personal rights."[48] Arguably, such rights do not belong to the unborn after *Roe*.

---

[40] Section 2 of the Housing Act of 1949, 42 U.S.C. § 1441 (1970).
[41] Section 2 of the Food Stamp Act of 1964, 7 U.S.C. § 2011 (1970).
[42] 410 U.S. 113 (1973).
[43] *Id.* at 158.
[44] *Id.* at 157.
[45] 402 U.S. 62 (1971).
[46] Bolling v. Sharpe, 347 U.S. 497, 499 (1954).
[47] 381 U.S. 479, 492 (1965).
[48] *Id.* at 486, 492-96.

In summary, the right to be born intellectually unimpaired, asserted by an unborn child, has at present no constitutional grounding in the fifth, ninth or fourteenth amendments. Although an unborn child, viable or not, may retain common law rights based on tort[49] or property[50] theories, even these rights depend for vindication upon the child's parents or guardians *ad litem*.[51] Nevertheless, providing common law recovery for a mother on behalf of her unborn child against a wrongdoer is different in kind, and not merely in degree, from recognizing constitutional rights for the unborn when these are in direct opposition to the asserted constitutional rights of the child's mother. The Court might react differently to a constitutional claim pressed in unison by the unborn child and the mother joining forces against the controllable, but hostile, environment.[52] For example, were any state or federal court to approve without notice or hearing the seizure of the contingent property rights of the unborn, with the seizure obviating future devolution of the property to the unborn, the courts would probably provide due process protection.[53]

The apparent firmness with which the Supreme Court resolved the issue of fourteenth amendment personality, however, makes uncertain this possibility of resurrecting the child's constitutional rights in alliance with the mother's. It is probably preferable for the mother of a potentially retarded child to assert any fifth, ninth, or fourteenth amendment rights primarily on her own behalf, but also derivatively for the fetus growing in her womb. In addition, infants and small children, acting through parents or guardians *ad litem*, might seek to assert the right to remain normal under the fifth, ninth, and fourteenth amendments.

In terms of the constitutional right to due process, neither a pregnant woman nor her child is, in the constitutional sense, being deprived of life, liberty, or property because of the state's failure to supply sufficient income, food, medical care, or a living environment free of hazards to a growing fetus or a child's brain. The concept of deprivation without due process, like that of denial of equal protection, requires a component of state action or involvement in taking away some previously state-granted entitlement.[54] Denial of due process requires a state-initiated, -authorized, -sanctioned, or -encouraged deprivation. Without a deprivation or removal of something previously bestowed by the state, there is no fifth or fourteenth amendment due process violation. Deprivation by inaction is, to date, not cognizable deprivation at all.

Had a pregnant woman previously been receiving welfare and had her benefits been arbitrarily terminated on the ground that she was not pregnant, without a prior hearing on the facts, she would as a matter of due process be entitled to continued

---

[49] *See, e.g.,* Bonbrest v. Kotz, 65 F. Supp. 138 (D.D.C. 1946). *See generally* W. PROSSER, HANDBOOK OF THE LAW OF TORTS 335-38 (1971).

[50] Louisell, *Abortion, The Practice of Medicine and the Due Process of Law,* 16 U.C.L.A. L. REV. 233, 235-38 (1969).

[51] *Id.*

[52] *But see* Murrow v. Chifford, Civil No. 114-73 (D.N.J., June 12, 1973), *vacated and remanded,* 502 F.2d 1066 (3d Cir. 1974).

[53] *See* Fuentes v. Shevin, 407 U.S. 67 (1972); Sniadach v. Family Finance Corp., 395 U.S. 337 (1969). *But see* Mitchell v. W. T. Grant Co., 416 U.S. 600 (1974) (virtual overruling of *Fuentes*).

[54] *See* Boddie v. Connecticut, 401 U.S. 371, 384-85 (1971); Goldberg v. Kelly, 397 U.S. 254, 262 (1970).

payments until a fair hearing could be held and a decision rendered.[55] Were she renting safe and sanitary housing only to be faced with an eviction notice falsely claiming that she was in violation of the lease, without an opportunity to present her case in an administrative forum, as well as in court, prior to eviction, her right to due process might again be vindicated.[56] But when she never received welfare in the first instance or never lived in decent housing, due process contentions are of no avail. They cannot secure welfare or housing she never had because there was no arbitrary exercise of governmental power against some entitlement, right, or property she already enjoyed. If there is not an existing constitutional or statutory entitlement, due process cannot obtain it. Due process can prevent exclusion from a program, but it cannot provide admission.

The ninth amendment is, if anything, weaker ground upon which to construct a right not to be mentally retarded. The Supreme Court, through the majority opinion of Justice Douglas and the concurrence of Justice Goldberg, resurrected the ninth amendment in *Griswold v. Connecticut.*[57] The majority opinion nourished the ninth amendment with minimal content, deriving from its emanations, as well as those from the first, third, fourth, and fifth amendments, a nebulously defined right of privacy and no more.[58] The concurrence would expand the amendment to embrace all "'those fundamental principles of liberty and justice which lie at the base of all our civil and political institutions.'"[59] This open-ended concept of "justice" would encompass the right to be intellectually unimpaired, but the Court has ignored the ninth amendment in the intervening years, never once referring to it in connection with welfare, food, housing, or health needs, and ultimately rejecting it in favor of the fourteenth amendment's concept of personal liberty as the basis for the very right of privacy which brought it back into judicial use.[60]

Equal protection is a third constitutional standard to which the right to nutritional subsistence sufficient to avoid malnutrition, and environmental protection and health care sufficient to avoid brain toxic effects, could attach. But here as well the claims of right are gossamer because the governing law is unfavorable to the creation of this right. State action is easier to establish in this context because, although the federal and state governments may not directly cause the lack of adequate nutrition, health care, and environmental protection, the government does operate income, health, and housing programs and is responsible for creating two classes of persons: those receiving the subsidies or benefiting from the programs and those being denied them. Although the marketplace rather than the government may be chargeable with the discrimination between those who can afford the proper diet and a safe home and those who are unable to purchase these commodities without assistance, clearly the government decides who shall be governmentally assisted and who shall

[55] *See* Goldberg v. Kelly, 397 U.S. 254 (1970).

[56] *See* Caulder v. Durham Housing Authority, 433 F. 2d 998 (4th Cir. 1970), *cert. denied,* 401 U.S. 1003 (1971); Escalera v. New York City Housing Authority, 425 F. 2d 853 (2d Cir.), *cert. denied,* 400 U.S. 853 (1970). *See also* U.S. Dep't of Housing & Urban Development, Grievance Procedure in Low Rent Public Housing Projects (HUD Circular RHM 7465.9, 1971).

[57] 381 U.S. 479 (1965).

[58] *Id.* at 484-86.

[59] *Id.* at 493, *citing* Powell v. Alabama, 287 U.S. 45, 67 (1932).

[60] Roe v. Wade, 410 U.S. 113, 153 (1973). *But see* 410 U.S. at 210 (Douglas, J., concurring).

not. The excluded mothers and children are neglected by reason of governmental choice in delineating the boundaries of eligibility. Nevertheless, state action in itself is not enough to establish a denial of equal protection of the laws.

Probably dispositive of the equal protection claim is the near impossibility of convincing the present Supreme Court to subject the exclusion criteria to searching review. The Court's decision upholding the validity of Texas' system of school financing in *San Antonio Independent School District v. Rodriguez*[61] makes it likely that the present Court would reject any "compelling state interest" test under either "the suspect classification" or the "fundamental interest" rubric.

The state action discriminates between two classes of indigents, not against indigents in general. Some indigents are given the food, medical attention, or housing they need to avert poverty-induced mental retardation. Some are not. This disadvantage, however, does not rise to the constitutionally condemned status of "suspect." The test of suspectness used by the present Court in applying the equal protection clause requires the existence of absolute deprivation of a desired benefit, not mere diminution in its quality or quantity.[62] According to the Court's review of its prior decisions, in each instance in which it found a suspect classification involving the poor, the poor who were involved had no other means of securing their goal, no adequate substitute for what they sought.[63] Strict application of the fourteenth amendment seems to rest upon the distinction between a claimant who wants something in place of the nothing he is receiving and a claimant who wants more of what he already has.

The state of knowledge about mental retardation is not, and may never be, precise enough to predict which pregnant women who are poor and who do not receive adequate food, medical, or housing assistance will inevitably give birth to retarded children or which children, if not retarded at birth, will invariably become so. Evidence that proves the absolute deprivation of the opportunity to be normal flowing from the discriminatory denial of assistance is what the Supreme Court seems to demand in order to find invidious discrimination against a class of indigents. Such evidence would also point to the "suspicious" creation of an immutable characteristic determined at birth, involving the state itself in the development of a suspect class.[64] But presenting evidence of this sort is, at the moment, an unsustainable burden.

As long as some uncertain, but nonetheless cognizable, percentage of poor pregnant women not housed or fed by the government bear normal children, the full force of the equal protection clause does not come into play. Mere rationality will suffice to uphold the line-drawing attendant upon establishing eligibility standards. As long as the poor can purchase some food or find some shelter, no suspicion

---

[61] 411 U.S. 1 (1973).

[62] *Id.* at 25.

[63] *See id.* at 20-22. As Justice Marshall noted in his dissent, 411 U.S. at 88-89, 117-20, neither Griffin v. Illinois, 351 U.S. 12 (1956), nor Douglas v. California, 372 U.S. 353 (1963), fit this mold since some appellate review was still available to both appellants.

[64] *See* Frontiero v. Richardson, 411 U.S. 677, 686 (1973), where Brennan, J., in announcing the opinion of the Court, grouped sex, race, and national origin together for fourteenth amendment strict judicial scrutiny purposes as immutable characteristics "determined solely by the accident of birth."

attaches to the government's classification of those whose purchases are governmentally augmented and those whose purchases remain minimal enough to trigger the potential (but only potential) danger of retardation. The resultant mental retardation is an ineradicable stigma, a permanent disability. But the operative governmental classification is not predicated on the retardation that may ensue. The government is not acting or failing to act on the basis of anyone's present status as mentally retarded.

The argument can be made that the right to be born and remain intellectually unimpaired and its constituent rights to be adequately fed, housed, and medically attended are fundamental, but the argument is not likely to succeed in the near future. The present Court has determined that it will not make the value judgments necessary to rate in importance various social and economic needs for purposes of applying stringent judicial scrutiny in equal protection analysis. What is "fundamental" in the sense of realistically important may not be the same as what is "fundamental" for purposes of judicial review of legislation.[65]

The need for income is obviously vital to life. Under the due process clause, the Court has recognized that "welfare provides the means to obtain essential food, clothing, housing and medical care,"[66] and that its loss "may deprive an eligible recipient of the very means by which to live."[67] Under the equal protection clause, the Court has acknowledged that "public welfare assistance . . . involves the most basic economic needs of impoverished human beings."[68] But no matter how important welfare benefits are to the poor, the Court has refused to require states to supply benefits or to justify refusal to supply them by advancing a compelling state interest.[69]

Food assistance in the form of food stamps or commodities or, for infants, special nutritional packages or food certificates is a "significant personal interest,"[70] or a basic human need. Nonetheless, it is not explicitly or implicitly protected by the Constitution and its denial will not presently be subjected to strict scrutiny.

The Court has expressly refused to "denigrate the importance of decent, safe, and sanitary housing. But the Constitution does not provide judicial remedies for every social and economic ill. We are unable to perceive in that document constitutional guarantee of access to dwellings of a particular quality. . . ."[71] A state's refusal to supply decent shelter is supportable by mere rationality.[72]

Finally, the Court in the course of its due process analysis in *Goldberg v. Kelly*[73] noted that the loss of welfare could also result in the equally serious loss of participation in medical programs. But the argument that medical care would be jeopardized

---

[65] San Antonio Independent School Dist. v. Rodriguez, 411 U.S. 1 (1973).
[66] Goldberg v. Kelly, 397 U.S. 254, 264 (1970).
[67] *Id.* at 264.
[68] Dandridge v. Williams, 397 U.S. 471, 485 (1970).
[69] *See* Jefferson v. Hackney, 406 U.S. 535 (1972); Dandridge v. Williams, 397 U.S. 471, 485 (1970); King v. Smith, 392 U.S. 309, 334 (1968). But a state may not deny a governmental benefit that is "necessary to basic sustenance," such as welfare assistance or medical care, simply to penalize persons who have migrated to that state. Memorial Hosp. v. Maricopa County, 415 U.S. 250 (1974).
[70] San Antonio Independent School Dist. v. Rodriguez, 411 U.S. 1, 37 (1973).
[71] Lindsey v. Normet, 405 U.S. 56, 74 (1972).
[72] *Id.* at 74.
[73] 397 U.S. 254 at 264 n.11 (1970).

if the Texas system of percentage reductions in calculating welfare benefits for persons with outside income were approved, because Medicaid benefits were dependent upon the receipt of AFDC cash assistance, was summarily ignored in *Jefferson v. Hackney.*[74]

None of the subsidiary rights of the right to be normal is fundamental. It is true that, in *Dandridge v. Williams*[75] there was no absolute loss of financial aid and that the litigation was only over the difference between $ 296.15 and $ 250; or that in *Jefferson v. Hackney*[76] the persons whose benefits were denied by application of the percentage reduction factor to the standard of need prior to subtraction of their earned income still had some earned income to live on; or that those who were paid only 75 percent of their standard still obtained that much aid; or that in *Lindsey v. Normet*[77] there was no showing that no alternative housing was available to the evicted tenant; or that in *James v. Valtierra*[78] no form of subsidized housing other than public housing was affected by the referendum requirement. But neither the fact of absolute deprivation of income, food aid, medical care, or housing nor the absolute certainty of retardation to be caused by such deprivation is likely to be provable in any individual case.

The Court probably will not soon soften its position: A right is either in the Constitution on its face, fairly derivable therefrom, or it does not exist for purposes of guaranteeing equal protection of the laws.

The constitutional expedition has concluded without any quarry or, at best, with a negative catch: The right to be born and remain intellectually unimpaired presently cannot be successfully pressed through constitutionally based litigation.

LEGISLATIVE AND COMMON LAW RELIEF: THE UNENFORCEABILITY OF CLAIMS

If the right to be born and remain normal does not have a constitutional basis that a majority of the current Supreme Court would find acceptable, then the sole alternative for protecting the fetus and the infant from poverty-connected mental retardation involves implementing whatever legislative or common law claims are available.

For the unborn child and the infant, welfare, food aid, and health care are minimal prerequisites. But the statutory "right" to welfare is narrowly compartmentalized by the limited availability of aid to families with dependent children (AFDC) and is absolutely denied to pregnant women in 35 states, pending the outcome of multiple litigation on the issue. Even when received, the aid is likely to be insufficient. The statutory "right" to food aid is not restricted according to

[74]406 U.S. 535 (1972).
[75]397 U.S. 471 (1971).
[76]406 U.S. 535 (1972).
[77]405 U.S. 56 (1972).
[78]402 U.S. 137 (1971).

family status or the source of earnings, but is difficult to secure because of substantial practical and fiscal barriers, and once obtained, the level of assistance is inadequate. Programs that might fill the gap have been enacted, but have never been fully utilized. The statutory "right" to health care depends upon qualifying for welfare, upon the hazards of geographical location, and upon program funding.

The Unborn Child, The Pregnant Mother, and Welfare

The statutory right of the unborn child to welfare that is paid to his mother in order to benefit him is dependent initially upon the mother's marital status (father must be continually absent from the home in 26 states)[79] and, secondarily, upon his father's employment (in the other 24, his father may be present in the home, but only if employed for fewer than 100 hours a month).[80] Yet even if both tests are satisfied, there is no guarantee of the receipt of aid because 32 states refuse to recognize a fetus *in utero* as a "dependent child" within the meaning of section 406(a)(2) of the Social Security Act.[81]

In 1971, the 17 states that did provide aid to the unborn child through his mother furnished funds to only 53,400 unborn children, about two-fifths of them in California.[82] California changed its program in September 1972, limiting but not eliminating financial help for the unborn, thereby reversing a 23-year-old policy of assisting the unborn on the same basis as children. The regular $190 grant to a pregnant woman living alone with no other children remained intact, but for pregnant women who were married or single with other children the state attributed a $65 in-kind contribution of rent, utilities, and food from each pregnant woman to her fetus and, accordingly, lowered the grant to $125. As a partial offset for this reduction, an across-the-board $9 monthly dietary allowance was granted, but the cutbacks remained, with their legality subject to challenge in state court.[83]

The federal welfare statute does not indicate the minimum age to which coverage extends.[84] The term "dependent child," which is used in the section that defines the persons for whom states may receive federal matching for aiding and

[79] *See* 42 U.S.C. § 607 (1970) (added in 1961, and created the AFDC-UP program as an option available to the states). As of January 1973, 26 states were not exercising the option. *See* Table 8—Aid to Families with dependent children, unemployed-father segment, January 1973, in OFFICE OF INFORMATION SCIENCE, NATIONAL CENTER ON SOCIAL STATISTICS, PUBLIC ASSISTANCE STATISTICS (U.S. Dep't of Health, Education & Welfare, Pub. No. (SRS) 74-03100, Nov. 1973).

[80] 45 C.F.R. § 233.100(a)(1)(i) (1974).

[81] 42 U.S.C. § 606(a)(2) (1970). The states that refuse to provide such aid include Oregon, Utah, Arizona, Colorado, Wyoming, Texas, Nebraska, Iowa, Indiana, Ohio, Missouri, Arkansas, Florida, Georgia, Vermont, Alaska, North Carolina, Maine, Virginia, Delaware, Kentucky, Tennessee, Minnesota, Michigan, New Jersey, South Carolina, Mississippi, South Dakota, Connecticut, Massachusetts, West Virginia, and New Hampshire. New York allows fetuses in on a limited basis. Puerto Rico and the Virgin Islands also deny aid entirely to unborn children.

[82] SENATE COMM. ON FINANCE, SOCIAL SECURITY ACT AMENDMENTS OF 1972, S. REP. No. 1230, 92d Cong., 2d Sess. 467 (1972).

[83] 3 CNI WEEKLY REPORT, Jan. 11, 1973, at 7. *See* California Welfare Rights Organization v. Brian, 31 Cal. App. 3d 265, 107 Cal. Reptr. 324 (1973), *vacated,* 11 Cal. 3d 237, 520 P.2d 970, 113 Cal. Rptr. 154 (1974).

[84] 42 U.S.C. § 602(a)(10) (1970).

which is incorporated by reference in the section 402(a)(10) mandate to furnish aid to all eligible individuals, suggests no age floor. An unborn child can be just as "dependent" as a one-year-old in the statutory sense of being needy, living with certain individuals, and having a continually absent or unemployed parent, as well as (in the sense of the declared objective of the Social Security Act) requiring "parental care and protection." [85]

It is uncertain, however, whether a fetus can be labeled a "child" prior to its birth. The constitutional precedents discussed previously would suggest not. But in this instance it is a statute that is being interpreted, an ameliorative statute designed to strengthen people's ability to become independent. This purpose would certainly not be furthered by denying aid to an impoverished pregnant woman (with no other children and thus not otherwise eligible for aid), thereby increasing the potential of retardation in her child when born. Furthermore, in terms of the traditional "plain meaning" approach to interpreting legislative intent, an unborn child is unmistakably, in the language of the statute, "under the age of eighteen."

In the absence of any other clear-cut indicia in the statute itself of whether or not the term "child" was meant to embrace the unborn and in view of a complete silence on the matter in the legislative history of the 1935 Act, it is necessary to turn to administrative practice. Since 1941, HEW has permitted federal matching of state expenditures to the mother as a grantee on behalf of the unborn child, but has maintained that state dispensation of benefits to the unborn is purely optional. [86] In February 1971, this permission became a program regulation stating that "Federal financial participation is available in . . . [p]ayments with respect to an unborn child when the fact of pregnancy has been determined by medical diagnosis." [87] The same regulations also authorize 50 percent federal cost-sharing of "expenses incurred in establishing eligibility for AFDC, including expenses incidental to obtaining necessary information to determine the existence of . . . pregnancy of a mother."[88]

Although HEW has consistently considered this provision of aid optional, not mandatory, this is by no means determinative of the right to such aid. In a series of cases including *King v. Smith,*[89] *Townsend v. Swank,*[90] and *Carleson v. Remillard,*[91] the Supreme Court concluded that when a state eligibility standard either contravenes a federal eligibility standard explicitly set forth in section 406(a)(2) of the Social Security Act, or, in the absence of any such express federal standard, excludes persons eligible for federal matching assistance, that standard violates the command of section 402(a)(10) that "aid to families with dependent children shall be furnished with reasonable promptness to all eligible individuals."[92]

Carleson v. Remillard,[93] the most recent of the cases, is controlling here. The

[85] 42 U.S.C. § 601 (1970).
[86] U.S. Dep't of Health, Education and Welfare, Handbook of Public Assistance Administration, pt. IV, § 3142.
[87] 45 C.F.R. § 233.90(c)(2)(ii) (1974).
[88] 45 C.F.R. § 233.90(c)(3) (1974).
[89] 392 U.S. 309 (1968).
[90] 404 U.S. 282 (1971).
[91] 406 U.S. 598 (1972).
[92] 42 U.S.C. § 602(a)(10) (1970).
[93] 406 U.S. 598 (1972).

term "absence" relating to a parent was undefined in the statute, but HEW read it to include absence due to military service, whereas California refused to extend benefits that far. The Court ordered California to include military orphans as AFDC beneficiaries. Similarly, the 35 states' refusal to treat the unborn child as a "child" should be judicially overridden in light of 32 years of HEW matching practice.

The courts that have considered the issue have split, with 11 district courts[94] and 2 circuit courts[95] upholding the rights of the unborn to welfare assistance and 3 district courts disagreeing.[96] In December 1972, the Federal District Court for the Northern District of Illinois in *Wilson v. Weaver*[97] found no congressional authorization for excluding the unborn, a burden of proof placed upon resisting states in *Remillard*. On the other hand, the Federal District Court for the Northern District of Georgia held early in January 1973 that mere inclusion in HEW regulations did not per se require payment of benefits and that the silence of the act itself indicated that mandatory coverage was not intended.[98] Essentially, the Georgia court reversed the *Remillard* burden of production, assuring no coverage despite liberal HEW regulations in the absence of some showing derived from the statute or legislative history that coverage was intended. The remaining 14 federal court cases essentially follow either the Illinois or Georgia pattern, with the great majority, including both the Fourth and Eighth Circuits in February and March 1974, supporting the Illinois line.[99] The Supreme Court has resolved this issue in *Burns v. Alcala*, 95 S. Ct. 1180 (1975). It held the term "dependent child" to mean an individual already born.

Whatever the intent of the Congress might have been in 1935, by 1971 and 1972 it had become hardended against the unborn. In May 1971, the House Ways and Means Committee stated that under the Family Assistance Program of Welfare reform, a generally expansionary proposal from the point of view of eligibility passed by the House later in June, it wanted "to make clear that an unborn child would not be included in the definition of a child" to preclude the practice in some states of "establishing a 'family' even before the child is born."[100] The Senate Finance

---

[94] Welling v. Westby, Civil No. 5093 (D. So. Dak., Jan. 17, 1974); Wisdom v. Norton, 372 F. Supp. 1190 (D. Conn. 1974); Alcala v. Burns, 362 F. Supp. 180 (S. D. Iowa 1973), *aff'd,* 494 F.2d 743 (8th Cir. 1974); Carver v. Hooker, 369 F. Supp. 204 (D.N.H. 1973), *aff'd,* 501 F.2d 1244 (1st Cir. 1974); Doe v. Lukhard, 363 F. Supp. 823 (N.D. Va. 1973), *aff'd,* 493 F.2d 54 (4th Cir. 1974); Green v. Stanton, 364 F. Supp. 123 (N.D. Ind. 1973), *modified,* 499 F.2d 155 (7th Cir. 1974); Harris v. Miss. Dept. of Pub. Welfare, 363 F. Supp. 1293 (N.D. Miss. 1973), *aff'd,* 504 F.2d 861 (5th Cir. 1974); Jones v. Graham, Civil No. 73-1-235 (D. Neb., Sept. 20, 1973); Tillman v. Endsley, Civil No. 73-1476 (S.D. Fla., Oct. 1, 1973); Whitfield v. Minter, 368 F. Supp. 798 (D. Mass. 1973); Wilson v. Weaver, 358 F. Supp. 1147 (N.D. Ill. 1973); *See also* Fletcher v. Lavine, 75 Misc.2d 808, 349 N.Y.S. 2d 43 (Sup. Ct. 1973).

[95] Alcala v. Burns, 494 F.2d 743 (8th Cir. 1974), rev'd, 95 S. Ct. 1180 (1975); Doe v. Lukhard, 493 F.2d 54 (4th Cir. 1974).

[96] Mixon v. Keller, 372 F. Supp. 51 (N.D. Fla. 1974); Murrow v. Clifford, Civil No. 114-73 (D.N.J., June 12, 1973), *vacated and remanded,* 502 F.2d 1066 (3d Cir. 1974); Parks v. Harden, 354 F. Supp. 620 (N.D. Ga. 1973), *rev'd* 504 F.2d 861 (5th Cir. 1974).

[97] Wilson v. Weaver, 358 F. Supp. 1147 (N.D. Ill. 1972), *modified,* 499 F.2d 155 (7th Cir. 1974).

[98] Parks v. Harden, 354 F. Supp. 620 (N.D. Ga. 1973), *appeal pending,* Civil No. 37-1855 (5th Cir.).

[99] *See* cases cited notes 94-96 *supra.* A New York court has upheld inclusion, but only on a restricted basis pursuant to New York rules, after the fourth month of pregnancy, contrary to the permissive HEW regulations which refer to the doctor's diagnosis as the trigger date. Boines v. Lavine, 71 Misc. 2d 259, 335 N.Y.S.2d 731 (Sup. Ct. 1972). *Remillard* would invalidate the delay occasioned in New York, a delay that might well permit malnutrition to take some toll.

[100] HOUSE COMM. ON WAYS AND MEANS, SOCIAL SECURITY ACT AMENDMENTS OF 1971, H.R. REP. No. 92-23, 92d Cong., 1st Sess. 184 (1971).

Committee echoed these sentiments in September 1972, incorporating the same provision in its bill limiting aid to those "who have actually been born"[101] and reciting the tale of a New York woman who unsuccessfully sought a retroactive payment for her second child when she gave birth to twins. [102]

Were the eligibility of the unborn to be clearly established by the courts (apparently not by the Congress), the remaining question is how many poor pregnant women would be benefited and to how great an extent. Numbers are uncertain, but it is reasonable to estimate that less than one-half of the nation's poor women each year (approximately 640,000 according to 1970 census data) would receive help because of AFDC's categorical restrictions, which now use the concept of "dependent" to deny aid to over half of the small children living in impoverished families. Every one of the recipients would receive less income than the eligibility limitation for food stamps (which is $6,000 for a family of four)[103] and food stamps are, by statutory definition, available only to persons who are unable to purchase a nutritionally adequate diet on their own.[104]

The Unborn Child, The Pregnant Mother, The Infant, and Food Aid

Food aid is not as hamstrung by categories and hard eligibility lines as welfare, but there are other hurdles to its receipt that at times amount to absolute barriers. In terms of income, at least 37 million individuals (with annual income under $6,000 for a family of four) and more likely in the vicinity of 50 million individuals are or shortly will be eligible to receive food stamps, unless they live in the few remaining counties that distribute commodities.[105] However, there are no more than 13.6 million recipients, or 37 percent of those eligible.[106] The reasons for the discrepancy are manifold and thoroughly canvassed in *Hunger USA Revisited*, a report by the Citizen's Board of Inquiry into Hunger and Malnutrition in the United States on the progress in feeding the poor from 1968 through 1972.[107] They amount to a nonlegal exclusion of one-half of those eligible.

Food stamps themselves may satisfy the nutritional needs of some groups in the population (small children up to 12 years of age and persons 55 and over), but they cannot furnish the level of food intake pregnant and nursing women require in order to maintain the nutrition of the children whom they are raising. According to March 1974 figures it appears that a pregnant woman must eat $44.10 a month worth of food merely to approximate the Economy Food Plan and a lactating woman, $51.20. [108] Yet each of them, if they are in a family of four, will receive, as of July 1, 1974, only

[101] SENATE COMM. ON FINANCE, SOCIAL SECURITY ACT AMENDMENTS OF 1972, S. REP. No. 92-1230, 92d Cong., 2d Sess. 467 (1972). *See also* H.R. REP. No. 92-231, 92d Cong., 2d Sess. 184 (1972).
[102] *Id.*
[103] 7 C.F.R. § 271.3(c)(3) (1974), *incorporating* FSP No. 1973-1, 38 Fed. Reg. 8287 (1973).
[104] 7 U.S.C. § 2014 (1970).
[105] JOINT EC. COMM., STUDIES IN PUB. WELFARE No. 14, PUB. WELFARE AND WORK INCENTIVES: THEORY AND PRACTICE 5, JT. COMM. PRINT., 93d Cong., 2d Sess. (1974).
[106] U.S.D.A. REPORTS, FOOD PROGRAM PARTICIPATION FOR MONTH OF MARCH, U.S.D.A. News Release 1397-73 (May 3, 1973).
[107] CITIZENS' BOARD OF INQUIRY INTO HUNGER AND MALNUTRITION IN THE UNITED STATES, HUNGER USA REVISITED 17-19, 25-26, 33-34 (1972).
[108] *See* note 5 *supra.*

$ 37.50 worth of nourishment from the use of stamps.[109] The Economy Food Plan itself is designed only for temporary, emergency use and is deficient with respect to the amount of vitamins B-6 and B-12, as well as folic acid and magnesium, that can be purchased within its framework.[110]

There are other small-scale federal feeding programs aimed at target populations that coincide with those in which mental retardation is most likely to occur. In late 1968, the Department of Agriculture developed, in response to a 1967 congressional mandate, a nutritional supplement package for pregnant and lactating women and children up to age six which was designed to provide them with essential nutrients, regardless of what they did with their food stamps or commodities.[111] The program received the President's endorsement in May of 1969 and proceeded, with much public fanfare, to try to involve county health departments in writing prescriptions for food for these specified groups.[112] By April 1970, budgetary stringency had substantially reduced the protein, vitamin A, vitamin C, calcium, and riboflavin contents of the package, had removed children over age one from the eligibility list, and had trimmed the service goal of 400,000 to the actual high service figure of 157,144 in October 1972, which was itself a reduction of 45,000 from the previous year and still 2 million shy of the nationwide total of impoverished infants and pregnant and lactating women.[113] The program was momentarily revived in late 1971 as part of the price of securing the vote of Senator Robert Griffin (R.-Mich.) to confirm Earl Butz as Secretary of Agriculture,[114] but now seems doomed to stagnation and ultimate elimination. As of April 1974, it was scheduled to be phased out, as the Department of Agriculture removed itself from the role of commodity purchaser.[115]

A companion pilot program was begun in 1970 to test the efficacy of giving the same groups certificates (similar to stamps) enabling mothers to purchase up to $ 5.00 of milk monthly for themselves and $ 10.00 of milk or iron-fortified formula and instant baby cereal for their infants. No more than 12,000 people in 5 counties received certificates at any one time. The Department of Agriculture has frozen the use of certificates at that level because they simply extended family income by permitting the replacement of cash expenditures with certificates, without ensuring the purchase of any greater quantities of milk or formula.[116]

The sole remaining program to feed pregnant women and infants was saved from being stillborn in the summer of 1973, but may still die an untimely death in 1975. In the course of the Senate debate over the 1972 National School Lunch Act Amendment, Senator Hubert Humphrey (D-Minn.) proposed an infant feeding program. The program authorized the Department of Agriculture to grant up to $20 million in customs receipts during fiscal year 1973 and 1974 to state health departments, which were to

[109]7 C.F.R. § 271.5 (1974), *incorporating* FSP No. 1973-1, 38 Fed. Reg. 8287 (1973).
[110]Deposition of Dr. R.L. Rizek, in Appendix to Appellants' Brief at 143a, Rodway v. United States Dep't of Agriculture, 482 F. Supp. 722 (D.C. Cir. 1973), *reproduced in Senate Select Comm. Hearings,* 92d Cong., 2d Sess., pt. 3B, at 761 (1972).
[111]CITIZENS' BOARD OF INQUIRY INTO HUNGER AND MALNUTRITION IN THE UNITED STATES, *supra* note 107, at 23.
[112]*Id.*
[113]*Id.*
[114]*Id.*
[115]N.Y. Times, April 28, 1974, at 51, col. 1 (city ed.).
[116]CITIZENS' BOARD OF INQUIRY INTO HUNGER AND MALNUTRITION IN THE UNITED STATES, *supra* note 107, at 23.

use local agencies to make supplemental foods available to infants and pregnant and lactating women with high nutritional risk.[117] The provision, which became law in September 1972 as part of Pub. L. No. 92-433, also contained a major medical evaluation component intended, as the conferees on the bill stated, "to obtain sufficient data . . . to medically identify and define the benefits that are provided through this program in combating and abating any physical and mental damage that otherwise might be caused to infants [by] malnutrition."[118]

For nine months the program existed on paper, but nowhere else. It took HEW until February 1973 to decide not to administer the program on delegation from Agriculture, and Agriculture was passing time with a task force developing program guidelines until the leisurely process was effectively short-circuited in June 1973 by the filing of a lawsuit on behalf of women, infants, and children who needed, but were unable to obtain, benefits from the program.[119]

They successfully challenged Agriculture's reluctance to issue regulations or to spend any money in fiscal year 1973 or more than a projected $6 million in fiscal year 1974. They obtained both a consent order,[120] pursuant to which Agriculture agreed to release program regulations and to process and approve applications by health clinics to participate, and litigated orders[121] requiring that the full $40 million Congress authorized for the program for fiscal years 1973 and 1974 be made available during fiscal year 1974.

The result has been the approval for operation of 255 projects, including 20 doing detailed medical evaluations, which have just begun in the spring of 1974 to make available to children under one year of age thirty-one 13-fluid-ounce cans of iron-fortified infant formula, three 8-ounce packages of infant cereal, and two 46-fluid-ounce cans of fruit or vegetable juice and to pregnant women, children up to age four, and women breastfeeding a child up to one year of age, and all women for a period of six weeks postpartum, thirty-one 13-fluid-ounce cans of whole fortified fluid milk, 30 eggs, six 46-fluid-ounce cans of fruit or vegetable juice, and four 8-ounce packages of iron-fortified cereal.[122] The quantities of food available to participants should satisfy the nutrient needs of infants, but will fall short for every other category. The continuation of the program in fiscal year 1975 depends upon expanding its authorization and appropriation and upon the results of the overall medical evaluation.[123]

The Fetus, The Infant, The Pregnant Mother, and Medical Care

Medical care for the poor throughout pregnancy and health services for every impoverished child from birth are as unrealized as statutory "rights" as is access to

[117] 118 CONG. REC. S11684-85 (daily ed. July 25, 1972) (remarks of Senator Humphrey); 118 CONG. REC. S13712-15, S13724-27 (daily ed. Aug. 16, 1972) (remarks of Senator Humphrey).
[118] H.R. REP. No. 1387, 92d Cong., 2d Sess. 7 (1972).
[119] Dotson v. Butz, Civil No. 1210-73 (D.D.C., filed June 20, 1973).
[120] Id., order of June 20, 1973.
[121] Id., orders of Aug. 3, 1973 and of Dec. 6, 1973.
[122] 7 C.F.R. §§ 246.1 et seq., esp. §§ 246.13 [(initial regulations, 38 Fed. Reg. 18447-51 (1973), and proposed revised regulations, 39 Fed. Reg. 13166-69 (1974)].
[123] The authorization may be raised to $131 million in fiscal year 1975. See S. 3388, 93d Cong., 2d Sess. (1974) (sponsored by nine senators).

welfare and food aid. Approximately 640,000 poor women give birth to children every year. In large cities it is estimated that up to one-half of these women deliver with little or no prenatal care, with an even higher proportion of such women in rural and inner-city areas having no contact at all with medical personnel prior to giving birth.[124]

The major sources for maternity care are Medicaid[125] and Title V of the Social Security Act,[126] which provides for maternal and infant care projects. Medicaid at best offers inpatient hospital care (rarely used by pregnant women until their infants are born) and, in 30 states, clinical services, which may or may not include preventive maternal health checkups.[127] Even this limited range of services may be reduced by the states under the provisions of the 1972 Social Security Act Amendment.[128] Medicaid eligibility, even for these few services, is restricted to those pregnant women who are eligible for AFDC (which revitalizes the argument about the status of the unborn), or, at each state's option, to those who are classified "medically needy," which may include expectant mothers in intact families in which the father is working full-time, but earning little.[129]

The 56 maternal and infant care projects sponsored under Title V of the Social Security Act through special project grants supplied comprehensive maternity care to approximately 141,000 women and 47,000 small children in selected geographic areas in fiscal year 1972.[130] The best of these projects offer thorough physical examinations, including health history, urinalysis, hemoglobin analysis, chest X rays, serologic testing for syphilis (a significant cause of mental retardation), and screening of infants for conditions such as phenylketonuria. The best projects, unfortunately, are few and far between. In fiscal year 1974 the project grants which have financed much of this effort were to have been incorporated into state allocations, but at the last moment Congress granted the projects a one-year reprieve until July 1, 1974 with $92.3 million in appropriations[131] or $700,000 less than in fiscal year 1973, which when coupled with inflation will result in a general diminution of available services. The projects are scheduled to be phased into state formula grants in fiscal year 1975.[132]

There is one increasing, rather than decreasing, source of health care for infants. Provisions of Medicaid[133] that have recently been endorsed and supported by Congress[134] mandate for eligible individuals such items as screening for lead poison-

---

[124] REPORT TO THE PRESIDENT—WHITE HOUSE CONFERENCE ON CHILDREN 156, 165 (1971).

[125] 42 U.S.C. § 1396 *et seq.* (1970).

[126] 42 U.S.C. § 701 *et seq.*, esp. § 708 (1970).

[127] *Medicaid—State or fiscal agent claims processing*, CCH MEDICARE AND MEDICAID GUIDE para. 14,931 (1972).

[128] *See* §§ 230 and 231 of Pub. L. No. 92-603 repealing §§ 1903(e) and 1902(d), respectively, of Title XIX of the Social Security Act, 42 U.S.C. §§ 1396b(e) and 1396a(d) (Supp. II 1972).

[129] 42 U.S.C. § 1396a(a) and 10(b) (1970).

[130] The Health Law Project, *A Poor Children's Health Crisis*, 7 CLEARINGHOUSE REV. 5 (1973); PUBLIC HEALTH SERVICE, U.S. DEP'T OF HEALTH, EDUCATION & WELFARE HEALTH SERVICES AND MENTAL HEALTH ADMINISTRATION, PROMOTING THE HEALTH OF MOTHERS AND CHILDREN, FISCAL YEAR 1972 (1973); 119 CONG. REC. H 5,386 (daily ed. June 26, 1973) (remarks of Representative Michel).

[131] *See* Act of July 1, 1973, Pub. L. No. 93-53, § 4(a)(6), 87 Stat. 135, *amending* 42 U.S.C. § 708(b); and Act of December 18, 1973, Pub. L. No. 93-192, 87 Stat. 746.

[132] THE BUDGET OF THE UNITED STATES GOVERNMENT, FISCAL YEAR 1975, at 387 (1974).

[133] 42 U.S.C. §§ 1396(a)(13)(B) & (C), 1396a(d)(1)-(3) (1970).

[134] 42 U.S.C. § 603(g) (Supp. II 1972), added by § 299F, Pub. L. No. 92-603, penalizes states for failing to implement the program by a reduction of 1 percent in the federal matching of AFDC costs.

ing, determination of nutritional status, and a developmental assessment of each child as early as possible in the child's life.[135] Unfortunately, this program is experiencing severe implementation problems, requiring administrative negotiations and lawsuits to guarantee results nationally and in each state.[136]

The pattern of access to welfare, food aid, and health care on behalf of the unborn and infants is consistent. The governing statutes state promises that range from the vague AFDC provisions for "Financial assistance . . . as far as practicable under the conditions in each state,"[137] and the maternal and child health services mandate to extend and improve "as far as practicable under the conditions . . . services for reducing infant mortality and otherwise promoting the health of mothers and children"[138] to the specific goals of using food stamps to alleviate hunger and malnutrition nationwide[139] and reducing "nutritional risk" with infant feeding.[140] But the statutory promise is hardly an enforceable legal claim. Like the pledge in the Housing Act of 1949 to furnish "a decent home and a suitable living environment for every American family,"[141] the promise merely states ideals that are useful as "a general guide to administration and interpretation of"[142] the relevant statutes, not as enforceable promises "by the government to the public to tax and appropriate as heavily as would be required to satisfy the ideal."[143]

The Infant and Lead Paint Poisoning

The right to safe and sanitary housing, and particularly the right not to be confronted with lead-based paint peeling from the ceilings, walls, window ledges, or other places in the interior, is perhaps the most significant right from the point of view of the infant who is born intellectually unimpaired and wishes to remain so. The evidence of brain damage induced by malnutrition is associated most clearly with harm to the fetus, rather than to the small child. But lead paint poisoning poses a serious threat to the brains of children aged 1 to 3 (85 percent of the cases of plumbism occur at this age level) who have an abnormal, compulsive desire to ingest non-nutritious and unnatural food substances, medically termed "pica." The nation's greatest source of lead-based paint is substandard housing built prior to World War II.[144]

The cost of eliminating this hazard is high, so high that most courts have shied away from imposing it on anyone other than a major unit of government

---

[135] 45 C.F.R. §§ 249.10 (1974). MEDICAL SERVICES ADMINISTRATION, U.S. DEP'T OF HEALTH, EDUCATION AND WELFARE, MEDICAL ASSISTANCE MANUAL, §§ 5-70-20(A)(4), (B)(1) & (12), (E)(7)(c), (1), & (m) (1969).

[136] See 5 THE HEALTH LAW PROJECT, MATERIALS ON HEALTH LAW—MEDICAID 296-99 (rev. ed. 1972).

[137] 42 U.S.C. § 601 (1970).

[138] 42 U.S.C. § 701 (1970).

[139] 7 U.S.C. § 2011 (1970).

[140] 42 U.S.C. § 1786 (Supp. II 1972).

[141] 42 U.S.C. § 1441 (1970).

[142] Michelman, *The Right to Housing*, in THE RIGHTS OF AMERICANS 43, 47 (N. Dorsen ed. 1971).

[143] *Id.*

[144] See generally Hearings on S. 3080, supra note 24; Senate Select Comm. Hearings, 91st Cong., 2d Sess., pt. 5 (1970); *Lead Paint Poisoning: Legal Remedies and Preventive Actions*, 6 COLUM. J.L. & SOC. PROBLEMS 325 (1970). According to the 1970 census, 40 percent of all American families occupy dwellings constructed before 1939, Chapman, *Housing Improved During '60s*. Washington Post, May 27, 1973, § A, at 7, col. 1.

and, even then, have usually permitted those units as much discretion in employing eradication techniques as possible. The cost factor is also responsible for the fact that Congress, the Department of Housing and Urban Development (HUD), and HEW have been quite hesitant to embark on any extensive program aimed at nationwide prevention of lead paint poisoning.

The goal could be achieved in various ways. The paint could be totally removed from the walls of the 7 million housing units in which a lead hazard is presented by using solvents, sanding, or burning, or by covering the surface with materials such as glass fiber, gypsum board, paper wall cover, or vinyl sheeting. The range of costs is from as low as $ 2 billion (based on reports of $ 300 as unit costs in Washington, D.C.) to $14 billion ($2,000 a unit in Chicago) to a high of $70 billion (National Bureau of Standards figures of $10,000 a unit).[145]

Measured only in terms of dollars, the cost of ending the threat is, on the surface, greater than the economic cost of the impact of the lead poisoning itself. Dr. Julian Chisolm of Johns Hopkins Medical School estimates that life institutionalization for a severely brain damaged child costs $ 225,000.[146] With over 800 children requiring institutionalization yearly because their brains have been crippled following the ingestion of lead paint, the annual cost is $ 200 million to which must be added the additional losses to other children who suffer, but suffer less.[147] Against this background of a total remedy which strictly in dollars terms appears to be more costly than permitting the harm to continue, subject to minor ameliorative efforts, it is easy to understand the usual reluctance of courts to compel landlords, paint manufacturers, or government agencies to act or pay for the damages caused by lead poisoning.

When landlords have been sued for damages for injuries caused by defects in their premises, they have been held liable only when they either (1) failed to perform a duty to avoid creating such defects imposed by a housing code or (2) failed to exercise reasonable care in correcting defects that they knew existed and which they could have reasonably foreseen would lead to such injuries.[148] These two tests have been strictly construed in the lead paint poisoning context so as to deny recovery in most instances, either by restricting the scope of the particular building code or by finding that the injury was not reasonably foreseeable.

In terms of the first theory of tort liability, the broad legal rule is that housing codes fix standards of conduct for landlords to which they must adhere upon penalty not merely of statutory fine, but also of tort liability. A subsidiary rule is that a code provision specifically requiring a landlord to repair his premises when confronted with peeling paint, or generally requiring him to maintain his apartments in a safe and sanitary condition, establishes a duty of care on his part in favor of the tenants, including children.[149] No court has specifically applied the rule to lead paint removal regulations, but the regulations exist in Chicago, Philadelphia, New York, Washing-

---

[145] *Hearings on S. 3080*, at 19-20, 217 (testimony of H. Finger & J. Sten); *Senate Select Comm. Hearings*, 91st Cong., 2d Sess., pt. 5, at 1548-53 (1970).

[146] *Hearings on S. 3080*, at 215.

[147] *Id.* at 118 (testimony of Representative Ryan).

[148] *See* Restatement (Second) of Torts §§ 357, 358 (1965).

[149] Whetzel v. Jess Fisher Management Co., 282 F.2d 943 (D.C. Cir. 1960); Ewing v. Balan, 168 Cal. App. 2d 619, 336 P.2d 561 (1959); Michaels v. Brookchester, Inc., 26 N.J. 379, 140 A.2d 199 (1958); Garcia v. Freeland Realty, Inc., 63 Misc. 2d 937, 314 N.Y.S.2d 215 (N.Y.C. Civ. Ct. 1970).

ton, D.C., and elsewhere, and at least one court in Chicago has suggested to a plaintiff, who mistakenly sought to hold the city responsible for nonenforcement of the code, that he should assert his cause of action against the landlord who violated the ordinance. [150]

The common law concepts of "notice" and "reasonable foreseeability" have been the undoing of most damage actions brought in the state courts based on the second theory of tort liability. Although the New York State Supreme Court did award $ 4,320 in damages from the landlord to a child victim of lead paint poisoning, the court stressed that the landlord had notice the walls were composed of peeling and falling paint and plaster. The conditions were, in fact, "in violation of the section of the Multiple Dwelling Laws requiring the owner of such premises to keep each and every part thereof in proper repair at all times."[151] The court further noted that the landlord should have foreseen that children, who often have cravings to put the most unusual things in their mouth, might pick up and eat any pieces of plaster left lying around, which, in turn, would lead to poisoning because of the well-known fact that old plaster contains dangerous quantities of lead.

One court has permitted the tenant to recover from the landlord both the cost of materials and a minimum hourly wage to reimburse the tenant for his efforts to re-plaster and repaint two rooms. The court found the father's work essential to protect his children from plaster and paint the landlord knew were peeling but failed to repair.[152] One law firm in Chicago has settled out of court two tenant suits against landlords for $125,000 and $33,000.[153] But to date only the New York State Supreme Court has been willing to recognize the legitimately linked, reasonably foreseeable circumstances (children will eat anything, including plaster; plaster contains lead; eating plaster will poison the child) in the context of awarding damages against the landlord.[154]

In all of the other damages cases, the courts have found some means of releasing the landlord from liability. In *David v. Royal-Globe Insurance Co.,*[155] the Louisiana Supreme Court questioned the quality of plaintiff's proof when the plaintiff showed that his child ate paint for only two weeks before convulsions began leading to permanent retardation. Physicians testified that ingestion of paint with such a calamitous outcome must take place over a period of six to eight months, and the landlord claimed that he had never used lead paint since he acquired the apartment in 1948. In *Montgomery v. Cantelli,*[156] another Louisiana court found no landlord liability where a child picked dry and flaking paint from the front door because "such gastronomic culinary impulses are, to say the least, abnormal and unexpected, and could not reasonably be anticipated by the lessor," and because the landlord had no duty to maintain the outside of his property in light of the great burden this would impose upon him given the New Orleans climate. In *Kolojeski v. Deisher,*[157] the Pennsylvania

---

[150] Stigler v. City of Chicago, 48 Ill. 2d 20, 268 N.E.2d 26 (1971).
[151] Acosta v. Indank Realty Corp., 38 Misc. 2d 859, 238 N.Y.S.2d 713 (Sup. Ct. 1963).
[152] Garcia v. Freeland Realty, Inc., 63 Misc.2d 937, 314 N.Y.S.2d 215 (N.Y.C. Civ. Ct. 1970).
[153] M. Moskowitz, *A New Threat — Lead Poisoning of Slum Children,* 3 CLEARINGHOUSE REV. 92 (1969).
[154] *See* Acosta v. Indank Realty Corp., 38 Misc. 2d 859, 238 N.Y.S.2d 713 (Sup. Ct. 1963).
[155] 257 La. 523, 242 So. 2d 839 (1970), *cert. denied,* 403 U.S. 911 (1971).
[156] 174 So. 2d 238, 240 (La. App. Ct.), *review denied,* 247 La. 1082, 176 So. 2d 143 (1965).
[157] 429 Pa. 191, 239 A. 2d 329 (1968).

Supreme Court found that the landlord was not negligently responsible for a child's death from lead paint poisoning because the landlord had no knowledge that the paint was dangerous and was not supposed to be an expert in the content of such substances. Finally, in *Weaver v. Schneider Realty Co.*,[158] the Missouri Supreme Court refused to attribute to the landlord the duty to foresee that an unattended child would eat paint chips in the common hallway of an apartment building.

There are to date no reported instances of a tenant's defending against eviction for nonpayment of rent on the ground that the landlord breached an implied warranty of habitability by permitting peeling paint or plaster to go unattended, but this defense is foreseeable in the District of Columbia and other jurisdictions that recognize such a warranty.[159] A district court in Pennsylvania has held that HUD as a seller of homes breached the implied warranty of habitability by selling homes containing quantities of lead-based paint that were in excess of standards set by the city code.[160]

Injunctive actions against landlords requiring them to comply with a housing code or specifically to perform their implied covenants of quiet enjoyment or implied warranties of habitability appear promising. A New York court, in light of state public health laws placing the burden on dwelling owners to remedy all conditions conducive to lead poisoning, has issued a preliminary injunction ordering a landlord to make the repairs necessary to de-lead a dwelling unit.[161] Given the existence of a specific building code, courts should be able to issue injunctions based on a finding of imminent, irreparable injury with no adequate remedy at law.

Tenants could also look to paint manufacturers to secure redress on the negligence theory that the manufacturers failed to warn the users of the danger, or on a theory of strict liability for sale of an unreasonably dangerous product.[162] The bar of the usually brief torts statute of limitations supplies a legal obstacle that can be overcome if the tort is held not to have occurred until the time of the injury.[163] Reality poses an even more insuperable hurdle because of the difficulty of ascertaining from whom the 1940s landlord bought his paint. Of course, there are situations in which batches of more recently manufactured interior house paint have been found to exceed the toxic level of lead. But these appear to be aberrations, with the exception of custom-mixed paints to which leaded tint has been added by the retailer, who might, under such circumstances, be liable in the absence of a warning label.[164]

Suits against a city mandating that it strictly enforce its housing code and crack down on landlords who refuse to repair their premises have met with mixed success. The cities seem loathe to enforce their laws aggressively. The reasons are legion: Cities cannot afford enough inspectors; local codes often require the intervention of a licensed physician; criminal penalties for noncomplying landlords are so minimal as to make a mockery of the cities' efforts; landlords often abandon inner-city units

---

[158] 381 S.W.2d 866 (Mo. 1964) (en banc).
[159] *See, e.g.,* Javins v. First Nat'l. Realty Corp., 428 F.2d 1071 (D.C. Cir., 1970), *cert. denied*, 400 U.S. 925 (1970).
[160] City Wide Coalition Against Childhood Lead Paint Poisioning v. Philadelpha Housing Authority, 356 F. Supp. 123 (E.D. Pa. 1973).
[161] Graham v. Wisenburn, Cir. No. 134 (N.Y. Sup. Ct. Albany City, N.Y. April 21, 1972).
[162] *See Lead Paint Poisoning: Legal Remedies and Preventive Actions, supra* note 144, at 327-28.
[163] *See* White v. Schnoebelen, 91 N.H. 273, 19 A.2d 185 (1941).
[164] *See Hearings on S. 3080, supra* note 24, at 26 (testimony of H. Finger).

when confronted with expensive repair orders; and any number of other good or bad reasons why housing codes normally lie dormant.[165]

Courts seem uncertain as to what level of law enforcement they should compel. The Illinois Supreme Court would not require the city of Chicago to enforce a lead paint removal ordinance adopted in 1968 against a 1966 injury-causing hazard and refused to hold the city liable for the injury itself.[166] The New York City courts have given the New York City Health Department as much leeway as it sought in enforcing the city's lead paint elimination law by refusing to compel the health department to order a landlord to remove all lead-based paints from interior walls.[167] The department had allowed him to even out wall surface irregularities after removing hazardous peeling paint and apply a new coat of lead-free paint on top, although the best available scientific data indicate that repainting does not eliminate the hazard from surfaces on which the leaded coats may be eight or ten layers deep.[168]

The Philadelphia Housing Authority recently negotiated a consent decree with various civic organizations representing parents and children living in properties subject to the housing authority's jurisdiction who had been subjected to lead paint poisoning caused by the condition of those properties. The decree provided that the housing authority would inspect all properties over five years old to determine the presence of lead paint and remove all such paint wherever found, up to a height of five feet and wherever else such paint might be accessible to small children.[169]

State and federal agencies have been as lax as the courts in dealing with lead paint poisoning. Only three states have statewide laws instituting programs to prevent and control lead poisoning. In 1971, a Massachusetts law established a state laboratory for detection and analysis purposes and a massive screening program for children under six. The statute compels landlords to remove all lead-based paint at heights and in places where children can reach. Compensatory and treble punitive damages can be levied against landlords who do not comply.[170] New York prohibits the use of lead paint on surfaces children are mostly likely to touch, including toys, furniture, sills, porches, and interior surfaces, and provides for abatement proceedings with penalties and appointment of an interim receiver in the event a demand to discontinue dangerous paint conditions is not complied with.[171] Maryland bans the use of lead-based paint on any interior surface and any exterior surface to which children may be commonly exposed.[172] From the other states: silence.

Since October 21, 1972, HUD has prohibited, through the inclusion of appropriate provisions in contracts and subcontracts, the use of lead-based paint on

[165] See generally Lead Paint Poisoning: Legal Remedies and Preventive Actions, supra note 144, at 338-39.
[166] Stigler v. City of Chicago, 48 Ill. 2d 20, 268 N.E.2d 26 (1971).
[167] In re Waters, 161 N.Y.L.J., Jan. 23, 1969, at 2 (N.Y. Sup. Ct. 1969); Scurry v. Department of Health, 162 N.Y.L.J., Dec. 5, 1969, at 16 (N.Y. Sup. Ct. 1969).
[168] See Hearings on S. 3080, at 45-46 (testimony of Dr. Chisolm).
[169] City Wide Coalition Against Childhood Lead Paint Poisoning v. Philadelphia Housing Authority, 356 F. Supp. 123 (E.D. Pa. 1973).
[170] Mass. Ann. Laws ch. 111, §§ 190-99 (Supp. 1972).
[171] N.Y. Pub. Health Law §§ 206(1)(n), 608(1)(g), 1370-76 (McKinney 1971).
[172] Md. Ann. Code art. 43. § 117 A (Supp. 1972).

interior and exterior surfaces accessible to children of any residential structure thereafter constructed or rehabilitated under any federally assisted program, including public housing.[173] The directive emerged over one and a half years after the passage of the Lead-Based Paint Poisoning Prevention Act of 1971, Pub. L. No. 91-695, which mandated that such action be taken with respect to any residential building erected after its date of enactment.[174]

HUD regulations also require HUD to remove lead paint from all of the properties it owns, but, because of the financial burden involved, HUD has construed the regulations narrowly to compel this process only where the paint is cracking, scaling, peeling, or loose and not where it remains intact on the wall.[175] On January 23, 1973, the District Court for the Eastern District of Pennsylvania issued a preliminary injunction against HUD preventing HUD from selling any residential housing structure located in Philadelphia until it completely removed lead-based paint from interior and exterior surfaces of the premises.[176] Compliance was ensured by enjoining the transfer of property title in the absence of an inspection by the City Department of Public Health. The thrust of the decision was not only to make HUD comply with its own limited regulations on paint removal, but with the more extensive complete removal provisions applicable to all other Philadelphia homeowners by virtue of Philadelphia public health regulations.

Effective January 1, 1973, HEW, through the Food and Drug Administration, has issued regulations requiring paints for interior residential surfaces to contain no more than 0.5 percent lead.[177] This order, in conjunction with the Federal Hazardous Substances Act, has the additional effect of banning the manufacture of any toy or other article intended for use by children which bears or contains paint with a greater lead content. But the order has no effect at all upon walls or items currently containing lethal quantities of lead. It even manages to weaken the normal refund right under the Federal Hazardous Substances Act (applicable to all banned articles whether or not so banned at the time of sale) by limiting repurchase only to hazardous substances shipped in interstate commerce after January 1, 1973.[178]

Given the reluctance of courts, state and local governments, and federal agencies to act vigorously and effectively against present demonstrated dangers of lead paint poisoning, it is not surprising that Congress sat idly by, watching its 1971 Act expire on June 30, 1972, with nothing to replace it. The Act was finally revived in the fall of 1973 by Pub. L. No. 93-151, the Lead-Based Paint Poisoning Amendments of 1973, which extended the old law and added new authority for the secretary of HUD to implement a research and demonstration program to determine the nature and extent of the problem of lead-based paint poisoning in the United States, particularly in urban areas, and to established procedures to eliminate the hazards of lead poisoning in housing covered by HUD mortgage insurance or housing assistance payments that was constructed prior to 1950.[179]

[173] 24 C.F.R. §§ 35.1 *et seq.* (1974).
[174] 42 U.S.C. § 4831 (1970).
[175] 24 C.F.R. § 35.3(e) (1974). *See also* 42 U.S.C. § 4811 (a)(2) (1970).
[176] City Wide Coalition Against Childhood Lead Paint Poisoning v. Philadelphia Housing Authority, Civil No. 72-1515 (E.D. Pa., March 12, 1973).
[177] 21 C.F.R. § 191.9(a) (197).
[178] *See* § 15(a)(3) of the Federal Hazardous Substances Act, 15 U.S.C. § 1274 (1970).
[179] Act of November 9, 1973, Pub. L. No. 93-151, 87 Stat. 560 (esp. § 4).

Lead paint poisoning is not the only serious lead poisoning hazard that confronts small children. In December 1972, the Environmental Protection Agency reported evidence that people who lived near heavy automobile traffic had greater concentrations of lead in their blood than people who lived where there were fewer cars. Citing the problem of children living in homes coated with lead-based paint, the report concluded that "lead in the air and consequently in the dust and dirt present additional sources of exposure which may contribute to and aggravate this problem . . . [and] . . . excessive lead exposures among children have approached what many consider an epidemic proportion."[180]

The threat from lead in the air and dirt, primarily attributable to gasoline, is substantial. According to Dr. Daniel B. Fisher of the National Institute of Mental Health, "one-third or more of the lead in city dwelling Americans comes from inhalation of airborne lead from automobiles."[181] Samples of soil from Los Angeles and New York City have contained nine or ten times the maximum permissible daily intake of lead in small children.[182] New York City's Environmental Protection Agency promoted an Air Pollution Control Code, adopted in 1971, which called for a step-by-step reduction in the lead content of gasoline sold in the city to a no-lead level after January 1, 1974.[183] The Environmental Protection Agency, in the fall of 1973, imposed a structured reduction in the average amount of lead in fuel, starting with 1.7 grams per gallon as the upper limit in refined gasoline as of January 1, 1975 and culminating in 0.5 grams by January 1, 1979.[184]

CONCLUSIONS

The potential incidence of mental retardation in children due to their inability to obtain adequate food, income, medical care, and living conditions is substantial. The cost in human life and mental functioning is great. The ability or willingness of the government to respond affirmatively to the situation appears minimal. The courts are limited by present constitutional interpretations. Congress is limited by either lack of sympathy for the particular programs or operational difficulties. The executive branch fails to implement enacted programs aggressively.

Unfortunately, this is the present status of the right to be born and remain intellectually unimpaired and the constituent rights to be fed adequately, to be provided suitable prenatal and pediatric health services, and to live in an environment free from retardation-producing pollutants. A mentally retarded citizen may have a right to go to school, receive special training, or to receive habilitative care if institutionalized. But this is all after the fact, after the retardation is irreversibly established. The right not to be mentally retarded currently has no meaningful judicial, legislative, or executive foundation. As usual, the most meaningful legal remedies are created long after the damage has been done. The practice of preventive law awaits development.

[180]N.Y. Times, Jan. 3, 1973, at 18, col. 1.
[181]*Hearings on S. 3080,* at 207 (paper by Dr. Fisher).
[182]119 Cong. Rec S1450 (daily ed. Jan. 29, 1973) (statement of Senator Kennedy).
[183]Bird, *City is Adamant on Limiting Lead,* N.Y. Times, Feb. 17, 1973, at 21, col. 5.
[184]*See* 40 C.F.R. § 80.20(a)(1) (1974) (38 Fed. Reg. 33, 735, Dec. 6, 1973).

Reaction Comment

LOUIS Z. COOPER

FORMER PRESIDENT NIXON'S goal of reducing the incidence of mental retardation by one-half within this century is realistic and can be reached, but only if some of the legal hurdles outlined by Kramer can be overcome. In most instances medical scientists are unable to identify the etiology of mental retardation. Even when the cause is known, biological labels can be given in only about one-fourth of the cases. An even smaller percentage of mental retardation is well defined in terms of specific environmental causes. Beyond a doubt, however, self-perpetuating poverty is the single most important common denominator as an environmental cause of retardation. Obviously, it is not the only cause, but its magnitude gives it first place in terms of significance. Not only is cultural-familial retardation (that which relates to not having sufficient and proper environmental stimulation) too frequently a result of poverty, but there are in addition well-defined and easily measured biological events leading to retardation to which the poor are especially vulnerable. Although we may not have the resources or ability to tackle the whole cycle of poverty and mental retardation at once, we can make major progress. With our present knowledge and abilities, we can break the chain of poverty and mental retardation at a number of discrete points, if we have the will.

As Kramer points out, infants in a healthy environment normally experience a rather sharp increase in brain development during the last few months of pregnancy and during the first year or so after birth. The growth of neurons is particularly rapid in this period along with a variety of cells that provide support, extension, and covering for the nerve cells. Brain weight approximately doubles during the first year, brain waves increase rapidly, and there are important enzymatic changes. The brain is particularly susceptible prenatally through the first year following birth to a host of factors that can have a detrimental effect upon its proper development. The effect of malnutrition upon the fetus and infant is discouragingly predictable; the brain is robbed of its potential. There is no way to compensate for the loss of the cells that do not develop. They either grow during this crucial period or they fail to grow at all. For this reason malnutrition certainly can be labeled a major cause of mental retardation; and the relationship between malnutrition and poverty has become increasingly well documented during the last few years.

Another important relationship that is all too evident is the fact that poor maternal nutrition can lead to poor maternal health with consequent poor fetal growth. The result is a high incidence of premature births among poor mothers. Also, it is now recognized that the premature infant who is born in a poor community has a much greater risk of becoming mentally retarded than an infant of the same birth weight born into a middle- or upper-class family. Once again, the victim can easily become trapped in a cycle of poverty and mental retardation.

Another major cause of mental retardation is infectious diseases, of which rubella (German measles) is the best known. Rubella begins in pregnancy as a consequence of maternal illness that can be mild or even unapparent: The mother may not even know that she is sick. The virus enters the placenta from the mother's blood stream and passes through the placenta into the developing fetus; it can infect any part of the unborn child. When the infection attacks the brain, mental retardation is often the result.

Of course, infectious diseases can strike anywhere in the economic spectrum, and rubella was found among all income groups before a vaccine was licensed in 1969. Since then the incidence of rubella has become concentrated in those socio-economic groups with limited access to education, preventive health care, and medical services. Once again, there is a cycle of poverty and mental retardation.

We may not be in a position immediately to eliminate poverty in our society, but it is now evident that even limited increases in the delivery of health care can dramatically reduce the incidence of mental retardation. Pilot projects throughout the country have demonstrated that the cycle can be broken. The result is a tremendous saving in both human resources and money.

That mental retardation is a causal result of poverty is more than mere abstraction. It is a daily reality for thousands of our citizens. I know of a young lady who lives in the Bedford-Stuyvesant section of New York City. She became pregnant for the first time at the age of sixteen and gave birth to a severely damaged rubella baby. Shortly thereafter she became pregnant again and had an attractive, healthy little boy. But the family lived in a home painted with sweet-tasting, lead-based paint. While still an infant the little boy became mentally retarded from eating the peeling paint; he is a victim of lead poisoning. About two years later the mother gave birth to a healthy girl, and one cannot but wonder how the third child will fare. This young woman is a classic example of what can happen to the poor. She did not have adequate access to family planning, contraceptives, health education services, or prenatal care. Hopefully, we are a little wiser now and will be able to help her protect her daughter.

The tragic paradox is that we presently have the knowledge to prevent most mental retardation, but our funds and attention have focused on habilitation of the individual after he has become retarded. Unfortunately, one gathers from what Kramer has written that the judicial system is not likely to provide the needed solutions within the scope of its present constitutional interpretations. Effective legal relief apparently must come legislatively, if it is to come soon. In the legislative arena, the legal profession can make a significant contribution to the field of mental retardation. If attorneys can make their impact felt with well-conceived legislation and adequate funding, we will have gone a long way toward eliminating the environmental causes of mental retardation.

CHAPTER 3

Guardianship and Limitations Upon Capacity

Kindred presents a call for reform of guardianship law, both in its formal legal statement and in its utilization. Noting a number of social and legal developments that render ancient guardianship concepts inadequate, he offers the principle of the right to the least restrictive alternative as the legal principle that should dominate this reform.

A major concern of the paper is the elimination of guardianship control when advice and the provision of social services will serve as well. In cases where some control is required, Kindred recommends the development and use of limited guardianship controls that are less restrictive than general guardianship. He notes the existence of a number of these controls now present in the legal system and suggests others that are needed. Limitations on the power of all guardians is also discussed in terms of decisions that are too personal to be made by any substitute decision maker. Kindred also develops a concept of facilitative guardianship, which would allow a guardian to confirm some decisions of his ward, but not to act in his place. Finally, the role of the state in providing guardianship is discussed in terms of safeguards against conflicts of interest.

Elkin's reaction directs attention to two problems. First, a variety of services, including counseling, must be available if the use of guardianship is to be limited. And second, guardians must not be viewed as having unlimited power over their wards. Elkin's focus on parent-guardians who have been allowed to decide their child shall die places this issue in sharp relief.

PRINCIPAL PAPER

MICHAEL KINDRED

THE DISTINCTION between guardianship and limitations upon capacity, reflected in the title of this chapter, is essential to the construction of a rational guardianship system. Limitations upon capacity provide one level of protection and restriction by removing certain legal powers from an individual;[1] guardianship provides a second level by transferring powers to a guardian.[2] The life of a mentally retarded individual can be greatly affected by either capacity restrictions or guardianship. Wald has dealt with the propriety of certain capacity restrictions[3] and the model that is appropriate to judge them.[4] This paper will focus on guardianship.

Guardianship is a legal mechanism for substitute decision making.[5] The guardian is distinguished from the adviser or social worker by his legal power to impose his advice or desires through the decisions he makes on behalf of his ward. Because guardianship is a control mechanism, a definition of its proper role and function must take account of the control characteristic. Some mentally retarded individuals need assistance and advice, but guardianship can properly be used only when the additional element of control is clearly required. Some individuals may require some control, but general and total guardianship can properly be used only when general and total control is clearly required. And some legal acts, such as marriage and making a will, are so personal that no guardian may ever be given the power to make them on behalf of any mentally retarded individual. This paper will examine less restrictive alternatives to guardianship, limited forms of guardianship, and safeguards that are required against the abuse of guardianship power.

The author is particularly indebted to his student assistant Marlin Harper for his research in connection with the writing of this paper. He also wishes to acknowledge the contributions made by Jeffery Glasgow, Steven Cox, J. Douglas Crowell, Lee Judy Johnson, and Anthony Lucia.

[1] Powers often removed include the capacity to contract, see 1 A. CORBIN, CONTRACTS § 6 (1963); the capacity to marry, see H. CLARK, THE LAW OF DOMESTIC RELATIONS § 2.15 (1968); and the capacity to make a will, see 1 T. HARRISON, WILLS & ADMINISTRATION § 123 (2d ed. 1961).

[2] R. ALLEN, E. FERSTER & H. WEIHOFEN, MENTAL IMPAIRMENT AND LEGAL INCOMPETENCY 71 (1968) [hereinafter cited as ALLEN].

[3] *See* pp. 7-9 (marriage), pp. 18-20 (contract), pp. 20-23 (work), and p. 25 (voting), Chapter 1 of this volume.

[4] *See* pp. 25-26 *supra*.

[5] The guardian's authority is defined by his statutory or judicial grant of power, rather than by his ward's desires. *See* Fratcher, *Powers and Duties of Guardians of Property,* 45 IOWA L. REV. 264, 292 (1960). The institution of agency provides a very different form of substitute decision making, in which the agent's powers are defined by the will of the principal who appointed him. W. SEAVEY, LAW OF AGENCY § 3 (1964).

Present guardianship law derives from the English common law[6] and still bears the marks of its origins. The concept of guardianship in the common law has proved a flexible one, serving diverse goals determined by the social, political, and economic structure of the time. In the feudal period, it reinforced the power of the feudal lord.[7] This power gradually disappeared, and the principle evolved that the guardian must serve the best interests of his ward.[8] Guardianship has continued to develop, however, with a focus on the preservation of the property of wealthy families against mismanagement and waste.[9] Although less affluent families with retarded family members no doubt have usually managed their affairs with little reference to guardianship law, a second system of control did develop to deal with the very poor. This system provides the roots from which present public guardianship[10] has grown. Initially, control was asserted over the poor, "paupers," without differentiation in terms of specific mental handicaps.[11] "Poor houses" were established, and "paupers" were committed to them. The director of the house had control over the residents placed with him.[12] In the nineteenth and early twentieth centuries, differentiation did occur, and special asylums and "schools" were established to isolate and control the mentally ill and the mentally retarded.[13]

This development of dual mechanisms for the control of persons thought to need protection and restriction has left the law well developed in some respects and underdeveloped in others. Rules relating to the powers and responsibilities of guardians when managing property are highly developed, yet little law has developed until recently concerning nonproperty decisions.

Several interrelated developments require a critical reappraisal of the ancient

[6] ALLEN 70.

[7] 3 W. HOLDSWORTH, A HISTORY OF ENGLISH LAW 512-13 (1908). For a description of the many forms of guardianship as they existed in feudal times, see H. TAYLOR, LAW OF GUARDIAN AND WARD 9-30 (1935).

[8] Id. See also THE MENTALLY DISABLED AND THE LAW (rev. ed. S. Brakel & R. Rock eds. 1971) [hereinafter cited as THE MENTALLY DISABLED].

[9] See, e.g., Emerick v. Emerick, 83 Iowa 411, 413 (1891). This point may be illustrated by an examination of present-day case law. A large number of cases for the appointment of a guardian which reach the appellate courts is brought by a family member who claims that the alleged incompetent is wasting his assets.

[10] The term "public guardianship" will be used in this paper to refer to the situation in which the guardian is a public official or a governmental employee with this designated function. It will be distinguished from "private guardianship," in which a private individual serves as guardian.

[11] See generally D. ROTHMAN, THE DISCOVERY OF THE ASYLUM 180-205 (1971).

[12] Id. Rothman reports that a Boston almshouse in the 1840s had a very strict regimen for its inmates. Boston's officials grouped all of the city's needy into one structure, a combination almshouse workhouse at Charlestown. They too made the heart of the program a rigid schedule and rigorous discipline. Exempting those under medical care from the several requirements, they expected all others to conform to a precise routine. An early morning bell would waken the inmates, another would signal the time for breakfast. Residents were to proceed immediately, but not in formation to the dining hall, take their assigned seats, and finish their meals in the prescribed time; those guilty of wasting or pilfering food would be punished by a decrease in rations, or at the superintendent's discretion, solitary confinement. After breakfast they were to enter workshops, and again the threat of reducing provisions and solitary confinement hung over anyone who might be slothful or sloppy in his labor. No one could leave the institution without the manager's permission; no one could come to visit without his formal approval. Those almshouse residents who faithfully obeyed the regulations would be allowed to remain with friends for a few days once every two months. Habitual violators would suffer curtailed rations or confinement and repeated offenses would bring still more severe punishments. The essence of the institution was obedience to its rules. Id. at 191.

[13] Id. at 130-54; Rothmna, pp. 407-11. Chapter 13 of this volume. See also A. DEUTSCH, THE MENTALLY ILL IN AMERICA (2d ed. 1949).

rules of guardianship. The first involves a change in social conditions. A guardianship system born in a feudal society and developed in an agrarian culture where the extended family provided support for dependent family members may be expected to require revision to satisfy the needs of a mobile urban society in which the nuclear family and social security have replaced the extended family and its responsibility. Preservation of family estates has become a less pressing social concern, and trust arrangements usually suffice to keep estates intact when this is an individual goal.[14] Qualification for training, employment, credit, and public benefits have taken on new importance. More choices are required of community members, and guardianship must satisfy new demands.

A second development is an increased emphasis on the legal rights and human potential of all members of society, with special emphasis on groups that have long been disenfranchised. The two most prominent movements of this sort relate to the rights of black Americans and the rights of women. Much of the success of these movements has been in the challenge to laws placing minority individuals and women in a restricted, disadvantaged position. Movements to establish the legal rights of the poor and of those charged with, or convicted of, crimes have also developed. Again, the focus has been on restrictive rules of law, and success has been gauged largely in terms of legal change. It is not surprising, therefore, to find a movement now gathering momentum that seeks to improve the legal status of the mentally handicapped. Nor is it surprising to find that the focus of this movement is upon changing legal rules that have restricted the participation of the mentally handicapped in community life. Guardianship rules are among those that must be scrutinized.

A third development is disenchantment with institutionalization as a mechanism to provide protection and control for mentally retarded citizens. News articles and television specials have exposed the inhumanity of the giant concentration camps called state institutions. Judicial decisions have placed limits on the availability of institutional placement.[15] Parents of mentally retarded individuals have begun to search for more acceptable solutions. Simultaneously, community education, training, and employment programs, and other services for the mentally retarded have slowly developed, making residence of most mentally retarded citizens in the community a feasible option. This trend away from the institutional "solution" places greater demands upon guardianship.

---

[14] For a discussion of the use of trusts for this purpose, see Effland, pp. 120-26, Chapter 5 of this volume.

[15] In Wyatt v. Stickney, 325 F. Supp. 781 (M.D. Ala. 1971), the first in a series of judicial orders to the Alabama commissioner of mental health, the court said: "The purpose of involuntary hospitalization for treatment purposes is *treatment* and not mere custodial care or punishment. This is the only justification, from a constitutional standpoint, that allows civil commitments to mental institutions such as Bryce." *Id.* at 384 (emphasis in original). In a later order, 344 F. Supp. 387 (M.D. Ala. 1972), the court proscribed the admission of any person whose retardation was only mild or borderline *Id.* at 396. And in Saville v. Treadway Civil Action No. 6969 (M.D. Tenn., March 8, 1974), the court held unconstitutional a Tennessee statute, TENN. CODE ANN. § 33-501 (Supp. 1973), which allowed commitment of the mentally retarded on consent of a parent or guardian accompanied by a physician's opinion that the individual is in need of care and treatment. In holding that the statute violates the due process clause of the fourteenth amendment, the court said "[W]here individual liberty is at stake to the extent it is in the instant case, it is absolutely essential that such confinement be preceded by adequate procedural safeguards." *Id.* at 4 (slip opinion). *See* Wyatt v. Aderholt, 503 F.2d 1305 (5th Cir. 1974), *See also* Lynch v. Baxley 386 F. Supp. 378 (M.D. Ala. 1974); Welsch v. Likins, 375 F. Supp. 487 (D. Minn. 1974).

Finally, knowledge about mental retardation renders simple distinctions between competent and incompetent individuals obsolete. Increasing recognition is given to gradations of competence and differential competences in different tasks and endeavors.[16] This view of the individuality of the mentally retarded citizen, when coupled with concern for the protection of his legal rights as a citizen, requires the development of more subtle and humane protective devices than total institutionalization or general guardianship.

Nevertheless, important and appealing policy goals are in tension in the guardianship area. The first policy goal is protection against exploitation of mentally retarded citizens. The second goal is freedom of the mentally retarded citizen, with opportunity to develop as an independent member of the community.[17] Extreme protection can sometimes be more onerous than moderate exploitation. For example, one can remove any danger of merchant exploitation by placing the person in an institution or a locked nursing house, where merchants cannot reach him. The individual, however, is then not only protected from his exploiters; he is also restricted from contact with honest and helpful storekeepers and the rest of the community—often a serious loss. The endeavor here will be to reconcile conflicting goals and to suggest measures that can provide optimum protection without unnecessary restrictions of freedom.

The legal principle that best expresses the theme of reconciliation of goals is the principle of the right to the least restrictive alternative.[18] This principle recognizes that there are public interests that justify restrictions on individual freedom. It requires, however, that these interests be precisely defined and that personal liberty be restricted only to the extent required by the defined public interest. The right to the least restrictive alternative is little more than a requirement that common sense and respect for the humanity and individuality of every person be the touchstone of the law.

SERVICES AS AN ALTERNATIVE TO CONTROL

The impact of guardianship law on mentally retarded citizens depends in large part on the life choices available to them. In a tightly structured society where care for dependent family members devolves upon the extended family, few choices are presented for the retarded individual and guardianship is likely to be used for control

---

[16] *See especially* INTERNATIONAL LEAGUE OF SOCIETIES FOR THE MENTALLY HANDICAPPED, SYMPOSIUM ON GUARDIANSHIP OF THE MENTALLY RETARDED 18-19 (1969) [hereinafter cited as SAN SEBASTIAN].

[17] This same policy conflict is present in decisions concerning mentally retarded citizens in the institutional setting (discussed in Chapters 13-18 of this volume), in the criminal system (discussed in Chapters 20-22 of this volume), and in the educational system (discussed in Chapters 8 and 9 of this volume). The resolution of this conflict is a primary challenge for the legal system in its treatment of the mentally retarded.

[18] The principle was outlined by the Supreme Court in Shelton v. Tucker, 364 U.S. 479 (1960).

In a series of decisions this court has held that, even though the governmental purpose be legitimate and substantial, that purpose cannot be pursued by means that broadly stifle fundamental personal liberties when the end can be more narrowly achieved. The breadth of legislative abridgement must be viewed in the light of less drastic means of achieving the same basic purpose. *Id.* at 488 (footnotes omitted).

For a comprehensive discussion of the application of the least restrictive alternative principle to the care of the mentally retarded, see Chambers, Chapter 16 of this volume. *See also* Murdock, *Civil Rights of the Mentally Retarded,* 48 NOTRE D. LAW. 133 (1972).

only when there is substantial property. In a society where the accepted "solution" to mental retardation is institutionalization, most choices are precluded by the institutionalization, and guardianship is little more than a convenient legal tool for shipping the individual to the far-off warehouse. Whenever a society opts for total control, formal or informal, guardianship does little to increase that control, although it may be one of the control mechanisms used. In contrast, social integration of mentally retarded citizens into society, or normalization, is characterized by choices and opportunities for mentally retarded citizens and presents more significant and difficult questions concerning the proper role of guardianship. The emphasis on individual potential contradicts a guardianship structure that invariably assumes general incompetence and imposes total control. On the other hand, the existence of choices renders decision making essential to the mentally retarded individual and suggests an increased role for guardianship in some cases.

The appropriate role for guardianship can be defined only in terms of the social services provided for mentally retarded individuals. Many mentally retarded individuals are such improper candidates for institutional confinement that the only "social service" they need in order to function independently is to be allowed to cope with society on their own. Many others, however, require a variety of social services in order to manage satisfactorily outside the institutional context. Guardianship is sometimes described as a social service, but unlike most services, guardianship's essential characteristic is that it removes choices from the mentally retarded individual (giving them to the guardian), whereas social services in the community expand choices. This section of the paper considers the extent to which noncontrolling social services can limit the need to use guardianship for control purposes. The thesis postulated is that management of most mentally retarded individuals does not require a choice between mismanagement and guardianship management. If society is willing to provide it, there often is a third choice: assistance and opportunities without control.[19]

Mentally retarded persons have the same basic needs for food, shelter, and recreation as other persons; the "social services" discussed here are directed to the fulfillment of these universal needs.

In a human society where mentally retarded citizens are accepted as full members, a complete range of supportive services is essential. Present community service systems for the mentally retarded, however, are archaic at best,[20] with scattered exceptions.[21] If adequate community services are developed, guardianship should be rarely needed. If the services are not developed, however, some form of

---

[19] *See* Chambers, *Alternatives to Civil Commitment of the Mentally Ill,* 70 MICH. L. REV. 1108, 1117 (1972).

[20] SENATE COMM. ON LABOR AND PUBLIC WELFARE, S. REP. No. 725, 90th Cong. 1st Sess. (1967), found in U.S. CODE CONG. & ADM. NEWS 2061 (1967).

[21] Several good illustrations of excellent community programs may be found in REPORT OF THE PRESIDENT'S COMM. ON MENTAL RETARDATION, MR 72; ISLANDS OF EXCELLENCE. One such example was that of Henry, who had spent 38 of his 46 years in the back wards of Beatrice State School in Nebraska. Henry's records showed that "he was totally incapable of functioning outside.

"Henry . . . moved into a hostel in Omaha, and was given five months of intensive vocational and social training. He has not missed a day of work nor been late once for his job as a dishwasher in an Omaha restaurant.

"He was almost late once, but that was during a blizzard. He walked through it and punched in on time." *Id.* at 43.

control is likely to be substituted and the strain on the guardianship system becomes intolerable.[22]

A first area of supportive services relates to the production of income for the sustenance of life. In the past, institutions maintained by the state have often provided this sustenance, however inadequate it may have been.[23] Where family members have had adequate means and inclination, they have provided sustenance through hired care in the community or private institutional placement.[24] The "normal" means of sustenance for all members of this society, however, is either employment or governmental assistance. To avoid the unacceptable choice between public institutionalization and dependence on the financial support of relatives, adequate income must be guaranteed mentally retarded individuals living in the community, either through employment opportunities or state assistance. In the absence of adequate financial resources, guardianship may seem to be needed to transfer an individual to a state institution or to compel the use of inadequate funds for what the guardian or family regards as "essentials."

A place to live—shelter—is essential to all persons. Mentally retarded individuals, like other individuals, have diverse tastes and needs in respect to residential services. A model providing a wide range of residential services is described elsewhere in this volume.[25] Where these services are provided in such a way as to serve both the physical and emotional needs of an individual, he will utilize them. No coercion is likely to be necessary. Like other persons, few mentally retarded persons will choose a hovel over a comfortable, well-furnished home with appropriate socialization and entertainment near at hand. However, if the choice is limited to a restrictive, medically oriented nursing home or institution on the one hand, and a hovel with some freedom on the other, a mentally retarded person—like many nonretarded persons—may choose the hovel. Coercion may then *seem* to be required.

Educational and training services also will have an impact on the apparent need for guardianship. Any individual excluded from job training, health training, dietary management training, behavior training, and the many other forms of training normally provided by society will have great difficulty functioning as even a semi-

---

[22] A good system of community services can serve two distinct functions, both of which reduce the need for a guardian. First, the community program can itself serve as a protector of the mentally retarded person, protecting both his personal and property interests. Second, and more important, the community service program can teach many functional skills, thereby preparing the mentally retarded person to better protect himself.

[23] In an unreported interim order in Wyatt v. Stickney, March 2, 1972, the court made a finding on the physical conditions at Partlow State School for the mentally retarded, a finding that was reiterated in Wyatt v. Stickney, 344 F. Supp. 387 (M.D. Ala. 1972):

> The evidence . . . has vividly and undisputedly portrayed Partlow State School and Hospital as a warehousing institution which, because of its atmosphere of psychological and physical deprivation is wholly incapable of furnishing [habilitation] to the mentally retarded and is conducive only to the deterioration and the debilitation of the residents. The evidence has reflected further that safety and sanitary conditions at Partlow are substandard to the point of endangering the health and the lives of those residing there, that the wards are grossly understaffed, rendering even simple custodial care impossible, and that overcrowding remains a dangerous problem often leading to serious accidents, some of which have resulted in deaths of residents. *Id.* at 390.

[24] Most states permit privately owned institutions to exist subject to state licensing requirements. *See, e.g.,* Ohio Rev. Code § 5123.16 (1970). These institutions are typically expensive and the care provided is sometimes not much better than in public institutions.

[25] *See* Glenn, pp. 505-14, Chapter 16 of this volume.

independent adult. Yet, many mentally retarded individuals are so excluded or are placed in educational and training programs that are not designed for, or responsive to, them. The absence of these services can make it seem that the only choice is to have someone else, an institution or a guardian, manage the functioning of the individual. The preferable choice, however, is to provide training that enables the individual to care for himself to the maximum possible extent.

In addition to physical resources such as housing, education, and employment, many mentally retarded individuals need supportive personal resources in order to function effectively. These needs, like the need for physical resources, are not unique to the mentally retarded. Most, if not all, individuals require and utilize an array of personal supportive services. Often, however, the personal services appropriate to the needs of mentally retarded individuals have not been made available. To take an illustration of the most common sort, dental services are needed by everyone, and each person's dental needs are different. Mentally retarded individuals, however, often have considerable difficulty in obtaining the dental services that other members of society take for granted.

Flexible and broad-ranging social work and homemaker services can be essential to an avoidance of formal controlling services. A mentally retarded individual may have difficulty budgeting properly. He may fail to pay his bills or run out of food before his next paycheck. Many nonretarded individuals in the community do the same. Proper supporting social services, providing advice on the planning of expenditures and access to banking mechanisms to facilitate money management, can alleviate this problem. With assistance the individual may become capable of managing reasonably well and of learning to manage with increasing independence. If these social support services are unavailable, however, a guardian may seem to be required. A mentally retarded individual may also require supportive advice in dietary planning. Without support, it may seem essential to restrict the freedom of the retarded individual. With support, the need for control may disappear. Social and sexual conduct, too, may require the supportive advice of a social worker. Without supportive service, external control can seem imperative; with support, the need for control can disappear. An endless list of illustrations could be provided, but the essential point is that the need for advice and assistance is very different from the need for control. Until a broad spectrum of supportive social services has been provided, it is impossible to determine an individual's real need for the control furnished by guardianship.

Another specialized personal service needed by many mentally retarded citizens is that of the advocate.[26] Services for the retarded do not magically appear from nowhere: They are the result of organized political and social pressure. Voluntary associations and individuals must advocate better social programs for the retarded, either at a general level or in response to the identified needs of an individual. Even where services exist, an advocate is often needed to secure access for his client or simply to locate the service within the bureaucratic maze. Where a guardian has been appointed, he has an obligation as an advocate to press the rights and needs

---

[26] *See generally* W. WOLFENSBERGER, TOWARD CITIZEN ADVOCACY FOR THE HANDICAPPED, IMPAIRED, AND DISADVANTAGED (rev. ed. 1971).

of his client upon society, but the advocacy role is distinct from, and does not depend on, the control that typifies guardianship.

A further distinct function is served by the "ombudsman" or "protector" of the retarded.[27] The San Sebastian Symposium on Guardianship recognized a difference between the need for guardianship services and the need for protective services.[28] It called for the establishment of an official body with the authority to monitor the performance of guardians' duties.[29] This need for counterchecks differs from the need for guardianship. There is an increasing awareness of the need for counterchecks on official functioning in many areas, and this need exists in the area of guardianship as well. The advocate may see such counterchecking as one of his functions, but there are additional ways to provide counterchecks. One such mechanism has been created in Ohio under the name of "protective services."[30] A "protector" is defined as "[an agency] acting with or without court appointment to provide guidance, service, and encouragement in the development of maximum self-reliance to a mentally retarded or other developmentally disabled person, independent of any determination of incompetency."[31] An additional very specific protective role is relegated to the Ohio Division of Mental Retardation by a recently enacted requirement that professionals report to the division for investigation any incident of suspected abuse or neglect of a mentally retarded adult.[32] The New York Mental Health Information Service[33] offers an additional model for a checking device.

Effective participation in today's complex industrial-technological society is a difficult cooperative endeavor. All citizens require a myriad of support from their fellow citizens. In this, as in so many other ways, mentally retarded citizens are more like than unlike the rest of the citizenry. They, too, need housing, education, training, and a variety of other support. Some of their needs are satisfied through the marketplace; others by their families and private organizations; still others through the agency of government. Their needs are individual needs and thus vary from person to person. If the basic needs of mentally retarded citizens are not met in a decent and effective manner, they will have difficulty participating in the life of society. It will appear necessary to manage their lives for them. General guardianship and/or institutionalization will seem to be the only "solution." If provision is made for their participation in society, the vast majority will manage adequately without the use of extensive control devices.

---

[27] For a discussion of the role of the ombudsman in helping the mentally retarded, see B. SWADRON, MENTAL RETARDATION—THE LAW—GUARDIANSHIP 167-68 (1972).

[28] SAN SEBASTIAN 18.

[29] Id. at 21.

[30] OHIO REV. CODE §§ 5119.85-89 (Supp. 1973).

[31] Id. § 5119.85(D).

[32] OHIO REV. CODE § 5123.98, found in OHIO AM. SUB. SENATE BILL 336 (effective July 1, 1975).

[33] The New York program is found in N.Y. MENTAL HYGIENE LAW § 29.09 (McKinney Supp. 1973-74). This program set up a commission whose duties are: (1) to study and review the admission and retention of all patients, (2) to inform patients and interested parties of patients' rights, (3) to assemble information for court proceedings, and (4) to provide service and assistance to patients and their families. For a discussion of this program, see Chapters 15 and 19 of this volume.

TOWARD THE REFINEMENT OF CONTROL MECHANISMS

Even if adequate social services are provided, some form of guardianship will be required for some mentally retarded individuals. When an individual is totally incapable of making choices, a guardian will have to be appointed to provide substitute decisions. In other cases, the assistance of a guardian may be needed to gain access for an individual to a service, program, or commodity the individual has decided he wants. This section examines alternative mechanisms that can be used to serve the needs for control and assistance.

General guardianship is the broadest and most comprehensive noninstitutional instrument for control. It transfers total transactional power to the guardian as substitute decision maker.[34] Some individuals are so profoundly mentally retarded and incapable of independent decision making that general guardianship is the only appropriate solution. Restrictive as it is, general guardianship is still conceptually less restrictive than institutionalization. The vast majority of mentally retarded individuals, on the other hand, are capable of making decisions, independently on some matters and with advice and assistance on others. For these individuals, general guardianship is an overly restrictive instrument and can stifle the realization of a mentally retarded individual's potential for independent living.

The major thrust of recent recommendations in the guardianship area has been for the development of more subtle, less restrictive forms of guardianship.

The President's Panel on Mental Retardation stated:

> For some, of course, a comprehensive guardianship will be needed. But we urge that, as far as possible, mentally retarded adults be allowed freedom — even freedom to make their own mistakes. We suggest the development of limited guardianships of the adult person, with the scope of the guardianship specified in the judicial order.[35]

The San Sebastian Symposium on Guardianship took the following position:

> The ability to assert one's rights or express one's wishes is seldom completely lacking. The retarded adult should be permitted to act for himself in those matters in which he has competence. The limitations of legal capacity inherent in guardianship

---

[34] The San Sebastian Symposium on Guardianship concluded that:

> Another serious difficulty arises because the law usually represents incompetence in simple black and white terms, with the result that most guardianships of the person are looked on as plenary guardianships. The effect is well expressed by the word *interdiction* (prohibition) which has until recently been in use in the statutes of many of the Latin countries. The person interdicted (declared incompetent) is deprived of the legal capacity to act in any way on his own behalf. Even though he may have a guardian appointed to exercise some of his rights, the emphasis usually is on the deprivation of rights rather than on implementing rights constructively through informed representation. Moreover, the idea that the person himself can properly retain and exercise some personal and even property rights, selectively, according to his individual capacity, is not adequately expressed in most existing statutes pertaining to guardianship. SAN SEBASTIAN at 11.

[35] THE PRESIDENT'S PANEL ON MENTAL RETARDATION, REPORT OF THE TASK FORCE ON LAW 25 (1963) [hereinafter cited as PPMR REPORT].

should not extend to these matters. It follows that a person whose mental retardation is characterized by impairments of social competence which are partial should enjoy a partial guardianship specifically adapted to his strengths and weaknesses.[36]

These recommendations call for the application of the principle of the right to the least restrictive alternative to guardianship law. Guardianship limited to the actual disabilities of the particular individual can be achieved in a variety of ways. Some involve greater utilization and development of established legal concepts; others require the development of new procedures and concepts.

Little, if any, change in the law would be required to provide for the rudimentary distinction between inability to manage financial affairs and inability to manage personal affairs. Guardianship has traditionally served the two interrelated functions of financial and social control, and this financial-social dichotomy is expressed in the legal distinction between guardianship of the estate, or conservatorship, and guardianship of the person. Guardianship of the estate is that legal creature which allows and requires the guardian to replace the ward in transaction dealing with management of property and income.[37] Guardianship of the person relates to a more amorphous group of problems, but is said to give the guardian the right to the custody of the ward; *i.e.,* to determine where and how he shall live and to take the responsibility for his education, training, and personal welfare.[38] Although courts presently have the power to limit their appointments to guardianship of the person or guardianship of the estate, this power seems to be rarely utilized.

Generally, once guardianship proceedings are begun, the appointment is a general one without limitations. A simple statutory reform would be to require courts to specify whether they are extending guardianship powers to financial matters, personal matters, or both. A further step would be to create a presumption that guardianship is limited to financial matters unless greater breadth is specified in the judicial order.[39] A further step in the same direction would be to presume that an unspecified guardianship relates only to the management of financial assets existing at the time the guardianship is created, thus excluding from the restriction income that may be earned by the individual subsequent to the guardian's appointment. A major goal of such presumptions would be to force judges to give more attention to the principal objectives sought through the appointment of a guardian and to require that the degree of control be related to these objectives.

In addition to the distinction between personal and estate guardianship, other existing legal mechanisms can be used to provide a limited degree of control and protection without the blanket restrictions of general guardianship. Effland has elaborated upon some advantages of the trust as an instrument to control the use of significant property inherited by a retarded individual from parents or other rela-

---

[36] San Sebastian 18-19. *Cf.* Lynch v. Baxley, 386 F. Supp. 378, 389 (M.D. Ala. 1974).

[37] For a general description of estate guardianship, see Fratcher, *supra* note 2.

[38] *See* Fraser, *Guardianship of the Person,* 45 Iowa L. Rev. 239 (1960). A fairly typical guardianship of the person statute is Cal. Prob. Code. § 1500 *et seq.* (1956).

[39] Some states have statutes that provide that if the powers of the guardian are not limited by the appointment order, then the guardianship is to be general, encompassing both the estate and the person. *See, e.g.,* Ohio Rev. Code. § 2111.06 (1969).

tives.[40] He emphasizes the flexibility of the trust as a legal mechanism.[41] Through terms of the trust instrument, or through precatory instructions to a trustee, the mentally retarded beneficiary of a trust can be given some decision-making power. The trust is a less restrictive and more normal device than general guardianship in other ways as well. Conceptually, a trust proceeds from the principle that an individual is entitled to dispose of his property upon such reasonable conditions as he may choose. The trust is a mechanism to control the use of the donor's own property; it is not an assertion of control over the life of the beneficiary. The beneficiary is free to make the same choices he could make in the absence of the trust. He is simply presented with additional choices that may be required if he wishes to enjoy the trust proceeds. Trusts are imposed on property by cautious donors and testators in a multitude of situations where some control is desired. It matters little that the beneficiary is a school, a church, a nonretarded individual, or a retarded person. Practically, it is less restrictive in that it provides control only for that property that is made part of the trust corpus, not for all assets of the trust beneficiary.

A related property control mechanism is that of the social security "representative payee."[42] In this case, the "donor" or "trustor" is the United States Social Security Administration (SSA). The SSA has created the representative payee system to provide assurances in some cases that social security benefits will be expended "properly." It is similar to the trust in that the restrictions apply only to specified funds, social security benefits, and are imposed by the payor of these funds, the SSA. A characteristic that differentiates it from most trusts, however, is the clear, direct involvement of the government. This governmental involvement brings into play, under the federal Constitution, standards of due process and equal protection.[43] On demand,[44] the SSA makes an investigation to determine whether it is in a person's

---

[40] *See* Effland, Chapter 5 of this volume.

[41] *Id.* at pp. 120-26. For a further discussion of the strengths and weaknesses of trusts and other estate planning devices as applied to property of persons labeled incompetent, see ALLEN 144-93.

[42] This system is discussed in ALLEN 114-28.

[43] The fourteenth amendment provides in part "[N]or shall any state deprive any person of life, liberty, or property, without due process of law; nor deny to any person within its jurisdiction the equal protection of the laws." U.S. CONST. amend. XIV, § 1.

For the fourteenth amendment to come into play, some action on the part of the state must be demonstrated; private, individual discrimination is not prohibited. The concept of state action was defined as long ago as 1879 in *Ex Parte* Virginia, 100 U.S. 339 (1879):

> The constitutional provision, therefore, must mean that no agency of the State, or of the officers or agents by whom its powers are exerted, shall deny to any person within its jurisdiction the equal protection of the laws. Whoever, by virtue of public position under a State government, deprives another of property, life, or liberty, without due process of law, violates the constitutional inhibition; and as he acts in the name and for the State, and is clothed with the State's power, his act is that of the State. This must be so, or the constitutional prohibition has no meaning. Then the State has clothed one of its agents with power to annul or to evade it. 100 U.S. at 347.

Although the fourteenth amendment speaks of state action, it is likely that the prohibition would also apply to actions of a federal agency such as the SSA. *See* Bolling v. Sharpe, 347 U.S. 497 (1954), a school segregation case from the District of Columbia in which the Supreme Court, applying the due process and equal protection standards to the federal government, stated that "[i]t would be unthinkable that the same Constitution would impose a lesser duty on the Federal Government." *Id.* at 500 (citing Hurd v. Hodge, 334 U.S. 24 (1947)).

[44] It is usually brought to the attention of the SSA by a relative or friend, or by the report of the institution where the person is confined. ALLEN 116-7.

best interest to have a "representative payee" appointed.[45] When such a payee is appointed, social security payments will be made to him on condition that he expend the funds only for the use and benefit of the beneficiary.[46] The "representative payee" may invest any of the funds not needed for the current support of the beneficiary,[47] but at the request of the administrator he must account for all funds received.[48]

Although the "representative payee" system serves a very useful purpose in many cases and is less restrictive than a general guardianship, it is also highly susceptible to abuse. The most serious problem stems from the procedure for determining when a "representative payee" is needed. A claims representative makes the determination to utilize a representative payee either on medical evidence or after a determination of legal incompetence.[49] Although due process of law requires at least that the alleged incapacitated person receive notice and a hearing,[50] no such safeguards are articulated in the relevant legislation or regulations. SSA's standards for appointment of a "representative payee" are also questionable on constitutional grounds. The authorization of the appointment of a "representative payee" to receive the benefits "regardless of the legal competency or incompetency of the individual entitled thereto"[51] may well deny a large class of people the right to the exclusive possession and use of funds to which they are entitled.[52] For an individual who is largely dependent on social security benefits, the appointment of a representative payee can have a major restrictive effect on his life. Nevertheless, little literature or case law has developed to refine the mechanism.[53]

Existing law provides these and other mechanisms for asserting partial control without the imposition of general guardianship and total control. Much of the need for reform may be in the greater utilization and refinement of these existing mechanisms with an understanding of the variable needs of mentally retarded individuals

---

[45] 20 C.F.R. § 404.1601 (1974).

[46] *Id.* § 404.1603.

[47] *Id.* § 404.1605.

[48] *Id.* § 404.1609.

[49] ALLEN 117.

[50] An analogy may be drawn between the SSA's "representative payee" system and certain state wage garnishment statutes which previously allowed wage attachment without a prior hearing. The Supreme Court, in Sniadach v. Family Finance Corp., 395 U.S. 337 (1969), held such garnishment statutes unconstitutional as violative of the fourteenth amendment's procedural due process requirements. The Court said:

> The result is that a prejudgment garnishment of the Wisconsin type may as a practical matter drive a wage-earning family to the wall. Where the taking of one's property is so obvious, it needs no extended argument to conclude that absent notice and a prior hearing . . . this prejudgment garnishment procedure violates the fundamental principles of due process. *Id.* at 341-42 (footnote and citation omitted).

> If these garnishment procedures violate due process, then certainly a procedure that allows the appointment of a "payee" to receive social security benefits without an opportunity for notice or hearing is also unconstitutional. This is particularly true in view of the facts that (1) a "representative payee" can be appointed regardless of whether or not the beneficiary is incompetent and (2) periodic social security benefits may be the only source of revenue for many people.

[51] 42 U.S.C. 405(j) (1970).

[52] *See* note 50 *supra.*

[53] *But see* ALLEN ch. 6.

and respect for their individual rights and their dignity as citizens. More extensive reforms are also needed, however, to develop a guardianship system that will meet the needs of mentally retarded individuals living in the community.

A "facilitative guardianship" should be developed as an alternative to present control guardianships. In his discussion of planning for the mentally retarded client, Effland suggests the use of a trust established by a mentally retarded individual to help the individual accomplish his own goals effectively.[54] Likewise, in a facilitative guardianship, the guardian's functions would be to assist the mentally retarded citizen to achieve his own goals, rather than to substitute the guardian's decisions for those of his ward.

Contracting is a part of everyday life. Minor contracts involve the purchase of food and sundries. Major contracts include: the purchase and repair of a car; the lease of an apartment or house; the contract for a vocational training program. These transactions can be as essential to mentally retarded citizens seeking to live a normal community life as they are to others. Because of others' questions about his competence to contract, however, the mentally retarded individual may need assistance in securing these contracts. A guardian can be of utility in this situation, but his role as facilitator requires much less than the full power of guardianship. The "facilitator guardian" would have no power to substitute his judgment for that of the ward, but would retain power and responsibility for supporting the ward in major decisions involving the use of the latter's contractual power. An intermediate position might permit the guardian to exercise independent judgment and withhold the supportive concurrent consent in cases where he felt the ward's decision was clearly unreasonable. He might then suggest alternatives to the ward, thus guiding and training him in wise decision making.

A final word on due process aspects of guardianship determinations must be added. The main thrust of this paper has been that reform of guardianship depends upon the recognition and use of less restrictive alternative mechanisms of management in place of comprehensive guardianship control. Nevertheless, basic due process requirements are also too frequently ignored in guardianship statutes[55] and procedures.[56] Suffice it to say here that a decision to establish guardianship over an individual involves a very significant restriction of fundamental rights and must be accomplished by procedural safeguards that recognize this fact. There must certainly be a hearing, and counsel must be appointed and required to expose all of the reasons militating against the guardianship appointment. Determinations must be based

---

[54] *See* Effland pp. 127-30, Chapter 5 of this volume.

[55] For a comparison of state incompetency statutes, see THE MENTALLY DISABLED AND THE LAW table 8.3. Although some states' statutes have been amended since 1971, there are still many state guardianship statutes that are silent as to the right to notice, the right to counsel, and the specific rights that must accompany the right to a hearing.

[56] Allen reports on the observation of combined hospitalization and incompetency proceedings held in a state hospital in Texas: "The hearing procedure followed a monotonous regularity to its inevitable conclusion. All of the proposed patients were ordered indefinitely committed and all were found to be incompetent. The hearings began at 2:00 p.m. and ended at 3:05 p.m., an hour and five minutes for 40 persons; about a minute and a half per patient." ALLEN 88. When *commitment* proceedings are held with so little regard for adequate procedural safeguards, it is not difficult to understand why guardianship proceedings are often so lacking in due process safeguards.

solely upon evidence that would be admissible in other court proceedings and that would clearly establish the need for guardianship. There must be a presumption against total guardianship; and the guardianship imposed must be fit to the particular limits on the capacity of the individual in question, as demonstrated by the evidence. Moreover, the performance of a guardian must be subjected to periodic review.

SUBSTANTIVE LIMITS ON GUARDIANS OF THE PERSON

Important as the powers of the guardian of the estate, the conservator, the trustee, and the representative payee may be, they are limited to the economic sphere. The guardian of the person, on the other hand, deals primarily in the noneconomic sphere (albeit sometimes with important economic consequences). The law must decide whether the guardian of the person shall have the power as substitute decision maker to vote on behalf of his ward; to enter into a marriage for his ward; to annul a marriage for the ward; to refuse life-saving medical care (*i.e.,* to kill his ward); to donate the ward's organs to another (before or after his death); and so on. Although the absurdity of granting some of these powers to a guardian is sufficiently obvious that one may safely say the power is withheld, the law is pitifully unclear with respect to some very basic issues.

The distinction made in the title to this chapter needs to be recalled again, for it is basic to the analysis that follows. Limitations upon capacity are imposed because our legal system posits a certain intellectual participation as essential to many legal acts. When an individual lacks the ability to provide this level of intellectual participation, the law declares that he lacks capacity to perform that act. It is a major additional step to provide that someone else shall be given the power to provide a substituted intellectual participation on behalf of the limited individual. Although a minimum capacity could theoretically be required for the exercise of the vote,[57] the franchise of the ward could not feasibly be exercised "on his behalf" by his guardian. The exercise of the vote is too personal and individual to be exercised by a substitute decision maker. The same assurance seems possible in terms of the decision to marry. Whereas the law may require a certain level of intellectual participation as a requisite to marriage,[58] a guardian cannot in his ward's stead make the decision for him to marry. Thus, there are certain legal acts so private, so personal, and so fundamental that they cannot be exercised at all unless the individual directly involve is able to provide the

---

[57] "[S]tates do have the power, within the framework of state and federal constitutional imperatives, to bar exercise of the franchise on appropriate grounds. This right of the state to regulate its elections forms the basis of laws which bar certain citizens, including incompetents from voting." ALLEN 364. *See also* THE MENTALLY DISABLED table 9.4, at 333. Recent cases, however, have held that voting is a "fundamental right," thus requiring the state to demonstrate a "compelling state interest" to support restrictions. *See* Harper v. Virginia State Bd. of Elections, 383 U.S. 663 (1966).

[58] ALLEN 299, *See also* THE MENTALLYDISABLED table 7.1, at 240, *But see* Loving v. Virginia, 388 U.S. 1, 12 (1967), where the court said: "Marriage is one of the basic civil rights of man; fundamental to our very existence and survival." Although this statement was not strictly necessary in the ultimate disposition of the case, any court considering marriage restrictions today might well apply the "compelling state interest" test. *Cf* Griswold v. Connecticut, 381 U.S. 479 (1965).

essential volition. Without attempting to provide a definitive catalogue, the following discussion will deal with some of the most pressing and current questions. Unfortunately, few of these questions are as simple as marriage and the vote.

The right to live is probably the most basic right held by citizens. At the end of life, all other individual rights are extinguished. The most stringent criminal penalties are reserved for those who take the life of another.[59] Thus, it might seem artificial to examine the question of whether a guardian has the right to decide to end the life of his ward. This is not, however, an artificial or hypothetical question, but rather one of immediate practical importance.

The Joseph P. Kennedy, Jr., Foundation pierced the shadows of medical practice in its film "Who Shall Survive?"[60] which reenacted an actual decision on the part of parents and doctors in a major hospital to allow their child, who had Down's syndrome,[61] to die although established surgical procedure could have saved it. A recent study of neonatal deaths at the Yale-New Haven hospital confirms the existence of a propensity to permit apparently mentally defective infants to die by withholding life-saving medical treatment that would be provided were it not for the mental abnormality.[62] The *Washington Post,* in a series of articles by B. D. Cohen, quotes the head of Georgetown University Hospital's intensive care nursery as saying that "about 20 times a year . . . he must tell a set of distraught parents that it is pointless to operate or continue treatment to save their child, for while the child may live for a few weeks, months, or even years, it will never lead a *meaningful* life."[63]

In other words, parent-guardians[64] have decided to allow their children to die by withholding consent to normal medical procedures.[65] Doctors and hospital administrators have also made a conscious decision not to interfere, indicating that at least a portion of the medical community has acceded to this parental assertion of guardianship power over the life of a child.[66] Although common hospital practice

---

[59] Although this is the case, it is a documented fact that juries are often very lenient in finding doctors and parents guilty of mercy killings. *See* Kamisar, *Some Non-Religious Views Against Proposed Mercy Killing Legislation,* 42 MINN. L. REV. 966, 1019-23 nn. 172-84 (1958).

[60] Joseph P. Kennedy, Jr., Foundation, *Who Shall Survive?* (film) (1971).

[61] Commonly known as Mongolism, one of a group of syndromes caused by chromosomal abnormality. Down's syndrome is often associated with physical, as well as mental, abnormalties, including congenital heart disease and duodenal atresia. L. HOLMES et al., MENTAL RETARDATION 151 (1972). *See also* Benda, *Mongolism,* in MEDICAL ASPECTS OF MENTAL RETARDATION 519 (C. Carter ed. 1965).

[62] Duff & Campbell, *Moral and Ethical Dilemmas in the Special Care Nursery,* 289 NEW ENGLAND J. MEDICINE 890 (1973).

[63] Cohen, *Life or Death for Infants,* Washington Post, March 11, 1974, at A10, col. 1 (emphasis supplied).

[64] The parent is often referred to as "the natural guardian" of the minor child. By this it is meant that the powers of guardianship are placed with the parent by operation of law where there is the basic pre-existing parental relationship. This natural guardianship, unlike other forms of guardianship, requires no special judicial act to establish. Indeed, it exists as a matter of law until majority of the child-ward, unless a judicial act intervenes to remove it.

[65] A distinction exists in the medical world between the use of ordinary and extraordinary medical procedures. The principle is to the effect that a physician has no moral obligation to sustain life by the use of extraordinary or experimental measures. The major problem is in determining which procedures are truly extraordinary. If a procedure would be ordinary when performed on a "normal" child, does it become extraordinary when the same procedure might be employed to sustain the life of a severely brain damaged child? *See* Gustafson, *Mongolism, Parental Desires, and the Right to Life,* 16 PERSPECTIVES IN BIOLOGY AND MEDICINE 529, 547 (1973).

[66] Reported instances to date have been limited to withholding medical care from children shortly after birth. An interview I conducted with the director of the nephrology unit of a Columbus, Ohio,

and legal requirements mandate a report to police when parents refuse to consent to medical care,[67] the child who is within some medical person's concept of "extraordinarily handicapped" is allowed to die.

Because of the lack of an advocate for the child and the concurrence of parents and medical personnel, litigation is rare, but recently one such case received widespread publicity. In *Maine Medical Center v. Houle,*[68] parents refused to give their consent for "nonheroic" life-saving surgery because the child was seriously physically impaired and there was a high likelihood of some permanent brain damage.[69] The court stated that "the most basic right enjoyed by every human being is the right to life itself"[70] and held "that the [parents] have no right to withhold such treatment and that to do so constitutes neglect in the legal sense."[71] The court then appointed a guardian *ad litem* to consent to the medical procedure.[72]

The court in the *Maine Medical Center* case has clearly stated that a guardian may not withhold consent for life-saving medical measures of a nonheroic nature, and that children suffering physical or mental impairments are as entitled to life as other children. The developing literature on the subject, however, identifies a further basic problem. As long as no one is willing to assert the right of the child to live, the parents' misuse of power will go unchallenged. The hospital context even provides

---

hospital indicates that the practice is not limited to infants. In response to an inquiry from another hospital about possible discrimination against the mentally retarded in the availability of kidney dialysis and transplant services, an interview was arranged.

I began the interview by indicating my interest in the general question of whether such discrimination exists. The director was quick to respond that mental retardation was indeed a factor that would have an effect in a decision about whether or not to make kidney dialysis or transplant treatment available. He recounted an incident in which parents of a Down's syndrome teenage girl with acute renal failure brought their daughter in to investigate the advisability of kidney dialysis. Since shortly after birth, the daughter had lived in a state institution that was, incidentally, also the place of employment of one or both parents. The director stated that he advised the parents against kidney dialysis with the knowledge that the child would die without medical intervention. He acknowledged that she would have been a satisfactory candidate for dialysis and transplant if she had not been mentally retarded and institutionalized. He indicated a hesitance about saving the child's life simply so that she could continue to live in the inhumane conditions of the state institution. He also expressed serious reservations about whether the institution would have provided adequate dietary supervision and treatment to accompany the dialysis treatment. According to the director, the decision not to provide dialysis was affected substantially by the child's mental retardation and by evidence of "inappropriate behavior," such as giggling and avoiding eye contact while she was present in the room where the director and the parents were discussing whether or not to provide the life-saving care.

The director related another incident in which a kidney transplant was performed on a mentally retarded girl referred to the hospital by an out-of-state doctor. The mother of the child wished to contribute one of her kidneys to save the life of her mentally retarded daughter. The referring doctor is reported by the director to have felt he needed to explain that he would not have referred a mentally retarded client for a kidney transplant were it not for the mother's desire to contribute her own kidney.

[67] Many states have so-called abuse and neglect reporting statutes which require all doctors, nurses, and school authorities who have reason to believe that a child has been neglected or abused to report their suspicions to the proper law enforcement officers. *E.g.*, OHIO REV. CODE § 2151.421 (Supp. 1974). Certainly refusal to consent to life-saving medical procedures would fall under the heading of abuse or neglect, and therefore, it is mandatory that these incidents be reported.

[68] Civil No. 74-145 (Super. Ct. Cumberland, Me., Feb. 14, 1974).

[69] *Id.*, slip opinion at 2.

[70] *Id.* at 4.

[71] *Id.*

[72] *Id.*

a prospect that a member of the hospital staff will act on behalf of the child and bring the matter to the attention of a court, but such action is infrequent and may be improbable. A step toward the protection of the child-ward is achieved by recognition of the problem and by the Maine court's forthright statement that the parents' power as guardian of the person does not extend to depriving a child of his life. One may seriously wonder, however, whether this single articulation is sufficient protection.

Related issues arise in another medical context, where the medical decisions do not relate directly to the life of the ward, but have an impact upon his health and bodily integrity. In *Strunk v. Strunk*,[73] the court considered whether the parent-guardian could consent to the removal of a kidney from a mentally retarded child for transplantation to his twin brother.[74] The court determined that this decision was beyond the power of the parent acting alone, but could be made with the concurrence of the court itself.[75] The court determined that the transplantation was in the interest of both brothers because of the deep affection of the retarded kidney donor for his twin brother. This case, unlike the decision about life itself, presents a situation in which some mechanism needs to be provided in order to allow the medical procedure. Safeguards must be established, however, to ensure that the interests of the ward are adequately protected. The court in the *Strunk* case recognized that the ward's interests were insufficiently protected by the parents themselves and added the requirement of court concurrence. Some may wonder whether this single additional requirement ensures full protection of the retarded citizen's interest.

Similar problems arise in the area of control of reproductive capacity.[76] The decisions to sterilize oneself, to have an abortion, or to use contraceptives are very personal decisions. The Supreme Court has recognized that they are within the realm of constitutionally protected privacy.[77] In such decisions, a guardian may have very distinct interests of his own which interfere with his ability to make decisions solely on the basis of the best interest of his ward. On the other hand, the decision that a person of limited intellectual development lacks capacity him-

---

[73] 445 S.W. 2d 145 (Ky. 1969).

[74] *Id.*

[75] *Id.* at 149.

[76] *See generally* Price and Burt, Chapter 4 of this volume.

[77] *See* Roe v. Wade, 410 U.S. 113 (1973) (abortion); Griswold v. Connecticut, 381 U.S. 479 (1965) (contraception); and Skinner v. Oklahoma, 316 U.S. 535 (1942) (sterilization). In *Skinner* the court said:

> Marriage and procreation are fundamental to the very existence and survival of the race. The power to sterilize, if exercised, may have subtle, far-reaching and devastating effects. In evil or reckless hands it can cause races or types which are inimical to the dominant group to wither and disappear. There is no redemption for the individual whom the law touches. Any experiment which the State conducts is to his irreparable injury. He is forever deprived of a basic liberty.

Since this case was decided before the development of the right to privacy concept, it is likely that a court today would hold that an individual has the right to decide on his own whether or not to undergo voluntary sterilization.

For a very recent case dealing with coerced sterilization of incompetents, see Relf v. Weinberger, 372 F. Supp. 1196 (D.D.C. 1974).

self to decide to be sterilized or have an abortion may contravene his personal interest. The Supreme Court has determined that the right to privacy permits a person to have an abortion in some instances,[78] and a pregnant mentally retarded woman may want to exercise this right. Similarly, many individuals are now deciding to use contraceptives or be sterilized in order to limit the size of their families, and contraception or sterilization may also be in the best interest of a mentally retarded individual.[79] The removal of this important and private decision from the power of a guardian without provision of a substitute mechanism has the effect of denying the mentally retarded individual the right to abortion or sterilization.

This dilemma is of sufficient gravity to impel the law to seek a refinement of guardianship that will permit sensible decisions about control of childbearing while at the same time protecting mentally retarded citizens from the usurpation of fundamental rights by others with conflicting interest. *Wyatt v. Aderholt,*[80] cited so often in this volume for its contribution to institutional reform and deinstitutionalization,[81] provides valuable assistance in this area as well. Following the right to habilitation and treatment decisions of the district court, plaintiffs' attorneys discovered that sterilizations were being performed with some regularity in the institution upon the sole decision of the superintendent. Because an Alabama statute authorized this procedure,[82] plaintiffs requested a three-judge federal panel to review its constitutionality. The three-judge district court panel, on December 20, 1973, declared the statute unconstitutional.[83] On January 8, 1974, Judge Johnson, upon a finding that "sterilization continues to be performed,"[84] issued a detailed order designed to protect the rights of institutionalized mentally retarded individuals, but not to prohibit completely the use of sterilization. The order implicitly recognizes that sterilization may be desired by some mentally retarded individuals and may be clearly in their best interest.

The court's order contains the following elements: (1) sterilization of persons under the age of 21 is completely barred, except in the case of medical necessity; (2) no sterilization is to be performed unless there has been a determination that no temporary measure for birth control or contraception will meet the needs of the resident; (3) with respect to persons capable of forming an informed consent, no sterilization is to be performed without such consent; (4) with respect to persons whose capacity to form an informed consent is unclear, no sterilization is to be performed unless the individual has formed "a clear desire" to be sterilized *and* a court has determined that sterilization is in the best interest of the individual to be sterilized; (5) an interdisciplinary review committee, composed of persons unaffiliat-

---

[78] Roe v. Wade, 410 U.S. 113 (1973).

[79] *See* Goodman, *Family Planning Programs for the Mentally Retarded in Institutions and Community*, in HUMAN SEXUALITY AND THE MENTALLY RETARDED 79 (F. de la Cruz & G. La Veck eds. 1973).

[80] 344 F. Supp. 387 (M.D. Ala. 1972); 344 F. Supp. 373 (M.D. Ala. 1972); 344 F. Supp. 1341 (M.D. Ala. 1971); 325 F. Supp. 781 (M.D. Ala. 1971); 503 F.2d 1305 (5th Cir. 1974).

[81] *See* Chapters 13-18 of this volume.

[82] CODE OF ALA. tit. 45, § 243 (1959) provides:
   The assistant with the advice and consent of the superintendent shall prescribe for the treatment of the inmates of the home, and if after consultation with the superintendent, they deem it advisable they are hereby authorized and empowered to sterilize any inmate.

[83] 368 F. Supp. 1382 (M.D. Ala. 1973).

[84] 368 F. Supp. 1383, 1384 (M.D. Ala. 1974).

ed with the institution, must approve any sterilization to be performed, with the approval coming only after interviews with the individual and others, a review of the consent or desire to be sterilized, and a determination that sterilization is in the best interest of the individual; (6) residents are to be represented at all stages of the procedure by special independent counsel, upon whom an ethic is imposed of ensuring "that all considerations militating against the proposed sterilization have been adequately explored and resolved"; and (7) no coercion in any form is to be utilized in obtaining consent for sterilization.[85]

Three innovative aspects of this procedure deserve to be stressed and emulated in a general reform of the power of guardians of the person to consent to acts affecting major aspects of the life of mentally retarded citizens. The first is the requirement of affirmative participation by the mentally retarded individual in the decision to sterilize. The order recognizes that some persons, though mentally retarded, are still capable of giving an informed consent to a major undertaking. It also recognizes that there are lesser levels of intellectual participation than that of informed consent, and thus the requirement of at least "a clear desire" to be sterilized is imposed. The unifying principle of this requirement is that the individual is a full human being with intellectual processes and that major decisions affecting his life should involve his participation to the greatest possible degree. Every effort is to be made to prepare the individual for participation in the decision, and at the very minimum no decision as important as sterilization is to be made over the individual's opposition. This concept of positive involvement by the mentally retarded individual is similar to the involvement suggested in the proposal for a "facilitator guardian" under "Toward the Refinement of Control Mechanisms," above.

The second important aspect of the order is the requirement for multiple layers of review before a decision as important as sterilization can be made. No sterilization is to take place until there has been an independent affirmative determination by (1) the retarded individual himself, (2) the director of the institution with which the individual is affiliated, (3) a special independent review committee, and (4) a court of competent jurisdiction in the case of a person whose competence to give informed consent is in question. In this requirement of multiple concurrence, the order departs from the facilitative model and employs a protective model, appropriate, in my opinion, for a decision as important as sterilization. The requirement of multiple concurrence recognizes the danger of conflicting interests and cooption in any bureaucratic scheme and creates a series of responsible bodies to provide checks and counterchecks against abuse. The need for checks and counterchecks is the aspect of the order that requires emulation. The number and type of checks may need adjustment depending on the nature of the decision to be made. A decision to utilize contraceptives or even to have an abortion might require different checks, but the principle has general vitality as an approach to providing genuine protection for mentally retarded citizens.

The third innovative aspect of the order relates to the use of counsel. Counsel is

---

[85] *Id.* at 1384-86.

to be appointed in all cases where sterilization has been recommended.[86] Further counsel is to be drawn from a specially designated list of attorneys who presumably will be chosen because of an interest in the protection of retarded citizens.[87] The attorney is directed by the order to play a special adversary advocacy role.[88]

The decision to place an individual in a closed institutional setting can have far-reaching effects on all other aspects of his life,[89] and it is used as a final illustration. Guardians and parents acting as guardians have traditionally had the primary decision-making role concerning whether or not a mentally retarded individual should be placed in a closed institution.[90] On March 8, 1974, a three-judge federal district court declared a typical state "voluntary" commitment statute unconstitutional because of its total delegation of power to the parent or guardian of mentally retarded individuals and its lack of due process protections.[91] The Tennessee statute in question[92] permitted the admission of mentally retarded individuals to state institutions upon the application of parent and guardian without hearing. Release was obtainable only upon the decision of the superintendent or a showing in a habeas corpus action that the individual was not mentally retarded. The court stated that individual liberty is at stake in the institutionalization process and noted that there exist "possible conflicts of interest between a mentally retarded child and even a parent."[93] The court enjoined further admissions pursuant to the statute.[94]

The potentially coercive effect of "voluntary" admission by parents and guardians is also recognized by newly enacted commitment legislation in Ohio.[95]

[86] *Id.* at 1385. *See also* Lynch v. Baxley, 386 F. Supp. 378, 389 (M.D. Ala. 1974) (counsel must be provided at all significant stages of the involuntary commitment process).
[87] 368 F. Supp. at 1385.
[88] *Id.*
[89] Even placement in the best institutional setting can have a devastating effect on the incarcerated individual. Once committed to an institution, the resident undergoes a process which, whether intended or not, strips him of most of the fundamental mechanisms which enable him to think of himself as a fully functional human being. Upon acquiring the label of "mentally disabled," the resident's every action is automatically assumed to be the product of a disordered mind. For an extended discussion of the effects of the total'institution, see E. GOFFMAN, ASYLUMS (1961). For an empirical test of Goffman's theoretical framework, see Roseham, *On Being Sane in Insane Places,* 179 SCIENCE 250 (1973), a report of a study of the "treatment" of eight sane volunteers who, after feigning insanity to gain admission to various mental hospitals, thereafter acted in a completely normal fashion, but were never recognized as sane by the staff.
[90] Most states label as voluntary an admission to an institution on the application of a parent or guardian. *See* THE MENTALLY DISABLED table 2.1.
[91] Saville v. Treadway, Civil Action No. 6969 (M.D. Tenn., March 8, 1974).
[92] TENN. CODE ANN. § 33-501 (Supp. 1973). allows the superintendent of the facility to admit a mentally retarded person to a hospital or school on one of the following procedures:
  1. Application to the superintendent by the parent or guardian or person having lawful custody of a mentally retarded minor or by the guardian of a mentally retarded adult or by a mentally retarded individual eighteen (18) years of age or over on his own behalf.
  2. Application to the superintendent by the spouse, adult child or other close adult relative of the individual, or by any health or by any public welfare officer, or school official, with the consent of the individual or his parent, guardian, or person having lawful custody of him, accompanied by a certificate of a licensed physician or a licensed physician and a licensed psychologist that he has examined the individual within thirty (30) days of the date on which admission is sought and that he is of the opinion that the individual is mentally retarded and is in need of care and treatment in a development center.
[93] Saville v. Treadway, Civil Action No. 6969 (M.D. Tenn., March 8, 1974) (slip opinion at 4).
[94] *Id.*, at 5.
[95] Ohio Amended Substitute Senate Bill No. 336 (1974) (enacting §§ 5123.67-98 of the Ohio Revised Code) [hereinafter cited as S. 336].

Under previous law, a parent or guardian could "voluntarily" admit a mentally retarded individual to a state institution.[96] Although persons who had provided their own volition for their admission had a right to release or hearing upon request,[97] where the parent or guardian had provided the volition, the right to release could be conditioned upon the consent of that person.[98] The new statute provides that the mentally retarded individual always has the right to release upon request,[99] unless the managing officer of the institution files a petition for involuntary admission within three court days.[100] Thus, the "voluntary" admission process is purified; active opposition to continued institutionalization negates voluntary status. In addition, a countercheck mechanism is provided in the form of a legal rights service independent of the state mental retardation administration.[101] The legal rights service is charged with informing individuals in state institutions of their legal rights. Presumably, a primary legal right to be communicated will be the right of "voluntary" residents to be released upon request. The legal rights service is also given another countercheck power. It can provoke a court hearing, even in the absence of protest by the resident himself, to determine whether the guardian's decision to place the mentally retarded individual in an institution is in the individual's best interest.[102] These countercheck mechanisms provide a further suggestive model for the development of a new guardianship system that provides safeguards against the misuse of the power.

The material in this section suggests that limitations on the power of guardians of the person are increasingly being recognized and imposed by the courts and the legislatures. This movement is in its infancy and the protections are still far from adequate; a systematic approach has not yet been developed by legislatures and courts. The creation of checks on the exercise of guardianship powers has several implications. The first is financial. The system created by *Wyatt* to deal with sterilization, and the legal rights service created by the Ohio legislature will both cost money. They call for additional advocacy personnel and additional court hearings to determine the propriety of proposed or challenged decisions. Although there may also be financial savings, such as the avoidance of improper institutionalization, services for and protection of mentally retarded citizens do depend on society's willingness to devote a portion of its resources to these purposes.

THE STATE AND ITS RELATIONS TO GUARDIANSHIP

The state has an important responsibility in the organization and delivery of services that will promote the independence and well-being of mentally retarded citizens.

---

[96] OHIO REV. CODE § 5123.311 (Supp. 1972).

[97] *Id.* § 5123.312.

[98] *Id.*

[99] *Id.* § 5123.70 (effective July 1, 1975). It is important to note that the right to release upon request does not depend upon the age of the person applying for release. Therefore, a minor child who was voluntarily admitted should be able to apply for and receive his own release.

[100] *Id.*

[101] *Id.* § 5123.94.

[102] *Id.* § 5123.69(c).

The effective discharge of this responsibility has major effects on the operation of guardianship.

A first major role of the state is to provide legal rules governing the institution of guardianship. It has been the contention of this paper that the state has not adequately performed this role and that additional substantive and procedural legal rules must be developed in the guardianship area.

Another important responsibility of the state is to provide a broad range of services for all citizens, including mentally retarded citizens. In the absence of education, training, employment, budgetary counseling, income maintenance, housing, and many other services, mentally retarded citizens will survive only marginally in today's society. The state has failed miserably in providing adequate services for mentally retarded citizens. Many children are excluded from state educational systems, and even if the mentally retarded individual is not excluded, the educational programs seldom maximize his developmental potential. Residential institutions are monuments to society's neglect of retarded individuals. Little has been done to provide satisfactory residential opportunities that are integrated into the rest of society. Income maintenance and job training programs are grossly inadequate. In short, the centuries of discrimination against, and neglect of, mentally retarded citizens have not yet ended. The technological capability to provide a full place in society for mentally retarded citizens has been developed, but the social willingness and political commitment to this end is still being born, or perhaps has been born still. A third role for the state in relationship to guardianship has also been previously discussed: the development of checking mechanisms to monitor the functioning of guardianship provided by others.[103]

The question to be addressed here is what special role the state has in the provision of guardianship itself. Although the state has long been directly involved in serving as guardian for individuals, considerable attention has recently been focused on the dangers of state guardianship. The most extensive guardianship involvement of the state in this society has been through state institutions for the mentally retarded. Statutes typically have given directors of institutions guardianship power over the institution's residents.[104] In 1917 Minnesota enacted a general public guardianship system for the mentally retarded, in which the director of public welfare could be given the guardianship of any mentally retarded individual, whether or not he was institutionalized.[105]

The major public policy declarations of recent years on guardianship and mental retardation have taken positions that suggest limits on the state's role. On the one hand, both the International League of Societies for the Mentally Handicapped and the United Nations have stated clearly that "[n]o person rendering direct services to the mentally retarded should also serve as his guardian."[106] The President's Panel on

---

[103] *Supra*, pp. 76-83.

[104] *See, e.g.,* OHIO REV. CODE § 5123.03 (1970).

[105] Minn. Sess. Laws 1917, ch. 344. For a thorough discussion of Minnesota guardianship, see R. Levy, *Protecting the Mentally Retarded: An Empirical Survey and Evolution of the Establishment of State Guardianship in Minnesota,* 49 MINN. L. REV. 821 (1965).

[106] INTERNATIONAL LEAGUE OF SOCIETIES FOR THE MENTALLY HANDICAPPED, DECLARATION OF GENERAL AND SPECIAL RIGHTS OF THE MENTALLY RETARDED, Article V (1968).

Mental Retardation stated: "We believe all retarded persons living in institutions, but not admitted on their own application, should have outside guardians who could check on the ward's treatment, care, and release possibilities."[107] The San Sebastian Symposium concluded:

> There are some persons who should not be considered as guardians because of the possibility of conflict of interest. These include a person who is performing some professional or other remunerated service for the ward — as physician, teacher, landlady, superintendent of an institution, attorney, etc. or who is employed in one of the service systems in which the ward is enrolled.[108]

The reason for these recommendations is simple enough. The primary standard governing the decisions of a guardian must be the best interests of the ward.[109] A manifest conflict of interest exists when guardianship powers are exercised by a service-providing individual or organization. A service provider makes some decisions in terms of the fiscal and political needs of his organization and is not in a position to give his sole attention to the best interests of the individual receiving the service. Because the state is a primary service provider, it is hard to reconcile state guardianship with these policy positions.

A contradictory theme, however, also runs throughout several of these major documents, reflecting a different policy imperative. In a society with limited extended family ties, in which many individuals have no family member willing to assume a guardianship role, either some societal guardianship mechanism must be provided or many individuals will have no realistic access to guardianship services. The President's Panel stated: "[t]he protection of guardianship should not be denied where there is no suitable relative available, or where the retarded person's financial assets are too small adequately to compensate a private person serving as guardian."[110] The Panel recommended that "[s]tudies be made to consider how best to deal with this problem," and suggested the possibility of utilizing either a state agency or specially chartered private nonprofit agencies or groups.[111] Both the International League and the United Nations Declaration of Rights state guardianship as a right of all mentally retarded individuals "when this is required to protect his personal well being and interest,"[112] thus apparently concurring in the position of the President's Pannel that guardianship should not depend on the availability of family members or financial resources. The San Sebastian Symposium also spoke in terms of a need for increased availability of guardianship to all who need it[113] and recognized that this would require the development of new sources of guardians.[114]

---

[107] PPMR REPORT 27.

[108] SAN SEBASTIAN.

[109] If the purpose of guardianship is the protection of the personal and property interests of the ward, the traditional justification for state guardianship statutes, then it is obvious that the guardian must act only in the best interests of the ward.

[110] PPMR REPORT 27.

[111] *Id.*

[112] INTERNATIONAL LEAGUE OF SOCIETIES FOR THE MENTALLY RETARDED, DECLARATION OF GENERAL AND SPECIAL RIGHTS OF THE MENTALLY RETARDED, Article V (1968). *See also* G. A. RES. 2856, 25 U.N. GAOR 368, U.N. DOC. A/8588 (1971).

[113] SAN SEBASTIAN 14.

[114] *Id.*

The tension between the need to avoid the conflict of interest inherent in having the guardian and service provider be the same person and the need to provide guardianship services to persons without either family or financial resources is strong. State services to the mentally retarded are provided through specialized administrative departments or agencies. Within the government structure these agencies generally have a monopoly on expertise and interest in the mentally retarded. If guardianship is to be provided through governmental efforts, it is natural to consider placing it within that department which has the greatest experience with the mentally retarded. It is exactly that department, however, which would experience most directly the conflict-of-interest problems.

Several states have begun to provide public guardianship services.[115] A few have begun to provide some checking mechanisms against exploitation of the mentally retarded.[116] No state has yet, however, successfully developed a mechanism for providing expanded guardianship services without creating serious conflict-of-interest problems.[117]

The policy conflict here is not a simple one to resolve, but various possibilities exist that have yet to be tried. The President's Panel, although limiting its concern about the conflict of interest to individuals in institutions and acknowledging the possibility of having a state agency provide guardianship services,[118] also recognized the alternative of chartering special private nonprofit agencies to provide guardianship services.[119] The San Sebastian Symposium apparently rejected the notion of direct state guardianship and proposed either the use of private guardians, with special efforts to develop a special profession of private guardians, or the use of specially created volunteer organizations whose establishment would be stimulated by existing associations of parents of mentally retarded individuals.[120]

The point that must be emphasized is that, in the structuring of social guardianship services either under government auspices or through the efforts of parent organizations, attention must be given to the conflict-of-interest problem and substantial efforts made to alleviate it. The use of specially organized and chartered non-profit organizations should be attempted. Legislation might prescribe the structure and conditions required of such an organization and provide a base of public funds for its operation. Another structural mechanism is available in most state

---

[115] *See, e.g.,* CALIF. HEALTH & SAFETY CODE §§ 416-416.20 (West 1970).

[116] New York has created a mental health information service. The duties of this commission are described *supra* at note 33. Ohio has recently made provisions for a legal rights service "to receive and act upon complaints concerning institutional practices and conditions" and to ensure that all persons in institutions or against whom institutionalization proceedings are brought are represented by counsel and fully informed of their rights. OHIO REV. CODE § 5123.94 (1974), found in S. 336. Although these services are definitely a step in the right direction, they are basically aimed only at institutions and the institutionalization process.

[117] *See* Levy, *supra* note 105. About Minnesota guardianship, Levy writes: "[T]he commissioner's powers are broad; his powers have been exercised; the Probate Code provides no postcommitment judicial review of any kind—even of a decision to institutionalize a ward; most wards do not have the sophistication to seek a method of testing the commissioner's use of his authority." *Id.* at 833 (footnote omitted). *See also* KAY, FARNHAM, KARREN, KNAKEL & DIAMOND, *Legal Planning for the Mentally Retarded,* 60 CALIF. L. REV. 438, where the authors, on the subject of state guardianship in California, report that "in cases in which the regional center is both the guardian and the proponent of institutionalization, the agency oversees itself and evaluates its own decisions." *Id.* at 527.

[118] PPMR REPORT 27.

[119] *Id.*

[120] SAN SEBASTIAN 23.

governments: the independent commission. Such a commission, although a part of the governmental structure, can be completely separate from the administrative department responsible for the delivery of services to the mentally retarded. Long staggered terms for commission members can provide an independence not found in the normal governmental structure.

Even if such "independent" mechanisms are utilized to provide guardianship, it is important that there be counterchecks on their exercise of responsibility. If special checking mechanisms are provided to prevent physical abuse of mentally retarded individuals, to provide advice and counsel to them, or to protect them within the structure of residential institutions, these agencies might also be given the power to challenge the exercise of responsibility by the guardianship commission or agency and to bring it under judicial supervision or to cause a revocation of its charge for legislatively specified abuses of duty.

CONCLUSIONS

Guardianship is a legal instrument that can do much to facilitate the fullest possible participation of some mentally retarded citizens in the life of society. It is also, however, a potential instrument of repression and dehumanization. In a society that regards mentally retarded individuals as citizens, mechanisms must be developed both to make guardianship available for all whose well-being requires it and to protect these persons and others from the potential abuses inherent in guardianship.

This requires the development of adequate services to provide mentally retarded citizens with opportunities for a full life. In the absence of such services, mentally retarded individuals and society as a whole will be dehumanized, and guardianship will be used as a means of placing mentally retarded individuals in a situation no human being could be expected to desire if he had any choice. Guardianship itself must be made more sophisticated and individualized, and limitations must be placed on an individual only in accordance with his demonstrated needs and following a hearing that satisfies stringent due process standards. Certain decisions must be placed beyond the power of any substitute decision maker; others require special precautions against abuse. Finally, any new structures created to make guardianship services more generally available must be designed to avoid any conflict of interest on the part of the person serving as guardian.

Reaction Comment

ELEANOR S. ELKIN

KINDRED has clearly distinguished the two basic categories of limitations upon capacity: those that transfer legal powers from one individual (the ward) to another (the guardian) and those that limit the capacity of an individual without vesting the power to act in any other individual. This response will discuss further which rights can properly be transferred to another person and which cannot.

Almost everyone seems to agree that a retarded person cannot manage an estate and that a guardian should be appointed to take care of his property and finances. This practice is thought to be necessary to protect the retarded citizen from exploitation and from having his resources dissipated. Yet hundreds of retarded persons are working and living in the community, paying their bills, and managing their lives without benefit of a guardian. Hundreds more will be moving into the community from the institution as residences become available for them there. Some of these citizens will be independent, some semi-dependent, and some dependent. Some of these citizens will earn regular salaries, some only a small amount. Some will receive public assistance, some social security payments. Should they all have guardians to manage their money and make their decisions for them?

If a mentally retarded person works, he should have the right to spend his earnings as he desires, even if the money is wasted in someone else's opinion. A woman reporting about several young men who had returned to her home town after living in an institution said that they were getting along well, but "somebody should keep their money for them." She was worried because she felt that "some of them don't know the value of money and other people might take advantage of them." She explained, "one fellow bought six watches and he can't even tell time." Do we all spend our money wisely? Do we never buy things that we do not need? The young man has the right to work and receive wages for his work. The money he earns is his to spend.

Trying to make your way in a strange new environment is confusing at times. Help may be needed with budgeting so that the rent gets paid and the individual can buy food and clothing and take care of personal needs. The opportunity to seek advice, perhaps from a social worker, should be readily available to him.

A retarded person may need a sponsor for some contracts, particularly those requiring the extension of credit. Kindred has proposed "a facilitative guardianship system" which would be available at the request of a person who is mentally retarded, perhaps upon the advice of a social worker or adviser, to provide a supportive signature or extra consent, but not to make decisions. This idea has merit. However, even here checks on the veto power of the facilitator are needed. This temporary guardian might be required to consult with the individual's social worker and get a second opinion before refusing to provide the backup signature.

Guardianship of the person raises more difficult questions of social support and decisions about where to live, education, training, and personal welfare. Certainly, a minor child needs someone to make these decisions for him. An adult who is profoundly retarded also needs someone who will be responsible for his welfare. Parents are the natural guardians or decision makers for their children. If the parents die or are unable to perform, then someone must be found to be guardian of the person of their minor child. Generally, other relatives are sought first and then friends, neighbors, the court, or the superintendent of an institution to act as surrogate parents. However, Professor Charles Murdock has pointed out the potential conflict of interest that may exist between parent and child.[1] He is not referring to the usual "problem parent" who is in conflict with his offspring because of a refusal to provide the money for the purchase of an automobile or to sanction his 17-year-old son's acting as personal guide for a 16-year-old girl's trip to Europe. The conflicts Murdock discusses involve basic rights such as the right to live in the community and even the right to live at all.

The case of the Down's syndrome infant born with an intestinal obstruction is an example of such conflict. Because the parents refused to permit corrective surgery, a sign was put on the baby's crib, "nothing by mouth," and the baby was allowed to die.[2] The decision of the parents to allow their baby to die of starvation because they did not wish to be burdened with raising a retarded child was indeed a conflict of interest.[3] It was also infanticide. There may be a conflict of interest in the decision of a parent or guardian to place a child or adult who is retarded in an institution. It is noted in *Wyatt v. Stickney* that:

> The parent may be motivated to ask for such institutionalization for a variety of reasons other than the best interests of the child himself, i.e., the interests of other children in the family, mental and physical frustration, economic stress, hostility toward the child stemming from the added pressures of caring for him, and perceived stigma of mental retardation. The retarded child's best interests may well lie in living with his family and in the community, but theirs may not lie in keeping him.[4]

A group of parents was asked to describe any advantages or disadvantages resulting from their child's placement in an institution. They listed "ability to devote more attention to other children." "freedom to leave the house without getting a sitter." "opportunity to work, to vacation, to finish college, safeguarding mother's health." Two of seven parents listed the care their child was receiving as an advantage. Disadvantages were "not being able to see the child as often as I'd like" and "the expense of keeping one's child in school."

Parents or guardians with children in public programs are sometimes unable to represent adequately the best interests of the retarded because of their inability to deal effectively with those who are providing the service. Presentation of reports about their son or daughter are often influenced by prejudgments. The rights of the resident are brushed aside.[5] They hesitate to question the quality of the service, be it educational, health, or residential, because of the threat (real or imagined) of exclusion or retaliation. Recently a mother told me that when she and her husband visited their son in a state institution they noticed that he had been beaten about the face. When they asked about what had happened, they were told that an aide had beaten their son, but there was no cause for alarm or worry. Their son would not be beaten by this man again because he (the aide) had been transferred to

---

[1] Murdock, *Civil Rights of the Mentally Retarded: Some Critical Issues,* 48 Notre D. Law.133 (1972).
[2] Joseph P. Kennedy, Jr. Foundation, *Who Shall Survive?* (film) (1971).
[3] Elkin, *The Right to Live* in The Record (National Association of Retarded Children, Winter, 1973).
[4] Wyatt v. Stickney, Alabama Right to Treatment, Amici Briefs, 1971.
[5] Crocker & Cushna, *Pediatric Decisions in Children with Serious Mental Retardation,* 19 Pediatric Clinics of N. America (1972).

another building. Later the same day they were asked if they would not like to have their son transferred to X State School, which is a little nearer their home. X State School has the well-publicized reputation of being overcrowded, under-staffed, dehumanizing, and lacking in programs.

The parent who says to the teacher, "You may punish my daughter by tying her or whatever you have to do; I can't handle her," does not adequately represent the child's best interests. This raises the question of which rights and powers become inoperative if the individual does not have the capacity to express them himself. Voting is one right that cannot be transferred. (Maryland, Pennsylvania, and Michigan have helped retarded people to exercise their voting rights.) Other rights such as marriage, birth control, and sterilization have been discussed by Kindred.

What about consent to participate in medical or pharmaceutical experimenta-tion? Can the individual's right to give this consent be transferred to somebody else? And what is informed consent? At Willowbrook State School admissions were closed, but there were "openings" in the hepatitis experimentation program. Des-perate parents could sign their child into this experimental program and they would be admitted to the institution.[6] Is this informed consent? At another institution young women were offered the opportunity for release to a community home and program if they agreed to take part in testing a birth control drug. Is this informed consent?

In Pennsylvania, testing of unlicensed vaccines for pneumonia, meningitis, and flu were administered to residents not only without parental consent, but without their knowledge. The experimenter received permission to test in the institution from either the superintendent or medical director, who considered themselves "guardians" for all the residents in their institution. Should anyone be allowed to make this decision for a retarded person? Is the experiment being conducted in the institution for the good of the resident or for the convenience of the experimenter or drug firm? It has been said that the retarded person should have the right to make a contribution to mankind. This, however, is another decision which is his to make and a power that cannot be transferred. Nobody has the right to volunteer another person for a dangerous mission.

Although there can be conflicts of interest between a parent and child, the parent does have rights, responsibilities, and interests that should not be ignored. Parents admitting their children to residential facilities are asked to sign a form permitting necessary medical and surgical treatment of their children. Most parents, wanting their children treated promptly when they are ill and immediately in emer-gencies, sign willingly. Nobody tells them that officials do not have to consult them about elective surgery. Operations can be performed on their children if the doctor considers it necessary for any reason. A distraught mother told me that her son, who is hydrocephalic and cannot walk, underwent leg surgery twice in one year without her knowledge. After the operations she was told by a social worker, "Your son is in the hospital recovering from surgery on his leg. You may visit him if you

---

[6] Adams & Cowan, *The Human Guinea Pig: How We Test New Drugs,* WORLD, December 5, 1972.

wish." This mother feels that there is no change in her son's condition since the operation and that it was experimental in nature. She was told that the form she signed permitted this surgery to be performed. Decisions for or against elective surgery should be made only after careful consideration by the individual, the parent/guardian, physician, and independent advocate.

The decision to live in the institution or in the community is also subject to conflicts of interest. Many parents do not want their children to leave the institution because they honestly believe they are safe and well cared for there. Other relatives confronted with this decision may object, too. A well-to-do matron said candidly, "I don't want my friends to see my retarded sister walking around town." The superintendent and his staff may find their feelings about the movement toward community-based facilities affecting their decision to release an individual. The supporters of group homes and the providers of this service may also find their eagerness a conflict. I recall meeting a young woman who had recently moved into a group home. She was pleased with her room, but seemed sad. Further conversation with her and with the houseparents revealed that she wanted to go back to the institution because she wanted to be with her sister who was still there. The girls had never been separated before, but the rules would not permit her 14-year-old sister to enter a home for those 16 and over. The United Nations Bill of Rights states that guardianship should not be provided by persons with responsibility for providing other services.[7] The individual should have the right to decide whether he wishes to leave the institution and live in the community residence to which he has been assigned . . . after he has had the benefit of advice from the social worker, parents/guardian, and advocate.

Worried parents ask, "What will happen to my child when I am no longer here?" What will happen to their other children? They need good advice to arrange for insurance, will, guardian, and so on. If the family has sufficient means, a trust can be set up to permit their retarded relative to live his lifetime in a private residential facility of their choice. However, it does require a substantial amount of money to fund the trust. There is also no guarantee of the permanence of the facility or continued quality or appropriateness of service. There should be provision for the guardian to remove the individual if it is in his best interest.[8]

Most parents know that when they die their retarded child must live either in a state institution or a publicly supported community residence. This does not relieve their worries. They may dread the institution, knowing of the inadequacy and inhumanity of this approach. They are uncertain of the quality of the community residences. They worry that their child may not receive proper guidance and protection in a community program. Parents say they want happiness for their children and they tend to equate happiness with a controlled, safe future. As Kindred has pointed out, it is clear that guardianship in itself cannot provide the answer. The crucial issue is provision of services to respond to the needs of the retarded indi-

---

[7] G.A. Res. 2856, 25 U.N. GAOR 368, U.N. Doc. A/8588 (1971).
[8] Diana & Pool, Human Rights for the Mentally Retarded, (Report of National Conference, School of Allied Health Professions, University of Texas Southern Medical School of Dallas).

vidual, rather than controlling choices. But the decision must be made as to where the retarded person will be in the complex of institutional and community services.

The retarded citizen must have the right to make his own decisions. Kindred's proposals for a guardianship system available upon request and with guardianship power tailored to the needs of the retarded citizen should be seriously considered. The retarded citizen may have unnecessary or even unjust limitations placed upon him by others who have powers of decision. Many parents see hope for the future in the concept of the nonguardian advocate whose job it is to help the retarded citizen continue to grow and develop. These advocates will help their retarded friend to learn to make decisions for himself and to learn that he must live with the consequences. They will help their friend to overcome failure.

Whether a citizen has a legal guardian or a nonguardian advocate it is the guardian's duty to see that needed services are available so that the individual may live his life as fully as possible wherever he may be residing.

CHAPTER 4

Nonconsensual Medical Procedures and the Right to Privacy

Editorial Introduction

*P*ublic law, once past the questions of what the state can force people to do, teems with issues of *consent,* from tort problems about consent to sexual relations, to the puzzling sequelae of the Supreme Court's decade of decisions regulating police conduct. Questions of what constitutes consent, the point at which coercion vitiates consent, and the identity and competence of surrogates who can consent to what the law otherwise forbids are part of any sophisticated discussion of intervention by government in the affairs of men.

Price and Burt consider the mechanisms and fictions under which mentally retarded citizens consent to confinement, treatment, and, especially, to the regulation of their sex lives. They examine the ironies of recent decades of reform: the irony in which involuntary sterilization has been replaced by the fiction of consensual sterilization; and the irony in which the fiction of consent to surgery will be replaced by consent to "self-regulating" contraception and abortion. They examine various safeguards against abuse of third-party consent, including in some circumstances the prohibition of reliance on it.

Appended to their paper is a recent court decision setting forth guidlines to deal with the problems raised by Price and Burt in the sterilization area.

Lebacqz' reaction comment emphasizes the profound ethical nature of the problems of involuntary and pseudovoluntary interventions that discriminate against mentally retarded citizens. She notes that these interventions extend to suggestions that some infants should be allowed to die because of the danger that they may be mentally impaired. She points out that these processes — so patently repulsive if seen as totally involuntary state action are also often disguised as "voluntary" with the volition being provided by parent and/or doctor. Lebacqz warns that decisions we make about others have an effect on all of society and each member of it.

PRINCIPAL PAPER

MONROE E. PRICE AND ROBERT A. BURT

THE LINE between proper and improper state intervention in the lives of individuals has never been adequately drawn. It is not surprising that this line is practically nonexistent, from the point of view of legal analysis, when the individuals subjected to intervention are considered mentally retarded. For many of these persons, medical and privacy rights are seldom recognized. There is a number of factors that account for this special fuzziness. There has been an absence of litigation, sometimes owing to the silence of possible plaintiffs, sometimes owing to the great difficulties involved in obtaining vigorous counsel. Also, there is a special context in which invasions of privacy and other rights take place. Intervention usually occurs under the cloak of medical care and habilitation, both of which are therapeutic and merciful aspects of state intervention. Because of this benign predicate, the nature and type of medical care the state provides, even involuntarily, has never been a welcome subject for judicial review.

Furthermore, the rights involved are often taken for granted by the population at large and are compromised only with respect to special groups. Examples of these rights include the right to have sexual relations; the right to marry and have children; the right to receive adequate medical treatment; the right to fair treatment in decisions on whether life support should be continued; and the right to personal dignity —to be fed, clothed, and sheltered in ways that are neither brutalizing nor shameful. These rights are diminished in offhand ways, often with a sense that nothing has been lost. The legal system has institutionalized techniques for depriving certain persons of these rights.

The focus in this paper is upon the technique of deprivation, rather than on the rights themselves.[1] The most flexible technique disguising the deprivation of rights

---

[1] These various rights, *qua* rights, are discussed elsewhere in this volume.

is the doctrine of consent and voluntariness. And the most peculiar aspect of the doctrine of consent—a doctrine that is repeatedly invoked in regard to the lives of mentally retarded citizens—is third-party consent, where the state is permitted to intervene because a person other than the subject has given approval. Frequently, the third person is a parent, but he or she may also be a physician, the superintendent of an institution, a guardian *ad litem,* or a conservator. By characterizing the transaction as voluntary rather than involuntary, constitutional, ethical, and moral questions are bypassed and the violation of taboos is avoided. Third-party consent is a miraculous creation of the law, adroit and flexible, capable of covering unseemly realities with the patina of cooperation.

Third-party consent has often justified admission to state hospital facilities, questionable forms of treatment, drug experimentation, and state control of sexual behavior. Indeed, third-party consent, whether by parent or by other surrogate, is probably the most frequent form of turning involuntary state intervention with respect to a mentally retarded person into a so-called voluntary action. Undoubtedly, the issue arises most frequently with respect to hospital admissions and various forms of medical treatment. This paper, however, will concentrate on third-party consent to control sexual behavior. Emphasis is placed primarily on this subject, rather than others, because there have been finely developed statutory approaches, judicial decisions, and public concern. Experience with the regulation of consent in this area might then justify generalized conclusions on deprivation of other rights.

FROM INVOLUNTARY INTERVENTION TO THIRD-PARTY CONSENT

Legal analysis sometimes falls behind events, which may be the case with respect to government intervention in the lives of mentally retarded persons. In any case, the forms of government control and intervention have changed and become more sophisticated and appealing—and more subtle. So delicate has this process been that at times government action seems immune from ordinary application of constitutional protection. Enlightened government policy with respect to mental retardation and mental illness is illustrative of these tendencies. When government intervention took the primary form of institutionalization, particularly compulsory institutionalization, the ideals of due process developed over decades in the criminal law system (with modifications, to be sure) could be brought to bear in order to increase the protection of the mentally retarded individual against arbitrariness. But times have changed and the philosophy of care has changed as well. It is now in budgeting and program planning that critical decisions are made, individual rights are affected, and new strategies of government intervention are fashioned. And new delivery strategies, particularly community care and the normalization of the environment, require novel approaches in ascertaining the appropriate balance between the state and the individual.

These new strategies are appealing; it is difficult to maintain a critical approach to them. But one should remember that when the asylum was founded in the nineteenth century as *the* answer to a major societal problem, delight in the approach obscured hazards. Today, as a result of enthusiasm which may be analogous, the community approach goes virtually unquestioned; the rhetoric of commitment is replaced with the rhetoric of encouragement; and voluntary family-centered approaches replace the cold hand of the state.

When the modern state decides to intervene, as in sterilization and certain forms of treatment, justifications also change. Positive eugenics is no longer in vogue. But—because of immense competition over tax dollars—hereditary considerations have been replaced by fiscal and psychological ones. Although the fear of "three generations of imbeciles," in Holmes' infamous phrase, was sufficient to uphold the constitutionality of intervention to sterilize a half century ago, people now talk confidently about "good parenting" or breaking the vicious cycle of three generations of welfare clients. Beyond these justifications, there is an additional one, the primary subject of this paper. Through adroit statutory change, and through nonstatutory efforts to confer the power to consent on persons other than the individual directly affected, the always thin line between involuntary and voluntary action has virtually been erased.

On a formal level, there is a vast distance between the voluntary and the involuntary in the law. Morally, ethically, and legally we separate and evaluate specially those interventions by the state carried out regardless of the consent of affected persons. In criminal law, a test of the validity of a confession is whether it was "voluntarily" given; if so, the confession may be considered on the question of guilt. To search a home, in most circumstances, the police need probable cause and must obtain a warrant unless an appropriate person "consents" to the search. Consent is an issue in tort and in contract. All are familiar with the efforts of physicians to shield themselves from liability by having their patients sign "consent" forms prior to an operation. Involuntary commitment of the mentally impaired is constrained and regulated in every state by means wholly distinguishable from voluntary admission to a hospital or treatment program. For an involuntary patient, the statute may state a limit on the length of stay and provide a standard for admission and release; the law provides a set of procedural safeguards (including, usually, court review) before a lengthy involuntary detention can be sustained. None of these safeguards is provided if a patient can be characterized as "voluntary."

Consent and voluntariness, then, are critical concepts—enormous consequences flow from them. Despite their importance, surprisingly little is known about the mechanism of consent and the forms states have utilized to delineate consent. Consent by a parent, legal guardian, or institution is *terra incognita,* but a survey of the statutes suggests that third-party consent is a familiar form for shifting an activity from the involuntary to the voluntary category. Since the ability to categorize an action as voluntary rather than involuntary has critical implications, one might expect that there would be an acceptable analytical framework by which one could test state approaches to determinations of voluntariness. Unfortunately, no such analytical framework exists.

To understand the role of the voluntariness issue with respect to control of sexual behavior, it is useful to take a short backward glance at the compulsory sterilization statutes and how they have functioned as perceptions of a positive genetic approach have changed. There are now 29 states that have statutes permitting compulsory sterilization. A Pennsylvania governor vetoed the first American sterilization legislation, passed in 1905. In 1907, Indiana became the first state to adopt an involuntary sterilization law.[2] The Association for Voluntary Sterilization reports that in the first half century of the operation of all state statues, approximately 60,000 people were compulsorily sterilized who were deemed a threat to themselves or to society, even though compulsory sterilization as a form of punishment was disfavored and declared unconstitutional as "cruel or unusual."[3] There have been intimations that a statute which compels sterilization because of a potential financial drain on society from impecunious wards might be a violation of the equal protection clause,[4] but the power of the state to compel sterilization for therapeutic or preventive reasons has been upheld.[5]

Today it is necessary to redirect attention to these laws and the motives behind them, in response to the new emphasis being placed on ending long-term institutionalization for mentally retarded persons, and opening to these individuals opportunities for more normal and productive community life. The motives persist for it is not self-evident that all who can live in the community and who are biologically capable of childbearing should in fact become parents. For some few there are serious genetic risks of bearing sadly limited children; but genetic risks are not the primary, nor the most widespread, concern. Among mentally retarded citizens who will be living in sheltered settings that give sufficient support for work and life in the community, it inevitably appears that some will lack social and emotional attributes that are considered optimal—or, for some, minimal—for childrearing. Many state laws give authority for compulsory sterilization based on assessments of either genetic or social incapacities.[6] Compulsory sterilization authority is not invoked as often as it once was: Sparse statistical data suggests that the number of persons compulsorily sterilized annually has declined by half in the last 20 years. Nonetheless, the continued existence of this legal framework may give the impression that American society has adequate genetic and social standards and sufficiently skilled personnel to predict in advance who among the population should not become parents—this impression is false.

CONTROL OF SEXUAL BEHAVIOR

Potential genetic or social incapacities for childrearing are not uniquely limited to mentally retarded individuals. State laws which single out the mentally retarded as specially unsuited for parenthood are derived more from community fear and prejudice than from any sensible view of the particular incapacities of mentally

---

[2]H. 364, [1907] Ind. Acts ch. 215.

[3]Mickle v. Henrichs, 262 F. 687 (D. Nev. 1918) ("cruel or unusual" under Nevada constitution). *Contra,* State v. Feilen, 70 Wash. 65, 126 P. 75 (1912).

[4]*See* Cook v. State, 9 Ore. App. 222, 495 P.2d 768 (1972).

[5]*See* Buck v. Bell, 274 U.S. 200 (1927); Cook v. State, 9 Ore. App. 222, 495 P.2d 768 (1972).

[6]*See, e.g.,* UTAH CODE ANN. § 64-10-7 (1953).

retarded citizens as a group. Nor is this special vulnerability to restrictions on sex and childrearing limited to the mentally retarded. Such restrictions are placed on prison and mental hospital populations and on other persons who are stigmatized and isolated as deviants. These restrictions begin with a rigid insistence on housing these populations in single-sex institutions with no opportunity for heterosexual contacts. (Compare European practices of providing some female staff within prisons for males and in permitting conjugal relations for prisoners.)[7] Indeed, about half of the state laws that authorize compulsory sterilization of mentally retarded persons have similar provisions for "hereditary criminals"; and virtually all state statutes apply both to the mentally retarded and to the mentally ill.[8]

The stereotypes projected onto groups that are seen as deviant—the mentally retarded, the mentally ill, criminals—are also remarkably similar in their attribution of sexual appetite and danger. The Supreme Court of Nebraska, in its 1968 opinion upholding the constitutionality of the state's compulsory sterilization law for institutionalized mental defectives, stated: "It is an established fact that mental deficiency accelerates sexual impulses and any tendencies toward crime to a harmful degree."[9] This statement, *which is not supported by empirical data,* illustrates popular prejudice regarding the mentally retarded, the mentally ill, criminals, and other stigmatized groups.

The prevalence of sexual imagery and fears regarding blacks in this country is a related phenomenon; the laws that forbade intermarriage among blacks and whites—rationalized by a potpourri of genetic and social arguments—have a kinship with restrictive laws applied to the mentally retarded. Indeed, one important attribute of slave status in this country (but, interestingly enough, not in the Latin American countries where slavery also flourished) was that slaves were forbidden to marry; familial ties between parent and child were disregarded as a matter of course.[10] Mentally retarded citizens also suffer from the popular perception that they are less than human. They, like other stigmatized groups, become the target and repository of a cluster of fears that are felt to assault society's "humanness" in general. Unabated sexual appetite ranks high among these fears.

This special vulnerability of mentally retarded individuals as members of an irrationally feared and stigmatized group has important legal implications. It means that, as a group, they warrant particular protection against the operation of legislation aimed at their sexual and childrearing behavior. Mentally retarded persons are, applying a legal analysis articulated by Chief Justice Stone in 1938, a "discrete and insular minorit[y]...[against whom prejudice] tends seriously to curtail the operation of those political processes ordinarily to be relied upon to protect minorities, and ... [on whose behalf] a correspondingly more searching judicial inquiry [may be called for]."[11] For blacks—another "discrete and insular minority"—the Supreme Court

[7] See N. MORRIS & G. HAWKINS, THE HONEST POLITICIAN'S GUIDE TO CRIME CONTROL 128-33 (1970).
[8] See THE MENTALLY DISABLED AND THE LAW ch. 6, at 183-97 (F. Lindman & D. McIntyre eds. 1961).
[9] In re Cavitt, 182 Neb. 712, 719, 157 N.W.2d 171, 177 (1968), appeal dismissed, 396 U.S. 996 (1970).
[10] See F. TANNENBAUM, SLAVE AND CITIZEN 75-82 (1946).
[11] United States v. Carolene Products Co., 304 U.S. 144, 152 n.4 (1933).

has increasingly done battle since 1938, deriving its task in part from a revised and clearer historical understanding of the purposes of the fourteenth amendment and in part from the vision of the role of the courts in protecting minority rights articulated by Chief Justice Stone. In this pursuit, the Supreme Court has ruled unconstitutional state laws prohibiting marriage between blacks and other races (for a plaintiff named Loving).[12] This result was dictated by a prior series of Supreme Court holdings invalidating any form of state action that singled out blacks as a group for special derogatory treatment.[13]

A similarly broad principle should be followed by the courts to protect mentally retarded citizens. Or, at the least, such citizens' rights to sexual freedom should be judicially protected.[14] The special status of family and sexual conduct in this society has been acknowledged in various Supreme Court cases as involving fundamental rights "to marry, establish a home and bring up children,"[15] the right to "privacy surrounding the marriage relationship,"[16] and "the right to satisfy [one's] intellectual and emotional needs in the privacy of [one's] own home."[17] These familial and sexual freedoms are drastically infringed upon by laws providing for sterilization and by marriage prohibitions directed against the mentally retarded.

Not all of the legislation, previously discussed imposes disabilities on all institutionalized mentally retarded individuals as such; some laws require sterilization, for example, only of persons who are considered "not capable of performing the duties of parenthood."[18] This standard—although it is no more precise than the standard which governs state interventions to redress child abuse or neglect in the general population—should be considered unconstitutionally vague as applied to a class composed exclusively of mentally retarded persons.[19] Ability to distinguish between, let alone predict, good and bad parents is uncertain, and this society and its officialdom are clearly moved by an irrational attitude regarding the sexuality of the mentally retarded. Officials share with most people in American society the incapacity to look at the retarded without irrational fear or pity. They are not able to regard them with sufficient clarity to permit sensible differentiation among them. Because the mentally retarded as a group are so readily victimized, because they are a vulnerable "discrete and insular minority," compulsory intervention in their childbearing activities, which might be tolerable for the general population, is constitutionally intolerable when limited to this group alone.

Justice Holmes' famous—indeed, notorious—opinion for the Supreme Court in 1927, upholding a state compulsory sterilization law with the aphorism "three generations of imbeciles are enough,"[20] wrongly failed to appreciate the special role

[12] Loving v. Virginia, 388 U.S. 1 (1967).

[13] The progenitor was Brown v. Board of Educ., 347 U.S. 483 (1954).

[14] *See* Burt, *Legal Restrictions on Sexual and Familial Relations of Mental Retardation: Old Laws, New Guises,* in HUMAN SEXUALITY AND THE MENTALLY RETARDED 206 (F. de la Cruz & G. LaVeck eds. 1973).

[15] Meyer v. Nebraska, 262 U.S. 390, 399 (1923) (dictum).

[16] Griswold v. Connecticut, 381 U.S. 479, 486 (1965).

[17] Stanley v. Georgia, 394 U.S. 557, 565 (1969).

[18] UTAH CODE ANN. § 64-10-7 (1953).

[19] *See* Burt, pp. 425-28, Chapter 14 of this volume.

[20] Buck v. Bell, 274 U.S. 200, 207 (1927).

for the courts in protecting a vulnerable minority. A 1942 Supreme Court case, invalidating a state's compulsory sterilization law for habitual criminals on the ground that it made irrational distinctions between criminals who should and those who should not be sterilized, suggests a different judicial attitude,[21] but the Court has not yet seen fit to administer the *coup de grâce* to compulsory sterilization laws.[22]

There are, then, an aggregate of ills surrounding involuntary sterilization imposed by the state. The laws are based on unsound, unscientific views and have the potential for being discriminatorily applied. But they have one attribute that might be a virtue, though its virtue is arguable. If the state is required to follow a stated statutory procedure to achieve its interventionist goal, certain side effects follow. It can be determined whether an individual has a right to a hearing before this particular form of intervention can take place. The courts can determine whether it is so serious a matter that there is a right to counsel. If the intervention is labeled as involuntary and a deprivation of basic human right, it may be that the state will have to demonstrate that there is no less restrictive alternative that will achieve the same purpose. Requiring an involuntary act to be so designated often provides a better grip on what is occurring, a recognition of the procedures that must be followed, a sharper record, in a sense, of the pattern of state intervention.

What is true here is true elsewhere in state intervention in the lives of the mentally ill and the mentally retarded. The flood of substantive reform in the care of mentally ill and mentally retarded persons has naturally led to a decline in the quantity of procedural safeguards. Such an approach may be defensible when the form of intervention itself is inherently less coercive. But in instances where it is indisputably clear that the intervention may be against the patient's interests, it is hard to justify it in the name of enlightened practice. And that indisputable likelihood may characterize sterilization, drug experimentation, and commitment to state institutions.

Yet, as could be predicted, the compulsory sterilization statues have largely fallen into disuse. Government has substituted more palatable techniques to achieve much the same result. Fears about empowering the state to engage in a eugenics program have been as strong as fears about childbearing by the mentally ill, the habitual criminal, and the mentally retarded. In a sense, there has been a search for a way to achieve a wanted result more covertly, more legitimately, or under a less sordid banner. Here the issue of consent arises, but it arises as one of several categories of possibility. *First*, there is the likelihood that "voluntary," or consensual, sterilization will become increasingly frequent. This is evident currently with sterilization being used as a prerequisite for deinstitutionalization. *Second*, it is possible that improved contraceptive counseling, including involuntary contraception, will be used to replace compulsory sterilization. And, in connection with improved contraception, reliance on therapeutic abortions may become more frequent. *Finally*, it is possible that public concern about the "parenting" qualities of the mentally retarded can be assimilated into general statutory enforcement powers concerning neglected children.

[21] Skinner v. Oklahoma, 316 U.S. 535 (1942).
[22] The Supreme Court agreed to review the Nebraska decision in *In re* Cavitt, 157 N.W.2d 171 (1968), but before the Court heard argument the Nebraska legislature repealed its compulsory sterilization statute. Act of April 11, 1969, ch. 825, § 1 [1969] Neb. Laws 3132; *see* 393 U.S. 1078 (1969); 396 U.S. 996 (1970).

CONSENT AND THE ROLE OF THE INDIVIDUAL

With the advance of community care, there is increased pressure to restrict mentally retarded persons in their right to procreate, and the restriction is increasingly through the use of sterilization by consent. It is here that the need for an analytical framework becomes paramount. There are degrees of retardation, degrees of understanding, and degrees of consent. At some point on the spectrum, the consent that is being considered cannot come from the person himself. Yet, it is quite clear, through the device of committees or guardians or through a recognition of the status of the parent, that "consent" is being obtained and sterilizations are being performed which do not comply with the regulations governing "involuntary" sterilizations. Some indication of the role that statutes perform in the development of the substitute consent idea may suggest the complexity of the issue.

In some states, the mentally retarded person must be consulted before a "voluntary" sterilization occurs. Here, questions arise that naturally lead to the issue of third-party consent. It is one thing to require the patient's consent; it is another to regard it as sufficient. It must be acknowledged that there will be a class of cases, perhaps a large class, wherein the consent of the retarded individual will not meet minimum standards of knowing consent. There are statutes that take each position, and they should be differentiated from statutes that render the wishes of the third person controlling regardless of the consent of the patient.

Under the California statute,[23] for example, consent is manifested in the following manner. When the superintendent decides that an institutionalized mentally retarded person can benefit from sterilization, he must notify the patient and other specified persons. If no objection is returned within 30 days, the patient is deemed to have consented. It appears from the statute that normally the written consent of the patient suffices if there is no written objection. The Maine statute requires, when a sterilizing operation is indicated, that the physician recommend to the target individual the advisability and necessity of the operation. At the outset, the patient himself may give written consent, but if the hospital seeks to proceed on the basis of this consent, a council of two doctors must be assembled to determine whether the person is "mentally capable of giving his consent."[24] In Michigan, the state can proceed to perform a sterilization when responsible officials have obtained the consent of a "defective person . . . of the age of 16 years or more and not otherwise incapable of giving consent," together with the consent of a guardian and near relative.[25]

Other statutes seem to suggest that a voluntary operation can occur without prior consultation with the patient. A Minnesota statute, for example, provides that the commissioner of public welfare may authorize a sterilization operation "with the written consent of the spouse or nearest kin" of the patient. The Connecticut statute similarly relies wholly on the responsible next of kin or guardian of the person

---

[23] CAL. WELF. & INST. CODE § 7254 (1972).
[24] ME. REV. STAT. ANN. tit. 34, § 2461 (1964).
[25] MICH. COMP. LAWS § 720.304 (1970). Cf. *In re* Eugene Weberlist, 79 Misc. 2d 753 (Sup. Ct. N.Y. 1974).

involved.[26] State statutes of this class usually place the burden on third parties to object to a state recommendation that sterilization take place or to initiate a request for sterilization or to "consent" to the operation. These third-party statutes are of various kinds. Minnesota serves as one pole since in that state the commissioner of public welfare serves as the legal guardian for institutionalized retarded persons.[27] Since he is the guardian, he may provide the exclusive consent where there is no spouse or near relative. In other states, a guardian *ad litem* must be appointed to provide specific consent to the operation. In some states, the objection of the third person (guardian or relative) is conclusive. In others, objection by third parties is only a factor to be considered by the board of the hospital and, later, by the court.

Legal authority to make such choices on behalf of mentally retarded persons appears available in the guardianship laws in all states, which authorize the appointment of custodians for, among others, mentally deficient persons who are not institutionalized but are nonetheless regarded as incompetent to handle some portion or all of their affairs.[28] The potential for abuse of these guardianship laws is clear. A case recently decided by the Kentucky Supreme Court should serve as a warning. In *Strunk v. Strunk*,[29] the court authorized the appointment of the mother as guardian of a 27-year-old institutionalized retarded person in order to permit her to consent, on his behalf, to remove one of his kidneys to donate to his otherwise doomed but intellectually normal older brother. The court did not seem troubled by the mother's necessarily ambivalent role in making this decision for her retarded son, nor by the value system (normal persons are "worth" more than retarded people) the ruling may reflect.

An early opinion of the Michigan attorney general holds that parental consent to a sertilization operation is null and void because "the right to possess and retain the power of pro-creation is second only to life itself among the rights . . . guaranteed by the Federal Constitution. It is a right that is personal to the child and is not merged with the right of control by the parent over the person of the child. . . ."[30]

How can it be determined in what circumstances a parent or guardian third party should be permitted to consent in the sense of taking the place of the individual? What are the factors to be considered?[31]

---

[26] CONN. GEN. STAT. ANN. §§ 17-19 (Supp. 1973).

[27] MINN. STAT. ANN. § 256.07 (1971).

[28] *See* THE MENTALLY DISABLED AND THE LAW, *supra* note 8, at 225-26, 230-34, 239-51.

[29] 445 S.W.2d 145 (Ky. 1969).

[30] 1921-22 MICH. OP. ATT'Y GEN. 229, 230 (1921).

[31] When a person is committed involuntarily to an institution or where, as in Minnesota, the commissioner of public welfare is the legal guardian of persons adjudicated as retarded under the relevant state statute, the state itself may prescribe certain treatment forms without obtaining consent from the patient or a third party. Where there is a state sterilization law, the procedure provided is undoubtedly the exclusive route by which a sterilization operation can be performed. But where a state has no such law and the institution considers the operation therapeutic, it is possible that the state can proceed without obtaining further consent. Sterilization aside, there seems to be extensive question about the kinds of treatment the state can unilaterally prescribe when it is the legal guardian. *See* Wade v. Bethesda Hospital, 356 F. Supp. 380 (S.D. Ohio 1973).

This problem of drawing the line between routine and more interventionist forms of treatment has had interesting outcroppings. A 1948 opinion of the Pennsylvania attorney general claimed that state mental hospitals could administer "electric shock and such other treatments, which in the exercise of reasonable skill and judgment, are indicated, after observation and diagnosis, as being necessary and proper for the patients' best welfare, without first obtaining written permission for such treatment from such patients, their friends, relatives, guardians or other persons who may be

One answer may be that "consent" should never be characterized as the justification for an operation when the individual involved has not provided informed consent or has been determined to be incompetent to consent.[32] But this answer may be too rigid. In *Strunk*, for example, there was evidence that the kidney transplant was a very low-risk surgical procedure for the donor and, as noted, essential for preserving the life of the recipient. Does it truly serve important social purposes to bar conclusively the incompetent donor from exercising the right that the "normal" population prizes as an ethical imperative—to give of one's self in order to help others? The right to elect sterilization is equally prized by many, and the Supreme Court's recent abortion decision would appear to give constitutional dimension to this or an analo-

---

legally entitled to give such consent on behalf of such patients. . . ." 1947-48 PA. OP. ATT'Y GEN. 120, 135 (1948), 64 Pa. D. & C. 14, 35 (1948). The Pennsylvania opinion may be qualified, however, since the department has now advised mental health facilities that electroshock treatments are no longer recognized as "routine."

The Wisconsin approach is more cautious. Given the "drastic nature of prefrontal lobotomy or psychosurgery, its permanent effects, as well as the fairly high mortality rates accompanying or following the procedure, and the rather limited percentage of cases resulting in improvement, [the attorney general has] . . . most strongly urg[ed] obtaining the consent of near relatives or guardians wherever possible. . . ." The opinion, however, continued to state that, "We wish to make it clear that this conclusion is in the nature of advice as to policy, and that as to the law relating generally to the care and treatment of insane persons in state institutions we subscribe to the view . . . that in the absence of express statutory provision the care and treatment of inmates in state mental institutions must be discretionary in the duly appointed officers of the institutions." 37 WISC. OP. ATT'Y GEN. 502, 510-11 (1948), *reprinted in* F. MILLER, R. DAWSON, G. PIX & R. PARNAS, CRIMINAL JUSTICE ADMINISTRATION AND RELATED PROCESSES 1664-68 (1971).

The California statute is odd and difficult to interpret on this issue. Section 7518 of the Welfare and Institutions Code provides that "the medical director of a state hospital with programs for developmentally disabled patients . . . may give consent to medical, dental, and surgical treatment of a minor developmentally disabled patient of the hospital and provide for such treatment to be given to the patient." The statute makes the director's consent binding if the patient's parent, guardian, or conservator does not respond within a reasonable time to a request for the granting or denying of consent. And the statute is silent as to the effect of a parental explicit refusal to consent.

California legislation for the mentally ill also provides an interesting technique for the distribution of authority to consent. When the Lanterman Petris Short Act was passed in 1969, it included a section or rights to patients. CAL. WELF. & INST. CODE § 5325 (1972). This section gave each patient the right to refuse lobotomies. The statute, however, indicated that when the medical director of an institution could give good cause, the rights of patients designated in the statute could be overridden. CAL. WELF. & INST. CODE § 5326 (1972). In 1973, the legislature. amended the relevant section to make the patient's determination on this treatment modality conclusive. Ch. 959, 1973 Reg. Sess. (West's Cal. Legislative Service).

[32] The debate over the testing of drugs in children may provide some guidance on the issue of third-party consent. Address by Dr. I. Ladimer, *Problems of Drug Evaluation in Infants and Children* 21-22, 58th Ross Conference on Pediatric Research, May 5-7, 1968 (available in pamphlet from Ross Laboratories, Columbus, Ohio):

The First National Conference on the Legal Environment of Medical Sciences held nine years ago sought to anticipate and meet many of these ethical problems. In particular, wrestling with the first and most compelling precept of the Nuremberg Code, "The voluntary consent of the human subject is absolutely essential," the working committee adopted this addition:

For those not capable of personal consent, permission of the parent or guardian is acceptable, provided:

1. The immediate and future welfare of the subject is not threatened in the light of established knowledge and provided the procedures are such that consent of a competent subject, under similar circumstances, could be readily presumed.

2. The subject or guardians are not subjected to economic sacrifice.

3. There is reasonable hope that such studies will contribute information of importance.

4. The applicability of these criteria be subject to review by a responsible and scientifically competent review body, not including the investigator.

The Nuremberg Code, the recognized father of the many current codes and guides, also

gous attitude.[33] It would thus be troubling, both in practice and in constitutional doctrine, for the state to identify some class of people who are "not competent" to make choices that the Constitution guarantees to others.

The state thus appears constrained by two competing commands regarding sterilization. It must scrupulously respect individual consent, but it must give adequate scope for individual choice to be expressed and to prevail. Third-party consent can have some role in charting a line between these commands, to help those who clearly need help in choosing. But no matter how scrupulously the required safeguards are applied, no person can ever stand wholly in another's place. Third-party consent will always be something of a fiction, will always be somewhat arbitrary, and thus must always be narrowly circumscribed.

The first line of defense against the dangers of this fiction is to forbid third-party consent to sterilization on behalf of full-time residents in state institutions. The reasons that lead to the rejection of state-commanded involuntary sterilization of institutionalized persons apply equally here. The weight of state coercion is too easily concealed behind a parent's choice to sterilize the institutionalized child. The documented practice of parents' admitting their children to Willowbrook State School in New York demonstrates that consent to a potentially harmful course of drug experimentation may be accepted by parents as the price for committing their children to state institutions. Furthermore, the deep-seated social prejudice against the mentally retarded—which supports the argument that they are a "suspect class" requiring protection against state-ordered sterilization—is often equally and even more passionately felt by parents of these children.

The general legal rule that parents may dictate their children's medical treatment is made tolerable by most parents' identification with their children and by powerful social attitudes against abuse of children. But for retarded children, and most particularly for those who are institutionalized, both of these constraints are often seriously eroded.

---

included the principle of consent based on free choice without coercion or duress which must be understood as applying to all types of consent. It did not however refer to "benefit" as such, but to fruitful results for society, and humanitarian importance, apparently considering that the subject or his representative would determine what significance to place on participation. The Declaration of Helsinki, which is endorsed by the A.M.A. and the pediatric societies, distinguishes between clinical research combined with professional care and non-therapeutic clinical research. I have never been convinced that this distinction is meaningful. The Public Health Service, guided by Helsinki, requires review bodies to evaluate among other things the "risks and potential medical benefits of the investigation," without defining these terms.

The American Medical Association, in adopting the Helsinki Code in 1966 added Ethical Guidelines for Clinical Investigation, which require consent in both therapeutic and non-therapeutic categories, except where deemed detrimental to therapy, in which case information withheld from the patient shall be disclosed to a responsible relative or friend where possible.

As to children the A.M.A. guidelines say minors or mentally incompetent persons may be used as subjects only if:

1. The nature of the investigation is such that mentally competent adults would not be suitable subjects.

2. Consent, in writing, is given by a legally authorized representative of the subject under circumstances in which an informed and prudent adult would reasonably be expected to volunteer himself or his child as a subject.

[33] Roe v. Wade, 410 U.S. 113 (1973).

A different line of defense to protect the retarded from sterilization might be considered. The question must be asked: Why should sterilization be permitted for any person—institutionalized or not—at parental direction? The availability of less drastic birth control techniques would suggest that individual autonomy regarding sterilization would be best protected by forcing postponement of this irreversible decision until the socially sanctioned "age of discretion" is reached, and only at that age might distinctions between "competent" and "incompetent" individual decision makers be drawn. By this standard, the unique character of sterilization as a bodily intrusion is highlighted—its irreversibility, its general inadvisability except as a last resort, its compelling psychological significance. Recent allegations that state officers coerced a welfare mother into consenting to her daughter's sterilization[34] suggest an added social reality that would dictate protecting children by conclusively banning sterilization of them.

CONTRACEPTION AND ABORTION

One alternative that has enormous appeal is to replace the cumbersome and taboo-laden practice of sterilization with an emphasis on systematic contraception. There is hope in some quarters that there will soon be approved a contraceptive (an injection for example) that will not rely on patient management. But zeal for technology has a way of converting counseling and encouragement to something more. A practice that is a virtue when elected may not remain so when compelled. The problem of voluntariness in contraception programs is no easier than the problem of voluntariness in sterilization. There are, of course, striking differences: contraception is not so drastic; it is reversible; it bears no stigma; it is being increasingly accepted and selected by the general population. But these reasons explain only why compulsory contraception is *more palatable* than compulsory sterilization; they do not prove that it is acceptable. Here, the problem of category rises again. In styling the reasons why mentally retarded persons are subject to a particular kind of involuntary treatment, reasons may be stated which apply to most of the population. Fiscal irresponsibility and "bad parenting" are reasons to *choose* contraception. They may not be reasons to *mandate* it or to mandate it for a stigmatized class such as mentally retarded persons. Involuntary (or semivoluntary) contraception will be used increasingly in the next decade as pharmacological advances are made and as emphasis on community placement of the mentally retarded grows. The trend must be viewed cautiously and with trepidation, both because of danger to the individual rights of mentally retarded citizens and because involuntary contraception creates bad precedents.

Involuntary or semivoluntary abortions present more difficult questions. The Supreme Court decision in *Roe v. Wade*[35] might have been heralded as a great victory for the right of a woman to decide whether to bring a child to term. How-

---

[34] Cox v. Stanton, 381 F. Supp. 349 (E.D.N.C. 1974). *See also* Relf v. Weinberger, 372 F. Supp. 1196 (D.D.C. 1974).

[35] 410 U.S. 113 (1973).

ever, it would be a strained extension that would consider that physicians or guardians or parents have the right to make this decision for a minor or ward. Minor children in many jurisdictions have the right, without parental consent, to obtain an abortion. But it is doubtful that there is a single jurisdiction in which a hospital would permit an abortion at the parent's wish and over the objection of a non-retarded child. Yet, though the ethical problems in abortion are greater (depending on one's definition of the status of the fetus) than in contraception, it is likely that the involuntary abortion will become increasingly common for persons who are mentally retarded, who formerly would have been institutionalized or sterilized, and who are now in the community.

CHILD NEGLECT STATUTES

A final less restrictive approach to the issues presented by sterilization and its alternatives involves child neglect statutes. Almost every state statute is broad enough to authorize compulsory removal of a child from a parent who, because of mental deficiency, is regarded as incapable of childrearing. The Minnesota child neglect statute, for example, authorizes the state to take custody of any child "whose . . . condition, environment or associations are such as to be injurious or dangerous to himself or others."[36] Inevitably, the fears and prejudices that stigmatize mentally retarded persons intrude on the judgment of courts and social agencies who apply these statutes. Open-ended statutes are invitations to abuse, abuse particularly of the mentally retarded. Numerous procedural guarantees — such as the right to counsel and the opportunity to rebut all adverse evidence — should be provided to all parents, including mentally retarded parents, who are subjects of child abuse or neglect proceedings. Still, it is doubtful that statutory standards for state intervention can be so narrowly defined as to eliminate the possibility of misuse, without inappropriately withholding the possibility of state intervention to help children in serious jeopardy from their parents.[37] The prophylactic principle that led to the argument that, for example, the compulsory sterilization laws should be overturned cannot properly be applied to invalidate the child abuse and neglect laws. The opportunity for victimizing the mentally retarded parent in the application of child abuse and neglect laws will probably, and regrettably, remain a reality.

This special vulnerability creates an obligation of defense on the part of those planning new modes of introducing mentally retarded persons into community life — by family planning, contraceptive counseling, and special plans for intensive childrearing services in heterosexual sheltered community living. These special childrearing programs may be more urgently required than similar programs for parents in the "normal" population who suffer childrearing disabilities. The label of mental

---

[36] MINN. STAT. ANN. § 260.015 (Supp. 1973). *See also* Paulsen, *The Legal Framework for Child Protection,* 66 COLUM. L. REV. 679, 693-94 (1964).

[37] *See* Burt, *Forcing Protection on Children and Their Parents: The Impact of Wyman v. James,* 69 MICH. L. REV. 1259 (1971).

retardation threatens loss to all who bear it. Childrearing programs are needed to protect them, as much as to protect those among the retarded population about whom there would be a very high degree of agreement that they are incapable parents.

Current thinking is not far removed, in time or in ideology, from Justice Holmes and *Buck v. Bell.* Society is now too sophisticated to talk eugenics, at least aloud; the language of fiscal responsibility and "parenting environment" has a more appealing cast then talk about "wards of the state" and menaces to society. But whatever the rhetoric, there is little need now, and there will be less in the future, to resort to compulsory sterilization. More modern and more acceptable interventions, contraception and abortion, will take its place. But it must be realized that larger issues are at stake, involving the permissible intervention of society to restrict or encourage childbearing. For Justice Holmes, the principle that supported compulsory vaccination supported the salpingectomy. It is not yet clear what the new-found principle of compulsory contraception of the mentally retarded will support.

TECHNIQUES FOR SELECTING THE THIRD-PARTY CONSENTER

Another critical element to be considered in regulating third-party consent to justify state-sanctioned intervention is the means for choosing the third party. For some "incompetents," namely, children, the law accepts parental consent for a vast range of interventions with virtually no external accountability—either before or after the decision. The law has embraced the notion that parents are more than adequately dedicated to their child's interest to exercise this power. But, as with the theory of the juvenile court, it is now patently clear that this view has little to recommend it in many important matters, and it serves little purpose except to obfuscate analysis. For mentally retarded children, for example, some people cling to the hope that parents can adequately act as surrogates for their children, though this hope is often scarcely warranted.

Aside from parents, the standard conservator is likely to be no different from the state itself. In Los Angeles, the public conservator is a huge bureaucracy, like other helping agencies. To say that, is not to say that it is bad, it is merely to acknowledge that third-party consent by an institutional conservator is virtually the same as involuntary intervention by the state. There is no indication that when the state prescribes commitment or sterilization it uses different standards from those an institutional conservator uses.

Yet, for all their potential abuses, it is clear that reliance on parents or on ordinary state bureaucracies to give consent for "incompetents" is sometimes appropriate. Propriety depends, it seems, on *what* is proposed, to *whom,* and *where.* Thus, for example, for children tonsillectomy might be at parental discretion, sterilization banned in any circumstance (where intended solely as birth control), and participation in drug experimentation at parental discretion only for children not residing in state institutions. And, for institutionalized children or for chronological but "retarded" adults new mechanisms must be created to provide adequate third-party consent for a wide range of interventions. For these persons, in these matters, parents are not reliable protectors; their personal involvement too readily obscures the proper perspective for their child. Similarly, the programmatic commitments of operating staff may mislead them and their charges. New arrangements are needed — in effect, agencies like public defenders, adequately staffed and trained to see the matter as closely as possible as an alter ego for the consented party. It is more comfortable, and less costly, to pretend that parents or current state employees can be trusted to act on behalf of their dependents in all the matters we have been discussing, but this is pretense.

A different question is presented in asking whether parents should be permitted to block an intervention even though they are empowered unilaterally to consent to it. Symmetry should not be seen as a requisite aesthetic standard in the development of legal rules. Just as there are good reasons to preclude parents from consenting unilaterally, there may be good reason to provide family and guardian with a substantial say if they wish to object to a particular operation. One might argue that a parental objection to an operation should have more weight than parental consent. The parent may be expressing a religious or philosophical view that is important to the family and to each member of it. The objection should be persuasive, though not conclusive.

On the issue of an appropriate tribunal, the resolution is still more confused. What is wanted is a panel that has no conflict of interest and that can separate the question of the desirability of the operation from the question of the capacity of the person to consent (as is stated in the Maine statute). The inappropriateness of involuntary sterilization, after all, is partly a consequence of the inappropriateness of any decision-making process which forces persons to make decisions incapable of ethical resolution.[38]

THIRD-PARTY CONSENT: SOME CONCLUSIONS

Control of sexual behavior is not the most pressing issue involving third-party consent for mentally retarded persons. Medical decisions relating to the giving or withholding of treatment, the form of treatment decided upon, drug experimentation,

---

[38] After this paper was written, the Alabama federal courts took action to regulate sterilization for residents of the state institution for retarded persons. First, a three-judge court ruled unconstitutional the state compulsory sterilization law. (Wyatt v. Aderholt, 368 F. Supp. 1383 (M.D. Ala. 1974).) Then, after remand, Judge Frank Johnson entered an order governing the availability of "consensual" sterilization in the institution. (368 F. Supp. 1383 (M.D. Ala. 1974).) The order specifies that no institutional resident under the age of 21 may be sterilized "except in cases of medical necessity"—that is, excluding sterilization solely for birth control purposes—and that adult residents may be sterilized only with their consent and with the protection of extensive review in forums both within and outside the institution. This order sensitively attends to the competing considerations adumbrated throughout this paper; it is reproduced in full as an appendix to the paper. *See also* Wyatt v. Aderholt, 503 F.2d 1035 (5th Cir. 1974).

and admission to hospitals raise problems that are more significant. Some aspects of the analysis of third-party consent in the sterilization issue can be applied to certain of these other issues.

The outstanding aspect of third-party consent is that it usually includes the hazards of involuntary state interventions without the cluster of safeguards that have been developed where state action, pure and simple, is found. Our prediction (not an empirically demonstrated conclusion) is that the move toward third-party consent will be seen to cover transactions that would once have involved pure state intervention. In circumstances which are among the most outrageous, a third-party can consent to an action that is forbidden when the state acts with proper procedural safeguards. Third-party consent may have been an attempt to humanize and render more informal and more individual a system that seemed rigid and unyielding, but in the course of development, the technique fostered unreviewable state intervention. Resort to third-party consent has, finally, become a way to avoid the analysis which follows from the requirement that government seek the least restrictive alternative.

Third-party consent to drug experimentation is not adequate when the experiment is not designed to benefit the patient as an individual. There is fear enough that disadvantaged populations such as the institutionalized mentally retarded are singled out for drug experimentation. Providing the opportunity for third-party consent makes it more likely that noncompetent groups will be increasingly the subject of such tests. If testing must take place, it should be according to ethical standards that are nondiscriminatory both in form and in application. Admission and status in hospitals also pose interesting issues. There is no suitable way to differentiate between third-party consent admissions and involuntary admissions unless it can be confidently assumed that the third-party is a fit and conflict-free surrogate for the patient. If one were able to design such a precise level of procedural safeguard, it would be possible to say that consent to involuntary admission is adequate when the third-party is harmoniously identified with the patient's best interests.[39] Even then, patients admitted under third-party consent should not have fewer review rights than persons who are involuntarily committed. It is an irony of the present system that persons "voluntarily" committed by a guardian or conservator may never have judicial review of their custody, whereas "involuntary" patients may even have limits on the length of their stay. Individuals admitted on fictional consent are "twice cursed." There is neither the assumed personal control over release and treatment that is the basis for regular voluntary status nor the growing set of protections for those involuntarily detained. Nothing in their status justifies this discrimination.

This is not to suggest that there is no room for third-party authorization of state intervention in the lives of persons who are mentally ill or mentally retarded. What is being suggested, rather, is that the identity of persons so authorized, the process

---

[39] Of course, this analysis presupposes that there are safeguards surrounding the involuntary admissions process. We appreciate that there is something formal about this analysis in that procedural standards in many jurisdictions are either inadequately developed or imperfectly administered. It is, however, most likely that third-party consent techniques are used most frequently in those states where involuntary admissions are the most difficult to obtain.

by which they come to have such power, and restrictions on the choices open to them must be closely analyzed. At present, third-party consent is a burgeoning fail-safe, to be resorted to more and more frequently as other routes to state intervention become difficult to follow. But current justifications for the practice suggest that there will be more and more attacks upon it in the future. Courts must begin to wonder who a guardian is, and how he is selected, and from where come his powers to deprive citizens of life and liberty.

Appendix

Court Order (January 8, 1974) Setting Standards to Govern
Sterilization of Institutional Residents
WYATT V. ADERHOLT, 368 F. Supp. 1383 (M.D. Ala. 1974)

ON DECEMBER 20, 1973, the three-judge court in *Wyatt v. Aderholt* declared that Tit. 45, § 243, Code of Alabama, is unconstitutional. As a consequence of that action, the three-judge feature of the case is now complete and that court has been dissolved. However, since it appears that sterilization continues to be performed in certain instances by the state health authorities, it is necessary that this Court promulgate adequate standards and procedural safeguards to insure that all future sterilizations be performed only where the full panoply of constitutional protections has been accorded to the individuals involved. Accordingly, it is ORDERED that the following standards be and they are hereby adopted and ordered implemented from this date for the sterilization of mentally retarded residents of the state retardation facilities:

1. (a) "Sterilization," as used in these standards, means any medical or surgical operation or procedure which results in a patient's permanent inability to reproduce.

    (b) A determination that a proposed sterilization is in the best interest of a resident, as referred to in these standards, must include a determination that no temporary measure for birth control or contraception will adequately meet the needs of such resident, and shall not be made on the basis of institutional convenience or purely administrative considerations.

2. No resident who has not attained the chronological age of 21 years shall be sterilized except in cases of medical necessity as determined in accordance with the procedures set forth below. No other resident shall be sterilized except in accordance with procedures set forth below.

3. No resident shall be sterilized unless such resident has consented in writing to such sterilization. Except as set forth below, such consent must be informed, in that it is (a) based upon an understanding of the nature and consequences of sterilization, (b) given by a person competent to make such a decision, and (c) wholly voluntary and free from any coercion, express or implied. It shall be the responsibility of the Director of the Partlow State School (with the assistance

of employees or officials designated by him) to provide the resident with complete information concerning the nature and consequences of sterilization, to assist the resident in comprehending such information, and to identify any barriers to such comprehension.

4. The Director shall prepare a report evaluating the resident's understanding of the proposed sterilization and describing the steps taken to inform the resident of the nature and consequences of sterilization. If the resident has been determined by a court of competent jurisdiction to be legally incompetent, or if the Director cannot certify without reservation that the resident understands the nature and consequences of sterilization, the sterilization shall not be performed unless (a) the Director sets forth reasonable grounds for believing that such sterilization is in the best interest of the resident; (b) the Review Committee described below approves such sterilization; and (c) it is determined by a court of competent jurisdiction that such sterilization is in the best interest of the resident.

5. No sterilization shall be performed without the prior approval of a Review Committee formed in accordance with this paragraph. The Review Committee shall consist of five members, and shall be selected by the Partlow Human Rights Committee and approved by the Court. The members shall be so selected that the Committee will be competent to deal with the medical, legal, social and ethical issues involved in sterilization; to this end, at least one member shall be a licensed physician, at least one shall be a licensed attorney, at least two shall be women, at least two shall be minority group members, and at least one shall be a resident of the Partlow State School (the foregoing categories are not mutually exclusive). No member shall be an officer, employee, or agent of the Partlow State School, nor may any member be otherwise involved in the proposed sterilization.

   Any fees or costs incurred by reason of services performed by the Review Committee, including reasonable fees for the physician and the attorney, shall be paid by the Alabama Department of Mental Health upon a certification of reasonableness by the Partlow Human Rights Committee.

6. Prior to approving the proposed sterilization of any resident, the Review Committee shall:

   (a) Review appropriate medical, social, and psychological information concerning the resident, including the report of the Director prepared pursuant to paragraph 4;

   (b) Interview the resident to be sterilized;

   (c) Interview concerned individuals, relatives, and others who in its judgment will contribute pertinent information;

   (d) Determine whether the resident has given his or her informed consent to the sterilization, or, if the resident is legally incompetent or the Director cannot certify without reservation that the resident understands the nature and consequences of sterilization, whether the resident has formed, without coercion, a genuine desire to be sterilized. In making such determination, the Review Committee shall take into consideration, *inter alia,* the report prepared by the Director pursuant to paragraph 4 and the interview required by paragraph 6(b).

   (e) Determine whether the proposed sterilization is in the best interest of the resident.

   If the Review Committee does not reach an affirmative determination as to the matters set forth in paragraphs 6(d) and (e), it shall not approve the proposed sterilization. Any doubts as to such matters shall be resolved against proceeding with sterilization.

7. Residents shall be represented throughout all the procedures described above by legal counsel appointed by the Review Committee from a list of such counsel drawn up by the Partlow Human Rights Committee and approved by the Court. Such counsel shall, *inter alia,* ensure that all considerations militating against the proposed sterilization have been adequately explored and resolved. No such counsel shall be an officer, employee, or agent of the Partlow State School, nor may such counsel be otherwise involved in the proposed sterilization.

8. The Review Committee shall maintain written records of its determinations and the reasons therefore, with supporting documentation. Such records shall be available for examination by the Partlow Human Rights Committee, the Court, and counsel of record in this cause. The Review Committee shall report in writing at least monthly to the Human Rights Committee, the Court, and counsel of record in this cause as to the number and nature of sterilizations approved and disapproved, the procedures employed in approving or disapproving such sterilizations, the reason for determining that such sterilizations were in the best interest of the residents involved, the number and nature of proposed sterilizations referred to courts of competent jurisdiction, and all other relevant information. The identity of residents sterilized or to be sterilized shall not be disclosed in such reports.

9. There shall be no coercion in any form with regard to sterilization of any resident. Consent to sterilization shall not be made a condition for receiving any form of public assistance, nor may it be a prerequisite for any other health or social service, or for admission to or release from the Partlow State School. Any individual having knowledge of coercion of any resident with regard to sterilization shall immediately bring such matter to the attention of the Partlow Human Rights Committee, the Court, or counsel of record in this cause.

    It is further ordered that the defendants, their agents, employees and those acting in concert with them be and each is hereby enjoined from failing to implement the standards hereinabove set out for the sterilization of mentally retarded residents of the Alabama retardation facilities.

    Done, this the 8th day of January, 1974.

Reaction Comment

KAREN LEBACQZ

THE REAL CONCERN here is well expressed by Price and Burt when they talk about erasure of the line between voluntary and involuntary intervention. Are we performing *unwanted* and perhaps *unwarranted* operations or medical interventions through subterfuge? Do we get away with things by calling them voluntary, because of third-party consent, when they would be illegal if considered involuntary procedures?

There is increasing pressure today to move mentally retarded persons out of institutions and into the community. This trend may be accompanied by an exacerbation of our fears of their sexual activities—fears that are fed by myths and stereotypes to which we all have subscribed at some time. These fears produce pressure to exercise control over the sexual activity of mentally retarded persons. In response to this pressure, will new forms of control be invented? Where we used to perform involuntary sterilizations, which had to be justified as such, will we now move to pseudovoluntary sterilization, or possibly pseudovoluntary contraception, all "justified" through third-party consent?

Since I am not a lawyer, I cannot respond to all of the legal subtleties involved in questions such as informed consent and procedural safeguards. But I do support the concerns that are expressed here, especially with regard to our fears of the mentally retarded person's sexuality and the probability that this society will move toward more subtle and insidious forms of control of persons who are mentally retarded.

Let me put these concerns in a somewhat broader context. First, the mentally retarded person has a right not to be subjected to unwanted and unwarranted medical intervention under the guise of voluntary consent by a third party, under the guise of medical care, or under any other guise.

Second, mentally retarded citizens should be guaranteed medical care where medical care is both needed and wanted. For example, an infant born with Down's syndrome who needs a life-saving operation has a right to the care which will save his life — even if his parents decide they do not want a child who is mentally retarded and therefore refuse to give permission for the operation. A physician responding to such a situation at Johns Hopkins Hospital was quoted as saying, "A different standard is used for mentally retarded babies. . . . It's a part of the American ethic." These cases are not unusual. One physician has gone on record as saying that in his opinion parents of children with Down's syndrome (mongolism) have the legal right to decide if their child should live or die (please note: not *all* parents are to have this right, but only parents of children with Down's syndrome).[1]

The question is whether life-saving operations should be performed on children or persons who are mentally retarded. The suggestion is being made now in some medical, legal, and theological circles that persons who are mentally retarded should be treated differently from persons who are called "normal." Increasing interest in euthanasia suggests a movement toward a point where mentally retarded persons will be "allowed to die" where normal persons would not be.

In other words, there must be, on the one hand, protection of the mentally retarded person from unwanted encroachment through medical intervention and, on the other hand, a guarantee to the mentally retarded person of needed medical, especially life-saving medical, care. At stake is a basic question of equal protection. Medical literature, legal literature, and theological literature reflect the encroachment of a new kind of ethic which is being called by its proponents a "quality of life" ethic. The "quality of life" ethic, in essence, rests on the principle that "some are more equal than others," that unequal capacity or potentiality provides grounds for discriminatory treatment. At stake here is the fundamental moral, and hence legal, equality of human beings as human beings.

[1] Shaw, *"Doctor, do we have a choice?"* New York Times Magazine, Jan. 30, 1972, at 44.

There are serious questions about what it means to operate according to such an ethic. Where does one draw the line on what "quality" must be present to justify discriminatory treatment? What degree of mental retardation must be present in order for the decision to be made that an infant shall be "allowed to die"? What *risk* of mental retardation must be present: Should the child born with a 40 percent chance of mental retardation be "allowed to die"?

Furthermore, the principle of unequal treatment in accordance with some standard of "quality" can be extended from mental and physical capacities to some other standard of "quality or meaningful life."[2] Price and Burt make an important point: It is extremely important to sort out the *categories* of people being considered and to avoid lumping all mentally retarded children or all persons with disabilities into the same category.

Third, we must focus on our *hidden agendas.* Price and Burt allude to this crucial issue in pointing to our sexual fears and fantasies and how these have influenced the treatment of mentally retarded persons. Operations are sometimes performed on mentally retarded children because it is better *for us* or better for the provider of medical care, not better for the individual. *Strunk v. Strunk*[3] provides an example: A retarded person's kidney was removed not for his benefit, but for the benefit of another. A clue to hidden agencies is the use of language. Some providers of medical care are beginning to talk about children in terms of "the product." One physician justifies prenatal diagnosis and selective abortion by putting it in the context of what society can do to "ensure as high quality a product as possible."[4] The fetus or child becomes a "product," and the aim of medical intervention is to yield the best product.

Finally, the issues raised here are issues of *social justice.* Predominantly, they have to do with the provision of legal protection and with the justice of the social order. But there is another side to justice: Justice is not only legal protection or justice in the social order; justice is not simply a matter of external relations and regulation of behavior. It is also an ordering of the various values, attitudes, and tendencies within the inner person. One of the issues which should be raised, therefore, has to do with the kind of people we want to be: What does it do to us as persons to violate the rights of other people, including mentally retarded people, and to create a world in which the moral community excludes whole categories of people? Do we not diminish as people when we participate in the myths and stereotypes that support this kind of unequal treatment?

All of us come to this discussion with good intentions, assuming that our hearts and our minds are in the right place and that it is our purpose to decide how we can help the mentally retarded. Perhaps we should ask what we have *to learn from* the mentally retarded, not simply what we have to give to them. So, when we talk about "humanizing," consider: Who is it that really needs the humanizing—is it the mentally retarded person, or is it us?

[2] Roe v. Wade, 410 U.S. 311 (1973).
[3] 455 S.W.2d 145 (Ky. 1969).
[4] Morison, *Implications of Prenatal Diagnosis for the Quality of, and Right to, Human Life,* in Ethical Issues in Human Genetics 201 (B. Hilton & D. Callahan eds. 1973).

CHAPTER 5

Trusts and Estate Planning

Editorial Introduction

Effland, distinguished author and expert on the law of property disposition, and Heckt of Minneapolis, a parent and busy specialist practitioner, outline in this chapter the complex and neglected problems of preparing for the personal and economic care of a retarded person after his primary providers die.

Effland explores the major questions involved, and the principal areas of client choice and attorney-client decision, in two contexts—the parent or provider as client and the retarded citizen himself as client. It is perhaps a rare situation when money is left after the death of a retarded dependent, but it is not unprecedented. Effland gives considerable attention to the amelioration of problems in states that have adopted the Uniform Probate Code, although recognizing that many other problems remain to be resolved.

Heckt's approach is that of an experienced draftsman. His learning and experience are brought into sharp focus by the fact that he states his opinions with a confident directness. His wariness of professional trustees as money managers for retarded persons, for example, is a view many lawyers of experience—and, needless to say, many bank trust officers—will dispute. The discussion should enrich and inform clients and lawyers as they make the difficult decisions that govern a beneficiary's economic fortunes.

Heckt and Effland take varying views on the wisdom of detailed explication in wills and trust instruments and the use of informal admonition rather than binding direction. They agree, however, on most major points, especially on the necessity for thought, collaboration with clients, and careful draftsmanship. Many lawyers will not share Heckt's optimism about evasion of creditors' and governmental claims through discretionary "spendthrift trusts." The discussion points up how impoverished the trust law of beneficiary protection is and how little its framers have considered the needs of retarded citizens and their families.

PRINCIPAL PAPER

RICHARD W. EFFLAND

AN EXAMINATION of the *Index to Legal Periodicals* for references on trusts and estate planning for mentally retarded citizens reveals few entries. Many entries can be found, on the other hand, on estate planning for the small businessman, the sole proprietor, the young professional, the migrant executive, the jet set, farm families, Americans residing abroad, the collector, and the real estate investor. Practitioners and legal scholars have given little attention to estate planning for the retarded person. There are a few recent articles concerned with estate planning for handicapped or incompetent persons in the broader sense, but these usually are concerned with planning for older citizens as they approach senility.[1] The specialized problems of the mentally retarded estator or beneficiary have received little attention.[2] This lack can be explained by various theses: (1) estate planning for the mentally retarded has no unique features, but is a facet of application of general principles of estate planning — devising and implementing a sound and economic plan in light of available assets, the needs of the beneficiary or beneficiaries, and the wishes of the client; (2) there is little money in planning for the mentally retarded, and estate planning, despite protestations of some of its proponents, centers around large estates for which dramatic tax savings can be demonstrated; (3) lawyers are not educated to be aware of mental retardation and hence not equipped to counsel families that have a retarded member. The truth behind the neglect of estate planning for the mentally retarded is probably a composite of all of these reasons.

---

[1] *See* Weaver, *An Analysis of Estate Planning Devices to Meet the Contingency of Incompetency*, in R. ALLEN, E. FERSTER & H. WEIHOFEN, MENTAL IMPAIRMENT AND LEGAL INCOMPETENCY 144 (1968); Corcoran, *The Revocable, Irrevocable Trust for the Incompetent Client*, 110 TRUSTS & ESTATES 96 (1971); Scoville, *Estate Planning for the Handicapped, Part III: Powers and Duties of Guardians Respecting Ward's Life Insurance*, 111 TRUSTS & ESTATES 614 (1972); Walkow, *Estate Planning for the Handicapped, Part II: Saving Taxes by Lifetime Gifts*, 111 TRUSTS & ESTATES 284 (1972).

[2] A few articles have been written on the subject, however: Daughrity, *Estate Planning for the Handicapped, Part I: Scope of the Problem — The Handicap Gap*, 111 TRUSTS & ESTATES 178 (1972); Wormser et al., *Planning for the Protection of Incompetents, Young and Old*, 6 U. MIAMI 1972 INST. ESTATE PLAN. ch. 72-15; Kay, Farnham, Karren, Krakel & Diamond, *Legal Planning for the Mentally Retarded: The California Experience*, 60 CALIF. L. REV. 438 (1972) (contains some material on planning by parents, but is primarily concerned with planning on the governmental level); Comment, *Planning for the Mentally Retarded: Guidelines for Lawyers*, 1962 WIS. L. REV. 686.

The present problem has two dimensions: (1) estate planning for the parents of a retarded child (whether a minor or adult child, "child" here describing a relationship) and (2) estate planning for the retarded person. The latter situation usually occurs because of a prior lack of planning by parents or relatives, with resulting inheritance of wealth by the retarded person. Of the two situations, the former undoubtedly is more important because it is more likely to occur. If the incidence of mental retardation is 3 percent of the population, the problem deserves attention. Moreover, many parents with a retarded child face a financial drain during their lifetime and are unable to accumulate substantial wealth. In this case careful planning is far more necessary than if the parents had a large estate to leave after death, just as budgeting is more vital at lower income levels.

One other preliminary comment is appropriate. Estate planning for the retarded is an area in which tax savings play an unimportant role and the human dimensions other than taxation become all important. This is not to say that in very large estates the planner can ignore the incidence of taxes, but rather that non-tax factors in the plan are dominant: maximization of the retarded person's potential; sound financial management of available assets; selection of fiduciaries (trustees, executors, guardians) who are both generally capable and are understanding of the special problems of the retarded beneficiary; and maximum flexibility to meet changing conditions in available services, relevant technology, and family attitudes.

PLANNING FOR THE PARENTS OR RELATIVES OF A RETARDED CHILD

Lawyer Skills

There is no simple or magic formula for estate planning when the clients are parents or other relatives of a mentally retarded individual. Among the many variables that must be considered are: the size of the estate; the amount of assets that the parents wish to devote to the care or support of the retarded child; the degree of retardation and the nature of any additional physical disabilities; the age and state of development of the child and his potential for partial self-support; benefits available under various government programs such as social security; the cost and availability of private or public institutions or alternative arrangements for care; and the general attitude of the parents and other family members toward the retarded person. Planning for a mildly retarded individual obviously presents completely different consideration from planning for a severely retarded person. With this wide range of variables, every plan must be individually contoured. This paper can only suggest possibilities and consider some of the special legal problems.

In one sense, the legal skills required are the same as in any estate plan: to gather all the relevant facts, guide decision making by the parents, offer legal alternatives for implementing the clients' wishes, and then embody the final plan in the necessary legal documents. However, one dimension of the problem is unique—and unfortunately this aspect is not always understood by either the parents or the lawyer counseling them: The beneficiary of the plan is handicapped and special attention must be given to the degree of his handicap. The medical and personal history of the child and a comprehensive professional interpretation of this material must be obtained. Parents often will be knowledgeable about the degree of retardation of their child and his potential for education and development. If they are not, the attorney should certainly suggest the services of an expert to assist in the development of an accurate picture of the retarded individual's capacity.

But more is needed. A retarded citizen has personal rights which must receive legal recognition. There must be sensitivity toward a plan that treats the mentally retarded person as a dignified, self-respecting human being with capacity to enjoy life. He is entitled to the treatment accorded any person who has needs for care, education, work assistance, marriage counseling — all dependent, of course, on his individual potential. One lawyer reported a case of very wealthy parents who, in setting up a trust for their retarded son, refused to make any provision for the son's wife or children if he were to marry. This was well intentioned and motivated by a desire to protect the son from a fortune hunter, but the potential for great resultant hardship is obvious. Therefore, in order to counsel wisely, the lawyer needs to have some understanding of the problems of mental retardation and the interests of the retarded person. The training received by most lawyers rarely provides the requisite background.

Decisions About Personal Care

Parents who are responsible for a mentally retarded child are concerned about more than financial provision for support of the child after the parents are dead. They are also concerned about who will take their place in making decisions on behalf of the child, or helping him make his own decisions, and in seeing that the child is being cared for in the best manner possible in light of the child's capacity and physical condition and current developments in education and care. After the parents die, only a legally appointed guardian can make such decisions. The amount of control the parents have over selection of a guardian depends on the law of their domicile. In many states, statutes authorize the parents to nominate the child's guardian by will.[3]

---

[3] See R. Schlesinger, *Testamentary Guardianships for Minors and Incompetents*, in CALIFORNIA WILL DRAFTING ch. 10 (1965); 1 H. WREN, CREATIVE ESTATE PLANNING § 402, at 232-37 (1970); Comment, *The Nonresident Testamentary Guardian*, 43 TEX. L. REV. 541 (1965).

A suggested clause might read: "My son Junior presently lacks sufficient understanding to make responsible decisions concerning his person, and I expect this condition to continue throughout his lifetime. Accordingly, if I am not survived by my wife, or if my wife dies after me without making a different appointment by her will, I hereby appoint my [brother, sister, relative or friend] _____ _____ as guardian of the person of my son Junior. He [she] has agreed to serve in this capacity, but if for any reason he [she] is unable to serve or declines appointment, then I appoint my [other named relative or friend]_____ as guardian instead." In the California study on legal planning for the mentally retarded, brothers and sisters of the retarded child's parents were the most frequent choice as guardian. Kay et al., *supra* note 2, at 495. *See also* Hodgson, *Guardianship of Mentally Retarded Persons: Three Approaches to a Long Neglected Problem*, 37 ALB. L. REV. 407 (1973), considering other possible solutions.

Unfortunately, the existing statutes in most of these states are far from satisfactory. Many do not permit selection of a nonresident of the state. Most do not permit testamentary nomination of a guardian for an incapacitated adult child; the testamentary nomination statutes typically deal only with a child under the age of majority. Finally, in most states the parents merely *nominate* a guardian; there must be a legal proceeding after the deaths of both parents to *appoint* the nominated person as guardian and vest him with legal powers.

The Uniform Probate Code, now adopted in 5 states[4] and under consideration in at least 14 others, contains a simple procedure for testamentary appointment. The procedure permits appointment of a nonresident as guardian of an adult child who is incapacitated, as well as of a minor child. Under the Uniform Probate Code, the will containing appointment of a testamentary guardian can be informally probated (a simple administrative proceeding without advance notice). Seven days' notice of the testamentary appointment of the guardian must be given to the retarded child and any person taking care of him, or to his nearest adult relative. The guardian then files with the probate court an acceptance of the appointment,[5] and the appointment is complete. No court action is necessary; a lawyer would not have to be retained because no guardianship proceeding is called for. The code does permit the child, if over 14 years of age, to file a written objection if he does not approve the guardian selected by the parent; in this event, the nonjudicial guardianship can be terminated.[6]

Whatever the law on appointment, selection of the proper person to be guardian is vital. Often a brother or sister or other relative is capable and willing to serve. If not, then the parents may seek help through a local association for the mentally retarded or a specialized agency. The person or persons to be named in the will should be consulted to determine their willingness and ability to serve, as well as their understanding of retardation in general and the potential of the individual in particular. Several persons should always be named as possible guardians in the will, in succession, so that if the first person named as guardian predeceases the parents, or because of changed circumstances is no longer willing to serve, the next person nominated can become guardian.

Selection of a guardian who is sensitive to the needs of the mentally retarded individual is only the beginning. The wishes of the parents and the interests of the child on matters such as institutionalization and special education must also be dealt with. In this respect, planners may well shy away from expression of detail in the will, lest it straitjacket the future. It may be wiser to prepare a separate letter that states the wishes of the parent in light of present circumstances, but makes it evident that the guardian has the personal responsibility for making decisions in the best interest of his ward in light of future possibilities. For example, parents who have cared for a

---

[4] Alaska, Arizona, Colorado, Idaho, and North Dakota (effective July 1975). In addition to the features discussed in the text, the Code contains another section of special interest to parents of a retarded child. Section 5-401 permits a parent (or guardian) to delegate his powers for a limited period. Thus, parents traveling abroad might wish to delegate power to handle emergencies, such as medical treatment, for a retarded child.

[5] UNIFORM PROBATE CODE § 5-301 [hereinafter cited as UPC]. Comparable provisions applicable to minor children generally are found in § 5-201 *et seq.*

[6] UPC § 5-301(d). In the event of court proceedings, the person nominated by will has priority under § 5-311(b) over all except a spouse or an adult child of the incapacitated person.

retarded child in their home for many years may see no alternative to institutional care after they are dead. The general practice has been to place the name of the child on a standby or waiting list of the institution they prefer. This precaution, of course, is particularly important if the assets available for support of the child are inadequate, and public institutional care appears to be the only avenue open. But the lawyer should be aware that other possibilities, such as community based group care facilities, are becoming available and generally are a preferred placement. Hence, the guardian should be left free to decide about care, although this does not mean that the parent who wants to impose some mandatory duties, such as a duty to inspect and review care arrangements at specified intervals, should not do so. A parent who can afford specialized education should be advised to make clear the obligation to educate, but leave details to the discretion of the guardian.

Financial Provisions for the Support of the Retarded Child

If the parents have sufficient wealth to provide adequately for the support of the child after their death, a plan for continued support must be designed. Outright gifts by will to the mentally retarded child would probably result in appointment of a conservator (sometimes called "guardian of the property," in contrast to guardian of the person). Most lawyers recommend strongly against such an arrangement because of its cost and lack of flexibility.[7] If the amount is small, one alternative is to leave the property to a relative or friend, along with a letter expressing the desire of the testator that the property be used for the retarded child. This method may have undesirable tax consequences for the devisee; it is always risky because the letter may be "precatory," that is, not legally binding. By all odds the best device is a gift in trust for the retarded child. The trust has many advantageous features:

1.   It provides management of funds and property to see that maximum income consistent with safety of principal is produced.

2.   It can provide a mechanism for expenditure of funds, with the trustee paying bills, contracting for care, and, as appropriate, paying modest amounts of cash directly to the retarded beneficiary. In some cases this feature may eliminate the need for a guardian. The trustee can perform most of the functions a guardian would.

3.   The trust can provide maximum flexibility in use of both principal and income by resting broad powers and discretion in the trustee, such as a power to accumulate income when not needed and to invade principal when income is inadequate for current needs.

4.   The trust can be adapted to the individual situation in light of the assets, the needs of other members of the family, and the desires of the parents.

5.   On termination of the trust, the remaining funds can be distributed to other family members without death taxes or probate expense.

---

[7] Weaver, *supra* note 1, at 148-50; Wynn, *A Vacuum in Our Law: Management of Property of Quasi-Incompetent Persons*, 95 TRUSTS & ESTATES 879 (1956).

No plan is any better than the people chosen to design and implement it. The laywer must either be knowledgeable about mental retardation or obtain background information prior to designing a plan. Then, the selection of a capable trustee becomes a key to proper implementation of the whole estate plan. Here individual lawyers have their own preferences, some favouring corporate fiduciaries, some favoring individual trustees, some preferring a combination of corporate and individual co-trustees. Even if lawyer preferences are discounted, no general rule can be drawn. Much depends on the quality and availability of competent trustees in the particular community. A corporate trustee usually has the advantage of providing expert investment and property management services. If a corporate trustee is chosen, its trust officer should be acquainted with the nature of the beneficiary's mental retardation and be left a separate letter of instructions as to the desires of the parents, but the trustee should be given broad discretion in the trust terms to deal with the future as conditions change. The trust instrument may also name an individual as co-trustee or as "adviser" to the trustee on expenditure of funds;[8] the adviser or co-trustee should be a disinterested person, not a brother or sister to whom unexpended funds will go and who, therefore, has a conflict of interest. An adviser with current expertise in the field of mental retardation, who understands services available to the mentally retarded, would be especially desirable. If a guardian is to be appointed, his role in deciding upon and receiving trust expenditures should be defined.

The living trust, created during the lifetime of the settlor and revocable and amendable by him, is preferable to a trust created by will. This is because the need for a mechanism to provide prompt care for the retarded child on death of both parents may be more acute than for nonretarded children. The trustee of a living trust is in a position to provide immediate funds for care and education so that there is a minimum of disruption. This can of course be done to some extent by an allowance in probate, but in most states that requires a court order and involves some delay and expense. Here the fact that there is no disruption in flow of income is even more important than the usual savings in cost which the living trust enjoys over probate of a will with a testamentary trust. Both of these types of trusts can receive assets from a will, as well as life insurance proceeds.

Whether the estate plan of parents who have a retarded child and one or more other dependent children should call for a single trust for all of the children or a separate trust for each child (or a single trust with separate shares for each child, which has the same effect) depends, among other considerations, on the amount of assets. If the family desires private, highly specialized care for the retarded child, and if we estimate that a fund of $200,000, say, is needed to provide income adequate for this purpose, then the requirements of the other dependent child or children must be calculated also to determine what resources are available. If there is an estate of approximately $300,000, the attorney may well recommend a single trust with power in the trustee to pay out all income, and to invade principal if necessary,

---

[8] Comment, *The Trust Advisor*, 78 HARV. L. REV. 1230 (1965).

to support and educate all of the children until the youngest nonretarded child reaches a stated age (21, probably, rather than the age of majority which now is 18 in many states), or completes his college-level schooling and can be self-supporting. Thereafter, the trustee could use as much of the income as is necessary for the retarded child's support and pay the balance to the other children. Or the trust can provide for partial distribution of principal to the nonretarded children when the youngest reaches a specified age. It would normally be unnecessary, and unsound for tax purposes, to give the trustee power to accumulate surplus income. (The trust would then become a "complex trust" and be subject to undesirable throwback income tax rules, for both accumulated income and capital gain.)[9] The possibility that another child might become handicapped through illness or accident can be met by giving the trustee discretion to provide full support for such a child.

If there is a separate trust for the retarded child, either because he is an only child or because assets are ample enough to provide separately for each of the children, a lawyer may want to recommend discretion in the trustee to accumulate surplus income to guard against future emergencies or inflation in costs of care. Here the fact that the accumulated income will be taxed on future distribution and throwback, as will capital gains, is not determinative.[10] A separate share for the retarded child will also insulate the shares of the other beneficiaries from the consequences of the throwback rules.

Regardless of the apparent adequacy of trust income to meet the current needs of the mentally retarded beneficiary, the trust instrument should include a discretionary power to invade principal. No one mindful of economic changes over the past few decades can be confident of his ability to foresee the future. Nothing can be lost by inserting a provision for invasion. It can be tied to a defined standard, but the standard should not be too restrictive.

One difficult problem for the trustee, and the draftsman mindful of the trustee's dilemma, is determining who should receive the trustee's annual accountings. Court accountings are expensive. Although the trustee may wish a court approval of his accounts at periodic intervals, he would not wish to burden the trust estate with unnecessary costs. Therefore, trust instruments where the beneficiary is not mentally retarded often expressly provide that the trustee will furnish the income beneficiary with an annual statement of his accounts and that consent of the income beneficiary in writing, or failure to object in writing within a stated period (such as 60 days), should be deemed approval of all matters shown by the statement. Such

---

[9] INT. REV. CODE OF 1954 §§ 665-69. *See* D. KAHN, E. COLSON & G. CRAVEN, FEDERAL TAXATION OF ESTATES, GIFTS AND TRUSTS pt. 3, ch. 5 (1970); Halbach, *Another Look at Discretionary Trusts: Income Tax Avoidance Under the 1969 Tax "Reform" Act,* 5 U. MIAMI 1971 INST. ESTATE PLAN. ch. 71-5.

[10] Even the adverse effects of throwback may possibly be avoided by creating a separate trust to which surplus income is distributed annually. Thus, the principal trust is required to distribute all of its income annually and qualifies as a "simple" trust to which the Internal Revenue provisions on throwback are inapplicable. *See* INT. REV. CODE OF 1954 §§ 651, 652, 665(B). The second trust can accumulate the income, and capital gain on investments in the principal trust would not be subject to throwback, even though accumulated income and capital gain in the split-off trust would be. *See* INT. REV. CODE OF 1954 §§ 661, 662; Treas. Reg. § 1.665(a)-(o)(1972).

approval is usually made binding on all other (non-income) beneficiaries as well. There are nice legal questions lurking under this type of accountability provision.[11] Although the law recognizes a doctrine of representation, the income beneficiary often has an interest which conflicts with the remaindermen.[12] Nevertheless, the rights of all beneficiaries are those conferred by the settlor, and he should be able to shape these rights as he wishes. If the trust is a living trust, and thus not under continuing supervision of the probate court as a testamentary trust would be in many states, most trustees are willing to rely on, and therefore follow, directions for non-judicial accounting.

Special problems arise in securing approval of trustee accounts if the beneficiary is mentally retarded. Even if the beneficiary is not legally incompetent, and even if he can understand the process, the settlor and the trustee might hesitate to burden him with the task of examining a statement of accounts. If a guardian of the person has been appointed, the guardian does have an incentive, if not a duty, to monitor the trustee's accounts because adequate performance of the guardian's functions depends upon funds from the trust. He also has a general concern for the well-being of his retarded ward. Hence, the guardian is a logical person to approve accounts, and he should be encouraged to seek competent advice if he feels personally unqualified to analyze them. In some estates the account may in fact be so simple that there is no problem. If no guardian is contemplated, there is no apparent reason why the settlor cannot select a member of the family or a concerned friend as the person authorised to approve accounts on behalf of the mentally retarded individual.

Some attention should be given to the drafting of a spendthrift or other protective clause, to guard against voluntary alienation and claims of creditors. Here one enters a legal jungle. Although most states uphold these clauses, there are wide variations in what type of clause is most effective, what exceptions to the general rule of validity are to be made regarding particular types of claims, and whether the judicial policy favors or disfavors creditors when the issue before a court involves construction of language.[13] The result is that particular case holdings may have limited authority value outside their jurisdiction. Nevertheless, some generalizations about these protective provisions are helpful. First, the fact that the beneficiary is retarded and therefore in special need of protection should be a persuasive factor in favor of upholding clauses. Second, the draftsman who explains the need for protection and carefully delineates the purpose of the trust avoids the risk that a court will twist the purpose of the clause in the process of "construing" the language employed in the instrument. Third, if the claimant is the state or a public institution, there is a policy element to be reckoned with, sometimes embodied in a

---

[11] Fleming, *Settlement of Trustee's Account Without Court Proceedings*, 5 U. MIAMI 1971 INST. ESTATE PLAN. ch. 71-6 contains an excellent discussion of the reasons for, and effectiveness of, informal accounting. *See also* Westfall, *Nonjudicial Settlement of Trustees' Accounts,* 71 HARV. L. REV. 40 (1957); A.B.A. Probate and Trust Law Division, Committee on Trust Admin. and Accountability of Trustee, Subcommittee Report on *Settling Trustees Accounts*, 102 TRUSTS & ESTATES 979 (1963).

[12] Beneficiaries are entitled to the principal.

[13] *See* G. G. BOGERT & G. I. BOGERT, THE LAW OF TRUSTS AND TRUSTEES §§ 222-36 (2d ed. 1965); 2 A. SCOTT, THE LAW OF TRUSTS §§ 151-58 (3d ed. 1967); Wormser, *Spendthrift Trusts as Part of an Estate Plan,* 5 U. MIAMI 1971 INST. ESTATE PLAN. ch. 71-9.

statutory preference for claims by the state for the costs of care.[14] Finally, a trust in which the beneficiary's interest rests on the discretion of the trustee (rather than one in which the beneficiary has an absolute right to income or principal), or in which the beneficiary's interest is subject to forfeiture if assigned or subjected to legal process by a creditor, has a better chance of success against creditors than a trust in which the beneficiary has full right to income (or income and principal) with a simple prohibition against voluntary and involuntary transfer.

Various types of spendthrift or protective provisions are likely to be effective against voluntary assignment by the mentally retarded beneficiary and against commercial creditors, even assuming the retarded beneficiary has sufficient legal capacity to make a transfer or incur a debt. Claims of a public institution for support furnished to a beneficiary of a trust are treated somewhat differently.[15] One should carefully distinguish a trust set up for the purpose of furnishing support from one set up to furnish special benefits or services supplementing public support. In the first type of trust, a court can construe a spendthrift (or support) clause as intended only to bar claims other than those for support; and even if a trust is discretionary, a claimant may succeed on the grounds that it is an abuse of discretion for the trustee to shift the obligation of support to the public. When, on the other hand, a trust is set up with limited assets to provide supplemental care beyond that regularly provided out of state funds, there is respectable authority for denying a state claim against trust funds.[16] If the state is allowed to recover, the trust purpose is thwarted. (Of course, this argument would support any spendthrift clause, and so it has to be discounted to some degree.)

A trust ought to be drafted with a clear and detailed statement of the purpose for which trust funds are to be used. The effectiveness of spendthrift clauses cannot be guaranteed absolutely since courts may decide on grounds of public policy that state claims override the intent of the settlor. Nevertheless, the draftsman can and must make clear the intent of the settlor if the settlor wants the interest of a mentally retarded beneficiary to be free from any state claim for state support furnished the beneficiary. Every trust for a mentally retarded beneficiary ought to include a spendthrift or other protective clause; draftsmen must avoid reliance on standard wording and draft specific language calling attention to the special need for protection and the settlor's purpose in limiting the ownership interest of the beneficiary.

There is general agreement that the toughest problem of estate planning is that of planning the use of assets that are inadequate for projected needs. Dean Tom Shaffer has bemoaned the neglect of this area, which he calls "Planning the Non-

---

[14] E.g., N.Y. MENTAL HYGIENE LAW § 24 (1) (McKinney 1971); WIS. STAT. § 701.16(5) (1973).

[15] See Annot., 92 A.L.R.2d 838 (1963). RESTATEMENT (SECOND) OF TRUSTS § 157(b) (1959) states the broad rule that the interest of the beneficiary of a spendthrift or support trust can be reached to satisfy a claim by the state or by any claimant who has furnished necessary services or supplies to the beneficiary.

[16] Estate of Rackmann, 156 Cal. App. 2d 674, 320 P.2d 186 (1958); Bridgeport v. Reilly, 133 Conn. 31, 47 A.2d 865 (1946), noted in 60 HARV. L. REV. 312 (1946); In re Wright's Will, 12 Wis. 2d 375, 107 N.W.2d 146 (1961). Cf. Randolph v. Roberts, 346 Mass. 578, 195 N.E.2d 72 (1964) (town claim for welfare payments not effective against discretionary trust).

Estate."[17] A couple with a mentally retarded child usually has a heavy drain on their resources during their lifetime. If the family has very limited assets, parents are not likely to think in terms of a trust. But even couples of modest means usually have two assets worth planning: one is their life insurance, the other is their home. Typically, life insurance will be payable to the surviving spouse, and the home will be owned in joint tenancy. Further planning is necessary, however, in terms of the disposition of assets when both husband and wife have died. If the mentally retarded child is an only child, the parents undoubtedly would want the child supported from these assets. If they have other children, then they may decide to devote all or most of their assets to the retarded child or to make no provision for the retarded child, placing the burden of support on existing government programs; they may, however, want to use limited funds for "extras" for the child and leave the balance to the other children.

Assuming provision is to be made for the retarded child, the trust is really the only adequate device. The plan might take various shapes, although the basic concept is to provide for the surviving spouse first and, after the deaths of both parents, for the retarded child. One simple way to accomplish this is by changing the beneficiary of the life insurance policies to a trustee as secondary beneficiary if the wife predeceases the insured husband, and by the husband and wife executing separate wills devising the home and any other property to the trustee. In several states, the trust can be a testamentary trust, with the terms set forth in the will. However, in a state where life insurance cannot be made payable to a testamentary trustee, or where there is serious doubt as to the effectiveness of such a designation as being nontestamentary,[18] it may be necessary to create an insurance trust, usually a revocable trust with the policy payable to the trustee, while the parents are still living. Both parents can then execute "pour-over" wills so that on the death of the survivor the home and other assets will be added to the trust assets.[19] The insurance trust in this situation would make full provision for the wife if she survived the husband, and only assets remaining at her death would be used for the retarded child. The wife, as survivor, could be given as much control (power to withdraw, power to appoint by will) as may be desired and as is consistent with the special needs of the retarded child and tax considerations.[20]

---

[17] T. SHAFFER, THE PLANNING AND DRAFTING OF WILLS AND TRUSTS 59 (1972); Shaffer, *Nonestate Planning,* 42 NOTRE D. LAW. 153 (1966).

[18] T. SHAFFER, *supra* note 17 at 245-46. Dean Shaffer suggests that a "funnel" trust might be set up; the insured would make the insurance policy payable to a named person in trust to transfer the proceeds to a trustee named in the will as soon as the latter received his letters of trusteeship from the probate court.

[19] Almost all states now allow a pour-over to an insurance trust, either by enactment of the Uniform Testamentary Additions to Trusts Act or similar legislation, or by judicial decision. 8 UNIFORM LAWS ANNOTATED: ESTATE, PROBATE AND RELATED LAWS 629 (Master ed. 1972) lists 43 states as having adopted the Uniform Act. *See also* Note, *The Testamentary Life Insurance Trust,* 51 MINN. L. REV. 1118 (1967).

[20] If the wife is given a general power of appointment, the trust would be subject to estate taxes on her death, of course, under INT. REV. CODE OF 1954 § 2041. She may be given a special power of appointment or a power to withdraw $5,000 or 5 percent of the trust principal annually, without adverse tax consequences. And the trustee may have power to pay her all or part of the principal in his discretion, with or without a defined standard. *See* W. BOWE, ESTATE PLANNING AND TAXATION §§ 3.5-3.14 (1957); J. TRACHTMAN, ESTATE PLANNING 201-11 (1968); Lauritzen, *Drafting Powers of Appointment—Problems and Suggestions,* 12 TAX COUNS. QUART. 363 (1968). Of course, if the wife is part owner of the life insurance policy, as is likely in community-property states, half of the proceeds would be taxed at her death. These estate tax problems are not serious in view of the $60,000 exemption in the wife's estate and our assumption that we are dealing with a small estate.

Under either basic plan the insurance proceeds and the residence eventually become part of a trust which can provide the features already considered for the larger estate. There are variations of these two basic plans, depending on use of settlement options for the life insurance. But most people at moderate economic levels prefer a simple plan, probably based upon wills creating a trust.

When assets are limited, there are tough decisions to be made. There may be insufficient funds to care for a mentally retarded child and also for other dependent children, requiring that the retarded child or his siblings be preferred. In many states, upon the death of a surviving parent, the cost of public institutional care for the retarded child can be legally shifted in its entirety to the state, even though the parent, while living, may be charged with part of the cost. Should the siblings be preferred by a plan to utilize public institutional care, if the retarded child qualifies? Should principal as well as income be consumed over a shorter period of time to care for and educate all the children, in the hope that the future will fortuitously provide an answer to the problem of the retarded individual or that educated brothers and sisters will take over the burden of support once they are embarked on their own careers? Is it fair to thrust this responsibility on them? Do they want it? The lawyer can only ask these kinds of questions and encourage the parents to seek the answers intelligently.

One problem in a small estate situation is obtaining a trustee willing to serve. Most corporate fiduciaries refuse trusts under a minimum size (*e.g.*, $100,000). If the trust is smaller than this amount, an individual must serve as trustee. In such instances special provisions to simplify the trustee's investment function (allowing him, for example, to keep funds invested in insured savings accounts or insured building and loan association shares or government bonds) may help. A clause exonerating the trustee for acts done in good faith also may be appropriate. Probably the trustee should have discretion to retain or sell the residence, depending on all the circumstances. If the degree of retardation is mild or moderate, the family residence suitable, and other funds sufficient for support, retention of the residence for use by the retarded person may be desirable as a way to avoid or postpone institutionalization. In other situations, sale of the residence may be necessary to provide investment assets to produce income.

In summary, the important guidelines, regardless of estate size, include these:

1. Find the best person to look after the personal care of the mentally retarded child; nominate or appoint this person guardian if guardianship is appropriate and he is willing to serve. If guardianship is inappropriate, make him co-trustee or adviser, so that he can check on the trustee and see that funds in the trust are properly used for the best interests of the child.

2. Select a trustee who can manage the trust assets effectively and who understands the personal problems of the particular retarded beneficiary.

3. Give the guardian and trustee as much discretion as possible so that the use of funds will enable the mentally retarded person to realize his greatest potential, with flexibility to take advantage of new concepts of care and education within the least restrictive environment.

ESTATE PLANNING FOR THE RETARDED PERSON
AS CLIENT

Another kind of estate planning occurs when a mentally retarded person needs legal services to plan for property he owns. This need almost always arises because the retarded person has inherited property outright. In other words, the situation occurs either because of a prior default in planning the estate of an ancestor or other relative, or because a deceased person has made the judgment that the retarded individual can manage his own affairs. One objective of estate planning for the retarded person as client may be immediate. The client may need protective management of his property, in which case the choice is between appointment of a conservator (guardian of the property) and the creation of a living trust. A testamentary objective may be a desire on the part of the retarded person to have his property go at his death to some member of his family (or a friend or an organization) other than his legal heirs.[21]

Initially, there is a capacity problem. It must be determined whether the mentally retarded person lacks the degree of capacity required by law to understand the nature of the transfer. The capacity to make a will is a minimal capacity, less than that required to enter into contracts, for example.[22] A person may be under guardianship or conservatorship and still have the capacity to make a will.[23] Basically, all that is required is that he know his property, the persons who are the natural objects of his bounty, and the disposition he desires made of his property, with some appreciation of the relation among these elements. The mentally retarded testator is aided by certain judicial attitudes. There is a presumption of capacity, which is a formal way of saying that the law favors a finding of capacity whenever possible. There is the repeated dogma that all capacity cases depend on the facts and circumstances of each individual case, so there is no hard-and-fast rule. A disposition which is reasonable, such as one favoring a person who has provided care and attention to the testator while close relatives have not, influences a court to find capacity even though, theoretically, personal relationships may be irrelevant.[24]

There are few cases dealing directly with this problem. One illuminating case,

---

[21] If very large amounts of money are owned by the retarded person, there may be tax savings to be achieved by making present gifts or creating trusts for others. Because this situation rarely arises, such a large estate will receive only this passing mention.

[22] THE MENTALLY DISABLED AND THE LAW 305-06 (rev. ed. S. Brakel & R. Rock eds. 1971). *See* T. ATKINSON, HANDBOOK OF THE LAW OF WILLS § 51 (2d ed. 1953); 1 W. PAGE, THE LAW OF WILLS § 12.15 *et seq.* (rev. ed. W. Bowe & D. Parker eds. 1960).

[23] T. ATKINSON, *supra* note 22, at 239; 1 W. PAGE, *supra* note 22, § 12.42; Annot., 89 A.L.R. 2d 1120 (1963). For recent cases applying this rule, see Rossi v. Fletcher, 418 F.2d 1169 (D.C. Cir. 1969), *cert. denied*, 396 U.S. 1009 (1970) (construing legislation voiding all property transfers after appointment of a conservator as not applicable to a will); *In re* Estate of Thomas, 105 Ariz. 186, 461 P.2d 484 (1969) (capacity to revoke will after adjudication of incompetence); *In re* Estate of O'Laughlin, 50 Wis. 2d 143, 183 N.W.2d 133 (1971).

[24] *See* Green, *Proof of Mental Incompetency and the Unexpressed Major Premise,* 53 YALE L.J. 271 (1944).

however, is *In re Teel's Estate*, decided by the Arizona Court of Appeals in 1971.[25] The testator in this instance was a mentally retarded person, described in the findings as functioning at a mental level of 10-12 years. He could do simple manual tasks and drive a car. He executed a will prepared by an attorney, which disinherited his brother and left his property to a woman who was a half cousin by marriage and who had a "close relationship" with the retarded testator and his mother over many years. A guardian was appointed for the testator ten months after the execution of the will. The court affirmed the finding of the trial court that the testator had the necessary mental capacity to execute his own will.

Oddly, the standard legal treatises on trusts relegate to other authors the question of the capacity required for a person to create a revocable living trust.[26] Although it is recognized that the revocable living trust is nontestamentary for many purposes, it can be revoked and is, in reality, a will substitute. Only form preserves the theoretical difference between a will and a revocable living trust; this difference is that the will has no legal significance during the life of the testator, whereas the trust immediately transfers legal or beneficial title, or both. This difference in form should not mask the reality that the revocable living trust in which the settlor is entitled to all the income has the same ultimate consequences in terms of property disposition. It should require no more capacity to understand a simple living trust document than to understand a will. A contract competence standard is inappropriate; unlike execution of a contract, execution of a living trust can be undone by revocation. A deed competence standard may or may not be helpful. Some courts apply a higher standard of mental capacity to execute a deed than to execute a will, but this results from a failure to analyze the difference in the nature of deed transactions, whether the deed conveys property in exchange for a commercial consideration, conveys property but reserves a life estate, or transfers property to the trustee under a completely revocable trust. Many courts recognize that some deeds are analogous to wills and hence apply similar principles in determining capacity.[27]

Even if the individual's degree of mental retardation raises serious doubts about his capacity to execute a revocable living trust, little is lost by performing the formalities of execution. At worst, the deed is voidable, and in most cases no one is likely to challenge the execution. The trustee, of course, must be willing to accept the trust under the circumstances, but he is unlikely to incur adverse consequences by doing so. Third parties dealing with the trustee will, as a practical matter, not raise the issue of validity. The trust instrument can be drawn so that no member of the family can have any interest in setting it aside. (If the trustee is charging excessive fees or improperly administering the trust, the expectant heirs may have motivation to challenge the trust but may have no legal standing *per se*.) All income would be payable to, or applied for, the benefit of the settlor (the mentally retarded person), or

[25] 14 Ariz. App. 371, 483 P.2d 603 (1971). *But see* 1 W. PAGE, *supra* note 22, at 623: "If the highest mental age achieved by those in the moron class is somewhere around twelve, it may be doubted that anyone in the moron class could have testamentary capacity."

[26] *See* G. G. BOGERT & G. I. BOGERT, *supra* note 13, at § 42 (2d ed. 1965); 1 A. SCOTT, *supra* note 13, at § 19. Neither authority differentiates revocable trusts from irrevocable trusts on the issue of capacity necessary for creation.

[27] *E.g.*, Jensen v. Jensen, 84 Cal. App. 2d 754, 192 P.2d 55 (1948) (deed reserving life estate executed shortly before appointment of guardian); McCoy v. McCoy, 360 Mo. 199, 227 S.W.2d 698 (1950); Lastofka v. Lastofka, 339 Mo. 770, 99 S.W.2d 46 (1936).

accumulated in the trust. The principal and any accumulated or unexpended income could be made payable to the settlor's estate. This sort of trust can provide management during the settlor's life.

The problem of informal approval of accounts, previously discussed for the situation in which parents create a trust for the retarded child, recurs here. The client, assisted by the attorney, should select a disinterested and capable person to review trustee accounts regularly and should make express provision for such review in the trust instrument. This is not a legal necessity, but it is a desirable check on the trustee in his operation of the trust. If no member of the family is capable or willing to review accounts, the attorney should explore possible advisers from local groups interested in mental retardation.

One other problem presenting legal difficulty relates to the validity of spendthrift or protective clauses designed to insulate the trust from future acts of the retarded person in assigning his interest or incurring debts. There seems to be agreement that a settlor cannot create a spendthrift trust for his own benefit.[28] Nevertheless, nothing is lost by inserting a clause purporting to prohibit voluntary assignment and legal process by creditors. The language may not withstand judicial attack, but it may have psychological value in dealing with assignees and creditors.

As in all trusts, provision should be made for disposition of the remainder at the death of the mentally retarded settlor. There are several possibilities. One is simply to provide that the remainder is payable to the settlor's estate. A variation of this provision may avoid probate costs by having the remainder payable to any person the settlor appoints by his last will and testament, and in default to his heirs. In some states a provision in a living trust purporting to create an interest in real estate in the settlor's heirs may create no interest in the heirs because of the Rule in Shelley's Case,[29] or because of a doctrine preferring a reversion, but in most states the limitation is valid if the document shows a clear intent to create a remainder in the heirs.[30] Under this type of disposition, the settlor of the trust can also execute a will appointing a favored person if he wishes, and the issue of capacity will then be raised at probate of the will.[31] No one has any motivation to attack the creation of the revocable trust on grounds of incapacity. Another kind of disposition would provide for transfer of the remainder on death of the settlor to another named individual or charity. This

---

[28] RESTATEMENT (SECOND) OF TRUSTS § 156 (1959); G. G. BOGERT & G. I. BOGERT, *supra* note 13, at § 223; 2 A. SCOTT, *supra* note 13, at § 156.

[29] The Rule in Shelley's Case is in force in only about one-fourth of the states. The rule is stated in RESTATEMENT OF PROPERTY § 312 (1940); L. SIMES & A. SMITH, THE LAW OF THE FUTURE INTERESTS § 1541 *et seq.* (1956).

[30] 1 AMERICAN LAW OF PROPERTY §§ 4.19-4.23, 4.40-4.51 (A.J. Casner ed. 1952); L. SIMES & A. SMITH, *supra* note 29, at §§ 1541-1613 (1956). The presence of a power of appointment is one factor leading courts to hold that the settlor of a trust intended a true remainder interest in default, and not a reversion. *In re* Burchell's Estate, 299 N.Y. 351, 87 N.E.2d 293 (1949).

[31] The ancient doctrine that the donee of a testamentary power of appointment can execute the power by a will even though he lacks capacity to transfer his own property by will may never have applied to any incapacity except that of the married woman and has not been followed in the United States. 5 AMERICAN LAW OF PROPERTY § 23.42 (A.J. Casner ed. 1952); L. SIMES & A. SMITH, *supra* note 29, at § 971. *But see* RESTATEMENT OF PROPERTY § 345 (1940). In any case where the person of questioned capacity creates the power for himself, it would involve a curious bootstrapping doctrine to allow him to exercise the power without capacity. The attack would then shift to the issue of capacity to create the power.

type of disposition may invite litigation by expectant heirs if they learn of the trust provisions, unless the named individual is also the only expectant heir.

A final problem, perhaps of even lesser importance, is the trustee's dilemma if the settlor tries to revoke the trust.[32] The problem is common to other trusts created by the "not quite incompetent" settlor. One hopes that the trustee's reluctance to comply with an attempted revocation hopefully stems not from self-interest but from concern that the settlor does not really understand the consequences of revocation, so that a carefully constructed protective mechanism is being discarded with threat to the financial safety of the assets. The problem is partly legal (satisfying counsel for the trustee that the settlor is competent to revoke) and partly nonlegal (being reasonably sure that the revocation is really in the best interests of the retarded person). One can envision situations in which the abilities of the mentally retarded person have dramatically improved since the creation of the trust. But the trustee is even then likely to be concerned about undue influence, as well as about the individual's ability to deal with financial matters which people with no retardation often handle inefficiently.

Another approach to the problem of property conservation and management, rather than creation of a trust, is appointment of a conservator (also called "a guardian of property" or a "committee"). Lawyers almost universally regard conservatorship proceedings with horror and recommend them only as a last alternative, because of several aspects of most state laws.[33] In the first place, the existing statutes are often archaic and mix guardianship of the person with guardianship of the property, and there usually must be a judicial declaration that the person is "insane" or "incompetent" before the court will act. No one wants to impress this stigma if it can be avoided. Second, under existing laws in most states, the conservator or guardian has only the powers conferred by court and must usually petition the court for orders regarding management of the property, as well as for authority to expend funds. The result is a heavy cost in legal fees. Corporate fiduciaries are reluctant to assume such an appointment because the fiduciary serves such a limited role.

In the past decade attempts have been made to break through these legal barriers and to secure enactment of modern procedures for protection of the property of people who lack ability to manage their property effectively. Most significant of these is Article V of the Uniform Probate Code. It was described by a committee of the American Bar Association as follows:

> In an attempt to determine whether the public would benefit from the enactment of that portion of the Code dealing with conservatorships, this committee surveyed the conservatorship laws of representative jurisdictions around the country. One basic fact emerged — the conservatorship law of most states is a hodge-podge of historical anachronisms which make Article V of the Code seem like a refreshing breath of spring.[34]

[32] The settlor of a revocable trust cannot exercise a reserved power to revoke if he lacks capacity at the time he attempts to revoke. Albers v. Kemmerer, 121 N.E.2d 583 (Ohio C.P. 1954), *aff'd sub nom.* Kemmerer v. Kemmerer, 139 N.E.2d 84 (Ohio Ct. App. 1956). One solution in such a situation is petition by the trustee asking the court for instructions, as in Oak Park Trust & Savings Bank v. Fisher, 82 Ill. App. 2d 251, 225 N.E.2d 377 (1967).

[33] *See* Wynn, *supra* note 7.

[34] A.B.A. Committee on Problems Relating to Persons Under Disability, *Conservatorship: Present Practice and Uniform Probate Code Compared,* 5 REAL PROP. PROBATE & TRUST J. 507 (1970).

The salient features of this part of the Uniform Probate Code are:

1. No declaration of incompetence or insanity is involved.[35]
2. The conservator is vested with the title of a trustee and given broad fiduciary powers to manage the property.[36]
3. The conservator has power to expend income or principal without court authorization or confirmation.[37]

These provisions make the conservatorship highly acceptable as an alternative to creation of a trust. Indeed, the conservatorship has certain advantages: (1) there is no need to worry about capacity; (2) the court itself has some exceptional powers relating to the area of tax planning for large estates, which it can exercise directly or through the conservator; and (3) the court can make gifts of property[38] under a statutory codification of the judicial doctrine of "substituted judgment."[39] The court makes the kind of decision regarding gifts which the protected person would make if not under any disability. Thus, where assets far exceed any possible future needs of the person and members of his household, the court could direct a program of lifetime gifts to minimize estate taxes; (4) The court can "create revocable or irrevocable trusts of property of the estate which may extend beyond his disability or life."[40] Thus, it might be possible to utilize the Uniform Probate Code conservatorship as a stepping-stone in the creation of a trust where the capacity of the retarded person is in doubt. The attorney would have to use extreme caution in employing such a procedure, as courts will properly use such extraordinary powers with great reluctance. It may be simpler to create directly a carefully worded and fully detailed trust, specifically tailored to the needs of the mentally retarded individual, and hope it will not be challenged.

In creating a trust for the retarded person, or in counseling regarding a conservatorship, the attorney must be careful to identify his client and serve his interests faithfully.[41] Often the family of the mentally retarded person will select the attorney and accompany the retarded person for the interview. There is danger that the interests and wishes of the retarded person may be confused with those of the family. Although this danger is more acute in commitment and guardianship matters, it

---

[35] UPC § 5-401, requiring only a finding that the protected person is unable to manage his property and affairs effectively for reasons which include "mental deficiency."

[36] UPC §§ 5-420, 5-424.

[37] UPC § 5-425.

[38] UPC § 5-408.

[39] *See* A.B.A. Comm. on Legal Services for the Elderly and Their Estates, *Substitution of Judgment Doctrine and Making of Gifts from an Incompetent's Estate,* 7 REAL PROP. PROBATE & TRUST J. 479 (1972); Kane, *Application of the Substitution of Judgment Doctrine in Planning an Incompetent's Estate,* 16 VILL. L. REV. 132 (1970); Walkow, *Estate Planning for the Handicapped, Part II: Saving Taxes by Lifetime Gifts,* 111 TRUSTS & ESTATES 284 (1972); Comment, *The Development of the Substitute Judgment Rule and Its Application in New York as a Vehicle for Estate Planning for Incompetents,* 33 ALB. L. REV. 597 (1969); Note, *Guardianship: The Power of a Guardian to Make Gifts of his Ward's Property,* 18 HAST. L.J. 415 (1967); Note, *Making Gifts from an Incompetent's Estate Under the Doctrine of Substituted Judgment to Reduce Federal Estate Taxes,* 14 WM. & MARY L. REV. 186 (1972).

[40] UPC § 5-408(3).

[41] *See* Blinick, *Mental Disability, Legal Ethics and Professional Responsibility,* 33 ALB. L. REV. 92 (1968).

is also a subtle element in the drafting of a will or a trust document with dispositive provisions in favor of others. A person cannot serve two masters, and the lawyer must be sure he is serving the mentally retarded client, not the client's family.

There is the additional problem of the ethical responsibility of the attorney asked to prepare a will or revocable living trust for a retarded person whose capacity to execute the document is questionable. The attorney may have one degree of responsibility when drafting a revocable living trust that merely provides for the management of property and application of trust funds for the mentally retarded settlor's care, with no dispositive provisions for other persons, and another degree of responsibility when he prepares a will or living trust containing beneficial provisions for others. In the former situation, all doubts can be readily resolved in favor of capacity. But where the document alters the legal course of beneficial ownership, there is greater risk of inviting litigation, and the lawyer should be more cautious. Even here, unless he is convinced after careful investigation that the client lacks capacity, the lawyer should resolve doubts in favor of executing the document and letting the courts resolve the question of capacity when and if it arises.[42]

Trust and estate planning for mentally retarded citizens, or for families with a mentally retarded member, can be seen both as similar to and different from all other trust and estate planning. It is similar in that all planning, properly done, requires special attention to the unique problems and potentials of the person or family in question. The difference centers on the special problems and potentials related to mental retardation and the inexperience of many practicing lawyers in dealing with them. This is a deficiency which must be overcome for an attorney competently to assist a family or person with long-range planning in which mental retardation is a factor. This paper has attempted to indicate some of the personal, as well as legal, issues lawyers need to be aware of in this area of trust and estate planning.

Reaction Comment

MELVIN D. HECKT

TODAY, with few exceptions, this nation's legal profession — judges, law professors, and practicing attorneys — has paid little attention to the special problems of estate planning for the mentally retarded, developmentally disabled, or other substantially mentally or physically handicapped citizens.

Generally, and with few exceptions:

1. The organized legal profession does not realize that special problems exist.
2. Law schools do not teach, research, or recognize these problems.

---

[42] *Id.* at 104-05; Miller, *Functions and Ethical Problems of the Lawyer in Drafting a Will,* 1950 U. ILL. L.F. 415, 426.

3. Individual attorneys are not aware of the difficulties, or if they are aware, do not know where to get help.

4. There are few continuing legal education courses, workshops, bar association articles, or programs which focus upon these problems.

5. Even the specialist sees so few clients who have a retarded child that he is either ill-equipped to give sound advice or finds the effort required too great to be practical.

6. The few attorneys who know anything about mental retardation are either parents of a retarded child or members of associations for retarded citizens, who have in the past concentrated upon their own law practice and expended their volunteer efforts in building strong associations for retarded children, lobbying, or engaging in the development of services for the mentally retarded.

Effland's thorough scholarly treatment of these problems is a refreshing change and a great contribution. This reaction comment expresses the point of view of an attorney-parent who has worked on trust and estate plans for many families with a mentally retarded family member.

A mentally retarded person is a human being and a citizen. He is more normal than abnormal. He wants the opportunity for love, dignity, education, training, habilitation, treatment, care, and work, and the rights and responsibilities which other citizens take for granted. Although professionals sometimes broadly classify the mentally retarded as mildly, moderately, severely, or profoundly retarded, each retarded person must be looked upon as an individual entitled to dignity and respect.

The greatest and most distressing concern of older parents of a mentally retarded child is: What will happen to our child when we are both dead? Parents are primarily concerned about finding solutions to three questions:

1. How can we be reasonably certain that there will be a friend, advocate, and protector of our child's legal rights for his lifetime?

2. How can we distribute our assets fairly among our retarded child and our other children?

3. How can we be reasonably certain that the assets we leave for the benefit of our retarded child will best be expended for him and last for his entire lifetime?

THE BASIC ESTATE PLAN

Of the more than 200 estate plans I have prepared for parents of retarded children, most were for parents whose children were profoundly, severely, or moderately retarded; only a few were for parents whose children were mildly retarded. I have never prepared an estate plan that would permit the retarded person to inherit outright assets other than keepsake personal property of nominal value. For the following reasons, legal title to the parents' assets should not be allowed to vest in a retarded person, either through inheritance or gift:

1. Mentally retarded persons can often be taken advantage of by friends, fellow employees, relatives, service providers, businessmen, government personnel, and the unscrupulous.

2. Under most state laws government agencies will take all or almost all assets owned by a retarded person, if the government agency provides service to him. These agencies are quick to locate assets and initiate litigation to seek reimbursement. This consumes personal assets in a very short period of time, leaving the retarded person without private funds.

3. If the retarded person owns assets in excess of a very limited amount, he is disqualified from receiving some types of government assistance until his assets have been largely expended.

4. Mentally retarded citizens are unable to manage large sums of money or certain types of property. The profoundly retarded do not know what property is. Many severely and moderately retarded persons have been taught the differences among coins, but not the differences among $10, $100, and $1000, let alone larger sums. This is less often true of the mildly retarded person, who can learn to pay his rent, deposit his paycheck, keep a checking account, and attend to small purchases. Nevertheless, he may not comprehend the significance of larger sums and may be vulnerable to exploitation.

An attorney employed to plan the disposition of wealth for a family with a retarded child should initially schedule an office conference and mail to the parents for completion and return a form for describing family history, income, and assets. The form should request the names, ages, birthdates, social security numbers, addresses, phone numbers, and income of the parents, the mentally retarded child, and other children. It should also include a list of all assets of the parents, with indications of approximate evaluation, nature of ownership, and the party who furnished the consideration for any assets held in joint tenancy. The form should request the following additional information concerning the mentally retarded person:

1. Degree of mental retardation: profound, severe, moderate, or mild, with copies of professional diagnostic reports.
2. Education.
3. Other physical or mental handicaps.
4. Personality and behavioral traits.
5. Capabilities and limitations (*e.g.,* can he read, walk, talk, toilet, dress himself, take a bus, drive a car, make change or purchases?).
6. Interests (*e.g.,* does he enjoy music, television, radio, bowling, movies, reading, athletics, camping, dancing, swimming, fishing?).
7. Work history and earnings.
8. Assets (*e.g.,* bank accounts, government bonds). Are assets held in his name, in joint tenancy with another, or in fiduciary account for him?
9. Other financial provision: Has anyone other than the parents or the mentally retarded individual provided for the mentally retarded person through will, insurance, or in any other way? Frequently this is done with the best of intentions, but the form of ownership may have to be changed to avoid problems.
10. Personal legal status: Has legal guardianship of his person or estate been established? Is he a ward of the state?

The form should also request insurance policy information, including policy number, name of company, face amount, type, ownership, and primary and contingent beneficiary provisions for each policy owned by or insuring the life of either parent. This information is necessary since the primary or contingent beneficiary clause may need to be changed to the estate or trust, if a trust is established, in order to avoid vesting legal title to insurance proceeds in the retarded child. This procedure may avoid the necessity of having both a guardianship of the estate and a trust for the benefit of the retarded person.

After receiving this information, the attorney should meet with the parents and review it with them. It is only at this point that it is possible to help the parents determine the type of estate plan best suited to their needs and those of their mentally retarded child. Usually, they will choose one of three plans: (1) a simple will which excludes the retarded person; (2) a contingent testamentary trust will; or (3) a revocable living or testamentary trust.

Simple wills which exclude a mentally retarded child may be advisable for young parents with very limited assets that would be needed after their death for the maintenance of their other children. If this type of plan is initially adopted, if often will be changed in favor of one of the other types as the assets of the parents increase or as the needs of their nonretarded children decrease. This plan may also be advisable for older parents who have limited assets and desire to distribute them to a nonretarded adult child whom they believe will expend a fair proportion of these assets for the retarded sibling. Parents should be fully advised, however, of the documented possibility that greed, mental illness, death, divorce, or disability of the nonretarded child may prevent their expectations from being realized. Under this plan each spouse executes a will which provides that his or her entire estate is to be distributed to the other spouse if surviving and otherwise to the nonretarded children in equal shares, with the retarded child specifically excluded from inheriting by the will.

Even in this situation, where the mentally retarded family member is excluded from any property rights under the will, the attorney should discuss with the clients the advisability of naming guardians and successor guardians of the person of the retarded child, in addition to the guardians customarily nominated for the normal minor children. It may be advantageous to have such a guardian of the person with the legal power to act as friend, advocate, and protector of the retarded person's rights. In many states, however, this would require an adjudication that the retarded person is incompetent and unable to vote, marry, or contract. In the case of a person who is only mildly retarded, this would probably be an erroneous labeling, with multiple attendant adverse effects. The adjudication of incompetence can, and in many cases should, be avoided, especially if someone in the family (perhaps a sibling) can protect the legal rights of the retarded individual much as a guardian of the person would, without a court-administered guardianship being established.

The second possibility is to create a contingent testamentary trust will for each spouse. Under one version of this plan, each will provides that the estate is to be distributed to the other spouse if surviving. Upon the death of the surviving spouse, the entire estate is to be divided into two parts: one to be held in trust for the benefit of, or distributed to, the nonretarded children and the other to be held in a separate trust for the benefit of the retarded child. The trust created for the benefit of the retarded child should provide for discretionary distributions to the retarded child during his lifetime; at his death, the remaining trust assets may be distributed to the siblings or to other beneficiaries.

This plan is especially appropriate when death taxes are nominal or nonexistent, when all assets are owned by the parents in joint tenancy, or when for non-tax reasons the parents decide that the survivor should have complete ownership and control of the deceased spouse's estate without a trust being created until both spouses are deceased. Contingent testamentary trusts offer great flexibility by permitting the surviving spouse during his or her lifetime to eliminate the trust, amend the trust provisions, or change the portion of the estate that will be held in trust for the benefit of the retarded child. The ability to make such changes may be of great importance if the programs or policies of the government with respect to the mentally retarded, or the needs of the mentally retarded child, or the spendthrift trust law of the state should change during the life of the surviving spouse.

The separate trust for the mentally retarded person is desirable since it encourages the parents to focus upon the trust provisions, determine what portion of their assets are to be held for the benefit of the retarded child, and decide whether the trustees are or are not to have the power to expend trust assets for the benefit of siblings. Even when the attorney, in drafting the trust instrument, has done everything possible to prevent trust depletion, if creditors of the mentally retarded person should at any time legally able to reach trust assets held for his benefit, at least with separate trusts for the retarded and nonretarded children, creditors of the retarded persons should be limited to reaching assets held for the benefit of the retarded individual and not trust assets held for the benefit of other children.

The third type of plan involves revocable living or testamentary trusts. A trust is created either prior to or upon the death of a particular parent. The trust generally provides for the distribution of principal and income for the benefit of the surviving spouse (if any) during his lifetime and, upon his death, establishes a separate trust for the benefit of the mentally retarded child. This plan often also includes a marital trust and nonmarital trust (or parallel devices in a community-property state) when there is a surviving spouse and when the size of the parent's estate would create substantial death taxes. In such a situation the administrative costs and burdens of maintaining the tax-saving trust during the lifetime of the surviving spouse is outweighed by the savings in death taxes.

If one spouse is an experienced manager of assets and the other inexperienced, the experienced spouse may, in the absence of a trust, fear dissipation of family assets after his death. He may fear that no property will remain after the death of the surviving spouse for the benefit of the mentally retarded child. The first spouse to die may also be concerned that the other spouse, if he survives, would favor the nonretarded children to the detriment of the retarded child, or vice versa. Also remarriage and subsequent death of the surviving spouse may result in the elimination of any trust benefit for the retarded child. These factors argue for trust management of assets of the surviving spouse.

After selection of a plan, the parents should be advised that it should be reviewed at least every five years, as well as when there is a substantial change in their assets, one of them dies, or their knowledge increases concerning the capabilities of their retarded child. In addition to the usual reasons for review, there may be changes in the capabilities of the retarded child, changes in trust law—especially with regard to spendthrift provisions and discretionary powers—or changes in the liability of parents for the support of mentally retarded children, governmental financial assistance, and other benefits for mentally retarded persons. It is not uncommon to have parents first adopt a plan excluding their retarded child, later adopt testamentary trust wills establishing a trust for their retarded child upon the death of the surviving spouse, and, finally, adopt a plan with a marital trust providing for the establishment of a trust upon the husband's death for the lifetime of the wife, and thereafter, for the benefit of the retarded person. This ultimate trust may be further amended to increase the portion to be distributed to the trust for the retarded child after other children have been educated, attained their majority, and are independent.

Once the type of plan has been selected, it is essential to determine the fractional division between the mentally retarded child and other children. This is frequently difficult for parents. They want to be fair to their normal children and are correctly fearful that the state or county government may be able to take assets left outright to, or in trust for, their retarded child. They are sometimes erroneously advised by government employees who either do not know the law or intentionally discourage parents from making appropriate plans for their handicapped child. These officials often seek to take all of the child's assets and have the state assume responsibility for the retarded person when he is destitute. Parents must be properly advised about existing support and benefit laws. Parents must also realize that although a trust may operate for the lifetime of the retarded person, upon his death distribution can be made to other children or beneficiaries of their choosing.

Existing governmental financial assistance that may be available for the mentally retarded person must also be analyzed (social security, veterans benefits, supplemental security income for the aged, blind, and disabled, medical assistance, Medicare, Medicaid, and other rehabilitation and cost-of-care programs). Parents must be assisted in analyzing the costs of care for a child who is mentally retarded. The cost will vary tremendously depending upon the nature of the handicap and services available. For example, in Minnesota's state institutions the average cost of care now amounts to $600 per month. Its community residential services cost from $150 to $700 per month, exclusive of medical, dental, hospital, clothing, and other miscellaneous costs. It is impossible to know what the costs will be 10, 20, or 30 years from now, but it can easily be seen that only very wealthy parents can provide for the total cost for 40-60 years of care for a mentally retarded person. Thus, for the vast majority of parent clients, the trust cannot cover the basic necessities such as food, housing, medical, and dental care, but rather must be designed to provide a source of funds for purchasing those things that government agencies usually do not provide (spending money, radios, record players, television sets, extra food, personal clothing, movies, bowling, athletic contests, vacations, evaluations, and trips). All of these items can make the retarded person's life more enjoyable and normal.

The fractional division of assets among children may vary—from excluding the mentally retarded child when the parents are young and their assets are very limited to excluding nonretarded children when they are independently established. Generally, however, parents dislike either extreme. They base their decision on the estimated size of their estate after the death of both, the age of their children, their conception of fair play, the estimated needs of the retarded child for his lifetime, the quality of the legal advice given, and the strength of their state's spendthrift trust law.

SPECIFIC TRUST PROVISIONS

Whenever a trust is to be used as a part of the estate plan, great care is required in its drafting. A standard form of trust instrument should never be relied upon and no broad assumptions should be made concerning the trustee's ability to know how to provide for the needs of the mentally retarded beneficiary.

Determination of Trust Purposes

The trust instrument must be drafted in light of its general purposes, and should articulate these purposes for the guidance of trustees and of judges in case of dispute. Essential trust purposes include the following:

1. The trust is primarily for the benefit of the retarded person and only incidentally for the benefit of the remaindermen beneficiaries. This purpose should lead trustees to try to ensure that the corpus and income are expended for, and last the lifetime of, the retarded person, rather than try to increase or maintain the corpus for the benefit of the remaindermen beneficiaries.
2. The trust is intended to ensure that there will always be a friend, advocate, and protector of the legal rights of the retarded beneficiary.
3. The trust is intended to ensure that the retarded individual receives the services that will assist him in developing his maximum potential and in achieving a reasonable degree of normalcy and happiness.
4. Since in most instances the trust fund cannot be expected to cover the basic costs of care (such as food, lodging, medical, dental, or hospital care), the trust will usually be intended to supplement the mentally retarded person's earnings or governmental financial assistance.

Determination of Trustees

Because of the many difficult decisions that will be required in order to accomplish the trust purposes and maximize its benefit to the beneficiary, designation of proper trustees is of prime importance. A bank or corporate institution should never be designated as the *sole* trustee. Appointment of such an institution as a trustee may be important where the trust corpus is sizable, but one should try to ensure that there will always be an individual trustee or individual co-trustee to serve with any corporate trustee. In this regard, clients might consider relatives who have a personal interest in and affection for the retarded person. They may wish to name as the individual, or successor individual, trustee a person of approximately the same age as the retarded person. Frequently, one or more siblings will have a sincere love and interest in the welfare of their retarded brother or sister. Parents should be advised, however, of possible conflicts of interest in a sibling acting as trustee when he is also a remainder-man beneficiary in the trust. The corporate trustee may have a similar conflict: the larger the corpus, the larger its trustee fee.

Individual trustees should be appointed in succession, with the last given the power to appoint a successor for himself. It is also possible to provide that the then executive director of the local or state association for retarded children, or similar organization, shall become trustee upon the death or disqualification of all named individual trustees and shall have the power to appoint a successor to himself. If the executive director cannot act, he can then locate another person who could become an advocate and protector for the retarded person, as well as manage trust funds. Such a replacement might be a staff person or the parent or relative of another retarded person who lives in the same facility as the mentally retarded child. If a bank, corporation, or other institution is named as co-trustee, the individual trustees should whenever possible be given the power to substitute another bank or corporate trustee.

Before a corporate trustee is named, the amount of its annual fee and its willingness to accept the trust should be determined. Some banks are not interested in trusts with a small corpus (under $50,000 in some cases). Frequently, their annual fee is as high as one-half of 1 percent, with a minimum of $750.00 per year. There also may be additional initial and termination fees which effectively preclude the use of a corporate trustee as co-trustee. This should not, however, deter an attorney from utilizing the trust in his plan. I have prepared trust instruments where the estimated corpus was as low as $5,000. It does not take exceptional skill for an individual trustee to purchase bank certificates of deposit, open and maintain savings accounts, or purchase government bonds; the trust instrument can require that conservative investments of this sort be used.

Finally, it must be determined whether or not the trust should be court supervised. The primary factors for consideration are: (1) the estimated size of the corpus; (2) the identity of the trustees and their successors; and (3) the cost of court supervision. In order to minimize expense, it may be desirable to avoid court supervision of the named and successor-named trustees and to have court supervision beyond that point for the unnamed trustees who may be appointed by the named trustees, if this power of appointment is given. It also may be desirable to avoid court supervision entirely, except where a majority of the remaindermen beneficiaries demand supervision. Certainly, the advantages and disadvantages of court supervision should be explained to the client.

Expression of Trustees' Powers, Duties, and Instructions

In order to accomplish the trust purposes, it is important to be quite specific regarding the powers and duties of trustees. Some of the items that should be specified are discussed in this section.

1. Include in the trust instrument the strongest possible spendthrift clause. Much of the shape of the rest of the trust will depend on a judgment as to whether the spendthrift clause will be respected by the courts of the state in question.[1] An example of such a clause is:

    > "Neither principal nor income of this trust, nor any beneficiary's interest herein, while undistributed in fact, shall be subject to:
    > (a) alienation, assignment, encumbrance, appointment or anticipation by the beneficiary;
    > (b) garnishment, attachment, execution, or bankruptcy proceedings;
    > (c) claims for alimony or support, or any other claims by any creditor or person including the State of [   ] or any of its political subdivisions thereof against the beneficiary;
    > (d) any other transfer voluntary or involuntary from the beneficiary."

    In a state that does not strongly enforce spendthrift provisions, a trust may be inadvisable. If a trust is used in such a state, the instrument should clearly define its purposes and prohibit the trustees from expending income or principal for costs of basic care. Either the trustees should be empowered to terminate the trust and distribute the trust fund to the named remaindermen beneficiaries if they determine that legally enforceable claims for reimbursement for costs of care would defeat the purposes of the trust, or the instrument should provide for termination of the trust and distribution of its assets to remainderman upon a judicial determination that the trust fund was subject to liability for payment of such claims by the state, county, or other creditor providing such costs of basic care. Such provisions might be unnecessary in the exceptional case where the trust funds are clearly sufficient to pay all costs for the lifetime of the mentally retarded person.

2. Instruct the trustee to accumulate and add to principal the entire net income of the trust fund. This provision, in addition to a provision granting the trustee absolute discretion relative to expenditures from principal and the strongest

---

[1] *See In re* Estate of Moulton, 233 Minn. 286, 301-302, 46 N.W.2d 667, 675 (1951): "It is sufficient to say that the law on this subject is settled in this state and that, once it is established that a spendthrift trust exists, either by express provisions of the instrument or by implication, the beneficiary's interest can no more be reached in the hands of the trustee for alimony or support than for any other debt of obligation." Town of Bridgeport v. Reilly, 133 Conn. 31, 47 A.2d 865 (1946); Town of Randolph v. Roberts, 346 Mass. 578, 195 N.E.2d 72 (1964); Lamberton v. Lamberton, 229 Minn. 29, 38 N.W.2d 72 (1949). *See also* Erickson v. Erickson, 197 Minn. 71, 266 N.W. 161, *rehearing denied,* 267 N.W. 426 (1936); *In re* Wright's Will, 12 Wis. 2d 375, 107 N.W.2d 146 (1961).

The text uses the term "spendthrift trust" to describe trusts which have a disabling restraint on the alienation of trust income or principal *and* in which the beneficiary has no definable economic interest until the trustee exercises discretionary power of distribution in the beneficiary's favor. There are considerable variations in the statutory and case law in different jurisdictions. Draftsmen will, of course, want to research their local law before they undertake the drafting suggested in the text. 2 A. Scott, The Law of Trusts § 155 (3d ed. 1967) is a useful place to begin.

possible spendthrift clause, should make it clear that no one (the mentally re-tarded person, his creditors, the federal, state, county, or local government, or anyone else) has any right to, or claim against, the income or principal of the trust fund. The advantages of ensuring that the trust fund will last for the lifetime of the mentally retarded person, that it will be protected from the claims of governmental or other creditors, and that its income will not be considered the income of the retarded person exceed any tax disadvantages (such as a lower income tax exemption from $300 to $100 or the imposition of the "throwback" provision of the Internal Revenue Code with respect to capital gains of the trust).

3. In states that enforce strong spendthrift trust provisions, the trust can provide that the trustees, in their sole and absolute discretion, shall have the power to expend principal for the education, comfort, maintenance, livelihood, health, and general welfare of the mentally retarded person. In such a state, the trustees may or may not exercise their options, but no one can compel them to expend funds for the costs of basic care or to reimburse the government for having paid for such costs. If the trust becomes effective during the lifetime of the surviving spouse, the trustees can be empowered to expend principal for the cost of care of the retarded child only up to the amount which the living parent would be legally liable to pay the state or county for care of the retarded child. The reason for this latter type of provision is that the laws of many states provide that the parents are not liable to the state or county government for the cost of care after the retarded child attains the age of 21 or 18, but that the parents are liable for all or part of such cost of care for a child under the age of 21 or 18.

4. In states that enforce strong spendthrift trust provisions, the trust instrument may provide that trustees, in exercising their discretion with respect to making expenditures of principal, should first secure and expend all government finan-cial assistance benefits and the beneficiary's own earnings before expending trust principal for the costs of basic care. The trustees should encourage the re-tarded individual to maximize his earning potential for the sake of his own personal development.

5. Even in states that enforce strong spendthrift trust provisions, if the amount of principal and income are clearly insufficient to pay the lifetime costs of basic care (food, lodging, medical, dental, hospital, and clothing), one should consider inclusion of a clause in the trust instrument prohibiting or limiting the trustees from expending principal for such costs to the provider of such services, or to the government as reimbursement.

6. Empower and instruct the trustee to collect, expend, account separately, and not commingle with the trust fund all governmental financial assistance benefits to which the retarded person is entitled. If a parent covered by social security dies, retires, or becomes disabled, his normal minor child may be entitled to a social security payment or benefit until the child attains the age of 22. If the child is mentally retarded before age 22, however, and continues to meet the disability and other prescribed qualifications, he may continue to receive such social security benefits for his lifetime.[2] It should also be noted that an individual entitled to childhood disability benefits may become re-entitled if he is again disabled within a period of seven years after termination of benefits.[3] This stipulation would certainly assist retarded recipients who had marginal employ-ment capabilities. It should also be noted that the amount a childhood disability recipient may earn without loss of benefits was raised from $1,600 to $2,100

[2]42 U.S.C. § 402(d)(1)(G) (Supp. II 1972).
[3]*Id.* § 402(d)(6)(B).

annually and income above $2,100 will be reduced only by $1.00 for each $2.00 of earnings.[4] The Social Security Administration prefers to make payments to a spouse, parent, relative, legal guardian, or friend who will expend the funds for the benefit of the mentally retarded person. The administration lists the state agency or institution as a possible payee, but a state agency or institution frequently attempts not only to become payee, but to deposit all but a pittance of the payment in the state's general revenue fund. The lawyer's awareness of these practices is especially important when the client is poor or easily intimidated.

7.   Instruct and empower the trustees, in their discretion, to expend principal for needs that are not provided by governmental financial assistance and benefits or by the provider of services. These needs should be specified in detail. They may include spending money, additional food, health services not provided, clothing, radios, record players, television sets, camping, vacations, athletic contests, movies, trips, and money to purchase appropriate gifts for relatives and friends.

8.   Instruct and empower the trustees to deposit from time to time in a credit account to be used by the mentally retarded beneficiary (or on his behalf by an employee of the facility in which he resides) such trust funds as the trustees deem advisable.

9.   Provide that the trustee or his agent shall personally visit the mentally retarded person at his residence at least once every three months (more frequently if the trust fund can support the visits) to inspect his living conditions; to inquire of the staff and especially of the retarded person regarding his treatment and care by employees of the residential facility; to let him know he has a friend and advocate; to see that he has spending money for the things he wants; to know that he is receiving education, work training, and social and recreational programs; and to ensure that government assistance and trust funds are in fact being expended by or for him. Eternal vigilance is required. Provisions should be made for the payment of reasonable compensation to the trustee for these visits, if possible, and for all expenses of travel, meals, and lodging.

10.   Provide in the trust instrument that the trustees or their agents shall make or have made an annual evaluation of the mentally retarded beneficiary, including the following elements:

(a)   physical condition, determined by an independent physician;

(b)   educational and training program;

(c)   work opportunities and earnings;

(d)   recreational, leisure time, and social needs;

(e)   appropriateness of existing residential and program services;

(f)   laws and administrative practices relating to various governmental financial assistance and benefit program,[5] because unless the person has a reasonable chance of earning sufficient income to support himself, it is essential that these benefits be secured;

(g)   legal rights, including free public education, habilitation and treatment which meet minimal (constitutionally protected) standards, a minimum or fair wage for the work he performs, privacy, the right to vote and freedom to

---

[4]*Id.* § 403(f)(1), (3).

[5]The financial assistance and benefit programs currently in effect include the following:

Social Security Act: Supplemental Security Income for the Aged, Blind, and Disabled (replaced

marry. The trustee should base his annual evaluation on contacts with the mentally retarded person himself, his brothers or sisters, the employees of his residential facility, the county or regional social worker and employees, and volunteer members of the state or local association for retarded children.

11. Provide in the trust instrument for distribution of the trust fund, principal and accrued net income, upon the death of the mentally retarded person.

Professional discussion of this sort will, I hope, be of some assistance to the legal profession in recognizing and stimulating thought and action toward the solution of special problems in estate planning for parents of a mentally retarded child. Beyond their technical skills, attorneys must also learn that a mentally retarded person is a human being, a citizen entitled to the legal rights of citizenship, to the opportunity to perform the obligations and duties of a citizen, and to the opportunity for love and personal dignity.

Old Age Assistance and Aid to the Permanently and Totally Disabled, as of Jan. 1, 1974), 42 U.S.C. § 1381-85 (Supp. II 1972); Medicare, *Id.* § 1395; Medicaid, *Id.* § 1396.

The War Orphans' Educational Assistance Act, 38 U.S.C. §§ 1701-68 (Supp. II 1972), *amending* 38 U.S.C. §§ 1701-68 (1970).

Railroad and Retirement Act, 45 U.S.C. § 228(e) (Supp. II 1972), *amending* 45 U.S.C. § 228(e) (1970).

Rehabilitation Act of 1973, 42 U.S.C.A. §§ 701 *et seq.* (Supp. 1974).

Comprehensive Employment Training Act of 1973, 87 Stat. 839.

See also 7 APWA WASHINGTON REPORT, Nov. 3, 1972 (Am. Pub. Welfare Ass'n.). *See generally* U.S. DEP'T OF HEALTH, EDUCATION & WELFARE, PUB. No. (OS) 72-26, MENTAL RETARDATION FINANCIAL ASSISTANCE PROGRAMS OF THE DEPARTMENT OF HEALTH, EDUCATION AND WELFARE (1971).

CHAPTER 6

Insurance

The restoration of human dignity and legal rights to mentally retarded citizens has clear economic implications. In areas such as peonage, community treatment, and public assistance, those who benefit from unjust treatment of retarded persons will, in a more just order of things, gain less; the mentally retarded citizen will lose less. Society may find that it must readjust economic (and, for that matter, social) cost as it restores the flow of deserved benefits to the thousands of retarded workers, parents, and dependents who today suffer unjust deprivation.

Insurance is an obvious economic dimension, although it is often overlooked by concerned citizens and even by reformers. Follmann's paper is a detailed description of the scope of private and public insurance and assistance programs which benefit or fail to benefit mentally retarded workers, parents, and dependents. He assembles a formidable array of facts on coverage, numbers of persons affected, dollar amounts involved, and limitations, as they affect retarded citizens and their parents, siblings, and children in areas such as hospitalization insurance, life insurance, workmen's and unemployment compensation, and the typical welter of inadequate programs of federal and state assistance. Follmann's expertise is formidable, although his somewhat laconic and factual style leaves to the reader the expression of outrage that the facts may justify.

Smith describes insurance programs being sponsored or espoused by the National Association of Retarded Citizens and differs with Follmann's assessment of the availability of health insurance coverage for mentally retarded individuals. Smith argues that the cost of long-term custodial care and other catastrophic health costs cannot be covered successfully in voluntary insurance plans and recommends that this type of risk be covered under an involuntary system such as social security. Smith also points out the lack of firm data on mortality and morbidity experience among retarded persons and expresses the hope that an authoritative study will be carried out in the near future.

Friday describes mechanisms available to reduce the impact of a mentally retarded person's possible legal incompetence on the provision of adequate insurance coverage. He focuses attention on the inadequacies of present health care coverage for retarded citizens and on the close relationship between health insurance and insurance for the costs of custodial care. Friday challenges the insurance industry to provide coverage that is needed for retarded citizens.

PRINCIPAL PAPER

J. F. FOLLMANN, JR.

MENTAL RETARDATION, in economic terms alone, is costly both to a family unit and to society. Although precise measurement of cost is not possible, it includes not only the costs of care, education, and training, but also the income which can be lost to the individual and family, and the loss of a productive person to society.[1] Basic to such considerations is the fact that mental retardation, where it involves severe disability, is essentially a matter of long-term care and treatment.

Despite some progress during the past decade, sufficient consideration has yet to be given the subject of mental retardation by either the private or the public sector of the economy. Availability of needed services, the quality of such services, and the means for financing them remain inadequate from the standpoint of need and, in many instances, human decency. In part, this situation emanates from personal reaction to the presence of a retarded child in the family, frequently expressed by overprotectiveness. In large part, it flows from the fact that social concern for the mentally retarded citizen has been marked by a long history of neglect in which the retarded person was ejected from the walls of the city, incarcerated with criminals and the insane, or humorously tolerated as the village idiot. The vestigial scars of this long history remain in their legal status, in public attitudes, in legislative amphitheaters, in services made available, in attitudes toward education and training, and in employment practices. Even the attitude of friends and neighbors mirrors centuries of misunderstanding, neglect, and lack of human sympathy.

The federal legislation advocated by President Kennedy and first enacted by Congress in 1963 represented a forward step in overcoming certain deficiencies

---

[1] For a thoughtful treatment of this type, see R. CONLEY, THE ECONOMICS OF MENTAL RETARDATION (1973).

of the past.[2] The President's Committee on Mental Retardation has, since its establishment in 1966, played a significant role in focusing public attention on mental retardation and particularly on the need for services for the individual, for research, public information, and prevention. Concepts and approaches have changed. Attitudes have become more understanding and more humane. It is fair to say that this society has come a long way in its understanding of the problems related to mental retardation. It is also fair to say it has a long way to go.

This paper views the status of mentally retarded citizens in relation to insurance protection against health risks, loss of income, and loss of life. In so doing, it is necessary to distinguish between those retarded citizens who are essentially dependent on others and those (a far larger group) who are capable of physical, social, and economic independence. This distinction, in turn, is generally determined by the individual's degree of mental retardation and potential for habilitation.

Adequate insurance protection for mentally retarded citizens is necessarily intertwined with the social policies and practices that prevail in dealing with the mentally retarded. The legal aspects of these various problems are discussed elsewhere in this volume. To the extent society provides appropriate prenatal, postnatal nutrition and medical care to mothers and infants, the incidence of mental retardation, and thus the need for special insurance problems, can be reduced.[3]

As educational and employment opportunities for mentally retarded individuals are improved,[4] there is an increased likelihood that the individuals will receive health and other insurance coverage through employer and union group insurance plans. It is also less likely that there will be a question about an individual's capacity to contract for insurance or consent to payment in settlement of an insurance claim.

Insurance for mentally retarded citizens is a complex subject. It does not lend itself to simple answers, applicable in all cases. The viewpoints of insurers are continually qualified, depending upon the degree of mental retardation, the socioeconomic circumstances present, the forms of care being received, and the legal status of the individual. The challenges for insurers are (1) to seek practical and workable solutions to the unusual problems of mentally retarded persons and (2) to avoid assuming that special problems exist in the absence of adequate data to support this assumption.

COMPETENCE TO CONTRACT

The legal status of the mentally retarded citizen, traditionally beset by difficult questions, is mired in concepts which have come to be looked upon as outmoded

---

[2]Maternal and Child Health and Mental Retardation Planning Amendments of 1963, 77 Stat. 273 (1963), *as amended* 42 U.S.C. §§ 701, 702, 711, 712, 1391-94 (1970); Mental Retardation Facilities and Community Mental Health Centers Construction Act of 1963, 77 Stat. 282 (1963), *as amended* in scattered sections of 20, 42 U.S.C. (1970).

[3]For a discussion of this problem, see Kramer, Chapter 2 of this volume.

[4]*See* Herr, Chapter 9 of this volume; Bernstein, Chapter 10 of this volume.

and fallacious.[5] In some states the law expressly declares that institutional commitment itself does, and in others that it does not, establish legal incompetence; elsewhere statutes and hospital regulations prohibit residents of institutions from holding a driver's license, making a will, marrying, executing a contract, or having any power of management of property. The shortcomings and inadequacies of many states' statutes, combined with the expense and stigma of guardianship, have often made institutionalization a poor man's guardianship.

The legal competence of a mentally retarded individual has a direct bearing on his insurance protection. The right of the individual citizen to enter into legal contracts and to give a valid release for the payment of benefits is fundamental for insurance, since all private insurance is in large part a matter of contract. Where group insurance protection is involved, the question of competence to enter into the insurance contract may never arise, since the contract operates between an entity, such as an employer or an association, and the insurer. The matter of competence to give a valid release for payments, however, would remain. Contracting for an individual policy of insurance and acceptance of a payment in satisfaction of a claim both require legal competence; an insurer will not knowingly enter into an insurance contract with, or make payment to, an individual who lacks legal capacity to execute a binding contract. The insurer will insist on the appointment of a guardian for fear that the contract or payment may otherwise be invalid.

PRIVATE HEALTH INSURANCE

The private health insurance system in the United States includes insurance companies, Blue Cross plans, Blue Shield plans, dental service corporations, group medical and dental plans operating on a prepayment basis, plans that are self-administered by employers or labor unions, community plans, prepayment prescription drug plans, prepayment vision care plans, fraternal societies, and rural or consumer health cooperatives. Each has its distinctive approach.

At the beginning of 1972 private health insurance in the United States provided some form of protection for over 186 million persons under age 65. This number represents some 92 percent of the civilian noninstitutionalized population under that age. It is clear, then, that the vast majority of the American public have some form of private insurance protection. In 1971, expenditures surpassed $16 billion in benefits for these persons. Of those having such protection at the beginning of 1972, almost 107 million persons were covered by insurance companies. Blue Cross, Blue Shield, and medical society plans covered close to 71 million persons. The several hundred miscellaneous types of plans, including the prepaid group practice plans, covered about 8 million persons. Thus, of the total number of persons having private health insurance coverage, before allowance is made for duplication, 58 percent were protected by insurance companies; 38 percent by Blue Cross, Blue Shield, and medical society plans; and 4 percent by miscellaneous plans. The vast

[5] *See* Kindred, Chapter 3 of this volume; Wald, Chapter 1 of this volume.

majority of persons over age 65 are covered by the public Medicare and Medicaid programs.

Among the people under 65 who do not have private insurance protection — a steadily decreasing proportion — there are large segments covered by other financing arrangements provided by the public sector of the economy. There is a residual number of people under age 65, however, who do not have any private insurance protection and who do not appear to be beneficiaries of any of the several available public programs. Their number is not easily estimated; their characteristics are varied. Examination of the subject indicates absence of insurance to be more prevalent among the unemployed, the unemployable, the seasonally employed, non-whites, persons living in rural areas, farm workers, domestics, the employees of very small businesses, persons with low educational attainment, and persons from broken homes. The inescapable conclusion is that many do not have health insurance because they cannot afford it. These population groups may, of course, overlap. In any instance, they reflect the influences of interacting social and economic practices of this society. Where the absence of insurance results from insufficient income or other social or economic maladjustments, society would appear to have a degree of responsibility. This might take the form of overcoming social and economic imbalances. It might take the form of bringing such persons into existing public insurance programs to the degree necessary. Or it might take the form of providing or assisting in the purchase of adequate private insurance protection through a system of national health insurance.

The number of mentally retarded persons covered by the various types of private health insurers is not known because such statistics are not maintained. This is principally because under coverages written on groups of persons (as is the practice in most types of private health insurance coverage), the insurer has no knowledge of the presence of retarded people in the insured group. To a considerable degree, this is also applicable to coverages written on individuals.

The remainder of this section will be confined to protection provided by the insurance companies and the Blue Cross-Blue Shield plans. These two types of coverages fall into essentially two patterns: (1) basic in-hospital protection (covering hospital room and board and ancillary expenses, surgery, physicians' visits, and, frequently, out-of-hospital diagnostic X-ray examinations and laboratory tests) and (2) major medical expense insurance protection (covering both in-hospital and out-of-hospital care of nearly all types).

With respect to insurance company coverage today, three fundamentals are important to note:

1. Of more than 107 million persons covered by insurance companies, 82 million (76 percent of the total) are covered under group insurance plans. This fact is significant from several standpoints:

    (a) In the vast majority of cases, the employer shares in the insurance costs. In many, and in an increasing number of cases, the employer pays the entire cost of the insurance.
    (b) The coverage can be tailored to the needs or wishes of the group. This means that a high degree of consumer sophistication is brought to bear

on all decisions concerning the nature and scope of the health insurance coverage.

(c) The process benefits from the administrative, operational, and marketing cost savings made possible by the group approach, thus reducing the nonrisk-bearing costs to a minimum.

2. Over 43 million persons are covered by individually purchased health insurance policies. Many of these persons do not have group affiliations and would be uninsured were it not for this form of protection. In other instances, individual policies are used to supplement other forms of health insurance coverage.

3. Of the persons below age 65 covered by insurance companies, 73 percent have comprehensive protection under major medical expense insurance. This proportion has been growing steadily (it was 9 percent in 1955 and 37 percent in 1960) and will continue to increase. The maximum amount of benefits also has been steadily increasing, today ranging from $10,000 or $20,000 up to $30,000, $40,000, or even $250,000. The deductible amount can vary from $25 (zero with respect to hospital or surgical expenses) to $300 or higher, usually depending on whether some type of basic insurance protection is effective. The amount of coinsurance under major medical expense insurance is generally 20 percent. The spectrum of health services covered can be as comprehensive and complete as the purchaser desires.

In instances where the mentally retarded individual has insurance coverage, medical care and treatment expenses would be covered. If the coverage includes treatment of mental illness, some additional coverage would be available in the form of expenses for hospital and ambulatory psychiatric care. Some insurance companies include the cost of services of a clinical psychologist, others do not. In many instances, the psychologist must be referred by, or perform under the direction of, a physician. Generally, no costs of training, education, or custodial care (without active treatment) for a mentally retarded person are covered by health insurance since these services do not constitute medical care. In instances where the individual is confined to an institution, the insurance is not applicable unless the institution qualifies under the insurance company's definition of a "legally licensed hospital" and the care provided is other than essentially custodial.

Health insurance coverage for mentally retarded persons might come about through (1) coverage under group insurance, (2) coverage as a dependent of an insured person, or (3) coverage under an individually purchased policy of insurance.

In the 76 percent of the private health insurance coverages that are on *groups* of persons (most often employed groups), the contract is between the employer or association and the insurance company. Retarded persons who otherwise qualify for the insurance are automatically covered and, in fact, the insurer has no knowledge that the individual is mentally retarded. Thus, no distinction is made by the insurance company, and there is no added charge for coverage of the mentally retarded person. Under group insurance coverages, the privilege to convert to an individual policy upon leaving the insured group applies equally to a mentally retarded person and to others. Individual coverage is available to him without evidence of insurability, provided the conversion right is exercised in accordance with the terms of the contract. In some instances of insurance on small groups of employed people, there may be limitations applicable to the coverage of the mentally retarded individual, but he will not be excluded from coverage.

An important form of health insurance for mentally retarded persons is coverage as a *dependent* of a person insured under a group insurance contract. This coverage is particularly important to severely retarded individuals who are dependent and not capable of employment. Under group health insurance policies, mentally retarded dependents are covered on the same basis as other dependents. Furthermore, today it has become general practice to continue the dependent coverage to any age, as long as the original coverage remains effective and as long as the handicapped dependent is unmarried and not capable of being self-sustaining. This continuation of the coverage is automatic, and there is no special premium for the continuation of coverage on such incapacitated dependents. Should the group insurance coverage cease, for whatever reason, the mentally retarded dependent usually is eligible for conversion to an individual policy of insurance at standard rates and without evidence of insurability. If the dependent person is confined in an institution at the time the group insurance coverage becomes effective, the dependent coverage becomes effective after such confinement ceases. These group insurance provisions are also becoming general with respect to dependents under *individual* policies of insurance.

In September 1969, a committee of the Health Insurance Association of America made several recommendations to insurance companies for the improvement of health insurance coverage. Among these recommendations the following relate to coverage for dependents:

> That member companies be urged to encourage employers to permit continuation of coverage for physically and mentally handicapped children.
> That insurers encourage the continuation of group coverage to dependent survivors of a deceased insured employee with whatever qualifications appear necessary and reasonable, such as remarriage, or alternatively make the conversion privilege available on the death of the insured.
> That companies adopt a limited period of eligibility during which a dependent child no longer eligible for coverage as a dependent is eligible for an individual policy without evidence of insurability. Continuation of coverage for dependents following the death of the primary insured is being guaranteed today by some insurers, oftentimes with a built-in option to extend the coverage to higher levels without evidence of insurability at the additional premium required for the extra coverage. Insurance companies are encouraged to give consideration to use of such provisions, not alone in new issues but also in amending outstanding contracts.
> That the Association continue its present position of encouraging experimentation and liberalization of individual coverage as respects pre-existing conditions.

It is also of interest that today 33 states have laws pertaining to health insurance coverage for mentally retarded persons. In most instances, these laws are applicable to group and individual policies of insurance and to Blue Cross-Blue Shield plans. These laws have largely resulted from the joint efforts of the National Association for Retarded Citizens (NARC) and the Health Insurance Association of America to develop model legislation and to advance its progress. The model bill is drafted separately for group and individual policies, but they are essentially similar. The following is the group insurance provision:

A group hospital or medical expense insurance policy, hospital service plan contract, medical service plan contract, delivered or issued for delivery in this state more than 120 days after the effective date of this Act, which provides that coverage of a dependent child of an employee or other member of the covered group shall terminate upon attainment of the limiting age for dependent children specified in the policy contract shall also provide in substance that attainment of such limiting age shall not operate to terminate the coverage of such child while the child is and continues to be both (a) incapable of self-sustaining employment by reason of mental retardation or physical handicap and (b) chiefly dependent upon the employee or member for support and maintenance, provided proof of such incapacity and dependency is furnished to the insurer, hospital service plan corporation, medical service plan corporation by the employee or member within 31 days of the child's attainment of the limiting age and subsequently as may be required by the insurer corporation, but not more frequently than annually after the two year period following the child's attainment of the limiting age.

In certain instances, health insurance protection is available to mentally retarded persons on an individual policy basis, although not all insurance companies offer such coverage. Eligibility for insurance may depend on the degree of mental retardation as well as the presence or absence of accompanying physical complications or abnormalities. It is recognized that there are no clear lines of demarcation and that each case must be evaluated on the basis of all surrounding circumstances. Some insurers, for example, will accept a mildly retarded person as a standard risk. A moderately retarded person might be offered hospital and surgical insurance only or might be offered substandard insurance at an increased premium. No practical basis has been found for insuring severely or profoundly retarded persons. At least one large insurance company does not consider Down's syndrome a disqualifying factor, although underlying physical complications present an underwriting problem. In any case, the mentally retarded person cannot be confined in an institution at the time of application for the insurance. He must be legally competent and self-supporting. As an alternative, if the degree of retardation is not too serious, an individual is probably eligible for the hospital indemnity policy (which pays a flat amount per day, week, month during which the insured is hospitalized, regardless of the expenses incurred) at a substandard premium rate. In such cases, any period of hospitalization occurring during the first six months of the policy, which results from a preexisting condition, may not be covered.

There are 74 Blue Cross plans operating in the United States. All have a restricted geographic area in which they conduct their operations; some are statewide, others are limited to a region within a state, and a few are limited to a single community. Blue Cross plans were designed originally to provide hospitalization coverage, with preference for the type of accommodation to be used, usually a semiprivate accommodation. However, they now make available extended benefit coverages.

A few Blue Cross plans cover surgical and medical expenses through cash indemnity payments to the subscriber. With respect to hospital care benefits, the unique character of Blue Cross is a result of its relationship with the hospitals that render the service. Insurance companies indemnify the covered person in relation to the charges for the services received; Blue Cross reimburses the hospital in accordance with the terms of a contract it makes with the hospital. Although Blue Cross plans emphasize group enrollment, enrollment is available in some plans to the general public on an individual or nongroup enrollment basis at irregular intervals during the year. Other plans solicit nongroup enrollment on a continuous basis. Conversion to a nongroup enrollment is permitted the subscriber if he leaves the group.

.   There are presently 73 Blue Shield and 9 medical society approved plans. Blue Shield plans have been categorized in three types, according to the nature of the benefits offered: full service plans, straight indemnity plans, and a combination of these two. The full service contracts entitle the subscriber to complete payment of expenses incurred for the benefits listed in the contract, with payment made directly to the physician. Straight indemnity plans are cash benefit plans paying specific predetermined cash benefits to the subscriber for a listed schedule of procedures. The third and most prevalent type of contract offers a combination of the foregoing types. The subscriber is accorded the full service type of coverage if his income is below a fixed amount, which varies among plans. If his income is above this limit, he is subject to the same benefits used in the indemnity contract.

Medical society approved plans other than Blue Shield are physician-sponsored, nonprofit, prepayment, surgical-medical benefit plans. The types of contracts are similar to those for Blue Shield plans.

Blue Shield benefits are essentially for services: surgery and physicians' visits. In most cases, coverage is limited to in-hospital care. Usually, extended benefits are available, but these generally serve to make the contract benefits more effective, rather than to change the nature of the coverage. Persons enrolled in Blue Shield plans are covered predominantly on a group basis or as conversions to individual certificates after leaving a group.

Much of the earlier information in this paper concerning insurance company coverages for mentally retarded persons pertains to Blue Cross-Blue Shield coverages. The availability of coverage and problems presented are essentially the same.

In August 1972, the Blue Cross Association reported that 48 of the 74 Blue Cross plans covered handicapped dependent children to any age. Usually, it is required that the dependent be totally and permanently disabled, be incapable of self-sustaining employment, be unmarried, and that he reside with the insured person. In a few instances, there is an age limit to the coverage. Two plans relate the dependency status to "dependent for income tax purposes."

In summary, a considerable degree of private health insurance coverage is available to mentally retarded persons. For those with a mild degree of retardation who are beyond childhood, coverage can be acquired through group insurance policies at the place of employment or through the purchase of individual protection. If the individual is a child or is seriously retarded, he can often be continued indefinitely as a dependent under the insurance coverage of his parent or guardian. Upon cessation of the coverage, he usually can convert to individual coverage without presentation of evidence of insurability. The most compelling problem affects mentally retarded persons at lower socioeconomic levels. They do not enjoy private insurance coverage. Many are employed, or their providers are employed, in occupations where group insurance is not available. Their reliance, if any, is on public programs.

PUBLIC PROGRAMS

There are several types of publicly established programs concerned with the payment of health or medical care expenses. All are limited to specifically designated population groups. Mentally retarded individuals eligible under these programs would have coverage of some or all of their medical expenses, but in almost all instances the cost of education, training, and custodial or residential care is not covered. These costs, however, are sometimes borne by public funds in other ways, such as through the public school system, vocational training, employment placement, and institutions established for the care of the metally retarded.

Medicare

The Medicare program was enacted in 1965 and became effective in 1966.[6] Its purpose was to provide medical care, within limits, for most persons age 65 and over. It is administered by private health insurers. The hospital portion of the program (Part A) is financed by a federal tax levied equally on employers and employees. The medical care portion of the program (Part B) is paid for in equal amounts by a monthly premium from the aged person and by a subsidy from the federal government paid from general tax revenues. Part A is a compulsory program, and Part B is voluntary. Both function under the social security system. Under Part A, provision is made for inpatient hospital services and for care in extended care facilities. Under Part B, provision is made for physicians and certain services such as outpatient clinics.

At the present time, Medicare coverage is restricted to individuals 65 and over. Any mentally retarded individual of this age group can receive full coverage provided he is otherwise eligible.

Under a recent amendment, Medicare protection was extended to persons entitled for not less than 24 consecutive months to cash benefits under social security or railroad retirement programs because they are disabled.[7] Persons eligible include disabled workers at any age, disabled widows, and disabled dependent widowers between the ages of 50 and 65. Also covered are women 50 or older entitled to mother's benefits who, for 24 months prior to the first month they would have been entitled to Medicare protection, met all the requirements for disability

[6] Health Insurance for the Aged Act, tit. I, 79 Stat. 290 (codified in scattered sections of 26, 42, 45 U.S.C. (1970).
[7] 42 U.S.C. § 1395(c) (Supp. II 1972).

benefits except for the actual filing of a disability claim; people aged 18 and over who receive social security benefits because they became disabled before reaching age 22; and disabled qualified railroad retirement annuitants.[8]

Assuming that mental retardation would in many cases qualify as a disability under social security, this amendment to the Medicare program will provide hospital and medical expense coverage to some mentally retarded individuals not previously receiving any health insurance protection. Under the Medicare program, however, no payment may be made for health or medical care expenditures:

> (1) which are not reasonable and necessary for the diagnosis or treatment of illness or injury or to improve the functioning of a malformed body member.
> . . . .
> (6) which consitute personal comfort items;
> (7) where such expenses are for routine physical checkups, eyeglasses or eye examinations; . . . .
> . . . .
> (9) where such expenses are for custodial care;
> . . . .
> (12) where such expenses are for services . . . [related to] teeth or structures directly supporting teeth . . .[9]

CHAMPUS

In December 1946, the federal government instituted a program to finance medical care for dependents of active duty and retired uniformed services personnel (including Army, Navy, Air Force, Coast Guard, Geodetic-Survey, and Public Health Service). Medical care under Civilian Health and Medical Programs of the Uniformed Services, now known as CHAMPUS, is provided by civilian physicians, nurses, anesthetists, and therapists in civilian hospitals or government facilities for some 6 million persons. The covered care, administered by private insurance organizations, includes hospitalization (semiprivate room), surgery, acute medical care, obstetrical and maternity care, treatment of acute emotional disorders, prehospitalization and posthospitalization tests and procedures, and limited treatment of injuries on an outpatient basis; custodial care is not covered. Dependents receiving care in civilian facilities must share the costs.

In 1967 the treatment of mental illness and mental retardation was added to this program. Up to 45 days of hospitalization (subject to extension in certain cases) is provided for nervous, mental, and emotional disorders, and treatment on an outpatient basis for 2 visits a week is unlimited.

The program for the handicapped is available only to dependents of active duty personnel and dependents already in the program whose fathers were killed in action while eligible for hostile fire pay. Persons in the program who became incapable of self-support because of disability prior to age 21, including severely and profoundly retarded persons, continue to be eligible for benefits for the handicapped as long as one parent has active duty status.

---

[8] *Id.* § 426.
[9] 42 U.S.C. § 1395(y) (1970).

Under this program, institutional care can be provided. The CHAMPUS manual provides the following description:

> Institutional Care. Normally, this is residential care in private, nonprofit, public, or state institutions and facilities. Such institutions include, but are not limited to, schools for the deaf and blind and institutions for physically and/or mentally handicapped persons, and may include day care, night care, or extended outpatient care at such facilities. It includes a private room when ordered by the physician or when no other accommodations are available. Institutional care is not [generally] authorized in a private facility operated for profit.....[10]

The benefits are available only for treatment of moderate, severe, or profound mental retardation or for a condition identified as a serious physical handicap condition; coverage does not extend to mild mental retardation. Benefits are limited to $350 a month for diagnosis, long-term treatment, and institutionalization.

Workmen's Compensation

The workmen's compensation laws provide for the payment of certain medical care expenses if mental retardation is the result of employment. For instance, a worker who sustains a severe head injury causing mental retardation will receive all of the state workmen's compensation benefits available. Although the benefits differ from state to state, most state laws today provide for full medical care benefits, including physical rehabilitation and the cost of education and training. Some laws, however, do not cover custodial or residential care, although the majority do so when such care is required by an injury.

Medicaid

In 1965, the Medicaid (Title XIX) program was established to assist persons who would sustain a severe financial burden as a result of medical care expenses.[11] This program is financed by federal and state governments from general revenues, with counties contributing in some instances. It is administered by the states, each of which determines in part standards of eligibility for benefits and the nature and extent of medical care to be provided. Frequently, the amount paid for a particular service is limited. Federal funds are available under Medicaid for inpatient psychiatric services in a general hospital, outpatient hospital services, physician services, skilled nursing homes, clinical services, and prescribed drugs. Mentally retarded individuals who qualify for assistance as permanently and totally disabled, or who are adjudged "medically indigent" under the criteria established in their state, qualify for the covered types of medical care provided for under Medicaid in their state. However, costs of education, training, and custodial or residential care are never covered.

---

[10] Office of Information for the Armed Forces, & Uniformed Services Health Benefits Program (DOD PA-3B 1969).

[11] Pub. L. No. 89-97, 79 Stat. 343 (1965) *as amended* 42 U.S.C. § 1396 (1970).

Veterans Administration Program

The Veterans Administration (VA) program[12] has no health insurance benefits or any benefits of this type. Although medical care is provided to disabled veterans, as are physical and vocational rehabilitation services and custodial care, no health benefits are available to their families. The War Orphans Educational Assistance Act[13] does, however, provide educational opportunities for children of veterans who died or were permanently and totally disabled as a result of service in the armed forces. Mentally retarded children of these veterans are eligible for "special restorative training" from ages 14-23, if approved by the Veterans Administration. The sum of $130 per month for up to 36 months is available for this special training. The monthly sum may be increased for shorter training periods, but total educational benefits cannot exceed $4,680.

"Special restorative training" under the act is individualized and not geared solely toward a high school diploma. Benefits may be used to pay institutional charges if the institution is training the child. ("Institution" is loosely defined by the act to include hospitals, institutions for mentally retarded persons, or any other place where training is being given.) Training starts as soon as the individual is approved, and no one is placed in training without parental consent. The VA does not conduct the training, but a VA training officer provides supervision at least once every 30 days and may adjust the progress as needed.

PROPOSALS FOR NATIONAL HEALTH INSURANCE

Presently there are before Congress several proposals that would establish a program of national health insurance in the United States. Each proposal offers benefits to mentally retarded persons through comprehensive health insurance protection available to all citizens regardless of health or financial status. Yet none of the proposals provides for the costs of education, training, or custodial care.

PROTECTION AGAINST LOSS OF INCOME

An important form of insurance is that which provides protection against loss of income resulting from disability. This type of protection is important to mentally retarded individuals who are gainfully employed. Private insurance against loss of income resulting from disability has been made available by insurance companies

[12] 38 U.S.C. §§ 101-5224 (1970).
[13] War Orphans Education Assistance Act of 1956, 70 Stat. 411 (1956), *as amended* in scattered sections of 38 U.S.C. (1970).

in the United States for over a century. Today, 41 million persons in the work force have some insurance protection against this hazard. In addition, 17.5 million have protection through formal paid sick leave plans, and perhaps 7 million through other arrangements. In 1971, loss of income benefit payments by insurance companies exceeded $1.7 billion. The amounts paid to workers through informal sick leave arrangements are no doubt also substantial.

Private loss of income insurance is made available on both group and individual insurance bases. Through either approach, a wide range of benefits is available. Benefits might continue for periods of 13, 26, or 52 weeks, up to 5 or 10 years, or until retirement age or death. Amounts of benefits vary from very little up to 60 percent or 80 percent of earned income. The number of gainfully employed mentally retarded persons with loss of income insurance protection is not known.

The majority of persons protected against loss of income by insurance companies have protection through group insurance programs at their places of employment. Coverage of mentally retarded persons under group insurance programs follows essentially the same pattern as protection against the costs of medical care described in the second section of this paper. Mentally retarded individuals who otherwise qualify as eligible employees for insurance protection are covered on the same basis as all other employees. There is no special premium loading for mentally retarded employees. Usually such coverage pertains only to full-time employees. Where long-term disability benefits are involved, there is sometimes a preexisting condition exclusion; the practical effect of this is unclear, since the fact of employment provides substantial evidence that the preexisting mental retardation was not disabling.

Individual insurance protection is important for employed or self-employed mentally retarded persons who do not have insurance coverage on a group basis. Mentally retarded applicants for individual insurance who are self-supporting and gainfully employed are considered by insurers for coverage, subject to the eligibility requirements and underwriting rules of the particular insurer. Generally, individuals with a mild degree of retardation (typically the case among those employed) would be insured unless other conditions were present, and the standard premium rate would apply. The basic consideration is the presence of earned income on a full-time basis and the ability to make the necessary premium payments, a consideration in the evaluation of all applicants. The nature of the occupation also enters into underwriting considerations. If the degree of retardation is of a more serious nature, the payment of a special premium might be required or the individual could be denied coverage. Primary considerations are the need for assurance that the applicant can economically afford to pay the required premiums over a period of time and the need to avoid the hazard of adverse selection. Each insurer reaches its own decisions in these matters.

Publicly established programs for protection against loss of income resulting from disability are also available to mentally retarded persons. In some instances such programs are employment centered and pertain principally to mentally retarded persons who are employed and self-sustaining. In others, they serve to benefit principally the noninstitutionalized more seriously retarded individuals.

The effectiveness of these programs in assisting mentally retarded persons is not known. Under most programs, however, the income payments are minimal.

In 1956 a disability insurance benefit was added to the Federal Old Age and Survivor Insurance program (social security)[14] and the Railroad Retirement Act[15] for some workers, and in 1960 and 1972 the scope of the program was extended.[16] It is financed by the employer-employee social security tax, and most, but not all, workers are eligible if they meet a work period test. Two types of income benefits under this program are applicable to mentally retarded persons. One is a benefit for which a mentally retarded individual is eligible as a disabled worker. Disability is defined as inability to engage in any substantially gainful activity by reason of a medically determinable physical or mental impairment. The condition must be such that it is or can be expected to last for a continuous period of not less than 12 months. Disability must have existed for approximately five months before benefits commence. Although more than 35,000 disabled workers (of about 1.5 million beneficiaries) receive benefits as a result of mental, psychoneurotic, and personality disorders, including mental retardation, under this program the number whose primary diagnosis is mental deficiency is quite small—1,833 persons in 1968. The amount of benefits is minimal, although in 1972 supplemental income was made available to aged, blind, and disabled persons who have low incomes and can meet other stipulated conditions and who are not inmates of public institutions.

The other benefit under this program is one to which the retarded person is entitled as a childhood beneficiary of an eligible parent who retires, becomes disable, or dies. The benefits in such cases vary. A mentally retarded child is automatically entitled to benefits until he reaches age 18. When he becomes 18, he continues to be entitled to benefits if, or so long as, he is unable to engage in substantially gainful activity (in excess of $125 per month earnings) and is unmarried. About 22,000 handicapped persons, of whom approximately 12,000 are mentally retarded, presently receive these benefits.

Five states (Rhode Island, California, New Jersey, New York, and Hawaii) and Puerto Rico have enacted laws which provide income benefits for certain eligible workers who become temporarily disabled. The purpose of these laws is to protect only against loss of income resulting from temporary disability, and therefore benefits cease after a maximum of 26 weeks. In effect, these laws supplement unemployment compensation laws. The number of workers covered under these programs is usually about 70 percent of the total work force. Benefits are insured by insurance companies or by state funds, or are self-administered by employers. They are financed by payment of premiums by the employer and, some instances, employees. Under these programs there is no special premium rating for mentally retarded workers, but the benefits are not large. The benefits, of course, would be limited to mentally retarded persons meeting the required conditions of employ-

---

[14] Social Security Amendments of 1956, ch. 836, tit. I, 70 Stat. 815 (1956).

[15] Railroad Retirement Act of 1937, ch. 836, tit. II, 70 Stat. 836 (1956).

[16] Social Security Amendments of 1960, tit. IV, 74 Stat. 967 (1960); Railroad Retirement Act of 1937, tit. VII, 74 Stat. 997 (1960); Social Security Amendments of 1972, tit. I, 86 Stat. 1333 (1972).

ment. The number of such persons who benefit from these programs is not known.

The nature and extent of workmen's compensation insurance has been outlined in a preceding section. The principal benefit under workmen's compensation insurance is the replacement of income lost as a result of occupational accidents or diseases. The amounts and duration of benefits under the workmen's compensation laws vary from state to state. In 1971, $2,322 million was paid in benefits under these programs, exclusive of medical care benefits. Obviously, these statutory benefits can be important to retarded persons who are employed and suffer loss of income as a result of a work-related accident or disease.

About half of the states' workmen's compensation laws provide that an employer's liability for an industrial injury or disease shall be limited if the benefits payable for the industrial disability are substantially increased because of preexisting physical or mental impairment which, when added to the industrial impairment, increased the disability arising out of the industrial accident alone. If, for instance, a person with vision in only one eye sustained an injury to that eye and was totally blinded, the employer's liability would be for the loss of vision in one eye, not for loss of vision in both. The balance of the benefits would be paid to the employee out of a special fund assessing all workmen's compensation carriers. The losses paid by the special funds are then fed back into the insurance system for rate making purposes. This is an important function of workmen's compensation since it encourages the hiring of mentally retarded and physically handicapped citizens.

Federal-state public assistance programs also play a significant role in providing subsistence income for mentally retarded persons, particularly those with more serious conditions who are not employed or self-sustaining. The most important program is Aid to the Permanently and Totally Disabled (APTD), which came about through the 1950 amendments to the Social Security Act.[17] Its basic purpose is to ensure the essentials of living to needy individuals over age 17 who are permanently and totally disabled, regardless of their work experience. Residents of an institution other than one to provide medical care and residents of institutions for tuberculosis or mental disease are ineligible. Some 16 percent of APTD recipients had mental retardation as the primary diagnosis, and 3 percent had it as a secondary diagnosis. Mentally retarded children may also receive aid under the Aid to Families with Dependent Children program (AFDC). Of all childhood recipients of this program, 5 percent are reported to be mentally retarded, although this figure may be low.

The public assistance programs are financed jointly by federal and state governments using general tax funds. Each state establishes its own eligibility criteria and its own level of benefits, subject to federally established minima, and administration is by state public assistance agencies. About 10 percent of the disabled (from all causes) receive assistance from AFDC. The vast majority of persons receiving payments from such federal-state public assistance programs are those permanently and totally disabled or who qualify for AFDC. It is not clear how many of these involve mental retardation, but certainly mentally retarded persons not capable of employment and not institutionalized, or whose families are in need of financial assistance,

---

[17] Social Security Amendments of 1950, tit. XIV, 64 Stat. 555 (1950), *as amended* 42 U.S.C. §§ 1351-54 (Supp. II 1972).

would be aided by the public assistance programs. The benefits provided, however, are at the subsistance level.

It might be assumed that mentally retarded persons do not qualify for Veterans Administration disability income benefits since they would not have qualified for military service.[18] However, some mentally retarded children are eligible for benefits as the dependents of veterans who died or were permanently disabled as a result of military service after January 1, 1957. These benefits are referred to as Dependency and Indemnity Compensation (DIC).[19] The benefits for children are $80 a month for one child, $115 a month for two children, and $149 a month for three children, with $29 a month added for each additional child. DIC benefits continue to be available for dependents over age 18 who are helpless (permanently incapable of self-support). A legal custodian or court-appointed guardian is the payee on behalf of the mentally retarded individual. No figures are available on the number of mentally retarded persons who benefit from this program.

LIFE INSURANCE

Life insurance can be important to a mentally retarded person in two ways. The first is as a beneficiary under a life insurance policy on the life of another, usually a parent. The purpose of the insurance is to provide for the continued support of the beneficiary. The fact that the beneficiary is mentally retarded does not present a problem in and of itself (although the matter of legal competence to give a valid release could become significant). The second way in which life insurance can be important to a mentally retarded citizen is as an insured person. Here the purpose is the creation of an estate for the benefit of a parent, spouse, child, or other person with insurable interest. Such insurance might come about through either group insurance or individually purchased insurance or both.

Much of what has been written in the second and third sections of this paper with respect to protection of a mentally retarded person under group insurance coverage is equally applicable here. All that is required for the individual to be covered under a group life insurance program is that he qualify as a covered employee and make application for such coverage as soon as he becomes eligible to do so. If he delays, but desires to enter the program at a later date, evidence of insurability is required. Otherwise, the same underwriting rules apply to him as to anyone else, unless excessive amounts of insurance are requested. The right of conversion to an individual policy upon leaving the group would be available to the mentally retarded person, without having to present evidence of insurability.

With respect to coverage of a mentally retarded person under individually purchased policies of life insurance, applications are considered on an individual basis. Based on considerations of degree of retardation, ability to pay premiums over a

---

[18] Although the cut-off used on the Armed Forces Qualification test should exclude most mentally retarded individuals, it is likely that many individuals who at some point in their lives were classified mentally retarded do, in fact, enter the military service. For them, VA benefits would be available.
[19] 38 U.S.C. §§ 401-23 (1970).

period of time, and competence to enter into a legal contract, some individual policies are accepted, some are issued at special rates, and others are declined. In some instances the amount of the policy is limited, since the face amount issued is related to the earning capacity of the insured. Mentally retarded persons requiring supervisory confinement generally are not considered to be insurable. Because of the relative infrequency of applications that identify the insured as a mentally retarded person, it is difficult to present a generalized picture. Individual judgment is made with each application. If the applicant is a minor, his potential for becoming self-sufficient and self-supporting is a factor.

It is unlawful in Massachusetts to refuse to issue a policy of life insurance solely for the reason of mental retardation. A Massachusetts statute requires issuance of a policy of insurance on a mentally retarded person's life in an amount of $1,500, provided such insurance is desired, no other life insurance is in force or application pending, and the person to be insured has reached 3 years of age.[20]

The National Association for Retarded Citizens counsels that since most mentally retarded persons will not have responsibilities for providing for the financial support of dependents, they do not have need for life insurance and that "the family's insurance dollars are better spent for additional insurance on the life of the breadwinner."[21] NARC then notes, however, that "a retarded person of higher level, who will be responsible for the financial support of others, does need life insurance. His ability to support himself and others and the cause of his retardation will determine the premium which must be charged in his case."[22]

The more common place in life insurance for the mentally retarded person is as a beneficiary under a policy written on the life of another person, usually a parent. This occurs under group and individual life insurance policies. In either instance, the insured person essentially has the right to name his own beneficiary. A problem that can arise in this situation is the legal competence of the beneficiary to give a valid release for the payment of benefits. If, at the time the proceeds are to be paid, a mentally retarded person has a legal guardian, payment of the benefits would be made to the guardian. If there is no guardian, and if the insurer has reason to question the competence of the beneficiary, the company will request a statement from the beneficiary's physician regarding his competence. If competence is in doubt, appointment of a guardian or conservator will be requested. Some states, however, provide for a waiver of guardianship requirements if the amount involved is not great (generally less than $1,000). Many group life insurance contracts contain a provision enabling the insurer to select an individual, other than the payee, to receive payment in the event of incompetence of the payee. Furthermore, under group life insurance contracts that include dependent coverage, provision is sometimes made that dependents of covered persons are covered for rather small amounts of life insurance protection (*e.g.*, $1,000). In such cases, mentally retarded persons can be eligible on the same basis as anyone else. If such group coverage is terminated, a conversion privilege is available without discrimination.

There is some opinion that it is unwise for an insured person to designate a

---

[20] Mass. Ann. Laws ch. 175, § 120A (Supp. 1972).
[21] National Association for Retarded Children, How to Provide for their Future 15 (1968).
[22] *Id.*

mentally retarded individual as a beneficiary. The principal reason is that in some states the presence of life insurance benefits affects the levying of charges for care received in public institutions. However, life insurance benefits are not part of an estate dispensed by a will, nor are they part of any trust created by will, unless the life insurance is payable to the estate or the trust is named as beneficiary.

The National Association for Retarded Citizens has prepared a useful pamphlet, "How to Provide for Their Future," which discusses estates, establishment of trusts, making of wills, insurance programs, governmental benefits, guardianship, establishment of mental incompetence, and ownership of property by the mentally retarded individual. It summarizes as follows:

> You have many factors to consider in providing lifetime protection for your retarded children. You should obtain a judicial determination of mental incompetence before the age of 18. You may at the same time wish to have guardian appointed.
> It is vital that you prepare a will upon the advice of a competent attorney. Your will may create a trust that will make proper financial provision for all of your children, including your retarded child.
> Life insurance on your life is essential; the proceeds from it will enlarge your estate and increase the protection of your children. In planning both your life insurance and your total estate, you will not want to forget the benefits available to your retarded children under the Social Security Act and the various veterans benefits.
> Keep in mind that the various factors affecting your future plans for your retarded child are related and must be considered in an entire, overall, single picture.[23]

NARC makes available the NARC Protection Plan, a group life insurance plan devised for parents of mentally retarded children, which provides funds toward the care of the retarded person after the parent's death. Its purpose is to supplement benefits available for the mentally retarded individual under social security. It is available to the income-earning parent of a mentally retarded person, if either parent is a member in good standing of a local or state unit of the National Association for Retarded Citizens. The policy benefit under the plan depends upon the age of the insured parent at the time of death, and ranges from $ 1,250 to $ 15,000.

In the interest of completeness, it should be noted that with respect to both group and individual policies of life insurance, a waiver of premium benefit is commonly available to cover the contingency that the insured person becomes totally and permanently disabled.

GAPS IN ELIGIBILITY AND COVERAGE

Some mentally retarded individuals encounter barriers to eligibility under both private and public insurance. Many employed mentally retarded persons are engaged in part-time work, temporary or seasonal employment, domestic work, or farm

---

[23]NATIONAL ASSOCIATION FOR RETARDED CHILDREN, HOW TO PROVIDE FOR THEIR FUTURE 23 (1968).

labor, and as a result are not covered by, or are ineligible for, private group insurance or for publicly provided programs. Sound arguments can be advanced for particular eligibility restrictions, but the net result can be an absence of needed protection. A means must be found to overcome this vacuum. In the area of health insurance, one such means is a national health insurance program (see the section that examined proposals for this program). As to life insurance and protection against loss of income resulting from disability, reliance is still likely to be placed on the purchase of individual policies of insurance and improvement of workmen's compensation benefits. In 1972, the National Commission on State Workmen's Compensation Laws concluded that the protection furnished by these laws was "neither adequate nor equitable." The commission supported the concept of state workmen's compensation programs, but called upon the states to improve existing programs by 1975, principally along the following lines:

> Make such programs compulsory with no exemptions for certain employers, including eventually farm workers, household workers, and casual workers to the extent they are covered under OASDHI.
> Make cash payments adequate (at least two-thirds the worker's gross weekly wage) by July, 1973, and 100 per cent by 1975.
> Remove arbitrary limits on amount or duration of benefits for permanent total disability. [24]

There are also some essentially unresolved questions regarding the extent of the coverage under health insurance protection. Professional opinion differs as to inclusion of services by clinical psychologists and psychiatric social workers, particularly if they are functioning independently of a physician. Insurance coverage has not yet been extended to such services as vocational training and sheltered workshops.

Care provided in public hospitals or by public or voluntary agencies raises special problems of coverage since the patient frequently does not pay for such care or makes only partial payment of the costs. Public or private insurance of these costs raises difficult questions, principally because expanded coverage may mean considerably increased costs. This poses the question of what kinds of coverage the public wants and can afford. The practices among insurance companies vary, and differences are also evident among contracts issued by any one company. Such variation can result from the fact that group insurance coverages are largely determined by the purchaser of the insurance. Thus, the employer, or the labor union through collective bargaining, can decide whether or not the cost of such treatment is to be covered. In some instances, a public institution does not satisfy the definition of a hospital stipulated in the contract. Where coverage is provided in a publicly financed institution, the coverage may be specified in the insurance contract or may be provided by administrative decision (provided that the confinement is not primarily custodial in nature) even though the institution would not satisfy the definition of a hospital stated in the policy. In either instance, the coverage applies to those expenses or charges that are actually incurred by the

---

[24] THE REPORT OF THE NATIONAL COMMISSION ON STATE WORKMEN'S COMPENSATION LAWS 13-25 (1972).

covered person and for which he is legally liable under the statutes of the particular state. That is to say, coverage is provided where there is an unconditional requirement on the part of the patient to pay charges without regard to any rights against others. Coverage usually does not extend to those instances where charges are levied solely because of the existence of insurance.

A special problem of coverage for mentally retarded citizens that deserves emphasis is that of insurance for the costs of custodial care. Substantial custodial care is important to some mentally retarded persons who are very seriously impaired or have accompanying physical complications. This is a subject which has not been adequately evaluated in terms of insurance coverage.

A basic problem in approaching custodial care is that of a useful definition. Both private and public insurers have felt it important to separate custodial care from that which is clearly health care, but they have had some difficulty in providing an appropriate definition. Where definitions of custodial care are given, they frequently are related to other forms of care or conditions and thus are of restricted value. The subject has been aptly described as a shadow land between professionally recognized health services and the general helping services in a society. A 1972 publication of the American Psychiatric Association (APA), "Equal Coverage for the Mentally Ill," defines the custodial function of public mental hospitals as "providing the necessary supervision and meeting the basic human needs of patients such as food and housing, together with access to health services when needed."[25] The APA considers the responsibility for meeting custodial needs to fall increasingly within the province of welfare administrations.

Regardless of definition, custodial care can be burdensome for most individuals or families when the need arises and cannot be met in the home by the family. On the other hand, it appears that publicly provided custodial care in institutions often leaves much to be desired. In any instance, the supply is scarce, and frequently such institutions are not readily available. Services to provide custodial care in the individual's home are becoming increasingly available, with public and philanthropic support; charges are usually gauged to the individual or family's income. Home care is becoming an important alternative to institutional care.

Traditionally, custodial care has been considered as a form of care needed by many, but lying beyond the realm of what reasonably might be considered medical or health care. Private health insurers, therefore, have very largely limited their benefits or services to medical or health care. The same is true of such publicly provided programs as Medicare and Medicaid. Although this attempt to segregate medical care from custodial care has considerable merit, it is well known that the separation of the two is never clear. For example, much custodial care is provided in nursing homes, mental hospitals, and VA hospitals. Some agencies that provide noninstitutional services to those needing health care also provide custodial care services (*e.g.,* homemaker services, and meals-on-wheels). Therefore, an attempt to segregate the two types of care can be difficult. Here it might be noted that all of the proposals for national health insurance presently before the

---

[25] AMERICAN PSYCHIATRIC ASSOCIATION, EQUAL COVERAGE FOR THE MENTALLY ILL (1972).

Congress are limited to the payment of benefits for health and medical care. Custodial care is not included, and this omission is a major flaw in these proposals.

An attempt to come to grips with the subject of custodial care may take one of three approaches:

1. Increase the availability and accessibility of services, both in the home or institutionally, and subsidize such services where necessary with public funds so that individual payments for services can be related to the income of the individual or his immediate family, and thereby avoid an undue burden.
2. Increase public income replacement programs in instances where custodial care is required to an extent that the individual can then be expected to pay for the services received.
3. Include custodial care in all public and private health insurance programs, with commensurate increase in premiums and other necessary safeguards.

Like so many other issues raised in this paper, solutions will not come easily. The problem of inadequate insurance protection affects a great many more persons than those who are mentally retarded. It is essential to recognize, however, that this issue and others raised have a major impact on a great many people who are mentally retarded, as well as on their families and on society as a whole. Efforts must be expended toward adequate, viable, and humane solutions.

Reaction Comment

FRANKLIN C. SMITH

FOLLMANN does an outstanding job of discussing the various types of insurance protection which a retarded person needs and the problems he encounters in trying to obtain such coverage. But I believe that Follmann has understated the difficulty a retarded person has in obtaining medical and hospitalization insurance. Those children whose fathers or mothers participate in group plans at their places of employment are indeed fortunate. Also fortunate are those who are born into families already covered by family group contracts. However, judging from the volume of inquiries on this problem received by the Insurance Committee of the National Association for Retarded Citizens, I conclude that obtaining health coverages is the greatest insurance problem faced by parents of retarded persons.

Some companies in recent years have developed contracts for persons with a wide of variety of impairments, including mental retardation, with the premium rate depending upon the type of impairment. The contracts I have seen offer coverage to retarded persons at a premium approximately 10 percent higher than the premium for standard risks. However, the contracts are not available to all retarded persons, but only to those in school or to those employed in regular jobs or in job training programs. A large number of persons is thus left without any coverage available.

It is the contention of many parents of mentally retarded persons and of many professionals who serve retarded persons that as a group they do not incur greater medical expenses than corresponding "normal" groups. This raises the question of whether the actions and policies of the insurance companies are based on hard data or on what they surmise that the insurance risk might be. The special contracts mentioned have now been on the market for several years, providing an opportunity to collect reliable data. Yet the health insurance industry has not published a study based on these data. Such a study would give authoritative information on the degree of risk incurred in providing health insurance for retarded persons.

In the area of life insurance, companies have based the underwriting of applications on the lives of retarded persons on the degree of self-support which appeared to be possible. Thus, if the applicant appeared capable of supporting himself, the application was accepted at standard or nearly standard rates. On the other hand, a severely retarded person who had no hope of self-support was rejected. This result seems tenable because there usually is no need for life insurance for a person who does not provide support for those who may survive him. However, insurance companies have contended that high mortality rates among severely retarded persons was the reason for declining the applications. To my knowledge this rationale is supported only by some old statistics covering persons in institutions which showed mortality rates 10-12 times normal. The facts that these statistics are over 20 years old and are based upon an obviously low-level population discredit their continued application.

The lack of contemporary statistics highlights the need for a study of mortality among retarded persons. The results of such a study would also be useful for the purpose of financial planning and an assessment of the various age groups for whom services will be needed. There are several problems connected with such an investigation. First, like many other projects, one must look for sources of staff and financing. Second, the study should encompass noninstitutional populations for whom data would not be readily available. Various agencies now collect data for the purpose of determining the types and amounts of services which groups of retarded persons need, and they have assembled rather massive card and tape files. However, these records are routinely destroyed under certain conditions. The various degrees of mental impairment and the other handicaps often present with mental retardation present a third problem, since it is desirable that mortality investigations be made with homogeneous populations. These difficulties are not insurmountable, and since the results are needed for many purposes, I hope that such a comprehensive study can be carried out.

Returning to the subject of health insurance, I wish to support Follmann's statement that even when retarded persons are covered under health insurance policies, the day-to-day maintenance costs for such persons are not reimbursable expenses. A few years ago, an attorney called me asking for my recommendation that the National Association for Retarded Citizens appear as an amicus curiae in a suit against an insurer which refused to pay for such costs. I told him that, in my opinion, he had a weak case because the insurance company had not included expenses of this type in setting premium rates and could produce independent expert witnesses who would verify this.

I doubt whether it would be feasible to include coverage of this type in contracts offered by private insurers. It would be necessary to charge a higher premium if such coverage were included, and the prospective buyer would tend to buy the cheaper contract (without this coverage), rationalizing that this type of misfortune is something which happens only to other people.

A few years ago, the Annual Report of the President's Committee on Mental Retardation contained a section on the cost of residential services for retarded persons and proposed that these costs be added to the benefit structure of the Social Security System to be supported by an additional tax of about 0.2 percent to 0.3 percent of payroll. This was a sound proposal, and I regret that apparently it has been dropped.

The above type of analysis applies to all catastrophic health costs. In order for a system of voluntary insurance to be successful, it must cover a risk common to a large number of persons and a risk which causes financial hardship to those who do suffer a loss. It must also be possible to make these persons aware of the fact that they run this risk. This may be difficult to do if the chances are small that any given one of them will have a loss. This difficulty also works against the most efficient operation of the plan since the greater the spread of the risk, the smaller the margins for unexpected claims need to be. If two health contracts are available, one covering a catastrophic loss and one not covering it, the typical insurance prospect will reason that catastrophic events occur only to other people and will buy the cheaper coverage. If the unfortunate event then befalls him, he will naturally complain, and it is human nature that he will put the blame on everything except his own deliberate choice of the cheaper contract.

All persons, whether they believe it or not, risk catastrophic medical expenses. Since it is human nature to ignore this risk, it is my opinion that it can be managed only under a type of involuntary program such as the Social Security System. Under this arrangement, the few parents of retarded persons who face extraordinary medical expenses and the others who must seek residential facilities would have the needed financial resources. The average cost per person for this type of protection would be slight; the benefit would be substantial.

Reaction Comment

HERSCHEL H. FRIDAY

FOLLMANN's paper is thorough and well done and represents an up-to-date, accurate analysis of insurance coverage available to mentally retarded citizens. The topic of adequate insurance coverage for mentally retarded citizens is one concerning which judicial relief is unlikely to be of much benefit. If compulsion is necessary, it can be accomplished most effectively in the legislatures of the various states, where insurance is normally regulated, or in the Congress. Much, however, may be possible through voluntary action, once the issues are defined. Follmann's paper is a significant step toward this goal.

Before I discuss the broader subject of providing adequate coverage, some clarification is needed in the areas of capacity to contract and to execute releases, guardianship, and insurance protection. Difficulties regarding these matters cannot and should not be allowed to stand in the way of obtaining insurance for retarded persons. Legal competence to contract is not absolutely necessary in order to obtain an individual policy of insurance. Assuming incompetence under existing legal criteria, an insurance contract would be voidable by the incompetent and not inherently void.[1] If an insurance policy is written and a claim is made by, or on behalf of, the insured, the insurer cannot assert the insured's incompetence at the time of contracting as a defense.[2] The only apparent risk from the standpoint of the insurer would occur if an insured individual should sue to recover premiums on the ground that he was incompetent to contract.[3] If this risk is really a deterrent to providing insurance, legislation could be drafted to protect the insurer against such a suit.

Limitations upon competence to grant releases also should not serve to restrict coverage. In most instances the insurer can rely upon payment whether or not a release is or can be obtained. Payment is the satisfaction of an obligation according to its terms, whereas a release is the giving up, or abandonment, of a right.[4] Although some benefits might not be subject to precise determination, this is not usually the case. In the absence of a statute to the contrary, payment to an incompetent person will satisfy the debt owing to him. In the case of large sums of money, an insurer can always reduce any risk by requesting the appointment of a guardian and make payment under the protection of a court order.

Turning now to problems of adequate insurance coverage, the principal need is in the area of health insurance. The reasonable availability of life insurance and loss of income insurance, although certainly not unimportant, is far less important than the need of the retarded person for protection against illness and injury. The basic purpose of life insurance is to care for an insured's dependents after the insured dies, and severely mentally retarded persons are not likely to have dependents. As the degree of retardation decreases, both the likelihood of dependents and the availability of life insurance increase. Loss of income protection is applicable to persons who are employed or employable, and mentally retarded persons are in only slightly different circumstances from other persons in this regard.

Adequate health insurance is the greatest problem. As a first step, all health insurers should be encouraged to follow the lead of the few insurers who have adopted underwriting criteria for individual policies that increase the availability

---

[1] Field v. Koonce, 178 Ark. 862, 12 S.W.2d 772; Annot., 68 A.L.R. 1303 (1929); 41 Am. Jur. 2d *Incompetent Persons* § 66 (1968).
[2] 41 Am. Jur. 2d *Incompetent Persons* § 82 (1968).
[3] 41 Am. Jur. 2d *Incompetent Persons* § 80 (1968).
[4] 60 Am. Jur. 2d *Payment* § 1 (1972); 66 Am. Jur. 2d *Release* § 1 (1973).

of coverage to retarded persons. The fact that some insurers have adopted such criteria indicates its feasibility. The underwriting criteria can be evaluated periodically with an eye toward further improvements. Since the cost is not significant from an industrywide standpoint and the need to be served is so great to those affected, the insurers should be expected to let their overall operations subsidize premiums to some extent.

The National Association for Retarded Citizens (NARC) might, in cooperation with private insurers, devise a group health insurance plan which would be available by reason of retardation alone. The financing of such a plan would need to be studied, but a combination of premium charges to those who are able to pay, contributions to NARC for this purpose, and appropriations from NARC's funds (including perhaps a special dues assessment) might be sufficient to provide at least minimum coverage. Of course, any other group or organization could undertake a similar project.

Closely related to the need for health care insurance is the need for custodial care coverage. This need is not being, and cannot be, met under existing governmental and private programs. One solution would be to make the need insurable in all health insurance policies, and a logical place to start would be with group health insurance plans. At the outset, it would be difficult to estimate the cost, but experience would be accumulated in a relatively short time. If need be, restrictions could be inserted initially, such as limitations on the amount payable, restrictions concerning the severity of retardation as it relates to the extent of custodial care required, or other limitations necessary to make the coverage feasible. After experience is gained, some or all of the restrictions could be removed. The fact that the risk might be different from those presently insured under health insurance does not mean that these risks are not insurable, nor does it diminish the close relationship between health care and custodial care.

If broadened coverage on a feasible basis cannot be voluntarily accomplished, compulsory legislation should be considered. A good example of this is the model law[5] (which also applies to group policies in Arkansas[6] and in other states) discussed in Follmann's paper.[7] There are difficulties with compulsory legislation because insurers invariably proceed in accordance with the strict letter of the law (and sometimes only after court interpretation). For example, a problem has arisen with reference to the model law. Policies written under this law have required that proof of incapacity and dependence be furnished within 31 days of a child's attainment of the limiting age and annually following a 2-year period after the child's attainment of the limiting age. This provision has the effect of placing the consequences of inaction on the insured. There have been instances in which an insured person has neglected to provide the annual proof and coverage has lapsed. The statute itself does not require annual notice, nor does it place the consequences of inaction on either the insured or insurer. The law would be complied with just as well by policy provisions obligating the insured member to furnish the necessary proof

---

[5] Ark. Stat. Ann. § 66-3632.1 (Supp. 1973).
[6] Ark. Stat. Ann. § 66-3702 (Supp. 1973).
[7] *See* pp. 150-51 *supra*.

only after a request from the insurer to do so. In this event, inaction would leave coverage in effect. The necessary steps should be taken to remedy this feature, including an appropriate amendment to the model law if needed.

We must proceed on the basis that a dedicated cooperative effort on the part of persons interested in the cause of mentally retarded citizens can obtain broader insurance coverage to meet their needs at an acceptable cost to retarded persons or individuals acting on their behalf.

PART TWO

Rights of Mentally Retarded Citizens within Community Systems

CHAPTER 7

The Right to Community Services

Editorial Introduction

*I*n a broad inquiry into the right of mentally retarded citizens to community services, Gilhool emphasizes that the issues raised pertain not just to mentally retarded citizens. Rather, there is a broader question of the right of all citizens who are "different" in one way or another to receive publicly supported services they need. Gilhool's inquiry begins with a classification of services. Some services are required specifically and only by mentally retarded citizens because they are mentally retarded. Many other services are needed by, and provided to, members of society at large, and the only claim that is made by mentally retarded citizens is that they have the same rights as others in society to these services. With two intermediate categories, this model serves as Gilhool's framework for analysis. He illustrates that services such as education are made available to members of society in very diverse forms, so that the claim for education is a claim for a service generally available, not a special service for the mentally retarded, even though special educators may call it "special" education.

Scott, in his reaction comment, lauds the efforts of the legal profession to achieve for mentally retarded citizens their entitlement to community services. With a focus on the right to education, Scott then calls for a continuing alliance to seek adequate public resources to fulfill the rights proclaimed. He laments that present funding levels for urban school systems present only the choice between total exclusion of a child or inadequate provision for his educational needs within a bankrupt school. Scott, like Gilhool, notes that the deprivation applies not alone to mentally retarded children, but to all children.

Price presents a different kind of caution. Noting that advocates of remote institutions once heralded such institutions as a total solution to the provision of services to the mentally retarded, Price warns that a similar illusion can lead to false hopes for community programs. He is particularly concerned about the manipulation by state officials of the "normalization" concept and its advocates. Drawing from the California experience, Price points out that the movement toward de-institutionalization can lead to a closing of institutions without a corresponding development of adequate community services, unless the budgetary commitment to community services follows the programmatic commitment.

PRINCIPAL PAPER

THOMAS K. GILHOOL

THE CENTRAL ROLE OF FACT IN THE LAW

In 1923, writing for the Supreme Court in *Meyer v. Nebraska,*[1] Mr. Justice McReynolds sounded an essential theme in the American constitutional experience. He took as his counterpoint Plato's Commonwealth.

> For the welfare of his Ideal Commonwealth, Plato suggested a law which should provide: "That the wives of our guardians are to be common, and their children are to be common, and no parent is to know his own child, nor any child his parent. . . . The proper officers will take the offspring of the good parents to the pen or fold, and . . . will deposit them with certain nurses . . . but the offspring of the inferior, or of the better when they chance to be deformed, will be put away in some mysterious, unknown place, as they should be."[2]

I wish to express my appreciation to my brother. Robert K. Gilhool, who began my education in these matters, to the members of the Pennsylvania Association for Retarded Children, who have been my co-workers, and to Andrew L. Niven, a second-year student at the University of Southern Calfornia Law Center, for his delving.
[1] 262 U.S. 390 (1923).
[2] 262 U.S. at 401-02.

But, for the Court, Justice McReynolds declared:

> Although such measures have been deliberately approved by men of great genius, their ideas touching the relation between individual and State were wholly different from those upon which our institutions rest; and it hardly will be affirmed that any Legislature could impose such restrictions upon the people of a State without doing violence to both the letter and spirit of the Constitution.[3]

The constitutional presumption is integrative. It is essential to our constitutional scheme that judgments of Plato's sort — that some (invariably "they") are inferior and some (invariably "we") are superior — are disfavored. It is essential to our constitutional scheme that stereotyping of men by government is to be prohibited. and that stereotyping of men by men is not to be encouraged by government, but affirmatively to be discouraged.

On January 7, 1971, 13 retarded children went to federal court in Philadelphia, suing for themselves and for all retarded citizens in the commonwealth of Pennsylvania, seeking access to a community service provided other citizens, namely, a free public education.[4] Thereby they placed themselves in a very old tradition in the United States. It is the tradition of the use of the courts by citizens who are different to achieve social change, or, from the perspective of the citizen, to achieve justice. In going to court, the children placed themselves and other retarded and handicapped citizens in this tradition alongside the black, the poor, women, and the elderly.[5]

---

[3] 262 U.S. at 402.

[4] Pennsylvania Ass'n for Retarded Children v. Pennsylvania, 343 F. Supp. 279 (E.D. Pa. 1972) [hereinafter cited as PARC]. The history and meaning of this case, which marked the beginning of the affirmative use of the courts by retarded citizens, are treated in Gilhool, *The Uses of Litigation: The Right of Retarded Children to a Free Public Education,* 50 PEABODY J. EDUC. 120 (1973); Gilhool, *Education: An Inalienable Right,* 39 EXCEPTIONAL CHILDREN 597 (1973); variations of these papers are printed in U.S. DEP'T OF HEALTH, EDUCATION & WELFARE, PUB. NO. (OS) 73-86, CURRENT ISSUES IN MENTAL RETARDATION AND HUMAN DEVELOPMENT 27 (Stedman ed. Dec. 1972); 2 LEADERSHIP SERIES IN SPECIAL EDUCATION 167 (Univ. of Minn. 1973). The case is treated extensively in L. LIPPMAN & I. GOLDBERG, RIGHT TO EDUCATION (1973).

On the now extensive line of right to education cases, set out at note 47 *infra* and concerned with access to schooling and with hearings before and after the classification and assignment of children, see Dimond, *The Constitutional Right to Education: The Quiet Revolution,* 24 HAST. L.J. 1087 (1973); Dimond & Reed, *Rodriguez and Retarded Children,* 2 J. LAW & EDUC. 476 (1973); Herr, *Retarded Children and the Law,* 23 SYR. L. REV. 995 (1972); Kirp, *Schools as Sorters: The Constitutional and Policy Implications of Student Classification,* 121 U. PA. L. REV. 705 (1973); Kirp, Buss & Kuriloff, *Legal Reform of Special Education: Empirical Studies and Procedural Proposals,* 62 CALIF. L. REV. 40 (1974); Murdock, *Civil Rights of the Mentally Retarded,* 48 NOTRE D. LAW. 133 (1972). *See also* Note, *Equal Protection and Intelligence Classification,* 26 STAN. L. REV. 647 (1974); Note, *The Right of Handicapped Children to an Education: The Phoenix of Rodriguez,* 59 CORNELL L. REV. 519 (1974); Note, *Toward a Legal Theory of the Right to Education of the Mentally Retarded,* 34 OHIO ST. L. J. 554 (1973); Comment, *Public Instruction to the Learning Disabled; Higher Hurdles for the Handicapped,* 8 U.S.F.L. REV. 113 (1973). *See also* Sorgen, Chapter 8 of this volume; Herr, Chapter 9 of this volume.

[5] The tradition dates back at least to 1909, when W.E.B. DuBois and others founded the National Association for the Advancement of Colored People. From the beginning the NAACP was committed, among other strategies, to the use of the courts to secure the rights of black people. Vose, *Litigation as a Form of Pressure Group Activity,* 319 ANNALS 20 (1958); C. VOSE, CAUCASIANS ONLY: THE SUPREME COURT, THE NAACP AND THE RESTRICTIVE COVENANT CASES (1959). That effort culminated in the decision of the Supreme Court in Brown v. Board of Educ., 347 U.S. 483, 349

It is not mere historical accident which binds the members of these groups together. Rather, they have shared a common social experience. Each of them — the retarded, the handicapped, the black, the poor, the elderly, and women — have been subjected systematically to the judgment McReynolds decried: *They* are inferior and *we* are superior.[6] This judgment has two important social consequences.

First, it results in the attribution of stigma to the citizens who are on the wrong end of the judgment. It results in prejudice and in discrimination against them.[7] It means that they are not listened to, or if listened to, not heard, or if heard, not heeded.[8] Persons discounted by stigma, prejudice, and discrimination become nonpersons from both official and private perspectives. Finally, there is a tendency

---

U.S. 294 (1954). As the contemporary civil rights movement has flowered, of course, resort has frequently been made to the courts.

In the mid-1960's, significantly influenced by the strategies of the civil rights movement, as lawyers became more generally available to poor citizens through the Office of Economic Opportunity's Legal Services program, welfare recipients, low-income tenants, and low-income consumers turned to the courts. JOHNSON, JUSTICE AND REFORM (1974). Later, the women's movement turned to the courts, *Symposium—Women and the Law,* 23 HAST. L.J. 1-316 (1971); L. KANOWITZ, WOMEN AND THE LAW 150-96 (1969). And most recently, aged citizens have looked to the courts to secure their rights. *Cf.* Jennings, *Private Pensions and the Elderly: A Broken Promise,* 18 N.Y.L.F. 121 (1972). *See also* Bernstein, *Aging and the Law,* in 2 AGING AND SOCIETY (1969).

[6] On the proposition that the judgment of superiority is at the center of prejudice and political oppression, *see generally* G. ALLPORT, THE NATURE OF PREJUDICE 410-21 (1954); H. ARENDT, THE ORIGINS OF TOTALITARIANISM 232-36 (new ed. 1966); Reisman, *Some Observations on Marginality,* 13 PHYLON 113 (1951).

On the retarded, *compare* Martin Luther, *quoted in* Wolfensberger, *The Origin and Nature of Our Institutional Models,* in CHANGING PATTERNS IN RESIDENTIAL SERVICES FOR THE MENTALLY RETARDED 71 (R. Kugel & W. Wolfensberger eds. 1969) *and* L. KANNER, A HISTORY OF THE CARE AND TREATMENT OF THE MENTALLY RETARDED 7 (1964) *with* Buck v. Bell. 274 U.S. 200, 207 (1927) (Holmes, J.).

On blacks, *e.g., compare* David Hume *quoted in* W. JORDAN, WHITE OVER BLACKS 253 (1968) *with* Scott v. Sandford, 60 U.S. (19 How.) 393, 407 (1857) (Taney, C.J.).

On the poor, *e.g., compare* Walter Channing *quoted in* D. ROTHMAN, THE DISCOVERY OF THE ASYLUM 172 (1971) *with* City of New York v. Miln, 36 U.S. (11 Pet.) 102, 142-43 (1837).

On women, *e.g., compare* JOHN STUART MILL & HARRIET TAYLOR MILL, ESSAYS ON SEX EQUALITY 123 (Ross ed. 1970) *with* Muller v. Oregon, 208 U.S. 412, 421-22 (1908).

On the elderly, *see* S. DE BEAUVOIR, THE COMING OF AGE 3-4 (1972).

[7] The core meaning of "prejudice" is to judge beforehand, and of "discriminate," to have the difference marked. WEBSTER'S THIRD NEW INTERNATIONAL DICTIONARY 647, 1788 (1966).

"Stereotype" takes its meaning from the technology of printing: The purpose of "stereotyping" is to produce a printing surface that can be used for thousands of impressions without needing to be replaced. A stereotype is (1) simple rather than complex, (2) erroneous rather than accurate, (3) acquired secondhand rather than through direct experience with the reality it is supposed to represent, (4) resistant to modification by new experience. 15 INTERNATIONAL ENCYCLOPEDIA OF THE SOCIAL SCIENCES 259 (1968). *See also* Lusky, *The Stereotype: Hard Core of Racism,* 13 BUFFALO L. REV. 450, 451 (1964).

[8] *See* John Adams' observation, J. ADAMS, *Discourses on Davila,* in VI WORKS OF JOHN ADAMS 239 (C.F. Adams ed. 1851):

> The Poor man's conscience is clear; yet he is ashamed. . . . He feels himself out of the sight of others, groping in the dark. Mankind takes no notice of him. He rambles and wanders unheeded. In the midst of a crowd, at church, in the market . . . he is in as much obscurity as he would be in a garret or a cellar. He is not disapproved, censured or reproached; *he is only not seen. . . .* To be wholly overlooked and know it are intolerable.

Compare with R. ELLISON, INVISIBLE MAN (1952) (on the black) *and* M. HARRINGTON, THE OTHER AMERICA (1962) (on the poor).

to separate them out.[9] When public policy is made, they are excluded or omitted or wronged.[10]

Being on the wrong end of the judgment has a second consequence; it affects the self-regard of those subject to it. With the judgment played back again and again to those on the wrong end, by people and by institutions, often they come

---

[9]Slavery, segregation, and what has come to be called "institutionalization" are functional equivalents; they are for the retarded and the handicapped, as for Plato, the historic expression of the judgment of inferiority taken to its furthest conclusion; such has characterized the historical treatment of the retarded, as it has each of the groups.

A. DEUTSCH, THE MENTALLY ILL IN AMERICA 116-18 (2d rev. ed. 1949) records that:

 . . . Sick poor, old poor, able-bodied poor, infant poor, insane and feebleminded—all were grouped together under the same stigmatizing label, "paupers", and all were treated in very much the same manner. . . .

 The custom most shocking to modern thought, undoubtedly, was that of placing the poor on the auction block like so many chattel slaves. . . . [T]he system was at that time generally accepted with quite the same complacency that the average Southerner then showed toward the institution of slavery. As a matter of record, the custom of bidding off the poor persisted over a wide area throughout the 19th Century and survives to this day, in modified form, in at least one southwestern state. . . .

 The insane and the feebleminded are often most eagerly sought after, for "strong backs and weak minds" make good farm laborers—and the bidders are invariably farmers. . . .

 Whole families, pauperized through one circumstance or another, were frequently torn apart. . . .

In the 1820s and 1830s enslavement of the feebleminded gave way to a network of institutions (almshouses, poorhouses, or asylums) for the inclusive pauper class. See generally D. ROTHMAN, supra note 6. ". . . [S]ocietal responses toward retardation were not specific, but were part of a generalized pattern of response toward deviance." Wolfensberger, *The Origin and Nature of Our Institutional Models,* in CHANGING PATTERNS IN RESIDENTIAL SERVICES FOR THE MENTALLY RETARDED 66 (R. Kugel & W. Wolfensberger eds. 1969).

In the middle of the nineteenth century the retarded were separated into their own institutions— State Asylums for Idiots (New York); Institutions of Feebleminded Youth (Ohio); Schools of Imbeciles (Connecticut). L. KANNER, *supra* note 6, at 62-66.

In the early 1900s two "scientific" judgments damned the retarded. Social scientists, misinterpreting demographic statistics, concluded that "feeblemindedness is the mother of crime, pauperism and degeneracy," Fernald, *What is Practical in the Way of Prevention of Mental Defect,* PROC. NAT. CONF. CHARITIES & CORRECTIONS 192 (1915). Eugenicists, misapplying Mendel's rediscovered genetic studies, urged that the retarded not be allowed to reproduce, "to prevent our being swamped by incompetence," Buck v. Bell, 274 U.S. at 207. See, e.g., Goddard, *The Possibilities of Research as Applied to the Prevention of Feeblemindedness,* PROC. NAT. CONF. CHARITIES & CORRECTIONS 308 (1915). Three methods for preventing future generations of the retarded were advocated. (1) Exclusionary marriage laws—by 1914, 25 states prohibited marriage with a person characterized generically as "idiot," "imbecile," "feebleminded," etc. SMITH, WILKINSON & WAGONER, SUMMARY OF STATE LAWS ON MARRIAGE OF FEEBLEMINDED, ASEXUALIZATION, AND INSTITUTIONALIZATION FOR THE MENTALLY RETARDED (1914). (2) Eugenic sterilization—by 1947 nearly 25,000 mental defectives had been involuntarily sterilized under statutes in 28 states. See, e.g., DAVIES, THE MENTALLY RETARDED IN SOCIETY 52-53 (1960). See generally N. KITTRIE, THE RIGHT TO BE DIFFERENT 308-35 (1971). (3) Mass colonization—modeled on the Indian reservation. Barr, *President's Annual Address,* 2 J. PSYCHO-ASTHENICS 13 (1897). In England ". . . under the Mental Deficiency Act of 1913 many mental defectives were segregated in colonies for the years when they were most likely to bear children." Shaw & Wright, *The Married Mental Defective: A Follow-up Study,* THE LANCET 273 (Jan. 30, 1960).

On the pattern of legal disqualifications to which the retarded are subjected, see note 23 *infra.* Generally, on the historical experience of the retarded in the United States, see DEUTSCH, *supra* at 332-86, and Wolfensberger, *supra,* at 59-171(b). See also the testimony of Professor Ignacy Goldberg, Columbia Teachers College, in PARC, 343 F. Supp. 279 (E.D. Pa., 1972) and of Professor Gunnar Dybwad, Brandeis University, in Lebanks v. Spears, 60 F.R.D. 135 (E.D. La., 1973), and the Appendix to the Brief of Council for Exceptional Children, National Center for Law and the Handicapped et al., Amicus Curiae in Lori Case v. California, Civil Appeal No. 13127 (Cal. Ct. App. 4th Dist. 1973). Cf. Kriegel, *Uncle Tom and Tiny Tim: Some Reflections on the Cripple as Negro,* 38 AMERICAN SCHOLAR 412 (1969); ten Broek & Matson, *The Disabled and the Law of Welfare,* 54 CALIF. L. REV. 810-16 (1966).

John W. Davis, counsel for the state of South Carolina, predicated his argument in Brown

to internalize it.[11] They come to believe that they are inferior. They regard themselves with shame and with guilt. What they have from others they have by grace of others; they take it (as they are expected to) with gratitude. Before those others and before authority they are timid and unusually acquiescent.[12]

These social facts have a place in our jurisprudence. The most coherent statement of that place, by the late Chief Justice Stone, is in the famous footnote four

---

v. Board of Educ. upon the historic and functional similarity here noted. He commenced his argument for appellees by saying:

> May it please the Court, I think if appellants' construction of the Fourteenth Amendment should prevail here, there is no doubt in my mind that it would catch the Indian within its grasp just as much as the Negro. If it should prevail, I am unable to see why a state would have any further right to segregate its pupils on the ground of sex or on the ground of age or on the ground of mental capacity. If it may classify . . . for one purpose on the basis of admitted facts, it may, according to my contention, classify it [sic] for other. ARGUMENT 51 (L. Friedman ed. 1969).

The crux, of course, is, what are "admitted facts," see note 23 *infra*.

[10] This aspect of the common social experience is briefly, and, in terms immediately germane to our inquiry here, best put by E. GOFFMAN, STIGMA 5-6 (1963):

> The attitudes we normals have toward a person with a stigma and the actions we take in regard to him, are well known, since these responses are what benevolent social action is designed to soften and ameliorate. By definition, of course, we believe that a person with a stigma is not quite human. On this assumption we exercise varieties of discrimination, through which we effectively, if often unthinkingly, reduce his life chances. We construct a stigma-theory, an ideology to explain his inferiority and account for the danger he represents, sometimes rationalizing an animosity based on other differences. . . . We use specific stigma terms such as cripple, bastard, moron in our daily discourse as a source of metaphor and imagery, typically without giving thought to the original meaning. We tend to impute a wide range of imperfections on the basis of the original one, and at the same time to impute some desirable but undesired attributes, often as a supernatural case, such as "sixth sense" or "understanding." . . . Further, we may perceive his defensive response to his situation as a direct expression of his defect, and then see both defect and response as just retribution for something he or his parents or his tribe did, and hence a justification of the way we treat him.

[11] The already classic work on the self-perception of stigmatized persons and their relations with others, drawing its data from the experience of the handicapped, including mentally retarded persons and noting explicitly its similarity to the experience of the other groups under discussion here is E. GOFFMAN, STIGMA (1963). Compare the discussions of stigma in Scott v. Sandford, 60 U.S. (19 How.) 393, 409, 416 (1857); Anti-Fascist Comm. v. McGrath, 341 U.S. 123, 168 (1950); Wisconsin v. Constantineau, 400 U.S. 433, 435-36, 437 (1971).

On the impact of stigma on self-regard see A. KARDINER & L. OVESE, THE MARK OF OPPRESSION (1951); G. ALLPORT, *supra* note 6, at 150-53, 302 (1954); K. LEWIN, RESOLVING SOCIAL CONFLICTS 186-200 (1948). Self-image may suffer even among those who share in stigma only by association: Hart, *Frequently Expressed Feelings and Reactions of Parents Toward Their Retarded Children,* in DIMINISHED PEOPLE 47-71 (N. Bernstein ed. 1970); Schild, *The Family of the Retarded Child,* in THE MENTALLY RETARDED CHILD AND HIS FAMILY 431-42 (R. Koch & J. Dobsen eds. 1971).

Coping with degradation may, of course, take forms other than internalization of the stigma. *See* G. ALLPORT, *supra* at 142-50, 153-62; Edgerton & Sabagh, *From Mortification to Aggrandizement: Changing Self-Concepts in the Careers of the Mentally Retarded,* 25 PSYCHIATRY 263 (1962); R. EDGERTON, THE CLOAK OF COMPETENCE 144-71 (1967).

[12] The great decisions of the Court touching upon the groups here under discussion (Brown v. Board of Educ., 347 U.S. 483, 349 U.S. 294 (1954), King v. Smith, 392 U.S. 309 (1968), Shapiro v. Thompson, 394 U.S. 618 (1969), and Frontiero v. Richardson, 411 U.S. 677 (1973)) have had perhaps their most significant effect upon the self-regard of members of the groups. *See, e.g.,* Carter, *The Warren Court and Desegregation,* 67 MICH. L. REV. 237, 246-48 (1968); F. PIVEN & R. CLOWARD, REGULATING THE POOR 306-08 (1971); 1969 ANNUAL REPORT OF THE DEPARTMENT OF WELFARE, COMMONWEALTH OF PENNSYLVANIA 43. There are signs of a similar effect of court decisions upon retarded citizens and their families. See Gilhool, *supra* note 4, 50 PEABODY J. EDUC. 130; Gilhool, *supra* note 4, 39 EXCEPTIONAL CHILDREN 608-09. Prejudice exacts a considerable toll also—in unrealism, lost opportunity, guilt—from those who deem themselves superior. *See, e.g.,* CLARK, PREJUDICE AND YOUR CHILD 168 (1956) reprinting in part, *The Effects of Segregation and the Consequences of Desegregation: A Social Science Statement,* Appendix to Appellants' Briefs, Brown v. Board of Educ., 347 U.S. 483 (1954). *See also* Clark, *The Social Scientists and the Brown Decision,* in ARGUMENT XXXI-L (L. Friedman ed. 1969).

to *United States v. Carolene Products Co.*[13] Mr. Justice Stone there recited that legislative judgments are to be accorded the presumption of constitutionality unless the judgment is of such a character as to preclude the assumption that it rests upon some rational basis within the knowledge and experience of the legislators. And in particular, Justice Stone wrote, in the closing lines of the footnote:

> prejudice against discrete and insular minorities may be a special condition, which tends seriously to curtail the operation of those political processes ordinarily to be relied upon to protect minorities, and which may call for a correspondingly more searching judicial inquiry.[14]

The point can be stated at a level of still greater generality: The constitutional scheme, in its central concern that governmental action not be arbitrary, makes

---

[13] 304 U.S. 144, 152-53 n.4 (1938).

[14] For his prime source Mr. Justice Stone returned to McCulloch v. Maryland, 17 U.S. (4 Wheat.) 400 (1819) and the basic notions of republican government and the role of courts in a republic there expressed. Chief Justice Marshall had written:

> The only security against the abuse of [a government's] power, is found in the structure of the government itself. In imposing a tax the legislature acts upon its constituents. This is in general a sufficient security against erroneous and oppressive taxation.
>
> The people of a State . . . give to their government a right of taxing themselves and their property, . . . resting confidently on the interest of the legislator, and on the influence of the constituents over their representative, to guard them against its abuse. *Id.* at 428.

But when a person burdened by the law is *outside* the polity, the protection of the "ordinary political processes" may not be relied upon and the ordinary presumption of constitutionality shall not be accorded acts of the legislature. One may be outside the polity physically, or geographically, as were the plaintiffs in South Carolina Highway Dept. v. Barnwell Bros., 303 U.S. 177, 184-85 n.2 (1938), cited by Stone. One may be outside the polity because of restrictions upon one's right to vote, or to speak, or to organize politically, or to assemble. And one may be outside the polity by virtue of the operation of prejudice within the polity:

1. prejudice which closes to the minority access to instruments of political communication, either by direct prohibition against access by the minority or indirectly by so affecting the minority's view of itself that the minority avoids political activity and is thus foreclosed;

2. prejudice which, even with access, renders communication ineffective, either because the political actors, themselves dominated by stereotype, cannot hear, or because, hearing, they do not act lest they trouble the stereotype embraced at large in the polity and themselves incur the fear and hostility cloaked by stereotype.

In each event, the mechanisms that ordinarily work to ensure tolerably rational decisions, or to preclude nonrational judgments, do not. In each event, "more exacting judicial scrutiny," 304 U.S. at 152 n.4, is necessary and appropriate to ensure that legislative judgments are rational and that citizens are neither affected erroneously nor oppressed.

Mr. Justice Stone's footnote 4 is in most significant aspects the source of "the two-tiered equal protection paradigm of recent glory," Michelman, *In Pursuit of Constitutional Welfare Rights: One View of Rawls' Theory of Justice,* 121 U. PA. L. REV. 962, 1013 n. 148 (1973). The notion of "strict scrutiny" is often traced to Skinner v. Oklahoma, 316 U.S. 535, 541 (1942). *See, e.g., Developments in the Law—Equal Protection,* 82 HARV. L. REV. 1065, 1131 (1968); Fessler & Haar, *Beyond the Wrong Side of the Tracks: Municipal Services in the Interstices of Procedure,* 6 HARV. CIV. RIGHTS— CIV. LIB. L. REV. 441, 444 n.11 (1971); Gunther, *Foreword: In Search of Evolving Doctrine on a Changing Court: A Model for a Newer Equal Protection,* 86 HARV. L. REV. 1 (1972). Yet Skinner v. Oklahoma is at most the source of the "fundamental interest" trigger of strict scrutiny. The notion of strict scrutiny itself and the suspect class criterion for invoking more exacting judicial scrutiny had their first articulation in footnote 4. Certainly, Stone's formulation is still the soundest functional justification for the special judicial role. Indeed, it was to footnote 4 that Mr. Justice Blackmun and the Burger Court turned for rationale in Graham v. Richardson, 403 U.S. 365, 372 (1971) to bring alienage under the suspect class rubric. For a contemporary appreciation of the footnote—and an authoritative understanding of it, for Professor Lusky was law clerk to Mr. Justice Stone when footnote 4 was written, see Lusky, *Minority Rights and the Public Interest,* 52 YALE L. J. 1 (1942).

Another part of footnote 4 provides the rationale also for the preferred place given to first amendment freedoms and for the corollary requirement that legislation touching upon preferred freedoms select the "least intrusive" or the "least restrictive" modes of regulation. *See, e.g.,* Shelton v. Tucker, 364 U.S. 479, 488 (1960); Sherbert v. Vener, 374 U.S. 398, 407 (1963).

special insistence that fact should be separated from myth and that governmental action should be grounded in fact. In the same case, *Carolene Products Co.,* for example, the Court declared that: "the constitutionality of a statute predicated upon the existence of a particular state of facts may be challenged by showing . . . that those facts have ceased to exist."[15] More recently, in *Stanley v. Illinois,* the Court wrote, "when [a procedure] explicitly disdains present realities in deference to past formalities, . . . it . . . cannot stand."[16] In short, citizens, including mentally retarded citizens, are protected in the constitutional scheme from what Judge Skelly Wright has called "the arbitrary quality of thoughtlessness."[17]

This understanding of the place of fact in our scheme of laws — and the derivative requirement that the social and case-specific facts which characterize the experience of the retarded be marshaled and displayed—must serve as the touchstone of any analysis of the rights of retarded citizens to services in the community.[18]

Thus, for example, in one of the areas of service in the community with which there is great concern — education — statutes adopted from the 1930s through the mid-1950s provided education for some retarded children but excluded many others. These statutes reflected the then perceived "fact" (or the then perhaps reasonably thought to be "fact") that some retarded children could not learn.[19] But this "fact" has changed. The fact now clearly is that every child, whatever his handicap, can benefit from education.[20] The fact is that among every 30 retarded children, 29,

[15] 304 U.S. 144, 153 (1938).

[16] 405 U.S. 645, 657 (1972).

[17] Hobson v. Hansen, 269 F. Supp. 401, 497 (D.D.C. 1967), *aff'd sub nom.* Smuck v. Hobson, 408 F.2d 175 (D.C. Cir. 1969).

[18] This is not the place to seek systematically to parse the doctrinal origins of this focus upon fact nor to examine the doctrinal clothing in which this concern for fact is presently applied. For example, there are some who regard the *Carolene Products Co.* rule (see note 14 *supra*), if not footnote 4 itself, as a trace of the old substantive due process doctrine, *cf.* McCloskey, *Economic Due Process and the Supreme Court,* 1962 SUP. CT. REV. 34-37. Others divine in recent cases a "new," and proper, substantive due process, though they may prefer to call it the "newer" equal protection. Gunther, *supra* note 14, at 20-24, 41-43. Tribe, *Foreword: Toward a Model of Roles in the Due Process of Life and Law,* 87 HARV. L. REV. 1 (1973). Whether the rubric is equal protection with the Court increasingly applying "middle scrutiny"—*e.g.,* Reed v. Reed, 404 U.S. 71 (1971) (women); Weber v. Aetna Casualty & Surety Co., 406 U.S. 164 (1972) (illegitimates)—or due process with the Court engaging in an irrebuttable presumption analysis—*e.g.,* Stanley v. Illinois, 405 U.S. 645 (1972) (unmarried fathers); Vlandis v. Kline, 412 U.S. 441 (1973) ("nonresidents"); Cleveland Bd. of Educ. v. LaFleur, 414 U.S. 632 (1974) (women)—the trigger very often seems to be the presence of a footnote 4 class and the danger of stereotyping.

[19] Or, more properly, "could not be taught." *See, e.g.,* PA. STAT. ANN. tit. 24, § 13-1375 (1962) (children who are "uneducable and untrainable" may be excluded from schooling); PA. STAT. ANN. tit. 24, § 13-1304 (1962) (school directors may refuse to accept or retain children who have not yet attained a "mental age of five years"); PA. STAT. ANN. tit. 24, § 13-1330 (1962) (children who are "unable to profit" from further public school attendance may be excused). For the similar exclusionary provisions of the school codes of virtually every state, some two dozen of them now being contested in litigation, see DIGEST OF STATE AND FEDERAL LAWS: EDUCATION OF HANDICAPPED CHILDREN *passim* (E. Trudeau ed. 1971).

[20] The explosion of attention and resources in the education of the retarded and the discovery of new teaching techniques in the late 1950s and early 1960s changed the fact. For the fact of the educability of all, see, *inter alia,* Cohen, *Vocational Rehabilitation of the Mentally Retarded,* 15 PEDIATRIC CLINIC OF NORTH AMERICA 1021 (1968); Roos, *Trends and Issues in Special Education for the Mentally Retarded,* 5 EDUC. & TRAINING OF THE MENTALLY RETARDED 51 (1970); YATES, BEHAVIOR THERAPY 324 (1970); Council for Exceptional Children, *Policy Statement: Basic Commitments and Responsibilities to Exceptional Children,* 37 EXCEPTIONAL CHILDREN 421 (1971). *See generally* L. LIPPMAN & I. GOLDBERG, *supra* note 4; and the expert testimony presented in litigation, *e.g.,* PARC, 343 F. Supp. at 296; *see also* NATIONAL CENTER ON LAW AND THE HANDICAPPED, COLLECTION OF AUTHORITIES ON EDUCABILITY OF HANDICAPPED CHILDREN (1973).

with a proper program of education and training, have the potential to achieve self-sufficiency: 25, in the ordinary marketplace; 4, in a sheltered environment. The remaining 1 of every 30, with a proper program of education and training, is capable of achieving a significant degree of self-care.[21] In the face of these existing facts, as a matter of law, whether of the Constitution or of the statutes themselves,[22] each mentally retarded child must be accorded access to a free public education.

It is against this background—the central importance of fact to confront stereotype[23]—that I turn to the litigation seeking to discern principles which may guide the pursuit of the rights of retarded citizens to services in the community.

[21] See, e.g., PRESIDENT'S COMM. ON MENTAL RETARDATION, MR69: ANNUAL REPORT 17 (1969). See also PARC, 343 F. Supp. at 296.
  Rehabilitation Act of 1973 § 503, 29 U.S.C.A. § 793 (Supp. 1974), requiring every federal contractor of $2,500 or more to "take affirmative action to employ . . . handicapped individuals," enhances still further the significance of the new fact that all mentally retarded citizens are educable and lends pointed additional importance to the recognition and enforcement of the right of each to an education.

[22] As to the constitutional effect of these facts, see PARC, 343 F. Supp. at 296-97; as to the effect of these facts on interpretation of the exclusionary provisions of the statutes, see PARC, 343 F. Supp. at 307-08, 312-13. See also cases cited note 47 infra.

[23] Stereotype has bred a host of legislative and administrative disqualifications of mentally retarded persons, without regard to specific competence. The pervasive patterns of official disqualification, touching, inter alia, the capacity to contract, to hold property, to make wills, are set out in THE MENTALLY DISABLED AND THE LAW (rev. ed. S. Brakel & R. Rock eds. 1971); R. ALLEN, E. FERSTER & H. WEIHOFEN, MENTAL IMPAIRMENT AND LEGAL INCOMPETENCY 144-225 (1968). Yet social science studies repeatedly penetrate the stereotype, establishing that persons labeled retarded, far from being generally incompetent, possess a range of skills often approaching and sometimes exceeding the normal in the very activities from which they are excluded. The competence literature is reviewed in Goldstein, Social and Occupational Adjustment, in MENTAL RETARDATION 214-58 (Heber & Stevens eds. 1964) (supplemented annually in MENTAL RETARDATION RESEARCH ABSTRACTS).
  The literature as it pertains to learning and occupational competences, and the common disqualification by law, is reviewed in part elsewhere in this paper. Here, by way of example, note some of the studies indicating competence for marriage, for voting, and for driving, as to which, THE MENTALLY DISABLED AND THE LAW, supra at 226-29, 240-43, 308-09, 334-40, 308, the retarded are commonly disqualified by law. On marriage, see Baller, Charles & Miller, Mid-Life Attainment of the Mentally Retarded: A Longitudinal Study, 75 GENETIC PSYCHOLOGY MONOGRAPHS 235, 255-65, 310 (1967); Bobroff, A Survey of Social and Civic Participation of Adults Formerly in Classes for the Mentally Retarded, 61 AM. J. MENTAL DEFICIENCY 127, 128 (1956); Dinger, Post-School Adjustment of Former Educable Retarded Pupils, 27 EXCEPTIONAL CHILDREN 353, 355-56 (1961); Fairbank, The Subnormal Child—Seventeen Years After, 17 MENTAL HYGIENE 177, 182, 190, 196-97, 204 (1933); Hartzler, A Ten-Year Survey of Girls Discharged from the Laurelton State Village, 57 AM J. MENTAL DEFICIENCY 512, 516 (1953); Muench, A Follow-up of Mental Defectives After Eighteen Years, 39 J. ABNORMAL & SOCIAL PSYCHOLOGY 407, 412-14 (1944); Shaw & Wright, The Married Mental Defective: A Followup Study, THE LANCET, Jan. 30, 1960, at 273-74; MATTINSON, MARRIAGE AND MENTAL HANDICAP 180 (1971). On voting, see Baller, Charles & Miller, supra at 257; Bobroff, supra at 130-31; Dinger, supra at 356; Peterson & Smith, The Post-School Adjustment of Educable Mentally Retarded Adults Compared with Adults of Normal Intelligence, 26 EXCEPTIONAL CHILDREN 404, 406 (1960). On driving, see Baller, Charles & Miller, supra at 257, 260-66, 310; Bobroff, supra at 131-32; Fairbank, supra at 201; Peterson & Smith, supra at 406; Gutshall, Harper & Burke, An Exploratory Study of the Interrelations Among Driving Ability, Driving Exposure and Socio-economic Status of Low, Average and High Intelligence Males, 35 EXCEPTIONAL CHILDREN 43-47 (1968).
  Against this history of stereotype dominating fact, the recent gratuitous dictum of Mr. Justice Brennan, writing in Frontiero v. Richardson, 411 U.S. 677, 686 (1973) for four members of the Court who would have held sex a suspect criteria, that

   [w]hat differentiates sex from such non-suspect statutes [sic] as intelligence or physical disability, and aligns it with the recognized suspect criteria, is that the sex characteristic frequently bears no relation to ability to perform or to contribute to society, 411 U.S. at 686.

is outrageous. This dictum derives almost verbatim, as the opinion indicates, 411 U.S. at 686 n.18, from Developments in the Law—Equal Protection, 82 HARV. L. REV. 1065, 1173-74 (1969), where the notion was presented, uninformed and unanalyzed. Intelligence and physical disability are con-

LEGAL RIGHTS TO SERVICES

Despite the general welfare clause of the Constitution's Preamble and the guarantee of life in the fifth and fourteenth amendments, there is in the federal Constitution no presently recognized affirmative right to services for retarded citizens or for any citizens.[24] Recently, Professors Michelman and Sparer and others have suggested theories of "minimum protection" and of the "right to life," which would give constitutional underpinning to affirmative rights to services.[25] But recently the Supreme Court also has become explicit about the matter, seeming to say in *Lindsey v. Normet* that there is no constitutional right to housing,[26] in *Jefferson v. Hackney* that there is no constitutional right to welfare,[27] and in *San Antonio Independent School District v. Rodriguez* that there is no constitutional right to edu-

---

nected with "lack of merit or performance," not in the "common experience," as the Harvard note had it, but only in common stereotype. *See* Note, *Equal Protection and Intelligence Classification*, 26 STAN. L. REV. 647 (1974).

　　More recently, in Cleveland Bd. of Educ. v. LaFleur, 414 U.S. 632, 644-646 (1974), the Court held an "irrebuttable presumption of physical incompetency" embodied in a school rule imposing mandatory pregnancy leave to be "neither necessarily nor universally true" and, therefore, violative of the due process clause. In contrast to the *Frontiero* dictum, the *LaFleur* Court, in an opinion by Mr. Justice Stewart, found:

> While the medical experts . . . differed on many points, they unanimously agreed on one—the ability of any particular pregnant woman to continue at work past any fixed time in her pregnancy is very much an individual matter. Even assuming *arguendo* that there are some women who would be physically unable to work past the particular cut-off dates embodied in the challenged rules, it is evident that there are large numbers of teachers who are fully capable of continuing work longer than the . . . regulations will allow, 414 U.S. at 645 (footnote omitted).

Indeed, the *LaFleur* Court articulated its suspicion that maternity leave rules "rationalized" in physical incompetence terms have their source, rather, in stereotype:

> The records in these cases suggest that the maternity leave regulations may have originally been inspired by other less weighty considerations. For example, . . . [a] Superintendent . . . testified that the rule had been adopted in part to save pregnant teachers from embarrassment at the hands of giggling school children. . . . [S]everal members of the . . . Board thought a mandatory leave rule was justified . . . to insulate school-children from the sight of conspicuously pregnant women. One member . . . thought that it was "not good for the school system" for students to view pregnant teachers, "because some of the kid [sic] say, my teacher swallowed a watermelon, things like that."
>
> The school boards have not contended in this Court that these considerations can serve as a legitimate basis for a rule requiring pregnant women to leave work; we thus note the comments only to illustrate the possible role of outmoded taboos in the adoption of the rules. Cf. Green v. Waterford Board of Education, 473 F.2d 629, 635 (CA2) ("Whatever may have been the reaction in Queen Victoria's time, pregnancy is no longer a dirty world." 414 U.S. at 641 n.9.

[24] The constitutions of the several states almost universally guarantee rights to education and may eventually come explicitly to provide for other affirmative rights to government services. *See, e.g.,* Morris, *New Horizons for a State Bill of Rights,* 45 WASH. L. REV. 474 (1970).

[25] Michelman, *Foreword: On Protecting the Poor Through the Fourteenth Amendment,* 83 HARV. L. REV. 7, 14-16 (1969); Michelman, *The Advent of a Right to Housing: A Current Appraisal,* 5 HARV. CIV. RIGHTS—CIV. LIB. L. REV. 207 (1970); Sparer, *The Right to Welfare,* in THE RIGHTS OF AMERICANS 65, 83-84 (N. Dorsen ed. 1970); Karst & Horowitz, *Reitman v. Mulkey: A Telophase of Substantive Equal Protection,* 1967 SUP. CT. REV. 39, 55-56. *See also* Dworkin, *There Oughta Be a Law, reprinted in* SOCIETY AND THE LEGAL ORDER 632-33 (R. Schwartz & J. Skolnick eds. 1970). *But see* Winter, *Poverty, Economic Equality and the Equal Protection Clause,* 1972 SUP. CT. REV. 41, esp. 66-85.

[26] 405 U.S. 56, 74 (1972).

[27] 406 U.S. 535, 545-51 (1972).

cation.[28] These cases, however, are not conclusive,[29] and developmental work to support affirmative rights to services will undoubtedly continue.[30]

But the claims of retarded citizens to services in the community do not depend on these developments. One can construct from the social fact discussed previously and its place in our legal scheme, and from other places in the Constitution and in the laws, much of the dynamic necessary to secure and realize the rights of these citizens.[31] To be sure, since there is no recognized direct affirmative right to governmental services, what we are doing is something like pushing with a string.[32] Several strings are available to us: equal protection, due process, federal statutes (especially section 504 of the Rehabilitation Act of 1973), state constitutions, state statutes enforceable in mandamus, the common law of tort and contract, taxpayer suits, and, throughout, procedural due process and the structuring of relief.

Types of Services

Before a consideration of the uses of each of these doctrinal strands, four types of services need to be distinguished. This tentative typology of services will then be used in suggesting the analysis and argument appropriate in claiming each.

[28] 411 U.S. 1, 35 (1973).

[29] Indeed, in *Rodriguez*, 411 U.S. at 36-37, the Court explicitly left open the question of a constitutional right of *access* to education:

> Even if it were conceded that some identifiable quantum of education is a constitutionally protected prerequisite to . . . [the right to speak or to vote], we have no indication that the present levels of educational expenditure in Texas provide an education that falls short. Whatever merit appellees' argument might have if a State's financing system occasioned an absolute denial of educational opportunities to any of its children, that argument provides no basis for finding an interference with fundamental rights where only relative differences in spending levels are involved and where—as is true in the present case—no charge fairly could be made that the system fails to provide each child with an opportunity to acquire the basic minimum skills. . . .

> Similarly, although the welfare rules upheld in Jefferson v. Hackney, 406 U.S. 535, *rehearing denied,* 409 U.S. 898 (1972), and Dandridge v. Williams, 397 U.S. 471 (1970), did undoubtedly exclude some persons from *public assistance,* no one was denied an *income* altogether. By hypothesis (the Court majority's) the additional family members in *Dandridge* would share in the maximum grant. *See* 397 U.S. at 477, 480-81 ("*some* aid is provided to all. . . .") (emphasis supplied); compare the dissent 397 U.S. at 511-12. By definition of eligibility for public assistance those denied welfare under *Hackney* had *some*—indeed, according to the eligibility rule, too much—income, 406 U.S. at 540, 541 & n.8. Similarly, there was no showing in *Lindsey* that without the house in question plaintiff would have *no* house. These cases are about what a minimum might be, not about whether a minimum is constitutionally required. The minimum protection theory remains, neither rejected nor yet adopted.

[30] For the most recent approaches to a theory, see Michelman, *supra* note 14; Tribe, *supra* note 18.

[31] On the relationship between litigation and the other modes of petitioning the government for redress of grievances, see Gilhool, *supra* note 4, 39 EXCEPTIONAL CHILDREN at 599; *cf.* Gilhool, *supra* note 4, 50 PEABODY J. EDUC. at 125-27.

A recent and significant illustration of this relationship is the adoption of the Rehabilitation Act of 1973 §§ 503-04, 29 U.S.C.A. §§ 793-94 (Supp. 1974) (*see* text at note 111 *infra*).

[32] Without undertaking to articulate exactly the extent to which it succeeded or failed (and my view is that it has significantly succeeded) or why (*see* Sparer, *supra* note 25), the analogy is to the welfare litigation strategy pursued by various welfare rights groups. The final objective (on one view) was a guaranteed annual income (one view would add "or job," *cf.* Wexler, *Practicing Law for Poor People,* 79 YALE L.J. 1049, 1066 (1970)). The strategy was to transmute the public assistance program into a guaranteed annual income by shaving restrictive eligibility requirements (eliminating durational residence requirements, man in the house rules, liens and other repayment obligations, relatives responsibility rules and other non-need related requirements), by eliminating grant maximums, by effecting rising grant minimums, by evening (up) differences among grant levels, categorically and geographically, by ensuring privacy, independence, and respect (eliminating midnight searches, home visits, and service requirements and simplifying the eligibility determination process), and throughout by ensuring that all persons eligible know of their rights and, if they wish, claim them.

Type one services are those available generally, to all citizens, and which the retarded would use and enjoy in the same way as the rest of the citizenry: street cleaning, garbage collection, fire and police protection, and perhaps recreation, education, and employment services.

Type two are services available generally, to all citizens, and which the retarded would use in some special way. Access to public buildings, for example, is generally available to all citizens, but physically handicapped citizens if they are to partake of access will require special provisions. Some would identify recreation, education, and employment as type two services, but they are, it will be argued in this paper, more properly classified as type one services.

Type three are services available only to some citizens, classified on grounds that do not touch on retardation as such, and which the retarded would use as part of the "some" on the same terms as other members of the defined class. Public assistance, Medicare, Medicaid, or homemaker services, for example, are available to some, with eligibility defined categorically, and if the retarded would otherwise be among the "some," they would be eligible.

Type four are services available to mentally retarded citizens as such; for example, supervised residential services.

With respect to each of the four types of services, there are two quite different claims that can be made. One is for access to the service; the other is for quality of service. Each claim utilizes quite different analysis and argument.

The Constitutional Strands: Equal Protection and Due Process

It is in the equal protection argument that the social facts which characterize the historic experience of the retarded citizen have their most apparent effect. Past stigmatization, isolation, and irrational exclusion of the mentally retarded provide a strong basis for arguing that a legislative or administrative classification which excludes or differentially burdens retarded citizens is suspect, subject to strict scrutiny, and justifiable only by a compelling interest of the state.[33]

Even on a lesser standard — rational scrutiny, if that be its proper name[34]— this historic experience requires that the relationship of means to end be scrutinized warily, and the legislature's or administrator's judgment be measured against the true relevant facts.

Even on the least standard, minimum rationality, the effect of these social facts survives. On the one hand once a classification created under the distorting influence of those facts is deprived of the comfort of the distortion (as it may be by careful proof, even on this rational basis test), it is often seen to be starkly arbitrary without any justification even in reasonable speculation;[35] and on the other hand, under that distorting influence very often patently arbitrary things have been done.[36]

[33] *See* Wald, Chapter 2 of this volume.
[34] Gunther, *supra* note 14, distinguishes three equal protection standards and denominates them "strict scrutiny," "rationality scrutiny" and "minimum rationality."
[35] *See* text at notes 60-64 *infra.*
[36] *See* text accompanying notes 59-60 *infra.*

Two cases, one a claim for education and the other a claim for health services, may help by way of example to focus the analysis. The claim for education was framed, from the beginning, in terms of access[37] and education was treated as a type one service. In *McInnis v. Shapiro*[38] grievance about the quality of education and a claim for "special education" brought by ghetto children had been held to be nonjusticiable: There are no clear or authoritative standards, the court found, by which a judgment of quality or the match of "special needs" to "special education" may be tested, and since courts are in the business of making only principled decisions this claim could not be decided by the courts. The claim for *access* to a free public education accorded generally to all children, however, does not raise the *McInnis* problem.

However problematic the quality of education delivered to retarded children who were in school, a very great number of retarded children were not in school at all.[39] Furthermore, it was unnecessary to frame the claim for education in terms of some "special" education, since some governmental services, education, recreation, and employment services among them, although available to all, are by their nature special: Different people partake differently of these services, and the services themselves are designed more or less differently for different persons. The statutes of virtually every state provide, as does California's Education Code, section 8505, that "Any course of study . . . shall be designed to fit the needs of the pupils for which the course of study is prescribed."[40] Normative educational theory is uniformly in terms of fitting education to each child. Descriptively, education is varied things for various children. The legal definition of "education" has never been univocal. The briefest review of the cases shows that since its inception in the nineteenth century, public education has never been limited even to reading, writing, and arithmetic.[41] Education for the profoundly and severely retarded, the education most likely to be regarded as "different" from that accorded children generally, is not different. Teaching a child to walk is not functionally different from driver training; both are about mobility. Teaching a child to feed himself is not functionally dif-

---

[37] Contrast the access to type one services theory of the right to education cases with the McInnis-prone theory suggested in the creative, Hall, *The Politics of Special Education* 1970 Inequality in Education 17, 22.

[38] 293 F. Supp. 327, 335-36 (N.D. Ill. 1968), *aff'd sub nom.* McInnis v. Ogilvie, 394 U.S. 322 (1969). *See* text at notes 47-49 for alternate approaches to the quality of education. (In my opinion, standards for judgment of quality and of appropriateness—input and output standards—*may* be more readily ascertainable and more certain in the education of exceptional children than they are in general education and the justiciability problem of *McInnis* may therefore be less a problem in litigation about the education of exceptional children.)

[39] Some 13,000 out-of-school retarded children were located in the search after judgment in Pennsylvania. The 1970 census shows some 80,000 children, aged 7-15, not in school in California. *See* U.S. Bureau of the Census, Dep't of Commerce, PC(1) C6 California, Census of the Population: 1970 General Social and Economic Characteristics 6-421 (1972). The greatest number of these out-of-school children is probably handicapped. The Children's Defense Fund (1745 R Street, N.W., Washington, D.C.) has developed the methodology for deriving these census figures and is now field testing them in several jurisdictions.

[40] Cal. Educ. Code § 8505 (West 1969). Among the similar provisions of other states, *see, e.g.,* Conn. Gen. Stat. Ann. § 10-4a (Supp. 1973) ("suitable"); Ohio Rev. Code Ann. § 3301.07 (Supp. 1973) ("sufficient to meet the needs"); Ore. Rev. Stat. § 326.011 (1973) ("best suited"); Pa. Stat. Ann. tit. 24, § 15-1512 (1962) ("adapted to the age, development and needs").

[41] *See* the definitions of "education" collected in 14 Words and Phrases 123-27 (1952). *See also* Brief of Amicus Curiae in Lori Case v. California, Civil No. 13127 (Cal. Ct. App. 1973) (available from the National Center for Law and the Handicapped).

ferent from health, hygiene, or home economics. Toilet training is not functionally different from the self-control and self-care taught in health, hygiene, or physical education. Nor are the teaching techniques different from those used in "ordinary" education. Thus, the claim for education was a claim for education no more different or special than the difference or specialty already accommodated in the education delivered generally to all children. Retarded children were claiming no variation greater than the variation already accommodated in the service called education.

The strongest equal protection claim can be made for type one and type three services. For, in services extended generally to all or to some categorically defined, except for the retarded, the suspect classification or the patent irrationality of the exclusion springs starkly into relief. Relief in such a case (providing the retarded with services others already enjoy) smacks not at all of an affirmative constitutional right to services. Thus, it becomes important to cast what might on first glance seem to be type two services as what they really are, namely, type one services.[42] Education,[43] recreation, employment services,[44] and other services as well[45] can be readily demonstrated to be type one services. What is called for is an application of the

[42] The strongest, or at least the surest, case for type two services, and type four services, is a statutory case. *E.g.,* Washington Urban League, Inc. v. Washington Metropolitan Area Transit Authority, Civil No. 776-72 (D.D.C., June 29, 1973) (permanently enjoining the D.C. Transit Authority from constructing the District's subway until and unless it will accommodate physically handicapped citizens as required by the Act of March 5, 1970, Pub. L. No. 91-205, 84 Stat. 49, *amending* 42 U.S.C. § 4151). *See* text at notes 86-134 *infra.*
  This is not to say that there is not a sound constitutional case against treating equally persons who are situated unequally. Dissenting in Dennis v. United States, 339 U.S. 162, 184 (1950), Mr. Justice Frankfurter wrote, "[T]here is no greater inequality than equal treatment of unequals." *See, e.g.,* Selph v. City Council of Los Angeles, Civil No. 74-48DWW (C.D. Cal., filed Jan. 7, 1974) (seeking access to the polls for physically handicapped and elderly citizens).

[43] *See* text at notes 39-41 *supra.*

[44] *See* the Federal Employment Service Act, 29 U.S.C. § 49(b), (g) (1970), and the state employment acts adopted pursuant thereto.

[45] Although residential services in the sense of specially organized and supervised residences are undoubtedly type four services, many, if not most, of the significant difficulties encountered in the effort to realize these services for retarded citizens are type one difficulties and should be recognized and addressed as such.
  Zoning, for example, functions in significant part as gatekeeping, regulating entry to such type one services as street cleaning, parks, fire and police protection, and so on. The difficulty in exclusionary zoning cases is that legislators are doubtful about sharing these services and the amenities they support, available generally to all citizens, with the retarded. Apart from statutory approaches to exclusionary zoning and apart from equal protection challenges based on fundamental interests implicated by exclusionary zoning — the right to settle, *see, e.g.,* Corfield v. Coryell, 6 F. Cas. 546 (No. 3230) (C.C.E.D. Pa. 1823), and the right of citizens to associate freely together, Boraas v. Village of Belle Terre, 476 F.2d 806 (2d Cir. 1973), *rev'd,* 416 U.S. 1 (1974) (holding a zoning ordinance prohibiting unrelated persons from occupying a residence in an area zoned "one family," a denial of equal protection) — such exclusions may be fruitfully addressed as a denial to retarded citizens of access to type one services. So addressed becomes the crux of the matter the distorted, irrational factual judgments underlying the exclusion: that the retarded are prone to criminality, that the retarded require medical supervision, that the retarded are uneducable and unemployable. On the facts confronting the stereotype which haunts zoning regulation, see the Affidavit of Gunnar Dybwad, July 25, 1970, in Defoe v. San Francisco City Planning Comm. 1 Civil No. 30789 (Cal. Ct. App. 1st Dist. 1973), and on approaches to the zoning problem see Chandler and Ross, Chapter 11 of this volume. Stated still more globally, the point here is that exclusionary zoning is merely the flip side of the historic effort to separate the retarded, see note 8 *supra,* and the removal of zoning barriers is part and parcel of undoing the deprivation of liberty involved in remote institutionalization. The zoning cases, therefore, are very much at the boundary where equal protection and due process meet. *See* text at notes 80-89 *infra* and *cf.* Burt, Chapter 14 of this volume.
  Similar type one access questions are involved in challenges to restrictive safety and fire codes.

principle of normalization,[46] increasingly the reigning perspective in work in retardation, to the framing of the claims of retarded citizens.

Although equal protection claims for access to type one services are argued, the pursuit of service quality by litigation is not thereby abandoned.[47] Rather, quality is pursued in doctrinally distinct ways; for example, by structuring an administrative process and assigning questions of quality there in the first instance, with the traditionally familiar and institutionally comfortable review of these proceedings in the courts[48] or by redress through the common law forms of tort or contract.[49]

The crux of this approach through equal protection to rights to services in the community was clearly stated in *Brown v. Board of Education*,[50] in which the segregation of students by race was held unconstitutional. In a passage central to the access to education cases[51] and declared by the Court as recently as *Rodriguez*

For example, the successful administrative challenges to a proposed ruling of the Industrial Board, Department of Labor and Industry, under Pennsylvania's building and construction codes, which would have allowed residential facilities for the retarded only in stone and brick buildings with wide hallway and egress accommodations (thereby precluding the location of such residences in Philadelphia and numerous other Pennsylvania communities and consigning mentally retarded citizens again to remote territories), was based on the facts (*e.g.*, the small proportion of the retarded who are immobile) and on equal protection argumentation. *In re* Classification of Residential Facilities for the Retarded (Pa. Dept. of Labor and Indus., Indus. Bd. 1972).

[46] The most influential statement of the normalization principle is Nirje, *The Normalization Principle and Its Human Management Implications*, in CHANGING PATTERNS IN RESIDENTIAL SERVICES FOR THE MENTALLY RETARDED 179-95 (R. Kugel & W. Wolfensberger eds. 1969). *Cf.* ten Broek & Marson, *The Disabled and the Law of Welfare*, 54 CALIF. L. REV. 810, 815-16 (1966) (denominating normalization the "integrationist" perspective, as contrasted with the "custodial").

[47] In the right to education cases the federal courts have uniformly declared a standard of appropriateness: The access to education granted must be access to appropriate education. PARC, 343 F. Supp. at 302-03 ("[A] free preschool program of education and training appropriate to [the child's] learning capacities. . . ."); Mills v. Board of Education, 348 F. Supp. 866 (D.D.C. 1972) [hereinafter cited as Mills]; Lebanks v. Spears, 60 F.R.D. 135 (E.D. La. 1973); *In re* H.G., Civil No. 8930 (Sup. Ct. N.D., April 30, 1974); *cf.* Appeal of Riley Reid, No. 8742, at 6 (Commissioner of Education of the State of New York, Nov. 26, 1973).

The courts borrowed the appropriateness standard from state statutes. *See, e.g.*, the provisions collected at note 40 *supra*. In addition, the record in each case showed that placement of an exceptional child in an inappropriate program is tantamount to excluding the child from schooling. *Cf.* Lau v. Nichols 414 U.S. 563, 566 (1974). There, holding on Title VI grounds that Chinese-speaking children cannot be assigned to English-only classes, the Court found: "students who do not understand English are effectively foreclosed from any meaningful education. . . . [Their] classroom experiences [are] wholly incomprehensible and in no way meaningful."

[48] *See* text at notes 155-67 *infra*. Thus, in the right to education cases, enforcement of the appropriateness standard was not undertaken by the courts, but was assigned to the administrative process, with review in the state courts by way of narrow certiorari. *See generally* Dimond, *supra* note 4.

[49] *See* text at notes 144-47 *infra*.

[50] 347 U.S. 483 (1954).

[51] In 1960, in a working paper prepared for the White House Conference on Children and Youth, Gunnar Dybwad, then executive director of the National Association for Retarded Children (NARC), invoked the decision in *Brown* and noted that still "insufficient attention had been given . . . to the legal status of the mentally retarded child. . . ." G. DYBWAD, CHALLENGES IN MENTAL RETARDATION 210 (1964). *See also* Kay, Farnham, Karren, Krakel & Diamond, *Legal Planning for the Mentally Retarded*, 60 CALIF. L. REV. 438 (1972).

In 1955 Leopold Lippman had written in a letter to the editor, in Children Limited, June 1955, at 9 (NARC's newspaper), "that [Brown's] statement of equal opportunity applies to the handicapped as it does to minorities." Letter from Leopold Lippman to editor of Children Limited, June 9, 1955. Elizabeth Boggs wrote to the same effect in *Legal Aspects of Mental Retardation*, in PREVENTION AND TREATMENT OF MENTAL RETARDATION 407, 408 (Phillips ed. 1966). Compare John Davis' argument in *Brown, supra* note 9. No other members of the legal profession, however, paid heed until years later.

to have "lost none of its vitality,"[52] a unanimous Supreme Court said in *Brown*:

> [Education] is required in the performance of our most basic responsibilities. . . .
> It is the very foundation of good citizenship. Today it is a principal instrument
> in awakening the child to cultural values, in preparing him for later . . . train-
> ing, and in helping him to adjust normally to his environment. In these days,
> it is doubtful that any child may reasonably be expected to succeed in life if he is
> denied the opportunity of an education. Such an opportunity where the state has
> undertaken to provide it, is a right which must be made available to all on equal
> terms.[53]

If "it is doubtful" that an ordinary "child may reasonably be expected to succeed
in life if he is denied the opportunity of an education," how much clearer is it that
the retarded child denied an education may not be expected to succeed. For the
ordinary child may be expected to learn willy-nilly, wandering in the world, watching television, or riding the bus. The retarded child, however, if he is to learn to
his full capacities requires a formal, structured opportunity to learn. Furthermore,
the retarded child denied the opportunity to learn is in jeopardy not merely of success, but of liberty and of life itself.[54]

Given the present fact that all retarded children can learn, the purposes of
public education will not brook a classification denying retarded children access
to it.[55] Any exclusionary classification will be arbitrary. This is so whatever the equal
protection standard. To test this conclusion consider one purpose consistently
offered by the states to support exclusionary classification; namely, saving money.

On any full record, exclusion must be seen not to save but to squander. Absent
education, the retarded are very likely to be institutionalized.[56] The cost of institutional care, per year per person, averages $5,865, almost $400,000 for a lifetime.[57]
The cost of special education is 1.9 times the average per student cost, or $1,936
per year, for most retarded students; 3.5 times for some, 5.9 for a few, and 2.2 times
overall; the average lifetime cost of education for the mentally retarded student
is about $26,000.[58] Proper education not only avoids the costs of institutional care,

---

[52] 411 U.S. at 1295.

[53] 347 U.S. at 493.

[54] The rate of institutionalization, *cf.* note 6 *supra,* is significantly higher for retarded citizens who
have been denied schooling. And the death rate of these citizens, in institutions and outside, is
significantly greater than it would be if education had not been denied, by reason of the absence
of danger avoidance and self-help skills which education would bring. R. CONLEY, THE ECONOMICS
OF MENTAL RETARDATION 88-95 (1973) [hereinafter cited as CONLEY]. The equal protection analysis
here does not depend on those facts or upon the invocation of certain still unrecognized "fundamental interests." But neither can equal protection analysis easily escape them. *See* text at notes
80-89 *infra.* Again we are at the boundary between equal protection and due process.

[55] The present analysis sets to the side the question of fundamental interests. The passage from *Brown*
is invoked not for the fundamentality of education, but for its authoritative statement of the purposes
of education, against which a statutory classification must be measured. This is so out of deference
to *Rodriguez,* though as we have seen, *supra* note 28, *Rodriguez* leaves open the fundamentality of
access to education.

[56] *Cf.* CONLEY 298-300, 88-95, esp. 91 and the works cited therein, esp. Graliker & Koch, *A Study of
Factors Influencing Placement of Retarded Children in a State Residential Institution,* 1965 AM. J.
MENTAL DEFICIENCY 553. *Compare* CONLEY tables at 86 showing the school ages 5-19 as the predomi-
nant age of admission to institutions.

[57] CONLEY 96, 298, 322 (1970 figures).

[58] CONLEY 146-48, 289-97 (these costs may be slightly understated since Conley's number of years in
school is lower than one would expect). *See* CONLEY 284-89.

but it yields employment for the retarded, lifetime earnings ranging, at least, from $23,000 to $185,000, and, of course these earnings yield taxes.[59] Thus, on the middle standard of equal protection scrutiny, the exclusionary classification fails to serve, indeed it frustrates, its supposed purpose of saving money.

Furthermore, the records in each of the litigated access to education cases indicate that each out-of-school mentally retarded child has a functional twin who is being accorded a free public education. There is every reason to suppose this is so in each state. Exclusion of any particular retarded child thus becomes as patently arbitrary, even on minimum scrutiny, as excluding every red-headed child or excluding every other child.

And, finally, in a holding apparently applicable on any equal protection standard,[60] the Court announced in *Shapiro v. Thompson*[61] that protecting the fisc is never in itself a constitutionally sufficient ground for classification; any such classification must have an independently rational ground, other than saving money:

> [A] state has a valid interest in preserving the fiscal integrity of its programs. It may legitimately attempt to limit its expenditures, whether for public assistance, public education, or any other program. But a state may not accomplish such a purpose by invidious distinctions between classes of its citizens. It could not, for example, reduce expenditures for education by barring indigent children from its schools. . . . [A]ppellants must do more than show that denying . . . benefits . . . saves money. The saving of costs . . . cannot justify an otherwise invidious classification.[62]

Nor, constitutionally, may the fisc be protected by delay.[63] In *Watson v. City of Memphis,*[64] access to recreation services had been denied to black citizens. Finding an equal protection right to access, the Court wrote:

[59] CONLEY table 50, at 272-84, 292-97.

[60] In support of the proposition that follows, the *Shapiro* Court at 394 U.S. 618, 633 n.11 relied upon Rinaldi v. Yeager, 384 U.S. 305 (1966), a case regarded by Gunther, *supra* note 14, at 27, as at most a middle "rational scrutiny" case, and in its own terms a "some rationality" or minimum scrutiny case. *See* Note, *Legislative Purposes, Rationality, and Equal Protection,* 82 YALE L.J. 123 (1972).

[61] 394 U.S. 618, 633 (1969).

[62] *Id.* Occasionally, though not often in a courtroom, someone will suggest that education may be restricted only to persons who will return a contribution to the state. Or, faced with the fact of contributions by retarded citizens such as the income (and hence tax) data given in the text represent, they will say that education should go first to those who will contribute "most." At its most sophisticated, such a justification for exclusion is merely a variant on the principle of *triage* — the battleground axiom which would accord medical treatment first to those least injured. L. LEWIN, TRIAGE 136-37 (1973). Apart from its Hobbesian (and therefore presumptively repugnant constitutionally) roots, the problem with it is that education is not a "state insurance program," *cf.* Shapiro v. Thompson, 394 U.S. at 632-33. We do not exact or enforce a promise of performance before granting entry to school. Indeed, such a scheme would raise severe constitutional problems of its own, not unlike McReynolds' with Plato's.

[63] A number of states, *e.g.,* Arkansas, Colorado, and New Mexico, has responded to the decisions in *PARC, Mills,* and *Lebanks* by adopting statutes providing access to education to all exceptional children to be phased in over 5 years, or 6, or 10. *But see* Harrison v. Michigan, 350 F. Supp. 846, 847-48 (E.D. Mich. 1972) (indicating that 1 year, no more, is a reasonable time for effectuating the duty to provide access to all); Opinion No. 73-187 of the Arkansas attorney general (Sept. 7, 1973) (holding despite the statute's 6-year clause that the obligation to educate all handicapped children was effective immediately); *PARC,* (where access for some 13,000 previously out-of-school retarded children, was achieved within 16 months between the May 5, 1972 final order of the court and the opening of the school year in September 1973).

[64] 373 U.S. 526 (1963).

The rights here asserted are, like all such rights, *present* rights; they are not merely hopes to some *future* enjoyment of some formalistic constitutional promise. The basic guarantees of our Constitution are warrants for the here and now and, unless there is overwhelmingly compelling reason, they are to be promptly fulfilled.

The claims of the city to further delay in affording petitioners that to which they are clearly and unquestionably entitled cannot be upheld except upon the most convincing and impressive demonstration by the city that such delay is manifestly compelled by constitutionally cognizable circumstances warranting the exercise of an appropriate equitable discretion by the Court.

[V]indication of conceded constitutional rights cannot be made dependent upon any theory that it is less expensive to deny than to afford them.[65]

The second example of the equal protection analysis, a claim in the California courts for round-the-clock personal and individual nursing care, illustrates the present limits of constitutional argument before even the most venturesome of courts. It illustrates as well the relationship between constitutional and statutory argument and the importance of a thorough grasp and careful use of the statutory strand in seeking services in the community. The case, *Roberts v. Brian*,[66] will serve also as a paradigm for approach to type four services, those available to handicapped citizens as such.[67]

John Roberts, a citizen with myoclonic epilepsy, required individualized nursing care during all of his waking hours, for his seizures came frequently and unpredictably and in the absence of prompt assistance would bring his death. Roberts lived in a nursing home whose routine nursing service was reimbursed by Medi-Cal. Neither the nursing home nor Medi-Cal, however, provided the personal attendants his condition required. For some years the cost of these attendants had been advanced by Roberts' sister. After an administrative hearing in the department of health care services found that there was no provisions under Medi-Cal permitting payment for attendant care, John Roberts went to court.

The Superior Court of Los Angeles County scrutinized the Medi-Cal statue and regulations, but found no authority therein for "personal and individual nursing care . . . not less than fifteen hours per day.[68] Hurdling difficult equal protection problems and being moved, no doubt, by some basic notion of a right to life, Judge Pacht looked to the provision under department regulations of "pulmonary respirators and renal dialysis machines" to others with "unique forms of illness and conditions of disability" and found the denial of the individualized nursing care required for Roberts' "unique illness and condition of disability" to be a denial of the equal protection of the law.[69]

On appeal, the California Supreme Court did not reach the constitutional ground. Instead the court indulged a careful, broad, and creative reading of the Medi-Cal statute focused by the legislature's declared "intention, whenever

[65] 373 U.S. at 533, 537 (emphasis in original).
[66] 6 Cal. 3d 1, 489 P.2d 1378, 98 Cal. Rptr. 50 (1971).
[67] Or perhaps, of type three services, those categorically available to some. Courts may be more comfortable in viewing type four services as type three, and since the question is so much a matter of which rung of Plato's ladder of abstraction one chooses to perch on, counsel wisely so frames it. As the lower court in *Roberts* had it, personal and individualized nursing care for a person with myclonic epilepsy is surely the functional equivalent of a renal dialysis machine for another.
[68] Roberts v. Brian, 6 Cal. 3d at 1-4, 489 P.2d at 1378-80, 98 Cal. Rptr. at 50-52.
[69] *Id.*

feasible, that the needs of recipients of public assistance for health care and related remedial or preventive services be met."[70] The director of health care services argued that the Medi-Cal program commanded limited funds, insufficient to meet all medical needs of individual recipients; he must, he argued, therefore choose to fulfill some needs but fail to fulfill others.[71] The court lightly turned this argument with the characterization: "Respondent does not argue that aid to petitioner is financially infeasible, but simply that he has issued no regulations providing for such care."[72]

The director, having exercised his authority to "prescribe policies" under the statute and having created a series of classifications for treatment, evidently including pulmonary respirators and renal dialysis machines, urged that an eligible patient can receive only such medical treatment as comes within one or another of these categories. Roberts, he argued, suffers from a unique illness, with abnormal requirements.[73] The court, however, found a regulation establishing a categorical service within which personal and individual nursing service for a myoclonic epileptic must be encompassed.[74] In Title 22, California Administrative Code § 51215, setting standards for nursing homes, the director had provided that the facility must "employ staff sufficient in number and qualifications to meet the requirements of the patient accepted for care" and must "provide 24-hour nursing services adequate in quality amount to meet the needs of patients who are admitted."[75] In construing these regulations the court found:

> [The director] argues that nursing homes need only provide adequate general nursing services, and not the exceptional services required for [Roberts]. The regulation, however, does not speak in terms of meeting the prescribed needs of an average or typical patient, but clearly ordains that services meet the prescribed personal needs of the specific patients accepted for care.[76]

Indeed, the California Supreme Court noted that even absent the state regulations,

[70] CAL. WELF. & INST. CODE § 14001.1 (West 1972).
[71] The necessity of an independent rational ground for choice (*see* discussion of *Shapiro* in the text accompanying notes 61-63) other than limited funds appears as a canon of statutory interpretation, as well as a constitutional canon. Note that the director had cited Dandridge v. Williams, 397 U.S. 471, 487 (1970) in his support. Note also, in the text accompanying notes 75-78, the Roberts court's treatment of a second cost question, "provided . . . rates do not increase over-all program costs."
    Judicial treatment of cost objections in the face of well-framed claims for evenhandedness, whether framed in statutory or constitutional terms — that is to say, judicial steadfastness in pressing scrutiny to the point of a reality judgment — is surely one of those styles which distinguish the courts institutionally. *See* text accompanying notes 13-15 *supra*.
[72] 6 Cal. 3d at 5, 489 P.2d at 1381, 98 Cal. Rptr. at 53.
[73] In other words: "Roberts is claiming a type four service and for *this* type four service there is no statutory or regulation authority."
[74] In other words: "there is regulation authority, and, besides, it's a type three service."
[75] 6 Cal. 3d at 5, 489 P.2d at 1381, 98 Cal. Rptr. at 53.
[76] 6 Cal. 3d at 6, 489 P.2d at 1381, 98 Cal. Rptr. at 53. In their nature, the regulation nursing services (of a type three variety, like type one) are to be individuated, yielding the benefits of type four and type two services (*i.e.,* a fit to the individual). *Compare* discussion of education, etc., at notes 39-46 *supra*.
    Note also in the remainder of the *Roberts* opinion that a "needs" analysis which in other constitutional terms may be found by a court to present severe problems of justiciability, see McInnis v. Shapiro, 293 F. Supp. 327 (N.D. Ill. 1968), *aff'd sub nom.* McInnis v. Ogilvie, 394 U.S. 322 (1969), and discussion at note 38 *supra*, comes easily to a court engaged in unpacking a statute or a regulation. *See* discussion following note 47, *supra*.

the federal medical assistance law, framed in similar terms,[77] would require the same result.

Finally, recognizing that a nursing home need not accept any particular patient and that a home's decision will hinge upon whether the state must pay for the personal and individual nursing services, the court turns to construction of the payment provisions of the regulations. They provided:

> the per diem rate ... shall not exceed $14.00, except that the director may negotiate all-inclusive per diem rates ... for additional medically indicated covered services and provided that such negotiated rates do not increase over-all program cost.[78]

Considering the alternative costs, namely, the cost of hospitalization with special-duty nurses or intensive care,[79] the court held that $33 a day for personal and individual services in the nursing home would not increase overall program costs. Thus, the court concluded the director was in error in his finding that existing regulations provided no means by which Roberts could obtain the needed individualized nursing care. This service was ordered provided.

Before further consideration of nonconstitutional approaches to services in the community, consider how very much the equal protection arguments sound also of due process. It is not simply the doctrinal point made widely in contemporary discussions that the two substantive strands of the fourteenth amendment are significantly intertwined and perhaps interchangeable.[80] The similarity of equal protection and due process analysis here also reflects the fact that, for retarded citizens, behind every question of access to services in the community, and not distantly, is the question of institutionalization or liberty.

In a host of recent cases, courts have found a due process right to treatment; if a citizen is to be deprived of his liberty he must be provided treatment of the disabling condition.[81] Formulated originally in cases dealing with the commitment of persons found incompetent to stand trial[82] and not guilty by reason of insanity,[83] the right to treatment has been extended to the civilly committed mentally ill,[84]

---

[77] 42 U.S.C. § 1396(a)(26)(B)(ii) (Supp. II 1972): "a state plan . . . must provide—with respect to each patient ... adequate ... services ... to meet current health needs."

[78] 6 Cal. 3d at 7, 489 P.2d at 1382, 98 Cal. Rptr. at 54.

[79] The director had urged that hospitalization was not an alternative, on the ground that Roberts' condition could not be "successfully treated." The court held, however, that hospital "treatment" is not limited to "curing" of a disease: "persons with incurable diseases such as petitioner are often hospitalized to facilitate procedures which will alleviate their distress and prolong their lives. The Medi-Cal regulations do not limit hospitalization to cases of curable illnesses, but provide that the need for hospital care be determined in accordance with the usual standards of medical practice in the community." 6 Cal. 3d at 7-8, 489 P.2d at 1382, 98 Cal. Rptr. at 54-55.

[80] Michelman, *supra* note 25, at 7, 14-16; *cf.* Tribe, *supra* note 18; Winter, *supra* note 25, 100-02; McCloskey, *Economic Due Process and the Supreme Court,* 1962 Sup. Ct. Rev. 34.

[81] *See generally* Halpern, Chapter 13 of this volume; Burt, Chapter 14 of this volume.

[82] Ragsdale v. Overholser, 281 F.2d 943, 950 (D.C. Cir. 1960) (concurring opinion). *But see* Benton v. Reid, 231 F.2d 780 (D.C. Cir. 1956) (a tubercular citizen housed in "hospital wing" of the D.C. jail has right to treatment or release).

[83] Rouse v. Cameron, 373 F.2d 451, 453 (D.C. Cir. 1966).

[84] O'Connor v. Donaldson, 95 S.Ct. 2486 (1975), Lake v. Cameron, 364 F.2d 657 (D.C. Cir 1966); Nason v. Superintendent of Bridgewater State Hosp., 353 Mass. 604, 611-12, 233 N.E.2d 908, 913 (1968).

and to retarded citizens committed to institutions.[85] The due process right to treatment has the familiar due process corollary, the principle of the least restrictive alternative: the requisite treatment is to be delivered in the least restrictive setting.[86] If the injunction to provide treatment in the least restrictive setting were given operational meaning (and to date it has not been)[87] the result plainly would be services to the retarded in the community. At some point, equal protection claims to services and due process-least restrictive alternative claims merge.

Indeed, starting from a base of deprivation of liberty, the due process approach more easily (doctrinally at least) makes the crossover to affirmative rights to service. The practical difficulty is that the least restrictive alternative doctrine, or indeed any doctrine at all, may not be sufficient to carry the enormous practical burden of dismantling institutions. Furthermore, the due process doctrine extends only to persons *already* institutionalized, and perhaps only to persons involuntarily institutionalized. The question is whether the threat to liberty, historically always lurking for retarded persons not yet institutionalized is sufficient to give rise to the due process, least restrictive alternative right to services. Is the fact, for example, that the rate of institutionalization goes up as a function of the unavailability of community services sufficient to trigger an affirmative right to services? The very conceptual confusion of the preliminary opinion of the federal district court in *New York Association for Retarded Children v. Rockefeller,*[88] conveying exactly the opposite of the message it purports to convey, suggests that it may be. There the court refused, preliminarily, to extend the right to treatment to persons voluntarily committed, saying,

> At the outset, there is a difference in the nature of the commitment. In *Rouse,* the commitment of persons acquitted by reason of insanity was not only involuntary but mandatory. On the other hand, a large part of the residents of Willowbrook entered *because they had no alternative,* and none have been denied a right to release. There is a significant difference between the state requiring commitment as an alternative to criminal incarceration and the state providing a residence for the mentally retarded. *The residents of Willowbrook are for the most part incapable of existing independently unless they are habilitated.*[89]

[85] Wyatt v. Stickney, 344 F. Supp. 387, 344 F. Supp. 373 (M.D. Ala. 1972), 334 F. Supp. 1341, 325 F. Supp. 781 (M.D. Ala. 1971), *aff'd,* 503 F.2d 1305 (5th Cir. 1974). *See also* Halpern, Chapter 13 of this volume; Burt, Chapter 14 of this volume.
[86] Lake v. Cameron, 364 F.2d 657, 659-60, 661 (D.C. Cir. 1967). *See also* Covington v. Harris, 419 F.2d 617, 623-24 (D.C. Cir. 1969); Kesselbrenner v. Anonymous, 33 N.Y.2d 161, 168, 305 N.E.2d 903, 907, 350 N.Y.S.2d 889, 894 (1973). See Chambers, Chapter 16 of this volume.
[87] Horacek v. Exon, 357 F.Supp. 71 (D. Neb. 1973), where plaintiffs are claiming a right to services in the community, rather than in an institution, poses precisely this opportunity as may further proceedings in Wyatt v. Stickney.
[88] 357 F.Supp. 752 (E.D.N.Y. 1973). *See addendum, p. 213.*
[89] 357 F. Supp. at 759-60 (emphasis supplied). Apart from a well-grounded finding of a right to reasonable protection from harm, the conceptual confusions in the opinion are legion. After finding a difference between "involuntary mandatory commitments" and commitments "because they have no alternative," the court seeks further comfort in that "none have been denied a right to release," yet the court itself denies release: "The court cannot in fairness direct that any of the residents be released before they have been habilitated as far as possible." *Id.* at 768.
The most egregious of the other errors touch the claim of plaintiffs for education: The court mistakes an access claim for one of quality, *id.* at 762; misreads *Rodriguez, id.* at 763; mistakes a counterfactual conditional statement of Judge Friendly in McMillan v. Board of Educ., 430 F.2d 1145 (2d Cir. 1970) as unconditional and factual, *id.* at 763; and mistakenly finds a D.C. code ground for decision in Mills, *id.* at 763. Indeed, the court's preliminary holding on education is contrary to the decision of the New York commissioner of education in *Appeal of Riley Reid,* discussed in text at note 101 *infra.*

State and Federal Statutes and Regulations and State Constitutions

Roberts v. Brian illustrates well the uses and the strength of finely threaded state and federal statute and regulation based claims, albeit with some admixture of the constitutional to secure services in the community to retarded citizens.

In *Usen v. Sipprell* [90] a New York Supreme Court had before it two children, a welfare statute, a juvenile court statute, a family court statute, and claims for adequate care, treatment, and education. A moderately retarded and emotionally disturbed 15-year-old girl had need of psychiatric, educational, and residential services. A seven-year-old boy twice expelled from the first grade with severe learning disabilities and emotional disorders caused by brain damage from lead poisoning had need of educational, psychiatric, and medical services. One state facility had refused the boy services because he required long-term treatment and it provided only short-term intensive treatment; another refused services because his behavioral problems required more supervision than it could give. A judge of the family court testified that scores of children had similar disabilities and that no appropriate program of care, treatment, and education was available.

The statutes in *Usen* were those common to most of the states. The Social Services Law provided that:

> [a] public welfare district shall be responsible for the welfare of children who are in need of public assistance and care, support, and protection. [91]

With respect to handicapped children, the Social Services Law provided:

> [the commissioner of public welfare must] obtain admission to state and other suitable schools, hospitals, other institutions, or care in their own homes or in family free or boarding homes or in agency boarding homes or group homes for such children.... [92]

The Mental Hygiene Law provided:

> All mentally disabled persons not in confinement under criminal proceedings who are unable to care for and maintain themselves or who are in need of care and treatment in a hospital or institution or whose mental or neurological condition is such as to endanger his own person, or the person and property of others, shall, without unnecessary delay, be properly and suitably cared for and maintained.... [93]

Various other statues provided that the department of mental hygiene is respon-

[90] 71 Misc. 2d 633, 336 N.Y.S.2d 848 (Sup. Ct. 1972), *rev'd in part,* 41 App. Div. 2d 251, 342 N.Y.S.2d 599 (1973).
[91] N. Y. Soc. Welf. Law § 395 (McKinney 1966). This provision, the court held, controlled the construction of another provision, section 131(1), of the Social Services Law, which provides: "It shall be the duty of social services officials, insofar as funds are available for that purpose, to provide adequately for those unable to maintain themselves, in accordance with the requirements of this article and other provisions of this chapter." 71 Misc. 2d at 637, 336 N.Y.S.2d at 852. *But see Usen II* in text at note 97 *infra.*
[92] N.Y. Soc. Serv. Law § 398(4)(a) (McKinney Supp. 1973).
[93] N.Y. Mental Hygiene Law § 24(1) (McKinney 1971).

sible for the provision of sufficient facilities for the care and treatment of the mentally disabled. Yet these children had been provided nothing.

Observing that,

> There may be some who question the wisdom, or the ability, of the State to take on the[se] obligations, . . .   but since they are already stated in the statute, approved by the legislative and executive branches of government, we have no alternative but to interpret the obligations imposed by the aforementioned statutes,[94]

the state supreme court held: "In view of the existing statute law of this State, government must, unless the statutes are repealed, provide the facilities and services necessary for the care of these children and others so situated."[95] The court ordered the respondent officials and agencies to submit to the court within 20 days a plan for the temporary care and treatment of the two children, and within 60 days a plan for their care and treatment and for the provision of education and mental health services over the next 5 years.

This penetrating and arguably correct decision was shortly reversed in part by the supreme court's appellate division.[96] In particular, the appellate division seemed to hold that the respondents' duties under the statutes are limited by budget, and further, since giving the children the services they sought might require eliminating other services respondents deem essential, that respondents' judgments are to be respected unless so arbitrary as to be without any reasonable explanation. Nonetheless, observing that,

> The needs of the two children in this proceeding are indeed real, and our society may not, through its several agencies, nonchalantly assert that there is no way to care for them and that, therefore, because of their nature they . . . should be incarcerated for the protection of the public,

the court directed:

> [The] matter should be remitted for an evidentiary hearing to ascertain more particularly the needs of [the children] and the actual services which respondents are able to provide for them, and to determine whether respondents or any of them are acting arbitrarily or capriciously in denying to [the children] necessary available services.[97]

---

[94] 71 Misc. 2d at 638-39, 336 N.Y.S.2d at 854.

[95] 71 Misc. 2d at 639, 336 N.Y.S.2d at 854.

[96] 41 App. Div. 2d 251, 342 N.Y.S.2d 599 (1973).

[97] 41 App. Div. 2d at 258, 342 N.Y.S.2d at 606-07. The appellate division sent the case to family court for a hearing under the newly amended Family Court Act § 255, which gives the Family court authority to order any local or state agency "to render such information, assistance and cooperation as shall be within its legal authority. . . ."

Months later, in Kesselbrenner v. Anonymous, 33 N.Y.2d 161, 305 N.E.2d 903, 350 N.Y.S.2d 889 (1973), a unanimous New York Court of Appeals in an opinion by Chief Judge Fuld rejected a cost defense raised by the state to the application of the least restrictive alternative principle in the assignment of a civilly committed "dangerous" citizen, saying: "Implicit in the petitioner's resistance to the appellant's transfer . . . is the absence of funds to provide for civil placement of all civil patients. But the '[c]ontinuing failure to provide suitable and adequate treatment cannot be justified by lack of staff or facilities.'" Id. at 168, 305 N.E.2d at 907, 350 N.Y.S.2d at 894.

The result is a set of uncertain, even ambivalent opinions, not yet working the conflicting principles to a clear and sound resolution, but an advance.

In *In re Marc H. Leitner,*[98] *In re David H.,*[99] and *In re Held,*[100] actions brought by individual children and their parents, the courts ordered that education be provided the children, on statutory grounds. In the *Appeal of Riley Reid et al. and the New York Association for Brain Injured Children*[101] the class claims of New York City's excluded handicapped children for education, in and out and up and down in the federal courts on federal constitutional grounds,[102] were finally honored by order of the commissioner of education in a decision grounded in the state's education statute and regulations.

In *Washington Urban League, Inc. v. Washington Metropolitan Area Transit Authority,*[103] a federal district court enjoined the construction of the Capital Subway until it was fitted for physically handicapped persons as required by an act of Congress.[104]

In *Souder v. Brennan*[105] the 1966 Amendments to the Fair Labor Standards Act were declared by a federal district court to require the payment of a minimum wage to resident-workers in institutions for the mentally retarded and the mentally ill, and the Secretary of Labor was enjoined to enforce the act.[106]

These few recent cases make clear the enormously fertile field for staking claims to rights in regulations and statutes. Commonly intricate and obscure and occasionally even unavailable, these acts can, nevertheless, supply a firm basis for

[98] (Fam. Ct. Westchester Co., Nov. 6, 1972) (en banc) 168 N.Y.L.J., Dec. 5, 1972, at 1, col. 7-8 (holding that N.Y. FAMILY COURT ACT § 232 (McKinney 1963) and N.Y. EDUC. LAW § 4403(2) (McKinney 1963) require that autistic child for whom there were no suitable educational facilities in New York State be provided education at a school in Rhode Island with the cost not to exceed $12,500 to be borne equally by New York State and County).

[99] 72 Misc. 2d 59, 337 N.Y.S.2d 969 (Fam. Ct. Queens Co., 1972) (under the same statutes, directing City of New York to pay $2,500 tuition for education of physically handicapped schizophrenic child).

[100] Nos. H-2-71 and H-10-71 (Fam. Ct. Westchester Co., N.Y., Nov. 29, 1971) (ordering school district to pay tuition at private school since district did not have an appropriate program for child). *See also* Kivell v. Nemoitin, No. 143913 (Sup. Ct. Fairfield Co., Conn., July 18, 1972) (ordering school district to pay out-of-state private school tuition of $13,400 since district did not have an appropriate program).

[101] No. 8742 (Commissioner of Education of the State of New York, Nov. 26, 1973). In New York, the commissioner of education has quasi-judicial powers.

[102] Resulting finally in abstention: Reid v. Board of Educ., 453 F.2d 238 (2d Cir. 1971) (vacating district court's order of dismissal with direction to retain jurisdiction). *See also* McMillan v. Board of Educ., claim dismissed at district court level, *rev'd*, 430 F.2d 1145 (2d Cir. 1970) (finding a federal constitutional cause of action), *dismissed*, 331 F. Supp. 302 (S.D.N.Y. 1971) (court abstaining).

[103] Civil No. 776-72 (D.D.C., June 29, 1973). *See generally* Comment, *Abroad in the Land: Legal Strategies to Effectuate the Right of the Physically Disabled*, 61 GEO L.J. 1501 (1973).

[104] 42 U.S.C. § 4151 (1970). A significant portion, at least 78%, of the moderately and severely retarded are also physically handicapped. CONLEY 41-48.
    Note also the pending Civil Aeronautics Board rule-making proceeding on the transportation of handicapped persons. 36 Fed. Reg. 20,309 (1971).

[105] 367 F. Supp. 808 (D.D.C. 1973).

[106] Although the minimum wage and overtime compensation provisions, 29 U.S.C. §§ 206-07 (1970), are extended to resident-workers, the court notes (367 F. Supp. at 814) the availability under 29 U.S.C. § 214 (1970) of work activity exemptions. They are granted when a handicap is so severe as to make the worker's productive capacity "inconsequential" (in practice, where workers are unable to earn at least half of the minimum wage). *See* CONLEY at 340. The court's note underscores the importance of an orchestrated approach in claims for services.

claims of some rights. The first task, as it has been in the development of welfare rights,[107]is to marshall the full array of these regulations and statutes (federal bureau by federal bureau, state department by state department) which define, perforce, the conditions of much of life for the retarded, and from this array, to constitute an agenda for litigation and other action. Unhappily, I cannot offer here even a preliminary sketch of that agenda.[108]Some elements, however, are clear.

There must be litigation like *Usen* to resolve affirmatively the question of whether common statutory provisions like section 4201 of Pennsylvania's Mental Health-Mental Retardation Act:

> The department shall have power, and its duty shall be: (1) to assure within the State the availability and equitable provision of adequate mental health and mental retardation services for all persons who need them. . . .[109]

create a type four service categorically available to all retarded citizens regardless of limited resources.[110]

Similarly at the top of any agenda must be sections 503 and 504 of the Vocational Rehabilitation Act of 1973.[111] Section 504, entitled "Nondiscrimination Under Federal Grants," provides:

---

[107]After the first constitutional bloom, much welfare litigation has been the assiduous pursuit of decisions on the statutes and regulations. *E.g.,* Shea v. Vialpando, 416 U.S. 251 (1974); Carleson v. Remillard, 406 U.S. 598 (1972); Townsend v. Swank, 404 U.S. 282 (1971); Engelman v. Amos, 404 U.S. 23 (1971); Wyman v. Rothstein, 398 U.S. 275 (1970); Rosado v. Wyman, 397 U.S. 397 (1970); King v. Smith, 392 U.S. 309 (1968). *But see* United States Dep't of Agriculture v. Moreno, 431 U.S. 528 (1973); United States Dep't of Agriculture v. Murry, 413 U.S. 508 (1973); New Jersey Welfare Rights Org. v. Cahill, 411 U.S. 619 (1973); Graham v. Richardson, 403 U.S. 365 (1971).

[108]Kramer, Chapter 2 of this volume, presents more than a sketch of a significant portion of such an agenda.

[109]Pa. Stat. Ann. tit. 50, § 4201 (1969). *See also* Pa. Stat. Ann. tit. 50, § 4305 (1969). Unlike the N.Y. Soc. Serv. Law, § 131(1) (1973), the Pennsylvania provision and the similar provisions in the statutes of most states are *not,* on the face of it, limited by the "funds available."

[110]The prototype of such a statutory mandate is in the public assistance title of the Social Security Act. 42 U.S.C. § 602(a)(10) (1970) provides that "aid to families with dependent children shall be furnished with reasonable promptness to all eligible individuals." The Court has held that this statute requires aid to be furnished to one who is *eligible. E.g.,* Carleson v. Remillard, 406 U.S. 598, 600 (1972); Townsend v. Swank, 404 U.S. 282, 285-86 (1971); King v. Smith, 392 U.S. 309, 333 (1968). For the state statutes, the analogous interpretation is: If one *needs* services, services must be provided. Thus, unlike public housing, for example, if one is eligible for public assistance (or if one needs mental retardation services), one is entitled to receive the assistance (or services), not just a waiting list. In a sense such a mandate is the statutory analogue of the constitutional "present right." Watson v. City of Memphis, 373 U.S. 526, 533 (1962). *See* text at notes 65-66 *supra.*

A supplementary approach, making guarantees to services in the community operational, would borrow from Wyatt v. Stickney. In that case the court promulgated certain minimum quantitative standards (staff : resident ratios, for example) adopted from accreditation standards, holding that absent these standards being met, treatment duties could not be discharged. Similar threshold quantitative standards can and should be formulated for services in the community, from epidemiological data and model service schemes. Such standards could be promulgated legislatively or they could be used by courts to give content to statutory declarations of duty like Pennsylvania's. Operational standards of this sort are crucial if guarantees of community services are to be real, rather than "will-o'-the-wisp."

[111]29 U.S.C.A. §§ 793-94 (Supp. 1974). For committee and conference reports on sections 503 and 504 see 1973 U.S. Code Cong. & Adm. News 214-43, 2154. *See also Hearings on H.R. 8395, and Related Bills Before the Select Subcomm. on Education of the House Comm. on Education and Labor,* 92d Cong., 2d Sess. 113 (1972); 118 Cong. Rec. H 1257 (1972); 118 Cong. Rec. 1595 (1972) (remarks of Representative Vanik).

No otherwise qualified handicapped individual in the United States . . . shall, solely by reason of his handicap, be excluded from participation in, be denied the benefits of, or be subjected to discrimination under any program or activity receiving Federal financial assistance.[112]

Section 503(a), entitled "Employment Under Federal Contracts," provides:

Any contract in excess of $2,500 entered into by any Federal department or agency for the procurement of personal property and nonpersonal services (including construction) for the United States shall contain a provision requiring that, in employing persons to carry out such contract the party contracting with the United States shall take affirmative action to employ and advance in employment qualified handicapped individuals. . . . The provisions . . . shall apply to any subcontract in excess of $2,500 entered into by a prime contractor. . . . [113]

These provisions track, virtually verbatim, the declaratory provisions of Title VI of the Civil Rights Act of 1964[114] and of the executive orders on nondiscrimination in employment by government contractors and subcontractors.[115] Their po-

---

[112] 29 U.S.C.A. § 794 (Supp. 1974).

[113] 29 U.S.C.A. § 793(a) (Supp. 1974). Section 503(a) further provides: "The President shall implement the provisions of this section by promulgating regulations within ninety days after the date of enactment of this Section." *Id.* The regulations were due on Christmas Day 1973. Although the regulations under other parts of the Rehabilitation Act were promulgated by the appointed date, 39 Fed. Reg. 898 (1974), regulations implementing § 503 have yet to be promulgated. The President has delegated his section 503 authority to prescribe regulations to the Secretary of Labor, in consultation with the Secretary of Defense and the administrator of general services. Exec. Order No. 11,758, 39 Fed. Reg. 2075 (1974). And on June 11, 1974 an inadequate set of regulations was published. 39 Fed. Reg. 20565 (1974).

    Section 503(b) provides for complaint to, and assigns investigation and compliance duties to, the Department of Labor. See 29 U.S.C.A. § 793(b) (Supp. 1974).

[114] 42 U.S.C. § 2000d (1970). Title VI prohibits discrimination in federally funded programs on grounds of race, color, or national origin.

    Section 504, unlike Title VI, 42 U.S.C. § 2000d-1 (1970), does not carry express authority or direction to any agency to issue regulations for its implementation. Each statute establishing a federal grant-making program, however, delegates authority to issue regulations, and section 504 may be taken to establish a new standard that must be accommodated in the administration of these grant-making programs. Moreover, even without these collateral sources for rule-making authority to effectuate section 504, the authority and the duty to issue implementing regulations under section 504 would be implied. *See* K. Davis, ADMINISTRATIVE LAW TEXT § 6.04 (1959).

    The importance of such regulations is illustrated in Lau v. Nichols, 483 F.2d 791, 805 (9th Cir. 1973) (Hufstedler & Ely, J.J., dissenting), *rev'd,* 414 U.S. 563 (1974). One ground upon which plaintiffs proceeded in that case and the ground upon which the Supreme Court unanimously reversed, is a regulation issued under Title VI requiring:

Where inability to speak or understand the English language excludes national origin-minority group children from effective participation in the educational program offered by a school district, the district must take affirmative steps to rectify the language deficiency in order to open its instructional program to these students. 35 Fed. Reg. 11595 (1970).

    For my suggestion that, even before section 504 was adopted, HEW had authority and perhaps the duty to issue regulations requiring zero reject education, periodic review, and due process hearings as a condition of federal funding under the Education of the Handicapped Act of 1972, 20 U.S.C. § 1401 (1970), see Gilhool, *The Uses of Litigation: The Right of all Retarded Children to Access to Free Public Schooling,* CURRENT ISSUES IN MENTAL RETARDATION 27, 32 (U.S. Dep't of Health, Education & Welfare, Pub. No. (OS) 73-86, Dec. 1972).

[115] Exec. Order No. 11,246, 3 C.F.R. 173 (1973). The order is published also in the annotations to Title VII, 42 U.S.C.A. § 2000e (Supp. 1974). Title VII prohibits discrimination in private employment, 42 U.S.C.A. § 2000e-2 (Supp. 1974), and in federal government employment, 42 U.S.C.A. § 200e-16 (Supp. 1974) on ground of race, color, religion, sex, or national origin; the executive order prohibits discrimination and also requires affirmative action to ensure employment by government contractors without regard to race, color, religion, sex, or national origin. *See also* the Age Discrimination in Employment Act, 29 U.S.C. § 621 (1970).

tential impact upon the lives of retarded and other handicapped citizens cannot be overstated. At least 400,000 of the 690,000 adult retarded citizens who are currently idle or institutionalized, for example, could be employed.[116] As Ronald W. Conley writes in *The Economics of Mental Retardation,*

> A wide diversity of products increases the number of assembly-line operations, widening the variety of specialized and uncomplicated jobs . . . . When an economy becomes as specialized and as diverse as the American economy is, the vast majority of the retarded, including the physically and psychologically handicapped, can be placed on jobs in which their residual abilities can be utilized.[117]

Most of the additional jobs for the retarded, including those which must provide sheltered work, can and should be found in regular employment channels.[118] The employment of 400,000 at minimum wage would increase output by $1.6 billion annually.[119] The opportunity of employment, apparently guaranteed to "otherwise qualified handicapped" persons by section 503, underscores the importance of education for all, and must affect affirmatively the content and quality of education, particularly in the later vocational training years.[120] Employment would have a similar impelling and supportive effect on the availability of residential facilities in the community.[121] Section 504 can provide a basis for securing a great many services only problematically secure otherwise.

Whether these benign and rippling effects of sections 503 and 504 are realized depends upon whether remedies are fashioned which "give flesh to the word and fulfillment to the promise those norms embody."[122] Two questions, in particular, will be decisive. First, what is the reach of the affirmative action duty under section 503? Second, may the duties declared in sections 503 and 504 be enforced by private actions in the courts?

Affirmative action invokes a host of devices for increasing the representation of minority workers in a work force where they are underemployed: active recruitment efforts, advertising a policy of nondiscrimination, and (whether called "preferential hiring" or "quotas" or not) undertakings to achieve certain ranges of minority employment. As one court, upholding the requirements of the Philadelphia plan, wrote:

---

[116] CONLEY 336 and the studies cited therein at 332-53. Conley's estimate is avowedly conservative; he omits employment needs among mentally retarded teenagers, the desirability of upgrading the existing employment of retarded employees (1,542,600 retarded persons over 20 were employed in 1970, CONLEY 207), and, most significant, he omits for purposes of calculation the severely retarded, those persons attributed IQs from 20 to 35 or 40. The severely retarded are a significant portion of the employees in sheltered work and there is no doubt that with a properly structured work opportunity virtually all could be employed. *See* CONLEY 333-34.

[117] CONLEY 352.

[118] The distinction is between sheltered work in private and public employment settings otherwise normal and sheltered work in segregated often eleemosynary settings. The former is economically more productive, most certain, and preferable on normalization or integration grounds.

[119] CONLEY 371.

[120] *E.g.,* CONLEY 335.

[121] *Cf.* CONLEY 357-58.

[122] Dellinger, *Of Rights and Remedies: The Constitution as a Sword,* 85 HARV. L. REV. 1532, 1534 (1972).

The heartbeat of "affirmative action" is the policy of developing programs which shall provide in detail for specific steps to guarantee equal employment opportunity keyed to the problems and needs of members of minority groups, including when there are deficiencies [in the number employed], the development of specific goals and timetables for the prompt achievement of full and equal employment opportunity.[123]

For the handicapped, the attitudes of employers are not the only spring of discriminatory practices. For the full realization for the handicapped of the opportunity for employment three barriers must be overcome:

First, just plain prejudice.[124]

Second, the structure of work settings (for the physically handicapped, for example, physical barriers to access and to functioning at the work table; for the deaf, communication systems which rely on the spoken word rather than the written; for the blind, the reverse; for the severely retarded, the unsheltered nature of some work settings and the structure of superivision.)[125]

Third, the definition of job tasks themselves (mentally retarded persons with limited mobility may do such tasks as stuffing envelopes or assembling electrical appliances; retarded persons with impaired use of upper extremities may be messengers).[126]

That section 503 should reach each of these barriers is clear, for example, from the Supreme Court's statement in *Griggs v. Duke Power Co.*[127] of the Title VII obligation of nondiscrimination (a lesser obligation than affirmative action):

Under the Act, practices, procedures, or tests neutral on their face, and even neutral in terms of intent, cannot be maintained if they operate to "freeze" the status quo of prior discriminatory practices. . . .

Congress has now provided that tests or criteria for employment or promotion may not provide equality of opportunity merely in the sense of the fabled offer of milk to the stork and the fox. On the contrary, Congress has now required that the posture and condition of the job seeker be taken into account. It has — to resort again to the fable — provided that the vessel in which the milk is proffered be one all seekers can use. The Act proscribes not only overt discrimination but also practices that are fair in form, but discriminatory in operation.[128]

[123] Contractors Ass'n v. Secretary of Labor, 311 F. Supp. 1002, 1009 (E.D. Pa. 1970) *aff'd,* 442 F.2d 159 (3d Cir. 1970), *cert. denied,* 404 U.S. 854 (1971). Generally on affirmative action under the executive order program, and under Title VII, see *Developments in the Law—Employment Discrimination and Title VII of the Civil Rights Act of 1964,* 84 HARV. L. REV. 1109, 1291-1304 (1971), and the works cited therein at 1277 n.8. On the remedial use of affirmative action under Title VII see, *e.g.,* Carter v. Gallagher, 452 F.2d 315 (8th Cir. 1971), *cert. denied,* 406 U.S. 950 (1972).

[124] *Cf.* CONLEY 348.

[125] CONLEY 337, 338-53.

[126] *Cf.* CONLEY 349.

[127] 401 U.S. 424, 430-31 (1971).

[128] For a discussion of the statistical proof required to establish a prima facie case under Title VII, and of the business necessity and bona fide *occupational qualification* defenses, see Note, *Height Standards in Police Employment and the Question of Sex Discrimination: The Availability of Two Defenses for a Neutral Employment Policy Found Discriminatory Under Title VII,* 47 S. CAL. L. REV. 585 (1974).

Whether the affirmative action required by section 503 will reach each of these barriers depends upon the implementing regulations[129] and upon the course of enforcement and of litigation thereafter.

Neither section 503 nor section 504 expressly creates a private cause of action to enforce the rights created therein. Yet 32 year's experience with the executive order programs indicates that reliance upon administrative mechanisms for compliance is starkly ineffective.[130] And reliance upon administrative mechanisms for compliance with Title VI of the 1964 Civil Rights Act has been only marginally more effective.[131] Thus, finding a private cause of action under sections 503 and 504 so that retarded and other handicapped persons may attend directly to the enforcement of their rights is crucial.

The executive orders, upon which section 503 is in part modeled, have been held not to create a private cause of action.[132] But those cases emphasized the availability to plaintiffs of a private cause of action expressly created in Title VII of the Civil Rights Act of 1964 to achieve the same results sought in suits under the executive order.[133] Title VI of the Civil Rights Act, upon a part of which section 504 is modeled,[134] has been held to create an implied private cause of action.[135] In addi-

---

[129] Section 503 regulations should not only require affirmative recruitment efforts where there exist appropriately defined job tasks in settings fitted to persons with particular handicaps, but should also require, where task definitions (but not work settings) are appropriate, that work settings be fitted to the handicapped; and where work settings (but not job tasks) are appropriate, that job tasks be redefined; and where neither are appropriate, that both be redesigned.

In a separate regard section 503 may present a dilemma. If, as is not unlikely, employers seek to meet their affirmative action obligations by "creaming," by employing and advancing the mildly handicapped, there is considerable risk that these citizens will be subject to "labeling" and to continued stigma. Heretofore many mildly handicapped persons suffered labeling only during their school years and afterward integrated normally without label into the community. E.g., PRESIDENT'S COMM. ON MENTAL RETARDATION, THE SIX HOUR RETARDED CHILD (1970). Section 503 regulations, therefore, must in some fashion seek to control against labeling. If they cannot, then the question will be whether the economic and other benefits to the mildly handicapped of section 503 protection are worth the cost of continued stigmatization. And furthermore, who will make this judgment? And how?

Undoubtedly, coincident with the implementation of section 503, some address of the state employment services and vocational rehabilitation agencies, perhaps by way of litigation to enforce performance of their statutory outreach and monitoring duties, will be ripe. See CONLEY 350. See also Federal Employment Service Act, 29 U.S.C. § 49(g) (1970), providing that:

> Such plans shall include provision for the promotion and development of employment opportunities for handicapped persons and for job counselling and placement of such persons, and for the designation of at least one person in each State or Federal employment office, whose duties shall include the effectuation of such purposes.

And see the various state employment service statutes.

[130] See Developments in the Law—Employment Discrimination and Title VII of the Civil Rights Act of 1964, 84 HARV. L. REV. 1275-91 (1971) and the works cited therein. See also THE UNITED STATES COMM. ON CIVIL RIGHTS, THE FEDERAL CIVIL RIGHTS ENFORCEMENT EFFORT — A REASSESSMENT 1-12 (1973).

[131] See THE UNITED STATES COMM. ON CIVIL RIGHTS, THE FEDERAL CIVIL RIGHTS ENFORCEMENT EFFORT — A REASSESSMENT 1-12 (1973).

[132] Farkas v. Texas Instrument, Inc., 375 F.2d 629, 632-33 (5th Cir.), cert. denied, 389 U.S. 977 (1967); Farmer v. Philadelphia Electric Co., 329 F.2d 3, 8-10 (3d Cir. 1964) (dictum); cf. Gnotta v. United States, 415 F.2d 1271, 1275 (8th Cir. 1969), cert. denied, 397 U.S. 934 (1970).

[133] See Farkas, 375 F.2d at 633-34 & n.3; Gnotta, 415 F.2d at 1275; 42 U.S.C. § 2000e-5(e) (1970).

[134] Section 504 tracks exactly the declaratory provisions of Title VI, 42 U.S.C. § 2000d (1970), but omits the administrative remedies created to enforce Title VI, 42 U.S.C. § 2000d-1 (1970). This omission, if anything, strengthens the case for a private action under section 504.

[135] Lemon v. Bossier Parish School Bd., 240 F. Supp. 709, 715 (E.D. La. 1965), aff'd, 370 F.2d 847, 851-52 (5th Cir.), cert. denied, 388 U.S. 911 (1967). See Alvarado v. El Paso Independent School Dist.,

tion, the criteria usually invoked to determine whether a statute implies a private cause of action — chiefly, whether a private action is a "necessary supplement" to effectuate the social policy declared by the Congress[136] — seem clearly to require the implication of a private cause of action under section 504. And the same criteria invoked to find a private action to enforce section 504 and Title VI would seem to locate one in section 503.

Thus, conduct discriminating against the retarded and other handicapped persons has been proscribed by sections 503 and 504[137]; only an additional remedy is sought.[138] Implying a cause of action will increase the likelihood of compliance, giving victims incentive to assist in the enforcement of sections 503 and 504, and potential violators added reason to conform their conduct to the law. The sections create new duties that are generally without state statutory or common law analogues. Only a few states presently prohibit discrimination against the handicapped in employment and these prohibitions vary significantly in their effectiveness.[139] Section 504 confides no enforcement duties to any agency, unlike Title VI, where nonetheless a private cause of action has been implied. Section 503 does confide undefined enforcement duties to the Department of Labor, but to the extent that the duties track administrative enforcement under the executive orders, they are apt to be ineffective and inadequate, and to the extent that they track administrative enforcement under Title VI, they should create no problems precluding private judicial enforcement. The necessity of a private cause of action, if the purposes of sections 503 and 504 are to be fully effectuated, makes its implication appropriate.[140]

---

445 F.2d 1011 (5th Cir.), *rev'g*, 326 F. Supp. 674 (W.D. Tex. 1971); Green v. Kennedy, 309 F. Supp. 1127, 1132 (D.D.C. 1970), *appeals dismissed*, 398 U.S. 956 (1970), 400 U.S. 986 (1971); Hicks v. Weaver, 302 F. Supp. 619, 620-21 (E.D. La. 1969); Marable v. Mental Health Bd., 297 F. Supp. 291 (M.D. Ala. 1969).

[136] J.I. Case Co. v. Borak, 377 U.S. 426, 433-34 (1964). *See* Note, *Implying Civil Remedies from Federal Regulatory Statutes*, 77 HARV. L. REV. 285, esp. 291-96 (1963); Note, *The Implication of a Private Course of Action Under Title III of the Consumer Credit Protection Act*, 47 S. CAL. L. REV. 383, esp. 403-21 (1974). *See also* Bivens v. Six Unknown Named Agents of the Federal Bureau of Investigation, 403 U.S. 388, 395-97 (1971); Dellinger, *supra* note 23, esp. 1550-52. *See generally* H.M. HART & H. WECHSLER, THE FEDERAL COURTS AND THE FEDERAL SYSTEM 798-800 (2d ed. 1973).

[137] The legislative history, note 111 *supra*, makes clear that the sections are proscriptions. They embody the rules of law declared in the equal protection cases concerned with access to education, for example, and those concerned with employment, *e.g.* King-Smith v. Aaron, 455 F.2d 378 (3d Cir. 1972) (holding that a complaint alleging that a school district which refused employment to a blind teacher because of her blindness states a cause of action). *Cf.* Lemon v. Bossier Parish School Bd., 370 F.2d 709 (E.D. La. 1965).

[138] Under section 503, a remedy in addition to whatever administration remedies may be created in regulations; under section 504, a remedy period.

The treacherous nature of the most common statutory interpretation argument against implication, the maxim of negative inference: *expressio unius est esclusio alterius*, invoked, *e.g.*, in Farkas v. Texas Instrument, Inc., 375 F.2d 629, 633 (5th Cir. 1967), and arguably available against implication for section 503, is considered, and a recommendation against its use is made, in Note, *Implying Civil Remedies from Federal Regulatory Statutes*, 77 HARV. L. REV. 285, 290-91 (1963). *See also* J.I. Case Co. v. Borak, 377 U.S. 426, 433-34 (1964).

[139] ALASKA STAT. § 18.80.220(1) (1969); ILL. CONST. art I, § 19; IOWA CODE ANN. § 601D.2, 601F (1974); MASS. GEN. LAWS. ANN. ch. 149, § 24k (1972); N.M. STAT. ANN. § 4-33-7 (1973); N.C. GEN. STAT. § 168-6 (1973); WIS. STAT. ANN. § 111.325 (1974).

[140] Jurisdiction of section 503 or 504 actions, given a private cause of action, will lie under 28 U.S.C. §§ 1331 and 1343(3) (1970). With these additional heads of jurisdiction for section 504 claims, abstention problems such as these sometimes encountered in constitutional claims for education may be mitigated. *See* HART & WECHSLER, *supra* note 137, at 989. And with § 1343(3) jurisdiction in section

Torts and Contract

S. F. C. Milsom, in his *Historical Foundations of the Common Law,* writes:

> The life of the common law has been in the unceasing abuse of its elementary
> ideas. If the rules of property give what now seems an unjust answer, try obligation;
> and equity has proved that from the materials of obligation you can counterfeit
> almost all of the phenomena of property. If the rules of contract give what now
> seems an unjust answer, try tort. Your counterfeit will look odd to one brought
> up on categories of Roman origin; but it will work. If the rules of one tort, say
> deceit, give what now seems an unjust answer, try another, try negligence. And so
> the legal world goes round.[141]

"Change," Milsom concludes, "is largely brought about by re-classification."[142]

In *Peter W. Doe v. San Francisco Unified School District, et al.,*[143] a dyslexic
high school graduate, able to read at lower than a fifth-grade level, has sued the
district, the members of its board, and others for $500,000 in damages for his dimi-
nished earning capacity. The action is grounded in negligence and misrepresen-
tation. Peter Doe alleges that when his parents inquired whether he was having
problems in school, whether he might have a learning disability, the school district
represented to them that he was doing fine and had no special problem. Doe alleges
that the district negligently failed to use reasonable care in imparting basic academic skills to him. For example, the district negligently failed to take notice of his
reading disabilities and to design his schooling accordingly, despite school records
recording his difficulties; the district negligently assigned him to classes unfitted
to his reading abilities when its officials knew or should have known the class was

---

504 cases, any jurisdictional amount problem, or in a class action, any aggregation or membership
problem, see Zahn v. International Paper Co., 414 U.S. 291 (1973); Snyder v. Harris, 394 U.S. 332
(1969), is avoided.

In any such action the United States may intervene as a party. FED. R. CIV. P. 24(b). The United
States has appeared as *amicus curiae* in Lebanks v. Spears, 60 F.R.D. 135 (E.D. La. 1973) and Wyatt
v. Stickney, 344 F. Supp. 373 (M.D. Ala. 1972), *aff'd sub nom.* Wyatt v. Aderholt, 503 F.2d 1305 (5th
Cir. 1974), and it has recently intervened in New York Association of Retarded Children v. Rock-
feller, 357 F. Supp. 752 (E.D.N.Y. 1973).

Title VI, unlike Title VII, 42 U.S.C. § 2000e-5(k) (1970), does not expressly authorize the
payment of attorneys' fees to prevailing parties. (*But see* 28 U.S.C. 1617 (1970) expressly authorizing attorneys' fees in schools cases). Nor do Sections 503 or 504 expressly authorize attorneys
fees. They may nonetheless be awarded.

In *LaRaza Unida v. Volpe*, 57 F.R.D. 94, 98 (N.D. Cal. 1972), the court wrote:
The rule briefly stated is that whenever there is nothing in a statutory scheme which might be
interpreted as precluding it, a "private attorney general" should be awarded attorney's fees when
he has effectuated a strong Congressional policy which has benefited a large class of people,
and where the necessity and financial burden of private enforcement are such as to make the
award essential.

See generally, Note, *Allowance of Attorney Fees in Civil Rights Litigation Where the Action is Not
Based on a Statute Providing for an Award of Attorney's Fees*, 41 U. CIN. L. REV. 405 (1972); Note,
*Awarding Attorney's Fees to the Private Attorney General: Judicial Green Light to Private Litigation
in the Public Interest*, 24 HAST. L.J. 733 (1973). Note that attorney fees were awarded in Wyatt v.
Stickney, 344 F. Supp. at 408-11, and, under authority of CAL. WELF. & INST. CODE § 10962, in
Roberts v. Brian, 6 Cal. 3dy1, at 10 n.6, 489 P.2d at 1384 n.6, 98 Cal. Rptr. at 56 n.6 (1971).

[141] S.F.C. MILSOM, HISTORICAL FOUNDATION OF THE COMMON LAW xi-xii (1969).
[142] *Id.* at xii.
[143] No. 653312 (Cal. Super. Ct. for San Fransisco, filed Feb. 8, 1973).

inappropriate; the district negligently passed him on from grade to grade and graduated him from high school when its officials knew or should have known he was not so qualified. The action looks *inter alia* to certain provisions of California's Education Code for the standard of care:[144] for example, section 10759 requires that the schools keep parents advised of the child's progress; section 8505 requires that a child's course of study be designed to fit his needs; sections 1057 and 8002 require that members of the school board inspect the schools, and revise and adjust curriculum as appropriate; and section 8573, in force when Peter Doe graduated, required at least an eight-grade reading level for the award of a high school diploma.

The point is not the claim for money damages, for this remedy may be available in any suit, whatever the grounds of suit.[145] The point is the new ground in the developing common law for claims on public entities by mentally retarded citizens and, furthermore, the ground for articulating new rights for mentally retarded persons as among private persons by change in the common law which still largely regulates private relationships.[146] Again, the agenda for such change and its return to retarded citizens can now be perceived only dimly; the work remains to be done.

Taxpayer Suits and Other Approaches to Irrational Administrative Behavior

It is not only the perspective of a sometime Philadelphia lawyer which suggests still another ground for action — what shall be called generically a taxpayer action for waste. In *Price v. Philadelphia Parking Authority,* the Pennsylvania Supreme Court announced:

> [A] recognition of the need to subject the activities of public authorities to judicial scrutiny: As public bodies, they exercise public powers and must act strictly within their legislative mandates. Moreover, they stand in a fiduciary relationship to the public which they are created to serve and their conduct must be guided by good faith and sound judgment. . . . The mushrooming of authorities at all levels of government and the frequent complaint that such bodies act in an arbitrary and capricious manner in violation of existing law dictate that a check rein be kept upon them. . . . These considerations dictate that the independence of authorities from some of the usual restrictions on governmental activity not be extended so as to insulate them from judicial scrutiny through the medium of taxpayers' suits.[147]

---

[144] On the relationship between statutory standards and standards of care in negligence actions, see Thayer, *Public Wrong and Private Action*, 27 HARV. L. REV. 317 (1914).

[145] And the utility of a claim for damages is to be weighed, whatever the context. Apart from the importance of money relief to plaintiffs, the damage remedy may be thought to have some special utility in deterring particular behavior by defendants or by others similarly circumstanced. On the other hand, (and its possible cost stems from the same circumstance as its possible benefit) money damages may engage the "face" or the personal honor of a defendant in a manner dysfunctional to significant change in defendant's behavior. *Cf.* E. GOFFMAN, RELATIONS IN PUBLIC 11 (1973) (the distinctions among warning, promise, threat, and challenge).

[146] Again, the pioneering work is ten Broek, *The Right to Live in the World: The Disabled in the Law of Torts* 54 CALIF. L. REV. 841 (1966).

[147] 422 Pa. 317, 329, 221 A.2d 138, 145 (1966). Extensive citation, *inter alia*, to Jaffe, *Standing to Secure Judicial Review: Public Actions*, 74 HARV. L. REV. 1265 (1961); Davis, *Judicial Control of Administrative Action: A Review*, 66 COLUM. L. REV. 635 (1966); Note, *Taxpayers' Suits: A Survey and Summary*, 69 YALE L.J. 895 (1960), and many cases, is omitted in the quoted excerpt.

The point is not just that taxpayers have standing, for there is seldom a shortage of proper parties to raise claims for the mentally retarded.[148] Rather, an additional basis is provided for a state court claim that is especially telling in maters concerning the retarded, where authority judgments respond so often to counter factual stereotypes. Beyond taxpayer actions for waste, claims challenging irrational official behavior may be raised through judicial review, whether on broad or narrow certiorari, of any administrative decision or rule that is not well based in fact or in the record. Indeed, significantly fertile fields exist for interpolating into the fabric of state law those canons of rational well-grounded decision articulated under the federal Administrative Procedure Act and memorialized in Reich's *Law of the Planned Society*.[149] For example, such an action would lie against a state building or bonding authority which proposed to spend $20 million to expand the "bed" capacity of a state residential institution. Such a decision would be vulnerable to attack as economically irrational and wasteful, as well as contradictory of statutory duties to advance the care and well-being of mentally retarded persons.[150] And such an action would lie against a decision or rule of a state board of building standards, based on stereotypical and false notions of retarded persons and the conditions of "their safety", requiring prohibitively expensive or scarce materials or design in community residences.[151]

TRANSLATING LEGAL RIGHTS TO SERVICES INTO REALITY

Whatever the ground for claims to services in the community, a suit yielding a change in the rules is just the beginning. Orders must be enforced, institutions rearranged, and the behavior reliably altered. When the task is to fit things anew in the face of stereotype, it cannot be done by order of a court alone. Significantly, in the two paradigm cases discussed previously, the right to education cases and *Roberts v. Brian*,[152] the courts retained jurisdiction. And significantly, where as in these cases litigation has been prosecuted not in the air, but in close relation to the constituency of the suit, where the suit has been used by its constituents to organize, and where relief has been structured to invoke and to accommodate the attention and talents of the constituency, implementation has been most sure and change has held the prospect of being long lasting.[153]

---

[148] The most stereotype-shattering party, perhaps, is a retarded taxpayer plaintiff.

[149] Reich, *The Law of the Planned Society*, 75 YALE L.J. 1227 (1966). One federal court, for example, applied these canons to void as arbitrary the action of the Department of Defense in terminating tuition payments to learning disabled children under the Civilian Health and Medical Program for the Uniformed Services. West v. Secretary of Defense, C.A. No. 75-2589-DWW, (C.D. Cal. April 4, 1974).

[150] *See* CONLEY 354-60. *Cf.* Horacek v. Exon, 357 F. Supp. 71 (D. Neb. 1973). *See also* L. LIPPMAN & I. GOLDBERG, *supra* note 4, at 20-21.

[151] *Cf. In re* Classification of Residential Facilities for the Retarded (Pa. Dep't of Labor & Indus., Indus. Bd. 1972), discussed at note 45 *supra*.

[152] See text accompanying notes 66-79 *supra*.

[153] The orders in PARC, 343 F. Supp. at 302-06, in Lebanks v. Spears, 60 F.R.D. (E.D. La. 1973), and in Wyatt v. Stickney, 344 F. Supp. at 376, 392 (M.D. Ala. 1972), provided in varying form, for the prep-

When the task is to fit things right in the face of stereotypes, particular proce-dures for continuing oversight are necessary. In the education cases, for example, retarded children have been accorded the right to periodic review of the appro-priateness of their educational assignment and, upon any original assignment and periodically thereafter, the right to notice and the opportunity to be heard, lest assignment succomb again to stereotype. Colloquially, it is the right to a due pro-cess hearing.[154] Periodic review and formal opportunities to be heard are necessary if the integrationist axiom is to be fulfilled: that exceptional children should be in the most normalized setting consistent with meeting their needs.[155] It is necessary if the pains[156] and penalties[157] of misclassification are to be avoided.[158]

It has long been established that before a person may be deprived of any signif-icant interest by the state, he must first be given notice and the opportunity to be heard.[159] And recently, in *Wisconsin v. Constantineau,*[160] the Court made clear that the state may not allocate stigma without extending to its citizens the same oppor-tunity. A Wisconsin statute had provided that anyone publicly drunk too often could be "posted." The sheriff thought Ms. Constantineau too often publicly drunk and posted a notice in all retail liquor establishments forbidding sales to her because of "excessive drinking." The Supreme Court held the statute unconstitutional, writing:

> The only issue . . . here is whether the label or characterization given a person by "posting," though a mark of illness to some, is to others such a stigma or badge of disgrace that procedural due process requires notice and an opportunity to be heard. . . . [T]he private interest [here] is such that those requirements must be met.
>
> Only when the whole proceedings leading to the pinning of an unsavory label on a person are aired can oppressive results be prevented.[161]

---

aration and submission of plans for implementation, for state and local district task forces composed of official and constituency members with reporting systems and access by task force members to all necessary data and persons and processes to participate in formulation of plans and to oversee their implementation, and for recourse to masters, committees, and ultimately the court to resolve any extended controversy. Perforce, this configuration of the constituency dealt extensively also with legislatures, governors, universities, experts, professionals, agencies, and with newly visible members of the constituency itself, as well as with defendant bureaus and districts and the courts. *See* Pa. Dep't of Educ., Introductory Information and Instructions for the Right to Education Plan (May 1972); Pa. Dep't of Educ., Commonwealth Plan for Identification, Location and Evaluation (1972) (available from Pa. Right to Education Office, Harrisburg).

[154] The particular procedures required in the prior hearings are set out in PARC, 343 F. Supp. at 303-05, Mills, 348 F. Supp. at 880-83, and Lebanks v. Spears, 60 F.R.D. 135 (E.D. La. 1973). They are collated and annotated in Dimond, *supra* note 4, 1115-20. *See also* Wyatt v. Stickney, 344 F. Supp. at 376, 392.

[155] *Compare* PARC, 343 F. Supp. at 307 *with* Wyatt v. Stickney, 344 F. Supp. at 396.

[156] *See, e.g.,* the discussion of stigma, notes 7-12 *supra*; PARC, 343 F. Supp. at 293-95.

[157] Consider, *e.g.,* that for mentally retarded individuals misplacement is tantamount to no placement at all, to the denial of access itself, note 47 *supra*.

[158] *See, e.g.,* Garrison & Hammill, *Who are the Retarded?* 37 EXCEPTIONAL CHILDREN 13 (1971) (reporting that in 5-county metropolitan Philadelphia at least 25% and perhaps as much as 68% of the children in classes for the educable mentally retarded had been misclassified and misplaced). *See generally* J. MERCER, LABELING THE MENTALLY RETARDED (1973). *See also* PARC, 343 F. Supp. at 295; *cf.* Larry P. v. Riles, 343 F. Supp. 1306 (N.D. Cal. 1972), *aff'd*, 502 F.2d 963 (1974); Diana v. California State Bd. of Educ., Civil No. C-70-37 (N.D. Cal., Feb. 5, 1970).

[159] *E.g.,* Slochower v. Board of Higher Educ., 350 U.S. 551 (1956) (employment); Schware v. Board of Bar Examiners, 353 U.S. 232 (1957) (professional license); Dixon v. Alabama Bd. of Educ., 294 F.2d 150 (5th Cir. 1961), *cert. denied*, 368 U.S. 930 (1961) (public college education). *See* Bell v. Burson, 402 U.S. 535 (1971) (driver's license); Goldberg v. Kelly, 397 U.S. 254 (1970) (public assistance).

[160] 400 U.S. 433 (1971).

[161] 400 U.S. at 436-37.

As the Court had previously written in *Kent v. United States:*

> [T]here is no place in our system of law for reaching a result of such tremendous consequences without ceremony — without hearing, without effective assistance of counsel, without a statement of reasons. . . .[162]

The opportunity for a due process hearing established in the education cases serves the child — and all of us — by ensuring a proper education.[163] It serves the superintendent and the secretary of education by ensuring "feedback," the opportunity to know if rules and resources are doing as they should and to make corrections if they are not. It serves local administrators by providing a forum at the highest reaches of the education bureaucracy where they can raise in particular and vivid terms their resources needs. It serves the professional — the teacher, the psychologist — by providing a forum in which to assert the rights of his or her clients and to check his or her own judgment and the judgment of others.[164] It serves associations of retarded citizens by providing a forum in which they can exercise their skills at advocacy and oversight, deliver "hard goods" services to their membership, and thereby gather further strength to the association.[165]

Beyond this, due process hearings and litigation itself, like every opportunity to petition the government for redress of grievances, indeed, like every opportunity gathered in the protection of the first amendment, serve still other values, the value to oneself and to others — and to all of us — of expression. The pleasure of asserting oneself, of saying who one is, and in particular of saying to the world: I am a being with rights.

For citizens who are different, the claim is not only for services in the community. The claim is for recognition: not to be merely tolerated, or even cared for, but to be seen, and to see oneself, proudly and with regard.

If the uses of litigation are to be realized, two things are important for the near future. First is needed a framework for the continued gathering of retarded persons, their family and friends, their organizations, and their lawyers in the focussed pursuit of their rights, by litigation and otherwise, and their full realization of these rights in fact. One such framework is the formation, state by state, of centers for law and the handicapped, with associations for retarded citizens and associations of other handicapped citizens gathered in coalition, contributing, say, $10,000 each annually, to maintain a clutch of lawyers whose full time belongs to their constituencies.[166] The time when such coalitions and legal centers exist in every state can-

---

[162] 383 U.S. 541, 554 (1966). *See also In re* Gault, 387 U.S. 1, 57 (1967).

[163] *See* text at note 40 *supra*.

[164] There is increasing recognition of the rights of bureaucratized professionals to assert the interests of their clients. *See, e.g.,* Parrish v. Civil Serv. Comm'n, 66 Cal. 2d 260, 425 P.2d 223, 57 Cal. Rptr. 623 (1967); Chalk Appeal, 441 Pa. 376 (1971); Donahue v. Staunton, 471 F.2d 475 (7th Cir. 1972), *cert. denied*, 410 U.S. 955 (1973). A full statement of the protections necessary, and of the theory to support them, if professionals in the bureaucracy are to do so generally is beyond the scope of this paper. The due process hearing, however, provides one such protected opportunity.

[165] A preliminary analysis of the impact of *PARC, Mills, Larry P.,* and *Diana* in Kirp, Buss & Kuriloff. *Legal Reform of Special Education: Empirical Studies and Procedural Proposals*, 62 CALIF. L. REV. 40 (1974), underscores the importance of the hearings, *inter alia,* to the implementation of substantive rule change.

[166] GALANTER, WHY THE "HAVES" COME OUT AHEAD: SPECULATIONS ON THE SETTING AND LIMITS OF LEGAL CHANGE (Yale Program in Law and Modernization, working paper no. 7, (1972), distinguishes

not come soon enough.

Second, the gathering, around litigation and otherwise, of mentally retarded citizens to speak for themselves is vital.[167] As Mr. Justice Douglas said of children in *Wisconsin v. Yoder:*

> [C]hildren are "persons" within the meaning of the Bill of Rights. We have so held over and over again. . . .
>
> On this important and vital matter of education, I think the children should be entitled to be heard. While parents, absent dissent, normally speak for the entire family, the education of the child is a matter on which the child will often have decided views. . . . It is the student's judgment . . . that is essential if we are to give full meaning to what we have said about the Bill of Rights and of the right of [persons] to be masters of their own destiny.[168]

Nor can this come soon enough.

Reaction Comment

HUGH J. SCOTT

GILHOOL and his colleagues, who have pressed for the acceptance and implementation of the fundamental right of the mentally retarded child to receive a

---

the ability of litigants to use the legal system to secure redistributive change, marked by whether litigants are one-shotters (OSs), who resort to the courts only occasionally, or repeat parties (RPs), who engage in a large number of similar court suits over time. Galanter urges if have-not parties, now typically OSs, are to achieve change they must reconstitute themselves as RPs:

> Our analysis suggests that change at the level of rules is not likely in itself to be determinative of redistributive outcomes. Rule change is in itself likely to have little effect because the [legal] system is so constructed that changes in the rules can be filtered out unless accompanied by changes at other levels. In a setting of overloaded institutional facilities, inadequate costly legal services, and unorganized parties, beneficiaries may lack the resources to secure implementation; an RP (opponent) may restructure the transaction to escape the thrust of the new rule. Favorable rules are typically not in short supply to have-nots; certainly less so than any of the other resources needed to play the litigation game. Programs of equalizing reform which focus on rule-change can be readily absorbed without any change in power relations. The system has a capacity to change a great deal at the level of rules without corresponding changes in everyday patterns of practice or distribution of tangible advantages. Indeed rule-change may become a symbolic substitute for redistribution of advantages. . . .
>
> The organization of have-not parties into coherent groups [would] have the ability to act in a co-ordinated fashion, play long-run strategies, benefit from high-grade legal services, etc. An organized group is not only better able to secure favorable rule change (in courts and elsewhere) but is better able to see that good rules are implemented. It can expend resources on surveillance, monitoring, threats, litigation that would be uneconomic for an OS. *Id.* at 42-43, 37.

[167] *See, e.g.,* Nirje, *Towards Independence,* 22 MENTAL RETARDATION No. 2 (April 1972) (a report of the declaration and proceedings of retarded adults in convention in Scandanavia); OUR LIFE: A CONFERENCE REPORT (Ann Shearer ed. 1972). (First Conference of Mentally Handicapped People in the United Kingdom); LISTEN: WEEKEND CONFERENCE OF RETARDED ADULTS (Ann Shearer ed. 1973) (Campaign for Mentally Handicapped, London). In California, Maryland, Massachusetts, and Pennsylvania, at least, retarded adults have begun to convene in annual sessions parallel to the conventions of the Associations for Retarded Citizens.

[168] 406 U.S. 205, 243-45 (1972) (concurring in part and dissenting in part). *Compare* Horacek v. Exon, 357 F. Supp. 71, 74 (D. Neb. 1973).

publicly supported education, have accomplished what all educators worthy of the identification should have been seeking for all mentally retarded children. A debt of gratitude must be acknowledged to these attorneys and justices and those in other institutions and agencies who have effectively advocated for the legal rights of mentally retarded individuals.

It remains for this fundamental right to be translated into the provision of quality service programs for persons who are labeled mentally retarded. The full implementation of the rights of metally retarded citizens to publicly supported quality educational programs and services will require a vast outlay of additional resources — financial and personnel — to school systems which in many instances currently are confronting the negative consequences produced by insufficient funds to meet expanding needs. The children who are the easiest to teach and thus the least expensive to educate — based on the positive effects of environmental supports that stimulate and facilitate growth and development — constitute the majority of students in some school systems. However, this is not true in most urban school systems. The priorities established in terms of programs and services should be aimed at alleviating situations in which socioeconomic factors, academic deficiencies, deficiencies in the service system, and innate impediments to growth and development combine to present the most urgent challenges to public education. The quality, quantity, and concentration of resources should be in direct proportion to the extent of student needs. A school system can be effective only to the degree that there is a balance between the educational needs presented to the system and its programmatic response to such needs.

The provision of programs and services for students with exceptional needs is severely limited by the national shortage of trained and skilled personnel at all levels to carry out the specialized demands on professionals who are to serve mentally retarded children. The actualization of the rights of mentally retarded children will necessitate vast training and staff development programs to prepare the cadre of personnel needed to provide the required services. Such services must be provided in a manner that is compatible with the best contemporary understanding of human growth and development.

Along with the assertion of the rights of the mentally retarded, there must be a reformation in the conceptual thrust that directs intent and content of programs and services. The new thrust should stress continuity and appropriateness of programs and services as the principles upon which to make judgments as to whether or not a school system is fulfilling its responsibility. Legitimacy is established only through the provision of equal educational opportunity when it can clearly be demonstrated that each mentally retarded child is given every possible opportunity to develop his potentialities to the fullest. Anything less than this represents a denial of full access to equality of educational opportunity.

When the United States Court for the District of Columbia issued its decree in *Mills*,[1] I was among the defendants. This class action suit was brought against the Washington, D.C., Board of Education, the superintendent of schools, the

---

[1] Mills v. Board of Educ., 348 F. Supp. 866 (D.D.C. 1972).

mayor, and the District of Columbia because the plaintiffs believed that some students in need of special education services were being denied their rights to a publicly supported program of instruction. The defendants openly admitted their obligation to provide each child with an education suited to his needs and also admitted their failure to do so. The defendants offered the defense that sufficient funds did not exist to provide such services unless the Congress of the United States appropriated additional funds for the reconciliation of the identified unmet needs of the plaintiffs. The Court rejected this rationale, finding that constitutional rights must be afforded citizens regardless of the greater expense involved. The Court stated: "The inadequacies of the District of Columbia Public School System whether occasioned by insufficient funding or administrative inefficiency, certainly cannot be permitted to bear more heavily on the 'exceptional' or handicapped child than on the normal child."[2]

The Court's mandate made the means by which this issue was to be resolved quite clear. The Court's reasoning was:

1. Parents are required to send their children to school by the D.C. Code, and criminal penalties are provided for those who fail to do so. The board of education is therefore obliged to provide education for all children in order to make it possible for parents to comply with the law.
2. The Supreme Court in the 1954 decision on school segregation ruled that educational opportunity must be made available to all on an equal basis.
3. In *Hobson v. Hansen*,[3] Judge J. Skelly Wright ruled that the doctrine of equal educational opportunity was a part of the law of due process and that denying poor children an equal educational opportunity was a violation of the due process clause of the Constitution.
4. Denying handicapped children not only equal education but all education violates the due process clause. Due process also require a hearing before a child is expelled or given a special classification.[4]

Following the Court's mandate, programs and services to other students have been reduced or terminated in order to finance the cost of special education services for the identified but unserved student population with exceptional needs. The rights not only of students who are mentally retarded, but of all students, especially those who suffer from the consequences of the cumulative deficiencies in the acquisition of basic skills, are recognized as non-negotiable. Such rights, however, can never be fully implemented until sufficient funds are made available and distributed equitably. The greater the child's needs, the higher the per pupil cost of education. The past and present levels of funding to school systems have been grossly insufficient to provide a programmatic response to the needs of students with exceptional needs in a manner consistent with recognized standards in special education.

Children with exceptional needs which result from physical, psychological,

[2] *Id.* at 876.
[3] 269 F. Supp. 401 (D.D.C. 1967), *aff'd sub. nom.* Smuck v. Hobson, 408 F.2d 175 (D.C. Cir. 1969).
[4] 348 F. Supp. at 875.

or mental handicaps comprise neither the only nor the largest group of students being denied both equality and a quality education. In the public schools of the District of Columbia, more than one-half of the 95 percent black student population of 140,000 students require some form of additional services to compensate for those impediments to growth and development which are traced directly to a disadvantaged environment. The maturation of an individual's intellectual potentialities is strongly influenced by those variables in his environment which serve as depressants or stimulants to growth and development. Many nonretarded students are being denied true equality of educational opportunity because the resources and programs are not available to respond to their needs.

It is true that the right to equality of educational opportunity in publicly supported educational institutions for persons who are mentally retarded, especially those who are profoundly retarded, has been ignored in most of the school systems across this nation. The violation of the rights of mentally retarded individuals has perhaps been the most flagrant in scope and impact of all of the denials of public education in the United States. Yet, the establishment of the right of all mentally retarded school-age children to publicly supported education will mean no more than an exercise in futility unless the resources can be secured to provide the range of programs and services needed to provide quality instruction and noninstructional services.

The fierce struggle over funds for public education is not being won by those who are in the most dire need of additional funds to deal with the scope and complexities of their needs. Somewhere along the way, the lawyers and courts, along with interested educators, must join forces in a united effort to deal with equality of educational opportunity. If public education in this nation were to go bankrupt, it would be of no comfort to the mentally retarded children that the nonretarded also were deprived. The needs of one group cannot be singled out as more important than the needs of another when the basic issue remains that equality of educational opportunity is a non-negotiable right. I see no hope for meeting the educational needs of students, including the mentally retarded, as long as the major school systems in America are continually denied sufficient funds. A right that is not implemented is a right denied. The battle in the court is being won and the legal profession is to be commended in this regard, but the struggle to secure both resources and appropriate programs for all youth continues.

Reaction Comment

MONROE E. PRICE

I WOULD LIKE to start with a thought inspired by David Rothman, who, in *The Discovery of the Asylum,* wrote so movingly about the wide and deep hopes in the nineteenth century that reformists had for the great state institutions that were then built and that are now so completely and thoroughly condemned. We are persuaded now that what was seen than as promise was really illusion; that the rehabilitative dream of the last century could not be achieved through the course pursued. There was a time when people still believed in the utility of the fantastic rural fortress, dismayed only by the manner in which plans had been implemented. They are a shrinking number. For we now begin, collectively, to place great faith in a new asylum, the "asylum of the community." The community and community services are the point for renewal of our faith.

Is this new asylum also an illusion? Or, to put the question more moderately and accurately, what obstacles are to be expected as we move from one system of service delivery to another?

The most difficult issue, of course, is the fiscal aspect of the transfer. The reformer's zeal may have focused upon the city, but it is not clear that the legislature's appropriation will follow. Without great care, "normalization" or "community services" can be a technique to reduce state expenditure or to shift the burden of spending from one level of government to another. Much of this is true of the experience in California involving the closing of state hospitals providing care for mentally retarded persons. When the legislation was passed, a meticulous new structure was established for regional centers, for the exploration and development of local alternatives, and, as a last resort, state institutions. It was presumed that state institutions would be curtailed drastically as the local services developed. Following this blueprint and the general state policy to shift services to a community base, the state administration began a program of implementation by announcing the closing of certain state facilities. The response was surprising and overwhelming. The families of retarded children were knowingly concerned that the flag of community care might cover a shift from some security (though in a not entirely satisfactory setting) to an underdeveloped, uncertain, and therefore worrisome system of services. There was a realistic fear that community services might not grow adequately even though state alternatives declined.

An important aspect of Gilhool's statement is his illustration of lawyerly resilience, the ability of counsel to function in harsh and unfriendly circumstances. A change in the complexion of the courts or a drastic change in signals from appellate court judges does not result in a statement that courts are no longer an important forum for intervention and reform. This kind of conclusion is for the newspapers. Gilhool emphasizes the need to search out new theories, new approaches. There is the refinement of the equal protection analysis, the expansion of the due process theories, and the relatively new doctrines of representation and contract.

What this means, at bottom, is that lawyers like Gilhool are constantly defining and refining the relationship among men and between men and institutions of government. There is a translation of what is intuitively thought to be decent to a more formal kind of doctrine. It is amazing how necessary this function has become. No matter how much training an educator or a doctor or a hospital administrator might have, it still becomes necessary at rather frequent intervals to define and refine the purpose and role of the institution and its relationship to the persons it serves.

Put another way, an important role of the lawyer and the judge is to ask questions that are not asked frequently enough by the institution itself, or if asked, are not put in a context where more than a formalistic, bureaucratic answer is forthcoming. Why is it that we do not more searchingly and more certainly ask questions such as whether there is an obligation to provide education to all who could benefit from it? What the minimum public standards should be for medical care? What they shoud be for nutrition, for family care or its substitute? It is peculiar, in the sense that few societies have similar patterns, that in the United States it falls to a judge, aided by the contributions of counsel and the intellectual investment of groups like the President's Committee on Mental Retardation, to attempt to resolve such basic and important issues.

The *PARC v. Pennsylvania* litigation provides a superb example of what is extraordinary about the system. There was a rational, deliberate, careful, and articulate pursuit of answers to basic questions. What does the Constitution say about the right to education for children who are, in varying degrees, mentally retarded? What facts can be adduced to enlighten the process of decision? There was an orderly presentation of views and an intelligent judicial panel, unhindered and unbound, empowered to resolve the issue.

A fundamental consideration is how pervasive is the desire to ask such basic questions and answer them. This is a particularly important matter with respect to mental retardation, for the issues involved often touch quite sensitive matters. What is the commitment to life itself? How much help should there be to, and intervention in, the decisions of the family? What is the relationship between the goals of society and the financial commitment it is willing to expend in pursuit of these goals? The example given by Gilhool—the recent Medi-Cal case of an epileptic patient who sought reimbursement for round-the-clock care—is illustrative of the difficulties. The trial judge gave an answer to the question of the quality of care available that was too searching, that was founded on the Constitution and provided an answer that was, therefore, too certain for some. The Supreme Court, relying on the Medi-Cal regulations, reached the same result but in a way that admitted tentativeness and frustration about the basic economic issue. It is not known to what extent cost is a limit on society's desire to be humane, at what point talk must explicitly relate to an allocation of resources, rather than an absolute entitlement.

But the allocation question is always in the near background. Even when a court reaches the basic issues, as in the *PARC* case, the allocation of resources question still permits only qualified commitment to the result. In California, as indicated, there has been a rather firm legislative commitment to the principle of community mental health services. But the easier portion of the resulting action has been carried out more fully than the harder part. The state institutions are in the process of being closed without the correlative provision of adequate replacements in the community.

Finally, it is interesting that a measure of national willingness to have such fundamental questions asked is the commitment to a free and unfettered publicly financed legal services program. Of the approximately 40 cases pending, according to the President's Committee on Mental Retardation, over 30 have serious and important OEO-funded legal services participation. In the debates over the financing of legal services programs, this aspect of the benefit is seldom noted. The kind of work, the kind of probing and ameliorative litigation which Gilhool has fostered will be forthcoming in a systematic and pervasive way only if a network of publicly funded lawyers of high professional quality is maintained.

ADDENDUM TO FOOTNOTE 88, P. 192

Although the court initially rejected the right to habilitation concept in its memorandum granting preliminary relief, it has subsequently noted that:

> Somewhat different legal rubrics have been employed in these cases—"protection from harm" in this case and "right to treatment" and "need for care" in others. It appears that there is no bright line separating these standards. Entry of final consent judgment, New York Association for Retarded Children v. Carey, Civil Nos. 72C356, 72C357 (E. D. N. Y. entered, May 5, 1975).

CHAPTER 8

Labeling and Classification

Editorial Introduction

*T*he testing, labeling, and placement process has been carried out by schools to assign children to particular programs or tracks, purportedly in the best interests of the students. Over the years, school have used the law, school regulations, and traditional practices to establish special education programs, to construct a system for identifying and transferring students into such programs, and to exclude children from both regular and special programs. It has become increasingly evident that these programs and processes show minimal concern for the rights of the individual.

Sorgen's paper on labeling and classification has particular relevance for practicing attorneys, highlighting the cases and arguments that have been developed and utilized to help secure adequate educational opportunities for mentally retarded individuals. Certain points in the paper bear mentioning here to help establish a background. First, the classification "mentally retarded" embraces a very diverse group in which the majority of individuals need services similar to those required by other school children. The instruments used in the labeling and classification process are extremely prejudicial against children from the lower socioeconomic area, as well as against racial and cultural minority children. Sorgen emphasizes the stigma attached to the label of mental retardation and the extent to which the labeling and placement process is integral to a self-fulfilling prophecy whereby a child is not expected to do well and, in fact, does not do well in school. He explores the protection that must be afforded such children under the law and the legal safeguards necessary to minimize the broad dissemination of what is essentially a school-related label. Many of the legal precedents in this area come from court rulings in other areas, including racial segregation, employment, and civil rights.

214

Although the emphasis on litigation and the judicial process to redress obvious wrongs is the focus of Sorgen's paper, legislative relief also carries considerable promise in this area. Sorgen illustrates the great need for lawyers and mental retardation personnel to work at and achieve effective communication. The ease with which people with a common background or profession develop a special jargon mitigates against full understanding of ideas and concepts. Communication must be improved to ensure achieving the goal of the most appropriate service for the mentally retarded individual.

In her comments on Sorgen's contribution to this volume, Nordin emphasizes the impact of *In re Gault* on school actions in a system that purports to be serving the needs of children. She elaborates on the significance of several of the cases cited by Sorgen and highlights two correlating pressures—the reluctance of courts to move into areas that are not within their usual expertise and the need for educators to rectify the inequities that result from the testing, labeling, classification, and placement process before the courts, no matter how reluctantly or poorly, are forced to do so.

Bransford's reaction emphasizes the complexity of the educational system and of the classification problem, particularly in its discriminatory impact on minority children. Bransford comments on the limited impact of individual lawsuits on the total educational process. Although he concurs with some of Sorgen's suggested remedies, he takes exception to others. Bransford sees the problem as requiring a whole new set of attitudes in and toward public education. Individual prescription of programs to serve the needs of each child is essential. He sees this reorientation as having to occur within the educational system. Litigation may help, but the problem is complex and must be solved by a dramatic reorientation of the public education system itself.

PRINCIPAL PAPER

MICHAEL S. SORGEN

THE CLASSIFICATION PROCESS AND ITS CONSEQUENCES

The Classification

The relevance of law to classification, labeling, and stigmatization of persons as mentally retarded is just beginning to emerge from popular misconception. Two widely held erroneous notions are being, and must be, dispelled. The first is that the term "mentally retarded" refers to a homogeneous group. The second is the popular image that almost all mentally retarded persons are near the low end of the intelligence scale, facing a pitiful and practically nonfunctional existence.

A simple description of two prototypes of mental retardation serves to highlight the heterogeneity of the concept. The profoundly retarded person, whose deficiency is biological and who is nonambulatory, often requires almost constant care and supervision. He has little in common with the mildly retarded individual, whose condition may be environmentally caused and who is capable of living a normal personal life and holding a job. Even the traditional, though highly unsatisfactory, means of classifying by scores obtained on standardized intelligence tests stratifies the retarded into five groups: borderline (with IQ scores between 70 and 84), mild (55-69), moderate (40-54), severe (25-39), and profound (0-24).[1]

Because the standardized tests themselves raise serious legal problems,[2] it is more useful to elaborate the differences in terms of functional or adaptive ability. The profoundly and severely retarded, who constitute only a small portion of the groups, can learn basic self-care and improve their behavior control, language development, and physical mobility, although their economic productivity is quite limited. On the other hand, the educability and developmental potential of most mentally retarded persons far exceed current public expectations. Mildly retarded individuals can master some formal schoolwork and become self-sufficient as adults. Moderately retarded individuals can learn to take care of their physical needs and to perform manual skills.[3] They may live in a somewhat diminished world, but it is far better than is commonly believed. Any discussion of the social and civil rights of the mentally retarded citizen must be preceded by recognition of the diverse nature of persons classified mentally retarded.

Even more crucial in attaining recognition of the rights of the mentally retarded is the basic fact that the vast majority are at the upper range of the scale. Tarjan's bipartite division is both illustrative and instructive. Individuals with severe to moderate intellectual impairment, often accompanied by physical handicaps, constitute only 10 percent of all retarded persons. The other 90 percent, with IQs generally over 50, can make a reasonably adequate adjustment and, as adults, become absorbed into the general population well enough that perhaps they should cease to be labeled "mentally retarded." Members of this second group are rarely characterized by physical indicia of their condition and normally are not diagnosed as mentally retarded until they enter school.[4]

---

[1] Brison, *Definition, Diagnosis and Classification* in MENTAL RETARDATION—APPRAISAL, EDUCATION AND REHABILITATION 10 (A. Baumeister ed. 1967); Heber, *Modifications in the Manual on Terminology and Classification in Mental Retardation*, 65 AM. J. MENTAL DEFICIENCY 499, 500 (1961). The scores given in the text are on the Wechsler scale and vary slightly if the Stanford-Binet test is used.

The previous American Association on Mental Deficiency classification of "borderline" retardation has been dropped from the revised classification levels. H. GROSSMAN, MANUAL ON TERMINOLOGY AND CLASSIFICATION IN MENTAL RETARDATION 18 (1973).

[2] *See* pp. 229-35 *infra.*

[3] NATIONAL ASSOCIATION FOR RETARDED CHILDREN, FACTS ON MENTAL RETARDATION 4 (1971).

[4] Tarjan, *Research and Clinical Advances in Mental Retardation,* 182 J.A.M.A. 617, 618 (1962).

The Process

Diagnosis and classification of the more severely retarded tends to occur early in life.[5] Because a severely retarded child often places great stress on a family's emotional and financial resources,[6] the early diagnosis and classification may be misused to seek institutionalization when other forms of care might be more consistent with the child's best interest.[7] Notwithstanding these serious problems in classification and treatment of the severely retarded, legal activity in the classification area should focus in the immediate future on the much larger more adaptable group of less seriously impaired individuals for two reasons. First, the less evident nature of their handicap and the difficulty of diagnosis raise serious questions regarding the adequacy of the sorting devices used. Second, because persons with only moderate intellectual impairment have considerable learning capacity and social adaptability, the harm of misclassification is especially tragic. A child's potential may remain not only unrecognized, but also be stifled by a decision to exclude him from school or to place him in a special program not appropriate to his needs. When a right as elemental as human development hangs in the balance, the law must take a hard look at the most frequent perpetrator of harm—the public schools.

Schools have the primary role in labeling and stigmatizing the less severely impaired mentally retarded. It is in schools that most persons come into contact with their first societal evaluator. Children with learning difficulties are referred by teachers or administrators to school psychologists, who, on the basis of standardized tests and other considerations, classify the children on the purported basis of intellectual capacity. The schools label more persons as mentally retarded, and share their labels more widely, than any other formal organization in the community.[8]

Given the widespread use of labeling and classifying children in public schools,[9] it can be presumed that this process not only accords with educators' demands for the efficiency of categorization, but also serves some significant scholastic purposes. For example, narrowing the range of student abilities within a particular classroom may enable the teacher to adapt the pace and content of instruction better, so as to devote more individual attention to students.[10] But given the remarkably primitive

[5] Koch, *Diagnosis in Infancy and Early Childhood*, in PREVENTION AND TREATMENT OF MENTAL RETARDATION 45 (I. Philips ed. 1966).

[6] H. ROBINSON & N. ROBINSON, THE MENTALLY RETARDED CHILD 516-23 (1965); Begab, *The Mentally Retarded and the Family*, in PREVENTION AND TREATMENT OF MENTAL RETARDATION 71 (I. Philips ed. 1966).

[7] *See* Murdock, *Civil Rights of the Mentally Retarded: Some Critical Issues*, 48 NOTRE D. LAW. 133, 136-43 (1972).

[8] J. Mercer, The Labelling Process, October 16, 1971 (paper delivered at Kennedy International Symposium on Human Rights, Retardation and Research; Panel on the Use and Misuse of Labelling Human Beings: The Ethics of Testing, Tracking and Filing). *See also* Mercer, *Institutionalized Anglocentrism: Labelling Mental Retardates in the Public Schools,* in RACE, CHANGE AND URBAN SOCIETY 311 (P. Orleans & W. Ellis eds. 1971) [hereinafter cited as *Anglocentrism*].

[9] Rist, *Student Social Class and Teacher Expectations: The Self-Fulfilling Prophecy in Ghetto Education,* 40 HARV. EDUC. REV. 411, 414 (1970); Findley & Bryan, *Ability Grouping: Do's and Don'ts,* 9 INTEGRATED EDUC., Sept. 1971, at 31-36.

[10] M. GOLDBERG, A. PASSOU & J. JUSTMAN, THE EFFECTS OF ABILITY GROUPING 150 (1966) (offering a comprehensive review of the literature on this issue).

knowledge of the diverse needs of children,[11] the number and variety of differentiating characteristics among children, and the inability of schools to devise programs properly tailored to individual needs, the result must of necessity be gross simplification of the differences. Because of the rudimentary nature of criteria and techniques with which the decisions are made, schools frequently must make crude and incorrect classifications.

The Consequences

Questionable classification processes used by schools have significant short- and long-term effects. They often define what, if anything, the school will try to teach the child, and the character of his classmates. Too often the classification also determines what the child's role and status will be both during his school years and after the completion of his schooling.

For the child deemed uneducable and given a one-way ticket out of school, the injury is most apparent.[12] Exclusion from school ironically confirms the prediction that the child cannot be educated. The child most in need of special instruction and attention is the one most completely denied it. The child excluded because of his handicap is, in effect, sentenced to a lifetime of illiteracy and public dependence. He may even be relegated to total loss of liberty through institutionalization—civil or penal—as a result of a failure to learn the skills essential to life in this society.

The child assigned to a special class for the educable mentally retarded (EMR) fares only slightly better because of the limited design and minimal curriculum of most such programs.[13] These classes are frequently "dumping grounds" for children with whom the schools refuse to deal.[14] Studies indicating that classroom peer group composition has the highest correlation to pupil performance[15] make it seem doubtful that a marginally retarded child would benefit as much from isolation in an EMR class as from continuation in a regular class.[16] If the added financial and educational resources now devoted to EMR classes were redistributed to normal classrooms, the improvement in overall education might more than compensate for the difficulty of dealing with EMR children in the regular classroom.

It is in the EMR classroom that the social stigma attaches. Whether the children are called "retarded" or just "special," it is in fact a debilitating recognition which

[11] See, e.g., PROBLEMS AND ISSUES IN THE EDUCATION OF EXCEPTIONAL CHILDREN (R. Jones ed. 1971); L. DEXTER, THE TYRANNY OF SCHOOLING (1964).

[12] Cf. Kirk, Research in Education, in MENTAL RETARDATION 63-67 (H.A. Stevens & R. Heber eds. 1964).

[13] See, e.g., CAL. EDUC. CODE § 6902 (the purpose of EMR classes is to make such children "economically useful and socially adjusted").

[14] See H. GOLDSTEIN, J. MOSS & L. JORDAN, THE EFFICACY OF SPECIAL CLASS TRAINING IN THE DEVELOPMENT OF MENTALLY RETARDED CHILDREN (1965).

[15] See pp. 226-27 & note 61 infra.

[16] Dunn, Special Education for the Mildly Retarded: Is Much of it Justifiable?, in PROBLEMS AND ISSUES IN THE EDUCATION OF EXCEPTIONAL CHILDREN 382 (R. Jones ed. 1971); G. HOELTKE, EFFECTIVENESS OF SPECIAL CLASS PLACEMENT FOR EDUCABLE RETARDED CHILDREN (1966); S. KIRK, EDUCATING EXCEPTIONAL CHILDREN (1972). Hence, two recent cases create a presumption in favor of regular class placement with ancillary services unless the school can justify a special class. Pennsylvania Association for Retarded Children v. Pennsylvania, 343 F. Supp. 279, 307 (E.D. Pa. 1972) [hereinafter cited as PARC]; Mills v. District of Columbia Bd. of Educ., 348 F. Supp. 866, 880 (D.D.C. 1972) [hereinafter cited as Mills]; cf. Seal v. Mertz, 338 F. Supp. 945, 950 (M.D. Pa. 1972).

connotes abnormality and limited educability. Children and their parents are well aware of what the school's label means. Children assigned to EMR classes are "ashamed to be seen entering the 'MR' room . . . [and] dreaded receiving mail that might bear compromising identification."[17] One mother whose son had been in EMR classes for five years reported that "[i]t's as if they have a sign around their neck for everyone to read."[18]

In fact, the manner in which the same school treats different children may be a more significant determinant of pupil performance than are the initial bases for the classification decision.[19] There is, for example, substantial support in education literature for the hypothesis that low expectancy by the child's classroom teacher diminishes the motivation of children in low-ability groups. The child who receives signals that he is regarded as a school "failure," who is assigned to EMR classes, and who thereby feels ignored and inferior may respond in fact by doing more poorly than he would if there were greater expectations of him. Motivation and effort decline. As a result, the student fails to develop the skills which might bring a more positive response.[20]

As Judge Skelly Wright noted in *Hobson v. Hansen*:

> The real tragedy of misjudgments about the disadvantaged student's abilities is . . . the likelihood that the student will act out the judgment and confirm it by achieving only at the expected level. Indeed, it may be even worse than that, for there is strong evidence that performance in fact declines. . . . And while the tragedy of misjudgments can occur even under the best of circumstances, there is reason to believe that the track system compounds the risk.[21]

Voicing the hopeless conclusion that "these kids are dumb" or "retarded" and cannot be properly educated, schools assign students to EMR classes are permanently relegated to an education less stimulating and in most respects decidedly inferior to that offered other students. This placement virtually ensures that the initial prognosis will be proven true. Classified and subsequently treated as less than "normal," they are ". . . left behind as second-class citizens . . . find[ing] themselves in a predicament that they are poorly equipped to overcome. Dimly realizing the powerful odds against them, they soon, with few exceptions, succumb to hopelessness."[22]

Regardless of how one explains the consequences of mental retardation on an individual's life,[23] there is substantial support in psychological and sociological

---

[17] Mercer, The Labelling Process, *supra* note 8.

[18] *Anglocentrism, supra* note 8, at 312.

[19] *See, e.g.,* R. ROSENTHAL & L. JACOBSON, PYGMALION IN THE CLASSROOM (1968); Rist, *supra* note 9; Rosenthal & Jacobson, *Teacher Expectation for the Disadvantaged*, 218 SCIENTIFIC AMERICAN, April 1968, at 19.

[20] C. Jencks, The Coleman Report and Conventional Wisdom (Harvard Center for Educ. Policy Research, 1970); Comer, *The Circle Game in School Tracking*, INEQUALITY IN EDUC., No. 12, at 23, 25 (1972).

[21] 269 F. Supp. 401, 491-92 (D.D.C. 1967), *aff'd. sub nom.* Smuck v. Hobson, 408 F.2d 175 (D.C. Cir. 1969). *See also* Larry P. v. Riles, 343 F. Supp. 1306 (N.D. Cal. 1972), *aff'd,* 502 F.2d 963 (1974); Moses v. Washington Parish School Bd., 330 F. Supp. 1340, 1345 (E.D. La. 1971), *aff'd.,* 456 F.2d 1285 (5th Cir.), *cert. denied,* 409 U.S. 1013 (1972).

[22] Bettelheim, *Segregation: New Style*, 66 THE SCHOOL REV. 251, 265 (1958).

[23] *See generally* Dexter, *A Sociological Perspective on Mental Retardation Practice,* 16 MENTAL RETARDATION, Summer 1966, at 2; Dexter, *The Sociology of the Exceptional Person,* 4 INDIANA J. SOCIAL RESEARCH 31 (1963); R. EDGERTON, THE CLOAK OF COMPETENCE: STIGMA IN THE LIVES OF THE MENTALLY RETARDED (1967); B. FARBER, MENTAL RETARDATION: ITS SOCIAL CONTEXT AND SOCIAL

literature for the hypothesis that labeling a person mentally retarded seriously affects him throughout his life. Although some persons defined as retarded may eventually come to lead "normal" lives, many are characterized by marginal life roles.[24]

Certainly, the classification forecloses vocational options. Even when employed, the mentally retarded often are relegated to semiskilled, service, or unskilled occupations because of popular folklore about the label. Obtaining employment when one has no demonstrable skills is difficult enough, but when the job applicant has a past that tends to discredit him in the eyes of the potential employer, the difficulties are compounded. Obviously, few employers are looking for, or are willing to accept, employees who not only have little training and experience, but who also are labeled "mentally retarded."

In addition, a retarded person is usually denied participation in social activities that "average" citizens living in the community take for granted. He may be prevented from entering into a contract or obtaining a drivers' license; he may be arbitrarily excluded from insurance coverage; he may not be able to exercise the franchise to vote.[25] On the incorrect assumption that the retarded citizen is incapable of exercising the most elemental personal rights, he may be denied the right to marry or to retain care and custody of his children[26] or even to have children.[27]

As Robert Edgerton described it on the basis of his study of life styles of over 100 formerly institutionalized mentally retarded individuals:

> To find oneself regarded as a mental retardate is to be burdened by a shattering stigma. . . . These persons cannot both believe that they are mentally retarded and still maintain their self-esteem. . . . [T]he stigma of mental retardation dominates every feature of the lives of these former patients. Without an understanding of this point there can be no understanding of their lives.[28]

CONSEQUENCES (1968); L. FREEMAN, ELEMENTARY APPLIED STATISTICS: FOR STUDENTS IN BEHAVIORAL SCIENCE (1965); J. JASTAK, H. MACPHEE & M. WHITEMAN, MENTAL RETARDATION, ITS NATURE AND INCIDENCE (1963); Mercer, *The Meaning of Mental Retardation,* in THE MENTALLY RETARDED LIVING IN THE COMMUNITY (R. Koch & J. Dobson eds. forthcoming); Mercer, *Who is Normal? Two Perspectives on Mild Mental Retardation,* in PATIENTS, PHYSICIANS AND ILLNESS (E. Jaco ed. forthcoming); Mercer, *Social System Perspective and Clinical Perspective: Frames of Reference for Understanding Career Patterns of Persons Labelled as Mentally Retarded,* 13 SOCIAL PROBLEMS 18 (1965).

[24] *See generally* Baller, *A Study of the Present Social Status of a Group of Adults, Who, When They Were in Elementary Schools, Were Classified as Mentally Deficient,* 18 GENETIC PSYCHOLOGY MONOGRAPHS 165 (1936); Doll, *A Historical Survey of Research and Management of Mental Retardation in the United States,* in READINGS ON THE EXCEPTIONAL CHILD 21 (E.P. Trapp & P. Himelstein eds. 1962); Doll, *Social Adjustment of the Mentally Subnormal,* 28 J. EDUC. RESEARCH 36 (1934); Fairbanks, *The Subnormal Child—Seventeen Years After,* 17 MENTAL HYGIENE 177 (1933); T. JORDAN, THE MENTALLY RETARDED (2d ed. 1966); E. KATZ, THE RETARDED ADULT IN THE COMMUNITY (1968); R. KENNEDY, THE SOCIAL ADJUSTMENT OF MORONS IN A CONNECTICUT CITY (1948); Kennedy, *A Connecticut Community Revisited: A Study of the Social Adjustment of a Group of Mentally Deficient Adults in 1948 and 1960—An Abstract Prepared by Ruby Jo Kennedy,* in PERSPECTIVES IN MENTAL RETARDATION 353 (T. Jordan ed. 1966); Peterson & Smith, *A Comparison of the Post-School Adjustment of Educable Mentally Retarded Adults with That of Adults of Normal Intelligence,* 26 EXCEPTIONAL CHILDREN 404 (1960); G. SAENGER, THE ADJUSTMENT OF SEVERELY RETARDED ADULTS IN THE COMMUNITY (1957).

[25] Haggerty, Kane & Udall, *An Essay on the Legal Rights of the Mentally Retarded,* 6 FAM. LAW Q. 59, 63-64 (1972).

[26] *See, e.g., In re* Jeannie Q., 31 Cal. App. 3d 709, 107 Cal. Rptr. 646 (1973); *In re* McDonald, 201 N.W.2d 447 (Iowa 1972); *In re* Franklin, 201 N.W.2d 727 (Iowa 1972).

[27] *See, e.g.,* Buck v. Bell, 274 U.S. 200 (1927); *In re* Cavitt, 182 Neb. 712, 157 N.W.2d 171 (1968), *appeal dismissed,* 396 U.S. 996 (1970).

[28] R. EDGERTON, *supra* note 23, at 204-08.

The label itself almost guarantees a failure life pattern.

The stigmatized person is viewed, often unconsciously, as being unable to participate in life as a "normal" person and accordingly is forced to the periphery of all social situations he enters. It is as though society, in an effort to prove the correctness of its label, proceeds to narrow the life chances of the stigmatized person to the preconceived notions connected with the stigma.[29]

The Role of Law

Where classification schemes create disparities of educational opportunity and resultant differences in life roles after school, the equal protection clause of the fourteenth amendment is the traditional tool for scrutinizing the school sorting process. It provides an available means by which many incorrectly classified and labeled students may attempt to realize their legal rights.

Intellectual ability is a relevant, even basic, criterion for judging differences in virtually every educational system. It would not be irrational for school officials to recognize obvious differences between "retarded" and "average" children, for example, by instituting "special education" programs to deal more adequately with academic deficiencies. Even if it could be shown that homogeneous grouping of retarded children and structuring of their educational experiences to their present levels of proficiency stifle educational growth, an unwise policy is not necessarily an illegal one.

Recognizing their lack of finesse and competence in matters of education, courts intrude only with grave trepidation into the area of school classification. In the absence of bad faith, arbitrariness, or capriciousness, courts usually will not intervene.[30] As the court stated in *Connelly v. University of Vermont:*

> [T]he school authorities are uniquely qualified by training and experience to judge the qualifications of a student, and efficiency of instruction depends in no small degree upon the school faculty's freedom from interference from other noneducational tribunals. It is only when the school authorities abuse this discretion that a court may interfere with their decision to dismiss a student.[31]

Although the courts sometimes have reviewed school classification decisions to determine whether a student was treated arbitrarily under the school's operative standards,[32] there is no case in which demonstrated academic ability has been held constitutionally invalid as a criterion for educational selection. As the Supreme Court noted in *Carrington v. Rash*, "Mere classification . . . does not of itself deprive a group of equal protection."[33] And as the court declared in *Stell v. Savannah-Chatham*

---

[29] *See, e.g.,* E. GOFFMAN, STIGMA 5 (1963).

[30] *See* Wright v. Texas S. Univ., 392 F.2d 728, 729 (5th Cir. 1968); Lai v. Board of Trustees, 330 F. Supp. 904, 906 (E.D.N.C. 1971).

[31] 244 F. Supp. 156, 160 (D. Vt. 1965).

[32] *E.g.,* Pettit v. Board of Educ., 184 F. Supp. 452 (D. Md. 1960); Jones v. School Bd., 179 F. Supp. 280 (E.D. Va. 1959), *aff'd,* 278 F.2d 72 (4th Cir. 1960); Ackermen v. Rubin, 35 Misc. 2d 707, 231 N.Y.S.2d 112 (S. Ct. 1962).

[33] 380 U.S. 89, 92 (1965).

County Board of Education, " . . . [I]t goes without saying that there is no constitutional prohibition against an assignment of individual students to particular schools on a basis of intelligence, achievement or other aptitudes upon a uniformly administered program. . . ."[34] The court in *Miller v. School District No. 2, Clarendon County*[35] permitted the school district to separate students according to slow or accelerated sections and to center its vocational curriculum at one school for financial or pragmatic reasons. Even in *Hobson v. Hansen,* the most far-reaching judicial foray into school classification, Judge Wright meticulously pointed out that ability grouping could be reasonably related to the purposes of public education, and that the mere fact of differential treatment would not necessarily offend constitutional protections.[36]

Yet because of the serious consequences of the process that labels individuals "mentally retarded," and the fact that the process may be applied differentially to certain groups, the law must scrutinize school practices to some extent. By borrowing doctrine from other areas of law partially analogous to school classification, an analytical framework has begun to emerge.

A judicial role is traditionally found, for example, where school practices have resulted in racial disparities or racial separation. Failure to defer to school authorities in such cases can be explained by two factors. First, *Brown v. Board of Education*[37] made it undeniably clear that, morally and philosophically, racial separation is unacceptable and inherently unequal. Largely because of the formative role of education, the courts have consistently required racial mixture in the schools so as to lay the foundation of a society in which races are not separated, alienated, and hostile. Second, the willingness of courts to intervene where racial separation occurs can be explained by the implicit recognition that educational separation usually means inferior education for minorities and that the courts are often the only effective resort for vindication of the right to equality. Since the systematic labeling and classification of students in public schools invariably leads to disproportionate numbers of minority students in classes for the educable mentally retarded,[38] the existence of racial imbalance has been the the launching pad for judicial missiles aimed at school sorting processes.[39]

Another approach focuses on the educational harm occasioned by classification as "mentally retarded" and upon the attendant stigma and their implications in later life. Whether the immediate consequence is educational exclusion or

---

[34] 333 F.2d 55, 61 (5th Cir.), *cert. denied,* 379 U.S. 933 (1964).

[35] 256 F. Supp. 370 (D.S.C. 1966). *See also* Goss v. Board of Educ., 305 F.2d 523 (6th Cir. 1962), *rev'd on other grounds,* 373 U.S. 683 (1963); Board of Educ. v. Clendenning, 431 P.2d 382 (Okla. 1967).

[36] 269 F. Supp. at 511-12.

[37] 347 U.S. 483 (1954).

[38] *See* C. JENCKS *et al.,* INEQUALITY: A REASSESSMENT OF THE EFFECT OF FAMILY AND SCHOOLING IN AMERICA (1972).

[39] In the two categories of special education in California that rely most heavily on standardized intelligence tests for screening and placement, the state has consistently reported substantial racial imbalance. *See, e.g.,* CALIFORNIA DEP'T OF EDUCATION, RACIAL AND ETHNIC SURVEY OF CALIFORNIA PUBLIC SCHOOLS (1970-72). This result, consistent with that in most states, has given rise to significant challenges to the classification process.

　　A pending California case that deals with the disproportionate number of Spanish-speaking children in EMR classes is Diana v. State Bd. of Educ., Civil No. C-70-37 (N.D. Cal., Feb. 5, 1970) (unreported; Feb. 5 decree superseded by consent decree of June 18, 1973). Of the 13 children in the class for the educable mentally retarded in the Soledad Elementary School District, 12 were Mexican-American. Of the approximately 85,000 children in EMR classes in the state of California

assignment to a special class, courts have begun to recognize the significance of the labeling and placement process. Any such fundamental change in a child's academic status triggers the application of procedural due process safeguards to ensure the legitimacy of the classification itself and of the manner in which the school treats the individual child. Concomitant problems arise from school record-keeping practices which compound the stigmatization inherent in the negative label. Emerging notions of protection against defamatory connotations and of the right to privacy have relevance here.

Finally, and as counterpoint to the assorted injuries of such school classification, some frontier regions of legal doctrinal development are being explored with vigor. Although the contours are nebulous and the supports perhaps tenuous, these involve the most basic consideration—the right to an education which meets the individual child's real needs and enables him to achieve a life role consistent with his highest capabilities.

EQUAL PROTECTION AND THE CLASSIFICATION OF MENTALLY RETARDED CHILDREN IN THE PUBLIC SCHOOLS

The Burden of Proof in Discrimination Cases

The presence of extreme racial segregation in special programs for the educable mentally retarded serves to dramatize the serious risk of misclassification. Though there is little dispute that minority groups are proportionately overrepresented in special education classes, the causes are more uncertain, and therefore, so are the legal consequences. Whether because of aspiration and interest, biases inherent in the testing instruments and pupil assignment process, different home environment and cultural orientation, or teacher prejudice, substantial racial and ethnic isolation in public school classrooms often results from school classification. The judge's evaluation of the underlying reason for this isolation will be largely determinative of the school district's legal responsibility for it.[40]

---

during the 1966-67 school year, 26 percent were of Spanish surname, although students of this ethnic and cultural background constituted only 13 percent of the state's total public school population. Plaintiff's complaint, *Id.*

The complainant's uncontroverted statistics, adopted by the court in Larry P. v. Riles, 343 F. Supp. 1306 (N.D. Cal. 1972), *aff'd,* 502 F.2d 963 (1974), another California case challenging racial inequality in the EMR program, indicate an even larger statewide disproportion of black children in these classes. Although representing only 9.1 percent of the public school population, blacks constituted 27.5 percent of California's classes for the educable retarded. In the San Francisco Unified School District, where blacks constituted only 28.1 percent of the student population, more than 60 percent of the students in classes for the educable mentally retarded were black. The disparity was even greater in the elementary schools alone, where almost 70 percent of children in EMR classes were black, more than twice the proportion of blacks in the school district population.

[40] *See, e.g.,* Spangler v. Pasadena Bd. of Educ., 311 F. Supp. 501, 519-20 (C.D. Cal. 1970), *aff'd,* 427 F.2d 1352 (1970). The court in *Spangler* voided racially discriminatory school "tracking." The discrimination was attributed to a number of factors, including (1) culturally discriminatory tests, (2) assumptions by both counselors and teachers that black children will achieve poorly, and (3) deference to parental requests which favors the more assertive parents of middle-class children.

Without a convincing explanation in terms of cultural or racial differences, it would be expected that acute learning disabilities would be spread randomly throughout the population, irrespective of racial, ethnic, or socioeconomic background. For example, it would seem likely that the percentage of minority children with physical handicaps (*i.e.,* blind, deaf, and dumb, or perceptually handicapped) would approximate the proportion of minorities in the total school population. The same would seem to apply to emotional or psychological disabilities and to mental retardation, unless there are racial, genetic, or environmental factors which might account for a significant statistical difference among groups.

In racial discrimination cases, "statistics often tell much, and courts listen."[41] When a prima facie case of discrimination has been established, the result is a reversal of the traditional equal protection test in which the plaintiffs must prove the irrationality of a challenged classification. Instead, the burden shifts to the defendants to justify the apparently discriminatory result. This conceptual approach finds precedential support in cases involving public housing, employment discrimination, and jury selection, as well as school desegregation. Thus, if a greatly disproportionate number of blacks fails a job qualification test, the burden shifts to the employer to explain how the test is valid as a criterion for employment.[42] Similarly, where administration of an ostensibly neutral testing device results in large-scale exclusion of blacks and low-income people from jury lists, the burden shifts to the state to justify the selection criteria.[43] And when a school district's methods of delineating school boundaries result in student bodies that are substantially segregated, the school district must demonstrate the educational relevance and validity of its methods.[44]

Courts have been concerned primarily with the presumptive invalidity of racial classifications which "must be scrutinized with particular care, since they are contrary to our traditions and hence constitutionally suspect."[45] The court in *Larry P.,* analogizing from employment discrimination cases, embraced the presumption that statistical imbalance would not occur in the absence of discrimination:

> [F]or most unskilled or semi-skilled jobs, an ample pool of qualified or potentially qualified workers of both races exists; and if racial imbalance in the work force nevertheless occurs, it is likely to be the consequence of racial discrimination. The analogous assumption in the instant case would be that there exists a random distri-

---

[41] Alabama v. United States, 304 F.2d 583, 586 (5th Cir. 1962), *aff'd,* 371 U.S. 37 (1962); *accord,* Turner v. Fouche, 396 U.S. 345 (1970); Hawkins v. Town of Shaw, 437 F.2d 1286 (5th Cir. 1971); United States v. Board of Educ., 396 F.2d 44, 46 (5th Cir. 1968); Armstead v. Starkville Municipal Separate School Dist., 325 F. Supp. 560, 569 (S.D. Fla. 1971), *modified,* 461 F.2d 276 (1972).

[42] Griggs v. Duke Power Co., 401 U.S. 424 (1971). *See also* Gautreaux v. Chicago Housing Authority, 296 F. Supp. 907 (N.D. Ill. 1969), *aff'd,* 436 F.2d 306 (1971).

[43] Turner v. Fouche, 396 U.S. 345 (1970); Whitus v. Georgia, 385 U.S. 545 (1967); Carmical v. Craven, 457 F.2d 582 (9th Cir. 1971), *cert. denied,* 409 U.S. 929 (1972).

[44] *See, e.g.,* Hall v. St. Helena Parish School Bd., 417 F.2d 801 (5th Cir.), *cert. denied,* 396 U.S. 904 (1969); United States v. School Dist. 151, 286 F. Supp. 786 (N.D. Ill.), *aff'd,* 404 F.2d 1125 (7th Cir. 1968), *cert. denied,* 402 U.S. 943 (1971).

[45] Bolling v. Sharpe, 347 U.S. 497, 499 (1954). *See also* Loving v. Virginia, 388 U.S. 1 (1967); Korematsu v. United States, 323 U.S. 214, 216 (1944).

bution among all races of the qualifications necessary to participate in regular as opposed to EMR classes. Since it does not seem to be disputed that the qualification for placement in regular classes is the innate ability to learn at the pace at which those classes proceed, such a random distribution can be expected if there is in turn a random distribution of these learning abilities among members of all races.[46]

Still another reason that might support shifting the burden, but which was not discussed by the court in *Larry P.,* is the traditional doctrine ". . . that where facts pleaded by one party lie peculiarly in the knowledge of the adversary, the latter has the burden of proving it."[47] Once the statistical racial imbalance in classroom composition is demonstrated, the information necessary to account for the racial discrepancy is almost exclusively within the defendant school district's office files. Hence, the party with the power to produce the facts should be called upon to respond with an explanation of the perceived difference.

Thus, once a substantial racial imbalance in EMR classes is shown, school district officials ought to be required to rebut the inference that racial factors cause the disparity[48] and to demonstrate that significant educational benefits outweigh the resulting racial isolation.[49] If they fail to do either and if it cannot be shown that the testing and classification system accomplishes what it purports to accomplish, then there is neither pedagogical nor legal justification for the differing treatment of persons labeled educable mentally retarded. Those children unjustifiably confined in EMR classes should then be reassigned to regular classes and provided special assistance to facilitate their reintegration. They require the special assistance to compensate for deficiencies caused by the program, and without this help, are likely to fail, thus "proving" the accuracy of the original label.

The Extent of the School's Burden

For at least the last two decades, a dual standard of equal protection review has existed.[50] It is said that when a suspect classification is created,[51] or when a fundamental interest is infringed,[52] the state must come forward to show that its action is required by a compelling state interest. When the classification is not "suspect,"

---

[46] 343 F. Supp. at 1310 (citation omitted).

[47] C. McCormick, Handbook of the Law of Evidence § 318, at 675 (1954).

[48] *Cf.* Swann v. Charlotte-Mecklenburg Bd. of Educ., 402 U.S. 1, 26 (1971) (establishing a presumption against schools that are substantially disproportionate in racial composition). The presumption in *Swann* relates to the propriety of remedy and not to the finding of initial constitutional violation. *See* Fiss, *The Charlotte-Mecklenburg Case — Its Significance for Northern School Desegregation,* 38 U. Chi. L. Rev. 697, 701 (1971).

[49] *Cf.* Tinker v. Des Moines Independent Community School Dist., 393 U.S. 503 (1969) (burden is on school officials to demonstrate significant educational benefits outweighing students' right to free expression by wearing black armbands).

[50] *See Developments in the Law — Equal Protection,* 82 Harv. L. Rev. 1065 (1969).

[51] *E.g.,* Harper v. Virginia Bd. of Elections, 383 U.S. 663 (1966); McLaughlin v. Florida 379 U.S. 184 (1964).

[52] *E.g.,* Shapiro v. Thompson, 394 U.S. 618 (1969); Skinner v. Oklahoma 316 U.S. 535 (1942).

the state need advance only a rational justification.[53] It has become increasingly clear that "suspect classification" and "fundamental interest" are words of art, more notable for the judicial reactions they evoke than for their descriptive value.[54] There can be no doubt that education is fundamental. It is the central feature in the formative process; it is a prerequisite to vocational, professional, and social achievement. Although the United States Supreme Court recently determined that education was not a "fundamental interest,"[55] it went to great pains to reiterate the vast importance of education in this society.[56] Thus, education remains unchallenged as a fundamental interest in all but the most artful sense; and the following statement from *Brown* loses none of its validity:

> Today education is perhaps the most important function of state and local governments. Compulsory school attendance laws and the great expenditures for education both demonstrate our recognition of the importance of education to our democratic society. . . . It is the very foundation of good citizenship. Today it is a principal instrument in awakening the child to cultural values, in preparing him for later professional training, and in helping him to adjust normally to his environment. In these days, it is doubtful that any child may reasonably be expected to succeed in life if he is denied the opportunity of an education.[57]

Despite the Supreme Court's recent retreat from simplistic categorization of schooling as a "fundamental interest," there should be no hesitation in asserting that it is "the *sine qua non* of useful existence."[58] The determination of the Court that education is not a "fundamental interest" is bound up in a judicial trend, at least at the top, away from the expanding role of the so-called new equal protection, with its dual standard of review.[59] It is unlikely that interests or classifications will be adjudged fundamental or suspect by this Court if they have not already been so designated. It is equally unlikely, however, that any retreat will be made from the judiciary's total hostility to racial classifications.[60]

Moreover, the Supreme Court's primary rationale in *Brown* — the impact of classroom segregation on a child's motivation to learn — applies a fortiori to segregation of mentally retarded children. The United States Commission on Civil Rights found that black children suffer a particularly great feeling of stigma and inferiority when, though attending a predominantly white school, they "are accorded separate treatment with others of their race, in a way which is obvious to them as they travel through the school to their classes."[61] Imagine the following conclusion as it applies to children in separate classes for the educable retarded:

> If separation from faceless white students in other schools and other neighborhoods on the impersonal ground of residence is damaging to a Negro child's self-esteem,

---

[53] *E.g.,* Dandridge v. Williams, 397 U.S. 471 (1970); Williamson v. Lee Optical Co., 348 U.S. 483 (1955).
[54] *See, e.g.,* San Antonio Independent School Dist. v. Rodriguez, 411 U.S. 1 (1973).
[55] *Id.* at 35-37.
[56] *Id.* at 29-30.
[57] 347 U.S. at 493 (1954).
[58] Manjares v. Newton, 64 Cal. 2d 365, 375, 411 P.2d 901, 908, 49 Cal. Rptr. 805, 812 (1966).
[59] San Antonio Independent School Dist. v. Rodriguez, 411 U.S. 1 (1973).
[60] *See* Brown v. Board of Educ. 347 U.S. 483 (1954); Korematsu v. United States, 323 U.S. 214 (1944).
[61] 2 U.S. Commission on Civil Rights, Racial Isolation in the Public Schools 42 (1967).

the daily experience of being isolated from white students in his own school on the highly personal and pejorative ground of ability must be infinitely more so.[62]

Although school classification decisions are rarely presented as racially motivated, but rather purportedly are prompted by estimates of student ability, it is not necessary to find intentional acts of discrimination in order to assign responsibility to the school district. The Supreme Court sounded the death knell for the fading jurisprudential philosophy of de jure segregation[63] when it declared in *Alexander v. Louisiana*[64] that "affirmations of good faith in·making individual selections are insufficient to dispel a prima facie case of systematic exclusion." And, more recently, the Court reaffirmed:

> [A]n inquiry into the "dominant" motivation of school authorities is as irreievant as it is fruitless. . . . Thus we have focused upon the effect — not the purpose or motivation — of a school board's action. . . . The existence of a permissible purpose cannot sustain an action that has an impermissible effect.[65]

In numerous Supreme Court cases, where a grossly discriminatory impact results from a statute nondiscriminatory on its face,[66] or from a seemingly neutral test or other measure of competence (such as to perform adequately on a job[67] or to participate intelligently on a jury),[68] the lack of specific intent to discriminate could not offset the grossly discriminatory results of the criteria or standards. As the court stated in *Arrington v. Massachusetts Bay Transportation Authority:*

> It is not enough that the factors producing the classification and the consequent inequality are themselves, objectively neutral and without a background of even

---

[62] Goodman, *De Facto School Segregation: A Constitutional and Empirical Analysis,* 60 CALIF. L. REV. 275, 430 (1972).

[63] *See, e.g.,* Deal v. Cincinnati Bd. of Educ., 369 F.2d 55 (6th Cir. 1966), *cert. denied,* 389 U.S. 847 (1967); Springfield School Comm. v. Barksdale, 348 F.2d 261 (1st Cir. 1965); Bell v. School City, 324 F.2d 209 (7th Cir. 1963), *cert. denied,* 377 U.S. 929 (1964). *But see* United States v. School Dist. No. 151, 404 F.2d 1125 (7th Cir. 1968), *cert. denied,* 402 U.S. 943 (1971); Taylor v. Board of Educ., 294 F.2d 36 (2d Cir.), *cert. denied,* 368 U.S. 940 (1961).

[64] 405 U.S. 625, 632 (1972). Consider also, "[T]he purpose of the legislation was irrelevant because the inevitable effect . . . abridged constitutional rights." United States v. O'Brien 391 U.S. 367, 385 (1968). *See also* Palmer v. Thompson, 403 U.S. 217 (1971); Gomillion v. Lightfoot, 364 U.S. 339 (1960).

[65] Wright v. Council of City of Emporia, 407 U.S. 451, 462 (1972). This language is a bit difficult to reconcile with the majority opinion in Keyes v. School Dist. No. 1, Denver Colorado, 413 U.S. 189 (1973), *rehearing denied,* 414 U.S. 883 (1973), where the Court established a series of evidentiary presumptions in ascertaining segregatory intent. See the concurring opinion of Mr. Justice Powell in *Keyes,* accusing the Court of establishing a sectional double standard and asserting that the issue had already been resolved in *Wright,* viz. that intent is "irrelevant." *See also* Goodman, *supra* note 62, for a discussion of the "thorny questions" which arise in proving racial motivation at trial.

[66] Tate v. Short, 401 U.S. 395 (1971) (imprisonment for failure to pay a fine); Williams v. Illinois, 399 U.S. 235 (1970); Harper v. Virginia Bd. of Elections, 383 U.S. 663 (1966) (poll tax).

[67] Griggs v. Duke Power Co., 401 U.S. 424 (1971); Chance v. Board of Examiners, 458 F.2d 1167 (2d Cir. 1972) (involving supervisory personnel in the New York Board of Education); Carter v. Gallagher, 452 F.2d 315 (8th Cir. 1971), *cert. denied,* 406 U.S. 950 (1972).

[68] Carmical v. Craven, 457 F.2d 582 (9th Cir. 1971), *cert. denied,* 409 U.S. 929 (1972).

latent discriminatory purpose; when the effect is to deprive some citizens of rights that should be equally available to all, then there must be a compelling justification.[69]

Despite the widespread use of testing and classifying in American schools, there is very little consensus about its impact on the quality of education. Nevertheless, with full knowledge of the segregative consequences of the procedures, school authorities continue to categorize and separate minority students into classes for the mentally retarded. To perform an act with known consequences is to intend the consequences. Just as courts have examined areas of school officials' discretion in assignment of pupils and teachers,[70] constructing and locating schools and attendance boundaries,[71] or enforcing transfer and zoning policies[72] to find de jure acts of discrimination, so courts must make similar examinations in regard to testing and classification practices.[73]

In the context of testing and classifying, the supposed dichotomy between de facto and de jure segregation is simply not important. Where school officials have for some time employed testing devices in the assignment of pupils the testing instruments have been shown to be socially and culturally biased, and the result has been a continuing and consistently disproportionate assignment of minorities to EMR classes, discriminatory intent can be inferred from the natural, probable, and foreseeable effect of perpetuating racially identifiable classrooms.[74]

The prima facie showing of racial imbalance in classes for the mentally retarded and the presumption against such a result suffice to require school officials not only to prove the relevance of their screening and assignment criteria[75] but also to demonstrate that they serve a compelling educational need and that no less segregative alternatives exist to meet this need.[76]

---

[69] 306 F. Supp. 1355, 1358 (D. Mass. 1969); *accord,* Hobson v. Hansen, 269 F. Supp. 401 (D.D.C. 1967), *aff'd sub nom.* Smuck v. Hobson, 408 F.2d 175 (D.C. Cir. 1969).

[70] *See, e.g.,* Davis v. School Dist., 309 F. Supp. 734, 742-45 (E.D. Mich. 1970), *aff'd,* 433 F.2d 573 (6th Cir.), *cert. denied,* 404 U.S. 913 (1971); United States v. School Dist. No. 151, 301 F. Supp. 201, 228-31 (N.D. Ill. 1969).

[71] *E.g.,* Bradley v. Milliken, 338 F. Supp. 582 (E.D. Mich. 1971), *aff'd,* 484 F.2d 215, *rev'd,* 418 U.S. 717 (1974); Johnson v. San Francisco Unified School Dist., 339 F. Supp. 1315 (N.D. Cal. 1971), *vacated,* 500 F.2d 349 (1974).

[72] Cases cited note 71 *supra.*

[73] *See, e.g,,* Larry P. v. Riles, 343 F. Supp. 1306 (N.D. Cal. 1972), *aff'd,* 502 F.2d 963 (1974); Spangler v. Pasadena Bd. of Educ., 311 F. Supp. 501, 519-20 (C.D. Cal.), *aff'd,* 427 F.2d 1352 (1970); Hobson v. Hansen, 269 F. Supp. 401 (D.D.C. 1967), *aff'd sub nom.* Smuck v. Hobson, 408 F.2d 175 (D.C. Cir. 1969).

[74] *See, e.g.,* Davis v. School Dist., 309 F. Supp. 734 (E.D. Mich. 1970), *aff'd,* 443 F.2d 573, *rev'd,* 404 U.S. 913 (1971); Bradley v. Milliken, 338 F. Supp. at 592 (E.D. Mich. 1971), *aff'd,* 484 F.2d 215, *rev'd,* 418 U.S. 717 (1974): "[P]roof that a pattern of racially segregated schools has existed for a considerable period of time amounts to a racial classification by the state and its agencies which must be justified by clear and convincing evidence." *Cf.* Wright v. Council of City of Emporia, 407 U.S. 451 (1972).

[75] *Cf.* Carter v. Jury Comm'n., 396 U.S. 320 (1970); Turner v. Fouche, 396 U.S. 346 (1970). In these cases the Supreme Court approved the use of intelligence or education as legitimate criteria for jury service. But the court in *Carmical* restricts the use of screening devices such as intelligence tests, once a discriminatory effect is shown, unless they in fact measure what they purport to measure and unless no less discriminatory alternative is available. Carmical v. Craven, 457 F.2d 582 (9th Cir. 1971), *cert. denied,* 409 U.S. 929 (1972).

[76] *Cf.* Tinker v. Des Moines Independent Community School Dist., 393 U.S. 503 (1969).

The Means of Classifying the Mentally Retarded

The most frequent tool in diagnosing differences of intellectual endowment is the standardized intelligence (IQ) test. Test performance might indicate differences in mental capacity among persons who

> have had an equal opportunity to learn certain types of cognitive, linguistic and mathematical skills and to acquire certain types of information; if they were equally motivated to learn these skills and to acquire this information; if they are equally motivated to exert themselves in a test situation and equally familiar with the demands of the test situation; if they were equally free of emotional . . . and biological . . . difficulties which might interfere with their performance. . . .[77]

Unfortunately, however, all these factors are rarely equal, and the many variables can hardly be isolated effectively. For example, beyond simple reflex acts and basic organic processes, few human attributes or behaviors are culture free. Intrinsic interest in the test content, rapport with the examiner, drive to excel on tests, and past habits of problem solving vary and can all distort results.[78] The use of instruments like the Wechsler Intelligence Scale for Children or the Stanford-Binet (the most commonly used intelligence tests), which were normed and standardized primarily by testing members of the dominant culture[79] and whose content is inevitably culturally oriented, is especially inappropriate for children who have not had the same opportunities to acquire the skills and attitudes for successful test performance.[80]

Language is another factor which can seriously affect the extremely sensitive relationship of tester, child, and testing instrument. The grossest kind of linguistic handicap was evident in *Diana,* where children were tested in other than their primary language.[81] The problem is manifest in an even broader sense where the

---

[77] *Anglocentrism, supra* note 8, at 322.

[78] A. ANASTASI, PSYCHOLOGICAL TESTING 251 (3d ed. 1968).

[79] Both the Wechsler Intelligence Scale for Children and the Stanford-Binet Test, the two most commonly used, were standardized exclusively on Anglo-American children. The Peabody Picture Vocabulary Text was similarly standardized on a population of approximately 4,000 white children in the area around Nashville, Tennessee. No mention is made in any standardization sample of the inclusion of minority children. *See* L. TERMAN & M. MERRILL, STANFORD-BINET INTELLIGENCE SCALE: MANUAL FOR THE THIRD REVISION (1960); D. WECHSLER, WECHSLER INTELLIGENCE SCALE FOR CHILDREN: MANUAL (1949).

[80] In psychological terms we say the test is not "objective" because it fails to isolate extraneous factors such as race or culture. *See* R. HURLEY, POVERTY AND MENTAL RETARDATION — A CAUSAL RELATIONSHIP (1969); S. SARASON, T. ALDWIN & R. MASLAND, MENTAL SUBNORMALITY (1958); Neff, *Socioeconomic Status and Intelligence: A Critical Survey,* 35 PSYCHOLOGICAL BULL. 727 (1938). *See generally* Comment, *Segregation of Poor and Minority Children into Classes for the Mentally Retarded,* 71 MICH. L. REV. 1212, 1215-22 (1973) for a full discussion of inaccuracies in IQ testing.

[81] No. C-70-37 (N.D. Cal., Feb. 5, 1970). In response to *Diana* and to the urging of psychologists, the California procedure was amended so as to require translation of tests into the native language of the tested subjects. 5 CAL. ADMIN. CODE § 3401 (1971). *See also* Guadalupe Organization v. Tempe Elementary School Dist. No. 3, Civil No. 71-435 (D. Ariz., May 9, 1972); Darcy, *Bilingualism and the Measurement of Intelligence: Review of a Decade of Research,* 103 J. GENETIC PSYCHOLOGY 259 (1963); Torrance,

child's auditory perception is defective,[82] where the test uses words of increasing rarity,[83] where the child misunderstands the pronunciation of an examiner from another culture,[84] or where the child comes from a home in which verbalization occurs only infrequently.[85] As the court found in *Hobson:*

> The evidence shows that the method by which track assignments are made depends essentially on standardized aptitude tests which, although given on a system-wide basis are completely inappropriate for use with a large segment of the student body. Because these tests are standardized primarily on and are relevant to a white middle class group of students, they produce inaccurate and misleading test scores when given to lower class and Negro students. As a result,

---

Testing the Educational and Psychological Development of Students from Other Cultures and Subcultures, 38 Rev. Educ. Research 71 (1968). Because of experiential gaps among different cultures, efforts at cross-cultural testing have not met with success. *Anglocentrism* at 324-38. Even where alternate wording was utilized to adjust for culturally different meanings, additional problems arose in the clinical interpretation and use of the test results. Coyle, *Another Alternate Wording on the WISC,* 16 Psych. Reports 1276 (1965). Similarly, because of the cultural bias in content, experiments in relying more heavily on performance portions rather than verbal parts of tests produced no significant change for black children. *Anglocentrism, supra* note 8, at 324-38. Such modifications either fail to erase cultural variations or leave the evaluator without a normative framework from which he can interpret results.

[82] Weintraub & Abeson, *Appropriate Education for all Handicapped Children: A Growing Issue,* 23 Syr. L. Rev. 1037, 1038-39 (1972).

[83] *Anglocentrism, supra* note 8, at 325. *See also* Watson, *IQ — The Racial Gap,* 6 Psychology Today, September 1972, at 48.

[84] Efforts might be made to recruit and employ minority psychologists and psychometrists to conduct and interpret tests of minority children, but such efforts will prove fruitless in many areas because of the scarcity of minority professionals. Requirements of in-service training of personnel who administer tests or who evaluate and place children in special classes is also inadequate by itself because the cultural background and experience of personnel is only one of many variables affecting test performance. Attempts to substantiate test results with "adaptive behavior" measures of a child's functional performance or with investigation of the child's home environment are not objective if conclusions are colored by primary reliance on standardized tests. *See, e.g.,* the discussion in Larry P., 343 F. Supp. at 1311-12, of the inadequacy of Cal. Educ. Code § 6902.085 as a procedure for screening minority students.
   Another solution might be to use different norms for different ethnic groups. *See, e.g.,* Mercer, Pluralistic Diagnosis in the Evaluation of Black and Chicano Children, Sept. 3-7, 1971 (paper presented at meeting of American Psychological Ass'n, Washington, D.C.). This has been occasionally attacked as "reverse discrimination" and sometimes advocated as necessary to compensate for past inequities. However, the nature of psychological testing makes it possible, and in fact logically necessary, to use different norms for different ethnic groups, since identical cutoff points are inherently discriminatory. The principle has long been established by the use of different norms on intelligence tests for boys and girls, by different height and weight limits for men and women, and by different actuarial mortality tables for life insurance on males and females, not to mention differential rates according to occupation and area of residence (these differential rates work to the disadvantage of minorities). If this kind of pluralistic evaluation were utilized, a child's "intelligence" would be evaluated only in relation to other children who come from similar backgrounds and who have had approximately the same opportunity to acquire the skills necessary for success on the "Anglocentric" tests.
   Since the legal and moral justification for use of psychological tests is their presumed ability to predict performance, it would only be fair to predict as accurately as possible, that is, to use norms appropriate to each ethnic group. For the more widely used tests, the development of separate norms for ethnic groups would be just as feasible as are the gender-specific, residence-specific, and occupation-specific norms for insurance purposes, assuming, of course, our willingness to accept highly imprecise delineation of cultural boundaries for particular groups.
   Differential norms might be a means to achieve racial parity in classes for the retarded. When faced with a prima facie discriminatory situation, the courts clearly have discretion even to use mathematical ratios in order to achieve racial balance. *See, e.g.,* Swann v. Charlotte-Mecklenburg Bd. of Educ., 402 U.S. 1, 26 (1971).

[85] *See* R. Hurley, *supra* note 80, at 81-113. *See also Hobson* v. Hansen, 269 F. Supp. at 481 (D.D.C. 1967), *aff'd sub nom.* Smuck v. Hobson, 408 F.2d 175 (D.C. Cir. 1969).

rather than being classified according to ability to learn, these students are in reality being classified according to their socio-economic or racial status, or—more precisely—according to environmental and psychological factors which have nothing to do with innate ability.[86]

Furthermore, the tests may provide a professionally tenable screen for misclassification by removing the moral responsibility from teachers and school administrators for the decision to find a child unfit for normal classes.[87] Indeed, the teacher's decision to make the initial referral of a child as potentially retarded may be largely influenced by his low score on a group intelligence test, which causes the teacher's consequent low expectation and the child's inevitably poor school performance.[88] Perhaps the most significant distortive effect is that "scientific" test scores often are overly impressive to unsophisticated parents and, therefore, can be used to convince them that their children are mentally retarded.

In light of the dubious validity of many "intelligence" or "aptitude" tests, perhaps they simply should be returned to the laboratory for more adequate scientific development. An increasing number of organizations, although defending the instruments themselves, has recognized the pervasive abuses and has called for a moratorium on the use of such tests in identifying and classifying school children, at least until a more appropriate instrument can be developed.[89]

School officials might contend that the abolition of tests in the absence of suitable alternatives would be to burn down the barn to be rid of the mice. Although the tests are concededly inappropriate to measure innate mental ability, they have utility as predictors of subsequent school performance.[90] It has been demonstrated that slow work habits, emotional insecurity, low achievement drive, lack of interest in abstract problems, and other culturally linked conditions which tend to lower test scores are also likely to handicap the individual in his educational and vocational progress.[91] Although the correlation between grades and test

---

[86] 269 F. Supp. at 514.

[87] Consider the following statement:

> Advocates of testing point to the objectivity of tests as a check against the personal prejudices of interviewers and hiring personnel. Tests, however, introduce their own element of racial bias, and their results can provide a smoke screen for those who wish to discriminate. An employer of seven hundred who selects applicants by interview and recommendations alone will find the absence of Negro workers harder to explain than one who can point to a record of poor test scores to explain Negro rejections.

Note, *Legal Implications of the Use of Standardized Ability Tests in Employment and Education*, 68 COLUM. L. REV. 691, 744 (1968).

[88] *See* the Section, "The consequences," & note 21 *supra*.

[89] *E.g.*, The President's Committee on Mental Retardation, the California Association of School Psychiatrists, and the Bay Area Association of Black Psychologists have all suggested such a moratorium. *See also* A.B. 483, A.B. 665 Cal. Legislature, Reg. Sess. (1971-72). A more appropriate measure might be one that takes sociocultural variables into account and considers how well a person functions in school or job, home, and community rules. *See, e.g., Anglocentrism, supra* note 8, at 328-37.

[90] *Cf.* Chaney v. State Bar, 386 F.2d 962, 964 (9th Cir. 1967), *cert. denied*, 390 U.S. 1011 (1968). *Chaney* upheld the California bar examination as constitutionally valid because it tests "capacity to analyze general legal situations" and therefore ". . . has a rational connection with the capacity to practice law."

[91] A. ANASTASI, *supra* note 78. *See also* Wesman, *Intelligent Testing*, 23 AM. PSYCHOLOGIST 267-69 (1968).

scores is far from perfect, and despite the myriad subjective variables that in-fluence both results, there does seem to be a relationship.

Thus, school officials contend, since the real issue is abuse of the tests and not the instruments themselves: "To abolish the tests while ignoring the fact that different students (and different classes of students) perform differently is about as sensible as the ancient Greek practice of slaying the messenger who brings bad news."[92] The defect in the argument that test results predict school performance lies, however, in the carry-over effect, or self-fulfilling prophecy. Reliance on the results of culturally biased tests may cause the same racial and ethnic bias to manifest itself later in the classroom. It brings the discussion full circle back to Judge Wright's observation that "the real tragedy of misjudgments about the dis-advantaged students' abilities is the likelihood that the student will act out the judgment and conform to it by achieving only at the expected level."[93] Hence, the child who fails the test is the child who does poorly in school is the child who fails the test is the. . . .

To say, then, that "intelligence" is what intelligence tests measure, and that what the tests measure is important because intelligence is important, is to take the road which "leads through the looking glass" because "intelligence" can mean so many different things. It would be equally logical to assume that intelligence is of no more consequence in human life than are scores on intelligence tests.[94] The propriety of sorting children into stereotyped categories on the basis of 15-point differences on standardized tests must be reconsidered as must making success on such tests a rite of passage to positions of power and wealth in the society.[95]

The Legal Responsibility of the Public Schools

When children from low socioeconomic status or minority ethnic backgrounds consistently do poorly on standardized intelligence tests, and when educators rely on these instruments to sort, classify, and label children in the public schools, the educators are embracing a sort of genetic and cultural fatalism. The comparative failure of minority children should not lead to an operational acceptance of the notion that there are genetic differences in intelligence.[96] The evidence of genetic

---

[92] Kirp, *Schools as Sorters: The Constitutional and Policy Implications of Student Classifications*, 121 U. PA. L. REV. 705 (1973).

[93] Hobson v. Hansen, 269 F. Supp. at 491 (D.D.C. 1967), *aff'd sub nom.* Smuck v. Hobson, 408 F.2d 175 (D.C. Cir. 1969).

[94] *See* C. JENCKS, et al., *supra* note 38, at 56-57.

[95] *See, e.g.,* SCHWEBEL, WHO CAN BE EDUCATED? 75 (1968). Even a notable proponent of the concept of genetically conditioned differences in "intelligence" recognizes that equality of rights is a *moral axiom* which does not depend upon genetic differences, even if they could be scientifically proved. Jensen, *The Ethical Issues*, 32 THE HUMANIST, Jan./Feb. 1972, at 5.

[96] *See, e.g.,* Jensen, *How Much Can We Boost IQ and Scholastic Achievement?* 39 HARV. EDUC. REV. 1 (1969); Shockley, *Dysgenics, Geneticity, Raceology—A Challenge to the Intellectual Responsibility of Educators,* 53 PHI DELTA KAPPAN 297 (1972); Shockley, *A Debate Challenge: Geneticity is 80% for White Identical Twins' I.Q.'s,* 53 PHI DELTA KAPPAN 415 (1972). *But cf.* Cronbach, *Heredity, Environment, and Education Policy,* 39 HARV. EDUC. REV. 338 (1969); Hunt, *Has Compensatory Education Failed? Has It Been Attempted?,* 39 HARV. EDUC. REV. 278 (1969); Stinchcombe, *Environment: The Cumulation of Effects is Yet to be Understood,* 39 HARV. EDUC. REV. 511 (1969).

racial inferiority is too sketchy and too inconclusive to support such a finding,[97] even if political considerations allowed a school district to raise it. The court in *Larry P.,* having shifted the burden of proof to defendants, refused to assume any relationship between race and ability to learn in the absence of proof to that effect.[98]

But what if it could be shown that poverty, malnutrition, and a host of other environmental factors cause the disproportionate incidence of mental retardation among minority children? The racial separation would then result not from prejudice in the schools, but instead from the individual plight of the labeled child who comes from a ghetto family. Undoubtedly, children from poverty neighborhoods enter school less prepared than their middle-class counterparts in skills essential to "normalcy" as defined within the essentially white middle-class school system. Nevertheless, schools which exclude children from education altogether or relegate them to inferior classes and hence to the bottom ranks of society make a decision to perpetuate and reinforce, rather than to alleviate, the child's disadvantages. The issue is whether the schools have a legal duty to do otherwise.

There is still considerable controversy over whether a school district has any remedial obligation for children who, because of some handicap unrelated to state action, allegedly cannot benefit from public education. The Supreme Court in *Lau v. Nichols*[99] recently upheld, on statutory grounds, the plea of Chinese-speaking children for bilingual instruction. Other courts have responded in a positive manner to the harms suffered by non-English-speaking students.[100] Still greater difficulty arises in defining the extent of the state's remedial obligation. As Mr. Justice Frankfurter once wrote, "[T]here is no greater inequality than the equal treatment of unequals."[101] Thus, the provision of educational resources to mentally retarded children which are equivalent to those invested in average children may frustrate the ideal of equality by not responding to the special needs of the retarded. Educational need is a nebulous concept; it is a determination which courts might understandably be reluctant to make.[102] But the law is now

---

[97] *See* Cohen, *Does IQ Matter?* 53 COMMENTARY, April 1972, at 51; C. JENCKS et al., *supra* note 38, at 68-69.

[98] 343 F. Supp. 1306. *See also* Note, *Legal Implications of the Use of Standardized Ability Tests in Employment and Education,* 68 COLUM. L. REV. 691, 695 (1968).

[99] 414 U.S. 563 (1974). Although the Court did not reach the issue of what equal protection requires, it explicitly rejected as too facile the court of appeals view that:

> Every student brings to the starting line of his educational career different advantages and disadvantages caused in part by social, economic and cultural background, created and continued completely apart from any contribution by the school system. That some of these may be impediments which can be overcome does not amount to a denial by the Board of educational opportunities within the meaning of the Fourteenth Amendment should the Board fail to give them special attention. 483 F.2d at 497.

Mr. Justice Douglas said for the majority in *Lau* that ". . . there is no equality of treatment merely by providing students with the same facilities, text books, teachers and curriculum; for students who do not understand English are effectively foreclosed from any meaningful education." 414 U.S. at 566.

[100] *E.g.,* United States v. Texas, 342 F. Supp. 24 (E.D. Tex. 1971), *aff'd,* 466 F.2d 518 (5th Cir. 1972); Serna v. Portales Municipal Schools, 351 F. Supp. 1279 (D.N.M. 1972), *aff'd,* 499 F.2d 1147 (1974); Guadalupe Organization v. Tempe Elementary School Dist. No. 3, Civil No. 71-435 (D. Ariz., Jan. 25, 1972) (unreported).

[101] Dennis v. United States, 339 U.S. 162, 184 (1950) (Frankfurter, J. dissenting).

[102] *See, e.g.,* McInnis v. Shapiro, 293 F. Supp. 327 (1968), *aff'd sub nom.* McInnis v. Ogilvie, 394 U.S. 322 (1969); *cf.* Kurland, *Equal Educational Opportunity: The Limits of Constitutional Jurisprudence Undefined,* 35 U. CHI. L. REV. 583 (1968).

tackling this task, and problems of mentally retarded children are at the crux of pioneering efforts on this legal frontier. Recently, in *Mills v. Board of Education,* Judge Waddy ordered that no child can be excluded from a regular public school unless the school board provides adequate alternative educational services "suited to the child's needs" (which could include special education or tuition grants) and a "constitutionally adequate prior hearing and periodic review of the child's status, progress and the adequacy of any educational alternative."[103] The school district was mandated to provide "to each child of school age a free and suitable publicly supported education regardless of the degree of the child's mental, physical or emotional disability or impairment."[104]

What then of the mentally retarded child who has been properly classified and labeled and who is given access to some form of public education, but who claims that the special program to which he is assigned is not best adapted to his particular needs? A court may well be reluctant to review the appropriateness of the schooling provided, except in a limited manner. Here, the established constitutional doctrine of the least restrictive alternative[105] may have some viability. Thus, the court in *PARC* inserted such a requirement of least restrictive alternative into its injunctive decree:

> It is the Commonwealth's obligation to place each retarded child in a free, public program of education and training appropriate to the child's capacity, within the context of a presumption that among the alternative programs of education and training required by statute to be available, placement in a regular public school class is preferable to placement in a special public school class and placement in a

---

[103] 348 F. Supp. at 878 (D.D.C. 1972). *See generally* Dimond, *The Constitutional Right to Education: The Quiet Revolution,* 24 HAST. L.J. 1087 (May 1973).

[104] *Id.; accord,* PARC, 334 F. Supp. 1257 (E.D. Pa. 1971).

Any legal technicality, such as the school district's failure to follow its own standards and procedures, can be of advantage to the excluded child. Thus, the school's exclusion of handicapped children may be *ultra vires* if outside the authority delegated to it by the state. *See, e.g.,* Board of Educ. v. Goldman, 47 Ohio App. 417, 191 N.E. 914 (1934) (retarded child could not be excluded from school because the district had not properly received approval from the state department of education). *See also* GELHORN & BYSE, ADMINISTRATIVE LAW 84-85 (4th ed. 1960). State statutes or constitutional provisions guaranteeing free public education to *all* children may afford a remedy. *See, e.g.,* Wolf v. Utah, Civil No. 182646 (3d Dist. Salt Lake City) (unreported). The *Wolf* court relied on a typical constitutional provision: "The legislature shall make laws for the establishment and maintenance of a system of public schools, which shall be open to all the children of the state. . . ." UTAH CONST. art III, § 4. Where the school district cannot prove the child incapable of benefiting from public education and presents only an economic argument for exclusion, courts have determined that financial limitations are an insufficient basis for the denial of an education. *See, e.g.,* Hosier v. Evans, 314 F. Supp. 316 (D. St. Croix 1970); and the Supreme Court's dictum in Shapiro v. Thompson, 394 U.S. 618, 633 (1969) that a state "could not for example reduce expenditures for education by barring indigent children from its schools." Where the district had insufficient places for all brain damaged children, tuition grants for those unaccommodated by the public schools were held to violate equal protection because they were for a lesser amount than it would have cost the district to educate the child. McMillan v. Board of Educ., 430 F.2d 1145 (2d Cir. 1970).

[105] *See, e.g.,* Shelton v. Tucker, 364 U.S. 479, 488 (1960): "[T]hat purpose cannot be pursued by means that broadly stifle personal liberties when the end can be more narrowly achieved." Thus, the inquiry is whether the state's legitimate purposes might have been achieved by some other means which would have a less onerous impact on the individual. *See, e.g.,* Carrington v. Rash, 380 U.S. 89 (1965); Rinaldi v. Yeager, 384 U.S. 305 (1966); Struve, *The Less Restrictive Alternative Principle and Economic Due Process,* 80 HARV. L. REV. 1463 (1967).

special public school class is preferable to placement in any other type of program of education and training.[106]

Society too easily accepts the current classification approach, which too often leads to early labeling and educational isolation of mentally retarded children and others incorrectly labeled in an environment adapted to a static level of functioning. Such treatment reflects the baseless assumption that these children are basically unmodifiable; it is likely to perpetuate their low levels of performance.[107] The law as normative of social relationships must help society to reject this negativism, to reverse the pattern, and to adopt a new strategy aimed at augmenting the capacity of retarded citizens. Only then, freed from stigmatizing stereotypes and confining classifications, can the mentally retarded citizen realize his fullest capabilities and lead a fulfilling and productive life.

LEGAL SAFEGUARDS FOR THE CLASSIFIED AND THE MISCLASSIFIED

Procedural Due Process in Schools

"The history of American freedom is, in no small measure, the history of procedure."[108] The fourteenth amendment thus protects every individual from state-imposed injury by ensuring that no state shall . . . deprive any person of life, liberty or property without due process of law." *Any* child excluded from school, or even placed in a special class for the mentally retarded, is potentially harmed thereby. Action by a school district is "state action,"[109] and "liberty" has been construed to encompass a student's interest in obtaining an education.[110]

The requirement of procedural safeguards in the realm of school classification arises from two types of potential injury that may result from an improper or inappropriate classification decision. The loss of schooling itself is an injury for which the law has provided a hearing requirement.[111] Given the educational

---

[106] 334 F. Supp. at 1260. *Cf. In re* Held, Civil No. H-2-71, H-10-71 (Fam. Ct. Westchester Co., N.Y., Nov. 29, 1971) (unreported). The court in *Held* granted tuition payments for private schools on a showing that the public school program was not well adapted to the child's special educational needs.

[107] A. YATES, BEHAVIOR THERAPY 324 (1970) rejects "the pessimistic views, which have been so widely and for so long entertained regarding the ineducability of the mentally defective. . . ." *See also* Feuerstein, *A Dynamic Approach to the Causation, Prevention and Alleviation of Retarded Performance,* in SOCIOCULTURAL ASPECTS OF MENTAL RETARDATION (H.C. Haywood ed. 1968); BAUMEISTER, *Learning Abilities of the Mentally Retarded,* in MENTAL RETARDATION: APPRAISAL, EDUCATION AND REHABILITATION 181 (1967).

[108] Malinski v. New York, 324 U.S. 401, 414 (1945) (Frankfurter, J., concurring).

[109] Cooper v. Aaron, 358 U.S. 1, 16 (1958).

[110] Bolling v. Sharpe, 347 U.S. 497 (1954).

[111] *E.g.,* Williams v. Dade County School Bd., 441 F.2d 299 (5th Cir. 1971); Scoville v. Board of Educ., 425 F.2d 10 (7th Cir. 1970); Vought v. Van Buren, 306 F. Supp. 1388 (E.D. Mich. 1969).

injury suffered by children assigned to special classes for the mentally retarded or excluded entirely from school[112] and given the significance and relative permanence of the classification, some form of hearing must be held before the school can make so basic a change in the child's educational status.[113] The second type of potential injury is in the affixing of a stigma which seriously affects the life style and opportunities of the labeled person.[114] When the child is not only removed from the educational mainstream, but also placed in a program to which a debilitating label attaches, fairness dictates prior notice and hearing.[115]

In *Wisconsin v. Constantineau,* the Supreme Court ruled that a Wisconsin law requiring the posting of the names of alleged problem drinkers in taverns and package stores for the purpose of preventing the sale of liquor to them constituted stigmatization serious enough to require due process safeguards. Posting, under Wisconsin practice, was done without prior notice or hearing, at the request of any one of a number of minor officials, elected or appointed, or at the request of the spouse of the alleged drinker.[116]

The *Constantineau* reasoning was recently applied by a federal district court in Boston in denying a defendant's motion to dismiss a complaint which sought, in part, to require the Boston school system to provide a prior hearing for children classified as retarded.[117] And a Wisconsin district court ordered excluded children reinstated in public schools and a full hearing procedure prior to all future "medical" exclusions.[118]

The applicability of procedural due process to educational rights of the mentally retarded can no longer be in doubt after the two recent landmark federal court decisions involving education for the handicapped. In *PARC*[119] the court-approved consent decree required notice and hearing for any mentally retarded child recommended for any fundamental change in educational status. And in *Mills*[120] the court prohibited public school exclusion while mandating for any school placement decision "a constitutionally adequate prior hearing and periodic review of the child's status, progress and the adequacy of any educational alternative." Both courts spelled out procedural necessities in detail, but these can be more fruitfully examined after analysis of administrative obstacles inherent in school classification determinations.

A major problem in providing adequate procedural safeguards for handicapped children is the probable attitude of school officials. To them, procedural requirements mean not only the time-consuming task of rendering an academic

---

[112] *See* pp. 218-21 *supra.*

[113] *Cf.* Goldberg v. Kelly, 397 U.S. 254 (1970); Dixon v. Alabama State Bd. of Educ., 294 F.2d 150 (5th Cir.), *cert. denied,* 368 U.S. 930 (1961).

[114] *See, e.g.,* Wisconsin v. Constantineau, 400 U.S. 433 (1971) (requiring hearing before names of alleged problem drinkers would be posted in taverns and perhaps stores).

[115] Mills, 348 F. Supp. 866 (D.D.C. 1972).

[116] 400 U.S. 433.

[117] Stewart v. Phillips, Civil No. 70-1199-F (D. Mass. Feb. 1971).

[118] Marlegq v. Board of School Directors, Civil No. 70-C-8 (E.D. Wis. Sept. 18, 1970).

[119] 334 F. Supp. 1257 (E.D. Pa. 1971).

[120] 348 F. Supp. 866 (D.D.C. 1972).

decision comprehensible to laymen, but also the possibility of challenge to a decision jealously guarded as the school's special domain.

School officials often feel threatened when pupils and parents insist on access to school records or seek the benefit of advice and assistance from members of the community not affiliated with the school system. The usual arguments for not giving parents access to records will be raised: the need to safeguard, and prevent parents' misinterpretation of, records of a highly professional and technical nature; the desirability of preserving the professional freedom of expression of psychologists and other educators free from fear of libel suits and parental retaliation; and the danger of parents' seeing information critical of the home environment and of the child. In many school districts, it may be expected that parents will be refused access to their children's records, including test scores and diagnoses crucial to the proposed placement.

The unwillingness of school authorities to allow inspection of records further suggests that they would view any procedural requirements as too cumbersome, especially if applied to the vast quantity of minute and quotidian classification or evaluation decisions made in the schools. Not only would the reluctance of school personnel make the appearance of due process a cruel hoax for the parent and child, but there might even be a reverse impact, making the classification itself more difficult to overturn. The ostensible process of careful administrative review of a decision that the child is mentally retarded would appear to legitimize the substantive decision. Courts will be more apt to defer to the experts' determination when this decision is submitted to serious scrutiny at the school. Moreover, children will be substituting the inadequate ad hoc review of the accuracy of an individual assignment for the more sweeping and fundamental challenge to the propriety of the classifying process. Finally, when the school official's judgment is couched not in disciplinary terms, but as scholastic evaluation, and when there is no overt acknowledgment of potential inconsistency between the child's interest and that of the school, parents are probably ill-equipped to challenge the proposed assignment or even to recognize a possible misdiagnosis or stigma.

A student dissatisfied with a determination by school officials may be further coerced by a consenting parent who tends to accept the expert advice of school authorities regarding what is best for the child's further academic progress. Realistically, the parent may be aware that the cost of a private program is prohibitive and that the school can offer something much better than what the parent could provide at home. Hence, there can be an implicit conflict between the parent's view and the child's independent interest in his own schooling.[121]

The inability of many well-intentioned parents to deal with service-providing institutions is borne out by experience. In the past, ghetto parents rarely contested school placement decisions. "[They] would feel themselves incapable of arguing the

---

[121] *See, e.g.,* Wisconsin v. Yoder, 406 U.S. 205, 241 (1972) (Douglas, J., dissenting in part) (recognizing a child's independent interest in his own schooling); Chandler v. South Bend School Dist., Civil No. 71-S-51 (N.D. Ind. 1971).

point, even if they were aware of it."[122] In *Larry P.*, for instance, despite the overwhelming racial imbalance in classes for the educable retarded and the resulting presumption of culturally erroneous classification, fewer than 2 percent of parents in the 2 years prior to the hearing had refused consent to the placement.[123]

For school assignments of special or enduring educational significance to the child, the very least that is warranted is a full discussion between family and school authorities of the ramifications of the assignment. When a child is to be placed in a special class for the mentally retarded, the parents should be informed of the specific educational plan proposed, the temporary or permanent alternatives that are available,[124] and of the fact that the classification will be noted in a permanent school record. The parent should also be told that the testing and evaluation may not be appropriate and may result in mislabeling the child.[125] It should also be explained that the choice is entirely up to the family, that no action will be taken against them if they refuse placement, and that they may consult with independent authorities if they have any doubts about the school's evaluation.[126]

Obviously, the parent and independent consultant must have full access to the child's school records, including teacher comments, guidance notes, and other informal data placed in the student's file.[127] Periodic review of the child's progress with the aim of his eventual reintegration into regular classes should also be required, and the parent should retain the right to withdraw consent and revoke the placement at any time for any reason.[128]

Because of the anticipated difficulty in ensuring implementation of all these basic prerequisites to meaningful parental consent, it may be unwise to eliminate or ignore the right to adversary procedure. Perhaps it is preferable, after all, to leave these decisions to the "experts" so long as reviewability is facilitated by the existence

---

[122] Schafer & Polk, *Delinquency and the Schools,* in President's Commission on Law Enforcement and Administration of Justice, Task Force Report: Juvenile Delinquency and Youth Crime app. M, at 222, 241 (1967).

[123] Defendant's Answers to Interrogatories No. 4, at 3, Larry P. v. Riles, 343 F. Supp. 1306 (N.D. Cal. 1972), *aff'd* 502 F.2d 963 (1974).

[124] Mills, 348 F. Supp. at 880.

[125] *See* the section, "The Means of Classifying the Mentally Retarded," *supra.* A federal district court recently invalidated parental consent for children's participation in a drug abuser indentification test, finding lack of candor in the letter soliciting consent. The school omitted mention of possible negative consequences such as dissemination of test results to school personnel and possible misdiagnosis of potential drug abusers; hence, the solicitation letter did not lead to "informed" consent. Merriken v. Cressman, 364 F. Supp. 913 (E.D. Pa. 1973).

[126] The decree in Mills, 348 F. Supp. at 880-81, requires that the parent or guardian be informed "that the child is eligible to receive at no charge, the services of a federally or locally funded diagnostic center for an independent medical, psychological and educational evaluation. . ." and that the school authorities specify the name, address, and telephone of the appropriate independent evaluator.

[127] *Id.* at 881; *see* Johnson v. Board of Educ., 31 Misc. 2d 810, 220 N.Y.S.2d 362 (Sup. Ct. 1961); Van Allen McCleary, 27 Misc. 2d 81, 211 N.Y.S.2d 501 (Sup. Ct. 1961); Goslin & Bordier, *Record-Keeping in Elementary and Secondary Schools* in On Record: Files and Dossiers in American Life 29, 64-65 (S. Wheeler ed. 1969).

[128] There is some indication, however, that courts may be unwilling to deprive school authorities of the ultimate decision. The court in *Kivell v. Nemoitin,* No. 143913 (Super. Ct. Fairfield County, Conn. July 18, 1972), although directing the Stamford Board of Education to furnish a child special education, added the following caveat: "this court will frown on any unilateral action by parents in sending their children to other facilities. If a program is timely filed by a local board of education and accepted and approved by the state board, then it is the duty of the parents to accept said program. A refusal by the parents in such a situation will not entitle said child to any benefits from this court."

of an adequate stenographic record and a decision based on this record. The specific procedures outlines in *Mills* and *PARC,* adhering to the Supreme Court's pronouncement in *Goldberg v. Kelly*,[129] would at least stimulate significant parental participation in basic educational decisions affecting the child. At the very least, these procedures increase communication and minimize misunderstanding. At best, they have the salutory effect of reducing disastrous misclassifications. Despite the evident drawback that such safeguards might be somewhat cumbersome to school administrators, the poignant lesson of experience is that no less than complete due process safeguards are required to protect the rights of mentally retarded school children.

Record Keeping and the School's Responsibility

The Problem of Dissemination

The need for procedural safeguards is compounded by school records which chart the history of a student's career and project the stigma of the label throughout his entire life. Amelioration of the injustices of the testing and classification process as proposed in this paper would also have salutory effects on the mentally retarded person's life chances after school. Computers further complicate the problem because of the qualitative changes in the nature and availability of information. The easier and more economical it is to store data, the more curiosities can be satisfied with less attention paid to the quality of the record. The computer has an air of infallibility.

It has become commonplace to assert that computer-based information systems may prove to be as significant to the progress of mankind as the advent of movable type.[130] It is already known that the machines can print out a 20-page dossier on every American from a single tape less than 5,000 feet long,[131] geometrically reduce the space needed for data storage,[132] dramatically cut the cost of data storage,[133] and speed retrieval and analysis by almost astronomical amounts. For example, a community college near Detroit has inaugurated a three-hour preadmission test, the results of which are processed on an IBM 210/50 computer and related to a chart called a "cognitive style map." This depicts characteristics and aptitudes of prospective students and presumably guides the school administrators in their admissions process.[134] A "Migrant Student Record Transfer Committee" now works through 137 teletypewriters, providing 7,000 schools with records on migrant workers' children. In addition to the identities of the children, the records contain

[129] 397 U.S. 254 (1970).

[130] *See, e.g.,* A. CLARKE, PROFILES OF THE FUTURE 212-27 (1962); H. KAHN & A. WEINER, THE YEAR 2000, at 88-98, 348-49 (1967); A. WESTIN, PRIVACY AND FREEDOM 158-68 (1967).

[131] *See* A. MILLER, THE ASSAULT ON PRIVACY 12 (1971).

[132] The makers of the Univac speculate that soon "the tax records of the nation may fit into one file cabinet." TIME, September 27, 1968, at 51.

[133] It has been predicted that it will soon be cheaper to store a page of English text in a computer than to preserve it on paper. Fano, *The Computer Utility and the Community,* in COMPUTERS AND COMMUNICATIONS — TOWARD A COMPUTER UTILITY 39, 44 (F. Gruenberger ed. 1968).

[134] COMPUTER WORLD, June 21, 1972, at 7.

data about their inoculations, urgent conditions, health, special interests, abilities, and academic status. The purpose is a "benevolent" one: to enable children to transfer to schools throughout the United States with an acceptable transcript. However, chances of "pigeonholing" a large population of children is greatly enhanced when 7,000 schools have access to their files,[135] which by their special nature separate them by racial and economic criteria from peers. Experimental programs have been launched in California high schools to automate fully the compilation and recording of attendance files.[136]

As the capacity of computers expands and school systems gain experience with automated data processing, most school will adopt some form of computerized record keeping. No doubt this will contribute to efficiency and perhaps even to imaginative use of records in improving education, but it also makes it imperative that special precautions be taken to ensure the accuracy of the data, to permit review of the material by the individual or the family, and to provide for the removal or correction of irrelevant or inaccurate data. Moreover, it dramatizes the need for clarity in laws relating to privacy and access to individual records.[137] School officials must know the extent of their authority or liability for releasing information.

State laws covering access to school records are in complete disarray. The majority of states have no statewide policy; determination of such matters is left to local school boards. And some school boards admit that they handle problems of access to students' records on an individual basis without formal policies.[138] In practice, formalized school policies regarding access to pupil records are almost nonexistent. On the basis of their survey of record-keeping practices in American elementary and secondary schools, Goslin and Bordier concluded that "[e]xpressed general policies vary greatly from district to district and . . . actual practices often deviate significantly, even from these broad guidelines."[139] They also found that schools frequently permit a variety of outside agencies and individuals access to pupils' records, without obtaining parental permission.[140]

In light of existing practices, one cannot expect any meaningful confidentiality of this information. Instead, the student labeled "mentally retarded" can expect that his file will be open to potential employers, and he can expect these school records to damage seriously his employment opportunities. Any remedy against the potential employer is tenuous.[141]

---

[135] *Id.,* June 14, 1972, at 12.

[136] *Id.,* July 28, 1972, at 11.

[137] *See, e.g.,* Project, *Computerization of Government Files: What Impact on the Individual?,* 15 U.C.L.A. L. Rev. 1371 (1968); Pipe, *Privacy: Establishing Restrictions on Government Inquiry,* 18 Am. U.L. Rev. 516 (1969).

[138] Goslin & Bordier, *supra* note 127.

[139] *Id.* at 56.

[140] *Id.* at 57, 64.

[141] Title VII of the Civil Rights Act, 42 U.S.C. §§ 2000e *et seq.* (1970), prohibits racial discrimination by private employers, however, and has been construed to forbid reliance on arrest records in denying a position, on the theories that (1) given the presumption of innocence, a record of mere arrest has no significance and (2) based on a showing that blacks are more frequently arrested than whites, reliance on such records amounts to racial discrimination. *See* Gregory v. Litton Systems, Inc., 316 F. Supp. 401 (C.D. Cal. 1970), *aff'd,* 472 F.2d 631 (9th Cir. 1972).

Legal Redress Against Government

Redress against the state is appropriate for unreasonable action which restricts the mentally retarded citizen's basic right to earn a livelihood.[142] Although the potential employer may draw mistaken inferences from state records, it is the state which devises, maintains, and promulgates the stigmatizing innuendo.[143] In *Watkins v. United States,* it was noted that:

> Those who are identified by witnesses and thereby placed in the same glare of publicity are equally subject to public stigma, scorn and obloquy. . . . That this impact is partly the result of non-governmental activity by private persons cannot relieve the investigators of their responsibility for initiating the reaction.[144]

Again, this evokes traditional notions of due process. Where the stigmatization and the potential for harm were created without proper procedure and without assurance of the accuracy of the record,[145] as with arrest records,[146] or school discipline in the absence of proper procedures,[147] the wrongfully labeled person may seek a court order of expungement of records maintained by the state. The judicial resolution would hinge upon whether any public good was accomplished by retention or dissemination of the record.[148] Relief should not, however, be conditioned on a showing of actual or imminent injury to the petitioner, because he may be unable to ascertain whether the records actually caused a rejection of employment applications.[149]

Another channel of legal rectification of injury lies in the law of defamation by the release of false information. According to William Prosser, defamation is a communication which "tends to injure 'reputation' in the popular sense; to diminish the esteem, respect, goodwill or confidence in which the plaintiff is held, or to excite adverse, derogatory or unpleasant feelings or opinions against him."[150] Certainly, release of inaccurate information labeling the student "mentally retarded" would not only embarrass and humiliate the individual, but also diminish his opportunity for employment and chances for acceptance in the community.

The sweep of the defamation argument is limited by the doctrine that a person with a legal, social, or moral duty is privileged to make good faith communication of an (otherwise) derogatory nature to others who have a corresponding duty or interest in the information. Thus, in *Iverson v. Frandsen,*[151] the court ruled that a

---

[142] *Cf.* Sniadach v. Family Finance Corp., 395 U.S. 337 (1969); Willner v. Comm. on Character and Fitness, 373 U.S. 96 (1962).

[143] *See* NAACP v. Alabama 357 U.S. 449, 463 (1958).

[144] 354 U.S. 178, 197-98 (1957).

[145] *Cf.* Wisconsin v. Constantineau, 400 U.S. 433 (1971).

[146] Wheeler v. Goodman, 306 F. Supp. 58, 65-66 (W.D.N.C. 1969), *vacated and remanded on other grounds,* 401 U.S. 987 (1971); United States v. Kalish, 271 F. Supp. 968, 970 (D.P.R. 1967).

[147] Breen v. Kahl, 296 F. Supp. 702, 710 (W.D. Wis.), *aff'd,* 419 F.2d 1034 (7th Cir. 1969), *cert. denied,* 398 U.S. 937 (1970).

[148] United States v. Kalish, 271 F. Supp. 968, 970 (D.P.R. 1967).

[149] *In re* Smith, 63 Misc. 2d 198, 310 N.Y.S.2d 617 (Fam. Ct. New York City, 1970).

[150] W. PROSSER, HANDBOOK OF THE LAW OF TORTS § 111, at 739 (4th ed. 1971).

[151] 237 F.2d 898 (10th Cir. 1956).

report filed by a psychologist with a child's school stating that the child was a "high-grade moron" was a professional report made by a public servant and that its contents were his best judgment of the situation. It is significant that the report went to school officials with an interest in, and responsibility to, the child. In *Kenny v. Gurley,*[152] the court held the physician and dean of women at the girl's school not liable for communicating to the girl's mother an incorrect diagnosis of venereal disease, particularly since malice was not proved. The court noted that the defendants had a duty to the student body, and when the school dismissed the girl, it was part of that duty to advise parents of the cause. In a similar case, *Basket v. Crossfield,*[153] a male student was charged with indecent exposure and the university authorities communicated this fact to the parents. The court held that this communication to the parents was within the authorities' privilege.

The classification and labeling process is somewhat different because of the invalidity of the testing devices used to measure students' "intelligence." It is highly probable that a diagnosis, evaluation, and any other information based on the test's results will be inaccurate. Nevertheless, it is doubtful under the present state of the law that the possible invalidity of the classification process is sufficient to impute to school officials "malicious intent" to publish false information or to hold them liable for transmittal of the stigmatizing information. Whether a prospective employer has a sufficient "interest" to warrant the school's invoking the doctrine of privileged communication is largely a matter of unsettled state law and reflects the need for statutory protection of the rights of individuals, including those classified as "mentally retarded." Irrespective of the accuracy or validity of records, the stigmatized individual may invoke statutory protection for confidentiality or non-dissemination of personal records.

In the absence of such statutory protection and regardless of the accuracy of the records, the individual may look to the relatively embryonic law of privacy as a further safeguard. For example, in *Melvin v. Reid*[154] the plaintiff had for several years been a notorious prostitute, and had been tried, though acquitted, for murder. After her acquittal she decided to reform, gave up her occupation, became rehabilitated, married, made friends, and took up a respectable position in society. Some eight years later the defendants published a movie which depicted true events in the plaintiff's earlier life as a prostitute. The film used the plaintiff's maiden name and was advertised as depicting her actual life-story. This action, of course, caused her great injury, and she brought suit for damages. The court held that a cause of action was stated and found a right of privacy inherent in Article 1, § 1 of the California Constitution, which protected the right of "pursuing and obtaining safety and happiness." The court assumed that the events depicted in the movie were true, but spoke of privacy as the right "to be let alone."[155] "The gravamen of the tort [of invasion of privacy] is ordinarily the unwarranted publication by the defendant of intimate details of the plaintiff's private life."[156] The facts disclosed may be

[152] 208 Ala. 623, 95 So. 34 (1923).
[153] 190 Ky. 751, 228 S.W. 673 (1920). *But see, e.g.,* Elder v. Anderson, 205 Cal. App. 2d 326, 23 Cal. Rptr. 48 (1972) (school district's responsibility for circular labeling plaintiff a "troublemaker").
[154] 112 Cal. App. 285, 297 P. 91 (1931).
[155] *Id.* at 289.
[156] Coverstone v. Davies, 38 Cal. 2d 315, 323, 239 P.2d 876, 880, *cert. denied,* 344 U.S. 840 (1952).

true and need not be necessarily embarrassing or incriminating.[157] They must simply be private and not subject to disclosure due to an overriding interest which creates a privilege.

Indeed, where it is the government which wrongfully discloses private facts, the right to privacy reaches constitutional dimensions.[158] So long as one has an expectation of privacy which society is prepared to recognize as reasonable,[159] any infringement by the government must be necessary[160] and accomplished by the least drastic means available to achieve the legitimate governmental purpose.[161] If one is protected against disclosure of his financial affairs[162] or the existence of a single criminal act in his past,[163] surely similar safeguards should be afforded the individual against the release of stigmatizing school records.

In *Doe v. McMillan,*[164] for example, the Supreme Court facilitated a right to privacy suit even against a congressional committee to restrain the publication of tests and disciplinary records of students in District of Columbia schools. And in a recent federal case, a program to detect potential drug abusers by means of a personality test was deemed an invasion of privacy because of the intimate nature of questions asked and the subsequent availability of test results to school personnel.[165] Resort to these remedies would not only safeguard citizens against unwarranted injury but should also lead school officials to reexamine their reasons for collecting and maintaining student records, and the basis for their release. It is of utmost concern that adequate rules and procedures be devised to ensure confidentiality of the information once it is inserted in the system. There must be written regulations promulgated in advance to govern access to records, providing for identification of persons authorized to use them, for informing the individual what use will be made of the data, for reviewing the accuracy of the data, and, most important, for obtaining consent prior to the release of any data to outside parties.

CONCLUSION

This discussion indicates that the law is discovering another oppressed minority, those citizens labeled as "mentally retarded." The parameters of a mentally retarded citizen's civil rights are just now taking shape. The "injunctive" or "prohibitive"

---

[157] Brex v. Smith, 104 N.J. Eq. 386, 146 A. 34 (Ct. Ch. 1929).

[158] *See* United States v. United States Dist. Court, 407 U.S. 297 (1972); Griswold v. Connecticut, 381 U.S. 479 (1965).

[159] Katz v. United States, 389 U.S. 347, 360-61 (1967) (Harlan, J., concurring); Nader v. General Motors, 25 N.Y.2d 560, 255 N.E.2d 765, 307 N.Y.S.2d 64 (1970).

[160] *See* Griswold v. Connecticut, 381 U.S. 479 (1965).

[161] *See* note 105, *supra.*

[162] *Compare* Reisman v. Caplin, 375 U.S. 440 (1964) *and* United States v. Harrington, 388 F.2d 520 (2d Cir. 1968) *and* Zimmerman v. Wilson, 81 F.2d 847 (3d Cir. 1936), *with* City of Carmel-by-the-Sea v. Young, 2 Cal. 3d 259, 446 P.2d 225, 85 Cal. Rptr. 1 (1970) *and* Brex v. Smith, 104 N.J. Eq. 386, 146 A. 34 (Ct. Ch. 1929).

[163] *See, e.g.,* Morrow v. District of Columbia, 417 F.2d 728 (D.C. Cir. 1969); Briscoe v. Reader's Digest, 4 Cal. 3d 529, 483 P.2d 34, 93 Cal. Rptr. 866 (1971).

[164] 412 U.S. 306 (1973).

[165] Merriken v. Cressman, 364 F. Supp. 913 (E.D. Pa. 1973).

realm of law acts as a restraint on zealous oversimplification of human differences and on the consequent deprivation of significant rights or privileges. Thus, the legal system provides a means to attack discriminatory or erroneous sorting techniques and procedures. The law attempts to preserve educational or employment opportunities which might be crippled or stifled by a mistaken categorization, a stigmatizing label, or the dissemination of potentially harmful information. Eventually, the law probably will assume a role of affirmative support, as a vehicle to guarantee each person the chance to attain a life style and role consistent with his maximum potentiality. No less noble a goal will permit the law to remain normative of social relationships and morality to remain normative of law.

Reaction Comment

VIRGINIA DAVIS NORDIN

THESE COMMENTS are intended to extend Sorgen's excellent survey of authorities and recent legal activity in the area of labeling and classification of mentally retarded citizens. The focus will, however, be from a slightly different perspective.

In re Gault[1] was based on the principle that the legal implications of social and educational policies (juvenile court procedures) would be judged by the actual effects of those policies, not by benevolent theories. The case has important teachings about due process and the right to individual consideration, which apply to labeling of individuals as mentally retarded.[2] Following the *Gault* reasoning, it is important to make clear to the educational community that the special education system, including labeling and its consequences, will be evaluated by courts as it actually works and not according to the theory and writings which may motivate those involved.[3]

An aspect of the suspect classification doctrine is the growing recognition of the need for more consideration of people as individuals as a matter of both legal and educational philosophy.[4] Education for the mentally retarded is decidedly different from most other need areas in that there is an absence of voices (no sit-ins, no disruptions). Therefore, the state might well be forced to let voices develop which will advocate the rights of individuals who may be harmed by the usual processes of the educational system.

---

[1] 387 U.S. 1 (1967).

[2] *See generally* GAULT: WHAT NOW FOR THE JUVENILE COURT? (V. Nordin ed. 1968). For discussion of the application of *Gault* doctrines to labeling, see Nordin, *Comment on "Labelling,"* in CONFRONTATION AND CHANGE: COMMUNITY PROBLEMS OF MENTAL RETARDATION AND DEVELOPMENTAL DISABILITIES 99, 102-03 (J. Cohen ed. 1971).

[3] *See* Clark, *Why Gault: Juvenile Court Theory and Impact in Historical Perspective,* in GAULT: WHAT NOW FOR THE JUVENILE COURT? 1, 6-12 (V. Nordin ed. 1968).

[4] *See In re* Gault, 387 U.S. at 16 (1967); Cruickshank, *Special Education, the Community and Constitutional Issues,* in SPECIAL EDUCATION INSTRUMENT OF CHANGE IN EDUCATION FOR THE '70's, at 3-10 (1971).

Sorgen's reference to the *Sniadach*[5] case, which requires the imposition of due process safeguards before garnishments of salaries are allowed, should be highlighted. If the social-legal system can tolerate the time and energy required to hold full due process hearings in these circumstances, surely educational systems can provide due process hearings for children who are to be labeled mentally retarded, thus incurring a stigma that may present a lifelong problem. Measured and objective description of the requirements surely answers the arguments that due process (or justice) is too slow or too expensive. The tragedies of labeling and classification are too severe to be justified by "administrative necessity," which too often means merely administrative convenience. Also, from a purely pragmatic approach, it would seem better for educational systems to provide a full and fair hearing initially than to risk lawsuits later. Threat of a lawsuit for damages does hold a potential for forcing realistic individual standards on reluctant administrators and agencies and for safeguarding rights of individual students.[6] The trend toward reliance on damage suits has a tremendous potential for redressing wrongs in this area.

The Supreme Court's decision in *Griggs v. Duke Power Co.,*[7] and especially its comment on testing, has implications for citizens labeled mentally retarded. *Griggs* holds that results of intelligence tests may not be used to deny someone a job, unless the tests relate to the skills and abilities required to do that job. This standard should have application to the legal validity of intelligence tests in schools. Sorgen reports that the majority of the mentally retarded population actually fall into the mildly retarded category, but the usual stereotype associated with any "retarded" person in this society is of a more limited individual with physical impairments. For most persons labeled mentally retarded during school years, intelligence tests actually are irrelevant to their life role, because most individuals classified as mentally retarded will, as adults, become indistinguishable from the general population. Are tests unnecessarily prejudicing school personnel, potential employers, and others? If so, the labeled individual's loss may be compensable.

A danger inherent in litigation in this area is the imposition of inappropriate educational standards by the courts.[8] *Hobson v. Hansen* is an example of a court plunging valiantly, if somewhat awkwardly, into the education process.[9]

[5] Sniadach v. Family Finance Corp., 395 U.S. 337 (1969); *see also* Sorgen, note 142, *supra*.
[6] *See* Nordin, *Comment on "Labelling," supra* note 2, at 108; Ross, DeYoung & Cohen, *Confrontation: Special Education Placement and the Law,* 38 EXCEPTIONAL CHILDREN 5 (1971).
[7] 401 U.S. 424 (1971).
[8] The issue of the use of sociological data is often discussed in connection with Brown v. Board of Educ., 347 U.S. 483 (1954). A relevant sampling of opinion is to be found in L. GARRISON & W. HURST, THE LEGAL PROCESS ch. 3 (C. Auerbach et al. rev. ed. 1961). *See also* Nordin, *Comment on "Labelling," supra* note 2, at 99-100. This problem obviously transfers to the area of special education and should be avoided by informed change outside the courts. The courts should be a last resort. There are, indeed, a few cases in which the courts have exercised judicial restraint, but I believe these are exceptions. *See* Conley v. Lake Charles School Bd., 303 F. Supp. 394 (W.D. La. 1969), *vacated and remanded sub nom.* Gordon v. Jefferson Davis Parish School Bd., 446 F.2d 266 (5th Cir. 1971); Whittenberg v. Greenville County School Dist., 298 F. Supp. 784, 790 (D.S.C. 1969). *But see* Stell v. Savannah-Chatham Bd. of Educ., 333 F.2d 55 (5th Cir.), *cert. denied,* 379 U.S. 933 (1964).
[9] 269 F. Supp. at 401. For a detailed analysis and explication of this thesis see Whelan & Jackson, *Labelling,* in CONFRONTATION AND CHANGE: COMMUNITY PROBLEMS OF MENTAL RETARDATION AND DEVELOPMENTAL DISABILITIES 63-67 (J. Cohen ed. 1971).

Educators must make a greater effort to inform themselves of the growing legal activity on labeling of mentally retarded children so they may clean their own houses before the courts do it, perhaps poorly, for them.

The total mixture of the racial and mental retardation issues in Sorgen's paper and elsewhere is a matter of concern. Since the illegality and social undesirability of racial discrimination is widely accepted, it is seductive to imply, if not assert, that the question of misclassification or labeling is always one of racial discrimination. It is not. As current cases indicate, *part* of the problem is racial discrimination,[10] but a very real part of the problem applies to children of all races and cultures who are "mentally retarded" and require individual attention. It helps neither racial nor ethnic minorities nor "special" children to coalesce these groups completely, even though it might make the legal battle easier. This society must face the problems, and the rights, of those citizens who function at below-average levels of intelligence. The classification of such individuals may be just as erroneous as the misclassification of children from a different culture with a different language. It is important not to lose sight of the general problem by subsuming it in the problem of minority groups subject to educational discrimination. The key to better special education is more individual consideration and due process safeguards, expensive as these goals may be.

Reaction Comment

LOUIS A. BRANSFORD

IT IS EVIDENT from the extensive litigation Sorgen cites that there is an intense interest in the implications of legal action to secure the rights of the mentally retarded citizen. What is not evident, although of particular interest, is the outcome of this litigation: How many classification cases have been decided by the courts? How many have been settled out of court? How many have been decided in favor of the defendant? What has been the "track record"? Whom do decisions affect? A report on special education and litigation published by the Institute for the Study of Mental Retardation and Related Disabilities states:

> In summary, it is important to note that only two cases have been decided in the courts, *Hobson* and *Spangler*. The others have been settled out of court or are still in the courts. As one looks at the cases in the Appendix, he may be surprised at the number of those which were settled out of court. Even though they can hold no legal precedent, these instances do show that school systems have felt the need to rectify the situation.[1]

---

[10] *See* Ross, Special Education Placement and the Law, A Review of Recent Cases (unpublished papers, Univ. of Mich., Institute for the Study of Mental Retardation and Related Disabilities, 1970). *See also* Lau v. Nichols, 414 U.S. 563 (1974).

---

[1] L. Burello, H. DeYoung & D. Lang, Special Education and Litigation: Implications for Educational and Professional Practice (Institute for the Study of Mental Retardation and Related Disabilities, Univ. of Mich., 1972). Although these statistics are dated, it remains true that many court cases in this area are settled by compromise, with agreed modifications of school procedures.

It is unclear what changes have been caused in the public schools by the recent emphasis on testing, labeling, and placement. The number of segregated classes for the mildly retarded has been reduced significantly in the past several years. Resource rooms and integrated classroom programs for exceptional children have increased at a significant rate. Changes of this sort can be demonstrated by a simple count of school programs in existence and training programs of a noncategorical nature in the universities. Nevertheless, facts such as these may indicate simply a symptomatic reaction to the social climate or a response to litigation, rather than a sincere concern for the mentally retarded.

Sorgen mentions the need for training programs that would teach minority group individuals to administer and interpret intelligence tests, thus minimizing the problems of testing, labeling, and placement. However, labeling and placement tests that have been found to have questionable validity for minorities will not assume greater validity if administered by a minority group individual. The tests will not have changed substantially, and regardless of the competence of the minority group individual in administering the test, test results must be questioned if the test itself is inadequate.

From all indications, training programs for school psychologists, counselors, and psychometrists have not been effective in the past, and there is very little evidence that substantial changes have or will take place in the future. Minority group individuals receiving training would essentially perpetuate the questionable practices that Anglo psychometrists have practiced in the past. In fact, the involvement of minority individuals could be even more devastating since minority group youngsters might overidentify with the examiner and be more accepting of test results. Studies have shown that Mexican-American teachers have the same prejudices as do Anglo teachers toward Mexican-American children in their classrooms and, in fact, deal even more harshly with them.[2] The biases of the American culture are learned by most people who are exposed to them, including professionals from minority groups. Even for the professional from a minority group with rapport, identification, and good training, the test results are questionable if the testing instrument is questionable. A recent report of the United States Commission on Civil Rights speaks to the issue of identification:

> In light of these findings, it is not surprising to have also found that Mexican American children participate less in class than do Anglos; they speak less frequently both in response to the teacher and on their own initiative.[3]

It is also interesting to note that:

> Mexican American teachers praise Anglo pupils considerably more than their Anglo colleagues. This results in a larger disparity in praise or encouragement from the Mexican American teachers in favor of Anglo students.[4]

---

[2]U.S. COMMISSION ON CIVIL RIGHTS, TEACHERS AND STUDENTS REPORT V: MEXICAN-AMERICAN EDUCATION STUDY 21-28 (March 1973).
[3]*Id*. at 43.
[4]*Id*. at 27.

A moratorium on testing has once again been suggested. In my opinion, this answer is not acceptable since it only postpones the inevitable. In one way or another, the educational system eventually will identify and place certain youngsters in programs outside the mainstream. In the meantime, the youngster with learning problems falls further behind. The further behind the youngster falls, the more difficult it is to overcome the disparity.

Sorgen refers to three approaches that have been suggested by others to minimize classroom inequities. He mentions racial ratios as the speediest solution to the placement problem. The primary advantage of racial ratios it that is places the burden of proof on the state to show that, when the ratios are significantly different between regular and special education classes, the agency must varify that appropriate criteria were used. Although such an approach may bring about parity, it does not solve the problem, because random placement based on a census ratio cannot guarantee that the youngsters not included in this racial ratio will be provided with educational programing designed to meet their needs.

Test translation has also been suggested. Supposedly, a test administered in the "mother tongue" would be less discriminatory to a youngster who speaks a foreign language in the home. This has been the rationale for programs in several states requiring that youngsters who speak a language other than English be tested in their primary language. The assumption that the translated tests are valid raises several concerns. The elementary difficulty of construction of translated tests is illustrated by the existence of many dialects of Spanish. However, the major problem with the use of translations is the assumption that the youngster is able to use his primary language in a formal, structured setting. Although the language used in a child's home may be of a different dialect from that used orally in the school by the examiner and different from that used on the test, the formal use of the language may be nonexistent for the child. For instance, the only formal language training that the majority of American Spanish-speaking youngsters have is in English. The assumption that Spanish-speaking youngsters have a formal command of Spanish is creating serious problems in many of the bilingual programs that have been developed.

A third proposal is the use of teachers' recommendations as a basis for placement. The suggestion is sound, but only if such recommendations are not used in isolation. To use only teachers as sorting agents is objectionable because many teachers are biased against certain groups or classes of students and are more likely to view them negatively. It is also likely that a primary criterion that teachers will use in sorting a child out of a class is overt aggression. Aggression is not a good indicator of mental retardation, and, in fact, may be a sign that the child is unwilling to adapt to a very oppressive system. Thus, the child with a discipline problem may be the first referral to a special class for the mentally retarded whereas an introverted child with more serious learning problems might remain in the regular classroom.

The most palatable recommendation refers to differential norms. Sorgen mentions specifically those adaptive behavior scales which use criteria other than a standard score as a basis for placement. Jane Mercer's "Multi-Ethnic Pluralistic Diagnosis" serves as an example of criteria-referenced assessment techniques in lieu of traditional standardized procedures.[5] For example, as Sorgen states, a young-ster with an IQ below 75 from a low socioeconomic minority setting would also have to score in the bottom 3 percent of his sociocultural group before a final placement could be made within the special education program. The assumption is that some other problem, such as language or cultural differences, was responsible for his low score on the test. This approach helps to isolate those youngsters in greatest need of special education programs, but does not ensure that all youngsters who score at a higher level in the adaptive behavior scale will receive an adequate educational program. There is a high risk that they will not, since the school system is designed primarily to meet the needs of the relatively small, well-motivated, educationally oriented group.

Sorgen also suggests that educational alternatives be developed and provided for youngsters unable to function within existing educational programs. But even this proposed alternative program does not provide youngsters with the skills required to cope with a system that, to date, has not provided suitable alternatives. As with many other programs designed for minorities, his suggested alternative might become a protective womb for youngsters which, in essence, postpones their inevitable entrance into a larger system where they will be required to cope with the unrestrained demands of society. Alternative programs in isolation are not fair to minority groups forced into them.

In discussing the legal aspects of labeling and classifying, the author suggested a number of legal issues that parents may be able to raise when their youngster has been inappropriately placed in a special class. I support such efforts, but believe that stronger test cases will be necessary in order to delineate more clearly the legal rights of the retarded in society today. The litigation to date has not proven sufficiently effective in bringing about the needed changes in the educational programs so that they do, in fact, meet the needs of a diverse student population and of individual students.

Legal efforts thus far have been minimally effective because of the focus on details or on specific cases. With the Pennsylvania case[6] as a possible exception, it is difficult to interpret at a policy level much of the discussion in this area. Concen-trating on specific suits and case details can lead to reactions focusing on details, rather than concepts or systems than can provide information to guide policy deci-sions or resource allocations. If the focus is only on individual cases, it may be expected that the process will have to be repeated next year when the younger brothers and sisters enter school. Labeling and classification problems are mani-festations and reactions to symptoms, and the need is to improve services, not react to symptoms.

Today, educational systems have become much more sophisticated, particularly in dealing with aggrieved parents. The threats, pressures, and intimidations that brought about changes five years ago have minimal impact today. Perhaps it is a case

[5]J. Mercer, Pluralistic Diagnosis in the Evaluation of Black and Chicano Children: A Procedure for Taking Socio-Cultural Variables into Account in Clinical Assessment (September 1971).
[6]Pennsylvania Ass'n for Retarded Children v. Pennsylvania, 334 F. Supp. 1257 (E.D. Pa. 1971).

of "overkill." It is evident that changes within the rigid educational structure are awkward and slow, often reflecting a reaction rather than a commitment. One statement might sum up the changes in programs for minorities: Five years ago we were raped in an educational sense. Today we are being seduced—seduced by special education programs and seduced by pseudolegal efforts. The outcome, however, is the same.

CHAPTER 9

The Right to an Appropriate Free Public Education

Editorial Introduction

*H*err's paper details the early development of the right of mentally retarded and other handicapped children to receive an appropriate publicly supported education. He articulates the factual premises and legal considerations that led federal courts, first in Pennsylvania and then in the District of Columbia, to require that appropriate educational programs be provided to all those who had traditionally been excluded from the school system as "uneducable." Herr also deals with the topic of due process procedures in the classification of children (an issue also discussed in Chapters 8 and 15 of this volume).

Herr reports that suits to enforce the right to education for mentally retarded children have been filed in at least 22 additional states and that several additional courts have followed the precedents established in the Pennsylvania and District of Columbia cases. Other courts have declined to rule in suits where state legislatures had recently enacted statutes designed to achieve the same goal.

Herr points out that the opinion of the United States Supreme Court in *San Antonio School District v. Rodriguez* explicitly notes that it does not reach the issue of total denial of educational services. Herr demonstrates the reasons why one should expect the Supreme Court to uphold the right to education for mentally retarded children and notes that one court has already articulated the factors that distinguish *Rodriguez* from this.

Herr closes by calling for federal legislative action to provide protection of the constitutional rights involved in the cases reviewed in his paper.

Bates voices general agreement with Herr's position and calls on professional educators to take strong action to provide appropriate education for all children. He notes that education is the job of educators, not lawyers, and calls for effective education to avoid the danger of legal overreaction to grossly deficient conditions.

Lippman places the legal battle for the rights of mentally retarded citizens in a broader historical and political context. Historically, he writes, parent organizations have had a major impact by bringing deficiencies to light and by developing model programs to demonstrate that education for mentally retarded children is not an unrealistic demand. He views their present and future role as one of securing and monitoring services, rather than providing them directly. Politically, Lippman notes that litigation is but one of several tools available to secure the rights of mentally retarded citizens. He calls for careful judgments about whether litigation, legislation, or administrative action is the most appropriate vehicle to use in any given case.

PRINCIPAL PAPER

STANLEY HERR

THE CHILDREN WHO WAIT

Across this country, many children are still without educational services from the public system. Countless numbers of American children are excluded from the very schooling which 48 states deem so important as to make compulsory for 10 years of every child's life.[1] Some of the excluded are classified (correctly or incorrectly) as mentally retarded, mentally ill, neurologically impaired, or learning disabled.[2]

---

[1] *See* Task Force on Children Out of School, The Way We Go to School: The Exclusion of Children in Boston (1970); F. Weintraub, A. Abeson & D. Braddock, State Law and Education of Handicapped Children (1971); J. Regal, R. Elliot, H. Grossman & W. Morse, The Systematic Exclusion of Children from School: The Unknown, Unidentified, and Untreated (1971); L. Lippman & I. Goldberg, Right to Education (1973); Gumpert, *Unequal Rights: Denial of Education to Abnormal Children Spurs Parent Protests,* Wall Street Journal, Mar. 27, 1972, at 1.

[2] Educational classification can drastically affect the life chances of a child. Both special educators and legal practitioners now recognize that classifications which result in special education placement impose a stigma and tend to isolate the child from his "normal" peers. *See* Garrison & Hammill, *Who are the Retarded,* 38 Exceptional Children 13 (1971); Goldberg, *Human Rights of the Mentally Retarded in the School System,* 9 Mental Retardation 3 (1971); Mercer, The Use and Misuse of Labelling Human Beings: The Ethics of Testing (unpublished essay presented at Kennedy International Symposium on Human Rights, Retardation and Research, Washington, D.C., 1971); President's Comm. on Mental Retardation, Placement of Children in Special Classes for the Retarded (1971); President's Comm. on Mental Retardation, A Very

Others are labeled "disciplinary problems" and are excluded through summary suspension proceedings or school-encouraged nonattendance.[3] All too often such exclusions are the result of informal and extra-legal processes. These practices belie the assumption that this society is one in which universal education is an accomplished fact and, more significant, offend basic constitutional principles of due process and equal protection. For the nearly 1 million handicapped children either excluded from public education or otherwise denied a free and suitable education, recent federal court decisions are requiring an end to such practices.[4]

Who are the children excluded from school? They are the "slow" "Garys," suspected of being mentally retarded, who are indefinitely suspended for alleged disciplinary infractions and whose parents are told to wait for a call from the principal when "our school has a small class for your child." They are the emotionally troubled "Derricks" who are shunted from one custodial institution to another while the public school system refuses to create special educational programs to serve them.[5] And they are the "Janes" who are so profoundly handicapped that public schools deny them admission to suitable learning programs (or to any program), leaving parents with the cruel dilemma of either institutionalizing their child and thereby, as in "Jane's" case, exposing them to injuries due to lack of adequate

---

SPECIAL CHILD (1971); PRESIDENT'S COMM. ON MENTAL RETARDATION, THE SIX-HOUR RETARDED CHILD (1969); HARVARD CENTER FOR LAW AND EDUCATION, CLASSIFICATION MATERIALS (1972); Hall, *The Politics of Special Education,* INEQUALITY IN EDUCATION 17 (March 1970); MENTAL HEALTH LAW PROJECT, BASIC RIGHTS OF THE MENTALLY HANDICAPPED 52 (1973).

[3] Mills v. Board of Educ., 348 F. Supp. 866, 869 (D.D.C. 1972) [hereinafter cited as Mills].

[4] *Id.;* Pennsylvania Ass'n for Retarded Children v. Pennsylvania, 343 F. Supp. 279, 334 F. Supp. 1257 (E.D. Pa. 1971) [hereinafter cited as PARC]; Lebanks v. Spears, 60 F.R.D. 135 (E.D. La. 1973); In re H.G., A Child, Civil No. 8930 (N.D. S. Ct., April 30, 1974); Maryland Ass'n for Retarded Children et al. v. Maryland, Equity No. 100/182/77676 (Cir. Ct. Baltimore Cty., April 9, 1974).

[5] Derrick is the fictitious name of a real child. What happened to him in his unhappy search for an education is a terrible indictment of the so-called child welfare "system."

Summarily suspended in the third grade, Derrick was to spend several years floating through Washington institutions before a federal judge compelled the school authorities to resume their educational responsibilities to him. By then he was 13 years old.

At the time of his expulsion, there had been great upheaval in Derrick's life. His father had recently died, he had problems with his siblings, and he was said to be "acting up" in school. One day he was told by his classroom teacher to get out and not come back anymore. Derrick's mother was to receive neither notice nor a hearing nor even the reasons for her son's dismissal.

Derrick's mother was left with an eight-year-old child to take care of and educate. As a working mother earning $4,000 to $5,000, what was she to do?

Eventually she went to the welfare department hoping to find a tuition grant for psychiatric-oriented schooling. The welfare department accepted Derrick as a ward, representing to his mother that the result would be therapeutic treatment, training, and an educational experience for Derrick.

Instead, Derrick was placed in Junior Village, a massive custodial "warehouse" for the District's dependent children. Four days after his arrival there, Derrick was sexually assaulted by other boys and ran home. When a ward runs away from a public institution, upon recapture, he can be transferred to a security facility. Thus, for nearly three months Derrick found himself behind the prisonlike bars and barbed wire fences of Oak Hill. Again, there was no educational program available to him. Although the very justification for declaring him a ward was his need for education, the outcome of this strategy was only a barren custodial care.

Before his plight was aired in Washington's daily newspapers and a congressional committee hearing, Derrick had made a most demoralizing odyssey: through three juvenile correctional institutions, St. Elizabeth's mental hospital, D.C. General Hospital, and Junior Village.

Having become a part of the *Mills* class action, Derrick became entitled to a tuition grant to a treatment-oriented facility with an educational component. He was so placed and, according to his mother, for the first time he is reading at grade level.

supervision, or bearing the burdens of 24-hour-a-day, 7-day-a-week care. When such parents are unaided by community agencies or when they lack funds for private care, the state imposes upon both child and parent a virtual house arrest.[6] Often, the only "option" left to these parents is commitment of their child to a public institution. Yet, in too many of these institutions — sorely overcrowded, under-funded and understaffed, improperly managed — living conditions are barely suitable for physical survival, let alone habilitation and education.[7]

The plight of these children is, in the words of one federal judge, a "human tragedy, unbelievable as it is in . . . the richest country on earth."[8] Most sadly, it is a tragedy which, given the necessary commitments by this country's educational bureaucracy, could be avoided. In May 1971, the United States commissioner of education, Dr. Sidney Marland, acknowledged that 6 out of every 10 handicapped children in this country fail to receive needed special educational services.[9] Commissioner Marland went on to declare that:

> The right of a handicapped child to the special education he needs is as basic to him as is the right of any other young citizens to an appropriate education in the public schools. It is unjust for our society to provide handicapped children with anything less than [the] full and equal educational opportunity they need to reach their maximum potential and attain rewarding, satisfying lives.[10]

Yet, at almost the same time that the commissioner was attempting to set in motion reforms for future generations of schoolchildren, researchers supported by the Department of Health, Education, and Welfare were calling attention to the wide-spread denial of the constitutional rights of *this* generation of exceptional children: "through legal, quasi-legal and extra-legal devices or through apathy, schools cause, encourage and welcome the lack of attendance in school of millions of American youngsters. Such activity by the educational system serves as a denial of civil rights as massive as the separate school systems maintained by law in prior years."[11]

---

[6]The harms of educational exclusion to the retarded child and his parents are incalculable. Dr. Elizabeth Boggs, chairman of the National Advisory Council in Development Disabilities, noted that:

> Each and all of the arguments for universal public education apply with even more intensity to exceptional children, deviant children, children whose needs are less well understood by parents or more difficult to meet than those of the normal child, whose risks of future dependency are greater, whose ability to profit from unstructured experiences is diminished, whose rejection by thoughtless peers is more frequent, whose self-image is more vulnerable. Yet it is these difficult children who are most frequently either misplaced in school or thrown back on their parents, who then are faced with a total responsibility beyond their bearing. To the child's initial handicap, which may have been beyond our human power to prevent, are then added two man-made injuries—the deprivation for the child of the benefits of any societal education and the burden to the parent which is greatly aggravated in the social, economic, and emotional senses. Mills affidavit, (para. 9).

[7]New York State Ass'n for Retarded Children v. Rockefeller, 357 F. Supp. 752, 756 (E.D.N.Y. 1973).
[8]Hobson v. Hansen, Ruling on Motion to Intervene, at 3 (unpublished opinion), Civil No. 82-66 (D.D.C. July 23, 1971) (Wright, J.).
[9]117 CONG. REC. 6749 (1971).
[10]*Id.*
[11]REGAL, ELLIOT, GROSSMAN & MORSE, *supra* note 1, at 15.

EQUAL ACCESS TO EDUCATION:
RECENT DECISIONS

Pennsylvania Association for Retarded Children v. Pennsylvania (cited as *PARC*)[12] was the first case to recognize the particular learning needs of the mentally retarded. On May 5, 1972, a three-judge federal district court permanently enjoined Pennsylvania officials from denying or postponing a free public program of education and training to any of the state's mentally retarded children.[13] In approving a consent agreement and stipulation as fair and reasonable to all members of both the plaintiff and defendant classes, the court acknowledged that every retarded child is capable of deriving benefit from education.[14]

The plaintiffs in *PARC* originally filed this civil rights class action as a challenge to a statutory scheme under which retarded children were being excluded from public schooling as persons deemed "uneducable" or "unable to profit" from further public school attendance.[15] The statutes also allowed denial of education to persons who had not attained a mental age of 5 years or were outside the compulsory school age of 8-17.[16] These issues would be resolved, however, by a judicially approved consent agreement of the parties. Following hearings at which some of the nation's most eminent experts in the field of mental retardation testified in support of the plaintiffs, the parties expressed their desire to settle the remaining disputed matters amicably. As the court was to note subsequently, Pennsylvania's willingness to negotiate essentially reflected "an intelligent response to overwhelming evidence against their position."[17]

The agreements reached were legal milestones in several respects. Since Pennsylvania explicitly acknowledged its responsibility to provide a free public program of education for all of its children, it agreed to place each mentally retarded child in a "free, public program of education and training appropriate to the child's capacity."[18] Accordingly, the state's attorney general would issue opinions so as effectively to foreclose use of the challenged statutes as exclusionary devices.[19] The agreement also required changes in the administration of two other statutes affecting the education of the retarded. The state would refrain from denying pre-

---

[12] 343 F. Supp. 279 (E.D. Pa. 1972).

[13] *Id.* at 302.

[14] Without exception, expert opinion indicates that:

> [A]ll mentally retarded persons are capable of benefiting from a program of education and training; [the vast majority] are capable of achieving self-sufficiency and the remaining few, with such education and training are capable of achieving some degree of self-care; that the earlier such education and training begins, the more thoroughly and the more efficiently a mentally retarded person will benefit from it and, whether begun early or not, that a mentally retarded person can benefit at any point in his life and development from a program of education. (*Id.* at 296; footnotes omitted.)

[15] PA. STAT. ANN. tit. 24, §§ 13-1375, 13-1330 (1962).

[16] *Id.* §§ 13-1304, 13-1326 (1962).

[17] 343 F. Supp. at 291.

[18] 334 F. Supp. 1257, 1260 (E.D. Pa. 1971).

[19] 343 F. Supp. at 285-86.

school educational opportunities to plaintiffs whenever they provided a preschool program to nonretarded children;[20] furthermore, plaintiffs would become eligible for tuition grant assistance for private school attendance on the same basis as other enumerated disability groups.[21]

After a process of identification, evaluation, and placement, an educational program would be provided to each plaintiff child by no later than September 1, 1972. Moreover, in accordance with the stipulation, no mentally retarded child (or child thought to be mentally retarded) would be assigned or reassigned to either a regular or special educational placement without notice and an opportunity for a due process hearing before a special hearing officer.[22] To review and approve the defendants' implementation plan, the court appointed two distinguished mental retardation specialists, one a social scientist and the other an attorney, to serve as special masters.

A consent agreement which binds the members of a class must secure express judicial approval. Hearings on such settlements require notice to the class of the proposed terms of the agreement.[23] Theoretically, the scope of such hearings is limited to an inquiry into the fairness of the settlement. Rarely are broad legal issues raised in such proceedings. *PARC,* however, proved to be an exception to this general pattern.

Opposing the agreements were several of the state's intermediate school districts, members of the defendant class. Initially, their objections focussed on the practicality of certain hearing provisions contained in the stipulations. After intensive negotiations and minor modifications, all but one intermediate district withdrew their objections. It was this dissenting defendant who pressed an attack, ultimately unsuccessful, on the court's jurisdiction to hear *PARC*

In upholding its jurisdiction, the court determined that a colorable constitutional claim under both the due process and equal protection clauses had been established. With respect to plaintiffs' due process contention, the court relied heavily upon the stigma which results from misplacement or exclusion. In reviewing the expert testimony and empirical studies, the panel recognized the stigma which society "unfortunately" attaches to the label of mental retardation.[24] The court applied the reasoning of the Supreme Court's decision in *Wisconsin v. Constantineau*[25] to the labeling of children: if "posting" an adult as a habitual drunkard required a prior hearing, branding a child retarded demanded no lesser safeguards.

Turning to the equal protection issue, the court, referring to *Brown v. Board*

---

[20] 334 F. Supp. at 1262.

[21] Under the terms of the consent agreement, the attorney general was required to issue an opinion construing the term "brain damage" as applied in Pa. Stat. Ann. tit. 24, § 13-1376 (1962) to include all mentally retarded children for purposes of rendering these children eligible for publicly supported tuition and maintenance grants to private schools.

[22] As an appointee of the state secretary of education, the special hearing officer is intended to be independent of the local school district.

[23] *See* Fed. R. Civ. P. 23(e).

[24] 343 F. Supp. at 293.

[25] 400 U.S. 433 (1971). A Wisconsin statute requiring the posting of the names of alleged problem drinkers in retail liquor establishments was deemed by the Supreme Court to impose a stigma serious enough to compel due process, including prior notice and an opportunity for a hearing. *See* PARC, 343 F. Supp. at 298.

of Education,[26] addressed the question of whether the commonwealth, in denying public education to some while providing it to others, could ground its exclusionary practices on some "rational basis."[27] It concluded that the evidence raised serious doubts as to the existence of any rational basis for such exclusions.

Mills v. Board of Education of the District of Columbia[28] unequivocally settled these constitutional questions. Finding the members of the plaintiff class to be entitled to a specialized education under the equal protection and due process clauses of the United States Constitution, *Mills* resolved any prior judicial uncertainties in favor of the exceptional child. Without limitation as to any particular disability, the *Mills* court extended the logic of *PARC* to all children and, furthermore, clearly based its decision upon constitutional grounds.

Nearly two years of legal work went into the planning and execution of the *Mills* litigation. Extensive fact finding, legal research, and resort to administrative and other judicial forums consumed nearly half that time.[29] Finally, on September 24, 1971, seven school-excluded children, their parents, Congressman Ronald V. Dellums, a local clergyman, and the District of Columbia Family Welfare Rights Organization, acting as next friends to institutionalized plaintiff children,[30] filed the class action suit. The named plaintiffs were children who, after being labeled emotionally disturbed, mentally retarded, behavioral problems, hyperactive, or otherwise impaired, were excluded entirely from educational programs. Each was black,[31] poor, and without financial means to obtain private instruction. The periods of exclusion ranged from two months to five years. The class they represented included all District of Columbia residents of school age who had been or might be excluded from a public school education or otherwise deprived of access to publicly supported education. Plaintiffs sought to require the District of Columbia, the board of education, and the social services administration and its public residential institutions to end their practices of denying handicapped and "disciplinary problem" (and any other) children the opportunity for publicly supported education.

Governmental omissions provided the gravamen of the *Mills* complaint. Over a number of years, the District of Columbia government had continued to ignore the alarming disparity between the number of handicapped children residing in the District and the number of such children having benefit of programs of specialized education.[32] Steps to narrow this disparity had proven either insufficient or mis-

---

[26] 347 U.S. 483 (1954).

[27] 343 F. Supp. at 297.

[28] 348 F. Supp. 866 (D.D.C. 1972).

[29] *Id.* at 870.

[30] These individuals and the District of Columbia Welfare Rights Organization filed as next friends for children who had been committed to the care of the District of Columbia as dependent wards. Similar suits have been maintained by nonrelated next friends to ensure that parentless children are properly represented.

[31] The class, however, was not defined by either race or poverty.

[32] TASK FORCE ON SPECIAL EDUCATION, REPORT OF THE SUPERINTENDENTS' TASK FORCE ON SPECIAL EDUCATION, at i (D.C. Public Schools 1971):

> In the city of Washington, the acknowledgement of the right of the handicapped child to public education has been honored more in the breech (sic) than by observance. The obscene nightmare of repetition from year to year continues for the parents of these children who must compete for placement and funds or accept the exclusion of their child from the opportunity to develop his human potential.

See also Mills file, affidavits of Robert L. Bostick, Rosalie Idarola, Bobbie McMahan, and Joy Chance relating to inadequacies in the District's diagnostic and placement processes.

directed. By the fall of 1971, there existed a waiting list of over 1,500 children identified as requiring specialized education. An even larger number of children remained "unknown" to the school system—children staying at home, living within public institutions, or attending wholly inappropriate classes.[33]

Nonetheless, for several reasons, the school system continued to overlook the gravity of the exclusion problem. The use of disciplinary suspensions to terminate the public schooling of mentally retarded and emotionally disturbed children was one such reason. Requesting parents to keep their children at home "until small classes" could be provided was another. As a result of such informal or illegal exclusionary devices, the system, as of October 1971, with 1,500 children on waiting lists and hundreds more at home, could not even identify those who had been so excluded or "excused." Moreover, it had ignored a statute requiring—for over four decades—an annual census of the school-age population.[34] The genesis of the case, as the court pointed out, could be found in the failure of the District of Columbia to provide publicly supported education and training to plaintiffs and other exceptional children and in the excluding, suspending, expelling, reassigning, and transferring of exceptional children from regular public school classes without affording them due process of law.[35]

Counsel for the school system and other defendants initially contended that the obligation to provide educational opportunities was moral, in nature, as applied to the plaintiffs.[36] Through investigation and discovery procedures, facts were uncovered which plainly established the legal and constitutional obligations of the defendants. For example, school system records showed that educational opportunities were being provided to other handicapped and "normal" children.[37] Additionally, board regulations and policy guidelines required that they be offered to all children.[38] However, District of Columbia reports to the United States Department of Health, Education, and Welfare and appropriations requests to Congress showed that defendants had failed to supply plaintiffs with publicly supported education programs.[39] Major responsibility for this failure rested with the District of Columbia Board of Education and its school administration. To the board, Congress had entrusted the responsibility of administering a system of publicly supported education for all the children of Washington. And to the board, not to social welfare or recreation agencies, exceptional children—the children of *Mills*—were entitled to turn for their education. Neither transfer to the makeshift programs of other public agencies, nor imposition

---

[33] The school system's failure to conduct a statutorily required school census or to even screen its enrolled population for handicapping conditions made it impossible to estimate accurately the numbers of children in such circumstances.

[34] "The precise number of [exceptional] children cannot be stated because the District has continuously failed to comply with [D.C. Code] Section 31-208 which requires a school census of all children aged 3 to 18 in the District to be taken." Mills, 348 F. Supp. at 868.

[35] *Id.*

[36] Defendants also contended by way of defense that financial constraints made it "impossible" to afford plaintiffs their requested relief. The *Mills* court, however, stated that it was "not persuaded by that contention." 348 F. Supp. at 875.

[37] *See* Task Force on Special Education, *supra* note 32.

[38] *See, e.g.,* Mills, 348 F. Supp. at 873-74.

[39] *Id.* at 868-69.

of educational costs on the financial resources of charities or parents, would properly discharge such a duty.

In the plaintiff's view, each day's delay on the part of the board of education in meeting its obligations constituted a further and irreparable injury to the constitutional rights of the plaintiff children.[40] Accordingly, a three-point request for preliminary injunctive relief had been filed with the plaintiffs' complaint. In this motion, plaintiffs requested that the named children be promptly admitted to suitable programs of public education. Furthermore, their motion asked that their counsel be provided with lists of all other children who remained excluded and that defendants initiate efforts to identify remaining "unknown" excluded children. The very day on which hearings were scheduled on plaintiffs' motion, defendants acceded to the requested relief.

On the basis of admissions of fact and affidavits from experts and concerned citizens, plaintiffs moved directly for summary judgment. The parents of named plaintiffs had submitted affidavits describing their child's educational deficits, manner of exclusion, and present status. Educational experts prepared affidavits, based on evaluations of these children, diagnosing their educational needs and attesting to their ability to benefit from suitable instructional programs. For institutionalized plaintiffs who were wards of the District of Columbia, the affidavits of social workers and the childrens' next friends described the conditions of their confinement. Spokesmen for local parents' association for exceptional children provided yet another type of affidavit detailing organizational efforts to obtain educational services for the exceptional child and the disheartening pattern of governmental evasion and unresponsiveness encountered. Last, the affidavits of nationally recognized authorities on the education of handicapped children underscored both the urgency and the feasibility of providing structured educational opportunities to all such children, setting forth the harms—social, educational, and economic—of denying such opportunities.[41] On March 24, 1972, after reviewing the affidavits and other exhibits and memoranda submitted, and after hearing lengthy oral argument, Judge Joseph C. Waddy granted summary judgment for the plaintiffs.

In its subsequently entered memorandum opinion, judgment, and decree, the court vindicated each of the plaintiffs' basic claims. Plaintiffs had contended, in view of the equal protection clause, that they, no less than other children, were entitled to a publicly supported education. Plaintiffs had argued that if disparities in the educational resources provided to poor children within a school district had been judged constitutionally impermissible, then the total exclusion of plaintiff

[40] Mills file, Memorandum in Support of Complaint, at 41, "Constitutional rights are rights in the here and now; deprivation generally requires immediate redress." Citing, *inter alia,* Watson v. City of Memphis, 373 U.S. 526, 532-33 (1963), Green v. County School Bd., 391 U.S. 430, 439 (1968). This memorandum from the *Mills* case can also be found at 2 PRACTISING LAW INSTITUTE, LEGAL RIGHTS OF THE MENTALLY RETARDED 897 (B. Ennis & P. Friedman eds. 1973).

[41] Mills file. The affidavits of Drs. Gunnar Dybwad, I. Ignacy Goldberg, Herbert Goldstein, James W. Prouty, Sue Tenorio, Nona Flynn, Merle Van Dyke, Joy Chance, and Ronald Conley, experts in various aspects of special education, were of inestimable value in highlighting the implications of school exclusion practices and policies.

children from the same public schools patently offended the requirements of equal protection. The court agreed. Citing *Hobson v. Hansen*,[42] the court declared:

> [T]he defendants' conduct here, denying plaintiffs and their class not just an equal publicly supported education but all publicly supported education while providing such education to other children, is violative of the Due Process Clause.[43]

Lack of fair assessment and placement procedures had been a direct cause of plaintiffs' exclusion or misclassification. Accordingly, their attorneys sought mechanisms to ensure accurate fact determinations prior to any substantial changes in educational assignment, as well as periodic review of such assignments. The court ordered many procedural safeguards, including notice and a hearing prior not only to a decision to suspend, but also to any decision to reassign a child to, or from, a special education program.[44]

Plaintiffs had included within their suit both children residing in public institutions and those living in the community. Wards of the District of Columbia, they argued, enjoy no less a right to the benefits of education than do other children; indeed, the government's obligation to educate is twofold. Beyond its general responsibility to provide educational opportunities to all children, the District of Columbia, by assuming a child's custody, incurs the special obligations that a guardian owes a ward.[45] In its opinion, the court pointedly reminded the social services administration, the District's public welfare agency, of this duty.[46] In construing provisions of the District's compulsory school attendance law,[47] the court found that the requirement that a child be regularly instructed applies equally to the social services administration as to any other guardian or parent.

Implementing the declared rights of the *Mills* children will plainly require a degree of interdepartmental coordination rarely seen in the District of Columbia. For reasons stemming from the District's unique lack of self-government and the peculiar Byzantine irresponsibility thereby engendered, the delivery of services to exceptional children has been alarmingly ineffective and even nonexistent.[48] Through endless referrals and overlapping and conflicting agency jurisdictions, "problem" children all too frequently are bounced between agencies, receiving inappropriate services or becoming hopelessly caught in the maze of bureaucracy. Finding no public school programs open to their child, indigent parents, for example, have been sometimes urged to declare their child "neglected" and to relinquish custody to the social services administration.[49] All the more tragically, parents com-

---

[42] 269 F. Supp. 401 (D.D.C. 1967).

[43] Mills, 348 F. Supp. at 875.

[44] *Id.*

[45] For an excellent discussion of these duties see D. C. Family Welfare Rights Organization v. Thompson, Civil No. 71-1150-J (Super. Ct. D.C., June 18, 1971).

[46] Mills, 348 F. Supp. at 876 n.8.

[47] D.C. CODE ANN. § 31-201 (1967). These provisions, similar to the compulsory school attendance laws of other states, require that every person residing in the District who has custody or control of a child between the ages of 7 and 16 years "shall cause said child to be regularly instructed in a public school or in a private or parochial school or instructed privately...." *Cf.* Mills, 348 F. Supp. at 877-83.

[48] *See, e.g.,* Mills file, affidavits of six parents; TASK FORCE ON SPECIAL EDUCATION, REPORT OF THE SUPERINTENDENTS' TASK FORCE ON SPECIAL EDUCATION (D.C. Public Schools 1971).

[49] *See, e.g.,* Mills file at 3-4, affidavit of Mrs. E.B., para. 14.

pelled to adopt this humiliating and desperate strategy might later find that only custodial institutionalization, not specialized instruction, had been provided.

The use of waiting lists posed perhaps the most Kafkaesque example of the fragmentation of the District's educational services. For a handicapped child or one so suspected, placement on a waiting list for evaluation in a department of human resources clinic in order to be placed on a waiting list for a board of education special education assignment was not uncommon. *Mills* sought to end this practice by positing ultimate responsibility for plaintiff's education in the board of education. Thus, the court emphasized that: "The lack of communication and cooperation between the Board of Education and the other defendants in this action shall not be permitted to deprive plaintiffs and their class of publicly supported education."[50] Accordingly, the court directed the board of education to present to it any "irresolvable issues" in the event that the District of Columbia "could not jointly develop the procedures and program necessary to implement" its decree.[51] Furthermore, should any such dispute involve questions requiring extrajudicial educational expertise, the court would appoint and utilize a special master.[52]

By proposing detailed remedies, plaintiffs had sought constitutional declarations which would clearly specify plaintiffs' rights and defendants' duties. Equally important was the creation of mechanisms to ensure enforcement of such rights and duties. Administrative assignment hearings were structured to provide a means by which questions as to what constitutes a "suitable education" for a particular child could be resolved.[53] In addition, a detailed order could also serve to educate school personnel and the general public as to the impropriety of any exclusionary dividing line, whether it be the child's degree of impairment or the school system's finances. Finally, through such an order, compliance could be monitored and misunderstanding or evasion minimized.

In view of the fundamental constitutional and human rights involved, the court mandated a strict implementation timetable. Within 30 days of the entry of the *Mills* judgment, defendants were to provide each previously identified member of the plaintiff class with a publicly supported education. For children subsequently identified by defendants (extensive media outreach having been ordered), an additional 20-days period was allotted for purposes of making an educational evaluation and placement proposal. Each parent or guardian of a plaintiff child would receive a notice stating, *inter alia*, that "such child has the right to receive a free educational assessment and to be placed in a publicly supported education suited to his needs."[54] Thereafter, a second notice would be forwarded to the parent or guardian advising him of defendants' proposal for his child's placement in an educational program, including compensatory educational services where required, and of the parent's right to object to such proposal and to have such objection heard by an independent hearing officer.[55] As to any child thought by any defendant, parent, or guardian to be in need of a program of special education, such child "shall neither be

[50] 348 F. Supp. at 876.
[51] *Id.* at 877.
[52] *Id.*
[53] *See* textual discussion accompanying notes 67-71 *infra.*
[54] 348 F. Supp. at 879, para. 8.
[55] *Id.* at 880, para. 13(e)(2).

placed in, transferred from or to, nor denied placement in such program" unless defendants first notify the parents of the proposed placement, the underlying reasons, and of their right to a due process hearing.[56] Moreover, the *Mills* decree, by requiring similar procedural safeguards for disciplinary suspension, closes a loophole through which many exceptional children had been removed from school. No suspension may be continued for longer than 10 school days from the date of the hearing.[57] The child's school principal is responsible for ensuring that he or she receives some form of educational assistance or diagnostic examination during the suspension period.[58] To provide judicial overview in the implementation and enforcement of its judgment and decree, the court retained jurisdiction.

"Access to education" suits similar to *Mills* and *PARC* are proliferating. Such litigation has been initiated in at least 22 other states, including California, Colorado, Connecticut, Delaware, Florida, Hawaii, Illinois, Kentucky, Louisiana, Maryland Massachusetts, Michigan, Minnesota, Nevada, New York, North Carolina, North Dakota, Rhode Island, Tennessee, Utah, Virginia, and Wisconsin. Caution, however, must be taken against hastily prepared and improvidently filed litigation. Successful suits are products of careful factual and legal investigation. Litigation should not be undertaken unless success is likely, and even then it is best viewed as one of a number of tactics.

Three recent suits are of particular significance. *Lebanks v. Spears*[59] attacked Louisiana's failure to provide education or instruction to large numbers of mentally retarded children in need of special education. This suit did not reach trial since the defendants agreed to a consent order providing a free public education for all children. The order has two additional features that are not found in *PARC* or *Mills*. The education provided must be oriented toward the goal of making every child self-sufficient or employable. In addition, it was agreed that education opportunities would be provided to mentally retarded adults who were not given educational services as children.

Maryland Association for Retarded Children, et al. v. State of Maryland[60] was a class action suit brought on behalf of mentally and physically handicapped children who were being denied access to free publicly supported education. The court relied upon state statutes and found that the state had an obligation to provide appropriate educational facilities and services for all persons between the ages of 5 and 20.

The Supreme Court of North Dakota is the highest judicial authority to date to recognize the right of mentally retarded children to equal educational opportunities. *In re H.G., A Child*[61] followed the lead of the earlier *PARC* and *Mills* decisions and concluded that the state constitution and the equal protection clause of the fourteenth amendment of the United States Constitution require the state to make educational opportunities available to all children.

[56] *Id.* at 880, para. 13(c).
[57] *Id.* at 883, para. 13(f)(16).
[58] *Id.*
[59] 60 F.R.D. 135 (E.D. La. 1973).
[60] Equity No. 100/182/77676 (Cir. Ct. Baltimore Cty., April 9, 1974).
[61] Civil No. 8930 (April 30, 1974).

The decisions in *Harrison v. Michigan*[62] and *Tidewater Society for Autistic Children v. Virginia*,[63] although nominally denying relief on *PARC-* and *Mills*-like claims, do so on very limited grounds. Neither court denies the validity of demands for publicly supported education for "exceptional" children. *Harrison*, in fact, explicitly affirms the contention that: ". . . providing education for some children, while not providing education for others (in this instance, handicapped children), is a denial of equal protection." In both cases the courts refused affirmative relief on the sole ground that the respective state legislatures had recognized the need for educating all handicapped children and had taken action to achieve this goal.[65] The decisions might be analytically subsumed under the rubric of "ripeness." Because the gravamen of the complaints addressed ongoing practices — that is, the relief requested was prospective in nature — and because intervening school district action under recent state enactments could vitiate the necessity for such relief, the courts determined that neither case was appropriate for adjudication. Repeatedly, the court in *Harrison* returned to its inability to provide a more speedy remedy than that effected legislatively.

> The state is already taking these steps. This could do no more than acting as a cheering section. . . . The actual issue in this case is whether a judicial remedy can eliminate the problem at an earlier date than the comprehensive program already adopted by the . . . legislature.[66]

Plainly enough, the rationale of these two cases is applicable only in states that have newly enacted provisions for the education of all handicapped children. Courts ought to be willing to fashion remedies, even in the face of partially remedial legislation, if the legislation does not meet basic constitutional requirements. A question of this nature was raised in *Harrison*, where the legislation did not specifically mandate a hearing process prior to special educational placement. The court refused to engraft such a requirement on the new law, assuming ". . . that the statute will be applied in a constitutional fashion . . . ."[67] and finding the matter premature because "the process of implementation is proceeding in good fashion."[68] Were the remedial legislation plainly incapable — by flat prohibition, for example — of achieving constitutionally required results, the assumption of constitutional application would obviously be inapposite. A final question raised by the cases is speed of the legislative remedy: How soon must it take effect to supplant judicial intervention to secure "present rights"? Although *Harrison*, as suggested previously, seems to insist on a remedy as speedy as that which could be effected by a court, *Tidewater Society* is more timid.[69] Clear lines are impossible to predict, but surely at some

---

[62] 350 F. Supp. 846 (E.D. Mich. 1972).
[63] Civil No. 426-72-N (E.D. Va., Dec. 26, 1972).
[64] 350 F. Supp. at 848.
[65] In *Harrison*, the state had enacted legislation requiring the education of all handicapped persons beginning in the 1973-74 school year.
[66] Harrison, 350 F. Supp. at 848.
[67] *Id.* at 849.
[68] *Id.*
[69] Civil No. 426-72-N (E.D. Va., Dec. 26, 1972). *See, e.g.,* slip opinion at 4-5.

level of legislative lassitude undue delay could be equated with avoidance and court action deemed appropriate.

APPROPRIATE EDUCATION AND CLASSIFICATION SAFEGUARDS

Educational assignment practices affecting persons thought to be retarded have also come under increasing scrutiny in the federal courts.[70] The focal points for judicial examination revolve around the decisions to transfer a child out of a regular education assignment and the opportunity to review periodically this determination. Labeling a child mentally retarded, as the court pointed out in *PARC*, attaches a degree of stigma which warrants procedural safeguards of notice and hearing to ensure that educational placement decisions will benefit, rather than harm. Detailed special education placement procedures, such as are mandated in *Mills* and *PARC*, are intended to provide a means by which the handicapped child and his parents may test the adequacy and suitability of a proposed or present education assignment. Moreover, these court decrees require that such assignments be made to the most "normalized" setting appropriate to the child's needs.[71] Accordingly, these courts have required that placement be made within the context of a presumption that among alternative programs of education, placement in a regular public school class with appropriate ancillary services is preferable to placement in a special school class.

A recent decision that generally supports these principles is *Larry P. v. Riles*.[72] In a class action suit, black elementary school children placed in classes for the "educable mentally retarded [EMR]" claimed that they were not in fact mentally retarded and did not require educational services that isolated them from their "normal" peers. They, therefore, argued that their placements, based on IQ tests allegedly biased against the culture and experience of black children, resulted in serious injury to their educational, social, and economic status and were violative of their equal protection rights under the fourteenth amendment. On plaintiffs' motion for preliminary relief, the court found that students who are wrongfully placed in EMR classes are irreparably harmed and required that the burden of proof shift to the defendants to show the rationality of this test-based classification. The court concluded that defendants did not demonstrate that IQ tests are rationally related to the purpose of segregating students according to their ability to learn in

---

[70] Lebanks v. Spears, 60 F.R.D. § 135 (E.D. La. 1973); Guadalupe Organization v. Tempe Elementary School Dist. No. 3, Civil No. 71-435 (D. Ariz., May 9, 1972); Larry P. v. Riles, 343 F. Supp. 1306 (N.D. Cal. 1972), *aff'd,* 502 F.2d 963 (1974); Stewart v. Phillips, Civil No. 70-1199-F (D. Mass., filed Feb. 8, 1971); Diana v. California State Bd. of Educ., Civil No. C-70-37 RFP (N.D. Cal., Feb. 5, 1970); Covarrubias v. San Diego Unified School Dist., Civil No. 70-394-T (S.D. Cal., filed July 31, 1972), *See generally* Sorgen, Chapter 8 of this volume.

[71] *See, e.g.,* Mills, 348 F. Supp. 866, 880 para. 13(a):

Each member of the plaintiff class is to be provided with a publicly-supported educational program suited to his needs, within the context of a presumption that among the alternative programs of education, placement in a regular public school class with appropriate auxiliary services is preferable to placement in a special school class.

[72] 343 F. Supp. 1306 (N.D. Cal. 1972).

regular classes, at least insofar as those tests were applied to the plaintiffs. Accordingly, the court enjoined the defendants from placing black students in EMR classes on the basis of criteria which place primary reliance on the results of IQ tests as they are currently administered, if the consequence of the use of such criteria is racial imbalance in the composition of such classes. Similar claims of misclassification have been vindicated as a result of cases brought by Spanish-speaking[73] and black children.[74]

To guard against improper placement, before a child can be classified as exceptional and consequently removed from, or denied admission to, the regular classroom, the school should have the responsibility of notifying the parents of the specific nature of the child's problem and of the reasons supporting its determination that he cannot be successfully served in the regular schoolroom. Any plans for, and results of, a medical, psychological, and educational assessment of the child (including test results relied upon) must also be relayed to the parents, and the child's educational needs in the interim period during such an assessment must be provided for. The parents must also be told of the specific educational plan for the child diagnosed as in need of special help. Periodic review of his progress, with the aim of eventual reintegration into regular classes insofar as possible, should also be required. If the parents believe the classification or diagnosis erroneous, they should be entitled to a hearing at which they can rebut the school's evidence and present their own. Such a procedure is vital to ensure that every child receives an adequate educational placement.

RODRIGUEZ: QUESTIONS NOT REACHED

Whatever the implications of *San Antonio School District v. Rodriguez*[75] for tax policy or interdistrict disparties in educational spending, it is plain that the Court did not consider the question of exclusion from free public education, the major issue posed by the plaintiffs in *Mills* and *PARC* and their counterparts in other states. As the Court pointed out:

> The argument here is not that the children in districts having relatively low assessable property values are receiving no public education; rather, it is that they are receiving a poorer quality education than that available to children in districts having more assessable wealth.[76]

Indeed, the state of Texas had repeatedly asserted in its briefs that it "now assured 'every child in every school district an adequate education.' "[77] In its *Rodriguez* opinion the Court, in apparent reliance on this assertion, never reached the question of the handicapped child's access to free public education. Because

[73] Diana v. California State Bd. of Educ., Civil No. C-70-37 RFP (N.D. Cal., Feb. 5, 1970).
[74] Stewart v. Phillips, Civil No. 70-1199-F (D. Mass., filed Feb. 8, 1971).
[75] 411 U.S. 1 (1973).
[76] *Id.* at 23.
[77] *Id.* at 24 n.59.

the state's assertion of universally available education was not controverted, the Court could conclude that "no charge fairly could be made that the [Texas school financing] system fails to provide each child with an opportunity to acquire the basic minimal skills necessary for the enjoyment of the rights of speech and of full participation in the political process." [78] Thus, the majority seems to be suggesting that some minimally adequate level of educational service requires constitutional protection. Whatever level this may be, one would reason that exclusion, as a non-level of education, must fail constitutional muster.

The analysis presented by this school finance decision did not contemplate the inequities and factors posited in the school exclusion cases, which include: (1) The discrimination inflicted upon the school-excluded child poses an absolute deprivation. [79] (2) The classification as an "uneducable" — and hence excludable — child affects a discrete, an insular, group, *i.e.,* the mentally retarded and other severely impaired persons. [80] (3) The system of discrimination against the mentally retarded displays all the "traditional indicia of suspectness," the retarded being persons saddled with disabilities and exposed to a history of prejudice, stigma, and purposeful unequal treatment. To put it in the terms used by the Supreme Court, the mentally retarded ought to be viewed as a group "relegated to such a position of political powerlessness as to command extraordinary protection from the majoritarian political process." [81] (4) Educating the handicapped, unlike matters of school finance and the impact of school expenditures, is *not* a matter upon which educational experts are in open and widely publicized disagreement. [82] To the contrary, the Council for Exceptional Children, the American Association on Mental Deficiency, and the Accreditation Council for Facilities for the Mentally Retarded (ACFMR) are in basic agreement that education must be provided to all, without regard to the citizen's degree of handicap or impairment. [83] (5) Nor would the vindication of the retarded child's rights entail any major upheaval in tax policy or drastic change in school administration on the scale posited in *Rodriguez* [84] Rather, the thrust of decisions like *Mills* and *PARC* is in conformity with long accepted principles of universal free education. These decisions and the constitutional mandate of 48 of the 50 states can require nothing less than the end of exclusionary practices for that minority of children whose educational entitlements are still withheld.

This point of view was recently adopted by the Supreme Court of North Dakota when it decided *In re H.G., A Child.* [85] In this decision the court discussed at some length the implications of *Rodriguez* and clearly held that with or without the shadow of *Rodriguez,* the fourteenth amendment of the United States Constitution

[78] *Id.* at 37.
[79] *Id.* at 23.
[80] *Id.* at 28.
[81] *Id.*
[82] *Cf.* 411 U.S. at 42.
[83] Lippman & Goldberg, *supra* note 1, at 24-25 (1973). The standards of the ACFMR are typical of expert opinion. Accreditation Council for Facilities for the Mentally Retarded, Standards for Residential Facilities for the Mentally Retarded 49 (1971): Standard 3,3,1 requires that "[e]ducational services . . . *shall* be available to all residents, regardless of chronological age, degree of retardation, or accompanying disabilities or handicaps." (Emphasis supplied.)
[84] 411 U.S. at 56.
[85] Civil No. 8930 (April 30, 1974).

entitles all of the mentally retarded children of North Dakota to an equal educational opportunity.

NATIONAL RESPONSES TO A NATIONAL TRAGEDY

The need for national action to resolve the problems raised in the education suits on behalf of the handicapped is apparent. Legislation has now been introduced in the United States Senate which would accomplish this objective. Sponsored by Senator Harrison A. Williams, Jr., of New Jersey, it seeks to "assure all handicapped children the right to a free appropriate public education."[86] In recognizing the responsbility of the states to provide education for all handicapped children, this bill attempts to provide federal assistance to the states to help underwrite this objective and to require mechanisms to prevent the improper testing and mislabeling of such children. To foster accountability, the bill would require that a school system produce in writing its individual evaluation of the child, the goals and objectives of its educational services, any ancillary services to be provided, and the estimated time frame for reaching specified goals and objectives. As a condition of eligibility for federal financial assistance, this bill would require states to establish operationally defined due process safeguards whenever a school system contemplates a change in educational placement for the child. At such time, the child's parents or guardian would be afforded the opportunity to raise any objections to such a change. This legislation offers a timely expression of authentic national concern for the quality of the lives of our most vulnerable natural resource, our children.

Judicial decision making is not a comprehensive process and is not in itself sufficient to ensure that all handicapped children will be accorded an appropriate public education tailored to meet their needs. Our children must not be deprived of educational opportunities until federal district courts of the 50 states have each ruled that their education is a present constitutional right. Waiting children need national legislation that will guarantee prompt placement procedures and funding to monitor and implement this right.

Reaction Comment

PERCY BATES

THE THRUST of Herr's paper is as unmistakable as it is unchallengeable: The mentally retarded citizen is entitled to all the legal rights and privileges available to any citizen, and the condition of mental retardation is not grounds for denial of educational rights. But if the legal profession is truly to achieve and maintain the

---

[86] S. 6, 93d Cong., 1st Sess. (1973).

best educational benefits for mentally retarded individuals, professional educators must actively participate in the movement.

As an educator, I find it somewhat embarrassing that in recent years attorneys have assumed leadership in obtaining equal educational opportunities for the mentally retarded. For too long educators have been mere spectators of change awaiting the results of special class legislation, administrative regulations, and right to education lawsuits. Too often we have been in the position of operating after the fact. Our lack of participation has created confusion within the profession, and, most tragically, delay in the delivery of services to children.

Special educators must get on with the business of educating children—all children. If we provide the educational services we should, we will be able to anticipate legal action and avoid most litigation. We will also be in a much better position to meet the increasing demands that will certainly be made on the profession. Educators must reassume leadership in the education of mentally retarded individuals.

The recent flurry of litigation has evidently brought us full circle from enacting legislation to provide services specifically for mentally retarded children back to a position that appears to curtail many of these services. The recent and rapid growth of special classes for the mentally retarded has come under attack. The attack is largely a result of the misuse of special education classes as dumping grounds for some children and of the total exclusion of others from public education. A growing number of courts and legislatures has recognized these abuses. This recognition is reflected in a growing demand that mentally retarded children be returned to "regular classes."

There is a real danger that this process is becoming an overreaction to past abuses and that in the stampede to return mentally retarded students to the regular classroom, the particular needs of individual students will be ignored. Schools that merely reassign such children on a wholesale basis without providing special help compound the harm of the original placement. Interim planning is essential whenever a student's educational placement is altered. This is especially true for students who have learning disabilities. The changing legal atmosphere, with its renewed reliance on the regular classroom, does not and should not relieve educators of the responsibility of providing the best possible educational services for mentally retarded children. Despite the national movement which supports massive and hasty curriculum changes, we must reaffirm our efforts to provide the best education we know for *every* child.

Reaction Comment

LEOPOLD LIPPMAN

IN THE 1950s parents of retarded citizens organized the National Association for Retarded Children (NARC)[1] and its local and state affiliates and stimulated public

---

[1] In 1973, the organization changed its name to the National Association for Retarded Citizens.

awareness of this group of citizens. And in the 1960s, starting with the aggressive and creative interest of the White House and the monumental work of the President's Panel on Mental Retardation, important federal legislation was enacted and comprehensive state plans developed. In the sixties, the focus of action was in the executive and legislative branches.

It looked as though the decade of the seventies would be the decade of the judiciary, but this perspective may already be somewhat out of date.[2] We must continue to use the courts as we are able to, but we must also use all other resources in a balanced attack on the many problems in the area of mental retardation.

Persons who care about asserting, establishing, and maintaining the rights of mentally retarded people must look at the process by which the favorable decisions came about in *PARC,* in *Mills,* in *Wyatt,* and in the other cases that have been successful. Self-organization has been the starting point, but it has not been the retarded themselves who have organized. Of all the disadvantaged minority groups in the United States, the mentally retarded are the least able to speak for themselves. But they do have advocates who can present their cases for them. Most parents care a great deal about their retarded children and are willing to work on their behalf.[3] So NARC and the state and local organizations of parents and friends of mentally retarded citizens are a mechanism that is essential to the process. Around NARC, and as partners with it now, are individual professionals and organizations of professionals, such as the American Association on Mental Deficiency, the Council for Exceptional Children, and other national and state professional groups.

The mounting of the case, the mobilization of resources, the gathering of facts, the searching of records to find documentation, the enlisting of witnesses — the whole routine of putting together the legal attack has been handled by a group of dedicated attorneys who have brought together a high level of professional skill and a concern for the rights of retarded persons, rights that some professionals in the mental retardation field were routinely and often callously violating. Publicity has been a very useful tool with respect to changing patterns. It has been especially important as the initial decisions have been handed down. As professionals have become aware of the impact of these rulings, there has been some evidence of change in the existing patterns of service, or nonpatterns of nonservice, for the mentally retarded. Political strategy and timing are other important considerations which must be fully integrated with court actions.

These observations about self-organization, mobilization of resources, the

---

[2] Countervailing decisions in similar cases have already been handed down by federal courts in various jurisdictions, and they are currently making their way through the lengthy and uncertain appeals procedure, perhaps ultimately to the Supreme Court of the United States. (See the recent issues of MENTAL RETARDATION AND THE LAW: A REPORT ON STATUS OF CURRENT COURT CASES, issued periodically by the U.S. Dep't of Health, Education and Welfare, and NEWSLINE, published by the National Center for Law and the Handicapped.)

Aside from substantive threats, two procedural devices utilized in the Pennsylvania and other pioneering cases are in jeopardy: Chief Justice Warren E. Burger, in his Report on Problems of the Judiciary to the American Bar Association in 1972, recommended the elimination of three-judge district courts; and, more recently, a severe constraint has been imposed on the use of class action suits. Eisen v. Carlisle & Jacquelin, 417 U.S. 156 (1974).

[3] *See* A. KATZ, PARENTS OF THE HANDICAPPED (1961); R. SEGAL, MENTAL RETARDATION AND SOCIAL ACTION (1970); Lippmann, *Community Organization: U.S.A.,* in MENTAL RETARDATION: AN ANNUAL REVIEW (J. Wortis ed. 1970).

use of publicity, and so on relate not only to litigation, but to the whole "lobbying" process. In the broad sense of the term, lobbying is important not only in the legislative halls for particular pieces of legislation, but also in the executive branch for administrative changes. It is appropriate that advocates for mentally retarded citizens press their views upon public school administrators and boards, for example.[4] This lobbying should include attempts to develop and secure new services in areas beyond the public school system and the departments of welfare, including services under voluntary auspices as well as public programs.

I share a view that NARC has maintained for years, that the responsibility of the friends and advocates of the retarded is to *obtain*, rather than *provide*, services. There are occasions when it is suitable for demonstration purposes for a voluntary agency to begin a service and to operate it, to show how it can and should be conducted; but NARC's primary function is to obtain the services from the proper agencies, both public and voluntary.[5] Just as the schools owe every child an education, community agencies owe every retarded individual those services they provide other people with similar needs.

Another matter for consideration is implementation, as neither laws nor court decisions are self-executing. The setting of standards, the monitoring, the whole evaluation process, the use of publicity, the efforts on the part of parents and professionals and other friends and advocates of the retarded to make it work are all required to turn into reality the glowing expressions found in legislation and court orders. In all this there is certainly a role for legal practitioners. Yet there are roles for many other kinds of professionals as well — for people in education, in psychology, in social work, in medicine, in rehabilitation, in all the fields that touch on mental retardation — and, of course, there are important functions for legislators, administrators, representatives of the communications media, writers, broadcasters, and filmmakers to perform. Finally, there is an important continuing role for the parents of mentally retarded citizens.

---

[4] *See* W. Wolfensberger, Citizen Advocacy for the Handicapped, Impaired, and Disadvantaged: An Overview (1972); A. Kahn, S. Kamerman & B. McGowan, Child Advocacy (1972).

[5] This is also the philosophy of the Riksförbundet för Utvecklingsstörda Barn (FUB), the national organization of parents of mentally retarded persons in Sweden. *See* L. Lippman, Attitudes Toward the Handicapped: A Comparison Between Europe and the United States 34-38 (1972).

CHAPTER 10

The Right to an Adequate Income and Employment

Editorial Introduction

Bernstein's paper is a broad review of the laws governing the income of both the economically productive and the nonproductive. Noting that many mentally retarded individuals are a part of the regular labor force, Bernstein searches for a principle and philosophy that will ensure that *all* members of society—because of their membership in society—are guaranteed a decent standard of living, whether or not they are economically productive. From an initial demonstration of the gross inequalities in income, he proceeds to an examination of the bases for allocating income to the employed (through wages, fringe benefits, and publicly supported services) and the disabled (through tort recovery, workmen's and disabled seamen's compensation, and social security disability payments). From this welter of programs, no policy emerges, only inconsistency and conflict.

Bernstein concludes that American society has no general policy of compensation—and certainly has no general policy governing compensation to the disabled. He then notes the great degree to which all members of the society profit economically from a common heritage, common societal assets, and a common endowment of natural resources. He articulates the notion of "the common unearned heritage" as the concept from which we can recognize that each member of society is entitled, as of right, to a share—to a decent standard of living even if so impaired as to be economically unproductive.

Finally, Bernstein examines the question of appropriate wage rates in the context of the Fair Labor Standards Act. Again noting a lack of conceptual purity in the law as written and applied, he suggests that the wages paid by employers might properly be geared to productivity—if reduced productivity of a handicapped worker could actually be demonstrated—but that "the common unearned heritage" or a straight social subsidy should be used to bring the total wages of the worker up to a level required for a decent standard of living.

Ferris, in his reaction comment, emphasizes the point that many mentally retarded individuals need only to be provided with the same employment opportunities available to other citizens in order to be able to earn a decent living in the world of competitive employment. Ferris describes some of the kinds of employment discrimination and disadvantages that force the mentally retarded to assume a false dependent role in society. He pleads for increased involvement of attorneys in the task of achieving better working conditions and the right of mentally retarded citizens to adequate income and employment.

Chambers explores the reasons why courts have been reluctant to develop a constitutional right to adequate income. He concurs with Bernstein's general approach of seeking the development of a consistent social policy through legislative action which would ensure adequate income and access to employment opportunities. He concludes by exploring nonconstitutional routes already open to retarded citizens, an area in which attorneys have a vital role to play.

PRINCIPAL PAPER

MERTON C. BERNSTEIN

THE DETERMINATION of proper wage rates for mentally retarded citizens necessitates ferreting out the principles governing the proper compensation of all members of society. This undertaking in turn requires an inquiry into the principles of compensation by which this society operates. If the principles appear unsatisfactory on the ground of appropriateness or efficiency, the inquiry must extend to what principles should govern compensation. Whatever principles emerge will be applied to the first issue: proper compensation for the mentally retarded.

The method of this inquiry is to describe and analyze the ways in which American society pays its working members and compensates the injured and the unemployed. The factors that emerge will be matched against some suggested social principles and considerations of efficiency to test the appropriateness of current compensation measures. The examples selected are chosen to provide the broadest group possible for which data are available.

INCOME, WAGES, AND SALARIES

Some Inequalities

Enormous inequalities of income exist between the highest and lowest paid individuals in the United States. In addition to higher cash income, the better compensated members of society enjoy more valuable fringe benefits than the lower paid. A considerable portion of the higher paid also benefit disproportionately from public programs which in turn improve the opportunities of their children to gain preferred employment. This section explores the dimensions of these inequalities and their justification for the individuals involved and for the proper functioning of the economy.

In 1970 over 25 million persons were members of families with incomes below the poverty level;[1] 17 million were children. In contrast a comparative handful of persons had annual incomes in the hundreds of thousands of dollars. This group heads a few mammoth corporations and presides over vast aggregations of property and income-producing institutions. One may wonder why they are "worth" 100 or 200 times the lowest paid individuals.

In 1969, families in the top 5 percent before-tax income bracket commanded 21.6 times the amount of the income of the lowest 5 percent income group.[2] Lucas and Thurow found that the disparities between the *relative* shares of income groups had narrowed between 1949 and 1969, but Peter Henle found a "slight but persistent trend toward inequality" between 1958 and 1970.[3] In any event, the disparities are very large and persist with surprisingly little variation in the distribution among the several income strata. Moreover, Professor Kuh points out that the top 10 percent income recipients own 56 percent of the national wealth.[4] The great majority of the physically and mentally handicapped find their fate in the low-income groups. However, the mentally retarded scion of a wealthy family has available to him far different opportunities from those available to a similarly handicapped child of a poor family.

Fringe benefits constitute a sizable income supplement for many of the employed. They may take the form of future income or current benefits, as in the case of hospital, surgical, and medical care insurance. These benefits, if not provided by the employer, would be purchased by some working citizens, especially those with

---

[1] U.S. Bureau of the Census, Dep't of Commerce, Statistical Abstract of the United States 329 (1972).

[2] L. Thurow & R. Lucas, The American Distribution of Income: A Structural Problem, (1972) *citing* U.S. Bureau of the Census, Dep't of Commerce, Current Population Reports: Consumer Income, P. 60, No. 75, Income in 1969 of Families and Persons in the United States (1970). Of course, considerable portions of the upper income group's income come from sources other than wages and salaries. Nonetheless, that income represents the allocation to them of the goods and services of our society.

[3] Henle, *Exploring the Distribution of Earned Income*, 95 Monthly Labor Rev., Dec. 1972, at 16.

[4] Kuh, *The Robin Hood Syndrome*, N.Y. Times, Mar. 5, 1973, at 29, col. 2.

more ample incomes. Coverage and benefits tend to be more expansive as wages and salaries rise.[5] But, in addition to wages, salaries, and income from investments, many workers receive benefits from tax-supported programs, which, even if not income in the taxable sense, represent services that might otherwise require purchase at substantial cost. Indeed, what could be better income than a desired nontaxable benefit?

Despite substantial disparities in per pupil expenditures between a crowded Mexican-American school district and a more sparsely populated Anglo school district, the Supreme Court has found the record of San Antonio School District v. Rodriguez[6] deficient in proof that districts with low per capita pupil expenditure are populated mostly by poor families and that the opposite is true for wealthy districts. The conclusion was based upon a Connecticut study that discovered "not surprisingly, that the poor were clustered around commercial and industrial areas — those same areas that provide the most attractive sources of property tax income for school districts." The dissenters seem to have arrayed at least equally persuasive data to the contrary.[7]

However the case may be for constitutional purposes, much data and common experience combine to demonstrate that wealthy suburbs manage to operate more modern schools with more varied curricula, a better teacher-student ratio, and a greater quality and quantity of support services than inner-city neighborhoods. The connection between money spent and the quality of education is unresolved. although it is not improbable that a curriculum offering wide choice is superior to one with limited choice, at least in so far as it has the potential for better meeting individual student needs. And it is demonstrable that, in general, children from wealthy families enjoy a larger per capita public school expenditure than poor children. Were such services purchased through private schools, they would be costly. Expenditures for education are the equivalent of additional income or, at the least, a substantial allocation of the community's wealth. This type of income supplement of the wealthy may be offset in part by the expenditures for private schools of city-dwelling upper income families, but the impact of this service cost is to be doubted given the reputed flight of white families with school-age children to the suburbs.[8]

It seems that higher family income correlates positively with lengthened school attendance.[9] In turn, length of school attendance confers greater opportunities for hiring into higher status[10] and better paying jobs.[11] Such an advantage seems

---

[5] *E.g.* Beier, *Incidence of Private Retirement Plans,* 94 MONTHLY LABOR REV., July 1971, at 37.

[6] San Antonio Independent School Dist. v. Rodriguez, 411 U.S. 1, 22-23 (1973).

[7] *Id.* at 65-67 (White, J., dissenting), 74-76, 80-81 (Marshall, J., dissenting).

[8] In 1970, slightly more than half the urbanized white population lived in "urban fringe" districts. U.S. BUREAU OF THE CENSUS, DEP'T OF COMMERCE, STATISTICAL ABSTRACT OF THE UNITED STATES table 16, at 16 (1972).

[9] C. JENCKS ET AL., INEQUALITY 216 (1972).

[10] *Id.* at 182, 191. Other factors also play a part.

[11] L. THUROW & R. LUCAS, *supra* note 2, at 24, 35-37. They observe that most job skills are learned on the job and question the relevance of "artificial credentials" such as duration of schooling. *Id.* at 37.

unearned and unfair in a society dedicated to the proposition that one's own capabilities alone should determine material rewards.

In this economy, differential pay is justified by the incentive it provides to train, expend energy, and be inventive. It is believed that the results redound to the benefit of society in greater production of desired goods and services. Although parts of this rationale have been criticized,[12] American society probably would be far less productive without any such incentives. But if the rewards are conferred not for ability, but for obtaining a particular badge (school diploma), the productive purposes of differential status and pay are not served. The unfairness is compounded when the badge goes to many individuals as an advantage conferred by the accident of birth.

The Classical Theories

The Subsistence Wage

Unwillingness to work and the consequent necessity of coercing labor by hunger are the basic suppositions of the early classical economists who addressed wage theory. A truly heartwarming proverb expressed the view neatly: "Need makes the old wife trot."[13] By "chance" it also was regarded as advantageous to manufacturers to pay low wages, this policy enabling them to market their wares at the lowest price and thereby assuring themselves an attractive slice of the business available where competition prevailed. High prices and large population would combine to goad the "lower orders" to industry and enable "the nation" to produce large amounts at prices beneficial to trade. Such an inhumane policy of exploitation requires just this kind of abstraction. The disadvantaged group requires no concern, for "the nation" (or perhaps the Reich) uses this policy to justify the subordination of the individual's interests. The corollary of the subsistence wage theory is that wages for the mass of workers should provide sufficient income to ensure that the workers are hungry, but not starving.

The Equalization Theory

Another classical formulation of wage theory is that wages, like prices, are governed by supply and demand. High wages reflect intense demand and inadequate supply. In response, more workers qualify themselves for highly compensated work, thereby enlarging the supply and lowering the wages. Low-wage jobs attract few new applicants, the supply diminishes, and the wages increase. In sum, wages tend to equalize over time. This formulation, however, describes no known economic

---

[12] Galbraith argues that today the wants are manufactured by the producers through advertising to match goods they produce. J. GALBRAITH, THE AFFLUENT SOCIETY 146-54 (1969).
[13] M. WERMEL, EVOLUTION OF THE CLASSICAL WAGE THEORY 3-7 (1939).

system because the knowledge, opportunity to train, and assumed worker mobility generally do not prevail.

Modern Wage Theories

Some modern wage theories seek to blend inductive methods with the abstract deductive approach of the classicists. One of the first concluded that wage and salary levels frequently reflect society's values.[14] For example, the arduousness and unpleasantness of garbage collecting arguably warrants a high wage, but in fact does not command it. Dirty work, in this and in other societies, is left to minority groups, recent immigrants (even in egalitarian Sweden), and the "untouchables." These individuals are paid at comparatively low rates for difficult, dirty, and often dangerous work.

One group of labor economists stresses the "institutional" setting as a factor in wage determination. Their analysis posits processes of great complexity and variability in which tactics, discretion, and many considerations other than maximized profits and minimized unit costs frequently play key roles.[15] Here again, societal values, including concepts about the appropriate use of human beings,[16] modify strictly market considerations in setting wage rates.

Modern Wage Practices

Whether collective bargaining affects long-range wage rates is a matter of dispute.[17] There is some evidence that varying degrees of organization result in achieving higher wages than would be forthcoming in its absence. Possibly 15 percent is the maximum increase of this sort, if it does indeed occur.[18] It it does, most of the difference probably is supplied by lower prices for products and services supplied by employees with the least bargaining and market power. A major union goal is standardization of wage rates among firms and within job classifications. To the extent that this goal is achieved, wages do not vary fully according to productivity, effort, or ability.

Some data support the proposition that similar work commands different wage rates in different industries.[19] For example, the work of actors and actresses performing in live plays requires equal talent and usually more effort than acting in televi-

---

[14] B. Wootton, The Social Foundation of Wage Policy (1955).

[15] New Concepts in Wage Determination *passim* (G. Taylor & F. Pierson eds. 1957).

[16] Goldfinger & Kassalow, *Trade Union Behavior in Wage Bargaining,* in New Concepts in Wage Determination 51, 77 (G. Taylor & F. Pierson eds. 1957) (wage incentive systems).

[17] John Burton neatly synopsizes the dispute in Burton, *Economic Impact of Unions,* in Labor Law: Cases, Materials and Problems 74 (B. Melzer ed. 1970).

[18] A. Rees, The Economics of Trade Unions 77-78 (1962).

[19] Watchel & Betsey, *Employment at Low Wages,* 54 Rev. Econ. & Statistics 121, 127 (1972).

sion productions. Nevertheless, television pays far greater salaries than theater, often to the same people, for what essentially is the same work.

Time and motion studies for wage settings lack consistent objective criteria for the key rates which form the basis for the often intricate construction of comparative rates. And the weighting of frequently used factors involves subjective assessments which reflect societal biases. Objective wage criteria have proven elusive for arbitrators and wage boards. Many elements of pay make market sense, but many are arbitrary. Compensation does not depend solely on potentially relevant characteristics such as effort, unpleasantness of job, and productivity. Even apart from racial and sex discrimination, which causes serious departures from set criteria, the disparity of wage scales is evident.

COMPENSATION POLICY IMPLICIT IN LEGAL AND SOCIAL PROGRAMS

The factors determining benefit levels in public programs tend to be as difficult to isolate as those in the private wage and salary sectors. Declarations of policy usually state considerations that compete, rather than provide mutual support. Such declarations reflect the conflicts that are presented to Congress and the state legislatures when different groups press their claims. For example, in the Fair Labor Standards Act "Findings and Declaration of Policy," the statute observes the existence "of labor conditions detrimental to the maintenance of the minimum standard of living necessary for health, efficiency and general well being" and asserts the policy "as rapidly as practicable to eliminate the conditions . . . without substantially curtailing employment or earning power."[20] Beyond such explicit recognition, public programs often compromise stated standards to take account of what the traffic will bear.

Many constituencies embrace heterogeneous groups with diverse enthusiasms, antipathies, and priorities — especially in the case of United States senators. So a "reformer" may trim his sails to the winds emanating from opponents of a particular measure. Few legislative victories are clear-cut. Thus, although the 1965 enactment of Medicare was a triumph for proponents of the view that government should provide the mechanism for health care services to the elderly on a no-needs-test basis, opponents (insurance companies and the organized medical profession) not only remained in charge of the medical delivery system, but received statutory confirmation and support of their preeminent role.[21]

The example of Medicare attests anew to the lack of doctrinal "purity" of the American political system and reveals much about social policy in the United States. Compromises are struck by a complicated unscientific process in which many elec-

[20] 29 U.S.C. § 202 (1970).
[21] *E.g.,* Pub. L. No. 89-97, § 1842, 79 Stat. 309-10 (1965).

ted officials assess the electorate's support for some features of a proposal and juggle competing and contradictory features to effect a rough balance that supposedly approximates the public's "philosophy," primarily as registered and represented by organized interest groups. Wrong guesses may result in the defeat of some officeholders and progress (or regress) toward a new balance. Administrators engage in similar juggling feats, carrying forward the elected executive's "program" — but with an eye windward to the legislature, which also must be considered lest it produce legislation detrimental to the executive-administrator's values. Courts establish rules and principles in the context of litigated disputes, a context which is certain to dramatize conflicting goals.

The law-making process is untidy and inconclusive. It makes it hazardous to try to infer coherent social policies from the tangle of statutes, administrative practices, and court decisions that make up our law of public compensation. Yet, some inferences are possible: It can be cogently asserted that if X represents a subsistence income for an adult in state Y and the legislature mandates a benefit of X minus i, some reasonable inferences may be drawn about the composite views and power distribution of that jurisdiction on the basis of the size of i and the strictness or laxity with which administrators and courts implement the proclaimed standard. This process of inference of principles from results will be utilized in examining several of the existing public compensation programs.

Tort Recovery

Compensation is the commanding principle of tort recovery.[22] Injury of one person through the negligence of another entitles the person wronged to compensation. "[T]his contemplates that damages [granted] for a tort should place the [innocent] injured person as nearly as possible in the condition he would have occupied if the wrong had not occurred."[23] Putting aside the considerable practical and theoretical difficulties in making good this principle, the principle itself dictates payment to the injured for all costs occasioned by the injury (*e.g.,* medical) and for loss of earnings, including discounted value of future losses, caused by the wrongdoer.

The principle requires payment for nonproduction, for this is what compensation for lost earnings comes to. It is essential to see that payment for nonproduction is exactly what the economy supposedly refuses to do for persons without the innate or developed capacity to produce. They are to be paid only in accordance with the market value of the goods or service they actually produce. Justification for such differing approaches (and their outcomes) is not immediately apparent. Persons meagerly endowed are to be paid little — because they produce little and so

---

[22] 2 F. Harper & F. James, Law of Torts 1299 (1956); C. McCormick, Handbook on the Law of Damages 560 (1935).

[23] C. McCormick, *supra* note 22, at 560.

are not "worth" higher wages.[24] On the other hand, persons injured by someone else's negligence and thereby rendered unproductive are to be compensated. Inconsistency toward the phenomenon of nonproductiveness must proceed from the notion that workers not only must be given incentives to produce when they are able, but also that they somehow are responsible for their capabilities. But many persons deserve little or no credit for their earning capacity. Endowments proceed from the environment, genetic inheritance, rearing of parents, access to schools that confer advantages, and other factors that lie outside the individual. Many inherit opportunities for preferment. In other words, capacity to earn is often largely unearned and yet is compensable in tort recoveries when lost.

It is unclear why the loss of capacity to earn in the future should be better compensated than is the absence of the ability to earn where the absence results from a developmental or other handicap. When a poorly and a richly endowed person both are deprived of their earning capacities through the fault of another, society decrees very different compensation although neither individual may be held responsible for his incapacitation and both are rendered nonproductive. Is it that the formerly more productive (more fortunate) person is "entitled" to a higher standard of living? Why should this be so? Surely, the notion that one is of finer and the other inferior clay is untenable. Perhaps the dependents of the more fortunate person require a higher standard of living. But why should certain nonproducers (wives and children of the more fortunate) be preferred over other dependent nonproducers? It is one thing to justify inequality on the ground of incentive to the potentially more productive worker, but the element of incentive has no role in tort compensation.

The tort system frequently overcompensates. It does not deduct certain income received (accident insurance, wage and salary payments actually granted although not currently earned) from the compensation payment. Innumerable studies attest to dramatic jury verdicts for pain and suffering, payments that are allowed despite their obvious lack of incentive potential.

Although the tort system assumes an innocent victim injured by a culpable defendant, the real world knows that some of the innocent contribute to their misfortune and many of the culpable do nothing worse than many other members of society (especially where the "fault" is an automobile driving lapse).

Nor do these payments come without cost to society, When payment actually occurs, usually the cost is borne immediately by an insurer through premiums paid by enterprises which build such costs into the price of products and services, where it is paid by the consuming public. In other words, the consumer and the produc-

---

[24] In his reaction comment, Milton Ferris observes that sheltered workshops tend to be poorly equipped. With modern facilities, he argues—and I agree—their output would command larger pay and often would be competitive. This pervasive lack tells us a great deal about the priorities placed upon enabling mentally retarded and other handicapped persons to be self-supporting. As I suggest later in this paper, retarded individuals especially can bring qualities of patience and perseverance to many tasks too repetitive and boring for the nonretarded. To withhold the means of becoming self-supporting is a terrible act of omission by society.

tive sector of the economy pay to support nonproducers at their former standard of living on the ground, frequently fictitious, that the victim is faultless.

Underlying this system is a belief in the correctness of paying for nonproduction, although some nonproduction is more valued than other nonproduction. Other interruptions to earnings and the ability to perform useful functions, however, are dealt with quite differently.

Workmen's Compensation

Operation of tort law for work-related injuries generated dissatisfaction throughout the working and employer sectors by 1910. The need to prove negligence attributable to the employer prevented recovery in many cases despite the high incidence of serious and fatal injuries at work. The first wave of remedial legislation, the employer liability acts, removed or modified common law employer defenses of assumption of risk, contributory negligence, and the fellow servant rule. But the tort system remained risky and slow, giving the employer (or its insurer) great bargaining power to beat down the claims of injured and necessitous workers.

By the turn of the century the British had adopted a workmen's compensation act with the essential feature of absolute but limited employer liability. The fact of job-caused injury made the employer liable to provide limited compensation to an employee. The stated purpose was to enable the workingman and his family to subsist during the period of work-caused disablement. The employee won dispensation from the need to demonstrate employer negligence and his own freedom from contributory negligence. In return, the employer's liability was limited to quite modest statutorily prescribed amounts instead of possibly large jury awards. Coverage for occupational disease (diseases with a special causal connection to particular occupations or industries) and mandatory medical care for such illness and work-connected injury were the next major developments.

The theory underlying this species of act is that work involves hazards of injury and illness and the enterprise that occasions exposure to the hazard should bear the cost of their occurrence. In turn, the consumers of the goods and services produced pay for the injury and illness incidental to their production. In one memorable formulation: "The cost of the product should bear the blood of the workingman."[25]

Society requires that the worker and his dependants be paid amounts to provide subsistence when he is not productive. And this is so even if the person receiving the payments caused the injury or contributed to its occurrence. By design, however, the amounts paid constitute less than full recompense: The reduction of benefits below full compensation is justified as a trade-off for absolute liability and as an incentive for the injured employee to return to productive activity. The deficit (which frequently brings compensation below the Spartan official poverty level)[26] also registers the

---

[25] H. SOMERS & A. SOMERS, WORKMEN'S COMPENSATION 28 n.16 (1954).

[26] In one recent year for which data were available, benefits fell below this level in 38 states. Berkowitz & Burton, *The Income Maintenance Objective in Workmen's Compensation,* 24 IND. & LAB. REL. REV. 14, 17 (1970).

degree of society's concern. As the blasé gift recipient observed: "It's something I always wanted — but not very much."

Significant segments of the economy allocate additional funds to supplement these meager statutory programs. Organized labor has won workmen's compensation supplements for many members in collective bargaining, and some segments of the business community make similar arrangements for white-collar or managerial employees. These supplements available to the more powerful members of the community reduce their demand for improvements in the program applicable to all.

In operation, the programs tend to provide a greater degree of wage replacement to the short-term disabled and proportionally less to the long-term disabled. This pattern developed accidentally, rather than by design, but its long continuation cannot be dismissed as accidental. Alteration of this pattern evidently has a low priority among persons with the knowledge and potential power to make a difference. Perhaps the pattern reflects society's willingness to prop up nonproductive workers' income through a nonfault system only for short periods.

Implicit in workmen's compensation is the notion that it is proper and desirable to pay the nonproductive employee, even those who cause their own disablement, but only enough for them and their dependents to subsist. This view contrasts to the full recompense approach of the tort system, whose operation is thought to be more unpredictable.

Programs for Seamen

In programs for seamen, several important types of absolute liability complement a negligence-based theory of recovery. For centuries the shipowner has owed the duty of providing "maintenance and cure" to ill seamen or to those injured without willful misbehavior while in the service of a vessel. The injury or illness need not be work-caused nor even occur while at work. Maintenance — continuation of food, shelter, and wages — lasts the duration of the voyage. Today "cure" means effecting as much return to physical soundness as medical care can achieve. Almost since the founding of the United States, special hospitals for seamen have been operated by the Public Health Service.

The concept of "unseaworthiness" also dates from the earliest days of this nation, but until 1903 it did no more than provide a valid excuse for a seaman to leave his vessel. Under this concept, the shipowner owes the seaman the duty to provide a seaworthy ship with equipment in proper order. Unseaworthiness does not require proof of negligence; inadequacy of the gear suffices. In 1903, the concept impliedly became a proper ground for the recovery of damages,[27] although the fellow servant rule then barred recovery where injury resulted from the negligence of another crewman or the master.

The LaFollette Seamen's Act of 1915[28] attempted to remove the fellow servant

---

[27] The Osceola, 189 U.S. 158, 175 (1903) (dictum).
[28] Seamen's Welfare Act ch. 153, § 20, 38 Stat. 1185 (1915), *as amended* 46 U.S.C. § 688 (1970).

doctrine as a defense, but the Supreme Court held the legislative attempt ineffective.[29] Congress, urged on by the Seamen's Union, responded with a provision[30] conferring upon seamen all the remedies available to railroad employees under the Federal Employer's Liability Act (FELA) of 1908. This provided a remedy for employer negligence which was reduced in proportion to the employee's contributory negligence, a concept totally alien to the unseaworthiness doctrine. The FELA also provided recovery where the employer's violation of a safety statute contributed to the employee's injury or death.

The Death on the High Seas Act of 1920[31] provides a remedy for death "caused by wrongful act, neglect or default." The act was construed to extend the remedy to death attributable to unseaworthiness regardless of the question of fault. As of 1944 the employer's duty became a "warranty" of seaworthiness.[32] It since has become the mainstay of seamen's recovery, providing a tortlike recovery through private suit with near absolute liability without fault for acts that closely resemble industrial accidents.

Social Security Disability

Under the Social Security Disability Insurance (DI) program, a person with strong labor force attachment (20 quarters of social security coverage during the 40 quarters preceding disablement) who is deprived of the capacity for any substantial employment by illness or injury receives a benefit computed like a retirement benefit; his dependents receive benefits as well. The disablement need have no work connection, and concepts like fault and contributory negligence are totally alien to the program. In 1972 Congress added Medicare benefits for disabled beneficiaries. The benefit is adjusted to increases in the cost-of-living index.

Policies Implicit in Compensation Programs

The melange of programs and policies just reviewed does not readily reveal any pattern of society's notion of proper treatment for the disabled. On the contrary, confusion seems the strongest element if the programs are viewed side by side. It might be said that the varying characteristics reflect differing circumstances and needs, but this hardly seems to be the case. Rather, the variety results from pressure groups at different stages of social and economic development seeking ameliora-

---

[29] Chelentris v. Luckenbach S.S. Co., 247 U.S. 372, 384 (1918).

[30] 46 U.S.C. § 688 (1970) (originally enacted as Act of June 5, 1920, ch. 250, § 33, 41 Stat. 1007, and known as the Jones Act).

[31] 46 U.S.C. §§ 761-68 (1970) (originally enacted as Act of Mar. 30, 1920, ch. 111, §§ 1-8, 41 Stat. 537).

[32] Mahnich v. Southern S.S. Co., 321 U.S. 96 (1944).

tion of their particular problems. New forms have emerged from the inadequacies of their predecessors without necessarily displacing the older programs. The DI program, which ought to be the quintessence of modern thought, appears as merely another patch upon the quilt. It does demonstrate, as workmen's compensation and the seamen's program did earlier, some concern for the social and economic situation of the disabled wage earner and his dependents. DI, however, simply ignores any theory of liability. Employees and employers pay contributions (payroll taxes) because this is a relatively easy and bearable way to finance a scheme of social insurance. Dependents need benefits when a wage earner is disabled, so benefits are provided for them. The system works satisfactorily because benefits, even though at a low level, come as of right and the employer has no stake in preventing or minimizing them.

The survey does establish that several enormous programs focus upon paying persons whose productivity is impaired or obliterated, in some instances even if they themselves caused their disablement. This peculiar situation occurs in an economy that believes in limiting its fruits to the producers and is tightfisted with nonproducers.

SUGGESTED STANDARDS FOR COMPENSATION

Precedents Provided by Payment and Compensation Patterns

The review of payment and compensation plans should be enlightening. The first clear conclusion to be drawn is that American society lacks a coherent philosophy about the value of human beings. Rather, there are innumerable standards of pay for work and of compensation for disability. These standards are inconsistent, wasteful, and, more important, unjust. Pay patterns do not match the changing needs of employees at various stages of life, and compensation patterns that are frequently inadequate to meet basic needs treat similar situations in bewilderingly different ways. Nor are societal needs well served. Some workers receive high pay for little effort or productivity while others render more value and expend greater effort for meager compensation.

These factors make suspect the present means for allocating society's products. Society seems almost vengeful to individuals with limited or no current work. Current inability to produce incurs penalties that ought to be inflicted, if at all, only upon the most culpable. In fact, deprivation of opportunity to produce frequently is caused by society (as with mandatory retirement, technological obsolescence, exclusion from job training programs, or government-approved rates of unemployment), as well as by chance, the effects of aging, other people's "genes," or inadequate prenatal care and nutrition.

Higher Productivity and The General Rise in Income

During the 60 years following 1889, the productivity of the American economy multiplied almost 5 times.[33] Of course, various sectors of the economy contributed in differing measures.[34] Assuming that the differentials existing in 1889 were "correct" (justifiable on some reasonable basis and assuming all other things equal),[35] does it follow that each occupation should earn five times in real dollars in the 1960s what that same occupation produced in the 1890s?

One could argue plausibly that to the producer belongs the fruits, so that each working group should obtain the full increment of its industry's productivity. Indeed, this view would seem to coincide with current philosophy — one lives at the level one earns for oneself. So, as a simple example, elementary school or college teachers, a group with little or no increase in productivity over the decades, "should" enjoy no more real income in 1960 than a teacher did in 1890. In contrast, some other group, such as engineers, to whose work one could attribute outputs 50 times that of their 1890 counterparts (not in units of their own, but in products attributable to their efforts), "should" be compensated at 50 times the rate of 1890s engineers. Arguably, this proposal is not only fair, but economically sound. Rewards should go to persons who "produce" most so as to encourage many more to enter the ranks of such prodigious productivity and draw them away from less productive pursuits.

But, this proposition is not generally viewed as fair or as necessary for progress. The disparity of rewards seems altogether disproportionate even if the different increases in output can be verified and measured. For one thing, the increased productivity of engineers is not attributable in equal measure to each engineer. The bulk of them build on the innovations of others, innovations of theory and technology that enable them to do more complicated things in less time. In effect, the modern practitioners of any art or science sit on the shoulders of their predecessors. This does not make the mathematicians and physicists of today the proper "owners" of all the fruits derived from their predecessors' advances. This is also true of every computer-served activity. Does the resulting phenomenal leap in output "belong" to those who made the latest innovation in computers or are the advantages to be more widely shared throughout society? By market mechanics the latter is the case to a degree; when improved productivity results in greater

---

[33] Using 1929 as a base of 100, the nation's productivity per man-hour went from 43.6 to 211.7 in 1957. U.S. BUREAU OF THE CENSUS, DEP'T OF COMMERCE, HISTORICAL STATISTICS OF THE UNITED STATES, COLONIAL TIMES TO 1957, at 599 (1960).

[34] Id. a 600-02. Differing measures for changes in productivity exist. Perhaps more relevant to our purpose are the figures for output per unit of (weighted) capital, i.e., money invested. Varying measures put this at 0.7 to 0.9 percent a year, which also produces impressive improvements during the same period. S. FABRICANT, BASIC FACTS ON PRODUCTIVITY CHANGE 5 (1959). Some believe it inappropriate to use output per man-hour, even weighted by wage rates, because this measure varies over the years and masks the contribution of improved educational attainments, achieved in considerable measure by the larger allocation of national resources to education.

[35] Of course, all things are not equal, notably population and the number of hours the average person works; and many new occupations have appeared.

output and lower prices, purchasers score a gain in living standard. But sharing in the gains depends in large measure upon one's purchasing power.

Lawyers provide another example. Since the turn of the century the productivity of this group has been increased very little or possibly not at all, given the increased complexity of any unit of what lawyers do. The implements of improvement have been those rudimentary tools (the typewriter, dictating machine, telephone, commercial airplane) which enable lawyers to avoid some time-consuming tasks. Yet, the legal profession has participated handsomely in the general advance of the economy over the last 30 years. For most years in the decade 1961-71 for which data are available, salaried lawyers almost matched the increases achieved by salaried engineers.[36]

The white-collar occupational groups experienced very similar advances, although the rates of advance varied from year to year during the 1960s. Although some differentials are expected and are tolerable, vast disparities in shared progress seen inappropriate. Recall that in the early 1960s the wage guideposts limited *all* workers to the general rate of productivity increase; exceptions were not contemplated for persons whose productivity exceeded the average. And, even though the guideposts were not always observed, their fairness was not seriously questioned.

It seems appropriate for all citizens to obtain a cost-of-living increase. Social security will soon provide automatic increases, although individuals directly benefited do not currently produce goods and services. Such increases are regarded as the irreducible minimum in collective bargaining and are begrudged by none — even to those whose productivity may be lagging, to use lawyers and teachers as examples again. It seems reasonable that no one should suffer financial demotion by the blind operation of the economy.

These illustrations add up to the implicit proposition that a considerable portion of the economy's progress is properly shared by individuals currently on the scene even though many of the participants have made little or no directly ascertainable contribution to the enlargement of the entire pie. It might be argued that these groups made possible today's and tomorrow's growth by their work yesterday and without the contribution of all or most working people productivity advances would not have been made or would have been smaller. Some groups, however, demonstrably or arguably slowed more efficient production; yet no such group is excluded from cost-of-living increases as employees or retirees. Nor does this argument apply to new jobholders who participate from their first day at work in the wage and salary increases won by the cost-of-living rationale. Participation in cost-of-living offset devices, however, is usually limited to persons who have worked for compensation and to their dependents.

Geographic Differentials

Although per capita annual income in the United States exceeds $ 4,000,[37] the residents of many less developed lands count their daily income in pennies, and their

---

[36] *See* U.S. Bureau of the Census, Dep't of Commerce, Statistical Abstract of the United States table 380, at 237 (1972).
[37] *Id.* at 319.

annual earnings are often below $100. Many perform prodigious labor for their pittance. Some Western Europeans match the incomes of their American counterparts, but most do not. The standard of living of Americans is determined not simply by the work they do individually, but also by their good fortune to be in a country with the most productive economy in the world. Canadians a few miles from Buffalo and Detroit have lower incomes than similarly employed American neighbors; Mexicans enjoy a living standard superior to that in most other Latin American countries, yet the contrast between Mexican and American earnings is extreme. Most people in the United States have not earned this unequaled opportunity; rather, it is our inheritance from forebears who departed less fortunate areas for a variety of reasons — most, but not all, creditable.

The Unearned Increment: A Common Heritage

The current United States population enjoys a standard of living far exceeding that available to earlier generations or to contemporaries throughout the world. Although all who work must do so to keep the system producing, most obtain a yield disproportionate to their own current contributions when measured against counterparts here, in former decades, and elsewhere, today. The advantages are built into the economy, the political system, and the natural resources of this country.

A very large part of the current production, then, represents the yield of a common heritage. As no one can claim credit for earning this economic element, no one person should have greater claim to it than any other. The common heritage should be shared equally.

It appears that American society has been approaching such a concept, but without the rationale suggested, which conceivably could affect and *should* affect many programs. The system of universal free public elementary and secondary education not only recognizes the need for an educated population, but supports this vast program (costing about $50 billion a year) from the common stores of society. To this enterprise almost all contribute. From the fruits of the common inheritance and current production (based in large measure upon the work and treasure accumulated by those who have gone before) provision is made for the young.

Similar provision is made through very different mechanisms for the elderly. Social security support for the retired elderly represents an allocation of current production to nonproducing groups in recognition that they have a claim upon the productive capacity of the nation. The size of the claim is measured only in part by their past contributions as producers of goods and services. Under the Prouty amendment, Congress decided to pay minimum benefits from general revenues to several millions who did not earn entitlement by contributions to the system. Realism requires the recognition that the recently instituted Medicare program immediately benefited millions who made no direct contribution to its financing (and to those fortunate enough to be in the position of providing the services). When Medicare is fully developed, all may share equally. This program and some of the compensation programs described earlier have achieved widespread acceptance. They are expressions of the concept that a part of current production should be allocated to current nonproducers as their share of a generally rich society's product. Our society sensibly provides a system of incentives to reward more production with more income, but it also provides current nonproducers and impaired producers with a share. This sharing is partly explained by the fact that many persons experience difficulties as a result of the hazards peculiar to an urban, industrialized, mechanized economy. It also recognizes common exposure to common hazards — aging and illness, for example. Society seems more willing to allot income and costly services where all citizens run similar risks.

Yet to be reached is the realization that congenital and other developmental defects are quite similar in nature. Just as most people do not expect to suffer a serious automobile accident, until it happens to them or someone very close, the tendency is to expect even less having a child with birth defects or impaired capabilities. But this, too, is a shared hazard.

Perhaps a new principle should be considered: The common heritage, unearned by the currently employed, requires sharing, as does any common inheritance. All members of the community have an equal claim upon it not conditional upon current ability to produce goods and services. The extent of the common inheritance, the size of individual shares, and when it is to be enjoyed all are issues to be considered. Given the fact that earning power so often does not coincide with needs (*e.g.*, lower earnings for young adults when family and childrearing expenses are highest), the common share may help supply the increments required at times of need. This principle should aid individuals whose earning power is reduced through degenerative disease, accidental injury (whether or not work connected), and developmental impairment. They do not need charity — they have a claim upon the common heritage as of right.

THE FAIR LABOR STANDARDS ACT

Purpose

Most legislation results from compromise. The Fair Labor Standards Act (FLSA) provides an example of a statute embracing conflicting policies. The battle for its original enactment reached epic proportions. All subsequent amendments of any substance also produced sharp conflict. Again and again significant groups in Congress have sought to eliminate low-wage competition but have had to compromise with groups that raised the fear of unemployment should the process be too abrupt.

New Deal economics regarded higher wages as a means of augmenting purchasing power for goods and thus stimulating production and expanding employment. As originally proposed in 1937, FLSA was designed primarily to promote this salutary process by eliminating wage cutting brought on by a few "chiselers" who reduced wages and thereby compelled other employers to follow suit. The measure proposed was to set minimum wages and a penalty rate for overtime to provide an incentive to hire additional employees. The humanitarian aspects of the legislation, ensuring a decent income and preventing overly long hours, ran second to the "recovery" thrust of the proposal.[38] Business and much of organized labor opposed the original measure for a variety of reasons. Employers feared the burdens of higher pay and the American Federation of Labor opposed government intrusion into the domain of collective bargaining. Many southern members of Congress expressed concern that regional wage differentials would be wiped out. Despite a large Democratic majority, the House recommitted the bill. In his 1938 State of the Union message, President Roosevelt shifted emphasis: "We are seeking only, of course, to end starvation wages and intolerable hours."[39] A modified bill remerged with a low minimum (25c an hour, scheduled over a 3-year period to increase to 40c) and emphasis upon "standards consistent with health, efficiency, and general well-being of workers and the maximum productivity and profitable operation. . . ."[40] The economic thrust of the original measure gave way in the enacted version to humanitarian emphasis upon "the health and welfare of the sweated worker."[41]

Increasingly, the minimum wage protections of FLSA have been seen as providing "a living wage"[42] and "a minimum standard of living for health, efficiency, and general well-being,"[43] criteria that go beyond subsistence. Belated recognition of poverty has brought with it some realization that the majority of the poor work, and work hard, but are paid too little. This in turn has led to fresh efforts to extend the protection of the act, whose coverage had enormous gaps, to new groups of the working poor. In the 1960s significant low-pay groups received FLSA coverage for the first time — by cautious stages, to be sure.

From the first, however, the Secretary of Labor was empowered to exempt learners and the disabled from full application of the act.[44] The Secretary determines and certifies the amount they may be paid below the statutory minimum. The legislative history of the 1938 Act does not explain these exceptions and the device adopted. But one may surmise that their work was regarded as less valuable to employers, and in the case of learners, that they were at a stage of life when they were not expected to be self-supporting. More recently, however, the manpower training programs, dealing with adult trainees, provide for training allowances no lower than the minimum wage.

Surely one function of minimum wage laws is to protect workers from the competition of others of equal competence with lesser needs for income (such as the young without family obligations) or with willingness to settle for low income

---

[38] Message to Congress from President Franklin D. Roosevelt May 24, 1937. S. REP. No. 884, 75th Cong., 1st Sess. 2-3 (1937). At that juncture Roosevelt also argued for a "fair day's pay for a fair day's work" by the "able-bodied."

[39] *Quoted in* F. PERKINS, THE ROOSEVELT I KNEW 261 (1964).

[40] H. R. REP. No. 2738, 75th Cong., 3d Sess. 15 (1938).

[41] G. Paulsen, The Legislative History of the Fair Labor Standards Act 280, 1959 (unpublished dissertation, Ohio State Univ.) (a splendid and fascinating play-by-play account upon which the opening paragraphs of this section are based).

[42] Testimony of Secretary W. Willard Wirtz, in *Hearings on S. 256, S. 879 & S. 895, Amends. to the Fair Labor Standards Act, Before the Subcomm. on Labor of the U.S. Senate Comm. on Labor & Public Welfare,* 89th Cong., 1st Sess. 32 (1965).

[43] H. R. REP. No. 1366, 89th Cong., 2d Sess. 2 (1966).

[44] 29 U.S.C. §§ 213(a)(7), 214(a) & (d) (1970).

due to necessity or societal conditioning (*e.g.*, women and minority group members). If set high enough, the minimum also offsets the geographical "advantage" of some workers (*e.g.*, Southerners with lower costs of living, notably for housing) so as to enable the employee with larger living costs (*e.g.*, in clothing and homes with insulation and heating in northern climates) to meet them. The minimum, then, interferes with market forces by preventing those who must, can, or are willing to tolerate low pay rates in the interests of protecting their livelihood and by ensuing a basically decent standard of living to other groups that Congress regards as deserving.

Establishment of a minimum wage embodies the proposition that employment should enable the worker to maintain a specified standard of living. Depending upon the rate chosen, it should be adequate for the individual or, if set higher, the individual with a family. In actuality, both coverage and the level of the minimum are determined by considerations of political power between persons seeking the protection and persons employing the seekers.

The Proper Determination of the Minimum Wage

For Whom — The Single Individual or
the Married Family Head?

Congress sets the minimum wage politically rather than scientifically. Congress has determined minimum wage levels over the years by a process that has combined considerations of poverty levels, increases in the cost of living since the rate was last set, and a feeling for what the political traffic will bear. Although these are likely to remain congressional guideposts, it might be possible to construct a benchmark against which the result of these factors can be measured.

A decision must be made at the outset as to how to grapple with the fact that many wage earners are heads of families who must regularly supply the staple needs of their families. The majority of these are men, but many are women. A growing number consists of married women whose earnings provide a "second" income. Indeed, there are more families in which both husband and wife work than in which only the husband works.[45] Yet another significant group, which may be growing proportionately larger as marriage loses its allure for some of the young, are unmarried men and women. Some of them contribute to the support of their families. Eventually some move into the married-with-children category, although perhaps at a slower rate and with fewer children on the average than heretofore. Subsequently, their children will leave the family to strike out on their own.

For whom and at what stage should "a living wage," or one adequate to maintain living "standards necessary for health, efficiency and general well-being" be provided? The answer depends upon what other social arrangements are in force. A society that ensures adequate medical care to all citizens need build into an

---

[45] *See* U.S. BUREAU OF THE CENSUS, DEP'T OF COMMERCE, STATISTICAL ABSTRACT OF THE UNITED STATES table 347 (1972).

income standard only the amount, if any, required as an insurance or social insurance contribution. Currently, however, most of the working population must earn enough to pay large and increasing premiums. Even "normal" medical care expenditures can lead to budget anemia, and a serious illness can overwhelm most budgets. Although this terribly important problem area remains far from solution, assume it away for purposes of this immediate discussion to focus on the non-health needs of the working population. (Such an assumption is doubly artificial because any shortfall in income will produce inadequate shelter, clothing, and nutrition which only exacerbate the needs for medical care. Bear in mind that when inadequate income generates the need for medical care, the medical cure may be more costly in dollars than prevention.)

Even with medical care aside, a society that gears the minimum wage to the married family head may "overpay" the single wage earner. On the other hand, if the minimum is designed only to meet the needs of the single person, family heads in minimum pay jobs will be unable to support their families and may abandon the task—a decision which this society imposes upon many men. Alternatively, the effort might be made to compel employers to pay larger wages to workers with dependents, a device that surely would result in undersirable descrimination. (In fact, married persons generally earn more than the unmarried. Workers with dependents may respond to their greater needs by greater work effort and also may constitute a group that more willingly assumes the obligations that enjoying a family entail.)

But discussion here focuses on individuals whose earning power cannot unaided by law command adequate compensation. It would be wholly unrealistic to attempt to impose childlessness upon them simply because their "ability" to earn does not correlate with their ability to be adequate or good parents. In any event, such attempts would be of dubious constitutionality and practicality. Moreover, as some engineers and hard scientists have learned in recent years, inability to earn at above-subsistence levels may afflict those who once possessed superior earning power.

The minimum wage answer is intimately related to how the rest of the economy is organized. Full employment policies reduce the pressure on the minimum wage as the need for employees persuades employers to hire and train persons otherwise regarded as submarginal employees. To the extent that such an economy is inflationary, a portion of the problem is exported to those otherwise on fixed incomes; but an expanding economy makes it easier to meet their needs and perhaps improve their absolute standard, although probably not their relative share. To the extent that an expanding economy means more potential pollution, it may intensify health problems and increase health care costs. Any program that fails to take account of these and other foreseeable interrelationships lacks rationality.

An alternative is to calibrate the minimum wage to meet an individual's basic needs *and* to meet otherwise unmet family needs by other devices. Actually, this is already done in some important and expensive ways. For over a century the United States has been committed to publicly financed primary education. Secondary education has been included in this commitment, and public financing subsidizes opportunities for advanced education to a considerable extent. Other direct and indirect aids, such as the deductibility of interest payments on home mortgages, subsidize families of middle and upper incomes primarily during their childrearing years. Public housing has been a haphazard and unequal attempt to do something similar for low-income families. School lunch programs, probably of disproportionate help to the nonpoor, are another example.

Other developments argue for the single earner approach. For several decades married women have been entering the labor market in larger numbers and at younger ages. More families may be expected to have two parents with current earnings even when children are present. Assuming that most families prefer to earn their own way, most will opt for employment-generated support, rather than direct subsidies if these are offered on a needs-test basis. Indeed, the furor over the 1972 reduction in federal day care funds demonstrates that a substantial group of women with young children deeply desire to earn their own living and work outside the home. They will not be denied. If society prefers to enable women not so motivated to work at home, children's allownces are an appropriate device.

But this approach to the minimum wage is hard on families with only one potential adult earner unless other supplements, especially a children's allowance, is readily forthcoming. Larger disability payments under social security and workmen's compensation probably constitute another need of such families. When all else fails, a guaranteed income or ample relief for both intact and one-parent families is needed.

A minimum wage designed for the individual, without adequate supplements for family needs, invites family disorganization and class and racial conflict. When large numbers of individuals are denied desirable roles in society, they will turn toward undesirable ones. With so many variables, this conclusion may not be demonstrable statistically, but a fairly persuasive nationwide experience supporting it seems to be going on.

Jobs Worth Doing Ought to Pay a Living Wage

The following is offered as a rebuttable presumption for further consideration: A job worth doing ought to enable a jobholder to earn a wage sufficient to support himself. If society desires a job to be done, it should expect to receive it without subsidy from the performer. Stated another way, the wage-price system is designed to provide incentive for self-support. When an individual has done as much as he can with ordinary effort, he should have earned self-support.

At any given time the great majority of the employed are under the necessity to support themselves and their dependents. Unless such needs are met, society cannot continue. A slave economy cannot do less. A free society, indeed any society, must renew itself in more than mere numbers. Growth requires that all activities of significance to the society be open to all, for no one knows from whence the needed energy and adaptability will come. If these elements are required by a healthy society, then all or the majority of the populace must enjoy something beyond subsistence. A decent standard of living will not short-circuit the ambitious and should enable most people to develop their talents. Indeed, one of the striking things to one whose memory reaches back into the pre-World War II era of depression is the abundance of talent and competence among the present younger generation.

Low wages, in contrast, mean inadequate clothing, shelter, and food, thereby increasing the need for social welfare, law enforcement, and penal expenditure while diverting many talents from desirable activities into efforts at beating the system.[46] A low level of real wages cannot fuel a high-production economy which requires mass consumption. Only totalitarian regimes attempt large-scale Spartan living in an industrial society.

Exceptions to the Minimum Wage?

Most of the existing exceptions to FLSA coverage involve traditionally low-paying jobs. Employers in this sector of the economy have had the political strength to persuade Congress that the industry could not afford the minimum. Happily, the exceptions are dwindling, but they exist, and workers in these jobs are among the most depressed and deprived of the citizenry.[47] Why should restaurant employees subsidize diners, or tobacco pickers subsidize cigar smokers, or Mexican-American children subsidize the consumers of table grapes? The payment of substandard wages to persons helping to provide luxuries and recreation seems especially indefensible. Until the right of all to a living wage is established, the weakest and most defenseless will remain third-class citizens.

Section 214 of the FLSA also exempts learners, messengers, full-time students, and handicapped workers. The Secretary of Labor is to control such submarginal wages by regulation. This represents a classic compromise between standards and job opportunities. In addition, departmental regulation is to set standards so as to minimize incursion on the employment of nonhandicapped adults.

Implicit in the arrangement is that the exempted categories produce goods and services worth less than the minimum wage. It also supposes, although often incorrectly, lesser financial needs by members of the specified groups. A sub-minimum wage constitutes an indefensible subsidy by those least able to provide it.

Where conditions of low-value production and needs less than those of an independent adult exist, exception seems in order, if a device can be found to shield other workers with need for adequate pay from job loss by virtue of the exception. This requires administrative regulation which, if effective, is neither simple nor cheap.

Applying the Minimum Wage Law to Mentally Retarded Citizens

The 1966 FLSA amendments[48] made specific the criteria to be used by the Secretary in setting subminimum wage rates for the handicapped (including the mentally

---

[46] That is surely among the lessons to be learned from THE AUTOBIOGRAPHY OF MALCOLM X (1965) and C. BROWN, MANCHILD IN THE PROMISED LAND (1969).

[47] See 29 U.S.C. § 213 (1970).

[48] 29 U.S.C. § 214(d) (1970) (originally enacted as Act of Sept. 23, 1966, Pub. L. No. 89-601, tit. V, § 501, 80 Stat. 842).

retarded).[49] The Secretary may establish subminimum rates "to the extent necessary in order to prevent curtailment of opportunities for employment,"[50] presumably of the handicapped. In essence, the lower wage is to be "commensurate with" (which presumably means proportionate to) that paid to "non-handicapped workers in industry in the vicinity for essentially the same type, quality, and quantity of work."[51]

In recommending the original version, the Senate committee report observed,

> The committee believes this amendment serves the purpose [sic] of improving the economic circumstances of handicapped workers, speeding their movement into fully productive private employment and assuring that such workers are not exploited through low wages ... [and also retains] ... flexibility which permits the employment of seriously handicapped workers at wage rates in proportion to their productivity.[52]

Logically, all three of this set of purposes could not be realized. For if the administrator (the Secretary's agent) formerly had set wages for the handicapped "too low," the amendments would require that they be raised; if they had been set "too high," "economic circumstances" of the handicapped would not be improved. One can understand that these several purposes are desirable but require balancing.

The standard of proportionality also may appear fair. It would seem to pay the handicapped worker what *he* is worth measured by productivity; *i.e.,* what *his product* is worth in the market. But this seemingly plausible conclusion may not be fully warranted. For one thing, as has been stated, in many instances pay to the unimpaired does not depend upon proportional productivity or social utility. More important, such proportional payment, if it is the total compensation, fails to pay the handicapped worker his worth as a person — all persons have value in their capacities other than as earners.

But it does not follow that the employer should pay the difference between the amount called for by the statute and the employee's due. As a measure of the employer's required contribution, the proportional measure seems reasonable and fair. But the worker ought to receive the minimum due him as a member of society. As this share is essentially unearned by anyone, it represents no burden to the taxpayer or anyone else; it simply is the share all can claim by virtue of being human beings, in an organized society. As with other subsidies for societal purposes, society at large (the federal treasury) should provide a supplement adequate

---

[49] 29 C.F.R. § 524.2(a) (1973).
[50] 29 U.S.C. § 214(d)(1) (1970).
[51] *Id.*
[52] S. REP. No. 1487, 89th Cong., 2d Sess. 23 (1966). The conference report described a somewhat revised version, but did not describe the purpose of the provision or the reasons for its revision. H. R. REP. No. 2004, 89th Cong., 2d Sess. (1966). Regulations governing "Application for a certificate" do not call for the information the administrator would need to make the determination based upon the policies described. 29 C.F.R. § 524.3 (1973). It does require a statement of the disability and the employer's proposed rate guarantee. If the administrator acts on these alone, it is the employer who makes the determination, a device which provides but dubious protection. Moreover, in some circumstances the products of the handicapped and the retarded are superior in quality to those of nonimpaired persons who lack their patience. It is both inaccurate and unfair to assume that the handicapped and retarded invariably produce inferior wares.

to bring wages up to the minimum. Whether the "unearned increment" paid out periodically as needed would be adequate for the needs of mentally retarded citizens cannot now be determined. It would, however, take this society part of the way toward providing adequate income and employment — how far remains to be seen.

Whether this formula properly applies to institutionalized and sheltered workshop employees presents special issues. In both instances the handicapped receive the benefits of facilities whose operation require substantial expenditure not covered by receipts. It is worth repeating that frequently the low productivity stems from inferior equipment or industrial practices, rather than inferior capability. The discussion here assumes that in some situations lower productivity may remain after adequate capital and program are provided.

One cannot blink at the fact that such facilities commonly receive insufficient funds and so, arguably, need the cheap labor of their clients to survive. This factor requires at least two observations. First, it must be recognized as a basic fact of life that the general populace regards the handicapped with considerable aversion. Moreover, "normal" individuals tend to desire a greater social distance between themselves and those with brain impairments than those with illness or physical disablement.[53] Understanding this phenomenon and overcoming it stand as towering preconditions of effective amelioration of the lot of the handicapped and especially of the mentally retarded. The problems have tangled psychological roots not readily amenable to reasoned discourse, but a new value system declaring that all human beings have substantial and irreducible rights as members of society may move this society toward the goal of understanding its uneasiness and overcoming it. Such efforts should have high priority. As long as the mentally retarded are shunned and regarded as subhuman, entitled only to a subminimum wage, few if any programs on their behalf can be adequate.

Public characterization of mental retardation will affect priorities assigned to dealing with the hardships of retardation. When the public recognizes that the way economic society operates causes a great proportion of the malnutrition and the insufficiency of medical care among the poor which in turn cause a large proportion of retardation, public responsibility may more readily be undertaken.

Although there are varying opinions as to who ought to bear the costs of institutions, the public pays the most extensive and costly ones — public schools. They benefit not only schoolchildren and their immediate families, but the community at large as well. They prepare the young to fill their roles in society, roles that are to be as productive as possible. In democratic theory at least (but certainly not in practice) public education must be equally available, through high school at the minimum, to all individuals regardless of variations in ability. This educational obligation toward the retarded is increasingly recognized, if not fully acted upon.[54] Although residential

---

[53] In a ranking of desired "social distance" among 20 conditions, test groups consistently placed mental retardation 19th, just behind the desired association with ex-convicts (18th); cerebral palsy also showed low acceptability, ranking 13th and 15th. Tringo, *The Hierarchy of Preference Toward Disability Groups,* 4 J. SPECIAL EDUC. 295 (1970).

[54] *See* Herr, pp. 252-64, Chapter 9 of this volume.

institutions and sheltered workshops are not the same as schools, it can be argued that their purposes are similar: maximization of an individual's utility to himself and the community and shaping of the individual to the society's basic standards.

CONCLUSION

These arguments move, rather hesitantly but steadily, toward the view that blameless physical or mental disability warrants community help. The rather spontaneous way in which the Senate added kidney treatment for all to the Medicare program evidences a widely shared community value, just as the Prouty amendment in the 1960s registered the commonly held view that old people without public pension income ought to receive some income at general public expense.

Increasingly, this society is coming to regard illness and physical misfortune as risks that are publicly insurable if private means prove inadequate. By these emerging standards institutional care and services are not chargeable to the blameless recipients. And if they are so chargeable in part, it would seem worth the cost to pay the working person the income "earned" by being a member of society and then taking payment from him for part of the value of the facility's service to him. The paying customer has more standing in everyone's eyes, especially his own, than the recipient of charity.

One can hope for the most widespread success for experiments in training institutionalized retarded citizens for self-sustaining community living, either alone or in groups. Full compensation on the scale argued for in this paper can only contribute to such efforts. If successful, this proposed approach probably will prove cheaper than most present institutional arrangements. Adequate compensation, then, constitutes part of the effort toward enabling the mentally retarded to use their full capabilities. Everyone would benefit.

Reaction Comment

MILTON W. FERRIS

THE RIGHT of retarded citizens to adequate income and employment has been well expressed by the United Nations' Declaration on the Rights of Mentally Retarded Persons: "The mentally retarded person has a right to economic security and to a decent standard of living. He has a right to perform productive work or to engage in any other meaningful occupation. . . ."[1] Whether this right remains a platitude or

---

[1] United Nations Declaration on the Rights of Mentally Retarded Persons, G.A. Res. 2856 Art. 3, 26 U.N. GAOR Supp. 29, at 93, U.N. Doc. A/8429 (1971).

becomes a reality will depend on whether or not attorneys join the fight on behalf of retarded citizens.

Bernstein advances several worthy approaches to the acquisition of economic security and a decent standard of living for the retarded citizen. His reference to the tort system suggests that many retarded citizens should be able to recover for the damages suffered through many years of neglectful and wrongful acts and omissions on the part of those responsible for their care and rehabilitation. It would not be difficult to prove that these acts of negligence have grossly affected retarded citizens' economic security and their right to a decent standard of living. Thousands of unemployed and unemployable retarded citizens are languishing in substandard living conditions in many public and private facilities, as well as in their own communities. They are living proof of the damage that is caused by the deprivation and misapplication of programs necessary for their public education, vocational education, and habilitation — all so necessary over and above the love and care which many have not received. The remedial effects of the popular class action suits are evident. Perhaps applying remedies of the tort system can also bring about improvements in the many programs and facilities that need a good jolt — where it is most effective — in the pocket book.

There are over 900 sheltered workshops, work activity centres, and similar vocational facilities in the United States with an average enrollment of 40 workers or clients per facility. Most of these 36,000 workers are engaged in quite similar work processes or operations, mainly hand sorting, hand assembling, hand packaging, foot press operation, and so on. The average pay rate is 40¢ per hour in work activity centers and 80¢ per hour in sheltered workshops.[2] In 20 years I have observed many retarded people working a steady 6 to 8-hour day to their fullest capability and producing good quality products in quantity. They are paid wage rates at special subminimum wage levels allowed by the United States Department of Labor.[3]

For over 40 years I have also observed nonretarded workers performing similar duties in private industry and government agencies. Many were not always working to their fullest capability or for a steady six to eight hours per day, nor were they producing greater quantity or quality than the retarded workers. This supports Bernstein's statement that similar work commands different pay in different industries; only the place of work is different — not the effort and certainly not the need. However, with nonretarded workers the minimum statutory wage rates were at least twice as high, and this minimum is often criticized as being too low.

The concept that a basic minimum wage is essential, regardless of productivity, has already been demonstrated by the proponents of the "guaranteed annual wage." Surely the right of retarded persons to perform productive work or to engage in any other meaningful occupation to the fullest possible extent of their capabilities should be readily accepted in a democratic society.

Before leaving the topic of the minimum wage and the expected decent standard of living, I would like to reinforce Bernstein's position further. The Fair Labor Stan-

[2]M. W. Ferris, NARC Survey for Sen. H. Humphrey, Dec. 10, 1971 (informal survey by the National Ass'n of Retarded Children Vocational Rehabilitation and Employment Comm.).
[3]Fair Labor Standards Act, 29 U.S.C. § 214(d) (1970).

dards Act establishes a minimum wage based presumably on that wage's ability to support a specified and acceptable standard of living. The rate set as the minimum wage for *nonhandicapped* workers is not determined by any benchmarks based on production or ability. Why then should the 5 million disabled,[4] including approximately 3 million mentally retarded, individuals who are in need of vocational rehabilitation, training, and employment have to endure special, lower minimum rates which are, in fact, established on the basis of special benchmark production levels in the profit-making sector of society?

This is extremely inequitable when we consider that these benchmark production levels are not truly comparable inasmuch as they have been achieved not by the private industry employee's ability to work faster or harder. On the contrary, they have been achieved through the advances made in tool design, processing techniques, and improved management skills. Perhaps lawyers can help interpret whether the special minimum wage for handicapped workers in rehabilitation facilities contradicts the right to perform productive work or to engage in any other meaningful occupation to the fullest extent of the retarded worker's capabilities.

Special minimum wages were established originally to help the mentally retarded and, especially, the sheltered workshops and work activity centers, which found it difficult to pay the regular minimum wage. Many will claim that under present circumstances, rehabilitation workshops and special on-the-job training programs have substantial and inherent expenditures for therapeutic and ancillary services which cannot and should not be covered by production receipts. Under existing conditions it is almost impossible for these types of rehabilitation facilities to pay the current regular minimum wage to clients/workers and also meet overhead costs.

Existing conditions, however, can and should be changed. The handicapped worker has little influence with regard to the decisions made to place him in training or employment situations or in sheltered work programs. He has no part in establishing the working conditions or his training and rehabilitation programs. As a result, many retarded workers are striving for a decent wage in job training programs and facilities that have not been improved or have not benefited by job simplification studies, technical tooling advances, job reengineering, quality control, or other advanced management techniques. It is significant that many of the skills to redress these imbalances lie with lawyers, especially those who specialize in labor law.

Bernstein indicates that in the seamen's program "the shipowner owes the seaman the duty to provide a seaworthy ship with equipment in proper order." The least other employers are expected to provide are good working conditions; this increases the worker's ability to increase the employer's profit, as well as his own income. This obligation should also be recognized in the search for employment opportunities for the retarded citizen. The operators or sponsors of vocational education facilities, work activity centers, and sheltered workshops, as well as employers involved in on-the-job training projects of the retarded, also should have the duty to provide an up-to-date facility with a realistic work atmosphere. They have an obligation to provide a crew of workshop technicians, directors, supervisors, and

---

[4] Vocational Rehabilitation Amendments of 1971, H.R. ˙8395 § 2(1), 92d Cong., 1st Sess. (1971).

administration and production personnel well experienced in the world of work and employment.

There is also reason to believe that many existing prevocational preparation and work training centers for the mentally retarded, at postschool level, do not achieve optimum results with their clients because they do not provide an environment that conveys to the trainees a positive feeling of their moving toward an adult status; moreover, the World Health Organization Committee on Mental Health, meeting in Geneva in 1967, felt, and this is the International Labor Office's experience, too, that work supervisors with experience in industry tend to be more successful in these situations than supervisors (teachers) who reflect a school atmosphere. In other words, a training center or sheltered workshop must try to simulate an industrial, rather than an educational or institutional, atmosphere and must as far as possible provide the conditions (hours of work, work procedures) usually found in normal industrial or commercial establishments.[5]

The sponsors and operators also have the duty to obtain and provide the type of work contracts, technical skills, and equipment that should profitably enhance the retarded worker's right to meaningful occupation, the right to economic security, and the right to a decent standard of living. The provisions of the Wagner-O'Day Act as amended in 1971,[6] the provisions of the Gude amendment of 1972 to the Small Business Investment Act,[7] and the little-known and even less frequently utilized provisions of the Vocational Rehabilitation Acts of 1968 and 1973[8] were enacted to improve rehabilitation and workshop facilities, employment opportunities, and the standard of living and wages for the retarded worker or trainee.

Given the choice, most retarded adolescents, adults, and their families would prefer to earn a decent wage and pay for necessary therapeutic and ancillary services, rather than continue their dependence on others.

Lawyers, while seeking to enforce existing laws, must persist in formulating new and beneficial laws designed to ensure the fullest possible level of independent living for mentally retarded citizens in this society.

Reaction Comment

DAVID CHAMBERS

BERNSTEIN'S PAPER advances no constitutional arguments for requiring the government to ensure economic security for retarded citizens. His omission is justifi-

[5] K. Kaplansky, Integrated and Sheltered Workshops for the Retarded, Oct. 1-6, 1972 (paper delivered at 5th International Congress on Mental Retardation, Montreal).
[6] 41 U.S.C. §§ 46-48(c) (Supp. I 1971).
[7] 15 U.S.C. § 636 (Supp. II 1972), *as amended* 15 U.S.C.A. § 636 (Supp. 1973).
[8] Vocational Rehabilitation Act of 1968, Pub. L. No. 90-391, §§ 7(a), (b), (d), 10, 82 Stat. 299; Rehabilitation Act of 1973, 29 U.S.C.A. §§ 701 *et seq.* (Supp. 1974) (originally enacted as Act of Sept. 26, 1973, Pub. L. No. 93-112, 87 Stat. 355, and repealed the Vocational Rehabilitation Act of 1968).

ed not merely by the alternative focus he has chosen, but also by the absence of any sound or vendible constitutional arguments to advance. There remain, however, important roles for attorneys.

THE MISSING CONSTITUTIONAL RIGHT TO MINIMUM SUBSISTENCE

With the magnanimity that a body without power can afford, the United Nations, in its Universal Declaration of Human Rights, has declared for individuals in all nations a right to a "standard of living adequate for . . . health and well-being" and a right "to work, to free choice of employment, and to just and favorable conditions of employment."[1] The United States has a Constitution with force but no comparable provisions. As originally adopted, the Constitution and Bill of Rights contained express protection for the economic interests of slaveholders and owners of other property but ignored the economic interests of others, mentally retarded or otherwise. Congress was authorized from the outset to "provide for the . . . general Welfare,"[2] but in 1789 few persons expected that Congress would distribute money or create job programs for persons in need and fewer yet would have believed that Congress had a constitutional obligation to do so.[3] Amendments adopted since the Civil War have ended slavery and authorized a graduated income tax, but have done little more for the economic interests of the citizen with modest income. The local governments and states within the United States assumed early on the function that England's Parliament had long imposed on its counties of providing relief for the worthy poor.[4] To date, however, no state court has held that its state constitution imposes an obligation on the legislature, enforceable by the courts, to guarantee a minimally decent standard of living or even an opportunity to work.

Despite the United States Constitution's silence, no great leap of imagination is required to devise arguments that either the state or federal government or both must ensure minimal levels of economic security to its citizens. It can, for example, be argued that ensuring a minimal level of subsistence is essential to the enjoyment of other rights explicitly guaranteed by the Constitution, such as the exercise of religion or free speech, although there is a textual difficulty here since these enumerated rights are defined only in terms of a right to be free from interference with speech or religion, not in terms of an obligation to foster speech or religion. It also can be argued that Congress' power to provide for the general welfare has become an obligation to do so as it has taken over more and more of the functions formerly performed solely by states. Finally, it can be argued that the equal protection clause of the

---

[1] United Nations' Declaration of Human Rights §§ 23-25, G.A. Res. 217, U.N. Doc. A/810, at 71 (1948).
[2] U.S. CONST. art. I, § 8.
[3] *See* C. BEARD, AN ECONOMIC INTERPRETATION OF THE CONSTITUTION OF THE UNITED STATES (1923). *See also* R. BROWN, CHARLES BEARD AND THE CONSTITUTION (1956).
[4] D. ROTHMAN, THE DISCOVERY OF THE ASYLUM 3-29 (1971).

fourteenth amendment (and its counterpart in the due process clause of the fifth) creates a governmental obligation to ensure access to the important elements of survival so long as others in the society have such access.

So far as I can find, no litigant in any case argued before the United States Supreme Court has advanced these arguments, though they have been discussed in the legal literature.[5] Litigants may have avoided such arguments because they believed them specious. Given the ardor and commitment of attorneys in the welfare rights movement of the last decade, however, it is more likely that they resisted these arguments and used narrower ones because they realized that the Court would have rejected broader ones.

The Supreme Court is simply not ready to declare a right to economic security, in the form of either grants or jobs, for all Americans or even for retarded Americans. Attorneys raising issues bearing on access to minimum security have generally cast the issues under the equal protection clause as narrow claims that two groups, equally needy, are being accorded unequal treatment under some governmental benefit program. Even in this narrow setting, the Court's attitude toward the judiciary's role in ensuring economic security for persons with low incomes can best be described as ambivalent. In one of the most important equal protection cases, *Dandridge v. Williams*,[6] for example, the Court upheld Maryland welfare legislation that granted to large families a lesser portion of their needs than it granted to small families. Acknowledging that the legislation involved "the most basic needs of impoverished human beings," the Court nonetheless could find no constitutional basis for applying a different standard to cases involving subsistence from the one it applied in equal protection cases involving purely commercial regulations; the discrimination, to be upheld, must merely be rationally related to the service of any imaginable legitimate government purpose. According to the justices, "the intractable economic, social, and even philosophical problems presented by public welfare assistance programs are not the business of this Court."[7]

The Court has explicitly reaffirmed its position in *Dandridge* in more recent cases involving cash benefits and access to decent housing,[8] but it has not uniformly rejected equal protection claims involving access to economic security. Perhaps irritated by Congress' motives, the Court, in 1973, struck down the exclusion from eligibility for food stamps of groups that included any person not related to at least one other within the group ("hippie communes" were on Congress' mind). The Court labeled the exclusion utterly irrational, although it was in fact no more irrational than the legislation upheld in the Maryland case three years before.[9] On the same day in 1973, the Court invalidated another statutory exclusion from the food stamp program, spinning a novel, potentially far-reaching, rationale under the due process clause:[10]

[5] For parts of these arguments, see Michaelman, *On Protecting the Poor Through the Fourteenth Amendment*, 83 HARV. L. REV. 7 (1969); G. Vlastos, The Human Right to Economic Assistance, Aug. 1969 (unpublished paper presented at Estes Park, Colorado). For an attack on them see Winter, *Poverty, Economic Equality and the Equal Protection Clause*, 1972 SUP. CT. REV. 41.
[6] 397 U.S. 471 (1970).
[7] *Id.* at 487.
[8] Jefferson v. Hackney, 406 U.S. 535 (1972); James v. Valtierra, 402 U.S. 137 (1971).
[9] United States Dep't of Agriculture v. Moreno, 413 U.S. 528 (1973).
[10] United States Dep't of Agriculture v. Murry, 413 U.S. 508 (1973). The exclusion is found in 7 U.S.C.A. § 2014 (b) (Supp. 1973).

The exclusion of the group (any household which includes a person eighteen or older who is claimed as a dependent by someone not a member of that household) was said to create a conclusive presumption that the members were not in need, without providing individuals within the group a chance to prove that they were indeed needy. Again, the case could just as easily have been analyzed under the equal protection clause and an opposite result reached under *Dandridge* (that is, even though the exclusion denied aid to some who were needy, it was a rational rough-and-ready tool for identifying many who were not.[11]

These recent decisions may indicate a reversal of field for the Court and foreshadow a period in which the Court will force more equitable distribution of government benefits. I doubt it, however. The Court's inconsistent concern for compelling equal treatment within programs that governments have already created hardly presages an era in which courts will try to force governments to create new benefits or opportunities where no program currently exists for anyone.

Why has the Court taken this constricted stand? It cannot be due alone to the absence of specific propelling language in the Constitution itself, for the Court has frequently found constitutional interests without explicit language. Consider, for example, the Burger Court's decisions regarding abortions or regarding denials of rights to aliens.[12] It appears that the Court's refusal to act is based in part on the fact that some justices lack genuine concern for the indignities suffered by persons of low income.[13]

For all the justices, whatever their level of concern, reluctance to act is probably reinforced by their perception, a perception that should give pause even to the most aggressive judicial activist, that no single judicial decision or group of decisions can resolve the issues. The justices can, with a flick of their robes, eliminate formal barriers to abortion or employment by aliens, but a direct holding, however unlikely, that all persons are entitled as of right to sufficient income or resources to subsist would place courts in an unwinnable struggle to force appropriations by state legislatures and Congress (and into the middle of struggles between the legislatures and the Congress). It would also require a constitutionalized and presumably organic definition of subsistence, a notion that would, if the line were drawn above the point of preventing literal starvation, involve as subjective a judgment as obscenity. Even a limited holding according added weight to the individual's interest in subsistence in equal protection cases would force the courts into repeated assessments of the acceptability of the justifications states would offer for restrictions and into the thicket of alternative mechanisms governments may claim to be using to achieve rough equality — tax laws, cash grants, in-kind programs, employment placement programs.[14]

[11] *Id.* at 522 (Rehnquist, J., dissenting).

[12] Roe v. Wade, 410 U.S. 113 (1973) (abortion); Graham v. Richardson, 403 U.S. 365 (1971) (aliens).

[13] For the prime example of insensitivity to the dignity of poor persons, see the Court's opinion in the case permitting the states to condition receipt of welfare benefits on recipient's willingness to permit visits into their homes to inspect for eligibility and for need for services. The Court there revived the old view of welfare as charity. Wyman v. James, 400 U.S. 309 (1971).

[14] For an example of a social scientist who advocates an employment strategy, see Packer, *Employment Guarantees Should Replace the Welfare System,* CHALLENGE, at 21 March-April 1974. The National Welfare Rights Organization has, on the other hand, consistently advocated a cash strategy for almost all support except for medical care. For a general review of strategies, see Jencks,

Thus, although neither prior case law nor the language of the Constitution compels or precludes the Court's finding a constitutionally based right to subsistence, courts probably would be wise to avoid declaring such a right until the time comes when they can draw upon a view widely accepted by the public of a specific approach to the elimination of gross inequalities of income. A struggle with legislatures today to force vindication of the right ("All right, Congress, we enjoin further expenditures on the National Guard until you provide for persons of low income") would certainly fail and would possibly erode the Court's powers in a variety of other areas. The foreseeability of a debilitating struggle thus not only makes the Court's reluctance understandable, it also probably vindicates it. The fact, however, that courts are ill-equipped to compel the assurance of adequate income should be viewed as redoubling Congress' duty to provide assurance — not as releasing Congress from any obligation to concern itself.

MORE PROMISING ROLES FOR COURTS AND LAWYERS IN ADVANCING THE ECONOMIC INTERESTS OF MENTALLY RETARDED CITIZENS

Even though economic security for America's retarded citizens is quite unlikely to be corrected through broad constitutional litigation, there remains much for attorneys to do. First, within a narrowly limited range, courts may be ready to use the Constitution to invalidate some state practices affecting the economic interests of the retarded. They may, for example, use the Constitution to put an end to forced uncompensated labor by residents of institutions.[15] They may aid long-term economic security of retarded persons through favorable holdings in right to education cases and in cases seeking to improve the quality of life at custodial institutions and to block unnecessary commitments to them.[16] They may also, if mental retardation is eventually held to be a suspect classification in equal protection cases, invalidate economic legislation openly discriminating against retarded persons as a named class.[17] These possible court actions are discussed elsewhere in this volume and some are already being pursued by attorneys.

Other actions lawyers might take turn largely on the degree of retardation of the person or persons being represented. The problems of economic security for the borderline or mildly retarded citizen who holds a job in the regular economy are likely to be the same as those of millions of other low-income Americans: The

---

The Poverty of Welfare: Alternative Approaches to Income Maintenance, 1 WORKING PAPERS FOR A NEW SOCIETY, Winter 1974, at 5.
PAPERS FOR A NEW SOCIETY, Winter 1974, at 5.

[15] Souder v. Brennan, 367 F. Supp. 808 (D.D.C. 1973). *See also* Friedman, Chapter 18 of this volume.

[16] *See* in this volume Herr, Chapter 9; Halpern, Chapter 13; Strauss, Chapter 15.

[17] *See* in this volume Gilhool, Chapter 7; Burt, Chapter 14. One discrimination that may or may not be benign is the provision of the minimum wage legislation that permits a lower minimum to be set for retarded persons. 29 U.S.C. § 214(d) (1970).

retarded person often works full time, year-round and still does not earn enough to sustain himself and his family at a decent income level. Take out a pencil and paper yourself and add up what you would consider the cost of a decent minimum level of subsistence for an urban family of four for a year. Include housing, utilities, food, transportation, clothing, entertainment, and so forth. (You may find it easier perhaps to break costs down by the week or month.) Have you jotted down your figures? Most persons who work out such a minimum budget arrive at a figure of at least $6,000, not including provision for taxes.[18] Now recall that a family head working full time at $2.20 per hour (which is the current minimum wage), will earn only $4,400 in a year. Many working borderline retarded persons earn substantially less. As it does for other poor Americans, the current federal public assistance system provides no cash benefits to retarded individuals unless they are totally disabled or part of a needy family unit including children and only one parent.[19] The single retarded person not totally disabled but not earning enough to sustain himself at a decent level can receive no federal funds. He may receive food stamps and, in some states, Medicaid benefits, but these often fail to erase his income deficit.

The lawyer's principal arena in seeking redress of these income imbalances will be the Congress. Bernstein has set forth some of the principal reasons why this nation, through its legislatures, should ensure an adequate level of income for all persons who work, without regard to what price their labor can command on the open market. His arguments are not of the sort that courts are likely to translate into constitutional doctrine. They are broad moral judgments that lawyers and others will need to prod Congress to act upon.

Until Congress acts, attorneys will be needed to secure the statutory benefits already available to lower income mentally retarded persons which state and federal agencies refuse to advertise and to secure procedural protections that the states begrudgingly extend.[20] The problem of inadequate awareness of available rights is acute for all persons of low incomes, but special efforts by lawyers tailored to inform retarded persons are probably called for.[21]

For the mentally retarded person who lives in the community, but who can work only in a sheltered setting, the lawyer's tasks will be compounded by further legal problems, some of which will be more traditional. Ferris, in his reaction comment, has outlined some of the problems encountered by persons working in special workshops. Lawyers can, for example, help draft articles of incorporation and grant applications, try to influence the development of regulations (or, if necessary, legislation) to shift the model of the workshop from a treatment center headed by a mental retardation specialist to a business venture headed by businessmen, and generally serve as legal advisers to a very specialized commercial enterprise.

[18]For a summary of surveys of public opinion on the income needed to "make do," see Rainwater, *Economic Inequality: A Proposal,* 1 WORKING PAPERS FOR A NEW SOCIETY, Spring 1973, at 50.

[19]42 U.S.C. §§ 606(a) & 1381 (1970).

[20]*See, e.g.,* Bell & Norvel, *Texas Welfare Appeals: The Hidden Rights,* 46 TEXAS L. REV. 223, 245 (1967).

[21]A particularly useful, if somewhat dated, publication is U.S. DEP'T OF HEALTH, EDUCATION & WELFARE, PUB. NO. (OS) 72-26 MENTAL RETARDATION FINANCIAL ASSISTANCE PROGRAMS OF THE DEPARTMENT OF HEALTH, EDUCATION, AND WELFARE (1971).

Lawyers also need to reach out and get to know well the mentally retarded population they are serving and the people who are already serving them. The latter group should include established business organizations like the chambers of commerce, the Small Business Administration, and labor unions.

For the retarded person who lives in the community but cannot obtain full employment, some public assistance benefits may be currently available. This citizen's economic security is likely to turn not merely on the extent of available cash assistance, but increasingly important as the level of retardation becomes more profound, on the quality of "in-kind income" available to him: housing, guardianship services, counseling services, and so forth. The lawyer's work in ensuring economic security thus shifts to the effort to secure adequate services, humanely provided, to persons who need them. The shift will be nearly total for attorneys working with individuals who live year-round in residential treatment centres and require long-term care and custody. For many of these persons, in-kind services will wholly replace earned or granted cash benefits as the basis for their material security, and arguments based on the right to habilitation or the right to be free of injurious treatment will be arguments for economic security in transmuted form.

We are in controversial territory when discussing economic security for severely and profoundly retarded persons, no matter where they live. For many of them, true security in the sense of reliable lasting freedom from the high probability of privation may be possible only at the cost of denying them all power to make important decisions for themselves. Such denial of free choice will also extend to many retarded persons living in the community with guardians. Disguised in the form of questions of fact about an individual's capacities will be questions of value about the right of individuals, if they wish, to make choices for themselves even when their choices may be viewed as grossly unwise by some external criteria. Economic security, like poverty, is best viewed as a relative concept. It is a nonabsolute measure of the overall quality of a person's material life through time, as viewed either by the person himself or by someone else making political judgments about its quality. It is not merely the sum of the calories poured into his body and the watertightness of the roof over his head.

Some retarded persons will feel secure only if they know that others will take care of them always. Others will feel secure only if permitted power to make some choices. Where choice is at issue, traditional civil liberties issues discussed elsewhere in this volume become important.

The civil liberties aspects of economic well-being are important. The point in this brief discussion is that for the increasing numbers of retarded persons who work in the free economy, these and other constitutional issues will be of far less importance than the gross disparity of incomes between the richest and poorest Americans, a disparity which the courts, even with the vaunted equal protection clause, will not reduce. Where the economic problems of mentally retarded citizens are different from those of low-income persons generally, they will still rarely be of constitutional dimensions. Lawyers who want to help need to get to know well those professionals like Milton Ferris who need legal help.

CHAPTER 11

Zoning Restrictions and the Right to Live in the Community

The nineteenth century movement which produced large, remote, secure institutions for mentally retarded people also produced land use control. Although the connection may not be obvious, one of the more subtle points of this chapter is that these two massive edifices of the law resemble one another. The instincts which call for pleasant places to live in also call for the exclusion of threatening and dissimilar people from one's pleasant neighborhood. The resemblance sets one thinking about institutions for retarded people, of course, and also about prisons, mental hospitals, juvenile homes, and ghettos.

Chandler and Ross, both vigorous, no-nonsense, law reform lawyers, analyze here an incredible welter of constitutional clauses, statutes, state and local administrative regulations, municipal ordinances, and judicial orders and opinions. They do it clearly and with single-minded intensity, concluding their essay (as one might expect of advocates) with a number of practical suggestions for lawyers and others who represent residential care operators and retarded citizens before local zoning authorities.

Opposition to small residential care facilities comes from the potential neighbors of these clients. The reaction comment by Deutch, a chemist speaking here as an objecting neighbor, presents the viewpoint of one who has been faced with the establishment of a group home in a single-family residential district. Deutch argues for recognition of the "costs" imposed upon neighbors by the establishment of group homes and for a consensus, rather than an advocacy approach to the problem.

Simmons also pursues the "social cost" analysis, but from a comparative view of general theories of such costs. He urges the recognition that group homes for mentally retarded citizens are distinguishable from ordinary single-family residences and probably from other congregate living arrangements as well. Simmons argues that an analysis of the distinguishing characteristics would further both policy making and advocacy.

PRINCIPAL PAPER

JO ANN CHANDLER AND STERLING ROSS, JR.

The Kallikak family presents a natural experiment in heredity. A young man of good family becomes through two different women the ancestor of two lines of descendants — the one characterized by thoroughly good, respectable, normal citizenship, with almost no exceptions; the other being equally characterized by mental defect in every generation. . . .

We find on the good side of the family prominent people in all walks of life and nearly all of the 496 descendants owners of land or proprietors. On the bad side we find paupers, criminals, prostitutes, drunkards, and examples of all forms of social pest with which modern society is burdened.

From this we conclude that feeble-mindedness is largely responsible for these social sores.

Feeble-mindedness is hereditary and transmitted as surely as any other character. We cannot successfully cope with these conditions until we recognize feeble-mindedness and its hereditary nature, recognize it early, and take care of it.

In considering the question of care, segregation through colonization seems in the present state of our knowledge to be the ideal and perfectly satisfactory method. (*Henry Goddard,* 1912)[1]

Today, of course, we know that most retarded adults make an adequate adjustment in the community, and that they are more likely to be the victims rather than the perpetrators of social injustice. It is also widely accepted that heredity is a relatively insignificant factor in the causation of retardation, as compared to maternal health and socio-cultural factors. (Wolf Wolfensberger, 1969)[2]

---

[1] H. Goddard, The Kallikak Family 116-117 (1912).
[2] Wolfensberger, *The Origin and Nature of Our Institutional Models,* in Changing Patterns in Residential Services for the Mentally Retarded 59, 129 (R. Kugel & W. Wolfensberger eds. 1969).

THE BACKGROUND OF CHANGING ATTITUDES
AND POLICIES

With the relatively recent acquisition of increased medical and behavioral knowledge about the condition of mental retardation, traditional theories are being eroded rapidly. In their place new models of care and treatment are being developed. Goddard represented the professional sentiment of his time. Between 1900 and 1915 the mentally retarded were the object of the most vituperative attacks:

> It has been truly said that feeble-mindedness is the mother of crime, pauperism and degeneracy. [3]

> For many generations we have recognized and pitied the idiot. Of late we have recognized a higher type of defective, the moron, and have discovered that he is a menace to society and civilization; that he is responsible to a large degree for many, if not all, of our social problems. [4]

> I do not think that, to prevent the propagation of this class it is necessary to kill them off or to resort to the knife; but, if it is necessary, it should be done. [5]

The authors of each of these invectives, including Dr. Goddard, had been, or became, presidents of what is now the American Association on Mental Deficiency. [6]

Though such verbal abuse decreased in the 1920s, large-scale institutional congregate care, offering only custodial supervision, was established as the prevailing approach to residential services for the mentally retarded. Many of this nation's large state hospitals for the mentally retarded were constructed in the years following World War I. It was not until the 1960s that the institutional theory of residential services was broadly challenged. In 1967 Blatt and Kaplan exposed, by photograph and narrative, the brutal reality of institutional "back wards." [7] Bengt Nirje, from Sweden, visited United States institutions for the retarded in 1969 and observed:

> They represent a self-defeating system with shockingly dehumanizing effects. Here, hunger for experiences is left unstilled; here, poverty in the life conditions is sustained; here a cultural deprivation is created — with the taxpayers' money, with the concurrence of the medical profession, by the decisions of the responsible political bodies of society. [8]

---

[3] *Id.* at 104 (*quoting* a statement by W.E. Fernald made in 1915).

[4] *Id.* at 102-03, *quoting from* Goddard, in PROCEEDINGS OF THE NATIONAL CONFERENCE ON CHARITIES & CORRECTION 307 (1915).

[5] *Id.* at 106, *quoting from* Johnson, in PROCEEDINGS OF THE NATIONAL CONFERENCE ON CHARITIES & CORRECTION 410-11 (1901).

[6] *Id.* at 105.

[7] B. BLATT & F. KAPLAN, CHRISTMAS IN PURGATORY (1967).

[8] Nirje, *A Scandinavian Visitor Looks at U.S. Institutions*, in CHANGING PATTERNS IN RESIDENTIAL SERVICES FOR THE MENTALLY RETARDED 51, 56 (R. Kugel & W. Wolfensberger eds. 1969).

The most important contribution of the Scandinavian influence has been Nirje's concept of "normalization."[9] The normalization principle "means making available to the mentally retarded patterns and conditions of everyday life which are as close as possible to the norms and patterns of the mainstream of society."[10] Translated into residential services, normalization prescribes the development of small-group homes which provide residents with as near a family environment as possible. Dybwad refines the normalization principle into the essential components of integration, dispersal, specialization, and continuity. Integration is the absorption of the retarded into the community; dispersal is the uniform distribution of residential facilities throughout the community; specialization is the limitation on the types of residents served in a certain facility and the services offered that resident; and continuity enables the handicapped individual to receive a broad range of specialized services and available care.[11]

As the maintenance of large-scale institutions comes under increasing legal, philosophical, and political attack, states are turning to foster or group homes for residential care of the handicapped. A foster or group home will generally house a small number of handicapped residents and be licensed by the state in categories which turn on the number of residents and the types of handicaps they possess. The operator of a licensed foster or group home for the handicapped is usually a private person who owns or leases a house and is paid by a state agency for the room and board provided. Treatment is usually not one of the services provided by the operator or the facility; treatment occurs off the premises or is provided by a specialist who comes into the home.

This new approach requires a flexible dispersal of foster homes for the mentally handicapped in geographic areas most conducive to normalization. Many cities and counties throughout the nation are attempting to prohibit dispersal. In most instances this prohibition assumes the form of exclusion of foster or group homes from residential zones. The problem faced by concerned citizens and interested attorneys is how to facilitate flexible placement. The issue is how to overcome discriminatory exclusion of family care homes for the mentally retarded from residential zones and particularly from single-family residential zones.

STATE TRANSFER TO THE PRIVATE SECTOR OF THE RESPONSIBILITIES FOR THE MAINTENANCE OF RESIDENTIAL SERVICES FOR THE RETARDED: THE CALIFORNIA SITUATION

In the same year that Nirje introduced his principle of "normalization" to this country, 1969, California enacted the Lanterman Mental Retardation Services Act. The major thrust of the law was to create a statewide system of regional centers.[12]

---

[9] *Id.* at 181-85.

[10] *Id.* at 181.

[11] Dybwad, *Action Implications, U.S.A. Today*, in CHANGING PATTERNS IN RESIDENTIAL SERVICES FOR THE MENTALLY RETARDED 383, 385-89 (R. Kugel & W. Wolfensberger eds. 1969).

[12] CAL. HEALTH AND SAFETY CODE § 38100 *et seq.* (West Supp. 1973).

A regional center is a private nonprofit corporation receiving state money for the purpose of evaluating a mentally retarded person and then placing him in an environment appropriate to his handicap. The regional center provides no services except evaluation and counseling. Program services are purchased by the regional center from private and public vendors. In this way, the regional center may favor the development of community programs it determines most beneficial. In addition, the center retains the freedom to revoke an individual placement if the services prove unsatisfactory. The center can therefore remain a continuing advocate for the retarded person. Because the regional center is run by a private board of directors and is directly responsible to a planning body of private individuals, private citizens determine the kind and quality of services which retarded individuals receive.

Admissions to state hospitals are through regional centers and are on a voluntary basis.[13] Judicial commitment of mentally retarded persons to state hospitals still exists if the person is "a danger to himself or others,"[14] but this form of commitment has greatly decreased in use since 1969. Regional centers will admit a person to a state hospital only if there is no satisfactory alternative. Most residential placements by regional centers are into foster care or "family care" homes licensed by the California Department of Social Welfare or the Department of Mental Hygiene.

Among the residential facilities licensed by the California Department of Mental Hygiene is the following:

> *Family Home (Mentally Retarded).*   "Family Home (Mentally Retarded)" is a facility intended solely for the admission of not more than six (6) mentally retarded patients who are provided with a program of services and protective supervision in a home setting.[15]

Though the definition indicates that a program is provided as a part of residential care, the fact is that licensees need no prior training or experience with the mentally retarded nor do they receive any instruction in mental retardation after licensing. Their function is solely to provide room and board. Nevertheless, an orientation and some training in mental retardation is seen as a very desirable factor in the licensees.

Regulations require "written zoning clearance or other satisfactory evidence of proper zoning" as a condition of department of mental hygiene licensing.[16] Restrictive zoning may make acquisition of a license impossible.

[13] *Id.* § 38150 (West Supp. 1973).
[14] *Id.* § 38002 (West Supp. 1973).
[15] 9 CAL. ADMIN. CODE § 29. Effective July 1, 1973, the licensing functions of the California Department of Mental Hygiene and Department of Social Welfare were consolidated into the Facilities Licensing and Certification Section of the new California Department of Health. CAL. HEALTH AND SAFETY CODE §§ 1250 *et seq.* (West Supp. 1973). Pursuant to this legislative reorganization, regulations are presently being promulgated to create a single licensing category for the small-group residential facility serving six or fewer handicapped persons.
[16] 9 CAL. ADMIN. CODE § 40(k). A proposed amendment to 9 CAL. ADMIN. CODE § 40(k) would eliminate the requirement of obtaining zoning clearance for "facilities serving six or fewer persons in a family care home located in an area zoned for a residential use." Approved for filing by California secretary of state, April 3, 1973. The amendment would eliminate the burden on the family home operator and at least shift the onus of going forward and trying to establish a zoning violation to the municipality.

The California State Department of Social Welfare also licenses family care homes under the following administrative definition:

> *Family Residential Care Home.*   A family residence in which room, board, and non-medical personal care services including supervision of and assistance with dressing, eating, personal hygiene, daily activity, health maintenance, transportation and protective safeguards for one to six adults are provided as needed.[17]

Though there is no explicit requirement that zoning clearance be obtained as a condition to department of social welfare licensure, compliance with local health and fire regulations is required. Local sanitation and fire officials often discover that zoning clearance has not been obtained. The planning commission is then promptly notified and compliance with the zoning ordinance is demanded.

Behind the legal framework for community placement of the mentally retarded is a philosophy of normalization in residential services. A report by the Assembly Ways and Means Subcommittee on Mental Health Services in 1965 found that community-located service alternatives to state hospital care were both necessary and desirable.[18] In 1969 there were 13,000 residents in California's state hospitals for the retarded; in 1973 there were 10,000. Increasing discharges and fewer hospital admissions because of the implementation of the Lanterman Act are the reasons for the significant decrease in resident population.

In 1971 legislation was passed to give the adult mentally retarded resident of a state hospital the right to a habeas corpus hearing on his request to leave the hospital. After an evidentiary hearing, the judge may discharge the petitioner if the petitioner is found not mentally retarded or, if found retarded, if the petitioner is found no longer in need of hospitalization and appropriate facilities exist in the community for his care. It is still too early to determine if this law will have a measurable impact on the hospital discharge rate. The potential for its broad application toward this end is apparent.

The changing face of residential services for the mentally retarded in California depends on the transfer to the private sector of the responsibility for the maintenance of residential facilities. By phasing out state hospitals in favor of private community-based foster care, the state avoids the costs of owning and operating large institutions. It has also tended to leave to private interests the burden of obtaining nondiscriminatory zoning ordinances, fire regulations, and health standards. The state should not espouse community integration of the mentally retarded and then abdicate its responsibility in attaining it. Later in this paper, an expanded role for governmental agencies in overcoming zoning barriers to normalization will be proposed.

---

[17] 22 CAL. ADMIN. CODE § 30011(a). *See* note 15 *supra.*

[18] Assembly Ways and Means Subcommittee on Mental Health Services, *A Redefinition of State Responsibility for California's Mentally Retarded,* vol. 21, no. 10, 1965 (Assembly of the State of California). *See also* Study Commission on Mental Retardation, *The Undeveloped Resource: A Plan for the Mentally Retarded of California* Jan. 1965 (a report to the governor and legislature, state of California).

ZONING OVERVIEW

Zoning is, in essence, the systematic regulation and control of the use and development of real property.[19] Modern zoning is the result of urbanization, industrialization, and population concentration. Traditional land use control devices, including zoning laws, are almost exclusively prospective and restrictive in concept. The word *zoning* emerges from the practice of dividing the municipality in question into various districts, or zones. Distinctions are made among parts of a city and the uses and restrictions that apply to each part. Zoning was at least initially calculated to enhance the general welfare through restrictions on the full exploitation of an owner's property. Zoning has sometimes had the additional effect of excluding certain groups of people, especially ethnic minorities and the poor, from particular residential areas.

The exercise of zoning authority has always been justified as an aspect of the police power. In *Village of Euclid v. Ambler Realty Co.,*[20] the Supreme Court of the United States said of the constitutionality of a comprehensive zoning plan: "The ordinance now under review, and all similar laws and regulations, must find their justification in some aspect of the police power, asserted for the public welfare."[21] The Supreme Court found that the use of zoning to implement planned development was consistent with the requirements of due process. Two years later, in *Nectow v. City of Cambridge,*[22] the Court reviewed and declared unconstitutional, under the due process standard, another zoning ordinance. Since 1928, however, the development of judicial interpretation and restriction upon zoning law has been left primarily to the states. Federal courts have only recently again begun deciding exclusionary zoning cases and applying federal constitutional standards. Every state has enabling legislation or constitutional provisions that grant to counties and cities, or to other political subdivisions, the power to zone for the general welfare. Most state statutes are patterned after the Standard State Zoning Enabling Act, which was published by an advisory committee of the Department of Commerce in 1926. The enabling statute delegates the power to zone and generally sets the minimum necessary requirements for zoning procedure. The state enabling statutes grant local units wide discretion; generally, the state statutes do not have clear substantive standards and require only that zoning ordinances prohibit things which are harmful to health, morals, safety, or welfare.

---

[19] One commentator has pointed out what he considers the four axioms of the legal theory of zoning. First, zoning is concerned with the control of private property; second, zoning is economic only in a negative sense and is primarily concerned with the traditional values of the police power: health, safety, and welfare of the community; third, zoning necessitates a balancing of private interest against an expanding concept of the public interest; and fourth, zoning is basically a negative construction of the concept of the public interest. Makielski, *Zoning: Legal Theory and Political Practice*, 45 J. Urb. L. 1, 14 (1967).

[20] 272 U.S. 365 (1926).

[21] *Id.* at 387.

[22] 277 U.S. 183 (1928).

One of the most perplexing and difficult problems for those seeking to understand or modify the relationship between zoning barriers and residential living for the mentally retarded is the extraordinary number of agencies that exercise zoning authority and the variation of restrictions which result from this division of authority. For instance, the Standard State Zoning Enabling Act names "legislative bodies of cities and incorporated villages" as the recipient of the power to zone. As a result of this delegation, more than 1,000 local units lay zoning rules in the Chicago area; approximately 1,400 units regulate the area surrounding New York City.

Provisions on zoning power in California illustrate the situation. The zoning power of counties and general law cities ordinarily comes from a state zoning law[23] which prescribes the procedure whereby entities shall enact, amend, or administer zoning laws. It also sets forth the substantive scope of zoning regulations permitted; this scope encompasses everything that may be regulated under current notions of zoning through the use of police power. Compared to the enabling legislation of other states, the California state zoning statute allows great flexibility to the localities. Although the California Constitution[24] provides that "a county or city may make and enforce within its limits all local, police, sanitary, and other ordinances and regulations not in conflict with general laws," the tendency has been to rely upon the state enabling act for the authority to zone, rather than upon the constitutional grant of home rule. This has been the tendency in most states.[25]

The state zoning law in California does not apply to a charter city unless adopted by the city.[26] Once a charter is framed and adopted by the city and approved by the state legislature, the city

> may make and enforce all ordinances and regulations in respect to municipal affairs, subject only to restrictions and limitations provided in their several charters and in respect to other matters they shall be subject to general laws. City charter... with respect to municipal affairs shall supersede all laws inconsistent therewith.[27]

Charter cities can adopt either their own zoning regulations and procedures or the procedures set forth in the state enabling statute.[28]

As a practical matter in California, it may not make much difference whether a city or country zones under charter, home rule power, or the state zoning law. No matter what the source of the power, no political subdivision has the authority to act in a matter of statewide concern unless there has been a specific delegation from the state, and in no event can a political subdivision zone in an unconstitutional manner. Nevertheless, since the source of zoning power may be significant in litigation that challenges a particular regulation as beyond the authority granted

[23] CAL. GOV'T CODE §§ 65800-65907 (West 1966).
[24] CAL. CONST. art. 11, § 7.
[25] D. MANDELKER, MANAGING OUR URBAN ENVIRONMENT 67 (1966).
[26] CAL. GOV'T CODE § 65803 (West 1966).
[27] CAL. CONST. art 11, § 5(a).
[28] The discussion of California zoning law derives substantially from D. HAGMAN, CALIFORNIA ZONING PRACTICE ch. 4 (1969) (Supp. Jan. 9, 1973).

to the political subdivision, a lawyer should always seek to identify the exact source of essential zoning power.

EXISTING ZONING BARRIERS

Ordinances or Administrative Interpretations That Exclude Foster or Group Homes for the Mentally Handicapped from Some or All Residential Zones

Residential zones are labeled according to the types of structures permitted within their bounds and the use to which these structures are put. In most Calfornia cities and counties an "R-l" notation indicates a single-family residential zone permitting one-family dwellings dedicated to residential use. [29] An "R-2" zone often denotes a a residential zone permitting two-family dwelling for "R-1" uses. "R-3," "R-4," and "R-5" zones frequently describe zones permitting apartment houses and multiple dwellings for "R-1" uses.

The most restrictive ordinances are those which define "family" as a housekeeping unit related by blood, marriage, or adoption; *e.g.,* "one or more persons each related to the other by blood (or adoption or marriage), together with such relatives' respective spouses, who are living together in a single-family dwelling and maintaining a common household." [30] Other ordinances limit "family" to a housekeeping unit of a limited number of unrelated persons; *e.g.,* "one person living alone, or two or more persons related by blood, marriage, or legal adoption, or *a group not exceeding four persons living as a single housekeeping unit.* " [31]

Foster or group homes licensed to serve the mentally handicapped are generally maintained by state funds. Municipal and county planning bodies frequently construe state licensing and support to designate the facility a business use of property for zoning purposes and limit such homes to commercial and industrial zones. In *Seaton v. Clifford,* [32] the court compared a family care home for the mentally retarded to a boarding house and held it to be a business use of property. Administra-

---

[29] *See* D. HAGMAN, *supra* note 28, at § 6.2 (1969). (Supp. Jan. 9, 1973) for a sample of a city zoning chart (Los Angeles) which depicts the various zones.

[30] City of Des Plaines v. Trottner, 34 Ill. 2d 432, 433, 216 N.E.2d 116, 117 (1966) (*quoting from* a Des Plaines ordinance). *See also* Marino v. Mayor & Council, 77 N.J. Super. 587, 187 A.2d 217 (1963); City of Newark v. Johnson, 70 N.J. Super. 381, 175 A.2d 500 (1961).

[31] Palo Alto Tenants Union v. Morgan, 321 F. Supp. 908, 909 (N.D. Cal. 1970) (emphasis supplied), *aff'd,* 487 F.2d 883 (9th Cir. 1973), *quoting from* PALO ALTO, CAL., MUNICIPAL CODE § 18.04.210. *See also* Anderman v. City of Chicago, 379 Ill. 236, 40 N.E.2d 51 (1942); Harmon v. City of Peoria, 373 Ill. 594, 27 N.E.2d 525 (1940); Robertson v. Western Baptist Hosp., 267 S.W.2d 395 (Ky. 1954).

The ordinances referred to in the following cases define "family" in terms of both consanguinity and unrelated persons constituting a housekeeping unit: Boraas v. Village of Belle Terre, 476 F.2d 806 (2d Cir. 1973), *rev'd,* 416 U.S. 1 (1974); Palo Alto Tenants Union v. Morgan, 321 F. Supp. 908 (N.D. Cal. 1970), *aff'd,* 487 F.2d 883 (9th Cir. 1973).

[32] 24 Cal. App. 3d 46, 100 Cal. Rptr. 779 (1972). *Seaton* was based upon a deed restriction limiting the property to residential uses. Restrictive covenants as a barrier to normalization are discussed in the concluding section of this paper.

tive bodies sometimes find that the mental condition of the residents indicates that a foster or group home is a use requiring medical supervision and should be limited to zones where municipal hospitals, nursing homes, or convalescent hospitals are permitted. The administrative interpretation challenged in *Defoe v. San Francisco City Planning Commission* [33] is of this type.

Ordinances That Grant Discretion to a Zoning Administrator or an Administrative Planning Body to Allow or Prohibit a Particular Use: The Special Exception or Conditional Use Permit

Most state zoning statutes provide for the existence of local variation in the kinds of uses which are permitted in a zone. An *exception* or *conditional use permit* is a grant of administrative permission for uses compatible with the prescribed zone, but which may be subject to regulation for the health and welfare of the residents.[34] Its purpose is to enable a municipality to exercise some measure of control over the extent of certain uses which "although desirable in limited number, could have a detrimental effect on the community in large numbers."[35] Names used in other jurisdictions are "special exception," "special permit," "land-use permit," and "unclassified use permit."[36]

Municipal ordinances often authorize the zoning administrator to impose conditions on certain uses of property as these are deemed necessary "to protect the public health, safety or welfare...."[37] If conditions do not satisfy the standard,

---

[33] 1 Civil No. 30789 (Dist. Ct. App. Cal., May 30, 1973). On May 30, 1973, the district court of appeal reversed and remanded the proceedings in *Defoe* to the superior court. The court stated that since significant new state legislation had been enacted after the decision of the superior court, the matter should be reconsidered in the light of the amended state statutes. The court noted that "It may well be that the amendments above discussed have eliminated any controversy between the parties as well as any need for injunctive relief." Slip opinion at 6. After the remand of the case to the superior court, the plaintiffs moved for summary judgment based on the state statutes which removed judgments about the location of foster and family care homes from the consideration of local zoning authorities. During the proceedings on the plaintiffs' motion, the city attorney conceded state law preempted the field, but indicated that no action contrary to the mandate of state law was presently being taken by any local zoning authorities. The plaintiffs argued that the mere existence of contrary local zoning ordinances was sufficient to justify a judicial declaration. The superior court refrained from acting, indicating that the plaintiffs should return to the judicial forum when, and if, activity of the local zoning authorities in contravention of the state statutes could be proven.

[34] D. HAGMAN, *supra* note 28, at 299 (1969).

[35] Van Sicklen v. Browne, 15 Cal. App. 3d 122, 126, 92 Cal. Rptr. 786, 788 (1971).

[36] *See* Gaylord, *Zoning: Variances, Exceptions and Conditional Use Permits in California,* 5 U.C.L.A. L. REV. 179 (1958). A variance is another method used to create local flexibility in land use planning. It differs from a conditional use permit in that

> An exception or conditional use permit is granted because that particular use, if subject to sufficient safeguards, is a compatible use in the zone, regardless of whether it is necessary to preserve the constitutional rights of the landowner. On the other hand, a variance is granted for a use even if it is compatible with the zone, because the zoning ordinance would otherwise create an unconstitutional hardship upon the property owner. The granting of a conditional use permit or exception permits a use contemplated by the zoning ordinance; a variance permits a use not contemplated by the ordinance except where necessary to avoid hardship. (*Id.* at 194.)

See also Mendelker, *Delegation of Power and Function in Zoning Administration,* 1963 WASH. U.L.Q. 60, 69-74.

[37] SANTA ANA, CAL., MUNICIPAL CODE § 9250.8(b) (1968).

the conditional use permit may be denied. The criteria for granting (or denying) a conditional use permit are generally based upon either a general welfare standard or a nuisance definition.[38] Though the criteria vary among cities and counties, they share a vagueness and generality which give great discretion to administrative bodies in passing on permit applications.

California municipal ordinances frequently provide that application for a conditional use permit must first be made to a planning administrator who recommends a disposition to the planning commission. When the planning commission receives the formal recommendation of the planning administrator, residents within a certain radius of the site of the proposed use are given an opportunity to appear and present objections to the application. In theory, the hearing provides the commission with the information to determine the limitations which necessarily must be imposed upon the use to achieve compliance with the ordinance standard. In reality, when the conditional use application of a prospective operator of a family care home for the mentally retarded is being examined, the hearing becomes an administrative reevaluation of the propriety of the use in the prescribed zone. That is, the hearing is not limited to gathering information about necessary conditions to be imposed upon the use, but asks whether the use is an appropriate one in the zone. In adopting the ordinance which prescribes the permitted zones for certain conditional uses, the legislative body has already made this determination. When it examines the propriety of the conditional use in the permitted zone, the planning commission in effect amends the ordinance and usurps a legislative function. It has been our experience that conditional use applications are denied because protesting residents express uneasiness about being near the mentally retarded. This discomfort is often couched in misconceived fears that the mentally retarded possess a high propensity for criminality, that they are oversexed, or that they are carriers of disease. Though these contentions are without support in scientific research or social experience, administrative bodies often use the general welfare standard to deny permit applications on these bases.

Appeal may be made from the planning commission to the city council, or to the board of zoning appeals, which acts as an administrative body. In California, the courts will not interfere with the denial of a conditional use permit "except upon a clear and convincing showing of fraud, illegality or abuse of discretion."[39] Only in one reported case in California has an abuse of discretion been found.[40] Judicial reluctance to review an administrative decision is partly attributable to the fact that by the time the matter is ripe for judicial review, it has already been examined at three administrative levels: the planning administrator, the planning commission, and the city council or board of appeals.

---

[38] GARDEN GROVE, CAL., MUNICIPAL CODE § 9214 (1971) is an example of the nuisance standard: "The characteristics of any such use shall not be unreasonably incompatible with the character of the City and its environs due to noise, dust, odors, or other undesirable characteristics."
[39] Gong v. City of Fremont, 250 Cal. App. 2d 568, 575, 58 Cal. Rptr. 664, 670 (1967).
[40] Gong v. City of Fremont, 250 Cal. App. 2d 568, 58 Cal. Rptr. 664 (1967).

JUDICIAL ATTACKS ON ZONING BARRIERS [41]

There is a number of procedural contexts in which a judicial challenge to the validity of a zoning ordinance or interpretation might arise. *First*, the judiciary could be asked to invalidate the restriction in a proceeding in which a property owner wished to devote his property to residential facility use or in which excluded retarded persons wished to secure satisfactory residential opportunities. The property owner would be the more conventional plaintiff and would probably seek a declaratory judgment that the designated use of his property would be valid or that the zoning restriction was invalid. He might also seek a writ of mandate from the court to direct a zoning official or board to issue an appropriate permit or zoning clearance. Although an action by mentally retarded citizens who were excluded from all community residential living because of the ordinance might not be directed at restrictions on a specific facility, individuals who had been assigned by a state agency to a particular residential facility could limit their challenge to that facility.

Second, challenge to the validity of the zoning restriction might occur when a property owner or operator of a group residence defended against an attempt by a local entity to impose a fine or other sanctions for violation of a zoning restriction. The restriction could also be challenged in defense against an action by neighboring property owners to enjoin a violation of the zoning ordinance.

There are certain fundamental points which should be kept in mind in any proceeding in which a zoning restriction is being challenged, whether one is taking the initiative or defending. An intriguing preliminary question is whether mentally retarded persons, standing alone, without the participation or intervention of property owners, have the requisite standing to challenge the validity of a local zoning ordinance. State courts have been reluctant to grant standing to excluded racial or economic groups to challenge zoning ordinance,[42] and these precedents may be difficult for mentally retarded individuals to overcome. It is difficult to imagine a situation, however, in which the intervention of some property owners (nonprofit organizations, for instance) who wish to devote their property to residential facility use cannot be obtained. The theoretical difficulty should be considered, nonetheless, and could influence the selection of plaintiffs and the decision of whether to seek relief in state or in federal court.

Another issue to be considered prior to seeking judicial relief is the effect of the doctrine of exhaustion of administrative remedies. The vagaries of this doctrine in any given jurisdiction may be considerable. For instance, some jurisdictions take the position that a person who seeks a permit or variance from an administrative body

---

[41] Litigation should always be viewed as the last resort in seeking to eliminate restrictive zoning and thus further normalization of residential living for the mentally retarded citizen. Litigation is a cumbersome, time-consuming, and risky undertaking. Not the least of its risks is the possibility that a courtroom victory will only increase neighborhood hostility, thereby eliminating, or substantially postponing, the real integration into the community which the litigation sought to accomplish.

[42] Comment, *Standing to Challenge Exclusionary Local Zoning Decisions: Restricted Access to State Courts and the Alternative Federal Forum,* 22 Syr. L. Rev. 598 (1971).

thereby admits the constitutionality of the underlying ordinance. The dangers posed by such an implied admission are clear. More fundamental, however, is the fact that many courts will not rule on a challenge to the application, or even on the validity, of a local ordinance unless all existing administrative remedies have been pursued. Exceptions to this doctrine are limited, and a party anticipating litigation would be well advised to evaluate and, in most cases, pursue administrative remedies.

Finally, it is imperative that litigants build a strong and detailed factual record in the court of first instance. The specific factual predicates will differ depending on the legal theory being utilized, yet these factual predicates must be fully analyzed prior to litigation and carefully laid in the lower court. The value of expert witnesses and commission reports cannot be overestimated.

Preemption of Local Zoning by State Statute

Let us assume that a state agency charged with the establishment and regulation of residential facilities for the mentally retarded wishes to issue a license (or certificate of authority to operate) to a facility in a residential district where a local zoning ordinance, if enforced, would preclude operation of the facility. It may be that the state statute on licensing residential facilities denies the authority of a political subdivision to interfere with the location of the facility through zoning regulation. In jurisdictions where political subdivisions of the state are still considered agents of the state which derive their authority from state delegation of power, the resolution of the conflict between the state statutes and the zoning ordinance is preordained. The state statute will prevail.

The potential problems arise in relation to home rule entities. Home rule, as a legal term, is usually understood as involving a grant of power to a local government to frame and adopt a charter of government, although occasionally it is employed also to refer to a direct constitutional grant of legislative power to local governments. More than half the states currently confer home rule powers upon at least some local governments, most frequently municipalities, but in some states counties as well. In approximately half of the states with home rule provisions, charter-making powers are conferred directly by the Constitution. Other states confer the power by statute, although generally in such states a constitutional provision authorizes legislative delegation of charter-making powers.

Those states operating under constitutional home rule are of particular concern here because of the tendency of such home rule provisions to contain a constitutional limitation upon the authority of the legislature to intervene in municipal affairs. For instance, the Colorado Constitution provides that home rule charters "and the ordinances made pursuant thereto in [local and municipal] matters shall supersede within the territorial limit and other jurisdiction of said city or town any law of the state in conflict therewith."[43] The California Constitution provides that "[C]ity charters . . . with respect to municipal affairs shall supersede all laws incon-

---

[43] COLO. CONST. art. 20, § 6.

sistent therewith."[44] Such constitutional texts, indicating an intention to limit state legislative power to interfere in the affairs of local government, exist in only a few states. They create an *explicit*, though ill-defined, area of municipal supremacy. Most constitutional home rule provisions require that local ordinances be consistent with the general laws of the state,[45] but courts in many of these states have nonetheless found an area of municipal autonomy and supremacy *implicit* in the constitutional provisions.[46]

The inquiry, in all constitutional home rule jurisdictions must be whether a state statute which precludes the operation of a local zoning ordinance invades the area of municipal affairs in violation of the state constitutional provision. If such a violation were found, the state statute would be void and the local ordinance could stand. The charter city of San Francisco raised, however inartfully, this claim in *Defoe v. San Francisco City Planning Commission.*[47] *Defoe* challenged a zoning restriction allowing only two mentally retarded children to live in state-licensed foster homes if the foster homes are located in R-1 R-1-D districts. The plaintiffs in *Defoe*, mentally retarded children and property owners who wished to operate foster homes in these districts, claimed that a state statute specifically precluded the use of local zoning ordinances to exclude foster homes from residential districts. The state statute relied upon provides in part: [A] state authorized, certified, or licensed family care, foster home, or group home serving six or fewer mentally disordered or otherwise handicapped persons shall be considered a residential use of property for the purposes of zoning. . . ."[48] San Francisco responded that the state statute cannot constitutionally regulate permitted zoning uses within a charter city. The California Constitution, San Francisco claimed, mandates that charter cities retain control over local municipal affairs, including zoning. The theory upon which the city relied is stated in *Cramer v. City of San Diego*: "A charter adopted [under the provisions of the California Constitution] is 'absolutely controlling and free from impairment by general law of the state, as to all "municipal affairs."'"[49] The court continued that insofar as the charter made provision relative to municipal affairs "'it is the supreme law, paramount to any law enacted by the State Legislature, and general laws enacted by the Legislature in regard thereto can have no application.'"[50]

The resolution of the *Defoe* issue depends upon whether the subject matter of

---

[44] CAL. CONST. art. 11, § 5(a). *See also* OHIO CONST. art. 18, § 3. In the Ohio Constitution, although "local police, sanitary and other similar regulations" enacted by home rule jurisdictions must not be in "conflict with general law," the grant of "all powers of local self government" is not restricted in the same way. There would thus appear to be an area of supremacy and independence from state legislative authority. *See* Simmons, *Home Rule and Exclusionary Zoning: An Impediment to Low and Moderate Income Housing*, 33 OHIO ST. L. J. 621 (1972).

[45] *See* MO. CONST. art. 6, § 19; OKLA. CONST. art 16, § 3(a).

[46] *See. e.g.,* Grant v. Kansas City, 431 S.W.2d 89 (Mo. 1968); State *ex rel.* Kansas City v. Lucas, 317 Mo. 255, 296 S.W. 781 (1927); Lee v. Norick, 447 P.2d 1015 (Okla. 1968).

[47] 1 Civil No. 30789 (Dist. Ct. App. Cal., May 30, 1973).

[48] CAL. WELF. & INST. CODE § 5116 (West 1972), *as amended* CAL. WELF. & INST. CODE § 5116 (West Supp. 1973).

[49] 164 Cal. App. 2d 168, 170-71, 330 P.2d 235, 237 (1958), *quoting from* Loop Lumber Co. v. Van Loben Sels, 173 Cal. 228, 232, 159 P. 600, 602 (1916).

[50] *Id.* at 171, 330 P.2d at 237-38 (1958), *quoting from* Loop Lumber Co. v. Van Loben Sels, 173 Cal. 228, 232, 159 P. 600, 602 (1916).

the state legislation is found to be exclusively within the realm of municipal affairs where the charter entity reigns supreme. San Francisco, and any other charter entity operating under a similar home rule provision, is essentially contending that, because zoning, at some time and in some circumstances, may be a municipal affair, a general state law which impinges on the exercise of zoning authority is unconstitutional. The critical phrase "municipal affairs" has been defined judicially in a flexible manner as "internal business affairs of the municipality."[51] The courts have also stated that nothing that is a matter of statewide concern can be a municipal affair.[52] Altered conditions of society can change what once was a municipal affair into a matter of general statewide concern.[53] Thirty years ago an authority could note that "the regulation of building and of the use of urban real estate is a phase of the police power which is of particular interest to cities and one which seems to be peculiarly local and intramural in operation and effect."[54] This view of urban land use policies would not be accepted today. The Supreme Court of California has given its solution to the problem by ruling that "general law prevails over local enactments of a chartered city, even in regard to matters which would otherwise be deemed to be strictly municipal affairs, where the *subject matter* of the general law is of statewide concern."[55] Whether the subject matter of the general law is of statewide concern, the court stated, must be determined from the legislative purpose of the state law in each individual instance.

As a general conclusion, it appears that very few matters outside the administrative and procedural aspects of local government have been held to be exclusively local or continually in the realm of municipal affairs. Examples of such procedural aspects are the conduct of municipal elections, the tenure of municipal officials, and the physical placement and removal of public buildings. The controlling inquiry is often said to be whether the matter under consideration has no effect on citizens of the state living outside the municipality whose charter and ordinances are involved.[56] If the legislature in our hypothetical jurisdiction has specifically precluded the operation of restrictive zoning ordinances concerning the location of residential facilities for the mentally retarded, it is likely that a litigant could show that the challenged local zoning ordinance did have an effect on citizens of the state living outside the municipality. A lawyer seeking to uphold the validity of the state legislation would have to demonstrate the interest of the state and the purpose of the statute; he could hope that there would be a declaration of intent included in the state legislation which would indicate the reasons for precluding local interference as to the location

[51] City of Walnut Creek v. Silveria, 47 Cal. 2d 804, 811, 306 P.2d 453, 456 (1957).

[52] *See, e.g.,* City of Pasadena v. Charleville, 215 Cal. 384, 10 P.2d 745 (1932); Horwith v. City of Fresno, 74 Cal. App. 2d 443, 168 P.2d 767 (1946).

[53] *See* Pacific Tel. & Tel. Co. v. City & County, 51 Cal. 2d 766, 771, 336 P.2d 514, 517 (1959); Hellmer v. Superior Court, 48 Cal. App. 140, 191 P. 1001 (1920).

[54] Sandalow, *The Limits of Municipal Power Under Home Rule: A Role for the Courts,* 48 MINN. L. REV. 643, 704 (1964).

[55] Professional Fire Fighters, Inc. v. City of Los Angeles, 60 Cal. 2d 276, 292, 384 P.2d 158, 168, 32 Cal. Rptr. 830, 840 (1953).

[56] It is impossible within the scope of this paper to begin to consider the variations of this problem which will emerge in different states. Even the California situation, despite several judicial pronouncements, is not susceptible of definitive conclusions. One observation is possible: the California courts are not sympathetic to claims of charter supremacy.

of group residences. Statements of past experience with exclusionary zoning, the necessity for dispersal and integration of group residences in all communities, the best interests of the mentally retarded in the state system designed for serving them may appear in legislative history, commission reports, or statements by legislators or administrators. Circumstantial evidence can be gained by statements from experts not involved in enacting or administering the legislation. Municipalities wth a less restrictive zoning ordinance might be willing to lend testimonial support to the state statute.

These considerations should be kept in mind by anyone litigating in constitutional home rule jurisdictions and by anyone proposing state legislation to preclude the interposition of zoning judgments by local municipalites.

Other difficulties arise if a state agency wishes to license a group residence prohibited by zoning ordinance, where there is a state statute arguably granting power to local entities to regulate the location of group residences. In this situation, the argument that state law preempts local power is not available.

The critical inquiry here might be whether the state licensing statute requires the express agreement of the local entity. In the *Defoe* case, San Francisco claimed local veto power. The city based its argument on a requirement in California's administrative regulations on licensing foster care homes; state regulations require that any person wishing to obtain a license for a foster home include in his license application a written zoning clearance or other satisfactory evidence of proper zoning.[57] The plaintiffs in *Defoe* argued that the requirement for a written zoning clearance is intended only to assure the licensing agency that the structure is in a residential district, as opposed to a commercial or industrial district. If such is not the interpretation given to a state regulatory provision such as California's, it appears likely that the local zoning restrictions will be enforceable, at least as to the location of residential facilities. Although a parallel exists in liquor licensing for municipal control over the location of state licensees,[58] there is nothing to gain from granting local municipalities this control over the location of residential facilities, and there is a great deal to lose. Even if it is desirable to grant political subdivisions some control over foster homes, this control should be something less than a veto power.

The final situation that might be faced by our hypothetical state agency is that the state has passed legislation dealing with the licensing and regulation of residences for the mentally retarded, but has not given an express indication of whether municipalties may also legislate in regard to the location of these facilities. This is the situation

---

[57] 9 CAL. ADMIN. CODE § 40(k).

[58] The exclusive power to prescribe the location of a state liquor licensee has been conferred on municipalities in various forms. For example, the licensing statute may grant a municipality the power

> . . . to regulate and control the sale of alcoholic beverages; may provide either a state license shall not issue to an applicant who intends to operate his business within a city zone where the sale of beer or liquor is prohibited by ordinance or that a city can establish zones within which the business of a state licensee cannot be located; or may provide that a state license shall not issue in contravention of a proper or valid zoning ordinance or an ordinance adopted pursuant to the zoning laws of the state.

Note, *Application of Local Zoning Ordinances to State-Controlled Public Utilities and Licensees: A Study in Preemption,* 1965 WASH. U.L.Q. 195, 200-01.

which will pose the greatest difficulties of interpretation both for the courts and for persons wishing to establish or live in a residential facility. It is also the form legislation tends to take when draftsmen are unaware of zoning difficulties. It seems fair to say that if the applicable state statute neither defers to the local ordinances nor expressly disallows their regulation, the validity of the local ordinance will depend upon judicial interpretation of legislative intent to preempt local authority. If the courts find an implied occupation of the field, the restrictive local ordinance will be of no effect; the license will be issued and will be judicially enforceable.

Before we look more carefully at the general doctrine of preemption by implication, the legislative scheme in California should be examined in some detail. The California situation is interesting in this context because prior to the most recent amendments to the statutes dealing with residential facilities for the mentally retarded, the state statutes seemed to imply preemption. (Recent amendments *expressly* occupy the field.)

In March 1970, the report of a study conducted by the Assembly Select Committee on Mentally Ill and Handicapped Children stated:

> One of the major obstacles to the development of local facilities for mentally disordered children — as well as other handicapped groups — is restrictive zoning ordinances which prohibit the establishment of residential treatment programs in many communities throughout the state.
>
> Because local treatment for children is preferable to care in remote facilities and because many local jurisdictions have chosen to ignore their responsibilities to foster the growth of such resources, it is proposed that the State Legislature declare its intent in this area by passing legislation to prevent local communities from discriminating against handicapped persons through restrictive zoning practices[59]

In response to the findings of the committee, Assemblyman Frank Lanterman introduced AB 2406 in the 1970 legislative session. In his summary of the bill prepared for presentation to legislative committees, Mr. Lanterman discussed the purpose of the measure:

> AB 2406 was developed as a result of the work of the Assembly Select Committee on Mentally Ill and Handicapped Children. In many ways it is one of the most important components of the legislative package which grew out of the study.
>
> AB 2406 declares that it is the intent of the Legislature to prevent local communities from discriminating against handicapped persons through restrictive zoning practices.
>
> The bill, which is supported by the California League of Cities, stipulates that a State licensed, authorized or certified family care home, foster home, or group home serving six (6) or fewer mentally disordered or otherwise handicapped persons, shall be considered a residential use of property. We feel that this provision will prevent the exclusion of these homes from residential areas solely because they are providing care to handicapped persons.[60]

---

[59] Arthur Bolton Associates, A Report to the Assembly Select Comm. on Mentally Ill and Handicapped Children March 1, 1970, at 180.

[60] The cited material appears at p. 30 of a text prepared by Assemblyman Lanterman to serve as the basis for his oral presentation of AB 2406 to various legislative committees in the 1970 legislative session of the California legislature, Sacramento.

As enacted into law, AB 2406 amended the Welfare and Institutions Code to provide:

> Section 5115. *Legislative intent*
>
> The   Legislature hereby finds and declares:
>
> (a) It is the policy of this State, as declared and established in this act and in the Lanterman Mental Retardation Act of 1969, that mentally and physically handicapped persons are entitled to live in normal residential surroundings and should not be excluded therefrom because of their disability.
>
> (b) In order to achieve uniform statewide implementation of the policies of this act and those of the Lanterman Mental Retardation Act of 1969, it is necessary to establish the statewide policy that the use of property for the care of six or fewer mentally disordered or otherwise handicapped persons is a residential use of such property for the purposes of zoning.
>
> Section 5116. *Property used for care of six or fewer handicapped persons or dependent or neglected children as residential use for zoning purposes.*
>
> Pursuant to the policy stated in Section 5115, a state-authorized, certified, or licensed family care home, foster home, or group home serving six or fewer mentally disordered or otherwise handicapped persons or dependent and neglected children, shall be considered a residential use of property for the purposes of zoning if such homes provide care on a 24-hour-a-day basis.[61]

AB 2406 passed the California assembly on a vote of 68 to 0, and the state senate, 25 to 2.

Cities and counties were soon faced with permit applications by operators of family care homes; by ordinance and administrative interpretation, local authorities attempted to limit the homes to multiple-dwelling zones. City zoning administrators argued that as long as family care homes were permitted in any one residential zone, the requirements of sections 5115 and 5116 had been met. Mr. Lanterman reacted to local obstructions in a letter dated November 6, 1972:

> Legislation I authored in 1970 (AB 2406) expressed legislative intent that mentally and physically handicapped persons are entitled to live in normal residential surroundings and that homes serving six or fewer handicapped persons shall be considered a residential use of property.
>
>   Unfortunately, several instances were brought to my attention where the intent of that law was being circumvented. In a few communities, family care and foster homes were excluded from single family zones (R-1) on the basis that my law only required that such homes be allowed in some residential neighborhoods, not necessarily R-1.
>
>   I view this practice as a deplorable and calculated effort to defeat the very clear intent of AB 2406
>
>   In order to insure that no potential legal loopholes can be used in the future to discriminate against the handicapped living in normal residential surroundings, I introduced and attained passage of AB 1856. . . . [62]

AB 1856 became law March 6, 1973. It amends Welfare and Institutions Code section 5116:

---

[61] CAL. WELF. & INST. CODE §§ 5115 & 5116 (West 1972).
[62] Letter from Frank Lanterman to Mr. Skip Tescher, Nov. 6, 1972.

5116. Pursuant to the policy stated in Section 5115, a state-authorized, certified, or licensed family care home, foster home, or group home serving six or fewer mentally disordered or otherwise handicapped persons or dependent and neglected children, shall be considered a residential use of property for the purposes of zoning if such homes provide care on a 24-hour-a-day basis.

Such homes shall be a permitted use in all residential zones including, but not limited to residential zones for single-family dwellings. Nothing in this paragraph shall be construed to prohibit any city or county from requiring a conditional use permit in order to maintain any home, pursuant to the provisions of this paragraph; provided that no conditions shall be imposed on such homes which are more restrictive than those imposed on other similar dwellings in the same zones unless such additional conditions are necessary to protect the health and safety of the residents. [63]

Though the law expressly indicates that application for a conditional use permit may be required of family care home operators, it is clearly not the intent of sections 5115 and 5116 that the conditional use system be used to deny an application. AB 1856 states that a family care home serving six or fewer handicapped residents is a *permitted use* in all residential zones. Limitations may be imposed upon the use in the discretion of the administrative planning body, pursuant to AB 1856, but the permit may not be denied. Many cities and counties in California presently employ the conditional use hearing and the general welfare standard to deny permits on the basis of the misconceived fears and irrational prejudices articulated by residents in the zone affected. AB 1856 makes unlawful the continuation of such local practices.

The criterion in a judicial finding of preemption by implication is legislative intent. This determination is often difficult since state legislatures seldom indicate their intention as clearly as was done in the California example. State legislative history is very seldom recorded. Rare cases hold that the state, by legislating in any area, automatically preempts it; but this is not a majority position. One writer has noted that perhaps the closest that a court can come to determining legislative intent is to inquire whether the ordinance substantially interferes with the effective functioning of the state statute. If the ordinance has such an effect, it should be invalidated on the theory that state legislation preempts local authority to make the ordinance. [64]

This interference concept was the basis for judicial invalidation of a village zoning ordinance which restricted residential placement of neglected and abandoned children in foster homes in the state of New York. In *Abbott House v. Village of Tarrytown*, [65] the zoning ordinance restricted to three the number of such children who could be placed in a foster home which had been approved by the New York State Board of Social Welfare as an agency boarding home. Under section 374-B of the New York Social Services Law, the maximum number of children allowed in a boarding home was six; the plaintiffs in the *Abbott House* case were authorized by the state agency to care for six children. The court pointed out that the purpose of this state law was "to give these neglected children a family atmosphere within which they can develop and mature," and that "[t]he whole program is supervised by the State Board of Social Welfare [and] financed in large measure by the State."[66] Moreover, "It is

---

[63] CAL. WELF. & INST. CODE § 5116 (West Supp. 1973).
[64] *See* Note, *Conflicts Between State Statutes and Municipal Ordinances,* 72 HARV. L. REV. 737, 745 (1959).
[65] 34 App. Div. 2d 821, 312 N.Y.S.2d 841 (1970).
[66] *Id.* at 822, 312 N.Y.S.2d at 843 (1970).

clear that this Zoning Ordinance has the effect of totally thwarting the State's policy, as expressed in its Constitution and Social Service Law, of providing for neglected children."[67] When ruling on a preemption by implication claim, the courts have also examined the scope of the regulatory power which has been conferred by state statute on state agencies, the public need for the facilities involved, the desirability for uniform regulation of the subject matter throughout the state, and the detail and completeness of the state statute.[68]

The case law of California is instructive, although in other jurisdictions the doctrine of preemption and the structure of state statutes will differ. The doctrine of preemption by implication in California had its origins in Art. 11, § 7, of the Constitution, which provides in material part that "a county or city may make and enforce within its limits all local, police, sanitary and other ordinances and regulations not in conflict with general laws." However, a local ordinance is invalid if it attempts to impose additional requirements in a field preempted by state law.[69] To determine whether the legislature intended to preempt a particular field to the exclusion of local regulation, the California courts will look to the "whole purpose and scope of the legislative scheme."[70] The legislators need not declare their intent in so many words, and the courts will look to several factors to determine the unstated legislative purpose. Among the factors are the detail of the state regulation, the quantity of that regulation, and the comprehensiveness of the state statute.[71] The decision in *In re Hubbard*[72] sets three alternative tests for determining when the legislature has preempted local regulation:

> (1) the subject matter has been so fully and completely covered by general law as to clearly indicate that it has become exclusively a matter of state concern:
> (2) the subject matter has been partially covered by general law couched in such terms as to indicate clearly that a paramount state concern will not tolerate further or additional local actions; or
> (3) the subject matter has been partially covered by general law, and the subject is of such a nature that the adverse effect of a local ordinance on the transient citizens of the state outweighs the possible benefit to the municipality.[73]

The plaintiffs in the *Defoe* case argued that the zoning ordinance of the city of San Francisco was void because the legislature had preempted the field. They relied on a legislative declaration of responsibility for the needs of California's mentally handicapped citizens[74] and upon the extensive licensing provisions.[75] In addition, the

---

[67] *Id.* It is not clear from the text of the opinion whether the court was exclusively relying on the preemption by implication doctrine or also considered that the ordinance was *ultra vires.*

[68] *See* Note, *Application of Local Zoning Ordinances to State-Controlled Public Utilities and Licensees: A Study in Preemption,* 1965 WASH. U.L.Q. 195, 209; Note, *Conflicts Between State Statutes and Municipal Ordinances,* 72 HARV. L. REV. 737, 745-46 (1959).

[69] Galvin v. Superior Court, 70 Cal. 2d 851, 859, 452 P.2d 930, 935, 76 Cal. Rptr. 642, 647 (1969); *In re* Hubbard, 62 Cal. 2d 119, 125, 396 P.2d 809, 812, 41 Cal. Rptr. 393, 396 (1964).

[70] *In re* Lane, 58 Cal. 2d 99, 102-03, 372 P.2d 897, 899, 22 Cal. Rptr. 857, 859 (1962).

[71] Comment, *The California City versus Preemption by Implication,* 17 HAST. L.J. 603, 605-07 (1966).

[72] 62 Cal. 2d 119, 396 P.2d 809, 41 Cal. Rptr. 393 (1964).

[73] *Id.* at 128, 396 P.2d at 815, 41 Cal. Rptr. at 399 (1964).

[74] CAL. HEALTH & SAFETY CODE §§ 38000 *et seq.* (West 1973).

[75] CAL. WELF. & INST. CODE §§ 7000-26 (West 1972).

administrative regulations promulgated under the licensing statute contained even more detailed state standards for the location and physical characteristics of structures to be used as small residential facilities.[76] Mr. Lanterman's statutes,[77] enacted in 1970, added substantial strength to the argument. The California legislative scheme has the detail, quantity, and comprehensiveness which the courts have found indicative of the legislative intent to preempt a field. In addition, it is demonstrable that to tolerate local municipal zoning power in this instance would thwart the purpose of state legislation, which purpose is to provide small residential facilities in all communities, near natural families, for mentally retarded children and adults. However, "the area of state-local conflicts is one in which very few principles have evolved that are capable of concrete application to specific cases. Indeed, the question may be raised whether the courts have even begun to develop the relevant criteria that must be used in deciding these conflicts."[78] The doctrine of preemption by implication has been criticized both for its lack of specific applicable criteria and for its tendency always to find the state legislative authority supreme and the local ordinance invalid. The vagueness of the criteria and the real difficulty of predicting judicial response render it imperative that state legislation eliminate the necessity for relying on the doctrine.

Traditional Statutory Interpretation of Zoning Ordinances

Zoning ordinances that limit the use of residential structures within certain districts to "single-family" use, without further definition, are a potential vehicle for the exclusion of residential facilities for the mentally retarded. The traditional definition of family is a group whose members are related either by marriage, blood, or adoption. Since the individuals living in a group residence for the mentally retarded are generally unrelated to each other, the municipality or the neighboring property owners would claim these people do not constitute a "family" within the meaning of the ordinance. This narrow definition of family is vulnerable to judicial challenge under traditional principles of statutory interpretation. Courts have and should continue to refuse to create narrow, exclusionary provisions by interpretation when the zoning ordinance itself does not further define the nature of a "family." A California decision interpreting Atherton zoning regulations illustrates the approach; the regulations provided:

> In one-family residential districts "A," "B," and "C" no lot or parcel of land, building, structure, or improvement shall be used, and no building, structure or improvement shall be hereafter erected, constructed, structurally altered or enlarged, except for a single-family dwelling and accessory buildings thereto. . . .[79]

---

[76] 9 CAL. ADMIN. CODE §§ 1-324.

[77] CAL. WELF. & INST. CODE §§ 5115 & 5116 (West Supp. 1973).

[78] D. MANDELKER, MANAGING OUR URBAN ENVIRONMENT 149 (1966).

[79] Brady v. Superior Court, 200 Cal. App. 2d 69, 71, 19 Cal. Rptr. 242, 243 (1962) (*quoting* from an Atherton, Cal. ordinance).

The ordinance defined a one-family dwelling as "a detached building designed for or occupied exclusively by one family." The Atherton approach was to zone by buildings, to define the buildings in terms of "family," and to leave "family" undefined. When the ordinance was challenged in litigation by unrelated individuals living in a structure, the lower court defined "single family" as follows:

> That the normal use and construction of the phrase "single-family" as used in the Zoning Ordinances means a unit that has a social status, a head who has a right, at least in a limited way, to direct and control those gathered into the household, a moral and legal obligation of a head to support the other members and a state of at least partial dependence by the other members for this support. [80]

On an appeal from a contempt citation, the district court of appeals disallowed the lower court's interpretation:

> We must interpret the words of the ordinance in their strict sense because, although Atherton could have endowed them with restricted or wide coverage, it did not do so; we can attach to them only their bare meaning. "Single-family dwelling" must mean, in our judgment, an individual or a group of persons living on the premises as a single housekeeping unit. We cannot concur with the trial court that the words necessarily require that the unit have a "social status" or "a head who has a right . . . to direct and control those gathered into the household" and who has a moral and legal obligation to support them. Nor does the definition require consanguinity or affinity of the members of the household. [81]

The court noted that the ordinance could really only "refer to the *use* of the premises as a family, or in a manner of a family. Such family use, again, would, and must be, a single and common use of the premises." [82] The *Brady* interpretation of "family" includes group residence for the mentally retarded, where facilities are designed and used as a family unit and individuals work, eat, sleep, and perform household chores as part of a common household. A familylike atmosphere is often mandated by the state directives establishing these facilities. In *Brady*, the court found that the restriction to "family" use could preclude the breaking up of the residence into separate tenancies, but a segregation of tenancies does not occur in a residential facility for the mentally retarded; the purpose of the residence is to prevent segregation and to create a community in which the retarded individual can reside as a member of a family. [83]

Another example is *Gloster v. Downeyside, Inc.* [84] Downeyside, a charitable corporation operated a group home for troubled youths in Holyoke, Massachusetts. Neighbors complained that the use being made of the premises violated a zoning

---

[80] Brady v. Superior Court, 200 Cal. App. 2d 69, 71, 19 Cal. Rptr. 242, 243 (1962). It might be well to note that a group residence for mentally retarded individuals could fit more easily into this definition of family than into one strictly in terms of blood, marriage, or adoption relatedness.

[81] *Id.* at 77, 19 Cal. Rptr. at 247.

[82] *Id.* at 77-78, 19 Cal. Rptr. at 247.

[83] For other liberal interpretations of zoning ordinances, see Carroll v. Miami Beach, 198 S.2d 643 (Fla. 1967); Robertson v. West Baptist Hosp., 267 S.W.2d 395 (Ky. 1954); Laporte v. City of New Rochelle, 2 N.Y.2d 921, 141 N.E.2d 917, 161 N.Y.S.2d 886 (1957); Missionaires v. Village of White Fish Bay, 267 Wis. 609, 66 N.W.2d 627 (1954).

[84] Docket No. 714 (Super. Ct. Hampden Co., Mass., June 1970).

ordinance which permitted only detached one-family dwellings. The court held that family meant "a group of people who lived together in one housing unit under the management or control of a directing head."   As applied to the group home:[85]

> The use of the premises contemplated by the respondent Downeyside, Inc., would come within that definition since the premises would be occupied by a group of persons sharing the benefits and responsibilities of living together and under the direction, management, discipline and control of a parental authority.[86]

The court refused to add a requirement that the members of a "family" be related by blood or marriage.[87]

In both *Brady* and *Downeyside* the difficulty was that the zoning ordinances failed to define "family" with specificity. If a court interprets a nonspecific zoning ordinance to allow the placement of residential facilities in a certain district, then persons wishing to exclude the facilities could seek amendment of the zoning ordinance. Once the zoning restrictions do define or are interpreted to define "family" with specificity, and thus exclude residences for the mentally retarded, the challenges which must at that point be mounted are likely to take on constitutional dimensions.

Constitutional Challenges to Restrictive Zoning

The due process clause of the fourteenth amendment to the Constitution of the United States has been the conventional route for attacking the validity of zoning ordinances. In *Nectow v. City of Cambridge*, the Supreme Court of the United States stated the basic principle:

> The Governmental power to interfere by zoning regulations with the general rights of the landowner by restricting the character of his use, is not unlimited, and other questions aside, such restriction cannot be imposed if it does not bear a substantial relation to the public health, safety, morals, or general welfare.[88]

The courts have traditionally presumed the validity of zoning ordinances and placed the burden of proof on the challenger. If the issue is debatable, the courts ordinarily will not intervene. The option open to the challenger is to show that the regulation is "clearly arbitrary and unreasonable, having no substantial relation to the public health, safety, morals, or general welfare."[89]

It is impossible to catalogue here all the zoning exclusions which might be

[85] Gloster v. Downeyside, Inc., Docket No. 714 (Super. Ct. Hampden Co., Mass., June 1970).
[86] *Id.*
[87] *Id.*
[88] 277 U.S. 183,188 (1928). As one federal court has recently noted, "in enacting zoning legislation the local authorities are vested with broad discretion. Ordinarily a court will intervene to declare a zoning ordinance to be a denial of due process only where it cannot be supported by a substantial public interest. Traditionally it may be justified by showing that it is related to such matters as safety, population density, adequacy of light and air, noise and necessity for traffic control, transportation, sewerage, school, park and other public services." Boraas v. Village of Belle Terre, 476 F.2d 806, 812 (2d Cir. 1973), *rev'd,* 416 U.S. 1 (1974).
[89] Village of Euclid v. Ambler Realty Co., 272 U.S. 365, 395 (1926).

vulnerable to a due process challenge. However, two illustrative restrictions can be described from the *Defoe* litigation. These illustrate how imperative it is that the factual record built by the litigants be detailed. In this context, factual detail aims to show that legislative judgments have no basis in fact or are irrational and arbitrary. In *Defoe*, the zoning administrator determined that a family care home for six or fewer mentally retarded children was a use "which required medical supervision" and that such a use was not permitted in R-1 and R-1-D zones of the city. In numerous expert affidavits submitted at the trial court level, the plaintiffs documented that foster home care for mentally retarded children was not a use requiring medical supervision.[90] The plaintiffs were also forced to attack as arbitrary and irrational an administrative interpretation that concluded that no more than two mentally retarded children could be cared for as part of a "family." The plaintiffs utilized expert testimony by state agency administrators and independent experts in the field of mental retardation to establish that since the number of children who could be cared for as members of the family was not limited to two, the zoning interpretation was arbitrary, irrational, and thus a violation of due process.[91] Restrictions of the sort encountered in *Defoe*, and any restriction that seeks to exclude residential facilities for the mentally retarded from a traditional single-family residential district, or from an entire municipality, may be challenged as lacking relation to the health, safety, and welfare of the community. It should be demonstrated to the courts that group residences for the mentally retarded serve the public welfare in the form of reduced cost to the state, to local communities, and to natural families of mentally retarded citizens. Mentally retarded citizens living in small residential facilities have increased potential for becoming productive members of the community. Thus, a value can be demonstrated both for society and for the mentally retarded resident of the community home.

The findings of the intermediate court in *Rogers v. Association for the Health of Retarded Children, Inc.*[92] illustrate the objective of a challenge to zoning restrictions on broad due process grounds. *Rogers* was an action to enjoin the association from using its real property as a school for mentally retarded children in an alleged violation of a zoning ordinance. The plaintiffs claimed, among other things, that the health, welfare, and safety of the neighboring community would be adversely affected by the presence of large numbers of mentally retarded children. The court found in part:

> That the health, welfare and safety of the plaintiffs were not adversely affected by the defendant's use of the premises; that the presence of mentally retarded children on the defendant's property did not cause hardship to the families of the plaintiffs;

[90] For instance, one of the plaintiffs' affidavits stated, "With reference to the issue as to whether family care of mentally retarded children is medical care, I can state unequivocally that family care of mentally retarded children is no different from family care of non-mentally retarded children. The presence of mental retardation in a child does not mean that this child needs medical care." Affidavit of Dr. Elias Katz, assistant director of the Center for Training in Community Psychiatry and Mental Health Administration, submitted in Defoe v. San Francisco City Planning Comm'n,1 Civil No. 30789 (Dist. Ct. App. Cal., May 30, 1973).

[91] Likewise, should a zoning ordinance attempt to exclude a residential home for mentally retarded adults on the basis that the home is a boarding or a lodging house, the restriction should be challenged on the same constitutional basis.

[92] 281 App. Div. 978, 120 N.Y.S. 2d 329, *aff'd,* 308 N.Y. 126, 123 N.E.2d 806 (1954).

that the method of education afforded by the defendant to mentally retarded children did not disturb the peace and quiet of the neighborhood, nor did those children cause damage to plaintiffs' property or bodily harm to anyone in the neighborhood.[93]

It is unlikely that the defenders of the local zoning restriction could create a record of anything more than fears over having mentally retarded people in the community. Fear is not sufficient to justify an exclusion based on the general welfare.

The likelihood of a successful due process challenge to zoning restrictions which limit the number of unrelated individuals permitted to live as a "family" in single-family dwelling zones has been considerably diminished by the recent decision of the United States Supreme Court in *Boraas v. Village of Belle Terre*.[94] In this case, the majority of the Court, although directly ruling on an equal protection challenge to the validity of a local zoning ordinance, reaffirmed a broad concept of general welfare and of the police power available to protect the general welfare. "The police power is not confined to elimination of filth, stench, and unhealthy places. It is ample to lay out zones where family values, youth values, and the blessings of quiet seclusion, and clean air make the area a sanctuary for people." [95]

This concept of general welfare, when combined with the notion that the legislation will stand as long as it is "fairly debatable" and not "wholly arbitrary,"[96] indicates that the Supreme Court is unlikely to invalidate, on due process grounds, zoning that distinguishes between single housekeeping units comprised of consanguineous families and those comprised of unrelated individuals.

It should be noted that *Village of Belle Terre* involved the facial validity of zoning restrictions, did not question the effect of the ordinance as applied, and also dealt with a broad zoning restriction, one which affected any and all nontraditional family living situations. The case does not preclude due process challenges to zoning actions which affect only group residences for the mentally retarded such as were raised in *Defoe* and *Rogers*.

The viability of these narrower challenges remains, based at least partially on the Supreme Court's citation, with approval, of its prior decision in *Seattle Title and Trust Co. v. Roberge*.[97] This decision dealt with a local zoning ordinance restricting the construction of homes for children or for the aged poor without the written consent of nearby property owners. The Court found that the maintenance and construction of the home was not shown "to work any injury, inconvenience, or annoyance to the community, the district or any person."[98] The type of demonstration made in *Rogers* offers, even after *Village of Belle Terre*, a potentially successful due process attack upon zoning restrictions.

The definition of "family" in zoning ordinances has provided the focal point for constitutional attack in the recent past. Many zoning ordinances define

---

[93] 308 N.Y. at 131, 123 N.E.2d at 808-09.
[94] 416 U.S. 1 (1974).
[95] *Id.* at 9.
[96] *Id.* at 5.
[97] 278 U.S. 116 (1928), *cited with approval* in Boraas v. Village of Belle Terre, 416 U.S. at 6-7.
[98] 278 U.S. at 122. The Supreme Court's decision in *Seattle Trust Co.* held that the delegation of a consent power to nearby property owners was the fatal flaw under due process, but the language of the decision is supportive.

"family" as one person living alone, or two or more persons related by blood, marriage, or legal adoption, or a group not exceeding a certain number (generally four or five) of unrelated persons, living as a single housekeeping unit. Any of these statutory definitions, when incorporated into the restrictions placed on single-family residential districts, may effectively exclude some or all residential facilities for the mentally retarded.[99]

Constitutional challenges to zoning restrictions which limit living arrangements for unrelated individuals have been advanced with increasing frequency over the past few years. The ordinances have generally been attacked on equal protection grounds and the results in the lower courts have been mixed. The decision of the Supreme Court in *Boraas v. Village of Belle Terre* is undoubtedly a setback for those who were anticipating a broad favorable equal protection ruling from the highest federal court. Whether the negative impact of the decision can be significantly limited by advancing a narrower factual context, specifically one concentrating on the rights of the mentally retarded, is yet to be determined.

Because *Village of Belle Terre* is an important decision in this context, it is worthwhile setting forth some of the details of the case. Belle Terre, New York, is a village on Long Island of 220 homes and 700 inhabitants; its land area is less than 1 square mile. The Court noted:

> It has restricted land use to one-family dwellings excluding lodging houses, boarding houses, fraternity houses, or multiple dwelling houses. The word "Family" as used in the ordinance means, "one or more persons related by blood, adoption, or marriage, living and cooking together as a single housekeeping unit, exclusive of household servants. A number of persons but not exceeding two (2) living and cooking together as a single housekeeping unit though not related by blood, adoption, or marriage shall be deemed to constitute a family."[100]

The Supreme Court noted that in *Euclid v. Ambler Realty Co.* the Court had sustained the zoning ordinance under the police power of the state:

> The main thrust of the case in the mind of the Court was in the exclusion of industries and apartments and as respects that it commented on the desire to keep residential areas free of "disturbing noises"; "increased traffic"; the hazard of "moving and parked automobiles"; the "depriving children of the privilege of quiet and open spaces for play, enjoyed by those in more favored localities.". . . The ordinance

---

[99] In this situation, group residences have encountered many of the same exclusionary practices confronting the growing number of communal residences. The case law and written commentary dealing with the constitutional problems have been directed to claims by these voluntary unrelated communal households, rather than by group residences for the handicapped. See the careful law review treatment of the problem of living arrangements for unrelated individuals in Note, *Burning the Housing to Roast the Pig: Unrelated Individuals and Single-Family Zoning's Blood Relation Criterion,* 58 CORNELL L. REV. 138 (1972); Comment, *All in the Family: Legal Problems of the Communes,* 7 HARV. CIV. RIGHTS—CIV. LIB. L. REV. 393 (1972). There are substantial tactical advantages in keeping group homes for the mentally retarded separate from communes or other social projects when facing legislative battles on a state or local level. The constitutional arguments attacking the restrictions on unrelated family units are broad and arguably would permit unlimited nontraditional living situations. Whether such an open-ended attack is unavoidable, as we believe, is an important issue, aptly noted by Professor Simmons. *See* note 7 to reaction comment by Simmons, p. 355 *infra.*
[100] 416 U.S. at 2.

was sanctioned because the validity of the legislative classification was "fairly debatable" and therefore could not be said to be wholly arbitrary.[101]

The Court concluded that in *Village of Belle Terre* it was still dealing "with economic and social legislation" and that the law would be sustained as long as it was reasonable, not arbitrary, and bore a rational relationship to a permissible state objective.[102] The Court set forth its views of the permissible objectives sought by the challenged zoning:

> A quiet place where yards are wide, people few, and motor vehicles restricted are legitimate guidelines in a land use project addressed to family needs. This goal is a permissible one within *Berman v. Parker, supra.* The police power is not confined to elimination of filth, stench and unhealthy places. It is ample to lay out zones where family values, youth values, and the blessings of quiet seclusion, and clean air make the area a sanctuary for people.[103]

Not only were the objectives held permissible; the Court also found none of the flaws which trigger a closer equal protection analysis of the legislation.[104] That is, the ordinance was not based on race, nor, held the Court, was it aimed at transients, nor did it involve any fundamental right guaranteed by the Constitution.[105]

---

[101] *Id.* at 5. The Supreme Court also noted that in Berman v. Parker, 348 U.S. 26, it had refused "to limit the concept of public welfare that may be enhanced by zoning regulations."

[102] 416 U.S. at 8.

[103] *Id.* at 9. The Second Circuit Court of Appeals, reversed by the Supreme Court, had taken a less benign view of the objectives and the methodology chosen to achieve them:
> It is suggested, for instance, that the ordinance is justified as a means of controlling population density. This contention is based on the assumption that the number of related persons in the conventional family unit (husband, wife, brothers, sisters, children, nephews, uncles, grandparents) tends to be "self-limiting," whereas in the absence of a regulation limiting the number of unrelated occupants, the "voluntary" family can be limitless in size. Another argument advanced by appellees is that the ordinance might avoid escalation of rental rates, which would price traditional families out of the market, since it is possible that unrelated groups would be willing to pay higher rentals than would consanguineal families. We are further asked to speculate that "voluntary" families would pose greater parking, traffic and noise problems than would traditional families and that there would be a greater degree of transiency on the part of the former than the latter, thus weakening the stability of the community. 476 F.2d at 816.

[104] The equal protection clause demands that classifications of people have a reasonable relation to a legitimate governmental objective. Single-family zoning ordinances often classify groups or related individuals one way and groups of unrelated individuals another. Related individuals, no matter what number, are able to live in single-family districts; unrelated individuals are excluded from such districts or are subject to a maximum limit for each household. Under a judicially developed "two-tiered" theory for testing classifications of people, stricter evaluation of governmental action applies if the classification is based on suspect criteria, such as race, or if the classification impinges on a fundamental interest. In this situation, the Supreme Court has held that the classification must be justified by a compelling state interest.

[105] 416 U.S. at 7-8. The Supreme Court's treatment of the equal protection challenge comports with the result reached in Palo Alto Tenants Union v. Morgan, 321 F. Supp. 908 (N.D. Cal. 1970), *aff'd,* 487 F.2d 883 (9th Cir. 1973) (per curiam). In his dissent, in *Village of Belle Terre,* Justice Marshall stated that rational goals have here been sought by irrational and unconstitutional means.
> It is claimed that the ordinance controls population density, prevents noise, traffic and parking problems, and preserves the rent structure of the community and its attractiveness to families. As I noted earlier, these are all legitimate and substantial interests of government. But I think it clear that the means chosen to accomplish these purposes are both over-inclusive and under-inclusive, and that the asserted goals could be as effectively achieved by means of an ordinance that did not discriminate on the basis of constitutionally protected choices of life styles. (416 U.S. at 18).

Numerous other court decisions, both state and federal, had reached contrary conclusions. These opinions emphasize that although there are solid policy reasons for the regulation of the intensity of land use — avoiding congestion, providing open land, providing adequate light and air, preventing traffic problems, and avoiding overburdening public facilities — it is almost impossible to demonstrate that restrictions of land use to single families, or to a maximum number of unrelated individuals, accomplish this purpose.[106] For instance, as one court observed:

> Family groups are mobile today, and not all family units are internally stable and well disciplined. Family groups with two or more cars are not unfamiliar. And so far as intensity of uses concerned, the definition in the present ordinance, with its reference to the respective spouses of persons related by blood, marriage or adoption, can hardly be regarded as an effective control upon the size of family units.[107]

In light of the Supreme Court's decision, the advocates for group residences for the mentally retarded may choose to emphasize the narrower, more distinctive characteristics of their clients to highlight both the nature of the rights being denied and the suspect nature of the exclusion. Aside from the rights of travel, association, and privacy, which have been advanced by others in this context, the fundamental relationship of group living situations to the "right to treatment and habilitation" should begin to receive emphasis. Similarly, although a zoning classification may be phrased in terms of traditional families, the courts should be shown that, because of an involuntary, unalterable, nonculpable status, the mentally retarded are far less likely than the nonretarded to be able to achieve a traditional family living situation. To exclude the retarded unless they are living in a consanguineous family is to exclude them with much greater finality and with less justice than others. Thus, the nature of the zoning exclusions as applied should be documented and challenged.

The most invidious zoning classification would be one which allowed unrelated nonretarded individuals to live in group settings and yet denied this opportunity to retarded citizens. The equal protection clause demands that a zoning ordinance bear a reasonable relation to a legitimate governmental objective. There is no necessity to look to the stricter equal protection test, the suspect criterion test, in order to invalidate an express segregation of retarded citizens. Express segregation is not fictional. In the *Defoe* case, the policy of the city of San Francisco provided:

> The City Planning Code makes no specific mention of foster children; nor has the Department of City Planning set forth any explicit policy in the past on this

---

106 Buckingham v. City of Dayton, Civil No. 45 (S.D. Ohio, Feb. 20, 1974); Timberlake v. Kenkel, 369 F. Supp. 456 (E.D. Wis. 1974); City of Des Plaines v. Trottner, 34 Ill. 2d 432, 216 N.E.2d 116 (1966). *See* Kirsch Holding Co. v. Borough of Manasquan, 59 N.J. 241, 281 A.2d 513 (1971).

107 City of Des Plaines v. Trottner, 34 Ill. 2d 432, 438, 216 N.E.2d 116, 119 (1966). Cases from state courts have indicated that these courts have considered the problems raised by single-family zoning in an equal protection context and have been seriously troubled by them even though they did not utilize an equal protection analysis to find the ordinances at issue invalid. *See* City of Des Plaines v. Trottner, 34 Ill. 2d 432, 216 N.E.2d 116 (1966); Kirsch Holding Co. v. Borough of Manasquan, 59 N.J. 241, 281 A.2d 513 (1971); Gabe Collins Realty, Inc. v. City of Margate City, 112 N.J. Super. 341, 271 A.2d 430 (1970).

subject. . . . The placement of foster children as part of a "family" should present no problem if kept within reasonable limits. Referral by a responsible public or private social welfare agency is deemed a sufficient guarantee of reasonableness.[108]

However, when dealing with the foster placement of *mentally retarded* children, the planning commission argued that

> the City Planning Code does not mention such family homes as permitted uses in single-family residential districts. . . . Nevertheless, the Code has been interpreted to allow supervisory home care under proper license as part of a "family" for not more than two mentally retarded children.[109]

In other words, referral by a responsible public or private social welfare agency "is deemed a sufficient guarantee of reasonableness" only with respect to non-retarded foster children. In California, the department of social welfare refers both retarded and nonretarded children for placements in family homes. The assumption that the agency will act responsibly in one case but not in the other is irrational and arbitrary.

All the constitutional attacks on zoning restrictions outlined in this paper have their difficulties. Not the least among these is the traditional and justifiable reluctance of the courts to invalidate legislation on constitutional grounds. Courts hesitate to rule that a particular act is for all time beyond the power of government. The next section suggests an attack on restrictive zoning regulations which is not based on constitutional challenge, nor on statutory interpretation, nor on the preemption doctrine.

Challenging Exclusionary Zoning as Beyond Municipal Authority

In order to set the framework for this discussion it is necessary to return briefly to the language of the home rule provisions. Under these provisions, municipalities are authorized to act in respect to "municipal affairs," or to enact laws and regulations "in respect to municipal affairs," to act concerning their "organization, government or affairs," or to "adopt and enforce within their limits . . . local police, sanitary and other similar regulations."[110]As discussed previously, restrictive municipal zoning ordinances might be challenged because they conflict with state legislation or attempt to regulate an area that the legislature has preempted for control at the state level. Judicial challenge is most difficult when the legislature enacts regulatory and licensing provisions for small residential facilities for the mentally retarded, but fails to indicate the degree of local control which will be allowed. The possibility of arguing preemption by implication may be minimal in such situations. However, the language of the grant of home rule may provide another basis for challenging exclusionary zoning as beyond the authority of the municipality.

[108]Defoe v. San Francisco City Planning Comm'n, 1 Civil No. 30789 (Dist. Ct. App. Cal., May 30, 1973).
[109]*Id.*
[110]Sandalow, *supra* note 54, at 643, 660 (1964) [hereinafter cited as Sandalow].

The theory of the challenge is that the language of the home rule grant, limited to power over municipal affairs, should be viewed by the courts as a limitation upon the authority of the municipality to zone restrictively both because of the extra-territorial impact of such zoning regulation and the basic interest at stake in the zoning. The courts would be urged to find that unless there has been an express delegation from the state of the power to zone in this restrictive manner, only the state has the authority to do it.[111] Under almost all existing home rule provisions, the courts have the authority to consider the impact of local legislation on the welfare of the state as a whole. When the court finds that the action of the municipality has a substantial negative impact upon the welfare of the state, the court may declare the legislation invalid as beyond the scope of municipal affairs.[112] The theory gives state courts a way to avoid constitutional determination. Courts may be more willing to invalidate local legislation than to declare that the action at issue is beyond the power of any governmental entity. Judges might prefer to impose a "suspensive veto" which leaves the ultimate determination to the state legislature. The theory would also provide a convenient mechanism for balancing the interests of the municipality against the interests of the state.[113] A litigant would still be required to demonstrate that there is a fundamental value or an established state policy which is threatened by the municipal action, and this burden might tend to merge with the constitutional considerations which have been raised in this discussion. Even though the issues raised would be similar, the litigant would be seeking only a limited interpretation of municipal power.

The argument that restrictive zoning threatens established state policies merges into arguments considered in preemption; one challenging municipal legislation is required to produce evidence of a state policy, and it is likely that the most persuasive evidence of that state policy would be contained in legislation. Still, the courts may be willing to consider state policy and the threat posed to it by municipal zoning restrictions, where they would not be willing to declare that the state has completely removed an area from the realm of municipal authority.

At least one case relied on a concept of limits to municipal authority in declaring an exclusionary zoning restriction invalid. In *City of Des Plaines v. Trottner*,[114] the Supreme Court of Illinois invalidated a zoning ordinance which defined family as

> one or more persons each related to the other by blood (or adoption or marriage), together with such relatives' respective spouses, who are living together in a single

---

[111] *See* Sandalow, *supra* note 54.

[112] Sandalow, *supra* note 54, at 703. The article suggests that cases dealing with the flow of intrastate commerce and with local legislation discriminating against nonresidents offer precedents for this approach.

[113] It should be noted that much criticism of the theory of preemption by implication has been directed at the lack of such a balancing of interests. In the preemption by implication doctrine, the interests of the state are almost always considered paramount. As Professor Sandalow summarizes this approach, "A use of governmental power which threatens fundamental values or established state policies might not be deemed a 'local' or 'municipal' affair for much the same reason that municipal regulations with too great an extraterritorial impact are not considered to be 'local' or 'municipal' affairs, the inadequacy of political processes at the municipal level to cope with such problems." Sandalow, *supra* note 54, at 717.

[114] 34 Ill. 2d 432, 216 N.E.2d 116 (1966).

dwelling and maintaining a common household. A "family" includes any domestic servants and not more than one gratuitous guest residing with said "family."[115]

The housekeeping unit which was challenged was composed of four young unrelated men who had rented the premises for a year. The court held that zoning ordinances which "penetrate so deeply . . . into the internal composition of a single housekeeping unit" were an overextension of local zoning power in the absence of express enabling legislation from the state.[116] The ordinance was condemned as a municipal usurpation of undelegated power. The court also noted that if the municipality were found to possess the power to regulate individual living arrangements, so extensively, this authority would "generate severe constitutional questions."[117]

It has become apparent that the restrictive zoning of municipalities in other contexts, particularly the exclusion of high-density residences, does have a severe extraterritorial effect. This extraterritorial effect is the other element which must be urged on the courts when the zoning restriction is attacked as beyond the scope of municipal authority. The most extensive attention was directed to this aspect of zoning in a series of zoning cases before the Pennsylvania courts. Although these cases have been resolved on due process considerations, rather than under the theory here at issue, the judicial language used in Pennsylvania is useful. In *Appeal of Kit-Mar Builders, Inc.,*[118] the Supreme Court of Pennsylvania found that exclusionary municipal ordinances which limited new housing to single-family homes on large lots conflicted with the general public interest:

> We . . . refused to allow the township to do precisely what we have never permitted — keep out people, rather than make community improvements. . . . [C]ommunities must deal with the problems of population growth. They may not refuse to confront the future by adopting zoning regulations that effectively restrict population to near present levels. It is not for any given township to say who may or may not live within its confines, while disregarding the interest of the entire area. If Concord Township is successful in unnaturally limiting its population growth through the use of exclusive zoning regulations, the people who would normally live there will inevitably have to live in another community, and the requirement that they do so is not a decision that Concord Township should alone be able to make.[119]

This is an appropriate place to emphasize that the difficulties involved in the operation of local restrictive zoning ordinances are primarily confined to that area where residential facilities are operated by the private sector. If the state has undertaken to establish and operate as state agencies such small residential facilities, under current legal theory, many of the problems discussed in this and preceding sections are obviated. State agencies are entitled to immunity from municipal

---

[115]*Id.* at 433-34, 216 N.E.2d at 117.
[116]*Id.* at 438, 216 N.E.2d at 120.
[117]*Id.*
[118]439 Pa. 466, 268 A.2d 765 (1970).
[119]*Id.* at 474-75, 268 A.2d at 768-69. *See also* Appeal of Girsh, 437 Pa. 237, 263 A.2d 395 (1970); National Land and Inv. Co. v. Kohn, 419 Pa. 504, 215 A.2d 597 (1965).

zoning regulations in the absence of consent to be governed by them. It may be necessary in some jurisdictions to determine whether this immunity is conferred only when the state agencies are performing "governmental," as opposed to "proprietary," functions. The definitions and the functions included within these two terms vary, and the vagueness of the distinction should make it possible to include the operation of small residential facilities within the more broadly immune "governmental" function area. The theoretical basis for this immunity is the concept that the state would not have intended for municipalities to be able to hinder or thwart the state or its agencies in performing a duty required by statute or by the general welfare. This immunity of state agencies from local regulation may, of course, be modified by state legislation.[120]

TOWARD EFFECTIVE ACTION

On the State Level

The direction that should be taken in the future by state legislatures raises new and difficult theoretical questions. These new issues suggest certain program needs and require legislative support. Group homes for the mentally handicapped should be integrated uniformly in residential zones throughout the state. State legislation must necessarily facilitate zoning authorization for their operation in all residential zones. The essential components of such legislation are:

1. A brief declaration of the need for normalizing the lives of mentally handicapped persons.
2. A description of how integration in residential zones meets this need.
3. A statement emphasizing that uniform integration can occur only through statewide legislation and that, therefore, the matter is one of statewide concern. (The relevant constitutional provisions and preemption cases of the appropriate jurisdiction should be consulted for suggested language.)
4. A provision making the statute expressly applicable to charter cities. (The home rule provisions of the state constitution should be consulted.)
5. The requirement that the foster home be a *permitted use* in all residential zones, including, but not limited to, single-family zones.
6. A grant of authority to the local entity to impose reasonable conditions on the use.
7. The type of home referred to in the statute, including the number of residents served and the range of handicaps which they possess, should be based on the licensing classification of small-group homes in the particular jurisdiction. Because in California the small-group residence is licensed as a family care home for six or fewer residents, the sample statute makes direct references to this classification.

---

[120] For a discussion and criticism of the immunity of state agencies from local zoning powers see Note, *Municipal Power to Regulate Construction and Land Use by Other State Agencies,* 49 MINN. L. REV. 295-301 (1965).

A statute might read:

Section ____ . *Legislative Intent*

(a) It is the policy of this state that mentally and physically handicapped persons are entitled to share with nonhandicapped individuals the benefits of normal residential surroundings and should not be excluded therefrom because of their disability.

(b) Pursuant to this policy it is the intent of the legislature that county and municipal zoning ordinances, and administrative interpretations thereof, should not deny the handicapped person the exercise of this right.

Section _____ .

(a) In order to achieve statewide implementation of the policy and legislative intent expressed in sections _____ , a state-authorized or -licensed family care home, foster home, or group home serving six (6) or fewer mentally retarded or otherwise handicapped persons shall be considered a residential use of property for the purpose of zoning and a permitted use in all residential zones including, but not limited to, single-family residential zones.

(b) Nothing in this paragraph shall be construed to prohibit any city or county from imposing reasonable conditions on such use consistent with the policy and intent of section ____ and necessary to protect the health and safety of the residents.

(c) The provisions of sections ____ and ____ shall apply to charter cities.[121]

[121] This model statute is only one of several alternatives for the reconciliation of state and local interests. Another model for this reconciliation is suggested in the area of public utility regulation. Generally, state statutes do not grant complete control to either the state or the municipality, but the statutes attempt to accommodate the powers of the utility and zoning commissions by requiring consideration by the state agency of all competing interests. The statutes provide that if the municipality denies a building permit to a public service corporation on the ground that the proposed structure would violate a zoning ordinance, the utility may petition the state public service commission for a determination that the structure is reasonably necessary for the welfare or convenience of the public, and hence exempt from the provisions of the local ordinance. The exemption, however, may not be granted until both the state and municipal interests have been considered and weighed. The provisions and operations of the statutes in the public utilities area are discussed in Note, *Application of Local Zoning Ordinances to State-Controlled Public Utilities and Licensees: A Study in Preemption,* 1965 WASH. U.L.Q. 195, 203-07.

State legislation modeled on this precedent could require that prior to or after the issuance of a state license, a licensee proposing the operation of a residential facility for the mentally retarded must obtain some form of zoning approval from the local entity. However, if such zoning approval were denied, the state licensee could appeal to a state appeals board to seek an exemption from the zoning clearance requirement. The municipality could present to the state appeals board the basis for its denial of a zoning clearance. The licensee, with the intervention of the state licensing agency, would present his case for the location of the facility at its proposed site. Obviously, some standards would have to be established guiding the decision of a state appeals board in order to avoid arbitrary or unreasonable decisions. The exact nature of these standards is a difficult problem and should be given serious consideration by authorities in both the social science and legal fields. Whether the burden of persuasion should fall on the licensee or on the municipality and what will be the required standard of proof are further questions which must be answered. Of course, prior to the institution of any such administrative appeal system, the delays inherent in such a procedure and the ultimate recourse to the courts in any event are also vital considerations. The need for the facilities under discussion is crucial, and the perhaps interminable delays of such a system, involving as it does the possibility for several appeals, might well render it undesirable.

Another possible model is found in state legislation, particularly in Massachusetts and New York, which provides for state-level overriding of local zoning ordinances which exclude low- and moderate-cost housing. The New York State Urban Development Corporation (UDC) may override local zoning and subdivision laws when they conflict with UDC findings that a particular site is appropriate for low- or moderate-cost housing. The statute provides that "when, in the discretion of the corporation, such compliance [with local laws concerning the construction of the housing] is not feasible or practicable," the projects will have to comply only with the requirements of

Some states, including California, made mandatory the adoption of a long-term general plan (or master plan) by general law and charter cities.[122] In California, the general plan must include specific elements enumerated in Government Code § 65302. Government Code § 65860(a) provides that county or city zoning ordinances must be consistent with the general plan of the county or city by January 1, 1973. Government Code § 65860(b) states that any resident or property owner within the city or county may enforce the provision. To encourage planning on the local level for the integration of group homes for the mentally retarded in residential zones, general plan specifications should be made to require in each general plan adequate provision for the flexible placement of group homes for the handicapped in all residential zones. The effect of such legislation in California would be to provide for the immediate amendment of inconsistent ordinances instead of waiting for group home applicants to request amendments on a case-by-case basis throughout the state.[123]

Inappropriate licensing of small-group residences for the mentally retarded is one of the major contributors to local opposition to their integration in residential zones. California creates a separate licensing classification for small-group residences called "family homes" or "family care homes." Many states, however, do not separately classify such homes, but require that they adhere to the same licensing standards which regulate the operation of large-group residences. It would be difficult, if not impossible, to devise a single set of regulations for all com-

---

the state building construction code. N.Y. UNCONSOL. LAWS § 6266(3) (McKinney Supp. 1973). The statute is designed to meet the needs of the state for low-income housing.

The Massachusetts statute provides that at least 0.3 percent of residential land of a community or 10 acres—whichever is larger—must be made available for development, for each year for a period of 5 years, upon application for zoning changes by eligible nonprofit or limited profit housing sponsors. MASS. ANN. LAWS ch. 40B, §§ 20-23 (1973). Refusal by a local jurisdiction to permit nonprofit or limited profit sponsors to proceed with development plans is subject to review by a special state zoning board of appeals.

Here again, the basic notion is one of the existence of a state agency empowered to override the restrictive zoning decision of a municipality. A rather strict mathematical formula is set up in the Massachusetts legislation. It is possible that a similar formula could be established which would define the obligation of a municipality to provide facilities that would care for a certain number of mentally retarded adults or children. The number of persons required to be cared for could be based upon the incidence of mental retardation in the state or upon a more specific evaluation of the incidence of mental retardation in the municipality or in the larger region surrounding the municipality. Until the municipality provided facilities for the care of the established number of persons, a presumption would operate that the proposed licensee should be exempt from the zoning restrictions of the municipality. This presumption could be overcome by a strong showing on behalf of the local government. Once the required number of facilities was present within the municipality. the presumption might be reversed until the need for a larger number of facilities was established at the state level.

A state statutory system designed with any of these models in mind would have the advantage of leaving some measure of control to the municipality, but would ensure that the local entities were aware that should their determinations regarding the matter be unreasonable or contrary to their obligation in the interest of the general welfare, their exclusionary decisions could be reversed at the state level. Such a statute would hopefully force municipalities to consider a broader range of interests when making zoning determinations. The political leverage granted the previously unrepresented interests of the mentally retarded would be considerable.

[122] CAL. GOV'T CODE § 65300 (West 1966). The provisions of sections 65300 et seq. on general plans were recently made applicable to charter cities. CAL. GOV'T CODE § 65700 (West Supp. 1973).

[123] See Haar, In Accordance with a Comprehensive Plan, 68 HARV. L. REV. 1154 (1955) (analysis of the legal effect of general plans in other jurisdictions).

munity residences for the mentally retarded. To be effective, quality controls on the physical configuration and ongoing operation of residential facilities must be based on the number of residents served and the types and severity of handicaps they possess. The answer to the licensing dilemma is not simply to make existing standards stricter. Onerous, irrational regulations may discourage reliable persons from seeking licenses. A balance must be struck, yielding standards which are strict enough to ensure the health and safety of the handicapped residents and neighbors yet not so unreasonable as to discourage license applications.

Another barrier to integration is the uneven distribution of homes within counties, cities, or neighborhoods. In California, licensing and placement agencies have taken no responsibility for the uniform dispersal of homes. Foster homes are most plentiful in areas which offer the least resistance to their existence. In urban areas where zoning is not an issue, housing is cheap, and health standards are permissive, applications for licenses are numerous. The granting of licenses and the placement of residents in group homes without sufficient attention to the locality of placement have produced high-density or "impacted" localities, frequently poor and urban. If the state adopts the treatment philosophy of normalization and relies upon private persons to provide the residential component, the state must ensure the concept's effective implementation. The licensing agency, therefore, should be prohibited by statute from granting a license when the issuance would substantially contribute to the uneven distribution of group homes for the mentally handicapped within a neighborhood, municipality, or county of the state. Regulations should define density restrictions with particularity. A personal inspection of the proposed site should be conducted by licensing officials. Maps showing the concentration of group homes within municipalities, counties, and the state should be available.

Finally, licensing officials, placement agency officials, or their representatives should appear in support of applicants for zoning permits in administrative hearings if the applicants are licensed or have met all licensing requirements except zoning approval. The officials should make licensing regulations available for inspection and reassure members of the zoning authority, and interested citizens, that effective quality controls exist upon the proposed use.

On the Local Level

Under existing administrative systems in most states, persons are given an opportunity to appear before administrative bodies in conditional use (or "special exception") hearings to suggest necessary controls for the proposed use. These hearings provide a forum for the expression of local concerns. Properly used, the conditional use system is a valuable mechanism for the resolution of state and local interests. Citizen participation in the process of normalization, however, should not be limited to administrative proceedings. Channels should be created through which the constructive suggestions of local residents concerning the operation of family care homes may be communicated to licensing and placement agencies.

Residents of municipalities should be consulted for their opinions prior to the adoption of licensing regulations. In instances in which residential facilities for the mentally handicapped have been organized into private nonprofit corporations, neighboring residents should be included on the corporate board of directors. Local participation in the integration of the mentally retarded in the community is essential both to communicate concern and to educate the populace. Public awareness of the problems and needs of the mentally retarded remains the major barrier to normalization.[124]

If an attorney seeks administrative relief from a restrictive ordinance by amendment, special exception, or variance, attention must be paid to methods of advocacy unique to this type of proceeding. Normal rules of evidence and procedure usually do not apply to hearings before administrative zoning bodies. The proceedings generally constitute nothing more than the presentation of individual testimony by interested persons. It is important that the attorney representing the permit applicant understand that the opposing party in a zoning proceeding is usually the public attitude toward retarded people. Methods of legal advocacy must suit the goal the attorney seeks to achieve. In contested zoning applications, the role of the attorney is more political that legal. It is necessary that each member of the administrative body be "lobbied" prior to hearing, unless local practices make such action inappropriate. Influential persons in the community who support the application should be called upon to testify. Representatives of state licensing and placement agencies should be present to describe the licensing controls placed upon the use. Testimony outlining the state's plan for integration and the purpose of integration should be presented. The media of the locality should be asked to help dispel popular misconceptions about mentally retarded people. Finally the attorney should request that letters from the municipality's representatives in the state legislature be directed to individual members of the administrative body.

THE PRIVATE RESTRICTIVE COVENANT:
A LOOK TO THE FUTURE

The subject of this discussion has been the restrictions placed by zoning ordinances on the location of small residential facilities for the mentally retarded. At the conclusion of this discussion it seems appropriate to consider another land use regulation which does or may result in similar restrictions—the uniform, mutually enforceable, restrictive private covenant contained in a deed or other instrument which results in a form of "private zoning." These covenants are generally established when the owner of a tract of land, perhaps a professional subdivider, prepares a "declaration of covenants, conditions and restrictions" which contains the limitations he wishes to impose on the use of the land he proposes to subdivide.

---

[124]The importance of community awareness and participation in the normalization process is emphasized and treated well in the reactions to this paper.

Sometimes the restrictions are recorded on a plat or as a separate instrument, and later incorporated by reference in deeds to individual lots in the tract. There are alternative procedures for establishing such restrictions, but the result is that a number of lots in the tract are conveyed subject to identical restrictions to produce a conformity of use within the tract. Each purchaser in the tract can enforce the restrictions against any other purchaser. The relationships between the purchasers are referred to variously as "equitable servitudes," "reciprocal negative easement," "negative easements," "equities," and "mutual, reciprocal, equitable easements of the nature of servitudes."

Although there is a variety of restrictions contained in reciprocal covenants, those of greatest concern here limit the use of a structure to single-family or residential use. The parties seeking to enforce a restrictive covenant are property owners whose lots are subject to the same restrictions. Although action by the state is relatively slight in such a situation, the parallels between this situation and racial restrictive covenants successfully challenged in *Shelley v. Kraemer*[125] should be apparent.

Before constitutional considerations are presented, it should be noted that a restrictive covenant containing a restriction to use as a single-family dwelling or "single-dwelling house,"[126] could be interpreted by a court as such restrictions have been interpreted in zoning cases. That is, a single housekeeping unit, such as is established in a small residence for the mentally retarded, is likely to fall within the definition of a single-family dwelling or single-family house and therefore not violate the covenant. Some cases support this theory. For instance, the restriction to a "single dwelling house and dwelling house purposes" was found to have a flexible scope and the covenant was not found violated by the group of priests living in the house.[127] However, in another case,[128] a nonprofit religious group which owned a structure and allowed five unrelated adults to live together for the purposes of this religious corporation was found to violate a restrictive covenant which limited the use of the property to that of one family. Even though the court found there was only one housekeeping unit, it found it could not stretch the definition of a family to cover the uses at issue for the purposes of a restrictive covenant.

Covenants restricting the uses of property to residential uses are even more troublesome. The problem has been adjudicated in one California case to date, *Seaton v. Clifford*.[129] Homeowners there sought injunctive and declaratory relief for enforcement of certain restrictions and protective covenants applicable to a tract housing development. The restrictions essentially limited the use of land to single-family dwellings for residential use. The defendant was alleged to be maintaining a business establishment in the nature of a facility for the care of the mentally retarded. The superior court granted summary judgment and permanently enjoined the defendants from "operating any business or commercial establishment or any facility for the care of the mentally retarded, mentally disordered or otherwise handicapped

---

[125] 334 U.S. 1 (1948).
[126] Boston Edison Protective Ass'n v. Paulist Fathers, 306 Mich. 253, 10 N.W.2d 847 (1943).
[127] *Id.*
[128] Simons v. Work of God Corp., 36 Ill, App. 2d 199, 183 N.E.2d 729 (1962).
[129] 24 Cal. App. 3d 46, 100 Cal. Rptr. 779 (1972).

persons."[130] On appeal, the defendant contended that her conduct did not violate the restrictions, that the restrictions were unenforceable as contrary to public policy, and that the restrictions violated the statutes of the state of California. The district court of appeal affirmed the judgment of the superior court, finding that the license, the employees, and the compensation that the defendant received were characteristic of a business enterprise. The defendant had admitted that she received $1,392 a month as compensation for the care of six handicapped individuals. The payments were supplied by the state of California under the Aid to the Totally Disabled program. The defendant had paid employees. The court found that the defendant was essentially maintaining a boarding house and that this was "not synonymous with 'residential purposes' as that latter phrase is commonly interpreted in reference to property use.[131] The court also emphasized that the persons living in the defendant's establishment were apparently transient. The court obviously took notice of, and approved, the reliance of the plaintiffs on the declarations contained in the restrictive covenants and found their desire to maintain the residential character of the neighborhood to be judicially enforceable. The court found the defendant's claim of violation of public policy not well taken.

The defendant urged upon the court the state statutory scheme for residential facilities for the mentally retarded, particularly sections 5115 and 5116 of the Welfare and Institutions Code. The defendant argued that "unless Sections 5115 and 5116 are permitted to override the restrictions [contained in negative covenants] people in all residential tracts could jointly agree to restrictions that would make it impossible for a mentally retarded home to operate anywhere in the state."[132] The court responded that under California law "a change in zoning restrictions in an area does not impair the enforceability of existing deed restrictions,"[133] and concluded:

> The state, for zoning purposes, has decreed that a home for the care of six or less persons is within the definition of residential zoning. . . . While Welfare and Institutions Code Sections 5115 and 5116 may operate as a shield to the operator of such a facility as against the attempted enforcement of its zoning regulations by a municipality, such an artificial and arbitrary attempt by the state at redefinition of terms cannot impair private contractual and property rights.[134]

The court dealt summarily with constitutional problems:

> The enforcement of the restrictions here does not violate public policy nor does it unconstitutionally discriminate against any group of persons. The restrictions are not aimed at the mentally retarded, they are aimed at the commercial aspects of the defendant's activity. The enforcement does nothing more than satisfy the reasonable expectancy of the other homeowners that the residential character of the neighborhood will be preserved.[135]

---

[130] *Id.* at 48-49, 100 Cal. Rptr. at 780.
[131] *Id.* at 51, 100 Cal. Rptr. at 781.
[132] *Id.* at 52, 100 Cal. Rptr. at 782.
[133] *Id.*
[134] *Id., citing* U.S. CONST. art 1, § 10; CAL. CONST. art 1, § 16.
[135] *Id.*

The approach of the *Seaton* court bodes ills for the success of challenges to restrictive covenants which are sought to be enforced against residential facilities for the mentally retarded. However, there are distinctions which could be raised in reference to factual situations in other cases, notably the court's emphasis on the transient nature of the defendant's clientele in *Seaton*.

Turning to the constitutional questions, the courts have exempted covenants from the constitutional criteria applied to zoning regulations unless the covenant imposed racial restrictions. As private contracts, goes the judicial litany, covenants are not subject to constitutional restraints, even though the designation of covenants as contracts is, in many respects, unrealistic.[136] Two methods of challenge to, and control by the courts upon, the enforcement of private restrictive covenants have been suggested. One would be to consider all deed covenants as "state action" and subject to constitutional review. The second would be to continue to call the covenants "contracts," but to hold them invalid, as a violation of public policy, where similar restrictions in zoning would be unconstitutional.[137] The usefulness of either of these approaches is dependent upon a prior judicial development of constitutional restraints upon similar zoning restrictions.

Reaction Comment

JOHN DEUTCH

I AM NOT an attorney and I am not expert in the history or present problems of mental retardation in the United States. I was invited to participate in this discussion because I was an active opponent in 1972 to the establishment of a residential prevocational life care program for mentally retarded young adults in the house next door to my home. During this period I considered the purposes of this type of program, the implications for my family and my neighbors, and the question of the process by which such a program should be established in a community. I also discussed the matter with many, including Mr. William Gorham, president of the Urban Institute of Washington, D.C., and a former assistant secretary of the Department of Health, Education, and Welfare. I sought Bill Gorham's counsel not only because he is a close friend and knowledgeable in matters of public policy, but also because he has a mentally retarded daughter and could be counted on to have insight into, and a deep concern with, problems of mental retardation in the nation. Although Bill Gorham should not be assumed to agree with the views I express here, he did suggest

---

[136] Note, *Validity Rules Concerning Public Zoning and Private Covenants: A Comparison and Critique,* 39 S. CAL. L. REV. 409, 436-37 (1966). The note is an excellent discussion of the problems of private restrictive covenants, although it is restricted to the more traditional questions of minimum lot size, architectural controls, etc. It should be consulted by anyone facing a problem with restrictive covenants.

[137] Both theories are discussed in Note, *Validity Rules Concerning Public Zoning and Private Covenants: A Comparison and Critique,* 39 S. CAL. L. REV. 409 (1966). *See* our earlier discussion of constitutional challenges to similar zoning restrictions in "Constitutional Challenges to Restrictive Zoning."

that my "challenging and somewhat iconoclastic view" might contribute to a stimulating and fruitful interaction. I accepted the invitation to participate in this discussion because I am not in principle opposed to residential programs for normalization of the mentally retarded and I would hope that to the extent that my comments have merit, they might contribute to better design of these important public programs.

Chandler and Ross' paper on zoning barriers to normalization provides a perfect vehicle for raising the issues that I think are important and too frequently overlooked. Many of my comments will be highly critical and I expect that there will be a tendency, certainly understandable, to dismiss these comments as those of one who, by his own admission, has been an opponent and is unknowledgeable in the law or problems of the mentally retarded. I hope that this impulse will be resisted and careful consideration given to the points I raise. There frequently is value in listening to a responsible critic. Advocates of programs for the mentally retarded, perhaps because they often have personal involvement, are frequently so immersed in their own point of view and the feeling that their cause is just that they do not see any merit in legitimate criticism. This not only is tactically unwise, but may in the long run be contrary to the public interest.

As the outset it is important to recognize that the basic objective of residential normalization is "the development of small-group homes which provide residents with as near a family environment as possible." Chandler and Ross view the problem as "how to facilitate the flexible placement" of residential homes for the retarded in "geographic areas most conducive to normalization" and in their paper examine zoning barriers to normalization and present legal efforts to overcome these barriers. Chandler and Ross have adopted a primarily legal approach for achieving their objective and this is unfortunate for several reasons. First, approaching the stated objective from the legal perspective is too narrow. A residential home for the retarded does not automatically become successful once a zoning barrier is overcome and the required special permit or other legal instrument obtained. The residential home will be successful if, and only if, it becomes an integrated part of the community; otherwise the facility is no more than a mini-custodial institution. The primary problem is a social problem of dealing with how people react, not how people ought to react, and the legal problem, even if favorably resolved, is only part of this problem. It is noteworthy that Chandler and Ross do not focus on the *neighborhood*. Yet acceptance by the neighborhood can yield the greatest benefit to residential normalization and it is also the neighborhood which can mount the most effective opposition to this type of program.

Another example of the limitation of the legal approach taken by Chandler and Ross is their proposal, as an alternative model for reconciliation of state and local interests, of the Massachusetts low- and moderate-income housing statute which provides for state-level overriding of local zoning ordinances. Chandler and Ross provide no empirical evidence for the success of this and similar approaches, and, indeed, it is my understanding that in Massachusetts this legal remedy has rarely been used and is likely to be used only infrequently. The reason goes beyond the high cost and long delays involved, to the reluctance of many committed supporters to bypass the accepted political and social mechanisms of the town. For example, this year in Lexington, Massachusetts, St. Brigid's Church sought approval for a zoning change from the Town Meeting to erect 16 moderate- and low-income housing units and did not receive the required two-thirds vote. I think it is understandable, in light of the expressed social and political attitudes of the town, that St. Brigid's has not sought relief under the Massachusetts statute.

In short, the most important barrier to residential normalization is not a zoning barrier; it is acceptance by neighbors. Chandler and Ross lose sight of the fact that the law reflects community attitudes and when one encounters opposition to a zoning change at the local level it is more worthwhile to develop a sensitivity to the community than to seek immediately to circumvent local opposition by state law.

The second important reason why the legal approach of Chandler and Ross is unfortunate is that it consists mostly of advocacy, rather than analysis. Our concern should extend beyond the consideration of tactics of how zoning barriers can be overcome to an assessment of the desirability of a public policy of residential normalization. We should attempt to determine the relative advantages and disadvantages to all parts of the community of the residential normalization program compared to alternative programs for the mentally retarded. Chandler and Ross assume that the mentally retarded are best served through residential normalization. However, they make the important further assumption, without supporting evidence, that when all the competing interests of society are considered, residential normalization is the preferred public policy. This latter assumption deserves more attention than it has received in their paper.

It certainly is not an easy matter to assess what is a desirable public policy. It is clear, however, that considerations other than the law enter. A useful shortcut for assessing alternative public policies is to ask "who gains and who pays" for each the alternative.

If we are asked to choose between well-run residential facilities and poor custodial institutions for the mentally retarded, the choice is simple. On the other hand, if we are asked to choose between well-run residential facilities and high-quality institutions, the problem is more difficult. Consider for a moment the hypothetical case in which a county or region could choose between a single institution or a number of smaller residential facilities that were determined to provide equal quality care for the mentally retarded. Under these circumstances the choice between the two alternative modes of care does not involve consideration of the interests of the mentally retarded, since, by assumption, the benefits they receive would be equal. Nevertheless, there remains the substantial question of determining which alternative is most desirable. The question, in this hypothetical situation, can be decided only by examining the costs and benefits to the non-retarded community of each of the alternatives. One must do a bit of imprecise social accounting to determine the net benefits to the community of the two alternatives.

I suggest that in this hypothetical situation, where the net benefits to the mentally retarded citizens are assumed equal in the two alternative modes, it might well turn out that the institutional mode would result in higher net benefits to the community. My reason for seriously considering this possibility is the difference in the distribution of how the "costs" (by which I mean social costs and not just financial costs) are borne by the community. In the first alternative of a state-run institution, the important "costs" are borne by the general tax levy. In the second alternative of a group of small residential facilities, the "costs" are redistributed to two groups — the neighbors of the residential facility, who will not, for right or wrong, wish to live near a group of retarded citizens, and the set of private individuals (presumably typically the family of retarded persons) who are ultimately responsible for the direct financing of the nonprofit residence. This redistributive effect of the "costs" in residential normalization is an important consideration in determining the net "benefits" in this hypothetical situation.

If it is admitted in this hypothetical situation that the institution is the more desirable alternative, it is a small, but painful, step to raise the question in the more realistic situation where one assumes that the interests of the mentally retarded are *not* equally served in the two alternatives. For then we face a situation in which an institution is more favorable from the public's point of view, whereas residential normalization is more favorable from the point of view of retarded citizens; some rational basis, beyond a legal process, for balancing these interests must be sought.

It seems to me that there is no reason in principle why an institution for the retarded cannot be designed to provide the desirable living conditions associated with residential facilities. As a practical matter perhaps we would all agree that institutions have not provided much beyond custodial care and consequently have been dehumanizing. This fact is an important reason for favoring residential normalization. It is important, however, to appreciate the implication of this shortcoming of state-operated institutions for the mentally retarded.

When a normal child is born to a family, it confers throughout its life a complicated set of costs and benefits to the parents and to society. Society provides all sorts of subsidies (*e.g.,* public education) to the child, presumably as an investment that will yield a return from the mature citizen. In contrast, when a mentally retarded child is born to a family, it confers throughout its life an entirely different set of costs and benefits to society. Fundamental considerations of social equity suggest that the state should assume a portion of the burdens from the parents and family and that these costs should be shared, as equally as possible, by more fortunate citizens. It is a sad fact that the state has not gone sufficiently far in providing this care — indeed it has not gone beyond providing custodial residences and some childhood special education programs. A responsible critic might well adopt the point of view that residential normalization has a stark economic motivation. The state is unwilling to bear the direct financial costs of adequate mental health care facilities and it is attempting to promote a different program, residential normalization, which shifts the financial and other costs to other groups in society. One might add that a similar interpretation can be given to a variety of other presently fashionable social residential programs, such as drug halfway houses, community youth facilities, and prison halfway houses. As concerned citizens we should resist the tendency to accept direct financial governmental costs as an adequate measure of the total social costs to the community. Our job is to understand as best we can what the social costs are and then to direct our efforts toward ensuring that governmental programs at the federal, state, or local level properly reflect these costs.

Chandler and Ross do not devote any attention to the question of "who gains and who pays" from residential normalization. They state that the private foster home is "paid by a state agency a per capita sum for the room and board provided" and that treatment "generally occurs off the premises." I would be most interested in knowing if the total state financial contribution is less in a residential normalization program than in an alternative regional state-operated institutional program. If this is so, and I suspect it is, I would be concerned that either the financial burden is, in effect, being shifted to private individuals or the net resources being devoted to the mentally retarded citizen are declining.

I should like to conclude this consideration of "who gains and who pays" for residential normalization by pointing to a very real "cost" that is borne by the normal neighbors of residential facilities for the handicapped. One important difference between an institutional program and a residential program is that in the latter a much larger number of normal families will be exposed on a day-to-day basis to the mentally retarded. Whether one likes it or not or whether it is right or wrong, one should anticipate that the neighboring normal families will not wish to be so exposed. They are being asked to bear a very real psychological cost of living in an atmosphere which is not normal, in the sense that their block or neighborhood will not reflect the ordinary composition of the community (which should include black and white, rich and poor, and a certain number of families with mentally retarded members). The residential normalization program redistributes these psychological costs to their backyard. Chandler and Ross apparently do not view this "general uneasiness" as a legitimate concern and indeed raise the false impression that the discomfort is based in "misconceived fears that the mentally retarded possess a high propensity for criminality, that they are oversexed, and that they are carriers of disease." The simple fact is that ordinary citizens seek a normal environment for their families that is in accord with the middle-class social mores and aspirations of the times. This seems perfectly understandable and legitimate to me. As a layman I am astonished when Chandler and Ross state that "there is no rational basis for the classification of the retarded as distinct from nonretarded." To me the preservation of traditional single-family neighborhoods is certainly a legitimate governmental concern, primarily because it is what the average citizen wants.

The most serious deficiency of the Chandler and Ross paper is an inadequate treatment of the question of "who gains and who pays" in residential normalization. In particular, the important point that a neighborhood is being asked to bear a perceived cost is missed. This perceived cost is not based in prejudice or ignorance, but on entirely normal reactions of good people who seek a particular quality of life for their families. When opposition arises in a neighborhood to a zoning change, it is based on this legitimate concern and not on abstract legal principles.

How should neighbors be compensated for this additional burden they are selectively being asked to bear? Certainly not by money transfers. Rather, it is important that every residential normalization program contain, both at the state and local level, explicit provisions that recognize the disproportionate social costs placed on the immediate neighborhood. These provisions should include (1) standards for the site and facility that ensure reasonable privacy to neighbors, (2) effective neighborhood participation in the management of the facility, and (3) a mechanism which guarantees that a residence will not be located in a neighborhood which has become "impacted" by other similar desirable nonresidential social uses.

The Chandler and Ross paper in large measure is directed toward assisting the interested citizen in overcoming zoning barriers to residential normalization. I have argued that this approach is too narrow. The zoning barrier is not a synthetic legal hurdle, it reflects legitimate concerns of people. In some ways the Chandler and Ross paper is a handbook of legal tactics. Nowhere is this more evident than in the section entitled, "On the Local Level: Effective Advocacy." My experience and the comments I have made would lead me to offer quite different advice.

The three pieces of advice I offer are not mentioned by Chandler and Ross: (1) Before legal and/or administrative zoning procedures are commenced, go into the neighborhood, talk to residents and abutters about the program and practical steps that can be taken to alleviate their concerns and reduce the unfavorable impact of the residence that they perceive. (2) Be sure that the residential facility is adequate for the purposes envisioned. It is quite likely that the two principal reasons for the failure of zoning applications are the absence of community support and the physical inadequacy of the facility. (3) In some jurisdictions, such as Massachusetts, linking the residence to a public school special education program may afford an effective alternative argument for the granting of a special permit in a single-family residential zone.

Two pieces of advice offered by Chandler and Ross appear poor to me. First, the suggestion that "each member of the administrative body (*e.g.,* zoning board of appeals) be 'lobbied' prior to hearing," seems to me both inappropriate and tactically unwise. Second, too much publicity in the media and from local political representatives, although it may serve to win the legal battle, may also effectively prevent local residents from speaking their mind. This may be costly in the long-term struggle to have the residential facility integrated into the community.

Finally, I would note that the "alternative models" mentioned by Chandler and Ross are of a strictly legal nature and present no real differences from the point of view of meeting legitimate neighborhood concerns.

As a concerned citizen my objective is to ensure that a reasonable life care program is established for all mentally retarded citizens. It is by no means clear to me that residential normalization is the preferred public program when compared to alternative programs from the perspective of the social costs and benefits to all parts of the community. When a zoning barrier is encountered in practice, it reflects a divergence in legitimate interest between local residents and those concerned with care for the mentally retarded. The issue should not be elevated to an emotional confrontation and cannot be resolved by legal brute force. The Chandler and Ross paper adopts too narrow a view of the problem. It is a useful statement of the legal status of zoning barriers, but it does not help us understand whether or not residential normalization is the relatively most desirable public policy and it does not indicate how to deal equitably with legitimate neighborhood concerns.

ADDENDUM

The preceding comments were directed to an early draft of the Chandler and Ross paper. The version appearing in this volume has the same basic thrust and remains largely unchanged. Certain modifications, however, have been added by the authors which partially meet some of the reservations expressed in my comments. Significant modifications occur in the section of the paper entitled "Toward Effective Action" and in the caveat added to the suggestion that board of appeals members be lobbied.

They add a commendable discussion of the responsibility of state licensing officials, including the suggestions that standards be established which strike a balance between handicapped residents and neighbors, that officials conduct personal inspections of the proposed site, and that officials assure interested citizens that effective quality controls exist. A most important new section entitled "Harmonizing Local Interests: Citizen Participation" is concerned with the role of private citizens in the planning and operation of residential facilities.

Although these new features of the Chandler and Ross paper are useful, they do not bridge the considerable gap between our points of view. Nevertheless, I am most pleased that they have been included. This may be a small example of how an improved design of a public program is achieved by careful and courteous attention to an opponent's views.

Reaction Comment

PETER SIMMONS

CHANDLER AND ROSS are enthusiastically engaged in an assault on the zoning barriers to normalization; their paper reflects the intensity and moral certainty of their commitment. As advocates they display a singularity of purpose — to promote acceptance of small-group homes within the *sanctum sanctorum* of American zoning laws, the single-family residential district.[1] As realists, they are aware that theirs is an uphill fight even though (or perhaps because) their opponents are moved by "misconceived fears and irrational prejudices." Because the struggle is meritorious and the opposition well entrenched, it is particularly important that

---

[1] Chandler and Ross seek admission of group homes to residential zones generally and single-family residential zones particularly. At no point do they explain why entry into single-family residential districts is important: Millions of people live perfectly normal lives in residential districts limited to multiple-family uses. Certainly, courts distinguish between exclusion of a use from an entire community and exclusion from a particular district, and Chandler and Ross ask a great deal of the courts if they seek to end distinctions based upon different kinds of residential uses.

their presentation be persuasive. These remarks are intended to identify opportunities for them to extend their analysis and strengthen their advocacy.

Three premises are imposed[2] upon the reader in the first section of the Chandler-Ross paper: *first*, that "large-scale institutional congregate care" which offers "only custodial supervision" for the mentally retarded is an inadequate and inappropriate answer to their needs; *second,* that the present system of institutional care is beyond reform; and *third,* that we must establish, in place of large-scale, publicly owned and publicly operated institutions, a system of privately owned, privately operated, small-group homes. Unless these premises are "self-evident truths," their proponents have the burden of establishing their merits. Moreover, it is not enough to demonstrate the shameful inadequacy of a system which offers "only custodial supervision" — and this *may* be a self-evident truth — in order to establish the validity of the two succeeding premises. An answer to large-scale institutions offering *only* custodial supervision might well be to ensure that such institutions offer more than custodial supervision. At a minimum, before Chandler and Ross enlist us in their assault upon the barriers of municipal zoning, they have an obligation to show that the attempt to improve the services of large-scale public institutions would be pointless, or worse, and that their alternative is the best answer available.

These citations of deficiency are not made because of abstract devotion to the niceties of formal debate, but because the failure to validate the premises involved tends to obscure one of the essential issues in the controversy: Does the entry of a group home for the mentally retarded into a single-family residential district (applying a traditional and restrictive definition of "family") impose costs upon the neighborhood? If the group home does impose costs upon its neighbors, then the inadequacy of the present treatment system and the unavailability of alternative means are important. The reasonableness of externalizing costs depends, at least in part, upon the magnitude of the public benefit and the unavailability of less burdensome alternatives. Thus, if there is no "problem" because present treatment systems are adequate, or if there are cost-free alternatives, there is little justification for imposing burdens upon otherwise innocent persons. Similarly, if group homes provide the only meaningful treatment context for the mentally retarded, or at least one substantially better than any other known alternative, the public benefit conferred by such a system may be sufficient to justify the burdens imposed upon neighboring residents. Even if Chandler and Ross do not find this analysis apt, their opponents are likely to raise it, in both judicial and legislative arenas; it deserves consideration on this basis alone.

Opponents are certain to claim, as Deutch does, that costs are transferred from

---

[2]The rhetorical flourishes of the opening section of Chandler and Ross' paper leave little room for questioning the desirability of substituting group homes for the present system of institutionalized care for the mentally retarded. Who but a hopeless and self-confessed misanthrope has even the semblance of a choice when the alternatives are, on the one hand, "segregation through colonization," "large-scale congregate care, offering only custodial supervision," and "the brutal reality of institutional 'back wards'"; and, on the other hand, "normalization . . . [which] prescribes the development of small-group homes which provide residents with as near a family environment as possible"?

the public sector or otherwise imposed upon the private sector in general, and neighboring landowners in particular, when group homes are substituted for centralized treatment facilities. This cost transfer provides a plausible basis for concern by those who are scheduled to become the neighbors of a group home. When Chandler and Ross assert that zoning barriers to normalization result from "misconceived fears and irrational prejudices"[3] on the part of neighboring residents, they assume either that a transfer of costs does not occur, or that if it does occur, it does not constitute a rational basis for concern. If a transfer of costs is not in itself objectionable, there is no reason to attempt to ascertain its existence, and the authors ought not be faulted for their failure to discuss the question. Therefore, it is appropriate to determine whether there is a reasonable basis for a neighboring resident's objection to a transfer of costs from the public sector to himself. If such a reasonable basis is found to exist, then it will be necessary to inquire whether a transfer does in fact take place or might reasonably be expected to occur.

There are two formal mechanisms for paying for goods and services provided by the government in our society; various policy considerations, including those of fairness and efficiency, influence which shall be used in a given case. *Direct user charges* are often imposed when it is possible to identify a particular group or class of persons who benefit from the governmental service in a manner distinguishable from the public at large and when it is possible to measure the amount of the service which each individual consumes. Thus, municipal utility services are often charged to the individual householder on the basis of the amount of service he uses during the billing period; the costs of improvements such as street paving and maintenance, sidewalk repairs, tree planting, curb and gutter installation, and street lighting are often assessed to the abutting property owners on the theory that they are the primary beneficiaries and it is thus fair that they pay for benefits they enjoy.

Other public goods and services are paid for out of *general revenue funds* derived from income, sales, and real estate taxes. Examples of this kind of financing include education, police and fire protection, welfare, and defense against foreign enemies. In some instances it is impossible to identify a benefit conferred upon a particular individual which differs from that conferred upon the public at large (*e.g.,* national defense); or it is deemed unwise to inhibit the use of the service by imposing user charges (*e.g.,* fire protection); or the benefits are both public and individual and the costs are split between user charges and general revenues (*e.g.,* public higher education). The main characteristic of the general revenue method of paying for public services is that the costs are distributed widely. To the extent that the income tax provides a substantial proportion of the revenue, cost distribution is "progressive" and serves a redistributive function; we are committed to

---

[3] If irrational prejudices result in a lowering of property values, are the fears of the neighbors really "misconceived"? The protection of property values is one of the historic goals of zoning. *See* Standard State Zoning Enabling Act § 3 (1926). In a more modern context, the protection of property values against what is sometimes "irrational prejudice" is the basis for so-called aesthetic zoning in those jurisdictions which uphold it. *See* United Advertising Corp. v. Borough of Metuchen, 42 N.J. 1, 198 A.2d 447 (1964). *See* Michelman, *Toward a Practical Standard for Aesthetic Regulation,* 15 PRACTICAL LAWYER 36 (1969), for a lucid exposition of the market basis for such regulation.

the principle that those who can best afford it ought to pay the largest share of the cost of the services which benefit all members of the public at large.

The problem, then, with the transfer of costs from the public sector to the neighbors of a group home — assuming for the moment that such a transfer takes place — is that the cost is distributed neither according to the principle that the party who benefits ought to pay nor broadly and progressively throughout all of society. Rather, it is imposed by happenstance upon those who, through no choice or fault of their own, find themselves with a new neighbor. This is not a problem unique to the establishment of group homes. It is well known that the government does not pay for all costs that it imposes upon private persons; each of us is required to absorb certain minimum costs of government as the price of living in "civilized society." Determining when the government ought to pay — that is, the dividing line between the police power and eminent domain — has perplexed the legal system for generations. We can identify an increasing sophistication about the obligation to compensate, based upon policy, if not upon constitutional mandate, when government action has externalized costs to the substantial disadvantage of particular private persons.[4] The consequences of shifting costs from the public to the private sector and the attempt to set limits upon the imposition of such burdens are major issues; it cannot be said that a landowner who is sensitive to such issues is acting irrationally; he may be acting out of self-interest, but this is hardly irrational in a society which prides itself on its market economy.

Having established the reasonableness of the neighbors' concern if a transfer from the public to the private sector occurs, let us now attempt to ascertain whether such a shift does or is likely to take place. In one limited sense Chandler and Ross recognize that an economic shift takes place:

> The changing face of residential services for the mentally retarded in California depends on the transfer to the private sector of the responsibility for the maintenance of residential facilities. By phasing out state hospitals in favor of private community-based foster care, the state avoids the costs of owning and operating large institutions.[5]

But what Chandler and Ross have identified here is a shift within the state budgeting process — from the capital improvement budget to the operating budget — rather than a transfer of costs from the private to the public sector. The state still pays for the services. Although taxpayers in general may have cause for concern if the change involves a reduction in cost effectiveness, there is no reason to believe that neighboring landowners have any special cause for concern because of this change in budgeting.

An obvious difference between the large-scale custodial institution and the

---

[4] For evidence of this development, see City of Buffalo v. George Irish Paper Co., 31 App. Div. 2d 470, 299 N.Y.S.2d 8 (1969), *aff'd,* 26 N.Y.2d 869, 258 N.E.2d 100, 309 N.Y.S.2d 606 (1970) (recognizing and providing protection against condemnation blight); Levin, *Dramatic New Uniform Relocation Assistance and Land Acquisition Policies,* in 1972 INSTITUTE ON PLANNING, ZONING, AND EMINENT DOMAIN 95, which details the increased benefits awarded to persons forced to relocate because of certain federally funded projects.

[5] P. 310 *supra.*

neighborhood group home, and a likely source of cost transfer, is that the former often creates its own environment, whereas the neighborhood facility takes advantage of surrounding uses. When the public institution is located in a rural setting, quite often it will not have immediate neighbors who will suffer in any way from its operation. Neighboring uses in rural (especially agricultural) communities may be less sensitive to the particular externalities of a public institution. When the large-scale institution is located in an urban setting, quite often it will have sufficient grounds so that its immediate neighbors are, at least in relative terms, at substantial distances. Often, when such an institution is found in an urban setting, it will be there because the city has grown up around it. What was originally a rural setting has undergone intensive development. Under such circumstances, neighbors have little to complain about. They chose to locate adjacent to an existing institution.

The group home, if qualified as a single-family use, would not carry with it more open space than other single-family residences. In most cases it would be an unanticipated use in a previously developed neighborhood; few, if any, of the established residential users will have purchased with notice that a group home was a potential use in the district. In fact, the definition of "single family" found in most zoning ordinances is designed to ensure that traditional family living will be the only group life style tolerated. Thus, establishment of group homes in single-family residential districts differs from the large-scale institutional facility in two regards: (1) the group home does not carry with it substantial open space to act as a buffer to neighboring uses and (2) it usually *comes to* an existing residential neighborhood, the neighborhood does not come to it. These two factors alone should be sufficient to demonstrate that there is a transfer of costs incident to the change from public institutions to group homes, unless it is argued that the group home is not unusual or objectionable in a single-family residential district. That is to say, neither the difference in open space, nor the difference in sequence of development, ought to matter if the group home is otherwise indistinguishable from its neighboring single-family uses.

Chandler and Ross are apparently of two minds on whether or not group homes are the equivalent of traditional single-family uses. On the one hand, they have little patience for those who see substantial differences between the two; they characterize their opponents as acting on the basis of "misconceived fears and irrational prejudices." Moreover, they say the objective of their mission is "to overcome discriminatory exclusion of family care homes . . . from single-family residential zones. . . ." The exclusion of group homes can be discriminatory only if they are not markedly different from traditional single-family uses. Thus, the authors are on record in support of the contention that group homes are the equivalent of traditional single-family uses.

But when one examines the definition of "normalization" which Chandler and Ross offer, and when their model statute is studied, an alternative and contradictory conclusion is possible. The definition of normalization adopted by the authors includes an attribute of "dispersal," which is "the uniform distribution of residential facilities throughout the community." If I understand the significance of dispersal, it includes the intention to avoid *impaction*—the clustering of group homes and other treatment facilities in one section of a residential neighborhood. Quite obviously it makes no sense to speak of dispersal unless there are two distinguishable ingredients, the medium and the substance to be dispersed; thus, the authors implicitly acknowledge that group homes can be distinguished from traditional single-family uses. An examination of their model statute reveals three features which distinguish the group home from other single-family residential uses. The statute protects only group homes that are (1) *authorized* or licensed by the state[6] and (2) serve *six or fewer* persons. And (3) the authors are agreeable that *conditions* be imposed as the price of protection. I am unaware of any zoning ordinance that imposes a state licensing requirement upon single-family residences or contemplates the requirement of a conditional use permit. Some zoning ordinances contain density standards for single-family districts, but most often it is the municipal housing code which establishes occupancy standards. (An ordinance that sets a number of occupants without regard to the size of the house or the number of sleeping rooms is so crude a mechanism for regulating density that it invites challenge on due process grounds.) Thus, it appears that Chandler and Ross not only recognize but adopt the position that group homes are distinguishable from ordinary single-family residential uses.

The internal inconsistency is troublesome. It contributes to a major weakness of their paper. If they overcame their ambivalence and openly conceded that group homes are not identical to ordinary single-family uses, they would be forced to explore the precise nature of the differences. This would permit them to accomplish two essential chores. First, they could then distinguish group homes for the mentally retarded from such other nontraditional forms of "family" living such as boarding houses, rooming houses, and halfway houses for alcoholics, drug addicts, sex offenders, thieves, as well as mini-dormitories and a wide variety of hippy pads and communes. If the logic of their argument compels courts and legislatures to remove barriers to all or even some of these applicants for family status, they are asking for more than is necessary and certainly more than is prudent when their clients are mentally retarded citizens. But Chandler and Ross invite such a catastrophe in failing to examine in detail the characteristics of group homes for the mentally retarded. This sort of analysis would provide detailed information and conceptualization so that they could distinguish the group homes which they wish validated from all others clamoring for admission to the sanctified district. Second, Chandler and Ross ought to concede that group homes are distinguishable from single-family residences because a detailed analysis of the differences would permit them to narrow their proposed delegation of authority to impose conditions.

---

[6]Location is not considered in the issuance of licenses; hence, the operation of group homes is customarily subject to local zoning clearance. Any assumption that the licensed operator of a group home is required, as a condition of licensure, to possess management skills or professional training such as would tend to improve the group home's relations with its neighbors is negated by the statement "that licensees need no prior training or experience with the mentally retarded nor do they receive any instruction in mental retardation after licensing." Thus, the fact that a group home is licensed should not, of itself, serve to alleviate neighbors' fears. Chandler and Ross do not explore the possibilities (1) of requiring the licensing agency to make an independent assessment of location or (2) of establishing minimum standards of training for operators.

They are aware that there is a danger that stringent conditions may be imposed as an indirect way to exclude group homes, yet their model statute does nothing to limit the authority of the administrative agency which controls the issuance of such permits. If they analyzed the costs which group homes threaten to impose on residential neighbors in sufficient detail, they would be in a position to draft a precise set of conditions which might be imposed under specific and enumerated circumstances. Their statute could then substantially diminish the scope of the authority it delegates; they cannot write precise performance standards unless they admit the special features of group homes.

Perhaps the state of the art will not permit Chandler and Ross, or anyone else, to identify *all* potential points of tension or instances in which costs are externalized when group homes enter a residential neighborhood. The answer may come as the product of persistent and precise analysis of applicable legal principles. More likely it will require the attorney to leave the confines of his office or library and study the actual settings in which such events occur. This might be a time-consuming and expensive undertaking, but it ought to lead to an accurate assessment of the external costs of group homes, offer needed reassurances to nervous neighbors, and enable a draftsman to narrow the statutory scope of administrative authority. Normalization is a recent reform movement. One publication provides a 133-page list of addresses of halfway houses for the mentally ill and alcoholics;[7] another includes a bibliography of the literature on halfway houses which runs to 387 items.[8] These leads may offer sufficient opportunity to interested scholars and advocates to complete this empirical research assignment before pursuing their cause in the courts.

---

[7] National Institute of Mental Health, Directory of Halfway Houses for the Mentally Ill and Alcoholics (1973).
[8] National Institute of Mental Health, Halfway Houses Serving the Mentally Ill and Alcoholics, 1969-1970, at 25-38 (1971).

CHAPTER 12

Quality Control of Community Services

Editorial Introduction

*T*his chapter addresses itself to the very difficult problem of providing adequate controls on the community services provided to mentally retarded citizens. Boggs takes the position that the problem of quality control of services is really the same whether one is discussing services provided in the community, *i.e.,* outside institutions, or those provided in institutions. Indeed, she prefers to view institutions, properly utilized and operated, as just one group of elements in a whole continuum of "community services." The chapter, therefore, addresses itself generally to the legal basis for quality control. (Chapter 17 is closely related to this chapter.)

Boggs argues for a nationally structured system of quality control, operated within the government, supplemented by voluntary accreditation. She discusses the great contribution to quality control that has been made by nongovernmental accrediting groups such as the Joint Commission on the Accreditation of Hospitals and its Accreditation Council on Facilities for the Mentally Retarded. She sees nongovernmental accreditation as continuing to have a vital role in improving the quality of services, but sees the public responsibility for maintaining minimum standards on behalf of the consumer as one that cannot be delegated to the nongovernmental sector.

Boggs draws on the experience in the fields of education and health services for ideas about the directions required for effective quality control and pays considerable attention to recent congressional attempts to establish an effective national quality control mechanism in the

356

health services area. Noting that these efforts have so far not come to fruition, Boggs nevertheless demonstrates the degree of concern about quality control within government.

Boggs concludes with a proposal that a national quality control mechanism be established by the federal government. She would have this national commission address itself not just to health services, however, but to the whole area of human services delivery systems. She notes that health care is just a small part of the continuum of services required by the mentally retarded and that a coordinated quality control is required of the various interlocking systems.

Caper's reaction supplements the position Boggs takes and argues that there is great need for quality control in the health services area. He notes that it is highly unlikely that quality control is less of a problem in other areas of human services for the mentally retarded.

Chu's reaction stresses the need to be aware of the danger that quality control mechanisms can become captives of the very groups they are to control. He also draws on the experience of the community mental health centers to ask that sanctions for noncompliance with standards be so structured that they can reasonably be expected to be invoked.

PRINCIPAL PAPER

ELIZABETH M. BOGGS

A CONTEXT FOR QUALITY CONTROL

In Chapter 7 of this volume, Professor Gilhool provides an excellent point of departure for a more detailed consideration of the role of the law in "quality control." His classification of community services specifies four types:

1. those generally available to all, in which the retarded also partake in the same way (*e.g.*, vaccination);

2. those generally available to all, in which the retarded partake in some special way or with special provision (*e.g.*, education);

3. those available to some, in which the retarded partake as part of the "some" (*e.g.*, vocational rehabilitation);

4. those available primarily to the retarded as such (*e.g.*, specialized day care, specialized residential care, specialized guardianship)[1]

[1] Gilhool, p. 183, Chapter 7 of this volume.

Gilhool also points out that the courts can better adjudicate rights of access to services than issues dealing with the level or quality of service.[2] He emphasizes that although courts have held that there is presently no federal constitutional right to many of these services, a federal issue of *access* may arise under the equal protection or due process clauses in the case of denial of an entitlement generally available.[3]

The federal courts are often able to speak dramatically on broad issues of rights of access to services, at the same time recognizing the limits on their ability to prescribe specific quality controls of these services. They draw upon broad "reservoirs of power" derived from the general concepts of the Constitution. They set a process of reexamination in motion. Judge Johnson, in *Wyatt v. Stickney*,[4] drew upon these reservoirs to announce a constitutional right to habilitation.[5] Judge Judd, in *New York Association for Retarded Children v. Rockefeller*,[6] on the other hand, initially declined to rule on the existence of a constitutional right to habilitation, but ruled that there clearly was a constitutional right to be kept free from harm in the institutional setting.[7] Judge Judd's approach may seem initially somewhat more conservative than Judge Johnson's, but the two approaches are consistent in initiating a review process by reference to the Constitution, without pretense of being able to regulate the minute details of institutional management.

"The emphasis in *Wyatt* was in assuring the existence of those conditions, which are a precondition to *any* kind of therapy—a humane physical and psychological environment, adequate staff, and individualized treatment plans. In this context, the court does not choose a specific treatment, but makes possible a range of treatment alternatives which persons rendering direct services can choose from."[8] Charles Halpern recently made the same point in different language when he told an American Association on Mental Deficiency audience: "The law is concerned not with telling professionals what to do, but in making sure that they can and do behave like professionals."[9]

In considering the more specific monitoring of the quality of community services, it is essential to recognize that many mechanisms other than litigation are available and essential. One such mechanism, upon which this paper will focus, is that of federal control of the quality of services through funding contingencies and administrative regulation under authority of law. In this connection it is worth noting that coverage has recently been extended to hospital and other

---

[2] *Id.* at 185.

[3] *Id.* at 181-82.

[4] 344 F. Supp. 387, 344 F. Supp. 373 (M.D. Ala. 1972), 334 F. Supp. 1341, 325 F. Supp. 781 (M.D. Ala. 1971), *aff'd sub nom.* Wyatt v. Aderholt, 503 F.2d 1305 (5th Cir. 1974).

[5] 325 F. Supp. at 784.

[6] 357 F. Supp. 752 (E.D.N.Y. 1973) [hereinafter cited as Willowbrook].

[7] *Id.* at 764. In entering a final consent judgment the *Willowbrook* court later noted that:

Somewhat different legal rubrics have been employed in these cases—"protection from harm" in this case and "right to treatment" and "need for care" in others. It appears that there is no bright line separating these standards. Entry of final consent judgment, Willowbrook Civil Nos. 72C356, 72C357 (E.D.N.Y. entered, May 5, 1975).

[8] MENTAL HEALTH LAW PROJECT, BASIC RIGHTS OF THE MENTALLY HANDICAPPED 23 (1973).

[9] Address by Charles Halpern, American Association on Mental Deficiency, Region 7 Conference, Nashville, Tenn., Nov. 30, 1972.

institutional employees (public and private) under the Fair Labor Standards Act Amendments of 1966,[10] thereby raising a presumption that such facilities are within interstate commerce and subject to federal regulation.

A number of generally accepted public policies justifies legislative and regulatory intervention in the control of the quality of human services for the mentally retarded. These include: (1) the principle of *parens patriae*, or society's responsibility to protect the weak and disadvantaged; (2) the responsibility for consumer protection, which can be considered as an application of the contract principle; (3) the responsibility to account for the prudent and efficient use of tax monies, which constitute a major portion of the dollar flow in support of community services; (4) the responsibility to mediate between interests; and (5) the responsibility to fix authority for the execution of the laws.

THE NATURE OF THE SERVICES TO BE REGULATED

In the delivery of services to human beings, there are many interests: primary consumers or clients, relatives and other surrogates of consumers, individual practitioners, organized providers (agencies), proprietors of facilities, managers, and payers (including government). There are conflicting interests within each group, as well as among groups—*e.g.,* conflicts between different professions and between levels of government.

Consumers and providers alike in the field of mental retardation are in general agreement on two principles. First, there is a continuum of human services needs, ranging from health to mental health, to social service, to rehabilitation (vocational and social), to education, and to recreation. The set of services required to meet these needs for mentally retarded citizens embraces all four of Gilhool's types, and, furthermore, requires mediation (or advocacy) services for the client if he is to benefit fully. Thus, comprehensive programing in this context means a program which includes whatever contributions are needed by the client from a great variety of community service systems, including health, education, and welfare. Second, from a program point of view, there is also a continuum between "residential" and "community" services. The only essential distinction between the two is that in residential services housing is provided on the same premises where the professional services are delivered.

Coincidentally parallel to this continuum are issues of custody and control. Because institutions historically have not only had responsibility for comprehensive programing for their residents, but have frequently held legal custody or authority for confinement as well, members of the legal profession often err in assuming that the essence of an institution lies in the manner of admission (*e.g.,* court ordered or voluntary) and authority to restrain, rather than in the range of services it is responsible for providing. The issues of programmatic quality control are, therefore, the same in residential and nonresidential settings. This unity of the quality control

[10] 29 U.S.C. §§ 203, 206-07, 213-14, 216, 255; 42 U.S.C. § 2000e-14 note (1970).

problem is fully recognized by such organizations as the Accreditation Council on Facilities for the Mentally Retarded (hereinafter ACFMR), the Joint Commission on Accreditation of Hospitals, and the United States Senate Subcommittee on Health. The discussion is this chapter will proceed on the same understanding.

Mentally retarded children and adults, in or out of institutions, share the basic need to have simultaneous access to several of the main components of human services systems. The facts that these systems are subject to separate and *not* equal criteria for eligibility, financing, and quality control and that these criteria are often arbitrary and incompatible create barriers to comprehensive quality care in addition to those that already exist *within* each of the segments. Some observers, taking a quick look at this confusion, have advocated the creation of a separate, self-contained services delivery system for the mentally retarded. The major drawback of this approach, however, is that it would be segregating rather than normalizing. The fact is that each mentally retarded person needs selective access to the full range of human services, some of which he can use generically and some of which he will require in an adapted or even a specialized form. The need for an *open system* (*i.e.*, access to all four of Gilhool's types), together with the need for specialized case management, follow-along, and advocacy services that are independent of the practitioners and agencies delivering specific health, education, social, and rehabilitation services (whether generic or specialized), was clearly addressed by the Technical Advisory Committee on Community Services, which has been developing standards for and with ACFMR.[11]

The problems in "putting it all together" for the client in the service systems have their analogue in the "quality control" field. Each of the generic components of the service system has its own traditions respecting standard setting, accreditation, and licensing, both for individual practitioners and for agencies and facilities. Moreover, each component has its own pecking order, lead disciplines, and games of "management monopoly." These are reflected in incompatible statutory bases for the various segments. In addition, there is increasing confusion as to the proper roles of voluntary and public bodies in standard setting and compliance assessment and the respectively appropriate roles of different levels of government.

THE ROLE OF ACCREDITATION AND LICENSURE IN QUALITY CONTROL

For purposes of this chapter, it is important to distinguish among accreditation, licensure, and certification. *Accreditation* is the process by which a *nongovernmental* agency or association evaluates a program, service, or facility and accredits, or recognizes, it as meeting predetermined standards or qualifications specified by the agency or association. *Licensure* is the process by which an agency of the *government* grants permission to an individual meeting predetermined qualifica-

---

[11] ACCREDITATION COUNCIL FOR FACILITIES FOR THE MENTALLY RETARDED, STANDARDS FOR COMMUNITY AGENCIES SERVING PERSONS WITH MENTAL RETARDATION AND OTHER DEVELOPMENTAL DISABILITIES (1973) [hereinafter cited as AGENCIES STANDARDS]; ACFMR STANDARDS FOR RESIDENTIAL FACILITIES FOR THE MENTALLY RETARDED (1971).

tions to engage in a given occupation or to use a particular title or grants permission to an institution or agency to perform specified functions or services. In our context, licensure is usually a state function.[12] *Certification* is a term variously used to signify recognition by an organization or agency (public or private) of an individual or facility. (Hospitals are certified for Medicare, social workers are certified by the National Association of Social Workers, teachers receive certificates from state departments of education, and so on). In our context, certification as applied to a facility is most commonly used to designate a facility whose services are reimbursable from federal funds or clients who have a federal entitlement to such services.

This paper focuses on accreditation and licensure of facilities and services. It must be remembered, however, that licensure of individuals — as doctors, teachers, administrators, or attorneys — is intimately related to quality control of service programs because the standards set for agencies frequently incorporate requirements relative to the qualification of personnel.[13] Thus, the term "qualified mental retardation professional," which has recently become important in standards for institutions, is a collective term encompassing individuals who have achieved a certain status in any one of a wide range of human services professions.[14]

Licensure, certification, and accreditation all presuppose standards. The relationship between standards appropriate for licensure and those which may be enunciated from time to time by accrediting bodies is currently a central issue in public policy in respect to quality assurance. The underlying issues are the same in "community" services as in residential facilities, including "institutions."

The federal government first faced this issue squarely with the advent of Medicare. Cashman and Myers, writing of the events surrounding its inauguration, had this to say:

> An attorney recently commented "... basic to government regulation is the fact that it must use objective standards uniformly applied and which can be interpreted by a court of law. Ultimately, you reach a point where it is the judges who determine whether or not an objective standard has been applied. To make it possible for judges to apply the standard it must be simple." While we do not fully agree with the basic tenet that government should not develop complex standards the fact remains that our standards were complex and subjective, and the statutory requirements were simple, objective and had the force of law. As July 1 approached, there was a notable reluctance to deny certification to any hospital that could meet the statutory requirement.
> . . . .
> There were times when it seemed as though every organization was either asked for or was offering advice. This is a desirable and essential part of the administrative process, particularly in a program such as Medicare. But decisions finally have to be made, and everyone's advice cannot be fully heeded . . . community influence on governmental policy certainly represents one of the major differences between accreditation programs and certification or licensure activities.[15]

[12] U.S. PUBLIC HEALTH SERVICE, STATE LICENSING OF HEALTH FACILITIES, 1968 (U.S. Dep't of Health, Education & Welfare Pub. No. (HSM) 72-1757, 1972).

[13] NATIONAL CENTER FOR HEALTH STATISTICS, STATE LICENSING OF HEALTH OCCUPATIONS (Public Health Service Pub. No. 1758, 1968).

[14] *See, e.g.,* Wyatt v. Stickney, 344 F. Supp. at 379.

[15] Cashman & Meyers, *Medicare: Standards of Service in a New Program—Licensure, Certification, Accreditation,* 57 AM. J. PUBLIC HEALTH 1107 (1967), *quoting from* J. Ludlam, Government Interest in Medical and Hospital Care, Can Voluntary Controls Do the Job? (Proceedings of the 7th Annual Symposium on Hospital Affairs, 1964.)

The following statement, taken from the preface to the aforementioned ACFMR standards, defines a role for accreditation:

> Uniquely American, voluntary accreditation differs from, yet complements, government regulation by means of licensure or certification. Government regulation is derived from public law. and the regulatory body is responsible to the public not only for determining whether the law has been adhered to, but also for initiating action when it has not been. Since accreditation, on the other hand, is not mandatory, but is a method of self-regulation, the accrediting body does not have the responsibility of enforcement. Thus, the accreditation survey is not an inspection, but an evaluation designed to provide educational and consultative benefits to the facility.
>
> A voluntary accreditation program provides for the continuing and objective outside evaluation of services rendered through a mechanism that minimizes domination or interference and provides freedom to experiment and innovate on the part of the agency, as well as freedom to refine and improve the mechanism and raise the standards of measurement on the part of the accrediting body. The voluntary accreditation programs of the Joint Commission and its Accreditation Councils are based on the development of nationally accepted, professionally valid standards, and on the use of valid and reliable procedures for measuring compliance with those standards.[16]

With respect to hospitals, this role has been filled since 1951 by the Joint Commission in Accreditation of Hospitals. Higher education has an even longer history of voluntary accreditation than health services.[17] The role of accreditation in higher education is currently undergoing review and evaluation. The experiences in the education field can, thus, provide important guidance on the uses and potential abuses of accreditation in other fields, such as that of services to the mentally retarded.

Three critical issues have emerged in the review of higher education accreditation. (1) Who should participate in the accreditation policy-making process, peers alone or representatives of other interests as well? (2) If government is to use, for purposes of dispensing public funds, the results of a voluntary accreditation process it does not control, what safeguards must be built in to protect the rights of the various parties involved, including the public? (3) If accreditation is carried out by experts in given subject areas, who review only components of the overall system, how can the interests of the whole be recognized as something more than the sum of its parts, and how can component accreditation processes be coordinated? These issues surfaced clearly during a recent "Study of Accreditation of Selected Health Educational Programs" (SASHEP) to such an extent that the commission conducting the study found it necessary to identify certain underlying principles applicable to all accreditation in higher education.[18] These principles can readily be translated into terms that are equally applicable to accreditation of human services programs.[19]

---

[16] AGENCIES STANDARDS at 4.

[17] F. DICKEY, ACCREDITATION: NEW ATTITUDES AND PARTNERSHIPS (National Comm'n on Accrediting 1973).

[18] Commission to Study Accreditation of Selected Health Educational Programs, Report § 2 (Washington, D.C. 1973).

[19] The study commission's statement of basic policies for accreditation, note 18 *supra,* with minor language substitutions to reflect attention to human services, rather than higher education,

It is of interest to note that several of the issues identified in higher education were at least partially anticipated by the actions which led to the establishment of ACFMR. Thus, even though the Joint Commission on Accreditation of Hospitals itself is still exclusively a combination of provider groups (composed of the American College of Physicians, American College of Surgeons, American Hospital Association, and the American Medical Association) the ACFMR, formed more recently as a component council of the commission, has a more mixed composition, including organizations that represent the interests of consumers.[20] As a result, some intensely interested laymen sit on the council. In seeking to become a "categorical council" of the joint commission, the interorganizational planning group that preceded and set up ACFMR also recognized the need to coordinate its activities with those of other accrediting bodies with contiguous or overlapping jurisdictions.

Some of the reforms in accreditation in higher education are arising in part

---

demonstrates the transferability of accreditation principles from one area to another and the unity of the problem of quality control. The following excerpts from the statement, with language changes in brackets, are illustrative of this fact:

I. Purposes and functions of accreditation
   A. Since the primary purpose of accreditation is to serve the needs of society by identifying those institutions or [service programs] that meet acceptable standards of . . . quality, accreditation should be sponsored and conducted only when there is a demonstrable social need.
   B. In serving the needs of society, accreditation should be soundly constructed and operated so that consideration is given to the interests of institutions [and agencies], to their [service] programs . . . , to members of the professions and others who have legitimate concerns with the [delivery of service], as well as to the concerns and responsibilities of the government. . . .

   . . . .

   D. Accreditation should be designed and conducted in such a manner that it serves as a guiding influence in the development, improvement, and operation of institutions and [service agencies].

II. Operations of accreditation
   A. Policies, procedures, and standards of accreditation should be established and applied on a national uniform basis.
   B. The policies, procedures, and techniques of all accrediting agencies and organizations should be adopted only after thorough analysis and validation, and should be subjected to continual analysis and review. . . .
   C. Accrediting agencies should make provisions on both their visiting committees and their review committees for persons with various competencies including those with intimate knowledge of the [service delivery technology in] the respective professional fields, as well as those directly aware of the concerns of [consumers] and [the general public].
   D. The policies, practices, and standards of accrediting agencies should recognize the interdependence of elements constituting [a comprehensive human service delivery system] and, therefore, should give adequate attention to the total [community service system] when considering one or more of its [service components].

   . . . .

III. Monitoring of accreditation
   A. Accreditation should be coordinated, monitored, and supervised by a national, independent body, governed by a policy board composed primarily of individuals who represent the public interest and, in addition, individuals who may be directly associated with [the service delivery system], the professions, and the civil government.

   . . . .

[20] Organizations represented on ACFMR include the National Association for Retarded Citizens and the United Cerebral Palsy Association, both of which reflect primarily a consumer viewpoint.

because of pressure from the United States Office of Education. The office still relies heavily on accreditation in determining eligibility for funding under the Higher Education Act and other authorities. But the National Council on Accrediting, the coordinating group for the many specialized accrediting activities in this field, is growing increasingly uneasy about the possible displacement of its goals.[21]

A helpful perspective on the origins of this discomfort is provided by the distinguished sociologist Amitai Etzioni. He makes the distinction among several forms of power, including "utilitarian" power and "social-symbolic" power. The former is characterized by material rewards, the latter by symbols of prestige and esteem accorded by peers to each other.[22]

> Students of the professions have pointed out that the autonomy granted to professionals who are basically responsible to their consciences (though they may be censured by their peers and in extreme cases by the courts) is necessary for effective professional work. . . . It is this highly individualized principle which is diametrically opposed to the . . . principle of administrative authority.[23]

Accreditation is a process by which peers exercise social-symbolic control over their collective activities. They sincerely believe that the public is thereby adequately protected. Quite aside from the question of whether all the professional consciences are indeed clear, this mode of control is not compatible with the machinery of government, which is administrative, demands accountability, and uses material rewards (grants, contracts, and fees for service) as its means for exercising control over providers.

It is not at all surprising, therefore, that federal reliance on voluntary accrediting bodies is becoming more controversial in other service fields as well. Of these, the health field is both the most institutionalized and the most chaotic at the present time. Child care (both residential and day) is another area in which peer consensus and public policy have not yet converged. This is partly because the massive flow of federal dollars for human services (other than higher education) is relatively recent and in any case has tended to depend on preexisting state government sanctions.[24] Another factor which tends to move a government agency toward licensure (as against reliance on accreditation) is the presence in the provider population of a significant proportion of proprietary facilities and agencies, as is the case in the nursing home and rehabilitation facility fields and more recently in "developmental" day care centers.

The staff of the United States Senate Subcommittee on Health has been probing these issues in the health care area from a national viewpoint in considerable depth

---

[21] DICKEY, *supra* note 17.

[22] A. ETZIONI, MODERN ORGANIZATIONS 59 (1964).

[23] *Id.* at 76-77.

[24] State licensure of facilities for the mentally retarded dates from the nineteenth century. In 1965 residential facilities were licensed in 42 states by 52 agencies. OFFICE OF MENTAL RETARDATION COORDINATION, MENTAL RETARDATION SOURCE BOOK 58 (U.S. Dep't of Health, Education & Welfare, Pub. No. (OS) 73-81, 1973). Specific authority for licensing day facilities is a more recent trend, exemplified by a comprehensive Minnesota statute covering both 24-hour and day facilities, which was enacted in 1971. Ch. 229 [1971] Minn. Laws. Reg. Sess. 436, *implemented by* Dep't of Public Welfare Rule 34, 1972.

over the past three years in connection with the effort to promote health maintenance organizations. The subcommittee's conclusions are reflected in a recent report which poses and then responds to a fundamental question:

> Who should undertake the assessment and regulation of health care on the basic of outcomes; should it be the Federal government; the states; or should public regulatory authority be delegated to a private, provider-controlled body?
>
> . . . .
>
> The delegation of public regulatory authority to a private, provider-controlled body would appear to create an inherent and essentially insurmountable conflict of interest. . . .
>
> The traditional systems of medical care delivery rely upon the leavening influence of competition among providers. It seems unlikely that competitors could successfully regulate each other and still remain competitors.
>
> This does not mean that professional expertise is not pivotal to the implementation of quality regulation. Scientific and technical expertise is essential and in most cases it can only be supplied by health care professionals.
>
> But, a quality regulatory system should be publicly accountable while relying upon professional expertise.
>
> There are also serious doubts about the constitutionality of delegating public regulatory power and grant-making authority to any private body.[25]

It should be added that many proprietary providers also prefer a public body, not only because such a body is more likely to be politically responsive, but because "due process" is more readily invoked where suspension of a license by a public body would lead to economic loss and hence to "deprivation of property."

Until 1972, Congress recognized accreditation by the Joint Commission on Accreditation of Hospitals, a private provider-controlled body, as a sufficient but not essential condition for certification of a hospital for purposes of reimbursement under Medicare. A facility could (and can) qualify as a hospital if it met the statutory conditions (section 1861 of the Social Security Act) even if it was not on the joint commission list. As of 1972 only about two of every three hospitals certified for Medicare participation were joint commission accredited. Dr. John Porterfield, executive director of the joint commission, has stressed this independence, as well as pointed up the strains which impinge on the joint commission by virtue of its public responsibilities.[26] Up to that time, moreover, Congress forbade the Secretary of Health, Education, and Welfare to set any standard higher than those of the joint commission. This provision was stricken by the Ribicoff amendment incorporated in Pub. L. No. 92-603 in 1972.[27]

The Ribicoff amendment not only freed the Secretary from the joint commission "ceiling" on quality; it also opened up the joint commission survey process to federal

[25]SENATE COMM. ON LABOR AND PUBLIC WELFARE, HEALTH MAINTENANCE ORGANIZATION AND RESOURCES ACT OF 1973, S. REP. No. 93-129, 93rd Cong., 1st Sess. 34-35 (1973) [hereinafter cited as S. REP. No. 93-129].

[26]Porterfield, *From the Director's Office,* PERSPECTIVES, No. 1, January 1973, at 1 (Joint Comm'n on Accreditation of Hospitals Bull.).

[27]42 U.S.C. § 1395bb(a)(4) (Supp. II 1972). The background of the amendment is discussed in the SENATE FINANCE COMM. REPORT ON THE SOCIAL SECURITY AMENDMENTS OF 1972, S. REP. No. 92-1230, 92d Cong., 2d Sess. 289-91 (1972).

validation.[28] This change resulted from court action in *Self Help for the Elderly v. Richardson,*[29] in which the plaintiffs successfully claimed that neither the Secretary nor the Congress could irrevocably delegate regulatory functions to a "non-accountable" private body. The Secretary is authorized, however, to delegate both his initial certification functions and his "validation" duties to an "appropriate" state (or local) public agency.[30] The essential "regulatory" functions at issue pertained to "health and safety," rather than to "quality of care."

At this time, the preponderance of evidence and opinion favors the position that accrediting bodies cannot have the best of both worlds. They cannot retain their "voluntary" character, their subjective "professional assessments," their self government and self-perpetuation, and, at the same time, be viewed as having the precision, responsiveness, accountability, and objectivity required of public agencies endowed with the full authority of the law. It remains important to stress that the functions of accreditation and licensure are still complementary and that each can contribute much to the other. The role of voluntary nongovernmental bodies in improving standards, securing consensus, and assisting providers to improve their performance is one which deserves the support of consumers, providers, and government itself. Public licensure, however, better responds to the ultimate demand for public accountability than does private accreditation.

FEDERAL-STATE RELATIONSHIPS AND QUALITY CONTROL

Recently, as the federal government has increased its participation as a purchaser of health, social, and rehabilitation services, the Congress has become more concerned about "quality control."[31] Except for Medicare, however, most ongoing federal funding for services runs through state treasuries. The commingling of state and federal funds has in most instances left the de facto leadership on program standards with the states. Some examples follow.

In the field of social services, even though the federal government pays 75 percent of the cost, amounting to some $2 billion a year, program standards beyond "definitions" are left to the states. The only major exception has been repeated controversial attempts to set federal standards for day care of children.[32]

Although the federal contribution is proportionately much less in the field of elementary and secondary education than in social services, the fear of "federal control of education has indeed limited federal specifications to the civil rights areas.

---

[28] 42 U.S.C. § 1395bb(b) (Supp. II 1972).

[29] Civil No. 2016-71 (D.D.C. Nov. 11, 1971).

[30] 42 U.S.C. § 1395aa(a), (c) (Supp. II 1972).

[31] In federalese this phrase is sometimes used to refer to procedures for limiting eligibility, utilization, or proliferation of services. In this paper, however, the term applies to maintenance of high standards of professional performance and management.

[32] *See* U.S. Office of Child Development, Dep't of Health, Education & Welfare, Federal Interagency Day Care Requirements (1972) and Guides for Day Care Licensing (1973).

This point is made not to minimize the effect of federal categorical funds, such as those for vocational education, in extending and improving the offerings in certain curricula, or in improving the quantity of services delivered to selected groups such as the handicapped. Rather, the example illustrates a real difficulty in establishing adequate federal control of human services, even where the services are financed in significant part from the federal treasury.

Vocational rehabilitation, an important component of any comprehensive service system for the physically and mentally handicapped, has long relied on federal dollars. Currently the federal contribution is 80 percent in the basic state programs. Such reliance contains a largely unrealized potential for federal intervention in respect to standards. Yet, as of this time, federal regulations are fairly explicit only on the content of the intake study (diagnosis and evaluation); with respect to other services, the state is merely required "to establish and maintain standards for the various types of facilities and personnel utilized in providing services. . . ."[33]

The Department of Health, Education, and Welfare has issued "Standards for Rehabilitation Facilities and Sheltered Workshops" based on the work of an official advisory body, the National Policy and Performance Council.[34] The standards are used in making project grants, but are not binding on the states with respect to their much larger expenditures of categorical federal funds.

THE HEALTH CARE FIELD AS A PROTOTYPE FOR EXPLORATION OF QUALITY CONTROL ISSUES

For various reasons, quality control in the health field currently offers by far the most visible and complex examples of the conflicting forces and ideologies in the whole area of quality control of human services. The evolution of policies and practices involving accreditation of health facilities has already been touched on. State-federal relations in this area are discussed in the McNerney report.[35]

---

[33] 45 C.F.R. § 401.42 (1972).

[34] NATIONAL POLICY AND PERFORMANCE COUNCIL, STANDARDS FOR REHABILITATION FACILITIES AND SHELTERED WORKSHOPS, (U.S. Dep't of Health, Education & Welfare, Pub. No. (SRS) 72-25010, 1972).

[35] U.S. DEP'T OF HEALTH, EDUCATION & WELFARE, REPORT OF THE TASK FORCE ON MEDICAID AND RELATED PROGRAMS 45-47 (1970) (emphasis in original):

Quality of Care

The Medicaid legislation contains numerous provisions intended to assure quality care for the needy and medically needy. Quality, however, is strongly influenced by the scope of services provided—i.e., the appropriate mix of services, the availability of these services and standards for providers of service.

In reviewing the policies on standards and their application, key factors noted were confusion, duplication of effort and inadequacy of surveillance of quality of care that have resulted from lack of coordination among Federal and State health programs. Some of this confusion arises from differing legislative requirements under various programs.

The function of Federal standards should be to establish consistent minimum requirements which States should be encouraged to exceed, according to their ability and resources to do so.

Concern with the related issues of economy and efficiency preoccupies the Office of Management and Budget. The Senate Finance Committee also worries about cost control in the health field and hence elaborates "utilization review" to prevent "too much" care.[36] States are concerned with overbuilding and "duplication." "Area wide planning" and "certificates of need" are the current jargon.[37]

Meanwhile, the Subcommittee on Health (which does not control the billions that flow through Medicare and Medicaid) of the Senate Labor and Public Welfare Committee has documented an overwhelming array of examples of shortcomings in moving the qualified professional and potential patient into affirmative interaction, and of variability in the "norms" of practice.[38]

> The Medicaid program must be more concerned than it has been with the quality of care which is purchased under the program. Establishment and implementation of reasonable standards of care is one means of accomplishing this. In providing standards, the Federal Government and the States must establish more effective mechanisms for communication and coordination of decisions on what goals they want to achieve, how best to implement standards, and their effect upon the resources of the health-care system. The Department should be closely concerned with coordination of those aspects of Medicaid and Medicare dealing with quality of care.
>
> *A legislative amendment is needed requiring uniform provisions and unified State standard-setting, certification, and consultation functions with respect to providers of service under both Medicaid and Medicare. (To the extent possible, also consistent with desired State flexibility to exceed Federal minimum standards, State-controlled licensure of health facilities and agencies should be integrated with those related functions.) The State agency with primary responsibility for health functions in the State should be responsible for all standards functions. Incentives, guidance and assistance should be provided to the States in bringing this about.*
>
> *Minimum requirements of training, experience and education for State surveyors for Medicaid and Medicare and their immediate supervisors should be developed by HEW. The Department should also be empowered to develop equivalency criteria to be used as a measure in determining whether individuals meet the minimum requirements for surveyors.*
>
> Medical Review
>
> Title XIX requires periodic inspections of all skilled nursing homes and mental hospitals within the State by at least one medical-review team of (a) the care provided in such homes and hospitals to recipients under the plan; (b) the adequacy of services available in particular nursing homes (or mental hospitals) to meet the current health needs and promote the maximum well-being of the patients, with respect to all patients receiving such care; (c) the necessity and desirability of their continued placement in such facilities; and (d) the feasibility of meeting their health-care needs through alternative institutional or noninstitutional services.
>
> Implementing policy requires that the medical-review team inspections include some personal contact with, and observation of, each patient receiving assistance in skilled nursing homes. Because of the many thousands of patients affected by this requirement, the conscientious implementation of the law would require States to make significant expenditures and use scarce personnel.
>
> The value gained in carrying out the present policy of medical review in comparison with the expenditure of necessary resources can be seriously questioned. Because the intent of the requirement is commendable, the solution to the above problem is to permit States greater flexibility in methods to meet successfully the intent of the law by coordinating medical reviews with the requirement for utilization review and certification activities.
>
> *The policy requiring periodic medical review and medical inspection in skilled nursing homes and mental hospitals should be amended to allow States more flexibility in meeting the statutory objective. At the same time efforts should be extended to prevent duplication of medical-review activities with those of utilization review and facility certification for program participation and with expanded visitation efforts by State and county welfare agencies.*

[36] STAFF OF SENATE COMM. ON FINANCE, 91ST CONG., 1ST SESS., MEDICARE AND MEDICAID: PROBLEMS, ISSUES AND ALTERNATIVES 105 (Comm. Print 1970).

[37] A. SOMERS, STATE REGULATION OF HOSPITALS AND HEALTH CARE: THE NEW JERSEY STORY (Blue Cross Ass'n 1973).

[38] S. REP. No. 93-129.

Questions of equal protection are raised by the fact that federal funds, derived from taxes levied on citizens in every state, are expended for health care on behalf of individuals in different states under different rules and contingencies, with the result that access to quality care may be available to a resident of one state but not to a resident of another, without rational distinction. As the federal government's direct role as a third-party payor becomes more prominent, reaching most of the elderly and many of the disabled (including adults disabled by mental retardation), the issues of equity and access will be raised more frequently.

The subcommittee's response, as expressed in Senate bill 14 (1973), is an innovative proposal for "quality assurance." It reflects a thoughtful analysis of the underlying legal and structural problems in the relationships between professionals and patients, between public and private interests, and between state and federal governments. For this reason the model proposed deserves attention in this discussion, even though the needs of the long-term patient, and especially the chronically disabled, are not well addressed in it. Moreover, an examination of the major provisions of Title XIII of the bill should assist in identifying issues common to standard setting and compliance in any human services field.

The subcommittee concludes, *inter alia*, that national norms need to be developed in the health care field, as they have been in occupational safety, food and drug standards, and many other fields where intrastate containment, and hence state autonomy, are no longer realities.

An examination of this proposition shows that although it can be supported in principle, its realization in practice is frought with a number of immediate difficulties. There is no set of definitive facts, and clearly no consensus regarding evaluation of facts, on the validity of any measures of outputs and benefits in the health care system and its components. Out of the recognition of the complexity of this problem—which only underlines the necessity for its being pursued on a nationwide basis with the attendant economies of scale—was born the proposal for a national commission on quality health care assurance, which would develop standards, or "norms," and output measures, assess compliance, research the process, and provide feedback on a continuing basis.

Additionally, Senate bill 14 incorporates an interesting restatement of the minimal federal obligation as affirmed by Judge Judd in relation to Willowbrook,[39] an obligation to assure a plaintiff relief from "harm" or imminent danger. The bill would provide that upon demonstration that imminent danger exists, the commission is empowered to file for an injunction against the provider. In recent years remedies have been sought by this route on several occasions on behalf of mentally retarded persons. The clause would add new avenues of relief to the extent that the prestige and resources of the commission could make the right of way more readily traversable, just as the advent of legal services agencies and "back-up centers" opened up to the mentally retarded avenues to the courts which had previously been cluttered by nonlegal barriers.

The proposal for a national commission is set forth and defended in some detail in the "Report of the Senate Committee on Labor and Public Welfare on the

[39] 357 F. Supp. at 764.

Health Maintenance Organization and Resources Act of 1973."[40] The Senate subsequently passed the bill (by a vote of 69-25) on May 15, 1973,[41] with several significant changes affecting the independence and scope of the commission. The bill was then amended by the House and enacted into law with a more conventional approach to quality control.[42] The proposal in Senate bill 14 to establish a commission was deleted. Instead, a study is to be undertaken by a private nonprofit organization, to be completed by January 1, 1976.[43] Therefore, the enactment of the provisions described here are clearly not imminent. The ideas do, however, deserve to remain current and to have a wider exposure than is usually given to congressional committee reports. For this reason, certain portions of the report, which explicate the commission proposal, are incorporated or paraphrased with comment in this discussion.[44]

Having concluded that a public regulatory body with national scope is needed in the health care field, the Senate Subcommittee on Health went on to examine

[40] S. REP. No. 93-129, at 81-83.
[41] 119 CONG. REC. S9132-40 (daily ed. May 15, 1973).
[42] 87 Stat. 914 (1973).
[43] Pub. L. No. 93-222 § 4, 87 Stat. 914, 934.
[44] S. REP. No. 93-129, at 81-83:

PART A — COMMISSION ON QUALITY HEALTH CARE ASSURANCE

Establishment of the Commission

[Section 403-new section 1301] Establishes a Commission on Quality Health Care Assurance as an independent agency in the Executive Branch. The Commission shall consist of eleven members who because of their experience or education are particularly qualified to serve. Membership shall include representatives of the health care delivery industry, private organizations developing quality health care standards, and consumers who are not related to the delivery of health care. Of the eleven, four must be consumers not related to the delivery of health care. Commission members shall serve a five-year term, except for the first eleven, who shall be appointed on a staggered basis. Members cannot serve more than two terms.

Duties and Powers of the Commission

[New section 1302] Sets forth the functions of the Commission. Requires the Commission to:

1. promulgate standards regarding personnel qualifications, medical group composition, and other characteristics dealing with the adequacy of facilities and equipment;

2. conduct research and experimental programs to develop:

(a) criteria for quality assurance systems; and

(b) norms regarding the processes, utilization, characteristics, and outcomes of health services provided;

3. require and monitor quality assurance systems for health care providers receiving assistance under the Public Health Service Act and the Mental Retardation Facilities and Community Mental Health Centers Construction Act of 1963. Such systems shall be intended to:

(a) improve and assess medical care quality;

(b) evaluate the inputs processes, utilization characteristics, and outcomes of health care in relation to those groups receiving such care; and establish relationships between such inputs, processes, characteristics, and outcomes;

(c) concentrate on those categories of disease which occur most commonly and on which the impact of medical treatment can be most effective;

(d) improve and assess the accessibility, availability and acceptability of health services provided by health care providers;

(e) develop procedures for quality assurance systems to report, through the health care providers policy making body, to the membership and the Commission;

(f) consider the need to include, on the decisionmaking body of the quality assurance system, consumers as well as representatives of the various health professions disciplines providing health services;

the location of the proposed commission on quality care assurance in the governmental structure. It asked: "Should the Commission be an independent regulatory body; what functions other than quality regulation, if any, should be included under the Commission's jurisdiction?"[45]

The subcommittee concluded that the issue was independence versus inclusion in the Department of Health, Education, and Welfare and opted for "independent" agency status. One substantive function now being performed by the Department of Health, Education, and Welfare is promotion of the industry, a task primarily carried out by the Health Services and Mental Health Administration. The committee questioned whether the government body whose main tasks include promotion of the health industry generally and investment in specific providers could simultaneously maintain the proper posture necessary to monitor and regulate the quality performance of this same industry effectively.[46]

Another important function of the Department, primarily carried out by two of its agencies, the Social Security Administration (SSA) for Medicare and the Medical Services Administration (MSA) for Medicaid, is that of third-party payor.

---

4. issue certificates of compliance to health care providers which certify that such providers are maintaining approved quality assurance systems and are otherwise meeting the requirements established by the Commission;

5. revoke or suspend certificates of compliance (after a hearing);

6. monitor health care provider reports on activities conducted under the Public Health Service Act and the Mental Retardation Facilities and Community Mental Health Centers Construction Act of 1963 to assure that such providers are conforming with the Commission's approved quality assurance system and norms;

7. publish statistical descriptions of norms;

8. conduct a research and development program to:
(a) improve the technology for assessing medical care quality emphasizing health care outcomes;
(b) assess and compare medical care quality provided under alternative health care delivery systems;
(c) analyze the effects of providing information to consumers and improve methods for disseminating information;
(d) analyze the impact of the quality assurance program on the level of health care; and
(e) coordinate existing information regarding quality health care assurance programs of government agencies;

9. collect, summarize, and distribute information on the impact of medical services and the health status of the United States population;

10. provide technical assistance to health care providers who are developing quality control programs;

11. study the levels, costs, and quality of health care provided under Federal health care programs;

12. administer the reinsurance program established under part B of new title XIII;

13. analyze the need to standardize medical records and facilitate the development of a standardized system of medical reference systems;

14. prescribe a schedule of reasonable contingent fees for attorneys representing health care providers who are claimants in malpractice arbitration proceedings (under new section 1309); and

15. report annually to the Congress on the activities conducted under this title and make recommendations for additional necessary legislation.

The Commission is required to consider the following when developing Quality Health Care Standards: (a) existing State regulations; (b) existing quality standards for Federal health agencies; and (c) results of the Federal Medical Malpractice Reinsurance Program and arbitration procedures (established under part B).

[45] S. Rep. No. 93-129, at 37.
[46] *Id.* at 37-41.

The committee was skeptical of lodging the quality regulatory function in the same department as the third-party payor function. The committee stated:

> The third-party payor may be concerned about the quality of those services that he purchases for others, but he is likely to be less concerned than if he were purchasing them for himself. More important, in the case of SSA and MSA, these agencies seem to be monitored particularly closely by Congress on their ability to hold down costs. Hence, their main interest is likely to be the containment of costs, and if forced to choose between lower cost/lower quality and higher cost/higher quality, then these agencies would appear to be placed in a most ambivalent situation.[47]

As noted earlier, the concept of an independent commission proposed by the committee did not survive the legislative process. However, during 1973-74 there was increasing evidence that HEW Secretary Weinberger recognized two issues: (1) the need to place responsibility for standards and for such control of assessment practices as are retained by the federal government vis-a-vis the states outside the agencies operationally responsible for reimbursement—i.e., elsewhere than in SSA and MSA—and (2) the need to develop consistency in the standards applied to similar facilities under Title XVIII (Medicare) and Title XIX (Medicaid), respectively. Responsibility in these areas was progressively assembled into the Public Health Service, where the Bureau of Quality Assurance became increasingly visible as the center of policy development with respect to health care standards generally, and the Office of Nursing Home Affairs emerged as the locus for resolving issues of enforcement specifically affecting skilled nursing facilities and intermediate care facilities. Operational duties relative to monitoring state performance, including approval of waivers for particular facilities, have now been delegated to the regional offices. Each regional office now has an Office of Long-Term Care Standards Enforcement headed by a director who reports directly to the regional director, who in turn reports directly to the Secretary.

It is well recognized by HEW watchers that the administrative distances between SSA, MSA, and PHS are even greater than their geographical distances (Baltimore, Washington; and Rockville, Maryland, respectively); thus, in practice if not in theory, the Secretary met some of the fundamental concerns of the Senate committee.

Moreover, the Secretary, unlike the committee, is in a position to make the major funding contingencies of Medicare and Medicaid supportive of his standards and enforcement procedures. Because of jurisdictional issues between the Senate Committee on Labor and Public Welfare and the Senate Committee on Finance (which has jurisdiction over all titles of the Social Security Act), the former could not set any conditions that would make Medicare or Medicaid reimbursements contingent upon certification by its proposed commission. The quid pro quo offered to providers to reward their compliance was the small carrot of "elective"

---

[47] 87 Stat. 914 (Dec. 29, 1973).

access to assistance under the Public Health Service Act[48] or the Mental Retardation Facilities and Community Mental Health Centers Construction Act of 1963[49] (which now includes the Developmental Disabilities Act[50]) for those "health care providers" who otherwise qualify under these acts. Since much of the Public Health Service Act funding goes for research or training or public health (as distinct from personal health care) and since only 3 or 4 of the 16 services enumerated in the Developmental Disabilities Act would be ordinarily delivered by "health care providers," the commission might find itself wielding only about 5 percent of the federal "persuasion" toward obtaining higher standards of quality. Thus, the power of the proposed commission would be more symbolic (in Etzioni's sense) than utilitarian.

The senate committee appears to favor a strong commission with nationwide influence and clout. Nevertheless, in addition to the tenuous reward system, other weaknesses appear. For reasons that must surely include political realism, the committee was prepared to have the commission delegate its compliance review functions and even its standard-setting functions to any state that would submit an acceptable "state plan." To quote the report:

> The concept of permitting the state agencies to develop their own standards and to enforce them, while giving the Commission evaluative authority over the state plan, is in keeping with the overall philosophy of the Committee. Where this is not possible, the Federal government has the obligation to the public to assume such responsibilities.[51]

This scarcely seems more powerful than the present arrangements by which the Department of Health, Education, and Welfare contracts with the states to certify nursing homes for Medicare reimbursements.[52]

STANDARDS FOR INSTITUTIONS FOR THE MENTALLY RETARDED—A SMALL VORTEX IN THE MAINSTREAM OF QUALITY CONTROL

Under Medicaid, the attenuation of federal influence can be even greater than in Medicare, since the program itself is state administered, with federal aid. Until 1974 "hard" federal requirements for state inspection and approval of inpatient facilities were minimal and more concerned with "life safety" than with programs. Millions of federal Medicaid dollars were flowing into Willowbrook and similar institutions which state agencies had approved for Medicaid funding as "skilled nurs-

---

[48]*E.g.,* 42 U.S.C. § 291a (1970).
[49]*E.g.,* 42 U.S.C. § 2662 (1970).
[50]42 U.S.C. §§ 2661-66, 2670-77c, 2691 & 2693-96 (1970).
[51]S. Rep. No. 93-129, at 46.
[52]Staff of Senate Comm. on Finance, 91st Cong., 1st Sess., *supra* note 37, at 92.

ing homes" or "intermediate care facilities." An intermediate care facility is an institution which provides (at less than a skilled nursing level) "health-related care and services" (above the level of room and board) to persons who require such care because of their mental or physical condition.[53]

Intermediate care, which had previously been authorized as an "income maintenance" expense under public assistance to the aged, blind, or disabled (ages 18-65), came under the Medicaid program effective January 1, 1972, as a result of provisions incorporated in Pub. L. No. 92-223 (1971).[54] The same act specified the circumstances under which a public institution for the mentally retarded or persons with related conditions could qualify as an intermediate care facility.[55] (Residents of a public institution, unlike those in private congregate care facilities, cannot qualify for public assistance, or supplemental security income, unless the facility is Medicaid eligible.) The Secretary was thus put under the necessity of promulgating standards for "ICF/MRs" which were specific to the needs of the retarded and not merely subsumed under the general standards applicable to various kinds of personal care homes for the elderly. The proposed regulations,[56] published in March 1973, were based on the ACFMR standards for residential facilities.[57] With some modifications, they reflected those items in the ACFMR list which were considered "essential" by the councilors. The proposal set entry levels, but called for convergence to full compliance within three years.

The reaction was mixed. Attorneys called for more explicit statements on "due process" and civil rights; state administrators called for more flexibility, particularly on staffing ratios and subdivision of sleeping rooms, which would have required major new investments; ACFMR councilors felt compromised. The new administrator of the Social and Rehabilitation Service, who joined the service after the proposed regulations were out, opined that the federal government should limit itself to "health and safety" and leave "program standards" to the states.[58] This position was not supported by other program-oriented operating agencies in HEW nor by the Civil Rights Division of the Department of Justice. The division had been involved in *Wyatt v. Stickney,*[59] and more recently has initiated its first case, against Rosewood State Hospital in Maryland.[60]

More than two years after Pub. L. No. 92-223 was signed, regulations were issued on January 17, 1974.[61] They, too, provide for a three-year escalation. The interim standards, for example, require a maximum bedroom occupancy of 12 except that existing buildings may be approved if altering them would cause "undue

[53] 42 U.S.C. § 1396d(c)(1) (Supp. II 1972).

[54] 85 Stat. 802 (1971); 42 U.S.C. § 1396d (a) (15) (Supp. II 1972).

[55] 42 U.S.C. § 1396d(d) (Supp. II 1972).

[56] 38 Fed. Reg. 5974, 5983-85 (1973).

[57] ACFMR, STANDARDS FOR RESIDENTIAL FACILITIES FOR THE MENTALLY RETARDED (1971).

[58] Conversation with James S. Dwight, administrator of the Social and Rehabilitation Service, August 17, 1973.

[59] 344 F. Supp. 387, 344 F. Supp. 373 (M.D. Ala. 1972), 334 F. Supp. 1341, 325 F. Supp. 781 (M.D. Ala. 1971), *aff'd sub nom.* Wyatt v. Aderholt, 503 F.2d 1305 (5th Cir. 1974).

[60] United States v. Solomon, Civil No. 74-181 (D. Md., filed Feb. 21, 1974).

[61] 39 Fed. Reg. 2219 (1974).

hardship"; effective in 1977, 4 will be the limit unless justified by "program needs of the specific residents."

All these events were paralleled and undoubtedly also influenced by the introduction by Senator Jacob Javits of New York (and others) on January 18, 1973, of Senate bill 458, somewhat misleadingly entitled "Bill of Rights for the Mentally Retarded." The main body of the bill provided for the enactment, as a part of the Public Health Service Act, of the ACFMR residential standards, word for word. Facilities were to be given five years to achieve compliance, under penalty of losing all federal aid. Discussion of the feasibility and propriety of legislating standards occupied a major portion of the testimony presented at the hearing before the Senate Subcommittee on the Handicapped on February 8.[62] Clearly, the administration hoped to head off such an administrative nightmare, by proving its good faith and competence under existing law, but Senator Javits was not appeased by the final ICF regulations; a modified version of his bill, with an updated form of the standards to reflect ACFMR's own revisions, appeared on April 24, 1974, as Title II of Senate bill 3378 to extend the Developmental Disabilities Act.[63]

This account cannot include the final scene in this drama of interaction among the Congress, the executive branch, a voluntary accrediting body, and various other actors including the courts. It is clear, however, that stiff and detailed federal standards cannot be successfully imposed on one element of the service systems without consideration of the impact on other components, particularly if the net effect is to cause a major exodus into unregulated "alternatives."

A PROPOSAL: A COMPREHENSIVE HUMAN SERVICES PERFORMANCE COMMISSION

None of the critical observations made earlier relative to the proposed commission on quality health care assurance negates the major merits of the grand design. Indeed, from the point of view of mentally retarded citizens, the design is not grand enough.

What seems to be required is not a health care commission in glorious isolation, but a college or joint commission composed of technical councils, each with a major component of the service system under its surveillance and a strong sense of community of purpose. The model is a public body, with both technical support and a global view of public policy, which overviews and monitors the entire direct service field encompassing health, education, and social rehabilitation services. A structure somewhat like the National Accreditation Council in higher education, or modeled on the Joint Commission on Accreditation of Hospitals, with its

[62] *Hearings on Developmental Disabilities Act Extension and Rights of the Mentally Retarded Before the Subcomm. on the Handicapped of the Senate Comm. on Labor and Public Welfare,* 93d Cong., 1st Sess. (1973).
[63] S. 3378, Title II, 93d Cong., 2d Sess. (1974).

multiple component subcouncils, but covering the entire human service field, with explicit provision for public and consumer input at a different level, could be considered as a starting point.

Perhaps then the national commission itself could be less concerned with jurisdictional definition (*i.e.,* what is and is not health care) and free itself to consider the total impact of the public (and private) investment in the human services delivery system upon the individual in need of habilitation. An "outcome" orientation as embodied in Senate bill 14 (1973) can be effective only when all the relevant input variables are taken into account. "Health care providers" provide only a fraction of the inputs for most people, including the mentally retarded.[64]

A FINAL CONCERN

Moreover, although the "total" institution does provide most of the inputs for those whom it accepts as residents, such facilities (specialized to the needs of the retarded) dominate the destinies of only 1-1.5 out of 1,000 people at any one time, perhaps 5 out of 1,000 at some time in their lives. For the rest of their lives and for

---

[64] In December 1973, the Secretary of the Department of Health, Education and Welfare promulgated proposed area assignments for 182 Professional Standards Review Organizations (PSRO), 38 Fed. Reg. 19270, 34944 (1973), thus implementing legislation enacted in 1972 as part of the Social Security Amendments of 1972 (Pub. L. No. 92-603). The PSRO requirements appear as Part B of Title XI of the Social Security Act and potentially affect all providers who may receive reimbursement under the act for services rendered to persons eligible for medical care under Medicare, Medicaid, or the Maternal and Child Health and Crippled Children's programs (Titles XVIII, XIX, and V). Payments under these programs now exceed $21 billion a year. PSROs have been described as "a program of tremendous significance that never has received much attention in Washington, and which will prod physicians to police quality and cost of medical care delivered by fellow physicians." Iglehart, *Executive-Congressional Coalition Seeks   Tighter Regulation for the Medical Services Industry,* 1973 NAT'L J. REP. 1684. In fact, the PSROs have considerable autonomy in deciding what services and facilities they will review. They are expected to start on hospitals and similar definable and quantifiable activities. The National Professional Standards Review Council, consisting of 11 physicians, has been convened and is meeting at frequent intervals, but its functions are primarily advisory to the Secretary and consultative to the PSROs. Thus, new and additional "quality control" mechanisms are being put in place which are peer controlled and highly decentralized; exclude participation by allied health professionals as well as consumer interests; reinforce the notion of "professional authority" as contrasted to "administrative authority" in the sense of Etzioni (*supra* note 22); and have a franchise broader than they are expected to elect to exercise. Section 1152(e) provides for PSROs eventually to replace any and all other review, control, certification, or "similar" activities otherwise currently required under any portion of the Social Security Act, on finding by the Secretary that the performance of the PSRO is such that other quality and cost control activities are superfluous. The administration expects PSROs to be the key to quality and cost control under national health insurance.

In the meantime, the health subcommittees in both House and Senate were trying various ploys, the boldest being contained in H.R. 12054 (1973). This would establish state health commissions with both planning and regulatory functions. Such bodies would be mandated to take charge of the licensure of health facilities and manpower and would, at state option, also have standard-setting responsibilities. Iglehart, *Stiff Industry Regulations Likely; Congress, HEW Near Agreement,* 1974 NAT'L J. REP. 163. In April 1974, a spate of variants on this bill was developing primarily in response to another of its provisions, relative to cost control by rate setting.

The implications of these developments for the character and appropriateness of those components of the human services delivery system needed by the mentally retarded in which physicians participate but do not dominate, and for the development of a well-rounded human services delivery system generally, have yet to be fully confronted.

all of the lives of the rest of the retarded, some other "less restrictive alternative" already prevails. Will malnutrition be the less restrictive alternative to the monotony of institutional food? Will the social suasion of the landlady be the alternative to the justicially sanctioned control of the superintendent? Will the lack of privacy of the dormitory be replaced by the solitude of the social isolate in an insensitive "community"? There is evidence that these are even now indeed the alternatives for many.[65]

In my view there are no easy answers. Better special services, better and more receptive generic services, more "normal" living arrangements, finely structured prescriptive diagnoses and individual treatment plans in place of "labels"—all are needed. But behind all the talk about normalization remains the fact without which there would be no need to talk about the mentally retarded and the law in any special way: the fact of impaired ability to cope, greater or lesser as the case may be.

To meet the special need implied by this fact in a new way, the agencies standards of ACFMR set forth as the first requirement of a "community" service system the provision of an independent specialized "individual support system," encompassing a cluster of activities to be undertaken on behalf of the individual independently of the service facilities which treat, train, or house the mentally retarded person. Included are personal advocacy, advising, protective services, personal guardianship to the extent needed, case management, and follow-along.[66] These activities imply some measure of intervention, some societal responsibility to give help when the recipient does not know how to ask for it. For these reasons they raise questions of civil and personal rights to which liberal attorneys are likely to have well-programed reactions. It is to be hoped that a collaborative stance may be developed through which professionals, parents, and attorneys, along with the mentally retarded individuals themselves, may be able to realize the legal and organizational framework for providing such social supports.

Reaction Comment

PHILIP CAPER

BOGGS HAS PROPERLY ARGUED that quality control of services for the mentally retarded is a complex, difficult, and high-priority problem. She has drawn upon experience in the fields of health care and education to demonstrate the very rudimentary state of the quality control art. It is probably fair to say that quality control is no better, and probably worse, in other areas of human services delivery than it is in the health care area. In order to urge further the need for dramatic

[65] Edgerton, *Stigma and the Quality of Life,* forthcoming in THE MENTALLY RETARDED AND SOCIETY: A SOCIAL SCIENCE PERSPECTIVE (M. Begab & S. Richardson eds.).

[66] AGENCIES STANDARDS § 1.

and effective movement toward quality control, this brief discussion will explore additional evidence in the health care field that quality control is presently grossly inadequate.

There is ample evidence that wide variation exists within the medical profession in techniques for diagnosing and treating human illness. The degree of uniformity in the quality of all health care services, as well as in the consumer's ability to evaluate the quality of health care services being delivered, appears to be far less than seems desirable. Experts have cast increasing doubts on continued reliance upon current methods of quality assessment, control, and regulation. An increasing number of studies suggests that although the quality of many individual medical procedures and practitioners is high, the overall quality of care provided in the present system appears to be lower than is generally understood. These studies support two broad conclusions. First, such processes often do not conform to predefined standards of "good medical practice." Second, there are wide variations between different providers in the rates at which laboratory tests, operations, and other medical procedures are performed.[1]

For example, the "Professional Activities Survey" has discovered that the use of antibiotics after tonsillectomies varies from 2 percent in some of its member hospitals to 96 percent in others.[2] Pearson and others found that "on the order of four times as many tonsillectomies are performed in New England as in Liverpool, England, or Uppsala, Sweden."[3] In summary, the authors concluded that interregional differences in the performance of individual operations are "real, large and important; they are found in most of the common operations. Some of the differences may be related to varying incidences of the conditions, but many are more likely to be caused by differences in the systems of medical care."[4]

These and other studies should not necessarily be interpreted to mean that the quality of medical care is universally low, but rather that it could probably be significantly improved through more widespread monitoring of the processes and outcomes of medical care. By measuring performance directly in terms of clinical outcomes, providers should be able to obtain feedback on the efficacy of medical procedures and techniques so that they can more readily improve the quality of medical care that they provide.

In an as yet incomplete study of manpower utilization, the American College of Surgeons—American Surgical Association have determined that 30.7 percent of all practicing surgeons in the United States are noncertified with the American Board of Surgery. According to the study, many of these surgeons are unquestionably dedicated skilled physicians, but some are undertrained, perform too few operations to retain their skills, and should not be performing surgery given the large number of highly competent surgeons available in the United States.[5]

---

[1] *See generally* Lewis & Hassanien, *Continuing Medical Education: An Epidemiologic Evaluation,* 282 NEW ENGLAND J. MEDICINE 254 (1970). *See also* a summary of surveys of medical care for teamster families in 98 THE MODERN HOSPITAL, May 1968, at 77.

[2] COMM'N ON PROFESSIONAL AND HOSPITAL ACTIVITIES, PROFESSIONAL ACTIVITIES, SURVEY REPORTER (Sept. 2, 1969).

[3] Pearson, *Hospital Caseloads in Liverpool, New England & Uppsala,* 2 THE LANCET 559 (1968).

[4] *Id.*

[5] American Surgical Ass'n, American College of Surgeons Study.

Osler Peterson and others conducted an extensive study of general practice in North Carolina in 1953-54. Among their findings, they concluded that the level of performance for general practitioners studied was quite variable.[6]

In short, then, whenever the level of medical practice has been studied, the data have shown it to be extremely variable. General agreement concerning the indications for particular procedures, as well as appropriate treatment once a diagnosis has been established, frequently does not exist. In most instances, satisfactory correlation between the process of medical care and the final outcome is absent.

The results are disappointing when one searches for a universally accepted, nationally effective means of monitoring the processes and outcomes of health care services. States license health care personnel based upon their training and certification and upon the results of examinations, which often have, at best, only a tangential relationship to the requirements of day-to-day medical practice. Facilities are almost universally licensed without respect to the events that occur within them, but rather with concentration upon their physical characteristics.

The closest approximation to a national standard-setting body which presently exists is the Joint Commission on Accreditation of Hospitals (JCAH). The JCAH is a profession-sponsored private voluntary body with minimal consumer representation,which, in the words of its executive director, Dr. Porterfield, "does not express any direct judgment in the medical care itself. . . . Accreditation implies . . . that a hospital, at whatever level it is, is progressing toward improvement in following whatever recommendations we make." [7]

The California Medical Association (CMA) has attempted to upgrade the level of hospital care provided in California hospitals through its 11-year-old program of medical staff surveys. CMA medical staff survey activities attempt to assess the quality of medical care practiced by a hospital's medical staff based upon the CMA's own criteria and standards. As of February 1972, approximately 15 percent of California's 631 hospitals had not requested a survey or been certified by the CMA.[8] Yet, in most instances, these hospitals have continued to remain licensed, have continued to participate in federal, state, and private health insurance plans, and have continued to enjoy the patronage of the public.

These specific examples raise troublesome questions. How is a consumer of health care services of any kind to evaluate accurately the quality of these services in the absence of publicly available benchmarks against which they may be measured? How many facilities throughout the country are operating virtually without accountability to anybody except the very small group of owner-investors or health care practitioners using them? At a time when an ever-larger proportion of personal health services is purchased on a collective, rather than individual, basis, what is the responsibility of the health professions to make their activities visible and accountable?

[6] *An Analytical Study of North Carolina General Practice 1953-54*, 31 J. MEDICAL EDUC., Dec. 1956, at 143.
[7] *Hearings on Physician's Training Facilities and Health Maintenance Organization Before the Subcomm. on Health of the Senate Comm. on Labor and Public Welfare,* 92d Cong., 2d Sess. 1901 (1972).
[8] *Id.* at 1624-52.

It is my belief that pressure for the development of generally applicable standards and criteria, accountable to the public at large, will continue to increase in the health care field. When promulgated, these standards will enable lay consumers, individually or collectively, to evaluate the quality of the health care services they purchase and will enable them to make priority decisions concerning appropriate allocation of their resources based upon the cost and effectiveness of the services they receive.

Medicine, other health care disciplines, and professions providing other human services must become more publicly visible in their activities and more publicly accountable for their processes and procedures. Ultimately, I believe the human services professions will have to stand accountable for the effectiveness of the services they are delivering to the public in terms of the impact of these services on the quality of life.

Reaction Comment

FRANKLIN D. CHU

BOGGS RAISES MANY complex and significant issues in her scholarly presentation. I will limit my response to three general comments.

Boggs quotes Charles Halpern's statement that "[t]he law is concerned not with telling professionals what to do, but making sure that they can and do behave like professionals." This is a vital role for the law to play, for the public can seldom depend on any professional group to police itself properly. A crucial assumption underlying the work of the so-called helping professions is that they first and foremost serve the interests of their individual clients. In the field of medicine this is sanctified in the Hippocratic oath, which, in theory, compels a doctor to do his best to help his patient and under no circumstances to act against the patient's best interests.

In many care settings for the mentally retarded, it is readily apparent that professionals do not function primarily as servants to individual clients. This failure is not due to venality or weakness on the part of professionals; rather, it results from the interaction of the individual with the structure of professional practice. In the one-to-one doctor-patient relationship in which an individual consumer seeks the help of a single practitioner, some people assume that the doctor acts in the interest of the individual. However, when professionals perform their duties in the employment of institutions—such as state institutions, community centers, courts, schools, and health facilities—conflicts frequently arise for the professional. Who is the professional serving: the individual client, the institution that pays the professional his salary, or another institution that has referred the client for help? No mechanisms for quality control can be effective without taking into account such conflicts. First, the professions must recognize the conflicts that influence their work. Second, these conflicts of interest must be made explicit to the public. And third, there must be third-party review of the most sensitive decisions of professionals.

In the certification and licensure of care facilities, realistic penalties should be assessed for noncompliance with standards and regulations. The federal community mental health centers program is an example of how not to hold facilities accountable by unrealistic penalties. Cutting off grant funds is the only manner in which federal officials can penalize individual centers for failure to comply with regulations. Since this drastic step is almost never taken, accountability is a farce. As a practical matter, centers continue to receive federal money whether they are doing good or ill for their patients. To avoid these mistakes, a quality control program for the care of the mentally retarded should include a graduated scale of penalties geared to the degree of noncompliance.

Finally, I would warn of the danger of turning accreditation, licensure, or certification into monopoly-granting procedures for professionals. These procedures often act as entry barriers to exclude volunteers and others from areas in which they are fully competent to provide services. In granting a license, accreditation, or certification, the granting agency or group must exercise great caution that it is certifying expertise and not enhancing prestige.

PART THREE

Institutionalization and the Rights of Mentally Retarded Citizens

CHAPTER 13

The Right to Habilitation

Editorial Introduction

*H*alpern presents a thorough review of the development of the legal concept of the right to habilitation. He places his analysis in the context of a legislative and institutional system that is antiquated in both time and scientific concept. Judicial intervention in the institutional care of the mentally retarded is seen as a response to a disgrace society has allowed to develop within itself. Halpern articulates the various constitutional bases upon which a legal right to habilitation is grounded. He notes that although the term "right to habilitation" is new, it is merely a shorthand way of indicating that the rights of due process, equal protection, and freedom from cruel and unusual punishment apply to mentally retarded citizens in institutions as they do to other citizens. He traces the recent case law development in this area. Halpern closes his paper by returning to the broader context of community attitudes and action— and the new issues that will arise as judicial action proceeds beyond the right to habilitation.

Rothman presents a historical review of the development of institutions in the United States. He notes the similarity between the development of institutions for the mentally retarded and those for the mentally ill and the criminal offender. The development of institutions was legitimized by the same high motives—rehabilitation and habilitation—which legitimize the development of the right to habilitation today. Rothman observes that every society goes through "moments of creation" when it critically evaluates major new efforts. Today is one of these moments, and he warns of the danger of taking an overly optimistic view of the new efforts. Rothman cautions against a primary danger inherent in the effort to establish a right to habilitation for the mentally retarded. This danger is that the process could serve to legitimize the use of massive, impersonal, geographically remote institutions, a use that can never be properly justified. He closes by suggesting some ways of safeguarding against this danger.

Gaver's reaction presents the viewpoint of one responsible for the administration of an institutional system. His emphasis is on the impetus that judicial intervention has provided for reform within the administrative and legislative branches of government. Gaver outlines some of the steps that he as an administrator has taken, and that other administrators can take, in response to the new awareness of legal rights of the mentally retarded. He sees the administrator as having the obligation—and the opportunity—to use this awareness to obtain additional funding and to begin a process of legislative reform, institutional development, community resource development, and public education. As Halpern does, Gaver closes on the note that litigation must be related to efforts to eradicate broad public fears and misconceptions about the mentally retarded.

PRINCIPAL PAPER

CHARLES R. HALPERN

IN OCTOBER 1970 a class action was filed in federal court in Alabama, alleging that the involuntarily confined mental patients at Bryce State Hospital were being denied their constitutional rights in that they were not being afforded adequate treatment. In August 1971 the class was enlarged to include the mentally retarded residents of the Partlow State School and Hospital. After lengthy hearings the court issued a series of orders in which it found habilitation to be inadequate at Partlow and set minimum constitutional standards for adequate habilitation. Thus, in *Wyatt v. Stickney*,[1] the constitutional right to habilitation for the mentally retarded was first articulated.

It is significant that this landmark decision regarding mentally retarded citizens developed literally from a footnote to a decision regarding the mentally ill.[2] The concept of a right to treatment for the mentally ill had been gestating during preceding years, beginning with the landmark decision in *Rouse v. Cameron*.[3] In *Rouse*, the Court of Appeals for the District of Columbia Circuit held that a person involuntarily confined in a public mental hospital had a judicially enforceable right to adequate treatment. Although the court based this ruling on a District of Columbia

---

[1] 344 F. Supp. 387, 344 F. Supp. 373 (M.D. Ala. 1972), 334 F. Supp. 1341, 325 F. Supp. 781 (M.D. Ala. 1971), *aff'd sub nom.* Wyatt v. Aderholt, 503 F.2d 1305 (5th Cir. 1974).
[2] Wyatt v. Stickney, 334 F. Supp. 1341, 1342 n.1.
[3] 373 F.2d 451 (D.C. Cir. 1966). *See* O'Connor v. Donaldson, 95 S. Ct. 2486 (1975).

statute, it enumerated constitutional provisions—due process, equal protection, the prohibition of cruel and unusual punishment—which could arguably compel the same result elsewhere.

The *Rouse* decision triggered much debate in legal and psychiatric circles about the concept of judicial review of the adequacy of treatment of the mentally ill.[4] Prior to that time, it was unchallenged dogma that the mental hospital administrator was in total control of the quality, kind, and quantity of treatment provided residents. Even though the involuntary confinement of the patients was the result of court orders, the courts had not assumed responsibility for ensuring that the promised treatment which justified confinement was in fact delivered. Notably absent from the professional discussion following *Rouse* was any consideration of the implications of the constitutional issues posed by *Rouse* for mentally retarded individuals.

The failure to make this logical extension of the right to treatment principle reflects, in large part, the ignorance of, and indifference to, the problems of mentally retarded citizens which have characterized the legal profession. At the time of the *Rouse* decision, numerous law schools offered courses in law and psychiatry, which focused on the legal problems of the mentally ill. Yet not one law school offered a course that dealt primarily with the legal problems of the mentally retarded.

As lawyers and judges come to understand mental retardation better, legal doctrine in the area can be developed with greater sophistication. Principles developed with respect to the mentally ill can be adapted and modified as appropriate. New concepts responsive to the peculiar needs of the mentally retarded can be developed; and legally sanctioned discrimination against the retarded, based on outmoded attitudes and discredited pseudoscience, can be discarded. The articulation of the rights of mentally retarded individuals in institutions is a step in this direction.

WAREHOUSING THE MENTALLY RETARDED— OUR INHERITED STATUTES AND INSTITUTIONS

To understand the development of the right to habilitation, one must first understand the institutions to which the mentally retarded are consigned and the statutory framework which gives legal sanction to these institutions.

After the "right to treatment" was firmly established in legal jargon, the shorthand term "right to habilitation" was coined to describe a constellation of legal

---

[4]*E.g.,* Tribby v. Cameron, 379 F.2d 104 (D.C. Cir. 1967); Nason v. Superintendent of Bridgewater State Hosp., 353 Mass. 604, 223 N.E.2d 908 (1968); Bazelon, *Implementing the Right to Treatment,* 36 U. Chi. L. Rev. 742 (1969); *Symposium: The Right to Treatment,* 57 Geo. L.J. 673 (1969); Note, *The Nascent Right to Treatment,* 53 Va. L. Rev. 1134 (1967); Note, *Civil Restraint, Mental Illness, and the Right to Treatment,* 77 Yale L.J. 87 (1967); Council of the American Psychiatric Association, *Position Paper on the Question of Adequacy of Treatment,* 123 Am. J. Psychiatry 1458 (1967).

rights which belong to retarded citizens who are confined in institutions.[5] The term, as usually used, refers to rights flowing from the Constitution, although it can also include rights defined by statute or administrative regulation. No general right to habilitation for mentally retarded persons who are not in institutions has yet been developed. Thus, even this progressive development in the law mirrors the archaic system of institutionalization which has been inherited.

The focus on the rights of the institutionalized mentally retarded, however, should not lead to acceptance of the legitimacy of institutionalization itself. It is impossible to discuss a right to habilitation intelligently if it is not recognized that the dichotomy between institution and community, with its implication of isolating the retarded in institutions, is antithetical to adequate habilitation. Judicial intervention which reinforces this inherited dichotomy does not enhance the welfare of the mentally retarded. The best modern thinking in the mental retardation field subscribes to the principle of normalization, a principle which urges that the mentally retarded should live a life style that is as normal as possible. A corollary of the normalization principle is that the treatment of the mentally retarded in large barrackslike institutions is inappropriate.

Statutes concerning the mentally retarded citizen provide a definition which purports to distinguish between two—and only two—classes of persons. They use language such as "feeble minded," "mentally inferior or deficient," "mentally defective person" to characterize a population of people who fail to meet some vaguely articulated criteria of intellectual and social competence.[6] The Alabama statute, for example, permits involuntary commitment of a person who has:

> Such a degree of mental defectiveness from birth, or from an early age that he is unable to care for himself, to manage his affairs with ordinary prudence, or is a menace to the happiness or safety of himself or others in the community, and requires care, supervision, and control either for his own protection or for the protection of others.[7]

The representative statute employs vague but absolute terms. It characterizes mentally retarded persons as being unable to survive in the community. It admits no nuances. Such a simplistic formulation precludes consideration of other questions that should be asked:

In what setting could habilitation services be delivered most effectively?

What habilitation program would entail the least interference with the retarded person's freedom?

What services would permit this person to continue to live in the community?

---

[5] Habilitation has been defined as "the process by which the staff of the institution assists the resident to acquire and maintain those life skills which enable him to cope more effectively with the demands of his own person and of his environment and to raise the level of his physical, mental, and social efficiency. Habilitation includes but is not limited to programs of formal, structured education and treatment." Wyatt v. Stickney, 344 F. Supp. at 395.

[6] *See* THE MENTALLY DISABLED AND THE LAW 98-102 (rev. ed. S. Brakel & R. Rock eds. 1971).

[7] ALA. CODE tit. 45, § 236 (1958).

Rather, the commitment process calls for a negative judgment: This person cannot make it on the outside. Furthermore, this judgment is not mitigated by temporal considerations. The statutory scheme does not invite consideration of temporary institutionalization for short-term skills training designed to return the mentally retarded person to the community with enhanced competence. Rather, commitment to an institution embodies a timeless judgment of the retarded person's incapacity.

The character of the institution in which the mentally retarded person is placed follows from this definition of the institutionalized population. Most of these institutions are hopeless places dedicated to the lifelong custodial care of residents. They are isolated from the larger community, often located in places difficult to reach and geographically remote from major population centers. They are discrete units, with no outreach and no coordination with the facilities that serve the mentally retarded in the community. They lack a habilitation commitment; indeed, the staff frequently feels that many or all of the residents are beyond habilitation. They are grossly underfunded, relying on uncompensated resident labor for bare maintenance. The people who staff such institutions, at professional and nonprofessional levels, do their dreary work without peer approval or public credit. Institutions of this character generate abuse and neglect of residents and cause deterioration of their physical and mental condition. Historically, these conditions have led to cycles of exposure, public outrage, and expressions of reformist enthusiasm, punctuating long periods of public neglect and indifference.

In every state, old-style institutions persist, and their mentally retarded residents suffer cruelly. The existence of these institutions is even more outrageous now than in the past. In recent years, attitudes toward mental retardation have changed radically and habilitation techniques have greatly improved. The giant institution set off in a rural community is no longer the preferred model for treating the mentally retarded. Systems which focus on community-based care—on group homes, day care centers, sheltered workshops, family counseling, respite care, and the like—can and should replace the older model.

Moreover, it has been recognized that the commitment process does not select only the mentally retarded most desperately in need of institutional care. Such vague criteria of social ineptitude as "inability to manage affairs with ordinary prudence" and "need for care, supervision, and control" import a wide range of extraneous considerations which have nothing to do with the mental competence of the person himself. A mentally retarded person in a family who can afford private nursing aid is far less likely to be institutionalized than a retarded person from a poor background. A person who has the good fortune to live in a community where supportive services for the mentally retarded are available is far less likely to be institutionalized than one who lives in a place without such community facilities. And the presence of physical defects in addition to mental defects is often a dispositive factor. Indeed, since many persons are committed to institutions in their infancy, the educational background, experiences, and ideology of a child's pediatrician are likely to be a major factor in whether the child is recommended for institutionalization. The heterogeneity of the institutionalized population is further increased because it includes the mildly retarded person who is institutionalized because it is thought that his antisocial behavior is more humanely dealt with through an institution for the retarded than through the criminal system.

The mentally retarded are a diverse group, with widely varying capacities. The range of habilitation services individuals in this group need is equally varied, yet the institutional and legal framework fails to recognize this diversity. The central question which must be confronted is: How can constitutional rights be ensured for the heterogeneous group that finds its way into the institutions, without adding to the legitimacy of such institutions? And, over the long run, how can the development of a full range of community-based habilitation facilities be encouraged?

The majority of mentally retarded persons now institutionalized should not be there at all; they should be living in the community. The effort to ensure habilitation in massive institutions for the mentally retarded should not deflect attention from the fact that these institutions themselves are an anachronism. This paradox must be borne in mind both by lawyers and mental retardation professionals as they utilize the new tools provided by judicial involvement for implementing the right to habilitation. It would be a tragedy if the net impact of right to habilitation litigation were to generate a misguided effort to turn massive institutions, which are beyond redemption, into suitable habilitation settings. Such institutions by their very nature—their size, their isolation, their impersonality, their tradition—are unsuitable for habilitation.

APPLYING CONSTITUTIONAL NORMS IN INSTITUTIONS FOR THE MENTALLY RETARDED

In retrospect, it seems inevitable that the courts would come to deal with the plight of the institutionalized mentally retarded citizen. At least since 1954, the date of the Supreme Court's decision in *Brown v. Board of Education*,[8] the federal judiciary has shown a special concern with the constitutional rights of minorities who are incapable of asserting their interests through the political process. More particularly, in recent years the courts have begun to delineate the constitutional rights of persons confined in total institutions—jails, prisons, mental hospitals, and juvenile detention facilities. Even so, the right to treatment concept has not been uniformly recognized, and the elaboration of a right to habilitation for the mentally retarded is still at a very rudimentary stage in the courts.

The following sections of this paper analyze the constitutional bases for the right to habilitation and discuss the *Wyatt*[9] decision and two other recent decisions in which federal district courts have considered the constitutional protections afforded the mentally retarded person in an institution, *Burnham v. Department of*

[8]347 U.S. 483 (1954).
[9]*See* note 1 *supra* for full citation.

Public Health[10] and *New York State Association for Retarded Children v. Rockefeller* (the Willowbrook case).[11]

Since *Wyatt* was decided, numerous cases have been filed all over the country concerning the right to habilitation for the mentally retarded.[12] At the present time no court above the trial court level has dealt with the right to habilitation. It is useful, therefore, to set out at some length the doctrinal bases for the right.[13]

Doctrinal Bases for the Right to Habilitation

The Constitution itself does not, of course, explicitly prescribe a right to habilitation. The right follows as a corollary from the guarantees of due process and equal protection and from the constitutional prohibition of cruel and unusual punishment.[14]

Civil commitment deprives a mentally retarded citizen of his personal liberty, an "interest of transcending value,"[15] on which other constitutionally protected rights depend. Civil commitment is one of those exceptional processes by which the government can incarcerate a person who has committed no crime, without the panoply of safeguards that surround the criminal defendant. This process, with its interference in the life of innocent citizens, must be closely scrutinized by the courts.[16] The due process clause of the fourteenth amendment is the starting point for such analysis.

Due Process of Law

Involuntary commitment to an institution for the mentally retarded is indisputedly confinement of a most onerous kind. Benevolent motivation for such confinement is overwhelmed by a harsh reality. The person confined is taken from his normal surroundings and often placed in a massive, isolated, prisonlike institution. The details of his life are regulated by an impersonal bureaucracy, and he is stripped of

[10] 349 F. Supp. 1335 (N.D. Ga. 1972), *rev'd*, 503 F.2d 1319 (5th Cir. 1974). The *Burnham* case was consolidated on appeal with *Wyatt*.

[11] 357 F. Supp. 752 (E.D.N.Y. 1973) [hereinafter cited as Willowbrook].

[12] These cases have been collected periodically and made available to the public by the Office of Mental Retardation, U.S. Dep't of Health, Education & Welfare, in MENTAL RETARDATION AND THE LAW (P. Friedman ed.).

[13] A thoughtful discussion of the right to habilitation appears in Welsch v. Likins, No. 4-72-Civ. 451 (D. Minn., Feb. 15, 1974). The constitutional basis for the right to treatment for the mentally ill was recognized in Donaldson v. O'Connor, 95 S. Ct. 2486 (1975).

[14] The following discussion draws heavily on the legal analysis in the brief in the court of appeals in the *Wyatt* case filed by amici curiae: American Association on Mental Deficiency, American Civil Liberties Union, American Orthopsychiatric Association, American Psychological Association, National Association for Mental Health, National Association for Retarded Children, and the American Psychiatric Association.

     Professor Robert Burt sets out an alternative legal analysis. *See* Burt, pp. 418-37, Chapter 14 of this volume.

[15] Speiser v. Randall, 357 U.S. 513, 525 (1958).

[16] *See* Covington v. Harris, 419 F.2d 617, 623 (D.C. Cir. 1969), Lessard v. Schmidt, 349 F. Supp. 1078 (E.D. Wisc. 1972), *vacated for entry of definitive decree,* 414 U.S. 473 (1974) (the Supreme Court made no ruling on the merits, but rather vacated the order below as being insufficiently specific in the formulation of its remedy), *clarified,* 379 F. Supp. 1376 (E.D. Wisc. 1974), *vacated on procedural grounds,* 95 S. Ct. 1943 (1975); *cf.* Wolf v. Colorado 338 U.S. 25-27 (1949).

his individuality and privacy.[17] For mentally retarded persons who enjoy very considerable autonomy before commitment, the deprivation is great. Others, because of the severity of their retardation and physical abnormalities, have relatively little autonomy in any event. For them, the deprivation attendant upon institutionalization will be relatively less severe; but, nonetheless, the isolation from family and familiar surroundings and the subjection to institutional routines and a barren environment constitute a deprivation.[18]

The Supreme Court has dealt with the due process yardstick by which involuntary confinement of the mentally impaired must be measured. In *Jackson v. Indiana*,[19] a mentally retarded man who was deaf and could not speak was found incompetent to stand trial and was confined to a mental institution where he was not provided treatment or habilitation suitable to his mental impairment or calculated to make him competent. The court held that his confinement for a period of three and one-half years without treatment violated his right to due process of law. The unanimous Court, speaking through Mr. Justice Blackmun, said: "At the least, due process requires that the nature and duration of commitment bear some reasonable relation to the purpose for which the individual is committed."[20] Under the *Jackson* decision, the due process clause imposes substantive requirements on the "nature" of confinement; there must be a "reasonable relation" between the nature of confinement and its purpose. Since statutes for the confinement of mentally retarded individuals are humane statutes intended to ensure adequate habilitation, any confinement without habilitation arguably violates due process. Habilitation is a necessary purpose for any constitutionally acceptable statute for the civil commitment of the mentally impaired. As the district court in *Wyatt* stated: "Adequate and effective treatment is constitutionally required because, absent treatment, the hospital is transformed 'into a penitentiary where one could be held indefinitely for no convicted offense.'"[21]

As a general matter, an individual can be deprived of his liberty only if (1) he has committed an act previously described as a crime and (2) he has the opportunity provided by a criminal trial to contest the allegations made against him.[22] In the commitment of the mentally retarded citizen, these traditional safeguards are removed. The constitutionally necessary exchange is the assurance that habilitation will be provided to the civilly committed person.[23] In *Martarella v. Kelley*,[24] the district court held that civil incarceration of nondelinquent children under primitive conditions without rehabilitative treatment violates due process:

[17] *See, e.g.,* E. GOFFMAN, ASYLUMS (1961); D. VAIL, DEHUMANIZATION AND THE INSTITUTIONAL CAREER (1966).
[18] This discussion refers to *involuntarily* confined retarded persons. The argument for treating all mentally retarded persons in institutions as involuntary residents is set out in the text. *See* pp. 396-99 *infra*.
[19] 406 U.S. 715 (1972).
[20] 406 U.S. at 738. *See also* McNeil v. Director, Patuxent Institution, 407 U.S. 245 (1972).
[21] 325 F. Supp. at 784.
[22] *See* Powell v. Texas, 392 U.S. 514, 533 (1968); *Id.* at 542-43 (Black, J., concurring).
[23] *See* Nason v. Superintendent of Bridgewater State Hosp., 353 Mass. 604, 233 N.E.2d 908 (1968); *cf.* Robinson v. California, 370 U.S. 660 (1962); Commonwealth v. Page, 339 Mass. 313, 159 N.E.2d 82 (1959).
[24] 359 F. Supp. 478 (S.D.N.Y. 1973), 349 F. Supp. 575 (S.D.N.Y. 1972).

> [E]ffective treatment must be the quid pro quo for society's right to exercise its *parens patriae* controls. Whether specifically recognized by statutory enactment or implicitly derived from the constitutional requirements of due process, the right to treatment exists.[25]

The court's holding in *Martarella* applies with equal force to the involuntarily committed mentally retarded individual. The concept of fundamental fairness, which is at the root of due process, forbids the denial of appropriate habilitation to the civilly committed retarded person.[26]

Cruel and Unusual Punishment

The nature of confinement in institutions for the mentally retarded must be measured against the eighth amendment proscription of cruel and unusual punishment, notwithstanding that the mentally retarded person is not confined for punitive purposes. Although confinement reflects a humanitarian intention to ensure adequate habilitation, the fact remains that "any deprivation of liberty, incarceration, or physical detention is, in reality, a form of punishment."[27] Hence, as the Court of Appeals for the First Circuit has recently held, the nature of confinement of the mentally impaired must be reviewed by the courts under the eighth amendment standard.[28]

The cruel and unusual punishment prohibition is not limited to physical torture or barbaric mistreatment; judicial interpretation has broadened the concept. Imprisonment of a narcotics addict for 90 days without treatment has, for example, been held to constitute cruel and unusual punishment.[29] Drug addiction, the court reasoned, is an illness, involuntarily contracted, and punishment for an illness is unconstitutional. In contrast, confinement for "compulsory treatment" would not violate the eighth amendment:

> It is unlikely that any State at this moment in history would attempt to make it a criminal offense for a person to be mentally ill, or a leper, or to be afflicted with a venereal disease. A State might require . . . that the victims of these and other

---

[25] 349 F. Supp. at 600. *See also* Nelson v. Heyne, Civil Nos. 72-1970, 73-1446 (7th Cir., Jan. 31, 1974) (involuntarily confined juveniles have constitutional right to adequate rehabilitative treatment); Stachulak v. Coughlin, 364 F. Supp. 686 (N.D. Ill. 1973).

[26] The fact that some mentally retarded persons may be thought to be dangerous to society does not relieve the state of its obligation to ensure adequate habilitation if they are committed to institutions for the retarded. *See* Tippett v. Maryland, 436 F.2d 1153 (4th Cir. 1971), *cert. granted sub nom.* Murel v. Baltimore City Crim. Ct., 404 U.S. 999 (1971), *cert. dismissed as improvidently granted,* 407 U.S. 355 (1972); Kent v. United States, 401 F.2d 408, 411-12 (D.C. Cir. 1968); Inmates of the Boys' Training School v. Affleck, 346 F.Supp. 1354 (D.R.I. 1972); Commonwealth v. Page, 339 Mass. 313, 159 N.E.2d 82 (1959).

[27] Hamilton v. Love, 328 F. Supp. 1182, 1193 (E.D. Ark. 1971).

[28] Rozecki v. Gaughan, 459 F.2d 6 (1st Cir. 1972). *See also* Cross v. Harris, 418 F.2d 1095, 1101 (D.C. Cir. 1969) ("Incarceration may not seem 'punishment' to the jailors but it is punishment to the jailed."); United States *ex rel.* Schuster v. Herold, 410 F.2d 1071, 1090-91 (2d Cir. 1969), *cert. denied,* 396 U.S. 847 (1969) (detailed comparison showing conditions in Massachusetts mental institution more restrictive than prison); Inmates of Boys' Training School v. Affleck, 346 F. Supp. 1354 (D.R.I. 1972); United States *ex rel.* von Wolfersdorf v. Johnson, 317 F. Supp. 66 (S.D.N.Y. 1970).

[29] Robinson v. California, 370 U.S. 660 (1962); Trop v. Dulles, 356 U.S. 86, 101 (1958) ("There may be involved no physical mistreatment. . . . There is instead the total destruction of the individual's status in organized society.").

human afflictions be dealt with by compulsory treatment, involving quarantine, confinement, or sequestration. But, in the light of contemporary human knowledge, a law which made a criminal offense of such a disease would doubtless be universally thought to be an infliction of cruel and unusual punishment in violation of the Eighth and Fourteenth Amendments.[30]

Under the reasoning of the Court in *Robinson*, incarceration of mentally retarded persons without adequate habilitation violates the eighth amendment ban on cruel and unusual punishment. Mentally retarded citizens suffer from an impairment which requires specialized habilitation. Confinement without such habilitation is indistinguishable from penal confinement.

There is another sense in which the cruel and unusual punishment prohibition of the eighth amendment is relevant to the institutionalized mentally retarded person. Regrettably, conditions in many institutions are substandard to the degree that confinement of the mentally retarded in them violates basic norms of decency. For example, conditions shown to exist in the *Wyatt*[31] hearing — the physical deprivation, the lack of basic sanitation, the overcrowding, the lack of physical exercise, the inadequate diet, the unchecked violence of residents against each other and of employees against residents, the lack of adequate medical and psychiatric care, the abuse of solitary confinement and restraint — constitute cruel and unusual punishment. Indeed, the conditions bear a close resemblance to conditions which have been held to violate this constitutional provision in cases involving convicted criminals and persons accused of crime.[32] A fortiori, these conditions subject the mentally retarded residents to cruel and unusual punishment.

Equal Protection of the Laws

The equal protection clause of the fourteenth amendment requires scrutiny of the standards by which persons are classified by law. The guarantee ensures that a minimal standard of equity and reasonableness constrains the process by which government regulation allocates burdens and benefits. Where fundamental rights are affected, the courts will scrutinize classifications closely. In such cases, the classification must be "measured by a strict equal protection test," and the government has the burden of showing "a substantial and compelling reason" for the classification in question.[33]

Classification of retarded citizens for purposes of institutionalization affects

[30] Robinson v. California, 370 U.S. 660, 666 (1962). The Supreme Court has cautioned against evasion of the eighth amendment standard by the adoption of sham treatment programs — "the hanging of a new sign reading 'hospital' over one wing of the jailhouse." Powell v. Texas, 392 U.S. 514, 529 (1968). *See also* Easter v. District of Columbia, 361 F.2d 50, 55 (D.C. Cir. 1966); Driver v. Hinnant, 356 F.2d 761, 765 (4th Cir. 1966) (incarceration of chronic alcoholics for status constitutes cruel and unusual punishment, but detention for treatment and rehabilitation is permissible).
[31] 334 F. Supp. at 1343; 344 F. Supp. at 393-94.
[32] *See* Haines v. Kerner, 404 U.S. 519 (1972), *aff'd*, 456 F.2d 854 (1972); Wright v. McMann, 387 F.2d 519 (2d Cir. 1967); Jones v. Wittenberg, 323 F. Supp. 93 (1 N.D. Ohio 1971); Hancock v. Avery, 301 F. Supp. 786 (M.D. Tenn. 1969).
[33] *See* Dunn v. Blumstein, 405 U.S. 330 (1972). *See also Developments in the Law — Equal Protection,* 82 HARV. L. REV. 1065 (1969).

the most fundamental rights of the persons committed.[34] Moreover, denial of the right to liberty necessarily infringes on other fundamental rights, including the right to travel and the right of free association.[35] The adverse impact of civil commitment of the mentally ill on these fundamental rights was forcefully stated by Professor David Chambers:

> Civil commitment does not merely penalize movement, as do welfare residency requirements, or somewhat curtail it, as do passport limitations. It eradicates it altogether. In the same manner, freedom of association — the right of "the people to gather in public places for social or political purposes," their right to associate with people of their own choice, protected under the first amendment — is drastically circumscribed. Suddenly, the sphere within which the ill person may travel or associate shrinks from the globe, or the state, or the city down to a day room of forty, or sixty, or two hundred others whom he did not choose to know. . . .
>
> And that is not the end of the commitment's curtailment of an ill person's liberties. His rights peaceably to assemble, to communicate and receive communications from others, to exercise his religious belief through ceremonies of his choice, and to enjoy his privacy in the company of his spouse, or even someone not his spouse, are all but totally ended.[36]

Since the classification of citizens as mentally retarded and committable so drastically impinges on fundamental rights, the closest scrutiny must be given to the classification and its alleged justification.

Classification Justified by the Need for Habilitation   Commitment statutes typically define mentally retarded people as a class in need of some kind of special habilitation service.[37] The basis for the classification of persons to be committed and the characteristic which sets the members of this class apart from the rest of the population is the fact that each one of them has been found to suffer from a degree of mental impairment which requires that special habilitation be provided. The mere fact that such persons are socially inept or incapable of looking out for their own welfare would not justify such classification and confinement. States have no general policy of providing involuntary care in incarcerative settings to citizens who are not mentally impaired, whether or not such care and treatment would be for their own welfare or the welfare of others. Mental retardation is a constitutionally permissible basis for a classification which affects fundamental rights *only* if the state provides persons in this class with suitable habilitation. It is the provision of such habilitation which would save this classification from challenge under the equal protection clause.

As the Supreme Court has held in another context, "equal protection does not require that all persons be dealt with identically, but it does require that a distinc-

---

[34] *Cf.* Speiser v. Randall, 357 U.S. 513, 525 (1958). *See also* Williams v. Illinois, 399 U.S. 235, 263 (1970) (Harlan, J., concurring); Chambers, *Alternatives to Civil Commitment of the Mentally Ill — Practical Guides and Constitutional Imperatives,* 70 MICH. L. REV. 1107, 1155-68 (1972).

[35] The Supreme Court has placed great emphasis on the right to travel. Papachristou v. City of Jacksonville, 405 U.S. 156, 163-64 (1972); Aptheker v. Secretary of State, 378 U.S. 500 (1964); Kent v. Dulles, 357 U.S. 116, 125 (1958). Similarly the Court has protected the right to free association. Coates v. City of Cincinnati, 402 U.S. 611 (1971).

[36] Chambers, *supra* note 34, at 1158-59, 1161 (footnotes omitted).

[37] *See* THE MENTALLY DISABLED AND THE LAW 66-71, 98-102 (rev. ed. S. Brakel & R. Rock eds. 1971).

tion made have some relevance to the purpose for which the classification is made."[38] For the mentally retarded people who are committed to institutions, "the purpose for which classification is made" is to provide habilitation. If the mentally retarded are confined without habilitation, "all semblance of rationality of the classification" purportedly based on the need for habilitation disappears.[39]

Failure to Provide Mentally Retarded Citizens the Protections and Services the State Extends to Others   Through a variety of regulations, the state protects the welfare of its citizens. Among these regulations are comprehensive requirements for the licensing of hospitals; certification of physicians who are qualified to practice medicine on its citizens; regulations for fire safety; and sanitary requirements necessary in institutions which serve food to the public.

Whether by statutory exempton, administrative practice, or simple neglect, this panoply of state regulations intended to protect the general citizenry is often denied to persons committed to institutions for the mentally retarded. Often state mental retardation institutions do not meet the standards for general hospitals in the state; the buildings are woefully out of compliance with the state's fire regulations; and the general sanitary conditions, particularly with regard to food service, fall below the standards which are otherwise required by the state. There is no compelling state interest which justifies the state's singling out this class of people and denying it the protections it affords to other persons.

The same analysis holds true for the state's failure to safeguard, as *parens patriae*, the welfare of institutionalized residents. State policy invariably shows an extreme solicitude for the welfare of children. Alabama statutes, for example, provide that custody of a child will be taken from parents or a guardian if "by reason of neglect, cruelty or depravity [such home] . . . is an unfit or improper place for such child," or if the child does not receive medical and other care necessary for his health and well-being.[40]

It is ironic that this solicitude for the welfare of children disappears in institutions which house mentally retarded children. This failure constitutes a denial of equal protection of the laws. The district court for Rhode Island followed this line of reasoning in holding that detention of juveniles in a substandard facility violated equal protection. The court stated:

> If a boy were confined indoors by his parents, given no education or exercise and allowed no visitors, and his medical needs were ignored, it is likely that the state would intervene and remove the child for his own protection. Certainly, then, the state acting in its *parens patriae* capacity cannot treat the boy in the same manner and justify having deprived him of his liberty.[41]

In *Mills v. Board of Education*, the district court for the District of Columbia held that failure to provide mentally retarded children (including children living

---

[38] Baxstrom v. Herold, 383 U.S. 107, 111 (1966).
[39] *Id.* at 115.
[40] ALA. CODE tit. 13, §§ 350 *et seq.* (1958).
[41] Inmates of Boys' Training School v. Affleck, 346 F. Supp. 1354, 1367 (D.R.I. 1972).

in mental institutions) a free public education constituted a denial of equal protection of the laws.[42] Equal protection demands that mentally retarded children in
institutions administered by the state be given educational opportunities suitable
to their needs.

Equal Protection and the Distinction Between "Voluntary" and "Involuntary" Status

Most of the preceding arguments relate to the right of the *involuntarily confined*
retarded person to receive adequate habilitation services in an institution. This
section presents the arguments for holding that, in terms of assessing constitutional
rights, all institutionalized retarded persons should be regarded as involuntary.

In institutions for the mentally retarded, there is usually no distinction made
between the care afforded to "voluntary" and "involuntary" residents. The two
groups are provided the same habilitation services, subjected to the same limitation on movement, and treated with the same impersonality. Both groups are
institutionalized by processes which do not involve their consent and, as the court
noted in *Willowbrook*, both "are held without the possibility of a meaningful
waiver of their right to freedom." [43] It would be incongruous if constitutional
doctrine were interpreted to require that one group was to receive substantially
different habilitation services from the other. Initial decisions recognizing the rights
of mentally retarded citizens in institutions have, in effect, rejected such a
distinction.[44]

State law often permits institutionalization of the mentally retarded individual
by two procedures, one involving some judicial involvement in the commitment
process. Typically the procedure which does not involve the judiciary is designated
as "voluntary." The applicable Alabama statute is fairly representative in this
respect. Alabama statutes provide for "involuntary" commitment under judicial
order, upon application by "any responsible person," including a parent or guardian;[45] the judge must have medical input before ordering commitment.[46] In the
alternative, parent, guardian, or adult next of kin may apply for "voluntary" admis-

---

[42] 348 F. Supp. 866 (D.D.C. 1972). *See also* Pennsylvania Ass'n for Retarded Children v. Pennsylvania,
334 F. Supp. 1257 (E.D. Pa. 1971).

[43] 357 F. Supp. at 764.

[44] This type of inequity was avoided by the United States District Court for the District of Massachusetts
(Ford, J.) when it denied (without opinion) the state's motion to dismiss for lack of jurisdiction. The
court rejected the state's contention that the quality of service provided by the state to voluntary
residents of the Belchertown State School was not of constitutional dimensions and therefore not
properly before the court. Ricci v. Greenblatt, Civil No. 72-469-F (D. Mass., Mar. 13, 1972). In *Wyatt*,
the court stated that its holding applied only to involuntary residents. (There were, as a practical
matter, only a few residents at Partlow who had been admitted to the institution by the procedure
denominated "voluntary.") The court, however, presumed that the right to habilitation applied to
all residents and stated that the institution had the "difficult burden" of proving that any particular
resident had not been involuntarily committed. 344 F. Supp. at 390 n.5. By this analysis, the court
implied that the right to habilitation is applicable to all residents, absent a showing of genuine
voluntariness.

In the Willowbrook case, the court held that *all* residents of Willowbrook should receive the
same protection without regard to the statutory procedure by which they were admitted. 357 F.
Supp. at 764.

[45] ALA. CODE tit. 45, § 239 (1958), § 252(a13) (Supp. 1971).

[46] *Id.* § 252(a13) (Supp. 1971).

sion of a person who, if found by the institution to be a mentally retarded individual, can be admitted.[47] In neither procedure does the person committed himself participate in the commitment decision, regardless of his age or capacity. He may vociferously object to institutionalization without effect in either proceeding. The "voluntary" proceeding probably deprives the mentally retarded individual of protection even more than the "involuntary" court proceeding, since the voluntary proceeding excludes even a modicum of judicial review and the necessity for independent medical judgment. Any concept of voluntariness in such a procedure is a fiction.

The retarded citizen voluntarily institutionalized can be discharged within 15 days by request of the person who sought his admission, but only if the superintendent does not file an objection with the court.[48] If objection is filed, an involuntary commitment proceeding will be initiated. Thus, the voluntarily committed individual is not free to leave, even if his parent or other committing person wants to take him out of the institution.

The parent or guardian's decision to commit a mentally retarded person to an institution should not be regarded as the equivalent of the consent of the retarded person. The closest analogy is to the parent's legal capacity to submit a child to medical or surgical treatment which may not be altogether in the child's best interests. Where there is any such potential conflict between the best interests of the child and other possible motives of the parent, the law has generally refused to allow the parent to make this choice for the child.[49] The general rule appears to be that when there is no question that the procedure is solely in the child's interest, the parent may give consent, but where someone else's interests might be paramount, the child must be separately represented by counsel or a guardian *ad litem* for valid consent.[50] This rule has been carried over to the sphere of parental consent to medical treatment of incompetents, regardless of age.[51]

Juvenile law, and by analogy the law of incompetents, does not assume an iden-

---

[47] *Id.* § 252(a9) (Supp. 1971).

[48] *Id.* § 252(a11) (Supp. 1971).

[49] *See, e.g., In re* Seiferth, 309 N.Y. 80, 127 N.E.2d 820, (1955) (minor can object to operation for cleft palate even though parents wish it); Frazier v. Levi, 440 S.W.2d 393 (Text. Civ. App. 1969).

[50] *See* Note, *Spare Parts from Incompetents: A Problem of Consent,* 9 J. FAMILY L. 309 (1970).

[51] *See* Strunk v. Strunk, 445 S.W.2d 145 (Ky. 1969) (parent needs court consent to donate retarded son's kidney for transplant to nonretarded brother).

In other kinds of juvenile court proceedings in which the parents' interests may be at odds with the child's, the law will not impute parental consent to the child, and separate representation for the child is required. Examples of this are proceedings involving the neglect and "beyond control" or "in need of supervision" jurisdiction of juvenile courts. *See* U.S. CHILDREN'S BUREAU, DEP'T OF HEALTH, EDUCATION & WELFARE, LEGISLATIVE GUDIES FOR DRAFTING FAMILY AND JUVENILE COURT ACTS § 14(b) (1969); D.C. CODE ANN. § 16-2305(b) (Supp. V 1972). When such a proceeding is initiated, the child is guaranteed counsel of his own, on the presumption that his interests may be antithetical to his parents'. U.S. CHILDREN'S BUREAU, *supra,* at § 25(a); D.C. CODE ANN. § 16-2304(a) (Supp. V 1972). *See also* UNIFORM JUVENILE COURT ACT § 26(a) (1968 version) (if interests of child and parents conflict, separate counsel must be provided for both); STANDARD JUVENILE COURT ACT §§ 37, 39 (6th ed. 1959) (counsel must be appointed for both if interests of child and parents conflict; appointment of guardian *ad litem* if interests of child and parents conflict); PRESIDENT'S COMMISSION ON LAW ENFORCEMENT AND ADMINISTRATION OF JUSTICE, THE CHALLENGE OF CRIME IN A FREE SOCIETY 87 (1967); PRESIDENT'S COMMISSION ON LAW ENFORCEMENT AND ADMINISTRATION OF JUSTICE, TASK FORCE REPORT: JUVENILE DELINQUENCY AND YOUTH CRIME 33-34 (1967) (counsel shall be appointed for a child as a matter of course whenever coercive action is a possibility without requiring any choice by parents or child).

tity of interest between the child and parent where institutionalization is at issue. The parent may be motivated to ask for such institutionalization for a variety of reasons other than the best interests of the child; *i.e.,* the interests of other children in the family, mental and physical frustration, economic stress, hostility toward the child stemming from the added pressures of caring for him, and perceived stigma of mental retardation. The mentally retarded child's best interests may well be met by living with his family or in another setting in the community, but the family's may be met by institutionalizing him.[52] In such a sea of human turmoil, the law cannot presume that the parent's voluntary act is also the child's voluntary act when the parent seeks to institutionalize his child.[53] The child must be presumed to be an involuntarily committed individual.[54]

Moreover, even if it is assumed that the mentally retarded person had himself made an informed and voluntary choice to seek institutionalization, he would still be as entitled to adequate habilitation as a court-committed individual. There can be no question that a person who voluntarily admits himself for institutionalized habilitation makes a substantial sacrifice of liberty, especially when, as is typically the case, he cannot leave at will. He is treated no differently from a court-committed resident.[55] Thus, his restraint is justified only if he secures the benefit of habilitation for which he sacrificed his liberty.

If a distinction in habilitation plans were made between voluntarily and involuntarily committed residents, the distinction would be susceptible to attack on equal protection grounds. The purpose of institutionalization of the mentally retarded person in all cases is care and habilitation, a purpose which bears no reasonable relationship to whether the resident entered voluntarily or involun-

[52] *See* R. ALLEN, LEGAL RIGHTS OF THE DISABLED AND DISADVANTAGED 13-14 (1970). A survey, by the Institute of Law, Psychiatry, and Criminology, of obstetricians, pediatricians, psychiatrists, and institutional superintendents showed that "there is a growing trend favoring home care of every young child whenever possible." *Id.* Though pediatricians and psychiatrists disagreed, obstetricians, the professionals first consulted by parents of retarded babies, tended to urge institutionalization of all retarded children when there were other children in the family. Professor Allen concluded:

Our laws seem to operate on the premise that institutionalization is for the benefit of the child; indeed many urge that institutionalization on parental application should be made as easy as possible. Yet, it would seem that a great many children are institutionalized less for their own benefit than for the comfort of others. Because it is believed that the retarded—including retarded children—do indeed have "rights," the author would be inclined to differ with the Task Force on Law of the President's Panel on Mental Retardation, and require judicial approval in any case in which institutionalization is based not on the needs of the child but on the needs of others, in order that appropriate resolution may be made of the perhaps conflicting interests of the child and his family, and that use of alternatives to residential care may be explored. *Id.* at 14.

[53] *See* Heryford v. Parker, 396 F.2d 393, 396 (10th Cir. 1968) (commitment of mental defective on mother's petition demands *Gault* protections).

[54] Indeed, it may well be that the parents' request for admission of a mentally retarded child may not be a truly voluntary decision by the parent where economic or physical and emotional resources have been exhausted and there is insufficient supportive help in the community to aid him in keeping the child at home.

See Murdock, *Civil Rights of the Mentally Retarded: Some Critical Issues,* 48 NOTRE D. LAW. 133, 139-43 (1972); Willowbrook, 357 F. Supp. at 762.

[55] R. ALLEN, *supra* note 52, at 18: "Our empirical data indicate that once a [retarded person] enters a public institution, his 'status' so far as the institution is concerned is that of 'resident', and it makes little or no difference whether he is a minor or adult, or whether he entered voluntarily or was committed."

tarily.[56] It would be totally irrational to run a mental retardation program in an institution which applied modern habilitation standards to court-committed residents and ignored them with respect to residents whose families had committed them. Under such a system, the child would be unjustly punished for his parents' decision. The therapeutic intent of voluntary admissions, to ease the emotional trauma of institutionalization for family and child, would be totally lost, and such admissions would be discouraged.[57]

The Decided Cases

The district court's decision in *Wyatt v. Stickney*[58] triggered renewed interest in the plight of the mentally retarded in institutions. The following three decisions regarding the right to habilitation illustrate the various judicial responses.

Wyatt v. Stickney

The significance of the *Wyatt* decision in focusing legal attention on the problems of mentally retarded citizens cannot be overestimated. It was the first major decision involving the constitutional rights of institutionalized mentally retarded persons. Since it was brought as a class action, it put in issue adequacy of treatment and habilitation provided throughout all of the mental institutions in Alabama.

In finding that the mentally retarded person who is involuntarily confined has a constitutional right to habilitation, the court relied heavily on its previous finding that the mentally ill had a right to treatment:

> Adequate and effective treatment is constitutionally required because, absent treatment, the hospital is transformed "into a penitentiary where one could be held indefinitely for no convicted offense. . . ." The purpose of involuntary hospitalization for treatment purposes is *treatment* and not mere custodial care or punishment.[59]

The court further stated:

---

[56] *Cf.* Baxstrom v. Herold, 383 U.S. 107 (1966).

[57] There is a fundamental policy in both federal and state law which strives to protect the growing and vulnerable child from neglect or abuse from any source.

    The duty of the state acting *in loco parentis* or as *parens patriae* in regard to one of its wards is to adhere to the same standards of care, training, and treatment that it imposes upon the child's natural parent or guardian. To allow any less is merely to substitute official community neglect for parental neglect. *See, e.g.* Creek v. Stone, 379 F.2d 106, 111 (D.C. Cir. 1967) (referring to the "legal right [of a ward] to a custody that is not inconsistent with a *parens patriae* premise of the law"); D.C. Family Welfare Rights Organization v. Thompson, Civil No. 71-1150-J (Super. Ct. D.C., June 18, 1971), 1 CCH POVERTY LAW REPORTER para. 4460 (1972), 5 CLEARING-HOUSE REV. 419 (1971) (the state must be held to a standard that is no less than the minimum required of a legal custodian).

[58] *See* note 1 *supra* for full citation.

[59] 325 F. Supp. at 784, *quoting from* Ragsdale v. Overholser, 281 F.2d 943 (D.C. Cir. 1960).

> In the context of the right to appropriate care for people civilly confined to public mental institutions, no viable distinction can be made between the mentally ill and the mentally retarded.[60]

The court concluded that the mentally retarded person had "an inviolable constitutional right to habilitation."[61]

There are many facets of the Wyatt decision which merit discussion: the standards of adequate habilitation it established; the impact of judicial intervention on a large state bureaucracy and on legislative areas of concern; the problems of implementing so large a decree.[62] The following discussion, however, focuses on the manner in which the court, in addressing the need for prompt redress of the horrible conditions in the institutions, simultaneously built into its order elements that would lead to reduction of the institutional population and return of its residents to the community. In this latter respect, the *Wyatt* decision incorporates current thinking among mental retardation professionals regarding habilitation. The court had the benefit of the *amicus curiae* participation of national mental health and mental retardation organizations. In addition, several experts in the field of mental retardation presented testimony to the court. In adopting the contemporary view that the mentally retarded person should live in conditions that are as close to normal as possible, the court rejected the old duality which treated the mentally retarded in the institution as a discrete class, clearly distinguishable from those who were considered fit to live in the community.

The standards adopted by the court set forth in detail the elements of an adequate habilitation program in the institution: a humane physical and psychological environment; an individual habilitation plan for each resident; and adequate staffing, in numbers and training.[63] Perhaps more important, the decision embodies the normalization principle and the notion that the mentally retarded should not in general be taken out of the community and placed in massive institutions at all.[64] In standard 3 the court states:

> (a) No person shall be admitted to the institution unless a prior determination shall have been made that residence in the institution is the least restrictive habilitation setting feasible for that person. (b) No mentally retarded person shall be admitted to the institution if services and programs in the community can afford adequate habilitation to such persons. (c) Residents shall have a right to the least restrictive conditions necessary to achieve the purposes of habilitation. To this end, the institution shall make every attempt to move residents from 1) more to less structured living; 2) larger to smaller facilities; 3) larger to smaller living units; 4) group to individual

[60] 344 F. Supp. at 390.

[61] *Id.*

[62] *See* Note, *Wyatt v. Stickney & the Right of Civilly Committed Mental Patients to Adequate Treatment,* 86 Harv. L. Rev. 1282 (1973).

[63] Immediately, at the end of the hearing on conditions at Partlow State School and Hospital, the court entered an interim emergency order to protect the physical safety of the residents. The order required the defendants to hire more than 300 additional aides and make provision for fire safety, effective regulation of drugs, and the like.

[64] The court's standards are set out in 344 F. Supp. at 395-407.

residence; 5) segregated from the community to integrated into the community; 6) dependent to independent living.[65]

In addition, standard 4 provides explicitly that no borderline or mildly mentally retarded person shall be a resident at Partlow. [66]Standard 10, stressing that institutionalization is not a final disposition of a hopelessly incompetent person, states that each resident shall have, upon admission, as part of his habilitation plan, an individual postinstitutionalization plan.[67] Standard 47 states that each resident discharged to the community shall have a program of transitional habilitation assistance.[68]

Thus, the court in *Wyatt* addresses the problem of ensuring adequate habilitation to institutional residents, at the same time avoiding the pitfall of continuing to accept a dualistic system which necessarily isolates the institution from the community. In addition, although not formally addressing itself to commitment procedures, the order ensures that the kinds of people who have been inappropriately placed in the institution in the past will not be institutionalized in the future.

Although progress has been disappointingly slow, the response of the Alabama Department of Mental Health in the period following the entry of the order has reflected an understanding of the need to improve habilitation in the institution while reducing population and developing community-based alternatives. On April 2, 1973, the Partlow Human Rights Committee, an independent citizen committee established pursuant to the court's order, filed a report on implementation of the order. The reported attitudes of the state administrators reflect an understanding that a primary response to the order must be rapid reduction of the Partlow population. Meeting the minimum physical standards for the institution was explicitly tied to a reduction in population. In the first year following the court's order, 500 residents were released, bringing the population down to 1,745. Further reductions to a level of approximately 700 residents were planned. At the same time, the number of qualified mental retardation professionals and the number of resident care workers were doubled, although the level of professional staffing remained woefully inadequate. The department began to develop a range of community services for the mentally retarded, including small-group homes.

The human rights committee noted progress in some areas within the institution, but there were still glaring inadequacies, particularly in the fundamental matter of medical care. The committee urged immediate attention to these inadequacies within the institution, but recognized that the long-term resolution of these problems could come about only through reduction of the institutional population and the transformation of the institution's very character.

The adequacy of habilitative services in the community is an issue which has yet to be explored adequately. It would be naive to think that community programs will escape all the problems that plagued Partlow. But the right to habilitation concept

[65]344 F. Supp. at 396.
[66]*Id.*
[67]*Id.* at 397.
[68]*Id.* at 407.

articulated in the *Wyatt* decision, recognizing the need for a continuum of habilitation services and the fundamental inadequacy of massive institutions, provides a framework in which the problems of the Partlow resident can be meaningfully addressed.

Burnham v. Department of Public Health

The *Wyatt* decision stands in striking contrast to the decision in *Burnham v. Department of Public Health*,[69] decided by a federal district court in Georgia in August 1972. The court in *Burnham* granted defendants' motion to dismiss before any evidence was heard. Petitioners in this case, inmates of the state's mental institutions, had alleged that they were not receiving adequate treatment and habilitation; specifically, that they were denied a humane psychological and physical environment, that staff was insufficient to provide adequate treatment, and that there were no individualized treatment plans. The district court refused to hold an evidentiary hearing. The court emphasized that the state of Georgia, unlike Alabama, was making large expenditures for its mental health programs, but this general fact could hardly establish that constitutionally acceptable habilitation and treatment programs existed in all the state's institutions.

For the reasons set forth previously, the equal protection and due process clauses and the prohibition on cruel and unusual punishment confer substantial protections on the institutionalized mentally retarded person. By dismissing plaintiffs' complaint without a hearing, the district court implied that these constitutional provisions could not be violated upon any kind of factual showing. Since the *Burnham* result has not been sustained,[70] the development of a right to habilitation by the federal courts continues.

New York State Association for Retarded Children v. Rockefeller

One year after *Wyatt*, a federal district court in New York entered a preliminary order in the *Willowbrook* case.[71] The plaintiffs, the state mental retardation association and individual parents, had filed suit alleging violations of constitutional rights and sought a preliminary injunction that would protect the residents of Willowbrook from harm while the decision on the broader issue of adequate habilitation was pending. A hearing was held in December 1972, and January 1973, on plaintiffs' request for preliminary relief. Unlike the district court in *Burnham,* in *Willowbrook* the judge refused to resolve the legal issues in the abstract, without looking at the facts, stating:

> It is very difficult to separate fact from law. And I think it is appropriate that I give the Plaintiffs a chance to present their picture so that I can decide the legal issues in light of the actual situation as presented.[72]

It is possible that the conditions of gross neglect and deprivation that he found at Willowbrook shaped his decision to order substantial relief. The judge stated such conditions "are hazardous to the health, safety, and sanity of the residents."[73] Based

[69] 349 F. Supp. 1335 (N.D. Ga. 1972), *rev'd,* 503 F.2d 1319 (5th Cir. 1974).
[70] *Burnham* was reversed, 503 F.2d 1319 (5th Cir. 1974).
[71] 357 F. Supp. 752 (E.D.N.Y. 1973).
[72] Transcript, Hearing on Preliminary Injunction, at 7.
[73] 357 F. Supp. at 765.

on this holding the court entered a wide-ranging decree in January 1973, granting most of the relief plaintiffs had requested. This included a ban on the use of seclusion; 'a requirement of substantial additions to professional and nonprofessional staff by May 31; and a requirement that appropriate provision for medical attention to acutely ill residents be made. The order went so far as to require that the starting salary for physical therapists be raised in order to permit effective recruitment.

The court noted that its order "may not exhaust the rights to which the federal constitution entitles residents of a place like Willowbrook."[74] Thus, the court held open the possibility that broader relief would be granted after a full hearing on the merits. Looking to the nature of the relief ordered, the judge's action in *Willowbrook* is analogous to the court's order for emergency relief entered immediately at the end of the Partlow hearing.

Although in its entry of a final consent judgment the *Willowbrook* court acknowledged that there is no bright line separating its own protection from harm standard from *Wyatt's* right to treatment for the mentally retarded, the conceptual basis for the court's decision to grant preliminary relief in *Willowbrook* is different from *Wyatt* court's. The initial decision in *Willowbrook* does not rest on a "right to habilitation." Rather, it finds in the due process, equal protection, and cruel and unusual punishment clauses a right of residents to be protected from harm. The court rejects any distinction between voluntary and involuntary residents for this purpose. The court notes that all the residents are treated alike in the institution[75] and that they "are for the most part confined behind locked gates; and are held without the possibility of a meaningful waiver of their right to freedom."[76] It further notes that conditions tolerable in prison, where punishment is permissible, may not be tolerable in institutions for mentally retarded citizens, where punishment is impermissible.[77] The underlying premise behind this analysis appears to be that the retarded residents should be treated as an involuntarily confined population.[78]

This conceptual justification gave the court a sufficient constitutional basis for purposes of the preliminary relief requested by plaintiffs. The court explicitly stated that it did not in its order address all the rights to which the federal constitution entitles residents of an institution for the mentally retarded.[79] The "protection from harm" standard, articulated for the first time in this opinion, is extremely open-ended. Does it apply to mental as well as physical harm? Is harm to the resident to be measured in terms of actual deterioration, or is it to be measured against the development which a retarded person would have had in an adequate habilitation

[74] *Id.* On May 5, 1975 the *Willowbrook* court entered a final consent judgment and therefore found no need
   to re-examine the constitutional standard properly applicable to Willowbrook's residents. Entry of final consent judgment, New York Association for Retarded Children v. Carey, Civil Nos. 72C356, 72C357 (E.D.N.Y. entered, May 5, 1975).
[75] 357 F. Supp. at 756.
[76] 357 F. Supp. at 764.
[77] *Id.*
[78] Noting that there may be a conflict between the interest of a parent in committing a retarded child and the best interests of the child, the court stated, "A 'voluntary admission' on the petition of parents may quite properly be treated in the same category as an 'involuntary admission' in the absence of evidence that the child's interests have been fully considered." 357 F. Supp. at 762.
[79] 357 F. Supp. at 765.

program? Many experts would argue that a resident in a large institution always suffers harm unless an adequate and appropriate habilitation program is developed for him; that without affirmative habilitation efforts, a retarded person necessarily regresses in the institution. Most important, a large number of experts would argue that confinement of many retarded persons in institutions like Willowbrook causes harm because of the very nature of the institution, regardless of the adequacy of staffing and programming. Would such confinement then "'shock the conscience' of the court" or offend "civilized standards of human decency"?[80] It is unclear how the court in *Willowbrook* would respond to these questions. Because of the present posture of the case (entry of a final consent judgment) the court found no need, "to re-examine the constitutional standard properly applicable to Willowbrook's residents."

Although the court initially rejected the right to habilitation concept in its memorandum granting preliminary relief,[81] it has subsequently noted that:

> Somewhat different legal rubrics have been employed in these cases—"protection from harm" in this case and "right treatment" and "need for care" in others. It appears that there is no bright line separating these standards. In the present posture of this case, there is no need for the court to re-examine the constitutional standard properly applicable to Willowbrook's residents. The relief which the parties agreed to will advance the very rights enunciated in the case law since this court's 1973 ruling.

It must also be noted that the *Willowbrook* opinion seems to accept the inherited system of treating the mentally retarded—the notion that the retarded person who is institutionalized should be thus confined. Indeed, the belief that there is "no place else to go" becomes an acceptable justification for institutionalization. However, this opinion was based only on plaintiffs' request for preliminary injunction. At a comparable stage in the *Wyatt* proceeding, the court was also concerned with the barbarous conditions in the institutions: the assaults on residents, the acute understaffing, the inadequacy of medical care. If the issue had been presented in full, the nexus between the institution and the community, the necessarily non-habilitative character of the massive institution, and the inappropriate institutionalization of most residents might have led the *Willowbrook* court to recognize that the plight of the mentally retarded resident cannot be dealt with simply by improving institutions.

THE RIGHT TO HABILITATION AFTER *WYATT*

It is perhaps premature to try to draw even tentative conclusions on the basis of the limited legal development in the area of mental retardation. The right to habilitation litigation has developed at a time when a questioning spirit is urgently needed. We have tolerated the continued existence of institutions which are shockingly incon-

---

[80] *Id.*
[81] 357 F. Supp. at 758. *Cf.* Entry of final consent judgment, Willowbrook, Civil Nos. 72C356, 72C357 (E.D.N.Y. entered, May 5, 1975).

sistent with our basic notions of human decency. We have put the retarded out of sight in places where it is literally impossible for them to develop their full human potential. Twenty-five years from now, after the establishment of a humane, flexible system for dealing with mentally retarded citizens, the habilitation cases may become a source of bemused wonder. But, taking the shorter view, it now appears that cases like *Wyatt* have provided a useful approach to an urgent problem.

In appraising the impact of the litigation, it is important to see litigation in context and not to have unrealistic expectations. The *Wyatt* decision illustrates some of the potency and limitations of litigation as a technique. The *Wyatt* order is not self-enforcing. It requires much more than a court order to move a large bureaucracy to solve a deeply rooted problem. No one would assert that all inappropriately placed residents of Partlow have been returned to the community or that adequate habilitation programs have been instituted. But a start has been made, and the orientation of the Alabama Department of Mental Health is significantly changed.

A judicial order recognizing the right to habilitation and setting out minimum standards is merely the beginning of a long and difficult task. The *Wyatt* decision has acted as a catalyst to mobilize public opinion, and effective implementation of the *Wyatt* order will require political action and continuing public attention to the problem.

There are, in addition, discernible secondary consequences which have flowed from judicial intervention in the area of the right to habilitation. It has helped generate a rethinking of the systems which purport to serve mentally retarded individuals and, superimposed on this system, an analysis that stresses the constitutional rights of the mentally retarded citizen. For mental retardation administrators, for parents, and for mentally retarded residents in state institutions, this emphasis on constitutional rights has had substantial consequences.

Mental retardation professionals have had to redefine their roles and professional responsibilities. The administrator of a state institution for the mentally retarded can no longer think he is fulfilling his responsibilities if he runs an adequate custodial program. The fundamental habilitation purposes of such institutions have again been reaffirmed. Many states are now in the process of revising their laws relating to the mentally retarded citizen. The perspectives reflected in recent judicial opinions have helped stimulate and shape such statutory revisions and have encouraged the development of entirely new legislation. Similarly, new administrative policies being developed within states in many instances are affected by judicial decisions. Several states have used the *Wyatt* standards to measure performance in their own systems. Indeed, the May 1973 conference on the legal rights of mentally retarded citizens sponsored by the President's Committee on Mental Retardation, bringing together experts in mental retardation with legal scholars and practitioners active in the field, would probably never have been held had it not been for the stimulation of recent judicial decisions.

The *Wyatt* decision has also underlined the need to develop community services as an alternative to institutionalization. It has raised the price of institutional warehousing and focused public attention on the inadequacy of institutionalization as a solution. It is likely that the next generation of litigation, building on the right to education litigation[82] and the emphasis of the *Wyatt* order on normalization,[83] will focus on the quantity and quality of services available to the mentally retarded person in the community.[84]

The most significant consequence of the recent judicial attention to the problems of the mentally retarded individual may be in raising new questions for exploration, rather than in providing answers. Probably the most important question raised by the recent decisions is how to ensure adequate community services for the mentally retarded citizen. If a state is to create group homes in the community and to move mentally retarded people into them and out of institutions, how can it ensure that the group homes provide an adequate habilitation setting? How can the public be reeducated with regard to its attitudes toward the mentally retarded members of this society?

Questions regarding conditions in the institutions themselves are no less difficult:

When can mentally retarded residents be subjected to sterilization?[85]

What should be regarded as "express and informed consent" by a mentally retarded resident? Is the consent of a parent sufficient for all purposes or are there situations in which such consent is inadequate?[86]

What constraints should be placed on experimentation with mentally retarded subjects?

What limitation should be placed on the use of behavior modification techniques on mentally retarded residents?

Should aversive conditioning be permitted and if so, under what circumstances? What limitations should be imposed to ensure that socially appropriate behavior is not extinguished in order to serve only institutional convenience?

The most alarming potential result of the recent litigation would be that nothing happens; and it must be stressed that this is a distinct possibility. Too often, important legal principles have been stated, but then have had little impact in the real world. Civil rights lawyers, welfare reform lawyers, and poverty lawyers have learned a lesson in recent years that people concerned with the mentally retarded have long known: Transitory victories and paroxysms of righteous indignation do not change institutions. Concerned communities, mental retardation professionals, and lawyers must have the energy, will, and stamina to seize the opportunity presented by recent judicial attention to the problems of mentally retarded citizens.

---

[82] *See* Herr, Chapter 9 of this volume.

[83] *See* Chambers, Chapter 16 of this volume.

[84] *See* Robinson v. Weinberger, Civil No. 74-285 (D.D.C., filed Feb. 14, 1974) (complaint alleging that patients improperly confined in mental hospital have constitutional and statutory right to placement in suitable community-based facility); Boggs, Chapter 12 of this volume.

[85] After entry of the court's main order in *Wyatt,* counsel for plaintiffs discovered that sterilizations were being performed at Partlow. The complaint was amended to challenge this practice. A three-judge district court held the state's mandatory sterilization law unconstitutional. Wyatt v. Aderholt, 368 F. Supp. 1382 (M.D. Ala. 1973). The district court established procedural and substantive standards, including right to counsel and an independent review mechanism, to ensure that sterilizations were not performed in violation of the residents' constitutional rights. Wyatt v. Aderholt, 368 F. Supp. 1383 (M.D. Ala. 1974).

[86] *See* Wald, Chapter 1 of this volume; Price & Burt, Chapter 4 of this volume.

Reaction Comment

DAVID J. ROTHMAN

THE QUESTIONS that Halpern has posed are the right ones, and I would like to address myself to one of them, to my mind the central one. He has asked: How can we protect the rights of persons inside the institutions without legitimating the institutions themselves? How can we argue for a right to habilitation behind the walls without encouraging legislatures, courts, and citizens to build the walls still higher? Or, put in its broadest form: How can we urge the idea of habilitation without producing unanticipated and mischievous results? To confront this issue, it is useful to adopt both a historical and a comparative approach. Tracing the history of incarceration over the past 150 years reveals all too clearly how the best of ideas can turn into the worst of realities. And to compare the experience of the mentally retarded with other incarcerated groups in this society, the mentally ill and the criminal offender, for example, is to recognize and understand many of the pitfalls that await those who enthusiastically and unwarily urge confinement for the sake of treatment.

The idea of habilitation was the critical element in the legitimation of institutionalization in the United States. Americans first built institutions to confine the deviant and dependent in the Jacksonian era, and central to this change was the notion of reform and cure. Moments of creation, the time when a society embarks on a new venture, are crucial moments, for it is then that a society most carefully examines its actions. New procedures, lacking the sanction of time and custom, can be challenged and changed most effectively. At this moment of creation, in the period from 1820 to 1850, when incarceration was novel and strange, when its survival was most in doubt, an incredibly inflated rhetoric of rehabilitation legitimated the entire enterprise. The promise of the asylums was so grand that no one doubted the wisdom and humanity of institutionalizing the unfortunates and the undesirables.

The process is dramatically clear in the history of American prisons. The first institutions were built with monumental grandeur—elaborate turrets, thick walls, costly private exercise yards—and paid for by legislatures that were as tightfisted with tax money as any known today. In effect, these institutions were monuments to the idea that the way to eradicate deviant behavior was to put people behind walls into a disciplined, regimented, and orderly setting. The same mode of thinking led to the establishment of the first insane asylums. A routine of punctuality and regularity would free the mentally ill from their maladies.[1]

This dedication to the ideal of cure and reform made procedural protections seem unnecessary. The mentally ill, reformers and psychiatrists insisted, ought to be

---

[1] *See generally* D. ROTHMAN, THE DISCOVERY OF THE ASYLUM (1971).

put into the asylums as quickly as possible, with the least amount of legal formality. Why have them languish on a courtroom bench while lawyers and judges discuss due process technicalities, if they can instead be inside the asylum being cured? This perspective, for many decades, really until the last several years, inhibited the growth of statutes protecting the rights of citizens against compulsory confinement in mental hospitals. The counterpart to this development in the criminal field was the very lengthy sentences that judges passed on convicted criminals. Reformers in the 1820s and 1830s urged magistrates to pass long sentences, not 1-2 years but 5-10 years; the penitentiary needed the time to reform the criminal. To this day, sentences in this country are two to three times longer than those in any other industrialized nation.

The history of the confinement of the mentally retarded individual belongs within this tradition. There is no suggestion that any natural resemblance links the mentally retarded to the insane or the criminal. But rather, to understand the dynamics of how American society reacts to the mentally retarded, one must reckon with the treatment of the insane and the criminal. One sad truth about American response to the mentally retarded individual is that it has generally followed the pattern set for deviant groups. The incarceration of the mentally retarded followed soon after the confinement of the insane and criminal. (In this instance, as in so many others, there was a lag in time. "Reform" for mentally retarded individuals came last, after all the other groups had been cared for.) In the 1850s, with the same inflated rhetoric, Americans built and administered separate institutions for the mentally retarded. For some of the founders, the venture promised nothing less than the eradication of retardation; others saw it as a way to equip the mentally retarded person for a successful return to the community. But everyone agreed that the incarceration of the mentally retarded person was a reform, a step representing progress.

The perspective of Samuel Gridley Howe, one of the innovators of this movement, represents his generation's viewpoint. Howe helped further the common school movement in Massachusetts, was one of the promoters of the state penitentiary, and was especially active in the origins of the insane asylum. These energies and outlooks brought him to advocate institutions for the mentally retarded. Inside them, Howe insisted, "the young can be trained to industry, order, and self-respect.... Shall we shrink from the higher task of transforming brutish men back into human shape?"[2]

The second stage in the history of incarceration opened in the 1850s and was fully apparent by the 1870s. In the post-Civil War period, it was obvious that the noble ideals of the founders were irrelevant to the operation of the institutions. Long after the rehabilitation ethic became irrelevant to the daily routine of the institutions. the practice of confinement persisted. By the 1870s, the prisons were modern (*i.e.*, brutal, corrupt, and overcrowded) and yet they remained central to the system of corrections. The insane asylums became warehouses, performing only a custodial function, and yet they, too, remained basic to the public response to mental illness.

---

[2]Wolfensberger, *The Origin and Nature of Our Institutional Models,* in Changing Patterns in Residential Services for the Mentally Retarded 93 (R. Kugel & W. Wolfensberger eds. 1969).

Why did institutions created in the name of reform and cure endure long after the rhetoric lost all connection with reality? Part of the answer involves functional considerations. After 1870, the asylums were filled with immigrants, aliens in all senses of the word, people who might be conveniently removed from the community without especial concern for their eventual fate. Moreover, the institutions were located at some distance from population centers. In the 1830s, reformers had urged this separation, eager to work their experiments without community interference. In the 1870s and thereafter, the isolation of the institutions meant that abuses would be that much more difficult to learn about and that much harder to publicize.

But such considerations are only part of the reason for persistence. Even more important were the negative effects of the lingering rhetoric of rehabilitation. Courtesy of this ethic, citizens did not have to ask themselves what they were accomplishing via incarceration. The answer was ready at hand: They were reforming. And, hence, when a scandal was uncovered, when some of the wretchedness and misery that existed inside these institutions came to light, the public assumed that it was an aberration, a momentary horror. The fault, they insisted, rested with a bad administrator, with an incompetent staff member, with a stingy legislature, but *not with the system itself*. Because of the rehabilitation ethic, abuses were understood as ad hoc, not endemic to incarceration. Because of this ethic, we have suffered the perpetual discovery and rediscovery of shortcomings, the spasm of public outcry, and the ensuing decades of neglect.

Once again, the fate of the institutions for the mentally retarded fit into this pattern. By the 1880s, they, too, had become warehouses and they, too, like the prisons and asylums, persisted long after the founding rationale had no meaning for institutional performance.

Indeed, it is worth noting, however briefly here, that the mischief worked in the name of rehabilitation extends also into the first efforts in the Progressive period to devise alternatives to incarceration. To choose one example, the origins of the practices of probation and parole demonstrate how reform ideology can legitimate a series of practices that may cause more harm than good. Probation and parole, as conceived of by reformers in the period from 1900 to 1920, was to reduce the numbers of convicted criminals incarcerated. Through intensive social case work methods, offenders would become readjusted to community life. But in fact, these new procedures did not substantially reduce institutional populations, and they did not cure the deviant. Instead, they made life that much easier for wardens (inmates had to obey or be denied parole) and for district attorneys (they could more easily persuade persons charged with crimes to plea bargain) and for judges (who could use the new discretionary powers to dispense justice as they saw fit). These functional considerations could not have won public support if not for the legitimating rhetoric that reformers supplied. And long after it should have become apparent that probation and parole increased the net amount of surveillance in the society and increased the time served by felons inside prisons, reformers supported these programs as rehabilitative.

Despite this grim record, it is easy to understand why individuals working in the field of mental retardation are reluctant to abandon the concept of habilitation.

For one, it is clear that professionals in this field can do things that wardens and psychiatric superintendents cannot. Mental retardation professionals have specific programs that work, in demonstrable ways, to improve the functioning of mentally retarded individuals. Wardens and psychiatrists do not have them. Second, and equally important, the attachment of retardation professionals to the idea of rehabilitation reflects a major difference in the history of the mentally retarded and the history of the insane and the criminal in this country. The major increase in the incarceration of the retarded came at the beginning of this century, from 1905 to 1920, and it came not because of any concern with rehabilitation, but because of a popular view of the mentally retarded as a primary menace to American civilization.

In 1890, there were 4,000 institutionalized mentally retarded citizens. By 1916 the number had mounted to 34,000. In 1890, there were 14 institutions for the mentally retarded in the United States. In 1910 there were 26; by 1923, there were 40. The ideology that brought about this vast increase in incarceration is well represented by this 1915 statement: "When we view the number of the feeble-minded, their fecundity, their lack of control, the menace they are, the degradation they cause, the degeneracy they perpetuate, the suffering and misery and crime they spread,—these are the burdens we must bear."[3]

The link between this attitude and the growth of incarceration was simple to forge. Writing in 1917, Walter Fernald argued: "The brighter classes of the feeble-minded, with their weak will power and deficient judgment, are easily influenced for evil and are prone to become vagrants, drunkards and thieves. . . . It is better and cheaper for the community to assume the permanent custody of such persons before they have carried out a long career of expensive crime."[4] Given this historical record, it is not surprising that those in the field of mental retardation have wished to emphasize the potential for habilitation.

Perhaps sensitivity to the risk of mischief in using the concept of habilitation can minimize it. Halpern certainly has this sensitivity and the *Wyatt* decision reflects it. But others who follow this strategy less cautiously may promote more harm than good, a danger that everyone in the field of mental retardation must be made aware of. They must recognize the possibility that arguing for habilitation inside institutions might lead courts to require, and legislatures to fund, newer, bigger, ostensibly better institutions, places that will become in the next 30 years just as dismal as the facilities they were designed to replace. And it is worth remembering that once funded, institutions have a way of persisting. Since 1925, the idea of the mentally retarded person as a social menace has declined, almost disappeared. Yet the institutions built under the influence of that ethos persist to this very day. Walled-in space seems to take on a life of its own.

In the fields of mental illness and crime, there are indications that the concept of rehabilitation could legitimate an overwide range of actions. A recent federal court decision on prisoners' rights argued that "a prison regulation restricting freedom of expression would be justifiable if its purpose was to rehabilitate the

[3] *Id.* at 102.
[4] Fernald, *The Growth of Provision for the Feebleminded in the United States,* 1 MENTAL HYGIENE 34, 42 (1917).

prisoner."[5] Another opinion contended that as soon as prison officials attempt to rehabilitate prisoners, "the best justification for the hands off doctrine will appear."[6] Indeed, some of the nightmarish possibilities of rehabilitation legitimating extension of sentences and wide-scale intervention are already apparent in Patuxent, the Maryland institution for defective delinquents.[7]

Halpern set forth some policy guidelines for ameliorative efforts. I would like to add to the list. Guidelines are important not only in determining strategies involving institutions, but also in devising alternative community-based programs.

Wherever possible, make programs voluntary. Build procedural protections around admissions. Use these procedures particularly when they appear least necessary, when you are most persuaded that you are doing good.

Use hard data when attempting to persuade a community of the efficacy of a program. Use performance as a measurement. Leave as little room as possible for inflated rhetoric.

Be concerned with the problem of supervising community facilities. To place a mentally retarded individual in a foster home setting without supervisory mechanisms may lead to a series of abuses; and one day someone may suggest consolidating all the boarding homes into one — in essence, rediscovering the asylum. Do not assume that a system of licensing will be effective or that state boards of charities will operate well. Innovations are very necessary here.

Make periodic reevaluations to be certain that programs are fulfilling their promises. Be particularly concerned with performance when the program is turned over to its second director, to the man who inherits the founder's design.

If there are hard choices, if one is forced to choose the lesser of two evils, choose the path out of institutions and into the community.

The field of mental retardation stands at a moment of creation and fresh departures. It is a dramatic, important, and highly significant moment. It is a moment when activists must be acutely sensitive to the precedents they are setting. Perhaps the legacy that is passed on to the next generation will be a good deal better than the one we have received.

Reaction Comment

KENNETH D. GAVER

HALPERN CONSIDERS the constitutional bases and the legal precedents relating to the right to habilitation for institutionalized mentally retarded citizens. He has illustrated the complexities of the right to habilitation and freedom from harm concepts.

[5] Carothers v. Follette, 314 F. Supp. 1014, 1024 (S.D.N.Y. 1970).
[6] Landman v. Royster, 333 F. Supp. 621, 657 (E.D. Va. 1971).
[7] See Rothman, Decarcerating Prisoners and Patients, 1 CIVIL LIBERTIES REV., Fall 1973, at 8.

My reaction is predicated on my position as a representative of the onerous bureaucracy that operates the massive institutions that are often referred to as the villains in discussions of the legal rights of the mentally retarded. It is my responsibility to increase the funds which have traditionally been made available to governmentally operated institutions for the mentally retarded. Furthermore, I have the questionable honor of being the titular head of the single largest bureaucracy in the state of Ohio, a good portion of which mans the massive institutions that have recently been receiving so much attention in legal circles. My response is that of an administrator who, although personally embracing the concepts, values, and advances promulgated in *Wyatt v. Stickney*,[1] must at the same time live with and attempt to administer programs mandated within the framework of law and funded under statutes that control the manner, mode, and utilization of the funds and personnel dedicated to the operation of the institutions.

In spite of an overt philosophy of advocating humaness, protection, kindness, concern, and a proper habilitation for the residents of these institutions, one finds it difficult not to straddle a fence between advocating all-out change in the institutions and attempting to create evolution within the existing system of care and services for the mentally retarded. It is difficult to attack the bureaucracy one heads and at the same time avoid mutiny and chaos within that bureaucracy.

Professionals who have worked many years in this field are aware that massive ill-planned changes in the structure and function of institutions not only augur for discontent among the staff of the institutions, but also result in regression and worsening of the plight of the residents of these institutions. In addition, it is not an easy task to move an elected bureaucracy and a sometimes complacent citizenry toward making a larger commitment of public resources to overcome the conditions to which the order in *Wyatt v. Stickney* so aptly addressed itself. The assignment of high priority and extra resources toward the proper care, treatment, and rehabilitation of the mentally handicapped citizen is hindered by the fact that such issues frequently have little inherent political reward.

It is not practical to deal comprehensively with all of the problems of implementation raised by *Wyatt* and related cases, so I shall address myself to five issues which seem to be most germane and important. They are the need for:

1. the revision of statutory law to conform to the principles of recent decisions relating to institutional admissions and commitment, and the rights of the mentally retarded;
2. the elaboration and implementation of the concept of "habilitation";
3. change and evolution in the institutions presently dedicated to care of the mentally retarded;
4. the development of community-based alternatives to institutionalization;
5. the mobilization of public interest, energy, and commitment toward recognizing the rights of mentally retarded citizens.

---

[1] 344 F. Supp. 387, 344 F. Supp. 373 (M.D. Ala. 1972), 334 F. Supp. 1341, 325 F. Supp. 781 (M.D. Ala. 1971), *aff'd sub nom.* Wyatt v. Aderholt, 503 F.2d 1305 (5th Cir. 1974).

REVISION OF STATUTES

The revision of an entire body of law which has been the basis for court and institutional practice over a long period of time is in itself an enormous task. In Ohio, a spin-off from *Wyatt* has been concern about the need for revision of Ohio's admission and commitment statutes consistent with the principles expressed in that landmark decision and other recent cases. Accordingly, in the fall of 1972 I convened a task force to recommend legislation to accomplish an appropriate revision of the statutes. In the charge to this task force, reference was made to the need to evolve statutory revisions which would meet the objectives of providing:

1. workable definitions of mental retardation for purposes of commitment;
2. means by which informed consent could be ensured;
3. due process procedures;
4. provision for the protection of individual civil rights;
5. assurances of adequate habilitation;
6. assurances of periodic review of the resident's status;
7. protection from exploitation;
8. the use of the least restrictive alternative.

The tactical problem of putting together such a task force was complicated by the broad range of representation required to take into account the diverse opinions and attitudes regarding clinical and habilitation practices. There was also great diversity in task force members' knowledge of constitutional and statutory law. A practical political consideration was to place on this task force persons who might have sufficient status to be influential in securing a favorable consideration of its recommendations by the legislative assembly. Thus, a broadly representative group was essential.

As a matter of fact, comparable revisions were called for in the fields of both mental illness and mental retardation. Therefore, a general task force comprised of some 50 persons was established with sub-task forces for mental health and mental retardation. The task force in mental retardation was composed of 14 persons, including legislators, probate judges, and professionals in mental retardation. Other areas represented included administrators from community mental retardation programs, representatives from the citizens' advocacy association, attorneys especially interested and skilled in the area, and administrators of institutions. A number of lawyers and law professors were appointed as consultants to the task force. Furthermore, representatives from the American Civil Liberties Union, legal aid services, and patients' rights organizations also were consultants. Persons instrumental in framing the original commitment laws now subject to revision were available to assist in the task.

The work product of the task force was two proposed new chapters of the Ohio Revised Code, which have been submitted to, and are under consideration by, Ohio's General Assembly.[2] Included in one of the chapters is a bill of rights for institutionalized mentally retarded citizens.

There are further practical problems of shepherding the bills through the general assembly, providing the legal research as backup for the bills, and establishing timetables of implementation. Moreover, there are enormous problems in estimating the impact of such changes, not only upon the institutions, but also upon probate courts throughout the state and upon the community as well. The implications to the community are substantial; the requirement for the least restrictive environment will necessitate the community's providing resources it may not currently have at hand. Furthermore, the ability of the community to rid itself of people who may be viewed as nuisances will be considerably hampered.

Without *Wyatt*, the advanced concepts incorporated in the bill would have been virtually unattainable. The level of public and professional awareness and conscience has been sufficiently raised by *Wyatt* to permit contemplation of the revisions noted previously.

ELABORATION OF THE CONCEPT OF HABILITATION

Extensive standards for the operation of Partlow School were ordered by the court in *Wyatt*. However, even these standards leave something to be desired in the determination of what constitutes an appropriate habilitation plan. I offer, therefore, the following concept of "habilitation." Active habilitation requires a written individualized plan:

1. based on a comprehensive assessment of the individual's social, psychological, health, and vocational capacities and liabilities;
2. based on the goals of improving the individual's adaptive capability and the ability to live independently;
3. based upon objectives related to these goals;
4. comprised of defined services, activities, or programs related to the objectives;
5. specific as to the responsibilities for the conduct of such services or activities;
6. specific as to a means to measure the progress or outcome;
7. clear as to periodic review and revision of the plan.

[2] Ohio S.B. 336, H.B. 984, 110th Gen. Ass. Reg. Sess. (1973).

THE EVOLUTION OF THE INSTITUTION

Most public institutions today cannot meet the requirements for an individualized plan for habilitation. Personnel simply do not have the information or skills which are presupposed in the definition proposed here. Furthermore, their established habits of thinking and their attitudes toward mentally retarded residents have tended to foster the dependence of the residents upon the institutional environment and have operated against the promotion of the individual adaptive capability and the development of skills conducive to community living. Most institutions, even if the staff would develop a written treatment and habilitation plan for each resident, still would lack the resources to carry out these plans.

Similarly, there is at present a shortage of resources to carry out habilitation plans effectively in the community. Professional information is available, technology is at hand, but the resources in sufficient amount are seldom organized into a truly effective program.

To accommodate modern concepts, an evolution of both community and institutional programs is required. There is a need for massive new changes in the areas of basic knowledge, education and training of personnel, numbers of personnel, revisions of physical plants, sufficient and appropriate supplies and equipment, patterns of administration, and patterns of communication within the community. Certainly, unless there is sufficient infusion of talent and resources, neither the community nor the institution will have the ability to respond promptly to such requirements.

THE DEVELOPMENT OF COMMUNITY-BASED ALTERNATIVES TO INSTITUTIONAL CARE

One of the primary considerations in *Wyatt* is the provision of the least restrictive environment that ensures an adequate opportunity for habilitation. In some instances, habilitative services of a quality available in institutions may not be available in the community, so that the pattern of institutional care may remain in spite of the desirable advantages of a less restrictive environment. However, in this instance, institutional placement must be of a specific and limited duration and established for the purposes of providing the individual specific rehabilitative services.

Services can be provided in many settings less restrictive than the large residential facility. Some of these include halfway houses, small-group homes, sheltered work training centers, sheltered workshops, day care centers, and activity centers.

The biggest problem, however, in community programs is the problem of access, including:

1. access to services such as recreation, health care, and dental care;
2. access to education in the public school, the vocational school, and the field of adult education;
3. access to transportation;
4. access to acceptable living quarters.

Perhaps the single largest constraint on the development of community-based alternatives to institutional care is restrictive zoning ordinances. This is the most troublesome issue in community residential care and is being attacked in the courts. Until there is a litigated resolution of this problem, even if money, personnel, and facilities are available, restrictive zoning ordinances and a rejecting public attitude frequently will hamper the implementation of these alternatives. Group homes often can be established only in the least desirable locations in the community.[3]

Furthermore, the issues of quality control of services in community care programs will constantly arise. It is essential to prevent the community group home from becoming a degrading, dehumanizing, small institution in its own right.

THE MOBILIZATION OF PUBLIC INTEREST AND COMMITMENT

The vast bulk of current funding decisions must now be made in the public, political arena. Thus, humane, decent, and constitutionally acceptable care of the mentally retarded individual needs to be made more politically appealing. Citizens preoccupied with other matters must become informed, responsive, and concerned. An active and informed constituency for the mentally retarded must be created. These imperatives may not fall within the concerns of constitutional protections for the mentally retarded, nor within the proper purview of the courts, but for the court decisions to be implemented effectively, they, too, must be met.

The mental retardation field is confronting new thought, new legal precedent, and new concern. Civil rights progress in similar fields has bettered the lives of many human beings in the past. The present directions of the law offer similar possibilities for bettering the lives of the mentally retarded and other handicapped persons in the years ahead. The law has become a prime mover in the search for dignity, humanity, self-respect, respect of others, and for the development of feelings of dignity and self-worth for the mentally retarded. The search for legal rights may, indeed, give great impetus to the search for human rights.

---

[3] *See* Chandler & Ross, Chapter 11 of this volume.

CHAPTER 14

Beyond the Right to Habilitation

Editorial Introduction

This chapter is an extension of the preceding chapter on the right to habilitation in that it explores an alternative theoretical approach that may assist mentally retarded citizens in their pursuit of a more fulfilling life. Burt's analysis is closely aligned to the reaction comment by Rothman in Chapter 13. Burt notes that the right to habilitation rationale for the *Wyatt* case risks an emphasis on improving institutional care, whereas the proper emphasis should be on deinstitutionalization and integration of mentally retarded citizens into the community. The *PARC* and *Diana* cases, both in the education arena, are utilized to develop an alternative analysis. Burt argues that *Wyatt* is consistent with *PARC* and *Diana* in that it attempts to redress an inequality between the services provided to most people in the community and those provided to the mentally retarded. He stresses the need for future court decisions to provide a means of preventing institutionalization or of returning mentally retarded citizens to the community where adequate programing is available, rather than maintaining better warehouses. He asks whether segregation of mentally retarded individuals in separate programs is not inherently unequal, as the courts have found to be true in the area of racially separate public services. He presents an analysis of the constitutional concept of "suspect classifications" and demonstrates the applicability of this concept to the classification of mental retardation as it is used to segregate the mentally retarded citizen in special institutions or classes.

The other critical point in Burt's analysis is the destigmatization process, a process which must occur before the mentally retarded citizen can ultimately function as an integral part of society. The only way to ensure that this class of citizens is treated like other citizens is to take away the stigma, and to this end, the mentally retarded individual must remain in the community and in the regular classroom. There will be difficulties and there may be penalties, but it must be recognized that what is occurring is a major attempt to destigmatize a group which has been stigmatized for centuries.

Clements challenges Burt's assumptions about the goals of litigation. Clements refers to a trend during the last decade of decreasing the proportion of mildly retarded individuals in institutions and of increasing the care and treatment of severely and profoundly retarded, multiply handicapped individuals. Although arguing for a gradual transition of institutions in the direction of integration into community service systems, he questions the feasibility of an approach that would require the use of integrated educational programing for the mentally retarded and nonretarded. The reader will want to compare Clements' position with that taken by Rosen in his reaction comment in Chapter 18. Clements holds out some hope for a future community in which segregation of mentally retarded citizens is the rare exception rather than the usual case.

The reaction by Dybwad brings into focus the extent to which "mental retardation" means what people want it to mean. He supports Burt's proposition that there is something highly suspect about the classification. He also emphasizes the need for applied and programmatic research to redress the current imbalance of research funding in the direction of basic research.

PRINCIPAL PAPER

ROBERT A. BURT

IN RECENT YEARS litigation against state agencies to improve services for mentally retarded citizens and those alleged to be retarded has had dramatic success. Three cases stand as landmarks. In *Wyatt v. Stickney,*[1] an Alabama federal court imposed detailed service standards at the state institution for mentally retarded individuals to vindicate the residents' constitutional right to habilitation. Through *Pennsylvania Association for Retarded Children v. Commonwealth of Pennsylvania,*[2] the state policy of excluding "uneducable" children from the public school system was reversed and the state was required to institute extensive

---

[1] 344 F. Supp. 387, 344 F. Supp. 73 (M.D. Ala. 1972), 344 F. Supp. 1341, 325 F. Supp. 781 (M.D. Ala. 1971), *aff'd sub nom.* Wyatt v. Aderholt, 503 F.2d 1305 (5th Cir. 1974). *See also* Halpern, pp. 385-407, Chapter 13 of this volume.
[2] 343 F. Supp. 279 (E.D. Pa. 1972) [hereinafter cited as PARC]. *See also* Herr, pp. 262-67, Chapter 9 of this volume.

remedial education programs for retarded children. *Diana v. State Board of Education*[3] invalidated the classification and standards procedures that a local California school district had employed to transfer Mexican-American children from regular classrooms into special classes for "slow learners." These three cases have spawned similar litigation in many other states. They have given promise of a new forum for forcing official and public attention on the multiple handicaps with which the state burdens the disabled. The cases also provide a new weapon for prying additional services from the public treasury for citizens with organic, psychological, and social disabilities.

The promise could, however, be short-lived. There is no assurance that federal district and appellate courts will continue to follow the *Wyatt-PARC-Diana* line in similar litigation.[4] And the Supreme Court's recent decision refusing to invalidate certain school financing laws[5] might appear to remove a portion of the doctrinal underpinnings of one or more of these cases. Thus, it cannot be assumed that a new era of judicial solicitude for mentally retarded individuals has arrived. It is, instead, necessary to reexamine critically both the persuasiveness of legal theories on which *Wyatt-PARC-Diana* were based and the usefulness for mentally retarded citizens of the remedies that were obtained in these cases.

This paper proposes several theses:

First, that the legal theory in *Wyatt* (institutionalized mentally retarded citizens have a constitutional "right to habilitation") may not be fully accepted and that the remedy most clearly following from this theory (conditions in residential institutions for the mentally retarded should be "improved") will not prove useful in working important improvements in the situation of retarded individuals;

Second, that *PARC's* legal theory (excluding mentally retarded children from public education is an unconstitutionally invidious discrimination) is persuasive and that a more helpful judicial remedy can be drawn from this theory (retarded children should not be segregated from the community or from regular public schools except in the rarest of cases);

Third, that future litigation must develop an extensive factual demonstration that the "retarded" label is stigmatizing, incapacitating, and unjust and that state agencies have a long history of imposing terrible burdens on the mentally retarded.

A REEVALUATION OF THE RIGHT TO HABILITATION

It may be that no matter what refinements are offered for *Wyatt-PARC-Diana*, courts will nonetheless refuse to invoke constitutional safeguards for the mentally

---

[3] Civil No. C-70-37 (N.D. Cal., Feb. 5, 1970) (unreported; Feb. 5 decree superseded by Consent Decree of June 18, 1973), *See also* Larry P. v. Riles, 343 F. Supp. 1306 (N.D. Cal. 1972), *aff'd,* 502 F.2d 963 (9th Cir. 1974).

[4] *See, e.g.,* Burnham v. Georgia, 349 F. Supp. 1335 (E.D. Ga. 1972), *rev'd,* 503 F.2d 1319 (5th Cir. 1974), New York Ass'n for Retarded Children v. Rockefeller, 357 F. Supp. 752 (E.D.N.Y. 1973).

[5] San Antonio Independent School Dist. v. Rodriguez, 411 U.S. 1, *rehearing denied,* 411 U.S. 959 (1973).

retarded. Hopefully, this result will not come, but there are some grounds for predicting it and some legal basis on which to rationalize it.

Some courts undoubtedly will cite Justice Powell's dicta in *Rodriguez,* the recent school financing case, that "difficult questions of educational policy . . . [are an] area in which this Court's lack of specialized knowledge and experience counsels against premature interference with the informed judgments made at the state and local levels."[6] This attitude is, however, more predictable than justifiable as a criticism of these cases. The state conduct complained of in *Wyatt, PARC,* and *Diana* was so grossly improper that no expert could disagree about the educational justification for requiring remedy. In *Wyatt,* no one alleged the educational merits of the medieval grotesqueries evidenced in the conditions at the Partlow State School and Hospital. In *PARC,* no one argued that totally excluding retarded children from school benefited them educationally. In *Diana,* no one argued the educational propriety of placing Spanish-speaking students in classes for the mentally retarded because they scored low on English language intelligence tests. One may contest the legal theories on which the courts based relief, but these cases were not wrongly decided on the ground that a federal judge lacked competence to evaluate competing educational claims in the controversy.

In these three cases, no one defended the challenged practices. In all three cases, the defendant state agencies admitted the inadequacies of their programs, and in all cases the remedy imposed was largely based on negotiated agreements between the plaintiffs and the challenged state agencies. In subsequent cases following these precedents, courts will likely be required to resolve disputes about remedies. At that point, judges can take evidence on general standards prevailing in the profession, and the standards agreed upon in *Wyatt, PARC,* and *Diana* will themselves be persuasive guides.

The way in which remedies were devised in this trilogy of cases suggests a different more troubling criticism. In *PARC,* for example, it appears that the federal court did not resolve a dispute between contesting parties, but instead ratified an agreement between advocates for children's services and professional service agencies to raid state treasuries for greater funds on behalf of their shared clientele. This poses a question of equal justice. The *PARC* court did not address itself to whether it is unfair to withhold public funds from a group of students who are difficult and expensive to educate. This question was answered by a District of Columbia federal judge who followed *PARC* to invalidate an educational exclusion law.[7] The D.C. school board concurred in the educational merit of the ruling requiring educational opportunities for mentally retarded children, but complained they had no funds to provide special educational programs. The court rejected this argument: If you have no special education funds, the court replied, then expenditures must be reduced on other educational programs so that all children at least share equally in inadequate schooling.[8] Similarly, the court in

---

[6]*Id.* at 42.

[7]Mills v. Board of Educ., 348 F. Supp. 866 (D.D.C. 1972).

[8]*Id.* at 876: "The inadequacies of the District of Columbia Public School System whether occasioned by insufficient funding or administrative inefficiency, certainly cannot be permitted to bear more heavily on the 'exceptional' or handicapped child than on the normal child."

Wyatt threatened to curtail state expenditures for such well-heeled programs as highways unless the state provided more funds from some source to meet the agreed professional standards for the residents of Partlow.[9]

The balance struck between majority and minority interests in these cases may be contested. But courts are not strangers to the task of evaluating competing definitions of equal justice. These three cases rest on norms of judicial equality. In all three cases, state agencies were giving different treatment to a class of citizens identified as "mentally retarded." The courts simply inquired whether the differences between mentally retarded citizens and other citizens are sufficient to justify the difference in state treatment. On the basis of this analysis, the *Diana* decision is clearly correct. Children in a local school district were being placed in "special" classes that segregated them from peers and subjected them to stigma, an impoverished curriculum, and diminished future educational and career opportunities. It is hardly innovative for a court to require that a state decision with such far-reaching individual consequences be made by standards and procedures that clearly ensure a reliable decision. The *Diana* decision requires no more than this. The school district justified special placement on the ground that "slow learners" require a slow track. Under *Diana* the school district must now show that their placement tests are in fact sufficiently accurate measures of educational capacity, rather than instruments of social or cultural bias, and that their placement procedures give full opportunity for adversary testing of placement decisions.

PARC also expresses a principle of equality. Pennsylvania, like most states, offered publicly funded education to some children and refused it to others. The ostensible ground for the refusal was that the excluded children were "uneducable." But the state in *PARC* properly conceded that this premise has no factual basis for any of the children excluded from public education by these state laws.[10] The most that can be said is that education is more difficult and more expensive for so-called "ineducable" children, and the possible educational attainments are more modest than for others. On this ground some may believe it rational to exclude these children from public education. For instance, if public commitment to educational funding is limited, and if public agencies choose to pursue the "excellence of the few," rather than developing individual capacities for the sake of the individual, then educational exclusion of the "mentally retarded" might be a justifiable policy.[11]

Before the Supreme Court's decision in *Rodriguez*, there were two techniques available to counter this reasoning. One was to argue that state policies regarding education were more rigorously and skeptically scrutinized by the courts than, for example, welfare policies. This, in essence, was the thesis of the courts that propounded a "fundamental right to education" in the Constitution. *Rodriguez*

---

[9] *See* 344 F. Supp. at 377.

[10] 343 F. Supp. at 296: "Without exception, expert opinion indicates that: [A]ll mentally retarded persons are capable of benefiting from a program of education and training; that the greatest number of retarded persons, given such education and training, are capable of achieving self-sufficiency and the remaining few . . . are capable of achieving some degree of self-care."

[11] Using similar reasoning, the Supreme Court has approved a state decision to reduce federal welfare funds from families with dependent children in order to provide greater benefits to the aged and the physically disabled. Jefferson v. Hackney, 406 U.S. 535 (1972).

rejects this proposition,[12] but this rejection does not mean that the rationale of the *PARC* decision is no longer valid. The *Rodriguez* opinion itself suggests one ground for justifying *PARC*. The Court stated that the argument for constitutional invalidity "might have [merit] if a State's financing system occasioned an absolute denial of educational opportunities to any of its children. . . ."[13] An ethical imperative is implicit in this suggestion, though its precise rationale is not clear. Perhaps the state is required to give some basic minimum education to all its citizens; perhaps the state is required to avoid imposing gross disadvantages by totally excluding some children from school in order to give some marginally greater services to remaining children. Whatever the rationale, it would be sufficient to justify *PARC*.

This interpretation of *Rodriguez* does not require a state to give precisely equal services or funds to every school district or school-age child; it does require that if public education is offered, some minimum opportunity for education be made available to everyone. Certainly, the practical importance of education and this country's traditional commitment to universal public education are sufficient to support a "fundamental right to public education" which invalidates state policy that totally excludes some as unworthy—even though capable—of benefiting from education.

Wyatt can also be justified by this norm of equality. Most of, if not all, the children residing at Partlow State School and Hospital came there by default, because of the absence of community-based educational and treatment facilities. But Partlow was emphatically not an alternative educational facility for these children. The record in *Wyatt* clearly established that Partlow sought only to give custodial care and did a dismal job of it.[14] The Alabama residents of Partlow thus stood exactly in the position of the Pennsylvania children excluded from the local schools before the *PARC* decision. In both instances the states gave community-based education to "normal" children and rendered no service remotely comparable to "retarded" children. The *Wyatt* order, requiring an educational program at Partlow and upgrading custodial facilities to a minimally humane environment, in effect demands for institutionalized children at least a minimum version of state educational programs for "normal" community-based children.

The *Wyatt* opinion does not explicitly rest on an equality norm and it has not been generally so considered. *Wyatt* instead speaks of a "constitutional right to habilitation" for mentally retarded citizens confined in state residential institutions.[15] This doctrine is, however, awkward in this setting. A constitutional right to treatment was first recognized for adults who were involuntarily committed to state mental institutions.[16] Since the state had sought confinement for mental illness, it clearly followed that the state was obligated to give treatment for this illness or establish some different justification for the confinement. By fortuity,

[12]411 U.S. at 35.
[13]*Id.* at 37.
[14]344 F. Supp. at 393-94: "[P]rimitive conditions . . . atmosphere of futility and despair which envelops both staff and residents . . . legislative neglect has been catastrophic; atrocities occur daily. . . . The gravity and immediacy of the situation cannot be overemphasized."
[15]*See* 325 F. Supp. at 784.
[16]*See* O'Connor v. Donaldson, 95 S. Ct. 2486 (1975); Rouse v. Cameron, 373 F.2d 451 (D.C. Cir. 1966).

most Partlow residents had been involuntarily committed under Alabama law,[17] and their status as involuntary residents supported recognition of the constitutional right to habilitation. But, for mentally retarded individuals, involuntary commitment status is usually a formality; most institutional residents have not been formally committed, but rather "voluntarily" placed by their parents.[18] Nonetheless, the right to habilitation for mentally retarded citizens has to date been confined to those actively detained by the state.[19] An attempt to broaden the right is struggling to gain firm footing, but it is not clear that even progressive courts will quickly extend the right and concomitant judicial intervention to all institutionalized populations. However, limiting the *Wyatt*-proclaimed right to habilitation to persons "involuntarily confined" makes a practical mockery of the right.

Furthermore, proposing a right to habilitation for institutionalized residents raises another doctrinal difficulty. If the state owes even minimal habilitation obligations (*i.e.*, medical care, food, clothing) to institutionalized citizens, why does it not owe the same obligations to all citizens?[20] Distinctions may be drawn to avoid this and other difficulties, but a more satisfactory alternative rationale for *Wyatt* is readily available. Subtle distinctions need not be drawn if the *Wyatt* right is conceptualized as a right to equal state services for all citizens. As in *PARC*, the court is not requiring the state to provide educational facilities for children in general. But if the state chooses to provide services for some, it must provide some such services to all. Under this rationale, the voluntary or involuntary commitment status of institutionalized children is irrelevant. The state was obligated to provide "habilitation"—that is, opportunities for cognitive and social growth—for mentally retarded children wherever they resided, because the state provided these opportunities—denoted "education"—for other children who cannot be treated so much differently from the mentally retarded.

Analyzing the right to habilitation as an equality norm has a further, even more important, consequence. This analysis highlights the central public policy issue at stake in providing special state services for institutionalized mentally retarded individuals. That issue is the degree to which or the circumstances in which separate state services for the mentally retarded are inherently unequal. The single greatest shortcoming of the *Wyatt* decision is its failure to address this issue. Elaborate standards for staffing ratios, recordkeeping, living conditions, disciplinary policies, and other aspects of institutional life are imposed in *Wyatt*.[21] But the basic question is never confronted: Can any large-scale, geographically remote, full-time residential institution beneficially affect the lives of its residents.?

Wyatt makes two explicit references to this question. Its standards recognize that every resident is entitled to "the least restrictive conditions necessary to

---

[17] 344 F. Supp. at 390 n.5.

[18] *See* Kay, Farnham, Karren, Knakal & Diamond, *Legal Planning for the Mentally Retarded: The California Experience,* 60 CALIF. L. REV. 438, 516 (1972).

[19] Judge Johnson, in the *Wyatt* opinion itself, spoke only of the right to treatment for persons "involuntarily committed." 344 F. Supp. at 390.

[20] *See* Lindsey v. Normet, 405 U.S. 56, 74 (1972) (housing); Dandridge v. Williams, 397 U.S. 471 (1970) (welfare).

[21] *See* 344 F. Supp. at 395 (Appendix A to the court's opinion).

achieve the purposes of habilitation"[22] and that "no borderline or mildly retarded person shall be a resident of the institution."[23] These are easily evaded generalities. "Least restrictive setting . . . necessary" is on its face an imprecise standard. Refusing admission for "borderline" individuals might appear more enforceable, but in practice a state can let too many retarded persons slip below the requisite "borderline" by simply withholding community services that would otherwise sustain and develop their capacities.

The *Wyatt* decision suggests, though only implicitly, a further pressure against institutional residence. The imposed standards requiring specified staffing, the payment of minimum wages to residents for performing institutional maintenance tasks, and other specified institutional amenities[24] may prove so expensive that the state will be led to close the institution or reduce its population dramatically. This prospect, however, seems remote. The *Wyatt* standards are not carved in stone; state budgetary constraints are a recurring reality that may erode the more stringent and expensive standards over time. And, in any event, if the institution becomes increasingly selective in its admission and nonselective in its release policies, or is closed, the result only forces the mentally retarded population into inadequate or nonexistent community programs. This has in fact been the result in other states where the slogan of "normalized community care" for mentally retarded or mentally ill individuals has been used to justify restricting access to large-scale institutions while providing no alternative community resources.[25] There is little guarantee that state or local agencies will design new programs to meet this need.

Approaching the Partlow problem by means of a constitutional right to habilitation was misleading. The approach permitted the court and parties to address institutional habilitation resources in isolation without forcing them to justify the very existence of the institutional habilitation modality. Neither the court nor the parties were ignorant of the inherent shortcomings of residential institutional care. Rather, they either failed to perceive or were unwilling to use a legal principle that would have brought this problem into the high visibility and relevance it properly deserved.

On this basis, the practical consequences of *Wyatt* and the recently decided *Willowbrook* case[26] seem disconcertingly similar. At first glance, the two cases appear poles apart. *Wyatt* resoundingly proclaims a constitutional right to habilitation and imposes wide-ranging standards to upgrade services and rehabilitative efforts at the Partlow State School and Hospital. The *Willowbrook* court initially held that there was no constitutional right to habilitation for the institutionalized

---

[22] 344 F. Supp. at 396.
[23] *Id.*
[24] *Id.* at 402-03, 406.
[25] *See* COMMITTEE ON MENTAL HEALTH SERVICES INSIDE AND OUTSIDE THE FAMILY COURT IN THE CITY OF NEW YORK, JUVENILE JUSTICE CONFOUNDED: PRETENSIONS AND REALITIES OF TREATMENT SERVICES 87, 96 (1972).
[26] New York State Ass'n for Retarded Children v. Rockefeller, 357 F. Supp. 752 (E.D.N.Y. 1973) [hereinafter cited as Willowbrook].

retarded,[27] although this court did find a constitutional right to be "protected from [state-imposed] harm." On this ground it promulgated standards of minimum decency (including additional staffing requirements) for Willowbrook State School.[28]

The more modest *Willowbrook* constitutional right and more modest remedy were drawn from recent cases forcing improvement in prison conditions to avoid unconstitutionally "cruel and unusual punishment."[29] With or without minimum standards of decency, a prison remains a prison and is basically a coercive, unnatural, and antitherapeutic place to live. Unlike *Wyatt,* the *Willowbrook* case does not aspire beyond this unpretentious characterization of the New York institution for the mentally retarded. But for all *Wyatt*'s greater ambitions, its imposed standards suggest the Alabama institution will remain a large-scale geographically and socially isolated residence for a scorned population. For this reason, it seems at least doubtful that *Wyatt* will provide any greater benefits to the institutionalized mentally retarded in Alabama than *Willowbrook* will give to its charges in New York. And *Willowbrook* at least calls a jail a jail.

AN ALTERNATIVE: MENTAL RETARDATION AS A SEMISUSPECT CLASSIFICATION

At first glance, the *PARC* legal theory appears to have the same limitations as *Wyatt* and *Willowbrook. PARC* rested on the premise that excluding mentally retarded children from public schools worked a wrongful inequality on them. If *PARC,* as qualified by the Supreme Court's dicta in *Rodriguez,* is based only on the notion that total deprivation of education is wrong, then it would appear that any minimum provision of educational opportunity would satisfy the constitutional requirement. Therefore, the marginal improvements in institutional education programs promised by *Wyatt,* or perhaps even by *Willowbrook,* might satisfy the dictates of equal treatment adequately. If *PARC* meant no more than this, there would be little to recommend it as an alternative constitutional theory for the right to habilitation.

But the *PARC* theory, properly developed, can mean much more than this. The *PARC* theory can and should mean that any state program that segregates

---

[27] 357 F. Supp. at 758. In the entry of a final consent judgment, however, the *Willowbrook* court noted:

> Somewhat different legal rubrics have been employed in these cases — "protection from harm" in this case and "right to treatment" and "need for care" in others. It appears that there is no bright line separating these standards. In the present posture of this case, there is no need for the court to re-examine the constitutional standard properly applicable to Willowbrook's residents. The relief which the parties agreed to will advance the very rights enunciated in the case law since this court's 1973 ruling. Entry of final consent judgment, Willowbrook, Civil Nos. 72C356, 72C357 (E.D.N.Y. entered, May 5, 1975).

Under similar circumstances a neighboring court has recently recognized the constitutional right to treatment. Martarella v. Kelly, 349 F. Supp. 575 (S.D.N.Y. 1972), *supplemented,* 359 F. Supp. 478 (S.D.N.Y. 1973).

[28] The court ordered hiring of additional ward attendants (specifying a staff/resident ratio of 1:9), 85 new nurses, 30 physical therapists (with starting salaries of $12,000, 10 percent above the "level at which present unsuccessful recruiting efforts are proceeding"), 15 additional physicians, and added recreation staff. The court further prohibited use of seclusion for discipline and required "repair of all inoperable toilets." 357 F. Supp. at 768-69.

[29] *Id.* at 764-65.

mentally retarded citizens as such from others is highly suspect and that courts will require states to treat mentally retarded persons indistinguishably from others, except in ways that are both very limited and very clearly beneficial to the individual. By this test, segregation of the mentally retarded in a remote large-scale institution could never pass constitutional muster, except perhaps for the very small number of profoundly retarded people who, after the state has provided years of painstaking, repeated, community-based training, are unable even to feed, clean, or clothe themselves.

The *PARC* theory is not based on the premise that the state has wrongfully given more funds and attention to the education of some children than others. *PARC* does not and, in light of the Supreme Court's decision in *Rodriguez*, cannot hold that the state must make available the same facilities or the same funds to all children in public education. But *Rodriguez* does not permit states to impose any differences that they might choose on children in public education. States may not differentiate between blacks and whites, as such, in public education.[30] Forms of discrimination by a state against aliens[31] and illegitimate children have been found to be unconstitutional.[32]

There are important analogues between these disfavored categories — blacks, aliens, illegitimates — and mentally retarded persons. The similarities are not so much in clearly applicable legal doctrine, though the doctrinal pathways can be traced adequately. The compelling similarities are found in historical social reality. A group of persons labeled "mentally retarded" in this society has been subjected to discriminations as brutal and dehumanizing as were imposed on the slave population. Contemporary students of slavery who strain to imagine conditions of life in slave-trading ships for human beings torn from (or delivered by) their families should visit institutions like Partlow State School and Hospital for the Retarded or Willowbrook State School.[33] No item in the catalogue of horrors from the slave trade is without its counterpart in these institutions. American society's willingness to confine retarded human beings in these terrible warehouses and even banish these warehouses from sight by their remote, often rural, locations is eloquent testimony that a class of persons has, like slaves, been made nonpersons.[34] If further confirmation is needed to demonstrate the brutal dehumanization this society has practiced on mentally retarded persons as a class, it as enough to consider the compulsory sterilization laws enacted during the first decades of this century[35] with the unjustified promise to cleanse the United States of "generations of imbeciles."[36]

---

[30] Brown v. Board of Educ., 347 U.S. 483 (1954).

[31] Graham v. Richardson, 403 U.S. 365 (1971).

[32] Weber v. Aetna Cas. & Sur. Co., 406 U.S. 164 (1972).

[33] For Partlow, see note 14 *supra*; for Willowbrook, the court found that "conditions are hazardous to the health, safety, and sanity of the residents." 357 F. Supp. at 756. There was expert testimony that "the situation was perhaps worse at Willowbrook" than Partlow. Slip opinion at 16 (not included in the opinion reported in Federal Supplement).

[34] *Cf.* Mr. Justice Brennan's conclusion that the eighth amendment requires that the state not "treat members of the human race as nonhumans, as objects to be toyed with and discarded," and his invalidation of the death penalty on this basis, Furman v. Georgia, 408 U.S. 238, 272-73, 290 (1972) (Brennan, J., concurring).

Further evidence of prejudicial discrimination against the mentally retarded is collected in THE MENTALLY DISABLED AND THE LAW (rev. ed. S. Brakel & R. Rock eds. 1971).

[35] *See* Ferster, *Eliminating the Unfit — Is Sterilization the Answer?* 27 OHIO ST. L.J. 591 (1966).

[36] Buck v. Bell, 274 U.S. 200, 207 (1927).

This social reality is the basic foundation that must and can be set out in future litigation to enlist judicial action. From this foundation, courts can be led to understand the social analogues between retarded persons, as a group, and other groups for whom the courts have done increasing battle in recent years. Regarding illegitimate children, for example, the Supreme Court has recently said that:

> [t]he status of illegitimacy has expressed through the ages society's condemnation of irresponsible liaisons beyond the bonds of marriage. But visiting this condemnation on the head of an infant is illogical and unjust. Moreover, imposing disabilities on the illegitimate child is contrary to the basic concept of our system that legal burdens should bear some relationship to individual responsibility or wrongdoing. Obviously, no child is responsible for his birth and penalizing the illegitimate child is . . . unjust. . . . Courts are powerless to prevent the social opprobrium suffered by these hapless children, but the Equal Protection Clause does enable us to strike down discriminatory laws relating to status of birth where . . . the classification is justified by no legitimate state interest, compelling or otherwise.[37]

Of aliens, the Court has said that "as a class [they] are a 'discrete and insular' minority . . . for whom . . . heightened judicial solicitude is appropriate" because they are a socially and politically vulnerable group, readily identifiable as such and readily made targets of unjust discriminations by popular majorities.[38]

Mentally retarded individuals have these same characteristics. As a rule they are the victims of birth or developmental defects for which they can bear no just blame, and, as a class, they are subjected to galling and brutal social discriminations. The *PARC* court itself noted the "stigma which our society unfortunately attaches to the label of mental retardation," citing compulsory sterilization laws for the mentally retarded, the history even of legislative "recommendation . . . [of] euthanasia," and "empirical studies show[ing] that stigmatization is a major concern among parents of retarded children. Some parents liken it to a 'sentence of death.'"[39]

Thus, there is ample evidence to show that retarded persons are an unjustly stigmatized, politically vulnerable group and that state policies — including compulsory sterilization, marriage prohibitions, exclusion from public education, and segregation in terrible human warehouses — have fanned popular social opprobrium. There is, furthermore, ample evidence that *all* mentally retarded persons can benefit from individualized educational programs. But existing large-scale geographically remote institutions cannot by their nature provide adequate programs to remedy the intellectual and emotional shortcomings and the galling social stigma that led the retarded residents to these institutions.[40] If this evidence is fully marshaled in litigation, courts can be led to rule that present patterns of state segregation of retarded persons for "habilitation" or "educational" purposes are impermissible.

---

[37] Weber v. Aetna Cas. & Sur. Co., 406 U.S. 164, 175-76 (1972).

[38] Graham v. Richardson, 403 U.S. 365, 372 (1971). In this case, the Court struck down a state law withholding welfare funds from aliens. Notwithstanding that the Court had authorized similar state action regarding ADC families (see note 11 *supra*), the Court here rejected the same "justification of limiting expenses" on the ground that it "is particularly inappropriate and unreasonable when the discriminated class consists of aliens." 403 U.S. at 376.

[39] 343 F. Supp. at 293-95.

[40] *See* note 10 *supra*. *See also* E. GOFFMAN, ASYLUMS (1961).

Courts can be led, that is, to force states to close the Partlows and Willowbrooks and, even more important, to require alternative programs for mentally retarded persons which treat them as indistinguishably as possible from other persons.

From this evidence, a legal theory can be drawn that will lead courts to enforce this remedy. That theory is, first, that special state categorization of "retarded persons" is (or comes perilously close to) a constitutionally suspect classification and, second, that state use of such classification for placement in socially and geographically isolated institutions is excessively harmful and unjustified.

Under current Supreme Court doctrine, both steps in this reasoning appear necessary to bring the desired result. The Court decisions mentioned regarding state action toward blacks, aliens, and illegitimates appear, at least at first glance, to require only the first step to justify judicial remedies. That is, each of these categories appears to be considered a constitutionally suspect classification and on this ground any state action explicitly limited to the suspect class is presumptively invalid.[41] To overcome this presumption, the state must mount a "compelling" case to demonstrate the need for categorically treating the suspect class differently from other citizens. In practice, the courts have been exceedingly reluctant to find an adequately compelling justification for suspect classifications.[42]

It would be preferable, for those advocating retarded persons' interests, if courts ruled that "retardation" is a constitutionally suspect class. The historical similarities between treatment of blacks and of mentally retarded persons suggest powerful arguments for this ruling. But it seems unlikely that courts will readily accept this argument. Judges and others can too easily argue that differences between blacks and whites are purely social, perpetuated solely by wrongful prejudice, but that differences between most (or many) (or some) retarded and other persons reflect true differences in endowment and potential, rather than prejudiced social artifact. Even if this argument is wrong, its rebuttal is a complicated, difficult undertaking.

Rebuttal has been made even more difficult by a dictum in a recent opinion by Mr. Justice Brennan. In arguing that sex should be added to the ranks of constitutionally suspect classifications, Justice Brennan stated:

> . . . [W]hat differentiates sex from such non-suspect statutes [sic] as intelligence or physical disability, and aligns it with the recognized suspect criteria, is that the sex characteristic frequently bears no relation to ability to perform or contribute to society.[43]

In this opinion, Justice Brennan spoke only for a minority of the Court. But his attitude indicates the skepticism that is likely to greet any argument that mental retardation is a suspect category. The skeptic will ask, "If the state may not make special stigmatizing classifications for mentally retarded persons, how then can

---

[41] *See, e.g.,* Graham v. Richardson, 403 U.S. 365, 376 (1971).

[42] *See* Gunther, *The Supreme Court 1971 Term — In Search of Evolving Doctrine on a Changing Court: A Model for a Newer Equal Protection,* 86 HARV. L. REV. 1, 8 (1972).

[43] Frontiero v. Richardson, 411 U.S. 677, 686 (1973).

the state, in its public schools, give stigmatizing low grades to students who fail to memorize spelling assignments?" In many cases the classification of mental retardation is not very different from the vast range of other state classifications based on test performance, such as school grades, admission to state universities, and state employment. It would, for example, be difficult for a state to make a "compelling" case for the accuracy and rationality of its admissions criteria to state universities.

There is, however, a response to this argument. State grading decisions, admissions decisions, employment decisions do not usually carry consequences so far-reaching or disastrous to individuals identified as less intelligent as the consequences imposed by the label of "mentally retarded." Moreover, the state's decision to warehouse persons labeled retarded in huge remote institutions clearly suffers the critical flaw identified by Justice Brennan. This state disposition "frequently bears no relation to ability to perform or contribute to society." To the contrary, this disposition virtually ensures that any ability or potential of the mentally retarded person will be irretrievably lost. The utter irrationality of state policy toward retarded citizens should be clear, even to a judicial skeptic, by considering the consequence imposed by the state following its diagnosis of "retardation."

There is, however, a further skeptical rejoinder to this position. Even admitting that state policy institutionalizing retarded persons is irredeemably foolish, it may be no more irrational or prejudiced than a host of other governmental activities such as the oil depletion allowance, the federal highway program, or the Vietnam war. What, in short, justifies the judiciary's correcting the irrationalities afflicting mentally retarded persons when it is unprepared to remedy other governmental irrationalities?

Unless one is prepared to accept that state action discriminating against mentally retarded persons is inherently suspect on constitutional grounds, there is no clear-cut doctrinally satisfactory way to answer this question. Such a position is strongly supported by the earlier discussion of the gross historical discriminations against mentally retarded persons, their continued social and political vulnerability, and their personal blamelessness for their status. But that discussion is repeated here in a narrower context. Even if retardation or low intelligence is not a constitutionally suspect category for all purposes, it surely is suspect when invoked to justify state action so grossly depriving and wholly irrational as consignment to Partlows or Willowbrooks.

The fact that this state-imposed classification often segregates children from regular public educational facilities is a further reason for judicial intervention. In *Brown v. Board of Education,* the Supreme Court noted the vital importance of education in American tradition, as a "principal instrument in awakening the child to cultural values,"[44] and suggested that quarantining black children in the name of education "generates a feeling of inferiority as to their status in the community that may affect their hearts and minds in a way unlikely ever to be undone."[45]

[44] 347 U.S. at 493 (1954).
[45] *Id.* at 494.

Imposing stigmatizing social isolation as a part of a state's educational policy taught a lesson to black children and today teaches a lesson to retarded children, which is directly inconsistent with a democratic ethos. Following *Brown,* the Court quickly indicated that state policies aimed at stigmatizing blacks were suspect whatever their context.[46] But the Court's choice of education for its first target was not accidental, for in that context the strongest case against stigmatizing state conduct could be made.[47] Even if the judiciary is not prepared to extirpate all stigmatizing state classifications for mentally retarded persons, courts should attack this stigma where it is most damaging and least justifiable.

The reasoning that a state classification may be constitutionally suspect for some purposes but not others, depending on the purposes which that classification serves, draws on some recent tentative developments in constitutional doctrine. Gerald Gunther has recently described these developments as "startling and intriguing" evolutions toward a "newer Equal Protection."[48] The trend is illustrated by the Supreme Court's decision in *Frontiero v. Richardson,*[49] where all of the justices but one agreed on the invalidity of an armed forces regulation imposing more stringent requirements on women than on men for obtaining dependency allowances. Four members of the Court, in the opinion by Mr. Justice Brennan discussed previously, concluded that the discrimination was invalid because sex was a constitutionally suspect classification.[50] Four other members rejected this analysis, but concurred in invalidating the discrimination essentially by proclaiming without explanation that the due process clause of the fifth amendment was violated.[51] As Professor Gunther observed regarding an earlier case relied on by the four concurring justices in *Frontiero,* "It is difficult to understand that result without an assumption that some special sensitivity to sex as a classifying factor entered into the analysis."[52] Nevertheless, the four concurring justices avoided stating this proposition.

Gunther has marshaled a significant number of similar cases found on the recent Supreme Court docket.[53] The doctrine emerging from these cases is "inchoate and fragmentary at present."[54] But the principle that Gunther attempts

---

[46] For Supreme Court opinions invalidating segregation in parks, golf courses, bath houses, and beaches, see New Orleans City Park Improvement Ass'n v. Detiege, 358 U.S. 54 (1958); Gayle v. Browder, 352 U.S. 903 (1956); Holmes v. City of Atlanta, 350 U.S. 879 (1955); Mayor & City Council v. Dawson, 350 U.S. 877 (1955).

[47] The *Brown* Court stated, "Such considerations [regarding stigma] apply with added force to children in grade and high schools." 347 U.S. at 494. *See* L. HAND, THE BILL OF RIGHTS 54 (1958). Compare the litigative strategy pursued by the NAACP to make "schools . . . the primary interest in this undertaking . . . of a coordinated effort to create civil rights precedents in the courts." J. GREENBERG, RACE RELATIONS AND AMERICAN LAW 37 (1959).

[48] Gunther, *supra* note 42, at 19.

[49] 411 U.S. 677 (1973).

[50] *Id.* at 688.

[51] *Id.* at 691-92. The four justices essentially relied on the Court's recent ruling in Reed v. Reed, 404 U.S. 71 (1971).

[52] Gunther, *supra* note 42, at 34.

[53] *See id.* at 18 n.88.

[54] *Id.* at 36.

to distill from these cases has a most useful and direct application to the issue here: the propriety of state resort to institutional placement for persons it labels "retarded." Gunther states:

> The model suggested by the recent developments would view equal protection as a means-focused, relatively narrow, preferred ground of decision in a broad range of cases. Stated most simply, it would have the Court take seriously a constitutional requirement that has never been formally abandoned: that legislative means must substantially further legislative ends. The equal protection requirement that legislative classifications must have a substantial relationship to legislative purposes is, after all, essentially a more specific formulation of that general principle. . . . Putting consistent new bite into the old equal protection would mean that the Court would be less willing to supply justifying rationales by exercising its imagination. It would have the Court assess the means in terms of legislative purposes that have substantial basis in actuality, not merely in conjecture. Moreover, it would have the Justices gauge the reasonableness of questionable means on the basis of materials that are offered to the Court, rather than resorting to rationalizations created by perfunctory judicial hypothesizing.[55]

Gunther's position that this newer equal protection principle may come to have wide application to all types of state action is possibly overstated.[56] But his discussion has clear applicability and attractiveness for judicial evaluation of state actions toward a vulnerable minority which might be considered at least a "semi-suspect class." It may be that courts will shy away from the implications of ruling that all state-imposed intelligence classifications are suspect. But if courts are given a doctrinal basis for inquiring why the label of mental retardation should lead a person to a Willowbrook, the essential foundation is laid for judicial action to aid the awful plight of institutionalized retarded persons. This doctrinal basis would permit courts to aim directly at the grossest injustices without serious danger of attacking unintended targets. With this assurance, courts can be persuaded to respond helpfully to the terrible conditions in institutions for mentally retarded citizens.

Although this argument seems most comfortably to fit current judicial predilections, the more muscular argument that retardation is in itself a suspect class should not be abandoned. Gunther's discussion and the cases he relies on assist this undertaking. That discussion and those cases reflect the considerable doctrinal tensions worked by judicial attempts to accommodate any state use of classifications that courts have clearly held "suspect."[57] The use of race to impose beneficial quotas is the most prominent and troubling example.[58] State denial of voting rights to aliens is a second, though less currently provocative, instance.[59] The Supreme Court's uneasy grappling with the illegitimacy status, striking down most

---

[55] *Id.* at 20-21.

[56] *Id.* at 37-46.

[57] *See, e.g.,* Burt, *Miranda and Title II: A Morganatic Marriage,* 1969 Sup. Ct. Rev. 81, 111-14, 118-21.

[58] *See, e.g.,* A. Bickel, The Least Dangerous Branch 57-65 (1962).

[59] *Compare* U.S. Const. art. 1, § 2 and amend. XVII (providing that qualifications for "Electors" to the House of Representatives and Senate shall be established by the states) *with* amends. XV and XIX ("the right of citizens of the United States" to vote shall not be abridged by race or sex).

such discriminations but never clearly explaining their doctrinal justification, is a third example.[60] Perhaps the newer equal protection cases cited by Gunther suggest that the Court is moving toward a more variegated and flexible analysis of the consequences of holding any classification inherently suspect. This possibility has useful implications for establishing "retardation" as a suspect classification. It can be argued that the use of race as a "beneficial" classification often, perhaps always, carries a stigmatizing implication.[61] Thus, to the extent that racial quotas are now court approved,[62] it is apparent that only the more gross or less justifiable stigmatizing uses of a suspect classification are disapproved. Similarly, a court might hold "intelligence" to be a suspect class, but invalidate its use only in imposing the most gross deprivations on the most vulnerable members of the class.

APPLICATION OF THE SEMISUSPECT
CLASSIFICATION ANALYSIS

A powerful case can thus be mounted that courts should command states to use extraordinary effort to avoid institutionalizing retarded citizens. By this analysis, *Wyatt* clearly was wrong in failing to address directly the adequacy of community alternatives to geographically remote residential institutional care. In this analysis, the adequacy of in-community resources is not an afterthought. It is central to the inquiry into whether separate treatment for the mentally retarded person is not inherently unequal just as racially segregated education was found inherently unequal in *Brown v. Board of Education.* The *Wyatt* court and parties should have spent more energy to determine what kinds of in-community resources should be mandated to achieve the greatest practical equality of opportunity for mentally retarded individuals, and less to determine how many baths each week were due the Partlow residents.[63]

It is irrelevant that many of the Partlow residents are older than compulsory school age. The state cannot discharge its obligation to redress past injustices in education and other areas by the fortuity that many of its victims cannot be fully compensated for those wrongs. The primary beneficiaries of this proposed judicial stance will be future generations of mentally retarded children who otherwise would be fated for institutionalized life. But remedies, however partial, are possible for currently institutionalized people to bring them much more into normal community life. Using the resourcefulness demonstrated in judicial orders to undo racial segrega-

---

[60] *Compare* Labine v. Vincent, 401 U.S. 532 (1971) *with* Weber v. Aetna Cas. & Sur. Co., 406 U.S. 164 (1972). *See* Gunther, *supra* note 42, at 31-32.

[61] *Cf.* Norwalk CORE v. Norwalk Bd. of Educ., 298 F. Supp. 213 (D. Conn. 1969), *aff'd*, 423 F.2d 121 (2d Cir. 1970).

[62] *Cf.* Swann v. Charlotte-Mecklenburg Bd. of Educ., 402 U.S. 1, 22-25 (1971).

[63] 344 F. Supp. at 404.

tion, courts can readily devise sensible remedies for the adult retarded population already victimized by unjust state policies.[64]

One special target for court attention under this theory should be the application of local zoning ordinances to forbid establishment of community group homes for retarded persons.[65] Exclusionary zoning practices have been attacked in litigation, without much success, as wrongful devices to perpetuate racial segregation.[66] This argument failed in part, however, because it cut too broadly. The challenged zoning practices did not exclude blacks as such, but typically excluded poor people by requiring single homes or large lots. Litigants did not request a special exemption for blacks, but rather sought to overturn the entire zoning pattern, thereby helping blacks, poor people, apartment dwellers, and others. Most courts have not accepted these arguments both because the link between past segregation and present zoning laws seems too tenuous and because the remedy could not be cleanly limited to the wronged class.[67] For the mentally retarded who are presently institutionalized, it seems more plausible to argue that the same communities whose public schools have practiced wrongful exclusion should now be required to make special provision for the specific institutionalized persons who have been victimized by that policy. The differences between the racial and retardation contexts are perhaps matters of degree, but such differences can be sufficiently great to permit differentiation in principle, at least to persuade courts properly intent on remedying past wrongs to the mentally retarded.[68]

The consequences of this constitutional analysis are not limited to requiring the end of remote large-scale residential institutions for mentally retarded citizens. The analysis suggests that state provision for education in special community buildings labeled "schools for retarded" might be as constitutionally suspect as state schools labeled "black." Even classrooms labeled "retarded" in a general school building might be suspect. This constitutional principle would not forbid special provision for the special educational problems of the retarded. But, if the analysis is applied, a powerful case would be required to prove that this special assistance necessarily required separating mentally retarded students from daily classroom contact with others. The *PARC* standards, as agreed by the parties, make a gesture in this direction by specifying that provision of public education for retarded children should favor

---

[64] *Compare* the following articles by Fiss: *Racial Imbalance in the Public Schools: The Constitutional Concepts*, 78 HARV. L. REV. 564 (1965); *Gaston County v. United States: The Fruition of the Freezing Principle*, 1969 SUP. CT. REV. 379; *A Theory of Fair Employment Laws*, 38 U. CHI. L. REV. 235 (1971).

[65] *See* Chandler & Ross, pp. 306-43, Chapter 11 of this volume.

[66] *See, e.g.,* Sager, *Tight Little Islands: Exclusionary Zoning, Equal Protection and the Indigent*, 21 STAN. L. REV. 767 (1969).

[67] The Supreme Court has not yet spoken directly to this issue, but its auguries are clear. *See* Lindsey v. Normet, 405 U.S. 56 (1972).

[68] The proposition that courts will require special remedial state action entailing considerable state favoritism toward a previously discriminated group is illustrated by United States v. Texas, 342 F. Supp. 24 (E.D. Tex. 1971), *aff'd*, 466 F.2d 518 (5th Cir. 1972), in which the state was ordered to institute substantial remedial bilingual instruction to undo the adverse effects of past state discrimination against Mexican-American students. *See* Lau v. Nichols, 414 U.S. 563 (1974).

regular classroom placements.[69] But in the implementation of the *PARC* decree, it appears that this specification has not been given much attention.

The issue of placement in special classes is complex. Respected professional opinion is virtually unanimous in opposition to isolated residential institutions for the mentally retarded. Opinion is more divided on the merits of separate facilities for the retarded in the community. Those favoring segregation speak of the special psychological vulnerabilities of the retarded, the deleterious effect on their self-esteem which direct comparison and competition with others would bring, and the greater efficiency in separate service delivery and consequent individualized attention. To a lawyer, these arguments do not seem conclusive. Similar arguments were advanced in the wake of *Brown* first to justify continued segregation and then to justify a snail's pace of desegregation. For example, so-called freedom of choice plans, which gave black parents an option to have their children enrolled in majority white or majority black schools were espoused on the ground that many black children and their parents would be uncomfortable in mixed racial settings and they should be given the choice to avoid these settings. The Supreme Court ruled, however, that reluctance among blacks to leave segregated facilities could well have been part of the legacy of deep-rooted social stigma imposed by past state discrimination against blacks. The Court held that extraordinary efforts must be undertaken to eliminate this legacy, noting that "freedom of choice" was not necessarily free enough of the past.[70]

Mentally retarded persons have been similarly and unjustly shut away from sight of the "normal" population. It appears equally suspect for a state to justify continued vestiges of segregation on the ground that the mentally retarded must be shielded from the social opprobrium fostered by its past segregative policy. It might also be argued that the presence of retarded children in a "mixed" classroom disrupts the pace of others' education. But, again, the desegregation experience might be instructive. Federal courts vigorously rejected school board arguments that the social upheaval accompanying desegregation unduly disrupted general education. Courts ruled that the disruption came from wrongful social stigma of past state segregation and could be no excuse for continued segregation.[71]

Certainly, the desegregation experience does not teach a single simple lesson. Black children brave enough to claim their just status were subjected to exceptional stress.[72] They bore the brunt of past injustices to be the vanguard of social reform. Courts were willing to force states to accept the sacrifices of these extraordinary children in part because there was no conceivable argument for separate educational facilities aside from adjusting educational policy in response to clearly unjust social stigma. For mentally retarded children, however, the solution is less certain. If classifications are sufficiently precise, these children do have demonstrable educational deficit and do require special educational support.

---

[69] 343 F. Supp. at 307: " . . . placement in a regular public school class is preferable to placement in a special public school class and placement in a special public school class is preferable to placement in any other type of program of education and training."

[70] *See* Green v. County School Bd., 391 U.S. 430 (1968).

[71] *Cf.* Cooper v. Aaron, 358 U.S. 1 (1958).

[72] *See* R. COLES, CHILDREN OF CRISIS (1967).

Several years ago *Hobson v. Hansen*[73] invalidated the District of Columbia school system's "educational tracking" practices by labeling them wrongful vestiges of the District's past history of segregation. But *Hobson* is not a clear-cut ruling against segregated facilities for all mentally retarded children; rather, it illustrates judicial ambivalence on this score. The *Hobson* opinion in fact appeared to permit the District to institute special classes for "slow learners" so long as the testing procedures were rigorous and retesting was frequent.[74] This was apparently permitted notwithstanding the likelihood that the overrepresentation of blacks, which the court found so offensive in the "tracking system," would recur in the new "slow learners" class.[75]

This approach was carried further by the California federal court in *Diana*. As noted previously, this case prescribed detailed procedures for administering special education placement tests, and the court ruled that specific placement tests then in use in the challenged district were not properly validated for the minority group population subjected to them. *Diana* accepted the assumption that placement tests could be adequately validated for minority groups; the case held merely that the particular tests before it did not pass muster.

There is, however, a growing body of professional opinion challenging this assumption. For legal purposes, two elements of this position have special importance: first, that a single instrument cannot be devised to compare the intellectual attainments of children raised in differing ethnic or cultural settings and, second, that tests of intellectual capacity have little intrinsic predictive value and social response to these tests creates a self-fulfilling prediction. If this argument is correct, the prospect offered by *Diana* is wrong because this decision used elaborate procedural safeguards to surround a testing process which has no educational justification.

By its very complexity, it seems unlikely that this argument will soon be resolved with the assurance that accompanies the argument against remote residential institutions. For a court concerned only with procedural regularity, this uncertainty is not troubling. If a responsible group of experts asserts that pupil placement tests are useful, it is enough for a court simply to ensure that these are applied in a manner consistent with their own internal premises, no matter how uncertain these premises are. For example, the *Diana* court's insistence that Spanish-speaking children be given intelligence tests in Spanish accepts a critical assumption of these tests—that adeptness in verbal manipulation is an adequate indicator of intellectual capacity. *Diana* merely holds these tests to their own stated premises: they are not English language comprehension tests but rather are general intellectual capacity tests.

---

[73] 269 F. Supp. 401 (D.D.C. 1967), *aff'd sub nom.* Smuck v. Hobson, 408 F.2d 175 (D.C. Cir. 1969).
[74] *Id.* at 512-14.
[75] The District of Columbia school board, in implementing *Hobson* apparently did not read the Court's opinion this permissively. Rather than institute special classes for retarded children who were considered unfit for regular placement, the board applied *Hobson,* with fine irony, to require the total exclusion of these children from the public school system. The *Mills* case, 348 F. Supp. 866 (D.D.C. 1972), successfully attacked this practice in the District.

Nevertheless, for a court intent on undoing the stigmatizing isolation that public school systems have imposed on disabled children, uncertainty about the underlying assumptions of intellectual capacity testing must be very troubling. The same court that is compelled to end remote residential isolation of disabled children might hesitate to forbid any educational testing in view of the complex professional argument surrounding the practice. But the court should not hesitate to ask what consequences must necessarily follow from different scores on these tests. Is it really necessary, for example, administratively to isolate for all or any part of the school day those children who score below 90 on an intelligence quotient test? Since there is uncertainty about their educational relevance, the court would be justified in demanding that these tests be used with great caution, if at all, as a basis for rigidly tracking students.

There may, however, be special justification for segregated classes in community facilities to redress the multiple disabilities of older children who have for many years been unjustly excluded from public schools as "uneducable" or for mentally retarded children who have been housed in state institutions and now are brought back into community life. The sacrifices asked of black children in previously segregated schools may be too great to be borne by other children, and some version of continued isolation may be reluctantly accepted in carrying out the *PARC* court's command.

But the *Diana* mandate goes much further. This case applied to testing procedures for children already in the regular public school system, including those who are just at regular school entry age. For these children, the need for specially solicitous isolation cannot be so convincingly argued, and the likelihood that their perceived "need" for solicitude is a stigmatizing social artifact cannot be easily ignored. For these children it would seem best to avoid isolating placement at all costs. The test results might mandate "enrichment programs," after-school tutoring, work with parents, and the like, but not social isolation.

The proposition that past unjust discrimination should be ended for the future, but only partially remedied for those who have already suffered from the discrimination, reflects the stubborn reality that courts cannot command the past to disappear. In *Brown II*, the Supreme Court bowed to this notion by mandating only that racial segregation be eliminated "with all deliberate speed." [76] Furthermore the present posture of *Brown*, a generation later, teaches that the principle may be satisfied even if some significant numbers of black children remain in all-black schools.[77] Thus, to acknowledge that 20 years from now it will still be necessary to place some profoundly retarded people in full-time specialized residential institutions does not establish that the *Brown* principle cannot apply to the mentally retarded. If the courts do battle for mentally retarded citizens, as they have done for blacks, a significant victory will have been won if the label of retardation does not carry an immediate implication of stigmatizing social isolation, if states make substantial efforts to avoid isolation for all the citizens whom it now casts away, and if many are thereby saved.

---

[76] 349 U.S. 294, 301 (1955).
[77] *See* A. BICKEL, THE SUPREME COURT AND THE IDEA OF PROGRESS 117-51 (1970).

Reaction Comment

JAMES D. CLEMENTS

AS ONE WHO IS NOT a member of the legal profession, I shall not attempt to argue law or question Burt's assessment of the constitutional impact of the various cases discussed in his paper. However, as an administrator who might be reponsible for the implementation of court decisions relating to the right to habilitation for the mentally retarded, I am concerned with some of the conclusions about previous and proposed litigation.

The nonlegal mind of this administrator is often confounded by the very essentials of our democracy. Thomas Jefferson wrote that all men were created equal, and although equality is the very basis on which this country was founded, it is a most confusing concept. Undoubtedly, neither Jefferson nor his ideological successors believed that all men were born with equal intellect and resources. Rather, they believed that government should not be an instrument of discrimination by establishing legal classes or social castes and that all should have equal protection under the law.[1]

Burt's first proposition is that improving institutional conditions will not result in improvements for mentally retarded individuals. His premise that there is no need for large-scale geographically and socially isolated institutions that serve as warehouses for large numbers of the mentally retarded is correct. These facilities should be phased out with the emphasis placed on development and utilization of more appropriate facilities and/or programs integrated with other community programs. It is not conscionable, however, to ignore the plight of those individuals remaining in the existing facilities, until this more appropriate alternative becomes reality. This, in my opinion, is the real intent and thrust of *Wyatt.*[2] Litigation alone will not achieve what I have interpreted as the "thrust" of *Wyatt.* A concentrated and focused effort to achieve systems change requires the combined work of administrators, professionals, consumers, and the executive and legislative branches of government.[3]

There is a small group of mentally retarded people, severely handicapped mentally, physically, and socially, who will continue to need, at least for certain periods of their lives, facilities of a special nature with a concentration of medical and other professional personnel.[4] A reconceptualization of the role of the institution to one of a more community-based, community-oriented, community-assisting

---

[1] *See* R. CARR, M. BERNSTEIN, W. MURPHY & M. DANIELSON, ESSENTIALS OF AMERICAN DEMOCRACY (1971).

[2] Wyatt v. Stickney, 344 F. Supp. 387, 396 standard 3c (M.D. Ala. 1972).

[3] Duncan, *An Administrator's Viewpoint,* in 3 LEGAL RIGHTS OF THE MENTALLY HANDICAPPED 1327 (B. Ennis & P. Friedman eds. 1973).

[4] Clements, *The Residential Care Facility, Indications for Placement,* 15 PEDIATRIC CLINICS NO. AM. 1029 (1968); THE PRESIDENT'S PANEL ON MENTAL RETARDATION, A PROPOSED PROGRAM FOR NATIONAL ACTION TO COMBAT MENTAL RETARDATION 137 (October 1962).

link in a chain of services is necessary. We must utilize the resources that we presently have and gradually redistribute them in a more meaningful, equitable, and useful manner. Many of the institutional resources will be either redistributed or shared with community-based programs. Before a mentally retarded individual is institutionalized, a habilitation plan should be developed for him. The plan should be based upon an analysis of the individual's capacity and needs and should set personal goals which the institution will help him achieve within a specific time. Each individual's progress must be monitored so that new goals in the habilitation process can be established as appropriate. Most important, institutionalization should be relied upon only when absolutely necessary and must always provide the most humane and normalizing environment possible.

In addition, the institution should provide certain emergency and temporary services, particularly related to the health needs of the severely and profoundly retarded, multiply handicapped citizen. It should provide respite care for families of the retarded and specialized outpatient services for mentally retarded persons not in residence in institutions. Research and demonstration projects that might have broad application in the field of mental retardation should be conducted on a small scale. The institution should provide public and parent education. It should train personnel to work in the general field of mental retardation and provide consultation, support services, and specialized training for personnel in alternative environments. In other words, institutions must not be warehouses for human beings. They must be an integral part of the system that provides needed services for mentally retarded citizens.

Burt's second thesis is that retarded children should almost never be segregated from the community, or from regular public schools, or even from the regular classroom. This concept deserves further cautious consideration. Results of past research relating to this premise are conflicting — possibly due to different methodologies and lack of control of the subject population.[5] In attempting the implementation of this concept, special provisions for those retarded individuals with lower functional abilities and multiple disabilities probably will continue to be needed.[6]

The third thesis Burt provides relates to labeling. Much study is needed to

---

[5] Johnson, *A Study of Social Position of Mentally Handicapped Children in Regular Grades* 55 AM. J. MENTAL DEFICIENCY 60 (1950); V. Cassidy & J. Stanton, An Investigation of Factors Involved in the Educational Placement of Mentally Retarded Children: A Study of Differences Between Children in Special and Regular Classes in Ohio, 1959 (U.S. Office of Education Cooperative Research Program, Project No. 043, Ohio State University); T. Thurstone, An Evaluation of Educating Mentally Handicapped Children in Special Classes and in Regular Grades, 1959 (U.S. Office of Education Cooperative Research Program, Project No. OE-SAE-6452, University of North Carolina); Bacher, *The Effect of Special Class Placement on the Self-Concept, Social Adjustment and Reading Growth of Slow Learners,* 25 DISSERTATION ABSTRACTS 7071 (1965); Carroll, *The Effects of Segregated and Partially Integrated School Programs on Self-Concept and Academic Achievement of Educable Mental Retardates,* 34 EXCEPTIONAL CHILDREN 93 (1967); B. Tilley, The Effects of Three Education Placement Systems on Achievement, Self-Concept and Behavior in Elementary Mentally Retarded Children (doctoral dissertation, University of Iowa) (available from University Microfilms, Ann Arbor, 1970, No. 71-5887); Knight, *The Self-Concept of Educable Mentally Retarded Children in Special and Regular Classes,* 27 DISSERTATION ABSTRACT 2121 (1966).
[6] Johnson, *Special Education for the Mentally Retarded,* 15 PEDIATRIC CLINICS No. AM. 1005 (1968).

determine how labeling affects the mentally retarded person. If Burt is correct in asserting that labeling may have a direct bearing on the denial of the constitutional rights of the mentally retarded citizen, major reforms in existing legislation, legal, and programmatic practices are required.

I realize that the theory of law must proceed to its eventual application.[7] We must avoid, however, inflexible decisions that ultimately may be harmful. "All or nothing," "either/or" practices based on inadequate information and experience must be avoided. A cooperative effort is needed between persons knowledgeable in mental retardation and those knowledgeable in law. This partnership can ensure that administrative and legislative resources and recourses are not ignored in the stampede for initiation of litigation and at the same time ensure that constitutional safeguards are provided for mentally retarded citizens.[8]

Reaction Comment

GUNNAR DYBWAD

BURT'S REFERENCE to mental retardation as a suspect classification finds substantial support in recent events. In 1959 a work group appointed by the American Association on Mental Deficiency (AAMD) completed a revision of the association's statistical and terminological manual, which was promptly published, widely distributed, and because of AAMD's unique status in the field was looked upon as the authoritative arbiter of all related questions. Besides some significant improvement and clarification in the medical classification system of mental retardation, the 1959 revision of the manual instituted a sweeping conceptual change: It decreed that henceforth the boundaries of mental retardation, its point of separation from the general, nonretarded population, should be placed at 1 standard deviation below norm on a recognized intelligence test (*i.e.*, at an IQ of 84 on the Revised Stanford Binet, where the standard deviation is at 16 points). As a result, the potential number of persons to be considered retarded more than doubled. Persons who previously had been described as being of borderline intelligence suddenly were moved into the realm of mental retardation, their status denigrated to one of borderline mental retardation.

A decade later another group was called together by the American Association on Mental Deficiency for yet another revision of this standard-setting document. This committee, however, took a radically different stance from the 1959 group and thus the *1973 Revision of the Manual on Terminology and Classification in Mental Retardation* pushed back the boundary lines of mental retardation to 2 standard deviations (*i.e.*, on the Revised Stanford Binet an IQ of 68) and specifically abolished the classification of borderline mental retardation. Thus, in 1973

---

[7] *See* MENTAL HEALTH LAW PROJECT, BASIC RIGHTS OF THE MENTALLY HANDICAPPED (1973).
[8] *See* THE COUNCIL FOR EXCEPTIONAL CHILDREN, LEGAL CHANGE FOR THE HANDICAPPED THROUGH LITIGATION (A. Abeson ed. 1973).

millions of American citizens were relieved of the burden of being presumed to be mentally retarded, albeit on the borderline level only, imposed on them 14 years earlier. Certainly, a classification which on the one hand can be so sweepingly changed by the mere publication of a book, but which on the other hand imposes so heavy a stigma and social burden on large numbers of citizens, warrants consideration as being suspect.

But this does not tell the whole story. In fairness to the authors of the 1959 revision it must be emphasized they also decreed another major change, namely, the requirement that in a finding of mental retardation two criteria must be considered: along with an impairment of intellectual functioning there must also be manifest an impairment in adaptive behavior. However, because intelligence can readily be assessed by means of tests widely accepted as authoritative, although instruments to measure adequately the degree of social adaptation have been available only most recently and are far from being generally recognized as essential parts of a psychological assessment, the day-to-day practice in schools, courts, social, health, and mental health agencies is to rely on IQ only. Certainly, a classification that depends on the existence of two criteria, of which in most cases only one is subjected to testing, merits being considered a suspect classification.

Professor Burt comments that more thought needs to be given to determine what kinds of in-community resources should be mandated as alternatives to institutional care. Unfortunately, one encounters here an amazing dearth of substantive knowledge because few studies have been made in the area of community care. As a result, we now witness that in several states, such as Pennsylvania, millions of dollars appropriated for the development of community alternatives remain unspent—the money is available but lacking is the knowledge of how to spend it, due to the lack of relevant exploratory and applied studies. For many years, large amounts of federal money have been available for research relating to mental retardation. Yet, unfortunately, the emphasis has been on basic research, and as a result there has not been enough applied or programmatic research. Presently there is a great need for research that should have been conducted 10 years ago. It was hoped that state governments and the universities would take up the slack by joining mental retardation professionals to help them evaluate what needs to be done now. But, by and large, this has not happened. Research seems always to be related to federal funding agencies' interests in basic or clinical areas.

Perhaps a personal experience can serve to show the general lack of interest in programmatic research. I was talking recently with the superintendent of a brand-new facility in Illinois. Nothing like this facility exists elsewhere in the country. It has free-standing cottages, with only four bedrooms for two children each; meals are cooked in the cottage; and the ratio of staff to residents is good. Four weeks after this facility opened I asked the superintendent whether there were procedures for evaluating the effectiveness of the new program. When he said there was no applied research taking place, I called one of my friends at a Chicago area university. He is a social scientist interested in mental retardation. I told him, "Right under your nose is one of the most interesting experiments in residential care that is going on anywhere in the country." He seemed interested, but three months later when I visited the program again, I found that the university had made only one contact and had never followed up with any applied research. This is not unusual.

The lack of applied research and program evaluation has serious consequences for present programing, particularly in terms of developing community programs. There is throughout the country a renewed interest in the problems of mentally retarded citizens. Much of this interest is reflected in an effort to close or change drastically large, warehouse-type institutions and provide instead community alternatives. This normalization process has been accelerated by litigation such as *Wyatt*, but because proper applied and programmatic research was not conducted previously, we are not well prepared to deal with the inevitable problems that will accompany community program development. Are group homes for 6 better than homes for 12 or 20? What types of professional and paraprofessional services are needed for community programs? What are the most effective methods of providing follow-up services for persons who were formerly institutionalized? How does the community provide services such as dental and medical care? These are not just rhetorical questions — they indicate difficult problems associated with the delivery of services in the community, to which the answers will not be forthcoming from basic or clinical research.

If the concept of normalization is to be implemented, we must refuse to let deficiencies in our precise knowledge of the details of optimum programing be used as an excuse to slow the normalization and deinstitutionalization processes. If the Partlows and Willowbrooks of the country are to be eliminated in favor of community alternatives, we must devote increased effort to the essential task of conducting applied program research. The current emphases on deinstitution-alization and normalization provide a signal opportunity for this needed research.

CHAPTER 15

Due Process in Civil Commitment and Elsewhere

Strauss provides a critical and sensitive analysis of the problems involved in ensuring due process in decisions affecting the lives of the mentally retarded. With commitment procedure and due process in the institutional context as a focal point, Strauss offers a general framework for analysis of due process problems of the mentally retarded. His perspective is cautious; he believes the judicial system should be used selectively. He makes it clear that commitment procedures in most states fall far short of what anyone could regard as due process of law. He details certain due process protections which he believes are essential, but eschews the full application of an analogy to criminal due process in the commitment procedure. Strauss characterizes most commitments as "avoluntary," that is, neither voluntary nor involuntary, and recommends strongly that independent advocacy systems be established to bring selected cases to the attention of the judicial system.

Ennis brings to his reaction the experience of having litigated many cases in this area. Although agreeing with Strauss' basic proposition that due process demands a great deal more protection for mentally retarded citizens than is provided by present state laws, Ennis takes sharp issue with Strauss' cautious approach. He analyzes his differences with Strauss as resulting primarily from different assumptions about mental retardation and about institutions. Ennis believes that a much greater and more regular involvement of the courts in the commitment process is required in order to implement the principle of the least restrictive alternative, the legal corollary of the social science principle of "normalization." He criticizes Strauss for seeing the issue primarily in diagnostic terms, whereas Ennis feels that the issue is generally not diagnostic, but social.

Judge Sprecher, the author of what Strauss calls "the most striking decision in this area," has limited his response in accordance with a policy of not defending his own opinion in a nonjudicial setting. Sprecher emphasizes the great need for legal reform in the commitment area and the necessity for federal court involvement to push legislators to take required corrective action. Although recognizing the case load pressure on federal courts, Sprecher insists that this is an area in which their involvement is clearly required.

PRINCIPAL PAPER

PETER L. STRAUSS

THE ANALYTIC BUILDING BLOCKS

Ten years have passed since the Task Force on Law of the Predident's Panel on Mental Retardation[1] made its eloquent report.[2] That report was infused with a sense of the problems mentally retarded citizens present for the law and those the law presents for retarded citizens. The broad range of personal disabilities encompassed in the concept "mental retardation" and the variety of possible responses to these disabilities present problems for the law, accustomed as it is to simple categorization.[3] The task force dealt with this complexity by recommending that discretion and initiative be granted to those who deal with the retarded — whether in programs open

---

The author is indebted to his students, James Cherney, Laura Drager, and Jonathan Mark, his colleagues, Professors Harvey Goldschmid, Walter Gellhorn, and Louis Henkin, and his wife, Joanna, for their assistance in the preparation of this paper.

[1] The President's Panel on Mental Retardation was appointed by President Kennedy on October 17, 1961. It was predecessor to the President's Committee on Mental Retardation.

[2] THE PRESIDENT'S PANEL ON MENTAL RETARDATION, REPORT OF THE TASK FORCE ON LAW (1963) [hereinafter cited as PPMR REPORT].

[3] *Id.* at 8-9, 14-15. The temptation to speak of "retarded citizens" as a single class with uniform interests and subject to uniform disabilities and risks is often overwhelming and contributes much to the all too prevalent stereotyping. State laws usually make no distinctions among retarded citizens on the basis of the degree of impairment they suffer. Murdock, *Civil Rights of the Mentally Retarded,* 48 NOTRE D. LAW. 133, 134-36, (1972); Michael J. Kuhlman, State Procedures for the Involuntary Commitment of the Mentally Retarded 13, April 23, 1973 (unpublished seminar paper, on file at the Ohio State University Law Library). A proposed Ohio statute limiting commitment to persons suffering moderate or greater retardation is a rare and welcome innovation in this respect. Ohio S.B. 336, 110th Gen. Ass., Reg. Sess. § 5123.01 (B)(12) (1973) [hereinafter cited as Ohio S.B. 336 (1973)]. *See also* Wyatt v. Stickney, 344 F. Supp. 387, 396 (M.D. Ala. 1972), *aff'd sub nom.* Wyatt v. Aderholt, 503 F.2d 1305 (5th Cir. 1974). Similar efforts at limitation or definition would contribute to the resolution of many of the problems discussed in the various chapters of this volume.

to all (such as public education) or in specialized services for the mentally retarded. "This means moving away from the formal towards the informal, from the organized towards the spontaneous, from higher levels of government towards the local, from the mandatory towards the encouraged, from 'strangers' towards 'kin,'[4] — and, one might add, from large institutions toward small community-based residences. "We would minimize mandatory requirements wherever voluntary compliance can be obtained."[5] The law's success could be significantly measured, the panel thought, by the extent to which it fostered this trend.

The panel did not believe that liberty for the mentally retarded citizen could be measured only by "the relative lack of physical confinement."[6] "To give a person liberty to choose between alternatives of which he [has] no appreciation is to defeat and mock the concept of liberty."[7] Restoration of capacity must be the primary objective, but where this is not possible "justice requires an effort at substitution. . . . [O]ccasions arise when a vitiated legal right must be excised and some substitution made. Protective intervention may be the device which maximizes liberty in such a case."[8]

The panel was emphatic that the question of due process could not be separated from the provision of adequate flexibility in legal response.[9] "The possibility of doing justice, and thus fulfilling the function of the law, turns upon at least two conditions: correct appreciation of the relevant circumstances, and a suitable range of possible dispositions. Failing the first, justice is truly blind; failing the second, it is impotent."[10] Yet law's "capacity to do good . . . can be dissipated in a system which demands needless formalities and which, through the abrasion of routine, dulls the professional acumen which should be the [mentally retarded citizen's] greatest defense. . . . The processes of commitment to mental institutions [in particular] are inadequate and wasteful. They actually impede justice."[11] In balancing the need for flexibility against the need for protection of the rights of mentally retarded citizens, the task force insisted that the way to the courtroom must always be kept open, but not by means of cumbersome formalities. It thought formal commitment appropriate only in the absence of voluntary placement by parent or guardian and, even then, only if the individual resisted placement or — more likely — was found incapable of forming the will requisite for consent.[12] Viewed as a whole, its recommendations stress accuracy in diagnosis and disposition and protection of personal dignity as the principal determinants of proper procedure. They accept not only the existence of mental retardation, but also a consequent need for benevolent intervention and the basic benevolence behind laws and institutions for the retarded.

Ten years later, acceptance of this benevolence was strongly questioned.

[4] PPMR REPORT at 12-13.
[5] Id. at 17.
[6] Id. at 13.
[7] Id. at 15.
[8] Id. at 15-16.
[9] Id. at 14.
[10] Id. at 16.
[11] Id. at 19.
[12] Id. at 28-31.

Reasoning from the Supreme Court's decision in *In re Gault*[13] and other auguries, lawyers have contended, and some courts have agreed, that the procedures for placing a mentally retarded or mentally ill person in an institution must be viewed as if they involved a determination of criminal guilt, so that the "accused" is given the benefit of every doubt and rigorous procedural protection before the finding can be made. A positive value is assigned to exclusion from the institution.

Gault rejected the claim that the stated beneficial purposes of juvenile delinquency statutes and dispositions justified the highly informal procedures then common in juvenile courts. The decision is the product of many factors — not the least of which was that the child stood accused of conduct that in an adult would have been criminal and was subject to a disposition viewed by the community and himself as punishment. But, in addition to noting that juvenile proceedings resemble criminal proceedings, the opinion also lays much weight on inadequacies in institutions, on the failure of the law's promise of beneficence, and on the central fact of deprivation of liberty. Courts in the mental health area have picked up these last themes, discounting the absence of any formal analogy to criminal law, and made them determinative of identical results in procedural disputes in that field.

One such case in which the criminal aspect plays a decided part is *Dixon v. Attorney General*.[14] *Dixon* concerned Pennsylvania's "medical certificate" procedure for commitment. This procedure authorized the indefinite hospitalization of an individual if two examining physicians certified that he was "mentally disabled and in need of care."[15] Although the hospital had discretion to refuse admission of the individual,[16] and the committed person was entitled to review of his commitment in a separate habeas corpus proceeding at any time,[17] the Pennsylvania statutes made no provisions for a hearing (except upon protest), assistance of counsel, or periodic review of mental status. In most settings the procedure resembles the nonprotesting admission which most medical and some legal commentators appear to favor,[18] but

---

[13] 387 U.S. 1 (1967).

[14] 325 F. Supp. 966 (M.D. Pa. 1971). The extended discussion of mental illness commitment cases and reliance on studies of the mental illness commitment process in this paper involve an assertion of comparability with commitment of the mentally retarded. This assertion has its weak points. Yet mental illness commitments have been far more widely studied and procedural points more fully litigated. Kuhlman, *supra* note 3, remarks that those states — a large minority — which have identical procedures for the mentally retarded and the mentally ill tend by this association to give the retarded greater procedural protection than they receive in states making special provision for the commitment of the mentally retarded.

[15] PA. STAT. ANN. tit. 50, § 4404 (1969).

[16] *Id.* at § 4404 (c). The operation of the system is described in R. ROCK, M. JACOBSON & R. JANOPAUL, HOSPITALIZATION AND DISCHARGE OF THE MENTALLY ILL 199-213 (1968) [hereinafter cited as ROCK, JACOBSON & JANOPAUL].

[17] PA. STAT. ANN. tit. 50, § 4426 (1969). ROCK, JACOBSON & JANOPAUL at 206-07 suggest that review on this basis was infrequent at best, and note that in another state, Kansas, "when serious legal resistance was manifested, the state dropped the case. . . . To have insisted on the admission of these few strongly resisting patients would simply not have made sense, for their admission would have been gained at the expense of a procedure that worked so well." *Id.* at 193.

[18] ROCK, JACOBSON & JANOPAUL at 38-40, 200, 263-65; THE MENTALLY DISABLED AND THE LAW (rev. ed. S. Brakel & R. Rock eds. 1971) [hereinafter cited as THE MENTALLY DISABLED]; SPECIAL COMMITTEE TO STUDY COMMITMENT PROCEDURES OF THE ASSOCIATION OF THE BAR OF THE CITY OF NEW YORK, MENTAL ILLNESS AND DUE PROCESS 22-24 (1962) [hereinafter cited as ABCNY SPECIAL STUDY]; N.Y. MENTAL HYGIENE LAW §§ 31.27, 33.27 (McKinney Supp. 1973). *But see* State *ex rel.* Fuller v. Mullinax, 364 Mo. 858, 269 S.W.2d 72 (1954); notes 21 & 53 *infra*.

the particular facts of *Dixon* were as unfavorable to the procedure as one could imagine. Plaintiffs were former state prisoners held at Farview, the state's only maximum security asylum. This institution, set in a remote corner of Pennsylvania, notably lacked psychiatric resources or programs.[19] Plaintiffs' prison terms had expired while they were "patients" in Farview. Physicians on the institution's staff — not psychiatrists — had then used the certificate commitment procedure to extend confinement. Neither the inmates nor their relatives or friends were consulted or heard, even by the examining doctors; no evaluation was made by independent practitioners.

That the court found *Gault* applicable and compelling is not surprising, given the relationship of the particular commitments to the criminal law and to societal judgments regarding social dangerousness. Unless commitment is voluntarily sought, the court ruled, one may be committed to Farview only under procedures which recognize a right to counsel (appointed if necessary), an independent examination if desired (possibly at state expense), a full formal hearing, a burden of proof close to the criminal standard, transcripts, and appellate court review. Finally, the court ruled, no commitment can be made for longer than six months.

The language of the opinion was not limited to the special circumstances of the case; it suggested that the court would have reached the same result on any application of the statute, without regard to prior criminal conviction or commitment to Farview.[20] The state attorney general, who consented to the entry of an order requiring the new procedures, regarded the order as overturning the medical certificate procedure. He has directed that all persons committed under this procedure be re-examined for possible discharge or for voluntary or involuntary admission.[21] Thus, *Dixon* could be understood to imply that procedures on the criminal model are required for any commitment that is not fully voluntary.

Lessard v. Schmidt,[22] the most striking of the recent decisions, is explicit on this point. The challenge there was to a commitment with few, if any, criminal overtones. Ms. Lessard appears simply to have been engaging in bizarre behavior suggestive of the mental disease which the state's doctors subsequently reported they found. When involuntary hospitalization was sought, she was able to find an attorney (not the usual

---

[19] Only 3 percent of the residents of Farview received any treatment whatever. 325 F. Supp. at 969.

[20] *Id.* at 972.

[21] Comment, 10 DUQUESNE L. REV. 674 (1972). The *Dixon* case did not discourage New York from enacting certification procedures for both the mentally ill and the mentally retarded in its new commitment law. N.Y. MENTAL HYGIENE LAW §§ 31.27, 33.27 (McKinney Supp. 1973). Under this New York procedure, judicial approval of a commitment by certificate must be sought after 60 days if no hearing has been demanded, but this approval may be based on the moving papers unless a hearing demand is made. *Id.* at §§ 31.33, 33.33.

Those who value the certificate form point to its speed, the medical character of initial decision making (thus freeing courts from decisions which, on the medical view of the commitment process, they are unequipped to make), and the absence of judicial hearing unless there is a protest (thus freeing courts from the need to appear to decide matters about which there apparently is no controversy). Unless the very low rate of protest experienced under such laws is to be discounted as the product of intimidation or ignorance of right, it would be more accurate to characterize the procedure as one for voluntary, or at least *a*voluntary, rather than involuntary, commitment. *See* note 53 *infra.*

[22] 349 F. Supp. 1078 (E.D. Wis. 1972), *vacated for entry of definitive decree,* 414 U.S. 473 (1974), *clarified,* 379 F. Supp. 1376 (E.D. Wisc. 1974), *vacated on procedural grounds,* 95 S. Ct. 1943 (1975).

court-appointed guardian *ad litem*) who mounted a vigorous and ultimately success-ful frontal assault on the state's commitment statutes.

Judge Sprecher's eloquent and learned opinion provides the point of departure for future reasoning about commitment processes. Its particular holdings on points of procedure are striking: No person may be detained more than 48 hours, even on an emergency basis, without a hearing on the probable cause for detention; and the detained person must be present at this hearing, free of medication and represented by counsel.[23] If further detention is ordered, a full hearing must occur within two weeks; notice of this hearing must include, *inter alia*, notice of the statutory right to jury trial,[24] of the standards to be applied at the hearing, and of the evidence to be presented in favor of detention.[25] Hearsay evidence may not be relied upon.[26] Com-mitment may not be ordered unless the state proves beyond a reasonable doubt that the individual is mentally ill *and* that, because of this illness, "there is an extreme likelihood that if the person is not confined he will do immediate harm to himself or others," based upon a finding of a recent overt act, attempt, or threat to do substan-tial harm to himself or another.[27] The state must also show, although perhaps not beyond a reasonable doubt, that the disposition sought is the least restrictive alterna-tive suitable for the patient.[28] The patient has the right to appointed counsel, as distinct from a guardian *ad litem*, who might view his role as advisory rather than adversary. Counsel must be appointed before the preliminary hearing and have

[23] *Id.* at 1091, 1092.

[24] There is presently no established federal right to a jury trial on commitment issues; *cf.* McKeiver v. Pennsylvania, 403 U.S. 528 (1971). Such right as is recognized in the states is generally statutory in nature. People *ex rel.* Keith v. Keith, 38 Ill. 2d 405, 231 N.E.2d 387 (1967). Although made popular in the nineteenth century through the crusade of a former mental patient who believed herself to have been railroaded into an asylum by scheming relatives, mandatory jury trial dis-appeared as a matter of state law in 1953. ROCK, JACOBSON & JANOPAUL at 16-18. Today, jury trial is available in civil commitment of the mentally ill, even on demand, in only 16 jurisdictions. THE MENTALLY DISABLED 53. Eight jurisdictions make juries available to retarded citizens in commitment proceedings. INSTITUTIONALIZATION OF THE MENTALLY RETARDED 90, 111-12 (R. Newman ed. 1967) [hereinafter cited as INSTITUTIONALIZATION]; Kuhlman, *supra* note 3, at 14 and Appendix.

    ROCK, JACOBSON & JANOPAUL at 17 characterize the "emphasis given jury trial . . . [as] a hysterical reaction to a more serious but unresolved set of problems: the shortage of mental health treatment facilities and the lack of sophistication in technique, accompanied by public horror of mental illness." Since the recent procedural developments, including *Lessard,* rest on a discovery that the same set of problems remains with us, still unresolved, one might expect a recrudescence of interest in jury trials. The Supreme Court has moved both away from and toward a jury right in recent years. McKeiver, 403 U.S. 528 (1971), found no right to jury trial on behalf of children charged with delinquency in juvenile court. In Humphrey v. Cady, 405 U.S. 504 (1972), the Court suggested that Wisconsin's refusal of a jury trial to one class of mentally ill persons (criminals), when this procedure was made available to all others, might offend the equal protection clause. Although it did not have to decide whether jury trial is constitutionally required absent a statute providing for it in the general run of commitment cases, dicta concerning the importance and function of the jury could be so interpreted. 405 U.S. at 510. Similar reason-ing may sometimes support a jury trial claim by retarded citizens, particularly if the commitment standard includes a nonmedical and potentially stigmatic criterion such as "dangerousness." *See In re* Gary W., 5 Cal. 3d 296, 486 P.2d 1201, 96 Cal. Rptr. 1 (1971); Kay Farnham, Karren, Knakel & Diamond, *Legal Planning for the Mentally Retarded: The California Experience,* 60 CALIF. L. REV. 438, 522-25 (1972).

[25] 349 F. Supp. at 1092.

[26] *Id.* at 1102-03.

[27] *Id.* at 1093-95.

[28] *Id.* at 1096.

access to all reports.[29] The court comes within a hair's breadth of announcing that counsel must be present at all psychiatric interviews, but suggests that the individual's rights may be adequately protected if the interviews are recorded and written results provided to counsel for his use.[30] Finally, the privilege against self-incrimination is said to apply: The individual is entitled to notice that anything he says may be used against him in the ensuing commitment proceeding and that he is not required to speak with examining psychiatrists.[31]

The arguments for a similar perspective in conjunction with the commitment of mentally retarded persons are easily developed. Even more than mental illness, mental retardation is a lifelong condition. Plainly, distaste, although not formal community condemnation, attaches to the label of mental retardation. Once institutionalized, few retarded citizens are released. Like mental hospitals and juvenile training schools, the larger institutions for the mentally retarded emphasize security and confinement, rather than programs of treatment or habilitation. Not a few are shockingly brutal. Some persons have forcefully argued that institutions which house the disadvantaged will always descend to this level because the safekeeping function is the only one society will finance over the long term for what most people see as a surplus population.[32] Most important of all, confinement in an institution for total care is a massive restriction on one's ability to wander the streets and do what one will. In sum, all the ingredients exist to produce a holding, as in *Lessard*, *Dixon*, or *Gault*, that due process requires the most formal of procedures when commitment of a mentally retarded citizen to a state institution is sought against his will.

The symbolic value of decisions like *Lessard* is great. They force attention to the outrages society perpetrates in the name of beneficent care at such places as Partlow School[33] or Willowbrook,[34] as well as to slipshod or antiquated procedures by which retarded citizens may be committed to a state school or subjected to other decisions having a major effect on their lives. Court decisions may galvanize welcome public pressure for the protection of human decency and dignity and jolt state legislatures into defining more appropriate procedures for these actions. Evidence of this impact can be found in such measures as a bill recently submitted to the Ohio state legislature for reform of procedures regarding the institutionalization of mentally retarded persons.[35] The bill details at considerable length a variety of innovative procedures and institutions[36] and clearly has more than a coincidental relationship to *Lessard* and other recent court decisions.

[29] *Id.* at 1097-1100.
[30] *Id.* at 1100.
[31] *Id.* at 1100-02.
[32] B. FARBER, MENTAL RETARDATION: ITS SOCIAL CONTEXT AND SOCIAL CONSEQUENCES (1968); D. ROTHMAN, THE DISCOVERY OF THE ASYLUM 264-91, (1971); *cf.* E. GOFFMAN, ASYLUMS 368-77 (1961).
[33] Wyatt v. Stickney, 344 F. Supp. 387 (M.D. Ala. 1972), *aff'd sub nom.* Wyatt v. Aderholt, 503 F.2d 1305 (5th Cir. 1974). *See also* Murdock, *supra* note 3, at 148-49 (1972).
[34] New York Ass'n for Retarded Children v. Rockefeller, 357 F. Supp. 752 (E.D.N.Y. 1973).
[35] Ohio S.B. 336 (1973).
[36] Ohio S.B. 336 (1973) § 5123.40 establishes a legal advocacy service to receive and act upon complaints arising from institutional practices and to see that all persons institutionalized or whose institutionalization is sought are fully informed of their legal rights and adequately represented by counsel. Section 5123.02 requires the legal advocacy service to review all "voluntary" admis-

Yet state legislatures, even when prodded into careful definition of commit-ment or other procedures, may be unwilling to accept all of the measures required by the *Lessard* court. The draftsmen of the Ohio bill did not provide, for instance, that retarded citizens could refuse, on "self-incrimination" grounds, to submit to the diagnostic process.[37] Other courts also may view some aspects of the problem differently. The specific due process questions raised by *Lessard* and other decisions, then, must be critically examined.

PRELIMINARY PROPOSITIONS

Retarded citizens unquestionably share equally with all others the constitutional right not to be deprived of life, liberty, or property except by "due process of law." The issue is not whether they enjoy this guarantee, but what it means in particular cases. It applies whenever government compulsion is brought to bear on the indivi-dual: compulsion to go to school or leave school; compulsion to go to special schools for the mentally retarded; compulsion to work in a sheltered workshop or live in a community home; or compulsion to live in Partlow School. "The requirements of due process are not static [but] vary depending upon the importance of the interests involved and the nature of subsequent proceedings."[38] Thus, passage of a statute imposing the obligation nearly suffices to compel attendance at school generally. Given society's right to impose the obligation, a proposition not questioned here, factual issues requiring individual decision (age? suitability of a proposed substi-tute?) occur only at the fringes. But more discriminating procedures are called for when a particular differentiating institution is pointed to—whether it be a special class, a sheltered workshop, or a large state "school." The due process question is: What is the constitutionally required minimum procedure for each such assignment? The answer may vary, in part, with the stringency of the restrictions imposed. One must resist the temptation to use "institution" as if it invariably meant a brutal state school, or "due process" as if that could mean only the protections associated with criminal trials.[39]

The complex assessment of what due process requires in various situations depends on a clear view of what procedures can and cannot accomplish. The prin-ciple of normalization, for example, suggests that procedures ought to produce a

---

sions where the volition was supplied by a parent or guardian and to request court hearings if the desirability of the admission is questionable. Section 5123.05 (B)(2) establishes the right to counsel and independent evaluation, at state expense in case of indigency. Section 5123.15 abolishes indeterminate commitment. Section 5123.29 details an extensive list of residents' rights, including the rights to a habilitation plan and habilitation. Section 5123.39 precludes the assignment of guardianship powers to any superintendent or staff member of an institution in which a retarded individual is a resident.

[37] Ohio S.B. 336 (1973) §§ 5123.11 (B) and (D) and 5123.14 permit refusal only when probable cause to believe the person retarded has not been shown.

[38] Lessard v. Schmidt, 349 F. Supp. at 1086; *accord,* Goldberg v. Kelly, 397 U.S. 254, 263 (1970); Hannah v. Larche, 363 U.S. 420, 442 (1960).

[39] *See* PPMR REPORT at 28.

vector pointing toward the least restrictive measure and toward integration into community life. Demanding standards and, perhaps, a demanding burden of proof might tend to reduce the number of mentally retarded citizens who are identified as requiring intervention at each level, and thus forward this goal. Similarly, the need to supervise institutional conditions and to ensure that necessary habilitation services are provided suggests the importance of periodic review of commitments. There may also be a need to limit the amount of time that may be taken involuntarily to accomplish habilitative goals for citizens able to live in the community without danger to themselves or others.[40]

It remains fundamentally true, however, that some retarded citizens require special services from the state. Most often this service is education or training, but occasionally it involves a sheltered place to live and work as an adult and, sometimes, total care. Appropriately, this volume stresses the need to devise legal means appropriate for forcing the provision of such services and controlling their adequacy.[41] We must not delude ourselves into believing that "inadequacy of treatment facilities . . . [can] be overcome by imposing legal controls on commitments. . . . Elaboration of procedural protection [is] probably successful in keeping people out of mental hospitals [and facilities of any nature for the retarded], but it [does] not necessarily keep the right people out or keep people out for the right reasons."[42] Indeed, requiring procedures on a criminal model runs the risk of legitimizing, at least unconsciously, the stigmatic labeling and prisonlike incarceration that are said to produce the requirement. Any tendency to respond to the demands of institutional improvement with a papering over of procedural reform must be scrupulously avoided.[43]

The conditions at Willowbrook or Partlow School are objectionable under any circumstances; no procedure can legitimate them. The unhappy conclusion that children must be kept out of special classes, institutions, or any other setting which, properly funded and administered, would provide the best available treatment for them—is a response to society's failures and not to the children's needs.

Nor is it clear how valid the law's distinction between "voluntary" and "involuntary" commitment is as applied to the mentally retarded citizen who needs specialized care. Many voluntary commitments are voluntary only in the most superficial sense. Statutes sometimes require the procedure and give the person

---

[40] *E.g.,* Ohio S.B. 336 (1973) § 5123.15 (H) and (I), *See also* S. 458, 93rd Cong., 1st Sess. (1972) (Senator Javits' "Bill of Rights for the Mentally Retarded"), notably §§ 1224 ("No individual whose needs cannot be met by the facility shall be admitted to it"), § 1226 (comprehensive evaluation before admission), and § 1227 (c) (annual review). On the interrelation of procedure and control over disposition and institutions, see Reisner, *Psychiatric Hospitalization and the Constitution,* 1973 U. ILL. L.F. 9.

[41] *See generally* Burt, pp. 418-37, Chapter 14 of this volume.

[42] ROCK, JACOBSON & JANOPAUL at 17-18. Institutions are not always unwanted by those who have the interests of retarded children at heart. See, for example, the remarks of the Association for Children with Retarded Mental Development, in responding to the Javits bill; S. 458, 93rd Cong., 1st Sess. (1972). As drafted, the bill stated as one purpose "to minimize inappropriate admissions to residential facilities." The association recommended adding "and to maximize necessary admissions." 119 CONG. REC. S910-11 (daily ed. Jan. 18, 1973).

[43] Procedural reform in response to institutional deficiencies—leaving the institutions essentially unchanged—has too often characterized juvenile justice reform. A. PLATT, THE CHILD SAVERS (1969); *cf. In re* Gault, 387 U.S. 1 (1967).

involved no option to waive it; and any such waivers would themselves be open to serious question. Conversely, many voluntary commitments involve no substantial volition on the part of the individual committed. He may be severely limited in his ability to understand what is taking place, or the admission may be made with the consent of his parent or guardian. For the mentally retarded, it is probably preferable to regard all commitments as *avoluntary*, rather than either voluntary or involuntary, and to develop a single procedure to protect all individuals from improper commitment.[44]

Attention must also be paid to ensuring procedures that are workable, both to air disputes and to foster attitudes which promote conscientious resolution of these disputes. Commitment hearings often have occurred essentially as a matter of routine, without regard to the existence of real dispute. Recent empirical studies of the commitment process have shown that routine judicial consideration of commitment has generally failed to generate significant decisional controls.[45] Whether or not judicial process is theoretically available, the basic decision has in fact been made medically. Routine hearings have served little purpose other than confirmation and, perhaps, influencing the presenting hospitals' choice of cases in which to press for commitment.[46]

---

[44] This problem is discussed more extensively at pp. 465-68 *infra*.

[45] *See* Kay et al., *supra* note 24; R. ALLEN, E. FERSTER & H. WEIHOFEN, MENTAL IMPAIRMENT AND LEGAL INCOMPETENCY (1968); ABCNY SPECIAL STUDY; Cohen, *The Function of the Attorney and the Commitment of the Mentally Ill,* 44 TEXAS L. REV. 424 (1966); Dix, *Acute Psychiatric Hospitalization of the Mentally Ill in the Metropolis: An Empirical Study,* 1968 WASH. U.L.Q. 485; Project, *The Administration of Psychiatric Justice: Theory and Practice in Arizona,* 13 ARIZ. L. REV. 1 (1971); Allen, *Legal Norms and Practices Affecting the Mentally Deficient,* 38 AM. J. ORTHOPSYCHIATRY 635 (1968).

ROCK, JACOBSON & JANOPAUL at 256-57 make this point repeatedly—and in striking fashion:

The deficiencies of judicial decision-making are not simply those arising from the fact that judges are not medically trained, but rather they arise from the manner in which courts work. Judicial decision-making is designed to resolve confrontations between conflicting interests and determine them in accordance with some general rule. In principle, the determination would hold for all similar cases, regardless of the idiosyncracies of each case. . . . Moreover, in the adjudicative process as it ordinarily occurs, the cases presented for judicial determination are those that remain unresolved after an intensive culling effected through negotiation and compromise. Presented for judgment in conventional adjudications are the cases in which consensual judgment has failed, and such cases are resolved, as a last resort, by fiat derived from legal rule. This is true of both civil and criminal cases in which only 10 to 15 per cent of the cases filed are actually tried.

In the judicial process as applied to commitment proceedings, both the matter for decision and the context in which the decision is made are quite different. The issue to decide is not squarely one of choosing between conflicting interests, but rather it is to assess the course of action that will best serve the interest of the patient while duly regarding the safety of the general community. Only in an artificial way can such a problem be formulated as one for decision according to some general legal rule. . . .

In addition to this difficulty, but related to it, is the fact that commitment decision-making does not ordinarily deal with those cases that cannot be disposed of by some preliminary process such as negotiation. It is concentrated instead on a flow of cases most of which are destined for routine disposition and few of which involve the confrontation that characterizes adjudication.

[46] ROCK, JACOBSON & JANOPAUL at 122. Kuhlman, *supra* note 3, notes that at least 17 states have formally placed effective control over the commitment process in hospital directors' hands by permitting them to refuse admission to a retarded citizen, whether or not he is committed. *See also* Kay et al., *supra* note 24, at 448-49, 514-15. Fewer than 10, however, provide that the commitment decision itself is to be administratively made. Kuhlman, *supra* note 3, at 11-12.

Making medical authorities select "clear cases" for their action is not an insignificant effect, although professional attitudes and limitations on available facilities will often point in the same

These observations are supported by a recently published study of California's commitment practices in dealing with the mentally retarded.[47] Four state hospitals for the mentally retarded were studied. One regularly required formal judicial commitment of all admittees; the other three required commitment only if no parent or guardian was available to apply for voluntary admission or when the retarded citizen approached majority.[48] In none of the four institutions did the judicial involvement or a lawyer's aid significantly control commitment or the agencies involved. Parents seeking help for their child and themselves went to doctors, teachers, and social workers—not lawyers—who referred them to the hospitals, which decided on medical grounds whether or not to accept the child. Parents, hospitals, and judges alike viewed the judicial proceedings as a mere formality. Less than one-fifth of the judges regularly sought to determine whether the parents in seeking commitment were acting for any reason other than the best interests of their child; only two recalled over hearing a contested case. None had ever refused to commit a child.

Is this rather typical result the product of a failure of judicial and lawyerly energy, much akin to the failures of dedication and resources which too often mark the institutions themselves? Certainly, such matters are often put in the charge of lower echelon judges. When lawyers are made available, they are provided under circumstances which make it extremely unlikely that careful representation will occur.[49] To some degree this reflects the low priority generally attached to the funding of such social service enterprises. It is also reflective of lawyers' awe at what appear to be specialist judgments. But, apart from this, mandatory hearings use trial procedures essentially for ratification, a function to which adversary processes are poorly adapted.[50] The result, as the task force noted, is procedures which "actually impede justice."[51]

---

direction. The question remains whether less cumbersome "procedures," such as availability of an advocacy service, would not produce the same result.

    Where commitment is sought by an incompetent's parents or guardians, formal procedures may also have the effect of lifting a psychological burden from them. Given the ineffectiveness of such hearings to protect the incompetent, however, the appropriateness of lifting this burden is unclear. *See* pp. 465-68 *infra*.

    As the least restrictive alternative comes to be a required part of any commitment setting, required judicial hearings might also prove effective in ensuring that this standard is met. Again, however, it may be that less cumbersome procedures would accomplish the same result as well or better.

[47] Kay et al., *supra* note 24.

[48] These are the only circumstances in which the task force had believed formal commitment appropriate. PPMR REPORT at 28-29. The number of initial commitments which arise under these circumstances is quite low—almost 90 percent of first admissions to institutions for the mentally retarded are 19 or younger. INSTITUTIONALIZATION at 200.

[49] *See, e.g.,* Cohen and Dix articles, *supra* note 45. The problem is partially one of resources: the private bar cannot supply effective representation at $10 per case. To this must be added the effect of appointment by cronyism or the like, which seems often to occur, and the effect of inexpertise, where mental health or mental retardation cases are put in the hands of general practitioners who lack both sophistication regarding the conditions they are asked to deal with and knowledge of available community resources.

[50] The ratification function may be an important one as it is in the case of guilty pleas or uncontested divorces. It has some tendency to prevent overbearing and to stress the seriousness of the act undertaken. It may lead to dispositional procedures requiring the exercise of substantial discretion. But, if ratification and disposition are the limited aims, a requirement of walking through an ostensible adversary hearing is hard to justify. Notice and an opportunity to register protest, and perhaps the right to counsel, would seem sufficient for the carrying out of any of these functions.

[51] PPMR REPORT at 19.

Finally, some attention must be paid to the limits placed by the Supreme Court on the criminal analogy. Even the most enthusiastic reading of *Gault* and the decision which followed it, *In re Winship*,[52] cannot obscure the Court's dependence on the fact that the children in question were being punished for committing acts that would have been criminal in an adult. The Court found and relied upon the formal stigmatic condemnation by the community for commission of a crime. The loss of liberty upon which it also relied was equally seen for its formal resemblance to adult punishment. In its footnotes the Court consistently eschewed any purpose to reach the prehearing or dispositional stages, the two stages which are most significant to the discussion here, or hearings involving children not accused of adult crimes.

DUE PROCESS REQUIREMENTS IN DECISIONS AFFECTING MENTALLY RETARDED CITIZENS

These propositions outlined, *Lessard* and *Dixon* can be examined as they bear on some of the major procedural issues affecting mentally retarded citizens.[53] The examination proceeds on the assumption that there are persons who *do* require residential care for particular purposes, as well as persons who do not. This framework has its own important procedural implications. The Supreme Court has stated, in the somewhat similar setting of procedures to determine incompetence for trial, that "due process requires that the nature and duration of commitment bear some

---

[52] 397 U.S. 358 (1970).

[53] Compilations of state statutes, showing their diversity and complexity, may be found in Kuhlman, *supra* note 3, and INSTITUTIONALIZATION. Comparable treatment of mental illness commitment statutes appears in THE MENTALLY DISABLED.

In some of the notes, for example note 24 *supra* on jury trials, an effort is made to suggest lines of development on issues not discussed in the text. One such omission is the matter of commitment by certification. As suggested at pp. 445-46 *supra*, such commitments are authorized by the certificates of medical examiners, usually two, without more. A hearing is available only on protest, but the opportunity to protest is very rarely taken. Absent such protest, judicial imposition of the commitment need never be sought. *See* note 21 *supra*.

The constitutional weaknesses of the scheme may include the use of a strictly medical standard (pp. 459-60 *infra*) and apprehensions about the reliability of the protest process. The main issue, however, is likely to be the use of a procedure which permits commitment to occur before any desired hearing has been held. Imposition of a sanction or disability *prior* to hearing has been said in a variety of contexts to be strictly the exceptional case; absent emergency or some similarly compelling factor, the opportunity to demand (and receive) a hearing, at least of preliminary character, must precede the action taken. *See* Goldberg v. Kelly, 397 U.S. 254, 260-61 (1970); Lessard v. Schmidt, 349 F. Supp. 1078, 1091 (E.D. Wis. 1972) *vacated for entry of definitive decree,* 414 U.S. 473 (1974), *clarified,* 379 F. Supp. 1376 (E.D. Wisc. 1974), *vacated on procedural grounds,* 95 S. Ct. 1943 (1975); State *ex. rel.* Fuller v. Mullinax, 364 Mo. 858, 865-66, 269 S.W. 72 at 76 (1954); Note, 75 HARV. L. REV. 847 (1962). *But see* Fhagen v. Miller, 29 N.Y.2d 348, 278 N.E.2d 615. *cert. denied,* 409 U.S. 845 (1972), *hearing pending on abstention,* 312 F. Supp. 323 (S.D.N.Y. 1970) ("protective shield of checks and balances" made unpersuasive the claim that preadmission hearings were mandatory).

In the bulk of cases concerning retarded citizens, an emergency requiring immediate action seems unlikely to be present. In the educational classification cases, for example, notes 62 *et seq. infra*, the courts generally forbade educational decisions to be put into effect until the opportunity to seek a hearing, or the hearing itself, had passed. Whatever its advantages where no protest is made, a certification procedure which does not provide for notice (and hearings where requested) prior to admission seems highly vulnerable to constitutional attack.

reasonable relation to the purpose for which the individual is committed."[54] Techniques for ensuring both proper placement and the quality of care and treatment are not readily comprehended in the criminal model.[55] For the problems under discussion, these assurances may be more important than the sometimes illusory alternative of freedom from any commitment.

In a number of respects, the analogy to criminal trials is unnecessary to the due process conclusions reached in cases like *Lessard* and *Dixon*. Increasingly, constitutional claims regarding required procedures have been decided on the basis of a particular analysis of the contending interests before the court, including both the characteristics of the parties and the nature of the controversies to be resolved.[56] Although a rule so generally stated leaves the judiciary considerable room for maneuver, the trend of recent decisions has been characterized by marked insistence on protection of individuals threatened by their government with any "grievous loss."[57] Elaborating on the premise that "the fundamental requisite of due process of law is the opportunity to be heard... at a meaningful time and in a meaningful manner,"[58] courts have described in detail the procedures constitutionally required in a variety of administrative settings, ranging from termination of welfare benefits[59] to suspension of driver's license.[60]

The strength of this approach is that it may be brought to bear on any governmental decision which might adversely affect the life, liberty, or property of a retarded citizen, whether or not it can be shown that the decision taken resembles conviction for crime, or that the outcome resembles imprisonment.[61] The decisions that will have to be made cover a broad range, from educational classification of children to guardianship decisions, to placements in sheltered workshops, and commitment to state schools. The recent litigation involving special education makes the classification decision a particularly useful example.

In Educational Placement

Special education faces many difficulties in this country. It is too often the financial weak sister in public education and is used as the dumping ground for disciplinary

---

[54] Jackson v. Indiana, 406 U.S. 715, 738 (1972).

[55] These techniques are provocatively explored in Chambers, *Alternatives to Civil Commitment of the Mentally Ill: Practical Guides and Constitutional Imperatives*, 70 MICH L. REV. 1107 (1972). Professor Chambers demonstrates with some force the nonapplication of the principle requiring exploration of alternatives to criminal dispositions. *Id.* at 1165-67. *See also* Chambers, Chapter 16 of this volume.

[56] *See* Goldberg v. Kelly, 397 U.S. 254 (1970); Cafeteria Workers, Local 473 v. McElroy, 367 U.S. 886, 895 (1961); Hannah v. Larche, 363 U.S. 420 (1960).

[57] *See, e.g.*, Fuentes v. Shevin, 407 U.S. 67 (1972); Board of Regents v. Roth, 408 U.S. 564 (1972); Perry v. Sinderman, 408 U.S. 593 (1972); Bell v. Burson, 402 U.S. 535 (1971).

[58] Goldberg v. Kelly, 397 U.S. at 267.

[59] *Id.* at 254.

[60] Bell v. Burson, 402 U.S. 535 (1971).

[61] To be sure, such showings are part of the calculus, although I believe that they lead more appropriately to a refusal to commit at all than to the conclusion that criminal standards apply.

problems and other students stigmatized by racial or cultural prejudice. In addition, the diagnostic tests employed sometimes measure a child's socioeconomic class or primary language group, rather than his inherent intellectual and socioadaptive abilities.[62] Yet substantial numbers of children do require special educational services in some form. For these children routine social promotion in normal schools, in the absence of special programing, can be an introduction to confusion, regression, and social maladjustment.[63] To place these children in a setting in which they have opportunity to grow is not punishment. To exclude them from the restriction on their liberty imposed by compulsory education laws is punishment.

Special education became the subject of litigation in *Pennsylvania Association for Retarded Children v. Pennsylvania*[64] and *Mills v. Board of Education.*[65] These suits were primarily intended to force the authorities to provide appropriate educational facilities to children who had been denied them.[66] But in each suit, the lawyers also requested and received the recognition of significant additional rights for their clients. These rights included a statement of detailed procedures for determining which children were to be sent to special facilities: advance notice of proposed action, with a recital of its basis; a right to an independent psychological reexamination at a federal or state testing and diagnostic center; the opportunity to have a full adversary hearing before educational officers other than those who had made the recommendation, with counsel present and school officials available for examination; a written decision on the record made at the hearing; and preservation of a transcript for use in judicial review.

The court's acceptance of these claims is not surprising. The consequences for the child of a wrong decision in either direction are severe. The risks of wrongful assignment to special education may be graver than those of social promotion, in light of public attitudes toward mental retardation and the probable economic and social consequences for a child removed from the normal track. At a time when the right to be heard in advance of adverse governmental action had received enor-

---

[62] Larry P. v. Riles, 343 F. Supp. 1306 (N.D. Calif. 1972), *aff'd,* 502 F.2d 963 (9th Cir. 1974). Further litigation addressed to this problem is reported in A CONTINUING SUMMARY OF PENDING AND COMPLETED LITIGATION REGARDING THE EDUCATION OF HANDICAPPED CHILDREN 43-51 (A. Abeson ed. 1973) [hereinafter cited as CONTINUING SUMMARY]. *See also* Sorgen, Chapter 8 of this volume; Ross, DeYoung & Cohen, *Confrontation: Special Education and the Law,* 38 EXCEPTIONAL CHILDREN 5 (1971); Sorgen, *Testing and Tracking in Public Schools,* 24 HAST. L. REV. 1129 (1973); Comment, *Separation of Poor and Minority Children into Classes for the Mentally Retarded by the Use of I.Q. Tests,* 71 MICH. L. REV. 1212 (1973); Note, *Constitutional Tests for Standardized Ability Tests Used in Education,* 26 VAND. L. REV. 789 (1973).
[63] Solomons, *Counselling Parents of the Retarded: The Interpretation Interview,* in PSYCHIATRIC APPROACHES TO MENTAL RETARDATION 455, 458 (Menolascino ed. 1970).
[64] 334 F. Supp. 1257, 343 F. Supp. 279 (E.D. Pa. 1972) [hereinafter cited as PARC].
[65] 348 F. Supp. 866 (D.D.C. 1972). This case and PARC are discussed at length in Dimond, *The Constitutional Right to Education: The Quiet Revolution,* 24 HAST. L. REV. 1087 (1973); Note *Due Process in Placement Hearings for the Mentally Retarded,* 41 GEO. WASH. L. REV. 1033 (1973).
[66] Other reported right to education litigation has a similar focus. *See Symposium, The Legal Rights of the Mentally Retarded,* 23 SYR. L. REV. 991 (1972); CONTINUING SUMMARY at 1-35. The claim of right to be compelled to undergo schooling with the rest of the juvenile community and, correlatively, to receive adequate schooling, seems far more central to retarded citizens' goals than the claim that this compulsion requires special procedures when this schooling is received in a special building or class.

mous impetus in public law generally,[67] recognition of children's interest in procedures which foster accurate classification and assignment to appropriate educational settings within general and special programs was only to be expected.

Two initial procedural stages—one implicit and one explicit in the opinions— are particularly important. The first stage is a conference with school officials at which they may explain informally the basis for their proposed action. The second is notice of the right to an independent reexamination at a state or federal testing and diagnostic center, at which the school's assessment may be confirmed or thrown into question. Sifting out, before hearing stage, those cases which involve no genuine controversy is an essential of efficient procedure. Hearings without controversy are destructive, not only because they needlessly consume resources and time, but also because their repetition ultimately anesthetizes the hearer to genuine controversy. Both the conference and retesting serve the sifting function well. In doing so, they protect the dignity of the individuals concerned—the children, the parents, and the sometimes harassed school officials. Before battle lines become too sharply drawn, the informal conference and the objective reevaluation by an outsider may lead officials to withdraw their initial decision or may lead parents to accept the recommended action.

Calling the parents' attention to their right to use federally- or state-funded testing and diagnostic centers is a particularly welcome measure. The child's capacity, the principal matter at issue, is determinable with greater precision by mental health and education professionals than by a hearing officer employing traditional adversary procedures.[68] Reexamination is useful both as a check on sometimes inadequate school procedures and as protection for parents likely to be overawed or mystified by "scientific" findings.[69] A further issue is whether the reex-

---

[67] *See* pp. 453-54 & notes 56 & 57 *supra*.

[68] The use of reexamination, rather than hearings, as the principal check on administrative action is well established, whether or not common, in setting requiring grading decisions. *See, e.g.,* U.S. ATTORNEY GENERAL'S COMMITTEE ON ADMINISTRATIVE PROCEDURE, ADMINISTRATIVE PROCEDURE IN GOVERNMENT AGENCIES pt. 7, *Administration of the Grain Standards Act, Department of Agriculture,* S. Doc. No. 186, 76th Cong., 3d Sess. 15-17 (1940). Such procedures have also been used when liberty is involved, as in medical classifications under the Selective Service System. 32 C.F.R. pt. 1628 (1972). Where veracity is not at issue, and the capacity of a hearing officer to make his own determination is limited, lawyers' instinctive reliance on the trial as the superior engine for determining the truth seems out of place. In the special education cases, the proposition need not be taken that far; reexamination was provided for, not as a form of appeal from the initial action, but as a litigative tool, to permit the parents an informed decision whether or not to challenge those conclusions and a basis on which possibly to do so.

In neither *Mills* nor *PARC* was the right to reexamination put on a constitutional footing. Each case relied on the existence of publicly financed testing and diagnostic centers and provided only that parents must be informed of the availability of these services. 348 F. Supp. at 880-81; 343 F. Supp. at 304. If such services were not available, one might argue that they must be provided or that the present state of the testing art is so uncertain that any decision based on a single test is fundamentally unfair. PARC, 343 F. Supp. at 295. *See also* Sorgen pp. 215-44, Chapter 8 of this volume. But the Supreme Court has drawn back from providing even elemental litigation services at public expense where loss of liberty was not involved, and so the constitutional impulse to this conclusion may be lacking.

[69] Larry P. v. Riles, 343 F. Supp. 1306 (N.D. Calif. 1972), *aff'd*, 502 F.2d 963 (9th Cir. 1974). *See also* the complaint in Stewart v. Philips, Civil No. 70-1199-F (D. Mass., Feb. 8, 1971), *noted in* MENTAL RETARDATION AND THE LAW 17 (P. Friedman ed., HEW Office of Mental Retardation Coordination, Feb. 1973). A means for checking and possibly combating official diagnoses and recommendations is made the more important by the frequent impossibility of knowing concretely what is wrong with a child other than that he is slow or retarded, by the effect on children of lowered expectations of them, and by the all too common deficiencies of special education facilities.

amination, once made available, should be given some force. If it may be suppressed by the parents, one risks endorsing only the adversary, and not the confirmatory, function of this innovation. No court has yet suggested that properly identified students have a right to remain in regular public school classes; the issue has been how to develop a reliable identification technique.[70] There may still be occasions for a hearing to resolve contentions regarding the appropriate disposition or the suitability of the proposed special education facilities. The reexamination technique, however, is likely to narrow significantly the range of disputes that will eventually result in a formal hearing.

Several substantive propositions with procedural implications are ably developed elsewhere in this volume. The first relates to a possible constitutional right to restrict governmental action to that with the least possible detriment.[71] The second, a corollary of the first, concerns the right to enjoy an educational setting as close to normal as the child and his classmates are able to profit from.[72] The procedural consequences of these substantive rights were forseen by the task force report in its remark that the "possibility of doing justice . . . turns upon [not only] correct appreciation of the relevant circumstances, [but also] a suitable range of possible dispositions."[73] Procedures must be adopted for ventilation of dispositional issues; the problem is what these procedures ought to be. It has been forcefully suggested that traditional adversary procedures are unlikely to ensure a meaningful search for alternatives to civil commitment.[74] In the educational setting, the need for flexibility of response and the very subtlety of the cascade approach argue against rigorous formality. Children are not necessarily well served if their parents are able to dissuade teachers from action by the threat of embroilment in cumbersome hearings, and any educational resources committed to these hearings are almost necessarily diverted from the primary business of education. A flexible response could be implemented by requiring state diagnostic centers to suggest suitable alternatives or by forming units similar to New York's Mental Health Information Service[75] to oversee the operation of special education in general. Finally, some provision for periodic reassessment probably is needed, with the dual purpose of identifying mistaken assignments and exercising a measure of control over the quality of individual services.

In Institutionalization: The Clear Minimum

Other decisions affecting mentally retarded citizens will each encompass its own set of procedures, varying with the function and gravity of the decision made.[76]

---

[70] Thus, the court in *Larry P.* refused to grant an order returning the plaintiffs to regular school classes. Instead, the school officials were enjoined to adopt selection procedures that would not have racially discriminatory impact. *See also* Hobson v. Hansen, 269 F. Supp. 401, 471-73, 511-15 (D.D.C. 1967); Sorgen, pp. 215-44, Chapter 8 of this volume.

[71] *See* Chambers, Chapter 16 of this volume. *See also* Chambers, *supra* note 55.

[72] *See* Herr, Chapter 9 of this volume.

[73] PPMR REPORT at 16.

[74] Chambers, *supra* note 55, at 1168-76.

[75] *See* pp. 468-70 *infra.*

[76] The appointment of a guardian is one event of particular importance to a retarded citizen, especially

The decision that will have the gravest impact, however, is the decision that a retarded person must live in a particular place, subject to a limited regime, with highly restricted rights of travel, social intercourse, and choice in all aspects of life. In a word, commitment. Although the frequent irrelevance of "voluntariness" in this area must be borne in mind, for the time being "involuntary" commitment will be the topic of discussion. And whereas commitment could be to a small, relatively open "group home," for the moment commitment to a large impersonal institution will be considered.

The pervasive character of the restrictions here imposed, which has consistently been given enormous weight in the due process calculus,[77] requires considerably more rigorous procedures than would be tolerated in assigning students to special classes. Although historically the commitment hearing has been marked by informality, *Lessard* and *Dixon* clearly reflect a movement toward greater procedural protection in the commitment process. A specific analogy to criminal proceedings, however, is of questionable validity and in some ways seems unnecessary, inappropriate, and potentially harmful. The potential harm arises from the inadequacy of the criminal model for a thorough exploration of dispositional alternatives, and from the danger that use of the criminal model may tend to justify, at least unconsciously, institutional neglect of persons committed. The criminal model may be inappropriate where the goals pursued by the state are indeed benevolent and protective, rather than punitive. These concerns about transposition of the criminal model to other areas are not new; they animated Justice Harlan's concurrence and dissent in *Gault*,[78] where the criminal law and its attitudes were a good deal closer.

Reaching for procedures that would ensure fundamental fairness, yet preserve the essential elements of the state's purpose, Justice Harlan identified three required procedures: timely and adequate notice of the proceeding and its possible outcomes; provision of counsel, appointed as necessary; and a written record, or its equivalent, to facilitate review. Interpreted with a view to what fairness requires for the mentally retarded citizen, these measures accomplish much.

Timely and adequate notice, in this context, easily bears the interpretation placed on it by *Lessard*, *Dixon*, *PARC*, and *Mills*: notice not only of date, place, time, and proposed action, but of the standard to be applied, the names of witnesses, and reports of all examinations.[79] Where the principle of the "least restrictive alter-

---

if, as the task force recommended, PPMR REPORT at 25, his guardian might be given authority to "consent" to his placement in an institution. Other useful starting points for consideration of the issues here are Murdock, *supra* note 3; R. ALLEN, E. FERSTER & H. WEIHOFEN, *supra* note 45; Levy, *Protecting the Mentally Retarded: An Empirical Survey and Evaluation of the Establishment of State Guardianship in Minnesota,* 49 MINN. L. REV. 821 (1965).

[77] *See, e.g.,* Morrissey v. Brewer, 408 U.S. 471; *cf.* Chambers, *supra* note 55, at 1155-64.

[78] 387 U.S. at 65.

[79] Lessard v. Schmidt, 349 F. Supp. at 1092. Whether the alleged retarded person must personally receive this notice and appear at the hearing has long been the subject of heated controversy (THE MENTALLY DISABLED at 51 *et seq.*) which *Lessard* resolves affirmatively. The withholding of notice because of "kindness" to the retarded citizen is in effect a prejudgment of the case and substantially undercuts any provision which might limit hearings to cases of actual protest. To be sure, the giving of notice must be handled with tact and understanding and where competence is in issue, a friend or relative must also be notified.

native" is used, notice would also be required of the alternatives considered and the disposition to be proposed. Each of these measures seems likely to reduce controversy.

With confinement at risk and competence at issue, the right to legal assistance is equally clear: "The Court has frequently emphasized [its] importance in proceedings in which an individual may be deprived of his liberty . . . ; this reasoning must include with special force those who are commonly inexperienced and immature."[80] Leaving aside for later examination the question of whether counsel may assume guardianship roles, adequate legal representation will require that counsel be independent of the court, the institutions, and individuals with possibly conflicting interests. His client must be the mentally retarded individual. He will also have to be appointed in sufficient time to evaluate and prepare his client's case adequately.[81]

Counsel's responsibility to assure his client an appropriate disposition[82] raises the issue of whether the right to counsel must be said to include a right to expert assistance and to an independent reexamination. *Dixon* asserts the right, but without explanation and in an essentially consensual setting; the *Lessard* court did not reach the question. Although the Supreme Court has rejected a similar claim in the criminal context, this occurred before the recent surge of interest in procedural matters and at a time when psychiatric testimony was considered more precise than it is thought to be today.[83] The ruling has been overruled for federal criminal prosecutions by statute,[84] and there are strong suggestions that the opposite constitutional result would be reached today.[85] On the present view of the psychologist's art, and given the central importance in our setting of both diagnosis and prognosis, the argument here seems a fortiori. Counsel without such resources will find it impossible to understand or carry out his role effectively. And, as the experience in California suggests,[86] provision for an independent expert view may be the most significant of safeguards.

At a minimum, diagnostic procedures must include measures to ensure the

[80] *In re* Gault, 387 U.S. 1 at 73 (Harlan, J., concurring in part and dissenting in part); *cf.* Heryford v. Parker, 396 F.2d 393 (10th Cir. 1968); Lessard v. Schmidt, 349 F. Supp. at 1097-1100; THE MENTALLY DISABLED at 55. Counsel is infrequently provided and less frequently required, as a statutory matter, even for involuntary commitments of mentally retarded citizens. Of the 49 jurisdictions surveyed by Kuhlman, *supra* note 3, only 9 require, and 7 others permit, the appointment of counsel in commitment proceedings. Another survey of mental illness statutes reports 24 and 12, respectively, as the comparable figures. THE MENTALLY DISABLED at 54.

[81] Lessard v. Schmidt, 349 F. Supp. at 1099-1100; *cf.* Geboy v. Gray, 471 F.2d 575, 579-81 (7th Cir. 1973); COLO. REV. STAT. § 71-1-8(1) (1963). The prevailing low level of legal representation in commitment cases, where any is afforded, is amply described in the articles by Cohen and Dix, *supra* note 45. Mental health or retardation advocacy programs, like public defender programs, may run some of the same risks as now attach to individual appointment of courtroom hangers-on: brief encounters with the client and dependence on the good graces of the judge or institution. If funded at a level that makes provision of services realistic, however, they offer compensating advantages. *See* pp. 468-70 *infra*; Chambers, *supra* note 55, at 1175-76.

[82] *See* Geboy v. Gray, 471 F.2d 575, 579-81.

[83] "Psychiatrists testified. That suffices." United States *ex rel.* Smith v. Baldi, 344 U.S. 561, 568 (1952).

[84] 18 U.S.C. § 3006 A (e)(1970).

[85] *See* United States v. Taylor, 437 F.2d 371, 383-84 n.6 (4th Cir. 1971) (Sobeloff, J., concurring in part and dissenting in part); Cooper v. United States, 337 F.2d 538, 539 (D.C. Cir. 1964), *cert. denied*, 382 U.S. 1029 (1966) (Wright, J., concurring); Goldstein & Fine, *The Indigent Accused, the Psychiatrist and the Insanity Defense*, 110 U.PA. L. REV. 1061 (1962).

[86] *Supra* p. 452.

integrity and independence of the diagnostician. Among the salient facts of *Dixon*, and sufficient to decide this case without generally condemning medical certification procedures, was that the examination and certification took place in the hospital where the plaintiffs were already confined and were made by doctors on its staff. In their role as staff doctors they were committed to social protection and hence should have been disqualified from the critical certification decision.

Lessard embodies the not strictly procedural judgment that the doctrine of "the least restrictive alternative" applies in the commitment setting.[87] Although this judgment springs from the same concern for liberty that animates many criminal procedures, it is the particular needs of the mentally retarded or the mentally ill, not some analogy from criminal procedure, which give strength to this constitutional argument. The right to the least restrictive alternative is least likely to be recognized in criminal proceedings,[88] and the procedures possible to vindicate it have no strong analogue there.[89] The importance of this right serves to underscore the dangers of uncritical reliance on the criminal procedure perspective.

Institutionalization: The Gray Areas

There is a number of respects in which *Lessard* appears to rely quite heavily on the criminal analogy, and it is in these respects that the procedural holdings seem more open to doubt and possibly of less real utility to the retarded citizen. The opinion categorically rejects the *parens patriae*, or helping, rationale of commitment laws: "The power of the state to deprive a person of the fundamental liberty to go unimpeded about his or her affairs must rest on a consideration that society has a compelling interest in such deprivation."[90] Willowbrook may be an institution of no help to its residents; if this is true, Willowbrook should be changed or closed. But the opinion's categorical position would strike equally at placement in a sheltered workshop or group home and ignores the truth acknowledged by the President's Panel on Mental Retardation — that some subjects of commitment proceedings may have no "fundamental liberty," but rather may be fundamentally dependent.[91] To insist that commitment procedures be viewed as deprivations without regard to the institution chosen may be further to obscure the obligation of help.

Discussing the right to be silent in the face of psychiatric inquiry, the *Lessard* court states:

> It may be expected that most patients, like Miss Lessard in the present case, will desire to talk to a person they believe they can trust. Basic fairness requires, though, that they be given notice of the fact that their statements may indeed tend to in-

---

[87] 349 F. Supp. at 1095-96. *cf.* ROCK, JACOBSON & JANOPAUL at 171; N.Y. MENTAL HYGIENE LAW § 33.27 (d) (McKinney Supp. 1973).

[88] Chambers, *supra* note 55, at 1165.

[89] *Id.* at 1168-82. *Lessard* places on the state the burden of showing compliance, 349 F. Supp. at 1096, but does not otherwise elaborate the procedures that might be followed.

[90] 349 F. Supp. at 1084.

[91] PPMR REPORT at 15.

criminate them in the eyes of the psychiatrist and the trier of fact in a civil commitment proceeding.[92]

That is, the patient, whose trust of her physicians is central to her recovery, is to be warned that they are her adversaries and thus not to be trusted. Deeply impressed with Justice Brandeis' warning that we must be most on guard to protect our liberties when the government's purposes are beneficent,[93] *Lessard* utterly rejects the procedural model of acting *for* the patient and insists that the state must treat him in all things, for procedural purposes, as an adversary.

Is the retarded citizen privileged, as *Lessard* would suggest, not to cooperate in the diagnostic process? Given the kind of inquiries which must be made in any commitment proceeding, to so hold would be virtually to stymie the process. Perhaps one may require a showing of probable cause before submission to an evaluation can be insisted upon;[94] but to suggest that the person need never submit on the basis of the Constitution's guarantee that no one "shall be compelled in any *criminal* case to be a witness against himself" is an unwarranted extention of the text.[95] It has been criticized strongly enough in the context of *Gault*, where the relation to criminal law was clear;[96] here, no condemnatory charge has been brought; arguably, none pends the outcome of the evaluation.

Its rejection of *parens patriae* reasoning also led the *Lessard* court to insist that mental illness alone was not a sufficient standard to support commitment. Responding to the frequent and forceful criticism of commitment laws, that they leave the definition of mental illness largely to the user[97] and make unwarranted assumptions of incompetence,[98] the court insisted that the state must prove dangerousness, defined as "an extreme likelihood that if the person is not confined he will do immediate harm to himself or others . . . based upon a finding of a recent overt act, attempt, or threat. . . ."[99] Must a similar standard be met in the retardation context or is greater precision in defining requisite degrees of dependence sufficient?

A limitation of commitment to "moderately," "severely," and "profoundly"

[92] 349 F. Supp. at 1101.
[93] *Id.* at 1103, *citing* Olmstead v. United States, 277 U.S. 438, 479 (1928). In uttering this famous sentiment, Justice Brandeis had no intent to call *parens patriae* legislation into doubt. The case concerned the admissibility of wiretap evidence obtained by illegal means which the government sought to justify on the ground of good faith in enforcing the laws. Hence Brandeis' response. It is apt for, say, the defendants' explanation of their conduct in the Watergate case. It was not a warning against laws intended to aid the unfortunate, even though it has acquired this force today.
[94] *See* Ohio S.B. 336 (1973) §§ 5123.11 (B), (D) & 5123.14.
[95] *Cf.* McNeil v. Director, Patuxent Institution, 407 U.S. 245, 250, 255 (1972), in which eight members of the court refused to reach the constitutional issue of self-incrimination under the fifth amendment in a case with clear criminal overtones.
[96] *See* 387 U.S. at 75-77 (Harlan, J., concurring in part and dissenting in part); Burt, *Forcing Protection on Children and Their Parents: The Impact of Wyman v. James*, 69 MICH. L. REV. 1259, 1294-1301 (1971).
[97] *See* Livermore, Malmquist & Meehl, *On the Justification for Civil Commitment*, 117 U. PA. L. REV. 75, 80 (1968). *See also* ROCK, JACOBSON & JANOPAUL at 8-10.
[98] *E.g., Hearings on the Constitutional Rights of the Mentally Ill Before the Subcomm. on Constitutional Rights of the Senate Comm. on the Judiciary*, 91st Cong., 1st & 2d. Sess. 271 (1970) (testimony of B. Ennis) [hereinafter cited as Ennis' testimony].
[99] 349 F. Supp. at 1093.

retarded citizens would create issues more suitable for diagnostic evaluation than speculative prediction about future behavior. Unquestionably, present commitment statutes define mental retardation imprecisely, permitting inappropriate institutionalization. No statutes presently differentiate degrees of mental incapacity, despite cogent suggestions that such differentiation is required.[100] Yet such differentiation would make clear what is ordinarily the case, that helplessness, rather than harmfulness, is the principal determinant of commitment. Indeed, if inappropriate institutionalization of the mildly or borderline retarded is the problem, the "dangerousness" approach may not be effective to avoid it; such a person may still appear "different" and hence "dangerous" to a juror or a judge.[101] And, to the extent words have power, application of the approach to the more severely retarded citizen may only reinforce unfortunate stereotypes. For retardation, as may not be true for mental illness, more precise definition of the conditions warranting commitment is possible. Such a definition, taken together with the requirement of measures imposing the least restrictive alternative consistent with the citizen's needs, provides the law with ample specificity.

With commitment restricted to the more serious degrees of retardation, the assumption that the class subject to it is generally incompetent to volunteer for help when help is needed seems fully warranted. In such circumstances, one cannot so easily deny the possibility of commitment for habilitative purposes. The proposed Ohio statute limits "involuntary" commitments to the moderately through profoundly retarded and allows commitment for habilitation purposes, subject to regular review and an overall five-year limitation.[102] The argument that even this proposal denies due process is less that directing a seriously retarded individual to undergo available habilitation training is inappropriate than that expecting such training ever to be provided is unreal, given the current level of society's commitment to support an appropriate resolution of the problem. This conclusion seems rather strong to engraft on a Constitution governing all 50 states and their many facilities.

With reference to the hearing itself, two difficult issues remain: first, the question of burden of proof; second, the manner in which medical evidence is to be presented. Regarding burden of proof, there is much to commend the *Lessard* position that "proof beyond a reasonable doubt" is required.[103] This position operates, to the extent the law can do so, to discourage parents and the community from too easily giving over their burden to the large state institutions, contributing to the vector pointing toward less restrictive alternatives. Yet the Supreme Court's analysis in the delinquency cases[104] suggests that somewhat less of a push may be

---

[100] *Supra* note 3. The new New York statute creates a class of "nonprotesting" admissions for the profoundly or severely retarded who are unable to volunteer, N.Y. MENTAL HYGIENE LAW § 33.25 (McKinney Supp. 1973), but does not similarly limit involuntary admissions. *Id.* §§ 33.27, 33.01. *See* 119 CONG. REC. S912 (daily ed. Jan. 18, 1973) (letter of R.A. Haslam, M.D.).

[101] See the incident recounted in Kay *et al., supra* note 24, at 519, where it is remarked that "the 'dangerousness' standard may prove even less a safeguard against improper commitment when applied to the mentally retarded than it has when applied to the mentally ill."

[102] Ohio S.B. 336 (1973) § 5123.15 (I).

[103] 349 F. Supp. at 1095. *See also In re* Ballay, 482 F.2d 648 (D.C. Cir. 1973).

[104] *In re* Winship, 397 U.S. 358 (1970). This form of analysis seems quite free of "criminal" connotation, at least as explained by Justice Harlan. 397 U.S. at 371.

constitutionally required. The Court sought to compare the effects and costs of error in either direction. If convicting the innocent were no more troublesome than acquitting the guilty, it said, a preponderance test would suffice. Of course, this is not so in the criminal context. But assume appropriate commitment standards here and, absent gross error, any mistake will involve a person who is either almost self-sufficient or nearly dependent. The radical discontinuity that exists between guilt and innocence is not present, and the claim to liberty may be illusory. Thus, commitment of the self-sufficient as against noncommitment of the dependent retarded person presents a much closer issue.[105] How the necessary comparison is to be made will depend on assessments of the adequacy of habilitation services available, the psychological effect of the determination on the person, the possibility of correcting any error at a subsequent reassessment, and so forth. If the least restrictive alternative approach is already incorporated in the standard to be applied, the balance is a fairly even one. The Supreme Court has suggested a sensible equation for determining the burden issue. The application of this equation leads to no clear answer, if one accepts the possibility of habilitation services.

The use of written medical evidence is put into doubt by the *Lessard* court's conclusion that, apparently as a constitutional matter, "close adherence" to the standard exclusionary hearsay rules is required in commitment hearings.[106] Here, choice of the criminal model would have striking consequences. The constitutional issue is not, as the *Lessard* court appears to state, whether any rules against hearsay testimony are a necessary component of due process. Rather, the issue is whether the commitment hearing is a proceeding in which the subject must be allowed to confront all adverse witness. In a strictly civil context, a hearing on a claim under the social security disability laws, the Supreme Court has held it proper for the government to proceed on the basis of medical reports, where the claimant had access to the reports in advance of hearing and the power to subpoena the examining doctors.[107] This gave ample protection to the hearing, yet recognized the state's compelling interest in avoiding unnecessary interruptions in medical practice. So here. Trained personnel in institutions for the retarded are too few as it is, and court appearances would effectively reduce their number. On the criminal analogy, however, neither this interest nor the possible admissibility of medical reports under well-recognized exceptions to the hearsay rule could control. The Court has repeatedly emphasized that "it is [the] literal right to 'confront' the witness at the time of trial that forms the core of the values furthered by the Confrontation Clause."[108] and the Court has refused to admit evidence which would have been admissible under recognized exceptions to the hearsay rule, but which offended constitutional values.[109] Whatever the costs of oral testimony, commitment hearings in which the government rested its case on medical reports, rather than live testimony, would be subject to attack if the criminal analogy were applied strictly in this area.[110]

---

[105] *See* pp. 449-50 & note 42 *supra.*
[106] 349 F. Supp. at 1102.
[107] Richardson v. Perales, 402 U.S. 389 (1971).
[108] California v. Green, 399 U.S. 149, 157 (1970).
[109] *Id.* at 155-56.
[110] *See* Denton v. Commonwealth, 383 S.W.2d 681 (Ky. 1964).

Perhaps the most sensitive questions of all concern the role of counsel. In what light is he to see his task, quasi-guardian for a dependent person, or counsel for the accused? Once counsel's independence of conflicting interests and responsibility to his client are made clear, and sufficient time is ensured for his work, it is a further step to impose on him the ethics of criminal law practice, as if retardation were guilt, treatment, punishment, and the "accused" entitled to every reasonable defense of his liberty regardless of counsel's knowledge of his needs.

A court that trusts the intentions and institutions of the law, if it can be put this way, may well allow counsel to blend the roles of advocate and guardian. This would permit him, on the basis of his assessment of his client's best interests, to determine when to insist upon full proceedings and when not to do so. The task force report reflected essentially this view 10 years ago, and it finds support in subsequent studies of the commitment process.[111] To protect a client's dignity, a lawyer may be obliged to convey the client's views to the hearing body; but he need not be put under an ethic of endorsing them or of refraining from counseling his client against a hearing when a hearing appears fruitless.

Introduce the proposition that commitment resembles imprisonment, and counsel's role and effectiveness become far more troublesome. In the area of juvenile delinquency, one commentator, torn between the view of counsel as guardian of the child's best interests and counsel as zealous defender of his client's liberty, concluded that not one but two representatives must be appointed for each child, one serving each function.[112] *Lessard* is similarly emphatic. Counsel's responsibility is to prevent incarceration, and this is inconsistent with a guardianship role. Indeed, *Lessard* seems quite explicit that protecting a resistant patient from "incarceration" is the measure of counsel's success.[113] If the patient's competence to decide whether or not to resist is in question, or if it is unclear what alternative disposition would be most favorable, the *Lessard* court, too, would apparently opt for the appointment of a second representative, to act as guardian and provide the attorney with any necessary instructions.

Any requirement of conscientious representation of the mentally retarded citizen gives rise to substantial additional costs, whatever view is taken of counsel's role. Lawyers, particularly competent lawyers, are neither in large supply nor inexpensive. Money paid for their services inevitably competes with demands for funds to improve services for the mentally retarded. It is doubtful whether an ethic of demanding hearings unless one's client is competent to agree to institutionalization and instructs one not to resist is a necessary or proper commitment of these resources. If the appropriate functions of the process are ensuring "correct appreciation of the relevant circumstances and a suitable range of possible dispositions,"[114] this ethic seems out of place. The pure advocacy ethic embodies, rather, the attitude that even the least restrictive disposition ought not be used. And the ethic denies a

[111] *E.g.,* Cohen, *supra* note 45, at 445, 447.
[112] Paulsen, *Juvenile Courts and the Legacy of '67,* 43 IND. L.J. 527, 536-40 (1968). *See also In re* Dobson, 125 Vt. 165, 168, 212 A.2d 620, 622 (1965).
[113] 349 F. Supp. at 1099.
[114] PPMR REPORT at 16.

function lawyers usually do perform — that of settling out the great bulk of cases that present no real issue for trial — and in this way threatens the integrity and workability of the hearing process.[115] Counsel must, of course, be aware of his own limits in resolving such issues and address the questions of disposition as well as commitment eligibility. The complexity and nonlegal character of the judgments to be made argue forcefully for the advantages of specialized counsel and suggest that finding competent legal counsel to do the job may be somewhat harder than tapping a pool of eager but inexperienced law students.[116] If, as seems true, the root problem is the deficiencies of particular institutions, then this matter should be addressed directly; the solution should not encumber all institutions with expensive formalities.

THE SO-CALLED VOLUNTARY COMMITMENT

Thus far only procedures for *in*voluntary commitment have been examined. People who wish to be where they are may seem to present no occasion for concern. Much recent writing about civil commitment has encouraged increasing use of voluntary or informal commitment processes.[117] Although the authors of *Dixon* might be startled to learn that 96 percent of the patients affected by their decision elected to remain in Pennsylvania mental hospitals on a voluntary basis,[118] the court gave no indication that it was unwilling to have them make this choice in the quite informal way that Pennsylvania law provides. Similarly, the *Lessard* court indicated that its procedures need not be followed for patients who agreed to change their status to voluntary commitment,[119] and appeared to say at another point that, indeed, the choice of undergoing hospitalization or not should be unsupervised unless the state could prove the person in question incapable of making it.[120]

This indifference to the voluntary commitment process is perhaps defensible when both voluntary and involuntary commitments are viewed as medical decisions, so that the underlying standard of admission to the institution is the same for involuntary commitment as for voluntary admissions. But on the *Lessard-Dixon* model, due process requires inquiries that examining physicians simply will not make of a voluntary admittee. Is there a clear and present danger of social or personal harm? Has this been shown clearly and convincingly or beyond a reasonable doubt? Clearly enough, some cases that would properly be accepted for voluntary treatment will escape compulsion; clearly enough, the courts intended this result, given their deep skepticism of the state institutions. It is hard to imagine that a court starting from the perspective of *Lessard* and *Dixon* could be indifferent, then, to

---

[115] *See* note 46 *supra.*

[116] *Cf.* Ennis' testimony, *supra* note 98, at 287-89.

[117] *E.g.,* THE MENTALLY DISABLED at 17; ROCK, JACOBSON & JANOPAUL at 34-38; *In re* Buttonow, 23 N.Y.2d 385, 244 N.E.2d 677, 297 N.Y.S.2d 97 (1968); *cf.* N.Y. MENTAL HYGIENE LAW § 33.21 (McKinney Supp. 1973).

[118] Comment, 10 DUQUESNE L. REV. 674 (1972).

[119] 349 F. Supp. 1103-04.

[120] *Id.* at 1094.

the procedures followed in "voluntary commitment" cases or to the individuals who are said to have elected that course in submitting to the identical institution.

Commentators adopting the medical model take an extraordinarily permissive view of voluntariness. It is enough to verbalize or understand that one is mentally ill, that one wants help for this condition, and that the hospital is a place to which one might come for this help.[121] As was the task force, many are willing to accept the consent of a parent or guardian for a child or incompetent adult unable to decide for himself, as would be done if an appendectomy were at issue.

Serious questions of validity of consent will be present in every ostensibly voluntary commitment proceeding of a mentally retarded person. Nor is this simply a matter of assessing the retarded person's ability to understand the process, the institution, and what it might be able to do for him. Part of the package to which he "agrees" may be an impaired right of release, making the commitment, once begun, a good deal less than voluntary.[122] His initial agreement, too, may have been the product of subtle compulsion—a threat that involuntary procedures will be invoked if agreement is not reached. The mentally retarded person's choice is then between voluntary or involuntary institutionalization, not institutionalization or freedom.[123] Perhaps most important, the choice is usually not his. Almost 90 percent of initial commitments are made during minority, when even without regard to the question of mental retardation consent is given by the child's parent or guardian.[124] Under the medical model, and in the task force report, such consent has been treated as sufficient to warrant treatment of the commitment as voluntary, requiring no further process.[125] But it may be intolerable to allow parents or guardians to place their children in surroundings so hopeless and cruel that the state could not put them there unless criminal standards of certainty were met.

Even the parental decision may not be free of subtle pressure partially ascribable to the state. The parent, unable to cope with full responsibility for his child, may not be presented with a wide range of possible alternatives from which the least restrictive may be selected. Often no alternatives to institutionalization exist, or the state may require that parents completely relinquish control to the state if the child is to gain access to any facilities.[126] The parent may fear to demand improved services lest he lose the little that is presently available or subject his child to possible retaliation.[127]

[121] See THE MENTALLY DISABLED at 19-20; ABCNY SPECIAL STUDY at 68; N.Y. MENTAL HYGIENE LAW § 33.15 (McKinney Supp. 1973).

[122] Murdock, *supra* note 3, at 154; Gilboy & Schmidt, *"Voluntary" Hospitalization of the Mentally Ill,* 66 Nw. U.L. REV. 429, 452 (1971); *see Ex Parte* Romero, 51 N.M. 201, 181 P.2d 811 (1947). The *Romero* court found such an agreement unenforcible, yet still gave the hospital two days to determine whether to seek involuntary commitment. The court's reasoning, heavily dependent on an inference of general incapacity from the fact of voluntary commitment, is suspect today.

[123] Gilboy & Schmidt, *supra* note 122, at 430, 439.

[124] INSTITUTIONALIZATION at 200.

[125] PPMR REPORT at 28-31; THE MENTALLY DISABLED at 19; INSTITUTIONALIZATION at 33-36.

[126] Kay et al., *supra* note 24, at 448, 480-83; Levy, *supra* note 76, at 838.

[127] Murdock, *supra* note 3, at 143-46. This vulnerability regarding dispositional alternatives makes parental consent on this issue especially suspect. When a parent presents his child for institutionalization, it may perhaps be assumed that he has had sound medical advice on the child's condition; few would present a child not so evaluated. But the pressures on his own life may lead him to accept whatever it is the state has to offer, and these options may be few. Since it is the child's interest,

Nor can one afford to ignore the possibility of conflicting interests between parent and child. Parents will be concerned not only for the child, but also for themselves and any other children they may have. Their assessment of these issues, of social and personal pressures for placing the child out of the family, of their own capacities and fatigue, may well lead to decisions, however well intended, contrary to the child's best interest.[128]

When one takes the view that institutions for the mentally retarded are places for detention, the impropriety of reliance on parental consent becomes particularly striking. Statutes exist for state disciplining of children in need of supervision in every state, and at least in some (New York, for example) parental complaints provide the principal occasion for invoking these statutes.[129] No one would think a parent could commit his child to a training school for delinquents without a full hearing on the *Gault* model. If facilities for the retarded are to be seen in the same light or sometimes used for the same purpose, the conclusion that parental consent is ineffective is virtually inescapable.[130]

The frequently cited decision of the United States Court of Appeals for the Tenth Circuit in *Heryford v. Parker*[131] points the same way. There, a mother as natural guardian for her retarded son sought and obtained his release from a state school on the ground that he had been denied counsel in involuntary commitment proceedings. The mother had initiated the proceedings by which the child was committed in 1945, when he was nine. In 1963, during a home leave, she decided not to return him and the state sought recommittal. In the original proceedings, he had not been represented by counsel (as the statute permitted), and the state claimed the mother had waived the right to counsel for the child. The court, finding that no express waiver had been made, decided (on analogy to *Gault*) that the child had been deprived of a fundamental right. The court remarked that even had the waiver of counsel been express, substantial doubt would have arisen whether the child's mother, "having set into motion the commitment machinery, represented such conflicting interests that she could not effectively waive her son's right to counsel."[132]

This discussion arrives at a point far removed from the task force's conclusion that the decisions of parents and guardians ought not to be questioned unless a wrong had been done so egregious as to constitute abuse or neglect. Although it is easy to agree with Professor Allen's early criticism that the possibility of conflicting

---

not the parent's, which is central here, some assurance must be given that all available possibilities have been canvassed. This assurance may not be given when the hospital providing treatment does the confirmatory examination. This need not be a legal procedure; if the state separates the functions of diagnosis and disposition from that of care (*see* Kay et al., *supra* note 24, at 513 *et seq.*), that should suffice.

[128] Murdock, *supra* note 3, at 139-40.

[129] State of New York, Eighteenth Annual Report of the Judicial Conference of the State of New York 390 (1973).

[130] *In re* H, 2 Cal. 3d 513, 468 P.2d 204, 86 Cal. Rptr. 76 (1970); *In re* Wretlind, 225 Minn. 554, 32 N.W.2d 161 (1948); *cf.* State *ex rel.* Richey v. Superior Court for King County, 59 Wash. 2d 872, 371 P.2d 51 (1962).

[131] 396 F.2d 393 (1968).

[132] *Id.* at 396.

interests cannot be so easily blinked[133] the task force recommendation nonetheless rests on a strong policy basis. Again and again, commitment procedures based on the assumption of possible controversy have proved meaningless when expected controversy failed to materialize. As the task force wisely foresaw and the California experience shows,[134] such procedures promote inefficiency; they become routine and tend toward the loss of protection in those few cases where it may be required. Unquestionably, the courtroom door must remain open, and hearings when sought must permit full and fair ventilation of all issues; but so much of the criminal model as appears to encourage hearings, or require them as hurdles in a commitment obstacle course, is equally overstated. The pure criminal model would inevitably undercut the quasi-consensual structure which characterizes the great bulk of actions today, with little, if any, real gain.

A less dramatic adjustment to the possibility of conflicting interests is the suggestion that a minor or other incompetent person committed by a parent or guardian must be given a right to protest. The protest would invoke involuntary hearing procedures or some less rigorous check of the parents' determination.[135] In the mental retardation setting, this right might prove illusory in some cases, if the capacity to protest were itself lacking. Alternatively or cumulatively, one may look for a public guardian or advocate for the child to perform a screening function, to determine in his interest whether or not proposed measures are to be opposed. Whether this is done through a state service such as New York's Mental Health Information Service or citizen advocates drawn from the community,[136] the essential is to identify a person or institution capable of assuming a responsibility to the committed person, one both knowledgeable and untainted by conflicting interests. Then the parental decision can be checked, without imposing the costs and risks of a full-scale involuntary commitment proceeding as a matter of routine in all cases. Such a representative should probably have authority to insist on independent reexamination, to pursue alternative placements, and to call for a hearing if need be.

THE ESSENTIALS OF PROCEDURAL PROTECTION

On the whole, stronger procedural protections clearly are required than typically have been provided in the past. There remains, however, substantial merit in the task force's refusal to abandon the helping model of mental retardation law and in its consequent insistence that procedures be realistically designed to protect against erroneous decisions without submerging hearing bodies in meaningless routine or assuming that the state and the retarded citizen are necessarily in an adversary posture. Particularly if one wishes to satisfy the needs of the child whose parents seek or agree to his institutionalization, the most fruitful direction may be toward

---

[133] R. Allen, Legal Rights of the Disabled and Disadvantaged 14 (1969).
[134] See p. 452 supra.
[135] The Mentally Disabled at 19; Rock, Jacobson & Janopaul at 34 n.2, 38-40.
[136] Murdock, supra note 3, at 145 n.38.

reducing, rather than increasing, the incidence of formal commitment proceedings. Formal commitment is not required when a child is taken to the hospital to have his tonsils removed. There must be effective consent to the operation, which the parent provides, but the hospital does not thereby acquire plenary authority over the child's life and freedom. Why is commitment associated with mental retardation any different? Surely institutions would not be threatened with collapse if the ultimate authority for the retarded person remained with his parents or with some public or private authority dedicated strictly to representation of the interests of the retarded person.

Both California and New York appear to be on the way to recognizing such a separation of functions as essential. The new California statutes place an almost exclusive emphasis on voluntary placement through regional treatment centers which, in collaboration with the parents or guardian of the retarded person, serve to determine what the most suitable habilitative setting would be.[137] Should it be a total institution, such as a state school, the facility receives a resident as any hospital would; it does not have plenary custody of the resident. New York, although not ostensibly altering the person's commitment to a particular institution, has effectively placed guardianship of all voluntary and involuntary mentally ill and mentally retarded patients in the hands of the state mental health information service.[138] That body receives regular reports of patient progress, is freely accessible to patients at all times (and must consider their cases in connection with periodic review of their confinement), and is empowered to act either *sua sponte* or as their representative in initiating proceedings to challenge their confinement or its conditions.[139]

The effect of the information service program on mental illness commitments in New York City has been dramatic. Previously, perhaps 50 commitment cases were processed each week in a meaningless routine of 5- and 10-minute hearings at Bellevue hospital. Lawyers usually did not know their clients and were unfamiliar with, and awed by, psychiatric matters. They were hardly in a position to illuminate possible alternatives to commitment or to ask more than perfunctory questions once conclusory medical testimony had been presented. Because its lawyers quickly become knowledgeable in matters of mental health law, the intervention of the information service has permitted a higher level of service before hearing. They help negotiate small matters which, if unattended, might balloon into major dis-

---

[137] The new statutes are described in Kay et al., *supra* note 24, at 511 *et seq.* The authors note the severe restrictions placed by the statutes on "formal" involuntary commitment, but question the effectiveness of the measure, given the authority of parents and guardians to "volunteer" dependent mentally retarded citizens, juveniles or adults, for institutional care. "If the reduction in commitments . . . is merely counterbalanced by an increase in the appointment of guardians whose function is to agree to their hospitalization, . . . [the] result may be a step backwards since guardianship, unlike commitment, unambiguously strips the ward of his legal and civil rights." *Id.* at 525.

[138] N.Y. MENTAL HYGIENE LAW §§ 29.09, 33.07 (McKinney Supp. 1973).

[139] The New York Mental Health Information Service has had little experience thus far with mentally retarded persons since it was only recently granted power in this area. Its operation in assisting the mentally ill under prior law is described in a number of articles, including Broderick, *Justice in the Books or Justice in Action — An Institutional Approach to Involuntary Hospitalization for Mental Illness*, 20 CATH. U. L. REV. 547, 620-27 (1971); Gupta, *New York's Mental Health Information Service: An Experiment in Due Process*, 25 RUT. L. REV. 405 (1971); Note, 67 COLUM. L. REV. 672 (1967).

putes, assess for the client the viability of his claim, and represent him in informal efforts to secure reexamination or a particular disposition that may obviate the need for suit. The frequency of hearings has also been dramatically reduced, from 50 each week to 2. The information service has ensured that those hearings which are held will command judicial attention.[140]

The commitment hearing is nonetheless unlikely to disappear. *Lessard* and the other cases discussed are invaluable sources of learning regarding both the notice of right, which ought to be given all persons subjected to avoluntary or involuntary control by the state, and the procedures which must be followed when they or others acting for them insist upon a hearing. If these procedures are to be effective, however, the lesson of history is that too much is not to be expected of them. Taken to excess, they anesthetize the decisional process. They are not a substitute for institutional reform. Indeed, to the extent people believe that they are, they may divert attention from the real problems and even seem to justify the treatment afforded persons who nonetheless are submitted to the state's benevolent care. For these reasons, reliance upon the criminal model and an ethic of automatically seeking hearings for a client whose competence is unclear seem essentially mischievous.

SOME POSTCOMMITMENT PROBLEMS

This paper does not attempt to provide more than this hint at issues which arise after commitment has occurred: How frequently and by what means must progress and continued commitment be reviewed? What procedures must attend unusual or harsh discipline or transfers to other programs or schools? What procedures must be available for possible release?

Periodic Review

Statutes provide only occasionally for regular review or renewal of commitments once made.[141] The constitutional supports for a claim to such procedures are limited to a dictum in a concurring opinion in the New York Court of Appeals[142] and, perhaps, the logic of the right to treatment cases and the principle of the least restrictive alternative. In the context of periodic review, the risk is particularly high that formal

---

[140] Similar impact may be anticipated from the new New York Mental Hygiene Law, which, by authorizing initial commitment on the basis of medical certification, requires a protest or hearing demand to activate a judicial hearing. N.Y. MENTAL HYGIENE LAW §§ 33.27, 33.31, 33.33 (McKinney Supp. 1973). *See* note 21 *supra.*

[141] Newman reports similar procedures in 11 states. INSTITUTIONALIZATION at 145-46, 184-95. *See also* N.Y. MENTAL HYGIENE LAW §§ 33.23, 33.33 (McKinney Supp. 1973); THE MENTALLY DISABLED at 136-39, 165 *et seq.*

[142] *In re* Buttonow, 23 N.Y.2d 385, 394, 244 N.E.2d 677, 682, 297 N.Y.S.2d 97, 104 (1968) (Keating, J., concurring).

judicial proceedings in individual cases would become another rubber-stamp exercise, rather than an occasion for meaningful intervention. The reality is that even judicial *discharge* is rarely a required procedure. Hospitals release thousands of individuals to the community yearly; courts, a relative handful.[143] The arguments for periodic review or renewal have least to do with the individual who is pressing for his release. A variety of other procedures is available to him, and the principal matter of importance is to keep the route to the courthouse open for use if need be.

Rather, periodic review or renewal prods the patient who has become too comfortable in his institutional setting (who does not care or have the energy to protest) and augments the right to habilitation. The review also fosters search for a less restrictive alternative by providing periodic indications to the outside world of what treatment is in fact being provided and with what success.[144] Both functions seem entirely sensible and desirable, although at least the first is not constitutional in dimension. But does either require formal judicial process in every case? Judicial controls in the past have been ineffective when too much chaff has been put before courts along with the wheat of a real dispute. It might be sufficient to require periodic reporting by the institution to the individual's private guardian or to a public guardian charged with maintaining standards of care in the institution. This would help to ensure contact with the mentally retarded person and permit him to seek judicial resolution of any complaint which could not be worked out among the parties concerned.[145]

Institutional Discipline and Transfers

Similar informality seems much less apt for questions of institutional discipline and for those transfers between programs which reflect a lowering of sights for the mentally retarded citizen's progress. Disciplinary measures sadly reflect the worst institutional abuses, and perhaps here the prison model is all too appropriate. The law of prison discipline which has emerged within the past several years emphatically insists upon procedural regularity and opportunity for a fair administrative hearing before heavy punishment is meted out. If an inmate of a penal institution, whose conviction and sentence exposed him to authoritarian controls, is protected against

---

[143] ROCK, JACOBSON & JANOPAUL at 234.

[144] *See* Dix, *Hospitalization of the Mentally Ill in Wisconsin: A Need for a Reexamination,* 51 MARQ. L. REV. 1, 34-36 (1967). Note that this is a function no less necessary for the "voluntary" resident placed with this parents' agreement than for the "involuntary" resident formally committed by court process. In the later case one may say that reexamination serves the additional function of ensuring that the mental condition which justified commitment continues to prevail. But how important this function is as an independent matter for a mentally retarded person once committed to institutional care under limited standards seems open to doubt.

[145] This is the mechanism embodied in the new N.Y. MENTAL HYGIENE LAW § 33.33 (McKinney Supp. 1973). The contrary argument, accepted by many, is that a requirement of formal, judicial recommitment is necessary to be ensured that any purported periodic review of a patient's status will be effective. THE MENTALLY DISABLED at 136-37, 139, 165. But the problem is less with the sentiment than its performance. If lawyers must go to court even if satisfied on the papers, judges will quickly tire of the process and it will lose its effectiveness as a sanction. This is another setting in which hearings must be available, but ought not be required.

harsh administration, how much more readily should a child, entrusted to medical care, be safeguarded against mistreatment?[146] Severe restraint of a retarded person, if permissible at all, should not be imposed without notification to some outside friend, who should then be permitted to participate on the person's behalf in whatever further institutional proceedings may be appropriate.

As for transfers involving a more restrictive setting or more limited program goals for the individual, one may wonder whether they reflect failures of the retarded person or of the institution. They clearly represent a recasting of the disposition which was a central part of the commitment process. Both factors make this a timely occasion for review of the commitment decision in all respects. The institution should be required to provide fully informative notice, including copies of relevant reports; an opportunity for independent examination and the appointment of counsel; and a hearing, if requested, before some independent judicial or administrative authority on the appropriateness of the proposed transfer. In effect, the same procedures that *PARC* and *Mills* held required to govern assignments from regular public school classes to special education classes properly govern institutional transfers to a more restrictive setting.

Revocation of Conditional Release

Finally, there is the issue of release. The issue is perhaps not release itself, since this rarely will be litigated, but the extent and duration of the authority the institution may retain over the released individual after his return to the community. The analogy which has regularly been used here is to parole from imprisonment. Release is made on conditions, and the violation of these conditions occasions prompt and essentially unreviewed administrative termination of the release privilege and return to the institution. In the case of criminals, return is to serve out the remainder of their term. For the mentally retarded or the mentally ill person, it may be to the full force of his or her commitment.

On the criminal analogy, procedures of considerable specificity must be followed before revocation can occur. In *Morrisey v. Brewer*[147] the Supreme Court was emphatic that parole revocation operated to deprive individuals of a measure of liberty and hence must be attended by timely and specific notice, an adjudicatory administrative hearing, and other accoutrements of administrative due process.[148] Similar reasoning could be said to control revocation of a conditional release from a facility for the mentally retarded.

Again, however, it may be preferable to approach this question without partic-

---

[146] *Cf*. Mills v. Board of Educ., 348 F. Supp. at 882. *Mills* does not leave the matter of hearing to parental demand in disciplinary proceedings, as it does where educational reclassification is proposed. The burden is properly placed on the school to justify its proposed discipline administratively in each instance.

[147] 408 U.S. 471 (1972).

[148] Two weeks earlier, the court had decided in Argersinger v. Hamlin, 407 U.S. 25 (1972), that counsel must be afforded all misdemeanor defendants threatened with imprisonment. It is noteworthy, and perhaps surprising, that the Court specifically declined to say in an otherwise explicit opinion whether there was any right to counsel at this hearing. 408 U.S. at 491 (Brennan, J., concurring).

ular reliance on the criminal analogy. The decision to place a person in an institution reflects a view of his mental capacity at a particular moment, a view which may be given (perhaps improperly) indefinite durational impact. But it is nonetheless only a view of the moment. If a retarded citizen is later found capable of life in the community, this more recent view should be given some force. A subsequent assertion that he has proved unable to live in the community seems to call for a fresh look at his present capacity, rather than blind reliance on a possibly ancient assessment. One would not wish to make life so inconvenient for the administrators of institutions that they would be discouraged from experimenting with the capacity for independence of a person they thought on the borderline. Short of this, however, the released individual has a strong claim to assessment of his *present* capacity before he is returned to his previous place. Certainly, the argument for requiring full commitment procedures becomes strong after a reasonable testing period (perhaps one year) has passed.[149] Even within that year, the retarded individual may be able to make a forceful claim for the independent examination which has been found to be central to so many issues, as well as to the administrative procedures suggested by *Morrisey*.

Requirement of new commitment procedures on this ground would have been a more forthright response to the *Heryford* case[150] than the court's reliance on the failure to afford counsel at the initial commitment hearing. That hearing had occurred in 1946, when the young man in question was nine years old. He was released to his mother's care in 1963 at age 29 and returned to the hospital 2 years later. Counsel's function in 1946 might truly have been of slight significance. Although Wyoming at that time required the formality of commitment proceedings in every case, the prescribed proceeding was in effect a voluntary one, with little expectation that counsel for a retarded child would have to guard vigilantly against parental malfeasance. But 20 years later the original proceeding was stale. Perhaps in the two years since his release, Heryford had relapsed, or his mother had proved herself unequal to the task of supervising him. But these questions, rather than the propriety of an ancient commitment order, are what ought to have been in issue.

CONCLUSION

In summation, any workable theory of proper procedures for institutionalization of mentally retarded citizens must take account of a number of limiting realities. Material resources and professional skills are limited; procedural devices are imperfect; institutional facilities are inadequate; the diagnosis of mental retardation is not static over time and must be open to review and reconsideration; decision makers are readily anesthetized to genuine dispute by the boredom of excessive routine; and many retarded citizens present indisputable claims for care and protection, against which traditional liberty is a cruel sham.

The argument has been presented that the effort to avoid mistakes, conflicts

---

[149] THE MENTALLY DISABLED at 135.
[150] 396 F.2d 393 (1968).

of interest, and excessive institutionalization by a uniformly formal hearing system and the adversary model of criminal procedures is not only costly, but doomed to failure as an instrument of protection. It is essential to structure the institutionalization process to expose conflicts of interest and improper efforts by the state or family members to abuse the weaknesses that may accompany mental retardation. It is essential to provide checks on, and a means of confirmation for, diagnoses and prescriptions for care that are necessarily uncertain. The courtroom door must remain open and access to legal assistance must be provided for those disputes that genuinely exist or ought to exist. It is another matter, however, to force the retarded person through procedural formalities and to direct lawyers into adversary postures, by an ethic which views every institution as an evil to be avoided at any cost and instructs counsel for questionably competent clients to resist institutional care fully whenever his client's competence to accept it does not clearly appear.

Reaction Comment

BRUCE J. ENNIS

ALTHOUGH I AGREE with many of Strauss' specific recommendations,[1] I disagree strongly with the thrust of his recommendations. He believes, in general, that procedures for the civil commitment of the retarded should not raise "procedural roadblocks" to institutionalization. Courts, lawyers, and all those troublesome paraphernalia of judicial process should be reserved for use in the small number of cases in which the mentally retarded person, his parents, or someone acting on his behalf actively oppose institutionalization. The majority of commitment decisions should be entrusted to parents and professionals. My disagreement is not with Strauss' legal analysis; his explication of the case law is intelligent and fair. The disagreement stems from the rather different attitudes and expectations I bring to bear upon this legal analysis.

Strauss seems bereft of hope for the mentally retarded and full of hope for drastic institutional reform. To him, mental retardation is primarily a diagnostic problem, a condition whose presence or absence is to be determined by experts. Accordingly, if the existence of mental retardation is "accurately diagnosed," commitment to an institution is not only appropriate, but also preservative of the retarded person's true freedom. It follows, in his view, that the legitimate function of judicial process is the rather limited function of providing an opportunity for contest and ensuring, in contested cases, that the diagnosis of mental retardation is "accurate."

In addition, Strauss seems to labor under the impression that the inhumanity of the Partlows and the Willowbrooks are gross exceptions to the rule. Unfortunately, they are not. Willowbrook is no worse than New York's Letchworth and

---

[1] "[T]he right to speed in initial determinations"; "provisions for extensive notice, including reports of all examinations"; "limiting the term of any commitment order"; "periodic assessment"; careful scrutiny of purportedly voluntary admissions; "citizen advocates," and the appointment of an independent representative for all persons subject to institutionalization.

considerably better than its Wassaic and Craig State Schools. New York spends less per resident for the 25,000 persons in its state schools for the retarded than it does per prisoner in its prison system. And New York probably spends somewhat more per resident than the national average. The reality is that only a handful of this nation's state institutions for the mentally retarded provide anything approaching education or habilitation. The vast majority provide, at best, only custodial care, the same food, clothing, shelter, and structured oppressive environment you could expect from a prison. And depressingly large number provides even less. Strauss' response to prisonlike institutions for the retarded is to reform them. This response is inadequate for two reasons: the *first* reason is that substantial reform may not come at all, and if it comes, it will not come for years. I am one of several lawyers who have been working almost full time for over a year to bring reform to Willowbrook. The effort has cost literally thousands of dollars. The result? An interim federal court ruling that the retarded presently do *not* have a constitutional right to education, treatment, or habilitation. They have a right to physical safekeeping and protection from harm, but no more.[2]

In effect, Strauss has recommended procedures to guard against the *abuses* of the system — the occasional brutality, the understaffed ward — but has failed to recognize that the system itself is abusive. At least for the foreseeable future, decent and humane custodial care is the best that can be expected from all but a handful of the state institutions for the retarded. In most, the conditions will continue to be so abnormal that they will be truly shocking. Placement in such settings has a deleterious effect on the residents. Over time their level of functioning deteriorates. And why not? Children locked for 5, 7, or 10 *years* in seclusion cells. Toilets without doors or toilet paper. Fourteen hundred serious physical injuries to 4,500 residents in less than 10 months. Forty or fifty nude men or women waiting in line for an hour or more to be hosed down with a rubber hose. A dayroom with one attendant caring for 61 severely retarded persons. That is Willowbrook today!

There are many Willowbrooks in this country and they will be around for some time to come. Commitment procedures will have to be designed with this fact in mind. There are, after all, degrees of deprivation of liberty, some of which are properly no concern of the law. Few would suggest that parents should be required to obtain judicial approval before placing their mentally retarded child for a weekend in a respite care center. But one would never allow parents to place their retarded child in a prison. The threshold question, then, is whether state institutions for the retarded are more like weekend respite centers or more like prisons. The answer, for now, is clear.

[2]New York Ass'n for Retarded Children v. Rockefeller, 357 F. Supp. 752 (E.D.N.Y. 1973). There has been a final consent judgment entered in this case, and in his accompanying memorandum Judge Orrin Judd noted that:

> Somewhat different legal rubrics have been employed in these cases — "protection from harm" in this case and "right to treatment" and "need for care" in others. It appears that there is no bright line separating these standards. In the present posture of this case, there is no need for the court to re-examine the constitutional standard properly applicable to Willowbrook's residents. The relief which the parties agreed to will advance the very rights enunciated in the case law since this court's 1973 ruling. Entry of final consent judgment, New York Association for Retarded Children v. Carey, Civil Nos. 72C356, 72C357 (E.D.N.Y. entered, May 5, 1975).

Second, even if state institutions for the mentally retarded are promptly and vastly improved, they will still be inappropriate residences for more than a very small number of the thousands of persons they now house. If anything has been learned in the past 10 years, it is that the best treatment for a retarded person is to provide him or her with an environment as close to normal as possible. Putting a a person in a state institution for the mentally retarded ensures that he will receive, at best, only second-class treatment. Such institutions, no matter how clean or well staffed, cannot provide a normal environment. It is not normal for retarded persons to have as their only peers other retarded persons. It is not normal to eat, sleep, go to school, work, and participate in recreation activities within the four walls of a single institution. This is not the way people normally live, and training retarded persons to adapt to this environment falls far short of training them to live in, and utilize the resources of, the community. It also helps ensure that they will have greater adjustment problems if a community placement is eventually attempted.

Now I wish to turn from this rather general discussion to a few more specific points.

WAIVER

Many of the rights Strauss would give the mentally retarded would be, at best, paper rights because they could be exercised only upon the affirmative demand of the retarded person. If the retarded person raised no objection, his theoretical right to have a court hearing or a lawyer, for example, could be deemed "waived." It is unrealistic to assume that the retarded, or persons acting on their behalf, will affirmatively exercise these theoretical rights. Even the mentally ill do not do so. At Bellevue psychiatric hospital in New York, for example, in 1966 there were nearly 12,000 *involuntary* admissions. All of these mental patients had the theoretical right to request a court hearing and a lawyer—but only 531 did.[3] It could be expected that an even smaller percentage of mentally retarded citizens would exercise their rights. The same Bellevue study, sponsored by the National Institute of Mental Health, showed that the act of requesting a hearing made a crucial difference. The discharge rate of persons who did request release was substantially higher than the rate of those who did not, and the study team could find no clinical differences in the two groups.[4]

---

[3] Kumasaha, Stohes & Gupta, Criteria of Involuntary Hospitalization, 1971, at 3 (unpublished report, Hospitalization Research Unit, New York University Medical Center). Of the approximately 12,000 admissions, 4,496 were placed on "two physician certificates" for extended confinement; of these, 531 requested a hearing.

[4] In 1966, 33.5 percent of persons requesting a hearing were discharged, compared with a 6.9 percent discharge rate for those who did not request a hearing. The discharge rates for the requesting and nonrequesting patients for 1967-69 were as follows: 1967, 34.5 percent—7.0 percent; 1968, 41.8 percent—14.9 percent; 1969, 49.3 percent—21.9 percent. By 1969, almost half the patients who requested a hearing were discharged. *Id.* table 2, Discharge Rates Among Hearing-Request Group and Non-Request Group.

JUDICIAL BOREDOM

Strauss is worried that routine use of judicial procedures will dull judicial sensibilities to the occasional real controversy. This argument would justify abolition of all the criminal courts, all the landlord-tenant courts, and all the family courts in this country. After all, most of what judges do is routine. The question is *not* whether judges might occasionally handle an unusual case in a routine manner. The question is whether judges are more likely to do this than are the superintendents and staffs of state schools for the mentally retarded. For administrative and professional sensibilities, too, may be dulled by routine. The judicial process, at least, has built-in safeguards to guard against routinization. The whole point of the adversary method, as opposed to the inquisitorial method, is to decide each case on the basis of the particular facts before the court. Judges and lawyers are trained to look for minute factual variations. This is their job. The adversary process makes it possible to ferret out those factual differences which might make a dispositional difference. The process works well when two lawyers present the strongest case that can be made for opposing points of view, and a judge, after hearing all the evidence, decides. It does not work well when one or both lawyers act as mini-judges, pre-judging the issues, because then the judge is denied the benefit of a full-scale presentation of the available evidence and options.

REAL CONTROVERSY

Professor Strauss also assumes that the decision to institutionalize a mentally retarded person raises a controversial issue in only a few cases. This might be true if, as seems to be his view, the only legitimate question is whether the diagnosis of retardation is "accurate." But, by taking this position he has allowed diagnosis to govern disposition. An accurate diagnosis of mental retardation is a necessary but not a sufficient prerequisite to institutionalization. *Every* institutionalization of a mentally retarded citizen raises at least the following controversial issues: (1) Does the retarded person want to be sent there, or would he if he were capable of forming and expressing preference? (2) What is the purpose for which he is sent there? Is it for medical treatment, education, toilet training, vocational training, or what? (3) Is the institution staffed and equipped to fulfill this purpose? (4) Is the confinement expected to be of short or extended duration? (5) Are there less drastic alternatives available in the community that would suffice? (6) Could adequate services be *purchased* in the community if the state would simply give the parents the amount it would cost the taxpayers to institutionalize their child?

LESS DRASTIC ALTERNATIVES

As Dr. Philip Roos notes in his reaction to Ms. Wald's paper,[5] the legal concept of the "least drastic alternative" is the vehicle for implementing the professional concept of "normalization." It might also be seen as the judicial equivalent of the "individualized" habilitation plan. Strauss says very little about these three concepts, and I think his recommendations suffer for it. Judicial hearings should be required before any long-term commitment, if for no other reason than to ensure that the parties recommending full-time institutionalization explore less drastic alternatives and demonstrate to the court that no less drastic alternative will suffice.

For some time now, lawyers and mental retardation professionals have been insisting that *institutions* prepare and provide an individualized developmental program tailored to the specific needs of each retarded person in the institution. This principle, so important in the institution, is perhaps even more important *before* institutionalization. Individualized programs within an institution are required because of the recognition that each mentally retarded person has unique strengths and weaknesses. Similarly, there should be a requirement for the preparation of an individualized program *before* institutionalization. This, in a nutshell, is what the principle of the least restrictive alternative is designed to do.

JUDICIAL INSTITUTIONALIZATION PROCEDURES AND THE RIGHT TO HABILITATION

If the role of the court in the institutionalization process is expanded, it might not be necessary thereafter to bring "right to habilitation" cases. At present, mentally retarded persons are institutionalized for the purpose of some vague and unspecified form of care, treatment, and habilitation. But it need not be this way. Legislatures could require courts to determine the *specific* purposes for which a retarded person is to be institutionalized and then determine, *before* institutionalization, if the institution is staffed and equipped to achieve this purpose. If the institution is not equipped to provide the specific service — say, two hours per day of physical therapy — the person would not be institutionalized. If it is, the institution would then be *ordered* by the court to provide the specific service.

At that point, whether the person is a "voluntary" or "involuntary" resident would not matter. Similarly, it would not matter whether there is or is not a constitutional right to physical therapy or to whatever specific services have been identified as required. The institution would be under court order to perform. Periodic

---

[5] *See* Roos, Chapter 1 of this volume.

review would be scheduled to ensure that the court order was, in fact, being carried out. In effect, the broad outlines of an individualized habilitation plan could be determined *before* institutionalization, and the institution could be directed to meet this plan or be subject to contempt. Under such a procedure, the institution might find itself in the unaccustomed but logical role of opposing institutionalization in specific cases on the ground that it was not equipped to provide the specified service.

There are obvious advantages to specifying the reasons for institutionalization. It makes little sense for the institution to provide a mentally retarded child with a full recreation program, physical therapy, and academic education, but not toilet training, when the parents would be willing and able to provide these services at home if their child were toilet trained. In other words, the court should determine what skills are required in order to keep the child in the community and should then order institutionalization only if (1) the institution is staffed and equipped to teach these skills and (2) community facilities are not.

As a corollary, the court could require that services which can be provided in the community must be provided in the community. The child might go to the institution to receive the benefits of sophisticated physical therapy equipment too expensive for communities to maintain, but might still go to school in the community. In other words, institutions should not, as at present, assume general responsibility for providing all needed services for persons in their custody. The court, following expert testimony, should determine which services the institution alone is equipped to provide. All others would be provided in the community.

There are problems with such a system, but it seems to me that if we are serious about "normalization," "developmental programing," and utilization of the "least restrictive alternative," we should begin to think in terms of expanded, rather than contracted, judicial participation in the institutionalization process.

Reaction Comment

ROBERT A. SPRECHER

WITH THE GROWING federal case load, no federal court would expand its jurisdiction or proliferate procedure unless forced to do so by utter necessity. Unquestionably, to require full-dress due process rights as a prerequisite to involuntary mental health and retardation commitment is to open a new floodgate above the already swamped plains of the judiciary. However, unless and until the states provide due process rights in their mental health and retardation legislation, the federal courts provide the only recourse.

There is no legal justification for depriving an entire class of persons of its freedom without due process. The purported justification based on the theory of *parens patriae* — that the state is the father of the country and of all its citizens — is pure fiction. It was based on the fallacious theological premise that God communicated to the citizenry only through the king and on a governmental premise, unacceptable in a democracy, of monarchy through a benign and benevolent ruler.

Although Sir Edward Coke had reminded James I of Bracton's words that "The King is subject not to men, but to God and the law,"[1] as late as 1765 Blackstone was writing about the divine right of kings, the royal prerogative, and the king's absolute perfection: "The king can do nothing wrong. . . . The king is not only incapable of doing wrong, but even of thinking wrong. In him there is neither folly nor weakness."[2]

In order to secure the rights of freedom, the founders changed all that and declared that "governments are instituted among men, deriving their just powers *from the consent of the governed.*" Mr. Justice Brennan, discussing sovereign immunity in a recent case, said:

> "We the People" formed the governments of the several States. Under our constitutional system, therefore, a State is not the sovereign of its people. Rather, its people are sovereign. Our discomfort with sovereign immunity, born of systems of divine right that the Framers abhorred, is thus entirely natural.[3]

Parens patriae in the sense implied in cases involving mental capacity or institutionalization was wholly discredited at the outset in democratic government.[4] Nevertheless, courts awed by the psychiatric mystique have acted as if the mentally retarded and the mentally ill had fewer rights than aliens or criminals. To compound the incredibility of the entire procedure, the common law of *parens patriae* as developed in England actually provided for some of the protections of due process, such as availability of habeas corpus, right to trial by jury, notice, and hearing, right to counsel and to cross-examination.[5]

The early commitment cases in this country restricted the basic constitutional rights of equal protection and due process for the individual on the fictional basis of a supposed common law power in the state. There was no basis in fact or in history for that power in this democracy. Even in its own monarchical setting, the courts had recognized and balanced individual rights.

The fiction of *parens patriae* was bound to disappear because of the reemerging sense of worth, meaning, and dignity of each human being and because the unchallenged psychiatric promise had failed to deliver. The present Supreme Court, like the Court before it, shows every sign of strictly enforcing the Constitution. In fact, the most strict constructionist has little difficulty in finding and applying the words "equal protection" and "due process of law." The Supreme Court has speci-

---

[1] T. PLUCKNETT, A CONCISE HISTORY OF COMMON LAW 49 (1929).

[2] BLACKSTONE'S COMMENTARIES ON THE LAW 111 (Gavit ed. 1941).

[3] Employees v. Missouri Public Health Dep't, 411 U.S. 279, 322-23 (1973) (Brennan, J., dissenting).

[4] The words have been used in a different sense to establish the right of a state to bring an original suit in the Supreme Court to prevent or repair harm to its quasi-sovereign interests pursuant to Art. III, § 2 of the Constitution. Hawaii v. Standard Oil Co. of California, 405 U.S. 251, 257-59 (1972).

[5] THE MENTALLY DISABLED AND THE LAW 5-6 (rev. ed. S. Brakel & R. Rock eds. 1971).

fically recognized these constitutional rights in mental health and mental retardation cases,[6] as it earlier did in juvenile cases.[7]

"We the people" have not consented to waive our full rights of equal protection and due process simply because we are characterized as mentally deficient or mentally retarded. The only constitutional justification for any deprivation of liberty of the mentally retarded is the police power, which is fully subject to due process requirements. It has now become apparent that each person must be presumed competent, as well as innocent, and that medical opinions finding mental retardation must be tested for accuracy by the adversary process, just as any expert opinion is tested.

The assumption may be made that professions and paraprofessions share a common goal to treat, habilitate, and restore to the community anyone needing or seeking treatment, habilitation, or training for mental illness or mental retardation. The harsh word "adversary" used by the legal profession strikes alarm in the medical profession, which seeks to comfort and ease, if not cure. The "adversary process does not create *adversity*."[8] It seeks the truth and it does so in a manner upon which no one has successfully improved. The legal process assigns adversary roles and permits each side to press his case as vigorously as possible and to present the documentary evidence and oral testimony that supports that case. In advance of trial each side is permitted to discover the facts upon which the other will rely and to prepare to rebut them. Witnesses are cross-examined to test their truthfulness and accuracy and to expose their bias. A number of jurors are selected for their impartiality and asked to reach a consensus of their views as to the facts.

It is understandable that persons seeking to commit other persons to institutions are not always willing or pleased to have their motives and purposes inquired into by this searching process. Nor are experts in the medical and psychiatric field always ready or eager to have their opinions as to mental retardation exposed to thorough testing. After all, it was so simple to tap someone on the shoulder and say, "you're institutionalized for life." Part of the *parens patriae* mystique depended upon another fiction — that institutions for the mentally ill and mentally retarded were pleasant places where one was continually trained and habilitated with the ultimate goal of restoration to the community.

The courts that exposed the fallacy of the *parens patriae* fiction have also torn away the pretense of benevolent and therapeutic habilitation of institutionalized citizens. The courts, of course, could have simply devastated the *parens patriae* theory as a matter of law, but the nature of mental retardation institutions was and is a

[6]*E.g.,* Murel v. Baltimore City Criminal Court, 407 U.S. 355 (1972); McNeil v. Director, Patuxent Institution, 407 U.S. 245 (1972); Jackson v. Indiana, 406 U.S. 715 (1972); Humphrey v. Cady, 405 U.S. 504 (1972); Specht v. Patterson, 386 U.S. 605 (1967); Baxstrom v. Herold, 383 U.S. 107 (1966).

[7]*In re* Gault, 387 U.S. 1 (1967); Kent v. United States, 383 U.S. 541, 554-55 (1966) ("The State is *parens patriae* rather than prosecuting attorney and judge [under the District of Columbia Juvenile Court Act]. But the admonition to function in a 'parental' relationship is not an invitation to procedural arbitrariness.").

[8]D. Bazelon, Psychiatry in Conflict, April 19, 1973, Helen Ross Lecture, Institute for Psychoanalysis, Chicago.

matter of fact and the courts have reacted to these facts in the normal course of adversary procedures. They have heard witnesses describe brutal and inhumane treatment. They have had presented to them documentary and carefully researched evidence of the crass warehousing of human beings. They have also heard of erroneous diagnoses of the mentally ill and mentally retarded by medical, psychiatric, psychological, and other experts.

Consequently, as Judge Bazelon recently said, "it's about time that we all understood that the Age of Mystique is almost over."[9] There is nothing about requiring procedural protections for the mentally retarded which "will appear to legitimate criminal treatment of those who are committed." To insist that institutionalized persons are entitled to constitutional habilitation at least equal to that given criminals is not to treat them as criminals. Actually they have been treated as worse than criminals precisely because they have been denied their constitutional rights. It is more accurate to consider that the mentally retarded should be given presidential treatment because the constitution entitles them to the same rights as a president.

It has been asked why, if the retarded who are subject to institutionalization are entitled to all the rights a criminal receives, those who volunteer for institutional habilitation should not be entitled to an adversary inquiry into the voluntariness of their submission, even as a criminal is entitled to an evidentiary hearing as to the voluntariness of his confession. One difficulty is that there is a limited amount of legal and judicial manpower, just as there is a limited amount of medical and psychiatric manpower. Although this fact does not justify withholding a constitutional right, the right is much less clear in regard to voluntary commitments than involuntary. If legal and judicial services are subject to rationing, the priority clearly lies with the involuntarily committed citizen. In the case of a coerced confession, a crime has been committed and an accused is on hand available for coercion. There is far less, if any, motive for an institution to coerce a waiver of rights from a voluntary resident who shows up at its gate. Presumably, institutions are not beating the bushes hunting for persons to commit. Law enforcement officers are doing just that.

Professor Strauss writes, "the authors of *Dixon*[10] might be startled to learn that 96 percent of the patients affected by their decision elected to remain in Pennsylvania mental hospitals on a voluntary basis." In contrast, within 90 days the *Lessard* decision[11] 41 institutions in Wisconsin reexamined 7,858 patients. Thirty-seven percent were converted by consent into voluntary patients, 27 percent were recommended for a return to court for a due process hearing on involuntary commitment, and the remaining 36 percent were processed for release into the community.

What accounted for the different results in Pennsylvania and Wisconsin is not known, but it is undoubtedly true that the possibility of and opportunity for coercion are greater at a reexamination than at the time of original commitment. Perhaps future courts will consider the possibility of at least the presence of a dis-

[9] *Id.*
[10] Dixon v. Attorney General, 325 F. Supp. 966 (M.D. Pa. 1971).
[11] Lessard v. Schmidt, 349 F. Supp. 1078 (E.D. Wis. 1972), *vacated for entry of definitive decree,* 414 U.S. 473 (1974), *clarified,* 379 F. Supp. 1376 (E.D. Wisc. 1974), *vacated on procedural grounds,* 95 S. Ct. 1943 (1975).

interested observer when voluntary consents are solicited in a massive reexamination caused by the invalidation of defective procedures. But this does not indicate a present need to question original voluntary commitments as they occur. The current implied court approval of voluntary commitments is based on the premise that some mentally retarded persons are presumed to be willing and able to make decisions about their lives. Thus, if someone chooses to go to an institution, no reason exists to dispute this desire. He has made a choice which should be respected (even if it is assumed that the person will actually receive little help in the institution). Institutions still have the authority to refuse to accept the voluntary admission if they believe it inappropriate.

Inasmuch as the requirements of due process are not static, some flexibility in judicial procedures may be needed when procedures tailored for the mentally ill are applied to the mentally retarded. On the one hand, it may be that definitions and standards of retardation are more precise and generally accepted than standards of mental illness, that diagnoses are demonstrably more accurate, and that a consensus of what amounts to total impairment of a person's ability to live in society is more readily attained. On the other hand, the likelihood of the insincerity of parents' motives in seeking institutionalization of a child may be greater than those of a third person in mental illness cases, and the range of possible treatment is far broader. These suppositions require close examination to determine the extent to which they are valid.

This would suggest that initial commitments of minors by the consent of parents may be suspect often enough and the kind of treatment required diverse enough to warrant a mandatory hearing on the need and justification for commitment, with the minor represented by counsel independent of the parents and guardians.[12] As a gratuitous by-product, shifting the onus of commitment from the parents to a court has therapeutic value to the parents. The emphasis in such a hearing should be upon (1) the parents' motives; (2) the kinds of possible habilitation; (3) the less drastic alternatives; and (4) the treatment facilities available in the community. Less attention may need to be given to the process of adversary testing of the medical findings.

It is conceded that there may be "cases of genuine controversy" in the commitment area. Whether these controversial cases, where persons may be unjustifiably incarcerated for the rest of their lives, are many or few is not relevant. If they exist at all, due process requires that the basis for commitments be tested. Even if the due process requirements were not mandatory, alternative procedures would not fill the void. Habeas corpus or judicial review procedures are not effective. Once the mentally retarded citizen is committed, the chance of his having the opportunity to communicate with a lawyer willing to assist him is reduced to close to zero. If he has the opportunity, then the complacency which often accompanies incarceration, or drugs, or both, may functionally diminish his motivation to seek judicial assistance.

---

[12] *See* Heryford v. Parker, 396 F.2d 393 (10th Cir. 1968); *cf.* Argersinger v. Hamlin 407 U.S. 25 (1972).

Anyone who finds himself in the service of the mentally ill or mentally retarded is a person of good will by definition. No one can dispute the need in the field of mental retardation for more funds, more facilities, more manpower, more dedication, devotion, and understanding, and more expertise in both the legal and medical professions. But there is no proven need for more commitments. The trend is, and must be, toward more temporary placement, community care, and fewer "life sentences."

The medical and psychological professions need assistance from the other professions and paraprofessions. Lawyers, particularly those in general practice who deal constantly with people, should be trained in counseling. After all, they represent themselves to be counselors. There is nothing about the adversary process which must make it a traumatic process. Seeing his lawyer should be a comforting and relieving situation for the client-patient. This is not to imply that lawyers either "play dead" or "play God," but simply that they should perform in the traditional role of advocate against the rest of the world yet treat their special client with compassion. It is also hoped that the more than 100,000 students now in law schools (constituting almost one-third of the present lawyer population) will supply enough legal manpower to ensure for the mentally impaired their rights in full measure. Perhaps judges who adjudicate cases involving the mentally ill and retarded should have special training. It will require their patience and understanding to ensure that these cases do not become a "waste and rote."

Enlightened programs in mental health and retardation conducted by state and private institutions have commenced and will grow because of the universal concern over these problems. The law will not impose obstacles to what proves to be both just and beneficial. It will promote these objectives. The judicial process can sharpen everyone's focus, correct mistakes, and hammer out justice. One hopes that the catalyst of court action will encourage state legislatures, state administrators, and professional people of all kinds to intensify their good efforts on behalf of mentally retarded citizens.

The Right to the Least Restrictive Alternative

Editorial Introduction

The material in this chapter is presented in a format slightly different from that of the material in other parts of the volume. Topically, it also overlaps some other chapters. The goal here is to explore a concept that may have special value and applicability to the legal rights of mentally retarded citizens. That concept is that the state must pursue its purposes by the least restrictive possible means appropriate to the achievement of its legitimate purposes.

The chapter begins with an exposition by Chambers of the technical legal nature of the principle of the least restrictive alternative. Professor Chambers draws upon his earlier work in this area to set forth the constitutional dimensions of the principle. He argues that the principle has the potential in constitutional litigation for securing relief for retarded citizens over a broad range of issues. He further argues that even when the constitution does not require the application of the principle, the principle may still provide a useful policy guide to legislators, to courts interpreting ambiguous statutes, and to administrators.

Chambers' analysis is followed by contributions from four mental retardation professionals who describe the potential for the application of this principle to four specific problems in which they have particular expertise: residential programing, education, guardianship, and law enforcement. These four discussions illustrate the versatility and value of the least restrictive alternative concept in dealing with innumerable policy and legal issues important to mentally retarded citizens.

THE PRINCIPLE OF THE LEAST RESTRICTIVE ALTERNATIVE: THE CONSTITUTIONAL ISSUES

DAVID CHAMBERS

THE PRINCIPLE OF THE LEAST RESTRICTIVE ALTERNATIVE

Mentally retarded people are people. When strong reasons exist to treat them differently from other people, they should be provided the necessary services, restraint, or protection through means that intrude as little as possible on their freedom to live the life that others are permitted to live. "Normalization" is the term professionals use to define the goal and the process of helping mentally retarded citizens lead a "normal" life. The attainment of this goal involves undoing the multitude of formal constrictions governments have typically placed on the retarded citizen's freedom: his place of residence, his schooling, his control over his own property, his freedom to marry —,in short, his freedom to do or be anything that others believe requires capacity to function "independently" and "responsibly."

The analysis here does not present data to demonstrate that normalization "works," but rather offers a legal resource to those who have found normalization does work and need help in securing its acceptance by courts and agencies.[1] The legal resource is the principle of the least restrictive alternative. The principle rests on the apple pie premise that people should in general be free to live as they please. If you accept this elementary moral premise, the principle of the least restrictive alternative easily follows; that is, when government does have a legitimate communal interest to serve by regulating human conduct it should use methods that curtail individual freedom to no greater extent than is essential for securing that interest. When you swat a mosquito on a friend's back, you should not use a baseball bat.

The principle of the least restrictive alternative is not only a useful guide to legislatures in deciding when and how to formulate new laws. It also has become a useful tool in constitutional litigation in working out rough accommodations between

---

[1] *See* Chambers, *Alternatives to Civil Commitment of the Mentally Ill: Practical Guides and Constitutional Imperatives,* 70 MICH. L. REV. 1107 (1972). Much of the paper that follows is a distillation of this article transplanted to the setting of mental retardation and applied to the range of official restrictions placed on retarded persons, rather than commitment alone.

constitutionally protected rights and weighty legislatively protected interests in the public's health, welfare, and safety. The Supreme Court of the United States, in the most frequently quoted recent statement of the principle, has declared that in judging governmental actions "even though the governmental purpose be legitimate and substantial, that purpose cannot be pursued by means that broadly stifle personal liberties when the end can be more narrowly achieved."[2]

Little can be said with confidence about how far the courts will go in applying the principle to regulations affecting the mentally retarded. Few courts have employed it yet in assessing regulations affecting the retarded. The Supreme Court has heard no cases posing the issue. Moreover, even if the principle is applied by courts, there are limits to what the principle can accomplish. Attorneys who employ the principle in the context of constitutional litigation can, however, develop strong arguments in three areas in which normalization efforts are proceeding: (1) in securing the broader use of already existing alternatives to constrictions upon the freedom of the retarded; (2) in securing individualized determinations, continually reexamined, of the current needs of each mentally retarded individual whose freedom is being curtailed; and (3) in securing the creation of a range of promising new alternatives that might be used to normalize the life style of retarded citizens. In the context of education, for example, the lawyer might strive to keep a mentally retarded child in the public school near her home or might seek to secure extra tutoring or special programing within the framework of the regular class. These efforts might avert later placement in a separate class or school for the mentally retarded. The lawyer may also seek to ensure that the child's needs are continually reassessed so that even limited special programing will continue no longer than necessary.

DRAFTING AND INTERPRETING STATUTES

Reliance upon constitutional safeguards will be unneeded if legislatures employ the principle of the least restrictive alternative or if courts interpret existing legislation to require application of the principle.

Emphasizing the treasures of a free life, the evidence of success for normalization programs, and the daily anxieties of persons who know that they do not appear "normal," attorneys need to encourage legislators to retain restrictive regulations for the mentally retarded only when informal noncoercive methods cannot achieve the same goals. When legislatures do continue restrictions, such as separate institutions, they should be urged for identical reasons to develop a full range of appropriate less restrictive regulations or settings. Legislatures are beginning to embody in new laws the concept of minimum intrusion into the lives of the mentally retarded. Tennessee, for example, has adopted legislation providing that, to the maximum extent possible, children are to be educated in the normal classroom setting.[3]

[2] Shelton v. Tucker, 364 U.S. 479, 488 (1960).
[3] TENN. CODE ANN. § 49-2913(B) (Supp. 1973).

Massachusetts has adopted a similar statute.[4] Nebraska, through flexible legislation, has developed an impressive range of residential treatment programs.[5] Several states explicitly authorize or compel their courts to use least restrictive alternatives in appropriate commitment cases.[6]

Even existing legislation not openly recognizing the principle can often be rendered more flexible through imaginative interpretation. No state, for example, requires the commitment of all mentally retarded persons. Courts can often sensibly interpret statutes, almost without regard to their operant language, to require the exploration and use of alternatives whenever the state's interest in securing adequate care and protection can be better served by other means. When confronted with vague or ambiguous statutory terms, attorneys can support arguments for the use of alternatives by pointing to the principle of the least restrictive alternative as an aid in interpreting legislative intent. That is, in the absence of convincing evidence to the contrary, legislation should not be interpreted to permit greater restrictions on personal freedom than are absolutely necessary to serve the state's interests. Attorneys also can brandish the constitutional arguments for the principle hereafter elaborated and invite the court to interpret the legislation as requiring the use of the least restrictive alternative "to save the constitutionality" of an otherwise offensive statute.[7] Even a guardianship statute that would appear to deprive a retarded individual of all of his legal capacity might be interpreted to permit or require the loss only of those specific powers that the retarded person was incapable of responsibly exercising.

Many statutes still in force that are grossly discriminatory against mentally retarded citizens were drafted at a time when most people were afraid of persons labeled as "idiots" or "naturals" and when even those who were concerned for the well-being of the mentally retarded person thought they needed absolute protection. Today, courts should wisely reinterpret their statutes, not only to achieve the state's original legitimate purposes, but also to achieve them in light of the new knowledge and public acceptance of successful less constricting alternatives for securing these purposes.

THE CONSTITUTIONAL ARGUMENTS FOR THE PRINCIPLE

On dozens of occasions the United States Supreme Court and state supreme courts have compelled state governments to achieve clearly legitimate goals by methods of regulation less constrictive of some important constitutionally protected interest than the methods being used. Though not yet applied by the Supreme Court to the mentally retarded, such precedents have obvious relevance to issues relating to mental retardation.

---

[4] Mass. Ann. Laws ch. 71 B, § 3 (Supp. 1972).

[5] Neb. Rev. Stat. §§ 83-1, 141-146 (Supp. 1969).

[6] New Mexico, for example, has adopted new legislation requiring courts to explore alternatives prior to commitment. N.M. Stat. Ann. § 13-14-39 (Supp. 1972).

[7] See Rouse v. Cameron, 373 F.2d 451 (D.C. Cir. 1966) (first case holding that patients in mental hospitals have a justiciable right to treatment; decided on statutory grounds with the court indicating that the Constitution was peering closely over its shoulder); accord, Townsend v. Swank, 404 U.S. 282, 291 (1971).

Two decisions of the Supreme Court offer illustrations.[8] In 1951, the Court struck down a ban placed by the city of Madison, Wisconsin, on the sale of milk processed more than 25 miles from the city.[9] The court invalidated the ordinance because it found that a less drastic method of inspection could fully serve the city's legitimate interest in protecting its citizens from spoiled or adulterated milk without entirely prohibiting the sale of nonlocal milk. In another case, decided in 1972, the Court examined a Tennessee statute requiring newcomers to reside in the state for 90 days before becoming eligible to vote.[10] Tennessee sought to justify the statute in part on the ground that it served to prevent fraud by persons who had not truly made the decision to become residents of Tennessee. Preventing fraud was a legitimate goal, but the 90-day residency requirement could not stand when there was an obvious alternative (checking places of former residence and checking drivers' licenses and car registrations) which did not deny constitutionally protected rights to bona fide new residents.

In terms of alternatives, this reasoning has obvious application to many of the regulations affecting the mentally retarded. For example, courts should not permit involuntary commitment if home care or a community group home can provide the needed protection and better equip the individual for independence. Courts and agencies should not permit placement in separate schools for mentally retarded children when extra assistance in regular public schools can properly educate the child and avoid the social stigma attendant upon segregation. Guardianship that denies a retarded citizen the right to make important life decisions should be avoided when the individual merely is incapable of handling one or two separable and specific kinds of responsibilities.

The application is obvious, but attorneys must leap one hurdle before they can be confident that courts and agencies will be required to apply the principle of the least restrictive alternative to state action affecting retarded citizens. The obstacle is that the Supreme Court and other courts do not apply the principle to all forms of regulations. The use of less restrictive alternatives is insisted upon only when the method of regulation used by the state affects interests that are considered especially sensitive under the Constitution, such as free speech, or are directed at groups against whom discrimination is regarded with especial suspicion by the Court, such as black Americans or aliens.[11] For example, courts will uphold a state regulation requiring sprinkler systems in apartment buildings without inquiring whether an

---

[8]Dunn v. Blumstein, 405 U.S. 330 (1972); Dean Milk Co. v. City of Madison, 340 U.S. 349 (1951). *See also* Police Dep't v. Mosley, 408 U.S. 92, 100-02 (1972); United States v. O'Brien, 391 U.S. 367, 377 (1968); Carrington v. Rash, 380 U.S. 89, 96 (1965); Shelton v. Tucker, 364 U.S. 479, 488 (1960); Butler v. Michigan, 352 U.S. 380 (1956); South Carolina State Highway Dep't v. Barnwell Bros., 303 U.S. 177, 190-91 (1938). For similar state court precedents, see City of Carmel-by-the-Sea v. Young, 2 Cal. 3d 259, 466 P.2d 225, 85 Cal. Rptr. 1 (1970); Schroder v. Binks, 415 Ill. 192, 195-201, 113 N.E.2d 169, 170-73 (1953); Altemose Constr. Co. v. Building and Constr. Trades Council, 449 Pa. 194, 212-13, 296 A.2d 504, 514-15 (1972) *cert. denied*, 411 U.S. 932 (1973). *See also* Chambers, *supra* note 1, at 1145-51; Wormuth & Mirkin, *The Doctrine of the Reasonable Alternative*, 9 UTAH L. REV. 254 (1964).
[9]Dean Milk Co. v. City of Madison, 340 U.S. 349, 354-56 (1951).
[10]Dunn v. Blumstein, 405 U.S. 330, 343, 347-49 (1972).
[11]*See* San Antonio Independent School Dist. v. Rodriguez, 411 U.S. 1, 18, 51 (1973); *rehearing denied*, 411 U.S. 959 (most recent elaboration on the circumstances in which the Court will and will not subject a state statute to rigorous examination).

alternative form of protection to tenants that is less costly for the landlord is available.[12] They will even uphold restrictive welfare legislation which discriminates against larger families without examining claims that narrower legislation not working such hardships would serve the state's interests.[13] The Madison milk ordinance imposed a burden on interstate commerce, an activity expressly protected in the Constitution. Tennessee's voting residency requirement affected two rights afforded special protection under the Constitution: voting in political elections and travel among the states. On the other hand, the laws requiring fire sprinklers and those providing a lesser portion of needs to larger families on welfare than smaller families were immune from inquiry into alternatives because they affected no constitutionally sensitive group or interest. Despite the fact that these laws were of critical importance to the individual's livelihood and sustenance, they were found to have no special place in the Constitution.

Thus, the first task for the court asked to find a constitutional obligation to use or explore alternatives to state regulations for retarded citizens is to ask whether the regulations affect a constitutionally preferred interest or constitutionally protected group. Elsewhere in this volume, contributors have presented arguments that answer this question affirmatively.[14] One of these arguments would eliminate most special regulations of the mentally retarded. It is, quite simply, that all laws which regulate the mentally retarded as a class should, like laws overtly based on race or legitimacy of birth, be regarded as constitutionally suspect and subjected to close judicial review. An essential point is that these arguments have considerable merit, but no court has yet accepted them, one court has rejected them,[15] and the most liberal members of the Supreme Court in some recent dicta seem to accept as nonsuspect regulations based on intelligence.[16]

If the Court *does* begin to treat as suspect regulation of the mentally retarded as a separate class, *all* special regulation adversely affecting the retarded should be subject to examination for less restrictive alternatives. If the Court refuses to recognize mental retardation as a suspect classification, arguments that courts should compel inquiries into alternatives (or order the creation of alternatives) must focus on special constitutional protections for particular forms of conduct. Arguments about some of these especially sensitive types of regulation are found elsewhere in this volume. For example, state laws limiting the freedom of retarded individuals to marry or procreate interfere with federally recognized rights to privacy in marital relations.[17] Courts appropriately might require case-by-case inquiry into the necessity of discriminatory curtailment to serve legitimate state interests.

Civil commitment of the mentally retarded also intrudes on the constitutionally

[12]Queenside Hill Realty Co. v. Saxl, 328 U.S. 80, 83 (1946).

[13]Dandridge v. Williams, 397 U.S. 471, 484, 486 (1970).

[14]*See* Gilhool, pp. 173-207, Chapter 7 of this volume; Burt, pp. 418-37, Chapter 14 of this volume.

[15]*See* New York State Ass'n for Retarded Children, Inc. v. Rockefeller, 357 F. Supp. 752, 767 (E.D.N.Y. 1973).

[16]Frontiero v. Richardson, 411 U.S. 677, 686 (1973).

[17]*See* Wald, pp. 7-15, Chapter 1 of this volume.

protected rights of travel and free association. Moreover, some Supreme Court decisions indicate a special sensitivity to regulations permitting incarceration, without reference to other specific freedoms that incarceration inhibits.[18] Reflecting this concern, three recent federal court decisions have held that prior to involuntary hospitalization of the mentally ill, the Constitution requires a demonstration that there are no suitable less restrictive alternatives.[19] In addition, the order entered by the trial court in *Wyatt v. Stickney* bars commitment of a retarded person to an institution "unless a prior determination shall have been made that residence in that institution is the least restrictive habilitation setting feasible for that person." [20]

Unfortunately, not all regulation of mentally retarded citizens affects activities considered especially sensitive by the Supreme Court. For example, at least under the United States Constitution, separate schooling for a retarded child may be permissible even though a less restrictive alternative is available, simply because the Supreme Court has found that the regulation of education, a subject nowhere mentioned in the Constitution, does not call for raised eyebrows in all cases.[21] State constitutional provisions establishing a system of public education may provide a basis for special judicial attention to regulations regarding education, but courts might well hold that such provisions at most require the state to offer some type of education to all children, retarded or otherwise, but carry no implications about the setting in which the education should occur.[22]

Similarly, government-condoned discrimination in employment (such as in the federal law permitting a lower than minimum wage for physically or mentally impaired workers)[23] does not seem to intrude on constitutionally protected rights, despite the fact that few aspects of a person's life are more important than the financial resources he needs to sustain himself. The possibility that discriminatory regulations in areas of vital importance to individual retarded citizens will be immune from invalidation on the ground of available less restrictive alternatives underscores the importance to attorneys for retarded citizens of inducing courts to view the mentally retarded as a suspect class.

[18] *See* Chambers, *supra* note 1, at 1180-1200 (arguments developed in the context of the mentally ill).

[19] Covington v. Harris, 419 F.2d 617 (D.C. Cir. 1969); Lessard v. Schmidt, 349 F. Supp. 1078 (E.D Wis. 1972), *vacated for entry of definitive decree,* 414 U.S. 473 (1974) (holding the trial court's order to be insufficiently specific and detailed under the Federal Rules of Civil Procedure), *clarified,* 379 F. Supp. 1376 (E.D. Wisc. 1974), *vacated on procedural grounds,* 95 S.Ct. 1943 (1975); Dixon v. Attorney General, 325 F. Supp. 966 (M.D. Pa. 1971).

[20] Wyatt v. Stickney, 344 F. Supp. 387, 396 (M.D. Ala. 1972), *aff'd sub nom.* Wyatt v. Aderholt, 503 F.2d 1305 (5th Cir. 1974).

[21] *See* San Antonio Independent School Dist. v. Rodriguez, 411 U.S. 1 (1973).

[22] *See* IND. CONST. art. 8, § 1 (providing that public schools shall be "equally open to all"); ILL. CONST. art 10, § 1 (providing for the educational development of all persons "to the limits of their capabilities"); N.J. CONST. art. 8, § 4, para. 1 ("through an efficient system of free public schools for the instruction of all the children in the state"); N.Y. CONST. art. 11, § 1 (public schools established so that "all children of this state may be educated"); WASH. CONST. art. 9, § 1 ("paramount of the state to make ample provision for the education of all children . . . without the distinction or account of . . . caste . . .").

[23] *See* Fair Labor Standards Act, 29 U.S.C. § 214(d) (1970).

THE MANY APPLICATIONS OF THE PRINCIPLE TO REGULATIONS AFFECTING THE MENTALLY RETARDED

Whenever it is properly applied, the principle of the least restrictive alternative requires first an articulation by the affected court or agency of the interests the state seeks to serve through the law (or regulation) at issue, for it is only through identifying the state interests that the court can determine what alternative methods may be substituted. In the process of articulating interests, courts are forced (if they act properly) to identify and reject impermissible interests that may have been the basis of the law. Thus, for mentally retarded citizens, alternatives to commitment should be assessed in terms of whether they provide needed protection or habilitation, not in terms of their effectiveness in serving the partially motivating, but improper, function of simply screening from sight persons who make others in society feel uncomfortable.[24] In defending its ban on milk processed at a distance from the city, Madison was similarly precluded from relying on its improper interest of protecting its local milk producers from outside competition.[25]

Once interests are identified, the principle can secure varied forms of relief. The most narrow, but perhaps most significant, relief is in the context of methods of regulation requiring case-by-case determination of a retarded person's need for differential treatment (*i.e.*, a civil commitment proceeding or a system for placement in a separate school). In such cases, the principle calls at a minimum for an individualized inquiry into the current availability of less restrictive alternatives that would serve the state's interests. This is the use to which the principle has been put in the context of the civil commitment of the mentally ill.[26] Irrespective of the system that exists and no matter how informally it operates currently, the principle can be used to demand an adequate unbiased inquiry into existing alternatives.

The principle (coupled with well-developed notions of due process of law)[27] also can properly be used to ensure that the search for less restrictive alternatives occurs before, and not after, the more restrictive placement occurs. Because mental retardation is rarely a condition with a sudden or insidious onset, hasty intervention should seldom be required and only in the rarest instance should a person whose only handicap is retardation be placed in a confining institution or a separate school prior to an inquiry into whether the placement is necessary at all.

---

[24] *Cf.* Papachristou v. City of Jacksonville, 405 U.S. 156, 170-71 (1972) (striking down, as unconstitutionally vague, a vagrancy statute aimed at "common night walkers," which served to round up "so-called undesirables"); Coates v. City of Cincinnati, 402 U.S. 611 (1971) (Ohio statute prohibiting "annoying" assembly by three or more people on sidewalk held violative of rights of free assembly and association).

[25] Dean Milk Co. v. City of Madison, 340 U.S. at 354-56.

[26] *See* Covington v. Harris, 419 F.2d 617 (D.C. Cir. 1969); Lessard v. Schmidt, 349 F. Supp. 1078 (E.D. Wisc. 1972) *vacated for entry of definitive decree,* 414 U.S. 473 (1974), *clarified,* 379 F. Supp. 1376 (E.D. Wisc. 1974), *vacated on procedural grounds,* 95 S. Ct. 1943 (1975); Dixon v. Attorney General, 325 F. Supp. 966 (M.D. Pa. 1971).

[27] *See* Goldberg v. Kelly, 397 U.S. 254 (1970); Chambers, *supra* note 1, at 1178-82.

A second extension of the principle would be to require case-by-case determinations where none are currently required. For example, the principle could be used to require individualized inquiries into and use of alternatives under statutes imposing absolute bans on marriage for institutionalized retarded persons.[28] Similarly, the principle can easily be used to compel individualized periodic reexamination of placements or restrictions to determine their continued necessity.[29]

Yet bolder uses of the principle lie in waiting. The principle may be a useful tool to lawyers in securing the removal of legal barriers to the use of currently available alternatives. For example, if a public or private agency is repeatedly blocked by zoning regulations from placing a group home in a residential area,[30] attorneys can argue that the state may not continue to confine retarded persons in institutions and retain their zoning regulations when group homes would adequately serve the needs of the institutionalized individuals. In such a case, a court striking down a zoning regulation would have to find either that the purposes underlying the zoning regulation would not be adversely served by permitting placement of the home or that (and here is an extension of the principle) the value of permitting the less restrictive home justified some intrusion in the state's interests in permitting restrictive zoning.[31]

Striking out even further, the principle may be used to compel the creation of new alternative programs or facilities (such as group homes in the community) even when no agency as yet stands ready to erect them. Many Supreme Court decisions have compelled states to choose between foregoing regulation of certain conduct altogether (such as the regulation of nonlocal milk) or adopting a new method of regulation not currently in existence.[32] Courts might similarly hold that states need not create systems of involuntary (or fictionally voluntary) commitment of mentally retarded persons, but if they do, they must create a full range of less confining residential settings so that no one is confined in a setting more restrictive of his freedom than is necessary.[33] The same argument can be made for compelling the creation of a diverse range of educational programs, so long as the state compels attendance of some mentally retarded children at segregated institutions. For institutionalized children, the creation of alternatives other than their own family homes, which may no longer be available, may be indispensable to their release.

The right to habilitation, developed in *Wyatt v. Stickney* and discussed elsewhere

---

[28] *See* Stanley v. Illinois, 405 U.S. 645 (1972) (Illinois forced to replace a system in which fathers of illegitimate children were barred absolutely from receiving custody of child with a system in which case-by-case determinations of fitness were made).

[29] Covington v. Harris, 419 F.2d 617 (D.C. Cir. 1969) (a case dealing with the degree of confinement within a hospital after the initial hospitalization had occurred long before).

[30] *See* Chandler & Ross, Chapter 11 of this volume.

[31] *See* Southern Pacific Co. v. Arizona, 325 U.S. 761 (1945) (openly weighing whether harm to state of having no regulation at all over train lengths was outweighed by value of protecting federal constitutional interest in unimpeded flow of interstate commerce).

[32] *See e.g.,* Shelton v. Tucker, 364 U.S. 479 (1960); Dean Milk Co. v. City of Madison, 340 U.S. 349 (1951).

[33] *See* Chambers, *supra* note 1, at 1180-1200 (arguments developed in the context of the mentally ill). A lawsuit has recently been filed in the District of Columbia through attorneys at the Mental Health Law Project seeking to force the creation of adequate alternatives to mental hospitalization for persons currently confined at St. Elizabeth's hospital. Robinson v. Weinberger, Civil No.

in this volume,[34] has in this context essentially the same potential for encouraging the creation of new programs. Under either rubric, courts have to assay the costs that government must pay as the price for continuing to incarcerate many mentally retarded citizens. In determining the forms of habilitation to be required, courts will find that experts disagree on the precise components of an adequate system of residential or educational alternatives for mentally retarded individuals. Courts may be even more puzzled by state claims that they cannot afford to create the alternatives but cannot humanely give up the institutions altogether. This seems in part to be Alabama's claimed dilemma in *Wyatt* argued through the veil (as seductive as Salome's) of the inappropriateness of judicial intrusion into this essentially legislative domain. But the judiciary has a duty to protect individual liberty, even if a consequence of this duty is to compel a redirection of funds away from programs not involving such constriction on individual liberty.[35] The effectiveness of the principle of the least restrictive alternative requires not only judicial boldness in framing an initial decree, but also steadfastness in overseeing its implementation.

Even beyond compelling the creation of alternatives to specific programs, the principle conceivably might be used to force the creation of preventive programs to ensure that institutionalization or separate education will not be necessary in the future. Phenylketonuria (PKU) testing programs, controls over lead-based paint, prenatal nutritional programs, and even broad income maintenance systems can all be justified by the principle so long as involuntary losses of freedom await some citizens who would become retarded without such programs. The costs of the development and implementation of such programs may possibly call into question the propriety of judicial use of the principle at all. For the principle brings with it an unbroken continuum of pressures on the state to avoid unnecessary deprivations of liberty. But drawing lines through undivided middles has been the magic of common law courts, and hopefully in the field of mental retardation, courts and future legislators will draw these lines toward the edge of the continuum where many current legislators still wince.

THREE PROBLEMS FOR ATTORNEYS

Three obstacles to successful application of the principle merit further consideration. The first two—state claims that placement in the restrictive setting is voluntary and that placement or regulation is the only avenue adequately serving the state's interest of maximum protection for the retarded person—may influence courts to hold that the principle does not apply at all or to apply the principle and still routinely permit the use of the most restrictive placement. The third obstacle—the inadequacy of current systems for exploring alternatives in individual cases—may not deter

---

[34] *See* Halpern, Chapter 13 of this volume; Burt, Chapter 14 of this volume.

[35] In a way, suits to compel the creation of new programs involve a dangerous bluff: The state can evade a court order by closing the attacked institution or school. Such closings may be disadvantageous for some residents or students if no other appropriate programs exist.

courts from holding that the principle applies, but may render useless any favorable holding that is reached.

The Myth of Voluntariness

States are likely to claim that participation in many forms of separate treatment for the mentally retarded is voluntary or that persons held are free to leave at any time.[36] If states permitted commitment to residential institutions or special schools for the retarded only when the individual voluntarily chose participation, courts might reject arguments that states must create new less restrictive alternatives (or even that they must explore existing ones). The courts might reason that the obligation to use alternatives that maximize freedom applies only when the government is seeking by force to remove an individual's freedom.

There are several responses to this position. In the first place, if courts accept the argument that disfavored treatment of persons labeled mentally retarded is constitutionally suspect, then establishing voluntary forms of segregation would arguably be as constitutionally unacceptable for the mentally retarded as the "freedom of choice" plans adopted by racially segregated school systems in response to court orders requiring elimination of racial segregation.[37] Continued reliance on the totally confining institution, even if it is operated on a voluntary commitment basis, unnecessarily perpetuates the stigma of mental retardation for both institutionalized and noninstitutionalized retarded citizens. However enticing the analogy to race discrimination may be, it is unlikely that courts will in fact borrow for the mentally retarded the full range of judicial techniques developed to attack racial segregation. Under the Constitution, racial segregation now occupies the lowest ring in hell, and courts have acted with greater aggression to uproot it than they are likely to display for any other form of institutionalized intolerance.

A more promising method of attack on claims that programs are "voluntary" is to argue that in reality the programs are "involuntary" in that they are chosen in an atmosphere of drastic governmentally threatened consequences or under misapprehensions about the consequences of not accepting such programs.[38] For example, a parent's seemingly voluntary choice of school placement might be considered involuntary if the alternative to separate placement were the child's removal from the school system. A parent's decision (or even the retarded person's own decision) might similarly be considered involuntary if not made with full disclosure about conditions and about the services provided in the school, available alternatives, and the reduced likelihood of the individual's reintegration into the community.

---

[36] *See* New York State Ass'n for Retarded Children, Inc. v. Rockefeller, 357 F. Supp. 752, 759-60 (E.D.N.Y. 1973).

[37] *See, e.g.,* Boson v. Rippy, 285 F.2d 43 (5th Cir. 1960). Even in the race area, freedom of choice plans carefully drawn to ensure that choice was voluntary and that the schools were not otherwise segregated by law have been sustained. *See* Stell v. Savannah-Chatham County Bd. of Educ., 333 F.2d 55, 65 (5th Cir. 1964), *cert. denied,* 379 U.S. 933 (1964).

[38] *See, e.g.,* Rogers v. Richmond, 368 U.S. 534 (1961).

Finally, a parent's "voluntary" decision should almost never be considered voluntary as to the child, for the interests of parents and child (especially when the parents are considering expelling him from their home) may conflict greatly.[39] The consequence of refusing to recognize the parent's choice as voluntary would be that courts or agencies would make an independent inquiry into alternatives. (The parents' own attitude about placing their child could, of course, still be considered as one important factor in judging the adequacy of a home-based alternative program.)

The State's Interest in Protecting the Retarded Person

Courts can be expected to require the use of the least restrictive alternative only when it serves the state's legitimate interests at least as well as (or, perhaps, not much less satisfactorily than) the more restrictive program the state is seeking to impose on the retarded person.

One goal of many governmental restrictions on the mentally retarded person is to protect him from his own inadequacies. The most restrictive form of regulation —for example, commitment to a distant institution or absolute guardianship—will nearly always maximize this protection. Judges who are often concerned solely or primarily with ensuring such protection[40] are understandably reluctant to run the risk that their failure to have ordered the most restrictive alternative will later lead to some incident for which they may be blamed. Thus, judges may honestly apply the principle and still reject the retarded person's plea for greater freedom.

Attorneys must be well prepared to respond to this defensive behavior. They must try to show that protection is not the only goal of the legislation in issue and point to other goals, if they exist, such as habilitation or maximizing capacity for independent decision making. Even accepting the primacy of a goal of protection, attorneys should try to show that many retarded persons need far less protection than is commonly believed and that a high degree of protective segregation will largely undermine the ability of the retarded person to develop personal independence. Attorneys should, in short, be sympathetic to the judge's concerns, but they also must show him that a greater degree of freedom best serves the judge's own goals.

The Need for Systems to Ensure That Alternatives Are Explored

Because the most likely use of the principle for the retarded citizen lies in compelling the use of existing less restrictive alternatives to institutional commitment or separate schooling, there is a need to emphasize the difficulties of ensuring that alternatives are actually explored even after courts decree that a search for alter-

---

[39] See Murdock, *Civil Rights of the Mentally Retarded: Some Critical Issues,* 48 NOTRE D. LAW. 133, 139-43, 154-55, 156-58 (1972).
[40] See Lake v. Cameron, 267 F. Supp. 155, 158-59 (D.D.C. 1967) (excessively protective attitude of federal district judge).

natives is mandatory. In 1966, the United States Court of Appeals for the District of Columbia Circuit ordered that alternatives to hospitalization for the mentally ill be explored in all cases and used where appropriate.[41] The government, according to the court, bore the burden of performing the search. In the vast bulk of commitment proceedings since conducted in the District, however, little or no exploration of alternatives has occurred because, at least until recently, there was no one to carry out the search. Attorneys were ignorant of the alternatives and too overworked to explore them, the committing authority and the reviewing court were understaffed, and the person who was being committed usually was unable to discover alternatives.

The same problem is likely to exist for the mentally retarded. Thus, a bare holding that alternatives to any compulsory procedure must be explored on a case-by-case basis is by itself of small value. Attorneys must seek to ensure that alternatives are in fact routinely assessed. The same court that holds that a retarded person has a right to the least restrictive suitable placement can appropriately hold that the right must be implemented by systems to ensure that alternatives are adequately brought to the attention of decision makers.

The appropriate system for exploring alternatives will vary with the nature of the issue (residential placement, guardianship, schooling) and the nature of the decision maker (judge, school official, institutional administrator). The task of seeking alternatives to implement court decisions might be entrusted to court personnel, just as probation officers now typically advise criminal and juvenile courts on community placement.[42] The analogy is more compelling than may initially appear. Specially trained court personnel could not only help locate community alternatives, but could also play a role in monitoring the progress of the retarded persons involved. They may also infuse judges with enthusiasm for developing new community programs. Another approach to implementing less restrictive alternatives would be the development of a separate agency with a staff of lay or professional advocates, perhaps attached to an agency providing legal representation. Already in use in some legal services agencies for the mentally ill, such an independent advocacy service can serve a similar function in the context of placements for mentally retarded persons.

In both commitment and educational decisions, the state may prefer to rely on an investigation of alternatives conducted by staff persons working for the agency operating the very restrictive placement the retarded person may wish to avoid. Because of the obvious conflict of interests between retarded citizens and those who are employed in the most confining and restrictive programs, exclusive reliance on such an arrangement should be avoided.

Whatever the system created, the important point is this: Any court that accepts the principle of the least restrictive alternative must also concern itself with the method for implementing the principle. Attorneys filing class suits or appealing

---

[41] Lake v. Cameron, 364 F.2d 657 (D.C. Cir. 1966). *See also* Chambers, *supra* note 1, at 1168-69 (discussion of implementation of *Lake*).

[42] *See* R. DAWSON, SENTENCING: THE DECISION AS TO TYPE, LENGTH AND CONDITIONS OF SENTENCE (1969) (describes the function of probation officers in sentencing).

individual cases need to address explicitly the abstract constitutional principle and its implementation as well.

THE LIMITATIONS OF THE PRINCIPLE AND
THE LIMITATIONS OF ATTORNEYS

The principle of the least restrictive alternative cannot alone, even if broadly accepted by courts, compel the development of the necessary variety of affirmative programs for mentally retarded citizens. Those who seek normalization walk a wobbly tightrope. To them, normalization does not mean the elimination of special programs for the mentally retarded. Rather, they seek elaborate but subtle special programs to help each mentally retarded person learn to live as nearly as possible at his own optimum level. The natural vector of the principle of the least restrictive alternative lies in the dismantling of restrictions. To the extent that it is a useful tool in arguing for the creation of community-based programs, its utility is premised on the continued existence of more restrictive programs. If acceptance of the concept of normalization of institutions and programs causes states to close their restrictive institutions and programs for the retarded, the principle would offer little aid in compelling the creation of new programs in the community. This emphasizes the point that the principle is not an affirmative right that can compel special programs if a state decides to do nothing. Today, while many restrictions remain, the principle of the least restrictive alternative can be very effective, but even today attorneys seeking special programs for the mentally retarded should couple the principle with statutory and constitutional arguments that are less intrinsically negative in their tone.

A broader warning is in order. The lawyer seeking alternatives for the mentally retarded, the mentally ill, or other segregated groups has a great responsibility. Class action lawsuits that fail may appear to vindicate current practices and impede efforts for change for the lawyer's own clients and thousands of others across the country. Class actions that succeed may produce hastily devised alternative placements or the release of institutional residents without the necessary community systems to support them. When lawyers seek to persuade courts to do what legislatures ought to have done, they bear a weighty burden to do what legislatures ought to do before they act. In this context, lawyers need to inform themselves about the varying capacities and needs of retarded citizens and the range and effectiveness of alternatives to whatever confining institution, program, or regulation they seek to dismantle. They need to visit the institutions and special programs for retarded persons and sit down and get to know some of their clients.

In some ways, attorneys involved in test cases are uniquely situated to act irresponsibly, often having no real client other than their own moral convictions, no accountability to an electorate, and no responsibility even to bear the brunt of a judicial opinion as their own. To date the attorneys who have been involved in the major litigation for retarded citizens have generally borne well the burden of becoming informed, keeping informed, and acting with caution. As lawsuits for the benefit of the mentally retarded proliferate, the legal profession must ensure that newly involved lawyers continue to meet the same high standards.

THE LEAST RESTRICTIVE ALTERNATIVE IN RESIDENTIAL CARE AND THE PRINCIPLE OF NORMALIZATION

LINDA GLENN

THE PRINCIPLE OF NORMALIZATION

Too often, as soon as an individual is identified as mentally retarded, he is placed in a group of individuals considered by this society as deviant or different. Individuals within such groups are expected to act deviantly and have as models only other handicapped persons. Thus, the labeled individual does act deviantly (reinforcing the initial perception of him as deviant) and, therefore, is maintained in deviant groups. The circle is endless. Even the associations and friendships established by the individual become a part of this culture. And often, staff who work within service programs add to this deviancy subculture (*e.g.,* unlicensed doctors, uncertified teachers, prisoners, persons with personal problems of their own). The managers of programs for the mentally retarded create a subculture of deviancy that will, in almost every case, trap a retarded individual for life.

Too often programs for the mentally retarded, especially institutional programs, interpret the label of mental retardation to mean that an individual needs sheltering in *all* spheres of his life. Total control is exerted in all areas: residence, recreation, worship, shopping, sex, marriage, education, training, and employment. Through such global provision of services and control, institutions strip mentally retarded citizens of all rights of self-determination and independence. Most retarded individuals are referred for services because they present a particular difficulty for important "others," such as parents, teachers, or neighbors. This difficulty is usually stated in terms of unacceptable behavior or the lack of behavioral competence in one or possibly two major spheres of life. An individual may have difficulty living independently and allocating leisure time appropriately, but be perfectly capable of competitive employment. Conversely, he may need a more sheltered and protective environment in which to work or receive educational or vocational training, but he may still be capable of living with his own family. By their very nature, however, institutions cannot allow mentally retarded residents to maintain their freedom of choice and independence in those areas in which they are capable. All aspects of institutional life are structured, controlled, and planned. Residential programs tend to be not the least, but the most, restrictive imaginable. If a mentally retarded individual needs only residential assistance, he should receive only that. If he needs only guidance in use of his leisure time in appropriate and accepted ways, he should receive this assistance and be left with the responsibility to exercise free choice in the other areas of his life.

This overcontrol, combined with attitudes toward mentally retarded people as nondeveloping organisms, rather than as the adaptive, developing persons that they are, has resulted in services which are supposed to meet the needs of every mentally retarded person. These programs usually group people according to age, degree of handicap, or some other global classification. The result can be seen in institutional services which in fact are not expected to and do not meet any individual's needs. An examination of widely divergent individual needs of mentally retarded persons emphasizes that such a scheme is not and cannot be satisfactory. The range of specialized needs is as wide, if not wider, in the field of mental retardation as it is among the nonretarded population. This phenomenon of building one box that everyone is supposed to fit into has resulted in the existing restrictions on the developmental growth of the mentally retarded. Services have been distorted. For example, a ward with 50 or more individuals may be locked at night because a single individual has a tendency to wander off or simply because it is easier to operate a ward when it is secured. Thus, *all* residents of the ward must sleep behind locked doors. The professional response has been to the lowest common denominator, a response which has not provided for developmental growth or individual self-determination.

The myth of staffing ratios is another example of responding to the lowest common denominator. There is a general misconception that high staffing ratios within programs are necessarily good. High staffing ratios in a classroom or residential facility are an indication to the clients, the staff, and the public that the clients are potentially very deviant and that they need controls more than support. If the facilities and programs are specialized and small, however, the need for a high staffing ratio diminishes and the program therefore can be seen as less restrictive. A high staffing ratio is usually necessary only for the most specialized (*e.g.*, behavior shaping, developmental maximization) services which are short-term and transitional in nature.

Understanding and applying the principle of normalization at an operational level is essential in the establishment of new service models, especially community residential facilities. Understanding the ramifications of program process and societal interpretation is also important. Historically, developmental opportunities and services given a mentally retarded person were determined in large measure by how he was perceived by others. The retarded citizen was perceived as an object of pity, a menace, a danger to society, and a danger to himself and others. Thus, the services focused on long-term care and custody in isolation from the rest of society. These perceptions and society's response to them have resulted in the large, overcrowded, understaffed, remote, and very protective institutions typical of present programs in many states.

Normalization, on the other hand, dictates that programing should be concerned with the individual's growth and with how he is interpreted to persons who work with him, ιο the public, and to himself. Of paramount concern is how programs can assist a person in presenting himself to others more acceptably. Unfortunately, in the field of human services this important interpretation dimension is not fully internalized, and the importance and effect it has on the mentally retarded individual's growth and community adjustment are not fully understood. Normalization dictates that program managers be not only clinically concerned with skill development, but also alert to ways of helping the client improve in areas that will make him more acceptable in the mainstream of his community.

The principle of normalization is deceptively simple, requiring that service delivery practices enable a person considered different by society to function within the acceptable norms of his community. Thus, the means employed for training should be as culturally normative as possible. The reason that some mentally retarded citizens are institutionalized is that they have not fit the acceptable norms of the community. It is the task of program managers and service advocates to help mentally retarded persons attain social approval by working with behavior, appearance, and intellectual functioning. If the ultimate goal is the individual's optimal level of self-sufficiency, then the program processes and content that are used should be as close as possible to those typically utilized in the normal culture. Only in this way will retarded citizens develop more normal adult behavior and improve their relations with others.

In terms of program practices in the field of mental retardation, the normalization principle has many specific implications.[1] These implications can be examined in five major areas: integration, appropriate interpretations and structures, specialization, developmental growth orientation, and quality of setting.

INTEGRATION

The ultimate goal of human management personnel is to enable clients to obtain acceptance and function as independently as possible in the community. Integration can be either physical or social, but the ultimate goal is social integration. Although physical integration is a prerequisite to social integration, physical integration alone does not mean that an individual is utilizing the available services effectively or is accepted by society as an individual with the right to receive these services. Physical integration requires that services and social opportunities be nearby and that the client have access to his own home and to a community which is not already saturated with persons who have special needs. Normalization assumes a normal environment.

Physical integration also requires that the size of the client population in any facility be small. As the clientele grows, programs tend to become inwardly oriented. Large numbers do not use outside resources well; they tend to bring things in.

---

[1] *See* W. Wolfensberger, Normalization (National Institute on Mental Retardation, Toronto, 1972); W. Wolfensberger & L. Glenn, Program Analysis of Service Systems (National Institute on Mental Retardation, Toronto, 1973).

Physically integrated clients go out and make friends among the general population, using resources available to all. Smaller facilities provide opportunities for a client to be perceived by the community as an individual, not as a deviant. For example, in an apartment building, one apartment used as a residential training site for mentally retarded adults would not be noticed and the persons living there would not be likely to be perceived as different, even in an intensive training program. A whole floor utilized in an apartment building (or a whole building) can stigmatize all individuals in the residence.

Once physical integration is achieved, program managers must be concerned with social integration. Several aspects of social acceptability involve the physical facility (*e.g.*, its name and the appearance of the building). If the building looks much different from any that surround it, those receiving services are going to be perceived as different, thus reducing their chances of social integration. The history of a facility is also important. If mentally retarded persons are served in a facility that traditionally was used for tubercular, emotionally disturbed, or aged persons, their chances of acceptance into the social mainstream of the community are greatly diminished. There must also be concern with the labels given to programs and facilities. Too often facilities have stigmatizing names that elicit pity (such as Hope, Haven, or Friendship) or are highly demeaning or point out the fact that they serve the handicapped. Programs that have been named "sheltered," or "workshop," or "program for the mentally retarded" are obvious. Persons using the services are automatically stigmatized. Public reaction to a person going to the same building would be much different if the building were identified as an "industry" instead of a "sheltered workshop," even though the same type of activities may be involved. Program managers must take responsibility for doing as much as possible to improve the image of persons being served. Often, pressure from program funding sources for visibility needs to be resisted in order to avoid stigmatizing designations.

In typical community life, daily social interaction provides innumerable occasion and role expectations that have implications for the normalization process. Normalization dictates that programs provide many opportunities in all aspects of the mentally retarded person's life for interaction with persons who are non-retarded. These opportunities should be part of his educational, vocational, recreational, and social activities.

Program structures must maximize contact with nonhandicapped persons for several reasons. First, normal behavior of the nonhandicapped serves as a model to help retarded persons develop appropriate behavior. Second, the societal interpretation of the retarded person is positively influenced by associations with persons who are nonretarded. Each person has the right to friendships and associations with persons who are not also in need of special assistance.

In the past, deviant clients have always been placed among other deviant clients, thereby reducing their range of social contacts. In addition, the problem often has been compounded by permitting some or even most of the staff working with deviant groups to be deviant themselves. A common phenomenon in human management is for deviant persons to drift into employment where they work with clients who are also considered deviant. A teacher who cannot cope with regular pupils or who is not licensed may be put in charge of a special education class. A physician who does not have a license to practice in the community is permitted to practice in institutions for the retarded or disordered. Prisoners are placed in training or work with the mentally retarded. Retarded workers may be placed as orderlies in homes for the aged. There is a real risk that, instead of the intended mutual benefits, all the involved parties may be socially hindered by reinforcing the appearance of a deviancy subculture.

Normalization requires that integrative social opportunities be provided in all spheres of a person's life. Handicapped children should be integrated into generic early education programs and into regular classrooms, instead of being placed in segregated schools or even segregated classes within a school. Vocational training also can be carried into generic programs, as well as the mainstream of business and industry; it need not always be conducted in special workshops. Retarded individuals can participate in recreational activities with other citizens, often without any special treatment. Special support and training will enable many handicapped persons to utilize community transportation, eliminating the requirement for special car pools and segregated buses. The list of opportunities for integration is virtually endless. Unfortunately, opportunities are too often limited by the lack of imagination in program creation and implementation.

Appropriate Interpretations and Structures

Normalization implies that an individual should be able to project a normal image. The rationale for this is twofold. First, as stated, an individual's image affects the way he is treated. A person perceived as different is very apt to elicit pity or to meet with rejection, persecution, and other behaviors which tend to diminish his dignity, adjustment, and growth. Second, the way an individual is treated by others will affect his self-image and shape his responses. Considerations of interpretations and structures must be based on the client's age, as well as normal cultural trends.

The issue of age-appropriate placement, so important in the field of mental retardation, is the one most commonly misunderstood or unconsciously violated. Unfortunately, mental retardation personnel have been bound by the concept of mental age, without recognizing the importance of appropriate chronological age interpretation of the person. Mental retardation personnel, especially when serving adolescents and adults, typically reinforce childlike behavior. This is done through a variety of means, including the types of facilities provided and the types of decorations and appointments used within the facility. Adult clients are not encouraged to value adult possessions. Adults are talked to as if they were children and are given childlike activities (*e.g.,* preschool educational materials for older adolescents, childrens' educational equipment for adults). Daily routines are more childlike and less demanding than necessary, and even recreational activities are inappropriately geared toward the lower mental age. Autonomy, legal rights, and sexual behavior appropriate for different age levels are ignored or repressed.

Programs must provide support systems and media which enable the client to look and behave appropriately and acquire an optimal amount of self-determination.

Normalization focuses on two aspects of cultural interpretations and structures which transcend the chronological age of the person: labels and personal appearance. The use of outmoded labels, such as "retardate," which stigmatize the client and make him appear more as a clinical object than a person, must be avoided. Culturally appropriate personal appearance relates to those issues which make an individual seem different: dress, mannerisms, and stereotyped behavior. Program managers should be so attuned to the importance of a person's appearance and how it affects his behavior as to provide inconspicuous prosthetic devices and allocate resources to cosmetic and corrective surgery. Some stigma are virtually insurmountable, but many can be reduced or eliminated. Failure to attend systematically and intensively to the reduction of stigma undermines the image of the client.

Specialization

Specialization refers to the interrelationships and coherence among many program and staff variables, with the central theme that all variables should combine harmoniously to meet the specific needs of each client at a given time in his life. Grouping of clientele should parallel comparable grouping of other citizens living in the community; in light of the group's function, consideration should be given to the size of the group, sex, and age range of members. The human management model, the program content, and the program process must be consistent with each other and designed to meet the specific needs of the population served. The program content should reflect the specialized skills and abilities of the staff. Specialization of program process allows for the development of continuums of program options. As a result, clients will be able to move toward receiving only those structures, services, and treatments they require.

Staff manpower identity should be consistent with the human management model. Persons skilled in child development should conduct child development services; medically trained personnel should conduct medically oriented services; and behavioral therapists should manage behavior shaping programs. Additionally, normalization dictates that staff functions be separated within a multifaceted system. A teacher in a child development program generally should not staff a residential unit in which the same children reside.

Developmental Growth Orientation

The developmental growth orientation of an agency program is manifested by the degree to which growth-oriented expectations placed upon clients are demanding and relentless, but also realistic and supported by kindness and warmth. Overprotective features (either physical or social) which detract from growth enhancing challenges and the intensity of the relevant programing are areas of concern.

Too often in programs for the mentally retarded, clients are perceived to be less developed, more infantile, less adaptive, or less trustworthy than they actually are. These lowered expectations manifest themselves in the removal of normative risk, denying human potential. Programs should place reasonably high physical and social demands for exposure to normative risk in order to enhance the dignity and growth of clients and to provide them with the learning that can occur as a result of opportunities to fail.

Intensity of relevant programing is considered in terms of the level of challenge, including near optimal amounts of client time, manpower interaction, and utilization of modern techniques and evaluative instruments to improve client movement. Programs should prepare persons for higher levels of programing which require reduced structure and support.

Quality of Setting

Unfortunately, managers of programs for the mentally retarded need to be reminded that the people they serve need the same quality and standard of program, facility, and staff as others. Quality of setting involves four elements: physical comfort, environmental beauty, individualization, and interactions. Physical comfort involves not only the facility (*e.g.*, comfortable furniture, carpeting, adequate warmth and cooling), but also a reasonable degree of cleanliness, the absence of noxious odors, quality food, and comfortable, seasonable clothing. Environmental beauty requires concern for the client's sense of aesthetics. Individualization is expressed in the degree to which programs encourage individualization and self-expression of the clientele in their own life space, with clearly defined life spaces and privacy provided. Interactions encompass quality staff-client relations and encouragement of appropriate client-client, client-public, and staff-public interactions. Programs should minimize any staff status and differentiation indicator (*e.g.*, staff toilets, separate eating areas).

THE NEED FOR A CONTINUUM OF RESIDENTIAL SERVICES

The normalization principle, when applied to the provision of residential services, is particularly specific and powerful in its influence on the growth, development, and societal acceptance of the individuals in residence.[2] The normalization principle and other considerations combine in arguing for the implementation of four highly interrelated concepts.

1. Integration (both physical and social) of the person into every aspect of community life.

[2] W. Wolfensberger, Normalization (National Institute on Mental Retardation, Toronto, 1972).

2. Dispersal of residential services across the state and within communities consistent with population patterns.

3. Specialization of residential settings and staffing patterns for clientele with particular management needs.

4. Continuity of services within a range of specialized residences and between residential and nonresidential services.

A continuum of residential options is mandatory for the progressive development of independent living skills. This continuum requires provision of many more options than now exist in most states. An adult client with limited skills should be able to start out in an intensive training residence, receiving training in the residence while attending vocational programing outside the facility. After attaining a certain level of independent living skills, he should be able to move to less structured residences. Options should include: board and room facilities, which provide only backup support; apartment living situations, with nonretarded peer models providing some assistance in refining independent living skills such as budgeting or cooking; or clusters of two or three apartments in a complex, with a nonretarded person(s) living in the same complex, providing backup support but not residing in the same apartment. Many additional alternatives for less structured, more advanced residential living are available. The most important issue in the development of a continuum of residential placements is for the agency to remain flexible, constantly reevaluating the specific needs of each client and responding to these needs.

Currently only three options appear to be present in most community-based service systems: living at home; living in a structured training hostel; or living independently with some support from an agency. Existing systems providing residential services for adult clients should actively pursue the development of several different models of apartment living residences. The major thrust of central administration personnel hired in adult residential services should be in the apartment living area, rather than the typical establishment of segregated group homes. Two compelling reasons for favoring apartments are that they are much more economical and that the apartment setting can be *at least* as productive for training aspects of residential living for most individuals as the group residence.

Children's residential programs have traditionally underutilized society's greatest potential for the provision of services — foster homes. Foster homes have not been fully utilized because there is a negative connotation due to their usual short-term nature, lack of a support system, and lack of training for potential parents to serve special children, and because service workers, expecting that they would fail at placing "hard-to-place" children, have let this expectation hinder attempts at foster home placements. However, experiments by many of the more dynamic agencies and individuals who were not aware of the "fact" that placement was "impossible" have succeeded. Developmentally and emotionally, family placement for children surpases group living situations.

The issue of backup support systems in any residential service system is vital. For instance, if a child in a developmental (foster) home or group residence demonstrates undesirable behavior patterns, these behaviors should not exclude the child from learning and experience opportunities, nor should they interfere with the development of other children. Specialized services for behavior shaping and control should be available. Whether these specialized services are rendered in the current residence or day program or in a separate facility is a determination which should be made in light of individual needs.

One recurring problem in systems of small residential units has been the feeling of isolation on the part of residential services staff. This is not an unusual problem in dispersed services, but it does require particular safeguards in the areas of staff training and backup support services and personnel.

Considering the present level of knowledge and experience in the development of residential services for the mentally retarded, I suggest the following components as developmental steps in a progressively less restrictive system of residential options. The primary need for any individual requiring residential services is a residence that affords him the greatest degree of independence possible while providing only necessary structure and controls. A range of residential and support services allows for movement as needed for any one individual. Specialized services should be short term and movement oriented. Too often, a highly specialized facility which may be clinically adequate is developed without other residential options necessary for movement into more normal settings. Components in a system of residential options are briefly described in the following sections.

Developmental Homes

A developmental home is a foster home, providing a residence for one child (or two) in an unrelated family. The home parents are screened and trained extensively by the service agency, the home is considered a long-term placement for the child (ideally to result in adoption), and a very strong support system is provided to assist home parents in the training and care of the child.

Children's Intensive Training Residences

For children who need initially extensive attention and individualized supervision, residences accommodating two to four children should be provided. Intense attention and home living skill training can be provided while the children attend public schools, specialized programs providing developmental training, or generic services in the community. Such residences are located in community homes and staffed with house parents and possibly house parent assistants. Emphasis in this setting would be on maintenance of a normal rhythm and routine of life with informal, as well as formal, training in the development of skills that would allow movement into more advanced, less supervised settings.

Adolescent Intensive Training Residences

Some adolescents need intensive services to correct behavioral problems or boost self-help skills. It is desirable to serve many of these individuals in small groups of two to four in local homes managed in the same fashion as the children's intensive training residences.

Family Living Residences

Group residences, when initially conceived, provided separate facilities for children, adolescents, and adults. Experience, however, has shown that this is neither normal nor best for the clients. Whenever possible, individuals should be grouped in a more normal configuration of a family living unit. Family living units should serve an age range of approximately 3-16 years, and the configuration of these units can attempt to place less impaired adolescents with younger children who are more impaired so that the adolescents can be of assistance to the house parents.

Intensive Adult Training Residence

An intensive adult training hostel is a short-term residence for mentally retarded persons over the age of 16 who are either actively involved in vocational training programs or working in the community, but who are in need of intensive training in independent living skills. Clients for this type of residence are those who need training away from the family unit in order to prepare for eventual self-sufficiency as adults. Because of the need for intensity in this unit, house parents and assistants provide the services. Each home in the community might serve up to 10 individuals.

Adult Minimum Supervision Residences

These units are for adults over the age of 16 who are able to function in competitive community employment or in vocational training, although they may still need some supervision and assistance in refining independent living skills or who may display periodic adjustment problems in community living. Minimum supervision residences function more like a rooming house with a landlady than a family living model with an intensive training unit. The size of such a facility may vary greatly, but small units are preferred.

Room and Board Homes

Adults who do not need intensive training should have the same residential options as anyone else in the community. Therefore, the agency should provide, coordinate, and maintain quality control of room and board homes. These homes need provide little training and are typically staffed only with a house mother whose function is to provide backup support.

Adult Boarding

Adult boarding is very similar to the developmental home concept, with one or possibly two adults living in a family home in the community. This family has the backup support of an agency, as well as training and quality control. Adult boarding, unlike children's developmental homes, however, is not considered long term. Training provided in the home and through the person's day training program should allow him to move into either a semi-independent or an independent living situation.

Cluster Apartments

Apartment living residences provide numerous options which may be used to vary the amount of independence and integration for which a particular person may be ready. An apartment cluster is composed of one apartment for staff members and one to four apartments for client residences, in relative physical proximity and functioning to some extent as a unit. As the most flexible of the apartment programs, the cluster offers many options for supervision, peer integration and normal living. The cluster will usually be in one apartment building or in neighboring buildings. Supervision of residents is varied according to their individual needs. Being part of a typical housing unit provides the client with opportunities for observing and participating in the normal interactions of nonretarded persons.

Co-Resident Apartments

The co-resident unit is a single apartment for two or three retarded persons and one or two staff residents, who should be nearly the same age as their mentally retarded roommates and who should either be working persons or college students. The co-resident apartment fosters as much independence on the part of the resident as possible and provides nonretarded peer models, with the eventual goal of eliminating the need for staff members. Each resident contributes to the payment of rent, utilities, and groceries. Through the sharing of activities and the normal peer interaction which this type of apartment fosters, interaction with nonretarded persons is much more likely. Intensive aspects of training can be carried out in this setting as effectively as in a group residence.

Counseled Apartments

A counseled apartment is a step less restrictive than a cluster or co-residence apartment because no staff members live in. A person may live alone in a counseled apartment or may share it with two to four mentally retarded adults. Residents in this situation require minimal supervision. Counseling is provided through residential service staff members and through the counseling division of the agency. Contact is as frequent as needed, but an attempt should be made not to provide any more assistance or support than in absolutely necessary. The desired culmination of the continuum movement through more independent living situations is severance from agency ties.

Independent Living (Counseling Available)

Independent living apartment arrangements are almost identical to counseled apartments, except that there is no systematic effort by the agency to intervene in the life of the person. Support and assistance is available from an agency, through counselors and the residential services division, but only if requested by the clients.

Five-Day Residences

Although many mentally retarded individuals live with their own families, some require residential facilities during the week due to special training needs or the distance between home and programs. Residences which operate only during the week allow residents to return home on the weekends. These residences, for children or adults, operate like the family living hostels, with the clients involved primarily for residence and secondarily for skill training.

Behavior Shaping Residences

Behavior shaping residences provide a very intense, specialized service needed by individuals who are severely or profoundly retarded with major behavioral problems such as destructiveness, self-mutilation, or low or minimal social or self-help skills. This unit provides a transitional residential and developmental program operated on a strict behavioral management methodology in order to prepare residents for more normalized day programs and residential settings. In these units a high staff-to-client ratio in a 24-hour-per-day program is provided in order to accelerate the individual's development and readiness for a more normalizing program.

   This unit is also available for residents who, because of behavior inadequacies or severe behavioral problems, would in all likelihood be placed in an institution or otherwise excluded from public schools and other community services. Much parent training must be involved with this unit in order to maintain skill development after the individual leaves the unit. Behavior shaping and other services that are provided through the behavior shaping unit would be operated by behavioral therapists.

Developmental Maximization Units

Maximization units are designed to serve severely and profoundly retarded individuals who, initially, may be nonambulatory and have multiple handicaps, such as seizures, physical impairments, and sensory problems. The medically oriented services provide combined residential and developmental programs for basic stimulation and to foster acquisition of needed skills. These services can be provided for individuals whose complex medical challenges require treatment or special therapy to supplement developmental potential. The purpose of the unit is to stimulate the client's development and to minimize or at least stabilize his medical problem. Care must be taken that this specialized service does not become a dumping ground for individuals whom other programs do not want to serve and that it does not become logjammed for lack of advanced residential options outside the maximization unit.

Crisis Assistance Units

One of the major reasons for institutionalization of mentally retarded citizens has been short-term crisis in the family (*e.g.,* illness or death). As an alternative to long-term institutionalization, crisis assistance units can be established. These very short-term units provide respite care for any individual who needs special emergency short-term residential services. This would be a homelike setting that would maintain the normal routine and rhythm of that person's life while he was resident.

Crisis Homes

Crisis homes are an extension to the crisis assistance unit and provide trained parents on standby to offer a home to a mentally retarded person on a short-term basis. Such homes may be used in lieu of a crisis residence or as a supplement to that service when the crisis assistance unit is at capacity or the person lives so far away that he could not continue to attend his normal day program.

Structured Correctional Residences

It may be necessary to establish several different types of residential services in order to provide mentally retarded offenders and delinquents with specialized training while protecting other persons and preserving the effectiveness of other programs. It is necessary to develop a residential service which utilizes a highly structured approach and intensive supervision. Such a residence should be designed for persons whose behavior has consistently been so aggressive, destructive, or antisocial as to endanger the safety of themselves or of others.

For those few individuals with difficult to manage or consistently antisocial, uncontrolled, or self-destructive behavior, a long-term residence which would segregate them from society may be necessary. This unit should provide sheltered work and training programs on the grounds. It should be supplemented by a second type of security residence, not isolated from the mainstream of society, appropriate for those individuals who may be behaviorally destructive or dangerous at present, but are not habitually antisocial or criminal. Since this group of individuals has a high likelihood of rehabilitation, provisions must be made for highly structured supervision within the community. This may imply court referrals or commitments in some cases. The unit should be short-term with an intensive correctional-rehabilitation-socialization program in residence. Services of this small facility should include education, rehabilitation, counseling, sheltered workshop, teaching a trade, providing a home, and structuring situations, probably directed by a person with training and experience in the field of corrections.

Structured Rehabilitation Residences

In contrast to individuals in need of supervision, the majority of mentally retarded offenders are neither dangerous nor a threat to public health and safety. They are individuals who need partial shelter, especially in the domiciliation area, but in many areas are capable of functioning at least semi-independently. Structured rehabilitation residences must be provided within the community to offer appropriate supervision while allowing the individual to take advantage of as many culturally normative opportunities as possible. These residences should be directed by mental retardation correction specialists who can train house parent assistants. Supporting assistance from correctional and vocational counselors can help provide a supervised residence while allowing variable outside education and training.

This listing is intended only as a summary of some necessary aspects of residential services to the mentally retarded in the community. Because of the wide variety of needs within any population, it is obvious that any system of services which proposes to serve the needs of all mentally retarded persons will need at least the majority of these 19 types of residential services.

COMPREHENSIVE COMMUNITY SERVICES— AN EXAMPLE

Nebraska provides a good example of statewide effort in the development of comprehensive community-based services. Massive and innovative changes in traditional mental retardation services have occurred in a relatively short period of time.

As late as 1968 there were only two alternatives in Nebraska for parents of mentally retarded persons: institutionalization or keeping the individual at home with no services. Parents could send a child to the state's only public institution for the mentally retarded, which was typical of most state institutions: remote, understaffed, professionally isolated, and overcrowded, with more than 2,300 residents in a facility constructed to hold approximately half that number. Or, if parents were wealthy enough, they could send their child to a private institution even farther away from his family and his home community. If parents rejected institutionalization as an alternative, they were left with virtually no support in the community to assist them in learning how to work with unique problems and demands of children with special needs.

After only five years, it is difficult to believe that this situation ever existed in Nebraska. Currently, fewer than 1,200 individuals reside at the state public institution, and the waiting list has all but been eliminated. Local services of extremely high quality have sprung up in every community across the state. These services are not only providing a comprehensive continuum of services for mentally retarded citizens within communities, but, as rapidly as possible, are returning institutional residents to their home communities.[3] There are 29 adult vocational training centers serving approximately 1,300 clients. Twenty developmental day care centers have been established to serve children excluded from public schools due to age or multiple handicapping conditions. Because of the activism of the parents and professionals in the development of educable and trainable classes within the public schools, these centers are serving almost all the children who need preschool and developmental services. In addition to these developmental centers, several regional offices are utilizing generic early education and preschool programs to serve the mentally retarded preschool population. The state has also developed adult training residences, staffed apartments, independent living apartments, children's and adolescents' group homes, foster homes, behavior shaping units, and other types of residential options.

In addition to the direct program services, regional offices provide many administrative and backup support services. Among these are social services, coordination of recreation services, specialized services (e.g., speech and language therapy, occupational therapy, physical therapy, medical and psychiatric consultation, and psychometric services), volunteer services, and transportation.

Contrary to popular belief, data are available which document that in most instances the provision of services in the community is less costly than institutional services. Immediate cost reductions result from a lessened need for attendant personnel, reliance on existing community generic services (e.g., medical care and recreation), and lower staff ratios in specialized programs. The provision of extensive services on the local level in Nebraska has proven to be less expensive and more effective than traditional institutional services.

Long-run savings are realized as individuals move through the residential services continuum and become more self-sufficient. From childhood to adulthood,

---

[3] *See* Wolfensberger & Menoloscini, *Reflections on Recent Mental Retardation Developments in Nebraska,* 8 MENTAL RETARDATION, Dec. 1970, at 20.

costs decrease dramatically. In addition to program savings, mentally retarded individuals who move into community employment contribute to the local economy and tax base.

More than a theoretical concept, the principle of normalization is a concept that works. As an alternative to traditional institutions for the mentally retarded, a continuum of community service programs is the least restrictive, most effective, most humane, and least expensive method of normalizing the lives of the mentally retarded citizens who need these services.

EDUCATION FOR HANDICAPPED CHILDREN IN THE LEAST RESTRICTIVE ENVIRONMENT

ALAN ABESON

DISCUSSION OF the least restrictive alternative concept in relation to the delivery of educational services to mentally retarded children must be based upon the emerging legal principle that *all* children have a right to public education.[1] Although this legal mandate might seem only to ensure access to education, analysis of the early right to education decisions reveals that the courts have in fact discussed appropriateness of educational programs in a manner that relates directly to the least restrictive alternative concept.

In dismissing a right to education suit, in *Harrison v. Michigan,*[2] on the ground that the state legislature had just taken effective action on the issue presented, the court noted that the new Michigan "education for all" law[3] required that "a special education plan must be implemented which will provide for the delivery of special education programs and services *designed to develop the maximum potential* of every handicapped person."[4] In *Mills v. Board of Education of the District of Columbia,*[5] the court held "[t]he District of Columbia shall provide to each child of school age a free and *suitable* publicly-supported education regardless of the degree of the child's mental, physical, or emotional disability or impairment,"[6] and "the Board of Education has an obligation to provide *whatever specialized instruction that* [sic] *will benefit the child*."[7] The court in *Pennsylvania Association for Retarded Children v. Commonwealth of Pennsylvania,*[8] the first right to education suit, in

---

[1] *See* Herr, pp. 252-67, Chapter 9 of this volume.
[2] 350 F. Supp. 846 (E.D. Mich. 1972).
[3] MICH. COMP. LAWS ANN. § 340.298c (Supp. 1973).
[4] 350 F. Supp. at 848 (emphasis supplied).
[5] 348 F. Supp. 866 (D.D.C. 1972).
[6] *Id.* at 878 (emphasis supplied).
[7] *Id.* at 874 (emphasis supplied).
[8] 334 F. Supp. 1257 (E.D. Pa. 1971), *modified,* 343 F. Supp. 279 (1972).

addition to holding the state responsible for providing every child with a suitable public education held that:

> It is the Commonwealth's obligation to place each mentally retarded child in a free, public program of education and training appropriate to the child's capacity, within the context of a presumption that, among the alternative programs of education and training required by statute to be available, placement in a regular public school class is preferable . . . to placement in any other type of program of education and training.[9]

By establishing that the preferred setting for educating mentally retarded children is the regular public school class, the court in essence called for the implementation of the least restrictive alternative concept.

This approach to service delivery is also being embodied in the laws of several states. In 1972, a comprehensive Tennessee law regarding the education of handicapped children specified that:

> To the maximum extent practicable, handicapped children shall be educated along with children who do not have handicaps and shall attend regular classes. Impediments to learning and to the normal functioning of handicapped children in the regular school environment shall be overcome by the provision of special aids and services rather than by separate schooling for the handicapped. Special classes, separate schooling or other removal of handicapped children from the regular educational environment, shall occur only when, and to the extent that the nature or severity of the handicap is such that education in regular classes, even with the use of supplementary aids and services, cannot be accomplished satisfactorily.[10]

Equally comprehensive legislation, passed in Massachusetts during 1972, provides that "[u]ntil proven otherwise, every child shall be presumed to be appropriately assigned to a regular education program and presumed not to be a school age child with special needs or a school age child requiring special education."[11] A 1973 Wisconsin statute requires that "[p]reference is to be given, whenever appropriate, to education of the child in classes along with children who do not have exceptional educational needs. Where it is not desirable to educate the child who has exceptional educational needs with children who do not have such needs, the child shall be provided with whatever special education is appropriate."[12]

Implementation of these legal directives has been interpreted by some to mean that all mentally retarded children, regardless of the severity of their handicap, are to be placed for their education in regular class programs. To others, these mandates mean that all mentally retarded children are to be placed in self-contained special education classes. Neither is correct, for what is required is the availability of a continuum of program alternatives that provide for meeting specific individual needs of children. Implementation of the least restrictive alternative forces educators, who make placement decisions, to "presume" at the outset that all

[9] 334 F. Supp. at 1260.
[10] Tenn. Code Ann. § 49-2913(B) (Supp. 1973).
[11] Mass. Ann. Laws ch. 71 B, § 3 (Supp. 1972).
[12] Ch. 89, § 1(4), [1973] Laws of Wis. (Wis. Legislative Service 256, ch. 89, § 1(4) (West 1973).

children can benefit from a regular education. Such thinking is implemented by making decisions that bring services to the child in the regular classroom, rather than taking the child to the services. The guiding assumption is that it is far more beneficial to the child to teach him in as normal an environment as possible than to remove him from that environment and then struggle to obtain a meaningful and stigmaless reentry. Equally important to this concept is the practical matter that the movement of a child from a less restrictive to a more restrictive environment must be governed by relevant evidence, adherence to due process safeguards, and the availability of a program appropriate to the child's needs.[13]

Special educators, in response both to legal mandates and to acceptance of the merits of the least restrictive alternative, have conceptually and pragmatically begun implementation. One of the most popular conceptual schemata is the "Cascade System."[14] This system presents nine educational program alternatives beginning with a regular classroom in a regular school, which is the desired setting for the majority of children. Progression through the remaining settings, in which gradually smaller numbers of children are placed, is determined by the increasing severity of children's handicaps and the consequent need for greater amounts of instructional and support resources. The most extreme setting in the cascade, where the fewest number of children will be served, is the hospital.[15]

As an example of the progression, a child who possesses a visual handicap may simply need corrective glasses which, when provided, enable the child to participate as a nonhandicapped child in a regular education program. Another visually handicapped child, however, may need instruction in braille, requiring the services of an itinerant teacher who periodically takes the child from the regular classroom to provide instruction in the use of braille. Finally, a child with a congenital visual problem may require surgery and long-term hospitalization, in which case his educational experience must be brought to his bedside. The decision to place a child on any level of the cascade should be made only on the basis of individual examinations which assess the child's ability to learn, his need for special services, and the likelihood that these services can be provided in a particular setting.

The flow of services in the cascade progresses from minimal to maximal, with the regular classroom being the setting in which the least amount of special resources is needed. Three modifications of regular classroom procedures can be made relatively easily, and they allow the minimally handicapped child the maximum opportunity to obtain and participate in a normal educational experience. Modification I provides the regular classroom teacher with opportunities to obtain consultation from a number of educational and related specialists in areas such as instructional materials, reading, psychology, guidance, and speech. In this situation

---

[13] *See* Sorgen, pp. 235-39, Chapter 8 of this volume; Strauss, pp. 453-70, Chapter 15 of this volume.

[14] *See* Reynolds, *A Framework for Considering Some Issues in Special Education,* 28 EXCEPTIONAL CHILDREN 367 (1962).

[15] *See* Abeson & Weintraub, *Appropriate Education for All Handicapped Children: A Growing Issue,* 23 SYR. U.L. REV. 1037 (1972), from which the following discussion of the "Cascade System" is adapted.

the regular classroom teacher searches for a better understanding of the child and the problems presented by the learning environment and seeks improved instructional and management techniques. Modification II involves itinerant specialists and differs from I in that these individuals supplement the classroom teacher by directly instructing the child. Modification III includes the primary placement of the child in a regular classroom, but with some time spent in a special resource area where specific remedial instruction occurs. Specialists working in this area confer with the classroom teacher, and together they plan a total appropriate program for the child. In all three of these approaches, the regular classroom teacher ultimately is responsible for the student.

Children who cannot participate or achieve in one of these three modifications of the regular classroom can divide their school day by spending part in the regular class and the remainder in a special class. In this program option, the special class is staffed by a trained special educator who works with the child in a special adaptation of the regular classroom program, as well as in other specialized instructional areas. The special education and regular classroom teachers confer and jointly plan to ensure that the child is provided with meaningful coordinated education. In this situation, responsibility for the student is shared.

If a child is unable to participate successfully in most regular classroom activities, he may be placed in a special education class, where most of his education will be provided. Usually, the student will be integrated with regular class students for such nonacademic areas as physical education, art, home economics, and music. In this placement, the total curriculum is adapted to each child's individual needs. The special class teacher in this program ultimately is responsible for the child.

Special day schools for handicapped children offer facilities and programs generally unavailable in the regular school for more severely handicapped individuals. These include adaptive physical education, smaller pupil-teacher ratios, and greater availability of support personnel. The children live at home and frequently are transported from within relatively large geographic areas extending beyond a single school district.

The residential school is reserved for children so severely handicapped that they cannot live at home because they require full-time supervision and maintenance. Education programs for these children focus on enabling them to improve their capacity for dealing with basic needs, including toileting, eating, and communicating. Wherever possible, these children should receive their education in settings outside the institution. Although educational programs in residential institutions most often are not directed by the state education agency, there are legislative and judicial trends to support this transition so that education can be provided equally to all in all settings as a responsibility of the state education department. For some severely handicapped children who possess major medical problems, an educational program provided by a trained special educator can occur only in a hospital. Like all special education programs, the goals and programs must be flexible and determined by each child's needs.

Implementation of the Cascade System is predicated upon the concept that handicapped children must not be removed any further from the normal setting than is absolutely essential for the effective delivery of services. Thus, if a mildly retarded child can be educated effectively in a part-time special class, there can be no justifiable reason for placing and retaining this child in a full-time special class. Similarly, if a child can be treated effectively in a community day facility, there can be no basis for condemning this individual to a residential institution. At no time can administrative or logistic difficulties justify denying children the opportunity to participate in the most normal education program available.

Implementation of all the cascade levels is rarely found in a single school district. Self-contained special classes are most frequent, but movement to the part-time placement of retarded children in regular programs is increasing. As the need for providing a continuum of program alternatives is recognized by individual school districts which cannot alone provide all the options for (relatively) limited numbers of children, various forms of cooperation among districts will be used. These include contracting, regionalization, and the creation of special school districts. A major impediment to the provision of program cascades by local education agencies in many states is that state funding formulas are based solely on the provision of education to handicapped children in self-contained special class units. Under such a formula, the only structure funded by state dollars is the segregated special classroom. Intermediate, less restrictive and more desirable, alternatives are not rewarded.

Providing mentally retarded children with an education in a system of alternative settings requires that decisions regarding the services to be provided and settings to be used not be intractable. The basic assumption underlying the entire effort to educate, rehabilitate, and treat is that the handicapped person should progress toward normalcy. Assuming that progress will occur, provision must be made for mobility up the cascade toward less restrictive settings. Building in the capability for upward mobility requires that periodic reevaluations be made to determine attainment of objectives and necessary changes in teaching strategies. The continuation of an individual in any setting must be based on systematically and frequently collected evaluative data.

Emphasis must be placed on upward mobility toward less restrictive programs because in too many situations, assignment to a level on the cascade is equivalent to a life sentence with no thought of upward movement. James Gallagher reported on data collected by the United States Office of Education and indicated that "[i]n a number of large city school systems far less than ten per cent of the children placed in special education classes are ever returned to regular education."[16] Lifetime placement often occurs in states where an agency other than a department of education is responsible for services to subgroups of handicapped children such as the trainable mentally retarded. Operationally, once a child is labeled to meet the requirements of a department of welfare or mental retardation, removed from the education system, and placed under the jurisdiction of the other department

[16]Gallagher, *The Special Education Contract for Mildly Handicapped Children,* 38 EXCEPTIONAL CHILDREN 527 (1972).

for specialized programing, there is virtually no likelihood of reentry into the less restrictive environment of the education track maintained under the state department of education.

Implementation of the cascade requires also that provision be made for movement toward more restrictive environments since occasionally, even in the best of situations, an individual child may not progress and alternative program efforts will need to be undertaken. Decisions to move children away from the mainstream must be viewed as being of great consequence and must occur only on the basis of clear evidence of need of the individual and not of the system.

To date, educational placement decisions made in many local education agencies have been arbitrary and capricious, providing for little or no involvement of the child and his family and little or no explanation by the public schools of the educational justification for the placement. Recently, however, the courts and state legislatures have acted to ensure that when placement decisions are made, children and their families must be provided with the full protection of due process of law.[17] Essentially, due process requires that before a child's status in a public education program can be altered, there is a right to a fair hearing, a right to receive notice of the hearing, and a right to have counsel present at the hearing.[18]

The emphasis on due process has caused many states to reexamine their statutory and regulatory requirements regarding placement decisions and subsequent reviews, since the availability of alternative educational settings for children with different needs becomes meaningless in the absence of proper identification procedures. Analysis of these regulations by the State-Federal Information Clearinghouse for Exceptional Children[19] reveals extensive variability among the states. Depending on the state, reviews are required continually, once a semester, routinely within three years of initial placement, or not at all.

In part, the emphasis being placed by courts, legislatures, parents, and professionals on providing mentally retarded children with an education in the least restrictive environment and on the use of due process procedures in determining placement has evolved into a new form of educational "planning," designated as the special education contract or the individually written program.[20] The basis of the individually written program is that, when a child is identified by the public schools as being in need of a special educational program, a formal contract is established between the child, his parents or legal guardian, and appropriate public school officials which binds all parties to the delivery of an individually determined educational program within a defined time period. Specific provisions would include at

---

[17] *See* Lebanks v. Spears, 60 F.R.D. 135 (E.D. La. 1973); Mills v. Board of Educ., 348 F. Supp. 866 (D.D.C. 1972); Pennsylvania Ass'n for Retarded Children v. Pennsylvania, 334 F. Supp. 1257 (E.D. Pa. 1971), *modified,* 343 F. Supp. 279 (1972); CONN. GEN. STAT. ANN. § 10-76(h) (Supp. 1973); MASS. ANN. LAWS ch. 71B, § 3 (Supp. 1972); TENN. CODE ANN. § 49-2947 (Supp. 1973).

[18] *See, e.g.,* Mills v. Board of Educ., 348 F. Supp. 866, 881 (D.D.C. 1972).

[19] COUNCIL FOR EXCEPTIONAL CHILDREN, STATE LAWS AND ADMINISTRATIVE PROCEDURES RELATING TO THE PLACEMENT OF EXCEPTIONAL CHILDREN (1973).

[20] *See* Gallagher, *The Special Education Contract for Mildly Handicapped Children,* 38 EXCEPTIONAL CHILDREN 527 (1972).

least: (1) the specific and measurable objectives to be realized by the child; (2) the criteria and methods for determination of the achievement of these objectives; (3) the specific activities that will be undertaken by all parties to the contract to achieve the desired objectives; (4) the allocation of people and other resources to achieve the objectives; (5) the schedule for the measurement of short- and long-term objective attainments as established in the individually prescribed program; and (6) the penalties to be applied to any parties to the contract failing to execute their responsibilities.

Use of the individually written program has many advantages including: delivering educational services to the child in response to specific needs; grouping by objective, thus eliminating the necessity for assigning potentially negative labels; allocating and requesting resources on the basis of specific child and teacher needs; making available specific cost-benefit and educational growth data; and effectively involving parents and the child not only in the establishment of the individually written program, but also in the evaluation and realization of goals. Finally, the individually written program provides the basis for an effective and continual process of individually assessing the child's needs, bringing services to the child in the least restrictive environment, and repeatedly evaluating the child's performance for the purpose of improving the teaching-learning setting. Most important is that all of this must occur with the parents and the child involved as fully as possible in all aspects of the program.

Regardless or whether the delivery system created to provide educational services to retarded children is called a cascade or something else, the emphasis must be placed upon educational attainment which contributes to normalization. The crux of the solution is that the planning of delivery systems must create one integrated system of alternatives open to all children, not one for the so-called normals and another for the mentally retarded. There must be one system which is and remains basic for all children and serves as the junction for bringing to retarded children the services they need. The implementation of this approach will enhance the feelings of self-worth of mentally retarded children, their teachers, and families, improve the educational achievement of the children, and ultimately foster their assimilation as adults into society.

THE LEAST RESTRICTIVE ALTERNATIVE AND GUARDIANSHIP

LEOPOLD LIPPMAN

IN THE PAST (and in the area of mental retardation the past starts with the earliest recorded history and continues to perhaps 8 or 10 years ago, and even up to this moment in some respects), the concept underlying guardianship was always one of total dependence. Whatever the reason for the presumed personal inadequacy — whether it was age, mental subnormality, gross physical impairment, or extreme emotional distress — the assumption was that the individual could not take care of himself and (therefore) that he needed someone to do everything for him. Either a person could take care of himself or he could not. If he could not, then he had to have total care, and the key word was *guardianship*. Moreover, the emphasis was almost universally and exclusively on guardianship of "the estate," that is to say, on protection of property and other assets.

Most often, if the retarded person lived in the community, the parent would serve as guardian; and if this was not feasible, the court would designate some other responsible individual or corporate institution as the agent of society in protecting the estate. If the retarded person was confined in a public institution, often the superintendent assumed the responsibility (and frequently also the title) of guardian. Indeed, in some states it was a routine and virtually automatic procedure for the superintendent to be named guardian. This practice gave the public official, who had intimate and continuing authority over every aspect of the retarded resident's life, total control, under the law, over his financial assets as well.

Clearly, this administrative arrangement took no account of the welfare of the retarded individual as a person, but it did concentrate in the hands of one official a range of responsibilities and powers over every aspect of the resident's life, including his financial assets. It must be obvious that no one gave much thought to who was representing the interests of the retarded person in relation to the "total institution" in which he lived. In this context, the idea of "guardianship of the person" is perhaps the outstanding feature of the new California guardianship plan that I will describe here.

When California confronted the problem of guardianship during the period 1965-68, several other plans and programs were already in effect in other states. The oldest had been operating since about 1921 in Minnesota, where the public welfare department was guardian for thousands of retarded persons, including most of those in institutions and many in the community. The Minnesota program worked quite well in some ways, better than any program any other state had. There were, however, some major inadequacies, which were described and analyzed in detail by Professor Robert Levy.[1]

In the state of Washington, in the 1950s and early 1960s, the parents of mentally retarded children and adults were concerned with providing protection for their children when the parents themselves would no longer be able to do so. Through their organization, the Washington Association for Retarded Children, they explored various ideas, including voluntary arrangements and legislative action. Alternative approaches were reviewed in a series of articles in the association's quarterly news-letter, *HOPE for Retarded Children*, which were later reprinted in a brochure entitled

---

[1] Levy, *Protecting the Mentally Retarded: An Empirical Survey and Evaluation of the Establishment of State Guardianship in Minnesota,* 49 MINN. L. REV. 821 (1965).

Lifetime Planning for the Retarded Child.[2] The various articles dealt with the uses of life insurance and trust arrangements, the proper writing of a will or bequest, and the legal guardianship arrangements which were then available in Washington. The brochure is now out of date, but it was advanced thinking when published.

The organized parents in Washington promoted the enactment of legislation which became known as the Co-Custody Law.[3] It was a great work of draftsmanship, and it reflected a marvelous concept — but no one used it. The idea was that the parent would designate an individual, a church, or some other organization as "co-custodian" for the retarded child and the designee would then assume primary responsibility for the retarded person's well-being when the parent was no longer able to bear it.

Another approach was enacted into law by the Washington legislature in a subsequent session. This was called the Parental Successor Law.[4] It incorporated some of the same principles and turned out to be slightly more workable. Even so, rather few parents attempted to use the Parental Successor Law for their children.

In Massachusetts, there is the MARC Retardate Trust, which is essentially a fiduciary plan offering financial protection. In Louisiana, whose laws developed under the Napoleonic Code, there is statutory provision for a "tutor," a variant of the court-appointed guardian. Ohio has still another version of "protectorship." New York has yet a different plan, authorized by statute but implemented by families working through voluntary organizations, notably the New York State Association for Retarded Children.[5]

California's approach was different from all the others. Guardianship came under active consideration in California in 1965 because of a decision made earlier on another issue. The earlier decision, echoing the thinking of the President's Panel on Mental Retardation, was: It is better to have retarded people living and receiving service in the community than in a remote residential facility. The principle was embodied and elaborated in the final report of the California Study Commission on Mental Retardation, *The Undeveloped Resource: A Plan for the Mentally Retarded of California.*[6] Within months after the study commission report was published, bills were enacted, signed, and moved toward implementation. The goal was to make services available as close to a person's home as possible.

California opted for community services and developed less restrictive approaches to the provision of services, but it also focused on a new problem. If the retarded were to remain in the community, there must be provision for protecting them insofar as they need protection. The study commission had been unable to handle the problem in the time available to it, but one of its high-priority recom-

[2] Washington Ass'n for Retarded Children, Lifetime Planning for the Retarded Child (1958).

[3] Rev. Code Wash. Ann. §§ 26.40.010-100 (1962).

[4] *Id.* § 72.33.500-590 (1962).

[5] *See* United Cerebral Palsy Association, Proceedings, Conference on Protective Supervision and Services for the Handicapped, New York City (1966).

[6] California Study Commission on Mental Retardation, The Undeveloped Resource: A Plan for the Mentally Retarded of California 76-77 (1965).

mendations for further study and action was the issue of guardianship. Accordingly, there was brought into existence, under the newly created California Mental Retardation Program and Standards Advisory Board, a committee on guardianship.[7]

The committee on guardianship looked at the variety of plans and proposals around the country, seeking to discover their strong points as well as their flaws. The essence of the committee's approach was that California was already committed to serving retarded people in the community. The word "normalization" was not in use at that time, but it was the concept on which the committee proceeded.

The approach the committee took to guardianship was that protection should be provided through the least restrictive mechanism appropriate to the individual case. One of the central features of the committee's proposal was that a retarded person would not be declared incompetent unless this was clearly required by the circumstances. Rather, three levels of guardianship were proposed. One was guardianship in the conventional sense, including the appointment of an agent of the court with substantial control over the retarded individual's financial resources and personal life. This arrangement was to be applicable in some cases to persons in institutions and in some cases to persons in the community, but not automatically to any class of cases. The committee felt that full guardianship of this type was necessary only for persons so severely impaired that they really could not manage any significant aspect of their own lives.

For retarded persons with less severe problems, the committee recommended less restrictive arrangements. The lowest level of intervention, the least restrictive, was in essence an advisory relationship, a service that might appropriately be called guidance, not guardianship. For this purpose, the committee recommended use of an existing mechanism, already in existence as a product of the work of the study commission on mental retardation. The study commission had called for, and the legislature had created, a program which subsequently developed into a statewide network of regional diagnostic, counseling, and service centers. The regional centers were to be operated under diverse local auspices, by contract with the state department of public health. They were to provide diagnosis and counseling and to help retarded persons and their families find the appropriate services to meet current needs. As permanent locally based agencies funded by the state, they were also to provide a continuity of concern about each retarded individual from the time he first came to the regional center. To the concept of the regional center, the committee on guardianship added the provision that when the retarded person's parents or present guardian were no longer able to care for him, the state of California, through the staff of the regional center, should be available to fulfill the protective functions of the parent. The assumption of the role was to be by prearrangement, at the request of the parent or guardian, to take effect when the need arose. With respect to those retarded persons evaluated as requiring minimal protection or only occasional guidance and assistance, the committee proposed that the necessary

---

[7] See Dinkelspiel, *Recent Legislative Acts for the Benefit of the Mentally Retarded,* 44 CAL. ST. B.J. 219 (1969); Kay, Farnham, Karren, Knakel & Diamond, *Legal Planning for the Mentally Retarded: The California Experience,* 60 CALIF. L. REV. 438 (1972).

services be provided through a staff member, usually a social worker or public health nurse, with the minimum of formalization and without a court declaration of incompetence.

In between the least restrictive level and total guardianship, was what was called the protectorship, a role envisioned as being formalized by court action, but without a declaration of incompetence. The committee originally proposed that the function be assigned to a new state office called the personal surrogate, with the responsibility delegated to, and exercised by, the staff of the regional center nearest the residence of the retarded person. As eventually enacted, the program became the responsibility of the state director of public health, and he in turn has carried it out through the regional centers.

Through this mechanism, then, the state, operating through local agencies, would provide whatever the retarded individual needed in the way of protection, guidance, supervision, and control where appropriate, but no more. Thus, for example, if he was capable of holding a job, capable of voting, capable of managing his financial affairs, but lacking in the ability to make appropriate judgments in personal matters of such importance as marrying and having children, then he would do for himself all those things that he could do, and the protector or conservator would be available to counsel him on personal matters of great magnitude. If the retarded person lost his job, the regional center staff would be available to counsel him, to help him find new employment. Similarly, if the house he was living in burned down, the regional center would be at hand to help him find suitable new housing—but again, only if he needed such help. In other words, the regional center would be a standby resource at any of the crisis points in the life of the retarded person, whether these were normal times of change, as from childhood to adolescence or from school years to work years, or the unpredictable events such as loss of a job or a place to live. These are points in life at which many persons, not only retarded persons, need help or support.

The court-designated protective services of the regional center could of course also include conservation of a retarded individual's financial resources. If he were entitled to social security or other benefits, the conservator could help him fill out the necessary papers and otherwise expedite appropriate action.

This is the essence of the idea, but I must add one phrase that I consider illuminating. One member of the committee developed a concept that was worked into the preamble to the law as finally enacted; it seemed to us to epitomize what we were after. The concept was that the guardian, conservator, or counselor should act "as a wise parent"—not just any parent, but a *wise* parent. This is not to imply that the retarded individual is, or acts as, a child; he is a person, but in some aspects of his life he may still need someone to help him in the role of the wise parent.

Since the California innovations, other states have experimented with new forms of, and alternatives to, traditional guardianship concepts. The essential point of this description of the California program is that the principle of the least restrictive alternative is crucial to guardianship reform and can provide a much richer mix of legal mechanisms to meet the variable and usually limited needs for protection on the part of mentally retarded citizens.

THE LEAST RESTRICTIVE ALTERNATIVE AND THE POLICE INVESTIGATORY PROCESS

DOLORES NORLEY

THE CONCEPT OF normalization, which the Scandinavians have used successfully as a philosophical base for more than a decade, is increasingly important in the United States. Stated simply, normalization means that if a procedure is right for the average citizen, it is right for the mentally retarded citizen.

Application of the principle of normalization by using less restrictive alternatives need not entail the granting of special privileges. In the context of law enforcement, police handling of retarded citizens should be neither more nor less restrictive than handling of nonretarded citizens. The optimal relationship between police official and citizen always requires that the citizen under observation or questioning be treated with dignity, respect, and all processes due under law. This must be the norm for police interaction with mentally retarded citizens as well.

The many myths about mental retardation that are common among the general public are often shared by police officers. The result too often is precipitate, and therefore frequently inappropriate, intervention due to misinterpretation of a mentally retarded individual's conduct or reactions. Retarded individuals do not get into trouble with the police. Usually, their trouble stems from a nonunderstanding society, and the police simply are the officials at the critical interface. Police are eager to know the facts about mental retardation. They do not enjoy being unsure, wary, fearful, or hostile in their approach. They properly see themselves as the guardians of safety and harmony and are appalled when faced with the possibility of an inappropriate intervention caused by their lack of understanding of a new situation.

Police cannot be expected to be clinicians or therapists, but they must often judge very quickly the actions of a person which may seem deviant in the context of the cultural norm. When appearance, gait, or behavior of citizens varies much from a narrow norm, it is likely to arouse police apprehension. Even with respect to police procedures short of arrest, it is important that the police be trained not to overreact. Misunderstanding has been the cause of countless unnecessary arrests, bookings, and trips to the police station for retarded citizens. The thrust of concern here is not arrest for violations of the law; in that situation police procedure is clearly defined. The risk that can be avoided is the risk that a retarded citizen will be subjected unnecessarily to complex and disturbing legal processes simply because he appears to be different or acts in an odd but harmless way. This is especially important when involvement with the legal-correctional system may result in a loss of rights and privileges that would not be suffered by a "normal" citizen.

For 15 years I have trained police personnel from 50 municipalities on the recognition and handling of mentally retarded citizens. There are four major questions law enforcement officers ask about mental retardation: (1) How do you recognize retarded individuals? (2) How do you approach and handle a retarded person? (3) Where do you turn for special help or advice in crises? (4) Are the mentally retarded violent? Discussion of these subjects provides a fair, though superficial, review of the basics of mental retardation.

There is, of course, no single way to recognize a mentally retarded individual, especially since retardation is usually not accompanied by physical symptoms. But quick estimates may be made by asking questions about schools, workshops, training centers, jobs held, knowledge of coins, transportation, and destinations. These are shallow, unscientific criteria, but they can yield information to a perceptive officer who is familiar with the community programs to which a retarded individual may make reference. False conclusions of mental retardation, based on superficial impressions created by epileptics, cerebral palsied, drugged, or emotionally unstable persons must be particularly guarded against. Retarded persons and intelligent partially spastic persons are sometimes picked up as suspected of being under the influence of drugs or alcohol.

No one has improved on the Golden Rule as an answer to the best way to handle individuals; an officer should handle a retarded citizen as he would like to be handled. The nuclear message is the essential fact that the mentally retarded individual is more like, than unlike, the average individual. His needs are the same as those of every other human being: to be respected, assured dignity, and treated as a worthwhile person. Objective kindness and official firmness is the proper approach, tempered by an understanding of the barriers caused by mutual fear and apprehension. Surely the burden of reducing the communication barriers produced by tension of an unfamiliar confrontation, in the presence of a menacing uniform, gun, and badge, should weigh more heavily on the side of the police officer in the dialogue.

The police officer must be made aware of the wide range of options he has in dealing with mentally retarded individuals. His use of options is most often a reflection of the stability and maturity of the officer. A relaxed officer, certain of his position and duties, is more likely to take the time to ask questions in a friendly fashion, then call or take the suspect or lost person home, to school, to work, to an agency, or back to the station house to get more referral help. An uptight, by-the-book officer will usually retreat into a role of official apprehension. One problem facing every police official is that from 5 P.M. on Friday to 9 A.M. on Monday, most social agencies and police stations act as if their responsibilities had ceased for the weekend. Ordinarily there is nowhere for the police officer to turn for help, unless agencies are wise enough in their planning to provide some weekend assistance.

The most frequently asked question in police training is whether mentally retarded individuals tend to be violent. Violence is in no way intrinsic to mental retardation. A retarded individual, however, may become violent in the same situations in which average persons are violent: when threatened, when upset, or when cornered and desperate. The age-old confusion of mental retardation with mental illness is the greatest threat to having retarded persons approached with dignity and calm assuredness. There are also the perennial myths of superstrength and elevated sexuality to be faced and educated away.

For the police officer, the application of the least restrictive alternative for mentally retarded citizens means treating the retarded person first as a citizen and then, if absolutely necessary, as a citizen with a handicap.

CHAPTER 17

Judicial, Legislative, and Administrative Competence in Setting Institutional Standards

Editorial Introduction

*J*ohnson and Wood note that all three branches of government have a vital role in the setting of institutional standards. The common needs for all branches are awareness of the developmental potential of mentally retarded citizens and information on how this development takes place and the kinds of resources it requires.

The optimal standards are those developed through a cooperative effort of administrative and legislative resources. The role Johnson and Wood see for the legislature is one of establishing fairly strict guidelines for administrators and then providing them with the financial resources to establish and implement proper standards. Within the administrative structure the authors recognize the essential role of persons responsible for running the institution, but argue for the creation of an independent administrative body to set and enforce standards.

The role of courts is seen as that of ensuring the proper discharge of legislative and administrative responsibilities. Courts will be required to intervene only when either legislators or administrators have failed. Intervention is required when there has been a failure to set appropriate standards, a failure to implement these standards generally in the institutions, or a failure to provide adequate habilitation programing to a single individual within a otherwise acceptable institutional program.

Johnson and Wood argue for an effective monitoring system, no matter who sets standards. They suggest the use of an inspector general for this function, or in the case of court-imposed standards, the use of a master. They discuss the mechanisms available to both courts and legislatures to secure the information necessary to set appropriate standards and refute the argument that courts should remain out of this area on the ground of "justiciability."

Acuff's reaction, from the point of view of an administrator of state institutions, stresses the administrative role in establishing adequate programs and program standards. He argues against overly specific legislative standards that impair the flexibility of administrators in using scarce resources imaginatively. He concurs in and reemphasizes the need for standards geared to produce "outcomes," rather than simply to prescribe inputs.

PRINCIPAL PAPER*

ROBERT H. JOHNSON AND JAMES JERRY ·WOOD, SR.

MOST OF the literature relating to the legal rights of mentally retarded citizens has been written by professionals in the field of mental retardation (or by lawyers specializing in the field); yet, in almost all cases the lawyers, legislators, and judges who will have to implement the right to habilitation will be laymen. It is these laymen, not the experts, who will make the decisions that fundamentally affect the quality of habilitation delivered in this country's institutions.[1] One goal is to indicate how

---

*Any opinions expressed in this paper are the authors' and do not necessarily represent those of the United States Department of Justice or the Alabama Mental Health Board.

[1] David Halberstam made this point most vividly in his recent book D. HALBERSTAM, THE BEST AND THE BRIGHTEST 40-41 (1972).

It was an extraordinary confluence of time and men, and many people in the know quoted Lyndon Johnson's reaction to them at the first Cabinet meeting. . . . They were all so glamorous and bright that it was hard to tell who was the most brilliant, but the one who impressed him the most was "the fellow from Ford with the Stacomb on his hair." . . . What was not so widely quoted in Washington (which was a shame because it was a far more prophetic comment) was the reaction of Lyndon's great and crafty friend Sam Rayburn, to Johnson's enthusiasm about the new men. Stunned by their glamour and intellect, he had rushed back to tell Rayburn. his great and crafty mentor, about them, about how brilliant each was, that fellow Bundy from Harvard, Rusk from Rockefeller, McNamara from Ford. On he went, naming them all, "Well, Lyndon, you may be right and they may be every bit as intelligent as you say," said Rayburn, "but I'd feel a whole lot better about them if just one of them had run for sheriff once."

these laymen can make appropriate, informed decisions and in what ways essential professional information can be channeled into their decision-making process.

This chapter is *not* a discussion of whether there is a "right to adequate habilitation," *nor* an attempt to define what constitutes "adequate" habilitation.[2] As Dr. Philip Roos has so aptly said: "Our challenge today is to evolve strategies of cooperation. The focus . . . is not on the content of desirable changes in an institution, but on the process of bringing about change."[3] We proceed on the assumptions that all three branches of government are capable of being made competent to formulate standards for mental retardation institutions[4] and that each branch has a vital role to play in ensuring that institutionalized mentally retarded citizens receive the care and habilitation they need and to which they are entitled.

The emphasis in the following pages is on the practical problems of effectively regulating institutions for mentally retarded citizens. However, this emphasis ought not to be viewed as expressing a technocratic approach to retardation: above all,

---

[2] This paper proceeds on the assumption that thousands of mentally retarded individuals in the nation's institutions will continue to be there involuntarily, either because they have been involuntarily committed or because the "voluntary" nature of their continued confinement resembles the voluntary nature of an enlistee's continued service in the armed forces. However, the possibility that institutions will become voluntary places of residence in the legal (if not the economic) sense of the term may be on the horizon.

Judge Bazelon has stated:

California has recently enacted legislation which promises virtually to eliminate involuntary hospitalization except for short-term crisis situations. . . . Only experience will reveal whether California can truly end involuntary commitments . . . and avoid the potential sequelae of voluntary commitments which are the product of subtle coercion.

But the careful drafting of the Lanterman-Petris-Short Act allows us all to hope. [*See also* Lanterman Mental Retardation Services Act, CAL. HEALTH & SAFETY CODE § 38002 (West Supp. 1973).] If its goals are achieved, the necessity for a right to treatment in its present form will wither away. If this happens, and I hope it will, the path will be cleared for society to confront the right to treatment in its more fundamental form. We should ultimately ground the right to treatment not in our duty to help the . . . person as a quid pro quo for confining him, but in our duty to help him as a troubled human being in our midst. . . . As a judge, it would be wholly inappropriate for me to predict the ways in which this more basic right to treatment may take root in the law. Bazelon, *Implementing the Right to Treatment,* 36 U. CHI. L. REV. 742, 753-54 (1969).

In any event, should the future alter or eliminate the present constitutional basis for the right to habilitation, the problems facing legislators and administrators in framing standards for adequate treatment will remain. Should "right to habilitation" statutes be passed, judges may still have to grapple with questions of adequacy. For an extensive discussion of the right to habilitation, see Chapters 13 & 14 of this volume.

[3] Address by Dr. Philip Roos, National Conference on Residential Care (sponsored by National Association for Retarded Children), in Houston, Texas, July 22, 1969, at 13.

[4] There is a good deal of discussion in the literature about the imperative need to think in terms of "residential services" instead of institutionalization. Although this chapter deals with institutions, to the exclusion of other treatment facilities and programs, we wish to emphasize that, at least with respect to the roles of the legislature and executive, the institution cannot be considered in a vacuum. Other issues, such as encouraging the training of more professionals in the relevant disciplines, commitment procedures, and certification and inspection of noninstitutional residential facilities, ought to be the focus of considerable governmental action.

Nonetheless, given the capital expenditures involved and the usual pace of change, institutions are going to be with us for a number of years. California, for example, recently backed off a plan to phase out state hospitals for the retarded by 1982 "because people got very scared of this date idea." The Sacramento Bee, April 17, 1973, § A, at 14, col. 1. The right to adequate habilitation is a "present" right and cannot await the destruction of state hospitals.

special care must always be taken to stress the individuality of our mentally retarded fellow citizens. The proper maintenance and staffing of institutions is not representative of ordinary governmental services such as paving roads or installing water and sewer lines. Rather, it "is the very preservation of human life and dignity."[5]

> ...[O]f immediate and paramount importance must be an all-out effort throughout the country to recognize the indisputable need for immediate adjustment of appropriations to make sure that in the future, institutions for the mentally retarded can buy enough clothing so that no resident needs to be naked, no child need be kept from playing out of doors for want of a pair of shoes or a sweater, no resident need freeze at night for lack of a blanket, and that essentials such as soap and toilet paper are available. Each of the examples just cited refer to actual situations in the recent past in the two richest states in this country. . . . The disgraceful conditions in our institutions for the mentally retarded . . . are related to the disgraceful salary level for basic care personnel. In one state, it was lower than that paid to exterminators of vermin; in another, lower than that of a disemboweler of chickens; and in a third, lower than that of an attendant of a public toilet.[6]

AN OVERVIEW OF STANDARD SETTING

Before the ink was dry on the court's opinion in *Rouse v. Cameron*,[7] a flood of controversy burst over the competence of government to ascertain and apply standards of adequacy to institutions for the mentally ill.[8] It is unlikely that extension of the right to adequate care to persons in institutions for the mentally retarded will halt the tide of commentary. Nonetheless, even the skeptical admit that, "a workable definition of responsible treatment [is needed] which judges can apply to curb negligent or palpably inappropriate treatment without unduly encouraging litigation or straitjacketing the medical profession."[9]

But what is a workable definition? Perhaps because the right to adequate habilitation for those committed to institutions for the mentally retarded is a conceptual stepchild of the right to treatment, recognized earlier for the mentally ill, most of the legal literature that may offer some guidance to officials seeking a yardstick for adequacy never mentions the word "retarded." (Hopefully, *Wyatt v. Stickney*[10] will initiate a needed change.) Thus, it may be productive to begin the discussion by pointing to a suggested set of "criteria" for determining the adequacy of treatment for the mentally ill which is an archetype of what *not* to recommend as "standards" to *any* governmental body.

---

[5] Wyatt v. Stickney, 344 F. Supp. 373, 377 (M.D. Ala. 1972), *aff'd sub nom.* Wyatt v. Aderholt, 503 F.2d 1305 (5th Cir. 1974).

[6] Dybwad, *Action Implications, U.S.A. Today,* in Changing Patterns in Residential Services for the Mentally Retarded 383, 411 (R. Kugel & W. Wolfensberger eds. 1969).

[7] 373 F.2d 451 (D.C. Cir. 1966).

[8] *See generally* Bazelon, *supra* note 2.

[9] Note, *Civil Restraint, Mental Illness, and the Right to Treatment,* 77 Yale L.J. 87, 105 (1967).

[10] 344 F. Supp. 387, 344 F. Supp. 373 (M.D. Ala. 1972), 334 F. Supp. 1341, 325 F. Supp. 781 (M.D Ala. 1971), *aff'd sub nom.* Wyatt v. Aderholt, 503 F.2d 1305 (5th Cir. 1974).

> The Council of the American Psychiatric Association . . . approved on February 6, 1967, the following seven basic considerations in determining the adequacy of treatment: (1) the purpose of hospitalization and related treatment programs; (2) the relevance of diagnostic procedures; (3) protecting the patient; (4) interrupting the disease process; (5) physical methods of treatment; (6) changing the emotional climate surrounding the patient; and (7) conventional psychological therapies. *These seven categories were designed to serve as criteria against which the adequacy of treatment might be assessed by courts and other agencies confronted with the problem of determining legitimacy and adequacy of treatment.*[11]

It appears evident that increasing numbers of officials, be they judges, legislators, governors, prosecutors, or simply private attorneys, *will* be "confronted with the problem of determining legitimacy and adequacy of treatment." Undoubtedly (and properly) they will be considerably reluctant to take over the job of administering institutions. Judges (who may have been patent lawyers, divorce lawyers, or securities lawyers) or legislators (who may be farmers, insurance salesmen, saxophone players, or car dealers) usually have a fairly honest view of their own lack of background in this highly specialized and complex field. Nonetheless, if the only standards furnished by the relevant professions are so vague as to be meaningless, or so laced with jargon as to be not understandable, at least some officials will put aside their reluctance and fashion their own standards. When faced with an effectively presented case that a particular institution is housing children in conditions "not distinctly different from the environment experienced by prisoners of war,"[12] many such officials will no longer tell themselves that medical, psychiatric, and psychological performance cannot be judged by mere mortals.[13] Even professionals have come to recognize the need for "workable standards."[14]

It is desirable that, insofar as possible, the standards of adequate habilitation for mental retardation institutions be set by the professions directly charged with this care. To a commendable extent, this has already been accomplished. The development of standards for institutional facilities for mentally retarded citizens has a relatively short history. It was not until 1952 that the American Association on Mental Deficiency (AAMD) first published a *Report of the Special Committee on Standards for Institutions.* In 1959, the AAMD's Project on Technical Planning in Mental Retardation started a major standards development project which resulted in the publication, in 1964, of *Standards for State Residential Institutions for the Retarded.* These standards were presented as *minimal* with an attainment projection of 5-10

---

[11] Cameron, *Nonmedical Judgment of Medical Matters,* 57 Geo. L.J. 716, 720-21 (1969), *citing* American Psychiatric Ass'n, *Position Statement on the Question of Adequacy of Treatment,* 123 Am. J. Psychiatry 1458 (1967) (emphasis supplied).

[12] President's Committee on Mental Retardation, Residential Services for the Mentally Retarded: An Action Policy Proposal, at v (1970).

[13] It should be noted for the record that the mental retardation professionals with whom we have dealt have, if anything, been eager to initiate interprofessional cooperation. The dialogues have been frequent, fruitful, and friendly. We are aware of no published opposition by mental retardation professionals to judicial involvement in assessing adequacy of treatment like that which emerged, *ex cathedra,* from the American Psychiatric Association after the decision in Rouse v. Cameron, 373 F.2d 451 (D.C. Cir. 1966). *Compare* American Psychiatric Ass'n, *supra* note 11, *with* President's Committee on Mental Retardation, President's Committee Sees Legal Breakthrough on Rights of Retarded in Institutions, April 12, 1973 (press release).

[14] Robitscher, *Courts, State Hospitals, and the Right to Treatment,* 129 Am. J. Psychiatry 79 (1972).

years, yet few institutions for the mentally retarded in the United States actually meet the majority of these standards even now.

In addition to AAMD, the American Psychiatric Association and the National Association for Retarded Citizens have been interested in the development of standards for residential facilities for retarded persons. After careful consideration and recognition of the desirability of having a single agency to establish, promulgate, and monitor standards leading toward accreditation, the National Planning Committee on the Accreditation of Residential Centers for the Retarded was formed in 1966. It included representatives of AAMD, the American Psychiatric Association, the Council for Exceptional Children, the National Association for Retarded Citizens, the United Cerebral Palsy Association, and the the American Medical Association. This group included mental retardation professionals, consumers, and lay persons.

After significant work by numerous multidisciplinary committees, the *Standards for Residential Facilities for the Mentally Retarded* were formulated and were adopted on May 5, 1971, by the Joint Commission of the Accreditation of Hospitals, Accreditation Council for Facilities for the Mentally Retarded (ACFMR). These standards are designed so that compliance can be objectively determined. They are prefaced with language indicating a continual review and revision to "maintain currency with the best thinking and with changing knowledge in the field, and in order to keep them clear, comprehensive, and challenging."[15]

Since the adoption of the ACFMR standards, courts have imposed standards of their own,[16] bills have been introduced in Congress to set standards for institutions for the mentally retarded,[17] and the Department of Health, Education, and Welfare has specified "conditions" that must be met by mental retardation facilities before they can receive reimbursement under Medicaid.[18] These various compilations of standards run the gamut from how many square feet of space ought to be required in multiresident rooms to how many times a week a resident's teeth ought to be brushed. By and large — at least to the lay reader — they represent a remarkable professional consensus. The "crunch" comes when attempts are made to set staffing standards.

Perhaps the most critical problem of standard setting facing any governmental

---

[15] ACCREDITATION COUNCIL ON FACILITIES FOR THE MENTALLY RETARDED, STANDARDS FOR RESIDENTIAL FACILITIES FOR THE MENTALLY RETARDED, at xii (1971).

[16] 344 F. Supp. at 379. *Wyatt's* standards are primarily based on the 1964 AAMD standards, principally because the court had indicated it wanted to consider specific "bare-bones" minimums with regard to staff needs. Note that the Fifth Circuit did not consider the standards ordered by the District Court in *Wyatt* because of stipulations entered into by the parties and *amici*. The holding on appeal focused on the existence of a right to habilitation. See also *New York State Association for Retarded Children v. Rockefeller,* 357 F. Supp. 752, 768-769 (E.D.N.Y. 1973), in which the court, while hinting that there was no "right to habilitation" nonetheless ordered the hiring of more personnel specifically adopting a ratio of staff to residents. In an analogous case involving juveniles who had been determined to be persons in need of supervision, a federal district court ordered standards, including staff-resident ratios, in *Martarella v. Kelly,* 359 F. Supp. 478, 484-486 (S.D.N.Y. 1973).

[17] S. 458, 93d Cong., 1st Sess. (1973); H.R. 76, 93d Cong., 1st Sess. (1973) [hereinafter cited as S.458 (1973) and H.R. 76 (1973) respectively].

[18] U.S. Department of Health, Education & Welfare Standards for Intermediate Care Facility Services in Institutions for the Mentally Retarded §§ 234.130 *et seq.,* 39 Fed. Reg. 2220 *et seq.* (1974).

body—be it executive, legislative, or judicial—is accurately determining the staffing necessary to enable a particular institution to be in a position to perform its functions adequately. By far the largest component of any institution's budget is staff salaries (about 62 percent of the operating budgets of California's state hospitals at the time of a 1965-67 study on staffing standards). Thus, it is not surprising that staff-resident ratios are a major concern of budget officers. Not only does staff represent the major component in an institution's budget, but its presence in adequate numbers is an indispensable precondition to attainment of all the other minimum standards. A humane environment presupposes clean buildings, and clean buildings require X amount of housekeeping time to stay that way. Individual habilitation requires individual evaluations, and evaluations require persons to perform them. Periodic review of habilitation programs requires records, and records imply that someone has to take the time to fill them out and to read and use them. Spot checks can tell an official whether or not buildings are in fact clean, whether or not evaluations have been made, and whether or not records are up to date. But once it is established that these tasks, to some greater or lesser degree, are not being performed, the official must determine how much more of various kinds of staff is needed to get the job done.

> Staffing standards may be expressed qualitatively or quantitatively. Quality standards specify the kind of person and the credentials needed for a particular job as: "this task requires a licensed physician with board certification in neuropathology" or "this task requires a doctoral psychologist."
>
> . . . .
>
> Most standards used by licensing and accrediting bodies are primarily qualitative. For example, a condition of licensure for a nursing home may be: "one or more registered nurses must be present on each shift in numbers sufficient to ensure health, safety and welfare of the patients." Determination of "numbers sufficient" is then left up to the intuitive judgment of the program manager or the licensing inspector. *Legislators and administrators who must make decisions about allocating financial and manpower resources need quantitative as well as qualitative standards, especially when they are dealing with large programs, or trying to evaluate program effectiveness.*[19]
> . . . [S]tandard-setting bodies, such as the Joint Commission on Accreditation of Hospitals, . . . various federal regulatory agencies, and the various state, local and other licensing and inspecting agencies, generally determine adequacy of a facility's staff through observation, and intuitive evaluation, of the quality of care rendered, with some restrictions about the qualifications of personnel employed. An exception has been the American Association on Mental Deficiency which, in 1964, published standard personnel ratios for various hospital treatment personnel and various categories of mentally retarded patients. Otherwise, authorities of the type mentioned have seldom ventured to specify numbers of personnel.[20]

Persuasive arguments can be advanced that such determinations can be made only on an ad hoc basis, taking into consideration such factors as building design,

---

[19] 1 CALIFORNIA COMMISSION ON STAFFING STANDARDS, STAFFING FOR PUBLIC MENTAL HOSPITALS 134-35 (Dep't of Mental Hygiene 1967) [hereinafter cited as CAL. STAFFING STANDARDS] (emphasis supplied).
[20] *Id.* at 26.

the degrees of disability in a given resident population, and the training, competence, and attitudes of individual staff members. Persuasive arguments can also be advanced, however, that there are certain irreducible minimums below which the delivery of adequate treatment at *any* institution is impossible even with the most brilliant and highly motivated staff.

Advocates of the former position argue that staff-resident ratios are meaningless as a measure of adequacy because different professionals can accomplish the same results with widely differing investments of their time. Such an argument is persuasive to a judge faced daily with the work product of attorneys who, though ostensibly qualified and often possessed of comparable training and experience, turn out papers ranging from models of draftsmanship to indecipherable garbage. To a legislator or administrator who deals with colleagues whose abilities, energy, and devotion cover a vast range, this argument is also telling.

Advocates of the latter position commendably advance the interest of administrative ease and are undoubtedly reluctant to argue at this seminal state of the right to habilitation that the Constitution requires in Institution *A* "different" things from those it requires in Institution *B*. (They tend to suspect, often with some reason, that critics of staff ratios are sophists, trying to protect their professional bailiwick against lawyers and judges.) Staff ratios are appealing because judges, legislators, and administrators generally are not personally conversant with mental retardation in a professional capacity, have heavy work loads of other matters, and are reluctant to get involved with the sticky business of rating the efforts of particular professionals.[21]

Insofar as the standards previously mentioned are concerned, they fall into the two "camps":

No Staff-Resident Ratios	Staff-Resident Ratios
ACFMR standards for professional staff [also S. 458 & H.R. 76]	ACFMR standards for resident care staff [also S. 458 & H.R. 76]
Medicaid standards for mental retardation facilities: professional staff	AAMD standards for *all* staff
	Wyatt standards for *all* staff
	Medicaid standards for mental retardation facilities—resident care staff [ratios after 3/18/77]

[21] Judge Johnson eloquently expressed the frustration of trying to apply vague standards to concrete situations in his comments to counsel during the hearing on Alabama's mental hospitals in *Wyatt*:

THE COURT: Gentlemen, I might state this to you for your guidance—it may be. It is not much assistance to the Court to offer expert testimony to the effect that these proposed regulations are minimal when practically all of them state that, "This shall be adequate in number," or, "This shall provide appropriate treatment," and that is what your regulations provide. And then to put an expert up here and say that these regulations provide minimal treatment, your

Actually, the two approaches are not mutually exclusive. There are two methods by which policy makers can frame workable staffing standards, which give due recognition to the valid points raised by both those who wish to assess staffing on an ad hoc basis and those who seek uniformity and ease of administration.   The first method is a modification of the staff-resident ratio approach which both takes into account the flexibility needed for various treatment modalities and variations in physical facilities and sets numbers against which compliance can be measured.

Instead of traditional staff-resident ratios, an aggregate number of representatives of the various professions required to provide adequate care might be established. Of this total, a minimum number of professional personnel within each discipline necessary to provide the specialized skills unique to the discipline would be set. The remaining professional personnel could be employed on the basis of skills, rather than discipline.[23] For example, assume that it was professionally established that a total of 20 psychiatrists, psychologists, physicians, nurses, and social workers was required to render adequate habilitation to a given population and that at least 1 representative of each profession ought to be employed. The permissible staffing pattern would be:

> 1 psychiatrist
> 1 psychologist
> 1 physician
> 1 nurse
> 1 social worker
> 15 of any combination of representatives
>   of the disciplines listed
>
> ―――――――――――――――――――――――――――――
>
> TOTAL: 20 qualified mental retardation professionals

Admittedly, this approach is no less intuitive than either staff-resident ratios or an individual professional's ad hoc judgment, but it does provide both fixed minimum staffing standards and the flexibility required for administration of a complex and changing program.

> In the ideal system, each unit should be described in terms of the functions required to accomplish the goals. An admissions unit, for example, might require a certain number of physical examinations, dental checkups, preparations of social history, and preliminary psychological examinations. These functions, described in terms of number of professional hours required, would then determine the number of physicians, dentists, social workers and psychologists required to staff the admis-

―――

minimal treatment, according to regulations, being adequate or appropriate, doesn't help me very much. . . . I am going to have to go further than that if I — if I render any judgment in this case that will be effective, either for the plaintiffs or the defendants. Hearing of Feb. 3-4, 1972, transcript at 153-54, Wyatt v. Stickney, Civil No. 3195-N (M.D. Ala. 1972).

[22] At this juncture we wish to note our joint opinion that the adoption by the district court of *all* the standards agreed to by the parties in *Wyatt* was a proper exercise of that court's authority to fashion a remedy. To protect the rights of both the plaintiff class and the defendants, the district court has retained jurisdiction and is open to modify its decree, if appropriate, as circumstances develop.

[23] Letter from Dr. Raymond D. Fowler, Jr., chairman, Dep't of Psychology, University of Alabama, to Robert H. Johnson, April 12, 1973.

sions unit. An exit unit might require little or no professional hours from physicians or dentists but could require the services of social workers to establish home and community contacts, psychologists to develop behavior shaping programs and vocational rehabilitation counsellors to assist in job placement. On many of the units between admissions and exit, the functions of group and individual counselling, activities planning, etc. could be provided by individuals from any one of several disciplines.[24]

A good deal of work has already been done to develop such a system. In 1965 the California senate passed a resolution[25] urging the department of mental hygiene to request the California Medical Association, the American Psychiatric Association, and such other professional organizations or persons as the department considered appropriate, jointly to evaluate the staff needs of the state hospitals for the mentally ill and mentally retarded. In response, the department created the California Commission on Staffing Standards for State Mental Hospitals, consisting of representatives of 11 professional associations.[26] In carrying out its duties, the commission was assisted by department staff, the Aerojet General Corp., representatives of the state department of finance, the California Legislative Analyst's Office, the California State Employees Association, and the California Pharmaceutical Association.[27]

As a result of its efforts, the commission submitted a two-volume report to the senate in February 1967, recommending the minimum staffing requirements it considered necessary to give the basic level of care for five "services"—ward (or nursing) services, medical services, psychological services, social work services, and rehabilitation services. Based on its standards, the commission concluded that the California institutions for mentally retarded people were operating at the following percentages of the staffing it considered acceptable:

Service	%
Ward services	71
Medical	22
Psychological	18
Social work	24
Rehabilitation	11
"Overall"	62[28]

The standards on which these findings were based were derived from five procedures. The first two — time studies and work sampling of the "on-ward" activities — were aimed at developing standards for what the ACFMR standards call resident-living staff. The third and fourth procedures — self-recorded diaries and detailed task inventories — were the basis for analyzing the medical, psychological, rehabilitative, and social work programs. The fifth procedure was a comparison of these

[24] Id.
[25] Cal. S.R. 166, State Sen. Reg. Sess. (1965).
[26] 1 CAL. STAFFING STANDARDS 2-3.
[27] Id. at v-vi.
[28] Id. at 5.

studies with other studies and with staffing patterns at other public and private institutions. [29]

As a result of the studies of ward services, a system was developed which uses computer programing to determine ward nursing service staff requirements. This system, called SCOPE (Staffing Care of Patients Effectively) was adopted in principle by the governor on February 23, 1968. [30]

In developing a computer program to determine staff requirements, an industrial engineering team made stopwatch measurements of the times that trained, experienced personnel required to do 55 different kinds of tasks — such as bathing, dressing, and feeding residents and preparing and dispensing medication. More than 3,500 such observations were recorded under actual working conditions with some activities evaluated more than 100 times. [31] It should be emphasized that the times measured were those a trained person *ought* to take to do the job right — not the time usually taken. [32] In conjunction with the time studies, work sampling was conducted on 104 wards considered representative of each hospital and the system as a whole. [33] In the studies, trained observers entered the wards and noted the activities of all personnel — classifying them in 1 of 30 different categories. The observations were made every few minutes at random intervals, 24 hours a day, over 7 days. [34]

The department of mental hygiene did *not* adopt the commission's recommended standards for the other four services. [35] Though no official explanation was given for the refusal to adopt the commission's recommendations with regard to these services, it was believed in capitol circles that although SCOPE represented a fresh, more precise approach to the problem of assessing staff needs, the commission's standards for the "professional" services essentially were an update of the staff ratios that had been used in the past. To be sure, they were substantially more sophisticated — focusing as they did on the time needed for various tasks thought necessary to provide adequate resident care. But they still represented essentially intuitive (and in that sense arbitrary) judgments by various professionals as to how long particular tasks ought to take. From an industrial engineering point of view, the self-recording diaries and task inventories did not provide the unassailable data base for the "professional" staff recommendations that the time studies and work sampling provided for the nursing staff recommendations. For this reason (and undoubtedly because of the difference between the then current levels of care and those recommended as adequate for the nonward services) it was much easier to sell SCOPE to the policy makers. [36]

[29] *Id.* at 21.

[30] The Sacramento Bee, Feb. 23, 1968, § B, at 1, col. 6.

[31] 1 CAL. STAFFING STANDARDS 21.

[32] Interview with Martin A. Naleway, industrial engineering specialist. Program Review Unit, Dep't of Mental Hygiene, in Sacramento, Cal., April 17, 1973 [hereinafter cited as Naleway interview]. Mr. Naleway designed the original SCOPE program for Aerojet. After July 1, 1973, when the department of mental hygiene merged into a new health department, he moved to the Outcome Measurement Section, Planning and Evaluation Program, Health Quality System of the California Department of Health.

[33] This sort of study shows how individuals distribute their working hours among various activities. It does not tell now long a person spends on an individual task or how well the task is done.

[34] 1 CAL. STAFFING STANDARDS 22.

[35] This fact was overlooked by the press at the time, as the decision *not* to adopt the standards for the other services was, to our knowledge, never publicly announced.

[36] Personal interviews by Robert H. Johnson with legislative and administrative sources.

SCOPE is so structured as to constitute a *fixed standard* yielding *variable* staffing patterns depending on the characteristics of different resident populations. This is possible because the tasks studied were timed for different resident types. For example, it takes an average of 4.3 minutes of ward staff time to arrange for the shower of a 115 + -pound self-bathing ambulatory resident. By contrast, the study indicated that 39.3 minutes ought to be allowed for bed-bathing a 115 + -pound bedfast patient.[37] Once it is decided how many times a week such patient ought to be bathed,[38] staff time needs for this particular task can be determined with a fairly high degree of accuracy simply by ascertaining how many residents fit into each time-per-task category.

Individual resident care of the wards ranges from 49 to 335 minutes per resident per day in the SCOPE program.[39] For those nursing services on which no time study was made, the time values were deliberately set low, because the commission felt that it had little measurable evidence of program results on which to base higher time values. Thus, for example, for mentally retarded residents, SCOPE provides only a "personal interaction allowance" ranging from 4 to 11 minutes per resident in every 24 hours after the first 30 days of institutionalization. "SCOPE does not provide a rich level of treatment programs[,] . . . [b]ecause the SCOPE allowances for the non-time studied activities have deliberately been kept 'lean.'"[40] The commission flatly stated that "any institution operating below the SCOPE levels of services does not afford its patients an adequate hospital level of care."[41]

To apply SCOPE to a particular resident population, a simple questionnaire is completed regarding 39 characteristics that affect the kind, number and frequency of nursing tasks necessary to give that type of resident adequate basic care. Direct care staff do *not* see where a particular resident falls into the time-to-be-spent categories to avoid the danger of self-fulfilling labels.[42]

Since the original survey, California's institutional residents have been surveyed once a year to update the staff needs. The commission, as such, ended its life with the publication of its report, but it continues to function — with many of the same members — as an advisory committee to the department of mental hygiene.[43]

Since SCOPE was developed, two states, Oregon and Indiana, have adopted a variation of the program. Seven others — Tennessee, Ohio, Missouri, Illinois, Pennsylvania, New Mexico, and Arizona — have tested or are testing their staffing patterns against the program.[44]

When SCOPE was first developed, the potential for expanding its approach to determine service levels for other treatment disciplines was recognized.[45] Now

---

[37] 2 CAL. STAFFING STANDARDS app. 1, at 3.
[38] The California staffing standards provide for thrice weekly baths for residents in the above categories; daily baths for other residents. *Wyatt*, on the other hand, requires daily baths for all residents "unless medically contraindicated." 344 F. Supp. at 404. Obviously, the computer program used in a SCOPE-type approach requires some policy judgments — but this would affect only the total staff time needed reflected on the printout, *not* the time it ought to take to perform the basic task.
[39] 1 CAL. STAFFING STANDARDS 37.
[40] *Id.* at 48.
[41] *Id.*
[42] *Id.* at 37.
[43] Naleway interview.
[44] *Id.*
[45] 1 CAL. STAFFING STANDARDS 38.

an effort is being made to do just that. In a project called PRU-72, the California Department of Mental Hygiene is updating the ward services program to reflect time studies that have been made of the "pure treatment" nursing activities. A new resident inventory form has been completed, and every resident in California's institutions was surveyed in May of 1973. It is intended that this survey will be used as the basis for future annual updates of ward staff needs and as a test of a new computer system for "professional" staff needs.

Since the original commission recommendations, more sophisticated industrial engineering techniques have been applied to the task of evaluating professional staff needs. Chief among these techniques has been the monitored "time-ladder." This device, quite similar in form to the legal billing systems which divide a day into 10- or 15-minute segments, is more precise than the self-recorded diaries used previously, for it requires the individual professional to keep track of what he is doing *as he does it,* noting the *exact* time he starts and stops. The "time-ladder" was validated in two ways: (1) trained monitors sought out each professional on the wards surveyed several times a day, at random, and did not leave this professional's side until his "time-ladder" was current and (2) whenever a professional was seen on a ward, the time he was seen and what he was doing was noted as an audit of his "time-ladder." Cooperation from the professionals was obtained because they were chosen as running a model ward (one with the best results, not necessarily the richest staff). As a consequence they were justifiably proud to have their efforts recognized and they responded with what the industrial engineer on the project termed the best cooperation he had ever encountered in the use of the "time-ladder" technique.[46]

The SCOPE approach has been discussed at length, not because we recommend its findings, but because the concept deserves serious consideration. We are not pleased with the fact that SCOPE, as adopted, did not contain a staffing yardstick for habilitation services. Nor does SCOPE take into consideration problems raised by inflexible civil service regulations, absenteeism and morale. For example, in one state hospital for the retarded in California, which has recently been converted to a mental retardation facility from an institution primarily housing the mentally ill, the difficulty of learning new skills coupled with an older than average work force, has led to high absenteeism, both for morale reasons and because the older work force takes more sick leave and has earned more vacation time. As is typical in some civil service contexts, the system has little ability to fill "temporary" vacancies. With the time-honored exception of the substitute teacher, most civil service jobs cannot be filled on a temporary basis. As a result, there are serious questions as to whether the state hospital mentioned above, which is supposed to have more than its full complement of positions required under SCOPE, actually is capable of delivering the services contemplated by the SCOPE staff-resident formula.[47] Any method

---

[46] Naleway interview.

[47] *Id.* The initial cost of determining which tasks ought to be measured and the necessary time studies for ward services alone was estimated to total about $200,000, $60,000 of which was paid to the outside consultant, Aerojet. Yet once the original time values are set, they retain their utility unless it is determined that there ought to be a material change in the way a particular task is done. Thus, assuming the validity of the time studies already made the time values developed therein would have national applicability.

that is adopted for assessing staff needs is by definition imprecise. National standards, developed by recognized professional associations, ought certainly to be the starting point for governmental action in this area. Nevertheless, before a consideration of the respective roles of the three branches of government in the standard-setting process, it ought to be emphasized that although detailed standards are necessary in order for government to assess an institutional or individual program of habilitation, the standards themselves are not rights. *Wyatt*, for example, ought not to be read as establishing a constitutional right to 80 square feet of living space.[48] Constitutional rights endure and are not, therefore, capable of being precisely defined by cementing current scientific thinking into law; when this has been attempted, the results have been absurd.[49] The 49-standard appendix to the court's order in *Wyatt* represents the remedy believed appropriate for that particular case; it is not the definitve definition of the *right* the order is designed to protect. It would be tragic, if in the efforts to bring governmental power to bear on the problems of the institutionalized mentally retarded population, the wrong concepts were carved into stone.

There must be a plan for continuing change. Long-range planning which gained considerable popularity during the past decade is at best tenuous. It must be open to continuing reevaluation and modification. Alternative plans and solutions must be developed, resisting the temptation of simplifying life by selecting a single answer to a problem.

For example, in designing buildings which will house services for retarded individuals, facilities should be built for a relatively short life span, for maximum flexibility, and for easy modification in order to incorporate variations so as to have a multitude of different models. There is danger, for instance, that the current emphasis on normalization will generate a plethora of "homelike" buildings throughout the land, just as the emphasis on efficiency decades ago led to construction of the massive warehouses which still house thousands of retarded persons in most states. By developing different architectural models we could evaluate the relative merits of each and research findings could be evaluated and incorporated in new designs. The past trend toward stereotyped uniformity in design should be avoided. Today's progressive ideas may soon be replaced by entirely different concepts. . . .

The very values underlying services to retarded persons are already in a state of change. For instance, the quality of programs has traditionally been evaluated by such indices as the ratio of staff to clients or the number of specific procedures performed. Standards developed by the American Association on Mental Deficiency during the mid-sixties to evaluate residential services relied heavily on such input measures, as do other accreditation standards. The underlying assumption is that if certain components are provided (e.g., specified numbers of nurses and physicians, specified numbers of psychological evaluations, specified square foot-

---

[48] 344 F. Supp. at 404.

[49] Some of the decisions following the first case to consider wiretapping provide good examples. One line of these cases afforded fourth amendment protection to conversations which were captured by means of a physical intrusion into a "constitutionally-protected area." *See, e.g.*, Goldman v. United States, 316 U.S. 129 (1942). The latest of this line, Clinton v. Virginia, 377 U.S. 158 (1964), temporarily provided the law with one of its more precise boundaries of constitutional police conduct. The sole difference between *Clinton* and *Goldman* was that in *Clinton* the offending microphone was thumbtacked to a party wall, whereas in *Goldman* the microphone was held against the wall by hand.

age of living area per resident) the service will be acceptable. This emphasis on input measures has already shifted to effectiveness measures based on output measures, that is, the measurement of *results*. Establishing a nurse/client ratio is now considered much less relevant than evaluating the changes occurring in the clients. Program effectiveness will soon be determined by objective quantification of changes in clients. The important consideration will be *what* is accomplished rather than *how* or *by whom* it is accomplished.[50]

STANDARD SETTING BY THE LEGISLATURE

It has been argued that legislative initiatives in setting institutional standard may prove fruitless because the projected extension of the rule in *Wyatt* will render unnecessary the "iron mold of a statutory remedy."[51] It is possible, however, that a state might go out of the involuntary commitment business with regard to the vast majority of residents in its mental retardation institutions.[52] This would avoid

[50] Roos, *Mentally Retarded Citizens: Challenge for the 1970's*, 23 Syr. L. Rev. 1059, 1060-61 (1972); *accord*, Wolfensberger, *The Origin and Nature of Our Institutional Models*, in Changing Patterns in Residential Services for the Mentally Retarded 59, 140 (R. Kugel & W. Wolfensberger eds. 1969).

[51] Fronzone, Kreglow & Weiss, *The Right to Treatment—Alternative Rationales*, 10 Duquesne L. Rev. 626, 627 (1972).

[52] *See* Lanterman Mental Retardation Services Act, Cal. Health & Safety Code §§ 38002, 38103, 38120-23 (West Supp. 1973). *See also* note 2 *supra*. It is unlikely that a state could escape the force of *Wyatt* simply by labeling its commitments "voluntary." But see, *Welsch* v. *Likins,* 373 F. Supp. 487 (D. Minn. 1974), where at page 494 the court distinguishes some of the narrow language in *New York State Association for Retarded Children* v. *Rockefeller,* 357 F. Supp. 752 (E.D.N.Y. 1973) on the grounds that Minnesota's commitment laws were more "circumspect" regarding the release of persons who have been civilly committed for mental reasons. Under former New York law, for example, "voluntarily committed residents were not permitted to leave for a minimum of 60 days after commitment. Fifteen-day notice was required and even then the superintendent could refuse to discharge the resident. Release could then be obtained only upon issuance of a court order. Law of April 11, 1961, ch. 504, §§ 14-15, [1961] Laws of N.Y. 1697 (repealed 1973). These provisions were substantially modified by N.Y. Mental Hygiene Law §§ 33.13-33.25 (McKinney Supp. 1973). § 33.13(b) provides that after notice, the director shall promptly release the "voluntary" resident. The director may retain the resident for three days after such application (notice); however, within these three days the director must apply to a court of record in the county where the school is located for an order authorizing the involuntary retention of the resident. § 33.13(a) gives the "voluntary" patient the right to a hearing to contest a mental health information service finding that he should be retained.

It is also questionable whether the "voluntary" character of a parent's decision to commit his child ought to be imputed to the child so as to cut off rights he would have were his commitment labeled involuntary. *Cf.* Strunk v. Strunk, 445 S.W.2d 145 (Ky. 1969) (parent needs court consent to donate incompetent retarded son's kidney for transplant to competent brother); *In re* Seiferth, 309 N.Y. 80, 127 N.E.2d 820 (1955) (minor can object to operation for cleft palate even though parents would permit it); Frazier v. Levy, 440 S.W.2d 393 (Tex. Civ. App. 1969) (mother-guardian cannot consent to sterilization of adult incompetent child). *See also* Note, *Spare Parts from Incompetents: A Problem of Consent,* 9 J. Family L. 309 (1970).

Most *current* "voluntary" commitments probably ought to be treated as involuntary for purposes of determining whether a particular resident has a *Wyatt*-based constitutional right, either because of the conflict of interest of the committing parent or the power of the state to convert his "voluntary" commitment into an involuntary confinement. It is not necessary to go further. *See* Strauss, pp. 465-68, Chapter 15 of this volume. Those who would label every entrance to an institution "involuntary" because of a "lack of viable alternatives," are needlessly pressing their luck. *See, e.g.,* Fronzone, Kreglow & Weiss, *supra* not 51, at 630 n.28. Calling an entry into an institution involuntary because the resident cannot afford to go elsewhere, in order to bring him within the rule of *Wyatt*, cheapens the constitutional precedent and will strike some as yet another attempt to gain preferential treatment for a desirable social goal by crowning it a right.

an obligation based on *Wyatt*.[53] There are other legal theories on which a right to habilitation for voluntary residents can be based. Chief among these is an "equal protection-right to adequate education" argument,[54] But the latest Supreme Court pronouncements on this subject may preclude such an approach if a state is providing school-age children voluntarily in its institutions with some educational services.[55]

Thus, for better or worse, those concerned with safeguarding the interests of the mentally retarded citizen cannot afford to ignore the legislative arena — if for no other purpose than obtaining a statutory right to habilitation which may be enforced in the courts. This may cause concern to some, who view legislatures as political bodies "primarily responsive to popular electoral passions, [which] cannot generally be relied on to act effectively" to protect the interests of the mentally disabled.[56] The elevation of the judiciary to the position of natural protector of civil liberties vis-à-vis the legislature undoubtedly has a basis in fact, but it overlooks those judges who are loath to get involved in *any* case in a developing area of the law, much less one as intricate as *Wyatt*.[57] Although we would not suggest that California has passed all the laws needed to protect the interests of the mentally disabled, it is generally recognized that the Short-Doyle,[58] Lanterman-Petris-Short,[59] and Lanterman Mental Retardation Services Acts,[60] among others, are giant steps in the right direction. This is not, however, the result of a legislature "rich" in the relevant professionals, or even in legislators experienced as laymen in the field.

> In the 1967 Legislature [which passed the Lanterman-Petris-Short Act], there were only four state senators (out of forty) and only one assemblyman (out of eighty) who were informed and active in this issue area. (The number of informed senators is reached by a generous count.) In the 1966 Legislature, the last elected before redistricting made "sure" contests into free-for-alls which returned an unusually high proportion of freshmen in each house, one could probably have added a second assemblyman to the total number of specialists. Even the specialists, though, did little in the way of routinely guiding legislative policy. There were no standing committees in either house with a jurisdiction uniquely, or even approximately, limited to mental health policy. The Senate Finance Committee and the Assembly Ways

[53] *Wyatt* expressly held that the decree dealt only with residents involuntarily committed. 344 F. Supp. at 390 n.5.

[54] *See generally* Burt, Chapter 14 of this volume.

[55] San Antonio Independent School Dist. v. Rodriguez, 411 U.S. 1 (1973). In most cases, even if a state provided such residents with an education costing as much as that furnished most "normal" children in the state, this expenditure would be inadequate to fund the special education services commonly needed by such children. Even Lau v. Nichols, 414 U.S. 563 (1974), does not reach its result on fourteenth amendment equal protection grounds. *Lau* found only San Francisco's failure to provide English instruction to non-English-speaking Chinese children to be a violation of section 601 of the 1964 Civil Rights Act, 42 U.S.C. § 2000d (1970), and HEW regulations, 33 C.F.R. § 4955. *See also* New York State Association for Retarded Children v. Rockefeller, 357 F. Supp. 752, 763 (E.D.N.Y. 1973).

[56] *See, e.g.*, Kenrick, *The Right to Treatment: Judicial Realism—Judicial Initiative*, 10 DUQUESNE L. REV. 609, 613 (1972). This attitude represents an interesting assessment of society's capacity for self-government.

[57] In one survey of attitudes of mental health professionals and selected lay groups toward mental health, judges ranked just behind nonpsychiatrist physicians as holding the most "traditional" attitudes. E. BARDACH, THE SKILL FACTOR IN POLITICS 74, table 8 (1972).

[58] Short-Doyle Act, CAL. WELF. & INST. CODE § 5600 (West 1972).

[59] Lanterman-Petris-Short Act, CAL. WELF. & INST. CODE § 500 (West 1972).

[60] Lanterman Mental Retardation Services Act, CAL. HEALTH & SAFETY CODE § 38002 (West Supp. 1973).

and Means Committee each had subcommittees that considered mental health along with all other matters of health, education, and welfare. In 1963 the Assembly appointed an interim subcommittee of the Ways and Means Committee to recommend solutions to the inadequate number of beds in the hospitals for the retarded. Two years later the subcommittee was reconstituted in order to study the problem of civil commitment to the hospitals for the mentally ill. In both cases the subcommittee's work was carried out mainly by two (and sometimes three) legislators (included in the enumeration above) and two or three full-time staff members.

A somewhat greater number of legislators took an interest in state hospital construction and payrolls. Like other public works, state hospitals are good for the local economy. . . . For the most part these legislators influenced mental health policy only inadvertently.[61]

Yet even the judge who wrote the seminal *Rouse* opinion calls appropriate legislation the "best hope" for the right to treatment, and Rouse's attorney concurs.[62]

> . . .[I]t is clear that inherent limitations of the judicial process require that the major stresses of scientific and technological advance be borne by legislative and administrative innovation. . . . *In large part, the relative freedom of these three branches of the legal system in acquiring and utilizing specialized knowledge must be recognized as duly reflecting their proper functions in the overall system.*[63]

It is beyond the scope of this paper to comment at length on legislative structure or reform, but a few observations on this general topic are required. The legislature has the potential to make enormous changes in the present system of habilitation delivery, but only insofar as it can collect and use relevant information. Many legislatures still meet in biannual sessions for very limited periods of time. Occasionally, these part-time legislators have some staff assistance, but all too often it is so minimal as to be of little or no use. The need for persons interested in mental retardation reform to join the fight for modern, well-staffed, full-time state legislatures cannot be emphasized too strongly.[64]

In any case, then, full-time representation before the legislature by an active mental retardation lobbyist is almost a precondition to progress. Mental health and mental retardation have been areas in which staff assistance has been of critical importance in shaping legislation and seeing it through the legislative obstacle course. Reform legislation in these areas faces not only the problem of gaining the acceptance of the lawmakers (the vast majority of whom have little or no experience with mental retardation and have a number of false preconceptions to overcome). Reform legislation also is the target for intense and

---

[61] E. BARDACH, *supra* note 57, at 26-27.

[62] *Compare* Bazelon, *supra* note 2, at 747, *with* Halpern, *A Practicing Lawyer Views the Right to Treatment,* 57 GEO. L.J. 782, 806 (1969).

[63] Korn, *Law, Fact, and Science in the Courts,* 66 COLUM. L. REV. 1080, 1116 (1966) (citations omitted) (emphasis supplied).

[64] *See* 2 CALIFORNIA J. 96, 114-15 (April 1971) (complete discussion of one legislature's staff resources). *See also* E. BARDACH, *supra* note 57, at 99 *et seq.*

Assemblyman Lanterman's efforts—and the enormous amount of staff effort—to pass the Lanterman-Petris-Short Act are set out in this chapter. Similar tactics (and staff resources) were used to pass the Lanterman Mental Retardation Services Act. Interview with Dennis G. Amundson, director, Minority Ways & Means Staff, Cal. State Assembly, in Sacramento, Cal. March 6, 1973 [hereinafter cited as Amundson interview].

often conflicting pressures from persons affected by the reform, not the least of whom are the institution employees.[65]

Clearly, the legislature has a vital role to play in the development of adequate standards for institutional programs. Paradoxically, that role is to facilitate the work of others in this area. The legislature must set guidelines and provide the resources to permit others to develop and implement appropriate specific standards.

> The transient nature of the future has significant implications for legislation bearing on handicapped persons. Legislation is likely to retain relevance and viability to the degree that it maintains flexibility, that it facilitates revision and change, and that it incorporates ongoing evaluation. Hence, by incorporating a system of ongoing review and planning at the federal and state levels, the Developmental Disabilities Services Act seems well suited to respond to changing conditions.[66]On the other hand, there is danger in incorporating within law fixed standards based on specific staffing ratios or other similar indices whose validity is likely to be highly transient.[67]

The establishment of legislative standards for institutions for mentally retarded citizens might be accomplished in several ways. A legislature, even a poorly staffed one, might commission an independent administrative agency or a consulting firm to conduct the sort of staffing analysis discussed in connection with the SCOPE system, so that the outcome of the traditional battle between the legislative abacus and the governor's computer would not be preordained. Such a project could be ad hoc[68] or continuing.[69]

Bills have been introduced in both Congress and the Pennsylvania legislature which point in this direction.[70] Both congressional bills provide for the creation of

---

[65]Memorandum from Dennis G. Amundson, director, Minority Ways & Means Staff, Cal. State Assembly, to Robert H. Johnson, April 6, 1973:

> In order to be in a position to make major policy decisions about institutional programs for the mentally retarded, the Legislature must have first-hand knowledge about the conditions in such institutions.
>
> The value of on-site visits and field inspections by individual legislators and legislative committees cannot be over-stressed.
>
> . . . .
>
> [Special] purpose investigative inspections are best conducted on an unannounced drop-in basis. Such investigations are particularly valuable because programs and hospital conditions can be observed as they really are without the red-carpet atmosphere that is sometimes falsely created on a guided tour.
>
> . . . .
>
> In addition to personal on-site inspections, legislative committees should also take the lead in encouraging impartial evaluations of such facilities by citizen, professional and parent association. Based upon many years' experience in California, it is clear that such associations contribute greatly to improving conditions in the state hospitals. Some are more effective than others and their work is not always appreciated by department personnel. They make waves; they raise questions; they interfere with smooth administrative practices; they introduce conflict and they have a capacity to embarrass program operators and administrators.

[66]Developmental Disabilities Services & Facilities Construction Act, Amendments of 1970, 42 U.S.C. §§ 2661-66, 2670-77c, 2691, 2693-96 (1970).

[67]Roos, *supra* note 50, at 1061-62.

[68]Arizona's legislature has received a grant to hire staff for the express purpose of reviewing mental health programs. Amundson interview, *supra* note 64.

[69]Both the General Accounting Office on the federal level and the California Office of the Legislative Analyst are examples of the ways in which a legislative body could approach the problem of obtaining independent fiscal advice (here on a very narrow scale).

[70]S. 458 (1973); H.R. 76 (1973); Pa. S.B. 158, Gen. Ass., Reg. Sess. (1969).

a national advisory council on standards for residential facilities for the mentally retarded. The bills provide that membership on this council would include representatives of the same organizations which presently make up the Accreditation Council for Facilities for the Mentally Retarded of the Joint Commission on Accreditation of Hospitals, and the National Association of Superintendents of Public Facilities for the Mentally Retarded. The bills stipulate that a majority of the members must be consumer representatives. The council would advise the Secretary of Health, Education, and Welfare regarding regulations which he would promulgate in the implementation of the minimum standards set out in the bills.[71] Failure to meet these regulations within five years from the passage of the act would result in a fund cutoff.[72] The proposed Pennsylvania right to treatment legislation also provides a formal structure for establishing standards, a mental treatment standards committee consisting of independent representatives of various professions.[73]

Whatever mechanism the legislature might choose, "the machinery created to carry out an administrative program is at least as important as detailed legislative guidance."[74] However, because "nebulous" statutes "typically promote only administrative chaos,"[75] it would be most desirable if the legislature would adopt nationally recognized standards concurrently with a statutory direction to an independent administrative body to develop regulations for the implementation of these standards.

Although the proposed Pennsylvania legislation is limited in its scope to the plight of the mentally ill, its thrust is susceptible to imitation in the area of mental retardation. Unfortunately the bill as proposed contains a grave defect which is inconsistent with a "right" to habilitation. The proposed bill provides that the "right to minimum standards of treatment provided by this act [almost exclusively staff ratios] shall not include the right to have reviewed the judgment, skill or care used by individual psychiatrist, physicians or clinical psychologists."[76] The exclusion is fatal, because right to habilitation includes not only the right to be housed in an institution capable of delivering adequate care; it must also include the right to actually receive such care.[77]

---

[71] S. 458 (1973) § 1209(b); H.R. 76 (1973) § 1109(b). As mentioned above, these standards are essentially those adopted by ACFMR in May 1971.

[72] S. 458 (1973) § 1206; H.R. 76 (1973) § 1106. *But see* S. 458 (1973) § 1207; H.R. 76 (1973) § 1107 (providing for extensions of time when appropriated funds do not meet the amount authorized in any given year).

[73] Furman & Conners, *The Pennsylvania Experiment in Due Process,* 8 DUQUESNE L. REV. 32 (1969). For text of the draft act see *id.* at 67-72 (§§ 3 & 4, dealing with the Mental Treatment Standards Committee, appear at 67-68).

[74] Bazelon, *supra* note 2, at 747.

[75] *Id.* at 746-47.

[76] Pa. S.B. 158, Gen. Ass., Reg. Sess. § 5(b) (1969), *cited in* Furman & Conners, *supra* note 73, at 67-72. *See also* Birnbaum, *Some Remarks on the "Right to Treatment,"* 23 ALA. L. REV. 623, 627-28, 637 (1971); Birnbaum, *A Rationale for the Right,* 57 GEO. L.J. 752, 753-55 (1969).

[77] Wyatt v. Stickney, 344 F. Supp. 387 (M.D. Ala. 1972), *aff'd sub nom.* Wyatt v. Aderholt, 503 F.2d 1305 (5th Cir. 1974); Donaldson v. O'Connor, 493 F.2d 507 (5th Cir. 1974), *vacated and remanded on the issue of immunity,* 95 S. Ct. 2486 (1975) and *Welsch v. Likins,* 373 Supp. 487 (D. Minn. 1974). *See also* Bazelon, *supra* note 2, at 745-46, 748; Halpern, *supra* note 62, at 790-92, 808-10; *cf.* Katz, *The Right to Treatment — An Enchanting Legal Fiction?* 36 U. CHI. L. REV. 755, 764 (1960).

Those who champion excluding the caliber of an individual resident's care from the adequacy equation are to be commended for their dual concern for the rights of all patients and the ease of administering the rights they espouse. But we are unaware of any other "rights" that are held jointly not severally — interests yes, but rights never. The need to focus on the individual as a unique human being is most urgent in the case of the mentally retarded. Too recent is the time when they were considered subhuman even by the professionals charged directly with their care.[78] A refusal to consider their right to habilitation as encompassing the individual right to adequate care is to repeat an ancient outrage; to embody this concept into law is folly.

Although the most difficult standard-setting task for any of the three branches of government is the development of certain "gross benchmarks"[79] against which an institution's adequacy can be measured, complete and up-to-date records must be required for each resident, including a detailed individualized habilitation plan. The design of the records system can appropriately be left to an administrative structure, but the keeping of proper records ought to be a statutory requirement.[80]

One final word of caution: It is entirely possible that with the drop in institutional population which should result from providing adequate habilitation, not only should the quality of services rendered dramatically improve, but the overall cost to the state in the long run should be substantially lowered. In *Wyatt*, there was highly persuasive evidence that adequate habilitation could be given in a community-based program at a substantial savings over the per capita cost of institutionalization.[81] Further savings are realized when the mentally retarded individual becomes self-supporting.[82] Nevertheless, care must be exercised, in presenting legislators with impressive-sounding cost-saving arguments, to recognize the dangers in over-reliance on cost savings as a reason for institutional reform. The large state institutions which are now abhored were founded as vehicles to achieve such savings, and institutional peonage, which is all too common, arose from the need to keep costs down.[83] Such cost arguments ought to be used as rebuttals to cries of impossibility, not as a justification which could be misconstrued as a guarantee. Governors, chairmen of appropriations committees, and judges do not enjoy being toyed with, and the credibility of mental retardation reformers could be seriously damaged.

It would also do the cause of reform a disservice if reformers pretended that adequate habilitation is simply a function of bigger budgets and better paid or larger staffs.

> It cannot be emphasized too strongly that the alleviation of dehumanizing and other undesirable management practices is ultimately more a matter of attitude,

---

[78] *See* Wolfensberger, *supra* note 50, at 100-29.

[79] Bazelon, *Foreword to Symposium on the Right to Treatment,* 57.GEO. L.J. 767, 768 (1969).

[80] *Id. See also* Bazelon, *supra* note 2, at 746; Halpern, *supra* note 62, at 794, 810.

[81] Hearing of Feb. 28-29 & Mar. 1, 1972, Transcript at 47-79, 364-402, Wyatt v. Stickney, Civil No. 3195-N (M.D. Ala. 1972) (testimony of Ms. Linda Glenn regarding Nebraska's community-based program for the retarded).

[82] *See* Murdock, *Civil Rights of the Mentally Retarded: Some Critical Issues,* 48 NOTRE D. LAW. 133, 163-65 (1972) and authorities cited therein.

[83] *See generally* Wolfensberger, *supra* note 50, at 99-100, 116-27, *accord,* P. ROOS, CURRENT ISSUES IN RESIDENTIAL CARE 12 (National Ass'n for Retarded Children 1969).

rather than of money as widely claimed. There have always been residential facilities that provided exemplary service at very low cost. Usually, such facilities are small, privately operated, and affiliated with religious organizations. On the other hand, one can point to public institutions in this country where even generous funding and high staff-to-resident ratios have failed to change old practices. Eight attendants can look at 75 residents from behind an unbreakable glass shield as easily as one attendant can, and I have known an institution where this was the sanctioned pattern.[84]

The staff has to be convinced that residents *can* be taught to wear clothes, that they *can* be engaged in purposeful activities, that they can learn to control their bladders. The staff has to believe that their "boys" and "girls" are men and women who can learn. Obviously, adequate funding and additional staff are vitally important. However, even more important, is the fundamental belief that each resident is a human being.[85]

STANDARD SETTING BY THE EXECUTIVE

Whereas this chapter does not attempt to discuss in detail the various national standards mentioned earlier,[86] a careful study of the standards shows them to be a reasonable formulation. The standards are realistic minimums and do not in any instance impose requirements that cannot be met. In applying these standards to specific programs and institutions within a given state, however, administrators are faced with a stark reality that the majority of residential institutions serving the mentally retarded in this country are underbudgeted, understaffed, and over-crowded. Many states are using buildings that were constructed over 50 years ago with attendant plumbing, electrical, heating, air-conditioning, sanitation, and space utilization defects. Given these problems, plus the factor of overcrowding, with some facilities housing twice the original projected capacity, the immediate adaptability of the 1971 ACFMR standards, or any other reasonable standards, takes on a troublesome dimension: How can most institutions be changed from what they are to what they should be?

The earlier discussion of national standards focused on input standards, and many of the observations point to a primary concurrent role for administrators in developing these standards. There is a consensus that certain minimum staffing levels exist below which adequate habilitation for institutionalized retarded citizens is impossible to provide. This is true of the other elements of an institution's program, both fiscally and in the physical facilities. A given physical plant can house X number of persons adequately. X number of persons can properly be fed, clothed, sheltered, and educated when expenditures are at a given level; below this level the provision for these persons cannot be adequate.

Nevertheless, it is the "bottom-line" output measurement which counts in the business world. Administrators ought to give the development of output measure-

---

[84] Wolfensberger, *supra* note 50, at 78.

[85] Murdock, *supra* note 82, at 148, *quoting* B. BLATT & F. KAPLAN, CHRISTMAS IN PURGATORY — A PHOTOGRAPHIC ESSAY ON MENTAL RETARDATION 22 (1966).

[86] *See* pp. 531-42 *supra*.

ments high priority, insofar as they can measure the *results* for the residents, in addition to calculating the required investments of time and money. Where a particular function is primarily habilitative, as opposed to custodial, the standard-setting agency *must* focus first on the development of output measures. Unfortunately, most institutions are so deficient in the provision of basic custodial care that lengthy consideration of "goals" may be an exercise in futility in the immediate future. Only limited debate is possible on how many baths a resident ought to be provided per week. No such limitation, born of consensus on ends and means, exists with regard to the more complex questions of habilitation. As institutions improve and begin to provide a modicum of safe custody, public officials will have to turn more of their attention to setting standards for services that are directly related to habilitation. Here the role of the executive becomes crucial, for even a court that is willing to issue sweeping orders regarding custodial practices may be quite reluctant to reach the question of what constitutes appropriate habilitation.[87]

If the right to habilitation is to have meaning to individual residents — other than as a right to sue — administrators will need to develop measurements reflecting changes in the lives of residents who, because of institutional programs, will be better able to cope and live productive and rewarding lives.[88] The executive branch, which is ultimately charged with overall responsibility for the proper operation of its mental retardation facilities, must take the lead in seeing that the legislature is

---

[87] Certain rough output indices may be available. With reference to mental hospitals, the defendants in *Wyatt* discussed some variables with the court:

> If Bryce Hospital's treatment programs are effective the following measurable indices should change:
>
> 1. The average length of stay of new admissions should decrease, compared with the average of the past.
> 2. The percentage of yearly admissions that are readmissions should decrease, for example, it should certainly fall below the current level of 40 to 50%.
> 3. The length of time between readmissions should increase, that is the rate of readmissions should decrease.
> 4. The length of stay upon readmission should decrease.
> 5. Inappropriate admissions would decrease, but valid admissions and discharges per year could well increase. This would mean that more people, and a broader range of people, might use brief hospitalization appropriately and effectively. Thus the turnover at Bryce Hospital would be higher than it presently is.
> 6. The hospital census should steadily decline. (Bryce Hospital's population has been declining at the rate of about 60 patients a month since September, 1970.)
> 7. Discharged patients should demonstrate ability to cope: self support or other support, staying out of trouble, living reasonably comfortably without undue isolation in current living arrangements, decrease in the manifestations of the symptoms that caused hospitalization or alienation from the society they lived in.
>
> These are all crude measures contaminated by uncontrolled variables, but they are better than none. Items (1) and (4) mean very little except that all of the other indices show improvement. The rest of the items, in turn, are not pure indices of hospital program effectiveness. They are influenced by chance factors, the effectiveness of community programs via the mental health centers, the right kind and amount of follow-up, and the Department's effectiveness in ameliorating attitudes toward mental illness that are held by families, physicians, judges and employers. Item (7) is the hardest to measure, as it must be measured in the field, but if it goes up then the other indices will reflect the change. Defendants' Report to the Court of June 10, 1971, at 2-3, Wyatt v. Stickney, Civil No. 3195-N (M.D. Ala. 1972).

[88] In this regard it will be important to study the new PRU-72 computer system, discussed *supra,* pp. 539-40, as much to ascertain what criteria were used to pick the "most effective" wards chosen for time studies as to note the staffing requirements yielded by PRU-72.

presented carefully drafted proposals reflecting the most current and appropriate concepts for providing services for mentally retarded citizens.[89]

Although an executive agency such as a department of mental retardation is charged with the actual day-to-day operation of institutions for the mentally retarded (and this agency must have input into any standards that are established), the actual standards should be set by an independent agency composed of highly qualified objective mental retardation professionals, other professionals such as lawyers and clergymen, consumers, and lay people. For true independence, this agency should be a creature of statute, providing for staggered long terms to ensure that no one governor can appoint all its members. With this framework it can be most responsive to the public at large and to appropriate changes in professional philosophy and methodology. The independent standard-setting agency can, ideally, be more objective than the department charged with the ongoing operation and administration of the institutions. There is less likelihood that such an agency will become myopic and calcified in its approach to proper standards.

The monitoring and enforcement of standards established for the operation of the institutions for the mentally retarded in a state can be handled in various fashions. An independent ombudsman or an inspector general ought to be created in order to address the questions of compliance with established standards effectively on a day-to-day basis.[90] Effective monitoring of retardation institutions cannot be left to complaint-oriented bodies alone, although they can play an important role. Because the process of institutionalization itself often has had a debilitating effect, too many residents of mental retardation institutions are in no position intellectually to voice their complaints cogently [91] At a minimum, the agency charged with administering institutions for mentally retarded citizens needs an effective inspector general to protect its own interests, by finding and correcting violations of standards before a public furor erupts. Preferably, this function should be performed by an independent body adequately staffed and empowered to investigate so that when a public furor ought to erupt, it will!

The inspector general concept in some states is operated through bureaus of licensure and certification of the state health departments. As a practical matter, the licensure and certification inspectors in many such departments are not able to do

---

[89] Adequate funding for institutions for the mentally retarded requires that the executive branch bring its institutions into at least minimal compliance with the mandatory requirements of the various funding agencies of the federal government. To a significant extent, the latitude of the executive branch in setting standards is circumscribed by these funding requirements. *See, e.g.,* U.S. Department of Health, Education & Welfare, Standards for Intermediate Care Facility Services in Institutions for the Mentally Retarded §§ 234.130 *et seq.,* 39 Fed. Reg. 2220 *et seq.* (1974). Although HEW funding regulations undoubtedly have some utility as measurements of compliance with minimum standards, certification for funding should *not* be construed as a "seal of approval." Like most such regulations, the latest revisions contain a waiver provision. Federal administrators traditionally face a tough decision when an institution is out-of-but-approaching compliance with minimum standards, for any fund cutoff not only impedes progress toward attainment of the minimum standards, but falls most heavily on the residents themselves.

[90] *Hearings Before the Subcomm. on Constitutional Rights of the Senate Comm. on the Judiciary,* 91st Cong., 1st & 2d Sess., at 65 (1969). *Cf.* Crampton, *A Federal Ombudsman?* 1972 DUKE L.J. 1.

[91] Halpern, *supra* note 62, at 795, 810. An interesting—and distressing—facet of institutionalization is that, given the choice, the residents may be so settled in that they refuse to leave. Fronzone, Kreglow & Weiss, *supra* note 51, at 639 n.69.

in-depth surveys of the institutions for which they are responsible. In fact, because of lack of staff or because of other pressing duties, the certification of the facilities, *especially* state-owned facilities for the mentally retarded, may be perfunctory, at best.

The executive branch is uniquely equipped to recognize the problems of inter-departmental coordination and cooperation. As with legislative staff, there are seemingly unrelated organizational matters which can have an unexpected impact on effective habilitation. In all states, the governor has overall responsibility for coordinating the activities of several hundred departments and bureaus. But if he does not have the power (or the desire) to exercise this responsibility, the actions of the many agencies whose responsibilities affect the mentally retarded can, if uncoordinated, have a serious negative impact on standard formulation and attainment within the mental retardation field. These agencies may include: the state personnel department, which is responsible for administering the merit system; the state building commission, which is responsible for the overall coordination of construction of public buildings; the state highway department, which may be responsible for maintaining the internal roads and parking lots at state institutions for the retarded; the state health department, which may be responsible for the health and sanitation programs within the institutions; and the state department of public welfare, which may be responsible for certain state and federal programs that provide funding for citizens within state institutions for the mentally retarded. The executive must carefully review all relevant legislative enactments and the various departmental regulations to establish a relatively simple and unencumbered format for the operations of the institutions for the mentally retarded. This may require the repeal of archaic, confusing, and conflicting statutory provisions that have accrued over the years. In order to implement the standards, the executive must ensure proper complements of professional and paraprofessional personnel are either recruited or trained. Possible difficulties in implementation are legion.

Another practical item that may be overlooked in standard setting is program budgeting for all mental retardation activities, even cutting across departmental lines if necessary. This has been tried with some success; it both promoted coordinated planning and released administrators from an artificial straitjacket.[92] It also has forced policy makers — particularly legislators — to take responsibility for ensuring that institutions receive adequate resources to do the job.

> Line-term budgeting (for most departments) at the state level [in California] was another constraint on flexibility in recruiting workers. If there were two positions authorized for psychiatric social workers but only one could be found, the second position remained vacant. This was especially irritating to an administrator if the nature of the tasks he would have assigned to the second psychiatric social worker were such that a psychiatric nurse or perhaps an especially able psychiatric technician could have performed them satisfactorily. . . . According to sources in the [California Department of Mental Health], the state legislature had resisted attempts by the department to prepare program budgets because the legislature did not wish to take responsibility for the inadequacy of staffing in the hospitals. As usual, the

---

[92] Amundson interview, *supra* note 64.

ostensibly managerial issue of choosing between program budgeting and line-item budgeting reflected an underlying political issue.[93]

Once the executive has an understanding and an overview of the operation of a state's facilities for mentally retarded citizens and once standards have been adopted, it is a relatively simple task to devise an action program that will bring the state program into compliance with these standards. This can be accomplished in stages through the proper use of program budgets, both capital and operational. It is a more difficult task to find the necessary tough-minded dedication to the shaping of a society in which every person has a realistic opportunity to achieve to his highest potential.

STANDARD SETTING BY THE JUDICIARY

In spite of the potential for legislative and administrative resolution of "standard setting" and implementation, experience has been that the potential is often not fulfilled. Standards for institutional programs for retarded citizens are, in many states, nonexistent, inadequate, or not implemented. This situation has resulted in increasing recourse to federal courts for the setting and enforcement of adequate standards. Because of the difficulties a court will naturally encounter if it attempts to set standards for mental retardation facilities, and because of the government's traditional separation of powers, some have argued that courts are not competent to set institutional standards. They assert that even if there is a right to habilitation, it is not "justiciable" because (1) ordering the provision of adequate treatment or habilitation to resident-plaintiffs may require an allocation of state funds, *i.e.,* "a political question," and (2) the determination of whether treatment or habilitation is adequate is too complex for a court.

The leading case articulating the "political question" doctrine is *Baker v. Carr,*[94] and the court in this case stated, "it is the relationship between the judiciary and coordinate branches of the Federal Government, and *not* the federal judiciary's relationship to the states, which gives rise to the 'political question.'"[95] Thus, a suit

---

[93] E. BARDACH, *supra* note 57, at 60-61 & n.21.

[94] 369 U.S. 186 (1962).

[95] *Id.* at 210 (emphasis supplied); *accord,* Powell v. McCormack, 395 U.S. 486, 516-18 (1969). Nowhere in the United States Constitution is the protection of eighth and fourteenth amendment rights committed solely to state legislatures. Other problems may be raised in the event a legislature refuses to appropriate the necessary monies to fund compliance with a federal court order. *See* Comment, *Enforcement of Judicial Financing Orders: Constitutional Rights in Search of a Remedy,* 59 GEO. L.J. 393 (1970) and authorities discussed therein. To be sure, in affirming *Wyatt,* the Fifth Circuit acknowledged that "state legislatures are ordinarily free to choose among various social services competing for legislative attention and state funds." The Circuit Court warned that this "does not mean that a state legislature is free, for budgetary or any other reason, to provide a social service in a manner which will result in the denial of individual's constitutional rights. . . . [T]he state may not fail to provide treatment for budgetary reasons alone." Nonetheless, the Fifth Circuit recognized the serious constitutional questions presented by federal judicial financing orders and indicated that such remedies are required to be considered by a three-judge district court. The Fifth Circuit even left open the question of whether—absent a stipulation—standard setting was within the province of a federal court (single judge *or* three-judge).

in federal court by a resident of a state institution could not raise a "political question" for a federal court.

Assuming that there is a federal constitutional right to habilitation for persons involuntarily committed to mental retardation institutions, and thus a suit to vindicate this right does not raise a political question, the more general question of justiciability must be faced.

> In deciding generally whether a claim is justiciable, a court must determine whether "the duty asserted can be judicially identified and its breach judicially determined, and whether protection for the right asserted can be judicially molded."[96]

This question will most frequently arise in the context of a class action attacking the adequacy of habilitation at an entire facility (or part thereof). Defendants will argue (correctly) that different individuals with different problems will not require the same type of habilitation. This argument misses the point. A class action of this sort must, by definition, involve *systemic* deficiencies in basic minimums necessary to provide habilitation to anyone, regardless of his affliction.[97]

At least insofar as involuntary civilly committed persons are concerned, the cases that have been cited for the proposition that adequacy of habilitation is solely a question for the state legislature do not support this position. For example, King v. Smith, 392 U.S. 309 (1968), dealt with Alabama's denial of welfare benefits pursuant to a substitute father regulation. In holding Alabama's action unlawful, the Court observed in passing that the level of welfare benefits was up to the state. However, in *King*, none of the plaintiffs was in the involuntary custody of the state. McGowan v. Maryland, 366 U.S. 420 (1961), is in no way applicable, dealing as it does with a Sunday closing law. Fullington v. Shea, 320 F. Supp. 500 (D. Colo. 1970) (three-judge court), *aff'd*, 404 U.S. 963 (1971), concerned income ceilings adopted by Colorado for receipt of Medicaid. Plaintiffs contended that such ceilings denied them the right to food, shelter, and necessities. This case, like *King*, is inapplicable because the *Fullington* plaintiffs were not in the involuntary custody of the state. Flemming v. Adams, 377 F.2d 975 (10th Cir.), *cert. denied,* 389 U.S. 898 (1967), is cited for the proposition that a right to education is not one of the rights secured by the United States Constitution. The plaintiff in *Flemming* was denied special education services for the handicapped because her application bore a certificate of eligibility signed by the chiropractor instead of a physician, as required by the Colorado State Board of Education. The Court ought to have disposed of the suit on the ground that the state *was* making available special education classes to all on equal terms, *i.e.,* that they furnish a certificate signed by a physician. In Peacock v. Riggsbee, 309 F. Supp. 542 (N.D. Ga. 1970), the plaintiff, who apparently failed out of Georgia Institute of Technology, asserted that he had a constitutional right to obtain a public higher education at the institution of his choice (*i.e.,* his right to the pursuit of happiness). This case does not apply because Peacock was in no way compelled to seek a higher education.

A state court, hearing a suit based on a state statutory or state constitutional right to habilitation, could refuse to order the kind of relief directed by Judge Johnson in the *Wyatt* case on the grounds that the level of habilitation involved a political question. As long as there is a federal right, however, even state courts must honor it under the "supremacy clause" of the Constitution, which provides, in part, that the "Constitution, and the laws of the United States which shall be made in Pursuance thereof; . . . shall be the supreme Law of the Land; and the Judges in every State shall be Bound thereby, any Thing in the Constitution or Laws of any State to the Contrary notwithstanding." U.S. CONST. art. VI, para. 2.

[96] Powell v. McCormack, 395 U.S. at 517, *citing* Baker v. Carr, 369 U.S. at 198.

[97] A court has broad discretion in determining whether a particular suit qualifies as a class action under Rule 23(a) of the Federal Rules of Civil Procedure, Gold Strike Stamp Co. v. Christensen, 436 F.2d 791 (10th Cir. 1970).

As required the class of plaintiffs in such a suit is generally "so numerous that joinder of all members is impracticable." Although Rule 23(a)(2) requires that "questions of law or fact common to the class" be present in order to maintain a class action, it is not required that *all* the questions of law and fact raised in the controversy be common to *all* members of the class.

In *Wyatt*, the court left the question of whether the treatment of particular individuals was appropriate or adequate in the hands of the defendants. The court held extensive hearings at which numerous nationally recognized expert witnesses testified regarding minimum professional standards by which the court could determine whether the institutions were providing minimally adequate treatment. This comports with established procedures for judicial inquiry into the medical and psychiatric treatment of incarcerated persons in parallel and related matters. Numerous courts have dealt with the constitutional protection of a prisoner's right to medical treatment.[98] Even more in point, numerous courts have evaluated (or remanded for a hearing on) psychiatric examinations, individual treatment plans (and their prospects for success), as well as conditions, staffing, and available programs at psychiatric or other treatment institutions.[99]

Thus, factual differences between members of a class are not fatal to a class action if common questions of law exist. Like v. Carter, 448 F.2d 798 (8th Cir. 1971), *cert. denied,* 405 U.S. 1045 (1972). The question of law (the right to habilitation) and the defense thereto is common to the class. The inability of the institution in question to provide adequate habilitation must be based on facts which are systemic in nature and affect the entire class. *See* Katz v. Carte Blanche Corp., 52 F.R.D. 510 (W.D. Pa. 1971).

The claims of the plaintiffs must be representative of other members of the class. FED. R. CIV. P. 23(a)(3). In construing this requirement, courts have found representative claims to be typical even though varying factual situations support the claim of other individual members of the class. Eisen v. Carlisle & Jacquelin, 391 F.2d 555 (2d Cir. 1968); Randle v. Swank, 53 F.R.D. 577 (N.D. Ill. 1971), *aff'd,* 95 S. Ct. 509 (1974). Where the same unlawful conduct (the denial of adequate habilitation) is the basis for relief, the varying fact patterns which underlie individual claims should not render the representative claims atypical. Gerstle v. Continental Airlines, Inc., 50 F.R.D. 213 (D. Colo. 1970), *aff'd* 466 F.2d 1374 (10th Cir. 1972).

Finally, the relief sought will undoubtedly benefit all other members of the class. Dierks v. Thompson, 414 F.2d 453 (1st Cir. 1969); Bailey v. Patterson, 323 F.2d 201 (5th Cir.), *cert. denied,* 376 U.S. 910 (1963).

Even the California Commission on Staffing Standards, which recommended the relatively flexible method for determining staff needs discussed *supra,* pp. 534-35, recommended its standards as:

> *... basic levels of treatment staff time that are necessary to furnish adequate medical care to anyone who is so seriously ... handicapped that they enter a hospital for the ... mentally retarded.*

1 CAL. STAFFING STANDARDS 4 (emphasis in original).

[98] Martinez v. Mancusi, 443 F.2d 921 (2d Cir. 1970), *cert. denied,* 401 U.S. 983 (1971); Tolbert v. Eyman, 434 F.2d 625 (9th Cir. 1970); Blanks v. Cunningham, 409 F.2d 220 (4th Cir. 1969); Riley v. Rhay, 407 F.2d 496 (9th Cir. 1969) (per curiam); Edwards v. Duncan, 355 F.2d 993 (4th Cir. 1966); Hirons v. Director, Patuxent Institution, 351 F.2d 613 (4th Cir. 1965); Hughes v. Noble, 295 F.2d 495 (5th Cir. 1961); Wood v. Maryland Cas. Co., 322 F. Supp. 436 (W.D. La. 1971); Jones v. Wittenberg, 323 F. Supp. 93 (N.D. Ohio 1971), *relief ordered,* 330 F. Supp. 707, *aff'd sub nom.* Jones v. Metzger, 456 F.2d 854 (6th Cir. 1972); Sawyer v. Sigler, 320 F. Supp. 690 (D. Neb. 1970), *aff'd,* 445 F.2d 818 (8th Cir. 1971); Black v. Ciccone, 324 F. Supp. 129 (W.D. Mo. 1970); Talley v. Stephens, 247 F. Supp. 683 (E.D. Ark. 1965).

[99] Humphrey v. Cady, 405 U.S. 504 (1972); Baxtrom v. Herold, 383 U.S. 107 (1966), *In re* Curry, 452 F.2d 1360, 1362-63 (D.C. Cir. 1971); United States v. Waters, 437 F.2d 722 (D.C. Cir. 1970); United States *ex rel.* Schuster v. Herold, 410 F.2d 1071 (2d Cir.), *cert. denied,* 396 U.S. 847 (1969); Dobson v. Cameron, 383 F.2d 519, 520-21 (D.C. Cir. 1967); Tribby v. Cameron, 379 F.2d 104, 105 (D.C. Cir. 1967); Millard v. Cameron, 373 F.2d 468, 472-73 (D.C. Cir. 1966); Lake v. Cameron, 364 F.2d 657 (D.C. Cir. 1966); Sas v. Maryland, 334 F.2d 506 (4th Cir. 1964), *on remand,* 295 F. Supp. 389 (D. Md. 1969), *aff'd sub nom.* Tippet v. Maryland, 436 F. Supp. 1153 (4th Cir.), *cert. granted sub nom.* Murel v. Baltimore City Crim. Ct. 404 U.S. 999 (1971), *cert. dismissed as improvidently granted,* 407 U.S. 355 (1972); Miller v. Overholser, 206 F.2d 415 (D.C. Cir. 1953); *In re* Jones, 338 F. Supp. 428, 429 (D.D.C. 1972); Dixon v. Attorney General, 325 F. Supp. 966 (M.D. Pa. 1971) (three-judge court); Clatterbuck v. Harris, 295 F. Supp. 84, 86 (D.D.C. 1968); *In re* Newton, 357 Mass. 346, 259 N.E.2d 190 (1970); Nason v. Superintendent of Bridgewater State Hosp., 353 Mass. 604, 233 N.E.2d 908, 913-14 (1968); Commonwealth v. Hogan, 341 Mass. 372, 170 N.E.2d 327 (1960); *In re* Maddox, 351 Mich. 358, 88 N.W.2d 470 (1958); Silvers v. People, 22 Mich. App. 1,

We would agree — in summary — with Chief Judge Bazelon of the District of Columbia Court of Appeals, who noted in a recent article:

> . . .[D]iffidence in the fact of scientific expertise is conduct unbecoming a court. Very few judges are psychiatrists. But equally few are economists, aeronautical engineers, atomic scientists, or marine biologists. For some reason, however, many people seem to accept judicial scrutiny of, say, the effect of a proposed dam on fish life while they reject similar scrutiny of the effect of psychiatric treatment on human lives. Since it can hardly be that we are more concerned for the salmon than the schizophrenic, I suspect the explanation must lie in our familiarity with judicial supervision of such matters as railroad rates, airplane design, power plant construction and dam-building.[100]

With the use of the tools available for compelling the production of evidence and expert testimony, courts *are* capable of identifying minimum professional and constitutional standards for adequate habilitation and ascertaining whether such care is being provided.

Rule 53 of the Federal Rules of Civil Procedure authorizes district courts to appoint a special master to assist the court in litigation pending before it in which "the issues are complicated" or "some exceptional condition requires it." Although reference to a master should be an exception and not the rule,[101] a trial judge can exercise his discretion and employ the services of a master where there are exceptional circumstances which justify it.[102] In a variety of contexts an expert has been appointed as a special master to assist the court to ascertain facts and arrive at a correct result.[103] Recently, expert penologists were consulted by the court in a civil rights suit brought by prisoners concerning conditions of life at the Rhode Island state penal institution.[104]

Even if the court does not wish to employ a master in its decisional process, the court will need specialized information. "Much has been written about the patent weaknesses of a system which provides for the presentation of such information by party-selected and compensated expert witness to an otherwise untutored and unassisted lay tribunal."[105] It has been suggested that expert assistants ("scientific" law clerks, as it were) might be appointed to aid lay judges on technical questions.[106] This

176 N.W.2d 702 (1970); People v. Bailey, 21 N.Y.2d 588, 237 N.E.2d 205, 289 N.Y.S.2d 943 (1968); People v. Kinney, 34 App. Div. 2d 728, 312 N.Y.S.2d 375 (1970); People v. Kearse, 28 App. Div. 2d 910, 282 N.Y.S.2d 136 (1967); People *ex. rel.* Chumley v. Mancusi, 26 App. Div. 2d 905, 274 N.Y.S.2d 477 (1966); People *ex rel.* Kaganovitch v. Wilkins, 23 App. Div. 2d 178, 259 N.Y.S.2d 462 (1965). *See also* cases cited note 98 *supra.*

100 Bazelon, *supra* note 2, at 743.

101 Bartlett-Collins Co. v. Surinan Navigation Co., 381 F.2d 546 (10th Cir. 1967).

102 Wilver v. Fisher, 387 F.2d 66 (10th Cir. 1967).

103 *See* Southern Agency Co. v. LaSalle Cas. Co. 393 F.2d 907 (8th Cir. 1968) (accountant): United States v. Cline, 388 F.2d 294 (4th Cir. 1968) (surveyor); Danville Tobacco Ass'n v. Bryant-Buckner Associates, Inc., 333 F.2d 202 (4th Cir. 1964), *cert. denied.* 387 U.S. 907 (1967) (tobacco marketing expert); Scott v. Spanjer Bros. Inc., 298 F.2d 928 (2d Cir. 1962) (neuropsychiatrist); Sutton v. Johnson Cotton Co., 114 F.2d 302 (4th Cir 1940) (auditor). *See also* Appeal of Mammoth Vein Consol. Coal Co., 54 Pa. 183 (1867) (reversing the trial court for granting excessive temporary relief) (two mining engineers).

104 Morris v. Travisono, 310 F. Supp. 857, 859 (D.R.I. 1970).

105 *See, e.g.,* Korn, *supra* note 63, at 1080.

106 *Cf.* Kaysen, *An Economist as the Judge's Law Clerk in Sherman Act Cases,* 12 ABA ANTITRUST SECTION 43, 45-46 (1958); Webster & Hogeland, *The Economist in Chambers and in Court,* 12 ABA ANTITRUST SECTION 50 (1958).

suggestion poses a problem, however, because the traditional trial concept pre-supposes a challenging, probing cross-examination and exploration of the sources of information being considered by the court. Although "some of our best friends" have been law clerks, we must admit to some personal apprehension about the effect of private conversations in chambers between a judge and his "expert" clerk on one of *our* cases. It would be preferable if, in addition to witnesses called by the adversary parties, neutral court-appointed "expert witnesses" were used, who would testify in open court and thus be subject to cross-examination by both parties.[107]

Even after the court has rendered its decision, it is difficult to monitor compli-ance with detailed standards touching the concerns of a dozen different disciplines. This may by itself pose such a complex problem of judicial administration as to con-stitute the sort of "exceptional condition" which would warrant the court's appoint-ing a master or masters.[108]

Whereas the *Wyatt* order provides that substantial changes in staff deployment from that ordered by the court's decree may be made with the prior approval of the court "upon a clear and convincing demonstration that the proposed deviation from this staffing structure would enhance the habilitation of the residents,"[109] and the court specifically retained jurisdiction,[110] it might be to the *defendants'* benefit in an appropriate case to have a readily available officer of the court to whom they could turn on an informal basis for interim approval of a deviation from a court order while preparing the necessary motion papers to obtain court permission to vary from the decree. From the plaintiffs' point of view, serious problems can arise almost over-night that demand contact with an officer of the court. Simple periodic reporting, though necessary and desirable, cannot fill this need. It would not, however, seem necessary to appoint a receiver to actually run an institution unless it became appar-ent that close monitoring of the implementation of the court's orders was not sufficient.

It has been suggested that the appropriate role for the court in standard setting

---

[107] It should go without saying that experts in some form are needed. However, shortly before the argument of the appeal in *Wyatt,* one of us was approached by a lawyer who had filed suit in a circuit that had not yet had a "right to treatment" case. His suit originally attacked his state's commitment statutes and now he was considering amending the complaint to allege a violation of the right to adequate treatment and habilitation. Because he was operating on limited funds, he seemed incredulous when it was suggested that he would need to prove the alleged inadequacy through expert testimony. But he quickly recovered his composure to ask about using as "expert" opinion the testimony of a college student (major unstated) who had recently been released after an involuntary commitment to one of the institutions in question. Such an approach is not recommended.

For a discussion of the practical problems encountered in obtaining expert witnesses see, Halpern, *supra* note 62, at 796-97.

[108] For example, in Pennsylvania Ass'n for Retarded Children v. Pennsylvania, 334 F. Supp. 1257 (E.D. Pa. 1971) [hereinafter cited as PARC], in which the court ordered appropriate free public education for all of Pennsylvania's mentally retarded children, two special masters were appointed "to implement the aforementioned relief and to assure that it is extended to all members of the class entitled to it." *Id.* at 1266. The extensive use of masters by the *PARC* court in the year following the decision is an excellent example of the utility of the master concept.

[109] 344 F. Supp. at 406.

[110] *Id.* at 395.

is analogous to the role it plays in reviewing administrative agency decisions.[111] Before the reader breathes a sigh of relief, it should be added that this is a suggestion that needs some qualification.[112] If taken literally, this approach runs counter to the historic interpretation of the Civil Rights Act of April 20, 1871.[113] It has not been necessary in other contexts to exhaust state legal or administrative remedies prior to proceeding to protect a constitutional right in federal court.[114] Any suggestion that mentally retarded plaintiffs be required to leap an administrative hurdle on the courthouse steps, when such an obstacle is not interposed between "normal" plaintiffs and judicial relief, will understandably be viewed by some as yet another example of discrimination against retarded citizens. It would seem anomalous indeed to allow a convicted murderer to go directly to federal court to complain of conditions in solitary confinement, but to require a civilly committed mentally retarded individual to exhaust his administrative remedies before complaining of the same conditions in his "therapeutic seclusion room." If the right is constitutional, the Civil Rights Act poses no "exhaustion" problem.

In *Wyatt*, Judge Johnson held that the right to treatment had at least three fundamental aspects: (1) humane psychological and physical environment, (2) qualified staff in numbers sufficient to administer adequate treatment, and (3) individualized treatment plans.[115] Though he did not similarly subdivide elements of the right to habilitation, Judge Johnson framed the general statement of this right along lines similar to those set out earlier for the right to treatment[116] and indicated that in "the context of the right to appropriate care, . . . no viable distinction can be made between the mentally ill and the mentally retarded."[117]

At least insofar as a resident asserts that he is housed in an inhumane psychological and physical environment, his complaint is analogous to that of a prisoner asserting he is subject to "cruel and unusual punishment,"[118] and no tenet of administrative review ought to hinder a court from swiftly and completely reviewing the resident's complaint de novo. However, although a humane psychological and physical envi-

---

[111] Covington v. Harris, 419 F.2d 617, 621 (D.C. Cir. 1969); Tribby v. Cameron, 379 F.2d 104, 105 (D.C. Cir. 1967); Nason v. Superintendent of Bridgewater State Hosp., 353 Mass. 604, 233 N.E.2d 908, 914 (1968); *accord,* Note, *The Nascent Right to Treatment* 53 VA. L. REV. 1134, 1154 (1967); Bazelon, *supra* note 2, at 743-45, 750; Note, *Guaranteeing the Right to Treatment,* 32 MARYLAND L. REV. 42, 47, 49 (1972). *See also* Note, *Civil Restraint, Mental Illness and the Right to Treatment,* 77 YALE L.J. 87, 115 (1967).

[112] Halpern, *supra* note 62, at 798 n. 73, 808 (1969). In all fairness to Judge Bazelon, it should be noted that he recognizes the problem: "[W]hen a constitutional right is directly involved, the court does not defer to the administrative agency: The expertise in that situation belongs to the judge." Bazelon, *supra* note 2, at 744.

[113] 42 U.S.C. § 1983 (1970) and its jurisdictional counterpart 28 U.S.C. § 1343 (1970) give federal courts jurisdiction to hear private suits asserting a deprivation of constitutional rights by action "under color of state law."

[114] McNeese v. Board of Educ., 373 U.S. 668 (1963); Monroe v. Pape, 365 U.S. 167 (1961). Exhaustion can be required, of course, if a right is *created* by statute.

[115] 334 F. Supp. at 1343-44.

[116] ". . . a constitutional right to receive such individual habilitation as will give each of them a realistic opportunity to lead a more useful and meaningful life and to return to society." 344 F. Supp. at 390.

[117] *Id.*

[118] Wheeler v. Glass, 473 F.2d 983 (7th Cir. 1973).

ronment is certainly basic to adequate habilitation, adequate habilitation can still be absent in an environment that is physically quite comfortable. At this point, the right to adequate habilitation — though it may be grounded on the eighth amendment in a particular case — diverges from the factual situations in which the "cruel and unusual punishment" clause has been applied in the past. When the resident's attack on the adequacy of his habilitation program focuses more on the care furnished him than on institutional deficiencies, courts probably ought to give considerable weight to the judgment of that institution's administrators.[119]

This is not the time in the development of the right to habilitation to urge that courts review institutional decisions as they do those of an agency set up to administer a regulatory scheme. However, the existence of adequate records, in-house peer review programs, and a complaint procedure by which residents can have the adequacy of their habilitation reviewed (including whether adequate staff is available) should be persuasive evidence that the institution is making a bona fide effort to deliver adequate habilitation. It would be inappropriate to require a resident to "exhaust administrative remedies" before suing, yet it is probably inevitable that to some extent the "right to habilitation" will be treated as a right to a professionally supportable program of habilitation. It is in this sense that the court's role is not unlike that which it plays in reviewing agency decisions.[120]

Because the potential plaintiffs in any right to habilitation suit are often indigent, incompetent, or both, the failure of an institution to meet recognized professional standards ought to have the following effect at the trial of such a case: Once a plaintiff has established by a preponderance of the evidence[121] that his institution fails in some significant aspect to meet recognized professional standards, a rebuttable presumption[122] should arise, shifting the burden of persuasion[123] to the defendants on the issue of the institution's adequacy. This shifted burden could be met only by the introduction of clear and convincing[124] evidence on this issue. Should the defendants

---

[119] Judge Bazelon himself contrasts the "gross benchmarks" used in assessing *institutional* adequacy with the administrative review standard used in assessing *individual* treatment programs. Bazelon, *Forward to Symposium on the Right to Treatment,* 57 GEO. L.J. 676, 678 (1969).

[120] Indeed, if an expert master is appointed to hear evidence and report in the case the net effect may be quite similar to "administrative review"—tacit though the recognition of this effect may be.

[121] A "preponderance" (more probable than not) of the evidence is the usual burden of persuasion that must be borne by a plaintiff in a civil case (contrasted with the "beyond reasonable doubt" burden borne by the prosecution in a criminal case). A middle level of proof, "clear and convincing," is sometimes required to be met by the party bearing the burden of persuasion on a particular issue in civil cases. *See* MCCORMICK'S HANDBOOK OF THE LAW OF EVIDENCE §§ 339-41 (2d ed. 1972) [hereinafter cited as MCCORMICK].

[122] A "presumption" is an assumption that the law *requires* be made by the "trier of fact" (either the court or jury, depending on the case). Presumptions are of two types: conclusive or rebuttable. Creation of a presumption may require a statute in a particular jurisdiction. *See* MCCORMICK § 342.

[123] "The burden of persuasion" is another name for what most people know as the burden of proof. The term "burden of proof" has sometimes been used to signify which party to a lawsuit has the obligation of producing evidence on a particular issue and which party must convince the judge or jury of its version of the truth in order to prevail on a particular issue. The terms "burden of persuasion" and "burden of producing evidence" were coined to avoid confusion. *See* MCCORMICK § 336.

[124] *See* note 121 *supra.*

meet this burden, the plaintiff could still show that despite the fact that the institution was capable of providing adequate habilitation to its residents, it was not doing so in *his* case. He would retain the burden of persuasion on this issue, however, and it would be met much as in a medical malpractice case.

This approach recognizes that (as formerly stated) the resident-plaintiff ought to be able to prevail on either of two theories: (1) that he is not housed in an institution capable of delivering adequate habilitation as a matter of course or (2) that in *his* case, bona fide efforts have not been made to provide adequate habilitation to *him*. There are at least four advantages to this approach.

First, the resident-plaintiff is spared substantial expense if his complaint is that he has been placed in a substandard institution. Judicial notice[125] of recognized professional standards might even be appropriate because these standards are verifiable facts.[126] The burden of producing enough evidence to persuade the judge that on a preponderance of the evidence the institution fails to meet recognized professional standards might well be met largely through interrogatories and subsequent requests for admissions.[127]

Second, if a state can demonstrate that the institution is capable of providing adequate care (*e.g.*, through clear and convincing expert testimony that the staffing is adequate), it may do so. Granted, it bears a heavy burden (as it should, if its institutions fail to meet recognized professional standards), but it has not automatically lost its case.

Third, the resident-plaintiff is still free to show that *he* is not receiving adequate habilitation (*e.g.*, there are no entries on *his* records, *he* does not have an habilitation plan), but he must prevail against the traditional assumption that due care has been exercised.

Finally, this allocation of the burden of persuasion mutes any implication of personal culpability on the part of the individual professionals at a given institution by focusing initially on institutionwide objective facts. Most professionals at mental retardation institutions are dedicated individuals, laboring under a heavy burden. An approach that spotlights institutional deficiencies without attacking efforts of individuals would seem to be desirable unless the plaintiff chooses to assume the burden of making a direct attack on individual decisions that have been made (or not made) in his particular case.

---

[125] "Judicial notice" excuses the party having the burden of persuasion on a particular fact from the necessity of producing testimony. *See* McCORMICK ch. 35.

[126] One of the instances in which courts have taken "judicial notice" of certain facts is when these facts could be "verified" by consulting materials in common use (here a document such as ACCREDITATION COUNCIL FOR FACILITIES FOR THE MENTALLY RETARDED, *supra* note 15). This basis for judicial notice has been frequently used to establish scientific facts, though it is not used if the "fact" is debatable among the scientists themselves. *See* Korn, *supra* note 63, at 1080, 1089-90, 1108. Korn discusses judicial notice of scientific facts and the weight that ought to be given judicially noticed facts of less than indisputable certitude.

[127] Interrogatories and requests for admissions are commonly used devices whereby lawyers may discover facts within the knowledge of the opposition prior to trial and secure the opposition's admission that the requested facts are true. Failure to grant a reasonable request for an admission is grounds for a court's requiring the party refusing the request to pay for the cost of proving the fact as to which an admission was requested. FED. R. CIV. P. 33, 36, 37(c).

CONCLUSION

Although this paper does not easily lend itself to summation, one point bears repeating: Affirmative public education is needed. When a judge or legislator drives over a bridge, he does not know how to construct the bridge or what the stresses are, but at least he knows *from past experience* that it ought to work. Government is not really any less competent to deal with the problems of mental retardation than it is to deal with a lawsuit or legislation involving construction of a bridge, the funding of bridge building, or, indeed, bridge building itself. Nonetheless, when an official who is not a mental retardation professional goes to a Partlow or a Willowbrook, it is difficult for him to resist the feeling that the problem is beyond solution. He does not have the past experience to tell him that habilitation will work. The prevailing attitude is that the subhuman conditions in many institutions are, like the floods in the Mississippi Valley, an act of God, and that the citizens in these institutions are helpless, hopeless, incurable, and untreatable.

Why? Because, like the residents of institutions, successful habilitation programs are all too often hidden from view. Massive efforts have recently been directed at telling the stories of institutional failures, and these efforts should not abate. But equally massive efforts are needed to offset the myth that mentally retarded citizens cannot be helped.

Reaction Comment

CHARLES ACUFF

JOHNSON AND WOOD recognize the need for administrators, professionals, consumers, and other citizens to be involved in setting standards for the care of the mentally retarded. This proposal certainly has merit. All too frequently it appears that recommendations of service administrators have been taken lightly when decisions are made about institutional standards. It seems wasteful not to make greater use of their experience and expertise. Regardless of standards applied, judgmental decisions are needed. Professionals responsible for the delivery of services are probably in an ideal position to make some of these decisions. They offer an effective and realistic way of professionally advising the courts or a state administration on the shortcomings of any particular program or institution and how these can be corrected. There is also a place for laymen, including professional people not directly involved in the field of mental retardation. Whereas most laymen do not have the background necessary actually to set standards, they are adept at suggesting desirable outcomes and reviewing programs to ensure that established standards are met.

Although it is very difficult to look at past standards, the thing we need to measure most is what is happening to individuals for whom we are providing services. Environmental standards, such as amount of space, cleanliness of space, number of people, and number of degrees staff hold, in no way ensure appropriate "outcomes." If we can measure outcomes for the individual, based on established goals (the goals must be set before the standards) and work toward the environmental requirements, much more meaningful programs can be developed. The starting point must be, however, what can optimistically, but reasonably, be provided for the resident to help him function at his optimum level. It does not make sense to start with standards by saying "with these standards we're going to get something; we're not quite sure we need or want it since we are not acquainted with the individual needs of the residents, but it's going to be good for them." This is especially true if the standards merely create a potentially good environment which should be conducive to a good program, but which offers no clue to success by measuring outcomes to individuals. "Outcome," not "input," is what needs to be emphasized.

There are two schools of thought on the application of standards to an institution. Some feel that minimum standards can be developed and applied to any institution. Others, including myself, believe each institution is unique and requires individual application of standards with flexibility for judgmental decisions by evaluators. The fallacy of relying on strict standards (without first looking at goals and outcomes for the particular institution involved) is demonstrated by our programs in Arkansas. Certainly we have room for improvement, just as do any other state programs, but we have a good program. However, we can maintain adequate institutional care for our mentally retarded citizens at standards below those set in *Wyatt v. Stickney*.[1]

How can we run a program with 16 registered nurses when *Wyatt* apparently would require 86? How can we run a program with 553 attendant personnel when *Wyatt* seems to indicate that we need over 1,300? Part of the answer is that we are organized on the developmental model and not the medical model. Also, we have an intensive in-service training program for attendant personnel. They are trained to carry out many functions formerly considered to be the responsibility of nurses, but not legally required to be performed by them. Attendant personnel also provide developmental activities for residents, even the severely and profoundly retarded. Not only do several hours spent each day in training and recreational activities relieve the need for some attendant personnel, but also the increased competence of the resident to assist in tending to his own needs decreases required personnel time. College students and volunteers also provide assistance. Maintaining a close tie with the home and encouraging summer vacations at home enable us to provide employee vacations without adding staff. The strict interpretation and application of standards would probably not permit this flexibility. Certainly we need more employees but not the number apparently directed by *Wyatt*. We neither have nor need the number of resident-living staff required by the standards of the Accreditation Council on Facilities for the Mentally Retarded.[2]

The type of program provided by the institution also affects resident-living-

---

[1] Wyatt v. Stickney, 344 F. Supp. 387, 344 F. Supp. 373 (M.D. Ala. 1972), 334 F. Supp. 1341, 325 F. Supp. 781 (M.D. Ala. 1971), *aff'd sub nom.* Wyatt v. Aderholt, 503 F.2d 1305 (5th Cir. 1974).

[2] ACCREDITATION COUNCIL ON FACILITIES FOR THE MENTALLY RETARDED, STANDARDS FOR RESIDENTIAL FACILITIES FOR THE MENTALLY RETARDED (1971).

staffing patterns. *Wyatt* and the Accreditation Council on Facilities for the Mentally Retarded standards do not give consideration to specific program activities and the effect these have on staffing needs. For example, relative to the *Wyatt* decision, Arkansas apparently has a greater number of educational personnel than would be required by that standard. These personnel, along with the recreation staff, relieve the attendant personnel of a significant amount of work throughout the day until about nine or ten o'clock at night. Therefore, our staffing ratios of attendant personnel do not have to be as high as some minimum standards would dictate. This sort of alternative should certainly be given consideration in evaluating a program.

Standards regarding space are further measures of the institutional environment and may be desirable, but also are unlikely to be directly proportional to outcomes.

It would be unwise to include institutional standards in federal legislation. Federal legislation should contain a bill of rights for mentally retarded citizens. General guidelines, with a mandate for standards to be developed by a governmental agency, would also be useful. I would rather have an agency establish institutional standards and regulations, which can be updated as the need is indicated, than to have standards rigidly "cast in bronze" in a federal law which required Congressional action to change. I do not believe that any standards, federal or state, should ever be embodied in legislation to the degree of detail that is now proposed in the bills mentioned by Johnson and Wood.[3] When institutional standards are established (regardless of by whom) they must be flexible enough to allow different service administrators in different types of programs to use them effectively.

[3] S. 458, 93d Cong., 1st Sess. (1973); H.R. 76, 93d Cong., 1st Sess. (1973).

CHAPTER 18

Peonage and Involuntary Servitude

Editorial Introduction

Protection against involuntary servitude is guaranteed under the thirteenth amendment to the Constitution of the United States and by specific laws and regulations. Friedman develops a detailed conceptual framework in which to view the problems of institutional peonage — a form of involuntary servitude — and the approaches that are available to the attorney to minimize and perhaps eliminate it. He also develops a clear picture of the paradox facing the institutional administrator in his efforts to separate therapy and peonage.

Friedman's material may be viewed in the larger context of the struggle to harness resources for the purpose of fostering the best possible life for those members of American society who are labeled mentally retarded — people who are put in institutional settings and then placed on work assignments which help maintain the institutions. When the legal remedies discussed by Friedman are viewed from this perspective, the question arises as to what will replace the system now characterized as peonage.

Friedman considers a variety of forces that come into play when payment for the work of institutionalized mentally retarded individuals is at issue. Different attitudes may be expected from labor unions, supervisors of institutions, academicians, the families of institutionalized persons, legislators, and administrators concerned with maintaining an institution. There will be many experienced voices whose suggestions will be diametrically opposed. Moreover, those who deal with legal remedies must concern themselves with the long-term impact of the results that may be achieved in the courts. Easy answers are not presented.

Isolated institutions developed because there were forces mitigating against community-based solutions. In remote, poorly funded, and poorly monitored settings, the movement toward the exploitation of residents through unremunerated labor is to be expected. The maintenance of institutions with insufficient resources has been possible only through the use of resident labor. Alternatives must be made available to institutional administrators, either through legislation, court' rulings, or administrative directives which eliminate peonage practices, or through increased fiscal program support which would obviate the need to use resident labor.

In her reaction paper, Tarr-Whelan, deputy director of program development for the American Federation of State, County, and Municipal Employees, presents the federation's view of institutional peonage. Her discussion of the problem from the labor unions' perspective indicates some of the long-run difficulties that will have to be faced as peonage is abolished and mentally retarded individuals are moved from institutions to community settings.

Rosen expresses the viewpoint of an experienced superintendent. Rosen addresses the institutional and community attitudes that have led to extended institutional placement and wage exploitation of individuals capable of residing in less restrictive environments. He highlights the need to develop community commitment to extensive community placement programs and the frequent absence of such commitment. Rosen's view of institutional attitudes, community programs, and deinstitutionalization provide an interesting contrast to the attitudes expressed in Clement's reaction in Chapter 14.

PRINCIPAL PAPER[*]

PAUL FRIEDMAN

OVERVIEW OF THE INSTITUTIONAL LABOR PROBLEM

The Nature and Extent of Institutional Labor in the United States

Throughout the United States, residents in institutions for the mentally handi-

*Copyright 1974 by The Harvard Law Review Association. This paper appeared as a comment in 87 HARV. L. REV. 567, where it was entitled "The Mentally Handicapped Citizen and Institutional Labor." The comment was an outgrowth of a paper on this topic presented by the author at the conference on the legal rights of the mentally retarded, sponsored by the President's Committee on

capped [1] are required to perform productive labor associated with the maintenance of the institution without adequate compensation. [2] One institutional psychiatrist has testified that large state mental hospitals employ a significant percentage of their patients without pay in kitchens, dining rooms, laundries, farms, and dairies, and as ward helpers, maintenance workers, and sanitary engineers; [3] and the National Association for Retarded Children has asserted that such practices are prevalent "in facilities across the country." [4] As yet, neither the United States Department of Labor nor any other organization has undertaken a comprehensive survey of the extent of patient labor in American mental institutions. Nonetheless, a 1972 study of 154 institutions in 47 states, which represent 76 percent of existing facilities for the mentally retarded, found that 32,180 of 150,000 residents were participating in a work program, 30 percent of these receiving no pay at all, and an additional 50 percent receiving less that $10 per week. [5] Research in Ohio indicates that as of January 1973, 1,237 out of 8,000 residents in facilities for the retarded were "working residents," laboring as a group over 40,000 hours per week. [6] And a 1969 study conducted by the Pennsylvania Department of Public Welfare disclosed a resident working

---

Mental Retardation, Columbus, Ohio, May 3-5, 1973. The views expressed herein are those of the author and do not reflect the policies of the Mental Health Law Project or the President's Committee on Mental Retardation. The author wishes to give special thanks for their assistance in the preparation of this paper to Rona Beck, Bruce Ennis, Margy Kohn, Gail Marker, George Solyanis, and Patricia Wald.

[1] Throughout this paper, the term "mentally handicapped" will be used to denote both the mentally ill and the mentally retarded. Although the treatment which is appropriate for the mentally retarded is different from that which is appropriate for the mentally ill, *compare* Wyatt v. Stickney, 344 F. Supp. 373, 379-86 (M.D. Ala. 1972) (adequate standards for treatment of mentally ill), *aff'd sub nom.* Wyatt v. Aderholt, 503 F.2d 1305 (5th Cir. 1974), *with* Wyatt v. Stickney, 344 F. Supp. 387, 395-407 (M.D. Ala. 1972) (adequate standards for treatment of mentally retarded), *aff'd sub nom.* Wyatt v. Aderholt, 503 F.2d 1305 (5th Cir. 1974), and is often referred to as "habilitation," "treatment" will be used to denote both regimens. Although the institutionalized mentally ill are usually referred to as "patients" and the institutionalized mentally retarded as "residents," "patients" and "residents" will be used interchangeably.

[2] For a history of the practice, see R. Kenney, The Prevalence of Peonage in State Supported Total Institutions for the Mentally Retarded, 1972, ch. 1 (unpublished thesis in Indiana University Library).

That many mentally handicapped persons are able to perform at least some kinds of work is now generally acknowledged. The President's Committee on Mental Retardation estimates that 87 percent of mildly retarded adult males—those with an IQ of 50-69—were employed in 1971, an employment rate only four points below that of adult males in the general population. PRESIDENT'S COMM. ON MENTAL RETARDATION, MR71: ENTERING THE ERA OF HUMAN ECOLOGY 27 (1971). Employment of the mentally retarded is especially common in federal governmental facilities. The United States Civil Service Commission reports that from 1964 to 1972, a total of 7,442 mentally retarded individuals were appointed to positions in 40 federal agencies located in every state. United States Civil Service Commission, An 8½ Year Record: Mentally Retarded Workers in the Federal Service 2, Nov. 1972. *See also* PRESIDENT'S PANEL ON MENTAL RETARDATION, REPORT OF THE TASK FORCE ON LAW 5-7 (1963). Fifty-three percent of these workers were still employed in federal agencies at the end of that period, "a figure which compares favorably with turnover rates for all employees in similar grades." United States Civil Service Commission, *supra,* at 2.

[3] Bartlett, *Institutional Peonage: Our Exploitation of Mental Patients,* ATLANTIC, July 1964, at 116.
[4] National Association for Retarded Children, Policy Statement on Residential Care 11-12, Oct. 1968.
[5] J. Richardson, A Survey of the Present Status of Vocational Training in State Supported Institutions for the Mentally Retarded 4, 11-12, July 18, 1972 (written for Dr. I. Ignacy Goldberg, Columbia University Teachers College).
[6] R. Benjamin, H. McCracken & J. Gardner, Operation of Farms on Ohio's Institutions for the Mentally Retarded, Mar. 1973 (Ohio Association for Retarded Children).

force of 3,040 out of a total population of 11,923 in 9 state schools and hospitals for the mentally retarded.[7]

Competing Interests in the Utilization of Institutional Labor

Several interests are served by a program which fairly compensates resident mental patients for the work they perform. First, there is the economic interests of the workers. Residents are injured most directly by their loss of income due to hospitalization. Compensation might enable such residents to pay part of the cost of room, board, and treatment, to purchase necessities and conveniences, to support a family, or to save enough money to ease their return to society. Uncompensated patients are also denied such collateral benefits of formal compensation as workmen's compensation, social security, and state retirement disbursements.

A second interest in such a compensation program is its therapeutic value. Denial of compensation adds the disability and stigma of poverty to the other handicaps which the patient and doctor must work to overcome, both in and out of the institution.[8] Forced employment without compensation may engender feelings of enslavement, exploitation, or persecution, undermining constructive attitudes and the sense of human dignity essential to therapeutic progress. [9]Appropriate compensation for work performed by patients serves as a meaningful "reward" which can motivate such patients to develop responsible work habits and behavior patterns vital to their eventual reintegration into the community.[10]

Although many hospital administrators appreciate the benefits of compensation, they are often forced by inadequate fiscal resources to perpetuate the current system of uncompensated labor assignments.[11]For example, a survey of 72 American mental institutions housing over 80,000 retarded patients estimated that the maximum reported salaries paid to the 20,000 patients working in those institutions

---

[7]Pennsylvania Dep't of Public Welfare, Calculation of Implied Savings for Nine State Schools and Hospitals as a Consequence of Utilization of Unpaid Patient Labor, June 17, 1969.

[8]*See* U.S. Dep't of Health Education & Welfare, Biometry Branch, Statistical Note 47: Admission Rates by Family Income Level—Outpatient Psychiatric Services—1969 (May 1971).

[9]American Psychiatric Association, Standard 32: Standards for Psychiatric Facilities 47-48, 1969; *see* Claimants' Post Trial Memorandum at 29-30, Dale v. New York, Cl. No. 51888 (N.Y. Ct. Cl., Mar. 30, 1973); L. Bartlett, Exploitive Work Programs in American State Hospitals 1-2, Oct. 12, 1971 (paper for International Conference on Productive Participation Programs for the Mentally Ill, Helsinki, Oct. 12-15, 1971).

[10]Record at 69, Dale v. New York, Cl. No. 51888 (N.Y. Ct. Cl., Mar. 30, 1973) (statement of Dr. Fox); *id.* at 350 (statement of Dr. Halpern); *see* D. Vail, Dehumanization of the Institutional Career 179 (1968), *citing* British Ministry of Health, 1964 Compendium of Standards; President's Committee on Mental Retardation and President's Committee on Employment of the Handicapped, These Too Must be Equal 12-13, 1969; Kenney, *supra* note 2, 17-18; Bartlett, *supra* note 9, at 1-2.

    Moreover, the guarantee of payment may constitute a safeguard against the possibility that mental institutions, motivated by fiscal necessity, will exploit productive resources by prolonging hospitalization. *See* Bartlett, *supra* note 3, at 119.

[11]Interview with Dr. Walter Fox, assistant commissioner of mental health for Arizona, June 25, 1972; interview with David N. Rosen, superintendent of Macomb-Oakland Residential Center, May 4, 1973; interview with Dr. Israel Zwerling, director of Bronx State Hospital, Jan. 24, 1972. *See* British Ministry of Health, *supra* note 10, *cited in* Vail, *supra* note 10, at 178-79.

would provide salaries of only $55.70 per month to the 5,000 staff members who would be necessary to perform their duties.[12] And the Pennsylvania study indicated that only one-third of the working residents in that state are performing tasks not essential to the maintenance of the institution;[13] total savings to Pennsylvania institutions as a consequence of the utilization of resident labor was estimated as $10,062,000 per year.[14] A hospital superintendent summarized the general condition in 1963: "The economy of a mental hospital is based on 'patient labor.' . . . [W]ithout it the hospital . . . would collapse."[15]

Even if they were not faced with fiscal barriers to compensation of resident workers, most hospital administrators would insist that institutions should not be required to provide compensation for work which represents a legitimate part of vocational training programs for the benefit of residents, or for worklike tasks which are part of a valid therapy program.[16] Yet the complex task of distinguishing between work which is primarily for the benefit of the patient and work which primarily benefits the institution further deters the establishment of any compensation program.[17]

A federal statute — the Fair Labor Standards Act[18] — and two constitutional provisions — the thirteenth amendment and the due process guarantee — offer alternative legal theories for resolving the conflicting interests of hospital administrators and mentally handicapped workers.

ALTERNATIVE LEGAL APPROACHES TO CHALLENGING THE ABUSES OF INSTITUTIONAL LABOR

Actions to Enforce the Fair Labor Standards Act

The Fair Labor Standards Act of 1938, as amended in 1966,[19] establishes minimum wages and overtime compensation for covered employees.[20] As interpreted by the Department of Labor,

[12] Kenney, *supra* note 2, at 108-09; *see id.* at 93, 100, 129.
[13] *See* Pennsylvania Dep't of Public Welfare, *supra* note 7.
[14] *Id.*
[15] Bickford, *Economic Value of the Psychiatric Inpatient*, LANCET, Mar. 30, 1963, at 714. *See also* Cumming & Cumming, *Social Equilibrium and Social Change in the Large Mental Hospitals,* in THE PATIENT AND THE MENTAL HOSPITAL 49 (M. Greenblatt, D. Levinson & R. Williams eds. 1957).
[16] *E.g.,* Interview with Dr. David Ray, assistant commissioner of mental retardation, Tennessee Dep't Mental Health, May 5, 1973; *see* Transcript, Meeting of the Subcommittee on Hospitals and Institutions of the Advisory Committee on Sheltered Workshops, Department of Labor, Application of the Fair Labor Standards Act to Working Patients in Hospitals and Other Institutions, Nov. 17, 1969; pp. 570, 576-78 *infra.*
[17] Interview with Dr. David Ray, assistant commissioner of Mental Retardation, Tennessee Dep't Mental Health, May 5, 1973. *See generally* Transcript, *supra* note 16.
[18] 29 U.S.C. §§ 201-19 (1970).
[19] Fair Labor Standards Amendments of 1966, Pub. L. No. 89-601, 80 Stat. 830 (codified at 29 U.S.C. §§ 203, 206-07, 213-14, 216, 218, 255 (1970)).
[20] 29 U.S.C. § 206 (1970).

the 1966 Amendments revised the definition of "enterprise" to make it clear that activities in connection with the operation of the following are "for a business purpose" within the meaning of the act:

(a) hospitals (excluding federal government hospitals),

(b) institutions primarily engaged in the care of the aged, mentally ill or defective who reside on the premises,

. . .

(d) schools for handicapped or gifted children.[21]

The act prescribes four methods for recovering unpaid minimum or overtime wages required under its various provisions: administrative action and repayment supervision by the Secretary of Labor;[22] legal action by the Secretary of Labor for payment of wages upon written request of an employee;[23] legal action by the Secretary of Labor or others to enjoin violation of the act;[24] and legal action by the employee for back pay, liquidated damages, attorney's fees, and court costs.[25]

Mentally handicapped persons have recently filed suits for wages and liquidated damages under the act against institutions in Florida,[26] Pennsylvania,[27] Delaware,[28] and Tennessee.[29] If successful, such actions would recover not only owed compensation but also damages.[30] And while injunctions are often ignored, requiring additional remedial action, money judgments are more easily enforced.[31] As a consequence, one or two successful class actions entailing substantial damage awards might effect reform of compensation policies ranging well beyond the specific institutions to which such awards are limited.[32]

In seeking compensation under the FLSA, however, litigants must confront the substantive problems of establishing both a right to compensation under the act and the extent of compensation under the act. Courts considering the question have found the act to authorize payment to mentally handicapped workers for at least

---

[21] U.S. Department of Labor, Publication 1282, Mar. 1971, *citing* 29 U.S.C. §§ 203(r)(1), (s)(4) (1970).

[22] 29 U.S.C. § 216(c) (1970).

[23] *Id.*

[24] *Id.* § 217.

[25] *Id.* § 216(b).

[26] Roebuck v. Department of Health, Civil No. TCA 1041 (N.D. Fla., filed July 6, 1972).

[27] Downs v. Department of Pub. Welfare, 368 F. Supp. 454 (E.D. Pa. 1973).

[28] Carey v. White, 375 F. Supp. 1327 (D. Del. 1974).

[29] Townsend v. Cloverbottom, Doc. No. A-2576 (Ch. Nashville and Davidson Counties, Tenn., May 22, 1973). Plaintiffs in *Townsend* had originally filed suit in federal court, Townsend v. Treadway, Civil No. 6500 (D. Tenn., Sept. 21, 1973). Their thirteenth amendment claims for injunctive relief and damages, see pp. 574-78 *infra,* were denied, and their claims under the FLSA were dismissed for lack of jurisdiction under the holding in Employers of the Dep't of Public Health and Welfare v. Missouri, 411 U.S. 279 (1973); see pp. 572-74 *infra.*

[30] 29 U.S.C. § 216(b) (1970).

[31] Ennis, *Litigation Strategies and Techniques,* in 3 Legal Rights of the Mentally Handicapped 1245, 1254 (Mental Health Law Project & Practising Law Institute eds. 1973).

[32] Such a class action might be brought on behalf of mentally handicapped workers by labor unions interested in either enlarging their membership or providing jobs to existing members by deterring institutions from utilizing noncompensated patient labor. With one important exception, however, no labor union has acted on behalf of resident workers. A spokesman for the American Federation of State, County, and Municipal Employees, which represents over 30,000 employees of state mental institutions, recently expressed that union's policy of seeking compensation for resident workers, both as a matter of right and as part of a larger union response to employment discrimination. Statement by Linda Tarr, President's Council on Mental Retardation Workshop, Columbus, Ohio, May 5, 1973. *See also* p. 573 & note 68 *infra.*

some kinds of labor,[33] and the language of the FLSA appears to support that conclusion. Section 6 of the act prescribes minimum wages[34] (or some percentage thereof to reflect the impaired productivity of handicapped workers)[35] for employees "engaged in commerce or in the production of goods for commerce."[36] Section 3 defines employee as "any individual employed,"[37] and defines employ as "to suffer or permit to work."[38] The 1966 amendments to the act, by defining the "commerce" phrase of section 6 to encompass employees "engaged in the operation" of institutions for the mentally handicapped,[39] would appear to require compensation for patient labor which serves institutional requirements.

Establishing the extent of compensation under the act, however, is a more complex problem. Labor which benefits an institution may also serve the therapeutic needs of the patient. Even such pedestrian tasks as sweeping floors, running errands, or shelling peas may be thought to have some therapeutic value. Tasks which are compensable under the act might thus be defined solely according to their effect upon the operation of the mental institution which assigns them; according to their effect upon the mentally handicapped laborer who performs them; or according to the purpose for which they are assigned. In practice, the alternative definitions suggest significantly differing compensation schemes. Requiring compensation for all tasks which concern or benefit the operation of the institution will compel payment even if such taks are also of therapeutic value. On the other hand, permitting compensation only for those labors which are not therapeutic may effectively preclude compensation, since most productive work is arguably therapeutic.[40] And permitting compensation only for those tasks assigned with the purpose of institutional maintenance poses difficult problems of proving the intent with which hospital administrators have assigned work.

The definition of compensable labor under the FLSA should depend solely upon the extent to which such labor benefits the institutional employer. The act itself makes no exception for labors which provide some collateral benefit such as therapy.[41] Moreover, in *Souder v. Brennan*,[42] decided in November of 1973, the federal district court in the District of Columbia explicitly addressed the question in the context of an action against the Secretary of Labor for enforcement of the FLSA, and concluded that the language of the FLSA requires compensation for institution-maintaining

---

[33] *See* Souder v. Brennan, 367 F. Supp. 808 (D.D.C. 1973); Wyatt v. Stickney, 344 F. Supp. 373, 381 (M.D. Ala. 1972), *aff'd sub nom.* Wyatt v. Aderholt, 503 F.2d 1305 (5th Cir. 1974); pp. 573, 579 *infra*.

[34] 29 U.S.C. § 206 (1970).

[35] *Id.* § 214(d); *see* 29 C.F.R. §§ 224-25 (1973).

[36] 29 U.S.C. § 206 (1970).

[37] *Id.* § 203(e).

[38] *Id.* § 203(g). "Work" has been defined as physical or mental exertion that is controlled or required by the employer and is pursued primarily for the benefit of the employer and his business. *See* Shupe v. Day, 113 F. Supp. 949, 952 (W.D. Va. 1953).

[39] *See* 29 U.S.C. §§ 203(r)(1), (s)(4) (1970).

[40] *See* Souder v. Brennan, 367 F. Supp. 808 (D.D.C. 1973). *But see* pp. 576-78 *infra*.

[41] Letter from Robert D. Moran, Workplace Standards Administrator, U.S. Dep't of Labor, to Dr. Walter Fox, president, Association of Medical Superintendents of Mental Hospitals, 1969-1970, Oct. 6, 1970.

[42] 367 F. Supp. 808 (D.D.C. 1973).

labor even if therapeutic.[43] The court found support for FLSA coverage in Congress' failure to exclude mental patients from the act's provisions;[44] in the opinion of those most closely concerned with the administration and enforcement of the act;[45] and in the act's provision for special wage rates for severely handicapped workers.[46] Observing that a standard of compensation based upon indices of therapy would be meaningless because any productive labor can be considered therapeutic,[47] and asserting that economic reality is the test of employment,[48] the court held that "[s]o long as the institution derives any consequential economic benefit the economic reality test would indicate an employment relationship rather than mere therapeutic exercise."[49]

Recognizing the financial burdens which a compensation requirement might impose upon institutions, some courts might instead sanction a construction of the FLSA authorizing compensation for only those institution-maintaining tasks that are not primarily therapeutic. But courts inclined to grant exceptions for therapeutic assignments should strictly scrutinize the institutional environment in which such assignments are made. Such scrutiny might reflect the three 1968 Department of Labor guidelines for determining the absence of an "employment relationship" under the FLSA: the task performed must be part of a program of activities professionally judged to have therapeutic or rehabilitative value to the patient; the assignment must not displace the functions of a regular employee or independent contractor of the institution or otherwise impair the employment opportunities of others; and work assignments for a period exceeding three months are presumed to establish an employment relations.[50]

A major substantive objection to the compensation of patient labor under the FLSA is that payment of wages would be meaningless because they could be "setoff" by the institution — recovered as payment for room, board, or treatment — either by deducting commitment costs from paychecks or by billing patients directly.[51] At

---

[43] *Id.,* slip opinion at 2-3.
[44] *Id.* at 3.
[45] *Id.* at 4.
[46] *Id.* at 4-5.
[47] *Id.* at fn. 3 n.21.
Most of the position papers on the subject by concerned organizations recognize the theoretic distinctions among institution-maintaining labor, therapeutic tasks, and general housekeeping duties. *See, e.g.,* American Association on Mental Deficiency, *Guidelines for Work by Residents in Public and Private Institutions for the Mentally Retarded,* MENTAL RETARDATION, Oct., 1973, at 59-62; American Psychiatric Association, Standard 32: Standards for Psychiatric Facilities 47-48; 1969; National Association for Mental Health, Position Statement on Standards for Labor Performed by State Mental Hospital Patients, June 16, 1972; National Association for Retarded Children, Policy Statement on Residential Care 11-12, Oct. 1968. But such papers generally suggest standards requiring compensation for all institution-maintaining labor regardless of therapeutic value, in light of the recognition that any other standard would permit institutions to contrive maintenance tasks arguably defensible as therapeutic, regardless of their propriety in terms of patients' particular handicaps. *See* American Association on Mental Deficiency, *supra*; National Association for Mental Health, *supra*; National Association for Retarded Children, *supra*.
[48] Souder v. Brennan, 367 F. Supp. 808 (D.D.C. 1973).
[49] *Id.*
[50] U.S. Dep't of Labor, Release No. G-874: Applicability of the Fair Labor Standards Act to Work Programs for Patients of Hospitals and Institutions Other Than Federal (Nov. 15, 1968).
[51] Ironically, the first assertions of a right to compensation for labor arose in the context of a claim, advanced in probate court, that patients' estates should be billed for the costs of institutionalization.

the outset it should be observed that any authorized setoff is likely to be only partial, since amounts owed an institution will rarely equal the amount of wages to which a patient is entitled.[52] Moreover, it is arguably a violation of the equal protection clause to assess those who are civilly committed as a substitute for criminal penalty, while declining to assess those who are penally committed, for the costs of institutionalization.[53] A line of cases in California has disallowed the assessment of costs against relatives of committed patients on the grounds that such procedures constitute arbitrary taxation and violate equal protection guarantees.[54] However, courts of no other jurisdiction have indicated an intention to hold unconstitutional the charge of a mentally handicapped patient or his relatives for the costs of his institutionalization.[55] In several actions by a state for costs, the constitutionality of the charge was not questioned,[56] perhaps because "at common law the estate of an incompetent was liable for necessities."[57]

But even if the costs of institutionalization constitutionally may be assessed against working residents, the administration of such assessment is regulated by many states in a manner which protects against the complete setoff of a working patient's wages and thus renders significant the payment of wages under the FLSA. Some state civil commitment statutes and regulations, for example, require a patient or his relatives to contribute only an amount commensurate with their ability to pay.[58] Such legislation frequently prescribes an income level below which there is no obligation to assume the costs of institutionalization.[59] Some residents com-

---

Heirs and relatives defended by seeking to reduce charges by the amount of compensation owed for labor. *See* Buck v. Thornley, 140 Iowa 355, 118 N.W. 530 (1908). *See also* Estate of Buzzelle v. Colorado State Hosp., 176 Colo. 554, 557, 491 P.2d 1369, 1370 (1971); State v. Newman, 140 Conn. 214, 99 A.2d 110 (1953).

[52] It has been estimated, for example, that the cost of taking care of the average working patient in Minnesota, including food, clothing, shelter, occasional entertainment, and minimal medical and nursing services, amounts to no more than $2 per day. Minnesota Dep't of Public Welfare, Mental Health Newsletter 1-2, Aug. 1964; *see* B. ENNIS, PRISONERS OF PSYCHIATRY: MENTAL PATIENTS, PSYCHIATRISTS, AND THE LAW 114 (1972).

[53] *See* People v. Brock, 57 Cal. 2d 644, 371 P.2d 296, 21 Cal. Rptr. 560 (1962). *But see* Grames v. Norris, 3 Ill. 2d 112, 115, 120 N.E.2d 7, 9 (1954).

[54] *See* Department of Mental Hygiene v. Kirchner, 60 Cal. 2d 716, 388 P.2d 720, 36 Cal. Rptr. 488 (1964), *vacated and remanded*, 380 U.S. 194, *as clarified*, 62 Cal. 2d 586, 400 P.2d 321, 43 Cal. Rptr. 329 (1965); Department of Mental Hygiene v. Bank of America, 3 Cal. App. 3d 949, 83 Cal. Rptr. 559 (Dist. Ct. 1970); County of Alameda v. Kaiser, 238 Cal. App. 2d 815, 48 Cal. Rptr. 343 (Dist. Ct. 1966).

[55] *See* Department of Pub. Welfare v. Haas, 15 Ill. 2d 204, 154 N.E.2d 265 (1958); Kough v. Hoehler, 413 Ill. 409, 109 N.E.2d 177 (1952).

[56] *See, e.g.,* State v. Woodworth, 4 Conn. Cir. 149, 227 A.2d 435 (Cir. Ct. 1966); State v. Dickinson, 4 Conn. Cir. 81, 225 A.2d 841 (Cir. Ct. 1966).

[57] Grames v. Norris, 3 Ill. 2d 112, 115, 120 N.E.2d 7, 9 (1954).

[58] *See, e.g.,* ILL. REV. STAT. ch. 91 1/2, § 12-12 (1971). *See also* ALASKA STAT. § 47.30.270(a) (1971). And, although the Washington code authorizes the assessment of institutionalization costs against the patient, WASH. REV. CODE ANN. §§ 72.33.180(2), 72.33 650-700 (Supp. 1972), state officials currently do not bill residents or their families for such costs. Conversation between Gail Marker, M.S.W., Mental Health Law Project, and William Lehman, Washington State Bureau of Mental Health, May 25, 1973.

[59] *See, e.g.,* MICH. COMP. LAWS § 330.658 (1948). Whereas the Michigan statute prescribes a cutoff of $4,999, the department of mental health permits patients in state mental health facilities to earn $7,000 before charging them for institutional costs. Conversation between Gail Marker, M.S.W., Mental Health Law Project, and Joe McCall, Information Service for the Michigan State Department of Mental Health, May 25, 1973.

pensated under FLSA requirements may never reach the statutory minimum, and others required to assume costs might retain a residuum of earning for their own use. Still others with independent sources of savings and income to satisfy cost obligations would be entitled to full compensation under FLSA provisions.

Moreover, even those patients required to return all of their wages to the institution may have the knowledge that they are earning their room and board, and are not mere wards of the state, knowledge which carries a sense of accomplishment, self-respect, and dignity of important therapeutic value.[60] Finally, an assessment of compensable wages under the FLSA will produce tangible economic benefits. By refusing to compensate working residents, or by paying them less than the statutory minimum, institutions deprive such patients of eligibility for, or cause a reduction of, work-related benefits such as social security, state retirement payments, and workmen's compensation.

Even if the substantive problems of FLSA damage actions may be overcome, there is a major practical impediment to bringing such actions: the Supreme Court's recent holding in *Employees of the Department of Public Health and Welfare v. Missouri*[61] that the eleventh amendment forbids a federal court to render judgment under the FLSA against a nonconsenting state. Recognizing that Congress has the power under the commerce and supremacy clauses to authorize these actions against the states in federal court, the Court found no such congressional intention in the language of the 1966 amendments to the FLSA.[62] Although the suit was brought by nonpatient employees of a state mental institution, the Court's holding certainly applies to working inmates as well. But several permissible FLSA damage actions survive the Court's ruling. First, mentally handicapped claimants may utilize federal forums to challenge the compensation policies of private institutions. Second, the Court appeared to sanction the initiation of FLSA actions against both private and state institutions in state courts, observing that the act "authorizes employee suits in 'any court of competent jurisdiction.' Arguably that permits suit in the Missouri courts but that is a question we need not reach."[63] Finally, the Court noted that its holding does not affect the act's authorization of suits against state institutions, brought on behalf of employees by the Secretary of Labor for unpaid wages or injunctive relief, since actions by the United States against a state are not constitutionally proscribed.[64]

However, the Department of Labor has in the past declined to enforce the FLSA on behalf of working residents of mental institutions,[65] as indicated by the Assistant Secretary of Labor in 1972:

---

[60] *See* p. 566 & note 10 *supra. See also* Frankel, *Preventive Restraints and Just Compensation Toward a Sanction Law of the Future,* 78 YALE L.J. 229, 257 (1968).

[61] 411 U.S. 279 (1973).

[62] *Id.* at 284-85.

[63] *Id.* at 287.

[64] *Id.* at 285-86, *citing* 29 U.S.C. §§ 216(c), 217 (1970). Although the *Employees* opinion would have no effect on the ability of the mentally handicapped to bring actions against federal institutions in federal court, the Fair Labor Standards Act expressly excludes federal institutions from its requirements. 29 U.S.C. § 203(d) (1970).

[65] Interview with Francis J. Costello, then assistant administrator, U.S. Dep't of Labor, Mar. 10, 1972.

While the Congress has made its intentions quite clear in extending coverage to employees of hospitals, the legislative history is silent as to the applications of the [1966 amendments to the] Act to work performed by patients in such institutions. Therefore, at this time the Department of Labor will take no enforcement action. However, the Department will carefully watch developments in this area and keep its position under continuous review and, if appropriate, modify its position at the proper time as a result of such developments.[66]

Department representatives have sought to justify a discretionary nonenforcement policy on the basis of several additional considerations: the futility of enforcement if institutions are entitled to recoup wages for the cost of institutionalization; the difficulty of defining which tasks are therapeutic or vocational and which are not; and the time required to investigate patient work programs in hospitals, schools, and other institutions for the mentally handicapped as compared to other Department investigations.[67]

In March of 1973, three mentally handicapped working residents of institutions, the American Association on Mental Deficiency, and the National Association for Mental Health filed suit in the District of Columbia to compel the Department of Labor to enforce the FLSA on behalf of working patients.[68] The claimants in *Souder v. Brennan* sought to require the Secretary of Labor and his subordinates to gather data concerning the wages, hours, and conditions of employment of the mentally handicapped and to enforce the payment of unpaid minimum or overtime compensation to which they are entitled under the FLSA.[69]

In addition to confronting the complex problem of defining compensable labor,[70] plaintiffs in *Souder* faced one other difficulty: Courts have often evidenced a fundamental unwillingness to disturb the exercise of an essentially discretionary function performed by administrative officials given a broad mandate and limited

[66] Letter from then Assistant Secretary of Labor R. J. Grunewald to author, Sept. 27, 1972.

[67] Affidavit of Benjamin P. Robertson, acting administrator, Wage and Hour Division, U.S. Dep't of Labor, para. 5, Souder v. Brennan, 367 F. Supp. 808 (D.D.C. 1973). An additional reason for the Department's reluctance to act may inhere in the FLSA requirement that the Secretary of Labor is empowered only to bring an action where there are no relevant unsettled issues of law. 29 U.S.C. § 216(c) (1970); *see* Mitchell v. Lancaster Milk Co., 185 F. Supp. 66, 73 (M.D. Pa. 1960). A determination that the act covers the labors of resident mental patients might remove this barrier if controlling throughout the federal judicial system. That the Department may now be willing to sanction such a determination is indicated by its Memorandum in Support of Motion for Summary Judgment in Souder v. Brennan, *supra*, which abandoned an argument that the act does not cover patient-workers in favor of an argument that enforcement on behalf of such workers would be difficult.

[68] Souder v. Brennan, 367 F. Supp. 808 (D.D.C. 1973). The American Federation of State, County, and Municipal Employees joined the action as intervenor-plaintiff in June of 1973. *Id.,* slip opinion at fn-3 n. 20; *see* note 32 *supra. See also* Jortburg v. United State Dep't of Labor, Civil No. 13-113 (S.D. Me., filed July 31, 1972).

The advantages of such an action are manifest. Successful litigation will accomplish in one action what would otherwise require a coordinated series of private actions within a single jurisdiction, since the issues in such a case do not concern specific instances of servitude, but relate solely to the scope of the FLSA and the obligation of the Department to enforce it. Moreover, states which have avoided initiating compensation programs in reliance upon the Department's current nonenforcement policy might move voluntarily to comply with judicially sanctioned FLSA requirements.

[69] The act generally authorizes representatives of the Wage and Hour and Public Contracts Division of the Department to investigate wage rates, hours, and other conditions of employment, by entering and inspecting establishments, transcribing records, interviewing employees, and taking whatever actions are necessary to discover violations of the Act. 29 U.S.C. § 211 (1970). *See* p. 568 *supra*.

[70] *See* pp. 569-70 *supra*.

resources to enforce legislation such as the FLSA.[71] Such judicial respect for administrative discretion may deter a court from directing the Secretary of Labor to undertake specific enforcement actions under the FLSA. But it did not prevent the *Souder* court from holding that working residents are generally entitled to compensation under the statute and that it would be an abuse of discretion to deny enforcement to an entire class of covered employees — leaving specific enforcement to administrative judgment.[72] Concluding that the language of the FLSA and its 1966 amendments requires compensation for working patients,[73] and that the Department's nonenforcement policy was grounded more in the administrative difficulties of enforcement than in its lack of propriety,[74] the court ordered the Secretary of Labor "to implement reasonable enforcement efforts applying the minimum wage and overtime compensation provisions of the Fair Labor Standards Act to patient workers at non-Federal institutions for the residential care of the mentally ill [and mentally retarded]."[75]

Thirteenth Amendment Suits

A second way to challenge the practice of employing institutional labor is to bring an action for injunctive relief and damages under the thirteenth amendment and statutes enacted thereunder,[76] claiming that resident mental patients have been

---

[71] *See, e.g.*, Wisconsin v. Federal Power Comm'n, 373 U.S. 294 (1963); McQueary v. Laird, 449 F.2d 608 (10th Cir. 1971); Powell v. Washington Post Co. 267 F.2d 651 (D.C. Cir. 1959).

[72] Souder v. Brennan, 367 F. Supp. 808 (D.D.C. 1973).

[73] *Id.* at 812-13.

[74] *Id.* at 814.

[75] *Id.* at 815.

[76] Three federal statutes apparently combine to create a private right of action for certain violations of the thirteenth amendment. *See* 42 U.S.C. § 1983 (1970) (permitting actions at law or equity for deprivations of civil rights under color of state law); 42 U.S.C. § 1985(3) (1970) (permitting damage actions for conspiracies to deny equal privileges and immunities) (upheld as constitutional under the thirteenth amendment in Griffin v. Breckenridge, 403 U.S. 88, 104-06 (1971); 42 U.S.C. § 1986 (1970) (damage action for knowing failure to prevent violation of section 1985). *See also* Brewer v. Hoxie School Dist., 238 F.2d 91, 103-04 (8th Cir. 1956) (authorizing injunctive actions under section 1985(3)). Other statutes more precisely codify the privileges of the thirteenth amendment without expressly providing for private rights of action or criminal sanctions. *See* 42 U.S.C. § 1982 (1970) (guaranteeing equal rights to hold and transfer property) (upheld as constitutional under the thirteenth amendment in Jones v. Alfred H. Mayer Co., 392 U.S. 409, 437-44 (1968)); 42 U.S.C. § 1994 (1970) (prohibiting peonage) (upheld as constitutional under the thirteenth amendment in Clyatt v. United States, 197 U.S. 207 (1905)). *See also* 42 U.S.C. § 1981 (1970) (guaranteeing equal rights in contracts, property, and judicial proceedings) (characterized as constitutional under the thirteenth amendment in Jones v. Alfred H. Mayer Co., 392 U.S. at 441-43 & n.78 (dictum)). But such statutes have been held to imply a private right of action for their violation. *See* Sullivan v. Little Hunting Park, Inc., 396 U.S. 229 (1969) (damage action under 42 U.S.C. § 1982); Jones v. Alfred H. Mayer Co., 392 U.S. at 414 n.13 (equitable action under 42 U.S.C. § 1982); Bryant v. Donnell, 239 F. Supp. 681, 683-86 (W.D. Tenn. 1965) ("civil liability" under 42 U.S.C. § 1994). Arguably, a private action for injunctive or compensatory relief lies for the violation of constitutional provisions, whether or not codified. The Civil Rights Cases, 109 U.S. 3, 20 (1883), granted federal courts the power to enforce the thirteenth amendment without statutory authority. *See* Bivens v. Six Unknown Named Agents, 403 U.S. 388 (1971) (damage actions under fourth amendment); Butler v. United States, 365 F. Supp. 1035 (D. Hawaii 1973) (damage actions under first and fifth amendments). Finally, several federal statutes prescribe criminal penalties for various violations of the thirteenth amendment. *See, e.g.*, 18 U.S.C. §§ 241, 242, 1582 (1970).

coerced into labor.[77] Such an action may constitute an important weapon against federal institutions, which are exempted from the provisions of the FLSA,[78] and may be brought against state institutions in federal court.[79]

Since successful litigants in thirteenth amendment actions may not automatically recover attorney fees,[80] working residents may have difficulty obtaining representation in such suits. Moreover, plaintiffs confront two significant substantive barriers to success on the merits in such actions — the difficulty of establishing that labors were performed involuntarily[81] and the greater difficulty of establishing that the assignment of such labors is not constitutional despite the thirteenth amendment because of the governmental objectives it serves.

Commitment to present-day institutions arguably subjects the mentally handicapped worker to environmental pressures which preclude his labors from being accurately characterized as voluntary. The claimant in *Dale v. New York*[82] described an experience which may not be atypical. According to Ms. Dale's testimony at trial, although she had refused to perform assigned tasks on several occasions, she had always returned to work out of the fear that her recalcitrance would result in reprisal.[83] Indeed, her hospital record establishes that during periods in which she refused assignments, her "honor card," permitting open ward privileges, was taken away.[84] In general, the prospect that patients may be labeled uncooperative or negative, resulting in the denial of privileges, the transfer to wards housing more seriously retarded or disturbed patients, and most frightening, the postponement of release may suggest an atmosphere of coercion in most institutions.[85] Of course, most

---

[77] *See, e.g.*, Townsend v. Treadway, Civil No. 6500 (D. Tenn., Sept. 21, 1973); Dale v. New York, Cl. No. 51888 (N.Y. Ct. Cl., Mar. 30, 1973); Stone v. City of Paducah, 120 Ky. 322, 86 S.W. 531 (1905). Although the immediate objective of the thirteenth amendment was the abolition of slavery, the notion of involuntary servitude has been construed to encompass "serfage, vassalage, villenage, peonage, and every other form of compulsory labor to mininster to the pleasure, caprice, vanity, or power of others." Railroad Tax Cases, 13 F. 722, 740 (C.C.D. Cal. 1883), *error dismissed*, 116 U.S. 138 (1885); *see* Bailey v. Alabama, 219 U.S. 219 (1911).

[78] *See* note 64 *supra*.

[79] *See* pp. 572-73 *supra*.

[80] No relevant federal statute provides for the award of attorney's fees for successful thirteenth amendment claimants. Courts, however, have held that the judge has discretion to award attorney's fees in actions under 42 U.S.C. § 1983 (1970). *E.g.*, Monroe v. Board of Comm'rs, 453 F.2d 259, 262-63 (6th Cir.), *cert. denied*, 406 U.S. 945 (1972).

[81] *See* Johnston v. Ciccone, 260 F. Supp. 553, 556 (W.D. Mo. 1966).

[82] Cl. No. 51888 (N.Y. Ct. Cl., Mar. 30, 1973).

[83] Record at 288, 290, Dale v. New York, Cl. No. 51888 (N.Y. Ct. Cl. Mar. 30, 1973).

[84] *Id.* at 192 (Claimant's Exhibit 1, Hospital Record). Despite such evidence, however, the trial court concluded that Mrs. Dale had volunteered to work.

[85]   Involuntarily confined mental patients live in an inherently coercive institutional environment. Indirect and subtle psychological coercion has a profound effect upon the patient population.

. . . .

The Law has always been meticulous in scrutinizing inequality in bargaining power and the possibility of undue influence in commercial fields and in the law of wills. It also has been most careful in excluding from criminal cases confessions where there was no clear showing of their completely voluntary nature after full understanding of the consequences. No lesser standard can apply to involuntarily detained mental patients.

Kaimowitz v. Department of Mental Health, Civil No. 73-19434-AW, slip opinion at 29-31 (Cir. Ct. Wayne Co. Mich., July 10, 1973) (citations omitted).

patients would probably prefer to undertake assigned labors than to succumb to the daily boredom of doing nothing. But such depressing alternatives would hardly appear to invoke a voluntary choice,[86] and it might be argued that a resident patient can work voluntarily only in an institution which offers meaningful alternative activities.[87]

Moreover, even compensated labor may be performed involuntarily within the meaning of the thirteenth amendment. That proof of compensation does not dispose of thirteenth amendment claims was the explicit conclusion of the United States Court of Appeals for the Fifth Circuit in 1944: "It is not uncompensated service, but involuntary servitude which is prohibited by the Thirteenth Amendment. Compensation for service may cause consent, but unless it does it is no justification for forced labor."[88] The thirteenth amendment and enforcing legislation proscribe, and award damages for, involuntary servitude, and although the wages owed may provide a convenient measure of damages in cases in which assigned tasks have not been compensated, the thirteenth amendment is no less transgressed when patients are forced to labor, even if they are rewarded.

Even if institutional labor is performed involuntarily, such labor will not constitute a violation of the thirteenth amendment if it serves compelling governmental interests.[89] Arguably, assignments which constitute therapy or vocational training for a patient serve the compelling purpose for which most patients[90] were originally

---

[86] Of course, the concept of voluntary consent is elusive when applied to mentally handicapped individuals. In many states, however, a finding of mental illness does not raise even a presumption that a patient is incompetent or unable to manage his affairs. *See, e.g.,* Winters v. Miller, 446 F.2d 65, 68 (2d Cir.), *cert. denied,* 404 U.S. 985 (1971); Sengstack v. Sengstack, 4 N.Y.2d 502, 151 N.E.2d 887, 176 N.Y.S.2d 337 (1958). In each case the court must decide whether a patient is capable of consent. *See* Winters v. Miller, *supra,* at 71. *But see* cases cited note 87 *infra.*

[87] *But cf.* United States v. Shackney, 333 F.2d 475 (2d Cir. 1964) (Friendly, J.), holding that an employer cannot be convicted under 18 U.S.C. § 1584 (1970) (making criminal the imposition of involuntary servitude) for threatening alien employees with deportation if they left his employ. The court reasoned that even if employees were led to believe that terminating employment would result in harsh consequences, they remained aware of a voluntary choice between continued service and freedom. *See also* Henry v. Ciccone, 315 F. Supp. 889, 891 (W.D. Mo. 1970), *appeal dismissed,* 440 F.2d 1052 (8th Cir. 1971); Parks v. Ciccone, 281 F. Supp. 805, 811 (W.D. Mo. 1968).

[88] Hefflin v. Sanford, 142 F.2d 798, 799 (5th Cir. 1944); *see* Taylor v. Georgia, 315 U.S. 25 (1942); Jobson v. Henne, 355 F.2d 129, 132 (2d Cir. 1966).

Of course, a court's willingness to hold that compensation demonstrates voluntary performance should very with the form and generosity of compensation. For example, institutions confronting fiscal difficulties may, consistent with the thirteenth amendment, reward labor with tokens to be exchanged at the institution's canteen. *But cf.* 29 C.F.R. § 531-34 (1973) (payment under FLSA must be in cash). However, if a patient must use such tokens for goods or services which the institution would otherwise be required to provide, payment in kind will not represent true compensation, but will be part of a system that coerces patients to work.

[89] It is unclear whether tasks performed involuntarily will not be characterized as servitude if they further compelling governmental objectives, or whether activities characterized as involuntary servitude will nevertheless survive a thirteenth amendment challenge if they further sufficiently important governmental interests. In any event, it is recognized that such governmental interests will defeat a thirteenth amendment claim. *See* Butler v. Perry, 240 U.S. 328, 333 (1916) (compulsory road work); Jacobson v. Massachusetts, 197 U.S. 11, 25-27 (1905) (vaccination); Hefflin v. Sanford, 142 F.2d 798, 799-800 (5th Cir. 1944) (military conscription); Crews v. Lundquist, 361 Ill. 193, 197 N.E. 768 (1935) (dictum) (jury service). *See also* Slaughter House Cases, 83 U.S. (16 Wall.) 36, 69-72 (1873).

[90] This is not to imply that commitment will always serve the compelling governmental purpose of treatment. Not all patients are committed for treatment, though most are. *See* Frankel, *Preventive Restraints and Just Compensation: Toward a Sanction Law of the Future,* 78 YALE L.J. 229, 234-45 (1968). And not all patients are committed for valid reasons.

committed.[91] Thus, the United State Court of Appeals for the Second Circuit reasoned in 1966:

> [M]any states . . . administer programs that are designed to supply institutional needs as well as provide therapy, . . . and we assume that mental institutions can constitutionally require inmate participation in these programs to the extent that the programs have a therapeutic purpose, or are reasonably related to the inmate's housekeeping or personal hygienic needs.[92]

However, the court's sanction of all therapeutic labor assignments appears to sustain an overly broad system for securing the benefits of civil commitment. Given the financial problems of mental institutions, permitting hospital administrators the unfettered discretion to assign any task which is even minimally therapeutic may result in the assignment of tasks primarily out of institutional requirements, regardless of alternative therapies more suited to a patient's needs.[93] Prohibition of required institution-maintaining tasks would still protect from judicial proscription a range of therapeutic assignments available to further the governmental objectives of commitment. Such a limitation on the constitutionality of involuntary "therapeutic" labor would also ensure that a patient's therapy regimen satisfied legitimate governmental, as opposed to illegitimate institutional, objectives.

Under current standards, however, successful litigants in thirteenth amendment actions may have to demonstrate that assignments which benefit an institution are not also therapy, and in the process overcome the belief that all productive labor is therapeutic.[94] The task of demonstrating that a given assignment is not therapy for the patient appears overwhelming, but several lines of argument may be advanced. Experts in *Dale v. New York* testified that work therapy can only be meaningful if performed voluntarily,[95] but such an argument would appear to be inconsistent with the conclusions of several courts that the performance of therapeutic tasks may be compelled.[96] Nevertheless, it may be asserted that some required tasks, especially those, like shelling peas, which are assigned primarily to meet institutional require-

---

[91] It may be argued that the governmental interest in a patient's treatment is outweighed by the constitutional protection against involuntary servitude. Analogous cases support such a conclusion. For example, a psychologist may decide that the litigious proclivities of a patient are reflective of a mental illness and that therapeutic goals would be furthered by prohibiting such a patient from petitioning courts for release from the institution. Yet such an action violates due process guarantees despite the habilitative purpose with which it is taken. *See* Hoff v. New York, 279 N.Y. 490, 493, 18 N.E.2d 671, 672 (1939). And the first amendment has been held to proscribe hospital psychiatrists from administering psychoactive therapeutic medication in certain circumstances to lawfully committed Christain Scientists. Winters v. Miller, 446 F.2d 65, 69-70 (2d Cir.), *cert. denied*, 404 U.S. 985 (1971).

[92] Jobson v. Henne, 355 F.2d 129, 132 n.3 (2d Cir. 1966). *See also* Krieger v. New York, 54 Misc. 2d 583, 283 N.Y.S.2d 86 (Ct. Cl. 1966). The *Jobson* court recognized, however, that mandatory programs may be "so ruthless in the amount of work demanded, and in the conditions under which the work might be performed, and thus so devoid of therapeutic purpose, that a court justifiably could conclude that the immate had been subjected to involuntary servitude." 355 F.2d at 132.

[93] *See* B. ENNIS, PRISONERS OF PSYCHIATRY: MENTAL PATIENTS, PSYCHIATRISTS, AND THE LAW 111-13, 118-19 (1972); *cf.* notes 10 & 50 *supra;* p. 579 & note 104 *infra.*

[94] *See* p. 569 & note 40 *supra.*

[95] *See* Claimants' Post Trial Memorandum at 28-29, Dale v. New York, Cl. No. 51888 (N.Y. Ct. Cl., Mar. 30, 1973).

[96] *See* cases cited note 92 *supra.*

ments, are "without therapeutic value."[97] Apart from their conviction that work must be voluntarily undertaken to be therapeutic, the claimant's experts in *Dale* adverted to a number of generally accepted professional standards for the proper assignment of work as therapy:[98] work assignments must be made only by qualified professional personnel, and only after careful physical and mental examination and diagnosis; work assignments must be dictated by a patient's particular therapeutic needs, as opposed to institutional requirements; work assignments must be part of a larger integrated and supervised therapy program; work assignments must be recorded; work programs must be regularly reviewed and adjusted; and patients must be fairly compensated for their participation in work programs.

Acceptance of a compensation requirement as a necessary attribute of work therapy would at least ensure that thirteenth amendment actions achieved results similar to those of FLSA actions. But courts unwilling to adopt such a requirement might accept the related assertion that compensation is a sufficient condition of therapy. Such a conclusion, which is supported by some medical opinion,[99] might permit institutions to avoid thirteenth amendment claims by compensating patients, an outcome which is progressive but which falls short of an outright prohibition of institution-maintaining work assignments which do not satisfy the other proposed criteria of therapy. The acceptance of such criteria would, however, help litigants to argue that, despite the contrary assertions of hospital administrators, some institution-maintaining assignments did not further the objective of therapy and thus violated the thirteenth amendment.

Actions Claiming Violations of the Right to Treatment

A third source of legal rights which may affect the utilization of institutional labor is the due process clause. Several cases have held that mentally handicapped individuals who are committed to an institution have a constitutional right under those clauses to some minimum level of therapy consistent with the treatment objectives of civil commitment.[100] Arguably, a patient's right to treatment is undermined by his subjection to labor assignments which are demonstrably harmful to his therapeutic progress, at least to the extent that such assignments push the therapeutic value of other institutional activities — and thus the patient's overall progress — below the constitutionally required minimum. And labor assignments which are not themselves harmful to therapeutic objectives may nonetheless undermine overall therapeutic progress by displacing activities necessary to meet constitutionally required levels of treatment.

---

[97] Bickford, *The Economic Value of the Psychiatric Inpatient,* LANCET, Mar. 30, 1963, at 714. *See* B. ENNIS, PRISONERS OF PSYCHIATRY: MENTAL PATIENTS, PSYCHIATRISTS, AND THE LAW 118-19 (1972); p. 566 & note 9 *supra*; p. 579 *infra. See also* Minnesota Dep't of Public Welfare, Mental Health Newsletter 1-2, Aug. 1964.

[98] *See* Claimants' Post Trial Memorandum at 18-35, Dale v. New York, Cl. No. 51888 (N.Y. Ct. Cl., Mar. 30, 1973).

[99] *See* p. 566 & note 10 *supra.*

[100] *See, e.g.,* Cameron v. Mullen, 387 F.2d 193 (D.C. Cir. 1967); Ragsdale v. Overholser, 281 F.2d 943, 950 (D.C. Cir. 1960); Eidinoff v. Connolly, 281 F. Supp. 191 (N.D. Tex. 1968). *But see* Burnham v. Department of Pub. Health, 349 F. Supp. 1335 (N.D. Ga. 1972). *rev'd,* 503 F.2d 1319 (5th Cir. 1974).

In *Wyatt v. Stickney*,[101] a federal district court in Alabama held that the right to treatment generally proscribes institutions from requiring patients to perform labor involving the operation and maintenance of the institution, presumably because "non-therapeutic . . . work assignments . . . [constitute] dehumanizing factors contributing to the degeneration of the patients' self-esteem."[102] Observing that patients may volunteer for institution-maintaining assignments for which they are entitled to compensation under the FLSA, the court stressed that patients may not be compelled to perform such tasks.[103]

Medical experts have agreed with the *Wyatt* court that institution-maintaining labor can be harmful to therapeutic objectives, if only by engendering an institutional dependence upon productive workers, prolonging their incarceration.[104] The *Wyatt* application of the right to treatment, however, appears to be limited to the visibly oppressive institutional conditions challenged in that case.[105] The *Wyatt* court offered no evidence for the assertion that all institution-maintaining labor is harmful to therapy and cannot be said to have suggested that the imposition of labor assignments necessarily pulls an overall therapeutic regimen below constitutional requirements. Nevertheless, the right to treatment approach to enjoining institutional labor remains an available judicial option to patients in institutions so preoccupied with institution-maintaining assignments as to ignore the minimum requirements of adequate and effective treatment.

CONCLUSION

Many mentally handicapped residents of institutions throughout the country are forced to perform, for at most token compensation, labors associated with the maintenance of the institution. Several legal theories are available to such patients which might require compensation for such labors or disallow their assignment altogether. The Fair Labor Standards Act arguably requires that institution-maintaining labor be compensated whether or not performed voluntarily, and whether or not such labor is also of therapeutic value. The thirteenth amendment proscribes forced work assignments of no therapeutic value and arguably proscribes institution-maintaining labor whether or nor it is also therapy or training. And a constitutional right to treatment ensures that work assignments will not undermine the minimum delivery of adequate and effective treatment.

Since test case litigation can at best play only a catalytic role in the development of new policies to eliminate institutional labor, however, effective progress may depend upon institutional reform. Hospital administrators and institutional superin-

---

[101] 325 F. Supp. 781 (M.D. Ala. 1971), *aff'd sub nom.* Wyatt v. Aderholt, 503 F.2d 1305 (5th Cir. 1974) *along with* 344 F. Supp. 373, 344 F. Supp. 387 (M.D. Ala. 1972).

[102] 344 F. Supp. at 375.

[103] *Id.* at 381. *See also* Wyatt v. Stickney, 344 F. Supp. at 402-03.

[104] *See* B. ENNIS, PRISONERS OF PSYCHIATRY: MENTAL PATIENTS, PSYCHIATRISTS, AND THE LAW 118-20 (1972); Bartlett, *Institutional Peonage, Our Exploitation of Mental Patients,* ATLANTIC, July 1964, at 116-17. *See also* p. 566 & notes 9-10 *supra.*

[105] *See* 344 F. Supp. at 390-91.

tendents who are concerned about the constitutional and statutory rights of working patients, but who nevertheless seek the flexibility to employ residents at therapy or training tasks without compensation, must recognize that any approach which permits such discretion, albeit for benevolent purposes, may eventually tend toward the pattern of abuse which characterizes too many institutions already. Administrators might begin compensating residents for all institution-maintaining work performed, with the recognition that fair compensation enhances therapy. But because of the great difficulty of ensuring that patient labor is performed truly voluntarily in an institutional setting, it might be wise to replace this approach with a flat ban on all institution-maintaining labor by patients.[106] Having patients perform labor which benefits the institution to any extent may create unavoidable conflicts of interest for financially burdened institutions charged with providing therapy and training to such residents.

If institutional reform is not forthcoming, administrative or legislative actions to control institutional labor may supplement the efforts of private litigants. For example, the assistant attorney general for the state of Washington recently issued a legal opinion indicating his belief that failure to compensate working mental patients would violate their rights under the thirteenth amendment and state law, a memorandum which prompted the promise of detailed regulations ensuring compensation.[107] And the states of New York and Indiana have recently passed legislation ensuring that resident mental patients will receive fair compensation for the work they perform.[108]

The control of institutional labor is of course only a first step toward eliminating a wider pattern of discrimination against the mentally ill and the mentally retarded. Test case litigation necessarily focuses upon obvious abuses. In the future, more subtle and perhaps more basic issues will be encountered, such as what to do to remedy job discrimination against patients released from institutions, and the even more vexing problem of how to ensure that mentally handicapped employees receive wages consistent with minimum living standards. Legislation will probably be required to compel employment by the private sector or to create government projects tailored to the needs of the mentally handicapped.[109] And although precise funding mechanisms would have to be arranged, all workers, the mentally retarded

---

[106] Institutions might thereafter contract out all vocational training to facilities in the community.

[107] Informal memorandum from Assistant Attorney General Paul J. Murphy, Washington, to Samuel L. Ornstern, chief, Office of Developmental Disabilities, Washington, Feb. 2, 1972. The views expressed in the memorandum will be formalized into rules and regulations under the state's Administrative Procedure Act. Interview with Donald Horowitz, senior assistant attorney general and chief counsel to Washington State Dep't of Social and Health Services, Dec. 8, 1973.

[108] N.Y. MENTAL HYGIENE LAW § 15.09 (McKinney Supp. 1973); IND. ANN. STAT. §§ 22-1315-1324 (Burns 1972). Both statutes state the general objective of protecting working residents from exploitation, but leave precise definitions of covered employees, compensable services, and wage rates to the future promulgation of rules and regulations. The Indiana statute, however, expressly exempts labors of therapeutic value from compensation requirements. IND. ANN. STAT. §§ 22-1315(h), 22-1321 (Burns 1972).

[109] *See* P. Wald, President's Commission on Mental Retardation Keynote Paper: The Legal Rights of People Within the Community: A Plea for Laissez Faire, May 4, 1973.

included, should be entitled to a minimum wage which will permit them to maintain a decent standard of life, regardless of nonwillful variations in productivity.[110]

Assuming these goals are ultimately recognized and pursued, legal challenges to the pattern of institutional servitude will be seen in perspective as only part of a larger affirmative societal obligation to guarantee meaningful employment opportunities for all citizens.

ADDENDUM

There have been several developments of significance since the publication of the foregoing paper.

1. Most important, Congress passed the Fair Labor Standards Amendments of 1974, Pub. L. No. 93-259, which became effective on May 1, 1974. A specific amendment to section 16(b) of the act attempts to overcome the effect of the United States Supreme Court decision in *Employees of the Department of Public Health & Welfare v. Missouri*, 411 U.S. 279 (1973), by providing that federal as well as state courts have jurisdiction over suits against nonconsenting states and state agencies. *See* text at notes 61-64 *supra*. Moreover, the 1974 amendments expand the scope of the FLSA to include "public agencies" as "employers" and government employees—both state and federal—as "employees" under sections 3(d) and 3(e) of the act. "Public agency" is defined under the amendments in section 3(x) as

> . . . the government of the United States; the government of a State or political subdivision thereof; any agency of the United States (including the United States Postal Service and Postal Rate Commission), a State, or political subdivision of a State; or any interstate governmental agency.

2. Congress passed the Rehabilitation Act of 1973, Pub. L. No. 93-112, which was approved by the President on September 26, 1973. The act grants a statutory right to the handicapped to be free from employment discrimination and requires certain employers to take affirmative action to employ qualified handicapped persons. In relevant part the act reads as follows:

> Sec. 503. (a) Any contract in excess of $2,500 entered into by any Federal department or agency for the procurement of personal property and nonpersonal services (including construction) for the United States shall contain a provision requiring that, in employing persons to carry out such contract the party contracting with the United States shall take affirmative action to employ and advance in employment qualified handicapped individuals as defined in section 7(6). The provisions of this section shall apply to any subcontract in excess of $2,500 entered into by a prime contractor in carrying out any contract for the procurement of personal property and nonpersonal services (including construction) for the United States.

---

[110] *See* M. Bernstein, President's Commission on Mental Retardation Paper: The Appropriate Wage Rates for the Mentally Retarded: An Essay on the Worth of a Person to Society and Vice-Versa, May 4, 1973..

The President shall implement the provisions of this section by promulgating regulations within ninety days after the date of enactment of this section.

(b) If any handicapped individual believes any contractor has failed or refused to comply with the provisions of his contract with the United States, relating to employment of handicapped individuals, such individual may file a complaint with the Department of Labor. The Department shall promptly investigate such complaint and shall take such action thereon as the facts and circumstances warrant, consistent with the terms of such contract and the laws and regulations applicable thereto.

Sec. 504. No otherwise qualified handicapped individual in the United States, as defined in section 7(6), shall, solely by reason of his handicap, be excluded from the participation in, be denied the benefits of, or be subjected to discrimination under any program or activity receiving Federal financial assistance.

The implementation regulations required under section 503(a) of the act are overdue and expected shortly.

3. (Addition to note 42 *supra.*) The time for filing an appeal in *Souder v. Brennan* passed without the government's filing a notice of appeal as required by Rule 4(a) of the Appellate Rules of Civil Procedure. The case should now be cited as *Souder v. Brennan*, 367 F. Supp. 808 (D.D.C. 1973).

4. (Addition to note 29 *supra.*) The Tennessee state court held that in a section 16(b) action under the FLSA, as amended in 1966, the doctrine of sovereign immunity did not bar an action by a state employee against the state of Tennessee. *Townsend v. Cloverbottom Hospital and School*, slip opinion no. 4-2576 (Tenn. Chancery Court, part 2, February 21, 1974). Reasoning from *Employees* and the 1966 amendments to the FLSA, the Tennessee court concluded that

> Congress having recognized the right to the protection of the Act for certain state employees, it is encumbent upon the Courts to insure that an alleged violation of some is not dismissed without the litigants' receiving the process due them under the Federal Constitution. This Court is, therefore, of the opinion that Congress, by the 1966 amendment, effectively lifted the states' immunity from private suit in the context of an FLSA action in a state forum. *Townsend* at 8.

The *Townsend* opinion, of course, preceded Congress' amendments to the FLSA restoring *federal* jurisdiction. See paragraph (1) *supra.*

Reaction Comment

LINDA Z. TARR-WHELAN

I AM health specialist for the American Federation of State, County, and Municipal Employees (AFSCME) and will present the federation's view of institutional peonage. AFSCME represents probably the only organized group of workers in mental retardation facilities. The federation has 40,000 members who work in state mental retardation facilities and it represents approximately twice that number.

Employees and their representatives have traditionally been "on the fence" with regard to the issue of peonage. Workers felt that jobs might be lost if residents were paid full wages, and yet they had a strong reaction to servitude. They are no longer on the fence. AFSCME has begun joining the suits which are being brought to compel adequate compensation for residents of mental retardation facilities and also patients in mental hospitals. The federation was a party in the *Souder v. Brennan* case.[1]

There are two reasons for this change of position. One is a philosophical reason that unions are in business to see that everyone gets paid adequately. A minimum wage is the right of any person who works. The second reason is not so philosophical, but is more pragmatic. AFSCME feels that many of the fears among workers regarding the payment of residents in institutions—fears that their jobs will disappear or that there will be no place for them—are misplaced. Our position now is that the employee and the resident have many of the same problems.

In fact, in many institutions AFSCME members (the majority of whom in retardation institutions are nonprofessional and technical workers) are dead-ended or prevented from moving upward in the system through formal, organized training programs or promotions or retraining. There is an economic justification for this: The employee who is the best aide stays the best aide rather than moving to a higher paid technical category. The same is true for residents. If residents were paid for the work they did in hospitals, this would cause an upward pressure for wages for the employees represented by the federation. Many AFSCME employees are practically at the minimum wage level right now and actually perform as supervisors of unpaid residents in such areas as the kitchen, housekeeping, and maintenance operations.

Another concern centers on definitions. There is a question as to whether a resident can be an employee, any more than an employee can be a resident. There may be a contradiction in terms. It may be that an individual who is capable of performing in a regular position, one that would normally be an employee-type position, has no place as a resident of that institution. A mentally retarded individual might need some services which the institution provides; he might even require residential placement. But perhaps the hiring facility should not be the one in which the resident was placed and where he was seen primarily as a resident. Employment in a different setting provides the co-workers with the image of the person as an employee.

There is an equality factor here as well. The resident-employee who is paid a minimum wage is provided housing and shelter, whereas nonresident-employees must pay for transportation, food, shelter, and so on. This is directly related to the setoff question discussed by Friedman.

As mentally retarded individuals become employees, full employees, their rights as employees must be considered. The New York Supreme Court considered in in *Ballentine v. Sugarman*[2] the situation of welfare recipients who were placed in

[1]367 F. Supp. 808 (D.D.C. 1973).
[2]74 Misc. 2d 267, 344 N.Y.S. 2d 39 (Sup. Ct. 1973).

positions within the New York City civil service system, without full employee rights. The question was whether or not this practice was peonage. In this case brought by the American Federation of State, County, and Municipal Employees and the New York Civil Liberties Union on behalf of three welfare recipients, the court held:

1. The assignment of home relief recipients to jobs does not constitute appointments and/or promotions in the civil service.
2. The legal situation is not altered because the work that the welfare recipients do might be similar to work performed by civil service employees.
3. The concept of work relief, by doing work for public agencies, would have no meaning if the jobs were exactly the same as those done by civil service employees because then civil service workers would be performing them.
4. It does not matter that civil service employees are not employed in greater numbers because of budgetary restrictions.[3]

The implications of this decision are: (1) the welfare recipients must fulfill the responsibilities of an employee in order to receive home relief welfare money; (2) they have no rights and privileges; (3) there is no civil service protection; (4) there is no promotion; and (5) there is no merit system. Questions such as pensions, fringe benefits, and other employees' rights will become increasingly important to the mentally retarded citizen who finds himself in essentially the same position.

In summary, the American Federation of State, County, and Municipal Employees supports the mentally retarded citizen in his fight to be paid minimum wage for his labors—to escape from institutional peonage. It should be recognized, however, that for the retarded individual to enjoy his full rights, a long battle will be required. (Cooperation between the unions and mentally retarded workers will be essential.)

There are specific concerns, however. One of the legal characteristics of a therapeutic program is supervision. Who supervises? In many institutions, the only supervision comes from minimally trained employees. Essentially, supervision is lacking for both employees and residents. AFSCME has been negotiating with the District of Columbia Department of Human Resources to develop a training program for dietary, laundry, and maintenance employees in a mental retardation facility. These employees, rather than doing the work themselves, supervise residents in doing the work. They have had no training in human relations and have no involvement in coordinating the work situation and other aspects of the resident's program. There is no contact between the kitchen in which the resident spends most of his time and the ward, where staff make notes on how the resident is progressing. Goal-directed supervision is a major problem now and it must be addressed. What is a work therapy program? Who trains and how are these individuals themselves trained?

A strong movement to decentralize large facilities is under way. The union is in favor of decentralization programs which improve care for people. AFSCME intends,

---

[3]*Id*. at 270-71, 344 N.Y.S. 2d at 43-44.

however, to be very vigilant with regard to whether decentralization plans are introduced for better care or for political and financial reasons. This causes tremendous problems for the union. Our workers are largely institutional employees. Work is going from the public sector to the private sector. AFSCME is in favor of decentralization when it is for the benefit of the patients or residents involved, as long as consideration is given to present institutional employees.

As decentralization accelerates, there will be very difficult problems in determining adequate staffing. The first phase of decentralization should result in a large-scale discharge of patients without any corresponding decrease in staff, since the staff ratios have been poor for many, many years. Staffing should begin to approximate the level required in a truly therapeutic environment.

As residents are moved into the community, two questions arise. For example, recently in Galesburg State Hospital in Illinois the issue of staffing was addressed. The institution has several hundred patients who are in a "work program," basically, maintenance of the institution. Residents are now working approximately the same number of hours that would be worked by 40 full-time employees. The institution is dropping about 160 people from its payroll. The hard question is : "What happens? Should 40 employees go, or should the work program go?" So far this problem has not been solved, and it is one that is going to occur more and more often. It will be very difficult to resolve the staff question while at the same time meeting the needs of both employees and residents. A second problem is the provision of care to remaining residents, who are frequently profoundly retarded, with staffs developed for a broader range of patients. Moreover, the care must be provided without resident assistance since those who heretofore worked without pay will normally be the first to reenter the community.

Reaction Comment

DAVID ROSEN

RETURNING mentally retarded individuals from institutional settings to the local community is a popularly espoused movement today. Like most concepts that promise more normal and healthy experiences, the benefits from living in a typical neighborhood are lauded by family members and those in the professional field alike. The effect has been significant, as community residential placements have been developed by the thousands.

Although some of these placements have proven to be unsatisfactory, the overwhelming majority result in relationships wherein retarded persons not only grow, but thrive, on freedoms not possible in the institution. These successful placements are testimony that differential program needs can be met if differential placements are developed, and practitioners are critical enough to be intolerant of inadequate ones.

With beautiful examples of retarded citizens prospering in the larger community, the question is: "Why do thousands continue to live in institutions?" "Why are so many retarded persons with the capability of contributing to the economy of a community kept within institutions?" Placements can be secured; this has been demonstrated. Institution administrators say that they have no desire to hold people in bondage; this is accepted. Why then are so many persons kept living and working in institutions when they might be living and working in the community? Why is peonage even an issue? Although the precise balance varies, the answer is usually found in an "overcommitment to program completion" within the institution and in a "token acceptance" of the retarded in the community.

"Overcommitment to program completion" is simply a policy that insists that an individual extract all the benefits from one program before pursuing another. The phenomenon is as prevalent as it is well meaning. And though it gives curriculum structure to educational objectives, it too often denies opportunity and freedoms. This "overcommitment" is seen in the institution in a moderately retarded man's working as a laundry helper to perfect "job habits and attitudes," which are alluded to but not taught, yet must be mastered before placement on a community job will be made. It is seen when a severely retarded girl is repeatedly passed over for placement consideration because she does not get along well with her housekeeping supervisor and is failing to make some undefined "adequate progress." And it is seen whenever men and women who are good workers are kept living within the institution for an indefinite period of time to refine "social skills." Examples abound; the retarded are denied return to the community because staff say there is still more to gain from the institutional program; the retarded are denied return to the community because they have not approached their ultimate skill development potential and further institutional stay might realize this goal.

These reasons cannot be accepted. There is no justification for keeping a person in an institution merely because he has not learned as much as he might. No retarded person should be denied a placement outside the institution because he has not perfected personal skills within the institution. No retarded person should be denied a placement outside the institution because he has not received maximum program benefit within the institution. No one of us is denied access to more desirable conditions for living, working, and leisure merely because the fullest exploitation of existing conditions has not been made. I have not. You have not. Why should the mentally retarded?

The irony is that the best programs, whether they are institutional or community based, can be expected to encourage learning in a fashion that best realizes or seeks to realize the individual's maximum potential. As clearly as skills increase, potential increases, and the retarded person is enough like most people that he never will reach his full potential whether he be in the community or the institution.

"Token acceptance" of the retarded is the attitude of communities that do little to facilitate the return of more than a token number of retarded persons. While lauding the desirability of deinstitutionalization, local agencies and civic groups seldom become actively involved in developing residential alternatives. Communities complacently rely only on existing program resources and justify their resistance to a substantial return of the retarded on the basis that support services are already taxed to the maximum. Besides, it would be better to have "those people" in another community, not here.

"Token acceptance" of the retarded is evident in areas where the citizens are apathetic about combating zoning ordinances that discriminate against the mentally handicapped. It is evident in communities that develop only a small number of group homes and foster homes for the most select retarded. It is evident in communities whose mildly and moderately retarded citizens are still residing in institutions with no plan for their swift return to the community.

"Token acceptance" of the retarded, whenever or wherever it inhibits the return of individuals who could genuinely profit from community living, must be denounced. No retarded person should be excluded from normal community life because a group home is not on the drawing board for the current fiscal year. No retarded person should be denied an opportunity to be part of the larger culture because his needs do not comfortably fit into existing community structures.

When consideration is given to placing or not placing the retarded, of any intellectual level, the professional has a fundamental responsibility to provide the least restrictive environment for all activities. In this regard the official rights statement of the American Association on Mental Deficiency (AAMD) is significant:

> Non-retarded adults have considerable latitude to control their own lives, particularly in terms of choosing place of employment and place of residence. Insofar as he or she is able to make these choices, a retarded adult should have the same freedom of choice. A classification of mental retardation is not, of itself, sufficient cause to restrict an individual's freedom of movement.[1]

The practices of "overcommitment to program goals" and token acceptance," which work against this goal of the AAMD, are not the exclusive property of institutions and communities, respectively. There are many examples of institutional programs that accept, in a "token" fashion, the retarded person's human desires for privacy, stimulation, and social interaction. Likewise, there are numerous examples of community programs that tenaciously remain "committed" to programs and placements that offer diminishing returns.

The causes of institutional peonage then, are rooted deep within the fabrics of both institutional and community philosophies and policies, and the leadership of each shares responsibility for the resolution. Let us examine a few of the efforts to resolve the problem of peonage.

Institutional admission of the mildly and moderately retarded, although still permitted in some states, is prohibited in several others. I am pleased that in the three states where I have worked as an institutional superintendent, New Jersey, Washington, and Michigan, persons classified as mildly and moderately retarded are not being admitted unless they exhibit extraordinary problems of behavior and unless alternative residences cannot be secured after exhaustive searching.

Admission policies such as these squarely place the responsibility for servicing

---

[1] American Association on Mental Deficiency, *Rights of Mentally Retarded Persons*, 11 MENTAL RETARDATION 56 (1973).

this segment of the population in home communities, which in 1973 is where it belongs, and reduce dramatically the possibility of institutional peonage. Such stringent admission policies also stimulate the creation of new neighborhood services that otherwise could be considered unnecessary. Without the threat of waiting lists, these policies also allow institutions the opportunity to concentrate on treating more severely limited persons with new efficiency, efficiency that now can be expected and demanded from the institutional programs.

Historically, one of the most advanced states in the area of resident payment and work assignments has been New Jersey, which 15 years ago began a program that over the years not only paid thousands of residents for routine tasks, but hired hundreds of them with full employee status. When the New Jersey plan to compensate residents was initially developed, it was decided not to discharge individuals from the program, since under existing state regulations they would not be able to receive room and board or medical care if they were discharged. They also would have been required to pay social security out of their trainees' salaries of $100.00 per month. Under this plan, each working individual received a private or semi-private room. Meals were provided in the employee dining room, and free movement into the community during off-duty hours was encouraged. Vacations and medical coverage were the same as those received by regular employees.

At the Vineland State School, in which I worked, each trainee was enrolled in social, vocational, and adult education programs a minimum of six hours per week, with most of the classes held during the working day. The combined hours of work and study did not exceed 40 hours per week. In the state of Washington, which adopted the New Jersey plan years later, adult education classes for the trainees were provided by the local community college.

The cases of these mildly retarded people were reviewed regularly. The majority of individuals were given the choice, after completing one year of training, of community placement or of civil service positions as food service workers, building service workers, laundresses, or attendants. Hundreds of people were hired; hundreds were placed.

One of the key factors in this program was that whenever a retarded member of the institutional work force was hired into a community job, a new position was allocated to the institution above and beyond the normal complement. Through this procedure, the success of the program in community placements in no way depleted the work force of the institution. Placement or the hiring of residents in the community was encouraged.

It should also be understood that both this program and the payment plan established for the severely and profoundly retarded resident, incorporated some years later, were under the direction of the professional vocational supervisor of instruction, who not only augmented the program with formal instruction, but also made regular reports on the working force to the central office, indicating the number of residents, the type of work, and the value of their contributions and compensation.

This program does well to point up that in the zeal to overcome the injustices that have been perpetrated on the retarded in institutions, care must be taken not to hamstring the residential facility in its efforts to provide appropriate, well-regulated training programs. In a number of states, for example, the payment of residents or patients is illegal. This is unfortunate, as we have seen many examples of severely retarded residents who achieved amazing degrees of occupational competency after being involved in well-designed training programs with monetary compensation.

Occupational training for the severely retarded in the average institution begins by the resident's learning work activities in his own living facility. In the facility, this training consists of mending, making beds, general housekeeping, assisting with meals, or taking care of the lawn. Although this could be considered peonage, these same training tasks in a group home or a foster home would invariably be seen as chores. The critical issue for the institutional program is whether or not the retarded person would be receiving the same kind of prevocational experience in a less restrictive community program; a community program that probably could developed with the manpower being used to do the training within the institution. Certainly there is enough wisdom to develop guidelines that would truly benefit the retarded in this regard.

A good example of a properly run job training program is one generated at the Woodbridge State School in New Jersey five years ago. Seventy-five mildly retarded individuals went through a 30-week training program in groups of 25. The program, funded by the New Jersey Vocational Rehabilitation Commission and the Federal Manpower and Training Act, included people between the ages of 17 1/2 and 30. The students, who were screened by the vocational rehabilitation commission, were given a stipend of $20 a week while going to classes 2 days per week and receiving on-the-job training for the other 3. The majority elected upon completion of the course to accept regular civil service positions at Woodbridge.

The state vocational rehabilitation agency has been working with the Macomb-Oakland Regional Center, a facility currently serving 100 severely and profoundly retarded persons in Michigan, to have 25-50 work training stations for the adult retarded living in the nearby community. If the facility's contemplated expansion develops, it will be able to serve nearly 300, and more work training stations can be maintained. Although this is seen as a very desirable effort, the intent is to be critical of this program and not allow it sacred status. It will have points of entry and exit so as to encourage all possible movement into the vocational community at large.

The center also has worked closely with other agencies and interest groups in its catchment area to encourage a mutual sense of urgency and a mutual trust in purpose. This effort has had significant results. In 8 months, 200 retarded persons have been returned to their local communities. They have been returned to model placements, each with a prescribed program, each with specific objectives, schedule evaluations, and aftercare from accountable sources.

During this eight-month period, four individuals were admitted to institutional residence at Oakdale, which was serving as a backup facility. This figure stands in contrast to the 45 persons admitted over the most recent similar period prior to the center's existence — an accomplishment secured through a joint effort by community and institution. It demonstrates that community placements are possible and that they have the effect of limiting institutional peonage.

What is the response to the question: "If the individual is capable of work, even supervised work, why is he in the institution at all?" I believe that the great majority of superintendents want to place the retarded — of all levels — but their problem is where to place them. Certainly, they have to become more involved in the development of new community residential and programing concepts and certainly more active in outreach efforts. Others besides superintendents, however, bear a share of the responsibility. It is sad to note that presently too many community leaders are insensitive to the needs of the retarded and to their role in deinstitutionalization.

It is true that thousands of persons have been placed, but many more thousands remain within institutions. In order to ensure a significant reduction in institutional populations, a few model group homes, some good foster care homes, some appropriate nursing homes are not enough. Local and county governments, as well as state governments, must make broad commitments. In many areas, even where state governments are committed, they are not only experiencing resistance to community placement from property owners but, more important, from professionals in key positions in the field of mental retardation who apparently are either lazy, irresponsible, or opposed to the cause.

Most state institution administrators and superintendents know better than anyone else that the programs and conditions of institutions were, and in many cases still are, unacceptable, but they frequently are not listened to (some, unfortunately, are thunderous in their silence). They have long known that those institutions which cannot be brought up to modern day standards should be closed. They agree that appropriate community placement is desirable — that many institutions, if needed at all, must be radically overhauled.

Most leaders in the field also are aware of the pitfalls in returning ill-prepared retarded people to ill-prepared communities and of the frequent absence of critical components for satisfactory placement programs. Without question, much of the policy that dictates return to the community is in need of as much modification and consĩstent public scrutiny as are institutional systems.

Somewhere the institutions and the community must come together. We have a responsibility, all of us in the field of mental retardation, to reject practices as inhumane as peonage, wherever they occur, and build new models for living and working in environments that are not restrictive and not retarding.

Until achievable goal-oriented programs are developed within all institutions and communities to ensure that each individual is given full opportunity for treatment, training, and therapy, and until it is certain that following the completion of prescriptive time-limited programs the individual is graduated to a less restrictive environment, in fact the person is still incarcerated. We need no reminder that, benevolent or not, incarceration is a repulsive alternative to freedom.

CHAPTER 19

Advocacy

Editorial Introduction

Cohen's paper focuses on what he calls case advocacy, the representation of a retarded citizen in a specific dispute. He argues that it is essential for an advocate to have a clear orientation toward his client or protégé and recommends that this orientation be generally in terms of a deprivation model, rather than a sickness model. Cohen emphasizes that the choice of a model is basically functional, so that the choice might need to be flexible depending on the goals sought.

In discussing the advocacy roles most commonly assumed by attorneys on behalf of mentally retarded individuals, Cohen distinguishes between law reform advocacy, which is directed toward the broad recognition of basic legal rights for the client group, and case advocacy. Case advocacy is seen as the representation of a specific individual in a specific dispute regarding incarceration, right to community services, or some other issue. Although Cohen views the law reform activities of the last several years favorably, he presents substantial data to indicate that the performance of attorneys as case advocates for the mentally impaired has been dismal. He reviews one of the most significant efforts in providing case advocates through a public agency, the New York Mental Health Information Service; his evaluation reflects hope tempered by great caution.

Cohen closes with a suggestion that non-attorneys may have a crucial role to play in providing the kind of case advocacy that attorneys frequently regard as their exclusive preserve. He urges experimentation with the use of volunteer lay case advocates, perhaps under the supervision of attorneys.

Burgdorf describes the activities and goals of the National Center for Law and the Handicapped, with which she is associated. She provides a perspective on some of the kinds of contributions a national legal advocacy office can make. Her description makes it clear that the center falls principally in what Cohen calls the area of law reform advocacy.

591

Wolfensberger offers a broader perspective on advocacy, and his contribution provides a useful context within which the more specific discussion of legal advocacy can be seen. He emphasizes the need for multiple safeguard systems to protect the rights and interests of mentally retarded citizens.

PRINCIPAL PAPER

FRED COHEN

ADVOCACY on behalf of the mentally retarded citizen is an idea whose time has come. Like many new arrivals, the advocacy idea has generated more enthusiasm than analysis, more discussion than implementation. Although the notion of advocacy for mentally retarded citizens, including the relatively narrow forms of case and law reform advocacy, is new, it follows an era of unprecedented expansion of the constitutional and statutory right to counsel and extraordinary reliance on the courts as agencies of reform.

In the area of criminal justice, the right to counsel has expanded in horizontal and vertical fashion. That is, it has moved from the most serious offenses to relatively minor misdemeanors and from total preoccupation with trial processes to some phases of the pretrial processes, to appeals, and now, to a limited extent, to the correctional process. A functional analysis is rapidly displacing reliance either on labels (criminal versus civil) or the professed goals of a system (punishment versus treatment) as the rationale for a counsel requirement.[1]

If one merely skims the surface of the right to counsel area, picking up helpful analogues and discarding the others, the case for lawyers acting on behalf of the retarded citizen facing confinement is classically simple: The retarded citizen faced with institutional confinement is confronted with a deprivation of liberty in its most basic sense. There are difficult questions of fact and law, particularly those involving questionable testing and diagnostic procedures, the dubious nature of the "help" to be imposed, and laws so vague that they offer decision makers no specific guidance and the confined no positive assurances. The alleged retarded person in most cases will be quite young, and this fact, when combined with the assumptions drawn from the supposed condition itself, suggests both great caution

---

[1] *E.g.,* Gagnon v. Scarpelli, 411 U.S. 778 (1973); *In re* Gault, 387 U.S. 1 (1967). *Gault* extended the right to counsel to a juvenile in a delinquency proceeding which might terminate with an order of incarceration. Although *Gagnon* refused to recognize a constitutional right to counsel in probation revocation hearings, the Court did suggest that states should provide counsel in cases where the probationer might have difficulty presenting his version of the facts. *See also* Heryford v. Parker, 396 F.2d 393 (10th Cir. 1968) (counsel and the mentally retarded).

in accepting consents or waivers, as well as a powerful case for representation. Thus, if juvenile delinquents and ordinary adult criminal defendants are entitled to counsel, the right to counsel for the retarded citizen facing a commitment follows a fortiori.[2]

One of the questions to be raised in this paper is whether the best interests of the retarded citizen will be served by a further expansion of a constitutional or statutory right to counsel or whether, in light of the experience gained in providing counsel to other persons, another direction is indicated. Before proceeding to a consideration of this question and the general problems of case and law reform advocacy, it is important to review the context into which advocacy for the mentally retarded is placed.

CHOOSING A LABEL: SICK, BAD, OR DEPENDENT-DEPRIVED?

The initial research in mental retardation and advocacy by this author began with a vaguely defined, yet overwhelming, sense of difference in the problems faced by the mentally retarded and other persons assigned to the categories of "sick," "bad," or "dependent-deprived." In fact, however, everything points to a depressing sense of similarity. There are some key terms which vary—the right to habilitation and the principle of normalization are leading examples of promotive terms unique to mental retardation—but the basic issues, at least those that are legally relevant, remain basically constant.

The laws governing the sick, the bad (in particular, after conviction), and the mentally retarded are vague and nearly always archaic: Goal clarification is virtually nonexistent; there is conceptual, definitional, and operational confusion; the areas are dominated by experts; conclusions are substituted for facts; the rhetoric of benevolence abounds; and official discretion is at its zenith. From another perspective, what is encountered is a persistent failure of theory and practice, the chronic unavailability of funds, degradation and abuse of clients, role confusion, swollen bureaucracies, and fragmentation in the delivery of what services there are.[3]

Despite this rather bleak picture, or perhaps because of it, this is an interesting, exciting, and terribly confusing time to be involved with the problems of those persons officially labeled as deviant and eligible for incarceration. Cynicism and enthusiasm appear to coexist. The most basic question (does mental illness exist?) is being raised in some quarters, while elsewhere such questions as an inmates's right to wear a mustache are hotly debated. There are calls for doctrinal

---

[2]There are other rather obvious embellishments — the harmful aspects of confinement, frequent conflicts of interest, the development of alternatives to confinement, seeking independent (or additional) expert testimony, and the like. The effort in the text is simply to provide a sketch of the argument. For a more extensive discussion, see Strauss, Chapter 15 of this volume.

[3]*See* Cohen, *Dangerous Humanitarianism*, THE HUMANIST 25 (July-Aug. 1971).

and procedural reform in every process for the deprivation of liberty, and even some tangible reforms. The language varies with the process, but the underlying concerns and objectives spill over.

In the area of criminal law and corrections, for example, some reformers insist that sentences must be imposed pursuant to articulated principles, that reasons be given and recorded, that sentences be subject to review, that incarceration become a choice of last resort and limited to persons who represent the greater danger of recidivism, and the correctional discretion be severely limited, if not totally abolished.[4] In civil commitment law, there is an emerging principle that the nature and duration of confinement must be strictly limited by the rationale for the intervention, and the longer the potential confinement, the more narrow the criteria and the more onerous the procedure.[5] As in the criminal process, the call is for incarceration only as a last resort, but with the added requirement that the decision maker be required to explore less drastic alternatives. A realization that the early right to treatment rhetoric gave away too much for too little, by conceding the right to treat within the walls of state hospitals,[6] has led to calls for appropriate care in the community with an emphasis on voluntarism in the selection of services.[7]

There is nothing new about the issues of overcriminalization and a more lenient approach to so-called victimless crimes. These issues are symptomatic of the larger concern that too much is asked of the criminal process, and that in the very asking the process loses its unique attributes, its concern for those acts or omissions which are most culpable or most productive of harm. The overreach of civil commitment law seems equally plain as manifested by the too easy reliance on conceptually and definitionally suspect categories to warehouse individuals who annoy us, as well as those who may be disabled but for whom society does not find it politically or economically expedient to create alternative care systems.

There are two themes, as yet unexpressed, which run through the observations just made. First, distinctions that are drawn between criminal law and civil commitment-therapeutic (or benevolent purpose) law are more formal than real. Second, within the latter category there are far more similarities among subcategories than differences. The subjects of these legal processes are the aged, the poor, the nonconforming young, the drunk, the narcotics addict, ethnic and racial

---

[4] *See* AMERICAN FRIENDS SERVICE COMMITTEE, STRUGGLE FOR JUSTICE, A REPORT ON CRIME AND PUNISHMENT IN AMERICA (1971). On the more difficult question of discretionary release see Kastenmeier & Eglit, *Parole Release Decision-Making: Rehabilitation, Expertise, and the Demise of Mythology,* 22 AM. U.L. REV. 477 (1973).

[5] *See* Jackson v. Indiana, 406 U.S. 715, 738 (1972) (competence to be tried in a criminal proceeding); *cf.* McNeil v. Director, Patuxent Institution, 407 U.S. 245 (1972).

[6] *See* Burt, Chapter 14 of this volume.

[7] Massachusetts has embarked on the most radical program for the decarceration of juveniles and, despite heated objections and attempts by system functionaries to derail the program, appears to be accomplishing its objectives. In an interview with Ed Budleman, an assistant commissioner with the department of youth services, I learned of the closing of all of the state's training schools and the plan to close immediately the smaller detention facilities. Some 200 community-based programs are substituted in their stead. For a general description of this program, see Massachusetts Dep't of Youth Services. A Strategy for Youth in Trouble (1973).

In Massachusetts, about 90 percent of the thousands of children in the care and custody of the department of youth services annually are members of families receiving some form of welfare aid. *Id.* at 2.

minorities, the mentally distressed — in a word, the powerless. The powerless are not going to be given power by a legal system which bends just enough to recognize that it is the community's conveyer belt for "sifting and sorting . . . by which the socially dead come to be effectively hidden from us."[8] However, there can be no alacrity and obviously no misguided notions of participation in a helping process. There can be only a sense of dread, of ultimate caution, and a willingness to endorse mechanisms which slow the process, make it more visible and accountable, and ease that task of removing more and more persons from the process at increasingly earlier points in time. And it is in this context that the need for advocacy, for effective and wholly partisan advocacy, begins to take shape. It is here also that one begins to detect the need to look beyond the immediate victory to the community and heed the cautions expressed so well by Price.[9] We must not aid unwittingly in the creation of community "institutions." And we must avoid the 30-mile isolation as well as the 300-mile isolation.

With the foregoing as backdrop, it appears that the mentally retarded do not easily fit within the traditional models used to organize and explain the utilization of deprivations of liberty or coerced treatment. That is, virtually all deprivations of liberty are legally based on a sick-bad paradigm. Sickness is viewed as a condition for which the individual is not responsible, but when it is of a particular nature (*e.g.,* psychosis) and degree (*e.g.,* creating a danger to the individual or others) the person may be involuntarily confined. Badness, on the other hand, is based on harm-producing conduct for which the individual is responsible and which may lead to enforced incarceration in a candidly penal institution.

The retarded may not be viewed as sick, although one encounters the not infrequent dual diagnosis of mentally retarded and mentally ill; nor are they viewed as bad, although some commit criminal offenses. Indeed, according to Professor Richard Allen, there are some 20,000 adult offenders who are substantially intellectually impaired.[10] Where neither mental illness nor criminal conduct is involved, and where the concern is with either a design for relief or the delivery of a service, a third model seems appropriate. This will be referred to as "dependent and deprived."

The utility of this third category is urged despite the fact that so distinguished an authority as Burton Blatt has written, "I believe that it may add perspective to the problem if we consider any child who has serious learning behavior disorders to be a sick child."[11] Blatt's position is that the term "illness" will be useful in escaping the consequences of the view that retardation as a "condition" refers to a static state in which it is implied that health is not attainable. Illness, on the other hand, implies a former condition of wellness and does not categorically preclude the possibility of either prevention or cure.

---

[8] Goffman, *On Cooling the Mark Out,* 15 PSYCHIATRY 451, 463 (1952).

[9] *See* Price, pp. 210-13, Chapter 7 of this volume.

[10] R. ALLEN, LEGAL RIGHTS OF THE DISABLED AND DISADVANTAGED 28 (1970).

[11] Blatt, *A Concept of Educability and the Correlates of Mental Illness, Mental Retardation, and Cultural Deprivation*, in DIMINISHED PEOPLE: PROBLEMS AND CARE OF THE MENTALLY RETARDED 7, 10 (N.R. Bernstein ed. 1970).

Used in this promotive fashion, and without regard to possible legal consequences, Blatt's suggestion is quite understandable. However, from a legal standpoint it may — like the right to treatment argument — give away too much in exchange for too little. For example, to the extent that one objective of advocacy — advocacy in the sense of system change — is to decarcerate incrementally and ultimately make it impermissible to confine totally any, except perhaps the manifestly dangerous or most profoundly retarded person, one is on more solid ground with the model of dependent and deprived than with the model of nonphysical illness.

The sick model, of course, can lead to important decisions like *Wyatt v. Stickney*, in which Judge Johnson held explicitly that

> In the context of the right to appropriate care for people civilly confined to public mental institutions, no viable distinction can be made between the mentally ill and the mentally retarded. Because the only constitutional justification for civilly committing a mental retardate, therefore, is habilitation, it follows ineluctably that once committed such a person is possessed of an inviolable constitutional right to habilitation.[12]

The case for avoiding the sick role, as well as the medical model as a design for relief, rests on avoiding or minimizing institutional isolation as a permissible option. A dependency model more nearly fits a social welfare design for relief with emphasis on the normalization principle: Patterns and conditions of everyday life for the mentally retarded should be as close as possible to the norms and patterns of the mainstream of society. By any criterion of normalization, the hundreds of thousands of persons in publicly supported institutions for the mentally retarded are denied its application, and by referring to them as sick, society may well impede progress toward their reintegration into normal living patterns.

Looking at the utility of "sickness" from yet another perspective, additional doubts arise. The sickness model, with its accompanying verbiage, carries too much ancient freight and contemporary mythology, including the imagery of contagion, a sense of peril, lack of control, and the potential for sudden and uncontrollable outbursts.[13] This fear — whether rational or irrational — is more easily translated into a policy of confinement and isolation than the more neutral and surely less frightening terminology of dependent and deprived. Illness, as well as dependence and deprivation, implies need, but in settling on a descriptive as well as a promotive model, one should have in mind ultimate objectives. In a very real sense, words have uses, not meanings. For legal purposes, then, the advocacy movement should avoid the sick model (and obviously the bad model) and adopt operative and descriptive words which express needs. The movement should provide the basis for the establishment of rights or entitlements and, most important, establish a predicate for the avoidance of total incarceration.

---

[12] 344 F. Supp. 387, 390 (M.D. Ala. 1972), *aff'd sub nom.* Wyatt v. Aderholt, 503 F.2d 1305 (5th Cir. 1974). *See also* Halpern, Chapter 13 of this volume; Comment, *Wyatt v. Stickney and the Rights of Civilly Committed Mental Patients to Adequate Treatment,* 86 HARV. L. REV. 1282, 1291-96 (1973).

[13] *See generally* D. ROTHMAN, THE DISCOVERY OF THE ASYLUM ch. 5 (1971). *See also* J. C. NUNALLY, POPULAR CONCEPTIONS OF MENTAL HEALTH 46 (1961), where field research led to the conclusion that "the mentally ill are regarded with fear, distrust, and dislike by the general public."

ADVOCACY IN GENERAL

Current descriptions of advocacy range from the relatively narrow confines of case representation to the virtually boundless arena of speaking and acting on behalf of the "client" group.[14] It should now be added that there is also considerable diversity when one comes to consider the role of the advocate and objectives of advocacy within a particular advocacy model. To illustrate the point and provide a further framework for the more detailed discussion of case advocacy, consider briefly two approaches to citizen advocacy.

Dr. Wolf Wolfensberger conceives of citizen advocacy as, "a mature, competent citizen volunteer representing, as if they were his own, the interests of another citizen who is impaired in his instrumental competency, or who has major expressive needs which are unmet and which are likely to remain unmet without special intervention."[15] On the other hand, the New York State Committee for Children views advocacy as, "a strategy to reduce the discrepancies between the services which are presently available to cope with problems. Advocacy is not a blueprint for the future, but a means of implementing better service systems for children."[16]

Whereas Dr. Wolfensberger (appropriately in my view) rules out agencies as well as professional persons, the New York proposal, although condemning the size, complexity, and fragmentation of existing delivery systems, proposes yet another state agency and ensures professional representation (although not a majority) on the proposed child advocacy commission. Furthermore, in interviews with members of the legal staff of the New York State Department of Mental Hygiene, it was strongly suggested that citizen advocacy should be directed to the broad category of youth and not simply to those who are retarded.[17] On the other hand, one suspects that the broader the definition and focus of citizen advocacy, the greater the dispersal of individual conviction and concern, and the less likely it is that any special group will receive the attention it deserves.

The structure, function, and operation of any advocacy program ultimately is dependent on the view of government held by the individuals who initiate the program. If the government—and in particular, those agencies directly involved with the retarded citizen—is viewed as an amiable giant in need of an occasional prodding or a friendly reminder, then the New York proposal for a strategy to reduce discrepancies between services and needs makes some sense. Agencies and advocates discover each other, link arms, and walk off into a glowing sunset of prospective good deeds.

On the other hand, if one adopts the government-as-enemy view and conceives of the paternalistic agencies of government as more often the enemy than the ally and to be feared most when desiring only to help, a very different concept of advocacy

---

[14] For a comprehensive discussion of "child advocacy" see A. KAHN, S. KAMERMAN & B. McGOWAN, CHILD ADVOCACY (U.S. Dep't of Health, Education & Welfare, Pub. No. (OCD) 73-18, 1972).

[15] W. WOLFENSBERGER, CITIZEN ADVOCACY FOR THE HANDICAPPED, IMPAIRED, AND DISADVANTAGED: AN OVERVIEW 12 (U.S. Dep't of Health, Education & Welfare, Pub. No. (OS) 72-42, 1972).

[16] New York State Committee for Children, A Child Advocacy System in New York State: Report to Governor Nelson A. Rockefeller 12 (1971).

[17] Interview with Martin Faust and staff in Albany, N.Y., April 16, 1973.

emerges. From this view a basic operating principle is that the greater the distance between the advocate and government the better. Furthermore, there is explicit recognition that an adversary situation exists, that expressions of a mutuality of interest must be viewed skeptically if not cynically. One might bargain or promote arbitration or mediation, but always with the recognition that the enemy has been met.

CASE ADVOCACY

Interviews with members of the legal department of the New York State Department of Mental Hygiene revealed agreement on the need for advocacy both to resist admissions and to follow the individual thereafter through the various testing and classification processes, alterations of status or place of confinement, treatment or habilitation programs, progress toward release, and eventual release. Yet the belief was expressed that there is far less need for advocacy (at least preadmission advocacy) on behalf of the retarded than there is for advocacy on behalf of the mentally ill. The asserted reasons were that (1) there is less doubt about whether or not a person is retarded and (2) New York has changed its admission policy and now does not accept "borderline" cases. In the past, institutionalization was used to "get rid of a troublesome, maybe low normal kid. But not now."[18]

Whether or not New York has changed its "troublesome kid" policy remains conjectural. However, whether or not the policy has been altered by administrative decision should not affect the need for case advocacy on behalf of those individuals facing confinement. It is by no means clear that mental retardation is easily diagnosed or that institutionalization should follow ineluctably from even an accurate diagnosis.[19] There now appears to be a consensus that whether a person is retarded is not always clear and that within the category of retardation there are great variances in cause, performance abilities, needs, and habilitation possibilities.[20]

Professor Murdock, in an excellent article, has written that, "the need for special advocacy is greatest in the institutional setting."[21] There can be no question that he is correct, particularly if it is clear that the focus on "institutional setting" is sufficiently elastic to include the development of resources and techniques to resist admissions and commitments and to make certain that institutionalization occurs

---

[18] Interview with Martin Faust and staff in Albany, N.Y., April 16, 1973.

[19] *See* Murdock, *Civil Rights of the Mentally Retarded: Some Critical Issues,* 48 NOTRE D. LAW. 133, 134-36 (1972).

[20] One recent study points out that despite the highly questionable scientific validity of IQ scores, such scores are devastatingly important in the outcome of juvenile proceedings. In the New York family court system if a child has an IQ score below 70 he probably will go to a state school for the retarded. If the score is between 70 and 90, the lawyer will have a difficult time avoiding a similar commitment. Private institutions rarely, if ever, will accept a child with an IQ score below 90, or even 100. Sussman, *Psychological Testing: Is It A Valid Judicial Function?* 107 N.Y.L.J., July 31, 1973 at 1, 4.

[21] Murdock, *supra* note 19, at 146.

only as a last resort. The Willowbrooks[22] and Partlows[23] tell their own horror stories in support of this proposition, but there is a quiet body of data which makes the point even more compelling.

Placement in an institution for the mentally retarded person, who nearly always will be under the age of 18,[24] in all likelihood will result in an extended stay. The mentally retarded have a current median institutionalization stay of almost 15 years.[25] About one-third of all such residents have a current length of stay of 10-19 years; another one-third have a current stay of 20 or more years.[26] Sixty-eight percent of the residents had no leave during the year,[27] and only 1 percent were expected to be discharged within 6 months.[28] Most mentally retarded persons will be found in large public institutions with a median population of 1,820[29] and with an average of $11.64 per day spent for their maintenance,[30] most of which is spent for attendants, matrons, and maintenance employees.[31]

Commitment statutes in all but six states provide for the involuntary confinement of the mentally retarded by special statutory provisions similar or identical to those used for the mentally ill.[32] Contested admission or commitment procedures are virtually nonexistent. The process will nearly always be a type of voluntary or substituted consent procedure with a relative or guardian initiating institutionalization, often following a physician's advice[33] (about 41 percent of the time according to one study).[34] Thus are the retarded brought to the closed world of the asylum, in silence, and until recently, in silence they would remain.

If the "lawyer representing a prospective patient in a typical [mental illness] commitment proceeding is a stranger in a strange land without benefit of guidebook, map, or dictionary,"[35] the lawyer for the retarded citizen is simply a stranger. For example, in a comprehensive study of California practices regarding the retarded, it was found that 38 of 40 judges responding to the question reported that counsel was never present at commitment hearings.[36] A few judges informed the parents of their right to counsel in the light of unnamed Supreme Court decisions, but the vast

---

[22] *See* New York State Ass'n for Retarded Children v. Rockefeller, 357 F. Supp. 752 (E.D.N.Y. 1973).

[23] *See* Wyatt v. Stickney, 344 F. Supp. 387 (M.D. Ala. 1972), *aff'd sub nom.* Wyatt v. Aderholt, 503 F.2d 1305 (5th Cir. 1974).

[24] U.S. DEP'T OF HEALTH, EDUCATION & WELFARE, PUB. NO. (OS) 73-81, MENTAL RETARDATION SOURCE BOOK 39, 47 (Sept. 1972) [hereinafter cited as SOURCE BOOK]. *See generally* Renelli v. Department of Mental Hygiene, 73 Misc. 2d 261, 340 N.Y.S.2d 498 (Sup. Ct. 1973) (tragic consequences of 12 years of confinement at Willowbrook).

[25] SOURCE BOOK 40.

[26] *Id.*

[27] *Id.* at 40, 51.

[28] *Id.* at 51.

[29] *Id.* at 39, 42.

[30] *Id.* at 13, 30.

[31] *Id.* at 13, 39-40.

[32] THE MENTALLY DISABLED AND THE LAW 37 (rev. ed. S. Brakel & R. Rock eds. 1971).

[33] *See, e.g.,* Kay, Farnham, Karren, Knakel & Diamond, *Legal Planning for the Mentally Retarded: The California Experience*, 60 CALIF. L. REV. 438, 447-48 (1972).

[34] SOURCE BOOK 39.

[35] Cohen, *The Function of the Attorney and the Commitment of the Mentally Ill*, 44 TEXAS L. REV. 424 (1966).

[36] Kay et al., *supra* note 33, at 460.

majority believed that an attorney was not only unnecessary, but also inappropriate.[37] Parents appeared to share the judges' views on counsel and none of the parents interviewed from one region either consulted an attorney or gave any thought to doing so.[38] The authors of the California study concluded that:

> it may be inferred from the almost total absence of attorneys in the commitment process and their low visibility as counsellors for the families of the retarded that this field is not perceived as one in which attorneys are particularly useful except as estate planners. Until very recently there was scant indication in professional legal journals that mental retardation is an area that attorneys should know about or that the mentally retarded and their families are potential clients whom attorneys should be prepared to serve.[39]

Justice Blackmun, discussing the broad power of the state to commit civilly and the large number of persons affected, remarked, "it is perhaps remarkable that the substantive constitutional limitations on this power have not been more frequently litigated."[40] The absence of legal challenges may come as a surprise to the uninitiated, but it is hardly remarkable. For the mentally ill, lawyers either are not involved or if involved appear to be ineffective as advocates.[41] For the mentally retarded citizen the fact that lawyers simply have not been involved goes a long way toward explaining the absence of appellate review. This situation, of course, is being reversed for the retarded person, and in a curious fashion.

In response to this author's inquiry, the National Center for Law and the Handicapped indicated that the center was unaware of any special legal services for the mentally retarded.[42] On the other hand, there are dozens of important civil actions that have been decided or are presently in the courts dealing with the denial of the civil rights of the retarded.[43] Thus, the current situation may be described as involving a flurry of legal advocacy for the retarded at the test case litigation level and virtually no case advocacy at the preadmission or admission level.[44]

The "granddaddy" case on lawyers for the mentally retarded was not decided until 1968. In *Heryford v. Parker*,[45] the Federal Court of Appeals for the Tenth Circuit held that under the due process clause of the fourteenth amendment, a

---

[37] *Id.* at 465.

[38] *Id.* at 481. That the parents are often reporting their own inability or lack of resources to deal with the child may go a long way toward explaining this phenomenon.

[39] *Id.* at 528.

[40] Jackson v. Indiana, 406 U.S. 715, 737 (1972).

[41] *See* Cohen, *supra* note 35. *Contra, e.g.,* Wenger & Fletcher, *The Effect of Legal Counsel on Admissions to a State Hospital: A Confrontation of Professions*, 10 J. HEALTH & SOCIAL BEHAVIOR 66 (1969). It should be noted, however, that effectiveness was measured by performance at the hearing and not in pursuing substantive or procedural issues through appeal.

[42] Letter from Ms. Marcia P. Burgdorf to Ernest Nagler (research assistant to the author), April 23, 1973.

[43] The Council for Exceptional Children, 1411 S. Jefferson Davis Highway, Suite 900, Arlington, Va. 22202, regularly publishes summaries of pending and completed litigation concerned with handicapped children. The point in the text will be illustrated by consulting any issue of this publication.

[44] Until the decision in *In re* Gault 387 U.S. 1 (1967), juveniles rarely had attorneys and very few cases ever were appealed. In the area of juvenile justice, efforts at case representation and test case litigation appear to be proceeding apace.

[45] 396 F.2d 393 (10th Cir. 1968).

mentally deficient youngster was entitled to legal counsel in a judicial proceeding initiated by the mother and leading to confinement in a state institution. It must be stressed that the Wyoming statutory procedure focuses on the court as the committing agency, whereas, for example, in New York the judiciary is relegated to a post-commitment role.[46] Thus, the matter of preadmission legal advocacy may in the first instance be determined by the nature of the commitment process.[47]

The commitment process used in *Heryford* is characteristic of the overwhelming number of cases leading to the confinement of the retarded: the process is denominated a voluntary admission—more accurately, a form of substituted consent—and is initiated by a close relative in the assumed interest of a young person. In *Heryford* the court found that there was not an explicit waiver of counsel and, although it recognized the issue, did not find the occasion to resolve the possibly conflicting interest of the person who initiated the process and the interest of the child.[48]

That the vast majority of commitments or admissions of the retarded involve children and are accomplished by the consent of a parent or guardian probably accounts for the fact that the right to counsel aspect of *Heryford* has received practically no subsequent judicial attention and little attention in the literature.[49] And yet, in my view, there is a vital role for case advocacy, whether it be performed by lawyers or nonlawyers acting as lay advocates, possibly in a guardian *ad litem* capacity.

An Ohio court of appeals recently confronted the right to counsel question in a civil commitment proceeding and was more articulate concerning the demands of advocacy than most courts.[50] The petitioner was committed without counsel and raised the denial of counsel question through habeas corpus. The state actually argued that, as a civil proceeding, no right to counsel attached. As one would expect, the court rejected the argument that the label was the controlling factor and chose to focus on the fact of involuntary confinement. Proceeding from there, the court established a constitutional right to be heard and reasoned that such right would be of little avail without a right to counsel.[51]

---

[46] *See* N.Y. MENTAL HYGIENE LAW §§ 33.01-33.35 (McKinney Supp. 1973).

[47] *Compare* New York *ex rel.* Rogers v. Stanley, 17 N.Y.2d 256, 217 N.E.2d 636, 270 N.Y.S.2d 573 (1966) *with* Briggs v. Arafeh, 411 U.S. 911 (1973), *aff'g mem. sub nom.* Logan v. Arafeh, 346 F. Supp. 1265 (D. Conn. 1972). The former case held that "an indigent mental patient, who is admitted to a mental institution, is entitled, in a habeus corpus proceeding (brought to establish sanity), to the assignment of counsel as a matter of constitutional right." 17 N.Y.2d at 256, 217 N.E.2d at 636, 270 N.Y.S.2d at 573. The latter case held that a statute permitting a 45-day emergency commitment without a hearing was valid when followed by a full hearing with a right to counsel.

[48] For a discussion of an indigent parent's right to counsel in child neglect and dependency proceedings, see *In re* B., 30 N.Y.2d 352, 285 N.E.2d 288, 334 N.Y.S.2d 133 (1972) (right of counsel upheld because of potentially serious consequences); *In re* Robinson, 8 Cal. App. 3d 783, 87 Cal. Rptr. 678 (Dist. Ct. 1970), *cert. denied,* 402 U.S. 964 (1971) (right to counsel denied because proceeding based on state's benevolent objectives).

[49] Virtually all the cases which make some use of *Heryford* are in the area of juvenile justice, with a sprinkling of cases in the area of mental illness. *See, e.g., In re Barnard,* 455 F.2d 1370, 1376 (D.C. Cir. 1971); Lessard v. Schmidt, 349 F. Supp. 1078, 1097-98 (E.D. Wisc. 1972), *vacated for entry of definitive decree,* 414 U.S. 473 (1974), *clarified,* 379 F. Supp. 1376 (E.D. Wisc. 1974), *vacated on procedural grounds,* 95 S. Ct. 1943 (1975).

[50] *In re* Popp, 33 Ohio App. 2d 22, 292 N.E.2d 330 (1972), *rev'd on other grounds,* 35 Ohio St. 2d 142, 298 N.E.2d 529 (1973). Although the case concerned a mental illness commitment, no distinction was made as to the mentally retarded.

[51] *Id.* at 26-28, 292 N.E.2d at 334.

> Just as in a criminal prosecution, effective participation in the hearing would require a knowledge of the law, both as to procedural and substantive prerequisites to a valid commitment order; a knowledge of the rules of evidence and the ability to examine and cross-examine witnesses; and the ability to construct and present a case as to factual issues. In addition, some acquaintance with current theories of mental illness might be necessary.[52]

This characterization of the function of counsel obviously is not unique. It flows from the recognition of a liberty-depriving situation as inherently adversarial and extracts from the many tasks that an advocate might perform for a client those which are at the most visible core.[53]

A natural question at this point is whether the same needs and functions apply in a situation where the loss of liberty is packaged in consensual form, where quite often the anguish of the parent or guardian and the impassive testimony of test scores seem reasonable assurance that there is no other choice, where any form of scrutiny or contentiousness would appear to inject needless suffering into an already painful situation. The author's response to this basic question—fully recognizing the reasonableness of disagreement—is contained in the following general rule:

> No person should be admitted to any institution for the mentally retarded [or the mentally ill] without having counsel or a counsel substitute available. Although the role of counsel or the counsel substitute may vary, in no event may representation be waived.
> A short-term emergency or observational confinement, which may not exceed 30 days, may be accomplished without representation, but the [agency with commitment authority] must be notified within 24 hours and a representative provided within 24 hours thereafter.

The principle, or standard, proposed here proceeds from the premise that for the purpose of obtaining an independent advocate or representative, there is no such thing as a voluntary admission to an institution for the mentally retarded.[54] There is tacit recognition that the interests of the moving party and the alleged retarded person may conflict and that, at a minimum, the person proceeded against requires the aid of a presumptively disinterested party with a clear and unequivocal duty to

---

[52] *Id.* at 29, 292 N.E.2d at 335.

[53] *See generally* F.R. MARKS, K. LESWING & B. FORTINSKY, THE LAWYER, THE PUBLIC AND PROFESSIONAL RESPONSIBILITY 9-10 (1972).

[54] The mentally retarded are to be found in three major types of institutions: public institutions for the retarded, private institutions for the retarded, and state mental hospitals. In 1969 there were 32,000 persons with a primary diagnosis of mental retardation in state mental hospitals and 33,000 persons in private institutions. *See* SOURCE BOOK 3. The principle, as stated, includes all facilities. There is a temptation to exclude private facilities, where one can reasonably assume a higher standard of care, a smaller number of residents, possibly a shorter stay, and generally a higher level of affluence enjoyed by the parents. If private facilities were excluded, however, one would be opting basically to give persons with money or some other form of influence a greater measure of control over the lives of others than those less fortunate. Should military schools or boarding schools for the exceptional and nonexceptional child also be included? Perhaps in logic they should. Indeed, opponents of the principle can extend this form of argument to parental insistence on one public school as opposed to another since this involves at least a temporary loss of liberty.

I have opted for one point on the extended continuum of loss of liberty, while at the same time attempting to leave untouched traditional areas of parental or guardian authority. It is one of many possible balances and others, hopefully, will be argued for. *See* note 86 *infra*.

represent the client. This representative must have the obligation to scrutinize, challenge, explore and develop alternatives, and, if need be, to be contentious, time-consuming, and untrusting.[55]

The role conceived here is what Justice Fortas had in mind, in *Kent v. United States,*[56] when he wrote,

> [w]e do not agree with the Court of Appeals' statement, attempting to justify denial of access to [a juvenile's social records], that counsel's role is limited to presenting 'to the court anything on behalf of the child which might help the court in arriving at a decision; it is not to denigrate the staff's submissions and recommendations.' On the contrary, if the staff's submissions include materials which are susceptible to challenge or impeachment, it is precisely the role of counsel to 'denigrate' such matter.[57]

The case advocate's mission includes the scrutiny and development of his client's position at every stage of the proceeding, including the circumstances of initiation (paying particular attention to the motives of the petitioning party and being alert to conflicts of interest) and examination and testing, making certain of the precise nature and extent of the claimed impairment, the availability and exploration of alternatives, and study of all the available records.[58]

Lawyers who function within the juvenile justice system face many of the same dilemmas which await counsel (or for that matter counsel substitutes) in the mental retardation field.[59] The Juvenile Justice Standards Project poses the questions in this fashion:

> To what extent should the defense attorney permit the child-client to define his own 'best interests' and confine his representation to attempting to secure that result for his client? Should he take a similar position, only deferring to the wishes of the parent rather than the child? Alternatively, are there circumstances in which the defense attorney must himself determine what is best for his client even though his opinion differs from that of the child or his parents? Or is there a middle course? For instance, might the defense lawyer's obligation be to supervise the court process to see that relevant information comes before the court and that the laws are properly applied?[60]

The report of the project does not attempt to answer these questions. However, it is made clear that the attitude of counsel toward the process is likely to be deter-

[55] *See* note 53 *supra.*
[56] 383 U.S. 541 (1966).
[57] *Id.* at 563. *See also* Anders v. California, 386 U.S. 738, 744-45 (concept of "active advocate" in the appellate process).
[58] *See* Andalman & Chambers, *Providing Effective Assistance of Counsel for Persons Facing Civil Commitment*, 45 Miss. L. Rev. 43 (1974), for an exhaustive discussion of the function of counsel and a recommendation that counsel's duties be statutorily prescribed.
[59] *Gault*, of course, obviates the need for a Supreme Court decision on the right of representation, at least where confinement is an issue. In the areas of persons in need of supervision, dependency, and neglect, where a change in custody is the most drastic judicial power, the need shifts to the parents, and back to the child where there is a conflict of interest.
[60] Institute of Judicial Administration, Juvenile Justice Standards Project: Final Report Planning Phase, 1971-72, at 299 (Feb. 1973) [hereinafter cited as Juvenile Justice Standards Report].

minative of the role assumed. That is, if the system is regarded as generally benevolent and likely to be helpful, counsel may be far less contentious and far more ready to override his client's desires than if the system is viewed as penal and harmful. In this regard the official policy of the family court branch of the New York City Legal Aid Society is quite interesting. According to that policy, lawyers in family courts (*law guardians* is the official designation) must act strictly as advocates for the wishes of their juvenile clients in delinquency and Persons in Need of Supervision (PINS) cases.[61] In child protection cases, however, law guardians are admonished to decide whether the child is capable of determining his best interests. If so, the law guardian slips into his role as advocate. If not, the law guardian does not try to decide what is best for the child, but instead acts as a kind of ombudsman or neutral monitor of the proceedings, making sure that proper procedures are followed and that all relevant facts, including any wishes expressed by the child, are made known to the court.[62]

It may be that cases involving the mentally retarded more closely resemble child protection cases than delinquency cases. In the latter type of case some form of misbehavior by the child must be shown, whereas in the former the child is more victim than offender. In the case of dependency, abuse, or neglect, all states have identified situations that will permit official interventions, usually court action, based on a failure to provide children with minimum standards of care.[63]

As the New York City law guardian approach suggests, one may recognize differences in the type of case for the purpose of how advocacy is to be performed and at the same time reaffirm the need for advocacy. For example, before a child is removed from the home, an advocate could explore homemaker services, counseling, or a limited form of foster care and could attend to nutritional or medical needs seemingly unrelated to the primary problem. The advocate for a child in a delinquency or dependency situation is confronted with the same institutional horrors as the advocate for a retarded person and it is this factor which must always shape his attitude toward the case.[64]

Thus far the question of case advocacy has been approached in terms of whether there is need and, if so, the possible functions to be performed. There is also the very basic question of how advocates might be provided. Should attorneys be selected on a case-by-case basis? If so, should they come from a community pool composed of lawyers with demonstrated interest and competence in the area? Should there be an agency — a retardation advocacy office — using only full-time personnel? Should such

---

[61] PINS refers to persons in need of supervision which, in turn, refers to juveniles who engage in noncriminal conduct — for example, running away from home, keeping late hours, or truancy — subjecting them to family court jurisdiction.

For a discussion of the difference between juvenile delinquents and persons in need of supervision, see *In re* C., 32 N.Y.2d 588, 300 N.E.2d 424, 347 N.Y.S.2d 51 (1973), holding that PINS may not be confined in a state training school with juvenile delinquents. A hearing under the Family Court Act is to determine if a delinquent is in need of supervision, treatment, or confinement; in a PINS case, such a hearing is to determine whether the child requires supervision or treatment only.

[62] JUVENILE JUSTICE STANDARDS REPORT 300.

[63] S. KATZ, WHEN PARENTS FAIL 57-58 (1971).

[64] *See generally* JOINT COMMISSION ON MENTAL HEALTH OF CHILDREN, CRISIS IN CHILD MENTAL HEALTH 283-85 (1970).

an agency be a statewide service, local, or mixed? Is it realistic to focus on attorneys as advocates or should one encourage experimentation with a form of lay advocacy, perhaps with attorney supervision?

Previously, I made an extensive study of commitment procedures in Texas and Colorado, with particular emphasis on the function of the attorney. Both states relied on an appointive counsel system but had no requirements of demonstrated interest or competence. The performance of the appointed attorneys was found to be perfunctory and practically useless. In assessing the possible causes for the lawyers' purely ceremonial role, it was suggested that nothing in the tradition of the legal profession provided even the rhetoric for lawyering in this area; the lawyers had no background or experience in the problems of the mentally ill; there were no incentives, financial or otherwise, to contest the process employed; identification with the client was wholly lacking; the system and its functionaries, particularly the equally confused judge, reinforced expectations of perfunctory performance; and the rhetoric of benevolence linked with the supposed hopelessness of the individual's condition caused the attorney to succumb to the experts and their unadorned conclusions.[65]

Other studies have reached far more optimistic conclusions about the effectiveness of legal representation in commitment proceedings. One study found that the "participation of lawyers in decision making regarding involuntary hospitalization of the mentally ill significantly increases the rate of out of court settlement and decreases the need for court hearings as a final recourse."[66] In another study, Wenger and Fletcher observed 81 commitment cases; in 66 the patient was not represented by counsel, whereas in 15 he was.[67] The results were striking: 61 of the 66 without counsel were admitted, yet only 4 of those with counsel were admitted.[68] The authors went further and attempted to determine whether counsel had affected the decision or whether individuals who were not mentally ill, or not within the statutory criteria, were more likely to acquire legal counsel. To accomplish this, the authors categorized each proposed patient prior to the hearing as to whether or not he met the legal criteria for commitment. Again, the results were striking. Twenty-three borderline cases without counsel all were admitted, whereas of the 6 borderlines with counsel, only 3 were admitted. A total of 23 individuals were judged by the authors not to meet the criteria, 15 without counsel and 8 with counsel. Ten of the 15 without counsel were admitted and *none* of those with counsel was admitted.[69]

There are, of course, the inevitable problems of methodology and omission. In the jurisdiction studied, counsel was allowed but not mandatory, and the authors did not know how a patient was informed of the right to counsel nor were they clear

---

[65] *See generally* Cohen, *supra* note 35. A subsequent study of commitments in Iowa reached similar conclusions. Note, *Contemporary Studies Project: Facts and Fallacies About Iowa Civil Commitment,* 55 IOWA L. REV. 895 (1970).

[66] Kumasaka & Stokes, *Involuntary Hospitalization: Opinions and Attitudes of Psychiatrists and Lawyers,* 13 COMPREHENSIVE PSYCHIATRY 201 (1972). I have described in detail the possible prehearing responsibilities of attorneys and indicated the importance of such tasks in reaching appropriate settlements. *See also* Cohen, *supra* note 35, at 452-55.

[67] Wenger & Fletcher, *supra* note 41, at 69.

[68] *Id.*

[69] *Id.* at 70.

on how counsel was provided or obtained. Whether or not counsel was the determinative factor in the results achieved depends heavily on the accuracy of the authors' determination of whether or not the prospective patient fit the typically vague statutory criteria. The reader is not told how the classifications were made, whether Wenger and Fletcher had previous experience at this most difficult task, or whether they attempted to replicate their ability to perform the diagnostic-legal task.

A most important factor in such a study is precise information on the regularity of the appearance of counsel. Except for the limited observations reported, no additional information was provided. The irregular appearance of attorneys in these proceedings may have been productive of affirmative results. That is, the mere presence of this unknown factor with the potential for asking difficult questions or disrupting schedules which are constructed on the speedy processing of proposed patients, was likely to result in settlements, discharges, or even a victory at the hearing. The regular appearance of counsel—certainly of the sort that I have observed and others have reported on—would quickly dispel the myth of professional competence and the prospect of challenge, and the system would probably settle into its comfortable regimen of routine and speedy processing.

A study conducted at the State University of New York at Albany's School of Criminal Justice involving the impact of counsel in juvenile delinquency proceedings in that "populous, northeastern New York County with urban and suburban characteristics," casts some doubt on the Wenger and Fletcher study. The data showed that juveniles with counsel were far more likely to be adjudicated delinquent and incarcerated than juveniles without counsel.[70] This result was unexpected and required rethinking the implications of the *Gault* [71] decision. It had been rather easy to assume that a basic objective of reform had been won when the Court extended the right to counsel to juveniles facing incarceration as delinquents, whereas in fact this confuses a technique with an objective, a question with a solution. The ultimate objective was not to secure a right to counsel. Nor was it, as Attorney Charles Garry likes to stress, the *assistance* of counsel.[72] The objective was, through the use of counsel, to assure young people a fair hearing, by requiring rigorous investigation, forcing the state to make its case, and avoiding the unknowing relinquishment of rights. As a result of the study, this ultimate objective seems elusive.

One tentative explanation for the result of the study suggested that adjudicative and dispositional outcomes were *not* related to the function performed by counsel. Rather, they were related to the judge's decision to ensure legal representation. In other words, when the judge decided that an adjudication or commitment was not called for, he had techniques to communicate this decision and ensure a waiver of counsel. On the other hand, when he was predisposed to adjudicate and commit, he made certain that counsel was present, partly in order to protect the validity of his decision. The decision having been made, counsel's presence was largely ceremonial and unlikely to be productive. The appointment of counsel, then, had become an effective device to protect the court and the record, but not the child.

---

[70] Duffee & Siegel, *The Organization Man: Legal Counsel in the Juvenile Court*, 7 CRIM. L. BULL. 544 (1971).

[71] *In re* Gault, 387 U.S. 1 (1967).

[72] *See* A. GINGER, THE RELEVANT LAWYERS 31 (1972).

Thus, the question to be asked of all studies which purport to show an affirmative impact when counsel is present relates to the process of how counsel and client come together. When counsel is always present there is a threat of cooption by a system committed to speedy processing, and when his presence is irregular one must be very cautious about causal statements without a full exploration of the dynamics of appointment, prehearing roles performed or not performed, and the location of the decision-making powers — a power which rarely will be effectively exercised at the point at which purported decision making is most visible

THE NEW YORK MENTAL HEALTH INFORMATION SERVICE

The New York Mental Health Information Service (MHIS) has been described as "history's first genuine legislative concern with providing effective legal safeguards for persons sought to be committed to mental hospitals."[73] It is of sufficient significance to warrant a special review in a study focusing on case advocacy for the mentally retarded. MHIS was established in 1965 largely in response to a study conducted by the Bar Association of the City of New York.[74] Although there has been substantial revision of the Mental Hygiene Law, effective January 1, 1973, including an expansion of the client population of MHIS to include the mentally retarded, the statutory duties assigned MHIS remain basically unaltered.[75]

---

[73] Gupta, *New York's Mental Health Information Service: An Experiment in Due Process*, 25 RUTGERS L. REV. 405, 410 (1971). *See also* literature cited at note 139, Strauss, p. 469, Chapter 15 of this volume.

[74] SPECIAL COMMITTEE TO STUDY COMMITMENT PROCEDURES OF THE ASSOCIATION OF THE BAR OF THE CITY OF NEW YORK, MENTAL ILLNESS AND DUE PROCESS 14 (1962).

[75] N.Y. MENTAL HYGIENE LAW § 29.09 (McKinney Supp. 1973):

(a) The mental health information service of the state in each judicial department of the supreme court is continued. The head of such service in each judicial department and such assistants and such staff as may be necessary shall be appointed and may be removed by the presiding justice of the appellate division of the judicial department. Appointments and transfers to the service shall comply with the provisions of the civil service law and, except for the head of the service in each judicial department, all such positions shall be in the competitive class of the civil service. Standards for the qualifications of the personnel in the service having duties requiring direct contact with patients and their immediate families shall be established in agreement with the commissioner.

(b) The mental health information service in each judicial department of the state shall perform the following duties subject to directions made and rules and regulations promulgated by the presiding justice of the appellate division of each department:

1. study and review the admission and retention of all patients.

2. inform patients and, in proper cases, others interested in the patients' welfare concerning procedures for admission and retention and of the patients' rights to have judicial hearing and review, to be represented by legal counsel, and to seek independent medical opinion.

3. in any case before a court, to assemble and provide the court with all relevant information as to the patient's case, his hospitalization, his right to discharge, if any, including information from which the court may determine the need, if any, for the appointment of counsel for the patient or the obtaining of additional psychiatric opinion.

4. provide services and assistance to patients and their families and to the courts having duties to perform relating to the mentally disabled or the allegedly mentally disabled, who are admitted pursuant to articles thirty-one, thirty-three and thirty-five of this chapter, as may be required by a judge or justice thereof and pursuant to the regulations of the presiding justice of the appellate division of each judicial department.

MHIS is assigned a preadmission role: providing the court with relevant clinical and social information as well as information relating to the possible need for counsel or additional psychiatric opinion. Beyond this, MHIS is to receive notice of such things as alteration in status and has the duty to review such actions and to seek postadmission hearings when appropriate.

The statute is sufficiently vague that MHIS could perform as a neutral agency, as an agent of the court, or as an agent of the resident or proposed resident. Interviews conducted with members of the legal department of the department of mental hygiene revealed that only one of the MHIS units, the First Department (New York City area), assumes the role of partisan advocate.[76] For the others, as one attorney expressed it:

> MHIS is part of the judiciary and is therefore a neutral agency: it represents neither the patient nor the hospital. . . . In the case of paranoid patients who feel that they have been 'railroaded' into the hospital, the service assures that they have been legally admitted.[77]

This may be of some comfort to the judiciary and the doctors, but it hardly represents an assurance of advocacy on behalf of patients or residents.

A study of the MHIS by Raj Gupta,[78] a staff attorney with New York University Medical Center, has disclosed some of the strengths and serious shortcomings of the agency. In practical effect MHIS is a branch of the judiciary, and in each of the state's four judicial departments there is a director responsible to the presiding judge of the department. The statute is silent concerning the qualifications of MHIS staff, and the scheme of appointments in each department reflects the personal philosophy of the presiding justice. The First and Second Departments—basically, New York City and its immediate environs—are staffed primarily by lawyers, whereas the Third and Fourth Departments—northeastern and northwestern New York — are staffed almost exclusively by social workers.[79]

Previous to the recodification, MHIS served only involuntary patients in state hospitals for the mentally ill, voluntary patients under the age of 21, and individuals who might require hospitalization during the criminal proces. Now MHIS is to serve all patients admitted to facilities for the mentally ill, residential care and treatment facilities for the mentally retarded, and facilities for the treatment of alcoholism. The 1973 legislature increased the appropriation for MHIS by 75 percent to provide additional staff and support resources.

[76] Interview with Martin Faust and staff in Albany, N.Y., April 16, 1973.

[77] *Id.*

[78] Gupta, *supra* note 73.

[79] *Id.* at 417. A more recent study shows the following staffing patterns by departments in 1973:

Staff	First department	Second department	Third department	Fourth department
Supervisory	2	5	2	2
Legal	21	41	2	0
Social work	4	3	5	14
Clerical	11	38	6	9
Total	38	87	15	25

Assembly of the State of New York, Ways and Means Committee, Willis H. Stephens, Chairman, Staff Paper: The MHIS: A Program Review and Suggestions for Reform 9 (July 31, 1973) [hereinafter cited as Committee Report on MHIS].

Although the First and Second Departments reflect a preference for lawyers and each services about the same number of admissions, the First Department commitment to advocacy results in a considerable difference in the service provided patients and prospective patients. First, a greater number of hearing requests originate in the First Department. Second, it appears that the higher the rate of requests for hearings, the higher the rate of discharge as a result of settlement. Indeed, patients in the group first asking for a hearing and then withdrawing the request had a 4 to 7 times better chance of discharge than those who obtained a hearing and judicial determination.[80]

Social workers were found to view their role as "helping" the patient. In trying to inform patients of their legal rights, they tended merely to transliterate orally statutory provisions as already set out in the notice to the patient.[81] In sum, in the Third and Fourth Departments there appeared to be less advocacy and thus less negotiation and open fighting for patients' rights.

The situation has not gone unnoticed in the New York legislature, with a dramatic increase in MHIS funding (75 percent) the not surprising occasion for reassessment. A report to the powerful Ways and Means Committee states that "unequal protection exists under current law."[82] The report concludes that:

> 1. The MHIS has not become the state-wide agency as originally envisioned due to the statutory departmental flexibility and decentralization of the MHIS. All patients in the State are entitled to the same services regardless of their geographical placement. Therefore, the MHIS should be centralized under the Administrative Board of the Judicial Conference, the central policy-making authority in the Judiciary. The Board would be charged with the duty to promulgate uniform rules and regulations, reporting procedures, staffing patterns and the overall administration of the MHIS.
> 2. In response to the changing legal and social expectations surrounding the question of patients' rights, a Mental Health Legal Assistance Panel (MHLAP) should be established. This panel of specialized attorneys would provide competent and continuous representation for patients who chose to be so represented. This is the most effective and practical way to insure that a patient receives an adequate and more than perfunctory safeguard of his constitutional rights.[83]

The MHIS model has been followed elsewhere[84] and has been proposed for Michigan and Ohio.[85] One wonders, however, if the role conflict will be recognized and avoided. The call here, once again, is for partisan advocacy and the avoidance of divided loyalties. It seems inherently unworkable to have a system whereby the same individuals must serve the court, inform or represent a client, and deal regularly with institutions. One of the great strengths of the legal profession lies in client

---

[80] Gupta, *supra* note 73, at 422.

[81] *Id.* at 442-43.

[82] Committee Report on MHIS, *supra* note 79, at 10.

[83] *Id.* at 16.

[84] On April 9, 1971, Maryland created a mental health information and review service. *See* Abrams, *Legislative Efforts to Reform Civil Commitment,* 1 MD. L. F., Summer 1971, at 12.

[85] Ohio S.B. 336, 110th Gen. Assembly, Reg. Sess. § 5123.02(B) (1973-74) requires that the service be notified and investigate in the case of an application for voluntary admission of a minor or incompetent person. *See* Andalman & Chambers, *supra* note 58, for a description of efforts to provide legal representation for the mentally ill in seven jurisdictions.

selection and independence and these strengths should be preserved in whatever system of advocacy ultimately is adopted.

A NEW ADVOCACY

At the beginning of this paper, it was stated that it was a rather easy task to construct a solid argument for a right to counsel by using the "helpful analogy" approach. It was also hinted that the issue properly posed may not be a right to counsel, but rather a right to assistance and representation and that an extension of the right to legal counsel may not be the best answer. If one answers the threshold question of a right to representation in the affirmative, then a series of specific implementation questions arises. The evidence is so scanty and confused on individual versus collective arrangements, state versus local, and part time versus full time that one must be candid and concede that whatever choice is made, it must be based primarily on surmise or intuition. Current proposals appear to favor a collective approach, based on the assumption that this approach will provide full-time attorneys with an advantage over private attorneys in terms of credibility, expertise, interest, and availability. One can hardly be sanguine about the performance of private attorneys, given the research previously reported here. On the other hand, the performance of the MHIS in the First Department suggests caution in any attempt to develop collective advocacy services.

At this point, the author will add another intuitive item to the possibilities noted earlier and express the strong belief that the future of representation for the retarded citizen is *not* in the legal profession, although there may be an important role for lawyers in the proposal that follows. As an introduction to this proposal, consider this excerpt from a previous article by this author,[86] dealing with prisoners' rights:

> Once it is shown, for example, that the right to counsel is critical at trial, by a parity of reasoning it can be shown that where counsel may not be required—say at interrogation or sentencing—there is a problem. The statement of the problem—typically in analogical form—carries with it the answer.
>
> Reasoning and argument by analogy is, of course, not unique to the legal profession. However, in fashioning litigation—particularly when the case involves a challenge to an existing practice—lawyers seem umbilically tied to the use of analogy. In the prisoners' rights area—indeed, in the entire correctional area—one of the dominant approaches can be reduced to a syllogistic type statement: Process A is virtually identical to process B. Process A requires an X while process B does not. Therefore process B should have an X.[87]

---

[86] Cohen, *The Discovery of Prison Reform,* 21 Buff. L. Rev. 855, 868-69 (1972).

[87] *X* may be counsel, notice, an impartial tribunal specificity in rules, and the like. The invested process (*A*) will be found by looking to virtually any situation—especially the pretrial and trial aspects of criminal law—where liberty or a "grievous loss" is involved. Process *B,* the one found lacking, is found by looking at almost any aspect of prison life and regulation. *See* Goldberg v. Kelly, 297 U.S. 254 (1970), requiring the rudiments of procedural due process before welfare benefits may be terminated. *Goldberg* has now become a necessary citation in any affort to extend procedural due process to prisoners' grievances, particularly those involving internal discipline.

The trap of excessive reliance on analogy is the limitation it imposes on the development of more creative solutions to the problem and the apparent tendency to accept on faith the inherent worth of the missing factor.[88] In the prisoner area, more and more courts are dealing with prisoners' grievances concerning disciplinary procedures. On the other hand, the grievances are real enough. Rules either are nonexistent or so vague as to be meaningless. The invocation and processing of alleged violations generally lacks even a semblance of procedural regularity.

Prisoners rightly complain about false charges, being accused and adjudged by the same person, the denial of notice of charges, and a fair opportunity to defend or explain before an impartial tribunal, lack of legal assistance and dozens of other similar items. If the automatic response to these grievances is the handiest analogue, once again the definition of the problem will be allowed to create the solution. For example, is the problem the right to legal counsel at disciplinary proceedings or is it better stated as the inability of most prisoners to adequately prepare and represent themselves even if given the chance?

Should the problem be defined as a lack of legal counsel, then the demand will be for counsel. It is exceedingly unlikely that lawyers in sufficient numbers in reasonable proximity to outlying institutions will even be available. If assistance and representation is the issue—and given the fact that the sixth amendment has not yet been moved into disciplinary proceedings—perhaps the search should be for a lay advocate or legal assistant-type program. Perhaps a better solution lies with a truly independent ombudsman along with the type of labor negotiation model being experimented with in the District of Columbia.[89]

Very much the same sort of analysis and questions applies to protecting the rights of the retarded citizen. Are there lawyers in sufficient numbers, with educational or experiential background in this area, who would be sufficiently motivated to devote their legal skills to the mentally retarded? Based on the legal profession's bleak performance in the area of mental illness and its questionable value in the juvenile process, and based on the long history of rather complete neglect of the mentally retarded, one should pause before attempting to extend a constitutional or statutory right to counsel. Since the question of the right to counsel remains open in many jurisdictions, there is opportunity for experimentation with a lay advocate program.

At the outset one must meet the problem of the lawyer's exclusive privilege to appear in court. This problem is not as difficult as might first appear. Courts have the power, often the obligation, to appoint guardians *ad litem* for a variety of persons unable to protect their best interests. A guardian *ad litem* is a special guardian appointed by the court to prosecute or defend on behalf of a person shown to be or believed to be under disability.[90] Although courts may appoint

---

[88] Consider the Alice in Wonderland faith and energy invested in the neutral and detached magistrate and warrant process, and the primary reliance on the exclusionary rule to alter police behavior. In the battle to control the police and bring a modicum of fairness to defendents, the objective tended to be submerged and the handiest solution adopted.

[89] The Center for Correctional Justice, funded by OEO, contracts with other agencies for civil and criminal legal services for inmates. The center's objectives are to negotiate binding agreements with institutional officials—indeed to do so with inmate negotiating teams—before litigation and surely before the Attica boiling point is reached. *See* Interview with Linda Singer, *Attica: A Look at the Cause and the Future,* 7 Crim. L. Bull. 817, 839-43 (1971).

[90] *See In re* Wretlind, 225 Minn. 554, 32 N.W.2d 161 (1948) (holding that a guardian should have been appointed for a retarded person whose mother initiated the proceeding); Application of Ciena, 8 App. Div. 2d 877, 187 N.Y.S.2d 59 (1959), *aff'd mem.,* 7 N.Y.2d 939, 165 N.E.2d 581, 197 N.Y.S.2d 740 (1960); Kossar v. State, 13 Misc. 2d 941, 179 N.Y.S.2d 71 (Ct. Cl. 1958).

attorneys to serve as guardians, there generally is not a requirement that they do so.[91]

I participated in a juvenile defender project in Austin, Texas, which made effective use of the guardianship concept. In 1965, and thus prior to *Gault,* an agreement was reached between myself and Judge Charles O. Betts, acting as juvenile court judge for Travis County, that youngsters facing delinquency proceedings should have representation and that law students were the best available resource. Texas had no statute or rule of court allowing law students to appear in court and so another device would have to be used. The judge agreed to appoint law students as guardians *ad litem* for the youngsters, first securing approval from the parents and the child. The appointment terminated with the disposition, although more often than not the law student maintained contact with his former "ward" and often acted as an advocate with school and welfare agencies.

The parties concerned were sensitive to the very real possibility of an ineffective assistance of counsel claim, but reasoned that a worthwhile service was being performed, an educational process was involved, and since neither the federal law nor Texas law had yet mandated a right to counsel, it was reasonable to proceed and face whatever challenge might be made. No challenges were forthcoming, so the question of effective assistance remained unresolved.

There are other examples which provide some support for the lay advocacy proposal. For example, prison inmates have established a right to lay advocates under certain conditions both in disciplinary proceedings[92] and in the preparation of petitions for habeas corpus when no legal assistance is available.[93] The Internal Revenue Service allows persons to practice before the IRS based on qualification by profession (lawyers and accountants, for example) and by qualification through examination. Parole boards often will allow nonlawyers to advocate an offender's case.

It is true that these examples except for the juvenile defender project in Austin and the preparation of habeas petitions for prisoners, all relate to administrative agencies. The point, however, is that lawyers may have something of an exclusive franchise on the courts, but they do not have an exclusive franchise on advocacy.

A jurisdiction interested in experimenting with a lay advocate program first would have to secure the consent of the judges involved. The judges would have to be persuaded to use the guardian *ad litem* device and thus to exercise appointive and supervisory power over the appointees. The availability of funds for such an operation also is an obvious hurdle. Foundation support for an experiment of this nature should not be difficult to obtain. It may be possible to treat the cost of the guardian *ad litem* as part of the costs of the case ultimately payable by whoever is

[91] *E.g.,* N.Y. Civ. Prac. Law & Rules Rule 1202 (McKinney 1963). *See also* R. Allen, E. Ferster & H. Weihofen, Mental Impairment and Legal Incompetency 99-112 (1968) (indicating a Minnesota practice of appointing law guardians).

[92] Landman v. Royster, 333 F. Supp. 621 (E.D. Va. 1971). *See also* Clutchette v. Procunier, 328 F. Supp. 767 (N.D. Cal. 1971), *modified,* 497 F.2d 809 (9th Cir. 1974).

[93] *See* Johnson v. Avery, 393 U.S. 483 (1969).

responsible for such costs. Typically, the cost will have to be borne either by the parents or, should they be impoverished, by the county.

It should be possible for the court and those who would initiate such a program to go even further. For example, it may be desirable to have an attorney in charge of the program and responsible for the initiation and conduct of a training program. Lay advocates could be drawn from the community in the same fashion as citizens involved in volunteer programs.[94] Training and educational materials could be developed to ensure a high level of understanding of mental retardation, judicial and administrative processes, investigatory techniques, the development of dispositional alternatives, and utilization of appropriate professionals, certainly including lawyers for estate planning, damage suits, and the like.

The possibilities are boundless and there undoubtedly are problems that have not been envisioned here. The plight of the retarded citizen, the need for representation, and the probabilities against obtaining lawyers in sufficient numbers all suggest that it is worth a try somewhere. There is a great reservoir of untapped citizen strength, representing an array of experience and talent that no single profession can match. For those who read this as an effort to treat the mentally retarded citizen as a second-class citizen, I can say only that this type of program might well bring a level of dedication and expertise rarely bought by the "first-class" citizen when he engages a private lawyer.

CONCLUSION

When one lists the rights either won or currently being litigated on behalf of the mentally retarded—the rights to treatment and habilitation, education, fair classification, custody of children, compensation for institutional labor, and damages for a failure to treat—it is a tribute to a small and dedicated group of attorneys. However, although test case litigation is demanding and the results thus far significant, the utilization of the class action in particular makes it plain that large numbers of lawyers are not required for this task. Certainly when compared with the need for precommitment case advocacy, the numbers required are infinitesimal. Test case litigation is obviously a form of advocacy, but it differs significantly from both case advocacy as conceived here and advocacy in the sense of providing a dependent person with a citizen advocate who represents his "protégé's" needs and interests on a continuing basis.

When attention is focused on issues beyond the institution, issues relating to keeping some individuals out of the institution, having others released, and human-

---

[94] The National Information Center on Volunteers in Courts reports 150,000 court volunteers in some 2,500 courts. This was estimated to be 50 percent of all juvenile courts and 20 percent of all adult courts. August 1971 is the date for these figures, which appear in S. Fox, Modern Juvenile Justice: Cases and Materials 807 (1972). How many child advocacy programs exist is difficult to determine. A. Kahn, S. Kamerman & B. McGowan, *supra* note 14, at 173-77, account for 103 operational programs.

izing the institution for others, the focus actually is on the vast majority of the retarded who are not and will not be institutionalized. Herein lies the broader concept
of advocacy. The lawyer's role in securing legal rights for the retarded citizen who
remains in the community—a striking example is securing a right to public education
suited to the varying needs of exceptional children—is clear and important. However, when the focus shifts to advocacy as a form of protective service, as an effort
to meet both instrumental and expressive needs, the advocate moves into a vast
new arena.

The arena is not without legal significance. Indeed, the various proposals
and programs concerned with child advocacy point to social service failures, as
well as legal failures, as having created the need. Dr. Wolfensberger has pointed
out that guardianship, conservatorship, and trust arrangements generally fail to
meet the full range of needs of the dependent handicapped individual.[95] The issue
is not whether the dependent and deprived have unmet needs, but who is going to
meet them and how.

In reviewing Kirkpatrick Sale's book, *SDS,* Wilson Carey McWilliams writes,
"Mass society can be warmed and humanized; it cannot be made either personal
or communal."[96] The most appealing proposals for citizen advocacy appear
implicitly to accept this view of society. With peace and love equally at home on
a biker's leather jacket and a flower child's blue workshirt, this society lacks
even the certainty of division by slogan. As the Cheerful Robot which C. Wright
Mills wrote about over a decade ago gains ascendancy[97]—as the legally unimpaired
are increasingly alienated from production, from work, from themselves and
others—what recourse is there for the legally impaired? If society cannot at this
stage be made personal then perhaps—and just perhaps—networks of personal
relationships can be established on behalf of those persons who have the greatest
need. The term "greatest need" is used here instead of the retarded citizen because
I suspect that an advocate-protégé relationship will be bilateral and that the
advocate stands to gain as much as the person whose needs are represented.

The problems of the mentally retarded citizen are depressingly similar to those
of all persons placed in a deviant status, who face the prospect of enforced incarceration, and who need help. With government and its agencies frequently the
enemy, it seems inconceivable to accept as valid those proposals for advocacy
which represent some form of partnership or collaboration. Building from the
premises that mental retardation is not a discrete entity, that it is diverse in cause
and effect, and that the most appropriate programing is itself diverse and as
conducive to a normal environment as possible, advocacy in its many forms becomes a valuable ally for the retarded citizen. Case advocacy has as its objective
the vigorous and undiluted representation of a proposed resident, whereas law
reform advocacy advances the legal rights of retarded citizens through the litigation and appeal process.

---

[95] W. WOLFENSBERGER, *supra* note 15, at 1-6.
[96] N.Y. Times, May 6, 1973, § 7 (Book Review Section), at 3.
[97] Mills, *On Reason and Freedom,* in IDENTITY AND ANXIETY 110, 115-16 (M. Stein, A. Vidich, &
D. White eds. 1960).

There is an important role for citizens in both of these functions: for example, experimentation with a lay advocacy program of the sort described in this article — providing data and pursuing implementation and evaluation tasks. When the concept of advocacy moves beyond case advocacy and law reform advocacy, the lawyer's possible role, as well as his knowledge, decreases accordingly. The concept of a concerned citizen volunteer, without material reward or agency connection, representing the instrumental and expressive needs of an impaired citizen until the volunteer is no longer required, is a beautiful idea. At a time when the most "competent" citizen may thirst for such a relationship, the appeal is particularly poignant.

As a general principle, the greater the distance from government and the professional establishment, the more likely it seems that an advocacy program will succeed. There is no political principle that rights are the equivalent of needs, and thus advocates scratch and claw to extract what is needed from an always reluctant government. Advocates without an institutional role to play and with the need to argue for a position and who (unlike most lawyers) accept the responsibility attendant upon having adopted it as their own can become potent actors. A sage observer was heard to remark that there are only two kinds of political problems: those that solve themselves and those that cannot be solved. Ultimately, the respect, dignity, and care offered the dependent and deprived citizen reflects the political texture of a nation.

Reaction Comment

MARCIA PEARCE BURGDORF

THIS PAPER will first consider advocacy in general. Then it will describe the National Center for Law and the Handicapped. Finally, it will consider some of the problems that handicapped persons have, their legal rights, and how a legal advocate goes about establishing and enforcing the legal rights of handicapped persons.

In a discussion of any of the various types of advocacy, a basic question must be, "for what are we advocating?" The answer is obvious: We are advocating for the good of handicapped people. The advocate is one who tries to obtain that which is beneficial for a handicapped person. To obtain any such benefit, the advocate employs any number of available tools. A professional person may select tools from his special areas of expertise; for a nonprofessional citizen advocate, the tools may involve simply his common sense, concern, and companionship.

One tool which may be used for the good of a handicapped person is the legal system. The use of this system in such a way as to benefit handicapped people is referred to as the process of legal advocacy. The legal structure in society is made up of a network of laws, legislators who make the laws, and the officials, courts, and lawyers who administer them. Legal advocacy may involve taking an active role as a lawyer in a courtoom or simply counseling a handicapped person as to his legal rights and liabilities, or it can involve writing, critiquing, or passing legislation that deals with the rights of handicapped people. Yet, the role of the legal advocate is a limited one. The attorney can really deal only with those things which are legal matters. A particular action or result may be clearly beneficial to a handicapped person, but it must also be required by the law or an attorney — *qua* attorney — can be of no help in obtaining it. The lawyer can befriend a handicapped person and function in the role of a citizen advocate, but this would not be legal advocacy. Legal advocacy is limited to functioning in the role of an attorney in the courts, in the legislature, in administrative proceedings, or in the giving of legal advice to effect beneficial changes in the lives of handicapped persons.

The National Center for Law and the Handicapped is a federally funded project located in South Bend, Indiana. The center was formed specifically to fight for and establish the legal rights of all handicapped persons. The center has four sponsoring agencies: the National Association for Retarded Citizens; the University of Notre Dame Law School; and American Bar Association, Family Law Section; and St. Joseph County Association for Retarded Children. The responsibility of the center is national in scope, and its interpretation of the term *handicapped* includes not only the mentally retarded, the mentally ill, and emotionally disturbed, but also persons with learning disabilities and the physically handicapped, blind, deaf, and so on — anyone who has been discriminated against because of a handicapping condition. The center is involved in legal advocacy on the national level, which includes providing supportive aid to citizen advocates as well as attempting to implement court decisions on a state-by-state basis.

The center's brand of legal advocacy is accomplished in a variety of ways, some of which are reviewed below.

INFORMING THE PUBLIC

The center publishes a newsletter designed to inform people from the grass roots level on up through professional groups concerning what the legal rights of mentally retarded persons are. The newsletter presents case reviews, recent developments, federal legislation, and so on to inform citizens about what is happening. The center staff is also heavily involved in many public speaking commitments, to communicate to the various national organizations representing handicapped persons that handicapped citizens have legal rights and that their legal rights can be enforced. The center is also putting together a syllabus and a bibliography for a course called, "The Handicapped Citizen and the Law." The course is presently taught at the University of Notre Dame Law School, and it is hoped that through publishing the syllabus and bibliography the course can be added to curricula of other law schools throughout the country.

LEGISLATION

The center offers a service whereby the staff will critique laws, rules, and regulations and will inform states or consumer groups whether or not legislation infringes on the rights of the retarded. If legislation is, in fact, discriminatory, changes are suggested. It is hoped that with an increase in staff, the center will be able to begin to write model legislation and rules and regulations as well. This service is available on the state level, as well as on the federal level, and the center has assisted not only consumer groups who represent the handicapped, but also state officials in their efforts to serve more effectively their handicapped clientele.

LITIGATION

Besides the educative and legislative activities of the center, the staff is authorized, when they find a problem that cannot be solved through the administrative process, to become involved in litigation. Litigation efforts by the center have taken various forms. The center may simply send briefs and background materials to attorneys in a particular case. The staff may also critique the formal documents (*e.g.*, a complaint) that will be filed with the court. The center may also work actively in the first instance by doing the investigation and groundwork or it may choose to join a case in the role of an amicus curiae or as counsel. Thus far, the center has entered as an amicus in federal court cases in Colorado, North Dakota, Wisconsin, California, Kentucky, and Nebraska and as co-counsel in a North Dakota case. The center is also working on setting up a network of attorneys throughout the country who are knowledgeable in the area of the rights of handicapped persons and who are willing to handle local problems and cases.

The center is taking an active role in analyzing the legal issues that relate to the everyday problems in the lives of handicapped persons. The issues that the center has focused on to date are the right to an equal educational opportunity for all people regardless of the degree of their handicap and the rights of persons who are in institutions. The center intends to expand its concern to other areas, including specifically the problems of the physically handicapped and the problems of sterilization.

Legal advocates are concerned with the legal rights of the people with whom they deal. These rights generally arise from the Constitution of the United States, state constitutions, and federal and state statutes. The Constitution guarantees to all citizens the right to equal protection and due process of law, in addition to other specific rights such as freedom of speech and freedom of religion. This means that the handicapped person has a right to education, for example, on an equal basis with other citizens. Legal advocates have made this principle a reality in several states through legal actions begun in federal and state courts. Court decisions favorable to the right of handicapped persons to an equal educational opportunity have been obtained in Pennsylvania, Michigan, Louisiana, the District of Columbia, New York, Wisconsin, Maryland, Colorado, and other jurisdictions. This concept of having equal rights with other citizens is also being tested in relation to handicapped persons' right to vote, right to marry, right to procreate, right to be free from involuntary sterilization, right to treatment and habilitation, right to access to the court, and numerous other rights.

Besides litigation, there are other ways of getting favorable rulings from the legal system. There exists federal legislation such as Pub. L. No. 90-480, which provides for the removal of architectural barriers in new or remodeled buildings that are built by the federal government or with federal funds. However, this legislation originally had no provisions for enforcement, and the law has not been followed in many instances. A recent law, Pub. L. No. 93-112, will solve the problem by adding an enforcement agency to make sure that builders comply with the legislation. Therefore, handicapped persons will have a means of recourse other than having to approach the courts to get a solution to their problem. New laws are being written to guarantee to handicapped persons the right to travel via public transportation and requiring transportation facilities to be adapted to meet their needs.

Another task of the legal advocate, besides establishing individual legal rights through legislation and the enforcement of these rights through litigation, is the communication of these rights, both to the handicapped person and to the community at large. Communication is probably one of the most important roles of a legal advocate because the proper functioning of our system presupposes that the citizen understands his legal rights.

This has been a very quick review of what one type of legal advocate does; that is, using the legal system as one of the tools to benefit and improve the everyday lives of handicapped persons in our society. Legal advocacy is only one of the channels that can be used to benefit handicapped citizens. Litigation in itself is not the sole answer; nor is legislation nor any of the other efforts of the legal advocate. There must be great cooperation among the legal advocates, citizen advocates, and all others interested in the rights of handicapped citizens in order actually to implement changes that will, in fact, benefit all handicapped persons.

Reaction Comment

WOLF WOLFENSBERGER

THE SAFEGUARDING of rights of the downtrodden is a concern of mankind perhaps as old as mankind itself. It has taken many, many forms over the years; sometimes the form has changed, sometimes only its label.

Although the word "advocacy," of course, has its historical denotation, the way in which it is used today and the intensity of its meaning are relatively new. In 1967, when the citizen advocacy schema was first conceptualized, people had little idea what I meant when I talked about "personal advocacy." Today, everybody uses the term "advocacy," to the point that it is beginning to lose its meaning. It reminds me of the television advertisement for Kraft cheese in which the viewer is advised to take any recipe, any meal, anything and "add Kraft cheese." So, you take any human services program, slap the label "advocacy" before, after, or on top of it, and then say "We're doing advocacy." This is unfortunate.

In order to clarify this concept, I would like to outline certain varieties; these are not exclusive by any means, but at least they are some of the major types of advocacy that are commonly encountered.

There are some advocacies which are valuable, but are not citizen advocacies. One of these is *collective advocacy*, in which a group of persons advocates for some other group. *Corporate advocacy* is the same thing, except that the advocacy group is incorporated. Associations for the retarded are corporate advocates; they have never been individual advocates.

A third type is *agency advocacy*, and today, unfortunately, this is what most people mean when they use the term advocacy. Child advocacy in particular is pure and simple professional, or agency, advocacy. The agency is paid, the staff is paid to perform some kind of advocacy function. One good aspect of this setup is, at least historically, that the agency often does nothing but advocacy and therefore has a certain freedom from conflicts of interest vis-à-vis other services.

The *ombudsman* system is essentially an agency advocacy — and a very desirable form of it. It is very important, but it is essentially an impersonal, agency-based operation; and so, of course, is the *staff advocacy* that is being set up inside many agencies.

Then there is a type I like to call *generic advocacy*: One person without conflicts of interest who represents an entire category of persons — someone like Ralph Nader, for example.

Citizen advocacy, very briefly, is advocacy in which a competent citizen volunteer represents — as his very own — the interests of another person who is in some way impaired or disadvantaged. This advocate would have the backup of an agency, but the backup performs purely logistical functions: recruiting people, getting them together, matching them up, providing guidance and counseling. The most important element to keep in mind here is that this advocate is a volunteer to the person, not to an agency, and he is not paid. He is free from conflicts of interest and he is unconditionally committed to the person. This feature emphasizes — and here rests a common misunderstanding — that the volunteerism practiced in many agencies is not advocacy.

The conflicts of interest that we must avoid tend to be of at least three types, to have at least three sources. One of these is payment. He who pays the salary determines what the employee does, unless the employee is prepared to quit, and we cannot assume that a large number of paid staff or professionals will give up their jobs on behalf of their clients. It happens very infrequently, and I want to emphasize one thing I feel very unhappy about: Professional morality is not very strong or high in *any* profession; it leaves much to be desired. Aside from the conflict of interest that is mediated by payment, there is another conflict of interest in loyalty to a supervisor or even loyalty to an agency beyond payment. There is, moreover, loyalty to professions, and professional loyalty can be very fundamental and identity defining to a professional, in a sense a religion.

Citizen advocacy, which does not have these problems, must take many forms, and I thoroughly agree with Cohen's assessment that in order to be a success, advocacy must be individualized and have many, many expressions, many forms. One of these is *dispersed advocacy*. In citizen advocacy we stress the necessity of a "near one-to-one" relationship. This means that one advocate may share two protégés, or one protegé may share two or three advocates, but this is the limit. Duration of the advocacy relationship also varies greatly: There are short-term, as well as long-term, advocacies. One very beautiful variant of citizen advocacy is advocacy by youth. Individuals as young as 14 years of age can play a very effective advocacy role, and such relationships may be not only very effective but may even be lifelong. They are unique, because youth can sometimes do and be things that adults simply will not or cannot do or cannot be.

There are also certain roles which are not citizen advocacy as such, but are related to it; these are referred to as *citizen advocacy associates*. Citizen advocacy associates are influential professionals, agency people, and friends who themselves are not advocates (maybe they do not have the time, or maybe they have conflicts of interest), but they are friends of the concept and support it. Many citizen advocacy offices in operation have such associates backing them up.

Throughout this volume there is discussion of the concept of the least drastic alternative or the least restrictive alternative, and in citizen advocacy we are also very much concerned with providing only such protection as is consistent with normalization concepts. It is interesting that when you provide more protection than a person needs, you diminish him. You are saying to him, "Well, you're not fully adult, you're not fully competent," and so on. Normalization implies the right to failure — offering a person as much risk as he is capable of handling, including the opportunity to fail — as everyone else fails. This is why any form of advocacy must be flexible and must recognize many distinctions. We have differentiated, for example, between instrumental and expressive advocacies: Instrumental advocacy fulfills a problem-solving function; expressive advocacy focuses on the relationship between advocate and protégé. Some persons need one and not the other form of advocacy and some persons need both. Different ways of filling advocacy roles are also extremely important; here, citizen advocacy subsumes many roles which already exist culturally — adoptive parents, guardianship successors, and so on.

A study in Hamilton, Ontario, confirmed something about guardianship that many people have suspected for some time. In this study, it was found that the need for guardianship was inversely related to the quantity and quality of available informal social supports. When there are strong informal and social supports, there rarely is a need for formal guardianship, and vice versa. This finding is highly supportive of the least restrictive alternative principle.

Implementation of citizen advocacy is much more widespread than most people are aware of. There are now state-level offices in nine U.S. states, as well as three province-level offices in Canada. On the local level, there are about 45 services, and there are 3 offices which are entirely youth oriented. In addition, many commitments to implement additional offices have been made. In short, the movement has grown considerably in a few short years.

Citizen advocacy, of course, is only one safeguard; by itself, it is not enough. It is of great significance, but we need multiple safeguards, perhaps even "safeguard overkill." In Table 1 I specify 17 safeguards needed by community services for the handicapped. We must avoid simply moving from a small number of very visible snake pits, state institutions for the mentally retarded, to thousands of snake pits, as we create thousands of new loci for community services.

TABLE 1

17 External Monitoring Mechanisms and Quality Safeguards for Human Services

A. Requiring Public Mandate
1. Responsibility vested in a "specialty point"
2. Effective regulatory control
3. Funding contingent upon externally evaluated performance
4. Special services backing up general ones
5. Institutionalization of ombudsman system
6. Prohibition of secret transactions

B. Realizable through Agency Initiative
7. Consumer participation in governance and committees
8. Written individualized objectives reviewed with client
9. Routinization of client feedback
10. Formalization of grievance management
11. Independent advisory committees
12. Routine external evaluation by experts
13. External consultancy
14. Written agreements on program operations

C. Under Voluntary Association Control
15. Independent watchdog committees
16. Systematic legal probing
17. Citizen advocacy

As Table 1 indicates, there are some safeguards that require public mandate and some that can be initiated within an agency, if the agency has the proper motivation. And then there are some safeguards that require voluntary association action.[1] These safeguards are, of course, for quality of service; they are for self-renewal; and they are for consumer voice and representation. At this point I want to make a very important distinction and emphasize it particularly for members of

[1] *See* W. Wolfensberger, The Third Stage in the Evolution of Voluntary Associations for the Mentally Retarded (International League of Societies for the Mentally Handicapped & National Institute on Mental Retardation, Toronto, 1973).

the legal profession; that is, the distinction between safeguards for systems and safeguards for persons. Most of the safeguards listed in Table 1 are safeguards for systems so that the system itself becomes self-renewing and functions properly. We are limited in our safeguards for persons. There are three that stand out particularly: the ombudsman system, the formalization of grievance management, and citizen advocacy. Citizen advocacy is so important precisely because it is a safeguard for individuals.

When funding is tied to proven performance and objectively and externally assessed service quality, we have a safeguard for the system. There has recently been developed an external evaluation system which has the potential for becoming a major systems safeguard. It is called PASS (Program Analysis of Service Systems).[2]

Many professionals, particularly social service and institutional professionals, have been hostile to citizen advocacy. Lawyers have not been hostile, but they have been cool, which puzzles me. They are not threatened in the sense that the social worker is often threatened by citizen advocates who assume powers vis-à-vis his client and confront him. I think lawyers have difficulty fitting citizen advocacy in somewhere because it involves legal action and formal legal roles only on relatively rare occasions. Thus, lawyers are not quite sure how citizen advocacy relates to their work, and so very few attorneys have involved themselves in any aspect of citizen advocacy to date, even as associates. I ask that attorneys take action to remedy this situation.

Some dissatisfaction among professionals over citizen advocacy is legitimate. Citizen advocates will be inconvenient; they have often been inconvenient to date. Yet, it is only through a process of painful change that things get better, and change without pain is unknown to me. We have to realize that there is a tremendous limitation in the capacity of paid human services professionals and attorneys to meet the needs of the handicapped. There is a lack of money and of dedication that can be bought with money to provide much needed services. And, of course, commitment cannot be bought — which returns us to the matter of professional morality. The child placement field, for instance, which I can describe best in terms of institutionalized dehumanization and sanctioned crimes against humanity, is a highly professionalized area; still, I often wonder just how many professionals in this field ever lose a single night's sleep over what they do to and with homeless children — or how they make homeless ones out of the nonhomeless.

We need alternative and additional human helping forms. We need the professional services of professional agencies, but we also need other forms, even though these may be overlapping. There are needs to be met, such as the need for continuity of relationship, which we cannot meet by paid employees. When services are tied to drawing a salary from an agency, provider-client relationships are temporary, and this discontinuity of relationship is one of the most wounding, most constant realities in the lives of retarded persons — the constant shift in residences, parental figures, work assignments, teachers, therapists, professionals — they dance in and they

---

[2] W. Wolfensberger & L. Glenn, PASS: A System for the Quantitative Evaluation of Human Services (National Institute on Mental Retardation, Toronto, 1973).

dance out. I think a human being is entitled to one relationship that endures across time, across distance, through all difficulties, and this relationship is more crucial, the more impaired the individual.[3]

In closing let me make a point about the law. The law is a powerful tool, but it cannot be wielded effectively without informed leadership. Moreover, provision must be made to implement the law, and the public must be made aware that the law seeks to ensure those rights to which *every* citizen is entitled. Despite the 1954 Supreme Court decision on integration, there is still segregation because enforcement has been slow and education to reshape public values even slower.

[3] For a more detailed description of citizen advocacy, see Citizen Advocacy and Protective Services for the Impaired and Handicapped (W. Wolfensberger & H. Zauha eds., National Institute on Mental Retardation, Toronto, 1973).

PART FOUR

The Mentally Retarded Citizen and the Criminal and Correctional Process

CHAPTER 20

The Criminal
Reform Movement

Editorial Introduction

*T*his chapter deals with some of the many current efforts to reform the criminal justice and correctional systems. The primary issue discussed is the extent to which mentally retarded offenders are or should be singled out in this movement for special treatment.

Fox surveys a number of the reform efforts and demonstrates that mental retardation is ignored in many situations where it has obvious relevance. It is clear from his discussion that there has been little input to most reform proposals by those sensitive to the needs and problems of mentally retarded citizens. Nevertheless, Fox is cautious about calling attention in the criminal law to the mentally retarded offender. Among the dangers he sees in such special attention is that of community fear and hostility toward the mentally retarded, with the resultant danger of further discrimination. He proposes a three-step approach to the problem: first, a thorough study of reform proposals to document systematically the extent to which they ignore special problems related to mental retardation; second, the development of a model criminal justice system from the viewpoint of the mentally retarded; and third, a strategic decision as to whether some or all aspects of the model should be actively pressed.

In his contribution, Fox discusses a proposal made some years ago by Allen for an exceptional offenders court. Allen's reaction responds in part to Fox's comments on this proposal; a reprint of that proposal is appended to the reaction comment. Allen also emphasizes some of the factors that tend to distort statistics on the number and nature of mentally retarded offenders, including the tendency of· parole boards to delay parole for retarded offenders and the likelihood that minor offenses by retarded individuals will not be prosecuted in the criminal court. Finally, Allen discusses the impact on the retarded offender of two important recent court decisions, *Jackson v. Indiana* and *United States v. Brawner*.

Golten's confident approach provides a sharp contrast to Fox's cautious exploration. Golten sees the present need for special attention to mentally retarded offenders as being clear, and he lists specific provisions that he feels should be enacted immediately.

PRINCIPAL PAPER

SANFORD J. FOX

THE REFORM MOVEMENT AND TACTICAL PROBLEMS

Even the casual observer would today affirm that the criminal justice process is in ferment. Almost every state has revised its substantive criminal code entirely or is in the process of doing so.[1] At one end of the process, police recruitment and training practices are being upgraded.[2] At the other end, many national, state, and local groups are dedicated to humanizing and rationalizing corrections.[3] The American Bar Association has undertaken the monumental task of stating standards of criminal justice in a 10-year, 17-volume project designed to improve the quality of justice from arrest to sentencing.[4] The influential report of President Johnson's Crime Commission in 1967[5] is being followed by the work of the National Commission on Criminal Justice Standards and Goals, which started to release its recommendations in January 1973.[6]

Fortunately, this is not the occasion to determine whether what appears to the casual observer as ferment would be seen by the more critical observer as progress

[1] *See* AMERICAN LAW INSTITUTE, STATUS OF SUBSTANTIVE PENAL LAW REVISION (April 1973), indicating enactment of 20 new codes; completed revisions, not yet enacted, in 16 more states, and revisions "well under way in still six more jurisdictions." Only Mississippi, Nevada, Wyoming, and the District of Columbia are in the class: "No over-all revisions planned."
[2] This can be readily observed from the annual planning and reporting documents published by the state planning agency responsible in each state for administering federal funds under the Omnibus Crime Control and Safe Streets Act of 1968, Pub. L. No. 90-351, 82 Stat. 197 (codified in various sections of 5, 18, and 42 U.S.C.) and the Juvenile Delinquency Prevention and Control Act of 1968, Pub. L. No. 90-445, 82 Stat. 462 (codified in various sections of 42 U.S.C.).
[3] *See, e.g.,* A.B.A. COMMISSION ON CORRECTIONAL FACILITIES AND SERVICES & COUNCIL OF STATE GOVERNMENT, COMPENDIUM OF MODEL CORRECTIONAL LEGISLATION AND STANDARDS pt. VIII, at 1 (1972) [hereinafter cited as COMPENDIUM].
[4] *See* Clark, *The American Bar Association Standards for Criminal Justice: Prescription for an Ailing System,* 47 NOTRE D. LAW. 429 (1972).
[5] PRESIDENT'S COMMISSION ON LAW ENFORCEMENT AND ADMINISTRATION OF JUSTICE, THE CHALLENGE OF CRIME IN A FREE SOCIETY (1967) [hereinafter cited as CHALLENGE OF CRIME].
[6] *See* Working Papers, National Conference on Criminal Justice, January 23-26, 1973.

or regress. All that must be affirmed here is that many people think the criminal justice system is being improved, bit by bit — with some loss of ground here and there, but with the overall result of qualitative improvement.

In view of this multifaceted attack on long-standing deficiencies of American criminal justice, the question to be raised in regard to the mentally retarded offender is whether he should throw in his lot with other offenders, reaping whatever benefits are forthcoming for *all*, in terms of a more efficient, fair, humane, and rational system, or whether he should seek some detailed and special consideration from the criminal justice system which would be responsive to the special circumstances of his mental retardation. Advocates for mentally retarded citizens must decide whether to address themselves to those engaged in the reform of the criminal justice system in terms of:

1.   Go on about your good works as if offenders were a homogeneous mass in regard to intelligence; or
2.   Stop! Before you go a semicolon further, remember that there are retarded offenders to whom you must pay some special attention when you rework the laws, administrative practices, personnel policies, facilities, and budgets.

And, if it is the second position which is to be adopted on behalf of the mentally retarded, it must be decided whether to propose a bit of tinkering here and there, for example, with the semantics of the insanity defense,[7] or to go further and propose creation of a completely separate system for dealing with the crime problem posed by offenders who are mentally retarded. It must be decided whether the whole conceptual and pragmatic machinery of justice for the mentally retarded offender should be moved completely out of the dominant system of criminal justice.

There may be appealing reasons for getting on the existing reform bandwagon and joining in the general reform of criminal justice, if this reform already includes particularly valuable changes for the retarded offender. There may be aspects of criminal justice reform that are of particular benefit to this class of offenders, above and beyond the benefits that flow to all persons caught up in the criminal justice system. Redefinition of kidnapping or provisions on police use of computers to identify stolen vehicles may be of little special interest in the context. But a new statute that would foreclose sending anyone, including mentally retarded persons, to a maximum security prison without providing treatment or habilitation is quite another matter.

It is important in the discussion that follows to keep in mind the empirical base on which these reform characteristics operate. The Brown and Courtless study indicated that on a national level, 9.5 percent of the prison population is mentally retarded, although this figure fluctuates substantially from region to region — almost 25 percent of the prisoners in the east south central states of Kentucky, Tennessee, Alabama, and Mississippi, for example, are classified as retarded.[8] Contrary to popular

[7] *See, e.g.,* Person, *The Accused Retardate,* 4 COLUM. HUMAN RIGHTS L. REV. 239, 256-66 (1972).
[8] Brown & Courtless, *The Mentally Retarded in Penal and Correctional Institutions,* 124 AM J. PSYCHIATRY 1164, 1166 (1968).

conception, one study indicates that retarded offenders within prison populations are disproportionately responsible for relatively serious offenses.[9] This disproportionate representation may be a function of intelligence, *i.e.*, the retarded offender is not as smart as his nonretarded colleague and so gets caught more easily, or it may be a function of how the legal-correctional system deals with the mentally retarded offender. These studies also serve to document that institutional programs and facilities specially designed for the mentally retarded offender are scarce or do not exist.[10]

Reform movements come and go, and some believe they are basically episodic and infrequent. There is no reason to suppose that the current interest in criminal justice reform will be different and last forever. In Massachusetts, for example, there is a proposed new criminal code before the legislature. It constitutes the first comprehensive reform of Massachusetts penal law since 1836.[11] After the code is adopted, a number of decades may pass before a fundamental reexamination is again undertaken. Unless a hard-nosed critical evaluation is soon undertaken of the various components of criminal justice reform, the opportunity to influence the directions and substance of the reform on behalf of mentally retarded offenders may well pass beyond the grasp of this generation. Now is the time for comprehensive and systematic questions to be put to the criminal justice reform program: What impact will it have on the retarded offender? What is society's interest in the fate of the retarded offender, as promised by these reforms? What additional reforms are required to deal best with the mentally retarded offender?

A REVIEW OF SOME GENERAL PROPOSALS FOR CRIMINAL JUSTICE REFORM

This section samples some of the reform programs with these questions in mind. Although the sample does not cover the whole range of criminal justice reform, it does permit the drawing of some tentative conclusions and presents the opportunity to analyze issues which may be of value in further comprehensive investigations.

Among the 17 volumes of the American Bar Association's *Standards of Criminal Justice* are several which relate to problems of mentally retarded offenders. In light of Professor Allen's observation that lawyers involved in criminal prosecutions rarely know whether the accused person is retarded,[12] not a few volumes are relevant. Consider first *The Prosecution Function and the Defense Function*, approved by the American Bar Association House of Delegates in 1971.[13] This volume includes

---

[9] Allen, *The Retarded Offender: Unrecognized in Court and Untreated in Prison,* 32 FED. PROBATION, Sept. 1968 at 22, 24-25.

[10] Brown & Courtless, *supra* note 8, at 1167.

[11] MASS. CRIMINAL LAW REVISION COMMISSION, PROPOSED CRIMINAL CODE OF MASSACHUSETTS (1972).

[12] Allen, *supra* note 9, at 25.

[13] A.B.A. PROJECT IN MINIMUM STANDARDS FOR CRIMINAL JUSTICE [hereinafter cited as A.B.A. PROJECT], STANDARDS RELATING TO THE PROSECUTION FUNCTION AND THE DEFENSE FUNCTION (approved draft 1971).

standards relating to plea negotiations. The prosecutor is enjoined by these standards to negotiate only with an accused's attorney, and if there is no attorney, he is urged to seek to have one appointed.[14] But he is also empowered to deal directly with the accused if the offer to provide defense counsel is refused.[15] There is no admonition to the prosecutor at this point that he should be alert to see if he is dealing with a retarded individual. The accompanying comment, however, states:

> . . . the prosecutor should be careful to determine that the defendant has made an effective waiver of his right to counsel and has not foregone the opportunity to be represented merely because the offer of counsel has not been made properly *or because he lacks the capacity to make an intelligent decision.*[16]

In the same vein, the volume on *Providing Defense Services*, approved in 1968, provides relevant cautionary language in its standard concerning waiver of the right to counsel. Standard 7.2 declares:

> An accused should not be deemed to have waived the assistance of counsel until the entire process of offering counsel has been completed and a thorough inquiry into the accused's comprehension of that offer and *his capacity to make the choice intelligently and understandingly has been made.* No waiver should be found to have been made where it appears that the accused is unable to make an intelligent and understanding choice because of his *mental condition*, age, education, experience, the nature or complexity of the case, or other factors.[17]

Suppose there is a mentally retarded defendant who accepts the offer of counsel. He is then asked by his lawyer how he would like to plead. Here the standards contain no caution to defense counsel regarding mentally retarded clients; they merely declare that the ultimate responsibility for deciding what plea to make rests with the accused, not with his lawyer.

Since an offer to plead guilty must be accepted by the judge before it can become effective, neither the defense nor the prosecution has the last say on pleading. The volume on *The Function of the Trial Judge* admonishes the judge not to accept a plea unless he first addresses the defendant personally and determines that the plea is "voluntary" and that the defendant understands what he is charged with and what rights his plea serves to waive.[18] No mention is made of what problems are presented by a "voluntary" plea from a mentally retarded person. The volume devoted exclusively to *Pleas of Guilty* places a similar emphasis on ensuring that the defendant is told what rights his plea waives, rather than on his capacity to waive any of them.[19] Capacity issues are barely discussed.

Since there is currently a widespread focus on the corrections-treatment part of the criminal justice system, the standards' concern for the retarded offender at the

---

[14] *Id.* § 4.1(b).

[15] *Id.*

[16] *Id.* commentary, at 106 (emphasis supplied).

[17] A.B.A. PROJECT, STANDARDS RELATING TO PROVIDING DEFENSE SERVICES § 7.2 (approved draft 1968) (emphasis supplied).

[18] A.B.A. PROJECT, STANDARDS RELATING TO THE FUNCTION OF THE TRIAL JUDGE § 4.2(a) (approved draft 1972).

[19] A.B.A. PROJECT, STANDARDS RELATING TO PLEAS OF GUILTY (approved draft 1968).

sentencing stage of the proceedings should be considered. Several volumes are relevant. The volume on *Probation* includes standards relating to the presentence report, the most material part of which provides that the contents of the report should include "the offender's medical history and, if desirable, a psychological or psychiatric report."[20] The comments to this standard say nothing further concerning special efforts to determine whether the offender is mentally retarded and to apprise the sentencing judge if he is. The related volume on *Sentencing Alternatives and Procedures*[21] makes no specific mention of mentally retarded offenders. It comes closest to dealing with the problem in its directives to individualize sentences and in its recommendation that "facilities be developed to provide special treatment for certain types of offenders, particularly the young, and that the court be authorized as a sentencing alternative to employ such facilities in appropriate cases."[22]

One of the difficulties facing an attorney representing a client known to him to be mentally retarded relates to the quantity and quality of cooperation he can expect to receive from his client in investigating the case, in constructing his defense strategy, and in being an advocate regarding the sentence. If this problem is extreme, he may want to consider a plea that his client is unfit to stand trial. But short of this, one avenue for compensating for this handicap would be via increased cooperation of the prosecution. This could have been treated in the volume entitled *Discovery and Procedure Before Trial,*[23] but nothing in this volume recognizes that there may be special discovery needs in cases of retarded offenders.

Passing from the American Bar's project on standards to substantive issues as they present themselves in the nationwide movement toward restating the penal law, it should be noted that mentally retarded persons often receive special attention in their roles not as offenders, but as victims of the antisocial conduct of others. They are, for example, declared to be incapable of consenting to sexual relations[24] or to confinement of their persons in kidnappings.[25] The new penal codes also undertake to restate the culpable states of mind which must accompany harmful conduct in order for there to be crime. Terms such as "purpose," "intention," "reckless," and so on are given statutory definitions designed to achieve a clarity which common law *mens rea* concepts notoriously lack. Consider the Model Penal Code's widely adopted definition of "recklessly":

> A person acts recklessly with respect to a material element of an offense when he consciously disregards a substantial and unjustifiable risk that the material element exists or will result from his conduct. The risk must be of such a nature and degree that, considering the nature and purpose of the actor's conduct and the circumstances known to him, its disregard involves a gross deviation from the standard of conduct that a law-abiding person would observe in the actor's situation.[26]

[20] A.B.A. Project, Standards Relating to Probation § 2.3(ii) (F) (approved draft 1970).
[21] A.B.A. Project, Standards Relating to Sentencing Alternatives and Procedures (approved draft 1968).
[22] *Id.* § 2.6(a).
[23] A.B.A. Project, Standards Relating to Discovery and Procedure Before Trial (approved draft 1970).
[24] *See, e.g.,* N.H. Rev. Stat. Ann. § 632:1, I (d) (Supp. 1972).
[25] *See, e.g.,* Conn. Gen. Stat. Ann. § 53a-91(1)(b) (1972).
[26] Model Penal Code § 2.02(2)(c) (proposed official draft 1962) [hereinafter cited as Model Penal Code]

There is nothing in the text of the Model Penal Code which deals with the question of how this is to be applied to a retarded person.

The issue most frequently raised when mental retardation is considered in the context of criminal law is the relationship of rules of criminal responsibility and mental retardation. Reformers generally have adopted the American Law Institute's (ALI) Model Penal Code formulation.

> A person is not responsible for criminal conduct if at the time of such conduct as a result of mental disease or defect he lacks substantial capacity either to appreciate the criminality (wrongfulness) of his conduct or to conform his conduct to the requirements of law.[27]

Even the Federal Court of Appeals in the District of Columbia recently abandoned the famous *Durham* rule, which it had adopted in 1954, in favor of the Model Penal Code formulation.[28] Both the ALI and *Durham* formulations include the term "mental defect," which is generally defined to include mental retardation.[29] (Under the traditional *M'Naghten* test of criminal insanity, mental retardation was generally held to be irrelevant.)[30] Thus, if he can meet the "capacity" and "result" tests, a mentally retarded person may avail himself of this defense.

If a retarded person has been found not criminally responsible under the criminal capacity rules, or if he has been found unfit to stand trial, he becomes subject to statutory provisions authorizing an indefinite commitment to a "hospital prison" pending his recovery.[31] These laws have had particularly harsh results in the case of mentally retarded defendants since there is little prospect for recovery from mental retardation. The result has often been a life sentence.

Three signs of change brought on by the criminal law reform movement need to be noted in this regard. One is new criminal code provisions that put some limit on the open-endedness of the commitments. New Jersey, for example, has a section in its penal code draft which would, at the end of 10 years, require the court either to release a person found not guilty by reason of insanity, or at that time initiate civil commitment proceedings.[32] Somewhat analogous is the provision concerning a person found unfit to stand trial. This provision authorizes the court to dismiss the case when it "is of the view that so much time has elapsed since the commitment that it would be unjust to resume the criminal proceedings."[33]

The second sort of change is found in the substantive definition of mental retardation which governs the issue of "recovery" in these circumstances. In Massachu-

---

[27] *Id.* § 4.01.

[28] United States v. Brawner, 471 F.2d 969 (D.C. Cir. 1972), *overruling,* Durham v. United States, 214 F.2d 862 (D.C. Cir. 1954).

[29] *See* McDonald v. United States, 312 F.2d 847 (D.C. Cir. 1962).

[30] *See* THE PRESIDENT'S PANEL ON MENTAL RETARDATION, REPORT OF THE TASK FORCE ON LAW 40-41 (1963) [hereinafter cited as TASK FORCE ON LAW]; Person, *supra* note 7, at 257-59.

[31] *See, e.g.,* MINN. STAT. ANN. § 631.19 (Supp. 1974).

[32] N.J. CRIMINAL LAW REVISION COMMISSION, 1 FINAL REPORT OF THE NEW JERSEY CRIMINAL LAW REVISION COMMISSION § 2C:4-8(f) (1971).

[33] *Id.* § 2C:4-6(c). *See also* Jackson v. Indiana, 406 U.S. 715 (1972), discussed by Allen *infra* at pp. 641-42.

setts, for example, a 1970 statutory definition speaks of the person's "ability to function in the community," rather than relying solely on a static impairment of intelligence as the central criterion for finding retardation.[34] If special training and education is available in a jurisdiction where "functioning in the community" is the touchstone of recovery, a significant change in the indeterminacy of commitment may be brought about.

A third aspect of the law relating to abnormal mental conditions and criminal responsibility has been fashioned largely in recent years by the courts, rather than the legislatures. The so-called doctrine of partial or diminished responsibility has come to be accepted by the great majority of courts that have confronted the issue.[35] This concept applies when an abnormal mental condition which falls short of establishing the insanity defense may, nonetheless, serve to raise a reasonable doubt concerning a specific state of mind which is an essential element of the offense charged, *i.e.*, the *mens rea* of the criminal law. For example, if a mentally retarded person charged with larceny can raise a reasonable doubt concerning his intention to deprive the owner permanently of his property (by evidence that he was too retarded to have such an intention), he is entitled to be acquitted of the charge. Of course, if there is a lesser included charge which does not require proof of the defendant's mental state, the retarded defendant may be convicted of the lesser crime. The most common example of this occurs when the charge involves a homicide and the evidence of mental abnormality negates the premeditation and deliberation required for first degree murder, leaving the defendant accused of second degree murder, or perhaps manslaughter. Criminal codes that have dealt with this issue have generally accepted the doctrine of diminished responsibility,[36] although most criminal codes are silent on the subject. Because the doctrine of diminished responsibility serves to *approve* the conviction of a mentally retarded offender, albeit for a lesser offense, it was rejected by the 1963 Task Force on Law.[37]

The subject of postconviction experiences is probably the most active area of reform in the whole corrections process. The reform process in corrections developed later than it did in other parts of the criminal justice system. Indeed, a persistent criticism of the federal programs in the late 1960s, largely emanating out of the 1967 report of President Johnson's Crime Commission, was that the whole field of corrections was greatly underplayed. This lack of emphasis on change in the corrections area was not, however, due to a similar lack of emphasis in the report of the crime commission in 1967. The report urged "careful screening and classification of offenders," a greater diversity of programs which would be outside large institutions and in a community setting, and a greater overall commitment of resources to the problems of corrections.[38] Few of these proposals were new; very soon after

---

[34] Mass. Ann. Laws ch. 123, § 1 (1972).
[35] *See, e.g.,* People v. Wolff, 61 Cal. 2d 795, 394 P.2d 959, 40 Cal. Rptr. 271 (1964).
[36] *See, e.g.,* Mass. Criminal Law Revision Commission, Proposed Criminal Code of Massachusetts ch. 263, § 27(a) (1972).
[37] Task Force on Law 38-39.
[38] Challenge of Crime 159-85.

prisons were instituted in America in the early nineteenth century, virtually the whole spectrum of prison problems became apparent. Prisoners subjected to solitary confinement went crazy; riots necessitated the use of troops, who came in and shot the convicts. Classification became an urgent need.[39] In more than a century and a half of experience with penal institutions, none of these problems has been solved. Over the decades, with the inability to find solutions, many observers came to believe that the mentally retarded prisoner was among the last to receive the specialized services he required, but among the first to be brutalized and victimized by both the prison administration and fellow inmates.[40]

There are, however, several unique features of the current wave of corrections reform. One is the participation of the courts, along with judicial willingness to take an active part in correcting some of the problems within the correctional system. The most obvious manifestations of this are seen in the success of federal court litigation designed to control, on fourteenth amendment grounds, disciplinary abuses inside the institutions[41] and in suits aimed at eliminating brutality by invoking the eighth amendment's prohibition against cruel and unusual punishments.[42]

A second singularity of current corrections reform is the role of the organized bar. The American Law Institute's approval of its Model Penal Code a decade ago included approval of substantial amounts of statutory material dealing with corrections.[43] The active interest of the American Bar Association in the field of corrections is evidenced by its recent formation of a special Joint Committee on Principles Relating to the Legal Status of Prisoners, its latest move to accelerate the participation of the bar in the corrections reform process.[44]

The third striking feature of corrections reform in our day is hardly a matter of newly arrived *dramatis personnae*. But the old players, the prisoners themselves, have assumed new roles. Self-help, unionization, participatory democracy — call it what you will — prisoners are a force to contend with in any change behind the prison walls. The novelty is not in some consideration being given to their interests and welfare, but rather in who it is who acts as advocates for them. Compare, for example, the rather quaint, nineteenth-century, and somewhat futile and impotent image evoked by the *Beacon Hill Ladies' Society for the Relief of Poor and Retarded Prisoners*, with the simple, powerful, and somewhat threatening ring of the *State Prison Inmates' Rights Committee*.

Perhaps the best way of gaining some insight into the specific types of corrections reforms which are being produced under these circumstances is to examine the *Compendium of Model Correctional Legislation and Standards*, published jointly in

---

[39] *See* W.D. Lewis, From Newgate to Dannemora (1965); S. Knapp, The Life of Thomas Eddy (1834).
[40] *See, e.g.,* Allen, *supra* note 9, at 27.
[41] *See, e.g.,* Morris v. Travisono, 310 F. Supp. 857 (D.R.I. 1970).
[42] *See, e.g.,* Lollis v. New York State Dep't of Social Services, 322 F. Supp. 473 (S.D.N.Y. 1970), *modified,* 328 F. Supp. 1115 (1971).
[43] *See* Model Penal Code pt. III.
[44] *See* News from the American Bar Association, #41273.

1972 by the American Bar Association and the Council of State Governments.[45] As Chief Justice Burger remarked in his forward to this publication: "For those examining virtually any facet of statutory improvement relating to corrections or offenders under correctional supervision, this work cannot help but contribute ideas, assistance and, where needed, convenient reference to original sources."[46] In other words, it fits our present purposes quite well.

The compendium is divided into 10 separate sections, dealing with such topics as the organization of corrections departments, probation and parole, and loss and restoration of civil rights. A number of relevant themes emerges from an examination of these materials. One is a repetition of the litany of individualization. The organization of the corrections bureaucracy, the structure of sentencing authority, and the administration of institutions are all admonished to pay close attention to the individual needs of convicted persons.[47] Second, there is a proposal (sometimes in the form of a recommendation, sometimes as a mandate) for the transfer of mentally retarded prisoners to a special facility or program of the corrections department or to the custody of the mental health department.[48] Third is the appearance in the legislation and standards relating to sentencing of authority to impose particularly stiff sentences on "dangerous offenders." Candidates for this classification are defined in various ways, but the succinct definition proposed by the "model sentencing act" is typical. Section 5 of this act speaks of persons who have committed serious offenses and are found by the court to be "suffering from a severe mental or emotional disorder indicating a propensity toward continuing dangerous criminal activity."[49] By the use of such language, these proposed statutes would become a substitute for many of the so-called defective delinquent statutes.

There are strongly asserted prohibitions on abuses of correctional authority. The compendium section on prisoner treatment and rights[50] contains absolute rules against physical brutality, verbal abuse, discrimination, and excessive solitary confinement as a disciplinary measure, as well as guidelines on how many calories a prisoner's diet must contain, and how frequently medical examinations must be conducted for each prisoner. There are also, as one might expect, recommendations for programs of an educational nature as part of the prison experience.

Certainly, this brief look at some aspects of modern penal law reform justifies no firm conclusions about whether the balance sheet shows a net gain or a net loss for the mentally retarded offender. But just as certainly, there are some distinct impressions that emerge which a more definitive investigation might bear in mind.

1. During the period of penal law reform in the first three decades of the nineteenth century, there were many advocates of a specialized system of justice for children which resulted in the House of Refuge movement and the development of

---

[45] COMPENDIUM, *supra* note 3.
[46] COMPENDIUM iii.
[47] *See, e.g., State Department of Corrections Act,* in COMPENDIUM pt. I, at 3.
[48] *E.g.,* Fourth United Nations Congress on Prevention of Crime and Treatment of Prisoners, *Standard Minimum Rules for the Treatment of Prisoners,* in COMPENDIUM pt. IV, at 15.
[49] COMPENDIUM pt. II, at 55.
[50] COMPENDIUM pt. IV.

specialized institutions for children and ultimately, in specialized juvenile courts and accompanying agencies of justice.[51] Except for Professor Allen's 1966 proposal, which will be discussed subsequently, there appears to be no such advocacy for a separate justice system for mentally retarded offenders.

2. A perusal of the American Bar Association's standards suggests there is only an insubstantial awareness of the problems presented by mentally retarded suspects to their defense counsel, to prosecutors, and to judges sitting in criminal cases. Revisions of the substantive penal law convey the same impression. For example, the evolution of the insanity defense was expanded early in the reform period so as no longer to exclude automatically the retarded offender, but it seems to have paid no further attention to the issue of mental retardation.

3. Relatively speaking, the greatest awareness of the special problems presented by mentally retarded offenders appears in the proposals for reform of the corrections system. But awareness is clearly a two-way street; along with demands for specialized programs and facilities for retarded offenders go law revisions which serve to perpetuate the predictions of "dangerousness" in the original defective delinquent laws.

THE EXCEPTIONAL OFFENDERS COURT

One of the most significant proposals of the reform movement is Allen's tentative suggestion for an exceptional offenders court.[52] A primary objective of this proposed court is the substitution of welfare considerations for punishment values for mentally retarded offenders. The court would be given jurisdiction only when there is a serious offense charged. The purpose of the initial court proceeding would be to determine whether there was a gross intellectual deficit as measured by a standard more flexible than an IQ assessment (such as an inquiry into whether the person is substantially impaired in his intellectual capacity to cope with the demands and responsibilities of normal adult life, or to conform his behavior to the requirements of law).[53] There would be a relatively informal determination of whether the offense was committed and whether the suspect was substantially mentally retarded. A positive finding on both these questions would then empower the court to assume broad supervisory powers over the mentally retarded person, including authority to commit him to a specialized institution, provided there was an additional finding that he was dangerous to himself or to others.

Allen's proposal was suggested in full recognition of the need to obtain additional facilities and trained personnel to implement the program. All of the elements of the proposal are based on a willingness to "accept the premise that the exceptional

---

[51] *See* Fox, *Juvenile Justice Reform: An Historical Perspective,* 22 Stan. L. Rev. 1187 (1970).

[52] Allen, *Toward an Exceptional Offenders Court.* 4 Mental Retardation 3 (1966) (reprinted in part as an addendum to Allen's reaction comment, pp. 643-45 *infra*).

[53] United States v. Brawner, 471 F.2d 969, 991 (D.C. Cir. 1972).

offender must be dealt with on the basis of what he is, and what he can become . . . if we are truly concerned with his rehabilitation and integration in the community."[54]

It would be a mistake to dismiss this proposal simply because juvenile courts have been the subject of recent criticism. To the extent that juvenile courts are no longer seen as a viable vehicle for dealing with delinquency, a court for mentally retarded offenders need not necessarily encounter the same fate. Much has been learned from the juvenile court experience which can help avoid such problems as the cavalier disregard of due process standards and the rhetoric of utopia that have plagued those courts.

Juvenile courts, like Allen's proposal, offer to deal with the persons before them on the basis of what they are and what they can become, rather than on the basis of what they have done. It is this repetition of juvenile court philosophy which the retarded offenders court idea invites us to embrace. There are, however, several philosophical differences which are important:

1. Strictly from a scientific point of view, the problem of diagnosis of juvenile delinquency appears to be more complex than the problem of recognizing whether an individual has a substantial degree of mental retardation.[55] Moreover, the issue of "what a child is" usually arises in a context broader than simply technical diagnosis. Family relations, peer group factors, school experiences — virtually all of a child's environment is normally seen as part of picture.[56] Some of this same breadth is evident in Allen's conception of what the retarded person is, but it appears that the relevance of environmental facts is more attenuated.

. An evaluation of a child proceeds with a substantial expectation that the child is malleable and that either he, or significant elements in his environment, can be changed. It is doubtful that the same tone of amelioration and optimism surrounds the evaluation when it is made of a mentally retarded person. Quite the opposite seems to be the case. There appears to be much more of the idea found in the distinction that the insanity defense now commonly makes between mental disease and mental defect: The former can be changed; the latter cannot.

3. The question of what a person *is* arises as a means of deflecting attention from what he has *done*. Hostility that may arise from focusing on what a person has done could interfere significantly with efforts to identify and meet the individual needs of that person. For a child, this is a relatively sound assumption. The movement of consciousness away from the harm that has been done is designed to arrive at a position that says: "He is, after all, just a child." The advantage of this approach is less clear in regard to the mentally retarded offender. Stripping away the matter of what he has done may leave dominant feelings of sympathy and love from many persons who work with the retarded, but it is doubtful that this would be the prevailing attitude of the public generally. There would likely be elements of fear and hostility which would be alien in the common conception of a child *qua* child.

---

[54] Allen, *supra* note 52, at 6.
[55] *See, e.g.,* A. FREUD, NORMALITY AND PATHOLOGY IN CHILDHOOD 114-18 (1965).
[56] *See* Rodman & Grams, *Juvenile Delinquency and the Family: A Review and Discussion,* in PRESIDENT'S COMMISSION ON LAW ENFORCEMENT AND ADMINISTRATION OF JUSTICE, TASK FORCE REPORT ON JUVENILE DELINQUENCY AND YOUTH CRIME (1967).

These three factors pose a serious question about adopting the philosophy of being, in place of the philosophy of doing, in constructing a policy position regarding mentally retarded offenders. A concentration on what the mentally retarded offender is causes serious and substantial risks that the system created for this individual will rely heavily on negative feelings and attitudes about the mentally retarded, on a hopelessness regarding the prospects for change, and on the view that the harm caused is entirely attributable to the retardation rather than being traceable, at least in part, to criminogenic factors in the environment. A system of this type, operating for a population of offenders who may be responsible for an inflated percentage of serious crimes, might easily become more punitive and brutal than is now the case with the present criminal system.

A RECOMMENDATION

The preceding analysis creates a dilemma. The general movement to reform the system of criminal justice appears flawed in its deficient awareness of the special needs posed by the mentally retarded offender. On the other hand, a look at some of the problems that might be created by concentrating attention on the uniqueness of the retarded offender gives reason for pause about movement in this direction. There are sufficient drawbacks to either alternative to make the other appear attractive.

The significant question is whether it is possible to enjoy the benefits of both alternatives. Can there be an increase in the sensitivity of the criminal justice system to mental retardation without risking a real deterioration of the retarded offender's role as victim of the system? A sense of the victimization of retarded persons generally appears to be at stake. If these citizens are, as a group, subject to deprivations, discrimination, and hostility wherever and whenever they come to the consciousness of the community, there is almost everything to lose and nothing to gain by focusing on mental retardation as an aspect of the criminal justice system. If, on the other hand, the dominant theme in the relations of mentally retarded individuals with society is one of benevolent concern and active care, a program to sensitize the criminal justice system makes a good deal of sense.

Whether the present day should be characterized as one of benevolence or hostility for the retarded population is a question that escapes a definitive answer. It is undoubtedly a difficult problem to solve, even for experts in the social problems of the mentally retarded. It is, however, on the assumption that hostility toward the mentally retarded is diminishing that the ultimate recommendations of this paper rest. First, a thorough study should be undertaken of the present criminal justice reform movement in order to identify where there is insufficient awareness of the special impact of mental retardation. Furthermore, a criminal justice model should be described which compensates for these insufficiencies. And, finally, some decisions will have to be reached concerning the social risks of implementing such a model.

Reaction Comment

RICHARD C. ALLEN

IN THE VERY FIRST ISSUE of *Mental Hygiene* (now *MH*), published in 1917, there appeared an article by Walter E. Fernald, M.D., superintendent of the Massachusetts School for the Feeble-Minded, which included the observation:

> The brighter classes of the feeble-minded, with their weak will power and deficient judgment, are easily influenced for evil and are prone to become vagrants, drunkards, and thieves. . . . As a matter of mere economy, it is now believed that it is better and cheaper for the community to assume the permanent custody of such persons before they have carried out a long career of expensive crime. The tendency to lead dissolute lives is especially noticeable in the females. . . . They either marry and bring forth in geometrical ratio a new generation of defectives . . . or become irresponsible sources of corruption and debauchery in the communities where they live.[1]

This kind of misinformation—so prevalent in the professional communities of the day—led to a system of lifelong custodial institutionalization for thousands of mentally retarded citizens who could have lived useful, productive, and fulfilling lives in their own homes and communities; of wholesale sterilizations; of deprivations of jural and civil rights; and of inhumane and repressive treatment of mentally retarded offenders.

The Institute of Law, Psychiatry, and Criminology at the George Washington University conducted a study of the mentally retarded offender and found that the proportion of mentally retarded individuals in prison is three times as high as in the general population and that the retarded are far more likely to be incarcerated for committing assaultive crimes, including homicide, than are the nonretarded.[2] It is not too surprising that these findings met with opposition, especially from persons who have for so long been trying to dispel the Fernaldian myth. The institute qualified its findings by observing that the retarded individual is more easily apprehended, more prone to confess, more likely to be convicted, will probably be incarcerated longer than the nonretarded offender, and is subject to a greater possibility of pretrial diversion if he is charged with a relatively minor offense against property.[3] These facts tend to inflate the figures upon which the study was based. But, bearing in mind the inadequacies of our institutional and community resources, it should not be surprising that mental retardation can be shown to have some causal relationship to crime.

---

[1] Fernald, *The Growth of Provision for the Feeble-Minded in the United States,* 1 MENTAL HYGIENE, Jan. 1917, at 34, 42.
[2] Allen, *The Retarded Offender: Unrecognized in Court and Untreated in Prison,* 32 FEDERAL PROBATION, Sept. 1968, at 22, 24.
[3] *Id.* at 25.

Nevertheless, the most basic truth is that mentally retarded citizens who commit criminal acts comprise a very small fraction of the total retarded population. It must be remembered also that mentally retarded citizens are the most discriminated against minority in our society. As juveniles, they may be denied access to public schools; community programs shun them; when they commit offenses which bring them to juvenile court, there is no total care institution in which they can get help; correctional agencies have no programs for them because they are retarded, and institutions for the retarded reject them because they are "acting out"; their crimes as adults may be frequently assaultive because they are blindly striking back against a world they do not understand and which has never tried to understand them.

If retarded citizens accused of crime are to continue to be dealt with under the present criminal justice system, then changes must be made in that system. As Fox points out, it is uncertain whether mental retardation comes within the prevailing court tests of insanity. Even where it does, in all probability the place to which a defendant found not guilty by reason of insanity must be committed will have neither the resources nor the trained personnel to meet the special needs of the mentally retarded individual. The determination of incompetency to stand trial (created to protect the impaired defendant against the unfairness of being required to answer criminal charges during a period of incapacity), with its resultant commitment "until recovery," has worked a virtual entrapment of retarded persons charged with criminal offenses, for whom "recovery," in the sense in which this term may be applied to the mentally ill, is simply not possible. And special procedures, like "sexual psychopathy" and "defective delinquency," have similarly resulted in lengthy commitments, without treatment, in institutions in which the retarded individual is again relegated to second-class citizenship—this time in subservience to the psychopath-sociopath-antisocial personality.

There is general agreement that the mentally retarded individual is inappropriately dealt with, and adversely affected by, the criminal correctional system. This situation prompted my 1966 proposal for an exceptional offenders court. The proposal was not intended to imply that the conduct which brings the offender before the law should be disregarded; such conduct is indeed the necessary precondition of coercive intervention by the state and may have very much to do with the determination of the individual's dangerousness and consequent need for institutional care. Nor did I intend to exclude the redemptive potential of punishment for retarded offenders. Rather, I was merely restating what had been said some three years earlier by the Task Force on Law of President Kennedy's Panel on Mental Retardation:

> Once it has been determined that an offender is mentally retarded to a degree and in a manner making it reasonable to believe his affliction caused the conduct in question, then we think it axiomatic that he should be treated according to his condition. For such persons, imprisonment for the sake of punishment is never appropriate. . . . The mentally retarded offender . . . requires rehabilitation addressed to the sources of his deviant behavior.[4]

[4] PRESIDENT'S PANEL ON MENTAL RETARDATION, REPORT OF THE TASK FORCE ON LAW 39 (1963).

I must respectfully dissent from Fox's observation that "Except for Professor Allen's 1966 proposal, ... there appears to be no such advocacy for a separate justice system for mentally retarded offenders." The proposal for diversion of mentally impaired offenders included in the final recommendations of the President's Commission on Law Enforcement and the Administration of Justice (the National Crime Commission) would seem to reflect just such a "separate justice system":

> Procedures are needed to identify and divert from the criminal process mentally disordered or deficient persons. . . . While recognizing the importance of the long-standing controversies over the definitions of criminal responsibility, insanity, and competence to stand trial, the Commission does not believe it has a substantial contribution to make to their resolution. It is more fruitful to discuss, not who can be tried and convicted as a matter of law, but how the officers of the administration of criminal justice should deal with people who present special needs and problems.[5]

And, it would call for the same kinds of judicial due process protection:

> Alternative ways of disposing of criminal cases that involve close supervision or institutional commitment without conviction, call for protections from their abuse, protections that should be roughly comparable to those of the criminal law.[6]

In June 1972, two decisions were announced which may have considerable impact on the plight of the mentally retarded offender. In *Jackson v. Indiana*[7] the United States Supreme Court reversed a determination of incompetency to stand trial and commitment "until sane" of a deaf mute with the mental age of a preschool child and no communicative ability other than through limited sign language. He had been charged with two counts of robbery (essentially pursesnatchings, involving property of the total value of $9 and was committed to the Indiana Department of Mental Health despite his counsel's protests that the commitment amounted to a life sentence without the suspect's ever having been convicted of a crime. The Supreme Court ruled:

> . . . a person charged by a State with a criminal offense who is committed solely on account of his incapacity to proceed to trial cannot be held more than the reasonable period of time necessary to determine whether there is a substantial probability that he will attain that capacity in the foreseeable future. If it is determined that this is not the case, then the State must either institute the customary civil commitment proceeding that would be required to commit indefinitely any other citizen, or release the defendant. Furthermore, even if it is determined that the defendant probably soon will be able to stand trial, his continued commitment must be justified by progress toward that goal.[8]

The decision in *Jackson* leaves a number of questions unanswered:

[5] President's Commission on Law Enforcement and Adiministration of Justice, The Challenge of Crime in a Free Society 133-34 (1967).
[6] *Id.*
[7] 406 U.S. 715 (1972).
[8] *Id.* at 738.

1. Can the constitutional proscription be asserted on behalf of someone less severely handicapped than was Mr. Jackson? The Court makes frequent reference to the degree of his disability (*e.g.*, "There is nothing in the record that even points to any possibility that Jackson's present condition can be remedied at any future time.")[9]

2. If there are defenses which can be asserted without the defendant's participation (*e.g.*, the running of the statute of limitations, defects in the indictment, lack of jurisdiction of the court, etc.), must the state permit them to be presented despite commitment of the defendant as "incompetent to stand trial"?

3. Is it constitutionally permissible to commit a mentally retarded defendant to a state mental hospital instead of to a facility for the mentally retarded?

4. How long is the "reasonable period of time necessary to determine whether [competency can be attained]"; and what is the maximum permissible period of detention once such determination has been made? Mr. Jackson had been confined for three and one-half years at the time of the decision.

Jackson does establish, however, a constitutional basis for protection against the practice of consigning mentally retarded citizens accused of crime to lifelong detention without prior establishment either of the fact of guilt of a criminal offense or the need for institutional care.

In *United States v. Brawner*[10] the United States Court of Appeals for the District of Columbia Circuit adopted the American Law Institute's Model Penal Code rule of criminal responsibility as a replacement for its much criticized *Durham* rule. In addition the decision adopts the rule of "diminished responsibility," under which mental impairment, though insufficient to exonerate, may nevertheless serve to reduce the degree of the offense. The court said: "Our rule permits the introduction of expert testimony as to abnormal condition if it is relevant to negative, or establish, the specific mental condition that is an element of the crime."[11] Since applicability of the insanity defense to the mentally retarded has been uncertain at best, the new rule for the District of Columbia affords a basis for introducing evidence of mental retardation to show that the defendant, for example, could not have premeditated and deliberated the act of homicide with which he is charged.

Hopefully, future court decisions will extend the right to treatment concept to the mentally retarded offender, who now receives nothing from the correctional system other than unrehabilitative custodial restraint. This right might be articulated in terms of the eighth amendment's prohibition against cruel and unusual punishment, or of the fourteenth amendment's guarantee of equal protection and right of due process. To implement these decisions, institutions housing criminally committed persons must be equipped with resources (*e.g.*, counseling, psychological testing, special education, and vocational training) that will afford the mentally retarded offender a chance for habilitation.

If all of this comes about, there may be no need for "special treatment" for the mentally retarded offender. But the development may be a long time in coming.

[9] *Id.* at 726.
[10] 471 F.2d 969 (D.C. Cir. 1972).
[11] *Id.* at 1002.

The exceptional offenders court concept was offered, not as a panacea, but as a new departure which might offer real hope for overcoming the neglect of the past. Fox has ably pointed to some of the problems in such a course; yet I cannot help but think that they are rather more surmountable practical obstacles than inherent conceptual defects.

My earlier proposal is included as an addendum here for the reader's convenience.

TOWARD AN EXCEPTIONAL OFFENDERS COURT *

The suggestion of an exceptional offenders court is offered, not as a considered judgment based on research findings, but simply as a possible area for exploration in our search for "new concepts."

The laws of most states have established special procedures outside the normal processes of the criminal law for defined categories of offenders: juveniles, youthful offenders, sex offenders, and defective delinquents, for example. Perhaps the closest conceptual model to the exceptional offenders court, among extant judicial institutions, is the juvenile court, with which there are at least two significant points of similarity: first, both are concerned with persons who are inadequately equipped to meet certain responsibilities of adulthood — in the case of the juvenile, because of his tender years, and in the case of the mentally retarded, because of his intellectual deficit; and second, like the juvenile court, the exceptional offenders court would have as a primary objective the welfare of retarded persons coming under its wardship, rather than imposing punishment for criminal offenses.

It has occasionally been suggested that the processes of the juvenile court should be made applicable to mentally retarded persons charged with crime (New Jersey Association for Retarded Children, 1958). More, however, is required than merely conferring jurisdiction on the juvenile court. A mentally retarded adult has different needs and presents different problems than a child of normal intelligence. Because of these differences, juvenile detention, probation, correctional and training facilities would be inappropriate for the adult retardate, and other dispositional alternatives, such as foster home placement, would be almost totally unavailable. Further, there is the problem of identification. While juveniles at the upper age ranges of jurisdiction of the juvenile court may look older than their years, most children are easily identifiable as children; whereas recognition of the retarded person as such is more difficult.

What is here suggested is a specially constituted court, empowered to assume wardship over any adult person shown to be substantially impaired in his intellectual capacity, who has committed an act which, if committed by an adult without such impairment, would constitute a felony or serious misdemeanor. It is suggested further that jurisdiction be transferred to such court at whatever point the existence of severe mental retardation is suspected — whether prior to trial on a criminal charge, or after conviction, sentence and incarceration for such offense.

Upon referral to such a court, there should first be a determination of the exist-

---

* Reprinted with permission from 4 MENTAL RETARDATION 3, 5-6 (1966).

ence of gross intellectual deficit. Such determination should be made by the judge, and should be based on expert evidence presented at a hearing at which the alleged exceptional offender is represented by a guardian *ad litem*. The criteria for such determination should be flexible.

It would be a mistake, for example, to legislate a fixed standard, such as IQ level. (The New York legislature has twice passed a bill bringing adult offenders with IQ's under 70 under their "Youthful Offenders" procedures. The Governor vetoed the proposed legislation principally on the ground that IQ is a "crude and inappropriate" criterion.) Rather, the statute should incorporate more general phraseology, such as "substantially impaired in his intellectual capacity to cope with the demands and responsibilities of normal adult life, or to conform his behavior to the requirements of law." In making such determination, the court should not consider evidence of commission of the offense with which the alleged exceptional offender has been charged (or of which he has been convicted in an adult criminal court).

After the foregoing determination has been made, any antecedent criminal proceedings should be voided, and a further hearing held, at which the alleged offender should be represented by counsel, to determine the operative facts of the offense with which he has been charged. The proceedings should be informal, and would render largely unnecessary such determinations as competency to stand trial, the admissibility of confessions, and criminal responsibility. There should, nevertheless, be observed elemental standards of due process of law, however, for it is not alone the existence of severe mental retardation that empowers the court to act, but also the fact of commission of what would otherwise constitute a criminal offense.

The court should have broad supervisory powers over all persons properly coming under its jurisdiction, including authority to commit exceptional offenders to appropriate specialized institutions for indeterminate periods. Institutionalization should, however, be based upon a finding of dangerousness to self or to others, and such orders should be subject to periodic review. Where the offender is capable of living in society under supervision, probation should be available, making use of group therapy, special education, and other techniques.

The court should also have authority to confer powers of guardianship (of the person, of the estate or both) on the probation officer, where the exercise of such powers is deemed necessary or desirable. Where a guardian had previously been appointed for the exceptional offender by another court, the exceptional offenders court should have authority to intervene in such proceedings, either to make the appointed guardian subject to its supervision, or to terminate the prior order of guardianship.

Following the analogy to juvenile court proceedings, it would perhaps be desirable to confer jurisdiction upon the court in cases of dependency and neglect as well — thus making it a court for exceptional adults rather than an exceptional offenders court. Indeed, such a court could be given exclusive authority over the institutionalization and guardianship of the mentally retarded.

The thoughts briefly presented here leave many unresolved problems, not the least of which is the need for additional facilities and trained personnel to implement such a program. It is believed, however, that answers can be found, if we accept the premise that the exceptional offender must be dealt with on the basis of what he is, and what he can become, and if we are truly concerned with his rehabilitation and reintegration in the community.

Historically, society has pursued three alternative courses with the mentally retarded offender: we have ignored his limitations and special needs; or we have sought to tailor traditional criminal law processes to fit them; we have grouped him with psychopaths, sociopaths, and sex deviates in a kind of conventicle of the outcast and hopeless. What is suggested here is a "fourth way," a way not of rejection and despair, but of acceptance and hope.

Reaction Comment

ROBERT J. GOLTEN

In 1966 Allen proposed a special system for the identified mentally retarded criminal suspect.[1] The prototype was the juvenile court system, with its *parens patriae* underpinning. Under the proposal, a threshold determination is somehow made as to whether a defendant is mentally retarded. If he is, informal proceedings are held to determine whether he committed the offense. Then, upon a finding of "guilt," and if also found to be "dangerous" to himself or others, he is committed to a special institution. The committing court is further empowered to establish a guardianship with broad powers over the retarded offender.

Allen candidly recognizes some unanswered questions, particularly with respect to the kind and number of facilities required for the mentally retarded offender. But he is sanguine about finding the answers, once the need to do so is made imperative.

Fox would reject such a specialized system. His antipathy toward it is based mostly on the fear that by isolating, and clearly focusing on, mentally retarded offenders, they will be more easily targeted for the deprivation, discrimination, and hostility too often their fate. On the other hand, Fox believes it is important to educate and "sensitize" the system to make special allowances and provisions for the exceptional offender. Thus, true to academic spirit, he would undertake "a thorough study" in order to identify those pressure points where not enough special consideration or awareness is given the retarded offender; he would establish a model that would compensate for these deficits; and he would analyze the "social risks" that might result from its implementation.

His proposal is suitably vague and inoffensive. Clearly, there is a need to identify the mentally retarded offender at the beginning and throughout his contact with

---

[1] Allen, *Toward an Exceptional Offenders Court*, 4 MENTAL RETARDATION 3, 5-6 (1966) (reprinted in part as an addendum to Allen's reaction comment, pp. 643-45 *supra*).

the criminal justice system and to afford him special protections. And one can quickly arrive at the kind of model that would make the sorts of allowances and special provisions which are required.

IDENTIFICATION

Upon a suspect's entry into the criminal justice system in the District of Columbia the D.C. Bail Agency (which acts as the court's screener in making bond recommendations) conducts narcotic analyses and attempts to detect problems of alcoholism and emotional illness in its offender-interviewees. This agency, and counterpart agencies in other courts, should be directed to undertake quick screenings for intellectual defect. Upon a tentative finding of a deficiency, the defendant would be subjected to a more thorough evaluation. If consistent with his pretrial bond status, this evaluation would be done on an outpatient basis.[2] On the other hand, if the defendant were denied pretrial release, the evaluation could be made promptly at a local detention facility or appropriate mental retardation institution. A standard determination of competency would be made: Does the offender know the nature of the proceeding and can he assist counsel in preparing a defense?

If found "incompetent," the mentally retarded offender should be promptly released or, if "dangerous" to himself or others, civilly committed to an appropriate institution.[3]

TRIAL

The defective offender who is not found incompetent[4] should be given special protection. First of all, the court should make special efforts to ensure that counsel is prepared to deal with the additional problems of the exceptional client. Perhaps a special proceedings panel of defense lawyers could be established to ensure that mentally ill or mentally defective defendants were provided with sophisticated counsel. A local public defender, such as the one in Washington, D.C., which has a mental health division, might be able to provide this specialized assistance by entering as co-counsel in the case.

Second, the prosecution would be obliged to open up its files more fully to counsel for the retarded offender (who is, by definition, less able to assist counsel).[5]

Third, purported confessions should receive the strictest scrutiny and the

[2] *Cf.* Marcey v. Harris, 400 F.2d 772, 774 (D.C. Cir. 1968).
[3] *See* Jackson v. Indiana, 406 U.S. 715, 738 (1972).
[4] The *incompetent* offender may be tried on the general issue ("did he do it?") with the understanding that a finding of "guilt" means only that the court can continue to exercise jurisdiction over him pending release or commitment, as stated. *See* People *ex rel.* Myers v. Briggs, 46 Ill. 2d 281, 263 N.E.2d 109 (1970).
[5] *Cf.* Wilson v. United States, 391 F.2d 460, 464 (D.C. Cir. 1968).

prosecution should be required to prove their validity beyond a reasonable doubt. There must be a knowing, intelligent, and truly voluntary waiver of the right to silence.

Finally, the fact finder (judge or jury) should hold the prosecution to an especially high burden of proof so as to exclude any hypothesis other than guilt.

DISPOSITION

If a trial determines a suspect's guilt, a special hearing should be held without a jury to determine whether the offender is so incapacitated as to be unable to form criminal intent. Experts would be called upon, perhaps not only as witnesses, but also as arbiters. Sophistication in decision making and uniformity in result might be facilitated by turning to a specialized panel of experts, such as the mental health commission used in the District of Columbia as an agent of the court in civil commitment cases.[6]

If lack of intent is found, then another determination should be made as to which nonpenal institution or community resource, if any, would lend itself to the offender's particular needs. If, on the other hand, a finding is made that sentence should be imposed (because the offender was capable of forming "criminal intent"), the individual should be specially classified to make clear and imperative to the correctional system the offender's special identity and problems.[7]

RELEASE

The mentally retarded offender who is "acquitted" because of incapacity, but then involuntarily consigned to a "treatment" facility, is entitled to, and should be provided, ongoing counsel (in the form of an appointed guardian or institutional ombudsman) who closely monitors his progress, protects his rights (*e.g.*, to habilitation), and urges his release whenever it can fairly be established that the client has been "rehabilitated" to the extent that he is not likely to jeopardize his own or the community's welfare.[8]

In short, the ideal model (which would be applicable to the mentally ill, as well as the mentally retarded, and indeed to other offenders with specialized problems such as alcoholism or drug addiction) would be: (1) immediate identification, through appropriate screening and testing devices at the entry point of the crim-

---

[6] D.C. CODE § 21-502 (1973).

[7] Of course, this presupposes the availability of (1) special community facilities and resources to deal with the problems of the retarded offender as well as (2) special facilities and resources *within* the prison setting for this category of convict.

[8] *Cf.* United States v. Simpson, 436 F.2d 162, 166-70 (D.C. Cir. 1970), *cert. denied*, 414 U.S. 873 (1973); Golten, *Role of Defense Counsel in the Criminal Commitment Process*, 10 AM. CRIM. L. REV. 385, 423-24 (1972).

inal justice system; (2) where retardation or deficiency falling short of incompetency is found, special counsel and broader pretrial discovery would be provided, there would be very strict surveillance by the court of purported "confessions," and a higher than normal burden of proof would be imposed on the prosecutor; (3) special disposition hearings after trial would be held if the defendant were found to have committed the offense, and appropriate classifications and diversions to specialized departments in the correctional systems would be made; and (4) special protections for the retarded inmate in the form of ongoing counsel to note and enforce his right to civilized confinement in the least restrictive alternative and to the earliest feasible release would be ensured.

The following case illustrates the problems faced by an attorney attempting to secure appropriate handling of a mentally retarded client. I recently represented a 30-year-old man who has an IQ of 57 (mild to moderate mental retardation). His record consisted of a 1961 assault, a 1962 attempted sexual assault, and then in 1966 again an attempted sexual assault. In the last offense, he was convicted and given a 4 — 12-year sentence. After five unproductive years in jail, it was determined in a habeas corpus action that he had been incompetent to stand trial. His prior conviction became a nullity.

The prosecution then tried to commit the man as a sexual psychopath. This route was ill-advised because he did not qualify as a sexual psychopath for various reasons, including a finding of "mental illness"[9] and the fact that he was charged with an offense (assault with intent to commit rape) that took him outside the statute.[10]

The prosecution, as a "holding" device, filed an appeal. It could not have invoked a civil commitment because the man was not mentally ill in the eyes of the psychiatrists at Saint Elizabeth's, the local (examining) mental hospital. There is a mental retardation statute that could have been tried, but it applied only to "non-acting out" retarded citizens. There was no proper pigeonhole.

The mentally retarded offender in the District of Columbia who is either incompetent or acquitted by view of his inability to form criminal intent has no place to go. He does not suffer from a "mental illness" and cannot be civilly committed (if incompetent) and if acquitted by reason of "insanity" could not be sent to a mental hospital.

The response to this vacuum has been to ignore the special problems of the retarded offender. This is what has happened in most places because of the lack of special community and institutional resources. The problem of inadequate rehabilitative and custodial resources lies at the crux of the criminal justice system and is dramatized clearly in the case of the mentally retarded offender.

[9] Millard v. Harris, 406 F.2d 964 (D.C. Cir. 1968).
[10] D.C. CODE § 22-3504(e) (1973).

CHAPTER 21

Cororrections

Editorial Introduction

Rowan's paper reviews the research conducted over the past decade on the lack of programing for mentally retarded offenders. She describes the current situation in which mentally retarded offenders receive little special education or counseling directed to their rehabilitation for community life. Correctional officials typically are frustrated by the obvious need for special attention among the mentally retarded. Official reaction, however, has not been to provide the needed special programs, but rather to despair and to delay in granting parole to individuals. Rowan documents the fact that the problem is not an insignificant one: The proportion of mentally retarded individuals in correctional institutions appears to be at least 7 to 9 percent nationally and as high as 30 percent in some states. The lack of responsive programs is demonstrated to be severe even in special institutions supposedly created for the specific purpose of providing rehabilitation to a broad category of "mentally disabled" persons.

Rowan also reports the recommendations made by recent studies. These include a number of steps aimed at alleviating this lack in the correctional system. The development of specialized programs and institutions for the mentally retarded offender is high on this list of recommendations. This preference arises as a consequence of the fact that retarded offenders receive the least appropriate programing of all inmates when placed in a general prison or mixed treatment center. Both general prison and regular institution placements for the mentally retarded are seen as being inappropriate for dealing with the problems of the mentally retarded offender. This preference for separate programing stands in contrast to recommendations of many contributors to this volume. In other papers, considerable emphasis is placed on eliminating special categorical distinctions between mentally retarded citizens and others.

Schwartz and Haywood, in their reactions, applaud Rowan's research review, but are sharply critical of the reported recommendations. Schwartz emphasizes Rowan's report that special institutions for "defective delinquents" have been the source of grave abuses and argues against further segregation of the mentally retarded offender. Schwartz is skeptical of society's ability and desire to provide truly rehabilitative treatment to offenders, whether mentally retarded or not. Haywood warns against the possibility of making mistakes similar to those made in segregated educational programs for the mentally retarded. Both Schwartz and Haywood emphasize the fact that most retarded offenders are only mildly retarded; they stress the dangers of overclassification and stigmatization. They both press for a reevaluation of prison programing and criticize the overuse of prisons in general.

PRINCIPAL PAPER

BEVERLY A. ROWAN

IN STATE PRISONS the proportion of individuals with low measured intelligence has been estimated at more than three times that in the general population.[1] Adding inability to function socially to intellectual disability, one-third of our country's prison population can be considered retarded.[2] Nevertheless, in most states appropriate institutional, probation, and other treatment resources for mentally retarded offenders do not exist, and these individuals receive little or none of the special rehabilitative care they need.

The care and treatment of mentally retarded offenders is one of the most consistently frustrating problems that confronts administrators of both correctional institutions and residential facilities for the retarded. Both types of facilities are geared to treat their predominant groups, and retarded offenders are misfits in both settings.

Mentally retarded individuals charged with, or convicted of, crimes have been committed to correctional institutions — as incompetent to stand trial or as insane — "until recovery" or "until sanity is restored."[3] In the case of mental retardation, there is little, if any, hope for recovery from the underlying condition. The most that can ordinarily be expected is a kind of social recovery in which the retarded individual becomes self-sufficient. But this "social recovery" anticipates appro-

---

[1] B. BROWN & T. COURTLESS, THE MENTALLY RETARDED OFFENDER (U.S. Dep't of Health, Education & Welfare, Pub. No. (HSM) 72-9039, 1971) [hereinafter cited as BROWN & COURTLESS].
[2] ACTION AGAINST MENTAL DISABILITY, THE REPORT OF THE PRESIDENT'S TASK FORCE ON THE MENTALLY HANDICAPPED 40 (1970).
[3] *But see* Jackson v. Indiana, 406 U.S. 715 (1972).

priate habilitation with adequate professional support, and retarded prisoners typically are confined to rural areas where it is difficult to find psychiatrists, psychologists, social workers, and other experts required to staff the necessary programs.

Recognition of mentally retarded offenders as a special group is only part of the battle. Awareness of the problem must be translated into programs designed to meet the particular needs of these individuals and into professional assistance essential to their reintegration into the mainstream of society.

Literature related to retarded offenders offers little concurrence, and there are vast differences of opinion as to definition, research methodology, interpretation of findings, and courses of action to be taken in coping with the problem. Although the Brown-Courtless survey estimated that the proportion of retarded prisoners across the United States was 9.5 percent.[4] an accurate determination of the percentage of criminal offenders who are actually mentally retarded is difficult to achieve because of the lack of clear guidelines for making estimates. Some institutions designate as retarded those people with IQs below 90; some, people with IQs below 85; some, below 80; and still others use IQ 75 or 70 as the cutoff point. Furthermore, tests defining mental retardation and its levels reflect some variation in IQ scores. For example, moderate mental retardation is said to be IQ 36-51 or IQ 40-54. Moreover, there is the very serious challenge to the use of intelligence tests for classifying people, and the open questioning of the meaning of any IQ score. This presents obvious difficulties for those who want to use these scores for either statistical or classification purposes.

Brown and Courtless discovered a bewildering array of tests used by institutions to measure intelligence, the most frequently employed being the Wechsler Intelligence Scale for Children (WISC) and the Wechsler Adult Intelligence Scale (WAIS).[5] Although about 75 percent of the institutions surveyed by Brown and Courtless reported that intelligence tests were administered by psychologists, it was found that other institutions used social workers, a few used classification officers, and 5 reported using inmates under the supervision of psychologists.[6]

Another distinction to be considered is that two basic categories of retardation are recognized, based on general etiology of the condition. Genetic retardation refers to a condition of organic or pathological origin; functional retardation refers to impairment of personal-social factors and involves elements of psychosocial or environmental deprivation. A score on the WISC or the WAIS does not permit the individual to be placed into either category; much additional information is required.

The results of any investigation should be examined in light of dissimilarities in testing situations among correctional and penal institutions across the country, including different IQ level definitions of mental retardation; the variety of instruments used to measure intelligence; the diversity of personnel employed to administer the tests; varying conditions under which the tests are administered; different stages of incarceration at which testing is conducted; and the validity of the test instrument in terms of the subject.

There have been two divergent views of mental retardation and crime: the

---

[4] BROWN & COURTLESS 25.
[5] *Id.* at 26.
[6] *Id.*

belief that every intellectually impaired person is a likely delinquent (prevalent about 50 years ago and still evident in the folklore of today) and the belief that mental retardation bears no causal relationship to crime. Both views are extreme and both have hindered effective action to solve the problems of retarded offenders.

Historically, three alternative courses have been pursued with respect to mentally retarded offenders: (1) their limitations and special needs have been ignored: (2) traditional criminal law processes have been twisted to fit their situations; or (3) they have been grouped with psychopaths, sociopaths, and sex deviants.

As early as 1894 workers in the field of mental retardation and criminal behavior were recommending separate legal and institutional handling of retarded offenders. Some saw segregation as a method of freeing society from the threat such people were thought to pose.[7] In 1906 J.W. Mulligan, a physician at the Illinois State Prison, suggested that separate institutions be developed to permit segregation of retarded offenders from ordinary offenders, not to provide the retarded with specialized treatment, but to ensure their segregation and commitment for life.[8] In 1912 H. H. Goddard, maintaining that penal institutions were inappropriate for the care of retarded offenders, asked the American Prison Association to recommend their segregation and transfer to more suitable facilities. It was his belief that at least two-thirds of these offenders came by their defects through heredity and that long-term colonization and segregation offered a partial solution to the problem.[9]

The first special facility established exclusively for defective delinquents in the United States was at Napanoch, New York, in 1921, where mentally defective male delinquents over 16 years of age were committed indefinitely. The program provided training, with an emphasis on industrial education and farming activities. Parole was possible, and 70 percent of those paroled were successful in adjusting to life outside the institution.[10] The Massachusetts State Farm at Bridgewater, a similar institution, opened in 1922. It provided treatment in the form of education, recreation, and industrial training within the framework of rigid discipline.[11] From the early 1920s through the 1950s, as a result of the belief that defective delinquents exerted a bad influence on ordinary delinquents, more and more demands were made for separate facilities to provide basic custodial care for retarded delinquents. In summary, until the 1960s, mentally retarded offenders were the subject either of intensely value-laden pressure for segregation or of total neglect by the correctional system. Little in the way of rehabilitative programing was provided.

Much of the recently renewed interest in mental retardation and criminal behavior has been generated by the legal community rather than criminologists. The American Bar Foundation, in 1961, published a study on the legal aspects of

---

[7] Clark, *The Relation of Imbecility to Pauperism and Crime,* 10 THE ARENA 788, 791 (1894). Martha Clark wrote that only by special segregation could society be free from the threat posed by the mentally retarded.

[8] Mulligan, *Mental Defectives Among Prisoners,* in PROCEEDINGS OF THE AMERICAN PRISON ASSOCIATION (1906).

[9] Goddard, *Feeblemindedness and Crime,* in PROCEEDINGS OF THE AMERICAN PRISON ASSOCIATION (1912).

[10] S. DAVIES, SOCIAL CONTROL OF THE MENTALLY DEFICIENT 138-43 (1930).

[11] *Id.* at 134-36.

mental disability,[12] and in the same year the late President John F. Kennedy appointed a panel of physicians, attorneys, scientists, judges, mental retardation professionals, and civic leaders to review the field of retardation. The report of the Task Force on Law of the President's Panel focused attention on the advisability of incarceration of mentally retarded offenders in correctional institutions and concluded that prisons in the United States were not able to provide special programs for inmates with significantly impaired intellectual ability.[13]

The current trend in correctional systems is to create a combined special handling category which includes certain sex offenders, psychopaths or sociopaths, and the mentally ill, together with the mentally retarded. This grouping is commonly referred to by some variation of the term "defective delinquent." Following criminal conviction, offenders falling into this broad category are, in most instances, subjected to a civil hearing and psychiatric examination to determine their eligibility for commitment to a specialized facility. A number of these facilities has been established in the United States within the last few years. Although their basic purpose is supposed to be specialized treatment, they have been subjected to increasing criticism.

Many state correctional systems have taken some minimal steps during the last 10 years to provide mentally retarded offenders with rehabilitation programing, but the meaningfulness or effectiveness of this "specialized" treatment remains open to considerable doubt.

RESEARCH AND RECOMMENDATIONS ON PROGRAMS FOR THE MENTALLY RETARDED OFFENDER

The Juvenile and Youthful Offender

Few retarded children who get into trouble with the law are severely or profoundly retarded. Some are moderately retarded, but the majority are either mildly retarded or near the borderline of ordinary intelligence.[14]

Although disposition of adult criminal offenders is often based primarily on the offense committed, the emphasis in juvenile court is supposed to be on the needs of the individual child. Thus, the philosophy of individualized justice is particularly relevant for the retarded juvenile delinquent.

Typically, a juvenile court judge seeks placement in an institution for the mentally retarded. In many states, however, he must first obtain permission from the institution to which commitment is sought, and the institutions are generally overcrowded already. Moreover, they are often reluctant to accept an individual who, in addition to being viewed as mentally retarded, is seen as a delinquent. Thus,

---

[12] THE MENTALLY DISABLED AND THE LAW (F. Lindman & D. McIntyre eds. 1961).
[13] PRESIDENT'S PANEL ON MENTAL RETARDATION, REPORT OF THE TASK FORCE ON LAW (1963).
[14] F. Dennis, The Mentally Retarded Public Offender and the Law, 1971 (Governor's Interdepartmental Committee on Mental Retardation, Tennessee).

failing an agreement among various agencies dealing with juvenile problems, it often is impossible to place children in these facilities. A judge may attempt commitment through the probate court, but in most instances this court has no more authority than the juvenile court to commit without approval of the designated institution. Foster home placement may be sought, but such placement is not easily accomplished. There is a reluctance to place mentally retarded children in institutions for delinquents, because they are easily victimized and exploited by their more intelligent peers; nevertheless, this is most frequently the placement finally chosen.[15]

The George Washington University Institute of Law, Psychiatry, and Criminology undertook a three-year study of both juvenile and adult retarded offenders in several states across the country from 1966 to 1969.[16] The study indicated that the handling of retarded juvenile offenders in five representative states demonstrates the mutual ineffectiveness of juvenile courts in placing retarded children in appropriate programs.

Even in those few states where transfer from correctional facilities to institutions for the mentally retarded is possible, the latter facilities are severely overcrowded, and there are extended waiting periods for admission. These waiting periods present peculiar problems, even assuming that admission is appropriate and can finally be accomplished. Some mentally retarded juveniles adjust fairly well in the correctional setting. If a child is functioning adequately and receiving some kind of academic and vocational training, the correctional facility is reluctant to transfer him out as retarded; and the child, having spent five or six months at such a facility, where the average length of stay is eight months, may react adversely to prospect of being transferred. Juvenile facilities in some states are sympathetic to this reaction, particularly in view of the fact that transfer to an institution for the retarded may result in a lifetime commitment. Thus, the application for transfer is often either withdrawn or not pursued, and the child is released to the community upon expiration of his original commitment.

Juvenile courts should be empowered to commit any child to the program or institution best suited to his needs, with some checks to prevent judges from erroneously labeling problem children as retarded and having them inappropriately committed to retardation facilities. Some middle ground must be reached between total arbitrary placement authority for juvenile courts and total admissions discretion for institutions for the mentally retarded. Otherwise, retarded juveniles will continue to suffer the grave inadequacies of a system that permits their exclusion from any appropriate rehabilitation programing.

If state institutions for the retarded are to remain virtually closed to juvenile offenders, alternative handling or placement must be sought. Possibilities include probation, probation augmented by remedial training, or placement in training schools for children with learning problems.

In order to compare youthful offenders of different intellectual achievement levels, more than 1,000 boys between the ages of 15 and 18 assigned to Tennessee

---

[15] E. Ferster & T. Courtless, All Men Are Not Created Equal, 1971 (unpublished manuscript, Washington, D.C.).

[16] *Id.*

institutions for delinquent youths were the subjects of a recent study in that state.[17] The results of this study demonstrate the importance of differential programing for mentally retarded juvenile offenders.[18]

The boys were placed in one of three categories: intellectually average or above; borderline; and mentally retarded. Through a series of personality probes, a number of variables was tested. It was found that mentally retarded youthful offenders have lower estimates of themselves than their more intellectually advantaged delinquent peers. The mentally retarded delinquents showed themselves to be more concerned about what they are, about their worth in relation to other people, and about their social interactions with others. Even after controlling for differences in intelligence, self-concept was an important variable in accounting for differences in both the institutional behavior and academic achievement of boys in the group. The higher the individual's self-concept, the less likely he was to become a disciplinary problem in the institution and the more likely he was to score higher on academic achievement tests.[19]

The data indicated that mentally retarded juvenile delinquents were more concerned about ease and comfort than about opportunity to learn. Also, the more intellectually disadvantaged youths tended to look to others for approval, judgment, and evaluation of their behavior, rather than to themselves. Mentally retarded offenders were much more likely to see what happened to them not as a result of their own actions, but as a result of chance or the whims of others. (This may be a very accurate perception.) Their conception of what happened to them as a result of their own behavior was not clear. Therefore, the issue of individual responsibility needs to be much more emphasized in the training of these youths.[20]

It was found that the disciplinary system at the state school was largely negative, and that the mentally subaverage boys bore the brunt of this system since they were the most disruptive and the most frequently disciplined. This provided systematic negative reinforcement within the correctional institution, which only served to accentuate the underlying emotional problems of these children.[21] Both the mentally retarded and borderline groups exhibited inadequate attentional skills and were more easily flustered and confused than the average group. It was concluded that social training at the state school was not equally effective for subgroups within the total population and that it was least effective with respect to the mentally retarded.[22]

Examination of school records revealed that delinquent boys in general were behind in academic achievement and that the borderline and retarded groups were even further behind. Conduct ratings differed significantly among the three groups

[17] F. Dennis, The Retarded Juvenile Offender Research and Demonstration Project, 1971 (Tennessee Department of Correction).

[18] Using IQ 69 as the upper limit of mental retardation, approximately 28 percent of the boys in Tennessee's correctional institutions score in the borderline retarded range; 9 percent score as mildly retarded; only a very few score in the severely retarded range. Department of Correction & Kennedy Center for Research on Education and Human Development, Our House, 1973 (A Report to Tennessee about the Mentally Retarded Juvenile Offender Project, Tennessee).

[19] F. Dennis, *supra* note 17, at 8.

[20] *Id.* at 9-10.

[21] *Id.* at 11-12.

[22] *Id.* at 12.

of boys, and these differences appeared as early as the first grade. Retarded boys in the sample consistently received more unsatisfactory conduct ratings than did boys from the other two groups, not only in the first grade, but in grades two and three as well. It was found that only 17 percent of the retarded and borderline groups had ever been placed in special education classes while attending public school. Thus, they were presented with a picture of progressive failure and alienation within the school system, culminating only after final removal from school despite numerous indications, some as early as the first grade, that special training was strongly indicated.[23]

Very few of the boys in any of the groups had ever been placed in alternative community programs; yet, as a total group they averaged more than one commitment to correctional institutions. Boys in the borderline group had been committed to the correctional system significantly more frequently than members of the other two groups.[24] The family variables examined indicated a high degree of cultural deprivation in the homes of delinquent boys, and this finding was accentuated for the two retarded groups.

It was the conclusion of the study group that a vast number of mentally retarded youths who would otherwise become juvenile offenders could avoid this fate if they acquired sufficient skills to meet the complexities of daily living and thus experience the rewards that community life has to offer.

In 1970, the Tennessee Legislative Council Committee recommended that, whenever feasible, care and treatment of mentally retarded offenders be provided in the community in cooperation with federal, state, and local agencies. "Our House" was a nonresidential community program developed in response to these recommendations. It was designed for boys with below-average IQ scores who had been sentenced to correctional institutions.[25] It offered a relatively effective way of rehabilitating boys while they lived at home instead of in an artificial institutional environment.

The program sought the most effective methods of teaching the boys academic and social skills while keeping them out of court. Building self-image was considered a prerequisite to teaching the boys how to learn that they could control what happened to them. Therefore, punishment tactics that undermine self-image and reduce performance were avoided by the staff.

One of the major functions of Our House was to instill self-confidence in the boys by building up their sense of success to the point that they were able to decide for themselves that they wanted to reenter the mainstream of society. The intent of the program was to emphasize all accomplishments and achievements, including improvements in behavior. Several assumptions were made: rules should be few and simple; appropriate behavior should be approved promptly; inappropriate behavior should be ignored; dangerous or destructive behavior should be interrupted and disapproved; self-confidence ensures a greater likelihood of success; and anyone can

[23] *Id.* at 12-14.
[24] *Id.* at 15.
[25] Department of Correction & Kennedy Center for Research on Education and Human Development, *supra* note 18.

be taught what he needs to know if it is broken down into very small sequential steps.[26]

Research data are presently being collected and analyzed to determine the effectiveness of Our House. Although funding for this unique program ended May 31, 1973, the results of the initial research analysis have encouraged proposed legislation that would establish other projects based on this model.

Another important project is a study that was done relative to all juvenile offenders received as new admissions by the Texas Youth Council during the 1969-70 fiscal year.[27] Of the 1,491 males for whom full-scale IQ scores existed, 192, or 13 percent, were determined to have scores of lower than 70; 58.3 percent of these males classified as retarded were black Americans, 32.3 percent were Latin Americans, and 9.4 percent were Anglo-Americans.[28] The most common offense committed by both retarded and nonretarded children was burglary. Finally, 24.6 percent of the nonretarded and 33.8 percent of the retarded had never attended school.[29]

Of the 175 females for whom full-scale IQ scores were available, 29, or 16.6 percent, had scores of lower than 70; 44.8 percent of those classified as retarded were black Americans, 41.4 percent were Latin Americans, and 13.8 percent were Anglo-Americans.[30] The most common offense for both retarded and nonretarded girls was running away from home. Twenty-four percent of the nonretarded and 31 percent of the retarded had never attended school.[31]

These studies and programs suggest that unjustified attitudes which advocate reliance on maximum security strategies for retarded juvenile offenders should be reevaluated. Programs in institutional care systems can be appropriately tailored to the needs of the retarded and borderline retarded by the use of carefully drawn and individualized behavioral objectives and educational programs, precision teaching techniques, positive reinforcement systems, token economy systems, and guided group interaction. The assumption that retarded children cannot be habilitated or rehabilitated as effectively as their more intelligent peers must be abandoned.

In 1969, the South Carolina Department of Corrections completed a survey of prisoners between the ages of 17 and 21.[32] From a population of 374 inmates in this age range, 131 tested in the retarded range.[33]

A primary concern facing the South Carolina judicial system, as in most states, has been what to do with retarded youthful offenders coming before the court. There are no facilities for retarded offenders at the three residential centers in South Carolina, and these young offenders are housed by various agencies in the state, such as state hospitals, county work gangs, and retardation centers. Retarded youthful

[26] *Id.* at 7-12.
[27] D. Kirkpatrick & J. Haskins, The Mentally Retarded Youthful Offender, A Preliminary Statistical Summary, 1971 (Texas Department of Mental Health and Mental Retardation).
[28] *Id.* at 3. *See* Sorgen, Chapter 8 of this volume, concerning the cultural bias that results from the use of standardized tests to label individuals as mentally retarded.
[29] Kirkpatrick & Haskins, *supra* note 27, at 3-8.
[30] *Id.* at 14.
[31] *Id.* at 14-16.
[32] W. Fries & S. LaBelle, File Y:35-83:0, A Plan for the Youthful Mentally Retarded Offender, 1969 (South Carolina Department of Mental Retardation).
[33] *Id.* at 6.

offenders initially were being sent to correctional schools, and it was only after such placement and preliminary testing that the nature of their disability became known. Even if the courts had had knowledge of their mental retardation prior to disposition of the cases, with the limited availability of special units on the grounds of the retardation centers, it is still questionable whether specialized services geared to their particular needs could have been provided. In many cases it was found that the courts did have such knowledge and became frustrated at their inability to find appropriate care and services for these offenders, many of whom were returned to the community on probation.[34]

The study group made the following recommendations:

> Organically impaired retarded offenders should be treated in mental retardation institutions, and culturally or socially deprived individuals, in correctional schools.[35]
>
> Special units for the care of youthful retarded offenders should be established on the grounds of residential centers for the retarded under the administration of the department of mental retardation. For a youthful offender to be assigned to such a unit, he would have to be evaluated as retarded and, in the court's opinion, require confinement. After referral by the court to the department of mental retardation, the individual's care, treatment, control, and disposition (including release) should be the sole responsibility of the retardation center. It was felt that courts, at disposition, should utilize local resources, such as special education classes, sheltered workshops, vocational rehabilitation, foster homes, and half-way houses.[36]
>
> In the event youthful retarded offenders are placed in these specialized units, they should be placed as retarded children and not as delinquents. Periodic evaluations should be undertaken in order to ascertain the development and effectiveness of rehabilitation programs, and the extent to which individualized programs are meeting the specific needs of each resident.
>
> After-care units should work with the parents of retarded offenders during treatment, prepare them for discharge of their children, and work with them after discharge. This unit should also obtain the help of other agencies, such as mental health, vocational rehabilitation, public welfare and public health. It was suggested that the youngsters and their families be followed for a minimum of one year after discharge.[37]

The Adult Offender

Using the American Association on Mental Deficiency's criteria for mental retardation, including an IQ of 69 as the upper limit of the mentally retarded range. the Brown-Courtless survey of all federal and state prisons in the United States found that 9.5 percent of the prison population could be classified as mentally retarded.[38] Impairment in adaptive behavior, the second element of the association's criteria, was inferred from the fact of institutionalization for antisocial behavior.

Of a sample of 500 males received and tested by the Texas Department of Cor-

---

[34] *Id.* at 5-7.

[35] *Id.* at 5-13. It may be important to determine the racial impact of distinguishing between "organically impaired" retarded individuals and those who are "culturally deprived."

[36] *Id.*

[37] *Id.*

[38] *A Manual on Terminology and Classification in Mental Retardation,* 64 AM. J. MENTAL DEFICIENCY (1959) (monograph supplement to vol. 64 no. 2, Sept. 1959).

rections during December 1970 and January 1971, 35 individuals, or 7 percent, were determined to have IQ scores below 70. Of those men scoring above 70, 25.8 percent scored between 70 and 84.[39]

In the Brown-Courtless study, the proportion of incarcerated offenders with measured IQs below 70 varied sharply with geographical region. For example, Kentucky. Tennessee, Alabama, and Mississippi had the highest proportion of retarded individuals in their prison systems — at 24.3 percent; following closely were Arkansas, Louisiana, Oklahoma, and Texas, with 20.6 percent of their prison population scoring as retarded; a low percentage was obtained among Washington, Oregon, California, Alaska, and Hawaii, which had 5.4 percent; and the lowest percentage was found in Montana, Idaho, Wyoming, Colorado, New Mexico, Utah, and Nevada, where only 2.6 percent of the prisoners had IQ scores below 70.[40]

For the Brown-Courtless investigation, questionnaires were mailed to all adult and juvenile penal and correctional institutions, other than diagnostic reception centers, in the United States correctional camps and farms, work houses, and detention facilities.[41] The goal of the study was to obtain data regarding the intelligence of incarcerated adult and juvenile offenders in the United States, together with information concerning offense patterns, management problems, and treatment programs affecting inmates with low reported intelligence. Responses were received from 80 percent of the institutions surveyed, housing some 200,000 serious criminal offenders. An intensive follow-up of a sample by psychologists indicated that on ca eful retesting. 75 percent of those inmates designated as retarded, based on institutional criteria, scored below IQ 70.

Thirty-eight percent of the institutions surveyed ranked breaking and entering and burglary as the offenses most frequently committed by mentally retarded offenders, whereas about 13 percent reported homicide as the most common offense. The category of crimes least frequently reported as the most common offenses was that of rape and other sexual offenses recorded (in 5 percent of all institutions responding). Property offenses (larceny, breaking and entering, burglary) were by far the most commonly committed offenses by inmates with low reported intelligence. Homicide was reported as more frequently committed by retarded prisoners than nonretarded segments of the institutional populations. It should be remembered that crimes reported in this survey related only to offenses committed by retarded prisoners and do not justify any generalizations made to the rank ordering of criminal offenses committed by retarded individuals in the total distribution of crimes committed in the United States.[42]

More than half (56 percent) of the institutions responding to a request to supply information relative to ongoing programs specifically designed for the retarded reported that no specialized programs of any kind were available. Only six institutions provided a full range of individual and group psychotherapy, as well as academic,

---

[39] D. Kirkpatrick, J. Haskins & C. Friel, The Mentally Retarded Adult Felon, A Preliminary Statistical Summary, 1971 (Texas Department of Mental Health and Mental Retardation).
[40] BROWN & COURTLESS 26-27.
[41] BROWN & COURTLESS.
[42] *Id.* at 27-28.

vocational, and special education programs. Of all institutions providing some special programs for the retarded, special and/or vocational education was the most frequently reported.[43]

A significant factor in the general lack of specialized programing for mentally retarded inmates was the lack of mental health manpower resources available to responding institutions. One hundred sixty-six institutions replied to questions concerning the numbers of psychiatrists and psychologists employed by them on a full-time or part-time basis. Six of these were specialized facilities for emotionally disturbed and/or mentally retarded offenders. These six special facilities, housing 6,825 inmates, employed 40 of 54 full-time psychiatrists and 11 of 93 full-time psychologists, whereas the other 160 institutions, housing 146,662 inmates, employed a total of only 14 full-time psychiatrists and 82 full-time psychologists.[44] The standards of the American Correctional Association provide that for each 600 inmates there should be 1 psychiatrist, 3 clinical psychologists, 3 case workers, and 4 counselors.[45]

An attempt was made to elicit data regarding the number of specially trained educational personnel who worked exclusively or primarily with retarded inmates. Unfortunately, the responding institutions reported all types of educational personnel, including inmates acting as teachers, so that it was impossible to arrive at a meaningful finding regarding this important aspect of institutional programing. However, the single most significant finding was that more than half the responding institutions offered *no* special programs of any kind.[46]

The Alabama Board of Corrections in 1972 surveyed its own correctional system, as well as others across the country, to determine the number of mental health personnel employed in these systems.[47] These findings strongly confirm those of the Brown-Courtless study. The need is highlighted when applying the American Correctional Association standards to the Alabama system, which houses a total of 4,048 prisoners. The Alabama study found that there were no psychiatrists or social workers, and only two psychologists[48] employed in the entire correctional system.[49] Although there is a high degree of interstate variability concerning mental health and retardation services, it is a safe general statement that the number of mental health and rehabilitation professionals presently employed in most correctional systems is abysmally substandard.[50]

The Brown-Courtless study sent follow-up questionnaires to each responding institution housing at least 1 inmate with an IQ lower than 55. These questionnaires were used to obtain supplementary information specifically geared to those offenders who were most clearly and significantly mentally retarded. Data were obtained on

---

[43] *Id.* at 28.

[44] *Id.* at 28-29.

[45] American Correctional Association, Minimum Mental Health Standards for Correctional Institutions (1967).

[46] *Id.* at 29.

[47] R. Fowler, Minimum Mental Health Standards for the Alabama Correctional System, 1972 (Alabama Board of Corrections).

[48] Although two psychologists are indicated, this figure represents one psychologist, one part-time consultant not employed by the correctional department, and another part-time consultant paid by the department.

[49] R. Fowler, *supra* note 47, at 10.

[50] *Id.* at 12-14.

964 adult offenders with reported IQs below 55 located in 26 different institutions.[51]

About 57 percent of those prisoners scoring below IQ 55 had been incarcerated for crimes against the person, including homicide, assault, and sexual offenses. However, the most frequent offense category for which they were committed was burglary/breaking and entering, which accounted for about 29 percent of all offenses. Interpretation of these findings regarding intelligence and criminal offense is difficult. The study group hypothesized that retarded offenders sentenced for criminal homicide might have been relatively easy to convict and might tend to remain in institutions for longer periods than those committed for other offenses. It was also believed that parole practices and policies for the retarded are more restrictive than for other offenders.[52]

Institutions were asked to report on any psychiatric or medical diagnoses made as a result of special testing or examination of inmates with IQs under 55. It was found that in only 11 of the more than 900 cases was such additional testing done and reported in the survey. Penal and correctional institutions did not frequently administer supplemental tests and examinations to inmates with low reported intelligence, instead they usually performed only routine admission examinations.[53]

Management Problems and Practices

Special attention was given in the Brown-Courtless study to penal administrators' problems and practices in managing mentally retarded inmates and their recommendations for appropriate handling and treatment strategies. The most common problem regarding management of the retarded was that they required constant and individual staff attention. Staffing arrangements were often stretched to the limit, and retarded inmates required an undue amount of staff time, thus taking away essential personnel service from the larger, nonretarded segments of the institutional populations. The second most frequent problem was that the retarded were often victims of exploitation by their more intelligent peers. Each of the responding institutions housed a minority of inmates who could be classed as mentally retarded. In attempting to manage and treat this minority with the manpower and physical resources available, prison administrators were faced with the possible consequences of inadequately covering the majority of their populations. Some institutions reported that they realized mentally retarded offenders often had difficulty in comprehending what was expected to them in terms of institutional rules and regulations, but that it was not possible to apply separate criteria. Thus, the rule violation rate among mentally retarded inmates was substantially higher than among other offenders. The very limited resources available to most prison systems could not be stretched to provide meaningful programs to both intellectually normal and retarded inmates, and the result was long-term custodial care for the retarded.[54]

From 1966 to 1969 a follow-up study to the Brown-Courtless survey was conduct-

[51] BROWN & COURTLESS 29-30.
[52] *Id.* at 30.
[53] *Id.* at 31.
[54] *Id.* at 31-33.

ed by the George Washington University Institute of Law, Psychiatry, and Criminology.[55] The study group selected adult correctional institutions in Colorado, Florida, Illinois, Maryland, Missouri, and Virginia for a further study of the characteristics of mentally retarded prisoners. The study used a field worker experienced in prison record systems and a clinical psychologist, who were sent to each of these states. The mentally retarded were found to be older and more poorly educated than the nonretarded, and there was a higher percentage of blacks among the retarded. The retarded had spent an average of 6.9 years in adult prisons, compared to 3.9 years for the nonretarded.[56]

There was often significant disparity in IQ scores between the test given on admission to the institutions and that administered by the study psychologist. The study group concluded, however, that institutional testing was a fairly reliable indicator of mental retardation. The subjects were poorly educated, came from lower socioeconomic backgrounds, and included a greater than average proportion of non-Caucasians. These are precisely the individuals who are at their greatest disadvantage in taking paper-and-pencil tests, where reading skills, comprehension, and some ability to conceptualize the demands of the test are required.[57]

It was also found that a significantly higher proportion of retarded inmates had been convicted of violent crimes against the person than had the general prison population. It was pointed out, in connection with this finding, however, that only a small proportion of mentally retarded citizens are arrested for breaking the law; however, when they are arrested, they are more likely to confess, easier to convict, and less likely to be paroled than nonretarded offenders.

The study concluded that even if effective mechanisms existed to identify significantly impaired persons in the criminal trial process, resources do not exist to ensure appropriate differential treatment.

The Mentally Retarded Offender Within United States Correctional Institutions

In 1972 the Texas Department of Mental Health and Mental Retardation undertook a survey to provide follow-up information regarding the study by Brown and Courtless and the effect of intervening programs on correctional systems in the United States.[58] Questionnaires were directed to each of the 50 states and the district of Columbia. Forty-three correctional systems responded, representing 81.2 percent of the total United States state prison population[59] and 84.3 percent of the original 51 correctional systems in the sample.

All 43 systems responded to a question concerning the use of psychometric intel-

---

[55] E. Ferster & T. Courtless, *supra* note 15.

[56] *Id.* at 385.

[57] *Id.* at 348.

[58] D. Kirkpatrick & J. Haskins, The Mentally Retarded Offender within U.S. Correctional Institutions, 1972 (Texas Department of Mental Health and Mental Retardation).

[59] NATIONAL PRISONER STATISTICS BULLETIN, PRISONERS IN STATE AND FEDERAL INSTITUTIONS FOR ADULT FELONS 1967 (U.S. Dep't of Justice, Bureau of Prisons, No. 44, July 1969).

ligence probes as part of initial diagnostic procedures. Only two systems indicated that they did not conduct any form of intelligence testing as a routine part of their initial processing. Two other states conducted testing, but employed general aptitude or personality inventory probes instead of intelligence tests.[60]

Two items in the survey inventory were designed to assess the manner in which intelligence tests were routinely administered and scored or interpreted, and responsive data were obtained from 39 of the sample systems. Custodial or correctional officers administered tests in two states, but were not involved in scoring or interpretation. Professionally trained staff members administered examinations in 30 states, and scored/interpreted the results in 38. Outside consultants administered tests in four systems, and functioned in the scoring and interpretation role in seven. Inmate assistants conducted examinations under direct professional staff supervision in eight diagnostic programs, and in six states without reported direct supervision. Inmates participated in test scoring and/or interpretation in seven states, and were employed for administration and scoring of group tests in two. Thus, professional staff members and/or trained outside consultants were utilized in administering nearly 77 percent of all testing and in more than 97 percent of all scoring and analysis.[61]

All 43 responding state level systems provided data concerning the manner in which prisoners identified as mentally retarded were handled within the institutions. Retarded offenders were not segregated from the general prison population in 29 of the states. Of these 29 systems, one indicated that a separate facility for the mentally retarded and the mentally ill was under construction; another indicated that the retarded were placed in "protective assignments to minimize abuse by other inmates"; a third reported a separate facility under construction which will house mentally retarded and physically handicapped offenders. In five of the responding systems, retarded inmates were segregated from the general prison population for work assignments only. In one they were segregated for work and housing, but otherwise retained in the general population, transferred to state hospitals for the mentally ill which have facilities for criminals, or transferred to state mental retardation schools if their IQ scores were below 50. Retarded offenders were transferred to special care facilities for the retarded or otherwise mentally defective offenders in only three reporting states.[62]

One study question was addressed to the importance placed on intelligence test results by each of the responding correctional systems, and usable data were obtained from 41 states. Intelligence quotients were not used in any initial classification decision by two reporting systems; in fewer than 50 percent of the decisions, by 17; in more than 50 percent of the decisions, by 12; and in every decision, by 10.[63]

Thirty-nine state systems provided meaningful data relative to the types of decisions upon which individual IQ scores have some bearing. Intelligence test results were reportedly utilized for work and job assignments in 36 states; housing assign-

[60] D. Kirkpatrick & J. Haskins, *supra* note 58, at § 4.3.

[61] *Id.* § 4.4.

[62] *Id.* § 4.5.

[63] *Id.* § 4.6.

ments in 2; custody and/or security grade assignments in 9; assignments to rehabilitative programs in 29; and educational program assignments in 36. They were also used to make assignments to group counseling in one state; to make assignments to vocational training and work release programs in another; and in inmate disciplinary hearings in a third.[64]

Sample correctional systems were asked to indicate the availability of treatment programs for the mentally retarded in the three principal areas of vocational rehabilitation, education, and psychological adjustment, and 39 provided usable data. Group special education programs were reportedly provided in 27 systems; programed instruction, individualized psychotherapy, and special vocational rehabilitation in 11 systems; individualized special education in 16; group psychotherapy in 9; and operant conditioning in 3. Four of the responding agencies indicated that they had no correctional treatment programs designed for, or available to, mentally retarded offenders.[65]

Since borderline retarded offenders constituted a large percentage of the 1963 national prison population,[66] another survey item was addressed to determining the number of correctional systems extending their specialized treatment programs to these individuals. Usable data were provided by 34 of the sample states. Specialized treatment programs were reportedly made available to borderline offenders in 26 of the responding systems, and one additional state indicated that such a program will be provided in the near future.[67]

Representative admissions data indicated that 4.1 percent of the current adult male offenders entering correctional facilities were mentally retarded; 18 percent were borderline.[68]

DEFECTIVE DELINQUENT STATUTES AND INSTITUTIONS

Several states have enacted legislation, commonly referred to as defective delinquent statutes, under which mentally deficient persons who commit crimes or who evidence a propensity toward the commission of crimes are subject to involuntary hospitalization. The first such legislation was enacted in Massachusetts in 1911.[69] Many of the legally formulated definitions of defective delinquents relate primarily to the notion of sexual psychopathology,[70] as it was for many years believed that sex

---

[64] *Id.* § 4.7.
[65] *Id.* § 4.8.
[66] BROWN & COURTLESS.
[67] D. Kirkpatrick & J. Haskins, *supra* note 58, at § 4.9.
[68] *Id.* § 4.10.
[69] Ch. 595, §§ 1-12 [1911] Acts & Resolves of Mass. 617; *repealed,* ch. 888, § 4 [1970] Acts & Resolves of Mass. 835. For a history of the amendments and revisions to the statutes, see MASS. ANN. LAWS ch. 123 §§ 113-24 (1965).
[70] *See, e.g.,* CAL. WELF. & INST. CODE § 6300 (1972).

crimes were committed by individuals demonstrating varying degrees of mental disability.

Sentencing under defective delinquent statutes, which is in lieu of the sentence provided by the regular criminal code, is usually for an indeterminate period. Release is usually predicated on a medical finding that the prisoner is cured or fully recovered and is no longer a psychopath or that he has improved sufficiently to be no longer dangerous to others. A common procedure is to place the individual on probation prior to granting him a complete discharge.

The Maryland defective delinquent statute and the Patuxent Institution, through which it operates, have been the subject of various articles written by individuals responsible for it, as well as by outside researchers. This experience may provide some insight into the effectiveness of this approach to dealing with mentally retarded offenders.

The Maryland statute was enacted in 1951. It defines a defective delinquent as

> an individual who, by the demonstration of persistent aggravated antisocial or criminal behavior, evidences a propensity toward criminal activity, and who is found to have either such intellectual deficiency or emotional unbalance, or both, as to clearly demonstrate an actual danger to society so as to require such confinement and treatment, when appropriate, as may make it reasonably safe for society to terminate the confinement and treatment.[71]

The Maryland statute provided for the establishment of the Patuxent Institution as a specialized facility designed to treat dangerous offenders who are emotionally disturbed and/or mentally retarded, not mentally retarded offenders alone. Patuxent utilizes the indeterminate sentence. The legislative research report on the statute was clear in its intent, giving as the primary purpose of the legislation the protection of society, with treatment of the individual being only secondary.[72]

Under the Maryland statute, only the courts can refer individuals to Patuxent after conviction and sentence. They refer for evaluation those whom they suspect might be defective delinquents, and the professional staff at Patuxent examines these individuals and makes recommendations for commitment. The court does not automatically accept the findings of the Patuxent staff, but commits only those persons found to be defective delinquents after court hearings. Of the 1,163 fully evaluated individuals recommended by the staff for commitment between January 5, 1955, and September 30, 1972, 187, or 16 percent, were found not to be defective delinquents and were not committed.[73]

Patuxent uses a graded tier system, which is a four-level system for developing behavioral controls. New inmates, with some exceptions, start at Level 1 and work their way to Level 4. Promotions within the graded tier system, earned by demonstrated cooperation with the goals of the institution, theoretically lead to more

[71] MD. ANN. CODE art. 31B, § 5 (1971).
[72] Research Division of the Maryland Legislative Council, An Indeterminate Sentence Law for Defective Delinquents, Dec. 1950 (Research Report No. 29, Governor's Commission to Study Medico-Legal Psychiatry).
[73] H. Boslow, Maryland's Defective Delinquent Statute, A Progress Report, Jan. 9, 1973, at 13 (Maryland Department of Public Safety and Correctional Services).

personal responsibility for behavior and decreasing levels of supervision and control. To be considered for leave or parole, an individual must have reached the third or fourth level and demonstrated his ability to adjust and improve while on these higher levels. Initially, retarded inmates were excluded from promotion to the fourth level. Some consideration was given to the development of a separate unit for the mentally retarded within the institution, but practical management considerations prevented implementation of the idea.[74]

In 1965 the director of Patuxent Institution undertook a study of the retarded segment of his population. At that time 27 percent of the population had IQs below 79; today the proportion of retarded prisoners is still approximately 27 percent.[75] The retarded were somewhat older than their nonretarded fellows, and the majority were urban blacks. Of the total retarded population at Patuxent, there were twice as many blacks as whites, just the reverse of the nonretarded population.[76]

According to the director, retarded individuals generally fare as well as the nonretarded in the graded tier system. This would seem to contradict another statement by the director that the retarded have a greater number of disciplinary problems, with the result that a higher percentage of their group is on the first level. It was also reported in the study that the retarded were discriminated against initially in that they were not even entitled to consideration for the upper tiers, which in turn automatically excluded them from eligibility for leave or parole. This was because it was "feared" by the staff (this staff allegedly educated in the particular problems of the mentally retarded and qualified to offer their expertise in this specialized area of corrections) that the retarded could not be rehabilitated and would never get out of Patuxent.

According to the director, each individual committed to Patuxent undergoes medical, psychiatric, psychological, and social service evaluations, as well as evaluations of his educational and vocational needs. With this information a treatment program is established around the combined educational, vocational, and psychotherapeutic needs of the individual.[77]

Prisoners at Patuxent are assigned to one of four treatment units, each of which functions as a small institution within the larger institution. Each unit has its own tier system, and the unit staff is responsible for coordinating the treatment programs of its prisoners, job assignments and job changes, disciplinary hearings, and promotions and demotions within the tier system.[78]

Each committed individual is offered formal psychotherapy which must be at least on a weekly basis. Individual therapy sessions are also scheduled depending on the needs of the inmate. Over 95 percent of all inmates are in psychotherapy; the remainder are newly committed individuals awaiting therapy assignments, and a few refusing psychotherapy.[79] The director's 1965 report pointed out that the retarded had not been included in psychotherapy programs for many years.[80]

[74] H. Boslow & A. Kandel, Psychiatric Aspects of Dangerous Behavior: The Retarded Offender (address delivered at American Psychiatric Ass'n Annual Meeting in New York, May 4, 1965).

[75] H. Boslow, *supra* note 73, at 14.

[76] H. Boslow & A. Kandel, *supra* note 74, at 4-5.

[77] H. Boslow, *supra* note 73, at 18.

[78] *Id.* at 19.

[79] *Id.* at 21.

[80] H. Boslow & A. Kandel, *supra* note 74, at 11.

There are programs to teach illiterate inmates how to read and write, and programs have been designed to bring those with IQs below 90 up to an eighth-grade level of education.[81]

Vocational training is said to be offered in automotive skills, clerical work, bookbinding, cooking, baking, meat cutting, food services, carpentry, masonry, painting, sheet metal work, plumbing, barbering, electronics, and circuit board repair; and classes are supplemented with appropriate job assignments within the institution. According to the director, the mentally retarded have participated in many of these programs and seem to progress as satisfactorily as the nonretarded. In vocational areas beyond the resources of the institution, the assistance of the state vocational rehabilitation agency is employed. When individuals earn work release on parole, professional assistance in obtaining employment is available.[82] The retarded are not mentioned at all in this area.

A significantly greater proportion of the retarded than the nonretarded remain committed longer than their original sentences. Although the retarded constituted 27 percent of the population in 1965, they accounted for 42 percent of those who remained beyond the length of their original sentences. The reasons given for the difference in length of commitment were unresponsiveness to treatment and lack of suitable community placement. Of 103 prisoners released on parole, 46 became parole violators, of whom 19 were retarded. Twelve of the 19 retarded men were returned to the institution, and in 11 cases their return was due to difficulty in community adjustment, rather than the commission of a new crime. The experience of the Patuxent staff has been that it is particularly difficult to find suitable jobs and home placements for mentally retarded inmates in the community. Once retarded individuals are paroled, they do fairly well; they are paroled, however, to a lesser degree than the general population.[83]

The director concludes that the retarded and nonretarded do well when integrated into a total institutional program. Although special efforts must be made for each group, particularly in the educational and therapy areas, it is his belief that the goal of returning the retarded to a nonretarded community is furthered by an integrated institutional program.

His conclusion does not seem to be supported by the facts. To summarize, the retarded are incarcerated for longer periods than the nonretarded. They stay on the first level longer and are returned to it more frequently because of disciplinary problems. They may also be held back because the staff does not expect them to do well and "fears they cannot be rehabilitated." They are not paroled as frequently as the nonretarded, and those paroled are often returned to the institution for the sole reason that suitable community placement cannot be found.

The facts suggest that mentally retarded offenders do not do well when they are integrated into a total institutional program. It seems they are, even in this "treatment" facility, once more low men on the totem pole. They remain second-class citizens and continue to be discriminated against in this specialized setting, allegedly designed to handle their specific treatment needs.

---

[81] H. Boslow, *supra* note 73, at 21.
[82] *Id.* at 21; H. Boslow & A. Kandel, *supra* note 74, at 8.
[83] H. Boslow & A. Kandel, *supra* note 74, at 10-11.

The indeterminate sentence is used as an instrument of inmate control, as it gives the institution complete power to release an inmate at any time or to keep him incarcerated for life. This type of sentence is fraught with potential for abuse, and there is a real danger that it can be used to punish political beliefs and views unpopular with the staff. Even when the sentence does not turn out to be for life, the result is a longer confinement than would have occurred had the inmate gone to a regular prison. The indeterminate sentence is just another device to hide society's dehumanizing treatment of criminals, particularly those who are mentally disabled.[84]

Despite claims that Patuxent is more like a hospital than a prison, it is a prison in every sense of the word. Each cell is sealed by a solid metal door with a window. These cells are "nine by six feet in size and are furnished with only a bunk having a drawer under it, a commode, a wash basin, and a table. Inmates can shower briefly once a week, and recreation is extremely limited."[85] According to the Patuxent patient handbook, "Cell searches and physical force by employees are authorized." [86]

Although placement in a "segregated confinement treatment facility" is supposed to be limited to 15 days,[87] confinement in "administrative segregation" is authorized on "an indeterminate basis."[88] This is true even though confinement in similar physical conditions under disciplinary segregation beyond the 15-day period was held to be cruel and unusual punishment by a state circuit court in *McCray v. Maryland.*[89] Without discussing the merits, an appellate court overturned the decision because the lower court lacked jurisdiction to make new rules and regulations for the institution.[90] Thus, *McCray* had only a temporary effect on the practice of forcing inmates to sit in dark and solitary, filthy, cagelike cells for months without even reading material to alleviate their boredom. This practice, known as negative reinforcement, is defended as part of the total treatment concept of the institution.[91]

Although officials at Patuxent play down discipline in their public reports, in fact the slightest infraction, the smallest offense, may not only result in loss of privileges, but may also be included in records and affect release dates. Prisoners can become so concerned with gaining freedom that they forget about everything else. All of their efforts are focused on trying to convince the therapist that they have improved, which makes it extremely difficult for them to experience the kind of therapeutic interactions essential for psychological growth.[92]

Individual therapy is virtually nonexistent, as there are simply not enough staff members to work with the total population of more than 550 men. Furthermore, group therapy provides the only way out of Patuxent. Not only must inmates attend, but they must comply with certain well-prescribed modes of behavior in therapy. They must recognize that they have been sick and gain insight into what their prob-

---

[84] Prettyman, *The Indeterminate Sentence and the Right to Treatment,* 11 Am. Crim. L. Rev. 7, 18-21 (1972).

[85] *Id.* at 22.

[86] Patuxent Patient Handbook, ch. X, paras. A, C, E.

[87] *Id.* at ch. XV, para. A(1)(b).

[88] *Id.* at ch. XVI, para. E(1)(b).

[89] Misc. Pet. No. 4363 (Cir. Ct. Montgomery Cty., Md., Nov. 11, 1971) (excerpts in 40 U.S.L.W. 2307), *rev'd*, 267 Md. 111, 297 A.2d 265 (1972).

[90] 267 Md. 111, 297 A.2d 265 (1972).

[91] Prettyman, *supra* note 84, at 23.

[92] *Id.* at 24-25.

lems have been and then evidence a strong intent to overcome the problems and become useful citizens. Clever inmates quickly discover what is expected of them, go through the motions, play the game, and fool the therapist. Thus, the indeterminate sentence structure encourages cunning offenders and is more favorable to them than to the less intelligent.[93] This places the mentally retarded inmates at Patuxent at still another disadvantage.

Treatment and habilitation are either token or nonexistent, and educational opportunities are poor. Also, there is not enough vocational training available to meet the needs of the inmates.[94] And when there is not enough vocational training to go around, the retarded are the first among those excluded.

As negative as the results are for the nonretarded segment of the population, they are that much more damaging for the retarded. Their frustrations are greater, and they are continually faced with their own inability to cope with structures and attitudes within the institution.

THE RIGHT TO TREATMENT

The right to treatment concept was first articulated in 1960 by Dr. Morton Birnbaum, attorney and physician. He argued that a person institutionalized solely because of mental illness should receive adequate medical treatment in order to regain his health and liberty as quickly as possible. It was also his belief that courts should support this concept through recognition and enforcement of the right to treatment as a necessary development of the right to due process of law.[95]

When a statute under which confinement is accomplished promises treatment, hospitalization, or rehabilitation, or prohibits confinement in institutions which are otherwise used as penal institutions, courts have little difficulty in justifying an inquiry into treatment actually provided. Even failing a statutory promise, courts have recognized that serious constitutional questions would be raised if confinement were condoned without investigation into either the adequacy of treatment or the appropriateness of the facility to meet the needs of the committed individual.

In *Rouse v. Cameron*[96] the court found a statutory promise of treatment for the plaintiff, who was involuntarily civilly committed to a mental hospital after being acquitted of a criminal charge by reason of insanity; and in *Nason v. Superintendent of Bridgewater State Hospital*[97] the court ordered that a program of appropriate treatment be determined and followed for the plaintiff, who was involuntarily committed to a mental hospital as incompetent to stand trial for an alleged criminal offense.

As illustrated by the situation at Patuxent Institution, commitment of defective delinquents and sex offenders to mental institutions and specialized facilities does

[93] *Id.* at 21, 25-29.
[94] *Id.* at 17-18, 30.
[95] Birnbaum, *The Right to Treatment*, 46 A.B.A.J. 499 (1960). *See also* Halpern, Chapter 13 of this volume.
[96] 373 F.2d 451 (D.C. Cir. 1966).
[97] 353 Mass. 604, 233 N.E.2d 908 (1968).

not ensure treatment, irrespective of the sincerity of legislative or judicial intentions. A federal court, in *Sas v. Maryland,* [98] held that the purpose of confinement of defective delinquents at Patuxent Institution provision of "such . . . treatment, when appropriate, as may make it reasonably safe for society to terminate the confinement and treatment,"[99] there is no requirement that they be given treatment unless same is "appropriate." The court upheld the facial constitutionality of the Maryland statute, stating:

> [T]he justification for the Act may not rest solely or even primarily on the theory that all defective delinquents will receive treatment or that the majority of the inmates who do will be greatly benefited or cured by treatment. . . . Many of the inmates will, therefore, in all likelihood, be confined for life on the premise that they are untreatable or incurable but, nevertheless, too dangerous either to life or to property to be released in a free society.[100]

Nevertheless, the court went on to say:

> But a statute though "fair on its face and impartial in appearance" may be fraught with the possibility of abuse in that if not administered in the spirit in which it is conceived it can become a mere device for warehousing the obnoxious and antisocial elements of society. Many of the inmates in Patuxent are there by reason of offenses against property rights. Many jurists and laymen would seriously question the wisdom of the practice of indefinitely confining young men under these circumstances. Deficiencies in staff, facilities, and finances would undermine the efficacy of the Institution and the justification for the law, and ultimately the constitutionality of its application.[101]

In *Millard v. Cameron*[102] the right to treatment was extended to a sexual psychopath confined in St. Elizabeth's hospital, the court holding that indefinite commitment under the sexual psychopathy law is justifiable only upon a theory of therapeutic treatment.

For juveniles, treatment should be the only justification for incarceration. The entire emphasis of the juvenile court is on treatment, and as a consequence certain due process requirements have been relaxed. It follows that if a juvenile is not receiving rehabilitative treatment, his incarceration is invalid. In addressing itself to the criteria to be applied in evaluating a juvenile's confinement, the court of appeals, in *Creek v. Stone,* [103] pointed out that the juvenile court is armed with broad statutory powers so that community resources may be marshaled to provide individualized care and treatment and held that the congressional objective comprehends psychiatric care in appropriate cases. Recognizing that full and imaginative use of these powers enables the juvenile court to fashion dispositional decrees tailored to meet the peculiar needs of a particular child, the court found the juvenile court obligated to conduct an appropriate inquiry when presented with a substantial complaint about commitment. [104]

---

[98] 334 F.2d 506 (4th Cir. 1964).
[99] *Id.* at 512.
[100] *Id.* at 513 (footnote omitted).
[101] *Id.* at 516-17 (footnote omitted).
[102] 373 F.2d 468 (D.C. Cir. 1966).
[103] 379 F.2d 106 (D.C. Cir. 1967).
[104] *Id.* at 111. The right to treatment, or habilitation for the mentally retarded, has received substantial impetus recently. For a full discussion of this development, see Chapters 13 and 14 of this volume.

The case of *Newman v. Alabama*[105] was a class action brought by state prisoners claiming that they were deprived of adequate medical treatment in violation of their rights guaranteed under the eighth and fourteenth amendments to the United States Constitution. The court held that failure of the board of corrections to provide sufficient medical facilities and staff to afford inmates basic elements of adequate medical care constituted willful and intentional violation of prisoners' rights. The issue was raised whether *mental* health standards were also appropriate topics for court examination. The court ruled that adequacy of care was to include both physical-medical services and mental health services, specifically stating:

> The fate of those many prisoners who are mentally ill or retarded deserves special mention. Mental illness and mental retardation are the most prevalent medical problems in the Alabama prison system. It is estimated that approximately 10 percent of the inmates are psychotic and another 60 percent are disturbed enough to require treatment. To diagnose and treat these almost 2400 inmates, the Board of Corrections employs one clinical psychologist, who works one afternoon each week. . . . There are no psychiatrists, social workers, or counsellors on the staff. . . . [T]he large majority of mentally disturbed prisoners receive no treatment whatsoever. It is tautological that such care is constitutionally inadequate.[106]

The *Newman* case could have a tremendous impact on correctional systems in this country. Alabama is not the exception, but the rule, in its lack of mental health manpower resources. As previously noted, in response to the Brown-Courtless survey, 166 institutions, housing more than 150,000 inmates, reported employing only 54 full-time psychiatrists and 93 full-time psychologists; and 6 of these facilities, housing only 6,825 inmates, employed 40 of the psychiatrists and 11 of the psychologists. These statistics dramatize the overwhelming inadequacy of diagnostic and treatment facilities within correctional institutions.

It has been suggested that if society can legitimately determine that certain people can be involuntarily treated for mental illness, all persons so classified are entitled to equal treatment, regardless of any other status, such as "criminal," that has been attached to them.[107] This reasoning applies with equal force to the mentally retarded. Proper treatment for mental illness or mental retardation does not depend on any status, such as "criminal," but on consideration of the diagnosis and pathology of the condition. Sentence-serving convicts are not afflicted with different mental illnesses or defects from those suffered by persons who are civilly committed, and they should therefore be entitled to habilitation or treatment equal to that received by civilly committed patients.[108]

There must be a justification for every deprivation of liberty or it becomes a deprivation without due process of law. If an individual has been found guilty in a criminal trial, confinement is usually limited to a definite period of time. One virtue of the criminal process is that the duration of penal incarceration typically has some maximum statutory limit. Any confinement beyond this limited period, as in those facilities which utilize the indeterminate sentence, must rest on the need for treatment. The promise of treatment is a quid pro quo for this potentially longer term

---

[105] 349 F. Supp. 278 (M.D. Ala. 1972), *rev'd,* 503 F.2d 565 (5th Cir. 1974).
[106] *Id.* at 284 (footnote omitted).
[107] Morris, *"Criminality" and the Right to Treatment*, 36 U. Chi. L. Rev. 784 (1969).
[108] S. Rubin, The Law of Criminal Correction 520-21 (1963).

imprisonment; and where no treatment is provided, the additional confinement is without due process of law. If the same individual has been found not guilty and committed to a mental institution, failure to provide him with treatment, at least during his confinement beyond the maximum sentence which would have been possible had he been found guilty, presents constitutional questions of due process, equal protection, and cruel and unusual punishment. In either event, it is questionable whether the courts must limit application of the constitutional standards to the period by which the term of indefinite confinement exceeds the maximum term of criminal punishment. Any length of confinement without treatment could be considered a denial of due process, for the defect which triggered the confinement, whether in a prison, a specialized facility, or a mental institution, purportedly rendered all criminal penalties or the traditional criminal punishment inappropriate. The justification for confinement is as lacking in the initial period as it is in the subsequent period.

Constitutional problems are also presented when an individual is considered "dangerous" and confined for the protection of society. Detention based solely upon prevention of future acts is not therapeutic and therefore must be punitive. If the danger is caused by some disease or defect, the detention arguably is a form of cruel and unusual punishment. Additionally, the tests for potential danger are presently so uncertain that the concept of dangerousness is impermissibly vague. Given this lack of adequate predictability and the correlatively increased potential for detaining nondangerous persons, all preventive detention is arguably rendered a deprivation of liberty without due process of law.

Newman points the way to the right to habilitation and treatment for mentally retarded and mentally ill prisoners. It remains to be seen how quickly other courts will act to enforce this right.

CONCLUSION AND RECOMMENDATIONS

Presently the penal system is a dismal failure for mentally retarded offenders. A statement by Dr. Karl Menninger concerning prisoners in general seems particularly applicable to the retarded: "I suspect that all the crimes committed by all the jailed criminals do not equal in total social damage that of the crimes committed against them." The most recent judicial expression of the right to treatment concept can be found in *O'Connor v. Donaldson.* [109] There the Supreme Court, dealing with the situation of a nondangerous individual involuntarily committed and denied treatment for his alleged mental illness, held:

> In short, a State cannot constitutionally confine without more a nondangerous individual who is capable of surviving safely in freedom by himself or with the help of willing and responsible family members or friends. [110]

This opinion leaves unanswered a number of critical questions concerning the extent

[109] 95 S. Ct. 2486 (1975).
[110] *Id.* at 2494.

and effect the constitutional right to treatment, but it certainly paves the way for further judicial development.[111]

In most states, appropriate institutional, probation, and other treatment facilities are not available for differential treatment of the retarded, and they therefore receive little or none of the special care needed if they are to be rehabilitated. This shortage of programs and services is a result of several factors: disagreement as to whether retarded offenders are most appropriately handled as part of an integrated prison system or in specialized facilities; a lack of manpower resources in the areas of special education, psychiatry, and psychology; a lack of alternative resources in the community; and a lack of coordination among and within the agencies dealing with mentally retarded offenders.

Undifferentiated handling has resulted not only in neglect of retarded offenders, but in positive damage to them. In these situations they vegetate in institutions, only occasionally participating in any programs at all. They are assigned to menial maintenance tasks having no vocational training potential and are required to conform to standard rules and share work assignments with more intelligent inmates. They tend to react by withdrawing from competition completely, thus making it more difficult to prepare them for life in the community.

Nor is specialized treatment a panacea. There is a danger that the existence of special facilities will imply a comparable existence of special expertise, encouraging society to leave to correctional institutions problems that should be handled elsewhere. Support among corrections professionals to build special facilities for the retarded seems prompted by a motive to reduce administrative problems, rather than a desire to habilitate these individuals.

Recognition of retarded offenders as a special group should neither excuse their behavior nor allow society to label them incorrigible and withhold appropriate services. Programs must be designed to compensate for their particular deficiencies; and professionals, agencies, and social institutions must provide continuing guidance geared to their special needs.

A suitable range of dispositional alternatives is necessary. For many retarded offenders, habilitation should be available under supervision in the community. Those individuals who exhibit persistent uncontrolled behavior which threatens the safety of others will require particular attention. The type of control and treatment most appropriate must undergo further study, since retarded offenders seem unsuited to both the typical prison environment and the typical institution for non-aggressive retarded individuals, and the specialized facilities into which they have been cast with sex offenders, psychopaths, and sociopaths have been disappointing in terms of treatment and habilitation results.

Most court decisions pertaining to the right to treatment of involuntarily institutionalized individuals have been made in the area of civil commitments. Nevertheless, where the basis of confinement is specifically stated as the necessity for treatment or habilitation, failure to provide meaningful treatment may warrant judicial intervention.

The mentally retarded are now, more than ever before in the history of correc-

---

[111] K. MENNINGER, THE CRIME OF PUNISHMENT 28 (1968).

tions, recognized as a significant and important element of the prison population which must be identified and afforded habilitation appropriate to their individual needs and impaired mental capacity. It is a long way from recognition of the problem to effective and meaningful habilitation alternatives, representing a substantial gap in services to the retarded. Most of the work remains to be done.

The recommendations of institutional administrators and suggestions and recommendations from numerous studies discussed in this paper are condensed in the material that follows.

After conviction, presentence investigations should be conducted and advice furnished courts so that judges can make intelligent and knowledgeable placement decisions for mentally retarded offenders. Additionally, courts should have the authority to commit these individuals to appropriate specialized institutions.

Institutionalization should be based on a finding of dangerousness to self or others, and periodic review should be required.

Screening and diagnostic resources should be strengthened and offenders classified and assigned according to their specific problems and needs. Operation of joint regional facilities or use of neighboring facilities on a contract basis should be undertaken where necessary.

Special facilities should be created to handle mentally retarded offenders in a more intelligent, humane, and effective manner. These facilities should be more secure than state institutions for the retarded, but free from the perverse influences found in standard training schools or prisons. They should be located near institutions of higher learning so that students, professors, and qualified corrections people will be available to assist with habilitation problems.

There has been too little scientific study done to permit decisions on what types of programs will be most effective in habilitating retarded offenders. Some individuals may best respond to correctional or penal handling; others will require some form of mental hospitalization; still others may be appropriately handled in training schools for the mentally retarded. Institutional programs for the retarded, especially in the areas of special education and vocational training, require considerable attention. A wider range of alternative programs should be available, including group therapy and counseling services, and qualified educational personnel must be attracted to correctional work so that needed programs can be offered.

Correctional personnel at all levels should be at least minimally equipped to work with mentally retarded inmates and should be given appropriate instruction on an in-service training basis. In addition to in-service training, more intensive education of correctional personnel should be directed toward assisting workers in their interaction with retarded offenders.

Community alternatives should be developed for those offenders who are in need of specialized treatment which can be provided outside the correctional environment. Communities have experienced extensive growth in day care centers, sheltered workshops, and a variety of educational settings for nondelinquent retarded citizens, and the possibility of using these facilities for selected offenders should be thoroughly explored. Among community programs which offer greater supervision and guidance than traditional probation and parole are guided group interaction programs, foster homes, group homes, prerelease guidance centers, intensive treatment programs, and reception center parole programs.

Probation and parole officials should be given supplementary education and training designed to assist them in working with the mentally retarded. Rather than placing total responsibility for an offender on a single officer, many persons should participate in the habilitative task, including teachers, vocational counselors, friends, family members, employers, and psychologists. The system should also draw from a variety of organizational resources, such as departments of mental health, education, mental retardation, youth services, and family services.

Organizational planning should include procedures to encourage collaboration between mental health professionals and corrections personnel. Additionally, cooperative efforts should be made by the American Association on Mental Deficiency and the American Correctional Association to establish standards for correctional programing for mentally retarded inmates. Cooperation between these two organizations could provide an excellent basis upon which to build more adequate and appropriate services for mentally retarded offenders within penal and correctional facilities.

Reaction Comment

HERMAN SCHWARTZ

ROWAN'S COMPREHENSIVE and insightful paper raises a host of difficult issues. These include the now well-known definitional problem, the criminality of the mentally retarded, the special problems they and the rest of us face because of their retardation, the implications of the Patuxent Institution, and the emerging right to habilitation.

The first problem is the "mental retardation" classification. Although the mentally retarded are often referred to as a group, there are subclassifications of mild, moderate, severe, and profound retardation. The mildly retarded account for the overwhelming majority of retarded persons both in and out of correctional institutions. Leaving them aside, there is a relatively small prison population of about 3,300 with a greater degree of retardation, according to the Brown-Courtless study. In discussing the "retarded prisoners" in correctional institutions, we must consider the differences between these categories.

This classification problem is compounded by the serious professional questioning about both IQ tests and about what, if anything, IQ scores actually mean. In this connection, it is no coincidence that the same group that does badly on IQ tests accounts for an overly large percentage of the mentally retarded — i.e., blacks, other minorities, and the poor. This is not just a matter of cultural deprivation, but to a large extent, a matter of cultural differentiation and of cultural bias in evaluation. Consequently, we should be extremely careful about pinning the label "retarded" on anyone and slow to suggest special treatment for certain people because they are labeled "retarded."

These considerations suggest that a broad definition of "retardation," particularly a definition relating to an "inability to function socially," should not be adopted in the correctional setting. Such definitions seem analytically wrong and potentially dangerous. The scope of stigmatizing classification should be narrowed, not broadened.

Similar considerations point also to excluding the mentally retarded from the class we have dehumanizingly labeled "defective delinquents."

Labels are functional; we use them to help highlight and identify problems. But it remains unclear to me what specific problems mentally retarded criminals raise. Given the frighteningly difficult management and exploitation problems already in prison, is there a significantly unique problem with mentally retarded inmates? Is there a significant difference between the adjustment of mildly retarded offenders and those more seriously impaired?

Rowan's paper does not satisfactorily answer these questions; it demonstrates principally that we have relatively little reliable information about the mentally retarded in conventional institutions.

We have learned, however, from a number of depressing studies, that prison programs rarely rehabilitate anyone.[1] Either because we will not or cannot rehabilitate, the fact is that with the rarest of exceptions, prison produces pain and nothing more. Special programs for rehabilitation remind me of Hamlet's smiling villains: hypocritical devices to hurt people while pretending to help them.

Labeling somebody "mentally retarded" in order to "help" that person impresses me as one of the worst things we can do. The chances are too great that the classification of mentally retarded offenders will result in more Patuxents and even more lifetime commitments to institutions for the mentally retarded. It is for this reason that the right of rehabilitation for retarded offenders strikes me as a dangerous concept, for the truth is we do not know how to rehabilitate prisoners. And even if we did know how, we probably would be unwilling to spend the necessary money.

Neither the mentally retarded nor the nonretarded prisoner has much chance of being rehabilitated in prison, and we should not think otherwise. Therefore, to classify a group of prisoners as mentally retarded is the first step in further segregating them into warehouses like Patuxent.

Perhaps my comments sound like something of an overreaction. I am not against trying to help people who are in trouble and have handicaps of one kind or another. Indeed, one wishes that the present national administration would demonstrate more compassion for those who are having a hard time because of their social and individual handicaps; it is my recollection that funds have been withheld and cut for some training programs of retarded people. We must always remember, however, how little we can do in the way of "habilitating" people, and we must adjust our hopes and proposals to these limitations. Although there may well be special problems with the mentally retarded in the criminal and correctional system, it is hard to identify them, which makes me wonder to what extent do they exist.

---

[1] Robison & Smith, *The Effectiveness of Correctional Programs*, 17 CRIME & DELINQUENCY 67 (1971); G. KASSEBAUM, D. WARD & D. WILNER, PRISON TREATMENT AND PAROLE SURVIVAL: AN EMPIRICAL ASSESSMENT (1971); Cressey, *Adult Felons in Prison*, in PRISONERS IN AMERICA 117 (L. Ohlin ed. 1973).

The severely retarded do not seem more criminal than the rest of the population. They do not seem to commit more serious crimes, although some studies indicate an unusually high incidence of homicide. The various findings on criminality in the Rowan paper provide rather mixed results.

I have three concluding observations:

1. We must be very careful about labeling individuals "mentally retarded," for we have very little to offer in return for damning them with such a stigma.

2. Very little is known about the types and magnitude of problems growing out of mental retardation and crime and particularly about the retarded in correctional institutions.

3. Compassion and realism counsel against special penal institutions for the mentally retarded offender, because experience indicates that separate institutions inflict harm, rather than provide help for the mentally retarded.

Reaction Comment

H. CARL HAYWOOD

THE CONCLUSION I draw from both Rowan's paper and Schwartz's reaction, and with which I agree, is simply that correctional systems are bad. The point I should like to add is that the system of institutions for the mentally retarded is probably worse. My reaction to Rowan's paper proceeds from this assumption.

Her paper underscores the confusion that results in trying to make generalizations about the characteristics of mentally retarded offenders. Studies made to date have been inconclusive and contradictory. This inconsistency is entirely explainable and not necessarily a bad thing. It is a result of the fact that retarded *offenders* do not constitute a class, just as mentally retarded *persons* do not constitute a class. It is a typical observation in behavioral research that there is more variability within a group of mentally retarded persons than between retarded and nonretarded persons.[1] This is a major statistical problem which must be dealt with in analyzing data in comparative studies. There is no homogeneity of variance. Mentally retarded persons are not alike, because mental retardation is not an entity. It is a collection of well over 200 syndromes that have only one element in common: relative inefficiency at learning by the methods and strategies devised for other people to learn.[2]

Rowan noted quite correctly that the number of retarded persons who are in the custody of adult and juvenile correction systems far outweighs their proportion in the general population. Whether it is 30 percent or 20 percent or whatever, it is

[1] Baumeister, *Behavioral Inadequacy and Variability of Performance*, 73 AM. J. MENTAL DEFICIENCY 477 (1968); Haywood, *Mental Retardation as an Extension of the Developmental Laboratory*, 75 AM. J. MENTAL DEFICIENCY 5 (1970).
[2] Haywood, *Intelligence, distribution of*, in 9 THE ENCYCLOPAEDIA BRITANNICA 672-77 (1974).

far more than the 3 percent figure cited frequently as the prevalence of mental retardation in the general population. This raises the question, "What is intelligence?" Intelligence is what mentally retarded persons are not supposed to have terribly much of.

It is useful to assume that intelligence is not a quality that inheres in the individual but, rather, a quality that is attributed to individuals by other people.[3] Mercer refers to this view as the social system perspective. In this sense it does not really matter whether those people who are in institutions and who have low IQs are really mentally retarded or not, but the fact of the matter is that they are *seen* as mentally retarded. Other people behave toward them according to some construct that inheres in the other people's minds about the nature of retardation and how one ought to behave toward mentally retarded persons. Once individuals have had this status assigned to them, they learn to play some of its associated roles. It is the responsibility of those of us who are concerned generally with the field of mental retardation to try to deal with the people to whom retardation is attributed and with the systems and individuals who apply the label to them.

Rowan has observed that many of the social conditions that are associated with delinquent behavior are the same conditions that accompany social-cultural or cultural-familial retardation. These are conditions of disrupted family life, poverty, limited access to social institutions and agencies, and restriction of social and educational opportunities. In the Tennessee study, this has certainly proved to be true.[4] The great majority of children who are committed to the department of correction in Tennessee come from the same population in which most of the mildly and moderately (cultural-familial) retarded citizens are found.[5] This correlation indicates that early attention to conditions of family life could be expected to reduce the prevalence of both delinquency and cultural-familial retardation.

For the mentally retarded offender, the problem remains of choosing the lesser of two evils: placement in prisons or in institutions for the mentally retarded. The Tennessee study, referred to in Rowan's paper, showed that mentally retarded persons in the corrections system and those in institutions for the mentally retarded are quite different even though they may have the same age, sex, and IQ. Those in prison are more competent than are those in institutions for the mentally retarded. They learn from their age peers not only delinquent behavior but also adaptive behavior. There are considerable data now to support the proposition that one learns a very large proportion of what one is going to learn in the developmental period from one's age peers. It is grossly discriminatory to prevent mentally retarded individuals from interacting with age peers who do not happen to have their disability. Segregation renders it impossible to capitalize developmentally on the powers of age-peer modeling.

---

[3] Mercer, *Sociocultural Factors in Labeling Mental Retardates,* 48 PEABODY J. EDUC. 188 (1971).

[4] F. Dennis, The Retarded Juvenile Offender Research and Demonstration Project, 1971 (Tennessee Department of Correction); Department of Correction & Kennedy Center for Research on Education and Human Development, Our House, 1973 (A Report to Tennessee about the Mentally Retarded Juvenile Offender Project, Tennessee).

[5] See H. Haywood & D. Stedman, Poverty and Mental Retardation (unpublished staff position paper prepared for President's Committee on Mental Retardation, Peabody College, 1969).

These observations support a "normalization" principle: Mentally retarded citizens should not be segregated and given different treatment *because they are retarded*, especially when the circumstances that require treatment may not be a result of the condition of retardation. A retarded child who has an infection does not necessarily need the attention of a specialist in mental retardation; he needs the services of a pediatrician, just as any other child would require these services. The attending pediatrician will need to know that his patient is retarded because of the association of mental retardation with some other conditions that may make the child more susceptible to certain illnesses. But in the great majority of cases the treatment will be the same as for nonretarded children. Similarly, a retarded child who breaks the law should be treated, whenever it is humane to do so, in the same ways prescribed for nonretarded offenders, once guilt and culpability have been established.

Since up to one-third of the population of correctional facilities may be at least psychometrically retarded, those whose professional interest is in mental retardation have a special responsibility for the corrections system. In discharging this responsibility they must not be content merely to construct laws that will relieve commissioners of corrections of the problems raised by mentally retarded offenders. They must address themselves to changing the corrections system so that it can provide more adequate services to mentally retarded offenders. Transferring mentally retarded persons out of correctional facilities may, in effect, impose upon them the life sentences that all too frequently are characteristic of institutions for the mentally retarded. Most such persons have been able to escape commitment to institutions for the mentally retarded and have made at least partially successful adjustments to community living. Serving six months or a year in a juvenile corrections facility is better than serving the rest of one's life in an institution for the mentally retarded. It is not the retardation that requires treatment, but the delinquent behavior; and this treatment should be provided by the juvenile justice system, by the education system, by the social welfare system, and by vocational rehabilitation. Grouping retarded persons together may intensify the maladaptive consequences of retardation while the delinquent patterns remain untreated. Very few retarded persons in correctional systems fall into the severely retarded range or even into the moderately retarded range. Mildly retarded persons can learn relatively easily that behavior has consequences, that the individual can frequently control these consequences, and that the key to the control of consequences is the regulation of one's own behavior. Furthermore, mentally retarded citizens have a right to be treated as nearly as possible like other citizens, and this right includes bearing responsibility for one's own behavior. Thus, there should be an insistence that present correctional facilities improve their habilitative procedures, incorporating nonsegregated programing for retarded offenders. These programs should focus on personal competence, reading skills, enhancement of self-concept, social skills, vocational training, and personal responsibility.

I offer the following recommendations:

1. Insist upon executive and legislative action (both preferable to litigation) that will focus responsibility for retarded offenders specifically within departments

of health, mental health, education, correction, vocational habilitation, and public welfare, depending on the individual's needs.

2. Do not commit the "special education error" of segregating individuals merely on the basis of diagnostic tests. Segregation is appropriate only when detailed individually constructed habilitation plans require it.

3. Object to the implicit assumption expressed in several state laws that the *necessity for institutionalization* can be determined, even by "experts." The term *necessary*, applied to institutionalization, implies a primary concern with the protection of society. The more reasonable approach is to ask what center or facility or treatment mode, in the individual case, is most likely to provide habilitation geared to the needs and capabilities of each individual.

4. Rowan has pointed out the difficulty that juvenile courts encounter in some states in getting retarded offenders admitted to residential institutions for the mentally retarded. I recommend that we *not* make it easier. I would insist that in most cases it is better to deal with delinquent behavior without attributing this behavior to mental retardation. Mentally retarded persons have a right to experience the consequences of their behavior, and most of them can assume the accompanying responsibility.

5. Resist movements to construct separate facilities for retarded offenders. Instead, we must devise habilitation and development programs for juvenile and adult offenders that are more habilitation oriented than existing ones, and treat retarded offenders within these more adequate systems. If the overall plans are based on individual needs and characteristics, retarded persons will be treated appropriately and in consequence will not receive de facto life sentences.

CHAPTER 22

Special Doctrinal Treatment in Criminal Law

Editorial Introduction

Morris has written at length on the problems created by special rules of competence to stand trial and of criminal responsibility. In this chapter he states succinctly the conclusions reached through his scholarship. Morris then proceeds to elucidate the experiential background for these conclusions. He notes that supposedly benevolent special rules often work great hardship on the mentally impaired individuals they are designed to help. He describes the effects of double stigmatization in terms of average longer periods of incarceration. Morris' paper argues for the equal application to mentally retarded citizens of the general rights to proof of specific criminal intent and a sentencing and correctional process that would provide proper services to the mentally retarded citizen because he is a citizen, rather than because he is mentally retarded.

Morris' theme has a different tone from that of Rowan (Chapter 21), although his proposals are not totally inconsistent with some presented there. Morris' skepticism of special "benevolent" diversions of mentally retarded citizens parallels that of Wald (Chapter 1) and Schwartz and Haywood (see reactions to Rowan's paper, Chapter 21).

Ziccardi strongly criticizes Morris' position, again from an experiential point of view. Ziccardi's approach is that of a criminal defense attorney and he is wary of giving up tools that may sometimes be used by an attorney in representing a person charged with a criminal offense.

PRINCIPAL PAPER

NORVAL MORRIS

THE THEME of this paper is the advocacy of a principle in relation to mental retardation and criminal law which at first blush may seem reactionary and punitive. It is this: The police power of the state should not be infected by the mental health power of the state. There should be no defense of insanity or mental retardation to a criminal charge; there should be no incompetency plea to stay the criminal trial of a mentally retarded person. The mentally retarded suspect should be accorded exactly the same rights and responsibilities under the criminal law and the same trial processes as any other citizen. Although the argument may appear paradoxical, such an approach will have beneficent and not punitive consequences.

The advocacy of this position in the criminal law is supported by a similar argument made so powerfully elsewhere in this volume in relation to civil law and mentally retarded citizens.[1] The principal in both civil and criminal law should be that special laws are not needed for the retarded citizen; the Constitution makes no mention of incompetents; and, legally and constitutionally, all citizens are equal before the law with respect to basic rights. It is not a lack of charity that supports rejection of the so-called humane and helping quality of special rules of law, civil and criminal, concerning the mentally retarded individual. Instead, experience has demonstrated that in practice these intended special benevolences stigmatize mentally retarded people and inflict on them more suffering than the rules of law from which they were to be protected. Therefore, the mentally retarded citizen should be tried for and, if convicted, held responsible for criminal conduct just like anyone else.

The incompetency plea should be abolished — not qualified, not modified with special commitment to follow, not protected or improved — but abolished. There may well be situations in which defense counsel will seek a delay in trial because of the accused's physical or mental condition. Likewise, in many cases the prosecution may decide that because of the physical or mental condition of the accused there is no purpose to be served by proceeding to trial. This is common and ordinary prosecutorial discretion. But, where the prosecution decides that it is necessary to pursue a given criminal allegation and the suspect is classified as mentally retarded, the law should make provision for trial of the accused. Of course, it makes sense to delay trial until the accused can play as large a role in his trial as possible, but this delay must be carefully defined so that it does not develop into permanent or prolonged incarceration of an untried suspect. Two proposals would prevent this undesirable development. First, before trial is ever delayed solely on the ground of a defendant's incompetency, a court should have to find specifically that there is a

---

[1] *See* Wald, Chapter 1 of this volume.

"substantial probability" that the defendant will be competent to stand trial "within the foreseeable future." Second, no trial should be delayed longer than six months solely because of a defendant's incompetency.[2]

Case law and practice support the view that the interests of both the permanently incompetent defendant and the state will be better served by abandonment of the traditional rule against trying incompetent defendants. Instead, incompetency should be ground for obtaining a short trial continuance, during which time the state must provide resources to assist the defendant toward greater trial competence. If trial competence is not achieved within six months, the state should be required to dismiss charges or to proceed to a trial governed, when necessary, by procedures designed to compensate for the incompetent defendant's trial disabilities.[3]

The defense of insanity also should be abolished.[4] The accused's mental condition should be relevant only to the question of whether he did or did not at the time of the act have the prohibited *mens rea* of the crime for which he is charged. Special rules like *M'Naghten*[5] or *Durham*[6] should be eliminated. Evidence of mental retardation would be admissible as to the *mens rea* issue to the same limited extent that deafness, blindness, a heart condition, illiteracy, "foreignness," drunkenness, and drug addiction are all now admissible.

At last a major legislative proposal has been made embodying this proposition.[7] Section 502 of the proposed federal criminal code reads:

> It is a defense to a prosecution under any federal statute that the defendant, as a result of mental disease or defect, lacked the state of mind required as an element of the offense charged. Mental disease or defect does not otherwise constitute a defense.[8]

Some commentators have interpreted this recommendation as just another indication of the punitive inclinations of a "law and order" society. They fail to realize that the defense of insanity is neither essential to the morality of punishment nor presently effective in reducing the social stigma of conviction and punishment. Nor do they understand that the perennial perseverations about the defense of insanity have impeded recognition of the great range of human wickedness and

---

[2] *See* Burt & Morris, *A Proposal for the Abolition of the Incompetency Plea*, 40 U. CHI. L. REV. 66 (1972), for a lengthy and analytic defense of these propositions. The article was precipitated by the Court's decision in Jackson v. Indiana, 406 U.S. 715 (1972), but it also had its roots in long observation of the abuse of the incompetency plea in Illinois.

[3] For proposed rules of court for granting trial continuances and for conduct of an incompetence trial, see Burt & Morris, *supra* note 2, at 93-95.

[4] This is, of course, not an original proposition. In Morris, *Psychiatry and the Dangerous Criminal*, 41 S. CAL. L. REV. 514 (1968) reference is made to support for this proposition by Lady Barbara Wootton, Professor H.L. A. Hart, Chief Justice Weintraub of New Jersey, Joel Feinberg, Dr. Thomas Szasz, and Dr. S.L. Halleck, all of whom have advocated its abolition, though for diverse reasons and with diverse substitutes for it. And Professors Katz and Goldstein have flirted most thoughtfully with this idea.

[5] *See* M'Naghten's Case, 8 Eng. Rep. 718(1) H.L. 1843).

[6] *See* Durham v. United States, 214 F.2d 862 (D.C. Cir. 1954).

[7] The bill, S. 1400, 93d Cong., 1st Sess. (1973), is the administration's proposed federal criminal code.

[8] *Id.* § 502.

human capacity for self-control that can be analyzed within ordinary criminal law principles. There is no need to establish a false dichotomy between the responsible and the nonresponsible. Mental retardation may well be important in the determination of the suitable punishment; it is irrelevant on the issue of guilt unless it leads to the same absence of specific criminal intent which would preclude the conviction of a person who is not mentally retarded.

My view toward the treatment of mentally retarded suspects is based largely on personal experience. Joseph Goldstein and I visited the Bridgewater Institution in Massachusetts in the 1950s, where we found a variety of retarded and generally harmless elderly gentlemen who should not have been there. We came across one particularly interesting case: a man in his late seventies who had spent a lifetime in Bridgewater because he had been found incompetent to plead to a criminal charge. The charge had not been a particularly serious one, and all the evidence concerning his alleged offense was, of course, now defunct. Had he been convicted he would have been at large for decades. However, in the 1950s, he was unable to return to the community for the persuasive reason that there was no one in the community who wanted him. We tried to get this man out of the institution. And we did, by finding someone who would take an interest in him. We managed to discover a long lost aunt, or some such relative, who needed a little extra money. It was cheaper for the state to place him with the relative and he was happier there. The story is a common one, and it is difficult to understand the benefit the community has conferred on a handicapped suspect by locking him up for perpetuity.

The next experience of this kind occurred during a visit to the psychiatric section of the Illinois Department of Corrections. Quite by accident I discovered that there were 18 unconvicted prisoners who had been sentenced to this institution between 1942 and 1944. Before 1942 suspects who were incompetent to stand trial went to prison; after 1944 the incompetents were committed to the department of mental health. The change in the commitment law was misinterpreted as being penal, rather than benevolent, and persons who had been previously found incompetent to stand trial were simply left in prison. They were not transferred to the department of mental health (or its predecessor in title) as they should have been. As a result, these 18 men were illegally detained in Menard Prison for more than 25 years each.

Incidentally, there was one delightful little aside when I found the numbers did not add up. I said, "Well, can I see these 18 men and may I talk to them, find out about them, look at their records?" They said, "Yes, of course, but how would we find them?" And I said, "Well, you know, we will look in the records, we will pick every record that has been here for more than 25 years. I would be prepared to sit down now and go through all such records." And they said, "How intelligent of you." These men were not only lost in the community; they were, in a very literal sense, lost in the prison. And one could find much the same situation today in many states throughout America, with only slight variations, in those facilities which are part of prison systems and are meant to be holding mentally ill and mentally retarded prisoners.

These men were not locked up because anyone was punishing them. They were locked up because people were being benevolent! The state was being nice to them; they were not capable of defending themselves; they were not capable of adequately advising counsel; and it would have been unfair to take them to trial. So, instead of being tried, they were incarcerated under processes that lacked both the protections of the criminal law and the protections of civil commitment.

I have learned that the views of parole boards toward the parole of individuals who are held in psychiatric facilities in prison are quite different from their views toward other prisoners. Indeed, when I first started taking an interest in the psychiatric division at Menard, prisoners were not paroled from there at all. Parole would be given only to those who were first transferred to another prison, because parole boards assumed that the mentally ill and the retarded were more dangerous than other people. So, the parole board waits until it is time for the mentally impaired to be sent back into the general population of the prison before these individuals will be considered for release. That there is absolutely no empirical support whatever for the assumptions that lead to this gross injustice troubles very few.

By and large, persons found to be incompetent spend a longer time in institutions than persons civilly committed or those convicted of the crimes of which they have been accused. Louis McGarry studied two reasonably comparable groups of criminal defendants in Massachusetts who had been found incompetent to stand trial. Persons in one group had been civilly committed following dismissal of charges and persons in the other group had been committed until competent to stand trial on the criminal charges which remained outstanding. McGarry found, over a 7-year observation period, that the average confinement of persons committed as incompetent was 61 months, whereas the average hospital stay of those who were civilly committed was only 14 months. One in six of the incompetent defendants had been returned to the community, but every member of the civilly committed group had been discharged to the community.[9] When an individual is so charged, he is doubly stigmatized: He is not only charged with a crime, but also the commitment power of the state is expanded on the basis of his mental retardation. The mentally retarded suspect has the worst of both worlds.

Hospital authorities are exceedingly reluctant to discharge or even to authorize brief community leaves for confined mental patients with criminal charges outstanding. In many states their release is specifically forbidden, and, in practice, hospital authorities must take the initiative in negotiating with prosecuting officials to arrange for the dismissal of charges. Even where release is not formally proscribed, the practical obstacles are formidable; only a zealous state hospital administrator has success in freeing a patient confined with criminal charges outstanding.

The thrust of cases like *Jackson v. Indiana*[10] and *Baxstrom v. Herold*[11] tends toward the constitutional prohibition of protracted or indeterminate commitment

[9]McGarry & Bendt, *Criminal and Civil Commitment of Psychotic Offenders: A Seven Year Follow-up,* 125 AM. J. PSYCHIATRY 1387, 1391 (1969).
[10]406 U.S. 715 (1972).
[11]383 U.S. 107 (1966).

of citizens on the ground of incompetency to stand trial or of their need for treatment. But the risk in *Jackson*[12] is that the civil commitment laws in most states are so flexible that it is easy for prosecutors and others manipulating the system, generally with benevolent intent, to use civil commitment processes instead of the incompetency plea to reach the same results. One way to minimize this risk is to insist that a pending criminal charge not be made an official basis for the civil detention of an allegedly incompetent person.

In relation to incompetency to stand trial the wrong questions are persistently asked: Is he fit for the trial; can he advise his counsel; does he know about the trial? If the answers are no, subject to *Jackson*, the suspect is locked up protractedly. The proper question is: If a period for defined inpatient or outpatient treatment is allowed, is the suspect likely to be *more* fit for trial? And only if this question is answered in the affirmative is there any benefit at all in denying the suspect bail, in denying him speedy trial, or in locking him up. If there is no advantage to the suspect in delay, he should be promptly tried and not committed under the guise of kindness.

At the trial, one should take into account, for procedural and evidentiary purposes, the reality of mental retardation and, by special rules of discovery, disclosure, and so on, assist the accused and his counsel. But the conclusion of the matter must be a decision as to guilt or innocence. And if the decision is guilt, then an attempt should be made to provide a rehabilitative setting, not on grounds of special benevolence or punitiveness, but on grounds that are exactly the same as in the cases of other convicts.

Similar experiences led me to the view that the defense of insanity should be abolished. This defense is pleaded extremely rarely except in homicide and a few other sensational and serious criminal charges. In most states it is only in relation to an extremely serious charge that is worthwhile raising the irresponsibility plea for the mentally retarded. The consequences of a successful plea can often be worse than the consequences of a conviction. Thus, the plea of not guilty on the ground of insanity is reserved for the isolated case, and mental disability among the mass of individuals who are run through the mill of the criminal court is seriously neglected.

Once capital punishment was made inoperative, in practice, the different consequences of the plea of not guilty on the ground of insanity and of a conviction became unimportant other than for purposes of stigmatization. This was so regardless of the terms in which the defense of insanity was to be tested, whether as the modified *McNaghten*[13] rule advocated by the American Law Institute[14] or whether phrased in

---

[12] In *Jackson* an Indiana court held that the petitioner was incompetent to stand trial and committed him for an indefinite period to a psychiatric institution under a less demanding procedure than ordinary civil commitment. Also, the petitioner was subjected to a more stringent standard of release.

The United States Supreme Court held that the Indiana indefinite commitment of a criminal defendant violated equal protection and due process. The state must either institute the usual civil commitment proceeding or release the defendant.

[13] 8 Eng. Rep. 718 (H. L. 1843).

[14] MODEL PENAL CODE § 4.01 (proposed official draft 1962):

Mental Disease or Defect Excluding Responsibility.

(1) A person is not responsible for criminal conduct if at the time of such conduct as a result of mental disease or defect he lacks substantial capacity either to appreciate the criminality [wrongfulness] of his conduct or to conform his conduct to the requirements of law.

(2) As used in this Article, the terms "mental disease or defect" do not include an abnormality manifested only by repeated criminal or otherwise anti-social conduct.

the broader terms of the lamentable experiment in the District of Columbia from *Durham* through *Brawner*.[15] The precise phraseology of the defense of insanity has involved nothing more than the application of an enormous amount of intellectual energy to a largely irrelevant question.

At last there are hints of a movement in the right direction in statutes and case law. As mentioned previously, a serious legislative proposal is before Congress advocating the abolition of the insanity plea and the substitution of ordinary *mens rea* principles. Also, in the *Wells — Gorshen — Conley*[16] doctrine in California, in the acceptance of the *Fisher*[17] doctrine in the District of Columbia, and in the general maturing and sophistication of *mens rea* analysis in the criminal law, there is a conceptual development which, in the long run, inexorably conflicts with the present defense of insanity. The moral question remains clear and simple: Did the accused — whether he was sick, well, blind, retarded, insane, or subject to any other social or personal pressures — intend the prohibited harm? This is all that should be determined.

Experience, as well as analysis, has convinced me of the proper relationship between the criminal law power and the mental health power of the state: There should be no relationship. They should be quite distinct jurisprudentially and should be kept apart. The convicted criminal had best be regarded as a citizen for all purposes of treatment whether he is mentally retarded or mentally ill. Whatever a generous or parsimonious state extends by way of mental retardation treatment facilities to its citizenry generally, it should extend equally and without differentiation to its convicted citizenry, whether they are confined in prison or allowed to be at large in the community.

Reaction Comment

VINCENT J. ZICCARDI

THE VIEWS Morris has presented in his previous law review articles, which he elucidates further in his paper for this volume, are extremely provocative. This reaction will first offer some material supportive of Morris' position that a reckless mixture of the mental health and criminal justice systems creates serious problems. I will then discuss my serious reservations about the kind of drastic surgery recommended by Morris. These reservations derive from my experiences and perspective as a criminal defense attorney.

Severe problems arise from mixing the criminal law with the mental health law. The courts are frightened by the mentally ill or retarded person. If the judge becomes aware that a person is mentally ill or mentally retarded, he treats that individual dif-

---

[15] United States v. Brawner, 471 F.2d 969 (D.C. Cir. 1972); Bolton v. Harris, 395 F.2d 642 (D.C. Cir. 1968); Washington v. United States, 390 F.2d 444 (D.C. Cir. 1967); McDonald v. United States, 312 F.2d 847 (D.C. Cir. 1962); Blocker v. United States, 274 F.2d 572 (D.C. Cir. 1959); Carter v. United States, 252 F.2d 608 (D.C. Cir. 1957); Durham v. United States, 214 F.2d 862 (D.C. Cir. 1954).
[16] See People v. Conley, 64 Cal. 2d 310, 411 P.2d 911, 49 Cal. Rptr. 815 (1966); People v. Gorshen, 51 Cal.2d 716, 336 P.2d 492 (1959); People v. Wells, 33 Cal.2d 330, 202 P.2d 53 (1949).
[17] Fisher v. United States, 328 U.S. 463 (1946).

ferently from other defendants in the system. Even where the courts are genuinely benevolent in intention, they usually do not know what to do with the person after conviction; there is no place to confine him beneficially or to send him for training or treatment.

Courts may want to help people with an identified handicap, but help, like beauty, is in the eye of the beholder. For example, I recently walked into a courtroom where one of our attorneys was representing a client at sentencing. The judge was saying to the attorney, "I want to help your client. I think he can be rehabilitated and he should learn a trade. I am going to send him to the state penitentiary for 5 to 15 years."

The defense attorney jumped up and said, "Judge, this man cannot be rehabilitated. What he needs is punishment. Send him away for 11½ to 23 months. He can never learn a trade."

This scene would be humorous if it did not occur so frequently. Unfortunately, "helping" a defendant, in the eyes of the court, often results in a person's being sentenced to a very long period of incarceration and seldom results in the provision of constructive services to him.

Other odd situations arise when the courts are forced to mix criminal law with mental health considerations. A client of our office was released from the Pennsylvania State Correctional Institution at Dallas after being granted a new trial following 16 years' incarceration for stealing a bicycle. (Dallas was created to house "defective delinquents.") Because this client had no place to live and no family whom we could locate, we arranged lodging for him at the House of Correction in Philadelphia. Through the superintendent of prisons we worked out a program for this man at the school run by the Pennsylvania Association for Retarded Children (PARC). He spent his nights at the prison and his days at the PARC school. On weekends the employees at the prison took him to ball games and other recreational events.

After a prison riot in 1969, the state attorney inspected the county prisons (the Philadelphia House of Correction is one of these). While examining the population records in an attempt to reduce prison populations, he found our client. The records showed that the man had been incarcerated for over 16 years and had not been tried. The attorney general ordered our client removed from the House of Correction and sent to a state hospital. Our office fought this order in an attempt to keep the man in prison. Our reasoning was that if he stayed in prison, he could, under the program set up between our office and the superintendent of prisons, attend the PARC school. If he were sent to Byberry State Hospital, he would not receive training of any sort. Because of the nature of the case, it attracted a lot of newspaper publicity. A brother of the client, who lived in Bethlehem, Pennsylvania, fortunately read the stories and found his brother, whom he had not seen in about 28 years. The brother volunteered to care for our client and to see that he continued receiving treatment. But for the brother's intervention, our client would probably have become another custodial patient whiling away his life in a state institution.

Despite these difficulties with any mingling of the health processes and the criminal justice system, as a criminal defense lawyer I am inclined to disagree with Morris' proposal that the plea of incompetence to stand trial be abolished. The insanity defense is really a matter of indifference since it is seldom used in the absence of the death penalty for major crimes.

The function of a criminal defense attorney is to move his client through the criminal justice system with the least harm to the client. What this means in practice is that the lawyer must assist his client in choosing the least harmful alternative available. As an example, a client charged with robbery may be incompetent to stand trial. The lawyer must determine whether a mental health commitment would result in more or less custody for the client. If the mental health commitment would result in a shorter period of "incarceration" (little or no rehabilitation or treatment results, in my view, from such commitment), the attorney would assist the client in choosing this alternative. We would not want to lose the lever of the incompetence avenue of escape from the criminal charge.

A major preliminary problem for attorneys who provide representation in criminal cases is that of identifying mental retardation, mental illness, and other handicapping conditions. If the attorney does not have this skill, problems develop. One of our attorneys was sitting in court one day, and a man came to the door of the court and smiled at the judge and said, "Hello, I am John Smith." The judge asked, "What are you here for?" The man smiled at the judge again and said, "Hello, I am John Smith"; he repeated this five, six, seven times. The judge became concerned about this behavior, so he asked our attorney to speak with the man to see what he could find out.

The attorney and the man went over to the side of the courtroom to talk. After a short period of time, our attorney advised the court that the only thing the man would say was, "Hello, I am John Smith." The judge, evidencing his strong concern, ordered an immediate psychiatric examination of the man. Upon examination, the court psychiatrist found that the man's responses were inappropriate and that he was unable to communicate. Upon receiving this report, the court committed the man to a state mental hospital for further examination.

About 2:30 that same afternoon a mother phoned me. She advised me that her son, who was deaf, had gone to court to watch the proceedings. She said she had taught him to smile and say, "Hello, I am John Smith." She felt in this way he could always get along in the world. Unfortunately, the attorney did not consider this possibility and the psychiatrist did not check the man's hearing and therefore treated him as either mentally ill or retarded.

For the criminal defense attorney who is aware of the existence of his client's mental retardation or mental illness, the crucial issue is whether he should reveal to the court the fact that the defendant is incompetent to stand trial, since hospital and other nonpenal institutional commitments are frequently much longer than a prison commitment. In most cases, the major thrust in the defense of a criminal case is not proving that the defendant did not commit the offense; it is stopping the prosecutor from proving your client did commit the offense. Defense testimony is not a very important aspect of most criminal cases. Frequently, acquittal is most likely if the defense attorney can keep his client off the stand, particularly if the client might be found incompetent to stand trial.

If an attorney reveals that his client is incompetent or that he believes his client incompetent to stand trial, the client is sent for a competence determination. This evaluation usually takes about 60 days, although additional delays often extend the elapsed time between arrest and trial to 7 or 8 months. If the defendant is found incompetent, the court in less serious cases will dismiss the case. If it is felt that the client needs inpatient treatment, the court will then proceed, at least in Pennsylvania, under civil commitment procedures. If the client requires outpatient treatment, we always try to work out the outpatient treatment. The court will, of course, order such treatment. Even the order for inpatient treatment allows the administrator of the hospital to transfer the defendant to outpatient treatment as soon as he feels him ready for it. I believe that the defense attorney has an obligation in this type of case to attempt to secure some community-based treatment program for his client after the trial is over. In our office we have a number of social workers and psychologists, as well as a psychiatrist. We are able, in drug cases at least, to come up with a drug treatment program for the client prior to going to trial. If we take a client into the court and he is in an ongoing program, he is less likely to be harmed by the court's disposition of the case. The court will continue him in the program, usually. In the areas of mental retardation and mental illness, if the attorney can place an individual in a community-based program, it is likely that charges against the client will be dismissed. We have been able to work out a number of programs for the retarded with PARC.

If the defendant is not dismissed, there is a problem. The scope of this problem depends on the kinds of programs available in various institutions. If the client is sent to a state mental hospital, he is usually housed in a segregated wing for criminal commited persons. In a great many ways, segregation limits the kind of program which can be offered the resident. People confined in this wing cannot be rewarded with going to the game room, which may be in another section of the institution, as can persons whose commitments are noncriminal. Moreover, hospital administrators worry that someone with a criminal charge against him will escape or be released and get into further difficulty. The administrators anticipate adverse publicity and thus are reluctant to release persons who have an outstanding criminal charge.

Public defenders, generally, are the gatekeepers to mental hospitals. Public defenders represent most of the poor people who have problems with either mental retardation or mental illness and who cannot afford private institutionalization. They come to the attention of the court when they are charged with an act of juvenile delinquency or a crime and because they are poor, counsel is provided for them in the criminal justice system. This counsel is usually the public defender. For this reason the public defender is in a key position in the system of criminal justice for ensuring the proper training and treatment of the mentally disabled.

I believe defense attorneys are well suited to work for the improvement of mental health and penal institutions. Our office, in conjunction with PARC, had a case involving the Hillcrest School. Hillcrest was a privately run school to which children were committed on an interim basis until a state facility became available. Hillcrest's history was a horror story. Children institutionalized there had died under suspicious circumstances and PARC found Hillcrest deficient in a number of aspects. Nonetheless, it was permitted to operate by the state. By filing a number of habeas corpus petitions claiming cruel and barbarous treatment, we were able to wear down the operators of the school. The petitions served a twofold purpose: (1) they required the operators, under oath, to describe their program and to be questioned by experts concerning its value and (2) they resulted in the removal of a number of children committed from Philadelphia. Because most of the school's commitments had previously come from Philadelphia, the removal of these children and the refusal of the court to make further commitments had a detrimental economic effect on the school. The operators sold the school shortly thereafter to a group whose program PARC found to be excellent.

Our office participated in another remedial matter. Hospitals in Philadelphia have set up "catchment areas" under the city mental health act. These catchment areas are the communities close by the hospital which are to be served by the hospital. The Philadelphia juvenile court had committed a number of children to these catchment area hospitals for evaluations. Although the hospitals had up to 75 beds available for the mental health program, they had only 3 or 4 beds available for children. There appeared to be a reluctance on the part of the hospitals to accept children: Children bring management problems into the hospitals and the hospitals wished to avoid such problems. Since these hospitals did not take children immediately, the courts were forced to order that the children be held in the Youth Detention Center until such time as the hospital could take them in. Frequently, the children would remain up to six or eight months at the detention center.

In order to motivate the hospitals to act sooner we threatened to request an injunction against the director of mental health, the administrator of the mental health program in Philadelphia, enjoining him from making payment under the mental health act to any of the hospitals in Philadelphia. The other hospitals named who could have been affected brought pressure on the guilty hospitals to open beds, and we were able to secure rapid evaluations of our client.

The defense attorney can also act as an advocate for reform of services that are provided. We have clients who are in custody because they cannot make bail and who need treatment for mental illness or training for mental retardation. We have been told by the administrator of the mental health act that these individuals can go to the catchment areas close to their homes. This answer does not take into account the problem that our clients cannot make bail and they are therefore not going to be released from jail to go to a hospital. Our office has started an action attempting to enjoin the administrator from spending any money under the act until he sets up a catchment area in the Philadelphia jails where these persons are confined. We believe we are going to be successful in this matter.

Much can be accomplished to improve services provided by state hospitals. I believe precedent has been developed in cases concerning prison programs and that this precedent can be employed in improving training and treatment programs. Public defenders have a great need to seek assistance from social workers, psychologists, and psychiatrists in pretrial diversion in cases involving the mentally ill or retarded. In addition, there is a very great need for educating lawyers both in the availability of facilities and recognition of the problems and symptomatology of the mentally ill and the mentally retarded. Finally, I believe there is a very strong need for concerted action on the part of relevant agencies and public defender offices throughout the country. If we fill these needs, we will be well on the way to solving some of the problems that now exist.

Table of Cases

693

Index